c. Overall conclusion/financial reporting objective
Based on your role in the case and the above information, conclude on whether the financial reporting will be more aggressive or conservative or somewhere in between. Note that aggressive accounting tends to overstate net income/assets and present the company in the best light. Conservative accounting ensures that net income/assets are not overstated and that all pertinent information (positive or negative) is disclosed.

2. Identification and analysis of the financial reporting issues

a. Issue identification
Read the case and look for potential financial reporting issues. To do this, you need to know the accounting principles and rules and have an understanding of the business and the business transactions. Issues are usually about deciding whether or not to **recognize** something (revenues, liabilities etc.), deciding how to **measure** financial statement elements (leave them as they are or write them down or off), or how to **present/disclose** these items in the financial statements (treat them as current or long-term, debt or equity, discontinued or continuing operations, etc.).

b. Ranking issues
Focus on the more important issues. In other words, focus first on the issues that are material to the users of the information (those that are more complex and/or those that affect any of the key numbers or ratios identified above). You should identify right away what you consider to be material.

c. Analysis
The analysis should consider both qualitative and quantitative aspects. It should also look at the issue from different perspectives. For example, in a revenue recognition issue, should the revenue be recognized now or later? Consider only the relevant alternatives.

Qualitative:
- Each perspective must be supported by making reference to GAAP and accounting theory (including the conceptual framework). For example, recognize the revenue now because... or recognize it later because...

- Make sure the analysis is case specific—i.e., that it refers to the facts of the specific case.

- Make strong arguments for both sides of the discussion. If the issue is a real issue, there is often more than one way to account for the transaction or event.

- Make sure that the analysis considers the substance of the transaction from a business and economic perspective.

Quantitative:
- Calculate the impact of the different perspectives on key financial statement numbers/ratios. Would this decision be relevant to users?

- Calculate what the numbers might look like under different accounting methods, if they are relevant.

3. Recommendations
After each issue is analyzed, conclude on how the items should be accounted for. Your conclusion should be based on your role and the financial reporting objective that you identified earlier.

Intermediate Accounting

NINTH CANADIAN EDITION

Intermediate Accounting

Donald E. Kieso, PhD, CPA
KPMG Peat Marwick Emeritus Professor of Accounting
Northern Illinois University
DeKalb, Illinois

Jerry J. Weygandt, PhD, CPA
Arthur Andersen Alumni Professor of Accounting
University of Wisconsin
Madison, Wisconsin

Terry D. Warfield, PhD
Associate Professor
University of Wisconsin
Madison, Wisconsin

Nicola M. Young, MBA, FCA
Saint Mary's University
Halifax, Nova Scotia

Irene M. Wiecek, FCA
University of Toronto
Toronto, Ontario

John Wiley & Sons Canada, Ltd.

Library and Archives Canada Cataloguing in Publication

Intermediate accounting / Donald E. Kieso ... [et al.]. — 9th Canadian ed.

Includes index.
ISBN 978-0-470-16100-5 (v. 1).—ISBN 978-0-470-16101-2 (v. 2)

1. Accounting—Textbooks. I. Kieso, Donald E

HF5636.I57 2010   657'.044   C2009-906922-9

Production Credits
Acquisitions Editor: Zoë Craig
Vice President & Publisher: Veronica Visentin
Vice President, Publishing Services: Karen Bryan
Creative Director, Publishing Services: Ian Koo
Marketing Manager: Aida Krneta
Editorial Manager: Karen Staudinger
Developmental Editor: Daleara Jamasji Hirjikaka
Media Editor: Channade Fenandoe
Editorial Assistant: Laura Hwee
Design & Typesetting: Lakeside Group Inc. (Gail Ferreira Ng-A-Kien)
Cover Design: Ian Koo
Cover Photo: ©iStockphoto.com/Felix Möckel
Printing & Binding: Quad/Graphics

References to the *CICA Handbook* are reprinted (or adapted) with permission from The Canadian Institute of Chartered Accountants, Toronto, Canada. Any changes to the original material are the sole responsibility of the author (and/or publisher) and have not been reviewed or endorsed by the CICA.

Printed and bound in the United States

5 6 7 8 9 QG 14 13 12

John Wiley & Sons Canada, Ltd.
6045 Freemont Blvd.
Mississauga, Ontario L5R 4J3
Visit our website at: www.wiley.ca

*Dedicated to accounting educators in Canada
and to the students in their Intermediate Accounting classrooms
as we step into a multiple-GAAP world.
Our discipline will be shaped by continuing change
as standards evolve,
making the future an exciting place to be.*

About the Authors

CANADIAN EDITION

Nicola (Nickie) M. Young, MBA, FCA, is a Professor of Accounting in the Sobey School of Business at Saint Mary's University in Halifax, Nova Scotia, where her teaching responsibilities have varied from the introductory offering to final-year advanced financial courses to the survey course in the Executive MBA program. She is the recipient of teaching awards, and has contributed to the academic and administrative life of the university by chairing the Department of Accounting, and membership on the Board of Governors and the Pension and other committees. Nickie was associated with the Atlantic School of Chartered Accountancy for over 25 years in a variety of roles, including program and course development, teaching, and program reform. In addition to contributions to the accounting profession at the provincial level, Nickie has served on national boards of the Canadian Institute of Chartered Accountants (CICA) dealing with licensure and education. She has worked with the CICA's Public Sector Accounting Board (PSAB) for many years as an associate, as a member and chair of the board, and as a chair and member of PSAB task forces. Nickie currently serves on the Board of Directors of the CICA and on its Education and Qualifications Committee. She and Irene Wiecek have also co-authored the *IFRS Primer: International GAAP Basics* (Canadian and U.S. editions).

Irene M. Wiecek, FCA, is a faculty member at the University of Toronto where she is cross-appointed to the Joseph L. Rotman School of Management. She teaches financial reporting in various programs including the Commerce Program (Accounting Specialist) and the Master of Management & Professional Accounting Program (MMPA). The Associate Director of the MMPA Program for many years, she co-founded and is Co-Director of the ICAO (Institute of Chartered Accountants of Ontario)/Rotman Centre for Innovation in Accounting Education, which supports and facilitates innovation in accounting education. Irene has been involved in professional accounting education for over 20 years, currently sitting on the Canadian Institute of Chartered Accountants (CICA) Financial Reporting and Governance Education Committee, as well as developing and directing the CICA IFRS immersion programs for practising accountants. She is an active member of the Ernst & Young Academic Resource Center where she is part of a team that authored a new IFRS curriculum for the Americas. In the area of standard setting, she has chaired the Canadian Academic Accounting Association CICA Financial Reporting Exposure Draft Response Committee. Irene co-authored the *IFRS Primer: International GAAP Basics* (Canadian and U.S. editions) with Nickie Young.

U.S. EDITION

Donald E. Kieso, Ph.D., C.P.A., received his bachelor's degree from Aurora University and his doctorate in accounting from the University of Illinois. He has served as chairman of the Department of Accountancy and is currently the KPMG Emeritus Professor of Accountancy at Northern Illinois University. He has public accounting experience with Price Waterhouse & Co. (San Francisco and Chicago) and Arthur Andersen & Co. (Chicago) and research experience with the Research Division of the American Institute of Certified Public Accountants (New York). He has done postdoctorate work as a Visiting Scholar at the University of California at Berkeley and is a recipient of NIU's Teaching Excellence Award and four Golden Apple Teaching Awards. Professor Kieso is the author of other accounting and business books and is a member of the American Accounting Association, the American Institute of Certified Public Accountants, and the Illinois CPA Society. He is the recipient of the Outstanding Accounting Educator Award from the Illinois CPA Society, the FSA's Joseph A. Silvoso Award of Merit, the NIU Foundation's Humanitarian Award for Service to Higher Education, the Distinguished Service Award from the Illinois CPA Society, and in 2003 received an honorary doctorate from Aurora University.

Jerry J. Weygandt, Ph.D., C.P.A., is Arthur Andersen Alumni Professor of Accounting at the University of Wisconsin-Madison. He holds a Ph.D. in accounting from the University of Illinois. His articles have appeared in *Accounting Review, Journal of Accounting Research, Accounting Horizons, Journal of Accountancy*, and other academic and professional journals. Professor Weygandt is the author of other accounting and financial reporting books and is a member of the American Accounting Association, the American Institute of Certified Public Accountants, and the Wisconsin Society of Certified Public Accountants. He has been actively involved with the American Institute of Certified Public Accountants and has been a member of the Accounting Standards Executive Committee (AcSEC) of that organization. He also served on the FASB task force that examined the reporting issues related to accounting for income taxes. He is the recipient of the Wisconsin Institute of CPAs' Outstanding Educator's Award and the Lifetime Achievement Award. In 2001, he received the American Accounting Association's Outstanding Accounting Educator Award.

Terry D. Warfield, Ph.D., is the Robert and Monica Beyer Professor of Accounting at the University of Wisconsin-Madison. He received a B.S. and M.B.A. from Indiana University and a Ph.D. in accounting from the University of Iowa. Professor Warfield's area of expertise is financial reporting, and prior to his academic career, he worked for five years in the banking industry. He served as the Academic Accounting Fellow in the Office of the Chief Accountant at the U.S. Securities and Exchange Commission in Washington, D.C., from 1995 to 1996. Professor Warfield's primary research interests concern financial accounting standards and disclosure policies. He has published scholarly articles in *The Accounting Review, Journal of Accounting and Economics, Research in Accounting Regulation*, and *Accounting Horizons*, and he has served on the editorial boards of *The Accounting Review, Accounting Horizons*, and *Issues in Accounting Education*. Professor Warfield has served on the Financial Accounting Standards Committee of the American Accounting Association (Chair 1995–1996) and the AAA-FASB Research Conference Committee. He currently serves on the Financial Accounting Standards Advisory Council of the Financial Accounting Standards Board. Professor Warfield has received teaching awards at both the University of Iowa and the University of Wisconsin, and he was named to the Teaching Academy at the University of Wisconsin in 1995. Professor Warfield has developed and published several case studies based on his research for use in accounting classes. These cases have been selected for the AICPA Professor-Practitioner Case Development Program and have been published in *Issues in Accounting Education*.

Preface

This is an edition of *Intermediate Accounting* like no other. Accountants are at the centre of very significant change and accounting educators are leading the charge to equip you with the tools needed to move forward into this exciting arena. The ninth edition has been shaped by the following themes:

- Change
- Choice
- Concepts and core
- Critical thinking
- Complexity

Let's start with the change theme as this one is the most obvious. Canadian accounting standards for publicly accountable enterprises are going global and being replaced by International Financial Reporting Standards (IFRS). This is energizing, especially for students' as it gives you a transferrable skill that allows you to go global as well. Accounting standards for private companies are moving to a "made-in-Canada" solution: the new private entity generally accepted accounting principles (PE GAAP). These standards are more flexible and responsive (from a cost-benefit perspective) to the needs of the numerous and varied private entities that make up much of the economy. Private entities will be able to choose to follow IFRS or PE GAAP. This edition integrates material from both sets of standards.

As more and more countries move to international accounting standards, the IFRS body of knowledge itself is undergoing unprecedented change. Not only are we moving to a new platform but that platform is shifting at a fairly rapid pace. We have accepted change as a constant in this edition. Although we have tried to ensure that we have the most up-to-date material, we acknowledge that we have to equip you to continue to be able to change with the standards after you leave us.

As always, the core of the textbook rests on foundational principles and concepts. Although these may change, they generally evolve more slowly and many of the basics endure. Much of IFRS and PE GAAP (and indeed U.S. GAAP) rests upon the same principles. We have attempted to highlight and focus on this core.

Because IFRS and PE GAAP are principles-based, we continue to encourage you to view things from differing perspectives and to develop professional judgement and critical thinking.

With change and more choice comes more complexity and so we have scaled back in some areas. For instance, in some chapters, we have moved some of the material to the textbook's website (such as that covering instalment sales and cost recovery methods). Many of the perceived complexities in accounting stem from the fact that many accounting students do not really understand the underlying economics and legalities. We have added material that will help you gain a greater understanding of these issues.

New Features

Several new features have been added in this edition.

COMPARISON CHARTS: Our end-of-chapter charts that identify the major differences between IFRS and PE GAAP are a key feature. These charts augment the more detailed charts that have been added to many chapters that also focus on differences. Where there is a new standard being proposed, we have added a column to the end-of-chapter charts so that you understand what may be in store in the future, or provide a Looking Ahead feature to alert you to upcoming changes expected.

Finance

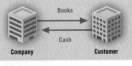

Law

FINANCE AND LAW ICONS: In order to help you integrate your knowledge of economics, finance, and law with accounting, we have added new finance and law icons. We have developed the material so that you gain an appreciation for these fundamentals before trying to account for them.

BUSINESS TRANSACTIONS BOXES/ICONS: Many chapters have a new business transactions box and icon. In most business transactions, you give something up and receive something. These boxes and icons are meant to help you understand what has been given up and what has been received in the transaction. As noted earlier, this is tremendously helpful when you are trying to decide how to account for a transaction or economic event.

SIGNIFICANT CHANGE ICON: These icons are meant to catch your attention. Everywhere there has been a significant change in the accounting standard or how it is applied, it has been highlighted with a giant asterisk in the margin.

END-OF-CHAPTER MATERIAL: While not a new feature, this material has been revised to ensure that you have ample opportunity to apply and practise the various methods and models that are acceptable under IFRS and PE GAAP. Case material allows you to analyze business transactions and situations and apply both IFRS and PE GAAP. We have added new research and writing assignment questions that allow you to explore the nature of GAAP differences and understand why standard setters choose different solutions when different groups of users are considered. New comprehensive coverage problems after chapters 5, 9, 12, 14, 17, and 23 combine material from the current chapter with previous chapters so that you understand how "it all fits together."

Significant Change

Continuing Features

Many things have contributed to the success of Kieso over the years. The following points outline just a few.

Helping Students Practise

The end-of-chapter material includes cases and integrated cases, which draw material from several chapters in order to help you build skills in identifying key accounting issues. In this edition, we have added more than 10 new cases overall and revised all solutions to incorporate IFRS and/or private entity GAAP. Further, a summary guiding you through the case study method appears inside the front cover of this text. This is in addition to the full Case Study Primer available on WileyPLUS and the Student Website.

Analysis doesn't have to be just part of the cases. Our Digging Deeper feature asks you to look more closely at the results you obtain in the problems and exercises. For instance, you might then be asked to comment on results or determine how things might be different if one of the original variables were to change. Digging Deeper questions are identified using the icon shown here.

Digging Deeper

Real-World Emphasis

Since intermediate accounting is a course in which students must understand the application of accounting principles and techniques in practice, we strive to include as many real-world examples as possible.

Real-World Emphasis

Reinforcement of the Concepts

Throughout each chapter you are asked What Do the Numbers Mean? and are presented with discussions applying accounting concepts to business contexts. This feature builds on

the opening feature stories in making the accounting concepts relevant to you. Through current examples of how accounting is applied, you will be better able to relate to and understand the material. The underlying concepts icons in each chapter alert you to remember that the issue under discussion draws on concepts identified in Chapter 2 as part of the conceptual framework. In addition, an Analysis section is present in most chapters. This section discusses the effect on the financial statements of many of the accounting choices made by corporate management, alerting you to look behind the numbers. Finally, the accounting equation appears in the margin next to key journal entries to help you understand the impact of each transaction on the company's financial position and cash flows.

**Underlying
Concept**

Integration of Ethics Coverage

Rather than featuring ethics coverage and problem material in isolation, we use an ethics icon to highlight ethical issues as they are discussed within each chapter. This icon also appears beside each exercise, problem, or case where ethical issues must be dealt with in relation to all kinds of accounting situations.

Ethics

A Complete Package

Kieso continues to provide the most comprehensive and useful technology package available for the intermediate course. Its Student Website continues to expand with new tutorials on bad debts, bonds, and inventory methods. Also featured are a case primer, demonstration problems, expanded ethics coverage, and more. The site can be accessed at www.wiley.com/canada/kieso.

A key feature of every accounting package produced by John Wiley & Sons Canada, Ltd. is *WileyPLUS*. This on-line suite of resources that includes a complete multimedia version of the text will help students come to class better prepared for lectures, and allows instructors to track students' progress throughout the course more easily. Students can take advantage of tools such as quizzes and tutorials to help them study more efficiently. *WileyPLUS* is designed to provide instant feedback as students practise on their own. Students can work through assignments with automatic grading or review custom-made class presentations featuring reading assignments, PowerPoint slides, and interactive simulations.

Currency and Accuracy

Accounting changes at a rapid pace—a pace that has increased in recent years. An up-to-date book is more important than ever. As in past editions, we have endeavoured to make this edition the most current and accurate text available. We have also ensured that new material subject to uncertainty has been vetted by subject matter experts.

The following list outlines the revisions and improvements made in the chapters of this volume.

Chapter 1 *The Canadian Financial Reporting Environment*

- Increased emphasis on standard setting in a global environment including the standard-setting process for the IASB
- Chart outlining GAAP responsibilities: who is responsible for setting which GAAP?
- New material on the GAAP hierarchy for both PE GAAP and IFRS

Chapter 2 *Conceptual Framework Underlying Financial Reporting*

- Material for the newly proposed conceptual framework model including new definitions for financial statement elements
- Expanded emphasis on analysis of assets and liabilities

- Comparison of existing and proposed definitions for financial statement elements
- New material on the definition of control
- New expanded section on the fair value principle
- New appendix on fair value measurements
- New link to present value module on the website

Chapter 3 The Accounting Information System

- Minor changes made

Chapter 4 Reporting Financial Performance

- New material on the nature versus function expense presentation choice
- Updated material for discontinued operations
- De-emphasis of extraordinary items since not allowed under IFRS and not mentioned under PE GAAP
- New IFRS/PE GAAP comparison chart
- Overview of new financial statement model being proposed

Chapter 5 Financial Position and Cash Flows

- New material highlighting different accounting policy choices under PE GAAP and IFRS including comparison chart
- Financial statements of Eastern Platinum Limited, which adopted IFRS early, included as sample statements

Chapter 6 Revenue Recognition

- New section on the economics and legalities of a business transaction
- New conceptual material on the contract-based approach (proposed model)
- Detailed comparison chart identifying differences in recognition and measurement under PE GAAP, current IFRS, and proposed IFRS
- New mechanics section that shows the journal entries under the various models
- New examples of how the approaches may be applied to certain types of transactions (such as layaways and bill and holds)
- New material on how to view accounting for long-term contracts in general

Chapter 7 Cash and Receivables

- Emphasis changed from calculating bad debt expense to determining the proper accounts receivable amount
- Summary T accounts that show the effects of all entries on the related receivable and bad debt accounts
- New section on straight-line amortization of premiums and discounts
- Change made to recognize notes receivable at the net amount received, rather than using a separate discount account
- New IFRS/PE GAAP comparison chart

Chapter 8 Inventory

- Traditional approach to inventory is now referred to as a "lower of cost and net realizable value" model
- Expanded discussion of net realizable value and fair value models permitted by IFRS for some inventories
- New IFRS/PE GAAP comparison chart
- Transferred Appendix on U.S. methods (LCM and LIFO) to the website
- New Appendix 8B, which provides a road map of primary sources of GAAP for different types of inventory
- Added borrowing costs and decommissioning costs to section on product costs because of IFRS requirements
- Reduced discussion of using NRV less a normal profit margin

Chapter 9 Investments

- Change in approach to investments material; a back-to-basics approach is used to describe three basic accounting models for (less than significant influence) investments: the cost/amortized cost model, the fair value with changes in value going through net income model (FV-NI), and the fair value with changes going through OCI model (FV-OCI)
- Removed references to held-for-trading, available-for-sale, and held-to-maturity classifications
- Less emphasis on FV-OCI for investments in debt securities
- FV-OCI model is explained with recycling (OCI to net income) and with no recycling (OCI directly to retained earnings)
- New impairment (required for investments at cost or amortized cost) section added with three approaches identified
- Non-controlling interest is now considered an equity item; bottom-line net income includes both parent company and non-controlling interest's share
- Updated section on non-controlling interest
- Choices allowed under PE standards are identified; update provided on IFRS
- New summary tables and comparison charts throughout the chapter
- Appendix 9A presents a summary table of pre-2011 Canadian GAAP for investments

Chapter 10 Property, Plant, and Equipment: Accounting Model Basics

- New sections on componentization; accounting for overhauls, inspections, and asset replacements, with examples; and costs incurred after acquisition
- New sections to explain the revaluation model and the fair value model
- Change in terminology from "amortization" to "depreciation"
- Removed investment tax credit coverage
- Updated contributed assets section
- Investment property explained as a specific type of asset under IFRS
- Reduced coverage of natural resource property; under IFRS, standing timber is an agricultural asset
- New IFRS/PE GAAP comparison chart

Chapter 11 Depreciation, Impairment, and Disposition

- Transferred less common depreciation methods to the website
- New section on which asset components are depreciated separately
- Increased emphasis on impairment and the two models in use: cost recovery approach (same as in eighth edition) and the rational entity approach
- New material on asset groups/cash-generating units
- New material on impairment and disposal of assets accounted for under the revaluation model
- New IFRS/PE GAAP comparison chart

Chapter 12 Intangible Assets and Goodwill

- New material on internally developed intangible assets that is far-reaching, with PE GAAP and IFRS almost identical
- Removed sections that are no longer relevant on R&D, development stage costs, organization costs, advertising costs, and other deferred charges
- Reorganized chapter to omit section on other internally developed intangibles and to cover impairment of goodwill in the section on goodwill
- Added section on prepaid expenses; omitted separate section on computer software costs and websites
- Increased emphasis on the similarities between the acquisition of PP&E assets and intangibles, as well as the impairment requirements
- Revised material on bargain purchase and "negative" goodwill
- New IFRS/PE GAAP comparison chart

Acknowledgements

We thank the users of our eighth edition, including the many instructors, faculty, and students who contributed to this revision through their comments and instructive criticism. In addition, special thanks are extended to contributors to our ninth edition manuscript and supplements.

Reviewers

Peter Alpaugh, George Brown College
Ann Bigelow, University of Western Ontario
Ralph Cecere, McGill University
Charles Cho, Concordia University
Robert Collier, University of Ottawa
Karen Congo, University of Western Ontario
Helen Farkas, McMaster University
George Fisher, Douglas College
Susan Fisher, Algonquin College
Ian Hutchinson, Acadia University
Stuart Jones, University of Calgary
Jocelyn King, University of Alberta

Cécile Laurin, Algonquin College
Douglas A. Leatherdale, Georgian College
Bruce McConomy, Wilfrid Laurier University
Songlan Peng, York University
Tom Pippy, Conestoga College
Gwen Roberts, Ryerson University
Zvi Singer, McGill University
Rik Smistad, Mount Royal University
Dragan Stojanovic, University of Toronto
Desmond Tsang, McGill University
Helen Vallee, Kwantlen Polytechnic University

Appreciation is also extended to colleagues at the Rotman School of Management, University of Toronto, and the Sobey School of Business, Saint Mary's University, who provided input, suggestions, and support, especially Peter Thomas, for his professionalism and wisdom and Martha Dunlop, for her expertise and review of the manuscript.

It takes many people and coordinated efforts to get an edition off the ground. Many thanks to the team at John Wiley & Sons Canada, Ltd., who are superb: Zoë Craig, Acquisitions Editor; Veronica Visentin, Publisher; Karen Staudinger, Editorial Manager, who has been an integral part of the last five editions; Karen Bryan, Vice President, Publishing Services; Channade Fenandoe, Media Editor, for managing this increasingly important aspect of the text; Deanna Durnford, Supplements Coordinator; and Aida Krneta, Marketing Manager. Their enthusiasm and support have been invaluable. The contributions of Alison Arnot, Laurel Hyatt, Zofia Laubitz, Gail Ferreira Ng-A-Kien and Julie van Tol are also very much appreciated. A special thank you goes to Daleara Hirjikaka, our Developmental Editor extraordinaire, who dealt cheerfully with us on an almost daily basis and kept everything on track.

We are particularly grateful to Ann Bigelow, Robert Ducharme, Allan Foerster, Ingrid McLeod-Dick, Anu Goel, and Rik Smistad for all their help with the end-of-chapter material and solutions. Thanks also go to Carole Clyne, Laura Cumming, Robert Ducharme, Helen Farkas, Helmut Hauke, Cécile Laurin, Ingrid McLeod-Dick, Richard Michalski, Peter Secord, Zvi Singer, Marie Sinnott, Rik Smistad, Dragan Stojanovic, and Glenys Sylvestre, who contributed so much to the related supplements.

We appreciate the continuing co-operation of the accounting standards group at the Canadian Institute of Chartered Accountants and of Ron Salole, Vice-President of Standards. The director and principals of the Accounting Standards Board have been as open and helpful as possible in all our dealings with them. For this ninth edition, a special thank you is owed to Tricia O'Malley and Ian Hague. We also thank the CICA itself for allowing us to quote from its materials and Eastern Platinum for permitting us to use its first-quarter 2009 financial statements prepared under IFRS for our specimen financial statements.

We thoroughly enjoy the challenges brought about by change and hope that we are able to transfer some of this enthusiasm to both instructors and students. We hope that this book helps teachers instill in their students an appreciation of the challenges, value, and limitations of accounting, encourages students to evaluate critically and understand financial accounting theory and practice, and prepares students for advanced study, professional examinations, and the successful and ethical pursuit of their careers in accounting or business. If so, then we will have attained our objective.

Suggestions and comments from users of this book are always appreciated. We have striven to produce an error-free text, but if anything has slipped through the variety of checks undertaken, please let us know so that corrections can be made to subsequent printings.

Irene M. Wiecek
TORONTO, ONTARIO
wiecek@rotman.utoronto.ca

Nicola M. Young
HALIFAX, NOVA SCOTIA
nicola.young@smu.ca

February 2010

Brief Contents

Contents

CHAPTER 11 Depreciation, Impairment, and Disposition   p. 677

CHAPTER 12 Intangible Assets and Goodwill   p. 743

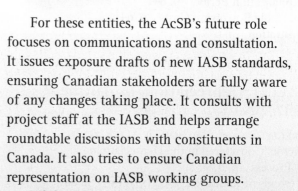

Going Global

As of January 1, 2011, all public companies in Canada will be preparing their financial statements according to International Financial Reporting Standards (IFRS). The decision to adopt IFRS was the result of a long consultation and deliberation process on the part of Canada's Accounting Standards Board (AcSB).

"The role of accounting in the allocation of capital is the underlying driving force for the Board's decision to adopt IFRS for publicly accountable entities in Canada," says Tricia O'Malley, Chair of the AcSB. The move will improve Canadian companies' access to capital markets and hopefully lower their cost of doing business internationally. "It's removing an impediment for Canadian companies to be considered by global investors," she adds.

Like any new development, there are inherent costs—for new systems, training, revising education curricula and resources, etc. But these are outweighed by the benefits. Global firms will save costs by having to prepare financial statements using only one set of standards, and they will be able to transfer employees among offices in different countries. This increased mobility is also an advantage for the individual accountant: "It significantly increases mobility and employment opportunities for accountants," says Ms. O'Malley.

For these entities, the AcSB's future role focuses on communications and consultation. It issues exposure drafts of new IASB standards, ensuring Canadian stakeholders are fully aware of any changes taking place. It consults with project staff at the IASB and helps arrange roundtable discussions with constituents in Canada. It also tries to ensure Canadian representation on IASB working groups.

While public companies must follow IFRS, private companies may follow private enterprise standards set by AcSB instead. "Every time IFRS change, we'll have to think about whether, and how, the private enterprise standards should change," Ms. O'Malley explains. For its private enterprise standards, every couple of years the AcSB will issue a single exposure draft encompassing all the changes necessary. She stresses that because the two sets of standards are built on the same conceptual framework, the fundamental differences between them are minimal.

Students will benefit from learning both sets of accounting standards. After all, the vast majority of businesses in Canada are private enterprises. However, as Ms. O'Malley says, "If you want to work for a big company and you're interested in international opportunities, learning IFRS opens the world for you." ∎

CHAPTER 1

The Canadian Financial Reporting Environment

Learning Objectives

After studying this chapter, you should be able to:

1. Describe the essential characteristics of accounting.

2. Explain how accounting makes it possible to use scarce resources more efficiently.

3. Explain the meaning of "stakeholder" and identify key stakeholders in financial reporting including what is at stake for each one.

4. Identify the objective of financial reporting.

5. Explain the notion of management bias in financial reporting.

6. Understand the importance of user needs in the financial reporting process.

7. Explain the need for accounting standards.

8. Identify the major entities that influence the standard-setting process and explain how they influence financial reporting.

9. Explain the meaning of generally accepted accounting principles (GAAP).

10. Explain the significance of professional judgement in applying GAAP.

11. Understand issues related to ethics and financial accounting.

12. Identify some of the challenges facing accounting.

Preview of Chapter 1

North American financial reporting systems are among the best in the world. Our commitment to keeping our financial reporting systems strong is as intense as ever, because in this changing business world, information must be relevant and reliable for our capital markets to work efficiently. This chapter explains the environment of financial reporting and the many factors that affect it.

The chapter is organized as follows:

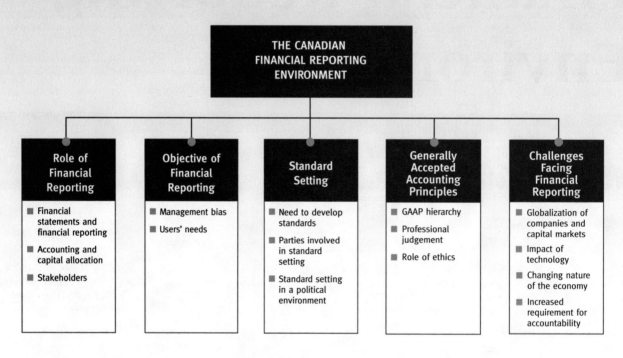

THE CANADIAN FINANCIAL REPORTING ENVIRONMENT				
Role of Financial Reporting	**Objective of Financial Reporting**	**Standard Setting**	**Generally Accepted Accounting Principles**	**Challenges Facing Financial Reporting**
■ Financial statements and financial reporting ■ Accounting and capital allocation ■ Stakeholders	■ Management bias ■ Users' needs	■ Need to develop standards ■ Parties involved in standard setting ■ Standard setting in a political environment	■ GAAP hierarchy ■ Professional judgement ■ Role of ethics	■ Globalization of companies and capital markets ■ Impact of technology ■ Changing nature of the economy ■ Increased requirement for accountability

ROLE OF FINANCIAL REPORTING

Like other human activities and disciplines, accounting is largely a product of its environment. This environment includes conditions, constraints, and influences that are social, economic, political, and legal, all of which change over time. As a result, accounting objectives and practices are not the same today as they were in the past. **Accounting theory and practice have always evolved and will continue to evolve.**

Over the past decade, the accounting landscape has changed dramatically, being shaped by such spectacular business failures as **WorldCom Inc.**, **Enron**, and **Arthur Andersen**, and market failures including the subprime lending crisis. The accounting profession is still dealing with the aftermath of these events.

Accounting is defined best by describing its three essential characteristics. It is the (1) **identification, measurement, and communication of financial information about** (2) **economic entities to** (3) **interested persons.** These characteristics have described accounting for hundreds of years. Yet, in the last 30 years, the size and complexity of economic entities have increased so much, and the interested persons have become so numerous and diverse, that the responsibility placed on the accounting profession is greater today than ever before.

Real-World Emphasis

Objective 1
Describe the essential characteristics of accounting.

Financial Statements and Financial Reporting

Financial accounting (financial reporting) is the process that culminates in the preparation of financial reports that cover all of the enterprise's business activities and that are used by both **internal and external** parties. Users of these financial reports include investors, creditors, and others. In contrast, **managerial accounting** is the process of identifying, measuring, analyzing, and **communicating financial information** to **internal** decision-makers. This information may take varied forms, such as cost-benefit analyses and forecasts that management uses to plan, evaluate, and control an organization's operations.

Financial statements are the principal way of communicating financial information to those who are outside an enterprise. These statements give the firm's history, quantified in terms of money. The most frequently provided financial statements are (1) the **balance sheet**, (2) the **income statement**, (3) the **statement of cash flows**, and (4) the **statement of owners' or shareholders' equity** or **statement of retained earnings**. In addition, **note disclosures** are an important part of each financial statement.

Some financial information cannot be expressed in the financial statements or is better expressed through other means. Examples include the president's letter and supplementary schedules in the corporate annual report, prospectuses, reports filed with government agencies, news releases, management forecasts, and descriptions of an enterprise's social or environmental impact. Such information may be required by an authoritative pronouncement or regulatory rule[1] or custom, or because management wants to disclose it voluntarily. The main focus of this textbook is the basic financial statements.

Accounting and Capital Allocation

Because **resources** are limited, people try to conserve them, use them effectively, and identify and encourage those who can make efficient use of them. Through an **efficient use of resources**, our standard of living increases.

Markets, free enterprise, and competition determine whether a business will succeed and thrive. The accounting profession has the highly important responsibility of **measuring company performance** accurately and fairly on a timely basis. The information provided by accounting enables investors and creditors to **compare** the income and assets of companies and thus **assess the relative risks and returns** of different investment opportunities. Based on their assessments, investors and creditors can then channel their resources (i.e., invest in these companies or lend them money) more effectively. Illustration 1-1 shows the process of capital allocation.

2 Objective
Explain how accounting makes it possible to use scarce resources more efficiently.

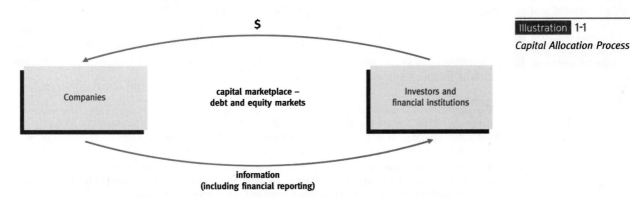

Illustration 1-1

Capital Allocation Process

---

[1] All public companies must disclose certain information under provincial securities law. This information is captured by the provincial securities commissions under the Canadian umbrella organization, the Canadian Securities Administrators (CSA), and is available electronically at www.sedar.com.

In Canada, the primary exchange mechanisms for allocating resources are **debt and equity markets**,[2] as well as **financial institutions** such as banks.[3] The debt and equity marketplace includes both public stock markets/exchanges and private sources.

Illustration 1-2 shows the sources of capital in Canada for various stages of company growth.

Illustration 1-2

Sources of Capital

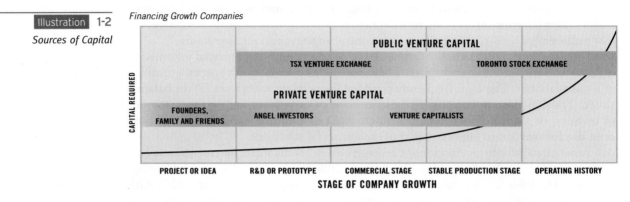

Financing Growth Companies

Source: www.tmx.com

An effective process of capital allocation is critical to a healthy economy as this promotes productivity, encourages innovation, and provides an efficient and liquid market for buying and selling securities and obtaining and granting credit.[4] Unreliable and irrelevant information leads to **poor capital allocation**, which has a negative impact on the securities markets and economic growth. The accounting numbers that companies report affect the **transfer of resources** among companies and individuals. Consider the fact that stock prices generally rise when positive news (including financial information) is expected or released. In addition, **credit rating agencies** use accounting and other information to rate companies' financial stability.[5] This gives investors and creditors **additional independent information** to use when making decisions. For companies, a good rating can mean greater access to capital and at lower costs.

Stakeholders

Objective 3

Explain the meaning of "stakeholder" and identify key stakeholders in financial reporting including what is at stake for each one.

Stakeholders are parties who have something at risk in the financial reporting environment; e.g., their salary, job, investment, or reputation. Key stakeholders in the financial reporting environment include **traditional users** of financial information as well as others. In the stakeholder context, **users** may be more broadly defined to include not only parties who are relying directly on the financial information for resource allocation (such as investors and creditors) but also others who help in the efficient allocation of resources (such as financial analysts and regulators).

[2] The largest, most senior equity market in Canada is the Toronto Stock Exchange (TSX). The junior market—the TSX Venture Exchange (formerly the CDNX Stock Market)—was created in 2001 to handle start-up companies. The Montreal Exchange, known as the Canadian Derivatives Exchange, is the main market for derivatives and futures trading.

[3] According to the Canadian Bankers Association website, based on total assets as at October 31, 2008, the six largest banks in Canada, from largest to smallest, are RBC Financial Group, TD Bank Financial Group, Scotiabank, BMO Financial Group, Canadian Imperial Bank of Commerce, and National Bank of Canada.

[4] AICPA Special Committee on Financial Reporting, "Improving Business Reporting: A Customer Focus," supplement in *Journal of Accountancy* (October 1994).

[5] For example, institutions such as Dominion Bond Rating Service, Moody's, and Standard & Poor's rate issuers of bonds and preferred shares in the Canadian and global marketplaces.

The broader definition of users includes anyone who **prepares, relies on, reviews, audits, or monitors financial information**. It includes investors, creditors, analysts, managers, employees, customers, suppliers, industry groups, unions, government departments and ministers, the public in general (e.g., consumer groups), regulatory agencies, other companies, and standard setters, as well as auditors, lawyers, and others. Illustration 1-3 shows the relationships among these stakeholders.

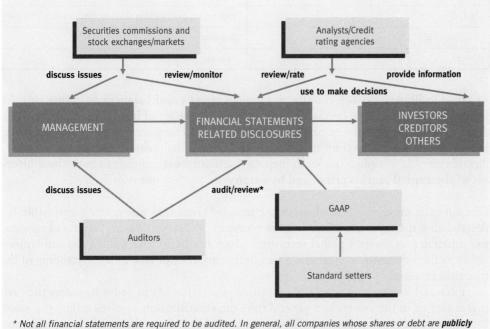

Illustration 1-3

Selected Key Stakeholders in the Financial Reporting Environment

* *Not all financial statements are required to be audited. In general, all companies whose shares or debt are **publicly traded** must have an audit and therefore comply with generally accepted accounting principles (GAAP). Private companies may decide not to have an audit but must have unanimous shareholder consent per Canada Business Corporations Act 163. For private companies, the decision to have an audit or not may depend on whether the users of the statements would find audited GAAP statements more useful.*

Various stakeholders have specific functions in the financial reporting environment. Company management **prepares** the financial statements. It has the best insight into the business and therefore knows what should be included in the financial statements. The statements are then **audited and reviewed** by auditors, who may discuss with management how economic events and transactions have been communicated in the financial statements. The value that auditors add to the statements lies in the auditors' independence. They act on behalf of the shareholders to ensure that management is accounting properly for the economic transactions. The auditors also **review** the information to ensure that it reflects sound accounting choices.

Investors and creditors **rely on** the financial statements to make decisions. It is up to these parties to carefully examine the information given. Standard setters **set generally accepted accounting principles (GAAP)**, which are often used to prepare the financial statements. GAAP helps **reduce management bias** by providing direction as to how events should be accounted for. Securities commissions and stock exchanges **monitor** the financial statements to ensure full and plain disclosure of material information and to determine whether the companies may continue to list their shares on stock exchanges. Finally, the credit rating agencies and analysts **monitor and analyze** the information produced by the company, looking for signs of change; i.e., an improved or weakened financial condition.

Illustration 1-4 identifies what is at stake for each stakeholder. This is not meant to be a complete list. Rather, it identifies the major stakeholder groups.

Illustration 1-4

What Is at Stake for Each Stakeholder?

STAKEHOLDER	WHAT IS AT STAKE?
Investors/creditors	Investment/loan
Management	Job, bonus, reputation, salary increase, access to capital markets by company
Securities commissions and stock exchanges	Reputation, effective and efficient capital marketplace
Analysts and credit rating agencies	Reputation, profits
Auditors	Reputation, profits (companies are their clients)
Standard setters	Reputation
Others	Various

As noted in Illustration 1-3, the system provides **checks and balances** to ensure that the people with capital—the investors and creditors—have good information to use when deciding where best to invest or allocate their capital. The system does not always work, however. Because the system involves people, human behaviour is often a key unpredictable variable. People often act in their own **self-interest** rather than in the **best interest of the capital marketplace, and by extension, the economy**.

What Do the Numbers Mean?

Consider the much-publicized subprime lending crisis that was partly responsible for destabilizing the capital markets and the economy. What was this all about and how did the situation precipitate a global recession? Much has to do with individuals and entities acting in their own self-interest and a lack of transparency or lack of understanding of the true risks involved.

Financial institutions regularly securitize pools of assets in order to access the cash that is tied up in the assets. As a general rule, the securitization involves selling the assets to a separate entity, often for cash. The entity then sells units or shares in the pool of assets to investors. The following summarizes the steps in a normal securitization of mortgage assets.

1. Lender lends money to customers to buy homes.

2. Lender sells pool of mortgage assets from above transaction to a separate entity (often referred to as a special purpose entity or SPE).

3. SPE sell units/shares in the pool of mortgages to investors.

There is nothing inherently wrong with this structure and it can work very well for all parties as long as they understand the risks involved. It is good for borrowers as it makes funds more accessible. It is good for lenders as they are able to get their cash out of the mortgage assets. It is good for SPEs as they earn interest on the pool of assets. Finally, it is good for investors as they earn a return on their investment. What went wrong in the subprime lending situation, then?

First, the lenders or their designated mortgage brokers loaned money aggressively (in hopes of higher profits) to borrowers who may not have been creditworthy in hindsight. Second, many of the loans were adjustable-rate notes, which meant that, initially, the interest rates were low (often below the prime lending rate) but, subsequently, the rates reset themselves according to the loan agreement, often becoming significantly higher. Therefore, even though the borrower may have been able to afford the loan payments initially, many could no longer afford them once the interest rates went higher. The borrowers borrowed the funds anyway because they wanted to buy houses even though they knew or should have known that they might not be able to keep up with the loan payments in future. Third, many investors in the SPE did not understand the risks they were taking on in investing in this type of pool of assets, which was systemically risky due to the creditworthiness of the borrowers and the structure of the mortgages (the interest rate reset feature).

Things began to unwind when the mortgages' interest rates were set higher. This caused many borrowers to default on the mortgages and lose their homes. These homes were repossessed and flooded the market, driving the prices of homes down. Many borrowers found that their mortgages were now higher than the value of their homes and then walked away from their debt, causing more homes to go on sale in an already depressed market. The investors in the SPE suffered large losses due to the defaulted loans. All this contributed to a depressed economy.

From a financial reporting perspective, a few lessons were driven home:

1. Many capital market participants act in their own self-interest to the potential detriment of others.

2. The amount and nature of risk is not always properly communicated to investors.

3. Investors do not always understand what they are investing in.

All stakeholders in the capital marketplace are working to ensure that this type of situation does not recur.

OBJECTIVE OF FINANCIAL REPORTING

To help establish a foundation for financial accounting and reporting, the accounting profession has put into words an overall objective of financial reporting by business enterprises.

The overall objective is to provide financial information that is useful to users (primarily capital providers such as investors and lenders) and that is decision relevant (i.e., will help them make decisions about allocating capital). The statements should communicate information about:

1. the entity's economic resources and claims to those resources and

2. changes in those resources and claims.[6]

Note the emphasis on **resource (or capital) allocation** decisions. The assessment of management stewardship is also important since users need to know whether management is doing their job to maximize shareholder value.[7] As a general rule, it is assumed that management stewardship is already taken into account in the resource allocation decision.

4 Objective
Identify the objective of financial reporting.

Management Bias

As previously mentioned, the company is responsible for preparing its financial statements and normally states this fact at the beginning of the financial statements. This makes most sense since management best understands the business and therefore is best suited to communicating information about the business to users. At **Eastern Platinum Limited (EPL)**, the interim statements are signed by David Cohen and Robert Gayton, directors of the company. The EPL statements are shown in Appendix 5B.

Care must be taken when using financial statements, however. Many companies have been accused of preparing **biased information**, which is information that presents the company in its best light. This is sometimes referred to as **aggressive financial reporting** (as compared with **conservative financial reporting**) and might take the form of

Real-World Emphasis

---

[6] This is taken from the IASB/FASB jointly published Exposure Draft. There is a slight shift in this wording to focus on investors and creditors as main users and capital allocation as the key use for the information. In addition, note that the information has a balance sheet focus, emphasizing resources and claims.

[7] Management's duty to manage assets with care and trust is also called its fiduciary responsibility.

Objective 5

Explain the notion of management bias in financial reporting.

overstated assets and/or net income, understated liabilities and/or expenses, or carefully selected note disclosures that emphasize only positive events.[8]

There are many reasons why financial statements might be affected by management bias. These include the fact that the statements give information to users about **management stewardship**, as previously mentioned, and the fact that managers are often compensated (i.e., paid) based on the company's net income or share value. There is also a strong desire to **meet financial analysts' expectations** as this affects a company's access to capital markets. Financial analysts monitor earnings announcements carefully and compare them with their earlier expectations. They and others (including certain stock markets) post what they refer to as "**earnings surprises**" each day on their websites. Earnings surprises occur when a company reports net income figures that are different from what the market expects (prior expectations). The focus is on net income or earnings. If net income is lower than expected, this is a negative earnings surprise and the market will generally react unfavourably, resulting in declining share prices.[9]

Another cause of financial reporting bias is management's desire **to comply with contracts** that the company has. Many lending agreements and contracts require that certain benchmarks be met, and these often relate to financial stability or liquidity. These requirements often state that the company must maintain certain minimum financial ratios. The lenders then monitor whether the company is respecting the contract by reviewing periodic financial statements that the company must submit.

An example of a restriction in a company contract that affects financial reporting is a debt covenant. The following is an excerpt from the financial statements of **Tim Hortons Inc.**'s 2008 financial statements and illustrates the existence of debt covenants, which focus on two financial ratios.

Illustration   1-5

Excerpt from Tim Hortons Inc.
Financial Statements

Real-World Emphasis

NOTE 14 TERM DEBT

Prior to March 2006, the Company was a wholly owned subsidiary of Wendy's. Accordingly, the Company did not historically seek significant external financing as its cash requirements were funded primarily by Wendy's.

On February 28, 2006, as amended on April 24, 2006, effective February 28, 2006, the Company entered into an unsecured five-year senior bank facility with a syndicate of Canadian and U.S. financial institutions that consists of a $300.0 million Canadian term loan; a $200.0 million Canadian revolving credit facility (which includes $15.0 million in overdraft availability and a $25.0 million letter of credit facility); and a US$100.0 million U.S. revolving credit facility (which includes a US$10.0 million letter of credit facility) (together referred to as the "senior bank facility"). The senior bank facility matures on February 28, 2011. The term loan bears interest at a variable rate per annum equal to Canadian prime rate or, alternatively, the Company may elect to borrow by way of banker's acceptances (or loans equivalent thereto) plus a margin. The senior bank facility contains various covenants which, among other things, requres the maintenance of two financial ratios—a consolidated maximum total debt to earnings before interest expenses, taxes, depreciation and amortization ("EBITDA") ratio and a minimum fixed charge coverage ratio. The Company was in compliance with these covenants as at December 28, 2008.

---

[8] This is not a new problem. David Brown, chairman of the Ontario Securities Commission (OSC), spoke at length on this topic in a speech in 1999 entitled "Public Accounting at a Crossroads." Arthur Levitt, chair of the Securities and Exchange Commission (SEC), discussed his concerns over this issue in "Numbers Game," a major address to New York University in 1998. Both the OSC and the SEC review financial statements and financial reporting practices to ensure that investors have "full and plain disclosure" of all material facts that are needed to make investment decisions. In their speeches, Mr. Brown and Mr. Levitt both cited specific cases where they felt that financial reporting practices were problematic.

[9] For instance, for quarterly earnings numbers released on August 21, 2009, the NASDAQ website notes that there were 27 positive earnings surprises and 5 negative earnings surprises. Positive earnings surprises included Barnes and Noble, which had higher earnings than expected, and Intuit, which had lower losses than expected. Selected negative earnings surprises noted for the same day included Footlocker, whose earnings were lower than expected and reported at $0, and Sears Holdings, whose earnings went from an expected 35 cents per share to a loss of 47 cents per share.

Users' Needs

The objective of financial reporting is to **provide useful information to users**. As noted in Illustration 1-3, investors and creditors are among the key users of financial information. Providing information that is useful to users is a challenging task since they have **different needs and levels of knowledge**. Institutional investors[10] hold an increasing percentage of equity share holdings[11] and generally put a lot of their resources into managing their investment portfolios. Can those who prepare financial information therefore assume that the average individual investor has the same needs and knowledge level as an institutional investor when it comes to business and financial reporting? Likely not.

    Meeting all user needs is made more challenging when linked with the potential for management bias. If the financial statements are aggressively prepared, they might be misleading to potential investors, who may want to see a company in its worst light **before** they decide to invest (as opposed to after). Generally accepted accounting principles assume that users have a **reasonable knowledge** of business and accounting.

6 Objective
Understand the importance of user needs in the financial reporting process.

STANDARD SETTING

Need to Develop Standards

The main controversy in financial reporting is this: "Whose rules should we play by, and what should they be?" The answer is not immediately clear. This is because the users of financial statements have both **coinciding and conflicting needs** for information of various types. A **single set** of general-purpose financial statements is therefore prepared with the **expectation** that the majority of these needs will be met by the statements. These statements are also expected to present the enterprise's financial operations fairly.

    As a result, accounting professions in various countries have tried to develop a **set of standards** that are **generally accepted** and **universally practised**. Without these standards, each enterprise would have to develop its own standards, and readers of financial statements would have to become familiar with every company's particular accounting and reporting practices. It would be almost impossible to prepare statements that could be compared.

    This common set of standards and procedures is called generally accepted accounting principles (GAAP). The term "generally accepted" means either that an authoritative rule-making body in accounting has created a reporting principle in a particular area or that, over time, a specific practice has been accepted as appropriate because it is used universally.[12] International GAAP is often referred to as International Financial Reporting Standards (IFRS). Although principles and practices have resulted in both debate and

7 Objective
Explain the need for accounting standards.

---

[10] Institutional investors are corporate investors such as insurance companies, pension plans, mutual funds, and others. They are considered a separate class of investors because of their size and financial expertise, and the large size of the investments that they hold in other companies. In general, for the reasons just mentioned, institutional investors have greater power than the average investor.

[11] The Canadian Coalition for Good Governance (CCGG) is a group of institutional investors that controls over $1 trillion in investments. Its members include many significant pension funds in Canada, such as Alberta Teachers' Retirement Fund, Ontario Teachers' Pension Plan, OPSEU Pension Trust, and Ontario Municipal Employees Retirement System, as well as many significant mutual funds and financial institutions such as Mackenzie Financial Corp., RBC Asset Management Inc., and TD Asset Management Inc. According to its website (www.ccgg.ca), CCGG was started in 2002 "to represent Canadian institutional shareholders in the promotion of corporate governance practices that best align the interests of boards and management with those of the shareholder." By working together, these shareholders, who represent many individual shareholders, can initiate positive change.

[12] The terms "principle" and "standard" are used interchangeably in practice and throughout this textbook.

criticism, most members of the financial community recognize them as the standards that over time have proven to be most useful. A more detailed discussion of GAAP is presented later in this chapter.

Parties Involved in Standard Setting

Objective 8

Identify the major entities that influence the standard-setting process and explain how they influence financial reporting.

Before 1900, single ownership was the most common form of business organization in our economy. Financial reports emphasized **solvency and liquidity** and were only for **internal use** or for banks and other lending institutions to examine. From 1900 to 1929, the growth of large corporations and their absentee ownership led to **increasing investment and speculation** in corporate stock. When the stock market crashed in 1929, this contributed to the Great Depression. These events emphasized the need for **standardized and increased corporate disclosures** that would allow shareholders to make informed decisions.

Several organizations play a role in developing financial reporting standards in Canada. The major organizations are:

1. Canadian Accounting Standards Board (AcSB): *www.acsbcanada.org*

2. International Accounting Standards Board (IASB): *www.iasb.org*

3. The Financial Accounting Standards Board (FASB): *www.fasb.org* and the Securities and Exchange Commission (SEC): *www.sec.gov*

4. Provincial securities commissions such as the Ontario Securities Commission (OSC): *www.osc.gov.on.ca*

The following chart shows how these organizations influence GAAP for Canadian entities. Each will be discussed in greater detail below.

Illustration 1-6

Various Entities Responsible for GAAP

	GAAP Responsibilities	Notes
AcSB	GAAP for private companies, pension plans, and not-for-profit entities	Private companies and not-for-profit entities may opt to use IFRS for periods beginning on or after January 1, 2011.
IASB	GAAP for public companies (referred to as IFRS, as previously noted)[13]	For periods beginning on or after January 1, 2011.
FASB	GAAP for U.S. entities (referred to as U.S. GAAP)	The FASB is working with the IASB toward convergence of standards.
Securities commissions	Not responsible for GAAP but often require additional disclosures for public companies	May grant Canadian public companies the right to adopt IFRS earlier or to use U.S. GAAP (in lieu of Canadian GAAP).

Canadian Accounting Standards Board (AcSB)

The first official recommendations on standards of financial statement disclosure were published in 1946 by the Canadian Institute of Chartered Accountants (CICA). Today, the Accounting Standards Board (AcSB) has primary responsibility for setting

---

[13] Technically, IFRS will be considered to be part of the Canadian *CICA Handbook* for legal reasons although the *CICA Handbook* as it relates to IFRS will exactly mirror the IASB standards. This was done as an interim measure as many Canadian laws refer to Canadian GAAP. At some point, these laws will be amended to reflect the fact that GAAP for public companies in Canada is IFRS per the IASB.

GAAP in Canada[14] and produces a variety of authoritative material, including the most important source of GAAP, the *CICA Handbook*. The *CICA Handbook* was originally published in 1968 and now consists of several volumes of accounting and assurance guidance.[15]

The AcSB's mission is as follows:

> to contribute to enhanced decision-making by continuously improving the quality of financial and other information about organizational performance reported by Canadian entities including profit oriented enterprises and not-for-profit organizations. The AcSB shall serve the public interest by developing and establishing standards and guidance governing financial accounting and reporting domestically and by contributing to the development of internationally accepted standards.[16]

Two basic premises underlie the process of establishing financial accounting standards: (1) the AcSB should **respond to the needs and viewpoints** of the **entire economic community**, not just the public accounting profession, and (2) it should **operate in full public view** through a "due process" system that gives interested persons enough opportunity to make their views known. The Accounting Standards Oversight Council (AcSOC) oversees AcSB activities. Its activities include providing input to the activities of the AcSB and reporting to the public, among other things. Members of the AcSB and the AcSOC come from a wide range of groups that are interested or involved in the financial reporting process.[17]

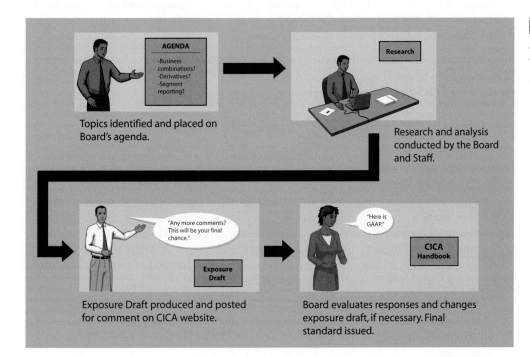

Illustration 1-7

Evolution of a New or Revised Canadian Standard

---

[14] The *Canada Business Corporations Act and Regulations* (CBCA) Part XIV Financial Disclosure and Part 8 (paras. 70 and 71), as well as provincial corporations acts, require that most companies incorporated under these acts prepare financial statements in accordance with GAAP per the *CICA Handbook*.

[15] The *Handbook* is also available to students and members on-line. With the rapid pace of change in standard setting, most members use the on-line source as their main source of GAAP.

[16] www.acsbcanada.org

[17] According to the CICA website, AcSOC membership consists of senior members from business, finance, government, academe, the accounting and legal professions, regulators, and the financial analyst community. The members have a broad perspective on the complex issues facing standard setters. The goal is to achieve full representation across the spectrum of stakeholders.

The steps in Illustration 1-7 show the evolution of a typical addition or amendment to the *CICA Handbook*.

Due process, by definition, is a lengthy process. To react more quickly to current financial reporting issues, the AcSB established the Emerging Issues Committee (EIC) in 1988. The EIC's original role was to study issues that were presented to it by interested parties, such as companies that need a ruling on an accounting issue that was not covered or sufficiently dealt with in the *Handbook*. After careful consideration, the EIC would produce EIC Abstracts, which would then be incorporated into the *Handbook*.[18]

The AcSB has historically been responsible for setting standards for public and private entities as well as not-for-profit entities (including some profit-oriented government entities). As noted in Illustration 1-6, starting in 2011, the AcSB will be responsible for setting standards for private enterprises, not-for-profit entities, and pension plans only. Standards for publicly accountable entities will be set by the International Accounting Standards Board. This approach makes sense for a number of reasons, including the following:

1. Public companies operate globally and often raise funds in global capital markets; therefore, it makes sense to have a common language for reporting financial position and performance so that users can compare companies.

2. Private companies often operate locally, have less complex business models and fewer users who are often close to the company, and can gain other information about the business first hand. Therefore, it makes sense to have a separate GAAP that is less complicated, has fewer disclosures, and is geared toward fewer users who have access to additional information about the company.

Note that there are some private companies that are global and complex. These entities have the option to use IFRS. Private entities that are looking to go public may find it easier to follow IFRS right from the beginning.[19]

International Accounting Standards Board (IASB)

Most countries agree that more uniform standards are needed. As a result, the International Accounting Standards Committee (IASC) was formed in 1973 to try to lessen the areas of difference. The IASC's objective in standard setting was to work generally to improve and harmonize regulations, accounting standards, and procedures relating to the presentation of financial statements. Eliminating differences is not easy: the financial reporting objectives in each country are different, the institutional structures are often not comparable, and there are strong national tendencies in most countries. Nevertheless, much progress has been made since the IASC's early days. In 2001, a new International Accounting Standards Board (IASB) was created.

According to the IASB website, its aims are as follows:

> Our mission is to develop, in the public interest, a single set of high quality, understandable and international financial reporting standards (IFRSs) for general purpose financial statements.

Illustration 1-8 shows the governing structure of the IASB. As shown in the diagram, the IASC Foundation monitors, reviews the effectiveness of, appoints members to,

---

[18] In 2009, the AcSB issued an Exposure Draft and concluded that all EIC Abstracts would be withdrawn once Canada moves to IFRS for publicly accountable enterprises in 2011. This will be discussed further in this chapter. For private entities, pension plans, and not-for-profit entities, any relevant material from the EIC has been incorporated into the respective *CICA Handbook* sections.

[19] Actually, there are six sets of GAAP in Canada. The CICA Handbook is divided into four parts: Part I - IFRS (for publicly accountable entreprises), Part II - Accounting Standards for Private Entreprises, Part III - Accounting Standards for Not-for-profit Organizations, and Part IV - Accounting Standards for Pension Plans. In addition, the Public Sector Accounting Standards Handbook contains GAAP for governments. Finally, as mentioned earlier, the OSC allows Canadian public companies who are U.S. reporting issuers to use U.S. GAAP.

and funds the IASB. Similar to the EIC, the **International Financial Reporting Interpretation Committee (IFRIC)** studies issues where guidance in IASB is insufficient or non-existent. If necessary, it produces additional guidance in the form of IFRIC interpretations, which are part of IFRS.

The **Standards Advisory Council (SAC)** is composed of various user groups, such as preparers of financial statements, analysts, auditors, regulators, professional accounting bodies, and academics. As its name suggests, it provides guidance and feedback to the IASB.

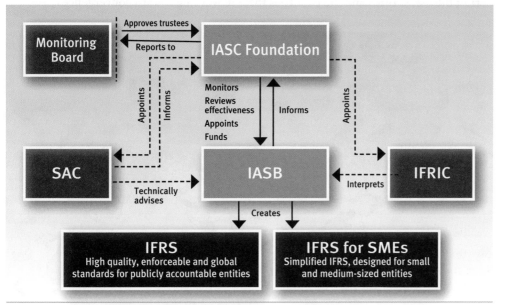

Illustration 1-8

How the IASB Is Set Up[20]

Illustration 1-9 shows the various stages in producing an international standard.

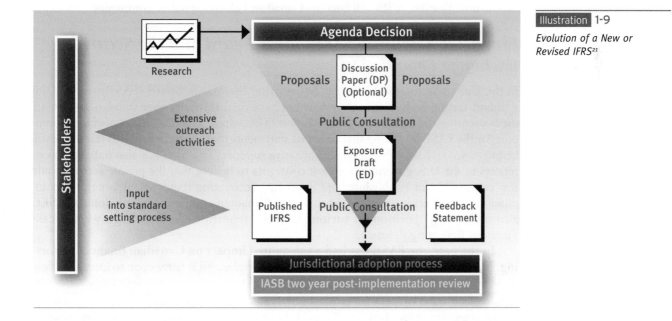

Illustration 1-9

Evolution of a New or Revised IFRS[21]

---

[20] International Accounting Standards Committee Foundation. 'How we are structured'. *Who we are and what we do*. July 13, 2009. Copyright © 2009 IASC Foundation.

[21] International Accounting Standards Committee Foundation. 'How we develop standards'. *Who we are and what we do*. July 13, 2009. Copyright © 2009 IASC Foundation.

Note that the process is very similar to the Canadian and U.S. processes. One difference is the existence and increased use of Discussion Papers (DP). DP are often the predecessors of Exposure Drafts (ED). When IFRS are being formulated, the IASB may issue a DP and ask for comment letters just as they do for ED. Therefore, by the time the proposed standard gets to the ED stage, many key decisions have already been made.[22]

The IASB is quickly becoming the dominant standard-setting body in the world. By the year 2005, over 7,000 companies in over 100 countries had adopted IASB standards and the list continues to grow. Illustration 1-10 shows the countries that have adopted or permit the use of IFRS and the countries that are working toward convergence.

Illustration 1-10

Countries that Allow or Use IFRS or Are Seeking Convergence[23]

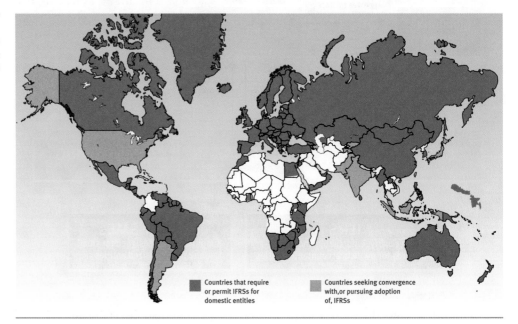

Countries that require or permit IFRSs for domestic entities

Countries seeking convergence with, or pursuing adoption of, IFRSs

As noted earlier, IFRS will become Canadian GAAP for public companies.

Financial Accounting Standards Board and the Securities Exchange Commission

In the United States, the Financial Accounting Standards Board (FASB) is the major standard-setting body, although it does not have final authority over standards—instead, the Securities and Exchange Commission (SEC) does. The SEC has confirmed its support for the FASB by stating that financial statements that conform to FASB standards will be presumed to have substantial authoritative support. The SEC has also indicated in its reports to the U.S. government that it continues to believe that the private sector should stay responsible for establishing and improving accounting standards, although the commission must oversee any changes. Like the Canadian securities commissions, the SEC also indicates its position on various financial reporting issues through what it calls Financial Reporting Releases.

In the past, the FASB has had a substantial impact on Canadian financial reporting. First, since Canadian GAAP is based on principles and is fairly open to interpretation,

---

[22] For instance, the IASB issued DP for revenue recognition, financial statement presentation, and fair value measurement and received 221, 227, and 136 comment letters, respectively. These comment letters were used to draft the subsequent ED.

[23] International Accounting Standards Committee Foundation. 'Since 2001, over 100 countries have required or permitted the use of IFRSs'. *Who we are and what we do.* July 13 2009. Copyright © 2009 IASC Foundation.

accounting professionals have often relied on the more rule-oriented, specific guidance provided in the FASB pronouncements. Second, many Canadian companies are also listed on U.S. stock markets and exchanges such as NASDAQ (National Association of Securities Dealers Automated Quotation) and the NYSE (New York Stock Exchange). To be listed on a U.S. exchange, these companies **must follow U.S. GAAP**[24] **or IFRS.**[25] As we move toward international harmonization in accounting standards, the U.S. standards will continue to influence Canadian and international standards due to the significant capital pool of these markets. This brings us to the third point. In October 2002, the FASB and IASB signed an agreement (the Norwalk Agreement) that formalizes their commitment to converge U.S. and international accounting standards. Thus, many new IFRS standards have been and will continue to be heavily influenced by the deliberations of the FASB.

Provincial Securities Commissions

Provincial securities commissions[26] oversee and monitor the capital marketplace. They ensure that participants in the capital markets (e.g., companies, auditors, brokers and dealers, and investors) respect securities law and legislation so that, ultimately, the marketplace is fair. For instance, the British Columbia Securities Commission (www.bcsc.bc.ca) states that its mission is to protect and promote the public interest by fostering:

• a securities market that is fair and warrants public confidence

• a dynamic and competitive securities industry that provides investment opportunities and access to capital

As part of ensuring that investors have access to the information that they need in order to make informed decisions, securities law and legislation requires that companies that issue shares to the public and whose shares trade on a Canadian stock exchange or stock market produce GAAP financial statements. The commissions generally rely on the CICA to develop GAAP and on professional accountants to use sound judgement as they apply GAAP.

Ontario is home to the largest stock exchange in Canada, the Toronto Stock Exchange (TSX), and most large public companies are therefore registered with the Ontario Securities Commission (OSC). The OSC reviews and monitors the financial statements of companies whose shares are publicly traded so that it can judge whether the

---

[24] U.S. GAAP is a mixture of more than 2,000 documents that have developed over the past 60 years or so. It includes items such as FASB Standards (SFAS), Interpretations, and Staff Positions; APB Opinions; and AICPA Research Bulletins. The body of knowledge is very prescriptive and detailed and therefore very complex and difficult to follow. In the past several years, the FASB has undertaken a process whereby all the standards have been collected in one database. The database has been resorted, reorganized, and the standards cross-referenced. This project is generally referred to as the Codification project. All standards have been renumbered under this new system and it is hoped that the body of knowledge will now be easier to access, research, and understand.

[25] Before 2007, Canadian companies that were listed on U.S. exchanges could use IFRS or Canadian GAAP but had to include a reconciliation to U.S. GAAP. This reconciliation was difficult and cumbersome and many Canadian entities decided to just use U.S. GAAP for their U.S. filings. The OSC allows Canadian reporting issuers to use U.S. GAAP or Canadian GAAP (subject to any reporting requirements under the company's incorporating legislation) per CSA National Instrument 52-107. For 2011, Canadian GAAP for public entities will be IFRS.

[26] In Canada, securities regulation is carried out by each province, with each of the 10 provinces and three territories being responsible for the companies in its jurisdiction. Many critics feel that this is cumbersome and costly, and are therefore lobbying for a national securities commission. There has been some movement in this direction. The provincial and territorial regulators have formed the Canadian Securities Administrators (CSA). The CSA is mainly responsible for developing a harmonized approach to securities regulation across the country (www.csa-acvm.ca). For now, the CSA collects and archives all filings that are required under the securities regulations of each province and territory (www.sedar.com).

statements present the financial position and results of operations of these companies fairly.[27] It also issues its own disclosure requirements, which inform companies about how the OSC interprets GAAP.[28] Stock exchanges, as well as securities commissions, have the ability to fine a company and/or delist the company's shares from the stock exchange, which removes a company's access to capital markets.

Standard Setting in a Political Environment

When it comes to influencing the development of accounting standards, the most powerful force may be the stakeholder. Standard-setting stakeholders are the parties who are most interested in or affected by accounting standards, rules, and procedures. Like lobbyists in the provincial and national government arena, stakeholders play a significant role. **Accounting standards result as much from political action as they do from careful logic or empirical findings.** As part of its mandate, the AcSB includes all stakeholders as its members, giving them a **formal voice** in the process. Furthermore, through due process, all interested parties can comment on proposed changes or new standards.

Stakeholders may want particular economic events to be accounted for or reported in a particular way, and they fight hard to get what they want. They know that the most effective way to influence the standards that dictate accounting practice is to participate in formulating them or to try to influence or persuade the formulator.

Should politics play a role in setting financial accounting and reporting standards? The AcSB and IASB do not exist in isolation. Standard setting is part of the real world, and it cannot escape politics and political pressures. That is not to say that politics in standard setting is necessarily bad. Since many accounting standards do have economic consequences,[29] it is not surprising that special interest groups become vocal and critical (some supporting, some opposing) when standards are being formulated. Given this reality, a standard-setting body must pay attention to the economic consequences of its actions; at the same time, however, it should not issue pronouncements that are motivated mainly by politics. While paying attention to its constituencies, standard setters should base their standards on sound research and a conceptual framework that is grounded in economic reality.[30]

The political nature of standard setting has become more of an issue as more and more countries have adopted IFRS. The IASB has 15 (soon to be 16 by 2012) members from 9 countries. It must consider the needs of all users when creating or changing standards. These user needs become more diverse as we consider the different political, cultural, economic, social, and legal settings of an increasing number of countries.

The IASB has committed to four principles to ensure that the nature and amount of funding for standard setting does not result in politicization of standard setting. The principles are as follows per the IASB website:

---

[27] The OSC has a Continuous Disclosure Team that regularly reviews public companies' financial statements and other regulatory findings. The team plans to review each company at least every four years. Results of the review are published on the OSC website.

[28] For instance, Rules 51-501 and 52-501 were issued in 2000 and deal with disclosures for annual and interim financial statements. In 2002, Staff Accounting Notice 52-303 on "Non-GAAP Earnings Measures" was issued.

[29] "Economic consequences" in this context means the impact of accounting reports on the wealth positions of issuers and users of financial information and the decision-making behaviour resulting from that impact. The resulting behaviour of these individuals and groups could have harmful financial effects on the providers of the financial information (enterprises). For a more detailed discussion of this phenomenon, see Stephen A. Zeff, "The Rise of Economic Consequences," *Journal of Accountancy* (December 1978), pp. 56–63.

[30] Politicization is a big issue for the IASB as more and more countries adopt IFRS.

Funding should be:

1. Broad-based: It should not rely on one or a few sources.

2. Compelling: Constituents should not be allowed to benefit from the standards without contributing to the process of standard setting.

3. Open-ended: Financial commitments for funding should not be contingent upon any particular outcomes that may infringe upon independence in the standard-setting process.

4. Country-specific: Funding should be shared by the major economies on a proportionate basis.[31]

GENERALLY ACCEPTED ACCOUNTING PRINCIPLES

GAAP includes **not only specific rules, practices, and procedures** for particular circumstances but also **broad principles and conventions that apply generally**, including underlying concepts.

9 Objective
Explain the meaning of generally accepted accounting principles (GAAP).

GAAP Hierarchy

The GAAP hierarchy identifies the sources of GAAP and lets users know which ones should be consulted first in asking the question: What is GAAP?

For private companies, pension plans, and not-for-profit entities, GAAP is divided into **primary sources** and **other sources**. Based on *Handbook*, Part II, Section 1100, the **primary** sources of GAAP (in descending order of authority) are as follows:

- *Handbook* Sections 1400 to 3870, including Appendices; and

- **Accounting guidelines**, including Appendices.

Other sources noted in Section 1100 include:

- **Background information and basis for conclusion documents issued by the AcSB**

- **AcSB implementation guidance**

- **Pronouncements** by accounting standard-setting bodies in other jurisdictions, although it is not necessary to comply with guidance in IFRS or other GAAP in order to comply with Canadian GAAP for private entities.[32]

- **Approved drafts of primary sources** of GAAP where no primary sources apply (e.g., exposure drafts)

- **Research studies**

- Accounting **textbooks, journals, studies, and articles**

- Other sources, including industry practice

---

[31] These principles were established in 2008. The 2009 budget was set at 18.4 million pounds sterling.
[32] *CICA Handbook*, Part II, Section 1100.20.

In general, primary sources must be looked at **first** for how to treat an issue. If primary sources do not deal with the specific issue, the entity should use accounting policies that are **consistent with the primary sources** as well as developed through use of professional judgement in accordance with the concepts in Section 1000 (the **conceptual framework**). As business is constantly changing and new business transactions and contracts are regularly being entered into, the other listed sources are also important sources of GAAP.

For public companies (under IFRS), GAAP incorporates:[33]

- IFRS

- International Accounting Standards (IAS) (these are standards that were issued by the IASB's predecessor[34])

- Interpretations (IFRIC or the former Standards Interpretation Committee [SIC]).

Where the above do not specifically apply, management uses professional judgement (in considering the applicability of similar IFRS in similar situations in applying the conceptual framework) as long as the resulting information is relevant and reliable. The following sources would be considered, in descending order:

- Pronouncements of other standard-setting bodies

- Other accounting literature

- Accepted industry practices

In essence, although the wording is different, both hierarchies are similar, as follows:

- They provide guidance that helps answer the question "What is GAAP?"

- They both rank sources and consider certain sources as more important.

- They are both grounded in the conceptual framework.

- They both establish the value of and envisage the use of professional judgement.

Professional Judgement

Objective **10**
Explain the significance of professional judgement in applying GAAP.

Professional judgement plays an especially important role in private entity GAAP and IFRS.[35] This is due to the basic philosophy of Canadian and international accountants on standard setting: the idea that **there cannot be a rule for every situation**. Private entity GAAP and IFRS are therefore based primarily on **general principles** rather than **specific rules**. The basic premise is that professional accountants with significant education and experience will be able to apply these principles appropriately to any situation.

In a principles-based standard-setting system, the conceptual framework underlies the standards. Therefore, accountants either apply specific standards that are based on the conceptual framework, or, if no specific standard exists, the accountant uses the conceptual framework and professional judgement to reason through to an answer, as noted previously as part of the GAAP hierarchy.[36] Chapter 2 examines the conceptual framework in

---

[33] IAS 8.

[34] The IASB decided to retain the old numbering system for these standards for familiarity and to signal that these standards are older and originated from the IASB's predecessor, the IASC.

[35] U.S. GAAP is often said to be more rules-based and more prescriptive, and provides significantly more detailed guidance.

[36] Neither Canadian GAAP for private entities nor IFRS is a perfect principles-based system. The conceptual frameworks for both were written after many of the other standards were written. Therefore, there may be inconsistencies. Standard setters are working to rid the body of knowledge of these inconsistencies.

greater detail. As can be seen from the previous discussion, the conceptual framework is foundational in terms of financial reporting.

Role of Ethics

In accounting, as in other areas of business, ethical dilemmas are common. Some of these dilemmas are simple and easy to resolve. Many, however, are complex, and solutions are not obvious. Management biases—either internally prompted (e.g., to maximize bonuses) or externally prompted (e.g., to meet analysts' earnings expectations)—are the starting point of many ethical dilemmas. These biases sometimes lead to an emphasis on short-term results over long-term results and place accountants (both inside and outside the company) in an environment of conflict and pressure. Basic questions such as "Is this way of communicating financial information transparent?", "Does it provide useful information?", and "What should I do in this circumstance?" cannot always be answered by simply staying with GAAP or following the rules of the profession. Technical competence is not enough when decisions have an ethical side.

Doing the **right thing** and making the right decision is not always easy. What is right is not always evident and the pressures to "bend the rules," "play the game," or "just ignore it" can be considerable. In these cases, self-interest must be balanced with the interests of others. The decision is more difficult because no consensus has emerged among business professionals as to what constitutes a comprehensive ethical system.

This process of **ethical sensitivity** and choosing among alternatives can also be complicated by time pressures, job pressures, client pressures, personal pressures, and peer pressures. Throughout this textbook, ethical considerations are presented to make you aware of the types of situations that you may encounter in your professional responsibility.

11 Objective
Understand issues related to ethics and financial accounting.

Expanded Discussion of Ethical Issues in Financial Accounting

CHALLENGES FACING FINANCIAL REPORTING

In North America, we have the most liquid, deep, secure, and efficient public capital markets of any place at any time in history. One reason for this success is that our financial statements and related disclosures have captured and organized financial information in a useful and reliable way. However, much still needs to be done. During 2001 and 2002, the future of the capital market system was challenged by several major corporate scandals, as mentioned earlier in this chapter. The resulting turmoil gave all stakeholders a chance to re-examine their roles in the capital marketplace and to question if and how they add value to the system.

In the United States, where many of the financial reporting problems occurred, the result was to increase government regulation in the capital marketplace. The *Sarbanes-Oxley Act* (**SOX**), enacted in 2002, gave more resources to the SEC to fight fraud and poor reporting practices.[37] The SEC was able to **increase its policing efforts** and approve **new auditor independence rules** and **materiality guidelines** for financial reporting. In addition, SOX introduced sweeping changes to the institutional structure of the accounting profession. The following are some of the legislation's key provisions:

- An accounting oversight board was established and given oversight and enforcement authority. It was mandated to establish auditing, quality control, and independence standards and rules, and is known as the **Public Company Accounting Oversight Board** or **PCAOB**.

12 Objective
Identify some of the challenges facing accounting.

Ethics

---

[37] *Sarbanes-Oxley Act of 2002*, H. R. Rep. No. 107-610 (2002).

- Stronger **independence rules** were made for auditors. Audit partners, for example, are required to rotate every five years.

- CEOs and CFOs must **forfeit bonuses and profits** if there is a restatement of their companies' accounting disclosures.

- CEOs and CFOs are required to **certify** that the financial statements and company disclosures are appropriate and fairly presented.

- Company management must report on **the effectiveness of the financial reporting internal control systems** and the auditors must assess and report on these internal controls.

- **Audit committees** must have independent members and members with financial expertise.

- Companies must disclose whether they have a **code of ethics** for their senior financial officers.

Stakeholders in the capital marketplace were faced with the question of whether similar reforms should be put in place in Canada. Companies that issue shares in the United States are bound by SOX[38] and these companies therefore have no choice. Many stakeholders feel that unless Canada matches the standard set by SOX, Canadian capital markets will be seen as inferior. As a result, many of the SOX requirements have now been put in place as follows:

- The **Canadian Public Accountability Board** (www.cpab-ccrc.ca) has been formed to look after similar issues as the PCAOB.

- The **CSA** has issued rules that, among other things, require company management to take responsibility for the appropriateness and fairness of the financial statements, public companies to have independent audit committees, and public accounting firms to be subject to the Canadian Public Accountability Board.[39]

- The **CSA** has issued a harmonized statement that requires much greater disclosures, including ratings from rating agencies, payments by companies to stock promoters, legal proceedings, and details about directors, including their previous involvement with bankrupt companies.[40]

- The **province of Ontario** has made amendments to its *Securities Act*.

The impact of these reforms on the North American capital marketplace has been to put **more emphasis on government regulation** and less on **self-regulation**.

Globalization of Companies and Capital Markets

Many companies list on foreign stock exchanges. Larger stock exchanges are encouraging these listings as on-line trading has made these markets (and through the markets, the companies) more accessible to investors. Trading now happens around the clock. The move is thus toward global markets and global investors. The financial reporting environment is no longer limited by Canadian borders and is not simply influenced by Canadian stakeholders.

---

[38] *Sarbanes-Oxley Act of 2002*, Section 106 (2002).

[39] CSA Multilateral Instrument 52-109, 52-110, and 52-108. A multilateral instrument is an instrument that has been adopted by one or more CSA jurisdictions.

[40] CSA revised National Instrument 51-102, "Continuous Disclosure Obligations." A national instrument is an instrument that has been adopted by all CSA jurisdictions.

As mentioned in this chapter, Canadian, U.S., and international accounting standards are becoming increasingly interrelated. All parties are committed to a convergence of standards, but there are still many issues that standard setters must deal with. One key issue is the **principles versus rules** debate regarding GAAP.

The **United States uses a rules-based approach**. In a rules-based approach—much like the Canadian tax system—there is a rule for most things. The result is that the body of knowledge is significantly larger. There is also a tendency for companies to interpret the rules literally. Many companies take the view that if there is no rule for a particular situation, they are free to choose whatever treatment they think is appropriate. Similarly, many believe that as long as they comply with a rule, even in a narrow sense, they are in accordance with GAAP. Unfortunately, this does not always provide the best information for users. This particular issue is a significant one in terms of the U.S. decision to adopt IFRS or not.[41]

Impact of Technology

Accountants are **providers of information**. They **identify, measure, and communicate useful information to users**. Technology affects this process in many profound ways. In its Report of the Inter-Institute Vision Task Force, the CICA concluded that we are presently in the third wave of computer technology. The first wave related to mainframes and the second wave related to personal computers. The third wave is driven by the use of networks and a convergence of computers and telecommunications technologies. Companies are now connected electronically to their banks, their suppliers, and regulatory agencies. The task force notes that in this third wave, automation focuses on stakeholders, distribution, and consumption. This gives stakeholders easy access to a significant amount of very timely company information.

As technology continues to advance at a dramatic pace, giving users **greater access to more and more information more and more rapidly**, the requirement for information that is more timely than annual and quarterly financial statements will rise sharply. Will this lead to **on-line real-time and/or continuous reporting**? Will this make users rely less on annual financial statements because they are not as timely and therefore relevant? Will this change the role of the public accountant?

The Internet's flexibility allows users to take advantage of tools such as search engines and hyperlinks and quickly find related information about a company. Financial reports are more relevant because the Internet allows companies to disclose more detail, which the user can then aggregate and analyze. From the company's perspective, providing information over the Internet gives the company access to a much larger group of users. Information can also be targeted to specific users, and costs are greatly reduced as well. This issue will be discussed further in Chapter 3.

Some of the main drawbacks concern accessibility: will all users have the knowledge and ability to access the information? Equal access is certainly important for a fair playing field. Another issue is the quality and reliability of the information, especially since the information may not be audited. Would certain sites and content be more reliable than others? Finally, would making information available in this way leave companies open to computer hackers?

A continuous reporting model is already being developed in the capital markets arena. Securities commissions and stock markets already require ongoing disclosures from public companies and monitor these disclosures. Companies can now file required disclosures electronically with securities commissions. Investors can log on to a website

---

[41] The SEC issued a Roadmap in 2008 to mandate a move to IFRS for public companies by 2016. It has subsequently backed off any definitive plans to mandate IFRS. Having said this, there is agreement between the IASB and FASB to work together toward convergence. Note that adoption of IFRS is not necessarily the same as convergence with IFRS. Under convergence, the two sets of standards might still exist side by side and have differing aspects.

and tap into conversations, including earnings calls, briefings with analysts, and interviews with senior management and market regulators. In the past, these conversations were not accessible to the average investor.

Changing Nature of the Economy

Real-World Emphasis

Much of North America is transforming from an economy based on traditional manufacturing and resource extraction to what has become known in the past decade as a **"knowledge-based" economy**.[42] In terms of the market value of publicly traded shares, such companies, including **IBM, Apple Inc.**, and **Hewlett Packard**, dominate the North American markets. What these companies all have in common is that a large percentage of the value given to their shares is linked to such factors as their **relationships with customers and suppliers, knowledge base or intellectual assets, ability to adapt to a changing technological environment, and skillful leadership**. This is different from the more traditional manufacturing and resource-based economy, where value was more closely linked to physical and tangible assets and financing.

Most of the assets of these "new economy" companies cannot be seen in the balance sheet, yet they are mostly responsible for the companies' value. As noted by the CICA:

> In light of these shifts [i.e., in the economy], to maintain its relevancy, the [accounting] profession must move beyond interpreting the past. Increasingly what matters is the ability for organizational decision-makers to be positioned for the future. This ability to look forward is driven by one's ability to measure organizational performance along an increasingly broad spectrum of measures, both financial and non-financial. … Chartered Accountants must provide decision-makers with the tools necessary to measure and report on organizational performance in all its aspects, not just the historical and financial.[43]

The knowledge-based companies that are beginning to dominate capital markets need **more relevant models for measuring and reporting value in order to evaluate assets that are currently not recognized on the balance sheet**. There has been little progress in this area so far because of the difficulty of objectively valuing these assets and their potential impact on future earnings. Despite this difficulty, underwriting firms such as **CIBC World Markets** are in fact valuing these types of companies all the time when there are securities offerings or mergers and acquisitions. The market also values these assets, and the companies that house them, through share prices. How, if at all, can these values be shown in the financial statements?

Increased Requirement for Accountability

There is a **growing number of institutional investors**, partly because more and more capital is being invested in pension plans and mutual funds. The impact is that investors have become **more sophisticated and knowledgeable**. Institutional investors, because of their size, have **greater representation in corporate boardrooms** and are thus more involved in running the companies they invest in. As a result, companies are being pushed toward **increased accountability**.

Financial performance is rooted in a company's business model (i.e., the earnings process, how companies finance the process, and what resources companies invest in). While historically, this has not always been the focus of financial accounting, a company's ability to articulate its strategic vision and carry out that vision affects financial performance. The

---

[42] R. McLean, *The Canadian Performance Reporting Initiative* (Toronto: Ontario Premier's Council and the CICA, ongoing), Chapter 2.

[43] *Report of the Inter-Institute Vision Task Force* (Toronto: CICA, 1996), p. 9.

accounting information system is also part of a larger system of information management—a system that contains a significant amount of non-financial information.

Will investors move **beyond the financial reporting model** to a more **all-inclusive model of business reporting**—one that includes not only financial information but other key indicators and measurements that help predict value creation and monitor an organization's performance? The CICA mandate includes a push to **develop and support frameworks for measuring and reporting information that is used for evaluating and improving an organization's performance.**[44] Changes in these directions would broaden the focus from financial reporting to business reporting.

The CICA also has several other initiatives in this area:

- The CICA's **Risk Management and Governance Board** (formerly the Criteria of Control Board) focuses on a practical, commercial approach to risk management and governance.

- The CICA's **Canadian Performance Reporting Board** has issued standards on Management Discussion and Analysis disclosures.

These and other initiatives take a broader view of an all-inclusive model of business reporting.

Related to this theme of "business reporting" is the development of a business strategy model called the **balanced scorecard.**[45] Used quite widely, this model notes that **financial measures are only one component of useful information that decision-makers need in order to make effective decisions about the company.** The model views the company from four perspectives: financial, customer, internal processes, and learning and growth. These four perspectives are linked to the company's strategic vision, and objectives are developed within each perspective. The objectives help the company achieve its strategic vision. Measures are also developed to determine whether the objectives are being met.

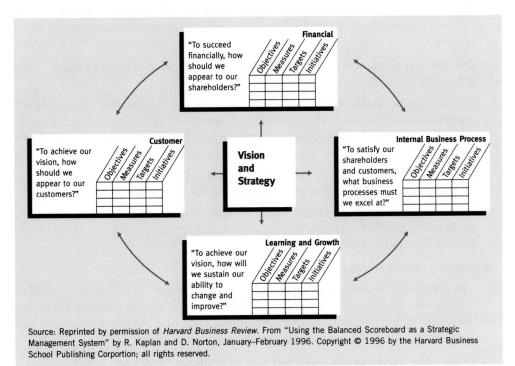

Illustration 1-11

The Balanced Scorecard Model

---

[44] J. Waterhouse and A. Svendsen, *Strategic Performance Monitoring and Management: Using Non-Financial Measures to Improve Corporate Governance* (CICA, 1998); and A. Willis and J. Desjardins, *Environmental Performance: Measuring and Managing What Matters* (CICA, 2001).

[45] R. Kaplan and D. Norton, *The Balanced Scorecard* (Boston: Harvard Business School Press, 1996).

Illustration 1-11 shows a **balanced scorecard model**. This model is used to help focus a company's internal efforts more effectively on meeting its strategic goals. The question is whether external users of financial statements also need to monitor these measures and whether companies should give external parties access to this information. If the information is important for company management in making decisions, is it not also important for external users?

We believe that the challenges presented by these changes must be met so the accounting profession can continue to provide the type of information that is needed for an efficient capital allocation process.

Conclusion

Financial reporting is standing at the threshold of some significant changes. Is the accounting profession up to the challenge? At present, we believe that the profession is reacting responsibly and effectively to correct the shortcomings that have been identified and to move forward with a new vision. Because of its great resources and expertise, the profession should be able to develop and maintain high standards and meet its mandate. This is and will continue to be a difficult process that requires time, logic, and diplomacy. Through a well-chosen mix of these three ingredients, however, and a measure of luck, the accounting profession will continue to be a leader on the global business stage.

WILEY PLUS
Glossary

KEY TERMS

Accounting Standards
    Board (AcSB), 12
Accounting Standards
    Oversight Council
    (AcSOC), 13
Canadian Institute of
    Chartered Accountants
    (CICA), 12
capital allocation, 5
CICA Handbook, 13
due process, 13
EIC Abstracts, 14
Emerging Issues
    Committee (EIC), 14
ethical dilemmas, 21
financial accounting, 5
Financial Accounting
    Standards Board
    (FASB), 16
financial reporting, 5
financial statements, 5
GAAP hierarchy, 19

Summary of Learning Objectives

1   Describe the essential characteristics of accounting.

The essential characteristics of accounting are the (1) identification, measurement, and communication of financial information about (2) economic entities to (3) interested persons.

2   Explain how accounting makes it possible to use scarce resources more efficiently.

Accounting provides reliable, relevant, and timely information to managers, investors, and creditors so that resources are allocated to the most efficient enterprises. Accounting also provides measurements of efficiency (profitability) and financial soundness.

3   Explain the meaning of "stakeholder" and identify key stakeholders in financial reporting including what is at stake for each one.

Investors, creditors, management, securities commissions, stock exchanges, analysts, credit rating agencies, auditors, and standard setters are some of the major stakeholders. See Illustration 1-4.

4   Identify the objective of financial reporting.

The objective of financial statements is to communicate information that is useful to key decision-makers such as investors and creditors in making resource allocation decisions (including assessing management stewardship) about the resources and claims to resources of an entity and how these are changing.

5   Explain the notion of management bias in financial reporting.

Management bias implies that the financial statements are not neutral: in other words, the preparers of the financial information are presenting the information in a manner that may overemphasize the positive and underemphasize the negative.

6 Understand the importance of user needs in the financial reporting process.

The financial reporting process is based on ensuring that users receive information that is relevant to decisions. This is a challenge as different users have different knowledge levels and needs. Management bias can make financial information less useful.

7 Explain the need for accounting standards.

The accounting profession has tried to develop a set of standards that is generally accepted and universally practised. Without this set of standards, each enterprise would have to develop its own standards, and readers of financial statements would have to become familiar with every company's particular accounting and reporting practices. As a result, it would be almost impossible to prepare statements that could be compared.

8 Identify the major entities that influence the standard-setting process and explain how they influence financial reporting.

The AcSB is the main standard-setting body in Canada for private companies, pension plans, and not-for-profit entities. Its mandate is from the CBCA as well as provincial acts of incorporation. For public companies, GAAP is IFRS as established by the IASB. Public companies are required to follow GAAP in order to access capital markets, which are monitored by provincial securities commissions. The FASB is also important as it influences IFRS standard setting.

9 Explain the meaning of generally accepted accounting principles (GAAP).

Generally accepted accounting principles are either principles that have substantial authoritative support, such as the *CICA Handbook*, or those arrived at through the use of professional judgement and the conceptual framework.

10 Explain the significance of professional judgement in applying GAAP.

Professional judgement plays an important role in Canadian GAAP since much of GAAP is based on general principles, which need to be interpreted.

11 Understand issues related to ethics and financial accounting.

When performing their professional duties, financial accountants are expected to note moral considerations and to make ethical decisions. Doing this is more difficult because no consensus has emerged among business professionals as to what constitutes a comprehensive ethical system.

12 Identify some of the challenges facing accounting.

Some of the challenges are globalization, leading to a requirement for international harmonization of standards; increased technology, resulting in the need for more timely information; the move to a new economy, resulting in a focus on measuring and reporting non-traditional assets that create value; and an increased requirement for accountability, resulting in the creation of new measurement and reporting models that look at business reporting as a whole.

Brief Exercises

(LO 1)   **BE1-1**   Briefly define accounting in your own words. What are the three main characteristics of accounting? Is accounting static or dynamic?

(LO 1)   **BE1-2**   Explain generally how financial accounting and managerial accounting are different from each other.

(LO 2)   **BE1-3**   How does accounting help the capital allocation process?

(LO 2)   **BE1-4**   Identify at least three major stakeholders that use financial accounting information and briefly explain how these stakeholders might use the information from financial statements.

(LO 1, 4)   **BE1-5**   What is the difference between "financial statements" and "financial reporting"?

(LO 4)   **BE1-6**   What are the major objectives of financial reporting?

(LO 7)   **BE1-7**   What is the value of having a common set of standards in financial accounting and reporting?

(LO 7)   **BE1-8**   What is the likely limitation on "general-purpose financial statements"?

(LO 8)   **BE1-9**   What are some of the developments or events that occurred between 1900 and 1930 that helped bring about changes in accounting theory or practice?

(LO 8)   **BE1-10**   Which organization is currently dominant in the world for setting accounting standards?

(LO 8)   **BE1-11**   Explain the role of the Canadian Accounting Standards Board (AcSB) in establishing generally accepted accounting principles.

(LO 8)   **BE1-12**   What is the role of the Ontario Securities Commission (OSC) in standard setting?

(LO 8)   **BE1-13**   What are some possible reasons why another organization, such as the OSC or the Securities and Exchange Commission (SEC), should not issue financial reporting standards?

(LO 8)   **BE1-14**   What are the sources of pressure that change and influence the development of accounting principles and standards?

(LO 8)   **BE1-15**   Some individuals have argued that the AcSB and the International Accounting Standards Board (IASB) need to be aware of the economic consequences of their pronouncements. What is meant by "economic consequences"? What are some of the dangers if politics play too much of a role in the development of financial reporting standards?

(LO 8)   **BE1-16**   Some individuals have argued that all Canadian companies should follow the same set of accounting principles. Explain why there are multiple sets of standards in Canada.

(LO 9)   **BE1-17**   If you were given complete authority to decide this, how would you propose that accounting principles or standards be developed and enforced?

(LO 9)   **BE1-18**   If you had to explain or define "generally accepted accounting principles," what essential characteristics would you include in your explanation?

(LO 9)   **BE1-19**   Explain the difference between primary and other sources of GAAP.

(LO 10)   **BE1-20**   The chairman of the Financial Accounting Standards Board (FASB) at one time noted that "the flow of standards can only be slowed if (1) producers focus less on quarterly earnings per share and tax benefits and more on quality products, and (2) accountants and lawyers rely less on rules and law and more on professional judgement and conduct." Explain his comment.

(LO 10, 12)   **BE1-21**   What is the difference between principles-based and rules-based accounting standards? In which category does IFRS belong? Canadian private entity GAAP? Explain.

(LO 11)   **BE1-22**   One writer recently noted that 99.4% of all companies prepare statements that are in accordance with GAAP. Why then is there such concern about fraudulent financial reporting?

(LO 11)   **BE1-23**   Some foreign countries have reporting standards that are different from standards in Canada. What are some of the main reasons why reporting standards are often different among countries?

BE1-24   How are financial accountants pressured when they need to make ethical decisions in their work? Is having **(LO 11)** technical mastery of GAAP enough to practise financial accounting?

BE1-25   What are some of the major challenges facing the accounting profession?   **(LO 12)**

BE1-26   The *Sarbanes-Oxley Act* was enacted to combat fraud and curb poor reporting practices. What are some key **(LO 12)** provisions of this legislation? Are these provisions in effect in Canada?

Writing Assignments

WA1-1   Some critics argue that having different organizations establish accounting principles is wasteful and inefficient. Instead of mandating accounting standards, each company could voluntarily disclose the type of information it considered important. In addition, if an investor wanted additional information, the investor could contact the company and pay to receive the desired information.

Instructions

Comment on the appropriateness of this viewpoint.

WA1-2   Some accountants have said that the development and acceptance of generally accepted accounting principles (i.e., standard setting) is undergoing a "politicization." Some use the term "politicization" in a narrow sense to mean the influence by government agencies, particularly the securities commissions, on the development of generally accepted accounting principles. Others use it more broadly to mean the compromise that results when the bodies that are responsible for developing generally accepted accounting principles are pressured by interest groups (securities commissions, stock exchanges, businesses through their various organizations, financial analysts, bankers, lawyers, etc.).

Instructions

(a) What are the arguments in favour of the politicization of accounting standard setting?

(b) What are the arguments against the politicization of accounting standard setting?

(CMA adapted)

WA1-3   Three models for setting accounting standards follow:

1. The purely political approach, where national legislative action decrees accounting standards

2. The private, professional approach, where financial accounting standards are set and enforced by private, professional actions only

3. The public/private mixed approach, where standards are set by private sector bodies that behave as though they were public agencies and the standards are mostly enforced through government agencies

Instructions

(a) Which of these three models best describes standard setting in Canada? Explain your choice.

(b) Why are companies, financial analysts, labour unions, industry trade associations, and others actively interested in standard setting?

(c) Cite an example of a group other than the AcSB that tries to establish accounting standards. Speculate on why such a group might want to set its own standards.

WA1-4   The increased availability and accessibility of computers and the Internet have had a major impact on the process of financial reporting. Most companies have websites and make available to stakeholders a significant amount of financial information, including annual reports and other financial data. This has sparked the question of whether companies should use a continuous reporting model instead of the current discrete model where financial statements are generally issued only quarterly and annually. Under a continuous reporting model, the company would make more information available to users in real time or perhaps on a "delayed" real-time basis (e.g., weekly).

Instructions

What are the pros and cons of a continuous reporting model? Consider the various stakeholders in the capital marketplace.

WA1-5   **Enron** and **WorldCom** are two companies that were accused of misstating their financial statements. The auditors for each company signed audit reports in which they stated that the financial statements of each company were fairly presented.

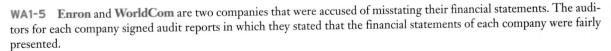

Real-World Emphasis

Instructions

How is it possible that a company can misrepresent its financial statements and still receive a "clean" audit opinion from its auditors?

Real-World Emphasis

WA1-6   The following information is from the Ontario Securities Commission (OSC) Statement of Allegation dated August 30, 2000, against **Philip Services Corp.** The allegation is about information in the company prospectus that included audited financial statements for the years ended December 31, 1995 and 1996.

The prospectus included an unqualified audit opinion, meaning that the auditors had concluded in the audit report that the financial statements presented the company's financial position and results of operations fairly and in accordance with GAAP. At the time, the company was a leading integrated service provider of ferrous scrap processing, brokerage, and industrial outsourcing services. The OSC alleged that the company failed to provide full, true, and plain disclosure in the prospectus of material facts about the company's restructuring and special charges.

Instructions

(a) Explain the meaning of the term "GAAP" as it is used in the audit report.

(b) Explain how to determine whether or not an accounting principle is generally accepted.

(c) Discuss the sources of evidence for determining whether an accounting principle has substantial authoritative support.

(d) Discuss how Philip Services Corp.'s auditors were likely able to issue a clean audit opinion even though the OSC alleges that the company did not fully disclose all material facts.

WA1-7   As mentioned in the chapter, the capital marketplace's reaction to recent corporate failures has been to increase the amount of government regulation.

Instructions

(a) Identify what steps Canada and the United States have taken to increase government regulation.

(b) What other options to strengthen the capital marketplace might have been available to stakeholders?

(c) What are the strengths and weaknesses of government regulation?

WA1-8   Effective 2011, Canada will have a two-tiered system for determining GAAP for private versus public companies. Private companies will follow private entity GAAP, as prepared by the AcSB, and public companies will have to follow IFRS. Private companies will be allowed to use IFRS if they choose.

Instructions

Discuss, noting the pros and cons of having this type of system versus a system where there is one set of GAAP for private and public entities.

Cases

WILEY PLUS
Case Primer

Refer to the Case Primer on the website to help you answer these cases.

CA1-1   When the AcSB issues new standards, the implementation date is usually 12 months after the issue date, but early implementation is encouraged. In this case, Paula Popov, controller, is discussing with her financial vice-president the need for early implementation of a standard that would result in a fairer presentation of the company's financial condition and earnings. When the financial vice-president determines that early implementation of the standard will lower the reported net income for the year, he discourages Popov from implementing the standard until it is required.

Instructions

Ethics   Discuss the ethical issues.

(CMA adapted)

Real-World Emphasis

CA1-2   The **T. Eaton Company** (Eaton's) was a private Canadian company that experienced cash flow difficulties and hired new management to turn the company around. The company then went public and the shares sold at $15. Within months, however, the share price plummeted and **Sears** bought out Eaton's when it was on the threshold of bankruptcy.

Instructions

Who were the stakeholders in this situation? Explain what was at stake and why and how they were affected when the share price plummeted.

CA1-3 In a *Financial Post* article dated September 17, 2002, it was reported that Standard & Poor's downgraded **Quebecor Media Inc.**'s credit rating by two levels from BB to B+. The credit rating agency was concerned about the company's ability to refinance portions of its debt. Both BB and B+ are considered "junk" bonds and are below the BBB− category, which is the lowest grade that many pension and mutual funds are allowed to hold.

Real-World Emphasis

   In the article, analysts said the company's financial profile had weakened due to tight debt covenants and resulting cash flow restrictions.

Instructions

(a) Discuss whether Standard & Poor's is a stakeholder from Quebecor Media Inc.'s perspective.

(b) Discuss any bias that Quebecor might have when it issues its financial statements.

CA1-4 **Quebecor Inc.**, the parent company of Quebecor Media Inc., is a public company whose shares trade on the TSX. Quebecor Inc. has debt covenants that limit the amount of debt and require that certain financial ratios be maintained. In 2011, the entity will have to present consolidated financial statements in accordance with IFRS. There is a risk for any company with debt covenants, that the covenants might be breached when the entity switches to IFRS.

Real-World Emphasis

Instructions

Discuss the risks associated with switching to IFRS and how the company might mitigate these risks.

Research and Financial Analysis

RA1-1 Ontario Securities Commission/Canadian Securities Administrators

The following is an excerpt from the Canadian Securities Administrators (CSA) Staff Notice 52-321 from the Ontario Securities Commission (OSC) website:

CSA STAFF NOTICE 52-321
EARLY ADOPTION OF INTERNATIONAL FINANCIAL
REPORTING STANDARDS,
USE OF US GAAP AND REFERENCE TO IFRS-IASB

Purpose

This notice updates the market on CSA staff's views on the issues addressed in CSA Concept Paper 52-402 *Possible changes to securities rules relating to International Financial Reporting Standards* (the concept paper), published on February 13, 2008, namely:

- use of International Financial Reporting Standards (IFRS) by a domestic issuer before January 1, 2011,

- use of US generally accepted accounting principles (US GAAP) by a domestic issuer that is an SEC issuer, and

- reference to IFRS as issued by the International Accounting Standards Board (IFRS-IASB) instead of Canadian generally accepted accounting principles (Canadian GAAP).

Background

We have reviewed the 42 comment letters and other feedback received in response to the concept paper. Based on that input, staff have further developed their views on the three issues addressed in the paper.

Early adoption of IFRS

Staff recognize that some issuers might want to prepare their financial statements in accordance with IFRS for periods beginning prior to January 1, 2011, the mandatory date for changeover to IFRS for Canadian publicly accountable enterprises. Staff are prepared to recommend exemptive relief on a case by case basis to permit a domestic issuer to prepare its financial statements in accordance with IFRS-IASB for financial periods beginning before January 1, 2011.

We expect an issuer contemplating the possibility of adopting IFRS before 2011 would carefully assess the readiness of its staff, board of directors, audit committee, auditors, investors and other market participants to deal with the change. An issuer should also consider the implications of adopting IFRS before 2011 on its obligations under securities legislation including those relating to CEO and CFO certifications, business acquisition reports, offering documents, and previously released material forward-looking information.

A domestic issuer may have previously filed financial statements prepared in accordance with Canadian GAAP or US GAAP for interim periods in the first year that the issuer proposes to adopt IFRS. In such cases, staff will recommend as a condition of the exemptive relief that the issuer file revised interim financial statements prepared in accordance with IFRS-IASB, revised interim management discussion and analysis, and new interim certificates.

Domestic issuers' use of US GAAP

Staff propose retaining the existing option in NI 52-107 for a domestic issuer that is also an SEC issuer to use US GAAP.

Reference to IFRS-IASB instead of Canadian GAAP

Staff have concluded that it is preferable for securities rules to require a domestic issuer to prepare its financial statements in accordance with IFRS-IASB after the mandatory changeover date, rather than Canadian GAAP, and require an audit report on such annual financial statements to refer to IFRS-IASB. However, we continue to consider issues relating to the availability of an appropriate French translation of IFRS and reference to both IFRS-IASB and Canadian GAAP.

Instructions

(a) Discuss the pros and cons of allowing Canadian public entities to follow IFRS prior to 2011 (when public companies are mandated to follow IFRS). Why would a company want to adopt IFRS early?

(b) Visit the OSC website (www.osc.gov.on.ca) and identify companies that adopted IFRS early.

(c) Canadian companies have been allowed to use U.S. GAAP for Canadian filing purposes where they are also SEC filers. Should this practice be allowed to continue after 2011? Discuss why companies might want to continue to be allowed to follow U.S. GAAP. Why might others want to get rid of this option?

(d) Another consideration is how GAAP for public companies is described in the financial statements starting in 2011. Should it be referred to as Canadian GAAP (with the understanding that GAAP for public companies is IFRS) or should it be explicitly referred to as IFRS?

RA1-2 IASB

Michael Sharpe, then deputy chairman of the International Accounting Standards Committee, made the following comments before the Financial Executives International 63rd Annual Conference:

There is an irreversible movement toward the harmonization of financial reporting throughout the world. The international capital markets require an end to:

1. The confusion caused by international companies announcing different results depending on the set of accounting standards applied. Recent announcements by Daimler-Benz (now DaimlerChrysler) highlight the confusion that this causes.

2. Companies in some countries obtaining unfair commercial advantages from the use of particular national accounting standards.

3. The complications in negotiating commercial arrangements for international joint ventures caused by different accounting requirements.

4. The inefficiency of international companies having to understand and use myriad accounting standards depending on the countries in which they operate and the countries in which they raise capital and debt. Executive talent is wasted on keeping up to date with numerous sets of accounting standards and the never-ending changes to them.

5. The inefficiency of investment managers, bankers, and financial analysts as they seek to compare financial reporting drawn up in accordance with different sets of accounting standards.

6. Failure of many stock exchanges and regulators to require companies subject to their jurisdiction to provide comparable, comprehensive, and transparent financial reporting frameworks giving international comparability.

7. Difficulty for developing countries and countries entering the free market economy, such as China and Russia, in accessing foreign capital markets because of the complexity of and differences between national standards.

8. The restriction on the mobility of financial service providers across the world as a result of different accounting standards.

Clearly, eliminating these inefficiencies by having comparable high-quality financial reporting used across the world would benefit international businesses.

Instructions

Research the issue using the Internet and answer the following questions:

(a) What is the International Accounting Standards Board and what is its relationship with the International Accounting Standards Committee?

(b) Which stakeholders might benefit from the use of international accounting standards?

(c) What do you believe are some of the major obstacles to harmonization?

RA1-3 Canadian Coalition for Good Governance

Real-World Emphasis

The **Canadian Coalition for Good Governance** was formed in 2002 and represents a significant number of institutional investors in Canada.

Instructions

(a) How does an institutional investor differ from other investors?

(b) In your opinion, what impact would the presence of a large number of investors have on management's financial reporting decisions?

(c) Go to the coalition's website (www.ccgg.ca) and identify the coalition's three largest member companies.

(d) Go to these member companies' websites and identify their major investments.

RA1-4 SOX

In 2002, the *Sarbanes-Oxley Act* was passed in the United States to strengthen the capital marketplace. In the following year, there were many debates in Canada about whether the securities commissions in Canada should adopt the same regulations. In the end, Canada did adopt a similar level of regulation.

Instructions

(a) Why was the Act issued and what are its key components?

(b) What impact do you think the Act had on the U.S. capital marketplace?

(c) Do you think there were any spillover effects in the Canadian marketplace? (Hint: look on the websites of the provincial securities commissions, the CICA (Canadian Institute of Chartered Accountants), the TSX, and the *Globe and Mail* and *Financial Post*. Key words might be "SOX," "corporate accountability," and "post Enron.")

RA1-5 Principles versus Rules

Canadian, international, and U.S. accounting standards are based on different philosophies. The AcSB and IASB use a principles-based approach while the United States uses a rules-based approach. The United States is currently studying the merits of the principles-based approach.

Instructions

(a) Identify the main factors that motivated the FASB to at least consider switching to the principles-based approach.

(b) Download and review the FASB Issues Proposal for a Principles-Based Approach to U.S. Accounting Standard Setting from www.fasb.org.

(c) In your own words, state the differences between a rules-based approach and a principles-based approach.

(d) Comment on which approach would be better, noting your thoughts on whether this issue will be a significant impediment to the United States moving to IFRS.

RA1-6 Financial Reporting Pressures

Ethics

What follows is part of the testimony from Troy Normand in the **WorldCom** case. He was a manager in the corporate reporting department and is one of five individuals who pleaded guilty. He testified in the hope of receiving no prison time when he was ultimately sentenced.

Q: Mr. Normand, if you could just describe for the jury how the meeting started and what was said during the meeting?

A: I can't recall exactly who initiated the discussion, but right away Scott Sullivan acknowledged that he was aware we had problems with the entries, David Myers had informed him, and we were considering resigning.

He said that he respected our concerns but that we weren't being asked to do anything that he believed was wrong. He mentioned that he acknowledged that the company had lost focus quite a bit due to the preparations for the Sprint merger, and that he was putting plans in place and projects in place to try to determine where the problems were, why the costs were so high.

He did say he believed that the initial statements that we produced, that the line costs in those statements could not have been as high as they were, that he believed something was wrong and there was no way that the costs were that high.

I informed him that I didn't believe the entry we were being asked to do was right, that I was scared, and I didn't want to put myself in a position of going to jail for him or the company. He responded that he didn't believe anything was wrong, nobody was going to be going to jail, but that if it later was found to be wrong, that he would be the person going to jail, not me.

He asked that I stay, don't jump off the plane, let him land softly, that's basically how he put it. And he mentioned that he had a discussion with Bernie Ebbers asking Bernie to reduce projections going forward and Bernie had refused.

Q: Mr. Normand, you said that Mr. Sullivan said something about don't jump out of the plane. What did you understand him to mean when he said that?

A: Not to quit.

Q: During this meeting, did Mr. Sullivan say anything about whether you would be asked to make entries like this in the future?

A: Yes, he made a comment that from that point going forward we wouldn't be asked to record any entries, high-level late adjustments, that the numbers would be the numbers.

Q: What did you understand that to mean, the numbers would be the numbers?

A: That after the preliminary statements were issued, with the exception of any normal transactions, valid transactions, we wouldn't be asked to be recording any more late entries.

Q: I believe you testified that Mr. Sullivan said something about the line cost numbers not being accurate. Did he ask you to conduct any analysis to determine whether the line cost numbers were accurate?

A: No, he did not.

Q: Did anyone ever ask you to do that?

A: No.

Q: Did you ever conduct any such analysis?

A: No, I didn't.

Q: During this meeting, did Mr. Sullivan ever provide any accounting justification for the entry you were asked to make?

A: No, he did not.

Q: Did anything else happen during the meeting?

A: I don't recall anything else.

Q: How did you feel after this meeting?

A: Not much better actually. I left his office not convinced in any way that what we were asked to do was right. However, I did question myself to some degree after talking with him wondering whether I was making something more out of what was really there.

Instructions

Answer the following questions:

(a) What appears to be the ethical issue in this case?

(b) Is Troy Normand acting improperly or immorally?

(c) What would you do if you were Troy Normand?

(d) Who are the major stakeholders in this case?

Mixed Measurement

THE INTERNATIONAL ACCOUNTING Standards Board (IASB) is reviewing its conceptual framework to create a solid foundation for future accounting standards that are principles-based, internally consistent, and internationally converged. One phase of this project focuses on measurement.

"We need to fill a gaping hole," says Ian Hague, principal in accounting standards at the Accounting Standards Board of Canada (AcSB). "There is almost no guidance on measurement."

One noted trend in the development of IFRS is the increased use of fair value measurement. "Twenty years ago, there was very little fair value in any standards," Hague points out. However, he adds, there is no intent to have a full fair value balance sheet. "The idea that IFRSs require more fair value measurement than Canadian standards is a misconception," says Hague. "There are really two areas where additional fair value is required." These are for agricultural activities and for some real estate investments.

The benefit of fair value measurement is that, for many assets, it makes information more visible in the financial statements, explains Hague. "Fair value measurements are arguably more relevant in many instances. They are always up to date and more comparable." The drawback with this form of measurement is that, in a large number of cases, fair value is difficult to determine, and it is subject to market volatility. However, in times of volatility, one should expect the financial statements to be volatile as well. "Fair value is not the only thing that puts volatility in the income statement," he points out.

While IFRS allow for more fair value measurement, they don't require it. Historical cost measurements still have a place on the balance sheet, says Hague. "IASB is not moving fundamentally to fair value measurement. It is developing a mixed-measurement accounting model." ■

CHAPTER 2

Conceptual Framework Underlying Financial Reporting

Learning Objectives

After studying this chapter, you should be able to:

1. Describe the usefulness of a conceptual framework.

2. Describe the main components of a conceptual framework for financial reporting.

3. Understand the objective of financial reporting.

4. Identify the qualitative characteristics of accounting information.

5. Define the basic elements of financial statements.

6. Describe the foundational principles of accounting.

7. Explain the factors that contribute to choice and/or bias in financial reporting decisions.

8. Discuss current trends in standard setting for the conceptual framework.

After studying Appendix 2A, you should be able to:

9. Understand in greater detail how fair value is measured.

Preview of Chapter 2

Users of financial statements need relevant and reliable information. To help develop this type of financial information, accountants use a conceptual framework that guides financial accounting and reporting. In this chapter, we discuss the basic concepts that underlie this conceptual framework.

The chapter is organized as follows:

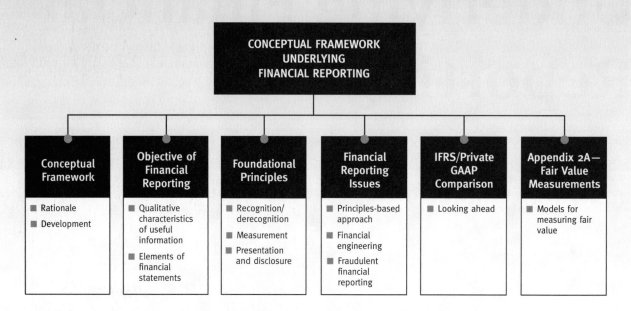

CONCEPTUAL FRAMEWORK

A **conceptual framework** is like a constitution: it is a "coherent system of interrelated objectives and fundamentals that can lead to consistent standards and that prescribes the nature, function, and limits of financial accounting and financial statements."[1] Many observers believe that the real contribution of standard-setting bodies, and even their continued existence, depends on the quality and usefulness of the conceptual framework.

Rationale for Conceptual Framework

Objective 1
Describe the usefulness of a conceptual framework.

Why is a conceptual framework necessary? First, to be useful, **standard setting should build on an established body of concepts and objectives.** Having a soundly developed conceptual framework as their starting point, standard setters are then able to issue additional **useful and consistent** standards over time. The result is a **coherent** set of standards and rules, as they have all been built upon the same foundation. It is important that such a framework **increase** financial statement users' **understanding** of and **confidence** in financial reporting, and that it **enhance the comparability** of different companies' financial statements.

---

[1] "Conceptual Framework for Financial Accounting and Reporting: Elements of Financial Statements and Their Measurement," FASB discussion memorandum (Stamford, CT: FASB, 1976), page 1 of the "Scope and Implications of the Conceptual Framework Project" section.

Second, by referring to an existing framework of basic theory, it should be possible to solve **new and emerging practical problems** more quickly. It is difficult, if not impossible, for standard setters to quickly state the proper accounting treatment for highly complex situations. Practising accountants, however, must solve such problems on a day-to-day basis. By using **good judgement** and with the help of a **universally accepted conceptual framework**, it is hoped that accountants will be able to decide against certain alternatives quickly and to focus instead on a logical and acceptable treatment.

Development of the Conceptual Framework

2 Objective
Describe the main components of a conceptual framework for financial reporting.

Over the years, many organizations, committees, and interested individuals have developed and published their own conceptual frameworks, but no single framework has been universally accepted and relied on in practice. Realizing there was a need for a generally accepted framework, in 1976 the FASB issued a three-part discussion memorandum entitled "Conceptual Framework for Financial Accounting and Reporting: Elements of Financial Statements and Their Measurement." It stated the major issues that would need to be addressed in establishing a conceptual framework for setting accounting standards and resolving financial reporting controversies. Based on this, six "Statements of Financial Accounting Concepts" were then published. A seventh, on accounting measurement, was added in 2000. The AcSB and IASB followed the FASB's example and issued their own respective frameworks. At the time this text was going to press, the IASB and FASB were working on a joint conceptual framework to promote global consistency and comparability. This chapter incorporates ideas from the newly emerging framework. The AcSB has signalled that it will likely adopt the framework for private entities as well.

Illustration 2-1 shows an overview of a conceptual framework.[2] At the first level, the objectives identify accounting's **goals and purposes**: these are the conceptual framework's

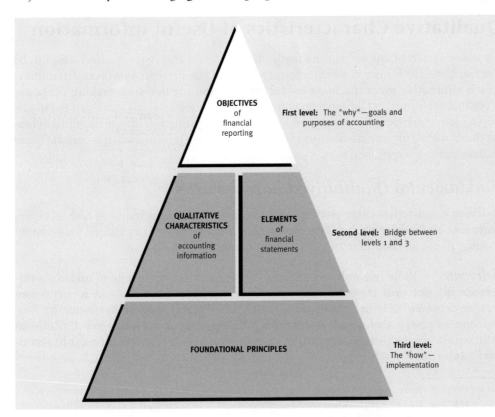

Illustration 2-1

Conceptual Framework for Financial Reporting

---

[2] Adapted from William C. Norby, *The Financial Analysts Journal*, March/April 1982, p. 22.

building blocks. At the second level are the **qualitative characteristics** that make accounting information useful and the **elements of financial statements** (assets, liabilities, equity, revenues, expenses, gains, and losses).[3] At the third and final level are the **foundational principles** used in establishing and applying accounting standards.

OBJECTIVE OF FINANCIAL REPORTING

Objective **3**
Understand the objective of financial reporting.

As we discussed in Chapter 1, the objective of financial reporting is to communicate information that is **useful** to investors, creditors, and other users in making their **resource allocation** decisions (including **assessing management stewardship)** about the economic resources and claims on them, as well as the financial performance.

Consequently, financial statements provide information about the financial position, changes in financial position, and the entity's performance.

The accounting profession provides this information to users of financial statements through **general-purpose financial statements**. These are basic financial statements that give information that meets the needs of **key users**.[4] The statements are intended to provide the **most useful information possible in a manner whereby benefits exceed costs** to the different kinds of users.

The objectives (the conceptual framework's first level) are about accounting's **goals and purposes**. Later, we will discuss how these goals and purposes are **implemented** (the third level). Between these two levels is another level: the second level is necessary as it provides certain **conceptual building blocks** that explain the **qualitative characteristics** of accounting information and define the **elements of financial statements**. These conceptual building blocks form a bridge between the *why* of accounting (the objectives) and the *how* of accounting (recognition and measurement).

Qualitative Characteristics of Useful Information

Objective **4**
Identify the qualitative characteristics of accounting information.

Choosing an acceptable accounting method, the amount and types of information to be disclosed, and the format in which information should be presented involves determining **which alternative gives the most useful information for decision-making purposes** (decision usefulness). The conceptual framework's second level has identified the qualitative characteristics of accounting information that distinguish information that is better (more useful) for making decisions from information that is inferior (less useful). These characteristics are explained next.

Fundamental Qualitative Characteristics

Relevance and representational faithfulness (sometimes referred to as faithful representation) are fundamental qualities that make accounting information useful for decision-making. Above all else, these two characteristics must be present.

Relevance.   To be relevant, accounting information must be capable of **making a difference in a decision**. If a piece of information has no impact on a decision, it is irrelevant to that decision. Relevant information helps users make predictions about the final outcome of past, present, and future events; that is, it has predictive value. Relevant information also helps users confirm or correct their previous expectations; it has feedback/confirmatory value.

---

[3] It is debatable whether other comprehensive income is a separate element of financial statements as it simply contains other elements such as revenues, expenses, gains, and losses. It is considered by some to be a subclassification of the income statement.

[4] Investors and creditors are assumed to be the primary or key users. For not-for-profit entities, key users include members/contributors rather than investors.

Representational faithfulness. Accounting information is representationally faithful to the extent that it reflects the underlying economic substance of an event or transaction. This notion of representing economic reality is sometimes referred to as transparency. If a financial statement user reads the financial statements, can they see what lies beneath the numbers? Information that is representationally faithful is **complete**, **neutral**, and **free from material error or bias**.

Completeness refers to the fact that the statements should include all information necessary to portray the underlying events and transactions. Care must be taken to ensure that pertinent information is included since it is possible to misrepresent something by not including all pertinent information.

Neutrality means that information cannot be selected to **favour one set of stakeholders over another**. Factual, truthful, unbiased information needs to be the overriding consideration when preparing financial information.

Livent Inc. was a Canadian company that produced and presented large Broadway-style musicals. In 1993, the company went public, listing its shares on the TSX. By 1998, it filed for bankruptcy protection while it was being accused of accounting irregularities, and in 2001 it was investigated by the Ontario Securities Commission. The following excerpt is from the OSC Notice of Hearing and Allegation about manipulation of the financial statements:

What Do the Numbers Mean?

> ... at the end of each financial reporting period, Livent accounting staff circulated to the Respondents a management summary reflecting actual results (including net income, on a show-by-show basis, compared to budget), as well as any improper adjustments carried forward from a prior financial period in connection with each show. Having regard to the actual results, the Respondents then provided instructions, directly or indirectly, to the Livent accounting staff specifying changes to be made to the actual results reflected in the company's books and records. In order to give effect to the Respondents' instructions, Livent accounting staff manipulated Livent's books and records by various means which did not accord with GAAP. The effect of the manipulations was to improve the presentation of Livent's financial results for the reporting period. Draft financial statements would then be generated for the reporting period incorporating the manipulations. These draft financial statements were then distributed to the Livent audit committee and, thereafter the Livent board of directors, for their review and approval. The Respondents attended meetings of the audit committee and the board of directors where these draft financial statements were discussed and ultimately approved. The Respondents did not disclose to the audit committee or the board of directors that, to their knowledge, the financial statements were false or misleading.

Among other things, management was charged with deliberately and systematically biasing the information. This contributed to the company's eventual downfall. Garth Drabinsky and Myron Gottlieb, co-founders of Livent, were found guilty in 2009 of two counts of fraud and one of forgery. Drabinsky's lawyers argued that he was not motivated by personal greed but rather by a desire to save the company.

Ethics

In practice, management needs to use many assumptions because of uncertainty in financial reporting. When choosing these assumptions, management must use its best estimates (management best estimate) in order to portray the economic reality.[5]

Significant Change

---

[5] How does the concept of **neutrality** fit with the notion of **conservatism**? Few conventions in accounting are as misunderstood as conservatism. In situations involving uncertainty and professional judgement, historically, the concept of conservatism has meant that **net assets and net income would not be overstated**. Conservatism acknowledges a **pre-existing tendency** of companies to overstate net assets and net income and acts to counterbalance this tendency. Users of financial statements are more tolerant of understated net assets and net income than overstated balances. Does the use of conservatism represent a bias? Many believe that it does. Biased information is tolerated much less now than in the past and the trend in financial reporting is away from any bias—including conservatism. The concept of conservatism is currently being downplayed in the conceptual framework in favour of neutrality.

There is also another aspect to neutrality: neutrality in standard setting. Some observers argue that standards should not be issued if they cause undesirable economic effects on an industry or company (the **economic consequences argument,** which was mentioned in Chapter 1). Standards must be free from bias, however, or we will no longer have **credible financial statements**. Standard setters must therefore choose the best standards regardless of economic consequences. If the accounting results in users changing their decisions, then by definition, the information is decision-relevant.

Freedom from material error/bias means that the information must be reliable. The task of converting economic events (which are constantly changing and difficult to measure) to numbers in a set of financial statements is a complex one. Management must make estimates and use judgement in determining how to portray events and transactions. Often, there is no correct or single right way to portray economic reality. Having said this, information is more useful if it is free from material error or bias, so every attempt must be made to achieve this.

Enhancing Qualitative Characteristics

Enhancing qualitative characteristics include **comparability, verifiability, timeliness,** and **understandability**.

Comparability.   Information that has been measured and reported in a similar way (both company to company and consistently from year to year) is considered comparable. Comparability enables users to **identify the real similarities and differences in economic phenomena** because these have not been obscured by accounting methods that cannot be compared. For example, the accounting for pensions is different in North America and Japan. In Canada and the United States, pension costs are recorded as incurred, whereas in Japan there is little or no charge to income for these costs. As a result, it is difficult to compare the financial results of General Motors or Ford with those of Nissan or Honda. It is important to remember therefore that **resource allocation decisions involve evaluations of alternatives** and a valid evaluation can only be made if comparable information is available. Although it is not a substitute for comparable information, a full disclosure of information sometimes allows users to overcome inconsistencies in how information is presented.

What Do the Numbers Mean?

In 2006, Nortel announced yet again that it would be restating its results for the past four years and delaying the filing of its annual report to no later than April 30. The restatement was in addition to the two previous restatements. In response to the announcement, there was a corresponding decrease in share price, as is normal when negative news is reported by a company. The previous restatements had occurred in November 2003 and January 2005. According to a newspaper article,[6] an analyst asked whether there were any additional skeletons in the company's closet. Nortel stated that the restatements did not affect its cash flows and that total revenues and cash flows over the period remained the same. However, when it restated the financial statements, the amount of revenues in a given period changed.

Toward the end of April 2006, information about the restated financial statements was released and it noted further adjustments. Interestingly, the share price did not decline as expected. The continuous restatements may have undermined the reliability or believability of the financial statements and made them less decision-relevant. In addition, the statements are no longer comparable.

Nortel declared bankruptcy in 2009 and the wireless operations were bought by Nokia Siemens.

---

[6] "Nortel Accounting Woes Continue," *Toronto Star,* March 11, 2006.

Verifiability.   Verifiability exists when knowledgeable, independent users achieve similar results or reach consensus regarding the accounting for a particular transaction. Some numbers are more easily verified than others; e.g., cash can be verified by confirming with the bank where the deposit is held. Other numbers—such as accruals for environmental cleanup costs—are more difficult (although not necessarily impossible) to verify, as many assumptions are made to arrive at an estimate. Numbers that are easy to verify with a reasonable degree of accuracy are often referred to as "hard" numbers. Those that have more measurement uncertainty are called "soft."

Timeliness.   Timeliness is also important. Information must be available to decision-makers before it loses its ability to influence their decisions. Quarterly reporting (involving the issuance of financial information every three months) provides information on a more timely basis. Thus, users have information throughout the year as opposed to having to wait until after the year end for the annual financial statements.

Understandability.   Users need to have **reasonable knowledge** of business and financial accounting matters in order to understand the information in financial statements. However, financial information must also be of sufficient quality and clarity that it allows reasonably informed users to see its significance. This is the information's **understandability**. In addition, standard setters assume that users have the responsibility to review and analyze the information with reasonable diligence. This point is important: it means that the onus to prepare understandable statements and to be able to understand them rests with both the financial statement preparer and the user. This characteristic affects both how information is reported and how much is reported. Where the underlying transactions or economic events are more complex, the assumption is that users will seek the aid of an advisor.[7]

An excerpt follows from the notes to the financial statements of **Enron Corp.** for the year ended December 31, 2000. The complexity of the business arrangements makes it difficult to understand the nature of the underlying transactions. It contributes to a set of financial statements that lack transparency. The choice of words also makes the note difficult to read.

What Do the Numbers Mean?

> In 2000 and 1999, Enron sold approximately $632 million and $192 million, respectively, of merchant investments and other assets to Whitewing. Enron recognized no gains or losses in connection with these transactions. Additionally, in 2000, ECT Merchant Investments Corp., a wholly owned Enron subsidiary, contributed two pools of merchant investments to a limited partnership that is a subsidiary of Enron. Subsequent to the contributions, the partnership issued partnership interests representing 100% of the beneficial, economic interests in the two asset pools, and such interests were sold for a total of $545 million to a limited liability company that is a subsidiary of Whitewing. See Note 3. These entities are separate legal entities from Enron and have separate assets and liabilities. In 2000 and 1999, the Related Party, as described in Note 16, contributed $33 million and $15 million, respectively, of equity to Whitewing. In 2000, Whitewing contributed $7.1 million to a partnership formed by Enron, Whitewing, and a third party. Subsequently, Enron sold a portion of its interest in the partnership through a securitization. See Note 3.[8]

---

[7] This represents a subtle shift in the level of knowledge required. Prior to the joint IASB/FASB conceptual framework project, users were only expected to have a reasonable understanding of business and a willingness to study the statements.

[8] Consolidated financial statements of Enron Corp. for the year ended December 31, 2000.

Trade-Offs

In general, preparers of financial information should identify all **relevant** information, then consider how best to ensure that the financial statements are presented such that they reflect the economic substance (**representational faithfulness**). Both characteristics must be present in order to ensure the information is decision-relevant.

However, it is not always possible for financial information to have all the enhancing qualities of useful information. Trade-offs may exist. For instance, in the interest of providing more relevant information, a new standard may be applied prospectively. In this case, comparability (**consistency** year to year) is temporarily sacrificed for better information going forward.

The accounting profession is constantly striving to produce financial information that meets all of the qualitative characteristics of useful information.

Constraints

Materiality.   Materiality relates to an item's impact on a firm's overall financial operations. Information is material if including it or leaving it out would influence or change the judgement of a reasonable person.[9] In short, information must make a difference in the decisions being made; otherwise, it is irrelevant. When making the determination whether something is material or not, the amount in question is often compared with the entity's amounts of other revenues and expenses, assets and liabilities, or net income.

It is hard to give firm guidelines to decide when an item is or is not material because materiality depends on both a relative amount and relative importance.

For example, the two sets of numbers in Illustration 2-2 show relative size.

Illustration 2-2

Materiality Comparison

	Company A	Company B
Sales	$10,000,000	$100,000
Costs and expenses	9,000,000	90,000
Income from operations	1,000,000	10,000
Unusual gain	20,000	5,000

During the particular period, the revenues and expenses, and therefore the net incomes, of Company A and Company B have been proportional. Each has also had an unusual gain.

In looking at the abbreviated income figures for Company A, it does not appear significant whether the amount of the unusual gain is presented separately or is merged with the regular operating income. It is only 2% of the operating income and, if merged, would not seriously distort the income figure. Company B has had an unusual gain of only $5,000, but it is relatively much more significant than the larger gain recognized by A. For Company B, an item of $5,000 amounts to 50% of its operating income. Obviously, including such an item in ordinary operating income would affect the amount of that income materially. In this example, we can therefore see the importance of an item's relative size in determining its materiality.

Many companies and their auditors have historically adopted the general rule of thumb that any item representing **5% or more of income from continuing operations** (after tax) is considered material. This is not a hard and fast rule and is a fairly simplistic and one-dimensional view of materiality. The item's impact on other factors, for instance on key financial statement ratios and management compensation—in short, on

---

[9] IASCF, IAS 8.5, *Accounting Policies, Changes in Accounting Estimates and Errors.*

any sensitive number on the financial statements—should also be considered. In addition, both **quantitative** and **qualitative** factors must be considered in determining whether an item is material.

Qualitative factors might include illegal acts, failure to comply with regulations, or inadequate or inappropriate description of an accounting policy. Materiality is also a factor in a large number of internal accounting decisions. The amount of classification required in a subsidiary expense ledger, the degree of accuracy required in prorating expenses among the departments of a business, and the extent to which adjustments should be made for accrued and deferred items are examples of judgements that should finally be determined based on reasonableness and practicability; i.e., on the materiality constraint sensibly applied. Only by exercising good judgement and professional expertise can reasonable and appropriate answers be found.

Cost versus Benefits.   Too often, users assume that information is a cost-free commodity. But preparers and providers of accounting information know this is not true. This is why the cost-benefit relationship must be considered: the costs of providing the information must be weighed against the benefits that can be had from using the information. In order to justify requiring a particular measurement or disclosure, the costs must be justified by the benefits.

The difficulty in cost-benefit analysis is that the costs and, especially, the benefits are not always evident or measurable. The costs are of several kinds, including the costs of:

- collecting and processing
- distributing
- auditing
- potential litigation
- disclosure to competitors
- analysis and interpretation

The benefits are enjoyed by both preparers (in terms of greater management control and access to capital) and users (in terms of allocation of resources, tax assessment, and rate regulation). Benefits are generally more difficult to quantify than costs. The AcSB has taken some steps to reduce the cost of providing information by developing separate standards for private entities that are less onerous and costly. This model allows these companies to follow a simplified version of GAAP based on cost-benefit considerations. In many cases, the shareholders and creditors of private companies have greater access to information and do not necessarily rely solely on the external financial statements. In addition, for smaller private companies, the business and business model are not so complicated and therefore less complex accounting standards are required. Private entities have the option to use IFRS if they wish.

Elements of Financial Statements

An important aspect of developing any theoretical structure is the body of elements or definitions to be included in the structure. At present, accounting uses many terms that have specific meanings. These terms make up the **language of accounting and business.** There are many elements that users expect to find on the financial statements, including **assets, liabilities, equity, revenues, expenses, gains, and losses.** In addition, within each of these categories there are many subcategories, such as current and noncurrent

5 Objective
Define the basic elements of financial statements.

assets, cash, inventory, and so on. The conceptual framework's second level defines the basic elements so that users have a common understanding of the main items presented on the financial statements.

The basic elements of financial statements that are most directly related to measuring an enterprise's performance and financial status are listed below. Each of these elements will be explained and examined in more detail in later chapters.[10]

Assets

One important term is "**asset**." Is an asset something we own? How do we define "own"? Is it based on **legal title** or **possession**? If ownership is based on legal title, can we assume that any leased asset would not be shown on the balance sheet? Is an asset something we have the **right to use**, or is it anything of value that is used by the enterprise to generate revenues? If the answer is the latter, should the enterprise's management then be considered an asset? These are some of the questions that the framework seeks to answer.

Assets have two essential characteristics:

1. They involve present economic resources.

2. The entity has a right or access to these resources where others do not.

In order for something to be an asset, the entity must provide evidence that it represents an economic resource and then link itself to that resource. In other words, the entity must first prove that the item has economic value and then that the entity may lay claim to or access that value.

Economic resources are defined to include things that are **scarce and capable of producing cash flows** (and therefore have economic value) where the **right to access is an enforceable right** (by law or other means). The economic resource is the thing itself (such as a building or the right to use it) and not the future cash flows that will be generated by it (although the latter generally drive the value).

For instance, if a company owns a parcel of land on which it builds a manufacturing facility, the land and manufacturing facility are considered assets for the following reasons:

1. Present economic resource: The land and plant represent a present resource; i.e., the entity may sell or use the property now. In addition, the property is not freely available to all, so it has economic value: someone would pay something to acquire the property. If the land were freely available to all, it would not be considered to have economic value. Why would anyone pay for something that was available for free? For instance, consider the air we breathe. It is freely available to everyone so no one would pay for it; although it has value, it is not considered to have *economic* value. However, if the air becomes polluted and someone finds a way to clean it up, this clean air would have economic value if it was not otherwise freely available to everyone; that is, people would pay to have access to it. This leads us to the second part of the definition of an asset.

2. Right or access that others do not have: The entity has sole ownership of the property since it holds legal title. It therefore is connected to this specific economic resource and may lay claim to it. If everyone owns or has access to the land (such as public parklands), then no single entity or individual (except perhaps the government itself)

---

[10] Note that the specific definitions are currently the subject of much debate and, as such, are in transition. The definitions presented for assets and liabilities reflect the most current thinking of the standard setters and have been drawn from *Information for Observers* and other documents which essentially capture discussion from the meetings held by the IASB and FASB. Illustration 2-6 compares these definitions to the existing definitions that are currently in IFRS and the *CICA Handbook*. The definitions for the other elements reflect existing wording as the IASB and FASB are still in the stages of preliminary discussions on these (equity, revenues, expenses, gains, and losses).

can lay claim to it as an asset on their balance sheet even though they may derive benefit from using the land. Since the entity has legal title, access is enforceable under law.

Illustration 2-3 depicts the essence of an asset.

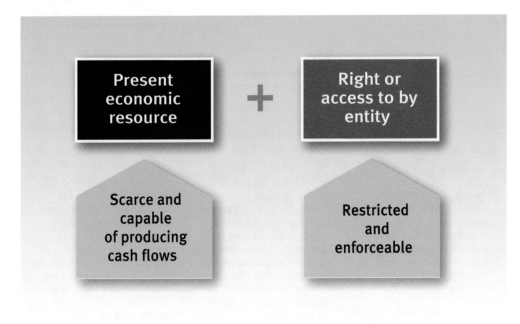

Illustration 2-3

The Essence of an Asset

Law

In the example above, the economic resource is represented by the legal rights to the property itself, which is a tangible asset. A resource may also be represented by a contractual or other right. For instance, a lottery ticket has value not only because it may win and generate cash flows in future but also because today it gives the present holder a contractual right to access those future winnings. It is an asset to the holder because possession of the ticket gives the holder restricted access to potential future cash flows.

Therefore, when determining if a present economic resource exists, care must be taken to review not only items such as inventory, cash, land, and patents (tangible and intangible properties) but also contractual and other rights (such as lottery tickets, forward contracts, insurance, and others). These rights may be conditional on a future event or unconditional or both. For instance, an insurance contract contains an ***unconditional right*** to recover insured losses from the insurance company. This has value even if no loss is suffered. Insurance transfers risk to the insurance company and the insured party is willing to pay a premium for that. This unconditional right is therefore an economic resource. In addition to this unconditional right, the insurance contract **also contains** a specific ***conditional right*** to receive compensation if a loss occurs. This is not a present economic resource since it does not exist until a loss occurs in the future. Therefore, although the contract contains both conditional and unconditional rights, only the unconditional rights represent economic resources (unless and until a loss occurs). The two rights are intertwined, however, since the conditional right can only legally be accessed by virtue of the unconditional right. Both are taken into account when measuring the asset. Note that it may be that the asset is measured at close to $0 in the end. Measurement is discussed further in this chapter and in Appendix 2A.

A summary of economic resources follows in Illustration 2-4.[11]

---

[11] The ideas were taken from the IASB *Information for Observers Paper* dated February 2007.

Item	Example	What Is the Economic Resource?	Explanation
Tangible items	Land	The land itself is a **present** economic resource. It may be sold or used currently.	The **future** cash flows are not the economic resource although they are considered in valuing the **present** economic resource.
Intangible items	Patents	The patent itself is a **present** economic resource. It may be sold or used currently.	Same as above
Contractual rights	Accounts receivable	The existing contractual right to receive the cash flows is the **present** economic resource.	Same as above
Contractual or other rights (statutory) that are **contingent on a future event** (other than or in addition to the passage of time)	Fire insurance contract (contains both an unconditional right to insurance coverage over a period of time and a conditional right to receive cash equal to the loss should a loss event occur).	The unconditional promise by the insurance company to provide coverage over the term of the insurance is a **present** economic resource to the insured (who has paid for this right). The conditional right to a specific amount of cash should a loss occur is not a **present** economic resource (since no loss has yet occurred).	The unconditional promise exists even though there may never be a loss from fire. The promise to pay a certain amount of money equal to the insured loss (if a fire occurs) is a conditional promise – this specific amount may or may not be paid out depending on if there is a fire. It would only become a **present** economic resource when and if a fire occurs and the entity is entitled to a payout.

Illustration 2-4

Present and Potential Economic Resources

Law

Right or access to the economic resource is generally evidenced by legal title or ownership. However, it may be evidenced by things other than legal title or ownership. For instance, a company may be in the process of refining a secret formulation for a new drug that has yet to be patented. If it is not yet patented, the entity does not own the secret formulation in a legal sense; however, it still has a right or access to it that is enforceable or protected by the company (by keeping it secret).

Liabilities

Liabilities have two essential characteristics:

1. They represent an economic burden or obligation.

2. The entity has a present obligation (which is enforceable).

Similar but opposite to an asset, a liability has a negative economic value and requires that the entity give up economic resources to settle the obligation. In addition, in order to meet the definition of a liability, the obligation must be enforceable through the application of the law or by other means.

Obligations may be conditional, unconditional or both (just like contractual and other rights). Unconditional obligations are sometimes referred to as stand-ready obligations. That is, the obligor "stands ready" to do whatever is required under the terms of the contract, agreement, or law. For instance, with an insurance contract, the insurer stands ready to pay out an amount equal to a loss that is covered under the insurance contract should the loss occur. Other examples include guarantees and warranties. Obligations where the entity agrees to provide a future service or deliver something in future are often referred to as **performance obligations**.

Illustration 2-5 depicts the essence of a liability.

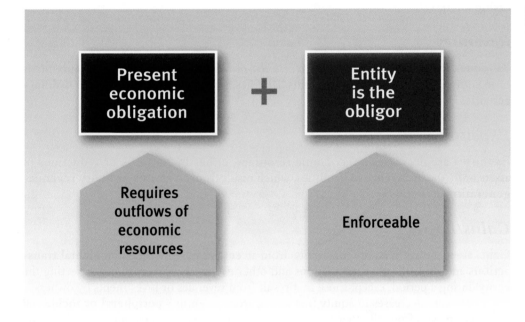

Illustration 2-5

The Essence of a Liability

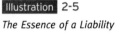 **Law**

Many entities must follow laws and/or regulations in the legal jurisdiction in which they operate. This duty for companies (and all citizens) to abide by the law may be seen by some as an unconditional obligation. Often it is not clear if a law has been violated and there are legal systems (courts, lawyers, judges, juries) that will help establish whether it has. The potential breaking of a law and/or regulation may be seen as a contingency and a conditional obligation may exist. If the law is violated, an economic burden exists to the company, which results in a present obligation that is enforceable under law. The uncertainty regarding whether a law has been broken and whether the company must pay a fine or settle a lawsuit is taken into account when measuring the liability (which results from the unconditional obligation). Note that it may be that the unconditional obligation, and hence the liability, is measured at an amount that is close to zero even when taking into account the conditional obligation.

Constructive obligations are obligations that arise though past or present practice that signals that the company acknowledges a potential economic burden. For instance, the entity might make a statement that it stands behind its products. Therefore, if a product is defective, even though the entity might not be **required to replace it under law or contract**, the expectation is that the entity will replace it. Care should be taken to ensure that constructive obligations are identified and properly accounted for if enforceable. These will be discussed further in subsequent chapters including chapters 13 and 16.

Liabilities may be further categorized by standard setters as financial (as defined in IAS 32, i.e., contractual obligations to deliver cash or other financial assets) or non-financial (everything else).[12]

---

[12] The terms "financial" and "non-financial" are somewhat vague and are meant to draw a line between liabilities that represent financial instruments (financial liabilities) and all other liabilities. Therefore, the term "non-financial" includes items such as contractual non-monetary performance obligations (such as warranties to fix assets or provide services) and non-contractual monetary obligations (such as lawsuits).

Equity

Equity/net assets is a **residual interest** in the assets of an entity that remains after deducting its liabilities (i.e., the net worth). In a business enterprise, the equity is the **ownership** interest.[13]

Revenues

Revenues are increases in economic resources, either by inflows or other enhancements of an entity's assets or by settlement of its liabilities, which result from an entity's **ordinary activities**.

Expenses

Expenses are decreases in economic resources, either by outflows or reductions of assets or by the incurrence of liabilities, which result from an entity's **ordinary revenue-generating activities**.

Gains/Losses

Gains are increases in equity (net assets) from an entity's **peripheral or incidental transactions** and from all other transactions and other events and circumstances affecting the entity during a period, except those that result from revenues or investments by owners.

Losses are decreases in equity (net assets) from an entity's **peripheral or incidental transactions** and from all other transactions and other events and circumstances affecting the entity during a period, except those that result from expenses or distributions to owners.

Other comprehensive income is made up of revenues, expenses, gains, and losses that, in accordance with primary sources of GAAP, are recognized in comprehensive income, but excluded from net income.

The financial statements include the following:

1. Income statement and/or statement of comprehensive income

2. Balance sheet

3. Statement of retained earnings or changes in shareholders' equity

4. Statement of cash flows

The term comprehensive income is a relatively new income concept and includes more than the traditional notion of net income. It includes net income and all other changes in equity except for owners' investments and distributions. For example, the following would be included as other comprehensive income in the new comprehensive income statement:

- unrealized holding gains and losses on certain securities

- certain gains and losses related to foreign exchange instruments

- gains and losses related to certain types of hedges

- other

---

[13] The IASB and FASB are looking at the definition of "equity."

Note that although the information must be presented in the statements, GAAP does not require companies to use the terms "Comprehensive Income" or "Other Comprehensive Income." This will be discussed further in Chapter 4.

Illustration 2-6 compares the definitions that exist now with the proposed definitions for assets and liabilities. The proposed definitions embody many of the same characteristics as the existing standards but the tighter wording is meant to provide additional guidance and reduce inconsistencies between the various standards. For most assets and liabilities, application of the respective definitions will yield the same accounting result.

Definitions	Existing Standards	Current Proposed Definitions (as discussed earlier in the chapter)
Assets	Assets are economic resources that have been obtained or are controlled by a particular entity as a result of past transactions or events from which future economic benefits may be obtained. They have three essential characteristics: 1. They embody a **future benefit**. 2. The entity can **control access** to this benefit. 3. The **transaction** or event that gives the entity access to this benefit **has occurred**.	Assets have two essential characteristics: 1. they involve **present economic resources** 2. to which the entity has a **right or access** where others do not.
Liabilities	Liabilities are obligations that arise from past transactions or events, which may result in a transfer of assets. Liabilities also have three essential characteristics: 1. They embody a **duty or responsibility**. 2. The entity has **little or no discretion to avoid** the duty. 3. The **transaction** or event that obligates the entity **has occurred**.	Liabilities have two essential characteristics: 1. they represent an **economic burden or obligation** 2. for which the entity has a **present obligation (which is enforceable)**.

Illustration 2-6
Comparison of Definitions

Significant Change

FOUNDATIONAL PRINCIPLES

The conceptual framework's third level consists of **foundational principles** that implement the basic objectives of level one. These concepts help explain which, when, and how financial elements and events should be **recognized**, **measured**, and **presented/disclosed** by the accounting system. They act as guidelines for developing rational responses to controversial financial reporting issues. They have evolved over time, and the specific accounting standards issued by standard setters are based on these concepts in a fundamental way.

Basic **foundational principles** underlying the financial accounting structure also include assumptions and conventions. It is often difficult to put a label onto the items noted below (and practice is varied), and so we have grouped them together. The specific label is not important—it is the substance of the concept and how it provides a solid foundation for accounting standard setting that is important. We will discuss the

6 Objective
Describe the foundational principles of accounting.

10 foundational principles under the groupings of recognition, measurement, and presentation and disclosure, as follows:

Recognition/Derecognition	Measurement	Presentation and Disclosure
1. Economic entity	5. Periodicity	10. Full disclosure
2. Control	6. Monetary unit	
3. Revenue recognition and realization	7. Going concern	
4. Matching	8. Historical cost	
	9. Fair value	

Recognition/Derecognition

Recognition deals with the act of including something on the entity's balance sheet or income statements. At a macro level, decisions need to be made on whether to consolidate investments in other entities. At a micro level, decisions need to be made on whether and when to include assets, liabilities, revenues, expenses, gains, and losses in the financial statements. In addition, once recognized, decisions need to be made on when to derecognize these elements (remove them from the financial statements). These are significant decisions.

The conceptual framework provides general recognition and measurement criteria, and underlying principles may be used to justify whether something should be reflected in the financial statements or not.

Historically, elements of financial statements have been recognized when:

1. they meet the definition of an element (e.g., liability),

2. they are probable, and

3. they are reliably measurable.

Significant Change

Finance

Presently under discussion is a model that requires recognition of these elements when:

1. they meet the respective definition, and

2. they are measurable.

Under this newer view, probability is incorporated through measurement. That is, the dollar value assigned to the element considers the riskiness and uncertainties of any related cash flows. Appendix 2A looks in greater detail at measurement models which incorporate uncertainty.[14] An entity must use all information to make a neutral decision as to whether the liability/asset exists or not (i.e., whether the definition is met) and then decide whether it is measurable.

Derecognition deals with the act of taking something off the balance sheet or income statement. In the past, derecognition criteria have been discussed in the context of financial instruments only (and primarily focused on financial assets). We will deal with derecognition as it pertains to financial instruments in Chapters 7 and 14. Having said this, just as the conceptual framework includes general recognition criteria for all elements, it makes sense that it should include general derecognition criteria for all elements. The standard setters plan to discuss the inclusion of derecognition criteria in the framework as a future project.

Several additional underlying principles help determine whether something should be recognized or not. A discussion of these follows.

---

[14] The issue of recognition criteria is also being debated currently. Do we need separate recognition criteria at all and, if so, what should they be?

Economic Entity Assumption

The **economic entity assumption** (or entity concept) allows us to **identify an economic activity** with a particular **unit of accountability** (e.g., a company, division, individual). If all the economic events that occur could not be separated in a meaningful way, there would be no basis for accounting. This concept helps accountants determine what to include or recognize in a particular set of financial statements (as well as what not to recognize).

For tax and legal purposes, the **legal entity** is the relevant unit for a company. Taxes are paid based on taxable income for each legal entity. GAAP, however, considers a broader definition when preparing consolidated financial statements. A parent and its subsidiaries are separate **legal entities**, but merging their activities for accounting and reporting purposes gives more meaningful information.[15] Thus, the consolidated financial statements are prepared from the perspective of the **economic entity**. This allows the company to recognize and group together the assets, liabilities, and other financial statement elements that are under the parent's **control** into one set of statements. Historically, the definition of control has been anchored in the number of common shares held in most cases.[16] However, the concept has recently been expanded.[17] This will be discussed further below.

Illustration 2-7 shows the notion of economic entity in regard to consolidated financial statements.

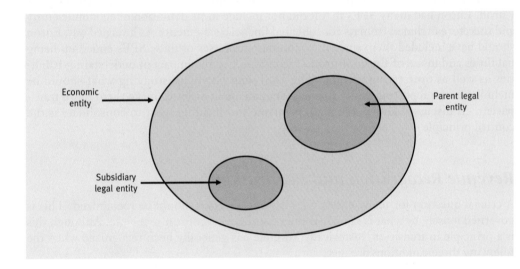

Illustration 2-7

Economic Entity as Defined for Consolidated Financial Statements

Control

Control is an important concept in determining which entities to consolidate and include in the financial statements. Things under the entity's control are generally included in the economic entity and the consolidated financial statements. What does control mean? There are several components to the concept of control, as follows:

---

[15] The concept of the entity is changing. For example, it is now harder to define the outer edges of companies. There are public companies with multiple public subsidiaries, each with joint ventures, licensing arrangements, and other affiliations and strategic alliances. Increasingly, loose affiliations of enterprises in joint ventures or customer-supplier relationships are formed and dissolved in a matter of months or weeks. These virtual companies raise accounting issues about how to account for the entity. See Steven H. Wallman, "The Future of Accounting and Disclosure in an Evolving World: The Need for Dramatic Change," *Accounting Horizons*, September 1995.

[16] That is, if the parent owns more than 50% of the (voting) common shares, it can exercise voting control.

[17] See joint IASB/FASB project on the conceptual framework (reporting entity).

Significant Change

1. There is power to direct the entity's activities. In order to include the entity in the consolidated financial statements, the reporting entity must be able to make strategic decisions for the entity.

2. Only one entity has the power to direct the activities of the entity in question. Control precludes the sharing of power.

3. Power need not be exercised or absolute. There is no requirement to have unrestricted, total control or power over the entity. For instance, the government may still exercise regulatory control over the entity. In addition, as long as the reporting entity has the **ability** to control the other entity, it need not exercise that control.

4. The reporting entity should have access to the benefits from the entity.

Consolidation is studied in advanced accounting courses and so is beyond the scope of this text.

What Do the Numbers Mean?

It is important to first **define the entity** for financial reporting purposes. Many companies use what are known as Special Purpose Entities ("SPE") or Variable Interest Entities ("VIE"). These are legal entities set up for a specific purpose; e.g., to hold leases, pension funds, or perhaps certain investments. Are SPEs part of the economic entity for consolidated financial reporting purposes? This was the centre of much of the controversy for Enron. Enron had many SPEs that it did not include in its definition of economic entity and therefore excluded from its consolidated financial statements. As it turned out, Enron should have included them since the liabilities and losses of these SPEs ended up being liabilities and losses of Enron. Enron's accounting had the impact of understating liabilities as well as overstating income. The IASB and FASB are studying what should be included in the reporting entity financial statements in order to make them more transparent. As discussed above, the main principle for deciding what to consolidate is the control principle.

Revenue Recognition and Realization

A crucial question for many enterprises is when revenue should be recognized. This is governed loosely by what is known as the revenue recognition principle. Although this is a principle in transition, historically, revenue has generally been recognized when the following three conditions are met:

1. **Risks and rewards** have passed or the **earnings process is substantially complete**.

2. **Measurability is reasonably certain**.

3. **Collectibility is reasonably assured** (realized or realizable).

Revenues are realized when products (goods or services), merchandise, or other assets are **exchanged** for cash or claims to cash. Revenues are realizable if the assets received or held can be readily converted into cash or claims to cash. Assets are readily convertible if they can be sold or interchanged in an active market at prices that are readily determinable and there is no significant additional cost.

As we will see in Chapter 6, an alternative contract-based view of this principle is emerging. It looks at revenue recognition in two stages: first, when to recognize the contract itself, and second, when to recognize the revenues.

Under the alternative contract-based view, any contract between the entity and a customer is recognized when:

1. the entity becomes **party to the contract** and

2. the resulting rights and obligations are **measurable,** including credit risk.

The resulting revenues are recognized when:

1. **control** over the goods passes and

2. performance **obligations are settled**.[18]

Significant Change

Matching

Assets such as long-lived assets contribute to a company's ability to generate revenues. Therefore, accounting attempts to match these costs with the revenues that they produce. This practice is called matching because it dictates that effort (expenses) be matched with accomplishment (revenues) whenever this is reasonable and can be done. It also illustrates the **cause and effect relationship** between the money spent to earn revenues and the revenues themselves.

It may be difficult to establish exactly how much of a contribution is made to each period, however, and so often an estimation technique must be used. GAAP requires that a **rational and systematic** allocation policy be used that will approximate the asset's contribution to the revenue stream. Selection of a rational and systematic allocation technique involves making assumptions about the benefits that are being received as well as the costs associated with those benefits. The cost of a long-lived asset, for example, must be allocated over all accounting periods during which the asset is used because the asset contributes to revenue generation throughout its useful life.

Costs are often classified into two groups: **product costs** and **period costs**. Product costs such as material, labour, and overhead attach to the product and are carried into future periods as inventory (if not sold) since inventory meets the definition of an asset. Period costs such as officers' salaries and other administrative expenses are recognized immediately—even though the benefits associated with these costs occur in the future—because no direct relationship between cost and revenue can be established and, more importantly, because the costs do not meet the definition of an asset.

In the past, accountants have argued that costs associated with producing revenues should be deferred, and recognized in the income statement when the related revenues are recognized. The following scenario provides an illustration of this.

Ethics

Livent Inc., mentioned earlier, followed the policy of deferring preproduction costs for the creation of each separate show until the show was opened. On opening night, the show would start to produce revenues and then the costs were amortized and matched with those revenues. Such costs included advertising, publicity and promotions, set construction, props, costumes, and salaries paid to the cast, crew, musicians, and creative workers during rehearsal. In short, anything to do with the production was deferred.

On the one hand, one might argue that this was a bit aggressive. One could also argue that this treatment was acceptable because of the direct and incremental nature of these costs in terms of future production revenues. The trouble began when the company started to reclassify some of these costs as fixed assets and also to reallocate these costs to different and unrelated shows that had higher revenue. The company even had spreadsheets to keep track of actual results as compared with those that were publicly reported.[19]

Real-World Emphasis

---

[18] IASB/FASB joint project on revenue recognition.

[19] OSC Notice of Hearing and Statement of Allegations concerning Livent Inc., July 3, 2001.

There are debates about whether or not "matching" is conceptually valid in terms of providing support for cost deferrals. A major concern is that matching permits certain costs to be **deferred and treated as assets** on the balance sheet when in fact these costs may not meet the definition of assets (no future benefits). If abused, matching can be used by a company to turn the balance sheet into a dumping ground for unmatched costs. There are no grounds for recognizing assets and liabilities that do not specifically meet the definitions of these elements under the current conceptual framework. If a cost or expenditure does not meet the definition of an asset, it is expensed (matching notwithstanding). Similarly, there are no grounds for deferral of revenues as liabilities in the name of matching.

Accounting standard setters are moving toward ensuring that the balance sheet elements are properly recognized and measured as a basis for measuring income (sometimes referred to as a balance sheet emphasis). Thus the concept of matching is not as central as it would be if the income statement were the main focus. In addition, the use of fair value in measuring assets renders the concept of matching—as historically defined—useless.

Significant Change

Measurement

Finance

Because **accrual accounting** is followed, many estimates must be used when preparing financial statements. Most numbers on a balance sheet and income statement are in fact quite "soft" and inexact. In order to communicate information about economic events, accountants must convert the economic events into the language of business: numbers. Some things are easy to measure, such as cash in the bank. Others are not so easy to measure. For instance, how do you measure the potential cost of environmental damage?

Too much uncertainty may make it inappropriate to recognize a financial statement element. As a general rule, **elements are recognized** in the financial statements if they meet the definition of elements and are **measurable** (i.e., amounts may be reasonably estimated). We will first discuss a few underlying concepts, such as periodicity, unit of measure, and going concern. Then we will look at basic measurement choices. The key for accountants is to **determine an acceptable level of uncertainty**, use **measurement tools** that help deal with the uncertainty, and **disclose enough information** to signal the uncertainty.

Periodicity Assumption

The most accurate way to measure the results of an enterprise's activity would be to do the measurement at the time of the enterprise's eventual liquidation. At that point, there is complete certainty about all of the company's cash flows. Business, government, investors, and various other user groups, however, cannot wait that long for such information. Users need to be informed about performance and economic status on a **timely basis** so that they can evaluate and compare firms. For this reason, information must be reported periodically. The periodicity assumption (or time period assumption) implies that an enterprise's economic activities can be divided into **artificial time periods**. These time periods vary, but the most common are one month, one quarter, and one year.

The shorter the time period, the more difficult it becomes to **determine the proper net income** for the period. A month's results are usually less reliable than a quarter's results, and a quarter's results are likely less reliable than a year's results. This is because more estimates are needed to accrue costs and revenues in accrual accounting when the time period is shorter. Investors want and demand information that has been quickly processed and distributed; yet the more quickly the information is released, the more likely errors become.

The question of what time period is appropriate is becoming more serious because product cycles are shorter and products become obsolete more quickly. Many observers believe that, given the advances in technology, more on-line, **real-time financial information** needs to be provided to ensure that relevant information is available. The issue of continuous financial reporting was introduced in Chapter 1.

Monetary Unit Assumption

The monetary unit assumption means that money is the common denominator of economic activity and is an appropriate **basis for accounting measurement** and analysis. This assumption implies that the monetary unit is the most effective way of expressing to interested parties changes in capital and exchanges of goods and services. The monetary unit is relevant, simple, universally available, understandable, and useful. Applying this assumption depends on the even more basic assumption that **quantitative data** are useful in communicating economic information and in making rational economic decisions.

In Canada and the United States, accountants have chosen generally to ignore the phenomenon of **price-level change** (inflation and deflation) by assuming that the unit of measure, the dollar, remains reasonably **stable**. This assumption about the monetary unit has been used to justify adding 1970 dollars to 2003 dollars without any adjustment. Only if circumstances change dramatically (such as if Canada or the United States were to experience high inflation similar to that in countries such as Zimbabwe) would the AcSB and FASB consider "inflation accounting." IAS 29 deals with hyperinflation.

Going Concern Assumption

Most accounting methods are based on the going concern assumption. This is the assumption that a business enterprise will **continue to operate for the foreseeable future**; i.e., that it will not be forced to end its operations. Although there are many business failures, experience indicates that companies do have a fairly high continuance rate. While accountants do not believe that business firms will last indefinitely, they do expect them to last long enough to fulfill their objectives and commitments. Management must assess the company's ability to continue as a going concern and take into account all available information, looking out at least 12 months from the balance sheet date.

The implications of this assumption are profound. The **historical cost principle** would have limited usefulness if **liquidation** were assumed to be likely. Under a liquidation approach, for example, asset values are better stated at **net realizable value** (sales price less costs of disposal) than at **acquisition cost**. Amortization and amortization policies are justifiable and appropriate only if we assume some permanence to the enterprise; this is what justifies allocating the costs of the amortized assets to future periods to match them against future revenues. If a liquidation approach were adopted, the **current versus noncurrent classification** of assets and liabilities would lose much of its significance. Labelling anything a **fixed or long-term** asset would be difficult to justify. Indeed, listing liabilities according to their likely liquidation would be more reasonable.

The going concern assumption applies in most business situations. The only time when the assumption does not apply is when **there is intent to liquidate the company's net assets and cease operations or cease trading in the company's shares or when the company has no realistic alternative but to liquidate or cease operations.** In these cases, a total **revaluation** of assets and liabilities can provide information that closely approximates the entity's **net realizable value.** The accounting problems that arise when an enterprise is in liquidation are presented in advanced accounting courses. In order to illustrate the going concern concept and the question of liquidation, consider the situation of **Air Canada.**

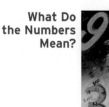

On April 1, 2003, Air Canada filed for bankruptcy protection under the *Companies' Creditors Arrangement Act* (CCAA) due to cash flow difficulties. The CCAA provides a safe harbour for companies in distress, giving them the opportunity to reorganize their financial affairs in a systematic manner while at the same time holding off creditors. Air Canada's protection was granted for the period ending June 30. This was subsequently extended to September 30, 2003. In the meantime, the company issued its first quarter results.

Should the statements have been prepared on a **liquidation basis** or a **going concern basis**? Air Canada prepared the statements on a going concern basis using certain assumptions:

1. that management was in the process of developing a plan to restructure operations under the CCAA,

2. that it had been able to obtain "debtor in possession" financing from General Electric Canada Finance Inc., and

3. that it expected the company to continue operating as a going concern.

The financial statements fully disclosed these facts. Companies are required to disclose any material uncertainties that may cast doubt upon their ability to continue as a going concern. As it turns out, the company successfully emerged from bankruptcy protection in 2004 but in 2009 was in the news, once again deliberating whether it needed to apply for protection under CCAA.

How do we measure things when we assume the entity is a going concern? Management must continually assess the likelihood of outcomes (e.g., whether a company will lose a lawsuit) based on history and supporting evidence. Often, companies rely on specialists such as lawyers and engineers for help with such assessments.

Measurability is a big issue for many financial statement elements. When there is a **variance** between the recognized amount and another reasonably possible amount, this is called measurement uncertainty. Accountants are continually working to develop and make use of **measurement tools** such as option pricing and discounted cash flow models, as well as others. When observable values are not available (e.g., market prices, cost), these models are used as a way of dealing with measurement uncertainty. There is a trade-off with uncertainty. Too much measurement uncertainty undermines the reliability of the financial statements. However, if the element is not recognized at all in the financial statements, then all relevant information has not been included and the statements are incomplete. A compromise is to measure and recognize the elements in the body of the financial statements and to disclose the measurement uncertainty and its significance in the notes to the financial statements.

Historical Cost Principle

Transactions are initially measured at the amount of cash (or cash equivalents) that was paid or received or the fair value that was ascribed to the transactions when they took place. This is often called the historical cost principle. The historical cost principle generally has three underlying assumptions:

1. It represents a value at a **point in time**.

2. It results from a reciprocal exchange (i.e., a two-way exchange).

3. The exchange includes **an outside party**.

Initial recognition.   For non-financial assets, the value includes any laid-down costs; i.e., any cost that is incurred to get the asset ready (whether for sale or for generating income by using it). Inventory, for instance, might include the **cost of material, labour, and a reasonable allocation of overhead**. Similarly, for a self-constructed asset, cost would include any cost incurred to get the asset **ready for its intended use,** including transportation and installation costs.

Sometimes it is not possible to determine **cost or fair value.** Transactions that have some or all of the following characteristics present challenges:

- Non-monetary or barter transactions where **no cash or monetary consideration** is exchanged. Here it may be more difficult to determine the value of the assets exchanged.

- Non-monetary, non-reciprocal transactions where there is **no exchange**, such as donations.

- Related party transactions where the parties to the transaction are not acting at arm's length (i.e., there is **no outside party**). In these cases, the exchange price may not reflect the true value of the assets exchanged.

In certain cases, an attempt is made to estimate the **fair value** if possible, and this may become the cost basis going forward.

The historical cost principle also applies to financial instruments. Bonds, notes, and accounts payable and receivable are issued by a business enterprise in exchange for assets, or perhaps services, that have an **agreed-upon exchange price** or **economic value.** This price, established by the exchange transaction, is the "cost" of the financial instrument and gives the figure at which the instrument should be recognized in the financial statements as long as it is equal to fair value.

Subsequent remeasurement.   Historical cost has an important advantage over other valuation methods. Because it generally comes from an **arm's-length transaction** or exchange, it represents a bargained, fairly arrived-at value at a specific point in time. When it is first recognized, cost usually represents fair value. Over time, however, it often becomes irrelevant in terms of **predictive value.** Later remeasurements also have limitations, however. They can be based on different measurement values, such as fair value, and give information that is more relevant, but they often involve **measurement uncertainty.** Furthermore, because there is often no external exchange (i.e., exchange with an outside party), the values may be **subjective.**

Despite these limitations, the trend is toward an increasingly **mixed valuation model.** What used to be primarily a **historical cost-based model,** modified by the application of conservatism (i.e., revaluations occurred if the asset's value declined below cost), is moving more toward a **market valuation model.** The use of fair value will be discussed below.

Fair Value Principle

GAAP has increasingly called for the use of standardized fair value measurements in the financial statements. This is an emerging principle which we will call the fair value principle. Fair value information may be more useful than historical cost for certain types of assets and liabilities and in certain industries. For example, companies report many financial instruments, including derivatives, at fair value. Brokerage houses and mutual funds prepare their basic financial statements using fair value.

Fair value is defined as "the price that would be received to sell an asset or paid to transfer a liability in an orderly transaction between market participants at the measurement date."[20] Accordingly, fair value is an exit price (a price to sell/transfer). Exit price

Significant Change

---

[20] See definition from FASB ASC 820-10 and IASB Exposure Draft on fair value. The term "market" refers to any mechanism where by parties objectively determine price, usually through bargaining and supply and demand. Examples of markets include capital markets (such as stock exchanges), commodities markets (such as futures exchanges), or other markets such as financial markets, which establish things such as interest and foreign exchange rates.

refers to a selling price (as opposed to an "entry price," which reflects the entity's potential purchase price). According to the definition, fair value is also a **market-based measure,** as opposed to an **entity-specific measure**. As such, it is meant to be more objective. It seeks to determine value by looking at how market participants would value the item in question. It does not look at value from the perspective of the entity itself and as such it does not consider company-specific synergies.[21]

Illustration 2-8 illustrates the various ways to define "value" or price.

Illustration 2-8

Defining Value or Price

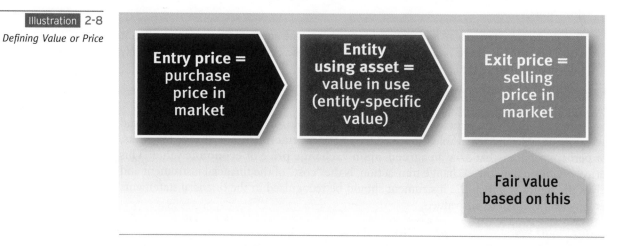

For instance, if an entity has a manufacturing facility that is integrated into its other facilities, the entity might successfully argue that the facility has synergistic value and is worth more to the specific entity. That is, the asset's value is higher to the entity because it interacts with the entity's other assets. However, the market would generally value the facility based on what it was worth without the entity-specific synergies. That is, someone buying the facility would not have access to these entity-specific synergies and so would not attribute any excess value to them.

Which value is better for use in the financial statements? Good question. There is a trade-off. Entity-specific value may be more relevant for operating assets where the entity plans to hold onto them and use them to produce revenues, but it is more subjective. As noted above, the market-based view is more objective and verifiable.

At initial acquisition, historical cost generally equals fair value. In subsequent periods, as market and economic conditions change, historical cost and fair value often diverge. These fair value measures or estimates often provide more relevant information about the expected cash flows related to the asset or liability. For example, when a long-lived asset declines in value, a fair value measure may be used to help determine a potential impairment loss.

Significant Change

In order to encourage increased use of fair value and simplify accounting, standard setters have given companies the option to use fair value for most financial instruments (e.g., cash, receivables, non-strategic investments, payables) where certain conditions are met, as an accounting policy choice. This is referred to as the fair value option. Standard setters feel that fair value is more relevant for most financial instruments as it reflects the current cash equivalent value. In addition, markets exist for many financial instruments, thereby providing independent, objective evidence of value. As a result, companies have the option to measure assets and liabilities such as receivables, payables, and investments at

---

[21] This is different from historical views of fair values, which often consider the value from the entity's perspective including any company-specific synergies. The objective of moving to a market-based fair value measure is to reduce subjectivity. An entity will usually believe that the asset is worth more than it actually is and often attributes this to past entity-specific synergies, which are difficult to prove.

fair value (with gains and losses being booked to income). In addition to the more general fair value option, certain standards under IFRS explicitly allow the use of fair value for non-financial assets such as investment properties and property, plant, and equipment. The fair value options will be expanded upon in future chapters.

Fair value is also discussed in greater detail in Appendix 2A.

Presentation and Disclosure

Full Disclosure Principle

Anything that is relevant to decisions should be included in the financial statements. This is referred to as the full disclosure principle. The principle recognizes that the nature and amount of information included in financial reports reflects a series of judgemental trade-offs. These trade-offs aim for information that is:

- **detailed enough** to disclose matters that make a difference to users, but

- **condensed enough** to make the information understandable, and also appropriate in terms of the **costs** of preparing and using it.

More information is not always better. Too much information may result in a situation where the user is unable to digest or process the information. This is called information overload. Information about a company's financial position, income, cash flows, and investments can be found in one of three places:

1. in the **main body of financial statements**

2. in the **notes to the financial statements**

3. as supplementary information, including the **Management Discussion and Analysis (MD&A)**

The financial statements are a **formalized, structured way of communicating financial information**. Disclosure is not a substitute for proper accounting.[22] Certain numbers, such as earnings per share, send signals to the capital marketplace. For example, cash basis accounting for cost of goods sold is misleading, even if accrual-based amounts have been disclosed in the notes to the financial statements. As mentioned in Chapter 1, and earlier in this chapter with regard to Nortel, the market watches and listens for signals about earnings in particular and does not usually react well to earnings surprises—especially negative ones.

The notes to financial statements generally **amplify or explain** the items presented in the main body of the statements. If the information in the main body of the statements gives an incomplete picture of the enterprise's performance and position, additional information that is needed to complete the picture should be included in the notes.

Information in the notes does not have to be quantifiable, nor does it need to qualify as an element. Notes can be partially or totally narrative. Examples of notes are:

- **descriptions** of the accounting policies and methods used in measuring the elements reported in the statements

- **explanations** of uncertainties and contingencies

- **statistics and details** that are too voluminous to include in the statements

---

[22] According to GAAP, recognition means including an item in one or more individual statements and does not mean disclosure in the notes to the financial statements. Some critics might argue, however, that if markets are assumed to be efficient, then as long as the information is disclosed, the market will absorb and use the information in pricing the shares.

The notes are not only helpful to understanding the enterprise's performance and position—they are essential.

Supplementary information may include details or amounts that present a different perspective from what appears in the financial statements. They may include quantifiable information that is high in relevance but low in reliability, or information that is helpful but not essential. One example of supplementary information is the data and schedules provided by oil and gas companies: typically they give information on proven reserves as well as the related discounted cash flows.

Supplementary information also includes management's explanation of the financial information and a discussion of its significance in the **MD&A**. The CICA MD&A *Guidance on Preparation and Disclosure* lays out six general disclosure principles.

MD&A's should:

- enable readers to **view the company through the eyes of management**;
- **complement** as well as **supplement** financial statements;
- be **reliable, complete, fair, and balanced**, providing material information; that is, information important to an investor, acting reasonably, in making a decision to invest or continue to invest in the company;
- have a **forward-looking** orientation;
- focus on **management's strategy for generating value** for investors over time;
- be **written in plain language**, with candour and without exaggeration, and embody the qualities of understandability, relevance, comparability, and consistency over reporting periods.

Thus, the MD&A is a step toward a more broadly based business reporting model that also contains forward-looking information. The guidance also includes a framework that identifies five key elements that should be included in the MD&A:

1. the company's **vision, core businesses, and strategy**

2. **key performance drivers**

3. **capabilities** (capital and other resources) to achieve the desired results

4. **results** (historical and prospective)

5. **risks** that may shape and/or affect the achievement of results

Hopefully, these additional disclosures will give users of the financial information a greater insight into the company's business.[23]

The content, arrangement, and display of financial statements, along with other facets of full disclosure, are discussed specifically in Chapters 4, 5, and 23, and more generally throughout the text.

Illustration 2-9 presents the conceptual framework discussed in this chapter. It is similar to Illustration 2-1, except that it gives additional information for each level. We cannot overemphasize the usefulness of this conceptual framework in helping to understand many of the problem areas that are examined in later chapters.

---

[23] Although MD&A disclosures are mandated for public companies, the CICA *Guidance*, in its executive summary, notes that the MD&A can also be used by other organizations to communicate more effectively.

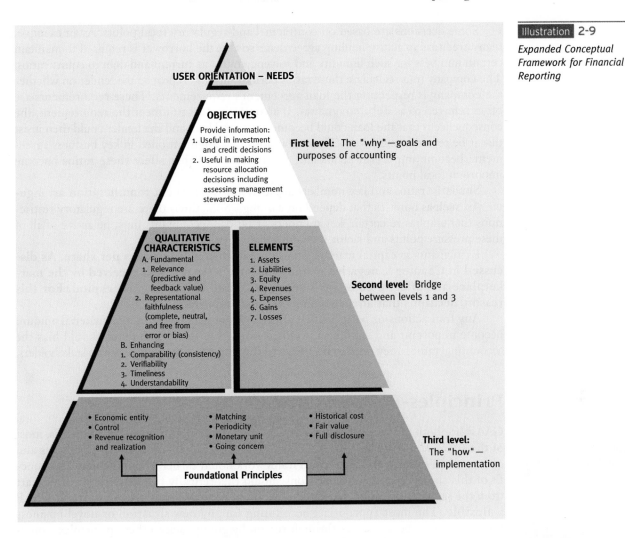

Illustration 2-9

Expanded Conceptual Framework for Financial Reporting

USER ORIENTATION – NEEDS

OBJECTIVES

Provide information:
1. Useful in investment and credit decisions
2. Useful in making resource allocation decisions including assessing management stewardship

First level: The "why"—goals and purposes of accounting

QUALITATIVE CHARACTERISTICS

A. Fundamental
1. Relevance (predictive and feedback value)
2. Representational faithfulness (complete, neutral, and free from error or bias)
B. Enhancing
1. Comparability (consistency)
2. Verifiability
3. Timeliness
4. Understandability

ELEMENTS

1. Assets
2. Liabilities
3. Equity
4. Revenues
5. Expenses
6. Gains
7. Losses

Second level: Bridge between levels 1 and 3

- Economic entity
- Control
- Revenue recognition and realization
- Matching
- Periodicity
- Monetary unit
- Going concern
- Historical cost
- Fair value
- Full disclosure

Foundational Principles

Third level: The "how"— implementation

FINANCIAL REPORTING ISSUES

Making financial reporting decisions is a complex process. This section examines the factors that make this process challenging. As mentioned earlier in the chapter, the main objective of financial reporting is to **provide reliable, decision-relevant financial information** to users so that they can make well-informed capital allocation decisions. Capital that is invested in good investments fuels the economy and encourages job growth and wealth creation. To achieve this objective, well-judged choices must be made between alternative accounting concepts, methods, and means of disclosure. Accounting principles and rules must be **selected and interpreted and professional judgement must be applied**.

Because accounting is **influenced by its environment** (in many cases in a negative way) and by decisions made by individuals who often act in **self-interest** or in the interests of the company (at the expense of other stakeholders), it is unrealistic to believe that the financial reporting system will always work properly. Instead of wealth creation in the capital markets and the economy, financial reporting decisions sometimes lead to wealth and value destruction. Many stakeholders depend on the information to make key decisions. As a result, some numbers in the financial statements have a **higher profile and visibility** than others since they become the **focus for decision-making**.

Some decisions are based on contractual and regulatory focal points. As an example, many creditors structure lending agreements so that the borrower is required to maintain certain numbers for such liquidity and solvency ratios as current and debt to equity ratios. The company must calculate these ratios periodically and report to the lender on whether the company is respecting the loan agreement's requirements. These requirements are often referred to as debt covenants. If a company does not meet the requirement, the consequence is that the loan could become a demand loan and the lender could then insist that it be repaid immediately. Thus, any ratios that are mentioned in key business agreements become important ratios and any transactions that affect these ratios become important focal points.

Similarly, ratios and key numbers are used in **management remuneration arrangements,** such as bonuses that depend on earnings. Sometimes there are regulatory restrictions that emphasize certain key numbers or ratios. Accountants must be aware of all of these pressure points and factor them into their decision-making.

Participants in capital markets focus on **earnings and earnings per share. As discussed in Chapter 1, negative earnings surprises are not well received by the marketplace and affect a company's share price and ability to raise capital. For this reason, decisions that affect earnings are also important.**

Any transactions or balances that affect key numbers or ratios by a material amount become important and significant. This is not to say that accountants should bias the accounting; rather, they need to **be aware of the impact** of their decisions on stakeholders.

Principles-Based Approach

Objective **7**
Explain the factors that contribute to choice and/or bias in financial reporting decisions.

Ethics

GAAP (for both private and public entities in Canada) is **principles-based**; that is, most of the *CICA Handbook*, including IFRS, is based on a few foundational principles and concepts like those in the conceptual framework noted earlier in the chapter. The benefit of this approach is that all decisions should theoretically be **consistent** if they start from the same foundational reasoning.[24] Another benefit is that principles-based GAAP is **flexible.** The most appropriate accounting for any new situation or novel business transaction may be arrived at through reason by going back to these principles (sometimes referred to as first principles). However, principles-based GAAP is sometimes criticized for being too flexible. Some critics feel that it allows too much choice and therefore results in **lack of comparability**.

Care should therefore be taken to ensure that this flexibility is not abused. The key foundational concept of **neutrality** is of the greatest importance. **The conceptual framework developed in this chapter is the anchor that should ground all financial reporting decisions.** In the absence of specific GAAP guidance, an entity should adopt accounting policies that are:

(a) consistent with specific GAAP guidance; and

(b) **developed** through the exercise of professional judgement and the application of the conceptual framework.[25]

---

[24] Because the framework was developed after many of the standards, there may be some standards that are inconsistent with the framework. Note that the framework does not override any specific standard. The standard setters are working to get rid of inconsistencies between the older standards and the framework.

[25] The IASB and FASB continue to work on the new joint conceptual framework. It is an iterative process since they must continually test the concepts against the existing and constantly changing body of knowledge to ensure its robustness.

Financial Engineering

A practice known as financial engineering became more visible during the past decade. Financial engineering is the process of legally structuring a business arrangement or transaction so that it meets the company's financial reporting objective (e.g., to maximize earnings, minimize a debt to equity ratio, or other). This is often done by creating complex legal arrangements and financial instruments. These arrangements and instruments are created so that the resulting accounting meets the desired objective within GAAP. For example, a company that is raising debt financing might want the instrument structured so that it meets the GAAP definition of equity rather than debt. In this way, the debt to equity ratio is not affected.

Ethics

Many financial institutions developed and marketed these products to their clients. These arrangements are often called **structured financings**. Since Enron, this practice has been reduced. Are financial engineering and the practice of structured financings ethically acceptable? Financial engineering has moved from being an accepted (saleable) practice and commodity to a potentially fraudulent activity.

Illustration 2-10 looks at the various shades of grey in accounting for transactions.

Illustration 2-10

Choice in Accounting Decision-Making

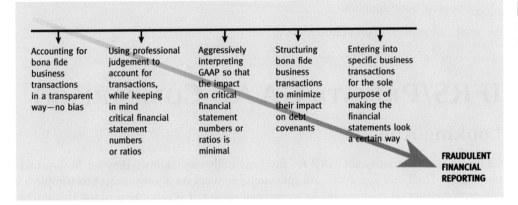

Illustration 2-10 contents:

- Accounting for bona fide business transactions in a transparent way—no bias
- Using professional judgement to account for transactions, while keeping in mind critical financial statement numbers or ratios
- Aggressively interpreting GAAP so that the impact on critical financial statement numbers or ratios is minimal
- Structuring bona fide business transactions to minimize their impact on debt covenants
- Entering into specific business transactions for the sole purpose of making the financial statements look a certain way

FRAUDULENT FINANCIAL REPORTING

Fraudulent Financial Reporting

The role of accountants who are responsible for preparing a company's financial records is to capture business and economic events and transactions as they occur and communicate them to interested parties. They should not use the financial statements to portray something that is not there. Similarly, good financial reporting should be a result of **well-reasoned and supported analysis** that is grounded in a conceptual framework. It should not be influenced by external pressures. Pressures in the capital marketplace are everywhere, however, and their potentially negative impact on financial reporting must be acknowledged. Pressures may arise from various sources, including the ones discussed below.

Economic or Business Environment

Sometimes a company experiences sudden drops in revenue or market share. The underlying reason may be unique to the company and due to some poor strategic and business decisions or it may result from an industry or economic downturn. This may put pressures on a company to "prop up" its revenues. There may be pressure to recognize revenues before they should be or to defer the recognition of some expenses.

Some companies use an industry or economic downturn as an opportunity to clean up their books and generally take large writedowns on assets such as inventory or goodwill.

Ethics

The markets expect a loss and the company's share price is therefore not overly affected in a negative way. This "purging" of the balance sheet has the positive impact of making future earnings look better.

Other Pressures

Budgets put tremendous pressure on company management. Since bonuses and even jobs depend on meeting budgets, sometimes this negative influence leaks inappropriately into accounting decisions.

Sometimes strong pressures build up because of debt covenants or analysts' expectations. These can be significant and may cause management to make biased decisions and misrepresent the company's financial position and operations.

If they are not monitored and controlled properly, these pressures are a major problem. In order to lessen the chances of fraudulent financial reporting, various controls and a solid governance structure may be put in place by a company. These could include:

Ethics

1. vigilant, knowledgeable top management

2. an independent audit committee

3. an internal audit function

4. other internal controls at lower levels

IFRS/PRIVATE GAAP COMPARISON

Looking Ahead

Objective 8
Discuss current trends in standard setting for the conceptual framework.

Canadian and international GAAP are fundamentally similar since they are both principles-based. The IASB and FASB are continuing to work on a joint project to complete a common conceptual framework. As mentioned earlier, it is the intent to use this framework in Canada for private entities as well. This chapter includes the work produced to date. The standard setters continue to work on definitions for financial statement elements and recognition/derecognition and measurement criteria. They also plan to work on issues related to presentation and disclosure and the status of the framework itself.

Glossary

KEY TERMS

assets, 46
basic elements, 46
comparability, 42
completeness, 41
comprehensive
    income, 50
conceptual framework, 38
conservatism, 41

Summary of Learning Objectives

1 Describe the usefulness of a conceptual framework.

A conceptual framework is needed to (1) create standards that build on an established body of concepts and objectives, (2) provide a framework for solving new and emerging practical problems, (3) increase financial statement users' understanding of and confidence in financial reporting, and (4) enhance comparability among different companies' financial statements.

2 Describe the main components of a conceptual framework for financial reporting.

The first level deals with the objective of financial reporting. The second level includes the qualitative characteristics of useful information and elements of financial statements. The third level includes foundational principles and conventions.

3 Understand the objective of financial reporting.

The objective of financial reporting is to provide information that is useful to individuals making investment and credit decisions.

4 Identify the qualitative characteristics of accounting information.

The overriding criterion by which accounting choices can be judged is decision usefulness; that is, the goal is to provide the information that is the most useful for decision-making. Fundamental characteristics include relevance and faithful representation. These two characteristics must be present. Enhancing characteristics include comparability, verifiability, timeliness, and understandability. There may be trade-offs.

5 Define the basic elements of financial statements.

The basic elements of financial statements are (1) assets, (2) liabilities, (3) equity, (4) revenues, (5) expenses, (6) gains, and (7) losses.

6 Describe the foundational principles of accounting.

(1) Economic entity: the assumption that the activity of a business enterprise can be kept separate and distinct from its owners and any other business unit. (2) Control: the entity has the power to make decisions and reap the benefits. (3) Revenue recognition: revenue is generally recognized when it is (a) earned, (b) measurable, and (c) collectible (realizable). (4) Matching assists in the measurement of income by ensuring that costs (relating to long-lived assets) incurred in earning revenues are booked in the same period as the revenues earned. (5) Periodicity: the assumption that an enterprise's economic activities can be divided into artificial time periods to facilitate timely reporting. (6) Monetary unit: the assumption that money is the common denominator by which economic activity is conducted, and that the monetary unit gives an appropriate basis for measurement and analysis. (7) Going concern: the assumption that the business enterprise will have a long life. (8) Historical cost principle: existing GAAP requires that many assets and liabilities be accounted for and reported based on their acquisition price. Many assets are later revalued. (9) Fair value principle: assets and liabilities are valued at fair value, that is, an exit price and viewed from a market participant perspective. (10) Full disclosure principle: accountants follow the general practice of providing information that is important enough to influence an informed user's judgement and decisions.

7 Explain the factors that contribute to choice and/or bias in financial reporting decisions.

Choice is the result of many things, including GAAP's basis of principles, measurement uncertainty, and increasingly complex business transactions. The conceptual framework is the foundation that GAAP is built on. If there is no primary source of GAAP for a specific decision, then professional judgement must be used, making sure that the accounting policies chosen are consistent with the primary sources of GAAP and the conceptual framework.

Financial engineering is the process of legally structuring a business arrangement or transaction so that it meets the company's financial reporting objective. This is a dangerous practice since it often results in biased information.

Fraudulent financial reporting often results from pressures on individuals or the company. These pressures may come from various sources, including worsening company, industry, or economic conditions; unrealistic internal budgets; and financial statement focal points related to contractual, regulatory, or capital market expectations. Weak internal controls and governance also contribute to fraudulent financial reporting.

8 Discuss current trends in standard setting for the conceptual framework.

The IASB and FASB will continue to work toward a common conceptual framework. The project on objectives and qualitative characteristics is essentially complete. The Boards are focusing on defining elements and the recognition/measurement frameworks.

Appendix 2A

Fair Value Measurements

Fair value as a basis for measurement was introduced in Chapter 2. This appendix goes into a bit more detail. Although the use of fair value may introduce greater relevance into the financial statements in many cases, it may also introduce more measurement uncertainty and subjectivity, especially where liquid markets are not available to provide evidence of fair value. In order to measure fair value, an entity must determine the following:[26]

9 Objective

Understand in greater detail how fair value is measured.

1. The particular asset being measured: Consider the specific nature, condition, and location of the asset being measured.

2. The valuation premise: Will the asset be valued by the market as part of a group of other assets as an "in-use" asset (for instance as part of a manufacturing facility) or on a stand-alone basis? Generally, the asset is valued based on what is referred to as its highest and best use in the market **regardless of how the entity is actually using the asset.** The highest and best use concept values the asset based on the highest value that the market would place on the asset considering uses that are physically possible, legally permissible, and financially feasible. For example, if the entity is trying to measure the fair value of a piece of land zoned as residential, it would not consider a value that assumed that the land was zoned as a commercial property (since commercial development is not legally permissible at the measurement date).

3. The most advantageous market: The measurement would consider the value based on the market that would pay the most for the asset. Many entities buy and sell in different markets and this concept assumes that the value would be based upon the most profitable market price (which would normally be the same as the price on the principal market that the entity would transact in).

4. The availability of data: Use the valuation technique appropriate for the measurement considering the availability of data used for inputs into the valuation model. In many cases, a liquid market for the asset will be available and this would represent fair value. In other cases, however, a valuation technique or model would be used (such as discounted cash flow or an option pricing model) to value the asset. If a model is used, then the entity would have to select inputs to use (including things such as discount rates, future cash flows to be generated by the asset, and other). Illustration 2A-1 looks at this. Inputs that are observable in the market (for instance, prime interest rate) are better than those that are not, as the observable inputs are more objective.

inputs ⟶ model ⟶ output
(observable inputs   (fair value
are the best)   measurement)

Illustration 2A-1

Measuring Fair Value

---

[26] Ideas and concepts taken from IASB *Exposure Draft: Fair Value Measurement*, May 2009.

Illustration 2A-2 illustrates the various levels of inputs and different models in the fair value hierarchy.

	Market Model	Income Model*	Cost Model
Level 1 inputs	Quoted prices in active market (no need to adjust)	Not applicable	Not applicable
Level 2 inputs	Quoted prices for similar assets, other market inputs/data (start with inputs and calculate value by adjusting)	Current market expectations about future, using as many objectively determined market inputs as possible	Quoted prices for similar assets in similar condition. May not be able to buy the exact same asset in same condition; i.e., if the asset being valued is a machine, use prices from supplier for a replacement machine.
Level 3 inputs	May include entity's own data or assumptions about how the market would value (start with inputs and calculate value by adjusting)	Current expectations about future, using whatever inputs are available, including management estimates	Estimates of prices for similar assets
		* (use time value of money and cash flow projections to value)	

Illustration 2A-2

The Fair Value Hierarchy

As the illustration indicates, level 1 inputs provide the most reliable fair values because these inputs are based on quoted prices in an active market for the exact same item (for instance, if we are valuing a company's shares, level 1 inputs to the valuation would include the actual price of shares trading on the TSX at a certain point in time; the actual price would be the fair value). Level 2 is the next most reliable and considers evaluating similar assets or liabilities in active markets or using observable inputs such as interest rates or exchange rates. Level 3 is the least reliable level since much judgement is needed based on the best information available. This often includes management judgements about how the markets would value the asset. As we move away from level 1 inputs, we are generally using a model to value the item; i.e., start with the inputs and adjust them. This introduces more measurement uncertainty. Additional disclosures are required as you move away from level 1 inputs.

Models for Measuring Fair Value

Finance

The second column in the illustration looks at income models. Where market prices are not available for the item, a valuation technique is used. As a general rule, the valuation technique should use all the input variables that are available from external market sources and rely as little as possible on internally generated variables. This allows the model to produce more objective, and more reliable, fair value estimates. Valuation models include discounted cash flow (discussed below) and options pricing models (discussed in Chapter 16).

Fair value estimates arrived at by using discounted cash flow models incorporate one or more of the following components:

(a) Estimates of cash flows: Management makes its best estimates of expected cash flows incorporating contractual cash flows as well as estimated cash flows.

(b) Time value of money: An interest rate is used to discount the cash flows. This rate may be the risk-free rate or it may be a risk-adjusted rate.

(c) Uncertainty or risk: Since not all cash flows are the same in terms of amount, timing and riskiness, discounted cash flow models reflect the risk or uncertainty by adjusting either the cash flows or the discount rate but generally not both in the same calculation. Uncertainty may be reflected in the numerator by applying probabilities to various cash flow scenarios. It may be incorporated in the discount rate by applying a risk premium such that the rate exceeds the risk-free rate.

Discounted Cash Flow Models

The **discounted cash flow model** is a very robust, widely accepted tool for dealing with uncertainty and the time value of money.

Present Value Concepts

Two approaches are generally accepted:

1. Traditional approach: The discount rate reflects all risks in the cash flows but the cash flows are assumed to be certain.

2. Expected cash flow approach: A risk-free discount rate is used to discount cash flows that have been adjusted for uncertainty.

Traditional Approach. Under the **traditional approach**, the stream of contracted cash flows is discounted, and the discount rate is adjusted to accommodate the riskiness of the cash flows. This model is best used where the cash flows are otherwise fairly certain. The discount rate would be adjusted for the credit risk that is associated with the party that is paying the cash flows. This method is useful for instruments where the cash flows are specified in the contract, such as fixed interest and principal payments. It is not very useful for more complex instruments where the cash flows may be variable for other reasons than the credit risk.

Assume that Company A has issued a 10% bond that is due in 10 years and has a face value of $100. Assume further that the risk-adjusted market rate that reflects the credit risk of Company A is 10%. This rate would be the rate that the market would demand of Company A, given the specific credit risk. The bond's present value would be calculated as follows:

$$\text{PV } \$1 \text{ at } 10\% \times \text{Principal} + \text{PV of an annuity for 10 years at } 10\% -$$
$$\text{All discounted at } 10\% = \$100$$

Expected Cash Flow Approach. Under the **expected cash flow approach**, the discount rate is the risk-free rate and the cash flow uncertainty is dealt with by using probabilities. The projected cash flows reflect the uncertainty in terms of amount and timing using probability weighting. This model is more flexible and is useful where the financial instruments have variable cash flows.

In this case, assume that the instrument has a variable cash flow. Assume that there is a 20% chance of a payment in three years of $30 and an 80% chance of a payment in three years of $60. If the risk-free rate were 5%, the expected cash flows (incorporating the credit risk) are as follows:

$$20\% \times \$30 + 80\% \times \$60 = \$54$$

$$\text{PV } \$54 \text{ at } 5\% \text{ in three years} = \$54 \times 0.86384 = \$46.65$$

Note that these methods may be used for valuing items at fair value, estimating liabilities, or conducting impairment tests. Subsequent chapters will examine these uses in greater detail.

Summary of Learning Objective for Appendix 2A

KEY TERMS

expected cash flow
    approach, 71
discounted cash flow
    model, 71
traditional approach, 71
highest and best use, 69
most advantageous
    market, 69

9 Understand in greater detail how fair value is measured.

Fair value measurement is a market-based approach which incorporates the specific attributes of the asset/liability being measured, the valuation premise (how the asset/liability is to be used), the most advantageous market, and the availability of data. Since market prices are not always available, valuation models are used to measure the value. Inputs to these models are either observable in the market or not. Observable inputs are most useful since they are more objective. The fair value hierarchy establishes three levels of inputs, with level one being the highest/best type of input (based on market prices which are observable). Because level three inputs are more subjective, additional disclosures are required. Valuation models include discounted cash flow and options pricing models.

Note: All assignment material with an asterisk (*) relates to the appendix to the chapter.

Brief Exercises

(LO 4) BE2-1   Indicate the qualitative characteristic of financial information being described in each item below:

(a) Financial statements should include all information necessary to portray the underlying transactions.

(b) Financial information should make a difference in the decision-making of a user.

(c) Financial information should not favour one user or stakeholder over another.

(d) Financial information should reflect the economic substance of business events or transactions.

(e) Financial information should help users assess the impact of past, present, or future events.

(f) Financial information must be reliable and without errors or omissions.

(g) Financial information should help users confirm or correct their previous expectations.

(h) Financial information should be reported and measured in a similar way within a company and between different companies.

(i) Financial information should be of sufficient quality and clarity to permit reasonably informed users to assess the information's significance.

(j) Financial information should be available to users before it loses its ability to be decision-useful.

(k) Knowledgeable, independent users should be able to achieve similar results and consensus when accounting for a particular financial transaction.

(LO 4) BE2-2   Identify which qualitative characteristic of accounting information is best described in each item below. (Do not simply use relevance and representational faithfulness.)

(a) The annual reports of Melissa Corp. are audited by public accountants.

(b) Able Corp. and Mona, Inc. both use the straight-line depreciation method.

(c) Swedish Corp. issues its quarterly reports within five days after each quarter ends.

(d) Philips Inc. disposed of one of its two subsidiaries that were included in its consolidated statements for prior years.

(e) The CFO of WebDesign stresses that factual, truthful, unbiased information is the overriding consideration when preparing WebDesign's financial information.

(f) EB Energy Inc. appreciates that financial information may be misrepresented or misinterpreted if all pertinent information is not included.

(g) Wright Industries exercises due care and professional judgement in developing all estimates and assumptions used to prepare its financial information.

BE2-3   What principle(s) from the conceptual framework does Master Limited use in each of the following situations?   **(LO 4, 6)**

(a) Master includes the activities of its subsidiaries in its financial statements.

(b) Master was involved in litigation with Kinshasa Ltd. over a product malfunction. This litigation is disclosed in the financial statements.

(c) Master allocates the cost of its tangible assets over the period when it expects to receive revenue from these assets.

(d) Master records the purchase of a new packaging machine at its cash equivalent price.

(e) Master prepares quarterly financial statements for its users.

(f) In preparing its financial statements, Master assesses its ability to continue to operate for the foreseeable future.

(g) Master records revenue when risks and rewards are passed to the purchaser.

(h) Master records its agricultural inventory at fair value. The company feels that this market-based value is more relevant, objective, and verifiable.

BE2-4   Discuss whether the following items would meet the definition of an asset currently proposed by the IASB and   **(LO 5)**
FASB. If so, explain with reference to the appropriate criteria.

(a) Corporate fleet of cars for senior management.

(b) Franchise licence to operate a Tim Hortons store.

(c) Customized manufacturing machinery that can only be used for one product line and for which there is a small and limited customer market.

(d) The parent company has guaranteed the operating line of credit of its subsidiary. Is the guarantee an asset for the subsidiary?

(e) FreshWater Inc. bottles and sells the spring water from a natural spring near its property. Is the natural spring an asset of the company?

(f) Mountain Ski Resort Ltd. often has to use its snow-making machine to make snow for its hills and trails when there is not enough natural snowfall. Is the snow an asset for Mountain Ski?

BE2-5   Discuss whether the following items would meet the definition of a liability currently proposed by the IASB and   **(LO 5)**
FASB. If so, explain with reference to the appropriate criteria.

(a) Environmental remediation after a chemical spill has occurred. This spill has violated an existing law and statute. Does a liability for cleanup exist?

(b) Environmental remediation after a chemical spill has occurred. No existing law or statute has been broken. Does a liability for cleanup exist?

(c) As part of its contract with the government, a logging company must replant one tree for each tree it cuts. Does a liability for replanting exist?

(d) A logging company has a corporate policy of always replanting trees and advertises this fact in its corporate and marketing brochures. Does a liability for replanting exist?

BE2-6   Assets are the cornerstone of financial reporting; often it is unclear whether an expenditure is an asset or an   **(LO 5, 6)**
expense. For each of the transactions described below, consider if the item should be recorded as an asset or as an expense. Be sure to include a discussion of the specific criteria in your response. Assume all items are material.

(a) Akamu Corp. pays legal fees of $2,500 in purchasing land to be used as a parking lot.

(b) Pratt, Inc. pays $7,000 to pave the driveway to its office building.

(c) On January 1, Alan & Cheng, Chartered Accountants, pay six months' office rent to cover the month of January and the next five months.

(d) Mattamy Inc. pays $190,000 to workers for construction of a building to be used as its corporate headquarters.

(e) Vaccine Inc. incurs legal fees of $5,500 for registering a patent for its product.

(f) Delhi's Florists pays wages of $2,100 for November to an employee who drives its delivery truck.

(g) Delhi's Florists pays $4,500 for flowers to be delivered to its premises.

(LO 5) BE2-7 For each item that follows, indicate which element of the financial statements it belongs to:

(a) Retained earnings

(b) Sales

(c) Acquired goodwill

(d) Inventory

(e) Depreciation

(f) Loss on sale of equipment

(g) Interest payable

(h) Dividends

(i) Gain on sale of investment securities

(j) Issuance of common shares

(LO 6) BE2-8 For each item that follows, identify the foundational principle of accounting that best describes it:

(a) For its annual reports, Walsberg Corp divides its economic activities into 12-month periods.

(b) JustPens, Inc. does not adjust amounts in its financial statements for the effects of inflation.

(c) Kiran Ltd. reports current and noncurrent classifications in its balance sheet.

(d) In preparing its consolidated financial statements, Bobby Corporation assesses if it has the power to direct the other entity's activities.

(e) Jayden Corporation reports revenue in its income statement when it is earned even if cash has not been collected.

(f) Duong Enterprises normally includes business transactions in its general ledger when the item meets the definition of an element (as defined in the conceptual framework) and the item is measurable.

(g) Gomez, Inc. provides information about pending lawsuits in the notes to its financial statements.

(h) Douglas Farms reports land on its balance sheet at the amount paid to acquire it, even though the estimated fair value is higher.

(i) McDonald Corporation uses fair value measurements for its financial instruments portfolio.

(j) Magnificent Inc. assumes that it will continue to operate into the foreseeable future.

(LO 3, 4) BE2-9 What is the objective of financial reporting? For each of the situations discussed below, explain the qualitative characteristics of financial information that help provide decision-useful information to users.

(a) Marcus Corp. has a management bonus plan based on net income. Marcus only records revenue once the risks and rewards have passed to the customer.

(b) Sosa Ltd. is a real estate company that holds land for eventual sale to developers. Sosa provides fair value information on its property holdings to its users.

(c) Mohawk Inc. has entered into a rental agreement that will eventually transfer ownership of the manufacturing equipment to Mohawk at the end of three years. Irrespective of the legal documentation, Mohawk will account for this transaction based on its economic impact to the company.

(d) Standard setters must ensure that accounting standards do not favour one entity over another or one industry over another.

(LO 9) *BE2-10 Medici Patriarchs purchased the following investments during 2010:

(a) 1,000 shares of Private Limited, a start-up company. The value of this investment was based on an internally developed model.

(b) 5,000 shares of CIBC, a public company listed on the TSX.

(c) $15,000 of corporate bonds. Although these bonds do not trade in an active market, their value closely resembles movements in the Bank of Canada bond rate.

Based on the discussion in Appendix 2A, indicate at which level in the fair value hierarchy these investment values will fall.

*BE2-11 Lucky Enterprises is using a discounted cash flow model. Explain how Lucky might estimate discounted fair **(LO 9)** value under each scenario:

Scenario 1: Cash flows are fairly certain
$100/year for 5 years
Risk-adjusted discount rate is 6%
Risk-free discount rate is 3%

Scenario 2: Cash flows are uncertain
75% probability that cash flows will be $100 in 5 years
25% probability that cash flows will be $75 in 5 years
Risk-adjusted discount rate is 6%
Risk-free discount rate is 3%

Exercises

E2-1 (Qualitative Characteristics) The conceptual framework identifies the fundamental and enhancing qualitative **(LO 4, 7)** characteristics that make accounting information useful.

Instructions

Answer the following questions related to these qualitative characteristics.

(a) Which quality of financial information makes it possible for users to confirm or correct prior expectations?

(b) Identify some of the trade-offs and constraints in financial reporting.

(c) The U.S. Securities and Exchange Commission chairman once noted that if it becomes accepted or expected that accounting principles are determined or modified in order to achieve goals that do not involve economic measurement, we risk a serious loss in confidence in the credibility of our financial information system. Which qualitative characteristic of accounting information should ensure that this situation will not occur?

(d) Owens Corp. chooses to account for a transaction based simply on its legal form. Is this acceptable?

(e) Companies in the mining industry defer losses on their properties because recognizing such losses immediately could have adverse economic consequences for the industry. Which qualitative characteristic of accounting information is not followed?

(f) Only Once provides overly complicated descriptions and explanations in its statement notes and provides only aggregated totals on the face of its financial statements. Which qualitative characteristic of accounting information is not followed?

(g) Baskins does not issue its first-quarter report until after the second quarter's results are reported. Which qualitative characteristic of accounting information is not followed?

(h) Predictive value is an ingredient of which qualitative characteristics of useful information?

(i) Vittorio Inc. is the only company in its industry to amortize its plant assets on a straight-line basis. Which qualitative characteristic is not present?

(j) Green Gable Corp. has tried to determine the replacement cost of its inventory. Three different appraisers arrive at substantially different amounts for this value. The president then decides to use the middle value for external reports. Which qualitative characteristic of information is lacking in these data? (Do not use reliability or representational faithfulness.)

(k) The controller at Owens Inc. noticed that a material transaction was not included in the year-end financial results. Which qualitative characteristic is not present?

E2-2 (Elements of Financial Statements) The elements that are most directly related to measuring an enterprise's **(LO 5)** performance and financial status follow:

Assets	Expenses	Liabilities
Gains	Equity	Revenues
Losses		

Instructions

(a) Indicate which element is being described below:

1. Arises from peripheral or incidental transactions.
2. Obliges a transfer of resources because of a present, enforceable obligation.
3. Are increases in the ownership interest.
4. Declares and pays cash dividends to owners.
5. Characterizes items by their service potential or future economic benefit.
6. Decreases in assets during the period for the payment of taxes.
7. Arises from income-generating activities that are the entity's ongoing major or central operations.
8. Is the residual interest in the enterprise's assets after deducting its liabilities.
9. Increases assets during the period through the sale of a product.
10. Decreases assets during the period by purchasing the company's own shares.

(b) Indicate which element listed above is being illustrated in the examples that follow:

1. MusiCo. has a written contract to receive money from the sale of copies of future recordings of music yet to be written.
2. FastMart Inc. has inventory out on consignment at a local retailer waiting for sale to the final customer.
3. Songs Unlimited Corp. has a written contract to deliver a percentage of future music revenues (royalties) from the sale of existing recordings.

(LO 6)   E2-3   (Foundational Principles) The foundational principles of accounting are as follows:

Recognition/Derecognition	Measurement	Presentation and Disclosure
1. Economic entity	5. Periodicity	10. Full disclosure
2. Control	6. Monetary unit	
3. Revenue recognition and realization	7. Going concern	
4. Matching	8. Historical cost	
	9. Fair value	

Instructions

For each situation that follows, identify by its number the foundational principle above that best describes it.

(a) Allocates expenses to revenues in the proper period.

(b) Indicates that market value changes after the purchase are not recorded in the accounts. (Do not use the revenue recognition principle.)

(c) Ensures that all relevant financial information is reported.

(d) Is why plant assets are not reported at their liquidation value. (Do not use the historical cost principle.)

(e) Related to the economic entity principle, defines the entities that should be consolidated in the financial statements.

(f) Indicates that personal and business record keeping should be separately maintained.

(g) Separates financial information into time periods for reporting purposes.

(h) Permits the use of market value valuation in certain specific situations.

(i) Requires passing of risks and rewards, measurability, and collectibility before recording the transaction.

(j) Assumes that the dollar is the measuring stick for reporting on financial performance.

(LO 6)   E2-4   (Foundational Principles) The following are operational guidelines and practices that have developed over time for financial reporting.

1. Price-level changes are not recognized in the accounting records.
2. Financial information is presented so that reasonably prudent investors will not be misled.
3. Property, plant, and equipment are capitalized and depreciated over the periods that they benefit.
4. There is no intent to liquidate the company's operations or activities.
5. Market value is used by companies for the valuation of certain securities that are regularly bought and sold.
6. After initial acquisition, the entity values land at its original transaction price.

7. All significant post–balance sheet events are reported.

8. Revenue is recorded at the point of sale.

9. All important aspects of bond indentures are presented in financial statements.

10. The rationale for accrual accounting is stated.

11. The use of consolidated statements is justified.

12. Reporting must be done at defined time intervals.

13. An allowance for doubtful accounts is established.

14. Goodwill is recorded only at the time of a business combination.

15. Sales commission costs are charged to expense.

Instructions

Select the foundational principle that best justifies each of these procedures and practices.

E2-5 (Foundational Principles) Examples of some operational guidelines used by accountants follow: (LO 1, 4, 6)

1. The treasurer of Sweet Grapes Corp. would like to prepare financial statements only during downturns in the company's wine production, which occur periodically when the grape crop fails. He states that it is at such times that the statements could be most easily prepared. The company would never allow more than 30 months to pass without statements being prepared.

2. The Land Holding Company has purchased a large amount of property, plant, and equipment over several years. It has decided that because the general price level has changed materially over the years, it will issue only price-level-adjusted financial statements.

3. Pyramid Manufacturing Ltd. decided to manufacture its own widgets because it would be cheaper than buying them from an outside supplier. In an attempt to make its statements more comparable with those of its competitors, Pyramid charged its inventory account for what it felt the widgets would have cost if they had been purchased from an outside supplier. (Do not use the revenue recognition principle.)

4. Cargo Discount Centres buys its merchandise by the truckload and train carload. Cargo does not defer any transportation costs in calculating the cost of its ending inventory. Such costs, although they vary from period to period, are always material in amount.

5. Quick & Healthy, a fast-food company, sells franchises for $100,000, accepting a $5,000 down payment and a 25-year note for the remainder. Quick & Healthy promises for three years to assist in site selection, building, and management training. Quick & Healthy records the full $100,000 franchise fee as revenue when the contract is signed.

6. Mustafa Corp. faces a possible expropriation (i.e., takeover) of its foreign facilities and possible losses on sums that are owed by various customers who are almost bankrupt. The company president has decided that these possibilities should not be noted on the financial statements because Mustafa still hopes that these events will not take place.

7. Maurice Morris, owner of Rare Bookstore, Inc., bought a computer for his own use. He paid for the computer by writing a cheque on the bookstore chequing account and charged the Office Equipment account.

8. Brock Inc. decides that it will be selling its subsidiary, Breck Inc., in a few years. Brock has excluded Breck's activities from its consolidated financial results.

9. Wilhelm Corporation expensed the purchase of new manufacturing equipment.

10. A large lawsuit has been filed against Mahoney Corp. Mahoney has recorded a loss and related estimated liability that is equal to the maximum possible amount that it feels it might lose. Mahoney is confident, however, that either it will win the suit or it will owe a much smaller amount.

Instructions

(a) Discuss the usefulness of a conceptual framework.

(b) For each of the situations above, list the foundational principle or qualitative characteristic of financial information that has been violated.

E2-6 (Qualitative Characteristics) In general, financial information should include all relevant information that faith-fully represents the economic substance of business transactions.   (LO 4, 7, 6)

Instructions

Discuss whether it is possible for financial information to have all of the qualitative characteristics.

(LO 4, 5, 6) E2-7   (Conceptual Framework—Comprehensive) The following are transactions recorded by Sugar Corporation during the current year:

1. Ordinary operating maintenance on capital assets was recorded as follows:

| Capital Assets | 2,000 | |
| Accounts Payable | | 2,000 |

2. The company received an advance on a custom order for merchandise that will be shipped during the next accounting year.

| Cash | 18,000 | |
| Sales Revenue | | 18,000 |

3. Sugar Corporation is holding inventory on consignment for Steamers Ltd. Sugar will only pay Steamers when a sale is made to a customer. It has made the following entry for the inventory.

| Inventory | 15,000 | |
| Accounts Payable | | 15,000 |

4. On the last day of the accounting period, a 12-month insurance policy was purchased. The insurance coverage is for the next accounting year.

| Insurance Expense | 4,000 | |
| Cash | | 4,000 |

Instructions

For each transaction, determine which component of the conceptual framework (i.e., qualitative characteristic, element, or principle) was violated, if any, and give the entry that should have been recorded if there was a violation.

(CGA-Canada adapted)

(LO 6) E2-8   (Full Disclosure Principle) The following information is for Brittany, Inc.

1. To be more concise, the company decided that only net income should be reported on the income statement. Details on revenues, cost of goods sold, and expenses were also omitted from the notes.

2. Equipment purchases of $270,000 were partly financed during the year by issuing a $110,000 note payable. The company offset the equipment against the note payable and reported plant assets at $160,000. No information has been provided in the notes.

3. During the year, an assistant controller for the company embezzled $50,000. Brittany's net income for the year was $2.3 million. Neither the assistant controller nor the money has been found. No information has been provided in the notes.

4. Brittany has reported its ending inventory at $2.7 million in the financial statements. No other information on inventories is presented in the financial statements and related notes.

5. The company changed its method of amortizing equipment from the double-declining balance to the straight-line method. This change is not mentioned anywhere in the financial statements.

Instructions

(a) Explain the meaning and implications of the full disclosure principle and how such information may be provided to users.

(b) For each of the situations above, discuss whether Brittany, Inc. has followed acceptable accounting and disclosure practices.

(LO 6) E2-9   (Going Concern Assumption)

Instructions

(a) Explain the meaning and implications of the going concern assumption in financial accounting.

(b) If the going concern assumption did not apply in accounting, how would this affect the amounts shown in the financial statements for the following items?
   1. Land
   2. Unamortized bond premium

3. Depreciation expense on equipment

4. Merchandise inventory

5. Prepaid insurance

E2-10   **(Revenue Recognition Principle)** The following independent situations require professional judgement for   **(LO 6, 8)** determining when to recognize revenue from the transactions:

1. Air Temiskaming sells you an advance purchase airline ticket in September for your flight home at Christmas.

2. Giant Lion's Furniture Stores Inc. sells you a home theatre on a "no money down, no interest, and no payments for one year" promotional deal.

3. The Centurions Baseball Team sells season tickets to games on-line. Fans can purchase the tickets at any time, although the season doesn't officially begin until April. It runs from April through October.

4. Belle Vallée Wools sells you a sweater. In August, you placed the order using Belle Vallée's on-line catalogue. The sweater arrives in September and you charge it to your Belle Vallée credit card. You receive and pay the Belle Vallée bill in October.

Instructions

(a) Explain when revenue is historically recognized under the current revenue recognition principle.

(b) Explain how revenue would be recognized under the alternative contract model.

(c) Identify when revenue should be recognized in each of the above situations under the current revenue recognition model.

(d) Identify whether revenue would be recognized differently for each of the above situations under the contract model.

*E2-11   **(Fair Value Principle)** Meerkat Industries would like to value its manufacturing facility in London, Ontario.   **(LO 9)** The facility consists of land, building, and manufacturing equipment.

Instructions

(a) Identify some of the considerations that are involved in a fair value measurement.

(b) Explain the various levels of input in the fair value hierarchy.

(c) Using the fair value hierarchy, discuss the level one, two, and three types of inputs Meerkat could use to value its facility.

Problems

P2-1   Foundational principles of financial reporting may be grouped into four categories: recognition, measurement, presentation, and disclosure.

Instructions

Briefly describe what is meant by these terms.

P2-2   DownUnder issues audited financial statements to its creditors and is required to maintain certain covenants based on its debt to equity ratio and return on assets. In addition, management of DownUnder receives a bonus partially based on revenues for the year. Information related to DownUnder, Inc. follows:

1. Depreciation expense on the building for the year was $45,000. Because the building was increasing in value during the year, the controller decided to charge the depreciation expense to retained earnings instead of to net income. The following entry was recorded:

Retained Earnings	45,000	
Accumulated Depreciation—Buildings		45,000

2. New legislation was discussed by the government that would require new pollution control technology for companies such as DownUnder. In anticipation of this legislation being passed next year, DownUnder has booked the following entry:

Property, Plant, and Equipment	21,000	
Accounts Payable		21,000

3. During the year, the company sold certain equipment for $285,000, recognizing a gain of $69,000. Because the controller believed that new equipment would be needed in the near future, the controller decided to defer the gain and amortize it over the life of the new equipment that would soon be purchased.

4. An order for $61,500 has been received from a customer on January 2, 2010, for products on hand. This order was shipped f.o.b. shipping point on January 9, 2010. The company made the following entry in 2009:

Accounts Receivable	61,500	
Sales		61,500

Instructions

(a) Discuss the reporting objectives of the users of DownUnder's financial statements.

(b) Comment on the appropriateness of DownUnder, Inc.'s accounting procedures and their impact on the company's financial statement users.

(c) Discuss whether there are alternatives available under IFRS to provide the reporting desired by DownUnder's management.

P2-3 Transactions from Lucky Bamboo, Inc.'s current year follow:

1. Lucky Bamboo, Inc. thinks it should dispose of its excess land. While the book value is $50,000, current market prices are depressed and only $25,000 is expected upon disposal. The following journal entry was made:

Loss on Disposal of Land	25,000	
Land		25,000

2. Merchandise inventory that cost $630,000 was reported on the balance sheet at $690,000, which is the expected selling price less estimated selling costs. The following entry was made to record this increase in value:

Merchandise Inventory	60,000	
Revenue		60,000

3. The company is being sued for $500,000 by a customer who claims damages for personal injury that was apparently caused by a defective product. Company lawyers feel extremely confident that the company will have no liability for damages resulting from the situation. Nevertheless, the company decides to make the following entry:

Loss from Lawsuit	450,000	
Liability for Lawsuit		450,000

4. Because the general level of prices increased during the current year, Lucky Bamboo, Inc. determined that there was a $16,000 understatement of depreciation expense on its equipment and decided to record it in its accounts. The following entry was made:

Depreciation Expense	16,000	
Accumulated Depreciation		16,000

5. Lucky Bamboo, Inc. has been concerned about whether intangible assets could generate cash in case of liquidation. As a result, goodwill arising from a business acquisition during the current year and recorded at $800,000 was written off as follows:

Retained Earnings	800,000	
Goodwill		800,000

6. Because of a "fire sale," equipment that was obviously worth $200,000 was acquired at a cost of $155,000. The following entry was made:

Equipment	200,000	
Cash		155,000
Revenue		45,000

Instructions

In each of the above situations, discuss the appropriateness of the journal entries in terms of generally accepted accounting principles. For purposes of your discussion, assume that the financial statements, particularly net income, will be used by the court in a divorce settlement for the compny president's wife.

P2-4 Accounting information provides useful data about business transactions and events. The people who provide and use financial reports must often select and evaluate accounting alternatives. The conceptual framework that was discussed in this chapter examines the characteristics of accounting information that make it useful for decision-making. It also points out that various limitations that are part of the measurement and reporting process can make it necessary to trade off or sacrifice some of the characteristics of useful information.

Instructions

(a) For each of the following pairs of qualitative characteristics, give an example of a situation in which one of the characteristics may be sacrificed for a gain in the other:

1. Relevance and verifiability

2. Relevance and comparability

3. Relevance and timeliness

4. Relevance and understandability

(b) What criterion should be used to evaluate trade-offs between information characteristics?

P2-5 You are hired to review the accounting records of Sophia Corporation before it closes its revenue and expense accounts as at December 31, the end of its current fiscal year. The following information comes to your attention.

1. During the current year, Sophia Corporation changed its shipment policy from f.o.b. destination to f.o.b shipping point. This would result in an additional $50,000 of revenue being recorded for fiscal 2010.

2. The estimated useful life of its manufacturing equipment was increased by five years. This reduced Depreciation Expense by $50,000 during fiscal 2010.

3. When the balance sheet was prepared, detailed information about the amount of cash on deposit in each of several banks was omitted. Only the total amount of cash under a caption "Cash in banks" was presented.

4. During the current year, Sophia Corporation purchased an undeveloped piece of land for $320,000. The company spent $80,000 on subdividing the land and getting it ready for sale. A property appraisal at the end of the year indicated that the land was now worth $500,000. Although none of the lots were sold, the company recognized revenue of $180,000, less related expenses of $80,000, for a net income on the project of $100,000.

5. For several years, the company used the FIFO method for inventory valuation purposes. During the current year, the president noted that all the other companies in the industry had switched to the moving average method. The company decided not to switch to moving average because net income would decrease by $830,000.

6. During fiscal 2010, new government legislation was passed requiring companies like Sophia, to install additional health and safety devices in their offices by 2015. Although Sophia does not intend to retrofit the required new devices until 2015, an accrual for $375,500 has been established in the year-end financial statements for the future installation costs.

7. To maintain customer goodwill, Sophia voluntarily recalled some products during the year. Sophia has not established an accrual and is recording the returns as they happen.

Instructions

State whether or not you agree with each of the decisions made by Sophia Corporation. Explain your reasoning and, wherever possible, support your answers by referring to the generally accepted accounting principles that apply to the circumstances.

P2-6 The following transactions fall somewhere in the continuum of the shades of grey among the choices in accounting decision-making that are shown in Illustration 2-10.

1. The company president approaches one of the company's creditors to ask for a modification of the repayment terms so that they extend beyond the current year. This would make the liabilities long-term rather than short-term and would improve the company's current ratio.

2. The controller determines that significant amounts of capital assets are impaired and should be written off. Coincidentally, the company is currently showing lower levels of net income, but expects better results in the following years.

3. The company management decides to use FIFO as opposed to weighted average since it more closely approximates the flow of costs.

4. The vice-president of finance decides to capitalize interest during the self-construction of only one of its properties. This policy will increase net income and several profitability ratios.

5. The business owner enters into an arrangement with a business associate whereby they will buy each other's merchandise before year end. The merchandise will then be shipped to customers after year end from the holding company's warehouse.

6. The assets and liabilities of an investment have been consolidated into Maher Company's annual financial statements. Maher Company does not have power to direct the investee's activities.

Instructions

For each situation, state where it falls in the continuum of choices in decision-making.

P2-7   The AICPA Special Committee on Financial Reporting proposed the following considerations for businesses in preparing their financial statements and other such financial reporting:

1. Business reporting should exclude information outside of management's expertise or for which management is not the best source, such as information about competitors.

2. Management should not be required to report information that would significantly harm the company's competitive position.

3. Management should not be required to provide forecast financial statements. Rather, management should provide information that helps users forecast for themselves the company's financial future.

4. Other than for financial statements, management need report only the information it knows. That is, management should be under no obligation to gather information it does not have, or does not need, in order to manage the business.

5. Companies should present certain elements of business reporting only if users and management agree they should be reported—a concept of flexible reporting.

Instructions

For each item, explain how the proposed consideration or constraint addresses the cost and benefits debate for financial reporting.

P2-8   Recently, your Uncle Waldo, who knows that you always have your eye out for a profitable investment, has discussed the possibility of your purchasing some corporate bonds that he just learned of. He suggests that you may wish to get in on the ground floor of this deal. The bonds being issued by Cricket Corp. are 10-year debentures, which promise a 40% rate of return. Cricket manufactures novelty and party items.

You have told Uncle Waldo, that unless you can take a look at Cricket's financial statements, you would not feel comfortable about such an investment. Thinking that this is the chance of a lifetime, Uncle Waldo has obtained a copy of Cricket's most recent, unaudited financial statements, which are a year old. These statements were prepared by Mrs. John Cricket. You look over these statements, and they are quite impressive.

The balance sheet showed a debt to equity ratio of 1:10 and, for the year shown, the company reported net income of $2,424,240.

The financial statements are not shown in comparison with amounts from other years. In addition, there are no significant note disclosures about inventory valuation, depreciation methods, loan agreements, and so on.

Instructions

Write a letter to Uncle Waldo explaining why it would be unwise to base an investment decision on the financial statements that he has given you. Refer to the concepts developed in this chapter.

Writing Assignments

WA2-1 Roger Chang has some questions about the theoretical framework in which standards are set. He knows that standard setters have been trying to develop a conceptual framework for the formulation of accounting theory. Yet Roger's supervisors have said that these theoretical frameworks have little value in the practical sense—in the real world. Roger did notice that accounting standards seem to be established after the fact rather than before—in other words, after problems occur. He thought this meant the theory could be poorly structured but he never really questioned the process at school because he was too busy doing the homework.

Roger thinks that he might feel less anxious about accounting theory and accounting semantics (the terminology) if he could identify the basic concepts and definitions that are accepted by the profession and then consider them in light of his current work. By doing this, he hopes to develop an appropriate connection between theory and practice.

Instructions

Help Roger recognize the purpose and benefit of a conceptual framework.

WA2-2 In the standard-setting conceptual framework, the word "reliability" has been replaced with "faithful representation." This has caused much discussion among preparers of financial information. This change has led to other implications related to substance over form, neutrality, conservatism and the ability of entities to "override" a standard in very rare circumstances.

Instructions

Discuss the following questions. (You may find the IASB's *Basis for Conclusions to the Exposure Draft: Conceptual Framework for Financial Reporting: The Objective of Financial Reporting and Qualitative Characteristics and Constraints of Decision-Useful Financial Reporting Information*, of May 29, 2008, helpful in your discussion. It is available on the IASB website at: www.iasb.org.co.uk and go to Projects on Conceptual Framework – Phase A.)

(a) "Faithful representation" has replaced the term "reliability" as a fundamental qualitative characteristic of financial information. What does faithful representation mean and how does this differ from reliability? Why was the term "reliability" replaced?

(b) What does "substance over form" mean? Give examples of where this might be relevant.

(c) How does "conservatism" conflict with the meaning of "faithful representation"?

(d) In IAS 1, a company is allowed, in rare circumstances, to override an accounting standard if applying the standard would not result in a "true and fair view." How does this support faithful representation? Are there any enhancing characteristics that might be violated by this? If you were a financial statement user of a company that had decided to use this override, what information would you like to have disclosed in the financial statements? Why?

WA2-3 An accountant must be familiar with the concepts involved in determining the earnings of a business entity. The amount of earnings that is reported for a business entity depends on the proper recognition, in general, of revenues and expenses for a specific time period. In some situations, costs are recognized as expenses at the time of product sale; in other situations, guidelines have been developed for recognizing costs as expenses or losses by other criteria.

Instructions

(a) Explain the rationale for recognizing costs as expenses at the time of product sale.

(b) Explain how the matching principle might contradict the definition of an asset. Give examples of where this might arise. What should take precedence: the matching principle or the asset definition?

(c) What is the rationale that makes it appropriate to treat costs as expenses of a period instead of assigning them to an asset? Explain.

(d) In what general circumstances would it be appropriate to treat a cost as an asset instead of as an expense? Explain.

(e) Some expenses are assigned to specific accounting periods based on a systematic and rational allocation of asset cost. Explain the rationale for recognizing expenses in this way.

(f) Identify the conditions in which it would be appropriate to treat a cost as a loss.

(AICPA adapted)

*WA2-4 The fair value hierarchy establishes three levels of input, with level one being the best type, as it uses the most objective inputs, and level three using the most subjective inputs.

Instructions

For each of the following scenarios, identify the level of fair value input and the method that has been used and what disclosure should be provided to assist the user's understanding.

(a) A company uses the fair value method for reporting its investment property. The company hired a building appraiser who reviewed prices for sales of similar buildings in the neighbourhood to determine the property's fair market value.

(b) A company recently purchased a trademark from another company. The trademark was valued using the royalty-based approach. This approach involves estimating the amount of royalties that would have had to be paid on future sales forecasts, if the company did not own the trademark itself. Sales are estimated for the year, then royalty costs are estimated based on these sales and discounted to determine the present value of the trademark.

(c) The company owns 1,000 shares in RX Limited, a publicly traded company. The RX Limited shares were valued by looking at their closing price at the reporting date.

(d) The equipment's fair value was determined using details from a supplier price list for the replacement equipment.

(e) The company valued one of its brand names using the discounted cash flow method. The sales and costs were forecast for the next five years based on management's plans. The terminal value was determined to be 3% based on market growth rates anticipated for North America. All of the future cash flows were discounted using the company's weighted average cost of capital.

WA2-5 The definition of a liability is a "present economic obligation for which the entity is the obligor." These terms can be further expanded as follows (as taken from IASB Board meeting minutes):

"Present" means at the report date that an economic obligation exists.

"Economic obligation" is an unconditional promise to incur an economic burden and is enforceable by legal or equivalent means.

Instructions

Using the definition of a liability, discuss whether or not the following scenarios would result in the recognition of a liability. (The following situations are adapted from examples provided in FASB board meetings on the Conceptual Framework—Elements Phase of June 25, 2008, and May 7, 2008.) Also explain how you might use probabilities in each scenario.

(a) Silverstrike Mines has purchased the right to mine for silver in two countries. In Country X, the environmental regulations require the company to completely fill in mining shafts greater than 15 metres when the mining operations cease or pay a fine of 250,000 euros per shaft. In Country Y, there are no environmental laws, but Silverstrike has signed a contract to fill in any mine shafts greater than 15 metres, in return for which the local government would grant it exploration rights within a 200-kilometre radius of the existing mine. It is December 31, 2010, and the company now has four operating mining shafts in Country X that are 17 metres deep. In Country Y, the company has six shafts that are only 10 metres deep. However, the company will have to dig down to 17 metres in Country Y to hit silver, and this should be completed by December 2011 with 95% certainty.

(b) Zion Limited has an employee benefit plan that will pay for medical and dental coverage after an employee leaves the company, provided the employee has worked for 15 years for the company. If the employee is terminated or leaves voluntarily before the 15 years is completed, then the company will not pay for any benefits. Historically, the company has found that only 15% of employees leave before the 15 years has passed. At the reporting date of December 31, 2010, there is one employee who is still currently employed and has been with the company for 11 years. How would the liability for this employee's benefits be determined?

(c) Beatonville's soccer team has just finished building a new soccer stadium and is now trying to raise corporate funds to help pay for the centre. The team has recently signed a contract with Masonry Limited, a large employer in the area, for sponsorship. The agreement states that in return for $2 million to be paid today, the team will allow Masonry to have its corporate name and logo on the building for eight years. At the end of eight years, the contract can be renewed, or the team will seek another sponsor.

Cases

Refer to the Case Primer to help you answer these cases.

Case Primer

CA2-1   **Bre-X Minerals (Bre-X)**, a small mining company, announced in the early 1990s that it had discovered a fairly significant gold deposit in Indonesia. The company's shares skyrocketed from pennies a share to over $280 per share. Subsequently, it was discovered that the company had been "salting the samples"[1] and that there was little, if any, gold there. This information was not disclosed to the market until long after it was discovered that there was no gold. Certain parties who had access to this information benefited; however, many investors lost a significant amount of money.

Many investors lost millions of dollars including the Ontario Municipal Employees Retirement System and the Ontario Teachers Pension Plan. Investors sued the company and its management for providing misleading information.

Real-World Emphasis

Instructions

Using the conceptual framework, identify and analyze the financial reporting issues.

CA2-2   **Bennett Environmental Inc.** operates in North America. Its basic business is high-temperature treatment services for the remediation of hydrocarbon-contaminated soil. In its 2008 financials, the company had a loss of $4.6 million (accumulated deficit of $63.7 million) and a cash outflow from operating activities of $0.6 million.

In the notes to the financial statements, the company deferred certain transportation costs and recorded them as assets. These costs relate to shipping contaminated materials to the treatment plant. They are reimbursable under the terms of the contract.

In addition, the company received a subpoena from the U.S. Department of Justice regarding conspiracy to commit fraud with respect to the bidding process on a government process. The company pleaded guilty to the charge in 2008.

Ethics

Instructions

Assume that the financial statements must be issued prior to the resolution of the lawsuit. Discuss the financial reporting issues.

Real-World Emphasis

CA2-3   The statement that follows about Timber Company appeared in a financial magazine:

> The land and timber holdings are now carried on the company's books at a mere $100 million (U.S.). The value of the timber alone is variously estimated at $1 billion to $3 billion and is rising all the time. The understatement of the company is pretty severe, conceded company management, who noted "We have a whole stream of profit nobody sees and there is no way to show it on our books."

Instructions

Act as an analyst and discuss the financial reporting issues.

---

[1] The term "salting" refers to the practice of someone tampering with the samples (and adding in some, or more, gold).

Research and Financial Analysis

RA2-1 Teck Resources Limited

Obtain the (restated) 2005 financial statements of **Teck Resources Limited** (formerly **Teck Cominco Limited**) from SEDAR (www.sedar.com) posted on May 19, 2006.

Instructions

(a) Using the notes to the consolidated financial statements, determine the company's revenue recognition policy. Comment on whether the company uses an aggressive or conservative method for reporting revenue.

(b) Give two examples of where historical cost information is reported in the financial statements and related notes. Give two examples where fair value information is reported in either the financial statements or related notes.

(c) Why did the company restate the financial statements? Comment on this. Argue both sides of the reporting issue; in other words, how the company treated the item before and after the restatement. (Hint: See the definition of cash and cash equivalents in the *CICA Handbook*.)

(d) Read note 3(e) (i) regarding stripping costs. Argue both sides of the debate on how to treat stripping costs. Comment on the impact of both treatments on the financial statements.

RA2-2 Air Canada

Going concern is one of the basic principles related to measurement. During a recession, the assessment of going concern becomes much more difficult. Companies are required to disclose if going concern is an issue, and why they have decided that the statements will still be prepared on a going concern basis.

Instructions

Access the 2008 annual report for **Air Canada** for the year ended December 31, 2008, from the company's website or SEDAR (www.sedar.com). Read Note 1 (c) Liquidity risk and answer the following questions.

(a) What is liquidity risk and how does Air Canada manage it?

(b) Why is the company concerned about liquidity risk?

(c) What initiative did the company take in 2008 and plan to continue in 2009 with respect to managing its liquidity risk?

(d) What additional risks is the company concerned about?

(e) Is Air Canada still reported as a going concern?

RA2-3 Retrieval of Information on Public Company

There are several commonly available indexes and reference products that help individuals locate articles that have appeared in business publications and periodicals. Articles can generally be searched by company or by subject matter. Several common sources are *Canadian Business and Current Affairs* (*CBCA Fulltext Business*), *Investex Plus*, *The Wall Street Journal Index*, *Business Abstracts* (formerly the *Business Periodical Index*), and *ABI/Inform*.

Instructions

Use one of these resources to find an article about a company that interests you. Read the article and answer the following questions. (Note: Your library may have hard copy or CD-ROM versions of these sources or they may be available through your library's electronic database.)

(a) What is the article about?

(b) What specific information about the company is included in the article?

(c) Identify any accounting-related issues that are discussed in the article.

RA2-4 Fair Values

Using fair values has come under attack in light of the recent credit crunch and the related financial crisis. Some have even accused fair value accounting of exacerbating the crisis. Access the following articles:

"Discussing the Credit Crunch," *IASB INSIGHT Journal*, Q1 and Q2 (from www.iasb.co.uk), and "Fair Values: When the Engine Overheats, Don't Blame the Oil Light," by Paul Cherry and Ian Hague, *CA Magazine*, June/July 2009 (from www.camagazine.com).

Instructions

Using the articles, address the following questions:

(a) What impact does using fair values to report assets and liabilities have on the financial statements?

(b) Why do some believe that using fair values is not appropriate for financial reporting? Discuss this in light of the financial crisis that began in 2007.

(c) What are the arguments to support using fair values in financial reporting?

(d) Do you think fair value accounting should be used in the preparation of financial statements?

RA2-5 OSC Report on Weak Areas of Disclosure

Annually, the Ontario Securities Commission (OSC) issues a report that summarizes its findings with respect to disclosure in the filing documents of companies. Download the report entitled: "OSC Staff Notice 51-706 Corporate Finance Branch Report 2008," available at the OSC website (www.osc.gov.on.ca). Pay particular attention to section 4, Discussion of Operational Results.

Instructions

(a) What common areas did the OSC find to have weak disclosure in its review of corporate reports? Provide the supporting examples.

(b) For each specific industry, highlight the risks that are associated with it. How do these risks affect disclosure requirements for users? What were the specific weak areas of disclosure that the OSC reported? Industries to discuss are mining, manufacturing and retail, real estate, and entertainment and communications.

Extensive Innovations in Accounting Information Systems

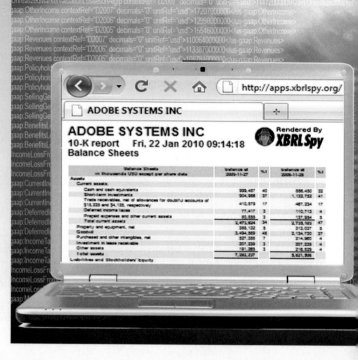

gaap:RealizedInvestmentGainsLosses contextRef="D2006" decimals="0" unitRef="usd">106600000</us-gaap:RealizedInv
gaap:RealizedInvestmentGainsLosses contextRef="D2005" decimals="0" unitRef="usd">341000000</us-gaap:Realizedinve
UnrealizedMarketValuationLossesonAigfp contextRef="D2007" decimals="0" unitRef="usd">1472000000</us-gaap:Unrealize
gaap:OtherIncome contextRef="D2007" decimals="0" unitRef="usd">17207000000</us-gaap:OtherIncome>
gaap:OtherIncome contextRef="D2006" decimals="0" unitRef="usd">12998000000</us-gaap:OtherIncome>
gaap:OtherIncome contextRef="D2005" decimals="0" unitRef="usd">15546000000</us-gaap:OtherIncome>
gaap:Revenues contextRef="D2007" decimals="0" unitRef="usd">110064000000</us-gaap:Revenues>
gaap:Revenues contextRef="D2006" decimals="0" unitRef="usd">113387000000</us-gaap:Revenues>
gaap:Revenues contextRef="D2005" decimals="0" unitRef="usd">108781000000</us-gaap:Revenues>

THE ELECTRONIC COMMUNICATION language XBRL, or eXtensible Business Reporting Language, is revolutionizing how businesses report their accounting information. Developed by XBRL International, a non-profit consortium, XBRL is an open standard, without any licence fees.

Instead of treating financial information as a block of text, XBRL provides a unique identifying tag for each item of data, such as company net profit. These XBRL tags allow for automated data processing. Computers can treat XBRL information "intelligently"–they can select it, analyze it, store it, and exchange it with other computers. XBRL thus increases the speed with which financial data are used, reduces the possibility for error, and permits automated checking of information. It can handle data in different languages and with different accounting standards.

XBRL Canada's role is to create and maintain XBRL taxonomies based on Canadian reporting standards and to increase awareness and understanding of XBRL and its uses in Canada. Taxonomies are the dictionaries that define the specific tags for individual items of data. XBRL Canada has created two taxonomies designed to enable preparation of XBRL-based financial statements that conform to Canadian GAAP: the Primary Financial Statements taxonomy, which covers the balance sheet, income statement, and statement of cash flows; and the Notes taxonomy, for preparing the notes to the financial statements. XBRL Canada is also working on a project to help companies with the 2011 convergence with IFRS, which will result in a taxonomy that conforms to IFRS as used in Canada, along with tools that will cross-reference existing Canadian GAAP and IFRS.

With XBRL, companies can save costs and streamline financial information collecting and reporting, while consumers of financial data–investors, analysts, financial institutions, and regulators–can receive, find, compare, and analyze data more quickly and efficiently.

In fact, the Canadian Securities Administrators (CSA) is considering whether to make filing in XBRL format a requirement. Until it does, XBRL financial statements will not be a substitute for financial statements required to be filed under Canadian securities legislation; issuers must continue to file in PDF format.■

Sources: www.xbrl.ca; www.xbrl.org; www.securities-administrators.ca/industry_resources.aspx?id=54

CHAPTER 3

The Accounting Information System

Learning Objectives

After studying this chapter, you should be able to:

1. Understand basic accounting terminology.

2. Explain double-entry rules.

3. Identify the steps in the accounting cycle.

4. Record transactions in journals, post journal entries to ledger accounts, and prepare a trial balance.

5. Explain the reasons for preparing adjusting entries.

6. Prepare closing entries.

7. Explain how inventory accounts are adjusted at year end.

8. Prepare a 10-column work sheet and financial statements.

After studying Appendix 3A, you should be able to:

9. Identify adjusting entries that may be reversed.

Preview of Chapter 3

The purpose of this chapter is to explain and illustrate the features of an accounting information system. Even though most companies have sophisticated computerized and automated accounting systems, it is still important to understand the mechanics of bookkeeping. How do transactions get captured in the system and how and when are the financial statements produced?

The chapter is organized as follows:

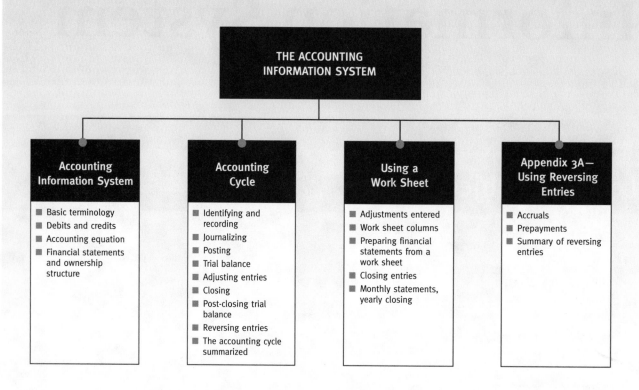

ACCOUNTING INFORMATION SYSTEM

The system of collecting and processing transaction data and making financial information available to interested parties is known as the accounting information system.

Accounting information systems can be very different from one business to another. Many factors shape these systems, including the type of business and the kinds of transactions it engages in, the firm's size, the amount of data that are handled, and the kind of information that management and others need to get from the system.

Basic Terminology

Financial accounting is built on a set of concepts (discussed in Chapters 1 and 2) for identifying, recording, classifying, and interpreting transactions and other events relating to enterprises. It is important to understand the **basic terminology** that is used in **collecting** accounting data.

BASIC TERMINOLOGY

Event.   A happening of consequence. An event generally is the source or cause of changes in assets, liabilities, and equity. Events can be external or internal.

Transaction.   A transaction is an **external event** involving a transfer or exchange between two or more entities or parties.

Account.   A systematic arrangement that accumulates transactions and other events. A separate account is kept for each asset, liability, revenue, and expense, and for gains, losses, and capital (owners' equity).

Permanent and temporary accounts.   Permanent (real) accounts are asset, liability, and equity accounts; they appear on the balance sheet. Temporary (nominal) accounts are revenue, expense, and dividend accounts; except for dividends, they appear on the income statement. Temporary accounts are periodically closed; permanent accounts are left open.

Ledger.[1]   The book (or electronic database) containing the accounts. Each account usually has a separate page. A general ledger is a collection of all the asset, liability, owners' equity, revenue, and expense accounts. A subsidiary ledger contains the details of a specific general ledger account.

Journal.   The book of original entry where transactions and other selected events are first recorded. Various amounts are transferred to the ledger from the book of original entry, the journal.

Posting.   The process of transferring the essential facts and figures from the book of original entry, the ledger accounts.

Trial balance.   A list of all open accounts in the ledger and their balances. A trial balance that is taken immediately after all adjustments have been posted is called an adjusted trial balance. A trial balance taken immediately after closing entries have been posted is known as a post-closing or after-closing trial balance. A trial balance can be prepared at any time.

Adjusting entries.   Entries that are made at the end of an accounting period to bring all accounts up to date on an accrual accounting basis so that correct financial statements can be prepared.

Financial statements.   Statements that reflect the collecting, tabulating, and final summarizing of the accounting data. Four financial statements are involved: (1) the balance sheet, which shows the enterprise's financial condition at the end of a period; (2) the income statement, which measures the results of operations during the period; (3) the statement of cash flows, which reports the cash provided and used by operating, investing, and financing activities during the period; and (4) the statement of retained earnings or statement of changes in shareholders' equity, which reconciles the balance of the retained earnings and other equity accounts from the beginning to the end of the period. Comprehensive income is generally shown in a separate statement—the statement of comprehensive income (starting with net income)—or as part of the income statement.

---

[1] Most companies use accounting software systems instead of manual systems. The software allows the data to be entered into a database and various reports can then be generated, such as journals, trial balances, ledgers, and financial statements.

Closing entries. The formal process for reducing temporary accounts to zero and then determining net income or net loss and transferring it to an owners' equity account. Using closing entries is also known as "closing the ledger," "closing the books," or merely "closing."

Debits and Credits

Objective 2
Explain double-entry rules.

The terms **debit** and **credit** refer to the left and right sides of a general ledger account, respectively. They are commonly abbreviated as Dr. for debit and Cr. for credit. These terms do not mean "increase" or "decrease." The terms "debit" and "credit" are used repeatedly in the recording process to describe where entries are made. For example, the act of entering an amount on the left side of an account is called **debiting** the account. Making an entry on the right side is **crediting** the account. When the totals of the two sides are compared, an account will have a debit balance if the total of the debit amounts is more than the credits. Conversely, an account will have a credit balance if the credit amounts exceed the debits. The procedure of having debits on the left and credits on the right is an accounting custom. We could function just as well if debits and credits were reversed. However, the custom of having debits on the left side of an account and credits on the right side (like the custom of driving on the right-hand side of the road) has been adopted in Canada. This rule applies to all accounts.

The equality of debits and credits is the basis for the double-entry system of recording transactions (also sometimes called double-entry bookkeeping). Under the **double-entry accounting** system, which is used everywhere, the two-sided (dual) effect of each transaction is recorded in appropriate accounts. This system gives a logical method for recording transactions. It also offers a way of proving the accuracy of the recorded amounts. If every transaction is recorded with equal debits and credits, then the sum of all the debits to the accounts must equal the sum of all the credits.

All **asset** and **expense** accounts are increased on the left (or debit side) and decreased on the right (or credit side). Conversely, all **liability** and **revenue** accounts are increased

Illustration 3-1

Double-Entry (Debit and Credit) Accounting System

Normal Balance—Debit

Asset Accounts

Debit + (increase)	Credit − (decrease)

Expense and Dividend Accounts

Debit + (increase)	Credit − (decrease)

Normal Balance—Credit

Liability Accounts

Debit − (decrease)	Credit + (increase)

Shareholders' Equity Accounts

Debit − (decrease)	Credit + (increase)

Revenue Accounts

Debit − (decrease)	Credit + (increase)

on the right (or credit side) and decreased on the left (or debit side). Shareholders' equity accounts, such as Common Shares, and Retained Earnings, are increased on the credit side, whereas Dividends is increased on the debit side. The basic guidelines for an accounting system are presented in Illustration 3-1.

Accounting Equation

In a double-entry system, for every debit there must be a credit, and vice versa. This leads us to the basic accounting equation shown in Illustration 3-2.

Illustration 3-2

The Basic Accounting Equation

Illustration 3-3 expands this equation to show the accounts that compose shareholders' equity. In addition, the debit/credit rules and effects on each type of account are shown. Study this diagram carefully. It will help you understand the fundamentals of the double-entry system. Like the basic equation, the expanded basic equation must balance (total debits **must** equal total credits).

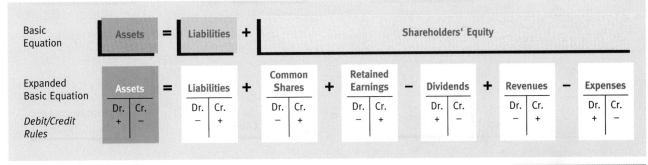

Illustration 3-3

Expanded Basic Equation and Debit/Credit Rules and Effects

Every time a transaction occurs, the elements in the equation change, but the basic equality of the two sides remains. To illustrate, here are eight different transactions for Perez Inc.:

1. Owners invest $40,000 in exchange for common shares:

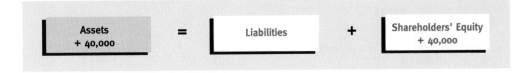

2. Disburses $600 cash for secretarial wages:

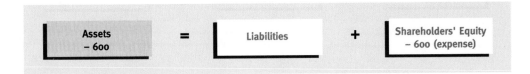

3. Purchases office equipment priced at $5,200, giving a 10% promissory note in exchange:

4. Receives $4,000 cash for services rendered:

5. Pays off a short-term liability of $7,000:

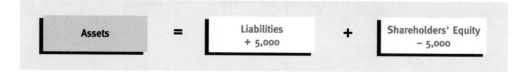

6. Declares a cash dividend of $5,000:

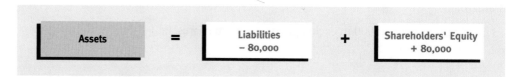

7. Converts a long-term liability of $80,000 into common shares:

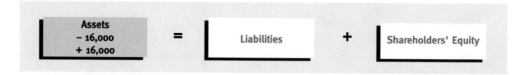

8. Pays $16,000 cash for a delivery van:

Financial Statements and Ownership Structure

Common shares, retained earnings, and accumulated other comprehensive income are reported in the shareholders' equity section of the balance sheet. Dividends are reported on the statement of retained earnings. Revenues and expenses are reported on the income statement. Revenues and expenses are eventually transferred to retained earnings at the end of the period while other comprehensive income is transferred to accumulated other comprehensive income.[2] As a result, a change in any one of these items affects shareholders' equity. The relationships to shareholders' equity are shown in Illustration 3-4.

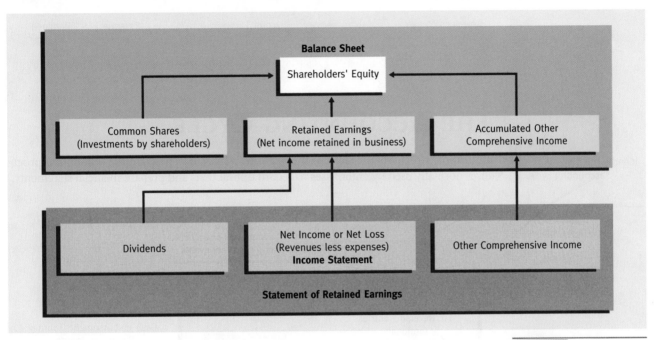

Illustration **3-4**

Financial Statements and Ownership Structure

The type of ownership structure that a business enterprise uses determines the types of accounts that are part of the equity section or that affect it. In a **corporation**,[3] **Common Shares, Contributed Surplus, Dividends, Retained Earnings**, and Accumulated Other Comprehensive Income are commonly used accounts. In a **proprietorship** or **partnership**, a **Capital** account is used to indicate the investment in the company by the owner(s). A **Drawings** or withdrawal account may be used to indicate withdrawals by the owner(s). These two accounts are grouped or netted under **Owners' Equity**.

Illustration 3-5 summarizes the transactions that affect shareholders' equity and relates them to the temporary and permanent account classifications and to the types of business ownership.

---

[2] A balance sheet account that accumulates the other comprehensive income—it is similar to the retained earnings account.

[3] Corporations are incorporated under a government act such as the *Canada Business Corporations Act*. The main reason for incorporation is to limit the liability for the owners if the corporation gets sued or goes bankrupt. When companies are incorporated, shares are issued to owners and the company becomes a separate legal entity (separate and distinct from its owners).

Illustration 3-5

Effects of Transactions on Owners' or Shareholders' Equity Accounts

		Ownership Structure			
		Proprietorships and Partnerships		Corporations	
Transactions Affecting Owners' Equity	Impact on Owners' Equity	Temporary Accounts	Permanent Accounts	Temporary Accounts	Permanent Accounts
Investment by owner(s)	Increase		Capital		Common Shares and related accounts
Revenues earned Expenses incurred Withdrawal by owner(s)	Increase Decrease Decrease	Revenue ⎫ Expense ⎬ Drawings ⎭	Capital	Revenue ⎫ Expense ⎬ Dividend ⎭	Retained Earnings/ AOCI

THE ACCOUNTING CYCLE

Objective **3**
Identify the steps in the accounting cycle.

Illustration 3-6 charts the steps in the **accounting cycle**. These are the accounting procedures normally used by enterprises to record transactions and prepare financial statements.

Illustration 3-6

The Accounting Cycle

WILEY PLUS
Accounting Cycle Tutorial

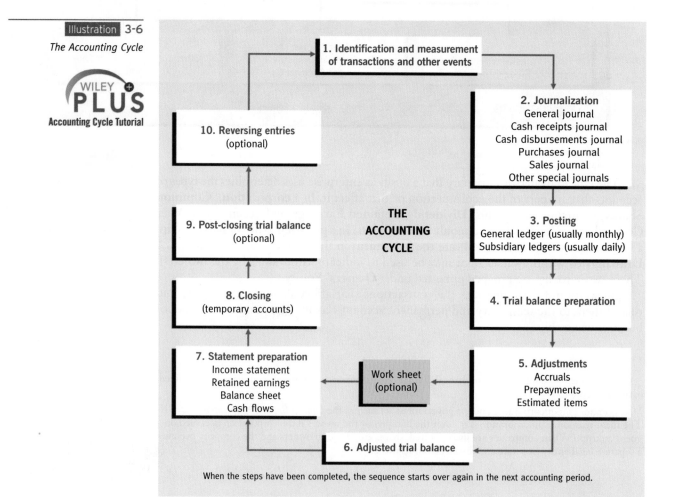

When the steps have been completed, the sequence starts over again in the next accounting period.

Identifying and Recording Transactions and Other Events

The first step in the accounting cycle is to **analyze transactions** and other selected **events**. The problem is determining **what to record**. There are no simple rules for whether an event should be recorded. It is generally agreed that changes in personnel, changes in managerial policies, and the value of human resources, though important, should not be recorded in the accounts. On the other hand, when the company makes a cash sale or purchase—no matter how small—it should be recorded. The treatment relates to the accounting concepts presented in Chapter 2. An item should be **recognized** in the financial statements if it meets the definition of an **element** (e.g., liability, asset), and is **measurable**. Where there is uncertainty about the future event occurring or not (e.g., potential loss from lawsuit), the entity must use all available information to make a neutral decision as to whether the liability/asset exists or not. The uncertainty would be taken into account when the element is measured. Recognition and measurement criteria were discussed in Chapter 2.

Information about transactions and other events and circumstances is captured and recorded in the financial statements. Events are of two types:

- **External events** involve interaction between an entity and its environment, such as a **transaction** with another entity, a change in the price of a product or service that an entity buys or sells, a flood or earthquake, or a competitor's improvement in its technology.

- **Internal events** occur within an entity, such as using buildings and machinery in its operations, or transferring or consuming raw materials in production processes.

Many events have **both** external and internal elements. For example, acquiring the services of employees or others involves exchange transactions that are external events. The employee provides services and the company remunerates the employee. Using those services (labour), often from the moment they are acquired, is part of production, which is internal. Events may be initiated and controlled by an entity, such as the purchase of merchandise or the use of a machine, or they may be beyond its control, such as an interest rate change, a theft or vandalism, or the imposition of taxes.

As a particular kind of **external event**, a **transaction** can be an exchange in which each entity both receives and gives up value, such as a purchase or sale of goods or services. Alternatively, a transaction can be a transfer in one direction (i.e., be non-reciprocal) in which an entity incurs a liability or transfers an asset to another entity without directly receiving (or giving up) value in exchange. Examples include distributions to owners, the payment of taxes, gifts, charitable contributions, uninsured losses, and thefts.

In short, as many events as possible that affect the enterprise's financial position are recorded. Some events are not recorded because of tradition or because measuring them is too complex. The accounting profession in recent years has shown signs of breaking with age-old traditions and is more receptive than ever to accepting the challenge of measuring and reporting events and phenomena that were previously viewed as too complex and immeasurable.[4] These areas will be studied in further depth in the rest of the textbook.

Journalizing

The varied effects of transactions on the basic business elements (assets, liabilities, and equities) are categorized and collected in accounts. The general ledger is a collection of all the asset, liability, shareholders' equity, revenue, and expense accounts. A T account (as

4 **Objective**
Record transactions in journals, post journal entries to ledger accounts, and prepare a trial balance.

---

[4] Examples of these include accounting for defined future benefit pension plans and stock-based employee compensation. These will be covered in Chapters 20 and 17, respectively.

shown in Illustration 3-8) is a convenient method for showing the effect of transactions on particular asset, liability, equity, revenue, and expense items.

In practice, transactions and other selected events are not first recorded in the ledger. This is because each transaction affects two or more accounts, and since each account is on a different page in the ledger, it would be inconvenient to record each transaction this way. The risk of error would also be greater.[5] To overcome this limitation and to have a complete record of each transaction or other selected event in one place, a journal (the book of original entry) is used. The simplest journal form is a chronological listing of transactions and other events that expresses the transactions and events as debits and credits to particular accounts. This is called a **general journal**. The following transactions are presented in the general journal illustration that follows them:

Nov. 11   Buys a new delivery truck on account from Auto Sales Inc., $22,400.

Nov. 13   Receives an invoice from the *Evening Graphic* for advertising, $280.

Nov. 14   Returns merchandise to Canuck Supply for credit, $175.

Nov. 16   Receives a $95 debit memo from Confederation Ltd., indicating that freight on a purchase from Confederation Ltd. was prepaid but is the buyer's obligation.

Expanded Discussion of
Special Journals

Each general journal entry has four parts:

1. The accounts and amounts to be debited (Dr.)

2. The accounts and amounts to be credited (Cr.)

3. A date

4. An explanation

Debits are entered first, followed by the credits, which are slightly indented. The explanation begins below the name of the last account to be credited and may take one or more lines. The Reference column is completed when the accounts are posted.

In some cases, businesses use **special journals** in addition to the general journal. Special journals summarize transactions that have a common characteristic (e.g., cash receipts, sales, purchases, cash payments), which saves time in doing the various bookkeeping tasks.

Illustration 3-7

General Journal with Sample Entries

GENERAL JOURNAL PAGE 12

Date 2010	Account Title and Explanation	Ref.	Amount Debit	Credit
Nov. 11	Delivery Equipment	8	22,400	
	Accounts Payable	34		22,400
	(Purchased delivery truck on account)			
Nov. 13	Advertising Expense	65	280	
	Accounts Payable	34		280
	(Received invoice for advertising)			
Nov. 14	Accounts Payable	34	175	
	Purchase Returns	53		175
	(Returned merchandise for credit)			
Nov. 16	Transportation-In	55	95	
	Accounts Payable	34		95
	(Received debit memo for freight on merchandise purchased)			

[5] The transition to electronic bookkeeping systems and databases has dramatically changed the way bookkeeping is carried out. Much of the terminology and visual layout of the reports has been retained, however.

Posting

The items entered in a general journal must be transferred to the general ledger. This procedure is called **posting** and is part of the summarizing and classifying process.

For example, the November 11 entry in the general journal in Illustration 3-7 showed a debit to Delivery Equipment of $22,400 and a credit to Accounts Payable of $22,400. The amount in the debit column is posted from the journal to the debit side of the ledger account Delivery Equipment. The amount in the credit column is posted from the journal to the credit side of the ledger account Accounts Payable.

The numbers in the Ref. column of the general journal refer to the ledger accounts to which the items are posted. For example, the 34 placed in the column to the right of Accounts Payable indicates that this $22,400 item was posted to Account No. 34 in the ledger.

The general journal posting is completed when all the posting reference numbers have been recorded opposite the account titles in the journal. This means that the number in the posting reference column serves two purposes: (1) it indicates the ledger account number of the account involved, and (2) it indicates that the posting has been completed for that item. Each business enterprise chooses its own numbering system for its ledger accounts. One practice is to begin numbering with asset accounts and to follow with liabilities, shareholders' equity, revenue, and expense accounts, in that order.

The various ledger accounts in Illustration 3-8 are shown after the posting process is completed. The source of the data that have been transferred to the ledger account is indicated by the reference GJ 12 (General Journal, page 12).

Illustration 3-8

Ledger Accounts, in T Account Format

Delivery Equipment No. 8

Nov. 11	GJ 12	22,400			

Accounts Payable No. 34

Nov. 14	GJ 12	175	Nov. 11	GJ 12	22,400
			13	GJ 12	280
			16	GJ 12	95

Purchase Returns No. 53

			Nov. 14	GJ 12	175

Transportation-In No. 55

Nov. 16	GJ 12	95			

Advertising Expense No. 65

Nov. 13	GJ 12	280			

Trial Balance

A trial balance is a list of accounts and their balances at a specific time. Customarily, a trial balance is prepared at the end of an accounting period. The accounts are listed in the order in which they appear in the ledger, with debit balances listed in the left column and credit balances in the right column. The totals of the two columns must agree.

The main purpose of a trial balance is to prove the mathematical equality of debits and credits after posting. Under the double-entry system, this equality will occur when the sum of the debit account balances equals the sum of the credit account balances. A trial balance also uncovers errors in journalizing and posting. In addition, it is useful when preparing financial statements. The procedures for preparing a trial balance consist of:

1. Listing the account titles and their balances

2. Totalling the debit and credit columns

3. Proving the equality of the two columns

Illustration 3-9 shows the trial balance prepared from the ledger of Pioneer Advertising Agency Inc.

Illustration 3-9

Trial Balance (Unadjusted)

PIONEER ADVERTISING AGENCY INC.
Trial Balance
October 31, 2010

	Debit	Credit
Cash	$ 80,000	
Accounts receivable	72,000	
Advertising supplies	25,000	
Prepaid insurance	6,000	
Office equipment	50,000	
Notes payable		$ 50,000
Accounts payable		25,000
Unearned service revenue		12,000
Common shares		100,000
Dividends	5,000	
Service revenue		100,000
Salaries expense	40,000	
Rent expense	9,000	
	$287,000	$287,000

Note that the total debits, $287,000, equal the total credits, $287,000. In the trial balance, the account numbers of the account titles are also often shown to the left of the titles.

A trial balance does not prove that all transactions have been recorded or that the ledger is correct. Even though the trial balance columns agree, there can still be many errors. For example, the trial balance may still balance when:

1. a transaction is not journalized,

2. a correct journal entry is not posted,

3. a journal entry is posted twice,

4. incorrect accounts are used in journalizing or posting, or

5. offsetting errors are made in recording a transaction amount.

In other words, as long as equal debits and credits are posted, even to the wrong account or in the wrong amount, the total debits will equal the total credits.

Adjusting Entries

Objective 5
Explain the reasons for preparing adjusting entries.

In order for revenues to be recorded in the period in which they are earned, and for expenses to be recognized in the period in which they are incurred, adjusting entries are made at the end of the accounting period. In short, **adjustments are needed to ensure that the revenue recognition principle is followed and that proper matching occurs.**

The use of adjusting entries makes it possible to report on the balance sheet the appropriate assets, liabilities, and owners' equity at the statement date and to report on the income statement the proper net income (or loss) for the period. However, the trial balance—the first pulling together of the transaction data—may not contain up-to-date and complete data. This is true for the following reasons:

1. Some events are **not journalized daily** because it is not efficient to do so. Examples are the consumption of supplies and the earning of wages by employees.

2. Some costs are not journalized during the accounting period because these costs **expire with the passage of time** rather than as a result of recurring daily transactions. Examples of such costs are building and equipment deterioration and rent and insurance.

3. Some items may be **unrecorded**. An example is a utility service bill that will not be received until the next accounting period.

Adjusting entries are required every time financial statements are prepared. The starting point is to analyze each trial balance account to determine whether it is complete and up to date for financial statement purposes. The analysis requires a thorough understanding of the company's operations and the relationships between its accounts. Preparing adjusting entries is often a complicated process that requires the services of a skilled professional. In accumulating the adjustment data, the company may need to take inventory counts of supplies and repair parts. It may also be desirable to prepare supporting schedules of insurance policies, rental agreements, and other contractual commitments. Adjustments are often prepared after the balance sheet date, but the entries are dated as at the balance sheet date.

Types of Adjusting Entries

Adjusting entries can be classified as either **prepayments** or **accruals**. Each of these classes has two subcategories as follows:

PREPAYMENTS	ACCRUALS
1. **Prepaid Expenses.** Expenses paid in cash and recorded as assets before they are used or consumed.	3. **Accrued Revenues.** Revenues earned but not yet received in cash or recorded.
2. **Unearned Revenues.** Revenues received in cash and recorded as liabilities before they are earned.	4. **Accrued Expenses.** Expenses incurred but not yet paid in cash or recorded.

Specific examples and explanations of each type of adjustment are given later in this chapter. Each example is based on the October 31 trial balance of Pioneer Advertising Agency Inc. (Illustration 3-9). We assume that Pioneer Advertising uses an accounting period of one month. Thus, monthly adjusting entries will be made. The entries will be dated October 31.

Adjusting Entries for Prepayments

As mentioned above, prepayments are either **prepaid expenses** or **unearned revenues**. Adjusting entries for prepayments are required at the statement date to record the portion of the prepaid expense or unearned revenue that was actually incurred or earned in the current accounting period. Assuming an adjustment is needed for both types of prepayments, the asset and liability involved are overstated and the related expense and revenue are understated. For example, in the trial balance, the balance in the asset account Advertising Supplies shows only supplies purchased. This balance is overstated; the related expense account, Advertising Supplies Expense, is understated because the cost of supplies used has not been recognized. Thus, the adjusting entry for prepayments will decrease a balance sheet account and increase an income statement account. Illustration 3-10 shows the effects of adjusting entries for prepayments.

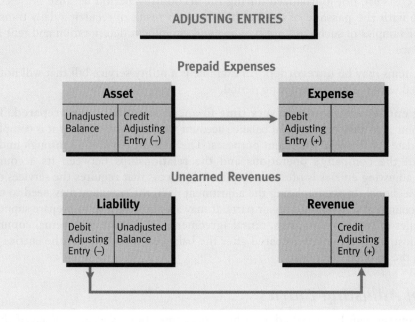

Prepaid Expenses.   As previously stated, expenses that have been paid in cash and recorded as assets before they are used or consumed are identified as **prepaid expenses**. When a cost is incurred, an asset account is debited to show the service or benefit that will be received in the future. Prepayments often occur for such things as insurance, supplies, advertising, and rent.

Prepaid expenses expire either with the passage of time (e.g., rent and insurance) or by being used and consumed (e.g., supplies). The expiration of these costs does not require an entry each day, which would be unnecessary and impractical. Instead, it is customary to postpone the recognition of such cost expirations until financial statements are prepared. At each statement date, adjusting entries are made to record the expenses that apply to the current accounting period and to show the remaining unexpired costs in the asset accounts.

Before adjustment, assets are overstated and expenses are understated. **Thus, the prepaid expense adjusting entry results in a debit to an expense account and a credit to an asset account.**

Supplies.   Several different types of supplies are used in businesses. For example, a CA firm will have office supplies such as stationery, envelopes, and accounting paper. In contrast, an advertising firm will have advertising supplies such as graph paper, colour ink cartridges, and poster paper. Supplies are generally debited to an asset account when they are acquired. During the course of operations, supplies are depleted or entirely consumed. However, recognition of the used-up supplies is deferred until the adjustment process when a physical inventory (a count) of supplies is taken. The difference between the balance in the Supplies account (the asset) and the cost of supplies on hand represents the supplies used up for the period (the expense).

Pioneer Advertising Agency purchased advertising supplies costing $25,000 on October 5. The debit was made to the asset Advertising Supplies, and this account shows a balance of $25,000 in the October 31 trial balance. An inventory count at the close of business on October 31 reveals that $10,000 of supplies is still on hand. Thus, the cost of supplies used is $15,000 ($25,000 − $10,000), and the following adjusting entry is made:

Oct. 31		
Advertising Supplies Expense	15,000	
Advertising Supplies		15,000
(To record supplies used)		

A   = L +   SE
−15,000   −15,000

Cash flows: No effect

After the adjusting entry is posted, the two supplies accounts, in T account form, are as shown in Illustration 3-11.

Advertising Supplies			Advertising Supplies Expense	
10/5 25,000	10/31 Adj. 15,000		10/31 Adj. 15,000	
10/31 Bal. 10,000				

Illustration 3-11

Supplies Accounts after Adjustment

The asset account Advertising Supplies now shows a balance of $10,000, which is equal to the cost of supplies on hand at the statement date. In addition, Advertising Supplies Expense shows a balance of $15,000, which equals the cost of supplies used up in October. **If the adjusting entry is not made, October expenses will be understated and net income overstated by $15,000. Moreover, both assets and shareholders' equity will be overstated by $15,000 on the October 31 balance sheet.**

Insurance.   Most companies have fire and theft insurance on merchandise and equipment, personal liability insurance for accidents suffered by customers, and automobile insurance on company cars and trucks. The cost of insurance protection is the amount paid as insurance premiums. The term (duration) and coverage (what the company is insured against) are specified in the insurance policy. The minimum term is usually one year, but three- to five-year terms are available and offer lower annual premiums. Insurance premiums are normally charged to the asset account Prepaid Insurance when they are paid. At the financial statement date, it is necessary to debit Insurance Expense and credit Prepaid Insurance for the cost that has expired during the period.

On October 4, Pioneer Advertising Agency Inc. paid $6,000 for a one-year fire insurance policy. The coverage began as of October 1. The premium was charged to Prepaid Insurance when it was paid, and this account shows a balance of $6,000 in the October 31 trial balance. An analysis of the policy reveals that $500 of insurance expires each month ($6,000/12). Thus, the following adjusting entry is made:

Oct. 31		
Insurance Expense	500	
Prepaid Insurance		500
(To record insurance expired)		

A   = L +   SE
−500   −500

Cash flows: No effect

After the adjusting entry is posted, the accounts are as in Illustration 3-12.

Prepaid Insurance				Insurance Expense		
10/4	6,000	10/31 Adj.	500	10/31 Adj.	500	
10/31 Bal.	5,500					

The asset Prepaid Insurance shows a balance of $5,500, which represents the unexpired cost of the 11 months of remaining coverage. At the same time, the balance in Insurance Expense is equal to the insurance cost that has expired in October. **If this adjustment is not made, October expenses will be understated by $500 and net income overstated by $500. Moreover, both assets and owners' equity also will be overstated by $500 on the October 31 balance sheet.**

Underlying Concept

The historical cost principle requires that depreciable assets be recorded at cost. Matching allows this cost to be allocated to future periods.

Depreciation/Amortization.   Companies typically own a variety of productive facilities such as buildings, equipment, and motor vehicles. These assets provide a service for many years. The term of service is commonly referred to as the asset's useful life. **Because an asset such as a building is expected to provide service for many years, it is recorded as an asset, rather than an expense, in the year it is acquired.** Such assets are recorded at cost, as required by the cost principle.

In order to match the cost of the asset with the revenues that it is generating, a portion of the cost of a long-lived asset should be reported as an expense during each period of the asset's useful life. Depreciation/amortization is the process of **allocating the cost of an asset** to expense over its useful life in a rational and systematic manner.

From an accounting standpoint, when productive facilities are acquired, the transaction is viewed essentially as a long-term prepayment for services. Periodic adjusting entries for depreciation are therefore needed for the same reasons described earlier for other prepaid expenses; that is, it is necessary to recognize the cost that has expired during the period (the expense) and to report the unexpired cost at the end of the period (the asset).

In determining a productive facility's useful life, there are three main causes of depreciation:

- actual use
- deterioration due to the elements
- obsolescence

Amortization

Oct. 1

Office equipment purchased; record asset ($50,000)

Office Equipment

Oct. $400	Nov. $400	Dec. $400	Jan. $400
Feb. $400	March $400	April $400	May $400
June $400	July $400	Aug. $400	Sept. $400

Amortization=$4,800/year

Oct. 31
Amortization recognized; record amortization expense

When an asset is acquired, the effects of these factors cannot be known with certainty, so they must instead be estimated. Thus, you should recognize that depreciation is an estimate rather than a factual measurement of the cost that has expired. A common procedure in calculating depreciation expense is to divide the asset's cost by its useful life. For example, if the cost is $10,000 and the useful life is expected to be 10 years, annual depreciation is $1,000.

For Pioneer Advertising, depreciation on the office equipment is estimated at $4,800 a year (cost of $50,000 less a salvage value of $2,000 divided by a useful life of 10 years), or $400 per month. Accordingly, depreciation for October is recognized by the following adjusting entry:

$$A = L + SE$$
$$-400 \qquad -400$$

Cash flows: No effect

Oct. 31		
Depreciation Expense	400	
Accumulated Depreciation—Office Equipment		400
(To record monthly depreciation)		

After the adjusting entry is posted, the accounts show that the balance in the accumulated depreciation account will increase by $400 each month.

Illustration 3-13

Accounts after Adjustment for Depreciation

Office Equipment		
10/1	50,000	

Accumulated Depreciation—Office Equipment		Depreciation Expense	
10/31	400	10/31 Adj.	400

Therefore, after journalizing and posting the adjusting entry at November 30, the balance will then be $800 in the accumulated depreciation account.

Accumulated Depreciation—Office Equipment is a contra asset account. A **contra asset account** is an account that is offset against an asset account on the balance sheet. In the case of accumulated depreciation, this account is offset against Office Equipment on the balance sheet and its normal balance is therefore a credit. This account is used instead of crediting Office Equipment so that the equipment's original cost and the total cost that has expired to date can both be disclosed. In the balance sheet, Accumulated Depreciation—Office Equipment is deducted from the related asset account (which is normally a debit), as shown in Illustration 3-14.

Illustration 3-14

Balance Sheet Presentation of Accumulated Depreciation

Office equipment		$50,000	
Less: Accumulated depreciation—office equipment		400	$49,600

The difference between any depreciable asset's cost and its related accumulated depreciation is known as its **book value**. In Illustration 3-14, the equipment's book or carrying value at the balance sheet date is $49,600. It is important to realize that the asset's **book value and market value are generally two different values**.

Note also that depreciation expense identifies that portion of the asset's cost that has expired in October. As in the case of other prepaid adjustments, **if this adjusting entry is not made, then total shareholders' equity and net income will be overstated and depreciation expense will be understated**.

If additional equipment is involved, such as delivery or store equipment, or if the company has buildings, depreciation expense is recorded on each of these items. Related accumulated depreciation accounts also are created. These accumulated depreciation accounts would be described in the ledger as follows: Accumulated Depreciation—Delivery Equipment; Accumulated Depreciation—Store Equipment; and Accumulated Depreciation—Buildings.

Unearned Revenues.   As stated earlier, revenues that have been received in cash and recorded as liabilities before they are earned are called **unearned revenues**. Such items as rent, magazine subscriptions, and customer deposits for further service may result in unearned revenues. Airlines such as **Air Canada** and **United Airlines** treat receipts from the sale of tickets as unearned revenue until the flight service is provided. Similarly, tuition fees received by a university before the start of a semester are considered unearned revenue. Unearned revenues are the opposite of prepaid expenses. Indeed, unearned revenue on the books of one company is likely to be a prepayment on the books of the company that has made the advance payment. For example, if identical accounting periods are assumed, a landlord will have unearned rent revenue when a tenant has prepaid rent.

Real-World Emphasis

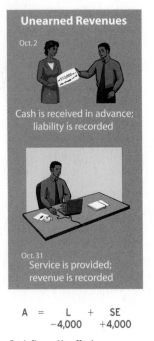

Unearned Revenues

Oct. 2

Cash is received in advance; liability is recorded

Oct. 31
Service is provided; revenue is recorded

A   =   L   +   SE
        −4,000   +4,000

Cash flows: No effect

When the payment is received for services that will be provided in a future accounting period, an unearned revenue account (a liability) should be credited to recognize the obligation that exists. Unearned revenues are later earned by performing the service for the customer (which discharges the liability). During the accounting period, it may not be practical to make an entry each day as the revenue is earned. In such cases, the recognition of earned revenue is delayed until the adjustment process. At that time, an adjusting entry is then made to record the revenue that has been earned and to show the liability that remains. In the typical case, liabilities are overstated and revenues are understated prior to adjustment. Thus, the adjusting entry for unearned revenues results in a debit (decrease) to a liability account and a credit (increase) to a revenue account.

Pioneer Advertising Agency received $12,000 on October 2 from R. Knox for advertising services that are expected to be completed by December 31. The payment was credited to Unearned Service Revenue, and this account shows a balance of $12,000 in the October 31 trial balance. When analysis reveals that $4,000 of these services have been earned in October, the following adjusting entry is made:

Oct. 31		
Unearned Service Revenue	4,000	
Service Revenue		4,000
(To record revenue for services provided)		

After the adjusting entry is posted, the accounts are as shown in Illustration 3-15.

Illustration 3-15

Service Revenue Accounts after Prepayments Adjustment

Unearned Service Revenue					Service Revenue		
10/31 Adj.	4,000	10/2	12,000			10/31 Bal.	100,000
		10/31 Bal.	8,000			10/31 Adj.	4,000
						10/31 Bal.	104,000

The account Unearned Service Revenue now shows a balance of $8,000, which represents the remaining advertising services that are expected to be performed in the future. At the same time, Service Revenue shows total revenue earned in October of $104,000. **If this adjustment is not made, revenues and net income will be understated by $4,000 in the income statement. Moreover, liabilities will be overstated and shareholders' equity will be understated by $4,000 on the October 31 balance sheet.**

Alternative Method for Adjusting Prepayments

So far, the assumption has been that an asset (e.g., prepaid rent) or liability (e.g., unearned revenue) is recorded when the company initially pays or receives the cash. An alternative treatment is to record the initial entry through the related income statement account and adjust it later. For example, if Pioneer Advertising Agency Inc. paid $6,000 for a one-year fire insurance policy on October 1, it could initially have recorded the whole amount in Insurance Expense. Thus at October 31, the adjusting entry would be as follows:

A   =   L   +   SE
+5,500   +5,500

Cash flows: No effect

Oct. 31		
Prepaid Insurance	5,500	
Insurance Expense		5,500
(To record unexpired insurance)		

The same could be done for other prepayments, such as supplies and revenues.

Adjusting Entries for Accruals

The second category of adjusting entries is **accruals**. Adjusting entries for accruals are required in order to record revenues earned and expenses incurred in the current accounting period that have not been recognized through daily entries. If an accrual adjustment is needed, the revenue account (and the related asset account) and/or the expense account (and the related liability account) are understated. Thus, the adjusting entry for accruals will increase both a balance sheet and an income statement account. Adjusting entries for accruals are shown in Illustration 3-16.

Accrued Revenues

Oct. 31

My fee is $ 2,000

Service is provided; revenue and receivable are recorded

Nov.

Cash is received; receivable is reduced

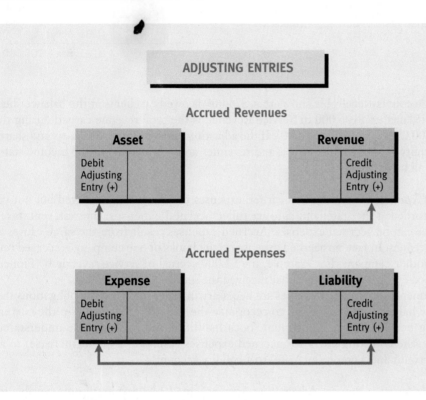

ADJUSTING ENTRIES

Accrued Revenues

Asset	
Debit Adjusting Entry (+)	

Revenue	
	Credit Adjusting Entry (+)

Accrued Expenses

Expense	
Debit Adjusting Entry (+)	

Liability	
	Credit Adjusting Entry (+)

Illustration 3-16

Adjusting Entries for Accruals

Accrued Revenues. As explained earlier, revenues that have been **earned but not yet received** in cash or recorded at the statement date are accrued revenues. Accrued revenues may **accumulate (accrue) with the passing of time**, as in the case of interest revenue and rent revenue. These types of accrued revenues are unrecorded because earning interest and rent does not involve daily transactions. Accrued revenues may also result from services that have been performed but neither billed nor collected, as in the case of commissions and fees. These types of accrued revenues may be unrecorded because only a portion of the total service has been provided.

An adjusting entry is required to show the receivable that exists at the balance sheet date and to record the revenue that has been earned during the period. Before adjustment, both assets and revenues are understated. Accordingly, an adjusting entry for accrued revenues results in a debit (increase) to an asset account and a credit (increase) to a revenue account.

In October, Pioneer Advertising Agency earned $2,000 for advertising services that were not billed to clients before October 31. Because these services have not yet been billed, they have not been recorded in any way. Thus, the following adjusting entry is made:

A = L + SE
+2,000   +2,000

Cash flows: No effect

Oct. 31		
Accounts Receivable	2,000	
Service Revenue		2,000
(To record revenue for services provided)		

Illustration 3-17 shows the accounts after the adjusting entry is posted.

Illustration 3-17

Receivable and Revenue Accounts after Accrual Adjustment

Accounts Receivable				Service Revenue		
10/31		72,000			10/31	100,000
10/31	Adj.	2,000			10/31	4,000
10/31	Bal.	74,000			10/31 Adj.	2,000
					10/31 Bal.	106,000

The asset Accounts Receivable shows that $74,000 is owed by clients at the balance sheet date. The balance of $106,000 in Service Revenue is the total revenue earned during the month ($100,000 + $4,000 + $2,000). If the adjusting entry is not made, assets and shareholders' equity on the balance sheet, and revenues and net income on the income statement, will all be understated.

Underlying Concept

Accrual accounting requires that expenses be accrued when they are incurred.

Accrued Expenses.   As indicated earlier, expenses that have been incurred but not yet paid or recorded at the statement date are called accrued expenses. Interest, rent, taxes, and salaries can be accrued expenses. Accrued expenses result from the same causes as accrued revenues. In fact, an accrued expense on the books of one company is accrued revenue to another company. For example, the $2,000 accrual of service revenue by Pioneer is an accrued expense to the client that received the service.

Adjustments for accrued expenses are necessary in order to record the obligations that exist at the balance sheet date and to recognize the expenses that apply to the current accounting period. Before adjustment, both liabilities and expenses are understated. Therefore, the adjusting entry for accrued expenses results in a debit (increase) to an expense account and a credit (increase) to a liability account.

Accrued Interest.   Pioneer Advertising Agency signed a three-month note payable for $50,000 on October 1. The note requires interest at an annual rate of 12%. The interest accumulation amount is determined by three factors:

- the note's face value

- the interest rate, which is always expressed as an annual rate

- the length of time the note is outstanding

In this instance, the total interest due on the $50,000 note at its due date three months later is $1,500 ($50,000 × 12% × 3/12), or $500 for one month. The formula for calculating interest and how it applies to Pioneer Advertising Agency for the month of October are shown in Illustration 3-18.

Illustration 3-18

Formula for Calculating Interest

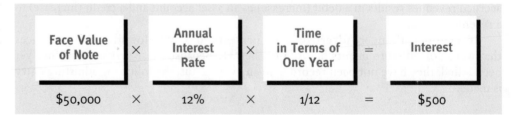

Note that the time period is expressed as a fraction of a year. The accrued expense adjusting entry at October 31 is as follows:

	Oct. 31		
Interest Expense		500	
Interest Payable			500
(To record interest on notes payable)			

A = L + SE
    +500   −500

Cash flows: No effect

After this adjusting entry is posted, the accounts are as shown in Illustration 3-19.

Interest Expense				**Interest Payable**	
10/31	$500			10/31	$500

Illustration 3-19

Interest Accounts after Adjustmentss

Interest Expense shows the interest charges that apply to the month of October. The amount of interest owed at the statement date is shown in Interest Payable. It will not be paid until the note comes due at the end of three months. The Interest Payable account is used instead of crediting Notes Payable in order to disclose the two types of obligations (interest and principal) in the accounts and statements. **If this adjusting entry is not made, liabilities and interest expense will be understated, and net income and shareholders' equity will be overstated.**

Accrued Salaries.   Some types of expenses, such as employee salaries and commissions, are paid for after the services have been performed. At Pioneer Advertising, salaries were last paid on October 26; the next payment of salaries will not occur until November 9. As shown in the calendar that follows, three working days remain in October (October 29, 30, and 31).

	October								November					
	S	M	Tu	W	Th	F	S		S	M	Tu	W	Th	F	S
		1	2	3	4	5	6							1	2	3
	7	8	9	10	11	12	13		4	5	6	7	8	9	10
Start of pay period	14	15	16	17	18	19	20		11	12	13	14	15	16	17
	21	22	23	24	25	26	27		18	19	20	21	22	23	24
	28	29	30	31					25	26	27	28	29	30

Adjustment period   Payday   Payday

At October 31, the salaries for these days represent an accrued expense and a related liability to Pioneer Advertising. The employees receive total salaries of $10,000 for a five-day workweek, or $2,000 per day. Thus, accrued salaries at October 31 are $6,000 ($2,000 times 3), and the adjusting entry is:

	Oct. 31		
Salaries Expense		6,000	
Salaries Payable			6,000
(To record accrued salaries)			

A = L + SE
    +6,000   −6,000

Cash flows: No effect

After this adjusting entry is posted, the accounts are as shown in Illustration 3-20.

Illustration 3-20

Salary Accounts after Adjustment

	Salaries Expense				Salaries Payable		
10/26		40,000				10/31 Adj.	6,000
10/31 Adj.		6,000					
10/31 Bal.		46,000					

After this adjustment, the balance in Salaries Expense of $46,000 (23 days times $2,000) is the actual salary expense for October. The balance in Salaries Payable of $6,000 is the amount of liability for salaries owed as at October 31. **If the $6,000 adjustment for salaries is not recorded, Pioneer's expenses will be understated by $6,000, and its liabilities will be understated by $6,000.**

At Pioneer Advertising, salaries are payable every two weeks. Consequently, the next payday is November 9, when total salaries of $20,000 will again be paid. The payment consists of $6,000 of salaries payable at October 31 plus $14,000 of salaries expense for November (7 working days as shown in the November calendar × $2,000). Therefore, the following entry is made on November 9:

A   =   L   +   SE
+20,000   −6,000   −14,000

Cash flows: ↓ 20,000 outflow

Nov. 9		
Salaries Payable	6,000	
Salaries Expense	14,000	
Cash		20,000
(To record November 9 payroll)		

This entry eliminates the liability for Salaries Payable that was recorded in the October 31 adjusting entry and records the proper amount of Salaries Expense for the period November 1 to November 9.

Bad Debts

Oct.31

Uncollectible accounts; record bad debt expense

Bad Debts. **In order to properly match revenues with expenses, a bad debt must be recorded as an expense of the period in which the revenue was earned instead of being recorded in the period when the accounts or notes are written off. So that the receivable balance shows its proper value, uncollectible, worthless receivables must be recognized.** Proper matching and valuation therefore require an adjusting entry.

At the end of each period, an estimate is made of the amount of current period revenue on account that will later be uncollectible. The estimate is based on the amount of bad debts experienced in past years, general economic conditions, how long the receivables are past due, and other factors that indicate uncollectibility. Usually it is expressed as a percentage of the revenue on account for the period. Or it may be calculated by adjusting the Allowance for Doubtful Accounts to a certain percentage of the trade accounts receivable and trade notes receivable at the end of the period.

To illustrate, assume that experience shows that a reasonable estimate for bad debt expense for the month is $1,600. The adjusting entry for bad debts is:

A   =   L   +   SE
−1,600   −1,600

Cash flows: No effect

Oct. 31		
Bad Debt Expense	1,600	
Allowance for Doubtful Accounts		1,600
(To record monthly bad debt expense)		

Illustration 3-21 shows the accounts after the adjusting entry is posted.

Illustration 3-21

*Accounts after Adjustment
for Bad Debt Expense*

Accounts Receivable

10/1		72,000	
10/31	Adj.	2,000	
10/31	Bal.	74,000	

Allowance for Doubtful Accounts			**Bad Debt Expense**		
	10/31 Adj.	1,600	10/31 Adj.	1,600	

Illustration 3-22

Trial Balance (Adjusted)

PIONEER ADVERTISING AGENCY, INC.
Adjusted Trial Balance
October 31, 2010

	Debit	Credit
Cash	$ 80,000	
Accounts receivable	74,000	
Allowance for doubtful accounts		$ 1,600
Advertising supplies	10,000	
Prepaid insurance	5,500	
Office equipment	50,000	
Accumulated depreciation— office equipment		400
Notes payable		50,000
Accounts payable		25,000
Interest payable		500
Unearned service revenue		8,000
Salaries payable		6,000
Common shares		100,000
Dividends	5,000	
Service revenue		106,000
Salaries expense	46,000	
Advertising supplies expense	15,000	
Rent expense	9,000	
Insurance expense	500	
Interest expense	500	
Depreciation expense	400	
Bad debt expense	1,600	
	$297,500	$297,500

Closing

Basic Process

The procedure that reduces the balance of temporary accounts to zero in order to prepare the accounts for the next period's transactions is known as the closing process. In the closing process, all of the revenue and expense account balances (income statement items) are transferred to a clearing or suspense account called **Income Summary**, which is used only at year end. Revenues and expenses are matched in the Income Summary account, and the net result of this matching (which is the net income or net loss for the period) is then transferred to an owners' equity account. For a corporation, this would be the Retained Earnings or Accumulated Other Comprehensive Income account. For

6 Objective
Prepare closing entries.

proprietorships and partnerships, this would normally be the capital accounts or owners' equity account. All **closing entries** are posted to the appropriate general ledger accounts.

For example, assume that the revenue accounts of Collegiate Apparel Shop Inc. have the following balances, after adjustments, at year end:

Sales revenue	$280,000
Rental revenue	27,000
Interest revenue	5,000

These revenue accounts would be closed and the balances transferred by the following closing journal entry:

A = L + SE
−312,000
+312,000

Cash flows: No effect

Sales Revenue	280,000	
Rental Revenue	27,000	
Interest Revenue	5,000	
Income Summary		312,000
(To close revenue accounts to Income Summary)		

Assume that the expense accounts, including Cost of Goods Sold, have the following balances, after adjustments, at year end:

Cost of goods sold	$206,000
Selling expenses	25,000
General and administrative expenses	40,600
Interest expense	4,400
Income tax expense	13,000

These expense accounts would be closed and the balances transferred through the following closing journal entry:

A = L + SE
−289,000
+289,000

Cash flows: No effect

Income Summary	289,000	
Cost of Goods Sold		206,000
Selling Expenses		25,000
General and Administrative Expenses		40,600
Interest Expense		4,400
Income Tax Expense		13,000
(To close expense accounts to Income Summary)		

The Income Summary account now has a credit balance of $23,000, which is net income. **The net income is then transferred to retained earnings by closing the Income Summary account to Retained Earnings**, as follows:

A = L + SE
−23,000
+23,000

Cash flows: No effect

Income Summary	23,000	
Retained Earnings		23,000
(To close Income Summary to Retained Earnings)		

Any items posted to Other Comprehensive Income would similarly be closed out to Accumulated Other Comprehensive Income, which acts like a second retained earnings account for certain gains and losses booked to Other Comprehensive Income.

Assuming that dividends of $7,000 were declared and distributed during the year, the Dividends account is closed directly to Retained Earnings, as follows:

Retained Earnings	7,000	
Dividends		7,000
(To close Dividends to Retained Earnings)		

$$A \quad = \quad L \quad + \quad SE$$
$$-7,000$$
$$+7,000$$

Cash flows: No effect

After the closing process is completed, each income statement account is balanced out to zero and is ready to be used in the next accounting period. Illustration 3-23 shows the closing process in T account form.

Illustration 3-23

The Closing Process

Inventory and Cost of Goods Sold

The closing procedures just shown assume that a perpetual inventory system is being used. With a perpetual inventory system, purchases and sales are recorded directly in the inventory account as they occur. Therefore, the balance in Inventory should represent the ending inventory amount, and no adjusting entries are needed. To be sure that the inventory amount is accurate, a **physical count** of the items in the inventory is generally done each year.

In the perpetual inventory system, since all purchases are debited directly to the Inventory account, there are no separate Purchases accounts. However, a Cost of Goods Sold account is used to accumulate what is issued from inventory. That is, when inventory items are sold, the cost of the sold goods is credited to Inventory and debited to Cost of Goods Sold.

7 Objective
Explain how inventory accounts are adjusted at year end.

Underlying Concept

Using a periodic inventory system instead of a perpetual one is an application of the cost-benefit concept since it is cheaper to maintain a periodic inventory system. Computers have greatly reduced the costs of maintaining a perpetual inventory system, however.

With a periodic inventory system, a Purchases account is used, and the Inventory account is unchanged during the period. The Inventory account therefore represents the beginning inventory amount throughout the period. At the end of the accounting period, the Inventory account must be adjusted by **closing out the beginning inventory amount** and **recording the ending inventory amount**. The ending inventory is determined by physically counting the items on hand and valuing them at cost or at the lower of cost or market. Under the periodic inventory system, cost of goods sold is therefore determined by adding the beginning inventory to net purchases and deducting the ending inventory.

To illustrate how cost of goods sold is calculated with a periodic inventory system, assume that Collegiate Apparel Shop has a beginning inventory of $30,000; purchases of $200,000; transportation-in of $6,000; purchase returns and allowances of $1,000; purchase discounts of $3,000; and ending inventory of $26,000. The calculation of cost of goods sold is as shown in Illustration 3-24.

Illustration 3-24

Calculation of Cost of Goods Sold

Beginning inventory			$30,000
Purchases		$200,000	
Less: Purchase returns and allowances	$1,000		
Less: Purchase discounts	3,000	4,000	
Net purchases		196,000	
Plus: Transportation-in		6,000	
Cost of goods purchased			202,000
Cost of goods available for sale			232,000
Less: Ending inventory			26,000
Cost of goods sold			$206,000

Cost of goods sold will be the same whether the perpetual or periodic method is used.

Post-Closing Trial Balance

We already mentioned that a trial balance is taken after the period's regular transactions have been entered and that a second trial balance (the adjusted trial balance) is taken after the adjusting entries have been posted. A third trial balance may be taken after posting the closing entries. The trial balance after closing, often called the post-closing trial balance, shows that equal debits and credits have been posted to the Income Summary account. The post-closing trial balance consists only of asset, liability, and owners' equity accounts (i.e., the permanent accounts).

Reversing Entries

After the financial statements have been prepared and the books have been closed, it is often helpful to reverse some of the adjusting entries before recording the next period's regular transactions. Such entries are called reversing entries. A reversing entry is made at the beginning of the next accounting period and is the exact opposite of the related adjusting entry made in the previous period. The recording of reversing entries is an optional step in the accounting cycle that may be done at the beginning of the next accounting period. Appendix 3A discusses reversing entries in more detail.

The Accounting Cycle Summarized

The steps in the accounting cycle follow a logical sequence of the accounting procedures that are used during a fiscal period:

1. Enter the period's transactions in appropriate journals.

2. Post from the journals to the ledger (or ledgers).

3. Take an unadjusted trial balance (trial balance).

4. Prepare adjusting journal entries and post to the ledger(s).

5. Take a trial balance after adjusting (adjusted trial balance).

6. Prepare the financial statements from the second trial balance.

7. Prepare closing journal entries and post to the ledger(s).

8. Take a trial balance after closing (post-closing trial balance).

9. Prepare reversing entries (optional) and post to the ledger(s).

   This list of procedures forms the complete accounting cycle that is normally performed in every fiscal period.

USING A WORK SHEET

To make the end-of-period (monthly, quarterly, or annually) accounting and reporting process easier, a work sheet is often used. A **work sheet** is a sheet of paper with columns (or computer spreadsheet) that is used to adjust the account balances and prepare the financial statements. Using a work sheet helps accountants prepare financial statements on a timelier basis. It is not necessary to delay preparing the financial statements until the adjusting and closing entries are journalized and posted. The **10-column work sheet** shown in this chapter (Illustration 3-25) has columns for the first trial balance, adjustments, adjusted trial balance, income statement, and balance sheet.

   The work sheet does not replace the financial statements. Instead, it is an informal device for accumulating and sorting the information that is needed for the financial statements. Completing the work sheet makes it more certain that all of the details of the end-of-period accounting and statement preparation have been brought together properly.

8 Objective

Prepare a 10-column work sheet and financial statements.

Adjustments Entered on the Work Sheet

The following items, (a) through (f), are the basis for the adjusting entries made in the work sheet in Illustration 3-25:

(a) Furniture and equipment is amortized at the rate of 10% per year based on an original cost of $67,000.

(b) Estimated bad debts are 0.25% of sales ($400,000).

(c) Insurance of $360 expired during the year.

(d) Interest of $800 accrued on notes receivable as at December 31.

(e) The Rent Expense account contains $500 of rent paid in advance, which is applicable to next year.

(f) Property taxes of $2,000 accrued to December 31.

The adjusting entries shown on the December 31, 2010, work sheet are as follows:

(a)	Depreciation Expense—Furniture and Equipment	6,700	
	Accumulated Depreciation—Furniture and Equipment		6,700
(b)	Bad Debt Expense	1,000	
	Allowance for Doubtful Accounts		1,000
(c)	Insurance Expense	360	
	Prepaid Insurance		360
(d)	Interest Receivable	800	
	Interest Revenue		800
(e)	Prepaid Rent Expense	500	
	Rent Expense		500
(f)	Property Tax Expense	2,000	
	Property Tax Payable		2,000

These adjusting entries are transferred to the work sheet's Adjustments columns and each column can be named by letter. The accounts that are set up from the adjusting entries and that are not already in the trial balance are listed below the totals of the trial balance, as shown on the work sheet. The Adjustments columns are then totalled and balanced.

Work Sheet Columns

Trial Balance Columns

Data for the trial balance are obtained from the ledger balances of Uptown Cabinet Corp. at December 31. The amount for Merchandise Inventory, $40,000, is the year-end inventory amount under a perpetual inventory system.

Adjustments Columns

After all adjustment data are entered on the work sheet, the equality of the adjustment columns is established. The balances in all accounts are then extended to the adjusted trial balance columns.

Adjusted Trial Balance

The adjusted trial balance shows the balance of all accounts after adjustment at the end of the accounting period. For example, the $2,000 shown opposite Allowance for Doubtful Accounts in the Trial Balance Cr. column is added to the $1,000 in the Adjustments Cr. column. The $3,000 total is then extended to the Adjusted Trial Balance Cr. column.

UPTOWN CABINET CORP.
Ten-Column Work Sheet
For the Year Ended December 31, 2010

Accounts	Trial Balance Dr.	Trial Balance Cr.	Adjustments Dr.	Adjustments Cr.	Adjusted Trial Balance Dr.	Adjusted Trial Balance Cr.	Income Statement Dr.	Income Statement Cr.	Balance Sheet Dr.	Balance Sheet Cr.
Cash	1,200				1,200				1,200	
Notes receivable	16,000				16,000				16,000	
Accounts receivable	41,000				41,000				41,000	
Allowance for doubtful accounts		2,000		(b)1,000		3,000				3,000
Merchandise inventory	40,000				40,000				40,000	
Prepaid insurance	900			(c)360	540				540	
Furniture and equipment	67,000				67,000				67,000	
Accumulated amortization— furniture and equipment		12,000		(a)6,700		18,700				18,700
Notes payable		20,000				20,000				20,000
Accounts payable		13,500				13,500				13,500
Bonds payable		30,000				30,000				30,000
Common shares		50,000				50,000				50,000
Retained earnings, Jan. 1, 2010		14,200				14,200				14,200
Sales		400,000				400,000		400,000		
Cost of goods sold	316,000				316,000		316,000			
Sales salaries expense	20,000				20,000		20,000			
Advertising expense	2,200				2,200		2,200			
Travelling expense	8,000				8,000		8,000			
Salaries, office and general	19,000				19,000		19,000			
Telephone and Internet expense	600				600		600			
Rent expense	4,800			(e)500	4,300		4,300			
Property tax expense	3,300		(f)2,000		5,300		5,300			
Interest expense	1,700				1,700		1,700			
Totals	541,700	541,700								
Depreciation expense— furniture and equipment			(a)6,700		6,700		6,700			
Bad debt expense			(b)1,000		1,000		1,000			
Insurance expense			(c)360		360		360			
Interest receivable			(d)800		800				800	
Interest revenue				(d)800		800		800		
Prepaid rent expense			(e)500		500				500	
Property tax payable				(f)2,000		2,000				2,000
Totals			11,360	11,360	**552,200**	**552,200**	**385,160**	**400,800**		
Income before income taxes							15,640			
Totals							400,800	400,800		
Income before income taxes								15,640		
Income tax expense			(g)3,440				3,440			
Income tax payable				(g)3,440						3,440
Net income							12,200			12,200
Totals							**15,640**	**15,640**	**167,040**	**167,040**

Illustration 3-25

Work Sheet

Similarly, the $900 debit opposite Prepaid Insurance is reduced by the $360 credit in the Adjustments column. The result, $540, is shown in the Adjusted Trial Balance Dr. column.

Income Statement and Balance Sheet Columns

All the debit items in the Adjusted Trial Balance columns are extended into the Income Statement or Balance Sheet columns to the right. All the credit items are also extended. The next step is to total the Income Statement columns; the amount that is needed in order to balance the debit and credit columns is the pretax income or loss for the period. The income before income taxes of $15,640 is shown in the Income Statement Dr. column because revenues exceeded expenses by that amount. Any other items would be closed out to Accumulated Other Comprehensive Income instead of Retained Earnings.

Income Taxes and Net Income

The federal and provincial income tax expense and related tax liability are calculated next. The company assumes a tax rate of 22% to arrive at $3,440. Because the Adjustments columns have been balanced, this adjustment is entered in the Income Statement Dr. column as Income Tax Expense and in the Balance Sheet Cr. column as Income Tax Payable. The following adjusting journal entry is recorded on December 31, 2010, posted to the general ledger, and then entered on the work sheet:

(g) Income Tax Expense	3,440	
Income Tax Payable		3,440

Next, the Income Statement columns are balanced with the income taxes included. The $12,200 difference between the debit and credit columns in this illustration represents net income. The net income of $12,200 is entered in the Income Statement Dr. column to achieve equality and in the Balance Sheet Cr. column as the increase in retained earnings.

Preparing Financial Statements from a Work Sheet

The work sheet gives the information that is needed to prepare financial statements without referring to the ledger or other records. In addition, the data have been sorted into appropriate columns, which makes it easier to prepare the statements.

The financial statements prepared from the 10-column work sheet are as follows: **Income Statement for the Year Ended December 31, 2010 (Illustration 3-26), Statement of Retained Earnings for the Year Ended December 31, 2010 (Illustration 3-27), and Balance Sheet as at December 31, 2010 (Illustration 3-28).**

Income Statement

The income statement in the illustration is for a trading or merchandising concern; if a manufacturing concern were illustrated, three inventory accounts would be used: raw materials, work in process, and finished goods.

Statement of Retained Earnings

The net income earned by a corporation may be retained in the business or distributed to shareholders by paying dividends. In Illustration 3-27, the net income earned during the year was added to the balance of Retained Earnings on January 1, increasing the balance to

$26,400 on December 31. No dividends were declared during the year. A statement of changes in shareholders' equity may be required instead of a statement of changes in retained earnings (for public companies, for instance). The statement of changes in shareholders' equity would include changes in all equity accounts, including Accumulated Other Comprehensive Income, Retained Earnings, and Common and Other Shares. This statement will be covered in more detail in Chapter 4.

UPTOWN CABINET CORP.
Income Statement
For the Year Ended December 31, 2010

Net sales			$400,000
Cost of goods sold			316,000
Gross profit on sales			84,000
Selling expenses			
Sales salaries expense		$20,000	
Advertising expense		2,200	
Travelling expense		8,000	
Total selling expenses		30,200	
Administrative expenses			
Salaries, office, and general	$19,000		
Telephone and Internet expense	600		
Rent expense	4,300		
Property tax expense	5,300		
Depreciation expense—furniture and equipment	6,700		
Bad debt expense	1,000		
Insurance expense	360		
Total administrative expenses		37,260	
Total selling and administrative expenses			67,460
Income from operations			16,540
Other revenues and gains			
Interest revenue			800
			17,340
Other expenses and losses			
Interest expense			1,700
Income before income taxes			15,640
Income taxes			3,440
Net income			$ 12,200
Earnings per share			$ 1.22

UPTOWN CABINET CORP.
Statement of Retained Earnings
For the Year Ended December 31, 2010

Retained earnings, Jan. 1, 2010	$14,200
Add net income for 2010	12,200
Retained earnings, Dec. 31, 2010	**$26,400**

Balance Sheet

The balance sheet prepared from the 10-column work sheet has new items created by year-end adjusting entries. Interest receivable, unexpired insurance, and prepaid rent expense are included as current assets. These assets are considered current because they will be converted into cash or consumed in the ordinary routine of the business in a relatively short period of time. The amount of Allowance for Doubtful Accounts is deducted from the total of accounts, notes, and interest receivable because it is estimated that only $54,800 of the $57,800 will be collected in cash.

In the property, plant, and equipment section, the accumulated depreciation is deducted from the cost of the furniture and equipment; the difference in the two amounts is the book or carrying value of the furniture and equipment.

Illustration 3-28

Balance Sheet

UPTOWN CABINET CORP.
Balance Sheet
As at December 31, 2010

Assets

Current assets			
Cash			$ 1,200
Notes receivable	$16,000		
Accounts receivable	41,000		
Interest receivable	800	$57,800	
Less: Allowance for doubtful accounts		3,000	54,800
Merchandise inventory			40,000
Prepaid insurance			540
Prepaid rent			500
Total current assets			97,040
Property, plant, and equipment			
Furniture and equipment		67,000	
Less: Accumulated depreciation		18,700	
Total property, plant, and equipment			48,300
Total assets			$145,340

Liabilities and Shareholders' Equity

Current liabilities			
Notes payable			$ 20,000
Accounts payable			13,500
Property tax payable			2,000
Income tax payable			3,440
Total current liabilities			38,940
Long-term liabilities			
Bonds payable, due June 30, 2012			30,000
Total liabilities			68,940
Shareholders' equity			
Common shares, issued and outstanding,			
10,000 shares		$50,000	
Retained earnings		26,400	
Total shareholders' equity			76,400
Total liabilities and shareholders' equity			$145,340

Property tax payable is shown as a current liability because it is an obligation that is payable within a year. Other short-term accrued liabilities would also be shown as current liabilities.

The bonds payable, due in 2012, are long-term liabilities and are shown in a separate section. (Interest on the bonds was paid on December 31.)

Because Uptown Cabinet Corp. is a corporation, the balance sheet's capital section, called the shareholders' equity section in Illustration 3-28, is a bit different from the capital section for a proprietorship. Total shareholders' equity consists of the common shares, which represent the original investment by shareholders, and the earnings retained in the business. Since there were no items booked to Other Comprehensive Income, there is no balance in Accumulated Other Comprehensive Income. This would normally be presented after retained earnings.

Closing Entries

The entries for the closing process are as follows:

GENERAL JOURNAL
December 31, 2010

Interest Revenue	800	
Sales	400,000	
Cost of Goods Sold		316,000
Sales Salaries Expense		20,000
Advertising Expense		2,200
Travelling Expense		8,000
Salaries, Office, and General		19,000
Telephone and Internet Expense		600
Rent Expense		4,300
Property Tax Expense		5,300
Depreciation Expense—Furniture and Equipment		6,700
Bad Debt Expense		1,000
Insurance Expense		360
Interest Expense		1,700
Income Tax Expense		3,440
Income Summary		12,200
(To close revenues and expenses to Income Summary)		
Income Summary	12,200	
Retained Earnings		12,200
(To close Income Summary to Retained Earnings)		

Monthly Statements, Yearly Closing

Using a work sheet at the end of each month or quarter makes it possible to prepare interim financial statements even though the books are closed only at the end of each year. For example, assume that a business that closes its books on December 31 wants monthly financial statements. At the end of January, a work sheet similar to the one illustrated in this chapter can be prepared to supply the information that is needed for the statements for January. At the end of February, a work sheet can be used again. Note that because the accounts were not closed at the end of January, the income statement taken from the work sheet on February 28 will present the net income for two months. To obtain an income statement for only the month of February, the items in the January income statement are simply subtracted from the same items in the income statement for the months of January and February together.

It is also possible to have a statement of retained earnings for February only by subtracting the January items. The balance sheet prepared from the February work sheet, however, shows assets, liabilities, and shareholders' equity as at February 28, the specific date for which a balance sheet is desired.

The March work sheet would show the revenues and expenses for three months, and the revenues and expenses for the first two months could be subtracted to supply the amounts needed for an income statement for the month of March only, and so on throughout the year.

Glossary

KEY TERMS

account, 91
accounting cycle, 96
accounting information
    system, 90
accrued expenses, 108
accrued revenues, 107
adjusted trial balance, 91
adjusting entries, 100
balance sheet, 91
book value, 105
closing entries, 112
closing process, 111
contra asset account, 105
credit, 92
debit, 92
depreciation/
    amortization, 104
double-entry
    accounting, 92
event, 91
financial statements, 91
general journal, 98
general ledger, 97
income statement, 91
journal, 91
periodic inventory
    system, 114
permanent accounts, 91
perpetual inventory
    system, 113
post-closing trial
    balance, 114
posting, 99
prepaid expenses, 102
reversing entries, 114
special journals, 98
statement of cash
    flows, 91

Summary of Learning Objectives

1 Understand basic accounting terminology.

It is important to understand the following terms: (1) event, (2) transaction, (3) account, (4) permanent and temporary accounts, (5) ledger, (6) journal, (7) posting, (8) trial balance, (9) adjusting entries, (10) financial statements, (11) closing entries.

2 Explain double-entry rules.

The left side of any account is the debit side; the right side is the credit side. All asset and expense accounts are increased on the left or debit side and decreased on the right or credit side. Conversely, all liability and revenue accounts are increased on the right or credit side and decreased on the left or debit side. Shareholders' equity accounts, Common Shares, and Retained Earnings are increased on the credit side, whereas Dividends is increased on the debit side.

3 Identify the steps in the accounting cycle.

The basic steps in the accounting cycle are (1) identification and measurement of transactions and other events, (2) journalizing, (3) posting, (4) the unadjusted trial balance, (5) adjustments, (6) the adjusted trial balance, (7) statement preparation, and (8) closing.

4 Record transactions in journals, post journal entries to ledger accounts, and prepare a trial balance.

The simplest journal form is a chronological listing of transactions and events that are expressed as debits and credits to particular accounts. The items entered in a general journal must be transferred (posted) to the general ledger. An unadjusted trial balance should be prepared at the end of a specific period after the entries have been recorded in the journal and posted to the ledger.

5 Explain the reasons for preparing adjusting entries.

Adjustments achieve a proper matching of revenues and expenses, which is necessary in order to determine the correct net income for the current period and to achieve an accurate statement of the end-of-the-period balances in assets, liabilities, and owners' equity accounts.

6 Prepare closing entries.

In the closing process, all of the revenue and expense account balances (income statement items) are transferred to a clearing account called Income Summary, which is used only at the end of the fiscal year. Revenues and expenses are matched in the Income Summary account. The net result of this matching, which represents the net income or net loss for the period, is then transferred to a shareholders' equity account (retained earnings for a corporation and capital accounts for proprietorships and partnerships).

7 Explain how inventory accounts are adjusted at year end.

Under a perpetual inventory system, the balance in the Inventory account should represent the ending inventory amount. When the inventory records are maintained in a periodic inventory system, a Purchases account is used; the Inventory account is unchanged during the period. The Inventory account balance represents the beginning inventory amount throughout the period. At the end of the accounting period, the inventory account must be adjusted by closing out the beginning inventory amount and recording the ending inventory amount.

8 Prepare a 10-column work sheet and financial statements.

The 10-column work sheet provides columns for the first trial balance, adjustments, adjusted trial balance, income statement, and balance sheet. The work sheet does not replace the financial statements. Instead, it is the accountant's informal device for accumulating and sorting the information that is needed for the financial statements.

Appendix **3**A

Using Reversing Entries

Objective 9
Identify adjusting entries that may be reversed.

The purpose of reversing entries is to make it easier to record transactions in the next accounting period. The use of reversing entries does not change the amounts reported in the previous period's financial statements.

Illustration of Reversing Entries—Accruals

Reversing entries are usually used for reversing two types of adjusting entries: accrued revenues and accrued expenses. To illustrate the optional use of reversing entries for accrued expenses, we will use the following transaction and adjustment data:

1. October 24 (initial salary entry): $4,000 of salaries expense incurred between October 1 and October 24 is paid.

2. October 31 (adjusting entry): $1,200 of salaries expense is incurred between October 25 and October 31. This will be paid in the November 8 payroll.

3. November 8 (subsequent salary entry): $2,500 of salaries expense is paid. Of this amount, $1,200 applies to accrued salaries payable at October 31 and $1,300 was incurred between November 1 and November 8.

Illustration 3A-1

Comparison of Entries for Accruals, with and without Reversing Entries

The comparative entries are shown in Illustration 3A-1.

Reversing Entries Not Used				Reversing Entries Used			
Initial Salary Entry							
Oct. 24	Salaries Expense	4,000		Oct. 24	Salaries Expense	4,000	
	Cash		4,000		Cash		4,000
Adjusting Entry							
Oct. 31	Salaries Expense	1,200		Oct. 31	Salaries Expense	1,200	
	Salaries Payable		1,200		Salaries Payable		1,200
Closing Entry							
Oct. 31	Income Summary	5,200		Oct. 31	Income Summary	5,200	
	Salaries Expense		5,200		Salaries Expense		5,200
Reversing Entry							
Nov. 1	No entry is made.			Nov. 1	Salaries Payable	1,200	
					Salaries Expense		1,200
Subsequent Salary Entry							
Nov. 8	Salaries Payable	1,200		Nov. 8	Salaries Expense	2,500	
	Salaries Expense	1,300			Cash		2,500
	Cash		2,500				

The illustration shows that the first three entries are the same whether or not reversing entries are used. The last two entries, however, are different. The November 1 reversing entry eliminates the $1,200 balance in Salaries Payable that was created by the October 31 adjusting entry. The reversing entry also creates a $1,200 credit balance in the Salaries Expense account. As you know, it is unusual for an expense account to have a credit balance; however, the balance is correct in this instance. It is correct because the entire amount of the first salary payment in the new accounting period will be debited to Salaries Expense. This debit will eliminate the credit balance, and the resulting debit balance in the expense account will equal the salaries expense incurred in the new accounting period ($1,300 in this example).

When reversing entries are made, all cash payments of expenses can be debited to the expense account. This means that on November 8 (and every payday), Salaries Expense can be debited for the amount paid without having to consider any accrued salaries payable. Being able to make the same entry each time simplifies the recording process in an accounting system.

Illustration of Reversing Entries—Prepayments

Up to this point, we have assumed that all prepayments are recorded as prepaid expenses or unearned revenues. In some cases, prepayments are recorded directly in expense or revenue accounts. When this occurs, prepayments may also be reversed. To illustrate the use of reversing entries for prepaid expenses, we will use the following transaction and adjustment data:

December 10 (initial entry): $20,000 of office supplies is purchased for cash.

December 31 (adjusting entry): $5,000 of office supplies is on hand.

The comparative entries are shown in Illustration 3A-2.

Reversing Entries Not Used				Reversing Entries Used		
Initial Purchase of Supplies Entry						
Dec. 10	Office Supplies	20,000		Dec. 10	Office Supplies Expense	20,000	
	Cash		20,000		Cash		20,000
Adjusting Entry						
Dec. 31	Office Supplies Expense	15,000		Dec. 31	Office Supplies	5,000	
	Office Supplies		15,000		Office Supplies Expense		5,000
Closing Entry						
Dec. 31	Income Summary	15,000		Dec. 31	Income Summary	15,000	
	Office Supplies Expense		15,000		Office Supplies Expense		15,000
Reversing Entry						
Jan. 1	No entry			Jan. 1	Office Supplies Expense	5,000	
					Office Supplies		5,000

Illustration 3A-2

Comparison of Entries for Prepayments, with and without Reversing Entries

After the adjusting entry on December 31 (with or without reversing entries), the asset account Office Supplies shows a balance of $5,000 and Office Supplies Expense shows a balance of $15,000. If Office Supplies Expense was debited when the supplies were first purchased, a reversing entry is made to return to the expense account the cost of the still unused supplies. The company then continues to debit Office Supplies Expense for additional purchases of office supplies during the next period.

It could be asked why all prepaid items are not simply entered originally into real accounts (assets and liabilities), as this would make reversing entries unnecessary.

Sometimes this practice is followed. Doing this is particularly useful for items that need to be apportioned over several periods (e.g., supplies and parts inventories). However, items that do not follow this regular pattern and that may or may not involve two or more periods are usually first entered in revenue or expense accounts. The revenue and expense accounts may not require adjusting and are systematically closed to Income Summary. Using the temporary accounts adds consistency to the accounting system and makes the recording more efficient, especially when a large number of such transactions occur during the year. For example, the bookkeeper knows that when an invoice is received for anything except a capital asset acquisition, the amount is expensed. This way, when the invoice is received, the bookkeeper does not have to worry about whether or not the item will result in a prepaid expense at the end of the period, because adjustments will be made at that time.

Summary of Reversing Entries

The guidelines for reversing entries can be summarized as follows:

1. All accrued items should be reversed.

2. All prepaid items for which the original cash transaction was debited or credited to an expense or revenue account should be reversed.

3. Adjusting entries for depreciation and bad debts are not reversed.

Although reversing entries reduce potential errors and are therefore often used, they do not have to be used. Many accountants avoid them entirely. Reversing entries add an extra step to the bookkeeping process. Also there may be instances where it does not make sense to use them. Assume a company with a December 31 year end has accrued six months' worth of interest on a bond (June 30 interest payment date) at year end. If the company releases financial information monthly, it would not make sense to reverse the entry in January since this would show a credit balance when the monthly reports are prepared.

Summary of Learning Objective for Appendix 3A

9 Identify adjusting entries that may be reversed.

Reversing entries are usually used for reversing two types of adjusting entries: accrued revenues and accrued expenses. Prepayments may also be reversed if the initial entry to record the transaction is made to an expense or revenue account.

Note: All assignment material with an asterisk (*) relates to the appendix to the chapter.
All references to Balance Sheet and Statement of Financial Position refer to the same financial statement.

Brief Exercises

BE3-1 For the following accounts, what are the differences between the trial balance before closing and the trial balance **(LO 3)**
after closing?

(a) Accounts Receivable

(b) Expense accounts

(c) Income accounts

(d) Retained Earnings

(e) Bank Advances

BE3-2 Transactions for Juan More Taco Inc. (JMT) for the month of May follow. Prepare journal entries for each **(LO 4)**
transaction. (You may leave out explanations.)

May	1	Owners invest $12,000 cash in exchange for common shares of JMT Inc., a small chain of fast food outlets.
	3	Buy ovens and computers on account for $4,500.
	13	Pay $800 to landlord for May rent.
	21	Bill $750 to Sub's Away for a staff function where JMT provided food and beverages.

BE3-3 One Wiser Corp. had the following transactions during the first month of business. Journalize the transactions. **(LO 4)**

August	2	Invested $12,000 cash and $2,500 of equipment in the business in exchange for common shares.
	7	Purchased supplies on account for $600. (Debit asset account.)
	12	Performed services for clients, collecting $1,300 in cash and billing the clients $670 for the remainder.
	15	Paid August rent, $600.
	19	Counted supplies and determined that only $270 of the supplies purchased on August 7 were still on hand.

BE3-4 On July 1, 2010, Blondie Ltd. pays $18,000 to No Claims Insurance Ltd. for a three-year insurance contract. **(LO 4)**
Both companies have fiscal years ending December 31. Prepare two sets of journal entries for Blondie for the July 1 entry
and the adjusting entry on December 31. Treat the expenditure as an asset in the first set and as an expense in the second.

BE3-5 Using the data in BE3-4, journalize the entry on July 1 and the adjusting entry on December 31 for No Claims **(LO 4)**
Insurance. No Claims uses the accounts Unearned Insurance Revenue and Insurance Revenue. Prepare two sets of jour-
nal entries: one where the initial cash receipt is treated as Unearned Insurance Revenue and one where it is treated as
Insurance Revenue.

BE3-6 On August 1, Secret Sauce Technologies Inc. paid $12,600 in advance for two years' membership in a global **(LO 4)**
technology association. Prepare Secret Sauce's August 1 journal entry and the annual adjusting entry on December 31.
Prepare two sets of journal entries, treating the initial August 1 expenditure as an asset in the first set and as an expense in
the second.

BE3-7 Store-it-Here owns a warehouse. On September 1, it rented storage space to a lessee (tenant) for six months for **(LO 4)**
a total cash payment of $12,000 received in advance. Prepare Store-it-Here's September 1 journal entry and the
December 31 annual adjusting entry. Prepare a second set of journal entries, assuming that the initial cash receipt on
September 1 is treated as revenue.

BE3-8 ABC Commerce Corp's weekly payroll totals $20,000 and is paid on Fridays every two weeks. The final payroll **(LO 4)**
for the year was December 24. The company pays full payroll during the holiday season. The next payroll was paid
January 7. To prepare for year end, employees were expected to return to work on the 28th. Prepare ABC's adjusting entry
on Friday, December 31, and the journal entry to record the $40,000 cash payment on Friday, January 7.

BE3-9 Included in Carville Corp's December 31 trial balance is a note payable of $20,000. The note is an eight-month, **(LO 5)**
12% note dated October 1. Prepare Carville's December 31 adjusting entry to record the accrued interest, and the June 1
journal entry to record the payment of the principal and interest due to the lender.

(LO 5)   **BE3-10**   Prepare the following adjusting entries at December 31 for Karpai Ltd:

1. Interest on notes receivable of $600 is accrued.

2. Fees earned but unbilled total $1,800.

3. Salaries earned of $1,200 have not been recorded.

4. Bad debt expense for the year is $900.

Use the following account titles: Service Revenue, Accounts Receivable, Interest Income, Interest Receivable, Salaries Expense, Salaries Payable, Allowance for Doubtful Accounts, and Bad Debt Expense.

(LO 5)   **BE3-11**   At the end of Rafael Limited's first year of operations, its trial balance shows Equipment $20,000; Accumulated Depreciation—Equipment $0; and Depreciation Expense $0. Depreciation for the year is estimated to be $4,000. Prepare the adjusting entry for depreciation at December 31, and indicate the balance sheet presentation for the equipment at December 31.

(LO 5)   **BE3-12**   Yeliw Enterprises purchases inventory amounting to $12,000. This is recorded as office equipment and the acquisition is recorded as a debit to Office Equipment. What would be the effect of this error on the statement of financial position and income statement of the same period as the purchase, assuming the inventory is sold during the year?

(LO 5)   **BE3-13**   Bashir and Homer (B&H), Accountants at Large, pay $1,200 to a landlord for one month's rent in advance for the month of May.

(a) Assuming that B&H records all prepayments in (permanent) balance sheet accounts:
1. Prepare the original journal entry B&H should record when it pays the rent on May 1.
2. Prepare the adjusting journal entry B&H should record at the end of May, when the month's rent has expired.

(b) Assuming the company records all prepayments in (temporary) income statement accounts:
1. Prepare the original journal entry B&H should record when it pays the rent on May 1.
2. Prepare the adjusting journal entry B&H should record at the end of May, when the month's rent has expired.

(c) Compare and comment upon the ending account balances for each alternative in parts (a) and (b).

(LO 6)   **BE3-14**   Ray Holiday is the maintenance supervisor for B Jay Insurance Co. and has recently purchased a riding lawn-mower and accessories that will be used in caring for the grounds around corporate headquarters. He sent the following information to the accounting department:

Cost of mower and accessories	$9,600	Date purchased	July 1, 2010
Estimated useful life	8 years	Monthly salary of groundskeeper	$1,100
		Estimated annual fuel cost	$150

Calculate the amount of depreciation expense (for the mower and accessories) that should be reported on B Jay's December 31, 2010, income statement. Assume straight-line depreciation.

(LO 7)   **BE3-15**   Willis Corporation has beginning inventory $76,000; Purchases $486,000; Freight-in $16,200; Purchase Returns $5,800; Purchase Discounts $5,000; and ending inventory $69,500. Calculate its cost of goods sold.

(LO 6)   **BE3-16**   Tiger Inc. has the following year-end account balances: Sales $928,900; Interest Income $17,500; Cost of Goods Sold $406,200; Operating Expenses $129,000; Income Tax Expense $55,100; and Dividends $15,900. Prepare the year-end closing entries.

(LO 9)   ***BE3-17**   Pelican Inc. made a December 31 adjusting entry to debit Salaries Expense and credit Salaries Payable for $2,700. On January 2, Pelican paid the weekly payroll of $5,000. Prepare Pelican's (a) January 1 reversing entry, (b) January 2 entry (assuming the reversing entry was prepared), and (c) January 2 entry (assuming the reversing entry was not prepared).

Exercises

E3-1 **(Transaction Analysis—Service Company)** Bill Rosenberg recently opened his legal practice. During the first **(LO 4)** month of operations of his business (a sole proprietorship), the following events and transactions occurred:

April	2	Invested $15,000 cash and equipment valued at $10,000 in the business.
	2	Hired a secretary-receptionist at a salary of $480 per week payable monthly.
	3	Purchased $1,200 of supplies on account. (Debit an asset account.)
	7	Paid office rent of $750 for the month.
	11	Completed the preparation of a will and billed the client $1,500 for services rendered. (Use the service revenue account.)
	12	Received a $4,200 retainer for future services.
	17	Received cash of $2,900 for services completed for Botticelli Limited.
	21	Paid insurance expense of $180.
	30	Paid the secretary-receptionist $1,920 for the month.
	30	A count of supplies indicated that $220 of supplies had been consumed.
	30	Purchased a new computer for $4,100 with personal funds. (The computer will be used only for business purposes.)

Instructions

Journalize the transactions in the general journal (omit explanations).

E3-2 **(Corrected Trial Balance)** The trial balance of Many Happy Returns Company, a sole proprietorship, does not **(LO 4)** balance. Your review of the ledger reveals the following: (a) each account had a normal balance; (b) the debit footings (totals) in Prepaid Insurance, Accounts Payable, and Property Tax Expense were each understated by $200; (c) transposition errors were made in Accounts Receivable and Service Revenue, and the correct balances are $3,290 and $8,860, respectively; (d) a debit posting to Advertising Expense of $300 was omitted; and (e) a $1,500 cash drawing by the owner was debited to Happy Tremblay, Capital, and credited to Cash.

MANY HAPPY RETURNS COMPANY
Trial Balance
April 30, 2010

	Debit	Credit
Cash	$ 4,800	
Accounts Receivable	3,920	
Prepaid Insurance	700	
Equipment		$ 8,000
Accounts Payable		4,500
Property Tax Payable	560	
Happy Tremblay, Capital		11,200
Service Revenue	8,680	
Salaries Expense	4,200	
Advertising Expense	1,100	
Supplies Expense		1,330
Property Tax Expense		800
	$23,960	$25,830

Instructions

Prepare a correct trial balance.

(LO 4)   E3-3   (Corrected Trial Balance) The trial balance of Blues Around the Corner Corporation does not balance.

BLUES AROUND THE CORNER CORPORATION
Trial Balance
April 30

	Debit	Credit
Cash	$ 3,238	
Accounts Receivable	15,799	
Supplies on Hand	1,122	
Furniture and Equipment	9,650	
Accounts Payable		$ 3,212
Wages Payable		850
Common Shares		6,000
Retained Earnings		9,450
Service Revenue		10,722
Wage Expense	3,000	
Office Expense	2,410	
	$35,219	$30,234

An examination of the ledger shows these errors:

1. Wages not yet paid amounting to $850 recorded to wages expense as $580.

2. Included in Accounts Receivable are sales of a concert recording amounting to $1,700 not recorded in income.

3. Funds received on account from a customer were recorded in Cash as $1,805 instead of the $1,850 actually received, which was properly recorded in Accounts Receivable.

4. A computer purchased for $1,200 was recorded as an office expense.

5. A payment from a customer was recorded as follows:

	Debit	Credit
Cash	$1,800	
Accounts Receivable	1,800	

Instructions

Use the information to prepare a correct trial balance.

(LO 4)   E3-4   (Corrected Trial Balance) The trial balance of Mis-Match Inc. does not balance.

MIS-MATCH INC.
Trial Balance
June 30, 2010

	Debit	Credit
Cash	$ 2,870	
Accounts Receivable	3,231	
Supplies	800	
Equipment	3,800	
Accounts Payable		$ 2,666
Unearned Service Revenue	1,200	
Common Shares		6,000
Retained Earnings		3,000
Service Revenue		2,380
Wages Expense	3,400	
Office Expense	940	
	$16,241	$14,046

Each of the listed accounts has a normal balance for the general ledger. An examination of the ledger and journal reveals the following errors:

1. Payment received from a customer on account was debited $570 to Accounts Receivable and cash was credited for the same amount. The amount collected was actually $750.

2. The purchase of a computer printer on account for $500 was recorded as a $500 debit to Supplies and a $500 credit to Accounts Payable.

3. Services were performed on account for a client for $890. Accounts Receivable was debited $890 and Service Revenue was credited $89.

4. A payment of $65 for telephone charges was recorded as a $65 debit to Office Expense and a $65 debit to Cash.

5. When the Unearned Service Revenue account was reviewed, it was found that $325 of the balance was earned before June 30.

6. A debit posting to Wages Expense of $670 was omitted.

7. A payment on account for $206 was credited to Cash for $206 and credited to Accounts Payable for $260.

8. A dividend of $575 was debited to Wages Expense for $575 and credited to Cash for $575.

Instructions

Prepare a correct trial balance. (Note: It may be necessary to add one or more accounts to the trial balance.)

E3-5 **(Transactions of a Corporation, Including Investment and Dividend)** LD Driving Range Inc. was opened on **(LO 4)** March 1 by Phil Woods. The following selected events and transactions occurred during March:

March	1	Invested $80,000 cash in the business in exchange for common shares.
	3	Purchased Tiger Mickelson's Golf Land for $68,000 cash. The price consists of land, $20,000; building, $32,000; and equipment, $16,000.
	5	LD sponsored an open house costing $6,800
	6	Paid $2,400 cash for a one-year insurance policy.
	10	Purchased golf equipment for $5,500 from VJ Ltd., payable in 30 days.
	18	Received golf fees of $3,700 cash.
	25	Declared and paid a $1,500 cash dividend.
	30	Paid wages of $1,900.
	30	Paid rent for the month of April in the amount of $2,500.
	31	Received $750 of fees in cash.

Woods uses the following accounts for his company: Cash; Prepaid Insurance; Prepaid Rent; Land; Buildings; Equipment; Accounts Payable; Common Shares; Dividends; Service Revenue; Advertising Expense; Rent Expense; and Wages Expense.

Instructions

Journalize the March transactions.

E3-6 **(Alternative Treatment of Prepayment)** At Sugarland Ltd., prepaid costs are debited to expense when cash is **(LO 5)** paid and unearned revenues are credited to revenue when the cash is received. During January of the current year, the following transactions occurred.

Jan.	2	Paid $3,600 for casualty insurance protection for the year.
	10	Paid $5,700 for supplies.
	15	Received $11,100 for services to be performed in the future.

On January 31, it is determined that $3,500 of the service revenue has been earned and that there is $2,800 of supplies on hand.

Instructions

(a) Journalize and post the January transactions. Use T accounts.

(b) Journalize and post the adjusting entries at January 31.

(c) Determine the ending balance in each of the accounts.

(LO 5) E3-7 (Alternative Treatment of Prepayment) Black-Eyed Pears Ltd. initially records all prepaid costs as expenses and all revenue collected in advance as revenues. The following information is available for the year ended December 31, 2010.

1. Purchased a one-year insurance policy on May 1, 2010, for $9,600 cash.

2. Paid $9,200 for five months' rent in advance on October 1, 2010.

3. On October 15, 2010, purchased 36 advertising spots on a local radio station at a cost of $9,000. The advertising spots were to be used over the next six months. At December 31, the company had used 18 spots.

4. Signed a contract for legal services starting December 1, 2010, for $4,500 per month. Paid for the first three months on December 1, 2010.

5. During the year, sold $1,500 of gift certificates. Determined that on December 31, 2010, $475 of these gift certificates had not been redeemed.

Instructions

(a) For each of the above, prepare a journal entry to record the initial transaction.

(b) Post each of the above transactions. Use T accounts (ignore the Cash account).

(c) Journalize and post the adjusting entries at December 31, 2010.

(d) Determine the ending balance in each of the accounts.

(e) How would the balances at December 31, 2010, be affected by Black-Eyed Pears deciding to initially record the payment of prepaid costs as assets and revenues collected in advance as liabilities?

(LO 5, 9) *E3-8 (Adjusting and Reversing Entries) On December 31, adjusting information for Big & Rich Corporation is as follows:

1. The estimated depreciation on equipment is $3,400.

2. Local business taxes amounting to $2,525 have accrued but are unrecorded and unpaid.

3. Employee wages that are earned but unpaid and unrecorded amount to $3,900.

4. The Revenue account includes amounts that have been billed to customers for services that have not yet been completed. The amount has been determined to be $5,500.

5. Interest of $200 on a $25,000 note payable has not been recorded.

Instructions

(a) Prepare adjusting journal entries.

(b) Prepare reversing journal entries.

(LO 5, 9) *E3-9 (Closing and Reversing Entries) On December 31, the adjusted trial balance of Domino Inc. shows the following selected data:

Accounts Receivable	$ 9,700	Service Revenue	$110,000
Interest Expense	12,800	Interest Payable	6,400

Analysis shows that adjusting entries were made for (a) $9,700 of services performed but not billed, and (b) $6,400 of accrued but unpaid interest.

Instructions

(a) Prepare the closing entries for the temporary accounts at December 31.

(b) Prepare the reversing entries on January 1.

(c) Enter the adjusted trial balance data in the four accounts. Post the entries in (a) and (b) and rule and balance the accounts. (Use T accounts.)

(d) Prepare the entries to record (1) the collection of the service revenue on January 10, and (2) the payment of all interest due ($6,400) on January 15.

(e) Post the entries in (d) to the temporary accounts.

*E3-10 (Adjusting and Reversing Entries) A review of the accounts of Tick and Bop Accountants reflected the fol- **(LO 5, 9)**
lowing transactions, which may or may not require adjustment at the year end of December 31.

1. The Prepaid Rent account shows a debit of $7,200 paid for the last month's rent plus the next five months' rent commencing October 1.

2. On November 1, Services Revenue was credited $2,400 for an amount paid by a client for audit services to be performed in January.

3. On June 1, a cheque in the amount of $6,000 was issued for a two-year subscription to a trade publication commencing June 1. The amount was charged to Memberships and Subscriptions.

4. Interest of $1,270 has accrued on notes payable.

Instructions

Prepare in general journal form (a) the adjusting entry for each item and (b) the reversing entry for each item, where appropriate.

E3-11 (Adjusting Entries) The ledger of Rainy Day Umbrella Ltd. on March 31 of the current year includes the fol- **(LO 5)**
lowing selected accounts before adjusting entries have been prepared:

	Debit	Credit
Prepaid Insurance	$ 3,600	
Supplies	2,800	
Equipment	25,000	
Accumulated Depreciation—Equipment		$ 8,400
Notes Payable		20,000
Unearned Rent Revenue		9,300
Rent Revenue		60,000
Interest Expense	–0–	
Wages Expense	14,000	

An analysis of the accounts shows the following:

1. The equipment depreciation is $350 per month.

2. One half of the unearned rent was earned during the quarter.

3. Interest of $550 is accrued on the notes payable.

4. Supplies on hand total $950.

5. Insurance expires at the rate of $300 per month.

Instructions

Prepare the adjusting entries at March 31, assuming that adjusting entries are made quarterly. Additional accounts are Depreciation Expense, Insurance Expense, Interest Payable, and Supplies Expense.

E3-12 (Adjusting Entries) Suli Mani opened a legal practice on January 1, 2010. During the first month of operations, **(LO 5)**
the following transactions occurred.

1. Performed services for clients represented by insurance companies. At January 31, $6,000 of such services was earned but not yet billed to the insurance companies.

2. Membership fees for the year to the Law Society incurred but not paid before January 31 totalled $720.

3. Purchased computer equipment on January 1 for $8,400, paying $2,000 in cash and signing a $6,400, one-year note payable. The equipment depreciation is $350 per month. Interest is $50 per month.

4. Purchased a one-year malpractice insurance policy on January 1 for $12,000.

5. Purchased $3,800 of office supplies. On January 31, determined that $500 of supplies had been used.

Instructions

(a) Prepare the adjusting entries on January 31. Account titles are Accumulated Depreciation—Computer Equipment; Depreciation Expense; Service Revenue; Accounts Receivable; Insurance Expense; Interest Expense; Interest Payable; Prepaid Insurance; Supplies; Supplies Expense; Membership Expense; and Accounts Payable.

(b) Prepare the adjusting entries on January 31 assuming that the law firm first records prepayments through the related income statement accounts (i.e., it uses the alternate method).

(LO 5)   E3-13   (Analyze Adjusted Data) A partial adjusted trial balance of Joy Limited at January 31, 2011, shows the following:

JOY LIMITED
Adjusted Trial Balance
January 31, 2011

	Debit	Credit
Supplies	$ 600	
Prepaid Insurance	2,400	
Salaries Payable		$ 800
Unearned Revenue		1,000
Supplies Expense	950	
Insurance Expense	2,400	
Salaries Expense	1,800	
Service Revenue		3,000

Instructions

Answer the following questions, assuming the company's fiscal year begins January 1:

(a) If the amount in Supplies Expense is the January 31 adjusting entry, and $650 of supplies was purchased in January, what was the balance in Supplies on January 1?

(b) If the amount in Insurance Expense is the January 31 adjusting entry, and the original insurance premium was for one year, what was the total premium and when was the policy purchased?

(c) If $2,500 of salaries was paid in January, what was the balance in Salaries Payable at December 31, 2010?

(d) If $1,600 was received in January for services performed in January, what was the balance in Unearned Revenue at December 31, 2010?

(LO 5)   E3-14   (Adjusting Entries) Alberto Rock is the new owner of Summer Computer Services Inc. At the end of August 2010, his first month of ownership, Mr. Rock is trying to prepare monthly financial statements. Information follows for transactions that occurred in August:

1. At August 31, Mr. Rock owed his employees $6,000 in wages that would be paid on September 1.

2. At the end of the month, he had not yet received the month's utility bill. Based on previous experience, he estimated the bill would be $900.

3. On August 1, Mr. Rock invested $60,000 of the company's funds with a local bank in a 180-day GIC. The annual interest rate is 5%.

4. Rent of $1,200 for September was paid August 31 and charged to rent expense.

Instructions

Use the information to prepare the adjusting journal entries as at August 31, 2010.

(LO 5)   E3-15   (Adjusting Entries) Selected accounts of Bang Bang Boom Fireworks Limited follow:

Supplies

Beg. Bal.	800	10/31	470

Accounts Receivable

10/17	2,400
10/31	1,650

Salaries Expense

10/15	800
10/31	600

Salaries Payable

10/31	600

Unearned Service Revenue

10/31	400	10/20	650

Supplies Expense

10/31	470

Service Revenue

10/17	2,400
10/31	1,650
10/31	400

Instructions

From an analysis of the T accounts, reconstruct (a) the October transaction entries, and (b) the adjusting journal entries that were made on October 31.

E3-16   (Adjusting Entries) The trial balance for Hanna Resort Limited on August 31 is as follows: **(LO 5)**

HANNA RESORT LIMITED
Trial Balance
August 31, 2010

	Debit	Credit
Cash	$ 6,700	
Prepaid Rent	3,500	
Supplies	1,800	
Land	20,000	
Cottages	142,000	
Furniture	16,000	
Accounts Payable		$ 4,800
Unearned Rent Revenue		4,600
Loan Payable		77,000
Common Shares		81,000
Retained Earnings		9,000
Dividends	5,000	
Rent Revenue		88,450
Salaries Expense	43,200	
Rent Expense	12,250	
Interest Expense	1,600	
Utilities Expense	9,200	
Repair Expense	3,600	
	$264,850	$264,850

Other data:

1. The balance in Prepaid Rent includes the payment of the final month's rent and August's rent.

2. An inventory count on August 31 shows $650 of supplies on hand.

3. Annual depreciation rates are cottages 4% and furniture 10%. The residual value is estimated to be 10% of the cost.

4. Rent revenue includes amounts paid for September rentals in the amount of $8,000. Of the Unearned Rent Revenue of $4,600, one half was earned prior to August 31.

5. Salaries of $375 were unpaid at August 31.

6. Rental fees of $800 were due from tenants at August 31.

7. The loan interest rate is 8% per year.

Instructions

(a) Journalize the adjusting entries on August 31 for the three-month period June 1 to August 31.

(b) Prepare an adjusted trial balance as at August 31.

E3-17   (Closing Entries) The adjusted trial balance of Serious Limited shows the following data on sales at the end of   **(LO 6)** its fiscal year October 31, 2010: Sales $1,250,000; Freight-out $18,000; Sales Returns and Allowances $4,000; and Sales Discounts $15,000.

Instructions

(a) Prepare the sales revenue section of the income statement.

(b) Prepare separate closing entries for (1) sales and (2) the contra accounts to sales.

(LO 6)   E3-18   (Closing Entries) Information follows for Shakira Corporation for the month of January:

Cost of Goods Sold	$228,000	Salary Expense	$ 61,000
Cash	62,000	Inventory	16,000
Advertising and Promotion	3,200	Interest Expense	1,200
Note Payable	33,000	Sales Discounts	7,000
Freight-out	9,000	Sales Returns and Allowances	1,000
Insurance Expense	12,000	Sales	364,000
Rent Expense	20,000		

Instructions

Prepare the necessary closing entries.

(LO 6)   E3-19   (Closing Entries) Selected account balances follow for Winslow Inc. as at December 31, 2010:

Merchandise Inventory	$60,000	Cost of Goods Sold	$222,700
Common Shares	75,000	Selling Expenses	26,000
Retained Earnings	45,000	Administrative Expenses	31,000
Dividends	18,000	Income Tax Expense	30,000
Sales Returns and Allowances	2,000	Sales	390,000
Sales Discounts	5,000		

Instructions

Prepare closing entries for Winslow Inc. on December 31, 2010.

(LO 7)   E3-20   (Missing Amounts) Financial information follows for two different companies:

	Pitbull Ltd.	Doberman Inc.
Sales	$192,000	(d)
Sales returns	(a)	$16,000
Net sales	162,000	65,000
Cost of goods sold	55,500	(e)
Gross profit	(b)	37,000
Operating expenses	35,000	23,000
Net income	(c)	14,000

Instructions

Calculate the missing amounts.

(LO 7)   E3-21   (Find Missing Amounts—Periodic Inventory) Financial information follows for four different companies:

	Pamela's Cosmetics Inc.	Dean's Grocery Inc.	Anderson Wholesalers Ltd.	Baywatch Supply Ltd.
Sales	$98,000	(c)	$144,000	$120,000
Sales returns	(a)	$ 5,000	12,000	9,000
Net sales	74,000	101,000	132,000	(g)
Beginning inventory	21,000	(d)	44,000	24,000
Purchases	63,000	105,000	(e)	90,000
Purchase returns	6,000	10,000	8,000	(h)
Ending inventory	(b)	48,000	30,000	28,000
Cost of goods sold	64,000	72,000	(f)	72,000
Gross profit	10,000	29,000	18,000	(i)

Instructions

Determine the missing amounts for (a) to (i). Show all calculations.

E3-22 **(Work Sheet)** Selected accounts follow for Kings Inc., as reported in the work sheet at the end of May 2010:   **(LO 8)**

Accounts	Adjusted Trial Balance		Income Statement		Balance Sheet	
	Dr.	Cr.	Dr.	Cr.	Dr.	Cr.
Cash	9,000					
Merchandise Inventory	80,000					
Accounts Payable		26,000				
Sales		480,000				
Sales Returns and Allowances	10,000					
Sales Discounts	5,000					
Cost of Goods Sold	290,000					
Wage Expense	62,000					
Interest Income		12,000				

Instructions

Complete the work sheet by extending the amounts reported in the adjusted trial balance to the appropriate columns in the work sheet. Do not total individual columns.

E3-23 **(Cost of Goods Sold Section—Periodic Inventory)** The trial balance of Jangles Corporation at the end of its   **(LO 7)**
fiscal year, August 31, 2010, includes the following accounts: Merchandise Inventory $22,800; Purchases $151,600; Sales $250,000; Freight-in $4,000; Sales Returns and Allowances $4,000; Freight-out $1,000; and Purchase Returns and Allowances $21,000. The ending merchandise inventory is $21,500.

Instructions

Prepare a cost of goods sold section for the year ending August 31.

E3-24 **(Work Sheet Preparation)** The trial balance of Airbourne Travel Inc. on March 31, 2010, is as follows: **(LO 8)**

AIRBOURNE TRAVEL INC.
Trial Balance
March 31, 2010

	Debit	Credit
Cash	$ 1,800	
Accounts Receivable	2,600	
Supplies	600	
Equipment	6,000	
Accumulated Depreciation—Equipment		$ 400
Accounts Payable		1,100
Unearned Ticket Revenue		500
Common Shares		6,400
Retained Earnings		600
Ticket Revenue		2,600
Salaries Expense	500	
Miscellaneous Expense	100	
	$11,600	$11,600

Other data:

1. A physical count reveals only $520 of supplies on hand.

2. Equipment is depreciated at a rate of $120 per month.

3. Unearned ticket revenue amounted to $100 on March 31.

4. Accrued salaries are $850.

Instructions

Enter the trial balance on a work sheet and complete the work sheet, assuming that the adjustments relate only to the month of March. (Ignore income taxes.)

(LO 8)   E3-25   (Work Sheet and Balance Sheet Presentation) The adjusted trial balance of West Kayne Company is provided in the following work sheet for the month ended April 30, 2010.

WEST KAYNE COMPANY
Work Sheet (partial)
For the Month Ended April 30, 2010

Account Titles	Adjusted Trial Balance		Income Statement		Balance Sheet	
	Dr.	Cr.	Dr.	Cr.	Dr.	Cr.
Cash	$17,672					
Accounts Receivable	8,520					
Prepaid Rent	3,280					
Equipment	18,050					
Accumulated Depreciation		$ 4,895				
Notes Payable		6,700				
Accounts Payable		4,472				
Bradley, Capital		34,960				
Bradley, Drawings	6,250					
Service Revenue		13,190				
Salaries Expense	8,040					
Rent Expense	2,260					
Depreciation Expense	145					
Interest Expense	83					
Interest Payable		83				

Instructions

Complete the work sheet and prepare a balance sheet as illustrated in this chapter.

(LO 8)   E3-26   (Partial Work Sheet Preparation) Lazy Dog Inc. prepares monthly financial statements from a work sheet. Selected parts of the February work sheet showed the following data:

LAZY DOG INC.
Work Sheet (partial)
For the Month Ended February 28, 2010

Account Titles	Trial Balance		Adjustments		Adjusted Trial Balance	
	Dr.	Cr.	Dr.	Cr.	Dr.	Cr.
Supplies	3,256			(a)1,500	1,756	
Accumulated Depreciation		6,682		(b) 257		6,939
Interest Payable		100		(c) 50		150
Supplies Expense			(a)1,500		1,500	
Depreciation Expense			(b) 257		257	
Interest Expense			(c) 50		50	

During February, no events occurred that affected these accounts. At the end of February, the following information was available and relates to the adjustments identified by letter in the work sheet:

(a) Supplies on hand, $1,756

(b) Monthly depreciation, $257

(c) Accrued interest, $50

Instructions

Reproduce the data that would appear in the February work sheet and indicate the amounts that would be shown in the February income statement and balance sheet.

Problems

P3-1 Transactions follow for Emily Cain, D.D.S., for the month of September:

Sept. 1 Cain begins practice as a dentist and invests $32,000 cash.
2 Purchases furniture and dental equipment on account from Dig Deep Drill Limited for $12,500.
4 Pays rent for office space, $1,300 for the month of September and October.
4 Employs a receptionist, Wanda Phillips.
5 Purchases dental supplies for cash, $900.
8 Receives cash of $1,960 from patients for services performed and $1,600 for referrals to specialists.
10 Pays miscellaneous office expenses, $680.
14 Bills patients $4,740 for services performed.
18 Pays Dig Deep Drill Limited on account, $6,300.
19 Withdraws $2,000 cash from the business for personal use.
20 Receives $2,100 from patients on account.
25 Bills patients $2,780 for services performed.
30 Pays the following expenses in cash: office salaries, $1,400; and miscellaneous office expenses, $85.
30 Dental supplies used during September amount to $330.

Instructions

(a) Enter the transactions in appropriate general ledger accounts, using the following account titles: Cash; Accounts Receivable; Prepaid Rent; Supplies on Hand; Furniture and Equipment; Accumulated Depreciation; Accounts Payable; Emily Cain, Drawings; Service Revenue; Rent Expense; Miscellaneous Office Expense; Office Salaries Expense; Supplies Expense; Depreciation Expense; Income Summary; and Emily Cain, Capital. Allow 10 lines for the Cash and Income Summary accounts, and five lines for each of the other accounts that are needed. Record depreciation using a five-year life on the furniture and equipment, the straight-line method, and no residual value.

(b) Prepare an adjusted trial balance.

(c) Prepare an income statement, balance sheet, and statement of owners' equity.

(d) Close the ledger. Post directly to the general ledger account without writing out the journal entry.

(e) Prepare a post-closing trial balance.

P3-2 Yancy Advertising Agency Limited was founded by Tang Min in January 2006. Presented below are both the adjusted and unadjusted trial balances as at December 31, 2010:

YANCY ADVERTISING AGENCY LIMITED
Trial Balance
December 31, 2010

	Unadjusted Dr.	Unadjusted Cr.	Adjusted Dr.	Adjusted Cr.
Cash	$ 10,750		$ 10,750	
Accounts Receivable	30,000		35,000	
Art Supplies	10,400		5,000	
Prepaid Insurance	11,600		2,200	
Printing Equipment	60,000		60,000	
Accumulated Depreciation		$ 28,000		$ 39,500
Accounts Payable		5,000		11,000
Interest Payable		–0–		650
Notes Payable		5,000		5,000
Unearned Advertising Revenue		17,800		20,600
Salaries Payable		–0–		9,600
Common Shares		10,000		10,000
Retained Earnings		3,500		3,500
Advertising Revenue		67,800		70,000
Salaries Expense	10,000		19,600	
Insurance Expense			9,400	
Interest Expense	350		1,000	
Depreciation Expense			11,500	
Art Supplies Expense			11,400	
Rent Expense	4,000		4,000	
	$137,100	$137,100	$169,850	$169,850

Instructions

(a) Journalize the annual adjusting entries that were made.

(b) Prepare an income statement and a statement of retained earnings for the year ending December 31, and a balance sheet at December 31.

P3-3   A review of the ledger of Rolling Resort Inc. at December 31, produces the following data for the preparation of annual adjusting entries:

1. Salaries Payable $0. There are eight salaried employees. Five employees receive a salary of $1,200 each per week, and three employees earn $800 each per week. Employees do not work weekends. All employees worked two days after the last pay period and before December 31.

2. Unearned Rent Revenue $415,200. The company began subleasing condos in its new building on November 1. Each tenant has to make a $5,000 security deposit that is not refundable until occupancy is ended. At December 31, the company had the following rental contracts that are paid in full for the entire term of the lease:

Date	Term (in months)	Monthly Rent	Number of Leases
Nov. 1	6	$ 4,100	5
Dec. 1	6	$10,300	4

3. Prepaid Advertising $16,200. This balance consists of payments on two advertising contracts. The contracts provide for monthly advertising in two trade magazines. The terms of the contracts are as follows:

Contract	Date	Amount	Number of Magazine Issues
A650	May 1	$7,200	12
B974	Oct. 1	9,000	24

The first advertisement runs in the month in which the contract is signed.

4. Notes Payable $80,000. This balance consists of a note for one year at an annual interest rate of 9%, dated June 1.

Instructions

Prepare the adjusting entries at December 31. (Show all calculations.)

P3-4   The completed financial statement columns of the work sheet for Canned Heat Limited follow:

CANNED HEAT LIMITED
Work Sheet
For the Year Ended December 31, 2010

Account No.	Account Titles	Income Statement Dr.	Income Statement Cr.	Balance Sheet Dr.	Balance Sheet Cr.
101	Cash			18,000	
112	Accounts Receivable			67,500	
130	Prepaid Insurance			1,800	
157	Equipment			98,000	
167	Accumulated Depreciation				28,600
201	Accounts Payable				31,600
212	Salaries Payable				7,200
301	Common Shares				80,000
306	Retained Earnings				66,800
400	Service Revenue		142,000		
622	Repair Expense	13,200			
711	Depreciation Expense	38,800			
722	Insurance Expense	8,800			
726	Salaries Expense	106,600			
732	Utilities Expense	3,500			
	Totals	170,900	142,000	185,300	214,200
	Net Loss		28,900	28,900	
		170,900	170,900	214,200	214,200

Instructions

(a) Prepare an income statement, statement of changes in owner's equity, and balance sheet. Canned Heat's shareholders made an additional $4,000 investment in the business during 2010.

(b) Prepare the closing entries.

(c) Prepare a post-closing trial balance.

P3-5 Noah's Foods has a fiscal year ending on September 30. Selected data from the September 30 work sheet follow:

NOAH'S FOODS
Work Sheet
For the Year Ended September 30, 2010

	Trial Balance		Adjusted Trial Balance	
	Dr.	Cr.	Dr.	Cr.
Cash	37,400		37,400	
Supplies	18,600		1,500	
Prepaid Insurance	31,900		3,600	
Land	80,000		80,000	
Equipment	120,000		120,000	
Accumulated Depreciation		36,200		41,000
Accounts Payable		14,600		14,600
Unearned Admissions Revenue		2,700		1,700
Mortgage Payable		50,000		50,000
N.Y. Berge, Capital		109,700		109,700
N.Y. Berge, Drawings	14,000		14,000	
Admissions Revenue		278,500		279,500
Salaries Expense	109,000		109,000	
Repair Expense	30,500		30,500	
Advertising Expense	9,400		9,400	
Utilities Expense	16,900		16,900	
Property Taxes Expense	18,000		21,000	
Interest Expense	6,000		12,200	
Totals	491,700	491,700		
Insurance Expense			28,300	
Supplies Expense			17,100	
Interest Payable				6,200
Depreciation Expense			4,800	
Property Taxes Payable				3,000
Totals			505,700	505,700

Instructions

(a) Prepare a complete work sheet.

(b) Prepare a statement of financial position. (Note: In the next fiscal year, $10,000 of the mortgage payable is due for payment.)

(c) Journalize the adjusting entries, using data in the work sheet.

(d) Journalize the closing entries, using data in the work sheet.

(e) Prepare a post-closing trial balance.

P3-6 The trial balance of Slum Dog Fashion Centre Inc. contained the following accounts at November 30, the company's fiscal year end:

SLUM DOG FASHION CENTRE INC.
Trial Balance
November 30, 2010

	Debit	Credit
Cash	$ 29,200	
Accounts Receivable	82,000	
Merchandise Inventory	105,000	
Store Supplies	8,600	
Store Equipment	225,000	
Accumulated Depreciation—Store Equipment		$ 86,000
Delivery Equipment	128,000	
Accumulated Depreciation—Delivery Equipment		39,000
Notes Payable		85,000
Accounts Payable		78,500
Common Shares		300,000
Retained Earnings		38,000
Sales		950,200
Sales Returns and Allowances	24,200	
Cost of Goods Sold	611,500	
Salaries Expense	150,000	
Advertising Expense	46,400	
Utilities Expense	24,000	
Repair Expense	32,100	
Delivery Expense	46,700	
Rent Expense	64,000	
	$1,576,700	$1,576,700

Adjustment data:

1. Store supplies on hand totalled $3,100.

2. Depreciation is $40,000 on the store equipment and $30,000 on the delivery equipment.

3. Interest of $9,000 is accrued on notes payable at November 30.

Other data:

1. Salaries expense is 60% selling and 40% administrative.

2. Rent expense and utilities expense are 90% selling and 10% administrative.

3. Of the notes payable, $35,000 is due for payment next year.

4. Repair expense is 100% administrative.

Instructions

(a) Enter the trial balance on a work sheet and complete the work sheet.

(b) Prepare a multiple-step income statement and retained earnings statement for the year and a classified balance sheet as at November 30, 2010.

(c) Journalize the adjusting entries.

(d) Journalize the closing entries.

(e) Prepare a post-closing trial balance.

P3-7 Second Hand Almost New Department Store Inc. is located near the shopping mall. At the end of the company's fiscal year on December 31, 2010, the following accounts appeared in two of its trial balances:

	Unadjusted	Adjusted
Accounts Payable	$ 79,300	$ 79,300
Accounts Receivable	95,300	95,300
Accumulated Depreciation—Building	42,100	52,500
Accumulated Depreciation—Equipment	29,600	42,900
Building	190,000	190,000
Cash	68,000	68,000
Common Shares	160,000	160,000
Retained Earnings	16,600	16,600
Cost of Goods Sold	412,700	412,700
Depreciation Expense—Building	0	10,400
Depreciation Expense—Equipment	0	13,300
Dividends	28,000	28,000
Equipment	110,000	110,000
Insurance Expense	0	7,200
Interest Expense	3,000	11,000
Interest Payable	0	8,000
Interest Revenue	4,000	4,000
Merchandise Inventory	75,000	75,000
Mortgage Payable	80,000	80,000
Office Salaries Expense	32,000	32,000
Prepaid Insurance	9,600	2,400
Property Taxes Expense	0	4,800
Property Taxes Payable	0	4,800
Sales Salaries Expense	76,000	76,000
Sales	718,000	718,000
Sales Commissions Expense	11,000	14,500
Sales Commissions Payable	0	3,500
Sales Returns and Allowances	8,000	8,000
Utilities Expense	11,000	11,000

Analysis reveals the following additional data:

(a) Insurance expense and utilities expense are 60% selling and 40% administrative.

(b) In the next year, $20,000 of the mortgage payable will be due for payment.

(c) Property tax expense and depreciation on the building are administrative expenses; depreciation on the equipment is a selling expense.

Instructions

(a) Prepare a multiple-step income statement, retained earnings statement, and classified balance sheet.

(b) Journalize the adjusting entries that were made.

(c) Journalize the closing entries that are necessary.

P3-8 The following accounts appeared in the December 31 trial balance of the Majestic Theatre:

	Debit	Credit
Equipment	$960,000	
Accumulated Depreciation—Equipment		$120,000
Notes Payable		186,000
Admissions Revenue		750,000
Advertising Expense	62,000	
Salaries Expense	80,000	
Interest Expense	9,000	

Instructions

(a) From the account balances above and the information that follows, prepare the annual adjusting entries necessary on December 31:

1. The equipment has an estimated life of 16 years and a residual value of $40,000. (Use the straight-line method.)

2. The note payable is a 90-day note given to the bank on October 20 and bearing interest at 10%.

3. In December, 2,000 coupon admission books were sold at $25 each; they can be used for admission any time after January 1.

4. Of the Advertising Expense balance, $1,100 is paid in advance.

5. Salaries accrued but unpaid are $11,800.

(b) What amounts should be shown for each of the following on the income statement for the year?

1. Interest expense

2. Admissions revenue

3. Advertising expense

4. Salaries expense

P3-9   The trial balance and the other information for consulting engineers Mustang Rovers Consulting Limited follow:

MUSTANG ROVERS CONSULTING LIMITED
Trial Balance
December 31, 2010

	Debit	Credit
Cash	$ 83,700	
Accounts Receivable	81,100	
Allowance for Doubtful Accounts		$ 750
Engineering Supplies Inventory	1,960	
Unexpired Insurance		1,100
Furniture and Equipment	85,000	
Accumulated Depreciation—Furniture and Equipment		6,250
Notes Payable		7,200
Common Shares		35,010
Retained Earnings		160,000
Service Revenue		100,000
Rent Expense	9,750	
Office Salaries Expense	28,500	
Insurance Expense	18,500	
Heat, Light, and Water Expense	1,080	
Miscellaneous Office Expense	720	
	$310,310	$310,310

1. Fees received in advance from clients, $6,900.

2. Services performed for clients that were not recorded by December 31, $7,300.

3. Bad debt expense for the year, $6,300.

4. Insurance expense included a premium paid on December 31 in the amount of $6,000 for the period commencing June 1, 2011.

5. Furniture and equipment, net of accumulated depreciation, are being depreciated at 9% per year.

6. Mustang gave the bank a 90-day, 12% note for $7,200 on December 1, 2010.

7. Rent is $750 per month. The rent for 2010 and for January 2011 has been paid.

8. Office salaries earned but unpaid at December 31, 2010, $2,510.

9. Dividends of $80,000 were declared for payment February 1, 2011.

Instructions

(a) From the trial balance and other information given, prepare annual adjusting entries as at December 31, 2010.

(b) Prepare an income statement for 2010, a balance sheet, and a statement of retained earnings.

P3-10   Brook Corporation was founded by Ronnie Brook in January 2003. The adjusted and unadjusted trial balances as at December 31, 2010, follow:

BROOK CORPORATION
Trial Balance
December 31, 2010

	Unadjusted		Adjusted	
	Dr.	Cr.	Dr.	Cr.
Cash	$ 7,000		$ 8,000	
Accounts Receivable	13,000		25,800	
Note Receivable	10,000		10,000	
Art Supplies	8,500		5,500	
Prepaid Insurance	3,250		2,500	
Prepaid Rent	6,000		4,000	
Printing Equipment	50,000		50,000	
Accumulated Depreciation		$ 27,000		$ 33,750
Accounts Payable		5,000		5,150
Unearned Service Revenue		7,000		5,600
Salaries Payable				1,500
Common Shares		15,000		15,000
Retained Earnings		4,500		4,500
Service Revenue		58,600		72,800
Interest Income				1,000
Salaries Expense	10,350		11,850	
Insurance Expense			750	
Depreciation Expense			6,750	
Art Supplies Expense	5,000		8,150	
Rent Expense	4,000		6,000	
	$117,100	$117,100	$139,300	$139,300

Instructions

(a) Journalize the annual adjusting entries that were made.

(b) Prepare an income statement and statement of retained earnings for the year ending December 31, 2010, and a balance sheet at December 31.

P3-11   The following information relates to Joachim Anderson, Realtor, at the close of the fiscal year ending December 31:

1. Joachim paid the local newspaper $335 for an advertisement to be run in January of the next year, and charged it to Advertising Expense.

2. On November 1, Joachim signed a three-month, 10% note to borrow $15,000 from Yorkville Bank.

3. The following salaries and wages are due and unpaid at December 31: sales, $1,420; office clerks, $1,060.

4. Interest of $500 has accrued to date on a note that Joachim holds from Grant Muldaur.

5. The estimated loss on bad debts for the period is $1,560.

6. Stamps and stationery are charged to the Stationery and Postage Expense account when purchased; $110 of these supplies remain on hand.

7. Joachim has not yet paid the December rent of $1,000 on the building his business uses.

8. Insurance was paid on November 1 for one year and charged to Prepaid Insurance, $1,170.

9. Property taxes accrued, $1,670.

10. On December 1, Joachim gave Alana Palmer a two-month, 15% note for $6,000 on account.

11. On October 31, Joachim received $2,580 from Tareq Giza in payment of six months' rent for Giza's office space in the building and credited Unearned Rent Revenue.

12. On September 1, Joachim paid six months' rent in advance on a warehouse, $8,300, and debited the asset account Prepaid Rent Expense.

13. The bill from Light & Power Limited for December has been received but not yet entered or paid, $510.

14. The estimated depreciation on furniture and equipment is $1,400.

Instructions

Prepare annual adjusting entries as at December 31.

P3-12   The trial balance follows of the Masters Golf Club, Inc. as at December 31. The books are closed annually on December 31.

MASTERS GOLF CLUB, INC.
Trial Balance
December 31

	Debit	Credit
Cash	$ 115,000	
Accounts Receivable	63,000	
Allowance for Doubtful Accounts		$ 9,000
Land	350,000	
Buildings	600,000	
Accumulated Depreciation—Buildings		40,000
Equipment	300,000	
Accumulated Depreciation—Equipment		120,000
Unexpired Insurance	12,000	
Common Shares		880,000
Retained Earnings		152,000
Dues Revenue		355,000
Green Fees Revenue		58,000
Rental Revenue		44,000
Utilities Expense	74,000	
Salaries Expense	90,000	
Maintenance Expense	54,000	
	$1,658,000	$1,658,000

Instructions

(a) Enter the balances in ledger accounts. Allow five lines for each account.

(b) From the trial balance and the information that follows, prepare annual adjusting entries and post to the ledger accounts:

   1. The buildings have an estimated life of 30 years with no salvage value (the company uses the straight-line method).

   2. The equipment is depreciated at 10% of it's year-end carrying value per year.

   3. Insurance expired during the year, $5,300.

   4. The rental revenue is the amount received for 11 months for dining facilities. The December rent of $4,000 has not yet been received.

   5. It is estimated that 24% of the accounts receivable will be uncollectible.

   6. Salaries earned but not paid by December 31 amounted to $3,600.

   7. Dues paid in advance by members total $9,900.

(c) Prepare an adjusted trial balance.

(d) Prepare closing entries and post to the ledger.

P3-13 The December 31 trial balance of Red Roses Boutique Inc. follows:

RED ROSES BOUTIQUE INC.
Trial Balance
December 31

	Debit	Credit
Cash	$ 18,500	
Accounts Receivable	42,000	
Allowance for Doubtful Accounts		$ 700
Inventory, December 31	80,000	
Furniture and Equipment	84,000	
Accumulated Depreciation—Furniture and Equipment		35,000
Prepaid Insurance	5,100	
Notes Payable		28,000
Common Shares		80,600
Retained Earnings		10,000
Sales		600,000
Cost of Goods Sold	398,000	
Sales Salaries Expense	50,000	
Advertising Expense	6,700	
Administrative Salaries Expense	65,000	
Office Expense	5,000	
	$754,300	$754,300

Instructions

(a) Create T accounts and enter the balances shown.

(b) Prepare adjusting journal entries for the following and post to the T accounts. Open additional T accounts as necessary. (The books are closed yearly on December 31.)

1. Bad debts are estimated to be $3,800 (the percentage of sales method is used).

2. Furniture and equipment is depreciated based on a 10-year life and no residual value.

3. Insurance expired during the year, $2,100.

4. Interest accrued on notes payable, $6,420.

5. Sales salaries earned but not paid are $8,000.

6. Advertising paid in advance is $750.

7. Office supplies on hand total $3,500 and were charged to Office Expense when they were purchased.

(c) Prepare closing entries and post to the accounts.

P3-14 The unadjusted trial balance of Clancy Inc. at December 31, 2010, is as follows:

	Dr.	Cr.
Cash	$ 37,740	
Accounts Receivable	103,000	
Allowance for Doubtful Accounts		$ 3,500
Merchandise Inventory	60,000	
Prepaid Insurance	4,620	
Investment in Casper Inc. Bonds (9%)	40,000	
Land	30,000	
Building	124,000	
Accumulated Depreciation—Building		12,400
Equipment	33,600	
Accumulated Depreciation—Equipment		5,600
Goodwill	26,600	
Accounts Payable		101,050
Bonds Payable (20-year, 7%)		180,000
Common Shares		121,000
Retained Earnings		21,360
Sales		200,000
Rental Income		10,800
Advertising Expense	22,500	

Supplies Expense	10,800	
Purchases	98,000	
Purchase Discounts		900
Office Salary Expense	17,500	
Sales Salary Expense	36,000	
Interest Expense	12,250	
	$656,610	$656,610

Additional information:

1. Actual advertising costs amounted to $1,500 per month. The company has already paid for advertisements in *Montezuma Magazine* for the first quarter of 2011.

2. The building was purchased and occupied on January 1, 2008, with an estimated life of 21 years. (The company uses straight-line depreciation.)

3. Prepaid insurance contains the premium costs of several policies including Policy A, cost of $960, one-year term, taken out on Sept. 1, 2009; and Policy B, cost of $1,980, three-year term, taken out on April 1, 2010.

4. A portion of Clancy's building has been converted into a snack bar that has been rented to the Ono Food Corp. since July 1, 2009, at a rate of $7,200 per year payable each July 1.

5. One of the company's customers declared bankruptcy on December 30, 2010. It is now certain that the $2,700 the customer owes will never be collected. This fact has not been recorded. In addition, Clancy estimates that 4% of the Accounts Receivable balance on December 31, 2010, will become uncollectible.

6. An advance of $600 to a salesperson on December 31, 2010, was charged to Sales Salary Expense.

7. On November 1, 2008, Clancy issued 180 $1,000 bonds at par value. Interest is paid semi-annually on April 30 and October 31.

8. The equipment was purchased on January 1, 2005, and has an estimated life of 12 years. (The company uses straight-line depreciation.)

9. On August 1, 2010, Clancy purchased at par value 40 $1,000, 9% bonds maturing on August 31, 2012. Interest is paid on July 31 and January 31.

10. The inventory on hand at December 31, 2010, was $90,000 after a physical inventory count.

Instructions

(a) Prepare adjusting and correcting entries for December 31, 2010, using the information given. (In solving this problem, record the adjustment for inventory in the same entry that records the Cost of Goods Sold for the year.)

(b) Indicate which of the adjusting entries could be reversed.

P3-15   The unadjusted trial balance of Imagine Ltd. at December 31, 2010, is as follows:

	Dr.	Cr.
Cash	$ 10,850	
Accounts Receivable	56,500	
Allowance for Doubtful Accounts		$ 750
Inventory	58,000	
Prepaid Insurance	2,940	
Prepaid Rent	13,200	
Investment in Legume Inc. Bonds	18,000	
Land	10,000	
Plant and Equipment	104,000	
Accumulated Amortization		18,000
Accounts Payable		9,310
Bonds Payable		50,000
Common Shares		100,000
Retained Earnings		80,660
Sales		223,310
Rent Revenue		10,200
Purchases	170,000	
Purchase Discounts		2,400
Transportation-out	9,000	
Transportation-in	3,500	
Salaries and Wages Expense	31,000	

Interest Expense	6,750	
Miscellaneous Expense	890	
	$494,630	$494,630

Additional information:

1. On November 1, 2010, Imagine received $10,200 rent from its lessee for a 12-month lease beginning on that date. This was credited to Rent Revenue.

2. Imagine estimates that 7% of the Accounts Receivable balances on December 31, 2010, will be uncollectible. On December 28, 2010, the bookkeeper incorrectly credited Sales for a receipt of $1,000 on account. This error had not yet been corrected on December 31.

3. After a physical count, inventory on hand at December 31, 2010, was $77,000.

4. Prepaid insurance contains the premium costs of two policies: Policy A, cost of $1,320, two-year term, taken out on September 1, 2010; Policy B, cost of $1,620, three-year term, taken out on April 1, 2010.

5. The regular rate of depreciation is 10% of cost per year. Acquisitions and retirements during a year are depreciated at half this rate. There were no retirements during the year. On December 31, 2009, the balance of Plant and Equipment was $90,000.

6. On April 1, 2010, Imagine issued at par value 50 $1,000, 11% bonds maturing on April 1, 2013. Interest is paid on April 1 and October 1.

7. On August 1, 2010, Imagine purchased at par value 18 $1,000, 12% Legume Inc. bonds, maturing on July 31, 2012. Interest is paid on July 31 and January 31.

8. On May 30, 2010, Imagine rented a warehouse for $1,100 per month and debited Prepaid Rent for an advance payment of $13,200.

Instructions

(a) Prepare the year-end adjusting and correcting entries in general journal form using the information given. Record the adjusting entry for inventory by using a Cost of Goods Sold account.

(b) Indicate the adjusting entries that could be reversed.

P3-16 Mona Kamaka, CGA, was retained by Downtown TV Repair Ltd. to prepare financial statements for the month of March 2010. Mona accumulated all the ledger balances from the business records and found the following:

DOWNTOWN TV REPAIR LTD.
Trial Balance
March 31, 2010

	Debit	Credit
Cash	$ 7,200	
Accounts Receivable	3,500	
Supplies	900	
Equipment	15,000	
Accumulated Depreciation—Equipment		$ 3,000
Accounts Payable		5,950
Salaries Payable		600
Unearned Fees Revenue		1,500
Common Shares		10,000
Retained Earnings		4,160
Repair Service Revenue		8,000
Salaries Expense	3,600	
Advertising Expense	800	
Utilities Expense	310	
Depreciation Expense	700	
Repair Expense	1,200	
	$33,210	$33,210

Mona reviewed the records and found the following errors:

1. Cash received from a customer on account was recorded as $570 instead of $750.

2. The purchase, on account, of a scanner that cost $900 was recorded as a debit to Supplies and a credit to Accounts Payable for $900.

3. A payment of $30 for advertising expense was entered as a debit to Utilities Expense $30 and a credit to Cash, $30.

4. The first salary payment this month was for $1,800, which included $600 of salaries payable on February 28. The payment was recorded as a debit to Salaries Expense, $1,800 and a credit to Cash of $1,800. The business does not use reversing entries.

5. A cash payment for repair expense on equipment for $90 was recorded as a debit to Equipment, $90, and a credit to Cash, $90.

Instructions

(a) Prepare an analysis of each error that shows (1) the incorrect entry, (2) the correct entry, and (3) the correcting entry.

(b) Prepare a corrected trial balance.

P3-17 Goliath Corp. began operations on January 1, 2010. Its fiscal year end is December 31. Samuels has decided that prepaid costs are debited to an asset account when paid, and all revenues are credited to revenue when the cash is received. During 2010, the following transactions occurred.

1. On January 1, 2010, Samuels bought office supplies for $4,100 cash. A physical count at December 31, 2010, revealed $1,900 of supplies still on hand.

2. Samuels bought a $6,000, one-year insurance policy for cash on August 1, 2010. The policy came into effect on this date.

3. On November 15, 2010, Samuels received a $1,200 advance cash payment from a client for architectural services to be provided in the future. As at December 31, 2010, one-third of these services had not been performed.

4. On December 1, 2010, Samuels rented out excess office space for a six-month period starting on this date, and received a $1,100 cheque for the first and last month's rent.

Instructions

(a) For each of the above transactions, prepare the journal entry for the original transaction and any adjusting journal entry required at December 31, 2010.

(b) In a business where there are several divisions or office locations where accounting is performed, is it possible that prepayments would be treated as assets in some offices and as expenses in others when initially recorded? Does the business have to have a consistent approach in all of its offices?

Digging Deeper

Research and Financial Analysis

RA3-1 Eastern Platinum Limited

Real-World Emphasis

The financial statements of **Eastern Platinum Limited** are presented in Appendix 5B. Complete the following instructions by referring to these financial statements and the accompanying notes.

Instructions

(a) What were the company's total assets at quarter end for the two periods that are presented?

(b) How much cash (and cash equivalents) did the company have at March 31, 2009?

(c) What were the company's revenues for the current and preceding quarter? What are the three main sources of revenues?

(d) Using the financial statements and related notes, identify the items that may result in adjusting entries for prepayments and accruals.

(e) What presentation currency has the company used? What is its functional currency? Why might the company use a different currency for presenting its financial statements?

RA3-2 Saputo Inc.

Real-World Emphasis

Saputo Inc. is the largest dairy processor and snack cake manufacturer in Canada, according to its website. Access its 2009 annual report through www.sedar.com and complete the following instructions.

Instructions

(a) On page 1 of the annual report, the company reports certain numbers that are meant to give an overview of the company's financial results. Are the numbers prepared in accordance with

GAAP? In your answer, also discuss why the company would present the information in this way and whether the information is useful to financial statement users.

(b) On page 42, there are two statements/reports. One is signed by company management and the other by the auditors. Briefly summarize the content of each statement and discuss why these statements provide important information to users. How much responsibility does senior management have for the creation and monitoring of the accounting information systems that produce the financial information?

RA3-3 Financial Statement Dates

Companies normally issue their annual financial statements within weeks of year end.

Instructions

(a) Identify the top five Canadian companies (by revenue) in the following industries.

    1. Banking   **2.** Insurance   **3.** Real estate   **4.** Biotechnology and pharmaceuticals

(b) For each company, identify its year-end date and the date that the financial statements were finalized (look at the auditor's report). Go to the company websites or SEDAR to find the statements.

(c) What is the likely reason that the banks have a different year end than the other companies?

(d) How many days does it take for the companies to produce the statements after their fiscal year ends? Look at the average time period for each industry. Within each industry, how close are the issue dates among companies? Comment on your findings.

RA3-4 Enterprise Resource Planning (ERP)

ERP software systems include bookkeeping systems as well as systems to monitor and manage human resource functions, quality control functions, and many other aspects of business. The software runs off a centralized database that services all company departments and functions.

Instructions

Research and write a one- to two-page summary that gives details about what ERPs are and why they have gained so much attention. Why do companies find them so useful? What are the pros and cons of these systems? (Hint: Search "Enterprise Resource Planning" on the Internet.)

RA3-5 Extensible Business Reporting Language

Extensible business reporting language (XBRL) is a financial reporting system that allows a company to "tag" each piece of financial information as it is input into the company's books of account. Information is tagged in the database according to a standardized tagging system (taxonomy). Users are then able to find and extract information about companies.

In the United States, use of XBRL will be mandatory for all public company filings with the SEC. In Canada, the Ontario Securities Commission (OSC) is discussing whether to make the use of XBRL mandatory for public companies.

The following is an excerpt from the XBRL website:

XBRL Canada is a not-for-profit consortium of leading Canadian companies and organisations, whose role is to create and maintain XBRL taxonomies based on Canadian reporting standards, to increase the awareness, knowledge and understanding of XBRL and its uses in Canada and to stimulate and promote the adoption of XBRL in Canada. XBRL Canada is a jurisdiction of XBRL International.

XBRL Canada has created two taxonomies designed to enable preparation of XBRL based financial statements that conform to Canadian Generally Accepted Accounting Principles (GAAP). The first is referred to as the Primary Financial Statements (PFS) taxonomy, and covers the Balance Sheet, Income Statement and Statement of Cash Flow. The second, the Notes taxonomy, is for the preparation of the Notes to the Financial Statements. Both taxonomies have been "acknowledged" by XBRL International and are available on this website for free download.

The organization has also conducted several seminars for companies and individuals wishing to learn about XBRL...

Currently, XBRL Canada is working on a project to assist companies with convergence to IFRS, which is currently scheduled to take place by 2011. The project, conducted in conjunction with the IASB Foundation, will result in a taxonomy that conforms with IFRS as used in Canada, along with tools that will cross-reference existing Canadian GAAP and IFRS.

Instructions

Discuss the following.

(a) What is XBRL?

(b) What are the pros and cons of mandating the use of XBRL for public filings with securities commissions?

New Standards for Private Performance

WHILE CANADA'S PUBLIC enterprises move toward International Financial Reporting Standards (IFRS), its private enterprises will have their own set of reporting standards. "Once the [Canadian] Accounting Standards Board made the decision to move to IFRS, the concern was that, because of the cost associated with gathering the information that's necessary to comply with the international standards, a substantial number of private companies would opt to issue forms of non-GAAP financial statements," explains Allan Foerster, a professor at Wilfrid Laurier University in Waterloo, Ontario, and a member of AcSB's private enterprises standards committee. "Rather than destroy a high-quality level of financial reporting for, quite frankly, the largest sector of Canada's economy, there was a strong motivation to develop standards that would be appropriate for private enterprises."

The process of developing the private enterprise standards involved a number of consultations over several months, followed by the issuing of an exposure draft in the spring of 2009. The committee, which made recommendations to the AcSB, first identified sections of the existing *CICA Handbook* that were irrelevant to private enterprises; for example, earnings per share. It then looked at the remaining standards and assessed what would be important for the users of the statements, predominantly credit issuers such as banks.

"We eliminated roughly 50% of the required areas of disclosure," says Professor Foerster. Examples of areas where the disclosure requirements were reduced include capital assets, pension plans, and financial instruments.

Although the International Accounting Standards Board has issued its own IFRS for SMEs (small and medium-sized enterprises), the AcSB will require the Canadian standards. "When we started the process of looking at GAAP for private enterprises in Canada, there was no indication as to a timeline associated with the international board releasing their standards for small and medium-sized enterprises, so we embarked on our own process," says Foerster. "There are a lot of similarities; there are also some significant differences." For example, IFRS for SMEs requires use of deferred taxes, while the Canadian standards allow taxes payable.

So private enterprises in Canada have two options: as of 2011, they can follow IFRS along with public companies, which may be necessary if they conduct any international business; or they can follow the new Canadian GAAP for Private Enterprises, applicable to the 2009 year end. The IFRS for SMEs will not be considered GAAP in Canada. ∎

CHAPTER 4

Reporting Financial Performance

Learning Objectives

After studying this chapter, you should be able to:

1. Identify the uses and limitations of an income statement.

2. Prepare a single-step income statement.

3. Prepare a multiple-step income statement.

4. Understand the difference between classifying expenses according to their nature versus their function.

5. Explain how irregular items are reported.

6. Measure and report results of discontinued operations.

7. Explain intraperiod tax allocation.

8. Explain where earnings per share information is reported.

9. Prepare a retained earnings statement.

10. Prepare a statement of comprehensive income.

11. Prepare a statement of changes in shareholders' equity.

12. Identify differences in accounting between accounting standards for private enterprises (private entity GAAP) and IFRS.

13. Identify the significant changes planned by the IASB regarding financial statement presentation.

After studying Appendix 4A, you should be able to:

14. Explain the differences between the cash basis of accounting and the accrual basis of accounting.

Preview of Chapter 4

The way items are reported in the income statement can affect how useful it is to users. Although the net income number (the bottom line) is a key focal point for many users, the other elements in the income statement have significant information content as well. This chapter examines the many different types of revenues, expenses, gains, and losses that are represented in the income statement and related information.
The chapter is organized as follows:

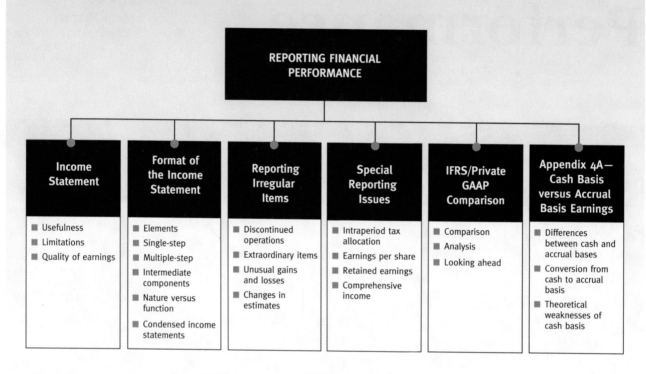

All business is based on the **business model** of getting cash, investing it in resources, and then using these resources to generate profits. This model can be broken down into three distinct types of activities:

1. **Financing:** Obtaining cash funding, often by borrowing, issuing shares, or (in established companies) retaining profits. Financing activities also involve the repayment of debt and/or repurchase of shares.

2. **Investing:** Using the funding to buy assets and invest in people. Investing activities also include divestitures.

3. **Operating:** Utilizing the assets and people to earn profits.

In performing these three types of activities, companies take on different levels of **risk** and find different **opportunities**. Companies must **manage** these risks in order to get the best performance and returns. Well-run companies develop strategies that will allow them to react to the best opportunities in order to maximize shareholder value. **Value creation** is central in any business model.

Since the objective of financial reporting is to communicate to interested stakeholders what the company is doing, the financial statements should capture these **fundamental**

business activities and communicate them appropriately. In general, the information is captured and communicated as follows:

- The **balance sheet** aims to capture the **financing and investing activities**.

- The **income statement** aims to capture the **operating and performance-related activities**.

- The **cash flow statement** looks at the **interrelationship** between the activities.

  Illustration 4-1 presents this overview of the business model.

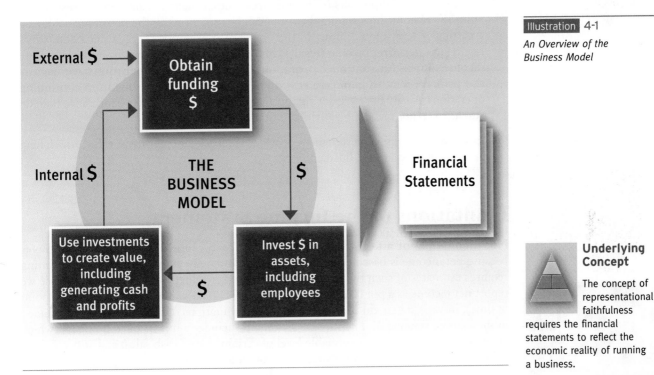

Illustration 4-1

An Overview of the Business Model

Underlying Concept

The concept of representational faithfulness requires the financial statements to reflect the economic reality of running a business.

INCOME STATEMENT

The income statement, often called the statement of earnings or statement of income, is the report that measures the success of a company's operations for a specific time period. The business and investment communities use this report to determine profitability, investment value, and creditworthiness. It provides investors and creditors with information that helps them allocate resources and assess management stewardship.

1 Objective

Identify the uses and limitations of an income statement.

Usefulness of the Income Statement

There are several ways in which the income statement helps financial statement users decide where to invest their resources and evaluate how well management is using a company's resources. For example, investors and creditors can use the information in the income statement to:

1. **Evaluate the enterprise's past performance and profitability.** By examining revenues, expenses, gains, and losses, users can see how the company (and management)

Company A   Company B

Revenues
–Expenses

$ Losses

Revenues
–Expenses

$ Losses

Which company did better last year?

performed and compare the company's performance with that of its competitors. (Balance sheet information is also useful in assessing profitability; e.g., by calculating return on assets. See Appendix 5A.)

2. **Provide a basis for predicting future performance.** Information about past performance can be used to determine important trends that, if they continue, provide information about future performance. However, success in the past does not necessarily mean the company will have success in the future.

3. **Help assess the risk or uncertainty of achieving future cash flows.** Information on the various components of income—revenues, expenses, gains, and losses—highlights the relationships among them and can be used to assess the risk of not achieving a particular level of cash flows in the future. For example, segregating a company's recurring **operating** income (results from continuing operations) from nonrecurring income sources (discontinued operations) is useful because **operations are usually the primary way to generate revenues and cash.** Thus, results from continuing operations usually have greater significance for predicting future performance than do results from nonrecurring activities.

In summary, the income statement provides feedback and predictive value, which help stakeholders understand the business.

Limitations of the Income Statement

You left something out!

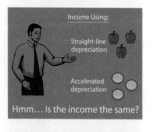

Hmm... Is the income the same?

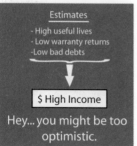

Hey... you might be too optimistic.

Net income is not a point estimate. Rather, it is a range of possible values. This is because net income is based on numerous assumptions. By definition, accrual accounting requires estimates of such things as expenses and asset values to be recorded. Because we report net income as a point estimate (i.e., a specific dollar value estimate at a single point in time), income statement users must know the limitations of the information contained in the income statement. The income statement includes a mix of **hard** numbers (which are easily measured with a reasonable level of certainty; e.g., cash sales) and **soft** numbers (which are more difficult to measure; e.g., provision for bad debt).

Specifically, the income statement has the following shortcomings:

1. **Items that cannot be measured reliably are not reported in the income statement.** Currently, companies are not allowed to include certain items in the determination of income even though these items arguably affect an entity's performance from one point in time to another. For example, contingent gains may not be recorded in income, as there is uncertainty about whether the gains will ever be realized.

2. **Income numbers are affected by the accounting methods that are used.** For example, one company may choose to depreciate or amortize its plant assets on an accelerated basis; another may choose straight-line amortization. Assuming all other factors are equal, the first company's income will be lower even though the two companies are essentially the same. The result is that we are comparing apples with oranges.

3. **Income measurement involves the use of estimates.** For example, one company may estimate in good faith that an asset's useful life is 20 years while another company uses a 15-year estimate for the same type of asset. Similarly, some companies may make overly optimistic estimates of future warranty returns and bad debt writeoffs, which would result in lower expenses and higher income. As mentioned above, when there is significant measurement uncertainty, the resulting numbers that are captured in the financial statements are called "soft numbers."

4. **Differing views of how to measure net income.** This is very important since many users focus on income and treat it as one of the most important numbers on the income statement, if not the most important. Earnings per share (EPS) numbers are generally based on net income. More recently, the concept of comprehensive income has emerged in GAAP.[1] Essentially, this newer measure of income includes all transactions aside from non-shareholder transactions and is therefore more "comprehensive," as its name suggests. Having these multiple views of income may confuse the marketplace. For instance, should EPS be based on comprehensive income instead of net income? Why does IFRS use the comprehensive income concept but private entity GAAP does not?

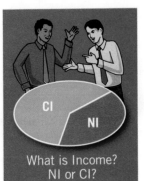

What is Income? NI or CI?

Comprehensive income was introduced in Chapter 2 and will be revisited in this and subsequent chapters.

Quality of Earnings

Users need **good information** about a company's earnings to make decisions; however, not all income statements provide this. We began to look at this issue above (through limitations of the income statement) and will examine it further here. When analyzing earnings information, there are two aspects that must be considered:

Underlying Concept

Higher-quality earnings have greater predictive value.

1. **Content**, which includes
   (a) the **integrity of the information,** including whether it reflects the underlying business fundamentals, and
   (b) the **sustainability of the earnings**

2. **Presentation**, which means a clear, concise manner that makes it easy to use and understandable

The **nature of the content** and the **way it is presented** are sometimes referred to as the quality of earnings.

From an accountant's perspective, the emphasis is on ensuring that the information **is unbiased, reflects reality, and is transparent and understandable**. From a capital market perspective, these factors are also important, but an additional focus is on whether the **earnings are sustainable**. With its current business model, can the company continue to generate or sustain these earnings in the future? Note that accountants acknowledge this additional perspective by segregating earnings on the income statement between those that are expected to continue and those that are not. For instance, the income statement shows income from continuing operations separately from income from discontinued operations. Even though the underlying business might be accurately reflected and understandable in the financial statements, the quality of the earnings might be judged to be low because the earnings are not sustainable.[2]

As suggested, earnings numbers may be judged to be of a **higher** quality or, conversely, a **lower** quality. Higher-quality earnings are more reliable, with a lower margin of potential misstatement, and are more representative of the underlying business and economic reality.

---

[1] In actuality, this concept has its roots in capital maintenance theory, which says that as long as capital is maintained from year to year, the rest is assumed to be income. Capital may be defined as financial (i.e., in terms of amount of dollars invested in the business) or physical (earnings potential of the income-generating assets).

[2] In assessing whether earnings are sustainable, a strategic analysis of the company's positioning within the industry must be performed, as well as an assessment of the business model's viability. This is beyond the scope of this course.

Companies with higher-quality earnings are attributed higher values by the markets, all other things being equal. Earnings that cannot be replicated and/or appear significantly biased are discounted by the markets.

Illustration 4-2 presents some attributes of high-quality earnings.

Illustration 4-2

Some Attributes of High-Quality Earnings

Ethics

High-quality earnings have the following characteristics:

1. Content
   - **Unbiased**, as numbers are not manipulated, and **objectively determined**. Consider the need to estimate, the accounting choices, and the use of professional judgement.
   - **Reflect the economic reality** as all transactions and events are appropriately captured.
   - **Reflect primarily the earnings generated from ongoing core business activities** instead of earnings from one-time gains or losses.
   - **Closely correlate with cash flows from operations.** Earnings that convert to cash more quickly provide a better measure of real earnings as there is little or no uncertainty about whether they will be realized.
   - **Based on sound business strategy and business model.** Consider the riskiness of the business, business strategy, industry, and the economic and political environments. Identify the effect of these on earnings stability, volatility, and sustainability.

2. Presentation
   - **Transparent**, as no attempt is made to disguise or mislead. It reflects the underlying business fundamentals.
   - **Understandable**

Can management control the quality of earnings? Looking at Illustration 4-2, we see that there are some factors that are under management control, such as the integrity of the information; i.e., what information is captured and **recognized**, how it is **measured**, and how it is **presented and disclosed**. Management may also have some control over how quickly cash is generated from operations and how closely this correlates with reported earnings; e.g., through the choice of sales and payment terms. Factors such as the economic and political environment are beyond the control of management for the most part, although management may certainly develop strategies to identify and minimize risks that lead to volatile earnings.

Ethics

Earnings management may be defined as the process of **targeting certain earnings levels** (whether current or future) or desired earnings trends and then **working backwards to determine what has to be done to ensure that these targets are met** (which can involve the selection of accounting and other company policies, the use of estimates, and even the execution of transactions). In many cases, earnings management is used to increase income in the current year by reducing income in future years. For example, companies may prematurely recognize sales before they are complete in order to boost earnings. Some companies may enter into transactions only so that the statements look better, and thus incur unnecessary transaction costs.

Earnings management can also be used to decrease current earnings in order to increase future income. Reserves may be established by using aggressive assumptions to estimate items such as sales returns, loan losses, and warranty returns. These reserves can then be reduced in the future to increase income. Earnings management activities have a negative effect on the quality of earnings. As long as there is full disclosure, an efficient market should see through these attempts to mask the underlying economic reality. Unfortunately, companies do not always disclose all important information and markets do not always operate efficiently.

Although many users do not believe that management intentionally misrepresents accounting results, there is concern that much of the information that companies distribute is too promotional and that troubled companies take great pains to present their results in the best light. Preparers of financial statements must strive to present information that is of the highest quality. Users of this information must assess the quality of earnings before making their decisions.

FORMAT OF THE INCOME STATEMENT

Elements of the Income Statement

Net income results from revenue, expense, gain, and loss transactions. Income can be further classified by customer, product line, nature, or function, or by operating and non-operating, continuing and discontinued, and regular and irregular categories.[3] The income statement presentation and classifications will be discussed later in the chapter.

More formal definitions of income-related items, referred to as the major **elements** of the income statement, are as follows:

ELEMENTS OF FINANCIAL STATEMENTS[4]

Revenues. **Increases in economic resources**, either by:
1. Inflows
2. Enhancements of an entity's assets
3. Settlements of liabilities resulting from the entity's ordinary activities

Expenses. **Decreases in economic resources**, either by:
1. Outflows
2. Reductions of assets
3. Creation of liabilities, resulting from an entity's ordinary revenue-generating activities

Gains. **Increases in equity (net assets)** from **peripheral** or **incidental transactions** of an entity and from all other transactions and other events and circumstances affecting the entity during a period except those that result from revenues or investment by owners

Losses. **Decreases in equity (net assets)** from **peripheral** or **incidental transactions** of an entity and from all other transactions and other events and circumstances affecting the entity during a period except those that result from expenses or distributions to owners

---

These are the same **elements** identified in Chapter 2 and the conceptual framework. **Revenues** take many forms, such as sales, fees, interest, dividends, and rents. **Expenses** also take many forms, such as cost of goods sold, amortization, interest, rent, salaries and wages, and taxes. **Gains** and **losses** also are of many types, resulting from the sale of investments, sale of plant assets, settlement of liabilities, and writeoffs of assets due to obsolescence, casualty, and/or theft.

Other comprehensive income is made up of certain specific gains or losses that may be required to be presented separately on the income statement (below net income). This classification, as well as comprehensive income, is presented in the income statement

Underlying Concept

Accounting standards for private enterprises differ from IFRS in many cases as the costs of the more complex set of standards (IFRS) outweigh the benefits to users of private entity financial statements.

---

[3] The term "irregular" is used for transactions and other events that come from developments that are outside the normal business operations.

[4] *CICA Handbook*, Part II, Section 1000 and IAS Framework.

under IFRS (but not under private entity GAAP) and includes unrealized **gains** and **losses** on certain securities, certain foreign exchange gains or losses, and other gains and losses as defined by IFRS.[5] Other comprehensive income is closed out to a balance sheet account that is often referred to as Accumulated Other Comprehensive Income, which acts as a type of retained earnings account. Accumulated Other Comprehensive Income is an equity account on the balance sheet.

Underlying Concept

The business model should be transparent.

The **distinction** between revenues and gains (and expenses and losses) depends to a great extent on how the enterprise's **ordinary** or typical business activities are defined. It is therefore critical to understand an enterprise's typical business activities. For example, when McDonald's sells a hamburger, the selling price is recorded as **revenue**. However, when McDonald's sells a deep fryer machine, any excess of the selling price over the book value would be recorded as a **gain**. This difference in treatment results because the hamburger sale is part of the company's regular operations while the deep fryer sale is not. Only when a manufacturer of deep fryers sells a fryer, therefore, would the sale proceeds be recorded as **revenue**.

The importance of properly presenting these elements should not be underestimated. For many decision-makers, the **parts of a financial statement may be more useful than the whole**. A company must be able to generate cash flows from its **normal ongoing core business activities** (revenues minus expenses) in order to survive and prosper. Having income statement elements shown in some detail and in a format that shows the data from prior years allows decision-makers to better assess whether a company does indeed **generate cash flows** from its normal ongoing core business activities and **whether it is getting better or worse at it**.

Companies are required to present the following items in the income statement.[6] Note that any items that are material and/or relevant to understanding the financial performance should also be presented separately. In addition, various other private entity GAAP and IFRS standards require specific disclosures. Judgement may be used to determine where these items are best presented (i.e., in the income statement or notes).

Significant Change

✳

Items Required in the Income Statement	
Private entity GAAP	IFRS
• revenues	• revenues
• amount of inventories recognized as expense for the period	• finance costs
• income from investments	• share of profits/loss for investees accounted for under the equity method
• government assistance	• tax
• amortization	• discontinued operations, net of tax
• impairment	• each component of other comprehensive income, net of tax
• compensation costs	• share of other comprehensive income for investees accounted for under the equity method, net of tax
• exchange gains or losses	
• interest expense	
• unusual items	• profit or loss attributable to non-controlling interests and owners of the parent
• non-controlling interest	
• income taxes	
• discontinued operations, net of tax	

---

[5] Each of these items will be discussed in greater detail in subsequent chapters. Basically, under private entity GAAP, there is no need for other comprehensive income to be presented since either the gains/losses do not exist under private entity GAAP due to accounting policy differences (e.g., under private entity GAAP, use of the revaluation method to measure property, plant, and equipment at fair value is generally not allowed) or the gains/losses are booked directly to equity (e.g., certain foreign exchange translation gains/losses).

[6] *CICA Handbook*, Part II, Section 1520 and IAS 1.

Illustration 4-3 shows the income statement of **Ballard Power Systems Inc.** for the year ended December 31, 2008, in accordance with Canadian GAAP before the changeover to IFRS for public companies and private entity GAAP for private companies. This statement has been chosen to illustrate the level of detail that is typical in the income statements of many public companies. Note that in this case, the company has no other comprehensive income gains/losses and so net income is equal to comprehensive income.

BALLARD POWER SYSTEMS INC.

Consolidated Statements of Operations and Comprehensive Income (Loss)

Years ended December 31,

(Expressed in thousands of U.S. dollars, except per share amounts and number of shares)

	2008	2007	2006
Revenues:			
Product and service revenues	$ 52,726	$ 43,352	$ 36,535
Engineering development revenue	6,854	22,180	13,288
Total revenues	59,580	65,532	49,823
Cost of revenues and expenses:			
Cost of product and service revenues	47,401	25,052	21,206
Research and product development	37,172	58,478	52,274
General and administrative	12,615	19,068	13,262
Marketing and business development	7,461	8,981	7,226
Depreciation and amortization	6,034	15,732	16,391
Total cost of revenues and expenses	110,683	127,311	110,359
Loss before undernoted	(51,103)	(61,779)	(60,536)
Investment and other income (loss) (note 19)	(186)	16,933	9,932
Gain on sale of assets (note 3)	96,845	—	—
Loss on disposal and write-down of long-lived assets (note 9)	(2,812)	(4,583)	(778)
Equity in loss of associated companies	(8,649)	(7,433)	(7,029)
Income (loss) before income taxes	34,095	(56,862)	(58,411)
Income taxes (recovery) (note 15)	16	(53)	(1,417)
Income (loss) from continuing operations	34,079	(56,809)	(56,994)
Loss from discontinued operations (note 4)	—	(493)	(124,143)
Net income (loss) and comprehensive income (loss)	34,079	(57,302)	(181,137)
Basic earnings (loss) per share from continuing operations	$ 0.40	$ (0.50)	$ (0.50)
Basic loss per share from discontinued operations	0.00	(0.00)	(1.10)
Basic earnings (loss) per share	$ 0.40	$ (0.50)	$ (1.60)
Diluted earnings (loss) per share	$ 0.40	$ (0.50)	$ (1.60)
Weighted average number of common shares outstanding – basic	84,922,364	114,575,473	113,390,728
Impact of dilutive options	840,843	—	—
Weighted average number of common shares outstanding – diluted	85,763,207	114,575,473	113,390,728

See accompanying notes to consolidated financial statements.

Illustration 4-3

Ballard Power Systems Inc. Statement of Operations and Comprehensive Income

 Real-World Emphasis

Single-Step Income Statements

Objective 2
Prepare a single-step
income statement.

In reporting revenues, gains, expenses, and losses, a format known as the single-step income statement is often used. In the single-step statement, only two main groupings are used: **revenues** and **expenses**. Expenses and losses are deducted from revenues and gains to arrive at net income. The expression "single-step" comes from the single subtraction that is needed to arrive at net income before discontinued operations. Frequently, income tax is reported separately as the last item before net income before discontinued operations to indicate its relationship to income before income tax.

Illustration 4-4 shows the single-step income statement of Dan Deines Corporation.

Illustration 4-4

Single-Step Income Statement

DAN DEINES CORPORATION
Income Statement
For the Year Ended December 31, 2010

Revenues	
Net sales	$2,972,413
Dividend revenue	98,500
Rental revenue	72,910
Total revenues	3,143,823
Expenses	
Cost of goods sold	1,982,541
Selling expenses	453,028
Administrative expenses	350,771
Interest expense	126,060
Income tax expense	66,934
Total expenses	2,979,334
Net income	$ 164,489
Earnings per common share	$1.74

The single-step form of income statement is widely used in financial reporting in smaller private companies. The **multiple-step** form described below is used almost exclusively among public companies.

The main advantages of the single-step format are that the **presentation is simple** and **no one type of revenue or expense item is implied to have priority over any other**. Potential classification problems are thus eliminated.

Multiple-Step Income Statements

Objective 3
Prepare a multiple-step
income statement.

Some users argue that **presenting other important revenue and expense data separately** makes the income statement more informative and more useful. For instance, additional information is communicated if there is separation between the company's operating and non-operating activities such as **other revenues and gains** and **other expenses and losses**. These other categories include interest revenue and expense, gains or losses from sales of miscellaneous items, and dividends received.

A multiple-step income statement separates **operating** transactions and **non-operating** transactions and **matches** costs and expenses with related revenues. It also highlights certain intermediate components of income that are used to calculate ratios for assessing the enterprise's performance (i.e., gross profit/margin).

To illustrate, Dan Deines Corporation's multiple-step income statement is presented in Illustration 4-5. Note, for example, that at least three main subtotals are presented that deal with operating activities: net sales revenue, gross profit, and income from operations. The disclosure of net sales revenue is useful because regular revenues are reported as a separate item. Irregular or incidental revenues are disclosed elsewhere in the income statement. As a result, trends in revenue from continuing operations (typical business activities) should be easier to identify, understand, and analyze. Similarly, the reporting of gross profit provides a useful number for evaluating performance and assessing future earnings. A study of the trend in gross profits may show **how successfully a company uses its resources** (prices paid for inventory, costs accumulated, wastage); it may also be a basis for **understanding how profit margins have changed** as a result of competitive pressure (which may limit the prices that the company is able to charge for its products and services). Gross profit percentage is a very important ratio in the retail business.

Finally, disclosing income from operations **highlights the difference between regular and irregular or incidental activities.** Disclosure of operating earnings may help in comparing different companies and assessing their operating efficiencies. Note that if Dan Deines had **discontinued operations or other comprehensive income**, these would be added to the bottom of the statement and shown separately. Income/losses from discontinued operations are by definition **nonrecurring** and therefore have **little predictive value.** They do, however, give **feedback value** on past decisions made by management. Net income that consists mainly of net income from continuing operations would be viewed as **higher quality**.

Underlying Concept

This disclosure helps users recognize that incidental or irregular activities are **unlikely to continue at the same level (i.e., it enhances predictive value).**

Illustration 4-5

Multiple-Step Income Statement

DAN DEINES CORPORATION
Income Statement
For the Year Ended December 31, 2010

Sales revenue			
Sales			$3,053,081
Less: Sales discounts	$	24,241	
Sales returns and allowances		56,427	80,668
Net sales revenue			2,972,413
Cost of goods sold			1,982,541
Gross profit			989,872
Operating expenses			
Selling expenses			
Sales salaries and commissions	202,644		
Sales office salaries	59,200		
Travel and entertainment	48,940		
Advertising expense	38,315		
Freight and transportation-out	41,209		
Shipping supplies and expense	24,712		
Postage and stationery	16,788		
Telephone and Internet expense	12,215		
Depreciation of sales equipment	9,005	453,028	
Administrative expenses			
Officers' salaries	186,000		
Office salaries	61,200		
Legal and professional services	23,721		
Utilities expense	23,275		
Insurance expense	17,029		
Depreciation of building	18,059		

continued on page 164

Depreciation of office equipment	16,000		
Stationery, supplies, and postage	2,875		
Miscellaneous office expenses	2,612	350,771	803,799
Income from operations			186,073
Other revenues and gains			
Dividend revenue		98,500	
Rental revenue		72,910	171,410
			357,483
Other expenses and losses			
Interest on bonds and notes			126,060
Income before income tax			231,423
Income tax			66,934
Net income for the year			$ 164,489
Earnings per common share			$1.74

Intermediate Components of the Income Statement

When a multiple-step income statement is used, some or all of the following sections or subsections may be presented:

INCOME STATEMENT SECTIONS

1. *Continuing Operations*
   (a) **Operating** Section. A report of the **revenues and expenses** of the company's principal operations.
      i. **Sales or Revenue** Section. A subsection presenting sales, discounts, allowances, returns, and other related information. Its purpose is to arrive at the net amount of sales revenue.
      ii. **Cost of Goods Sold** Section. A subsection that shows the cost of goods that were sold to produce the sales.
      iii. **Selling Expenses.** A subsection that lists expenses resulting from the company's efforts to make sales.
      iv. **Administrative or General Expenses.** A subsection reporting expenses for general administration.
   (b) **Non-Operating** Section. A report of revenues and expenses resulting from the company's secondary or auxiliary activities. In addition, special gains and losses that are infrequent and/or unusual are normally reported in this section. Generally these items break down into two main subsections:
      i. **Other Revenues and Gains.** A list of the revenues earned or gains incurred from non-operating transactions, and generally net of related expenses.
      ii. **Other Expenses and Losses.** A list of the expenses or losses incurred from non-operating transactions, and generally net of any related income.
   (c) **Income Tax.** A short section reporting income taxes on income from continuing operations.

2. *Discontinued Operations.* Material gains or losses resulting from the disposition of a part of the business (net of taxes).
3. *Extraordinary Items.* Atypical and infrequent material gains and losses beyond the control of management (net of taxes).[7]
4. *Other Comprehensive Income.* Other gains/losses that are not required by primary sources of GAAP to be included in net income. This section includes all other changes in equity that do not relate to shareholder transactions (net of taxes).[8]

Although the **content** of the operating section is generally the same, the **presentation** or organization of the material does not need to be as described above. Sometimes the expenses are grouped by nature instead of function. This is discussed below.

Usually, financial statements that are provided to external users have **less detail** than internal management reports. The latter tend to have more expense categories, and they are usually grouped along lines of responsibility. This detail allows top management to judge staff performance.

Whether a single-step or multiple-step income statement is used, **irregular transactions** such as discontinued operations, extraordinary items, and other comprehensive income are **required to be reported separately**, following income from continuing operations.

Presentation of Expenses: Nature versus Function

Whether the single-step or multiple-step method is used, consideration should be given to providing additional details about expenses. This helps ensure transparency. IFRS requires an entity to present an analysis of expenses based on either nature or function, as follows:

4 **Objective**
Understand the difference between classifying expenses according to their nature versus their function.

Significant Change

1. Nature (e.g., depreciation, purchases of materials, transport costs, employee benefits, and other). This method tends to be more straightforward since no allocation of costs is required between functions.

2. Function (e.g., cost of sales, distribution costs, administrative costs, and other). This method requires more judgement since costs such as payroll and amortization are allocated between functions. At a minimum, this method requires that cost of sales be presented separately from other costs. This presentation gives more insight into the various phases of operations (e.g., production, distribution, and other).

Under IFRS, entities are encouraged to present this in the income statement; however, it may be presented elsewhere. Under private entity GAAP, although this is not mandated, an

---

[7] Extraordinary items are not allowed under IFRS and no guidance is given under private entity GAAP (since the standard setters felt that private entities would likely not have any transactions that would qualify for separate line item presentation as extraordinary). Note that in the decade leading up to this point, it was relatively rare to find extraordinary items presented separately in the financial statements of Canadian and U.S. entities. The category is still allowed under U.S. GAAP. *Accounting Trends and Techniques – 2007* (New York: AICPA) indicated that only 4 out of 600 companies surveyed reported extraordinary items.

[8] This concept is not used under private entity GAAP, as previously discussed; however, it is utilized under IFRS and U.S. GAAP.

entity may choose to make such disclosures if it feels that the information is decision relevant. Which method is better? That depends on the nature of the business and industry. For instance, it is useful in the retail industry to focus on cost of sales and gross profit. Because information about the nature of expense is useful for predicting cash flows, this information must also be disclosed when the income statement presents expenses by function. Illustration 4-6 shows an income statement for **Air Liquide** with expenses presented by nature. An example of expenses presented by function is noted in Illustration 4-7 for Dan Deines. In this statement, the functions are cost of sales (production), selling (distribution) and administrative (other).

Illustration 4-6

*Air Liquide Income Statement
Classified by Nature
of Expense*

**Real-World
Emphasis**

CONSOLIDATED INCOME STATEMENT

FOR THE YEAR ENDED DECEMBER 31

In millions of euros	2007	2008
Revenue	11,801.2	13,103.1
Purchases	(4,547.9)	(5,547.1)
Personnel expenses	(2,037.8)	(2,176.8)
Other income and expenses	(2,485.5)	(2,437.4)
Operating income recurring before depreciation and amortization	**2,730.0**	**2,941.8**
Depreciation and amortization expense	(935.9)	(992.8)
Operating income recurring	**1,794.1**	**1,949.0**
Other non-recurring operating expenses	(5.3)	(30.2)
Operating income	**1,788.8**	**1,918.8**
Net finance costs	(179.4)	(214.4)
Other net financial expenses	(54.3)	(55.9)
Income taxes	(411.8)	(401.5)
Share of profit of associates	26.7	24.8
Profit for the period	**1,170.0**	**1,271.8**
Minority interests	46.9	51.8
Net profit (Group share)	1,123.1	1,220.0
Basic earnings per share (in euros)	**4.26**	**4.70**
Diluted earnings per share (in euros)	**4.22**	**4.67**

**Underlying
Concept**

This contributes to understandability as it reduces "information overload."

Condensed Income Statements

In some cases, it is impossible to present all the desired expense detail in a single income statement of convenient size. This problem is solved by including only the totals of expense groups in the statement of income and preparing **supplementary schedules** of expenses to support the totals. With this format, the income statement itself may be reduced to a few lines on a single sheet. In such instances, readers who want to study all the reported data on operations must give their attention to the supporting schedules.

The income statement shown in Illustration 4-7 for Dan Deines Corporation is a condensed version of the more detailed multiple-step statement presented earlier and is more typical of what is done in actual practice.

Illustration 4-7

Condensed Income Statement

DAN DEINES CORPORATION
Income Statement
For the Year Ended December 31, 2010

Net sales		$2,972,413
Cost of goods sold		1,982,541
Gross profit		989,872
Selling expenses (see Note D)	$453,028	
Administrative expenses	350,771	803,799
Income from operations		186,073
Other revenues and gains		171,410
		357,483
Other expenses and losses		126,060
Income before income tax		231,423
Income tax		66,934
Net income for the year		$ 164,489
Earnings per share		$1.74

An example of a supporting schedule, cross-referenced as Note D and detailing the selling expenses, is shown in Illustration 4-8.

Illustration 4-8

Sample Supporting Schedule

Note D: Selling expenses	
Sales salaries and commissions	$202,644
Sales office salaries	59,200
Travel and entertainment	48,940
Advertising expense	38,315
Freight and transportation-out	41,209
Shipping supplies and expense	24,712
Postage and stationery	16,788
Telephone and Internet expense	12,215
Depreciation of sales equipment	9,005
Total selling expenses	$453,028

Deciding **how much detail** to include in the income statement is always a problem. On the one hand, a simple, summarized statement allows a reader to quickly discover important factors. On the other hand, disclosure of the results of all activities provides users with detailed relevant information. Certain basic elements are always included, but they may be presented in various formats.

Underlying Concept

This is an example of a trade-off between understandability and full disclosure.

REPORTING IRREGULAR ITEMS

Objective 5
Explain how irregular items are reported.

Either the **single-step** or the **multiple-step** income statement may be used for financial reporting purposes, which means there is some flexibility in presenting the income components. In two important areas, however, specific guidelines have been developed. These two areas relate to what is included in income and how certain unusual or irregular items are reported.

What should be included in net income has been a controversy for many years. For example, should irregular gains and losses, corrections of revenues and prior years' expenses, and non-operating changes in equity be treated differently from ongoing revenues and expenses from operating activities? Should other comprehensive income be included in net income?

One option is to book these items directly to retained earnings or a separate equity section; i.e., not book them through the income statement. Another is to include everything in net income.

Currently, income measurement follows a modified all-inclusive approach. This approach indicates that most items, even irregular ones, are recorded in income.[9] Some exceptions include:

1. **Errors** in the income measurement of prior years

2. **Changes in accounting policies that are applied retrospectively**

Because these items relate to earnings that were already reported in a prior period, they are not included in current income. Rather, they are recorded as adjustments to retained earnings. Under IFRS, recall that certain gains and losses are included in other comprehensive income. Recall further that other comprehensive income is excluded from net income but included in comprehensive income (which is closed out to accumulated other comprehensive income). Thus comprehensive income is closer to a true all-inclusive approach than net income.

Some users support a current operating performance approach to income reporting. They argue that the most useful income measures are the ones that reflect only regular and recurring revenue and expense elements; i.e., normalized, sustainable earnings. Irregular items do not reflect an enterprise's future earning power since, by definition, they are irregular and atypical or nonrecurring. Operating income supporters believe that including one-time items such as writeoffs and restructuring charges reduces the income measure's basic **predictive value**.

In contrast, others warn that a focus on operating income potentially misses important information about a firm's performance. Any gain or loss that is experienced by the firm, whether it is directly or indirectly related to operations, contributes to the firm's long-run profitability. As one analyst notes, "write-offs matter. They speak to the volatility of (past) earnings."[10] In other words, they have **feedback value**. As a result, some non-operating items can be used to assess the riskiness of future earnings—and therefore have **predictive value**. Furthermore, determining which items are (regular) **operating** items and which are **irregular** requires judgement and this could lead to differences in the treatment of irregular items and to possible manipulation of income measures.

---

[9] The modified all-inclusive approach is substantially consistent with a capital maintenance approach to measuring income (if we ignore errors and changes in accounting policies) since comprehensive income is equal to a change in net assets excluding capital transactions.

[10] D. McDermott, "Latest Profit Data Stir Old Debate between Net and Operating Income," *The Wall Street Journal*, May 3, 1999.

Discontinued Operations

One of the most common types of irregular items relates to discontinued operations. Discontinued operations include **components of an enterprise** that have been **disposed of** (by sale, abandonment, or spinoff) **or** are classified as **held for sale.**[11]

What Do the Numbers Mean?

Companies might discontinue operations as part of a downsizing strategy to improve their operating results, to focus on core operations, or even to generate cash flows. For example, **Napster Inc**. (formerly Roxio Inc.), whose shares traded on NASDAQ, was the subject of much controversy for helping music lovers swap music for free. Until December 17, 2004, the company had two divisions: the consumer software division and the on-line music distribution division. The consumer software division was sold so that the company could focus solely on the on-line music distribution business. Its goal is to become a leading global provider of consumer digital music services. Currently, the company boasts that it is the only legal on-line advertising-supported service that offers free on-demand music listening. Since the sale, the company has devoted all of its resources to the on-line music business. In 2008, it was acquired by Best Buy for U.S. $121 million.

Separate Component

In order to qualify for separate presentation on the income statement, the discontinued business must be a **component of an entity** (a business component) where the **operations, cash flows, and financial elements are clearly distinguishable** from the rest of the enterprise. A component can be any one of the following:[12]

Significant Change

Private Entity GAAP	IFRS
• An **operating segment**. Operating segments engage in business activities, have their performance reviewed by management, specifically the chief operating decision-maker, and have discrete accounting information available.	• A separate major **line of business or geographical area of operations.**
• A **reporting unit** as defined in *CICA Handbook*, Part II, Section 3064, which deals with goodwill and intangible assets. A reporting unit is equal to an operating segment or one level below, the difference being that performance is reviewed by a lower level of management.	• A **business** that meets the criteria to be accounted for as held for sale upon acquisition.
• A **subsidiary** as defined in *CICA Handbook*, Part II, Section 1590. Subsidiaries are separate legal entities.	
• An **asset group** as defined in *CICA Handbook*, Part II, Section 3063 for impairment of long-lived assets. An asset group has cash flows that are largely independent of other cash flows from the business.	
• Operations without assets.	

---

[11] *CICA Handbook*, Part II, Section 3475.27 and IFRS 5.32.

[12] *CICA Handbook*, Part II, Section 3475.28 and IFRS 5.31. At the time of writing of this text, the IASB was revisiting the definition of discontinued operations.

Private entity GAAP is less restrictive, as IFRS generally allows only major lines of business or geographical areas to be included.

Depending on which GAAP is being followed, a component consists of a **unit of operation**, which may be as small as a hotel or an apartment building that is being rented out, or as large as a major subsidiary or geographical area. In terms of discontinued operations, when does the **disposal of an asset** constitute a **disposal of a component**? **The key elements are that the asset or group of assets generates its own net cash flows** (is a cash-generating unit) **and is operationally distinct (i.e., it operates as a separate unit).**

Illustration 4-9 gives a conceptual view of what constitutes a component in terms of discontinued operations under accounting standards for private entities.

Illustration 4-9

A Conceptual View of a Component of an Entity in Terms of Discontinued Operations for Private Entities

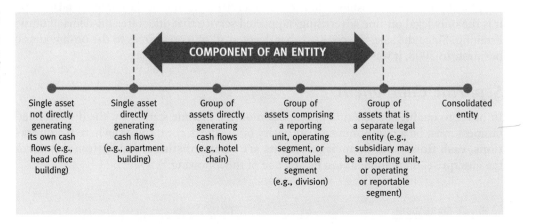

Under accounting standards for private entities, in order to be presented as discontinued operations, the operations and cash flows from the component must be eliminated from the ongoing operations and the entity must not have continuing involvement. Generally, this will be the case in a straightforward sale.[13]

Assets Held for Sale

If the component is not yet disposed of, an additional condition must be met before the transaction can be given a different presentation on the income statement. This condition is that the assets relating to the component must be considered to be **held for sale** by the company. Assets are considered to be held for sale when all of the following criteria are met:

- There is an **authorized plan** to sell.
- The asset is **available for immediate sale** in its current state.
- There is an **active program** to find a buyer.
- Sale is **probable** within one year.
- The asset is **reasonably priced** and actively marketed.
- **Changes** to the plan are **unlikely**.[14]

---

[13] Cash flows might not be seen to be eliminated, for instance, where the entity continues to sell products to the disposed component or to its customers. Continuing involvement might be evidenced where the entity retains an ownership interest in the disposed component or where it provides management services. Consideration would be given to the significance of the cash flows or continuing involvement.

[14] *CICA Handbook*, Part II, Section 3475.08 and IFRS 5.7 and .8.

In summary, for accounting purposes, assets may be considered as held for sale when there is a formal plan to dispose of the component. This ensures that only assets or asset groups for which management has a detailed, approved plan for disposal get measured and presented as held for sale. Note that assets that are held for sale might not (and do not need to) meet the definition of discontinued operations. Where this is the case, these assets, as noted below, would be measured and presented the same way (as if they were discontinued operations) on the balance sheet, but any related gains or losses would be recorded as part of income from continuing operations.

Measurement and Presentation

When an asset is held for sale, regardless of whether it meets the definition of a discontinued operation, the asset is **remeasured** to the lower of its carrying value and fair value less its cost to sell.[15] Note that if the value of an asset that has been written down later increases, **the gain can be recognized up to the amount of the original loss**. Once an asset has been classified as held for sale, **no further depreciation is recognized**.

Assets and related liabilities that are classified in this way are **presented** separately as held for sale in the balance sheet, and retain their original classification as assets (or liabilities) that are current or noncurrent under private entity GAAP.[16] Under IFRS, assets held for sale are generally classified as current assets.[17] If the asset meets the definition of a discontinued operation, the results of operations are shown separately on the income statement, net of tax for both the current and prior periods.[18] Otherwise, the writedown is treated like any other asset impairment charge on the income statement. The example that follows illustrates accounting concepts related to discontinued operations.

On November 1, 2010, top management of DeGrootes Corporation approves a detailed plan to discontinue its electronics division (a major line of business) at December 31, 2010. The plan, among other things, identifies steps to find a buyer and includes a timeline for disposition, along with a calculation of the expected gain or loss on disposition. The business is available for sale immediately.

As top management has approved the disposal and has stated in reasonable detail which assets are to be disposed of and how, a **formal plan** exists. The division is a separate business (being a division) that is therefore operationally distinct, with separate cash flows. Since it is a division, it will also have separate financial information and is thus a business component. Separate financial information is critical so that the gain or loss from discontinued operations can be properly **measured**. The company will have no continuing involvement in the electronics division after it is sold.

During the current year, the electronics division lost $300,000 (net of tax). DeGrootes estimates that it can sell the business at a loss of $500,000 (net of tax). The assets and liabilities relating to the division would be segregated on the balance sheet as follows under private entity GAAP, according to their nature:

- current assets: as "current assets held for sale/related to discontinued operations"

- noncurrent assets: as "noncurrent assets held for sale/related to discontinued operations"

- current liabilities: as "current liabilities related to assets held for sale/discontinued"

- long-term liabilities: as "long-term liabilities related to assets held for sale/discontinued"

---

[15] *CICA Handbook*, Part II, Section 3475.13 and IFRS 5.15.

[16] *CICA Handbook*, Part II, Section 3475.33–.35. These assets and liabilities would be classified as current only if they have been sold prior to the completion of the financial statements and the proceeds are expected to be received within the year.

[17] IFRS 5.3.

[18] *CICA Handbook*, Part II, Section 3475.30.

Significant Change

Under IFRS, the assets and liabilities would be presented as held for sale and classified as current assets and liabilities.

The information would be shown as in Illustration 4-10 on the current year's annual income statement (assuming $20 million of income from continuing operations).

Illustration 4-10

Income Statement Presentation of a Discontinued Operation

Income from continuing operations		$20,000,000
Discontinued operations		
Loss from operation of discontinued electronics division (net of tax)	$300,000	
Loss from disposal of electronics division (net of tax)	500,000	800,000
Net income		$19,200,000

Objective 6

Measure and report results of discontinued operations.

The company would stop recording depreciation on the division's assets and, in the following year, would show any operating losses or profits and/or revised gain or loss on disposal as discontinued operations. Estimated future losses would not be included in the loss from operations since they would already be implied (and therefore included) in the fair value estimate of the assets held for sale or sold. Note that the phrase "Income from continuing operations" is only used when gains or losses on discontinued operations or extraordinary items occur. Note that the company would, in addition to the detail shown on the income statement, make additional note disclosures including a description of the disposal. The detail shown on the face of the income statement (breakdown between earnings/loss from operations and gain/loss from sale) could also be shown in the notes.[19]

Extraordinary Items

Extraordinary items are material, nonrecurring items that are significantly different from the entity's typical business activities.[20] They are presented separately on the income statement in order to provide enough detail to have predictive value. The three criteria that must all be met for items to be considered extraordinary are as follows. They must:

1. be **infrequent**
2. be **atypical** of the company's normal business activities
3. not depend mainly on **decisions or determinations by management** or owners

What Do the Numbers Mean?

No event better illustrates the difficulties of determining whether a transaction meets the definition of extraordinary than the financial impact of the terrorist attacks on the World Trade Center on September 11, 2001. To many, this event, which resulted in the tragic loss of lives, jobs, and in some cases, entire businesses, clearly meets the criteria for unusual and infrequent. For example, airlines, insurance companies, and other businesses recorded major losses due to property damage, business disruption, and the suspension of airline travel and of securities trading. But, to the surprise of many, extraordinary item reporting was not permitted for losses arising from the terrorist attacks.

The reason? After much deliberation, the Emerging Issues Task Force of the FASB decided that measuring the possible loss was too difficult. Take the airline industry as an

---

[19] *CICA Handbook*, Part II, Sections 3475.36 and .37; IFRS 5.41 and .42.

[20] It is often difficult to determine what is extraordinary, because assessing the materiality of individual items requires judgement. However, in making materiality judgements, extraordinary items should be considered individually, and not together.

example. What portion of the airlines' losses after September 11 was related to the terrorist attack, and what portion was due to the ongoing economic slowdown? There was also concern that some companies would use the attacks as a reason for reporting as extraordinary some losses that had little direct relationship to the attacks. For example, shortly after the attacks, energy company AES and shoe retailer Footstar, both of which were experiencing profit pressure before the attacks, put some of the blame for their poor performance on the attacks.[21]

Real-World Emphasis

In addition to the criteria of unusual and infrequent, the third criterion for classifying an item as extraordinary looks at **management involvement**. The event must not depend on or result from a management or owner decision. This third criterion ensures that items that are classified as extraordinary items are beyond management control. Thus, decisions to sell assets at losses, or to downsize or restructure, and other similar expenses are not considered extraordinary.

In determining whether an item is extraordinary, the environment in which the entity operates is very important. The environment includes such factors as industry characteristics, geographic location, and the nature and amount of government regulations. Thus, a loss from hail damage is only treated as an extraordinary item for a tobacco grower's crops if severe damage from hailstorms is rare where the grower is located. And, frost damage to a citrus grower's crop in Florida does not qualify as extraordinary, because frost damage is normally experienced there every three or four years. In this environment, the criterion of infrequency is not met.

Extraordinary items are shown **net of taxes** in a separate section in the income statement, usually just before net income. Under IFRS, extraordinary items are not allowed, and under private entity GAAP, there is no guidance.

Significant Change

Unusual Gains and Losses

Unusual gains and losses are items that by their nature are not typical of everyday business activities or do not occur frequently. They include such items as writedowns of inventories and gains and losses from fluctuations of foreign exchange. They are generally presented as part of normal, recurring revenues, expenses, gains, and losses (as part of income from continuing operations). If they are not material in amount, they are combined with other items in the income statement. If they are material, they are disclosed separately, but are shown above "income (loss) before discontinued operations" and before the income tax provision. This separate presentation allows for greater transparency as the users are able to see the cause of major gains and losses.

Unusual items have been common in recent years and are especially prevalent in times of economic downturn. If the same types of gains/losses recur each year, then they are not really unusual and care must be taken to classify them with other gains and losses as normal transactions. Otherwise, it is misleading.[22]

---

[21] J. Creswell, "Bad News Bearers Shift the Blame," *Fortune* (October 15, 2001), p. 44.

[22] Some companies report items such as restructuring charges every year as unusual items. Research on the market reaction to income containing one-time items indicates that the market discounts the earnings of companies that report a series of nonrecurring items. Such evidence supports the argument that these elements reduce the quality of earnings. See J. Elliot and D. Hanna, "Repeat Accounting Write-Offs and the Information Content of Earnings," *Journal of Accounting Research* (Supplement, 1996).

Changes in Estimates

Another type of change involves changes in estimates. Estimates are inherent in the accounting process. Estimates are made, for example, of useful lives and salvage values of depreciable assets, of uncollectible receivables, of inventory obsolescence, and of the number of periods that a particular expenditure is expected to benefit. Often enough, as time passes, as circumstances change, or as additional information is obtained, even estimates that were originally made in good faith must be changed. Such changes in estimates are accounted for in the period of change if they affect only that period, or in the period of change and future periods if the change affects both.

To illustrate a change in estimate that affects only the period of change, assume that DuPage Materials Corp. has consistently estimated its bad debt expense at 1% of credit sales. In 2010, however, DuPage's controller determines that the estimate of bad debts for the current year's credit sales must be revised upward to 2%, or double the previous year's percentage. Using 2% results in a bad debt charge of $240,000, or double the amount using the 1% estimate for prior years. The expense is recorded at December 31, 2010, as follows:

A = L + SE	
−240,000 −240,000	
Cash flows: No effect	

Bad Debt Expense	240,000	
Allowance for Doubtful Accounts		240,000

The entire change in estimate is included in the 2010 income because it reflects decisions made and information available in the current year and no future periods are affected by the change. Changes in estimate are not handled retrospectively; that is, they are not carried back to adjust prior years.

All accounting changes (including corrections of errors) will be examined further in Chapter 21.

SPECIAL REPORTING ISSUES

Intraperiod Tax Allocation

Objective 7
Explain intraperiod tax allocation.

As previously noted, certain irregular items are shown on the income statement net of tax, which is a more informative disclosure to statement users. This procedure of allocating tax balances within a period is called intraperiod tax allocation. Intraperiod tax allocation relates the income tax expense or benefit of the fiscal period to the underlying income statement items and events that are being taxed. Intraperiod tax allocation is used for the following items: (1) income from continuing operations, (2) discontinued operations, (3) extraordinary items, and (4) other comprehensive income.

The income tax expense that is attributed to income from continuing operations is calculated by finding the income tax expense related to the revenue and expense transactions for continuing operations. In this tax calculation, the tax consequences of the items that are excluded from the determination of income from continuing operations are not considered. A separate tax effect is then associated with each irregular item.

In applying the concept of intraperiod tax allocation, assume that Schindler Corp. has income before income tax and discontinued operations of $250,000 and a gain from the sale of one of its operations of $100,000. If the income tax rate is assumed to be 40%, the information in Illustration 4-11 is presented on the income statement.

Income before income tax and discontinued operations	$250,000
Income tax	100,000
Income before discontinued operations	150,000
Gain from sale of discontinued operations net of applicable taxes of (40,000)	60,000
Net income	$210,000

Illustration 4-11

Intraperiod Tax Allocation, Discontinued Operations

The income tax of $100,000 ($250,000 × 40%) that is attributed to income before income tax and discontinued operations is determined from the revenue and expense transactions related to this income. In this income tax calculation, the tax consequences of items excluded from the determination of income before income tax and discontinued operations are not considered. The "gain from sale of discontinued operation" then shows a separate tax effect of $40,000.

Earnings per Share

Typically, the results of a company's operations are summed up in one important figure: net income. As if this simplification were not enough, the financial world has widely accepted an even more distilled and compact figure as its most significant business indicator: **earnings per share** (EPS). Many users focus primarily on the earnings per share number (rightly or wrongly) as a key indicator of the company's performance. While the earnings per share number yields significant information, it does not tell the whole story. This undue emphasis on earnings per share makes it a very sensitive number for companies. Note further that when comprehensive income is presented, it begs the questions as to why EPS is not based on this more "comprehensive" measurement of income.

8 **Objective**

Explain where earnings per share information is reported.

The calculation of earnings per share is usually straightforward. Net income minus preferred dividends (income available to common shareholders) is divided by the weighted average number of common shares outstanding to arrive at earnings per share. To illustrate, assume that Lancer Inc. reports net income of $350,000 and declares and pays preferred dividends of $50,000 for the year. The weighted average number of common shares outstanding during the year is 100,000 shares. Earnings per share is $3.00, as calculated in Illustration 4-12.

$$\frac{\text{Net Income} - \text{Preferred Dividends}}{\text{Weighted Average Number of Common Shares Outstanding}}$$

$$= \text{Earnings per Share (EPS)}$$

$$= \frac{\$350,000 - 50,000}{100,000}$$

$$= \$3.00$$

Illustration 4-12

Sample Calculation of Earnings per Share

WILEY PLUS
Additional Disclosures

Note that the EPS figure measures the number of dollars earned by each common share but not the dollar amount paid to shareholders in the form of dividends.

"Net income per share" or "earnings per share" is a ratio that commonly appears in prospectuses, proxy material, and annual reports to shareholders. It is also highlighted in the financial press, by statistical services like Standard & Poor's, and by Bay Street securities analysts. Because of its importance, public companies are required to disclose earnings per share on the face of their income statement. In addition, a company that reports a discontinued operation must report earnings per share for income before discontinued operations as well as per share amounts for discontinued operations either on the face of the income statement or in the notes to the financial statements.[23] Illustration 4-3 shows how earnings per share may be presented.

Many corporations have simple capital structures that include only common shares. For these companies, a presentation such as earnings per common share is appropriate on the income statement. In many instances, however, companies' earnings per share are subject to dilution (reduction) in the future because existing contingencies allow future issues of additional common shares. These corporations would present both basic EPS and fully diluted EPS.[24]

In summary, the simplicity and availability of figures for per share earnings lead inevitably to their being used widely. Because of the excessive importance that the public—even the well-informed public—attaches to earnings per share, this information must be made as meaningful as possible. Note that this area is of lesser relevance to private entities as most have shares that are closely held. Therefore, private entity GAAP does not include guidance on presentation of EPS numbers.

Retained Earnings

Objective 9
Prepare a retained earnings statement.

Retained earnings is affected by many variables and can be presented in many different ways. Net income increases retained earnings and a net loss decreases retained earnings. Both cash and share dividends decrease retained earnings. Retroactively applied changes in accounting principles and corrections of errors may either increase or decrease retained earnings. Information on retained earnings, including the changes it has undergone, can be shown in different ways. For example, many companies prepare a separate retained earnings statement, as shown in Illustration 4-13.

Illustration 4-13

Retained Earnings Statement

Retained Earnings Statement For the Year Ended December 31, 2010		
Balance, January 1, as reported		$1,050,000
Correction for understatement of net income in prior period (inventory error) (net of taxes of $35,000)		50,000
Balance, January 1, as adjusted		1,100,000
Add: Net income		360,000
		1,460,000
Less: Cash dividends	$100,000	
Less: Stock dividends	200,000	300,000
Balance, December 31		$1,160,000

The reconciliation of the beginning to the ending balance in retained earnings provides information about why net assets increased or decreased during the year. The association of dividend distributions with net income for the period indicates what management is doing with earnings: it may be plowing part or all of the earnings back into the business, distributing all current income, or distributing current income plus the accumulated earnings of prior years. Note that the retained earnings statement may be combined with the income statement by adding it to the bottom of the income statement. Illustration 4-14 shows such a combined statement for **Technicoil Corporation.**

---

[23] IAS 33.68.

[24] Earnings per share will be covered in significant detail in Chapter 17.

CONSOLIDATED STATEMENTS OF OPERATIONS AND RETAINED EARNINGS

Years ended December 31, 2008 and 2007

(Thousands, except per share data)	**2008**	2007
Revenue	$ **62,279**	$ 41,155
Operating expenses	**43,659**	27,700
Gross margin	**18,620**	13,455
General and administrative expenses	**3,230**	2,788
Stock-based compensation	**17**	346
Depreciation and amortization	**9,288**	8,329
Gain on sale of assets	**—**	(931)
Impairment of goodwill	**7,391**	—
Interest on long-term debt	**1,166**	1,459
Other revenue	**(288)**	(38)
Net (loss) income before income tax	**(2,184)**	1,502
Income tax (recovery) expense: *(note 11)*		
Current	**(39)**	(1,457)
Future	**1,235**	414
	1,196	(1,043)
Net (loss) income and comprehensive (loss) income	**(3,380)**	2,545
Retained earnings and cumulative comprehensive income, beginning of year	**21,782**	19,237
Retained earnings and cumulative comprehensive income, end of year	$ **18,402**	$ 21,782
(Loss) earnings per share: *(note 10)*		
Basic	$ **(0.05)**	$ 0.04
Diluted	$ **(0.05)**	$ 0.04

See accompanying notes to consolidated financial statements.

Illustration 4-14

Combined Income and Retained Earnings Statement for Technicoil Corporation

Real-World Emphasis

Changes in Accounting Principle

Changes in accounting occur frequently in practice, because important events or conditions may be in dispute or uncertain at the statement date. One type of accounting change is when a different accounting principle is adopted to replace the one previously used. Changes in accounting principle would include, for example, a change in the method of inventory pricing from FIFO to average cost. Accounting changes are only allowed if they are required by a primary source of GAAP or if they result in reliable and more relevant information. Under private entity GAAP, there are some exceptions to this principle. For instance, where private entity GAAP allows a choice of accounting policies such as accounting for income taxes, significant influence investment, or development costs an accounting policy change may be made without having to prove that the new policy is more reliable and relevant. This is because, in principle, private entity GAAP is meant to be more flexible and adaptable.

Changes in accounting principle are generally recognized through **retrospective restatement**, which involves determining the effect of the policy change on the income of prior periods that are affected. The financial statements for all prior periods that are presented for comparative purposes should be restated except when the effect cannot be determined reasonably. If all comparative years are not disclosed, a cumulative amount would instead be calculated and adjusted through the opening retained earnings amount.

To illustrate, Gaubert Inc. decided in March 2010 to change from the FIFO method of valuing inventory to the weighted average method. If prices are rising, cost of sales would be higher and ending inventory lower for the preceding period.

Underlying Concept

Retrospective application ensures consistency.

Illustration 4-15 shows what should be presented in the 2010 financial statements.

Retained earnings, January 1, 2010, as previously reported	$120,000
Cumulative effect on prior years of retrospective application	
of new inventory costing method (net of $9,000 tax)	14,000
Adjusted balance of retained earnings, January 1, 2010	$106,000

The journal entry would be:

A   = L +   SE
−14,000   −14,000

Cash flows: No effect

Taxes Receivable	9,000	
Retained Earnings	14,000	
Inventory		23,000

The example in the illustration assumes that no comparative data for prior years are shown. A note describing the change and its impact would also be required.

Comprehensive Income

Objective 10

Prepare a statement of comprehensive income.

Additional Disclosures

Comprehensive income includes all changes in equity during a period except for the changes that result from investments by owners, distributions to owners, correction of errors, and adjustments to retained earnings due to retrospective application of changes in accounting policy. Comprehensive income therefore includes all revenues and gains and expenses and losses reported in net income, and, in addition, gains and losses that bypass net income but affect shareholders' equity. These items that bypass the income statement are recorded in an account called **Other Comprehensive Income**. Comprehensive income is equal to net income plus other comprehensive income.

An example of one of the items that is included in other comprehensive income is unrealized gains and losses on revaluation of property, plant, and equipment under the revaluation model.[25] Why are they excluded from net income? There is little theoretical justification for segregating items such as this from net income, and over time, the category other comprehensive income will likely disappear and comprehensive income will hopefully be equal to net income. The creation of this separate and distinct category outside of net income serves to transition GAAP to a more all-inclusive concept of net income.

The statement of comprehensive income[26] shall be presented either:

1. in a single combined statement including revenues, expenses, gains, losses, net income, other comprehensive income, and comprehensive income, or

2. in two separate statements showing the traditional income statement in one and a second statement beginning with net income and displaying the components of other comprehensive income, as well as comprehensive income.

---

[25] The revaluation model will be discussed in greater detail in Chapter 10. Other examples of other comprehensive income are certain translation gains and losses on foreign currency and unrealized gains and losses on certain investments. Other comprehensive income is sometimes reclassified to net income over time (known as recycling). This will be reviewed in subsequent chapters.

[26] IAS 1.81.

By providing information on the components of comprehensive income, the company communicates information about all changes in net assets. With this information, users will be better able to understand the quality of the company's earnings. This information should help users predict the amounts, timing, and uncertainty of future cash flows.

Earnings per share information related to comprehensive income is not required.

Note that a company is not required to use the terms "Other comprehensive income" or "Comprehensive income."

Combined Income and Comprehensive Income Statement

To illustrate these presentation formats, assume that V. Gill Inc. reports the following information for 2010: sales revenue $800,000; cost of goods sold $600,000; operating expenses $90,000; and an unrealized holding gain on equity securities (fair value with gains/losses through other comprehensive income) of $30,000, net of tax.

The combined income statement format is shown in Illustration 4-16 below. The relationship of the traditional income statement to the comprehensive income statement is apparent because net income is the starting point in the comprehensive income statement.

V. GILL INC.	
Statement of Income and Comprehensive Income	
For the Year Ended December 31, 2010	
Sales revenue	$800,000
Cost of goods sold	600,000
Gross profit	200,000
Operating expenses	90,000
Net income	110,000
Other comprehensive income	
Unrealized holding gain, net of tax	30,000
Comprehensive income	$140,000

Illustration 4-16

Combined Income and Comprehensive Income Statement

The combined statement has the advantage of not requiring the creation of a new financial statement. However, burying net income in a subtotal on the statement is a disadvantage.

Statement of Shareholders' Equity

The statement of shareholders' equity reports the changes in each shareholders' equity account and in total shareholders' equity during the year, including comprehensive income. The statement of shareholders' equity is often **prepared in columnar form** with columns for each account and for total shareholders' equity. This is a required statement under IFRS. Under private entity GAAP, the statement of retained earnings is required instead (accompanied by disclosures of changes in share capital and surplus accounts).

To illustrate the presentation of the statement of shareholders' equity, assume the same information for V. Gill Inc. and that the company had the following shareholders' equity account balances at the beginning of 2010: Common Shares $300,000; Retained Earnings $50,000; and Accumulated Other Comprehensive Income $60,000. No changes in the Common Shares account occurred during the year. A statement of shareholders' equity for V. Gill Inc. is shown in Illustration 4-17.

11 Objective
Prepare a statement of changes in shareholders' equity.

Illustration 4-17

Presentation of Comprehensive Income Items in Shareholders' Equity Statement

V. GILL INC.
Statement of Shareholders' Equity
For the Year Ended December 31, 2010

	Total	Common Shares	Comprehensive Income	Retained Earnings	Accumulated Other Comprehensive Income
Beginning balance	$410,000	$300,000		$ 50,000	$60,000
Net income	110,000		$110,000	110,000	
Other comprehensive income[27]	30,000		30,000		30,000
Comprehensive income			$140,000		
Ending balance	$550,000	$300,000		$160,000	$90,000

Note that other comprehensive income is accumulated in an account called Accumulated Other Comprehensive Income, as shown in Illustration 4-18. This account acts like a second Retained Earnings account. Amounts in Accumulated Other Comprehensive Income will either be recycled through net income when realized or may be transferred directly to retained earnings.

Balance Sheet Presentation

Regardless of the display format chosen, the **accumulated other comprehensive income** of $90,000 is reported in the shareholders' equity section of the balance sheet of V. Gill Inc., as shown in Illustration 4-18.

Illustration 4-18

Presentation of Accumulated Other Comprehensive Income in the Balance Sheet

V. GILL INC.
Balance Sheet as at December 31, 2010
(Shareholders' Equity Section)

Shareholders' equity	
Common shares	$300,000
Retained earnings	160,000
Accumulated other comprehensive income	90,000
Total shareholders' equity	$550,000

IFRS/PRIVATE ENTITY GAAP COMPARISON

A Comparison of IFRS and Private Entity GAAP

Objective 12

Identify differences in accounting between accounting standards for private enterprises (private entity GAAP) and IFRS.

Illustration 4-19 sets out the major differences between GAAP for private entities and international accounting standards for publicly accountable enterprises.

---

[27] Details of other comprehensive income may not be presented in the statement of changes in shareholders' equity. This detail must be shown only in the statement of comprehensive income.

	Accounting Standards for Private Enterprises (Private Entity GAAP)—*CICA Handbook*, Part II, Sections 1400, 1506, 1520, 1521, 3251, and 3475	IFRS—IAS 1 and 8, and IFRS 5
Required presentation on face of income statement	As noted earlier in the chapter, private entity GAAP mandates a list of required items that must be presented.	As noted earlier in the chapter, IFRS mandates a list of required items (which are different from private entity GAAP) that must be presented.
Guidance on how to classify expenses (nature vs. function)	There is no guidance on how to or when to present expenses according to their nature or function. Entities are free, however, to present their income statements in a manner that is most transparent as long as they adhere to the required disclosures noted above.	IFRS requires that the entity present an analysis of expenses based on either their nature or their function.
Discontinued operations	Held-for-sale assets and liabilities are classified as current or noncurrent depending on the nature of the assets/liabilities unless the assets have been sold prior to the completion of the financial statements. The definition of a discontinued operation component includes operating segments, reporting units, subsidiaries, asset groups and operations with no assets. Additional guidance is provided noting that the operations and cash flows must have been or will be eliminated and the enterprise must have no significant continuing involvement.	Held-for-sale assets and liabilities are reclassified as current assets/liabilities. The definition of a discontinued operation component includes major lines of business or geographical areas and businesses acquired with an intent to resell.
Extraordinary items	Not mentioned in private entity GAAP since it's not felt to be relevant.	IFRS prohibits the use of the term and classification.
Other comprehensive income/comprehensive income	Not used in private entity GAAP. Transactions are either booked through net income or directly to a separate component of shareholders' equity (e.g., certain foreign currency gains/losses).	IFRS requires certain items be classified as either comprehensive income or net income. In addition, entities must prepare a statement of comprehensive income.
Earnings per share	Not mentioned in private entity GAAP since many private entities have closely held shareholdings by definition.	Basic and diluted EPS must be presented in the statements.
Statement of changes in retained earnings vs. statement of changes in shareholders' equity	The statement of retained earnings is one of the core financial statements. There is no requirement to present a statement of shareholders' equity, although changes in shareholder equity accounts must be disclosed.	The statement of changes in shareholders' equity is a required statement.
Accounting changes	Certain accounting policy choice changes do not have to meet the "must be reliable and more relevant" test.	For all accounting policy changes, the new policy must be reliable and more relevant.

Illustration 4-19

IFRS and Accounting Standards for Private Enterprises (Private Entity GAAP) Comparison Chart

Analysis

Financial analysts assess quality of earnings and factor it into their decisions. They are often looking to see what additional information the income statements provide in terms of valuing the company's shares. When valuing the shares, analysts look at how good the numbers are at the financial statement date and then they determine whether the company can continue to produce similar or better earnings in the future.

Some attributes of high-quality earnings were expressed in Illustration 4-2. To assess the quality of earnings, look for and analyze the following:

- **accounting policies**—aggressive accounting policies, soft numbers

- **notes to financial statements**—unrecognized liabilities and asset overstatement and in general measurement uncertainty

- **financial statements** as a whole—complexity of presentation or language (which may obscure the company's performance or financial position)

- **income statement**—percentage of net income derived from ongoing operations, to see whether the company can produce profits mainly from its core business

- **cash flow statement**—cash from operating activities versus net income, to get a sense of whether net income is backed by cash or not

- **balance sheet**—to see how the company is financed and what the revenue-generating assets are

- **other**—environmental factors such as the industry and economy. How is the company doing compared with its competitors? How is it positioning itself to take advantage of opportunities and manage risk? Where is the industry going? Are current earnings likely to be repeated in the future?

Companies often try to help users assess the results of operations and their financial position by providing modified GAAP information such as non-GAAP earnings. Non-GAAP earnings start with GAAP net income and add back or deduct nonrecurring or non-operating items to arrive at an adjusted net income number. Non-GAAP earnings are not bad per se. If the calculation of the non-GAAP earnings is **clearly disclosed and explained**, and is also reconciled to net income, it hopefully adds value to the decision-making process. The danger with these numbers is that there are no standards to ensure that the calculation is **consistently** prepared and **comparable** between companies.

Looking Ahead

Objective 13

Identify the significant changes planned by the IASB regarding financial statement presentation.

The IASB has been working on its *Performance Reporting* project since September 2001. In October 2001, the FASB also began to work on a similar project. There was concern that the two projects were diverging in focus, and so, in April 2004, the IASB and FASB decided to work together to come up with a joint, converged standard. In March 2006, the name of the project was changed to *Financial Statement Presentation* and it now consists of three phases:

Phase A—What constitutes a complete set of financial statements

Phase B—Presentation of information on the face of the statements

Phase C—Interim financial reporting

Phase A is complete and embedded in IAS 1. Working principles for Phase B, which have been agreed upon, state that the financial statements should:

- provide a cohesive financial picture of an entity,
- provide information to help users assess the liquidity of an entity,
- separate the financing activities from other activities,
- provide information about the measurement of assets and liabilities, and
- disaggregate information and present subtotals and totals.

The following was taken from a presentation of the preliminary views document issued by the IASB. The chart illustrates how information might be presented on the various statements.

Proposed format for the presentation of financial statements

Statement of financial position	Statement of comprehensive income	Statement of cash flows
Business • Operating assets and liabilities • Investing assets and liabilities	Business • Operating income and expenses • Investing income and expenses	Business • Operating cash flows • Investing cash flows
Financing • Financing assets • Financing liabilities	Financing • Financing asset income • Financing liability expenses	Financing • Financing asset cash flows • Financing liability cash flows
Income taxes	Income taxes on continuing operations (business and financing)	Income taxes
Discontinued operations	Discontinued operations net of tax	Discontinued operations
	Other comprehensive income, net of tax	
Equity		Equity

The IASB plans to issue a standard by 2011.

Summary of Learning Objectives

Glossary

1 Identify the uses and limitations of an income statement.

The income statement provides investors and creditors with information that helps them predict the amounts, timing, and uncertainty of future cash flows. It also helps users determine the risk (level of uncertainty) of not achieving particular cash flows. The limitations of an income statement are that (1) the statement does not include many items that contribute to the general growth and well-being of an enterprise; (2) income numbers are often affected by the accounting methods that are used; (3)

KEY TERMS

all-inclusive approach, 168
business component, 169
capital maintenance
    approach, 168

income measures are often estimates; and (4) there are differing views on how to measure net income.

2   Prepare a single-step income statement.

In a single-step income statement, there are only two groupings: revenues and expenses. Expenses are deducted from revenues to arrive at net income or loss; i.e., only a single subtraction is made. Frequently, income tax is reported separately as the last item before net income to indicate its relationship to income before income tax.

3   Prepare a multiple-step income statement.

A multiple-step income statement shows two additional classifications: (1) a separation of operating results from the results obtained through the subordinate or non-operating activities of the company; and (2) a classification of expenses by functions, such as merchandising or manufacturing, selling, and administration, or by nature (such as salary expense, depreciation and other).

4   Understand the difference between classifying expenses according to their nature versus their function.

IFRS requires entities to provide information about either the nature or function of expenses. When information is presented using function, additional disclosures should be made regarding the breakdown of the nature of expenses as the latter has good cash flow predictive value. The entity should choose the method that best reflects the nature of the business and industry.

5   Explain how irregular items are reported.

Irregular gains or losses or nonrecurring items are generally closed to Income Summary and are included in the income statement. They are treated in the income statement as follows: (1) Discontinued operation of a business component is classified as a separate item, after continuing operations. (2) Other items that are material in amount, are unusual or nonrecurring, and are not considered extraordinary are separately disclosed and are included as part of continuing operations. Extraordinary items are not allowed under IFRS and not referred to under private entity GAAP.

6   Measure and report results of discontinued operations.

The gain or loss on disposal of a business component involves the sum of: (1) the income or loss from operations to the financial statement date, and (2) the gain or loss on the disposal of the business component. These items are reported net of tax among the irregular items in the income statement.

7   Explain intraperiod tax allocation.

The tax expense for the year should be related, where possible, to specific items on the income statement in order to give a more informative disclosure to statement users. This procedure is called intraperiod tax allocation; i.e., allocation within a period. Its main purpose is to relate the income tax expense for the fiscal period to the following items that affect the amount of the tax provisions: (1) income from continuing operations, (2) discontinued operations, and (3) other comprehensive income.

8   Explain where earnings per share information is reported.

Because of the dangers of focusing attention solely on earnings per share, the profession concluded that earnings per share must be disclosed on the face of the income statement. A company that reports a discontinued operation must report per share amounts for these line items either on the face of the income statement or in the notes to the financial statements. EPS information is not required to be presented under private entity GAAP.

9 Prepare a retained earnings statement.

The retained earnings statement should disclose net income (loss), dividends, prior period adjustments, and transfers to and from retained earnings (appropriations). This statement is required under private entity GAAP.

10 Prepare a statement of comprehensive income.

Comprehensive income may be presented by expanding the income statement or by adding another separate statement. The concept of other comprehensive income is not relevant under private entity GAAP.

11 Prepare a statement of changes in shareholders' equity.

The statement of shareholders' equity is a required statement under IFRS and takes the place of the statement of changes in retained earnings. It shows all changes in all equity accounts including accumulated other comprehensive income.

12 Identify differences in accounting between accounting standards for private enterprises (private entity GAAP) and IFRS.

The chart on page 181 outlines the major differences.

13 Identify the significant changes planned by the IASB regarding financial statement presentation.

The IASB is planning to change the way financial statements are presented, with a new standard being issued by 2011. The major statements, including balance sheet, income statement, and statement of cash flows, will be classified according to business and financing activities.

Appendix 4A

Cash Basis versus Accrual Basis Earnings

Differences between Cash and Accrual Bases

Objective 14

Explain the differences between the cash basis of accounting and the accrual basis of accounting.

Most companies use the accrual basis of accounting: they recognize revenue when it is earned and recognize expenses in the period when they are incurred, which means that the time when cash is received or paid is not a factor in recognizing the transaction. Some small enterprises and the average individual taxpayer, however, use a strict or modified cash basis approach. Under the strict cash basis, revenue is recorded only when the cash is received and expenses are recorded only when the cash is paid. On the cash basis, income is determined based on the actual collection of revenues and payment of expenses, and the revenue recognition and matching principles are ignored. Consequently, cash basis financial statements do not conform with generally accepted accounting principles.

To illustrate and contrast accrual basis accounting and cash basis accounting, assume that Quality Contractor signs an agreement to build a garage for $22,000. In January, Quality Contractor begins construction, incurs costs of $18,000 on credit, and by the end of January delivers a finished garage to the buyer. In February, Quality Contractor collects $22,000 cash from the customer. In March, Quality pays the $18,000 that is owed to the creditors. Illustrations 4A-1 and 4A-2 show the net income for each month under cash basis accounting and accrual basis accounting.

Illustration 4A-1

Income Statement—
Cash Basis

QUALITY CONTRACTOR
Income Statement Cash Basis
For the Month of

	January	February	March	Total
Cash receipts	$-0-	$22,000	$ -0-	$22,000
Cash payments	-0-	-0-	18,000	18,000
Net income (loss)	$-0-	$22,000	$(18,000)	$ 4,000

Illustration 4A-2

Income Statement—
Accrual Basis

QUALITY CONTRACTOR
Income Statement Accrual Basis
For the Month of

	January	February	March	Total
Revenues	$22,000	$-0-	$-0-	$22,000
Expenses	18,000	-0-	-0-	18,000
Net income (loss)	$ 4,000	$-0-	$-0-	$ 4,000

For the three months combined, total net income is the same under both cash basis accounting and accrual basis accounting; the difference is in the timing of net income. The balance sheet is also affected by the basis of accounting. For instance, if cash basis accounting were used, Quality Contractor's balance sheets at each month end would appear as in Illustration 4A-3.

QUALITY CONTRACTOR
Balance Sheets Cash Basis
As at

	Jan. 31	Feb. 28	Mar. 31
Assets			
Cash	$-0-	$22,000	$4,000
Total assets	$-0-	$22,000	$4,000
Liabilities and Owners' Equity			
Owners' equity	$-0-	$22,000	$4,000
Total liabilities and owners' equity	$-0-	$22,000	$4,000

Illustration 4A-3

Balance Sheets—Cash Basis

Illustration 4A-4 shows what Quality Contractor's balance sheets at each month end would look like if accrual basis accounting were used.

QUALITY CONTRACTOR
Balance Sheets Accrual Basis
As at

	Jan. 31	Feb. 28	Mar. 31
Assets			
Cash	$ -0-	$22,000	$4,000
Accounts receivable	22,000	-0-	-0-
Total assets	$22,000	$22,000	$4,000
Liabilities and Owners' Equity			
Accounts payable	$18,000	$18,000	$ 0
Owners' equity	4,000	4,000	4,000
Total liabilities and owners' equity	$22,000	$22,000	$4,000

Illustration 4A-4

Balance Sheets— Accrual Basis

An analysis of the preceding income statements and balance sheets shows the following ways in which cash basis accounting is inconsistent with basic accounting theory:

1. The cash basis understates revenues and assets from the construction and delivery of the garage in January. It ignores the $22,000 of accounts receivable, which is a near-term future cash inflow.

2. The cash basis understates the expenses incurred with the construction of the garage and the liability outstanding at the end of January. It ignores the $18,000 of accounts payable, which is a near-term future cash outflow.

3. The cash basis understates owners' equity in January by not recognizing the revenues and the asset until February, and it overstates owners' equity in February by not recognizing the expenses and liability until March.

In short, cash basis accounting violates the theory underlying the elements of financial statements.

The **modified cash basis**, a mixture of cash basis and accrual basis, is the method often followed by professional services firms (doctors, lawyers, accountants, consultants) and by retail, real estate, and agricultural operations. It is the pure cash basis of accounting with modifications that have substantial support, such as capitalizing and amortizing plant assets or recording inventory.[28]

Conversion from Cash Basis to Accrual Basis

Fairly often, a cash basis or a modified cash basis set of financial statements needs to be converted to the accrual basis so it can be presented to investors and creditors. To illustrate this conversion, assume that Dr. Diane Windsor keeps her accounting records on a cash basis. In the year 2010, Dr. Windsor received $300,000 from her dental patients and paid $170,000 for operating expenses, resulting in an excess of cash receipts over disbursements of $130,000 ($300,000 − $170,000). At January 1 and December 31, 2010, she has the accounts receivable, unearned service revenue, accrued liabilities, and prepaid expenses shown in Illustration 4A-5.

Illustration 4A-5

Excerpt from General Ledger

	Jan. 1, 2010	Dec. 31, 2010
Accounts receivable	$12,000	$9,000
Unearned service revenue	–0–	4,000
Accrued liabilities	2,000	5,500
Prepaid expenses	1,800	2,700

Service Revenue Calculation

To convert the amount of cash received from patients to service revenue on an accrual basis, changes in accounts receivable and unearned service revenue during the year must be considered. Accounts receivable at the beginning of the year represent revenues earned last year that are collected this year. Ending accounts receivable indicate revenues earned this year that are not yet collected. Therefore, beginning accounts receivable are subtracted and ending accounts receivable added to arrive at revenue on an accrual basis, as shown in Illustration 4A-6.

Illustration 4A-6

Conversion of Cash Receipts to Revenue— Accounts Receivable

Cash receipts from customers	(− Beginning accounts receivable) (+ Ending accounts receivable)	=	Revenue on an accrual basis

Using similar analysis, beginning unearned service revenue represents cash received last year for revenues earned this year. Ending unearned service revenue results from collections this year that will be recognized as revenue next year. Therefore, beginning unearned service revenue is added and ending unearned service revenue is subtracted to arrive at revenue on an accrual basis, as shown in Illustration 4A-7.

---

[28] A cash or modified cash basis might be used in the following situations:

1. A company that is primarily interested in cash flows (for example, a group of physicians that distributes cash-basis earnings for salaries and bonuses)

2. A company that has a limited number of financial statement users (a small, closely held company with little or no debt)

3. A company that has operations that are relatively straightforward (small amounts of inventory, long-term assets, or long-term debt)

Cash receipts from customers	(+ Beginning unearned service revenue) (− Ending unearned service revenue)	= Revenue on an accrual basis

Illustration 4A-7

Conversion of Cash Receipts to Revenue—Unearned Service Revenue

Cash collected from customers, therefore, is converted to service revenue on an accrual basis, as Illustration 4A-8 shows.

Cash receipts from customers		$300,000
Beginning accounts receivable	$(12,000)	
Ending accounts receivable	9,000	
Beginning unearned service revenue	–0–	
Ending unearned service revenue	(4,000)	(7,000)
Service revenue (accrual)		$293,000

Illustration 4A-8

Conversion of Cash Receipts to Service Revenue

Operating Expense Calculation

To convert cash paid for operating expenses during the year to operating expenses on an accrual basis, you must consider changes in prepaid expenses and accrued liabilities during the year. Beginning prepaid expenses should be recognized as expenses this year. (The cash payment occurred last year.) Therefore, the beginning prepaid expenses balance is added to cash paid for operating expenses to arrive at operating expense on an accrual basis.

Conversely, ending prepaid expenses result from cash payments made this year for expenses to be reported next year. (The expense recognition is deferred to a future period.) As a result, ending prepaid expenses are deducted from cash paid for expenses, as shown in Illustration 4A-9.

Cash paid for operating expenses	(+ Beginning prepaid expenses) (− Ending prepaid expenses)	= Expenses on an accrual basis

Illustration 4A-9

Conversion of Cash Payments to Expenses— Prepaid Expenses

Using similar analysis, beginning accrued liabilities result from expenses recognized last year that require cash payments this year. Ending accrued liabilities relate to expenses recognized this year that have not been paid. Beginning accrued liabilities, therefore, are deducted and ending accrued liabilities are added to cash paid for expenses to arrive at expenses on an accrual basis, as shown in Illustration 4A-10.

Cash paid for operating expenses	(− Beginning accrued liabilities) (+ Ending accrued liabilities)	= Expenses on an accrual basis

Illustration 4A-10

Conversion of Cash Payments to Expenses— Accrued Liabilities

For Dr. Diane Windsor, therefore, cash paid for operating expenses is converted to operating expenses on an accrual basis as in Illustration 4A-11.

Cash paid for operating expenses		$170,000
Beginning prepaid expense	$ 1,800	
Ending prepaid expense	(2,700)	
Beginning accrued liabilities	(2,000)	
Ending accrued liabilities	5,500	2,600
Operating expenses (accrual)		$172,600

Illustration 4A-11

Conversion of Cash Paid to Operating Expenses

Illustration 4A-12 shows how this entire conversion can be presented in a work sheet.

Illustration 4A-12

Conversion of Statement
of Cash Receipts
and Disbursements to
Income Statement

DIANE WINDSOR, D.D.S.
Conversion of Income Statement Data from Cash Basis to Accrual Basis
For the Year 2010

	Cash Basis	Adjustments Add	Adjustments Deduct	Accrual Basis
Collections from customers	$300,000			
− Accounts receivable, Jan. 1			$12,000	
+ Accounts receivable, Dec. 31		$9,000		
+ Unearned service revenue, Jan. 1		—	—	
− Unearned service revenue, Dec. 31			4,000	
Service revenue				$293,000
Disbursement for expenses				
+ Prepaid expenses, Jan. 1		1,800		
− Prepaid expenses, Dec. 31			2,700	
− Accrued liabilities, Jan. 1			2,000	
+ Accrued liabilities, Dec. 31	170,000	5,500		
Operating expenses				172,600
Excess of cash collections over disbursements—cash basis	$130,000			
Net income—accrual basis				$120,400

Using this approach, collections and disbursements on a cash basis are adjusted to revenue and expenses on an accrual basis to arrive at accrued net income. In any conversion from the cash basis to the accrual basis, depreciation or amortization expense is an expense in arriving at net income on an accrual basis.

Theoretical Weaknesses of the Cash Basis

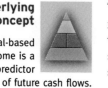

Underlying Concept

Accrual-based net income is a good predictor of future cash flows.

The cash basis does report exactly when cash is received and when cash is disbursed. To many people, that information represents something solid, something concrete. Isn't cash what it's all about? Does it make sense to invent something, design it, produce it, market and sell it, if you aren't going to get cash for it in the end? If so, then what is the merit of accrual accounting?

Today's economy is based more on credit than cash. And the accrual basis, not the cash basis, recognizes all aspects of credit. Investors, creditors, and other decision-makers seek timely information about an enterprise's future cash flows. Accrual basis accounting provides this information by reporting the cash inflows and outflows associated with earnings activities as soon as these cash flows can be estimated with an acceptable degree of certainty. Receivables and payables are forecasters of future cash inflows and outflows. In other words, accrual basis accounting aids in predicting future cash flows by reporting transactions and other events with cash consequences at the time the transactions and events occur, rather than when the cash is received and paid.

Summary of Learning Objective for Appendix 4A

WILEY
PLUS
Glossary

14 Explain the differences between the cash basis of accounting and the accrual basis of accounting.

KEY TERMS

accrual basis, 186
modified cash basis, 188
strict cash basis, 186

Accrual basis accounting provides information about cash inflows and outflows associated with earnings activities as soon as these cash flows can be estimated with an acceptable degree of certainty. That is, accrual basis accounting aids in predicting future cash flows by reporting transactions and events with cash consequences at the time the transactions and events occur, rather than when the cash is received and paid. The cash basis focuses on when the cash is received or dispersed, and therefore it is not the best predictor of future cash flows if the company has irregular cash flow patterns.

Note: All assignment material with an asterisk (*) relates to the appendix to the chapter.

Brief Exercises

BE4-1 Mega Inc. had sales revenue of $1.1 million in 2010. Other items recorded during the year were: **(LO 2)**

Cost of goods sold	$450,000
Wage expense	270,000
Income tax expense	115,000
Increase in value of company reputation	35,000
Other operating expenses	20,000
Unrealized gain on value of patents	60,000

Prepare a single-step income statement for Mega for 2010. Mega has 100,000 common shares outstanding. Include EPS calculation.

BE4-2 Taylor Corporation had net sales of $2,780,000 and investment revenue of $103,000 in 2010. Its 2010 expenses **(LO 2, 4)**
were as follows

Change in inventories	$ 380,000
Materials consumed	1,810,000
Cost of sales	2,190,000
Wages	175,000
Advertising and promotion	60,000
Entertainment	37,000
Selling expenses	272,000
Wages	142,000
Rent	48,000
Utilities	21,000
Administrative expenses	211,000
Interest expense	76,000
Income tax expense	40,000

Taylor has 10,000 common shares outstanding.

Prepare a single-step income statement showing operating expenses by nature. Include EPS calculation.

4)   **BE4-3**   Use the information in BE4-2 for Taylor Corporation to prepare a multiple-step income statement showing operating expenses by function.

(LO 6)   **BE4-4**   The Blue Collar Corporation had income from continuing operations of $12.6 million in 2010. During 2010, it disposed of its restaurant division at an after-tax loss of $89,000. Before the disposal, the division operated at a loss of $315,000 (net of tax) in 2010. Blue Collar had 10 million common shares outstanding during 2010. Prepare a partial income statement for Blue Collar beginning with income from continuing operations. Include EPS calculation.

(LO 5)   **BE4-5** The Big and Rich Corporation had income from operations before tax for 2010 of $7.3 million. In addition, it suffered an unusual and infrequent loss of $1,770,000 from a tornado. Of this amount, $500,000 was insured. In addition, the company realized a loss from the sale of a building amounting to $250,000. The corporation's tax rate is 30%. Prepare a partial income statement for Big and Rich beginning with income from operations. The corporation had 5 million common shares outstanding during 2010. Include EPS calculation.

(LO 5)   **BE4-6** Billy's Burgers (BB) is a franchisor that operates several corporate-owned restaurants as well as several franchised restaurants. The franchisees pay 3% of their sales revenues to BB in return for advertising and support. During the year, BB sold its corporate-owned stores to a franchisee. BB continues to monitor quality control in its franchised operations and franchisees must buy all products from it. Would the sale qualify for discontinued operations treatment under IFRS?

(LO 11)   **BE4-7** Your Pal Postcard Company Limited reports the following for 2010: sales revenues $900,000; cost of sales $750,000; operating expenses $100,000; and an unrealized holding loss on securities previously designated through Other Comprehensive Income for 2010 of $60,000. The company has January 1, 2010, balances in common shares of $600,000; accumulated other comprehensive income of $250,000; and retained earnings of $900,000. It issued no shares during 2010. On December 15, 2010, the board of directors declared a $300,000 dividend payable January 31, 2011. Prepare a statement of changes in equity. Ignore income taxes.

(LO 8)   **BE4-8**   Turner Limited had 40,000 common shares on January 1, 2010. On April 1, 8,000 shares were repurchased. On August 31, 12,000 shares were issued. Calculate the number of shares at December 31, 2010, and the weighted average number of shares for 2010.

(LO 8)   **BE4-9**   In 2010, I & T Corporation reported net income of $1.6 million. It declared and paid preferred share dividends of $400,000. During 2010, I & T had a weighted average of 120,000 common shares outstanding. Calculate I & T's 2010 earnings per share.

(LO 9)   **BE4-10**   Global Corporation has elected to adopt private entity GAAP in Canada. At January 1, 2010, the company had retained earnings of $529,000. Net income in 2010 was $1,646,000 and cash dividends of $660,000 were declared and paid. Prepare a 2010 retained earnings statement for Global Corporation.

(LO 9)   **BE4-11**   Use the information in BE4-10 to prepare a retained earnings statement for Global Corporation, assuming that in 2010 Global discovered that it had overstated 2007 depreciation by $25,000 (net of tax).

(LO 11)   **BE4-12**   On January 1, 2010, Rocket Corp. had cash and common shares of $60,000. At that date, the company had no other asset, liability, or equity balances. On January 2, 2010, it purchased for cash $40,000 of equity securities that it designated in such a way as to have gains and losses recorded in OCI until derecognition. It received non-taxable cash dividends of $18,000 during the year on these securities. In addition, it has an unrealized holding gain on these securities of $25,000 net of tax. Determine the following amounts for 2010: (a) net income; (b) comprehensive income; (c) other comprehensive income; and (d) accumulated other comprehensive income (end of 2010).

(LO 14)   ***BE4-13**   Renato Corp. had cash receipts from customers in 2010 of $152,000. Cash payments for operating expenses were $97,000. Renato has determined that at January 1, accounts receivable were $13,000 and prepaid expenses were $17,500. At December 31, accounts receivable were $18,600 and prepaid expenses were $23,200. Calculate (a) the service revenue and (b) the operating expenses.

Exercises

E4-1   (Calculation of Net Income) The following are all changes in the account balances of Brad Company Ltd. dur- **(LO 1)**
ing the current year, except for Retained Earnings:

	Increase (Decrease)		Increase (Decrease)
Cash	$ 90,000	Accounts payable	$ (76,000)
Accounts receivable (net)	70,000	Unearned revenue	22,000
Inventory	167,000	Bonds payable	82,000
Investments in trading securities	(27,000)	Common shares	125,000
		Contributed surplus	75,000

Instructions

Calculate the net income for the current year, assuming that there were no entries in the Retained Earnings account except for net income and a dividend declaration of $19,000, which was paid in the current year.

E4-2   (Calculation of Net Income) Selected information follows for Videohound Video Company during 2010: **(LO 1)**

Cash balance, January 1	$ 23,000
Accounts receivable, January 1	19,000
Collections from customers during year	200,000
Capital account balance, January 1	38,000
Total assets, January 1	75,000
Cash investment added, July 1	5,000
Total assets, December 31	101,000
Cash balance, December 31	20,000
Accounts receivable, December 31	36,000
Merchandise taken for personal use	11,000
Total liabilities, December 31	41,000

Instructions

Calculate the net income for 2010.

E4-3   (Income Statement Items) Certain account balances follow for Vincenti Products Corp.: **(LO 1)**

Rental revenue	$ 8,500	Sales discounts	$ 17,800
Interest expense	2,700	Selling expenses	79,400
Beginning retained earnings	114,400	Sales	490,000
Ending retained earnings	74,000	Income tax	31,000
Dividends earned	91,000	Cost of goods sold	384,400
Sales returns	22,400	Administrative expenses	82,500

Instructions

Based on the balances, calculate the following:

(a) total net revenue,

(b) net income or loss, and

(c) dividends declared during the current year.

E4-4   (Single-Step Income Statement) The financial records of Geneva Inc. were destroyed by fire at the end of **(LO 2)**
2010. Fortunately, the controller had kept the following statistical data related to the income statement:

1. The beginning merchandise inventory was $84,000 and it decreased by 20% during the current year.

2. Sales discounts amounted to $15,000.

3. There were 15,000 common shares outstanding for the entire year.

4. Interest expense was $20,000.

5. The income tax rate was 35%.

6. Cost of goods sold amounted to $420,000.

7. Administrative expenses were 20% of cost of goods sold but only 4% of gross sales.

8. Selling expenses were four-fifths of cost of goods sold.

Instructions

Based on the available data, prepare a single-step income statement for the year 2010 including EPS.

(LO 2, 3, 4) E4-5 **(Multiple-Step and Single-Step)** Two accountants, Yuan Tsui and Sergio Aragon, are arguing about the merits of presenting an income statement in a multiple-step versus a single-step format and operating expense disclosure in the nature or function of expense format. The discussion involves the following 2010 information for Singh Corp. (in thousands):

Administrative expense	
Officers' salaries	$ 3,900
Amortization of office furniture and equipment	3,560
Rent	16,200
Cost of goods sold	58,570
Goods purchased and sold	32,860
Change in inventory	25,710
Rental revenue	15,230
Selling expense	
Transportation-out	2,290
Sales commissions and wages	67,280
Amortization of sales equipment	6,480
Advertising and promotion	42,500
Sales	306,500
Income tax	9,070
Interest expense on bonds payable	1,860

Common shares outstanding for 2010 total 30,550,000.

Instructions

(a) Prepare an income statement for the year 2010 using the multiple-step form with expenses disclosed by function. Include EPS calculation.

(b) Prepare an income statement for the year 2010 using the single-step form with expenses disclosed by nature. Include EPS calculation.

(c) Which format do you prefer? Explain why.

(LO 2, 3, E4-6 **(Multiple-Step and Single-Step—Periodic Inventory Method)** Income statement information for Flett Tire
5, 12) Repair Corporation for the year 2010 follows:

Administrative expenses:		Transportation-in	$ 14,000
Officers' salaries	$ 39,000	Purchase discounts	10,000
Amortization expense—building	28,500	Dividend revenue	20,000
Office supplies expense	9,500	Inventory (beginning)	120,000
Inventory (ending)	137,000	Sales returns and allowances	15,000
Flood damage	50,000	Selling expenses:	
Gain on the sale of equipment	5,500	Sales salaries	71,000
Purchases	600,000	Depreciation expense—store equipment	18,000
Sales	930,000	Store supplies expense	9,000
Interest expense	9,000		

The total effective tax rate on all income is 34%. The company has elected to adopt private entity GAAP.

Instructions

(a) Prepare a multiple-step income statement for 2010.

(b) Prepare a single-step income statement for 2010.

(c) Discuss the merits of the two income statements, compared with each other.

E4-7 **(Combined Single-Step)** The following information was taken from the records of Presley Inc. for the year **(LO 2, 5, 12)** 2010:

Gain from expropriation	$ 95,000
Loss on discontinuance of Ace Division	75,000
Administrative expenses	240,000
Rent revenue	40,000
Loss from flood	60,000
Cash dividends declared	70,000
Retained earnings, January 1, 2010	600,000
Cost of goods sold	850,000
Selling expenses	300,000
Sales	1,900,000

The following additional information was also available: income tax applicable to income from continuing operations, $187,000; income tax applicable to loss on discontinuance of Ace Division, $25,000.

The company has elected to adopt private entity GAAP.

Instructions

(a) Prepare a single-step income statement for 2010.

(b) Prepare a combined single-step income and retained earnings statement.

E4-8 **(Multiple-Step and Unusual Items)** The following balances were taken from the books of the Big Track **(LO 3, 5)** Trucking Company Limited on December 31, 2010:

Interest revenue	$ 86,000	Accumulated depreciation—equipment	$ 40,000
Cash	51,000	Accumulated depreciation—building	28,000
Sales	1,380,000	Notes receivable	155,000
Accounts receivable	150,000	Selling expenses	194,000
Prepaid insurance	20,000	Accounts payable	170,000
Sales returns and allowances	150,000	Bonds payable	100,000
Allowance for doubtful accounts	7,000	Administrative and general expenses	97,000
Sales discounts	45,000	Accrued liabilities	32,000
Land	100,000	Interest expense	60,000
Equipment	200,000	Notes payable	100,000
Building	140,000	Loss from storm damage	150,000
Cost of goods sold	621,000	Depreciation expense	60,000

Assume the total effective tax rate on all items is 44%.

Instructions

Prepare a multiple-step income statement disclosing operating expenses by function, assuming 200,000 common shares were outstanding during the year. Include EPS calculation.

E4-9 **(Condensed Income Statement—Periodic Inventory Method)** The following are selected ledger accounts of **(LO 3, 4)** Holland Rose Corporation at December 31, 2010:

Cash	$ 185,000	Travel and entertainment	$ 69,000
Merchandise inventory (as of Jan. 1, 2010)	535,000	Accounting and legal services	33,000
Sales	4,275,000	Insurance expense	24,000
Advances from customers	117,000	Advertising	54,000
Purchases	2,786,000	Transportation-out	93,000
Sales discounts	34,000	Depreciation of office equipment	48,000
Purchase discounts	27,000	Depreciation of sales equipment	36,000
Sales salaries	284,000	Telephone sales	17,000
Office salaries	346,000	Utilities—office	32,000
Purchase returns	15,000	Miscellaneous office expenses	8,000
Sales returns	79,000	Rental revenue	240,000
Transportation-in	72,000	Loss on disposal of equipment	70,000
Accounts receivable	142,500	Interest expense	176,000
Sales commissions	83,000	Common shares	900,000

Holland's effective tax rate on all items is 34%. A physical inventory indicates that the ending inventory is $686,000. The number of common shares outstanding is 90,000.

Instructions

Prepare a multi-step 2010 income statement for Holland Rose Corporation, disclosing expenses by function. Include EPS calculation.

(LO 3, 4, 10)   **E4-10   (Multiple-Step Statement, Statement of Comprehensive Income, and Statement of Changes in Owners' Equity)** The following is information for Gottlieb Corp. for the year 2010:

Net sales	$1,300,000	Writeoff of inventory due to obsolescence	$ 80,000
Unrealized loss on investments		Loss on sale of equipment	35,000
designated through OCI	42,000	Amortization expense omitted by accident	
Cost of goods sold	780,000	in 2008	55,000
Selling expenses	65,000	Loss due to expropriation of land	60,000
Administrative expenses	48,000	Dividends declared	45,000
Dividend revenue	20,000	Retained earnings at December 31, 2009	980,000
Interest revenue	7,000		

The effective tax rate is 44% on all items.

Instructions

(a) Prepare a multiple-step statement of comprehensive income for 2010.

(b) Prepare the retained earnings section of the statement of changes in equity for 2010.

(c) Prepare the journal entry to record the amortization expense omitted by accident in 2008. Ignore IFRS EPS requirements.

(LO 6)   **E4-11   (Discontinued Operations)** Assume that PAC Inc. decides to sell SBTV, a reported segment of its operations, on September 30, 2010. There is a formal plan to dispose of the subsidiary and the sale qualifies for discontinued operations treatment. Pertinent data on the operations of the TV subsidiary are as follows: loss from operations from beginning of year to September 30, $1,900,000 (net of tax); loss from operations from September 30 to end of 2010, $700,000 (net of tax); estimated loss on sale of net assets to December 31, 2010 (net of tax), $150,000. The year end is December 31.

Instructions

(a) What is the net income/loss from discontinued operations reported in 2010?

(b) Prepare the discontinued operations section of the income statement for the year ended 2010.

(c) If the amount reported in 2010 as a gain or loss from disposal of the subsidiary by PAC Inc. becomes materially incorrect, when and how is the correction reported, if at all?

(LO 6)   **E4-12   (Discontinued Operations)** On October 5, 2010, Diamond in the Rough Recruiting Group Inc.'s board of directors decided to dispose of the Blue Division. A formal plan was approved. Diamond derives approximately 75% of its income from its human resources management practice. The Blue operating segment gets contracts to perform human resources management on an outsourced basis. The board decided to dispose of the division because of unfavourable operating results.

Net income for Diamond was $91,000 for the fiscal year ended December 31, 2010 (after a charge for taxes at 30% and after a writedown for the Blue assets). Income from operations of the Blue Division accounted for $4,200 (after tax) of this amount.

Because of the unfavourable results and the extreme competition, the board believes that it cannot sell the business intact. Its final decision is to auction off the office equipment. The equipment is the division's only asset and has a carrying value of $25,000 at October 5, 2010. The board believes that proceeds from the sale will be approximately $5,000 after the auction expenses. Currently, the estimated fair value of the equipment is $10,000. The Blue Division qualifies for treatment as a discontinued operation.

Instructions

(a) Prepare a partial income statement for Diamond in the Rough Recruiting Group and the appropriate footnote that relates to the Blue Division for 2010. The income statement should begin with income from continuing operations before income taxes. Earnings per share calculations are not required as Diamond follows private entity GAAP.

(b) Explain how the assets would be valued and presented on the balance sheet.

E4-13   (Earnings per Share) The shareholders' equity section of Emerson Corporation as at December 31, 2010,   **(LO 6, 8)** follows:

8% cumulative preferred shares, 100,000 shares authorized,	
80,000 shares outstanding	$ 4,500,000
Common shares, 10 million shares authorized and issued	10,000,000
Contributed surplus	10,500,000
	25,000,000
Retained earnings	177,000,000
	$202,000,000

Net income of $43 million for 2010 reflects a total effective tax rate of 44%. Included in the net income figure is a loss of $15 million (before tax) relating to the operations of a business segment that is to be discontinued.

Instructions

Calculate earnings per share data as they should appear on the financial statements of Emerson Corporation.

E4-14   (Earnings per Share) At December 31, 2010, Tres Hombres Corporation had the following shares outstanding: **(LO 8)**

10% cumulative preferred shares, 107,500 shares outstanding	$10,750,000
Common shares, 4,000,000 shares outstanding	20,000,000

During 2010, the corporation's only share transaction was the issuance of 400,000 common shares on April 1. During 2010, the following also occurred:

Income from continuing operations before taxes	$23,650,000
Discontinued operations (loss before taxes)	3,225,000
Preferred dividends declared	1,075,000
Common dividends declared	2,200,000
Effective tax rate	35%

Instructions

Calculate earnings per share data as they should appear in the 2010 income statement of Tres Hombres Corporation.

E4-15   (Retained Earnings Statement) The Holiday Corporation, a private company, began operations on January 1,   **(LO 9)** 2008. During its first three years of operations, Holiday reported net income and declared dividends as follows:

	Net income	Dividends declared
2008	$ 55,000	$ –0–
2009	135,000	30,000
2010	160,000	50,000

The following information is for 2011:

Income before income tax	$340,000
Prior period adjustment: understatement of 2008 amortization expense (before taxes)	57,000
Cumulative increase in prior year's income from change in inventory methods (before taxes)	37,000
Dividends declared (of this amount, $25,000 will be paid on January 15, 2012)	100,000
Effective tax rate	39%

Instructions

Prepare a 2011 statement of retained earnings for Holiday Corporation.

E4-16   (Comprehensive Income) Reach Out Card Company Limited Corporation reported the following for 2010:   **(LO 10)** net sales $1,200,000; cost of sales $750,000; selling and administrative expenses $320,000; gain from the disposal of property $250,000; and unrealized holding gains on investments designated as gains/losses through other comprehensive income $18,000.

Instructions

Prepare a statement of comprehensive income. Ignore taxes and EPS.

(LO 11) E4-17   **(Comprehensive Income)** Rainy Day Umbrella Corporation had the following balances at December 31, 2009 (all amounts in thousands): preferred shares $2,006; common shares $5,291; contributed surplus $2,225; retained earnings $13,692; and accumulated other comprehensive income $1,526.

During the year ended December 31, 2010, the company earned net income of $4,352,000, generated an unrealized holding loss on investments designated through Other Comprehensive Income of $348,000, sold common shares of $170,000, and paid out dividends of $23,000 and $7,000 to preferred and common shareholders, respectively.

Instructions

Prepare a statement of changes in equity for the year ended December 31, 2010, as well as the shareholders' equity section of the Rainy Day Umbrella Corporation balance sheet at December 31, 2010.

(LO 14) *E4-18   **(Cash and Accrual Basis)** Portmann Corp. maintains its financial records on the cash basis of accounting. As it would like to secure a long-term loan from its regular bank, the company asks you, as an independent CA, to convert its cash basis income statement data to the accrual basis. You are provided with the following summarized data for 2008, 2009, and 2010:

	2008	2009	2010
Cash receipts from sales:			
On 2008 sales	$320,000	$160,000	$ 30,000
On 2009 sales	–0–	355,000	90,000
On 2010 sales	–0–	–0–	408,000
Cash payments for expenses:			
On 2008 expenses	185,000	67,000	25,000
On 2009 expenses	40,000[a]	135,000	55,000
On 2010 expenses	–0–	45,000[b]	218,000

[a]Prepayments of 2009 expense
[b]Prepayments of 2010 expense

Instructions

Using the data above, prepare abbreviated income statements for the years 2008 and 2009 on:

(a) the cash basis

(b) the accrual basis

Problems

P4-1   Information for 2010 follows for Rolling Thunder Corp.:

Retained earnings balance, January 1, 2010	$ 1,980,000
Sales for the year	36,500,000
Cost of goods sold	28,500,000
Interest revenue	170,000
Selling and administrative expenses	4,700,000
Unrealized loss on investments designated through OCI	320,000
Impairment of goodwill (not tax deductible)	520,000
Income taxes for 2010	768,000
Assessment for additional 2008 income taxes (normal, recurring)	500,000
Gain on sale of investments (normal, recurring)	110,000
Loss due to flood damage	390,000
Loss on disposition of assets of discontinued operation (net of tax of $188,571)	440,000
Operating loss for wholesale division (net of tax of $38,571)	90,000
Dividends declared on common shares	250,000
Dividends declared on preferred shares	70,000

Instructions

Prepare a multiple-step comprehensive income statement disclosing expenses by function. Rolling Thunder decided to discontinue its entire wholesale operations and to keep its manufacturing operations. On September 15, it sold the wholesale operations to Dylane Corp. During 2010, there were 800,000 common shares outstanding all year. Include EPS calculation.

P4-2 The trial balance follows for McLean Corporation at December 31, 2010:

MCLEAN CORPORATION
Trial Balance
Year Ended December 31, 2010

	Debits	Credits
Purchase discounts		$ 10,000
Cash	$ 205,100	
Accounts receivable	105,000	
Rent revenue		18,000
Retained earnings		260,000
Salaries payable		18,000
Sales		1,400,000
Notes receivable	110,000	
Accounts payable		49,000
Accumulated depreciation—equipment		28,000
Sales discounts	14,500	
Sales returns	17,500	
Notes payable		70,000
Selling expenses	432,000	
Administrative expenses	99,000	
Common shares		300,000
Income tax expense	38,500	
Cash dividends	45,000	
Allowance for doubtful accounts		5,000
Supplies	14,000	
Freight-in	20,000	
Land	70,000	
Equipment	140,000	
Bonds payable		100,000
Gain on sale of land		30,000
Accumulated depreciation—building		19,600
Merchandise inventory	89,000	
Building	98,000	
Purchases	810,000	
Totals	$2,307,600	$2,307,600

A physical count of inventory on December 31 resulted in an inventory amount of $124,000.

Instructions

Prepare a single-step income statement and a retained earnings statement assuming McLean is a private company that has elected to adopt private entity GAAP. Assume that the only changes in retained earnings during the current year were from net income and dividends.

P4-3 Lanestar Inc. reported income from continuing operations before taxes of $1,790,000 during 2010. Additional transactions occurring in 2010 but not considered in the $1,790,000 are as follows:

1. The corporation experienced an insured flood loss of $80,000 during the year.

2. At the beginning of 2008, the corporation purchased a machine for $54,000 (residual value of $9,000) that had a useful life of six years. The bookkeeper used straight-line depreciation for 2008, 2009, and 2010 but failed to deduct the residual value in calculating the depreciation base amount.

3. The sale of securities held for speculative purposes resulted in a loss of $107,000.

4. When its president died, the corporation gained $100,000 from an insurance policy. The cash surrender value of this policy had been carried on the books as an investment in the amount of $46,000 (the gain is non-taxable).

5. The corporation disposed of its recreational division at a loss of $115,000 before taxes. Assume that this transaction meets the criteria for discontinued operations.

6. The corporation decided to change its method of inventory pricing from average cost to the FIFO method. The effect of this change on prior years is to increase 2008 income by $60,000 and decrease 2009 income by $20,000 before taxes. The FIFO method has been used for 2010.

Instructions

(a) Prepare an income statement for the year 2010 starting with income from continuing operations before taxes. Calculate earnings per share as it should be shown on the face of the income statement under IFRS. There were 80,000 common shares outstanding for the year. (Assume a tax rate of 40% on all items, unless they are noted as being non-taxable.)

(b) Assume beginning retained earnings for 2010 is $2,540,000 and that dividends of $175,000 were declared during the year. Prepare the retained earnings portion of the statement of changes in equity for 2010.

Digging Deeper

(c) How do the GAAP classification rules for the statements of income and retained earnings assist in the assessment of the quality of earnings?

P4-4 The following account balances were included in the trial balance of Reid Corporation at June 30, 2010:

Sales	$1,928,500	Depreciation of office furniture	
Sales discounts	31,150	and equipment	$ 7,250
Cost of goods sold	1,071,770	Real estate and other local taxes	7,320
Sales salaries	56,260	Bad debt expense—selling	4,850
Sales commissions	97,600	Building expense—prorated to	
Travel expense—salespersons	28,930	administration	9,130
Freight-out	21,400	Miscellaneous office expenses	6,000
Entertainment expense	14,820	Sales returns	62,300
Telephone and Internet—sales	9,030	Dividends received	38,000
Depreciation of sales equipment	4,980	Bond interest expense	18,000
Building expense—prorated to sales	6,200	Income taxes	133,000
Miscellaneous selling expenses	4,715	Depreciation understatement due to	
Office supplies used	3,450	error—2008 (net of tax)	17,700
Telephone and Internet—administration	2,820	Dividends declared on preferred shares	9,000
		Dividends declared on common shares	32,000

The Retained Earnings account had a balance of $292,000 at June 30, 2010, before closing. There are 180,000 common shares outstanding. Assume Reid has elected to adopt private entity GAAP.

Instructions

(a) Using the multiple-step form, prepare an income statement and retained earnings statement for the year ended June 30, 2010.

(b) Using the single-step form, prepare an income statement for the year ended June 30, 2010.

P4-5 A combined single-step income and retained earnings statement for California Tanning Salon Corp. follows for 2011 (amounts in thousands):

Net sales		$640,000
Costs and expenses		
Cost of goods sold		500,000
Selling, general, and administrative expenses		66,000
Other, net		17,000
		583,000
Income before income tax		57,000
Income tax		19,400
Net income		37,600
Retained earnings at beginning of period, as previously reported	141,000	
Adjustment required for correction of error	(7,000)	
Retained earnings at beginning of period, as restated		134,000
Dividends on common shares		(12,200)
Retained earnings at end of period		$159,400

Additional facts are as follows:

1. Selling, general, and administrative expenses for 2011 included a usual but infrequently occurring charge of $10.5 million for a writedown of inventory.

2. Other, net for 2011 included the results of an identified segment of the business that management had determined would be eliminated from the future operations of the business ($9 million). If the decision had not been made to discontinue the operation, income taxes for 2011 would have been $22.4 million instead of $19.4 million.

3. Adjustment required for correction of an error resulted from a change in estimate as the useful life of certain assets was reduced to eight years and a catch-up adjustment was made.

4. The company disclosed earnings per common share for net income in the notes to the financial statements. The company has elected to adopt private entity GAAP.

Instructions

(a) Determine from these additional facts whether the presentation of the facts in the California Tanning Salon Corp. income and retained earnings statement is appropriate. If the presentation is not appropriate, describe the appropriate presentation and discuss the theory that supports this change.

(b) Prepare a revised combined statement of income and retained earnings for California Tanning Salon Corp.

P4-6 A combined statement of income and retained earnings for DC 5 Ltd. for the year ended December 31, 2010, follows. (As a private company, DC 5 has elected to follow private entity GAAP.) Also presented are three unrelated situations involving accounting changes and the classification of certain items as ordinary or unusual. Each situation is based on the combined statement of income and retained earnings of DC 5 Ltd. and makes it necessary to revise the statement.

DC 5 LTD.
Combined Statement of Income and Retained Earnings
For the Year Ended December 31, 2010

Sales	$5,700,000
Cost of goods sold	2,900,000
Gross margin	2,800,000
Selling, general, and administrative expenses	1,800,000
Income before income tax	1,000,000
Income tax	300,000
Income before unusual item	700,000
Loss from tornado (net of taxes)	490,000
Net income	210,000
Retained earnings, January 1	700,000
Retained earnings, December 31	$ 910,000

Situation A. In late 2010, the company discontinued its apparel fabric division. The loss on the sale of this discontinued division amounted to $620,000. This amount was included as part of selling, general, and administrative expenses. Before its disposal, the division reported the following for 2010: sales of $1,200,000; cost of goods sold of $600,000; and selling, general, and administrative expenses of $450,000.

Situation B. At the end of 2010, the company's management decided that the estimated loss rate on uncollectible accounts receivable was too low. The loss rate used for the years 2009 and 2010 was 1.2% of total sales, and owing to an increase in the writeoff of uncollectible accounts, the rate was raised to 3% of total sales. The amount recorded in Bad Debts Expense under the heading Selling, General, and Administrative Expenses for 2010 was $68,400 and for 2009 it was $75,000.

Situation C. On January 1, 2008, the company acquired machinery at a cost of $500,000. The company adopted the diminishing balance method of depreciation at a rate of 20% for this machinery, and had been recording depreciation over an estimated life of 10 years, with no residual value. At the beginning of 2010, a decision was made to adopt the straight-line method of depreciation for this machinery to provide more relevant information. By mistake, however, the double-declining balance method was used for 2010. For financial reporting purposes, depreciation was included in selling, general, and administrative expenses.

Instructions

For each of the three unrelated situations, prepare a revised combined statement of income and retained earnings for DC 5 Ltd. The company has a 30% income tax rate.

P4-7 The equity accounts of Feeling Alright Vitamin Limited as at January 1, 2010, were as follows:

Retained earnings, January 1, 2010	$257,600
Common shares	600,000
Preferred shares	250,000
Contributed surplus	300,000
Accumulated other comprehensive income	525,000

During 2010, the following transactions affecting the above accounts took place:

Adjustment to correct error in prior years (gain – net of tax)	$ 48,000
Unrealized gains on investments designated through OCI	
(net of tax)	82,000
Dividends:	
Common shares	120,000
Preferred shares	62,000
Issue of equity:	
Common shares	300,000
Preferred shares	5,000
Net income	325,000

Instructions

Prepare a statement of changes in equity for the year ended December 31, 2010 (the company follows IFRS).

P4-8 Hamad Corporation commenced business on January 1, 2007. Recently the corporation has had several unusual accounting problems related to the presentation of its income statement for financial reporting purposes. The company follows private entity GAAP.

You are the CA for Hamad and have been asked to examine the following data:

HAMAD CORPORATION
Income Statement
For the Year Ended December 31, 2010

Sales	$9,500,000
Cost of goods sold	5,900,000
Gross profit	3,600,000
Selling and administrative expense	1,300,000
Income before income tax	2,300,000
Income tax (30%)	690,000
Net income	$1,610,000

This additional information was also provided:

1. The controller mentioned that the corporation has had difficulty in collecting on several of its receivables. For this reason, the bad debt writeoff was increased from 1% to 2% of sales. The controller estimates that if this rate had been used in past periods, an additional $83,000 worth of expense would have been charged. The bad debt expense for the current period was calculated using the new rate and is part of selling and administrative expense.

2. There were 400,000 common shares outstanding at the end of 2010. No additional shares were purchased or sold in 2010.

3. The following items were not included in the income statement:

    (a) Inventory in the amount of $112,000 was obsolete.

    (b) The company announced plans to dispose of a recognized segment. For 2010, the segment had a loss, net of tax, of $162,000.

4. Retained earnings as at January 1, 2010, were $2.8 million. Cash dividends of $700,000 were paid in 2010.

5. In January 2010, Hamad changed its method of accounting for plant assets from the straight-line method to the diminishing balance method. The controller has prepared a schedule that shows what the depreciation expense would have been in previous periods if the diminishing balance method had been used. Assume that this change results in more reliable and relevant presentation.

	Depreciation Expense under Straight-Line	Depreciation Expense under Diminishing Balance	Difference
2007	$ 75,000	$150,000	$ 75,000
2008	75,000	112,500	37,500
2009	75,000	84,375	9,375
	$225,000	$346,875	$121,875

6. In 2010, Hamad discovered that in 2009 it had failed to record $20,000 as an expense for sales commissions. The sales commissions for 2009 were included in the 2010 expenses.

Instructions

(a) Prepare the income statement for Hamad Corporation. Do not prepare notes to the financial statements. The effective tax rate for past years was 30%.

(b) Prepare a combined statement of net income and retained earnings.

(c) From the perspective of the reader of the financial statements, what is the purpose of intraperiod tax allocation for the statements of income and retained earnings?

Digging Deeper

P4-9   Faldo Corp. is a public company and has 100,000 common shares outstanding. In 2010, the company reports income from continuing operations before taxes of $2,710,000. Additional transactions not considered in the $2,710,000 are as follows:

1. In 2010, Faldo Corp. sold equipment for $140,000. The machine had originally cost $80,000 and had accumulated amortization of $36,000. The gain or loss is considered ordinary.

2. The company discontinued operations of one of its subsidiaries during the current year at a loss of $290,000 before taxes. Assume that this transaction meets the criteria for discontinued operations. The loss on operations of the discontinued subsidiary was $90,000 before taxes; the loss from disposal of the subsidiary was $200,000 before taxes.

3. The sum of $520,000 was received as a result of a lawsuit for a breached 2007 contract. Before the decision, legal counsel was uncertain about the outcome of the suit and had not established a receivable.

4. In 2010, the company reviewed its accounts receivable and determined that $54,000 of accounts receivable that had been carried for years appeared unlikely to be collected. No allowance for doubtful accounts was previously set up.

5. An internal audit discovered that amortization of intangible assets was understated by $35,000 (net of tax) in a prior period. The amount was charged against retained earnings.

Instructions

Analyze the above information and prepare an income statement for the year 2010, starting with income from continuing operations before income taxes. Calculate earnings per share as it should be shown on the face of the income statement. (Assume a total effective tax rate of 38% on all items, unless otherwise indicated.)

P4-10   Campbell Corporation management formally decided to discontinue operation of its Rocketeer Division on November 1, 2010. Campbell is a successful corporation with earnings of $150 million or more before taxes for each of the past five years. The Rocketeer Division, a major part of Campbell's operations, is being discontinued because it has not contributed to this profitable performance.

The main assets of this division are the land, plant, and equipment used to manufacture engine components. The land, plant, and equipment had a net book value of $96 million on November 1, 2010.

Campbell's management has entered into negotiations for a cash sale of the division for $87 million. The expected sale date and final disposal of the division is July 1, 2011. Campbell Corporation has a fiscal year ending May 31. The results of operations for the Rocketeer Division for the 2010–2011 fiscal year and the estimated results for June 2011 are presented below. The before-tax losses after October 31, 2010, are calculated without depreciation on the plant and equipment.

Period	Before-Tax Loss
June 1, 2010, to October 31, 2010	$(6,100,000)
November 1, 2010, to May 31, 2011	(3,900,000)
June 1–30, 2011 (estimated)	(750,000)

The Rocketeer Division will be accounted for as a discontinued operation on Campbell's 2010–2011 fiscal year financial statements. Campbell's tax rate is 40% on operating income and all gains and losses.

Instructions

(a) Explain how the Rocketeer Division's assets would be reported on Campbell Corporation's balance sheet as at May 31, 2011, based on IFRS.

(b) Explain how the discontinued operations and pending sale of the Rocketeer Division would be reported on Campbell Corporation's income statement for the year ended May 31, 2011.

(c) On July 5, 2011, Campbell Corporation disposes of the division assets at an adjusted price of $84 million. Explain how the discontinued operations and sale of the Rocketeer Division would be reported on Campbell Corporation's income statement for the year ended May 31, 2012.

Digging Deeper

(d) Assume that Campbell Corporation management was debating whether the sale of the Rocketeer Division qualified for discontinued operations accounting treatment under IFRS. List specific factors or arguments that management would use to suggest that the treatment should be as a discontinued operation. Why might management have a particular preference about which treatment is given? From an external user's perspective, what relevance does the presentation of the discontinued operation have in the interpretation of the financial results?

(CMA adapted)

P4-11 Amos Corporation was incorporated and began business on January 1, 2010. It has been successful and now requires a bank loan for additional working capital to finance an expansion. The bank has requested an audited income statement for the year 2010 using IFRS. The accountant for Amos Corporation provides you with the following income statement, which Amos plans to submit to the bank:

AMOS CORPORATION
Income Statement

Sales		$850,000
Dividends		32,300
Gain on recovery of insurance proceeds from earthquake loss (unusual)		27,300
Unrealized holding gain on equity investments designated as gains/losses through other comprehensive income		5,000
		914,600
Less:		
Selling expenses	$100,100	
Cost of goods sold	510,000	
Advertising expense	13,700	
Loss on obsolescence of inventories	34,000	
Loss on discontinued operations	48,600	
Administrative expense	73,400	779,800
Income before income tax		134,800
Income tax		53,920
Net income		$ 80,880

There are 100,000 common shares outstanding during the year.

Instructions

(a) Indicate the deficiencies in the income statement as it currently is. Assume that the corporation wants a single-step income statement.

(b) Prepare a revised single-step statement of income and comprehensive income.

P4-12   The following is from a recent income statement for Baring Corp (a public company):

Sales	$21,924,000,000
Costs and expenses	20,773,000,000
Income from operations	1,151,000,000
Other income	22,000,000
Interest and debt expense	(130,000,000)
Earnings before income taxes	1,043,000,000
Income taxes	(287,000,000)
Net income	$ 756,000,000

It includes only five separate numbers, two subtotals, and the net earnings figure.

Instructions

Digging Deeper

(a) Indicate the deficiencies in the income statement.

(b) What recommendations would you make to the company to improve the usefulness of its income statement?

(c) Why do some businesses provide only a minimal disclosure of financial statement elements on their income statement?

P4-13   Veselin Komel, vice-president of finance for Hand Corp., has recently been asked to discuss with the company's division controllers the proper accounting for items that are large but do not typify normal business transactions (due to either the nature of the transaction or the frequency of the transaction). Komel prepared the situations that follow to use as examples in the discussion. He understands that accounting standards mandate separate presentation of certain items, that these standards change over time, and that standards from different standard setters may require different things. He has decided to focus on general principles.

1. An earthquake destroys one of the oil refineries owned by a large multinational oil company. Earthquakes are rare in this geographical location.

2. A publicly held company has incurred a substantial loss in the unsuccessful registration of a bond issue. The company accesses capital markets very frequently.

3. A large portion of a cigarette manufacturer's tobacco crops are destroyed by a hailstorm. Severe damage from hailstorms is rare in this locality.

4. A large diversified company sells a block of shares from its portfolio of securities. The securities are currently treated as investments designated through Other Comprehensive Income. The company frequently buys and sells shares from this portfolio.

5. A company sells a block of common shares of a publicly traded company. The block of shares, which represents less than 10% of the publicly held company, is the only security investment that the company has ever owned. Gains and losses from investment in these securities are generally booked through other comprehensive income.

6. A company that operates a chain of warehouses sells the extra land surrounding one of its warehouses. When the company buys property for a new warehouse, it usually buys more land than it needs for the warehouse because it expects the land to increase in value. Twice during the past five years, the company sold excess land.

7. A textile manufacturer with only one plant moves to another location and incurs relocation costs of $725,000. Prior to the move, the company had been in the same location for 100 years.

8. A company experiences a material loss in the repurchase of a large bond issue that has been outstanding for three years. The company regularly repurchases bonds of this type.

9. A railroad experiences an unusual flood loss to part of its track system. Flood losses normally occur every three or four years. How would this be different if the company were to insure itself against this loss?

10. A machine tool company sells the only land it owns. The land was acquired 10 years ago for future expansion, but shortly after the purchase the company abandoned all plans for expansion and decided to keep the land as an investment that would appreciate in value.

Instructions

For each situation, determine whether the item should be classified as unusual. Explain the reasons for your position.

P4-14   In recent years, Grace Inc. has reported steadily increasing income. The company reported income of $20,000 in 2007, $25,000 in 2008, and $30,000 in 2009. Several market analysts have recommended that investors buy Grace Inc. shares because they expect the steady growth in income to continue. Grace is approaching the end of its 2010 fiscal year, and it looks to be a good year once again. However, it has not yet recorded warranty expense.

Based on prior experience, this year's warranty expense should be around $5,000, but some top management has approached the controller to suggest a larger, more conservative warranty expense should be recorded this year. Income before warranty expense is $43,000. Specifically, by recording an $8,000 warranty accrual this year, Grace could report an income increase for this year and still be in a position to cover its warranty costs in future years.

Instructions

(a) What is earnings management?

(b) What would be the effect of the proposed accounting in 2010? In 2011?

(c) What is the appropriate accounting in this situation?

P4-15   Joe Schreiner, controller for On Time Clock Company Inc., recently prepared the company's income statement for 2010. Schreiner believes that the statement is a fair presentation of the company's financial progress during the current period, but he also admits that he has not examined any recent professional pronouncements on accounting.

ON TIME CLOCK COMPANY INC.
Income Statement
For the Year Ended December 31, 2010

Sales			$377,852
Less: Sales returns and allowances			16,320
Net sales			361,532
Cost of goods sold:			
Inventory, January 1, 2010		$ 50,235	
Purchases	$192,143		
Less: Purchase discounts	3,142	189,001	
Cost of goods available for sale		239,236	
Inventory, December 31, 2010		41,124	
Cost of goods sold			198,112
Gross profit			163,420
Selling expenses		41,850	
Administrative expenses		32,142	73,992
Income before income tax			89,428
Other revenues and gains			
Unrealized gain on investments designated through OCI			36,000
Dividends received			40,000
			165,428
Income tax			56,900
Net income			$108,528

ON TIME CLOCK COMPANY INC.
Retained Earnings Statement
For the Year Ended December 31, 2010

Retained earnings, January 1, 2010			$216,000
Add:			
Net income for 2010	$108,528		
Gain from sale of long-term investments	31,400	$139,928	
Deduct:			
Loss on expropriation	13,000		
Correction of mathematical error (net of tax)	17,186	(30,186)	109,742
Retained earnings, December 31, 2010			$325,742

(Note: Retained earnings are extracted from the statement of changes in equity.)

Instructions

(a) Prepare a Statement of Comprehensive Income.

(b) Prepare the Retained Earnings and Accumulated Other Comprehensive Income (assume an opening balance in AOCI of $120,000) portion of the Statement of Changes in Equity.

P4-16   The following financial statement was prepared by employees of Klein Corporation:

KLEIN CORPORATION
Income Statement
Year Ended December 31, 2010

Revenues	
Gross sales, including sales taxes	$1,044,300
Less: Returns, allowances, and cash discounts	56,200
Net sales	988,100
Dividends, interest, and purchase discounts	30,250
Recoveries of accounts written off in prior years	13,850
Total revenues	1,032,200
Costs and expenses	
Cost of goods sold	465,900
Salaries and related payroll expenses	60,500
Rent	19,100
Freight-in and freight-out	3,400
Bad debt expense	24,000
Addition to reserve for possible inventory losses	3,800
Total costs and expenses	576,700
Income before extraordinary items	455,500
Unusual items	
Loss on discontinued styles (Note 1)	37,000
Loss on sale of trading securities (Note 2)	39,050
Loss on sale of warehouse (Note 3)	86,350
Tax assessments for 2009 and 2008 (Note 4)	34,500
Total unusual items	196,900
Net income	$ 258,600
Net income per common share	$ 2.30

Note 1: New styles and rapidly changing consumer preferences resulted in a $37,000 loss on the disposal of discontinued styles and related accessories.

Note 2: The corporation sold an investment in trading securities at a loss of $39,050. The corporation normally sells securities of this type.

Note 3: The corporation sold one of its warehouses at an $86,350 loss (net of taxes).

Note 4: The corporation was charged $34,500 for additional income taxes resulting from a settlement in 2010. Of this amount, $17,000 was for 2009, and the balance was for 2008. This type of litigation recurs frequently at Klein Corporation.

Instructions

Identify and discuss the weaknesses in classification and disclosure in the single-step income statement above. You should explain why these treatments are weaknesses and what the proper presentation of the items would be in accordance with recent professional pronouncements.

*P4-17   On January 1, 2010, Caroline Lampron and Jenni Meno formed a computer sales and service enterprise in Montreal by investing $90,000 cash. The new company, Razorback Sales and Service, has the following transactions in January:

1. Paid $6,000 in advance for three months' rent of office, showroom, and repair space.

2. Purchased 40 personal computers at a cost of $1,500 each, 6 graphics computers at a cost of $3,000 each, and 25 printers at a cost of $450 each, paying cash on delivery.

3. Sales, repair, and office employees earned $12,600 in salaries during January, of which $3,000 was still payable at the end of January.

4. Sold 30 personal computers for $2,550 each, 4 graphics computers for $4,500 each, and 15 printers for $750 each; of the sales amounts, $75,000 was received in cash in January and $30,750 was sold on a deferred payment plan.

5. Other operating expenses of $8,400 were incurred and paid for during January; $2,000 of incurred expenses were payable at January 31.

Instructions

(a) Using the transaction data above, prepare (1) a cash basis income statement and (2) an accrual basis income statement for the month of January.

(b) Using the transaction data above, prepare (1) a cash basis balance sheet and (2) an accrual basis balance sheet as at January 31, 2010.

(c) Identify the items in the cash basis financial statements that make cash basis accounting inconsistent with the theory underlying the elements of financial statements.

*P4-18   Dr. John Gleason, M.D., maintains the accounting records of Bones Clinic on a cash basis. During 2010, Dr. Gleason collected $146,000 in revenues and paid $55,470 in expenses. At January 1, 2010, and December 31, 2010, he had accounts receivable, unearned service revenue, accrued expenses, and prepaid expenses as follows (all long-lived assets are rented):

	January 1	December 31
Accounts receivable	$9,250	$16,100
Unearned service revenue	2,840	1,620
Accrued expenses	3,435	2,200
Prepaid expenses	2,000	1,775

Instructions

Last week, Dr. Gleason asked you, his CA, to help him determine his income on the accrual basis. Write a letter to him explaining what you did to calculate net income on the accrual basis. Be sure to state net income on the accrual basis and to include a schedule of your calculations.

Writing Assignments

WA4-1   Information about a corporation's operations is presented in a statement of earnings or a statement of comprehensive income. Income statements are prepared on either a current operating performance basis or an all-inclusive basis. Users of these income statements have different opinions about how material, non-recurring charges and credits should be treated.

Instructions

(a) Define "current operating performance" and "all-inclusive" as they are used above.

(b) Explain the differences in content and organization of a current operating performance income statement and an all-inclusive income statement. Include a discussion of the proper treatment of material, non-recurring charges and credits.

(c) Give the main arguments in support of each of the three statements: all-inclusive income statement, current operating performance income statement, and a combined income and retained earnings statement.

(d) Discuss what the category Other Comprehensive Income is based on as a concept.

(AICPA adapted)

WA4-2 Ernest Banks is the manager and accountant for a small company that is privately owned by three individuals. Banks has always given the owners cash-based financial statements. The owners are not accountants and do not understand how financial statements are prepared. Recently, the business has experienced strong growth, and inventory, accounts receivable, and capital assets have become more significant company assets. Banks understands generally accepted accounting principles and knows that net income would be lower if he prepared accrual-based financial statements. He is afraid, however, that if he gave the owners financial statements prepared on an accrual basis, they would think he is not managing the business well—they might even decide to fire him.

Instructions

Discuss the accounting and ethical issues.

WA4-3 Anikan Limited has approved a formal plan to sell its head office tower to an outside party. A detailed plan has been approved by the board of directors. The building is on the books at $50 million (net book value). The estimated selling price is $49 million. The company will continue to use the building until the new head office is complete. Construction has not yet started on the new building, but the company has begun to look for a buyer.

Instructions

(a) Discuss the financial reporting issues as described for the situation above.

(b) Assume it is now two years later and construction of the new building is now complete. The company has moved into the new building. Discuss the financial reporting issues under private entity GAAP and IFRS. What would be the presentation on the income statement and balance sheet? The book value is now $45 million and the fair value is $42 million.

WA4-4 Other comprehensive income is a category of comprehensive income that is made up of specific gains and losses that are reported separately after net earnings under IFRS. Under private entity GAAP, there is no such concept as comprehensive income or other comprehensive income, and only net income need be reported.

Instructions

(a) Discuss the rationale for excluding other comprehensive income items from private entity GAAP. Use examples of items that are currently reported under other comprehensive income and discuss their treatment under private entity GAAP.

(b) Under IFRS, earnings per share (EPS) is based on net earnings. Discuss the pros and cons of calculating EPS on comprehensive income instead.

WA4-5 Under IFRS, items of income and expenses are not allowed to be presented as "extraordinary" in the income statement or notes. Under private entity GAAP, the old accounting standards related to extraordinary items have been removed.

Instructions

Explain what reasons the accounting standard setters might have had to eliminate the separate reporting of extraordinary items.

WA4-6 Write a brief essay highlighting the differences between IFRS and accounting standards for private enterprises noted in this chapter, discussing the conceptual justification for each.

Cases

Refer to the Case Primer to help you answer these cases.

CA4-1 Allen Corp. is an entertainment firm that earns approximately 30% of its income from the Casino Royale Division, which manages gambling facilities. As auditor for Allen Corp., you have recently overheard the following discussion between the controller and financial vice-president:

VICE-PRESIDENT: If we sell the Casino Royale Division, it seems ridiculous to segregate the results of the sale in the income statement. Separate categories tend to be absurd and confusing to the shareholders. I believe we should simply report the gain on the sale as other income or expense without any details.

CONTROLLER: Professional pronouncements would require that we disclose this information separately in the income statement. If a sale of this type relates to a separate component and there's a formal plan to dispose of it, it has to be reported as a discontinued operation.

VICE-PRESIDENT: What about the walkout we had last month when our employees were upset about their commission income? Wouldn't this situation also be an extraordinary item?

CONTROLLER: I'm not sure whether that would be reported as extraordinary or not.

VICE-PRESIDENT: Oh well, it doesn't make any difference because the net effect of all these items is immaterial, so no disclosure is necessary.

Instructions

Discuss, assuming that the company is a private Canadian entity.

CA4-2   Anderson Corp. is a major manufacturer of foodstuffs whose products are sold in grocery and convenience stores throughout Canada. The company's name is well known and respected because its products have been marketed nationally for over 50 years.

In April 2011, the company was forced to recall one of its major products. Thirty-five people in Okotoks were treated for severe intestinal pain, and three people eventually died from complications. They had all consumed the same Anderson product.

The product causing the problem was traced to one specific lot or batch. Anderson keeps samples from all lots of foodstuffs. After thorough testing, Anderson and the legal authorities confirmed that the product had been tampered with after it had left the company's plant and was no longer under the company's control.

All of the product was recalled from the market—the only time an Anderson product had been recalled nationally and the only incident of tampering. People who still had the product in their homes, even though it was not from the affected lot, were encouraged to return the product for credit or refund. A media campaign was designed and implemented by the company to explain what had happened and what the company was doing to minimize any chance of recurrence. Anderson decided to continue the product with the same trade name and the same wholesale price. However, the packaging was redesigned completely to be tamper-resistant and safety-sealed. This required the purchase and installation of new equipment.

The corporate accounting staff recommended that the costs associated with the tampered product be treated as an extraordinary charge on the 2011 financial statements. Corporate accounting was asked to identify the various costs that could be associated with the tampered product and related recall. These costs are as follows (in thousands):

1. Credits and refunds to stores and consumers	$30,000
2. Insurance to cover lost sales and idle plant costs for possible future recalls	5,000
3. Transportation costs and off-site warehousing of returned product	2,000
4. Future security measures for other Anderson products	4,000
5. Testing of returned product and inventory	900
6. Destruction of returned product and inventory	2,400
7. Public relations program to re-establish brand credibility	4,200
8. Communication program to inform customers, answer inquiries, prepare press releases, etc.	1,600
9. Higher cost arising from new packaging	800
10. Investigation of possible involvement of employees, former employees, competitors, etc.	500
11. Packaging redesign and testing	2,000
12. Purchase and installation of new packaging equipment	6,000
13. Legal costs for defence against liability suits	750
14. Lost sales revenue due to recall	32,000

Anderson's estimated earnings before income taxes and before consideration of any of the above items for the year ending December 31, 2011, are $225 million.

Instructions

Play the role of the company controller and discuss the financial reporting issues. Assume the company is a private company.

CA4-3   As a reviewer for the Ontario Securities Commission, you are in the process of reviewing the financial statements of public companies. The following items have come to your attention:

1. A merchandising company overstated its ending inventory two years ago by a material amount. Inventory for all other periods is correctly calculated.

2. An automobile dealer sells for $137,000 an extremely rare 1930 S type Invicta, which it purchased for $21,000 ten years ago. The Invicta is the only such display item that the dealer owns.

3. During the current year, a drilling company extended the estimated useful life of certain drilling equipment from 9 to 15 years. As a result, amortization for the current year was materially lowered.

4. A retail outlet changed its calculation for bad debt expense from 1% to 0.5% of sales because of changes in its clientele.

5. A mining company sells a foreign subsidiary that does uranium mining, although the company continues to mine uranium in other countries.

6. A steel company changes from straight-line amortization to accelerated amortization in accounting for its plant assets.

7. A construction company, at great expense to itself, prepares a major proposal for a government loan. The loan is not approved.

8. A water pump manufacturer has had large losses resulting from a strike by its employees early in the year.

9. Amortization for a prior period was incorrectly understated by $950,000. The error was discovered in the current year.

10. A large sheep rancher suffered a major loss because the provincial government required that all sheep in the province be killed to halt the spread of a rare disease. Such a situation has not occurred in the province for 20 years.

11. A food distributor that sells wholesale to supermarket chains and to fast-food restaurants (two major classes of customers) decides to discontinue the division that sells to one of the two classes of customers.

Instructions

Discuss the financial reporting issues.

CA4-4   You are working on the audit team for December Inc., a client with multiple divisions and annual sales of $90 million whose shares trade on the national stock exchange. The company mainly sells electronic transistors to small customers and has one division (the October Division) that deals in acoustic transmitters for navy submarines. The October Division has approximately $18 million in sales.

It is an evening in late February 2011, and the audit work for the year ended December 31, 2010, is complete. You are working in the client's office on the report, when you overhear a conversation among the financial vice-president, the treasurer, and the controller. They are discussing the sale of the October Division, which is expected to happen in June of this year, and the related reporting problems.

The vice-president thinks that the sale does not need to be segregated in the income statement because separate categories tend to be abused and they confuse the shareholders. The treasurer disagrees. He feels that if an item is unusual or infrequent, it should be classified as an extraordinary item, and that this applies to the sale of the October Division. The controller counters that an item must be both infrequent and unusual to be extraordinary, not one or the other. He therefore feels the sale of the October Division should be shown separately, but not as an extraordinary item. Another alternative is to show pro forma income that excludes the October Division.

The sale is not news to you because you read about it in the minutes of the December 16, 2010, board of directors meeting. The minutes indicated plans to sell the transmitter plant and equipment by June 30, 2011, to the company's major competitor, who seems interested. The board estimates that net income and sales will remain constant until the sale, on which the company expects a $700,000 profit.

You also hear the controller disagree with the vice-president about the results of the strike last year and the sale of old transistor ovens. The ovens were formerly used in manufacturing, and the vice-president believes that both the effects of the strike and the sale of the ovens should be extraordinary items. In addition, the treasurer thinks that the government regulation issued last month that made much of their inventory of raw material useless would also be extraordinary. The regulations set beta emission standards at levels lower than those in the raw materials supply, and there is no alternative use for the materials.

After a long discussion that seems to be getting nowhere, the controller finally claims that the discussion is really just academic anyway. Since the net effect of all three items is immaterial, no disclosure is required, he says.

Instructions

Discuss the financial reporting issues.

Integrated Case

(Hint: If there are issues here that are new, use the conceptual framework to help you support your analysis with solid reasoning.)

IC4-1   United Manufacturing Company (UMC) recently filed for bankruptcy protection. The company manufactures downhill skis and its shares trade on the TSX. With the increased popularity of such alternative winter sports as snowboarding and tubing, sales of skis are sagging. The company has decided to start a new line of products that focuses on the growing industry surrounding snow tubing and snowboarding. At present, however, the company needs interim financing to pay suppliers and its payroll. It also needs a significant amount of cash so that it can reposition itself in the marketplace. Management is planning to go to the bank with draft financial statements to discuss additional financing. The company's year end is December 31, 2010, and it is now January 15, 2011. Current interest rates for loans are 5%, but because it is in bankruptcy protection, UMC feels that it will likely have to pay at least 15% on any loan. There is concern that the bank will turn the company down.

At a recent management meeting, the company decided to convert its ski manufacturing facilities into snowboard manufacturing facilities. It will no longer produce skis. Management is unsure if the company will be able to recover the cost of the ski inventory. Although the conversion will result in significant expenditures, the company feels that this is justified if UMC wants to remain a viable business. The shift in strategic positioning will not result in any layoffs as most employees will work in the retrofitted plant. The remaining employees will be trained in the new business.

The conversion to snowboard manufacturing facilities would not require selling the ski manufacturing machines as these machines can be used to produce snowboards. The company estimates the results and cash flows from its operation of selling skis to be a $20-million loss.

On December 15, 2010, the company entered into an agreement with LKT to sell its entire inventory in ski bindings to LKT. Under the terms of the deal, LKT paid $10 million cash for the inventory (its regular selling price at the time). The cost to UMC of this inventory was $6 million and so a profit of $4 million was booked pre-tax. In a separate deal, UMC agreed to buy back the inventory in January for $10,125,000.

Before filing for bankruptcy protection, the company was able to buy a large shipment of snow tubes wholesale for a bargain price of $7 million from a supplier that was in financial trouble. The value of the inventory is approximately $10 million. The inventory was sitting in the UMC manufacturing facility taking up a lot of space. Because the manufacturing facility was being renovated, UMC reached an agreement with its leading competitor, MMN. According to the contract, MMN agreed to purchase the snow tubes from UMC for $8 million and UMC shipped the inventory on December 31 to arrive on January 5. The inventory was shipped f.o.b. shipping point. UMC normally reimburses its customers if the inventory is damaged in transit. UMC has a tentative verbal agreement that it will repurchase the snow tubes that MMN does not sell by the time the renovations are complete (in approximately six months). The buyback price will include an additional amount that will cover storage and insurance costs.

The company pays taxes at a rate of 40%.

Instructions

Adopt the role of Mia Romano—the company controller—and discuss the financial reporting issues related to the preparation of the financial statements for the year ended December 31, 2010.

Research and Financial Analysis

RA4-1 Eastern Platinum Limited

The financial statements and accompanying notes of **Eastern Platinum Limited** are presented in Appendix 5B as they appear in the company's interim report.

Real-World Emphasis

Instructions

Refer to the statements and notes to answer the following questions.

(a) What type of income statement format does the company use: single- or multiple-step?

(b) What business is the company in? (Hint: Look at the Management Discussion and Analysis.) How is this reflected in the balance sheet and income statement?

(c) Is the income statement presented by function or nature? Why?

(d) What is included in other comprehensive income and what is the total of comprehensive income for the current year? How much of this loss is attributable to the shareholders of the parent and to the non-controlling shareholders?

(e) How has the EPS been calculated? How many EPS figures are presented and why? Where is the EPS disclosed?

RA4-2 Royal Bank of Canada

Obtain the 2008 annual report for the **Royal Bank of Canada** from the company's website or from SEDAR (www.sedar.com). Note that financial reporting for Canadian banks is also constrained by the *Bank Act* and monitored by the Office of the Superintendent of Financial Institutions.

Real-World Emphasis

Instructions

(a) Revenues and expenses are defined as arising from ordinary business activities. What are the bank's ordinary (core) business activities? What normal expenses must the bank incur in order to generate core revenues?

(b) Are the core business activities reflected in the income statement? (Hint: Look at the classification between revenues and other income/gains and expenses and other costs/losses.)

(c) Calculate the percentage of the various revenues/income streams to total revenues/income. Discuss the trends from year to year. In other words, are these revenue/income streams increasing as a percentage of the total revenue/income or decreasing? What are the main sources of the revenues/income?

(d) Describe the types of transactions that are included in the Statement of Changes in Equity.

RA4-3 Brookfield Asset Management Inc. and Mainstreet Equity Corp.

Instructions

Use the annual reports of **Brookfield Asset Management Inc.** for the year ended December 31, 2008, and **Mainstreet Equity Corp.** for the year ended September 30, 2008, to answer the following questions. These reports are available on SEDAR (www.sedar.com) or the companies' websites.

Real-World Emphasis

(a) What type of income statement format(s) do these two companies use? Identify any differences in income statement format between the two companies. Are the income statements presented by function or by nature?

(b) Look at the Management Discussion and Analysis and the annual report in general. What business are both companies in?

(c) What are the main sources of revenues for both companies? Are these increasing or decreasing?

(d) Is the nature of each business reflected in its balance sheet? (Hint: What is the main asset and what percentage of total assets is this asset?)

(e) Identify the irregular items reported by these two companies in their income statements over the two-year period. Do these irregular items appear to be significant? Comment on both presentations.

(f) What types of items are included in the other comprehensive income for each company?

RA4-4 Canadian Securities Administrators

Real-World Emphasis

The Canadian Securities Administrators (CSA), an umbrella group of Canadian provincial securities commissions, accumulates all documents that public companies are required to file under securities law. This electronic database may be accessed from the CSA's website: www.sedar.com.

Instructions
Visit the CSA website and find the company documents for **Bank of Montreal** and **Royal Bank of Canada**. Company financial statements may also be accessed through the company websites (www.bmo.com and www.rbcroyalbank.com). Answer the following questions:

(a) What types of company documents may be found here that provide useful information for investors who are making investment decisions?

(b) Locate the Annual Information Form. Explain the nature of the information that it contains. As a financial statement analyst, is this information useful to you? Why or why not?

(c) Who are the auditors of both banks?

(d) Which stock exchange(s) do the banks trade on?

(e) Go to the company websites directly. Look under Investor Relations. What type of information is on these websites and how is it different from what is found on the CSA website? Should these websites contain the same information as the CSA website?

RA4-5 Reporting Financial Performance/Financial Statement Presentation

The IASB and FASB are currently studying the issue of reporting financial performance. As noted in the chapter, Phase A of the project is complete and the standard setters were working on Phase B as this text went to press.

Instructions
Go to the IASB website (www.iasb.org) and download the Discussion Paper: Preliminary Views on Financial Statement Presentation from October 2008.

(a) Explain the proposed presentation model for the statement of comprehensive income. Why has the Board decided on this format? What are the main income statement categories that are being proposed? Discuss whether these categories will improve financial reporting.

(b) Why is disaggregation so important? What disaggregation is proposed? Give three examples of this disaggregation of operating revenue and expenses using the sample statements in the appendix to the report. Is this useful?

RA4-6 Quality of Earnings Research

Quality of earnings analysis is a very important tool in assessing the value of a company and its shares. The chapter presents a framework for evaluating quality of earnings.

Instructions
Do an Internet search on the topic and write a critical essay discussing the usefulness of the quality of earnings assessment.

Real-World Emphasis

RA4-7 Stora Enso Oyj and International Forest Products Limited

Two types of presentation of the expenses on the income statements are by nature and by function. Access the financial statements of **Stora Enso Oyj** for the year ended December 31, 2008, and

International Forest Products Limited for the year ended December 31, 2008. These are available from the companies' websites (www.storaenso.com and www.interfor.com).

Instructions

Use the financial statements to answer the following questions:

(a) What business are the companies in?

(b) Do they report expenses by nature or function? Give examples of the line items shown.

(c) What are the advantages and disadvantages of these types of presentation?

RA4-8 BCE Inc.

An excerpt from the annual report of **BCE Inc.** is shown below. The excerpt shows summarized financial information including calculations of earnings before interest, tax, depreciation, and amortization (EBITDA), adjusted net earnings, and free cash flows—all non-GAAP earnings measures. The company has also provided information on these calculations, which also is shown.

Real-World Emphasis

Instructions

Read the excerpts below. Discuss the pros and cons of management's decision to report additional earnings numbers outside of the traditional audited financial statements. In the case of this company, in your opinion, do you think that this presentation provides good, useful information?

BCE operations

	2008	2007	2006
Revenue (in millions)	17,698	17,752	17,554
EBITDA[1] (in millions)	7,004	6,994	6,790
Operating income (in millions)	2,864	3,479	3,314
Net earnings applicable to common shares (in millions)	819	3,926	1,937
Adjusted net earnings[1,2] (in millions)	1,811	1,884	1,676
Net earnings per common share	1.02	4.88	2.25
Adjusted net earnings per common share[1,2]	2.25	2.34	1.95
Dividends declared per common share	0.73	1.46	1.32
Common dividend payout ratio	71.7%	29.2%	60.4%
Free cash flow[1] (in millions)	1,689	1,960	1,810
Cash from operating activities (in millions)	5,912	5,733	5,357
Capital expenditures (in millions)	2,988	3,144	3,121
Capital intensity	16.9%	17.7%	17.8%

[1] The terms EBITDA, adjusted net earnings and free cash flow are non-GAAP measures. Refer to next page for descriptions.

[2] Before restructuring and other, net losses (gains) on investments incurred to form Bell Aliant.

NON-GAAP FINANCIAL MEASURES

This section describes the non-GAAP financial measures we use in the MD&A to explain our financial results. It also provides reconciliations of the non-GAAP financial measures to the most comparable Canadian GAAP financial measures.

EBITDA

The term EBITDA (earnings before interest, taxes, depreciation and amortization of intangible assets) does not have any standardized meaning according to GAAP. It is therefore unlikely to be comparable to similar measures presented by other companies.

We define EBITDA as operating revenues less cost of revenue and selling, general and administrative expenses, meaning it represents operating income before depreciation, amortization of intangible assets and restructuring and other.

We use EBITDA, among other measures, to assess the operating performance of our ongoing businesses without

continued on page 216

the effects of depreciation, amortization of intangible assets and restructuring and other. We exclude these items because they affect the comparability of our financial results and could potentially distort the analysis of trends in business performance. We exclude depreciation and amortization of intangible assets because it largely depends on the accounting methods and assumptions a company uses, as well as non-operating factors such as the historical cost of capital assets.

Excluding restructuring and other does not imply they are non-recurring.

EBITDA allows us to compare our operating performance on a consistent basis. We believe that certain investors and analysts use EBITDA to measure a company's ability to service debt and to meet other payment obligations, or as a common measurement to value companies in the telecommunications industry.

The most comparable Canadian GAAP financial measure is operating income. The following tables are reconciliations of operating income to EBITDA on a consolidated basis for BCE and Bell.

BCE	2008	2007	2006
Operating income	2,864	3,479	3,314
Depreciation and amortization of intangible assets	3,269	3,184	3,122
Restructuring and other	871	331	354
EBITDA	7,004	6,994	6,790

BELL	2008	2007	2006
Operating income	2,143	2,652	2,507
Depreciation and amortization of intangible assets	2,685	2,559	2,482
Restructuring and other	810	308	299
EBITDA	5,638	5,519	5,288

The following tables are reconciliations of operating income to EBITDA on a consolidated basis for Bell and for our Bell Wireline and Bell Wireless segments for the fourth quarter of 2008.

BELL	Q4 2008	Q4 2007
Operating income	520	557
Depreciation and amortization of intangible assets	715	643
Restructuring and other	146	141
EBITDA	1,381	1,341

BELL WIRELINE	Q4 2008	Q4 2007
Operating income	226	274
Depreciation and amortization of intangible assets	580	538
Restructuring and other	131	138
EBITDA	937	950

BELL WIRELESS	Q4 2008	Q4 2007
Operating income	294	283
Depreciation and amortization of intangible assets	135	105
Restructuring and other	15	3
EBITDA	444	391

Operating Income before Restructuring and Other

The term operating income before restructuring and other does not have any standardized meaning according to Canadian GAAP. It is therefore unlikely to be comparable to similar measures presented by other companies.

We use operating income before restructuring and other, among other measures, to assess the operating performance of our ongoing businesses without the effects of restructuring and other. We exclude these items because they affect the comparability of our financial results and could potentially distort the analysis of trends in business performance. Excluding restructuring and other does not imply they are non-recurring.

The most comparable Canadian GAAP financial measure is operating income. The following tables are reconciliations of operating income to operating income before restructuring and other on a consolidated basis for BCE and Bell and for our Bell Wireline and Bell Wireless Segments.

BCE	2008	2007	2006
Operating income	2,864	3,479	3,314
Restructuring and other	871	331	354
Operating income before restructuring and other	3,735	3,810	3,668

BELL	2008	2007	2006
Operating income	2,143	2,652	2,507
Restructuring and other	810	308	299
Operating income before restructuring and other	2,953	2,960	2,806

BELL WIRELINE	2008	2007	2006
Operating income	902	1,454	1,523
Restructuring and other	773	304	296
Operating income before restructuring and other	1,675	1,758	1,819

BELL WIRELESS	2008	2007	2006
Operating income	1,241	1,198	984
Restructuring and other	37	4	3
Operating income before restructuring and other	1,278	1,202	987

Adjusted Net Earnings

The term Adjusted net earnings does not have any standardized meaning according to Canadian GAAP. It is therefore unlikely to be comparable to similar measures presented by other companies.

We define Adjusted net earnings as net earnings before restructuring and other, net losses (gains) on investments, and costs incurred to form Bell Aliant.

We use Adjusted net earnings, among other measures, to assess the operating performance of our ongoing businesses without the effects of after-tax restructuring and other, net losses (gains) on investments, and costs incurred to form Bell Aliant. We exclude these items because they affect the comparability of our financial results and could potentially distort the analysis of trends in business performance. Excluding these items does not imply they are non-recurring.

The most comparable Canadian GAAP financial measure is net earnings applicable to common shares. The following table is a reconciliation of net earnings applicable to common shares to Adjusted net earnings.

	2008		2007		2006	
	TOTAL	PER SHARE	TOTAL	PER SHARE	TOTAL	PER SHARE
Net earnings applicable to common shares	819	1.02	3,926	4.88	1,937	2.25
Restructuring and other (1)	572	0.71	206	0.25	222	0.26
Net losses (gains) on investments (2)	420	0.52	(2,248)	(2.79)	(525)	(0.61)
Other costs incurred to form Bell Aliant (3)	—	—	—	—	42	0.05
Adjusted net earnings	1,811	2.25	1,884	2.34	1,676	1.95

(1) *Includes transaction costs associated with the formation of Bell Aliant. These costs relate mainly to financial advisory, professional and consulting fees. In 2006, we incurred $138 million ($77 million after tax and non-controlling interest).*
(2) *Amounts for 2006 include the recognition of a future tax asset of $434 million, representing the tax-effected amount of approximately $2,341 million of previously unrecognized capital loss carryforwards.*
(3) *Premium cost incurred by Bell Aliant on early redemption of long-term debt as a result of the formation of Bell Aliant. In 2006, we incurred $122 million ($42 million after tax and non-controlling interest).*

Free Cash Flow

The term free cash flow does not have any standardized meaning according to Canadian GAAP.

We define free cash flow as cash from operating activities and distributions received from Bell Aliant less capital expenditures, preferred share dividends, dividends/distributions paid by subsidiaries to non-controlling interest, other investing activities and Bell Aliant free cash flow.

We consider free cash flow to be an important indicator of the financial strength and performance of our business because it shows how much cash is available to repay debt and reinvest in our company. We present free cash flow consistently from period to period, which allows us to compare our financial performance on a consistent basis.

We believe that certain investors and analysts use free cash flow to value a business and its underlying assets.

The most comparable Canadian GAAP financial measure is cash from operating activities. The following table is a reconciliation of cash from operating activities to free cash flow on a consolidated basis.

	2008	2007	2006
Cash flows from operating activities	5,912	5,733	5,357
Bell Aliant distributions to BCE	290	282	309
Capital expenditures	(2,988)	(3,144)	(3,121)
Other investing activities	(726)	14	(3)
Dividends paid on preferred shares	(129)	(124)	(84)
Dividends/distributions paid by subsidiaries to non-controlling interest	(366)	(404)	(293)
Bell Aliant free cash flow	(304)	(399)	(383)
Telesat free cash flow	—	2	28
Free cash flow	1,689	1,960	1,810

"Cash Is Cash"

EASTERN PLATINUM LIMITED (Eastplats) is Canada's leading platinum group metals producer. Formed in 2005, it is engaged in the acquisition, development, and mining of platinum group metal deposits in South Africa.

While the first few years were not profitable as the company focused on expansion, there have been ebbs and flows in cash flow. "If you're looking at it from an operational point of view, our cash flows have generally been improving every quarter," explains Horng Dih Lee, Vice President, Finance, and Chief Financial Officer at Eastplats. "Overall, however, our cash flows also depend on what goes on at the corporate level, such as financings and acquisitions. When we're doing a financing, for instance, we'll have a positive line item on the cash flow statement."

This was the case in 2007 when the company raised over $200 million in capital by issuing shares. "We have never taken funds generated from operations out of South Africa," Mr. Lee emphasizes. "Instead, we've used the funds to improve our operations or to develop our other properties in South Africa." The company does not issue dividends to shareholders.

Significant expenditures in a given period can also affect overall cash flow. For example, cash flow dipped in December 2008, when

Eastplats acquired an additional interest in its Barplats Mine property.

"You've got to look at the three sections of the cash flow statement," says Robert Gayton, chair of the audit committee. "The operating section, which can be plus or minus, and, in the case of Eastplats, generally plus; then you may do some financing, and that becomes positive in the financing section; at the same time, you're always making capital expenditures and that's in your investing section. So every quarter, you have ebbs and flows because you're doing different things, particularly in the latter two sections of the statement."

Eastplats adopted International Financial Reporting Standards (IFRS) for the 2009 fiscal year, earlier than the 2011 deadline set by the Canadian Accounting Standards Board. With its operations in South Africa, which had already adopted IFRS, it made sense to change early.

While adoption of IFRS will result in changes to Eastplats' reported financial position and results from operations, it will not change the company's actual cash flows. "The cash flow statement isn't particularly influenced by IFRS or GAAP," says Dr. Gayton. "That's why that's the statement most people should read, because they'll understand it. Cash is cash, and moving from Canadian GAAP to IFRS doesn't change that!" ∎

CHAPTER 5

Financial Position and Cash Flows

Learning Objectives

After studying this chapter, you should be able to:

1. Identify the uses and limitations of a balance sheet.

2. Identify the major classifications of a balance sheet.

3. Prepare a classified balance sheet.

4. Identify balance sheet information that requires supplemental disclosure.

5. Identify major disclosure techniques for the balance sheet.

6. Indicate the purpose of the statement of cash flows.

7. Identify the content of the statement of cash flows.

8. Prepare the cash from operating activities section of the statement of cash flows.

9. Understand the usefulness of the statement of cash flows.

10. Identify differences in accounting between accounting standards for private enterprises (private entity GAAP) and IFRS.

11. Identify the significant changes planned by the IASB regarding financial statement presentation.

After studying Appendix 5A, you should be able to:

12. Identify the major types of financial ratios and what they measure.

Preview of Chapter 5

The **balance sheet** and **statement of cash flows** complement the income statement, offering information about the company's financial position and how the firm generates and uses cash. This chapter examines the many different types of assets, liabilities, and shareholders' equity items that affect the balance sheet and the statement of cash flows.

The chapter is organized as follows:

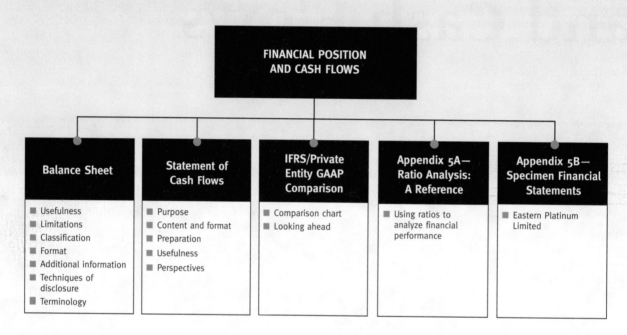

SECTION 1—BALANCE SHEET

The **balance sheet**, sometimes referred to as the **statement of financial position**, reports a business enterprise's assets, liabilities, and shareholders' equity at a specific date. This financial statement provides information about the nature and amounts of the following: investments in enterprise resources, obligations to creditors, and the owners' equity in net resources. It therefore helps in predicting the amounts, timing, and uncertainty of future cash flows.

Usefulness of the Balance Sheet

Objective 1
Identify the uses and limitations of a balance sheet.

Containing information about assets, liabilities, and shareholders' equity, the balance sheet becomes a basis for calculating rates of return on invested assets and evaluating the enterprise's capital structure. Information in the balance sheet is also used to assess business risk[1] and future cash flows. In this regard, **the balance sheet is useful for analyzing a**

---

[1] Risk means the unpredictability of the enterprise's future events, transactions, circumstances, and results.

company's liquidity, solvency, and financial flexibility, as described below, and helps also in analyzing profitability (even though this is not the main focus of the statement).

Liquidity looks at the **amount of time that is expected to pass until an asset is realized** (converted into cash or other monetary asset) or until a liability has to be paid. Does the company have enough cash on hand and cash coming in to cover its short-term liabilities? Certain ratios help assess overall liquidity, including the **current ratio, quick or acid test ratio**, and **current cash debt coverage ratio**. The liquidity of certain assets, such as receivables and inventory, is assessed through **turnover ratios**.[2] These ratios look at how fast the receivables or inventories are being collected or sold. Creditors are interested in **short-term** liquidity ratios, because these ratios indicate whether the enterprise will have the resources to pay its current and maturing obligations. Similarly, shareholders assess liquidity to evaluate the possibility of future cash dividends or the buyback of shares. In general, the greater the liquidity, the lower the risk of enterprise or business failure.[3]

Solvency refers to an **enterprise's ability to pay its debts and related interest**. For example, when a company carries a high level of long-term debt compared with its assets, it is at higher risk for insolvency than a similar company with less long-term debt. Companies with higher debt are riskier because more of their assets will be required to meet these fixed obligations (such as interest and principal payments). Certain ratios help assess solvency. These are often called "coverage" ratios as they refer to a company's ability to cover its interest and long-term debt payments.

Liquidity and solvency affect an entity's financial flexibility, which measures the **"ability of an enterprise to take effective actions to alter the amounts and timing of cash flows so it can respond to unexpected needs and opportunities."**[4] For example, a company may become so loaded with debt—so financially inflexible—that its cash sources to finance expansion or to pay off maturing debt are limited or non-existent. An enterprise with a high degree of financial flexibility is better able to survive bad times, to recover from unexpected setbacks, and to take advantage of profitable and unexpected investment opportunities. Generally, the greater the financial flexibility, the lower the risk of enterprise or business failure.

Air Canada filed for bankruptcy protection in April 2003. Factors such as outbreaks of severe acute respiratory syndrome (SARS), the Iraq war, and terrorism threats had severely reduced airline travel, and therefore airlines' cash inflows. At that time, Air Canada's total debt exceeded its total assets by $2,558 million, leaving it very little flexibility to react to changes in its environment. It was therefore very vulnerable to the decreasing demand for its services. Its current liabilities exceeded its current assets by $1,386 million, resulting in an inability to cover its day-to-day operating costs. By the end of the second quarter, the company had taken steps, while under bankruptcy protection, to ease the cash flow problems and increase flexibility. These included:

1. arranging for interim financing (called debtor in possession [DIP] financing) with General Electric Capital Canada Inc. (GE),

2. restructuring union contracts, and

3. renegotiating aircraft leases for 106 planes (with GE).

This DIP financing provided the company with an additional $700-million line of credit while the other two significant renegotiations helped reduce immediate cash needs

How quickly will my assets convert to cash?

Obligation Ocean

We are drowning in a sea of debt!

Can we afford the high payoff investment?

What Do the Numbers Mean?

---

[2] The formulas for these ratios and other ratios are summarized in Appendix 5A.

[3] Liquidity measures are important inputs to bankruptcy prediction models, such as those developed by Altman and others. See G. White, A. Sondhi, and D. Fried, *The Analysis of Financial Statements* (New York: John Wiley & Sons, 2003), Chapter 18.

[4] "Reporting Income, Cash Flows, and Financial Position of Business Enterprises," *Proposed Statement of Financial Accounting Concepts* (Stamford, Conn.: FASB, 1981), par. .25.

for salaries and lease/rent payments. Note that the line of credit, while providing short-term relief, increases total debt when it is used. The company announced that it hoped to emerge from bankruptcy protection by the end of 2003. It did not quite meet this target but did eventually emerge from bankruptcy protection on September 30, 2004. With a new strategy that included a competitive cost structure, a redesigned network, a new revenue model, and a new corporate structure, the company managed to turn a $258-million profit for its year end 2005 despite the increase in fuel prices. As at December 31, 2005, the long-term debt to equity ratio was still high at 6.6:1; however, this was a significant improvement over the previous year when the ratio was 32:1.

By 2008, Air Canada's long-term debt to equity ratio had risen to 8.6:1 and the company acknowledged the negative impact of weakening demand (again) from a recessionary environment, pension deficits, and volatile fuel prices as potential issues contributing to its significantly leveraged position. The company continues to actively manage its exposures by doing the following:

- ensuring that it has cash balances on hand, and access to additional capital if needed,
- hedging fuel prices, and
- controlling costs.

The liquidity risk is and will always be an ongoing concern for the company given the nature of the industry.

Limitations of the Balance Sheet

Timber at Historical Cost   Timber at Current Value

If we sell that land, we could get more than we paid.

Because the income statement and the balance sheet are interrelated, it is not surprising that the balance sheet has many of the same limitations as the income statement. Here are some of the major limitations of the balance sheet:

1. Many assets and liabilities are stated at their historical cost. As a result, the information that is reported in the balance sheet has higher reliability but it can be criticized as being less relevant than the current fair value would be. Use of historical cost and other valuation methods was discussed in Chapter 2. As noted there, as a general trend, we are moving toward greater use of fair value, specifically for things such as investments and biological assets.

Underlying Concept

"Soft" numbers are less reliable than "hard" numbers and have less predictive value because they are likely to change.

2. Judgements and estimates are used in determining many of the items reported in the balance sheet. This recalls the issue identified in Chapter 4 when discussing income statement limitations. As was stated there, the financial statements include many "soft" numbers; i.e., numbers that are significantly uncertain.

3. The balance sheet necessarily **leaves out many items** that are of relevance to the business but cannot be recorded objectively.[5] These may be either assets or liabilities. Recall again the discussion from Chapter 4. Because liquidity and solvency ratios worsen when liabilities are recognized, a company may be biased against including liabilities in the financial statements. Knowing this, analysts habitually look for and capitalize[6] many liabilities that may be "off–balance sheet" before they calculate key liquidity and solvency ratios. For example, when reviewing a company, analysts consider off–balance sheet liabilities such as certain types of leases. The information that

Balance Sheet

Hey... we left out the value of the employees!

---

[5] Several of these omitted items (such as internally generated goodwill and certain commitments) are discussed in later chapters.

[6] While the term "capitalize" is often used in the context of recording costs as assets, it is sometimes used differently: in the context here, it means recognizing the liabilities on the balance sheet.

is disclosed in the notes to the financial statements and the analyst's knowledge of the business and industry become critical in this context, as they make it possible to identify and measure off–balance sheet items that often represent either additional risk to the company or unrecognized assets.

Underlying Concept

Disclosing too much detail often obscures important information by creating information overload.

Classification in the Balance Sheet

Balance sheet accounts are **classified** (like the income statement) so that **similar items are grouped together** to arrive at significant subtotals. The material is also arranged so that important relationships are shown.

2 Objective

Identify the major classifications of a balance sheet.

As is true of the income statement, the balance sheet's parts and subsections can be more informative than the whole. Individual items should be separately reported and classified in enough detail so that users can assess the amounts, timing, and uncertainty of future cash flows, and evaluate the company's liquidity and financial flexibility, profitability, and risk.

Classification in financial statements helps analysts and other financial statement users by **grouping items with similar characteristics** and **separating items with different characteristics**. In this regard, the balance sheet has additional information content. Recall that many users use the information in financial statements to assess risk, including the company's financial flexibility, as noted earlier. Consider how the following groupings of assets and liabilities provide additional insight:

1. Assets that are of a different type or that have a different **function** in the activities of the company should be reported as separate items. For example, merchandise inventories should be reported separately from property, plant, and equipment. Inventory will be sold and property, plant, and equipment will be used. In this way, investors can see how fast inventory is turning over or being sold.

2. Liabilities with **different implications for the enterprise's financial flexibility** should be reported as separate items. For example, long-term liabilities should be reported separately from current liabilities, and debt should be separate from equity.

3. Assets and liabilities with different **general liquidity characteristics** should be reported as separate items. For example, cash should be reported separately from accounts receivable and property held for use is reported separately from that held for sale.

4. Certain assets, liabilities, and equity instruments have **attributes that allow them to be measured or valued more easily**. Reporting these separately takes advantage of this characteristic. Monetary assets, and liabilities and financial instruments are two such groupings. Each will be discussed separately below.

Monetary versus Non-Monetary Assets and Liabilities. Monetary assets represent either money itself **or claims to future cash flows that are fixed and determinable in amounts and timing**.[7] Because of these characteristics, they are said to be easier to measure, and they generally are. In addition, their carrying values (which approximate net realizable value) are more representative of reality as they normally are close to the amount of cash that the company will receive in the future. Examples are accounts and notes receivable. Likewise, liabilities that require **future cash outflows that are fixed and determinable in amounts and timing**[8] are also considered to be monetary and thus easier to measure. Accounts and notes payable and long-term debt are examples. In

Underlying Concept

With non-monetary assets, historical cost is often a more reliable measure where market values are not available.

---

[7] *CICA Handbook*, Part II, Section 3831.05.

[8] Ibid.

contrast, other assets—such as inventory; property, plant, and equipment; certain investments; and intangibles—are **non-monetary assets** because their value in terms of a monetary unit such as dollars is not fixed. There is therefore additional measurement uncertainty. These assets are often recorded at their historical cost (or amortized cost), which does not reflect their true value.

Law

Financial Instruments. **Financial instruments** are contracts between two or more parties. They are often marketable or tradable, and therefore easy to measure.[9] Many financial instruments are also monetary assets or liabilities. Financial assets include the following:

- **cash**

- **contractual rights to receive, or obligations to deliver, cash or another financial instrument**

- **investments in other companies**[10]

Contractual rights to **receive** cash or other financial instruments are assets, whereas contractual obligations to **pay** are liabilities. Cash, accounts receivable, and all payables are examples of financial instruments. These instruments are all monetary. Shares are also financial instruments. Current accounting standards on financial instruments require fair value accounting for certain types of financial instruments, including certain types of investments, especially where market values are readily available. This is due to the fact that fair value (often market value) is fairly easy to obtain and represents an objective view of the measurement of the instrument. In addition, GAAP generally allows an entity to choose to value financial instruments in certain situations at fair value as an accounting policy choice (with gains and losses booked through net income). This is referred to as the fair value option. Financial instruments should not be offset against each other on the balance sheet except under limited circumstances. The accounting and reporting of financial instruments is discussed more extensively in Chapters 7, 9, 13, 14, 15, and 16. Derivatives, a more complex type of financial instrument, will be covered in Chapter 16. Most monetary assets and liabilities are financial instruments.

The three general classes of items that are included in the balance sheet are assets, liabilities, and equity. They are defined below.

Significant Change

ELEMENTS OF THE BALANCE SHEET

1. *Assets.* **Present economic benefits** that the entity has rights or access to where others do not.
2. *Liabilities.* **Present economic burden or obligation** that is **enforceable.**
3. *Equity/Net Assets.* The **residual interest** in an entity's assets that remains after deducting its liabilities. In a business enterprise, the equity is the ownership interest.

These are the same definitions from Chapter 2 and the conceptual framework. Illustration 5-1 shows a standard format for presenting the balance sheet for many companies.

---

[9] Markets often exist or can be created for these instruments because of their nature and measurability. Liabilities are included because they represent the other side of an asset contract; e.g., accounts payable to one company represents accounts receivable to another. Accounts receivable contracts or pools are often bought and sold.

[10] See *CICA Handbook*, Part II, Section 3856, IAS 32, and IAS 39 for more complete definitions.

Illustration 5-1

Balance Sheet Classifications

Assets	Liabilities and Shareholders' Equity
Current assets	Current liabilities
Long-term investments	Long-term debt
Property, plant, and equipment	Shareholders' equity
Intangible assets	Capital shares
Other assets	Contributed surplus
	Retained earnings
	Accumulated other comprehensive
	income/other surplus

Although the balance sheet can be classified or presented in other ways, in actual practice the major subdivisions noted in Illustration 5-1 are closely followed, with exceptions in certain industries. When the balance sheet is for a proprietorship or partnership, the classifications in the owners' equity section are presented a little differently, as will be shown later in the chapter.

These standard classifications make it easier to calculate important ratios such as the current ratio for assessing liquidity and debt-to-equity ratios for assessing solvency. Because total assets are broken down into categories, users can easily calculate which assets are more significant than others and how these relationships change over time.[11] This gives insight into management's strategy and stewardship. Illustration 5-2 shows a classified balance sheet for **Air Canada**.

Financial Statement Analysis Primer

Illustration 5-2

Classified Balance Sheet— Excerpt from Air Canada's December 31, 2008, Financial Statements

Real-World Emphasis

CONSOLIDATED STATEMENT OF FINANCIAL POSITION
As at December 31
(Canadian dollars in millions)

		2008	2007
ASSETS			
Current			
Cash and cash equivalents	Note 2o	$ 499	$ 527
Short-term investments	Note 2p	506	712
		1,005	1,239
Restricted cash	Note 2q	45	124
Accounts receivable	Note 18	702	750
Aircraft fuel inventory		97	98
Fuel derivatives	Note 15	—	68
Collateral deposits for fuel derivatives	Note 15	328	—
Prepaid expenses and other current assets	Note 18	226	182
		2,403	2,461
Property and equipment	Note 3	7,469	7,919
Intangible assets	Note 4	997	952
Deposits and other assets	Note 5	495	488
		$11,364	**$11,820**
LIABILITIES			
Current			
Accounts payable and accrued liabilities	Note 18	$ 1,440	$ 1,226
Fuel derivatives	Note 15	420	—
Advance ticket sales		1,333	1,300

continued on p. 226

---

[11] This type of comparison is done by performing a **vertical analysis**, which calculates the percentage that a specific asset represents when divided by total assets. This number may then be compared with the same percentage from past years. The latter comparison is generally called **horizontal** or **trend analysis**. Horizontal and vertical analyses are discussed further on the Student Website under Financial Statement Analysis.

Current portion of long-term debt and capital leases	Note 6	663	413
		3,856	2,939
Long-term debt and capital leases	Note 6	4,691	4,006
Future income taxes	Note 7	88	88
Pension and other benefit liabilities	Note 8	1,407	1,824
Other long-term liabilities	Note 9	370	336
		10,412	9,193
Non-controlling interest		190	184
SHAREHOLDERS' EQUITY			
Share capital	Note 11	274	274
Contributed surplus		1,797	1,791
Retained earnings (deficit)		(703)	322
Accumulated other comprehensive income (loss)	Notes 21 &11	(606)	56
		762	2,443
		$11,364	**$11,820**

The accompanying notes are an integral part of the consolidated financial statements.
Commitments (Note 14); Contingencies, Guarantees, and Indemnities (Note 17)

Note that the total debt to equity ratio changed significantly from 2007 to 2008. The calculations for the ratio are as follows.

2007 = $9,193 million/$2,443 million = 3.76 to 1

2008 = $10,412 million/$762 million = 13.66 to 1

The worsening ratio is due, as previously discussed, to fuel costs and lessening demand for travel, among other things. The company was negatively impacted by the slowdown in the economy. Note that retained earnings have moved from a surplus number to a deficit. This in itself causes the ratio to be higher than the prior year as the denominator is lower.

Current Assets

Objective 3
Prepare a classified balance sheet.

Current assets are **cash and other assets that will ordinarily be realized within one year from the date of the balance sheet or within the normal operating cycle if the cycle is longer than a year**.[12] The operating cycle is the average time between the acquisition of materials and supplies and the realization of cash. Cash is realized through sales of the product that is created from the materials and supplies. The cycle begins with cash and then moves through inventory, production, and receivables, and back to cash. When there are several operating cycles within one year, the one-year period is used. If the operating cycle is more than one year, the longer period is used. Illustration 5-3 shows the operating cycle for manufacturing companies.

Illustration 5-3

The Business Operating Cycle for Manufacturing Companies

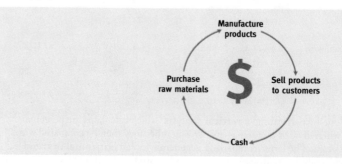

---

[12] *CICA Handbook*, Part II, Section 1510.01 and IAS 1.66.

For most industries, current assets are generally segregated and presented in the balance sheet in order according to their liquidity.[13] The five major items that are found in the current assets section are cash, short-term investments (including derivatives), receivables, inventories, and prepayments. Cash is included at its stated value, investments are valued at cost/amortized cost or fair value, accounts receivable are stated at the estimated amount that is collectible, inventories generally are included at the lower of cost and net realizable value, and prepaid items are valued at cost.

Cash.   Cash is often grouped with other cash-like liquid assets and reported as cash and cash equivalents. Cash and cash equivalents are defined as **cash, demand deposits, and short-term, highly liquid investments that are readily convertible into known amounts of cash and have an insignificant risk of changing in value.**[14] Illustration 5-4 details the cash and cash equivalents for **Astra Zeneca**.

Cash and Cash Equivalents

Cash and cash equivalents comprise cash in hand, current balances with banks and similar institutions and highly liquid investments with maturities of three months or less when acquired. They are readily convertible into known amounts of cash and are held at amortised cost.

Any restrictions on the general availability of cash or any commitments regarding how it is likely to be used must be disclosed and may affect whether the items are presented as current.

How much cash should a company hold? In general, a company needs enough liquid assets, including cash, to be able to settle its current liabilities in a timely manner; however, it must also ensure that its assets do not sit idle. Cash itself is generally non-interest-bearing and so does not contribute to net income. Too much cash can make a company a more likely target for a takeover bid.

Short-Term Investments.   Investments in debt and equity securities are presented separately and valued at cost/amortized cost or fair value. Those measured at cost are written down when impaired. Companies that have excess cash often have significant amounts of short-term investments. While deciding what to do with the money, they will temporarily invest it so as to generate some profits (instead of letting the funds sit idle as non-interest-bearing cash). In addition, the way a company does business can result in higher levels of investments. For instance, the business models of insurance companies, pension funds, and banks result in significant amounts of temporary as well as long-term investments. Insurance companies collect premiums up front and invest the money so that they have funds available to pay out future claims that arise under the insurance policies. Pension plans likewise collect money up front (through pension contributions from individuals) and invest it for future payout when the contributors retire. Money is a bank's inventory. The bank must decide how much of it should be invested and in which investments. Investment banks often trade short-term investments to maximize profits and manage risks.

---

[13] The real estate industry is an example that does not follow this approach. This is because the industry feels that a more meaningful presentation results when the most important assets are presented first. In most real estate development companies, the most important and largest asset is revenue-producing properties. This asset includes hotels, shopping centres, leased buildings, and so on that generate revenue or profits for the company. **Brookfield Properties Corporation** records this asset first on its balance sheet. On the liabilities side, the corresponding debt related to the properties is recorded. For Brookfield, this asset represents 77% of total assets. Many real estate companies follow specialized industry GAAP (Real Estate GAAP) as published by the Real Properties Association of Canada or REALpac (see www.realpac.ca). For different reasons, **Bombardier Inc.** does not classify its balance sheet. It operates in two distinct segments (aerospace and transportation) that have differing operating cycles and, because of this, the company feels that classification would not add value.

[14] *CICA Handbook*, Part II, Section 1540.06 and IAS 7.6.

Underlying Concept

Grouping these similar items together reduces the amount of redundant information on the balance sheet and therefore makes the information easier to understand.

Illustration 5-4

Balance Sheet Presentation of Cash and Cash Equivalents— Excerpt from Astra Zeneca December 31, 2008, Financial Statements

Real-World Emphasis

WILEY PLUS

Additional Disclosures

Receivables.   Accounts receivable should be segregated to show **ordinary trade accounts**, amounts owing by **related parties**, and other **unusual items** of a substantial amount. Anticipated losses due to uncollectibles should be accrued. The amount and nature of any nontrade receivables, and any receivables that have been designated or pledged as collateral, should be disclosed. Accounts receivable are valued at their net realizable value. Illustration 5-5 shows how **QLT Inc.** reported its receivables in Note 4 to its financial statements.

Illustration 5-5

Balance Sheet Presentation of Securities—Excerpt from QLT Inc.'s December 31, 2008, Financial Statements

Real-World Emphasis

4. ACCOUNTS RECEIVABLE

(In thousands of U.S. dollars)	2008	2007
Visudyne	$ 11,056	$ 11,609
Royalties	10,620	8,193
Sales milestones	3,000	—
Contract research and development	—	213
Eligard product shipments	6,315	5,049
Trade and other	105	318
Allowance for doubtful accounts	—	(125)
	$ 31,096	$ 25,257

Accounts receivable – Visudyne represents amounts due from Novartis and consists of our 50% share of Novartis' net proceeds from Visudyne sales, amounts due from the sale of bulk Visudyne to Novartis and reimbursement of specified royalty and other costs. The allowance for doubtful accounts at December 31, 2007 was provided for specifically identified accounts.

What Do the Numbers Mean?

QLT is a biotechnology company that specializes in the discovery, development, and commercialization of drugs, including light-activated drugs such as Visudyne. Visudyne is marketed through **Novartis Ophthalmics** (Novartis), the company's co-development partner. The companies share the earnings from distribution of the drug. Because of the relationship between QLT and Novartis, the latter is considered a related party[15] and the accounts receivable are therefore disclosed separately. Note also that because the company markets and distributes its main product through Novartis, almost all of its receivables come from one source and this creates a credit risk concentration. This is important information and is thus highlighted in Note 19 to the financial statements, which deals with financial instruments and concentration of credit risk. The category "Contract research and development" represents work done for other companies. Ordinary trade and other receivables represent a very small part of QLT's total receivables.

Inventories.   "Inventories are assets:

1. **held for sale in the ordinary course of business,**

2. **in the process of production for such sale, or**

3. **in the form of materials or supplies to be consumed in the production process or in the rendering of service.**"[16]

They are valued at the lower of cost and net realizable value, with cost being determined using a **cost formula** such as first-in, first-out (FIFO), weighted average cost, or specific

---

[15] The identification and measurement of related parties and related-party transactions will be covered in Chapter 23.

[16] *CICA Handbook*, Part II, Section 3031.07 and IAS 2.6.

identification (where items are not ordinarily interchangeable). It is important to disclose these details as this information helps users understand the amount of judgement that was used in measuring this asset. For a manufacturer, the stage of the inventories' completion is also indicated (raw materials, work in process, and finished goods). Illustration 5-6 shows the breakdown of QLT's inventory.

5. INVENTORIES

(In thousands of U.S. dollars)	2008	2007
Raw materials and supplies	$ 6,308	$ 12,653
Work-in-process	30,445	33,819
Finished goods	256	67
Provision for excess inventory	(2,471)	(3,020)
Provision for non-completion of product inventory	(3,735)	(4,613)
	30,803	38,906
Less: Long-term inventory, net of provisions	19,170	20,395
	$ 11,633	$ 18,511

We review our inventory quantities against our forecast of future demand and market conditions and if necessary, provide a reserve for potential excess or obsolete inventory. Our provision for excess inventory of $2.5 million, all of which was applied against our long-term Visudyne inventory, reflects our forecast of future Visudyne demand.

We record a provision for non-completion of product inventory to provide for the potential failure of inventory batches in production to pass quality inspection. During the year ended December 31, 2008, we charged $0.5 million against the provision for non-completion of product inventory as a result of batch failures. At December 31, 2008, $1.9 million of the provision for non-completion of product inventory was related to long-term inventory. We classify inventories that we do not expect to convert or consume in the next year as non-current based upon an analysis of market conditions such as sales trends, sales forecasts, sales price, and other factors (See Note 10 - Long-Term Inventories and Other Assets.)

Illustration 5-6

Balance Sheet Presentation of Inventories—Excerpt from QLT Inc.'s December 31, 2008, Financial Statements

Real-World Emphasis

QLT also discloses the following in its Significant Accounting Policy note:

Inventories

Raw materials and supplies inventories are carried at the lower of actual cost and net realizable value. Finished goods and work-in-process inventories are carried at the lower of weighted average cost and net realizable value. We record a provision for non-completion of product inventory to provide for potential failure of inventory batches in production to pass quality inspection. The provision is calculated at each stage of the manufacturing process. We estimate our non-completion rate based on past production and adjust our provision quarterly based on actual production volume and actual non-completion experience. Inventory that is obsolete or expired is written down to its market value if lower than cost. Inventory quantities are regularly reviewed and provisions for excess or obsolete inventory are recorded primarily based on our forecast of future demand and market conditions. We classify inventories that we do not expect to convert or consume in the next year as non-current based upon an analysis of market conditions such as sales trends, sales forecasts, sales price, and other factors.

What Do the Numbers Mean?

The **nature of the inventory is important in assessing value.** QLT's inventory consists mainly of manufactured pharmaceuticals, which must be made according to very high standards and demanding specifications. Because of this, QLT acknowledges the risk that the manufactured batches might not pass quality inspection. The company also has a provision for obsolescence since products may become "off-code"; i.e., unusable due to their age. Retailers would consider theft and out-of-date stock in assessing the value of their inventory. High-tech companies would consider obsolescence.

Finally, QLT classifies some of its inventory as long-term. Inventory is generally presented as a current asset since it will generally be sold within the year. Where QLT does not feel it will be able to convert the inventory to cash within the following year due to the specific nature of the inventory or market conditions, it has decided that it makes more sense to present it as long-term.

Which types of companies are likely to have significant inventory? Companies that sell and manufacture goods will normally carry inventory (as compared with companies that offer services only). How much inventory is enough or, conversely, how much inventory is too much? Companies must have at least enough inventory to meet customer demands. On the other hand, inventory ties up significant amounts of cash flows, creates storage costs, and subjects the company to risk of theft, obsolescence, and so on. Many companies operate on a just-in-time philosophy, meaning that they streamline their production and supply channels so that they can order the raw materials and produce the product in a very short time. Car manufacturers often follow this philosophy, thus freeing up working capital and reducing the need for storing inventory.

Prepaid Expenses.   **Prepaid expenses** included in current assets are **expenditures already made for benefits (usually services) that will be received within one year or the operating cycle**, whichever is longer. These items are current assets because cash does not need to be used for them again in the current year or operating cycle as they have already been paid for. A common example is the payment in advance for an insurance policy. It is classified as a prepaid expense at the time of the expenditure because the payment occurs before the coverage benefit is received. Prepaid expenses are reported at the amount of the unexpired or unconsumed cost. Other common prepaid expenses include rent, advertising, taxes, and office or operating supplies.

Companies often include insurance and other prepayments for two or three years in current assets even though part of the advance payment applies to periods beyond one year or the current operating cycle. This is done by convention even though it is inconsistent with the definition of current assets.

Noncurrent Investments

Noncurrent investments normally consist of one of the types shown in Illustration 5-7.

Illustration 5-7

Types of Noncurrent Investments

TYPES OF NONCURRENT INVESTMENTS	MEASUREMENT
Debt Securities	
Held to maturity	Amortized cost
Equity Securities	
Significant influence investments	Equity method
Subsidiaries	Consolidated
Non-consolidated subsidiaries	Fair value or at cost
Where no influence or control	Fair value or at cost
Other	
Sinking funds, tangible assets held as investments, other	Generally at cost

Long-term investments are usually presented on the balance sheet just below current assets in a separate section called "Investments." Many securities that are properly shown among long-term investments are, in fact, readily marketable. They are not included as current assets unless management intends to convert them to cash in the short term; that is, within a year or the operating cycle, whichever is longer.

Management may be holding some of these investments for strategic reasons (e.g., significant influence investments or non-consolidated subsidiaries). Investments that are held for strategic reasons are generally held for longer periods of time and are consolidated (subsidiaries) or accounted for using the equity method (significant influence investments). This will be examined in greater detail in Chapter 9.

Long-term investments carried at other than fair value must be written down when impaired.

Property, Plant, and Equipment

Property, plant, and equipment are tangible capital assets—i.e., properties of a durable nature—that are **used in ongoing business operations to generate income**. These assets consist of physical or tangible property such as land, buildings, machinery, furniture, tools, and wasting resources (e.g., timberland, minerals). They are generally carried at their cost or amortized cost. With the exception of land, most assets are either depreciable (such as buildings) or depletable (such as timberlands or oil reserves). IFRS allows an option to carry them at fair value using a revaluation or fair value method. Like all other assets property, plant and equipment are written down when impaired.

ClubLink Corporation has significant capital assets. In fact, in 2008, capital assets represented 93% of the corporation's total assets. This is not surprising as the company is one of Canada's largest golf club developers and operators. The bulk of these assets are in land (golf courses) and buildings. Illustration 5-8 shows the detailed breakdown of these assets, as presented in Note 3 to ClubLink's financial statements.

Illustration 5-8

Balance Sheet Presentation of Property, Plant, and Equipment—Excerpt from ClubLink Corporation's December 31, 2008, Financial Statements

Real-World Emphasis

3. CAPITAL ASSETS

(thousands of dollars)	Cost	Accumulated Amortization	2008 Net	Cost	Accumulated Amortization	2007 Net
Operating capital assets						
Golf course lands	$276,602	$ —	$276,602	$276,147	$ —	$276,147
Leased lands	12,857	2,137	10,720	12,893	1,854	11,039
Buildings	155,607	33,536	122,071	150,720	29,393	121,327
Roads, cart paths and irrigation	82,507	28,192	54,315	79,932	23,961	55,971
Maintenance equipment	25,838	15,891	9,947	32,170	21,347	10,823
Clubhouse equipment	27,279	16,220	11,059	29,824	18,269	11,555
Golf carts	16,446	7,847	8,599	16,446	7,370	9,076
Office and computer equipment	7,585	4,291	3,294	8,571	4,518	4,053
	$604,721	$108,114	496,607	$606,703	$106,712	499,991
Development capital assets						
Properties under construction			894			11,858
Properties held for future development			37,110			28,895
			38,004			40,753
			$534,611			$540,744

Interest of nil (2007 – $1,869,000) and direct project development and management costs of $138,000 (2007 – $822,000) have been capitalized during the year to properties under construction.

Certain capital assets have been assigned as collateral for long-term debt (note 7).

Costs to complete properties under construction (including capitalized interest and direct project development and management costs) as of December 31, 2008 total $5,578,000 (2007 – $7,513,000) and are expected to be incurred in 2009.

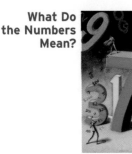

What Do the Numbers Mean?

Note that ClubLink further segregates its capital assets into **operating** and **development** assets. This helps users understand which assets are already producing revenues and which ones will be coming on stream to produce additional future revenues, and are therefore the company's current growth potential. The basis of valuing the property, plant, and equipment; any liens against the properties; and accumulated amortization should be disclosed, usually in notes to the statements.

Aside from companies in the golf club business, those based in real estate, manufacturing, resources, or pharmaceuticals also have large amounts of capital assets on their balance sheets. These types of companies are often referred to as being **capital-intensive** since they require large amounts of capital to invest in their long-term revenue-generating assets.

Intangible Assets

Intangible assets **are capital assets that have no physical substance** and usually have a higher degree of uncertainty about their future benefits. They include patents, copyrights, franchises, goodwill, trademarks, trade names, and secret processes. These intangibles are initially recorded at cost and are divided into two groups for accounting purposes:

- those with finite lives

- those with infinite lives

The former are amortized to expense over their useful lives. The latter are not amortized. Both are tested for impairment.

Intangibles can amount to significant economic resources, yet financial analysts often ignore them. This is because their **valuation and measurement are difficult**. Many intangible assets, especially those that are **internally generated** (e.g., goodwill), are never recognized at all on the balance sheet.

As Illustration 5-9 shows, a significant portion of **Biovail Corporation's** total assets is composed of goodwill and intangibles (51%).

Illustration 5-9

Balance Sheet Presentation of Goodwill and Intangible Assets—Excerpt from Biovail Corporation's Financial Statements (amounts in thousands of U.S. dollars)

Real-World Emphasis

	At December 31 2008	2007
ASSETS		
Current		
Cash and cash equivalents	$ 317,547	$ 433,641
Short-term investment	278	—
Marketable securities	719	3,895
Accounts receivable	90,051	111,114
Insurance recoveries receivable	812	62,942
Inventories	59,561	80,745
Assets held for sale	6,814	—
Prepaid expenses and other current assets	14,582	14,680
	490,364	707,017
Marketable securities	21,916	24,417
Long-term investments	102	24,834
Property, plant and equipment, net	148,269	238,457
Intangible assets, net	720,372	630,514
Goodwill	100,294	100,294
Deferred tax assets, net of valuation allowance	116,800	20,700
Other long-term assets, net	25,448	35,882
	$1,623,565	$1,782,115

A further look at the detail behind the amount for intangibles shows that Biovail's intangibles include trademarks and product rights for several pharmaceutical products. It makes sense that the company would have a large amount of money invested in intangibles since Biovail is in the business of developing products in the controlled-release drug-delivery sector. The drugs are patented by the company and become main revenue generators. Having stated this, the true value of **internally generated** patents is generally not reflected in the balance sheet. Instead, it is most often the **purchased** rights to drugs that show up as intangible assets since the value of these rights is measured through their acquisition.

What Do the Numbers Mean?

Other Assets

The items included in the Other Assets section vary widely in practice. Some of the items that are commonly included (if they are not included anywhere else) are noncurrent receivables, intangible assets, assets in special funds, future income tax assets, property held for sale, and advances to subsidiaries. The company should be careful to disclose these assets in enough detail for users to get a better idea of their nature.

Future income tax assets (deferred income taxes) represent the taxes that may be avoided or saved due to deductions that a company may take when it prepares its **future** tax returns. For instance, when a company buys an asset, it is allowed to deduct the cost of the asset from future taxable income. This represents a benefit, which is tax effected and recognized on the balance sheet. Future income taxes will be discussed in greater detail in Chapter 18.

Current Liabilities

Current liabilities are the **obligations that are due within one year from the date of the balance sheet or within the operating cycle, where this is longer.**[17] This concept includes:

1. Payables resulting from the acquisition of goods and services: trade accounts payable, wages payable, taxes payable

2. Collections received in advance for the delivery of goods or the performance of services, such as unearned rent revenue or unearned subscriptions revenue

3. Other liabilities whose liquidation will take place within the operating cycle, such as the portion of long-term bonds to be paid in the current period, or short-term obligations arising from a purchase of equipment

4. Short-term financing that is payable on demand (such as a line of credit or overdraft)

5. Derivative financial instruments

At times, a liability that is payable within the year may not be included in the current liabilities section. This may occur either when the debt will be refinanced through another long-term issue,[18] or when the debt is retired out of noncurrent assets. This approach is justified because the liquidation of the liability does not result from the use of current assets or the creation of other current liabilities.

Current liabilities are not reported in any consistent order. The items that are most commonly listed first are accounts payable, accrued liabilities, or short-term debt;

---

[17] *CICA Handbook*, Part II, Section 1510.08 and IAS 1.69.

[18] In Chapter 13, there is a more detailed discussion of debt.

those that are most commonly listed last are income taxes payable, current maturities of long-term debt, or other current liabilities. Any secured liability—for example, notes payable that have shares held as collateral for them—is fully described in the notes so that the assets providing the security can be identified.

The excess of total current assets over total current liabilities is referred to as working capital (sometimes called net working capital). Working capital is thus the net amount of a company's relatively liquid resources. That is, it is the liquid buffer (or cushion) that is available to meet the operating cycle's financial demands. Working capital as an amount is rarely disclosed on the balance sheet, but it is calculated by bankers and other creditors as an indicator of a company's short-run liquidity. To determine the actual liquidity and availability of working capital to meet current obligations, however, one must analyze the current assets' composition and their nearness to cash.

Long-Term Debt/Liabilities

Underlying Concept

Information about covenants and restrictions gives insight into the entity's financial flexibility and is therefore disclosed in respect of the full disclosure principle.

Long-term liabilities are **obligations that are not reasonably expected to be liquidated within the normal operating cycle but instead are payable at some later date.** Bonds payable, notes payable, some future income tax liabilities, lease obligations, and pension obligations are the most common examples. Generally, extensive supplementary disclosure is needed for this section, because most long-term debt is subject to various covenants and restrictions in order to protect lenders.[19] Long-term liabilities that mature within the current operating cycle are classified as current liabilities if current assets will be used to liquidate them.

Generally, long-term liabilities are of three types:

1. Obligations arising from **specific financing situations**, such as the issuance of bonds, long-term lease obligations, and long-term notes payable

2. Obligations arising from **ordinary enterprise operations**, such as pension obligations, future income tax liabilities, and deferred or unearned revenues

3. Obligations that **depend on the occurrence or non-occurrence of one or more future events to confirm the amount payable**, the payee, or the date payable, such as service or product warranties and other contingencies

It is desirable to report any premium or discount as an addition to, or subtraction from, the bonds payable. The terms of all long-term liability agreements (including the maturity date or dates, interest rates, nature of the obligation, and any security pledged to support the debt) are frequently described in notes to the financial statements. **Future income tax liabilities** (deferred income taxes) are future amounts that the company owes to the government for income taxes. Deferred or unearned revenues are often treated as liabilities because a service or product is owed to the customer (performance obligation). They may be classified as long-term or current.

The excerpt from **Empire Company Limited** in Illustration 5-10 is an example of the liabilities section of the balance sheet. The company owns Sobeys Inc. food stores.

---

[19] The rights and privileges of the various securities that are outstanding (both debt and equity) are usually explained in the notes to the financial statements. Examples of information that should be disclosed are dividend and liquidation preferences, participation rights, call prices and dates, conversion or exercise prices or rates and pertinent dates, sinking fund requirements, unusual voting rights, and significant terms of contracts to issue additional shares.

Illustration 5-10

Balance Sheet Presentation of Long-Term Debt—Excerpt from Empire Company Limited's 2009 Balance Sheet (in millions of dollars)

Real-World Emphasis

Liabilities

Current

Bank indebtedness (Note 11)	$ 45.9	$ 92.6
Accounts payable and accrued liabilities	1,487.1	1,348.4
Income taxes payable	—	15.5
Future income taxes (Note 18)	42.7	32.9
Long-term debt due within one year (Note 12)	133.0	60.4
Liabilities relating to assets held for sale (Note 9)	—	6.4
	1,708.7	1,556.2
Long-term debt (Note 12)	1,124.0	1,414.1
Employee future benefits obligation (Note 25)	118.4	110.7
Future income taxes (Note 18)	89.5	125.5
Other long-term liabilities (Note 13)	135.0	106.5
Minority interest	38.9	37.6
	3,214.5	3,350.6

Shareholders' Equity

Capital stock (Note 14)	324.5	195.7
Contributed surplus	1.7	0.5
Retained earnings	2,405.8	2,207.6
Accumulated other comprehensive loss	(48.5)	(21.5)
	2,683.5	2,382.3
	$5,898.0	$5,732.9

Guarantees, commitments and contingent liabilities (Note 23)

Subsequent events (Note 30)

Note that the company's long-term liabilities are mainly composed of long-term debt.

Owners' Equity

The **owners' equity** (shareholders' equity) section is one of the most difficult sections to prepare and understand. This is due to the complexity of capital share agreements and the various restrictions on residual equity that are imposed by corporation laws, liability agreements, and boards of directors. The section is usually divided into four parts:

1. **Capital Shares**, which represents the exchange value of shares that have been issued

2. **Contributed Surplus**, which may include items such as gains from certain related party transactions

3. **Retained Earnings**, which includes undistributed earnings, and is sometimes referred to as earned surplus

Law

4. **Accumulated Other Comprehensive Income**, which may include unrealized gains and losses on certain investments, certain gains or losses from hedging activities, gains or losses on revalued property, plant, and equipment, and other. This need not be called "Accumulated Other Comprehensive Income."

The major disclosure requirements for capital shares (or stock) are their authorized, issued, and outstanding amounts. Contributed surplus is usually presented as one amount. Retained earnings, also presented as one amount, is positive if the company has undistributed accumulated profits. Otherwise, it will be a negative number and labelled "Deficit." Any capital shares that have been reacquired by the company (treasury stock) are shown as a reduction of shareholders' equity.[20]

[20] In Canada, under the CBCA, shares that are reacquired must be cancelled. However, some provincial jurisdictions and other countries (e.g., the United States) still allow treasury shares to exist.

A corporation's ownership or shareholders' equity accounts are quite different from the equivalent accounts in a partnership or proprietorship. Partners' permanent capital accounts and the balances in their temporary accounts (drawings accounts) are shown separately. Proprietorships ordinarily use a single capital account that handles all of the owner's equity transactions.

Illustration 5-11 presents the shareholders' equity section from **Talisman Energy Inc.**

Illustration 5-11

Balance Sheet Presentation of Shareholders' Equity—Excerpt from Talisman Energy Inc.'s December 31, 2008 Balance Sheet (in millions of dollars)

Real-World Emphasis

Shareholders' equity		
Common shares, no par value (note 13)		
Authorized: unlimited		
Issued and outstanding:		
2008 – 1,015 million (2007 – 1,019 million)	**2,372**	2,437
Contributed surplus	**84**	64
Retained earnings	**8,966**	5,651
Accumulated other comprehensive loss (note 14)	**(272)**	(189)
	11,150	7,963

Note that the Accumulated Other Comprehensive Loss account is in a deficit position and hence the amounts are shown in parentheses. The company has chosen to show the details on the number of shares issued and authorized on the face of the balance sheet. Additional details are shown in the notes.

Balance Sheet Format

One method of presenting a classified balance sheet is to list assets by sections on the left side and liabilities and shareholders' equity by sections on the right side. The main disadvantage of this format is that it requires two facing pages. To avoid the use of facing pages, another format, shown in Illustration 5-12, lists liabilities and shareholders' equity directly below assets on the same page.

Illustration 5-12

Classified Balance Sheet

SCIENTIFIC PRODUCTS, INC.
Balance Sheet
December 31, 2010

Assets		
Current assets		
Cash		$ 42,485
Investments—trading		28,250
Accounts receivable	$165,824	
Less: Allowance for doubtful accounts	1,850	163,974
Notes receivable		23,000
Inventories—at lower of average cost and NRV		489,713
Supplies on hand		9,780
Prepaid expenses		16,252
Total current assets		$ 773,454

Long-term investments			87,500
Property, plant, and equipment			
Land—at cost		125,000	
Buildings—at cost	975,800		
Less: Accumulated amortization	341,200	634,600	
Total property, plant, and equipment			759,600
Intangible assets			
Goodwill			100,000
Total assets			$1,720,554

Liabilities and Shareholders' Equity

Current liabilities			
Accounts payable		$247,532	
Accrued interest		500	
Income taxes payable		62,520	
Accrued salaries, wages, and other liabilities		9,500	
Deposits received from customers		420	
Total current liabilities			$ 320,472
Long-term debt			
Twenty-year 12% debentures, due January 1, 2011			500,000
Total liabilities			820,472
Shareholders' equity			
Paid in on capital shares			
Preferred, 7%, cumulative—authorized, issued, and outstanding, 30,000 shares	$300,000		
Common—authorized, 500,000 shares; issued and outstanding, 400,000 shares	400,000		
Contributed surplus	37,500	737,500	
Retained earnings	102,333		
Accumulated other comprehensive income	60,249	162,582	
Total shareholders' equity			900,082
Total liabilities and shareholders' equity			$1,720,554

Additional Information Reported

SUPPLEMENTAL BALANCE SHEET INFORMATION

1. *Contingencies:* material events that have an uncertain outcome

2. *Accounting Policies:* explanations of the valuation methods that are used or the basic assumptions that are made for inventory valuations, amortization methods, investments in subsidiaries, etc.

3. *Contractual Situations:* explanations of certain restrictions or covenants that are attached to specific assets or, more likely, to liabilities

4. *Additional Detail:* expanded details on specific balance sheet line items

5. *Subsequent Events:* events that happened after the balance sheet data were compiled

Contingencies

A **contingency** is an **existing situation in which there is uncertainty about whether a gain or loss will occur and that will finally be resolved when one or more future events occur or fail to occur.**[21] In short, contingencies are material events that have an uncertain future. Examples of gain contingencies are tax operating loss carry-forwards or unsettled company litigation against another party. Typical loss contingencies relate to litigation against the company, environmental issues, or possible tax assessments. Contingencies are not recognized unless they meet the definition of an asset/liability.

Recall the material in Chapter 2 regarding financial statement elements. Sometimes, rights or obligations have two parts: an unconditional right/obligation (a "stand ready" right/obligation) and a conditional one. The unconditional right/obligation is recognized as long as it meets the definition of an asset/obligation. The conditional right/obligation is normally contingent upon some future event occurring or not. This uncertainty is taken into account through measurement of the asset/obligation.

For instance, where an entity has a warranty obligation, there is an unconditional performance obligation to provide coverage over the warranty period and a conditional performance obligation to fix the product under warranty should the product break. If sold separately, the warranty coverage would cost a certain amount and this amount would reflect the value of the company standing ready to honour any losses and the value of any actual losses that occur.

The accounting and reporting requirements for contingencies are examined fully in Chapter 13.

Accounting Policies

Accounting standards recommend disclosure for all significant accounting principles and methods that management has chosen from among alternatives or that are peculiar to a particular industry. For instance, inventories can be calculated under different cost formulas (such as weighted average and FIFO); plant and equipment can be amortized under several accepted methods of cost allocation (such as double-declining-balance, straight-line, and other); and investments can be carried at different valuations (such as cost, fair value, or using the equity method). Users of financial statements who are more informed know of these possibilities and examine the statements closely to determine the methods that are used and their impact on net income and key ratios.

Companies are also required to disclose information about their use of estimates in preparing the financial statements.[22] The disclosure of significant accounting principles and methods and of risks and uncertainties is particularly useful when this information is given as the first note or when it is presented in a separate summary that precedes the notes to the financial statements.

Contractual Situations

Objective 5
Identify major disclosure techniques for the balance sheet.

In addition to contingencies and different valuation methods, contractual situations should also be disclosed in the notes to the financial statements when they are significant. It is mandatory, for example, that the essential provisions of guarantees, lease contracts, pension obligations, and stock option plans be clearly stated in the notes. The analyst who examines a set of financial statements wants to know not only the liability amounts but also how the different contractual provisions (i.e., the terms and conditions) are affecting the company now, and will in the future.

---

[21] *CICA Handbook*, Part II, Section 3290.02 and IAS 37.

[22] *CICA Handbook*, Part II, Section 1508 and various other sections.

Commitments that oblige a company to maintain a certain amount of working capital, limit its payment of dividends, restrict its use of assets, or require it to maintain certain financial ratios must all be disclosed if they are material. Considerable judgement is necessary to determine whether leaving out such information is misleading. The axiom in this situation is, "When in doubt, disclose." It is better to disclose a little too much information than not enough.

The accountant's judgement should include ethical considerations, because the way of disclosing the accounting principles, methods, and other items that have important effects on the enterprise may reflect the interests of a particular stakeholder in subtle ways that are at the expense of other stakeholders. A reader, for example, may benefit from having certain information highlighted in comprehensive notes, whereas the company—not wanting to emphasize that information—may choose to provide limited (rather than comprehensive) information in its notes.

Underlying Concept

The basis for including additional information is the full disclosure principle; that is, the information needs to be important enough to influence the decisions of an informed user.

Ethics

Additional Detail

For many balance sheet items, further detail is disclosed to make it clearer. This has already been discussed under the various headings of the balance sheet: assets, liabilities, and equity.

Subsequent Events

Several weeks or months may pass after the end of the year before the financial statements are issued. This time is used to count and price inventory, reconcile subsidiary ledgers with controlling accounts, prepare necessary adjusting entries, ensure that all transactions for the period have been entered, and obtain an audit of the financial statements.

During this period, important transactions and events may occur that materially affect the company's financial position or operating situation. These events are known as **subsequent events**. Notes to the financial statements should explain any significant financial events that occur after the formal balance sheet date but before the financial statements have been issued.

Subsequent events fall into two types or categories:

Underlying Concept

There is a trade-off here. Timely information is more relevant but may not be as reliable because it takes time to verify the information to ensure that it is complete and accurate.

1. Events that provide further evidence of **conditions that existed** at the balance sheet date (financial statements must be adjusted for these)

2. Events that indicate **conditions that occurred after** the financial statement date (these must be disclosed in notes if the condition causes a significant change to assets or liabilities, and/or it will have a significant impact on future operations)

These will be covered in further detail in Chapter 23.

Techniques of Disclosure

The additional information that is reported should be disclosed as completely and as intelligently as possible. The following methods of disclosing pertinent information are available: explanations in parentheses, notes, cross-references and contra items, and supporting schedules, as will be explained next.

Parenthetical Explanations

Additional information is often provided by explanations in parentheses that follow the item. For example, shareholders' equity may be shown as it is in Illustration 5-11 in the financial statements of Talisman.

Using the parentheses makes it possible to disclose additional balance sheet information that is pertinent and adds clarity and completeness. It has an advantage over a note because it brings the additional information into the body of the statement where it is less likely to be missed. Of course, lengthy parenthetical explanations that might distract the reader from the balance sheet information must be used carefully.

Notes

Notes are used if additional explanations cannot be shown conveniently as parenthetical explanations or to reduce the amount of detail on the face of the statement. For example, the details for property, plant, and equipment of **Air Canada** are shown in Note 3 to its financial statements rather than on the face of the statement, as Illustration 5-13 shows. Including this level of detail on the face of the balance sheet would make it more difficult to read and to focus on the main groupings of assets.

Illustration 5-13

Notes Disclosure—Excerpt from Notes to Air Canada's Financial Statements (in thousands of dollars)

Real-World Emphasis

3. PROPERTY AND EQUIPMENT

	2008	2007
Cost		
Flight equipment, including spare engines (a)	$ 6,235	$ 5,433
Assets under capital leases (b)	1,940	1,899
Buildings, including leasehold improvements	643	603
Ground and other equipment	160	136
	8,978	8,071
Accumulated depreciation and amortization		
Flight equipment, including spare engines (a)	1,101	685
Assets under capital leases (b)	562	438
Buildings, including leasehold improvements	148	118
Ground and other equipment	49	35
	1,860	1,276
	7,118	**6,795**
Purchase deposits, including capitalized interest (c)	351	1,124
Property and equipment at net book value (d)	**$ 7,469**	**$ 7,919**

The notes must present all essential facts as completely and concisely as possible. Loose wording can mislead readers instead of helping them. Notes should add to the total information that is made available in the financial statements, not raise unanswered questions or contradict other parts of the statements.

Cross-References and Contra Items

When there is a direct relationship between an asset and a liability, this can be cross-referenced on the balance sheet. For example, among the current assets section of a balance sheet dated as at December 31, 2011, this might be shown as follows:

Cash on deposit with sinking fund trustee for redemption of bonds payable—see Current liabilities	$800,000

In the same balance sheet, in the current liabilities section would be the amount of bonds payable to be redeemed within one year:

Bonds payable to be redeemed in 2012—see Current assets	$2,300,000

This cross-reference points out that $2.3 million of bonds payable are to be redeemed currently, and thus far only $800,000 in cash has been set aside for the redemption. This means, therefore, that the additional cash will need to come from unrestricted cash, from sales of investments, from profits, or from some other source. The same information can be shown in parentheses if this technique is preferred.

Another common procedure is to establish contra or adjunct accounts. A **contra account** on a balance sheet is an item that reduces an asset, liability, or owners' equity account. Examples include Accumulated Amortization and Allowance for Doubtful Accounts. Contra accounts provide some flexibility in presenting the financial information. Use of the Accumulated Amortization account, for example, allows a statement reader to see the asset's original cost and its amortization to date.

An **adjunct account**, on the other hand, increases an asset, liability, or owners' equity account. An example is Premium on Bonds Payable, which, when added to the Bonds Payable account, describes the enterprise's total bond liability.

Supporting Schedules

Often a separate schedule is needed to present more detailed information about certain assets or liabilities because the balance sheet only provides a single summary item.

Terminology

Account titles in the general ledger often use terms that are not the most helpful ones for a balance sheet. Account titles are often brief and include technical terms that are understood only by accountants. Balance sheets, meanwhile, are examined by many people who are not familiar with the technical vocabulary of accounting. Thus, balance sheets should contain descriptions that will be generally understood and are less likely to be misinterpreted.

SECTION 2—STATEMENT OF CASH FLOWS

The balance sheet, the income statement, and the statement of shareholders' equity each present information about an enterprise's cash flows during a period, but they do this to a limited extent and in a fragmented manner. For instance, comparative balance sheets might show what new assets have been acquired or disposed of and what liabilities have been incurred or liquidated. The income statement presents information about the resources provided by operations, but not exactly the cash that has been provided. The statement of retained earnings shows the amount of dividends declared. None of these statements presents a detailed summary of all the cash inflows and outflows, or the sources and uses of cash during the period. To satisfy this need, the **statement of cash flows** (also called the cash flow statement) is required.[23]

6 Objective
Indicate the purpose of the statement of cash flows.

Cash Flow Statement Tutorial

---

[23] According to the *CICA Handbook*, Part II, Section 1540.03 and IAS 7.1, the cash flow statement should be presented as an integral part of the financial statements.

The statement's value is that it helps users evaluate liquidity, solvency, and financial flexibility, as previously defined. The material in Chapter 5 is introductory as it reviews the statement of cash flows' existence, usefulness, and the mechanics of calculating cash flows from operations. Note that Chapter 22 deals with the preparation and content of the statement of cash flows in greater detail.

Purpose of the Statement of Cash Flows

The main purpose of a statement of cash flows is to allow users to **assess the enterprise's capacity to generate cash and cash equivalents and its needs for cash resources.**[24]

Reporting the sources, uses, and net increase or decrease in cash helps investors, creditors, and others know what is happening to a company's most liquid resource. Because most people maintain their chequebook and prepare their tax return on a cash basis, they can relate to and understand the statement of cash flows as it shows the causes and effects of cash inflows and outflows and the net increase or decrease in cash. The statement of cash flows answers the following simple but important questions:

1. Where did cash come from during the period?

2. What was cash used for during the period?

3. What was the change in the cash balance during the period?

Content and Format of the Statement of Cash Flows

Objective 7
Identify the content of the statement of cash flows.

Cash receipts and cash payments during a period are classified in the statement of cash flows into three different activities: **operating, investing**, and **financing** activities. These are the main types of activities that companies engage in. These classifications are defined as follows:

1. Operating activities are the enterprise's main revenue-producing activities and all other activities that are not related to investing or financing.

2. Investing activities are the acquisitions and disposals of long-term assets and other investments that are not included in cash equivalents.

3. Financing activities are activities that result in changes in the size and composition of the enterprise's equity capital and borrowings.[25]

With cash flows classified into each of these categories, the statement of cash flows has assumed the basic format shown in Illustration 5-14.

Illustration 5-14

Basic Format of Cash Flow Statement

Statement of Cash Flows	
Cash flows from operating activities	$XXX
Cash flows from investing activities	XXX
Cash flows from financing activities	XXX
Net increase (decrease) in cash	XXX
Cash at beginning of year	XXX
Cash at end of year	$XXX

[24] *CICA Handbook*, Part II, Section 1540.01 and IAS 7.4.

[25] *CICA Handbook*, Part II, Section 1540.06 and IAS 7.6.

Illustration 5-15 shows the inflows and outflows of cash classified by activity.

Illustration 5-15

Cash Inflows and Outflows

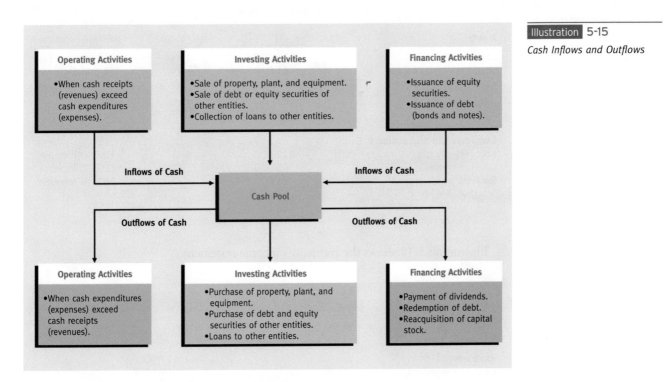

Preparation of the Statement of Cash Flows

Companies obtain the information to prepare a statement of cash flows from a variety of sources. These include the balance sheet, income statement, and selected transaction data—normally data in the general ledger Cash account. Because the statement is intended to include all cash transactions, the Cash account is an important source of information. Preparation of the statement requires the following steps:

1. Determine the cash provided by or used in operating, investing, and financing activities.

2. Determine the change (increase or decrease) in cash during the period.

3. Reconcile the change in cash with the beginning and ending cash balances.

In this chapter, we will use the following simple example to look briefly at how to calculate the cash provided by or used in operating activities. Assume that on January 1, 2010, in its first year of operations, Telemarketing Inc. issued 50,000 shares for $50,000 cash. The company then rented its office space, furniture, and telecommunications equipment and performed marketing services throughout the year. In June 2010, the company also purchased land for $15,000. Finally, it paid cash dividends of $14,000 during the year. Illustration 5-16 shows the company's comparative balance sheets at the beginning and end of 2010.

8 Objective

Prepare the cash from operating activities section of the statement of cash flows.

TELEMARKETING INC.
Balance Sheets

Assets	Dec. 31, 2010	Jan. 1, 2010	Increase/Decrease
Cash	$31,000	$–0–	$31,000 Increase
Accounts receivable	41,000	–0–	41,000 Increase
Land	15,000	–0–	15,000 Increase
Total	$87,000	$–0–	
Liabilities and Shareholders' Equity			
Accounts payable	$12,000	$–0–	12,000 Increase
Common shares	50,000	–0–	50,000 Increase
Retained earnings	25,000	–0–	25,000 Increase
Total	$87,000	–0–	

Illustration 5-17 shows the company's income statement.

TELEMARKETING INC.
Income Statement
For the Year Ended December 31, 2010

Revenues	$172,000
Operating expenses	120,000
Income before income tax	52,000
Income tax	13,000
Net income	$ 39,000

Additional information:
Dividends of $14,000 were paid during the year.

Cash provided by operating activities is the excess of cash receipts over cash payments for operating activities. Companies determine this amount by converting net income on an accrual basis to a cash basis. To do this, they add to or deduct from net income those items in the income statement that do not affect cash, such as credit sales, accrued expenses, amortization, and non-cash gains/losses. They then adjust net income for the items that affected the current year's cash but are related to the operating activities of prior years, such as the collection of the previous year's credit sales or payment of the previous year's accrued expenses. This procedure requires that a company analyze not only the current year's income statement but also the comparative balance sheet and selected transaction data (especially items affecting the Cash account). This analysis is important since, for instance, credit sales from last year that are collected this year (and were previously recorded as accounts receivable) will increase cash.

Analysis of Telemarketing's comparative balance sheets reveals two items that will affect the calculation of net cash provided by operating activities:

1. The increase in accounts receivable is a non-cash increase of $41,000 in revenues from credit sales. This amount would be included in net income as sales and so must be deducted in arriving at cash from operations.

2. The increase in accounts payable is a non-cash increase of $12,000 in expenses due to accruals. This amount would have been deducted in arriving at net income but, since these expenses did not require a cash outlay, they will be added back in arriving at cash from operations.

Therefore, to arrive at cash from operations, Telemarketing Inc. deducts from net income the increase in accounts receivable ($41,000) and it adds back to net income the increase in accounts payable ($12,000). Note that since there were no operations in the previous year, there is no need to adjust for items accrued last year that may affect cash this year. Furthermore, there are no non-cash gains/losses and no amortization. As a result of these adjustments, the company determines that cash provided by operations amounted to $10,000, as calculated in Illustration 5-18.

Net income		$39,000
Adjustments to reconcile net income to net cash provided by operating activities:		
Increase in accounts receivable	$(41,000)	
Increase in accounts payable	12,000	(29,000)
Net cash provided by operating activities		$10,000

Illustration 5-18

Calculation of Net Cash Provided by Operations

Telemarketing Inc.'s only investing activity was a land purchase. It has two financing activities: (1) the increase of $50,000 in common shares resulting from the issuance of these shares, and (2) the payment of $14,000 in cash dividends. Illustration 5-19 presents Telemarketing Inc.'s statement of cash flows for 2010.

Illustration 5-19

Statement of Cash Flows

Additional Disclosures

TELEMARKETING INC.
Statement of Cash Flows
For the Year Ended December 31, 2010

Cash flows from operating activities		
Net income		$39,000
Adjustments to reconcile net income to net cash provided by operating activities:		
Increase in accounts receivable	$(41,000)	
Increase in accounts payable	12,000	(29,000)
Net cash provided by operating activities		10,000
Cash flows from investing activities		
Purchase of land	(15,000)	
Net cash used by investing activities		(15,000)
Cash flows from financing activities		
Issuance of common shares	50,000	
Payment of cash dividends	(14,000)	
Net cash provided by financing activities		36,000
Net increase in cash		31,000
Cash at beginning of year		–0–
Cash at end of year		$31,000

The increase in cash of $31,000 that is reported in the statement of cash flows agrees with the increase in cash that was calculated from the comparative balance sheets. Note that not all of a company's activities involve cash; for example, the conversion of bonds to shares, an issuance of debt to purchase assets, and non-monetary exchanges. These activities should not be included in the body of the cash flow statement but should be disclosed elsewhere in the financial statements.

Note that the net cash provided by operating activities section begins with net income and reconciles to cash. This presentation is called the indirect method of presenting cash flows from operating activities. Another option is the direct method. The direct method normally presents the following information in the operations portion of the statement (the rest of the statement remains the same in both methods):

1. Cash received from customers

2. Cash paid to suppliers and employees

3. Interest paid/received

4. Taxes paid

5. Other

Under GAAP, either method is acceptable although the direct method is preferred. See Chapter 22 for a more detailed discussion.

Usefulness of the Statement of Cash Flows

Objective 9
Understand the usefulness of the statement of cash flows.

Although net income provides a long-term measure of a company's success or failure, cash is a company's lifeblood. Without cash, a company will not survive. For small and newly developing companies, cash flow is the single most important element of survival. Even medium and large companies indicate that controlling cash flow is a major concern.

Creditors examine the statement of cash flows carefully because they are concerned about being paid. A good starting point in their examination is to find **net cash provided by operating activities**. A high amount of net cash provided by operating activities indicates that a company was able to generate enough cash internally from operations in the most recent period to pay its bills without further borrowing. Conversely, a low or negative amount of net cash provided by operating activities indicates that a company did not generate enough cash internally from its operations and, therefore, had to borrow or issue equity securities to acquire additional cash.

Just because a company was able to generate cash flows from operating activities in the most recent period, however, does not mean that it will be able to do so again in future periods. Consequently, creditors look for answers to the following questions in the company's statement of cash flows:

1. How successful is the company in generating net cash provided by operating activities?

2. What are the trends in net cash flow provided by operating activities over time?

3. What are the major reasons for the positive or negative net cash provided by operating activities?

4. Are the cash flows sustainable or renewable; i.e., can they be repeated over time?

It is important to recognize that companies can fail even though they are profitable. The difference between net income and net cash provided by operating activities can be substantial. One of the main reasons for the difference between a positive net income and a negative net cash provided by operating activities is major increases in receivables and/or inventory. To illustrate, assume that in its first year of operations Hinchcliff Inc. reported net income of $80,000. Its net cash provided by operating activities, however, was a negative $95,000, as shown in Illustration 5-20.

Illustration 5-20

Negative Net Cash Provided by Operating Activities

HINCHCLIFF INC.
Net Cash Flow from Operating Activities

Net income		$ 80,000
Adjustments to reconcile net income to net cash provided by operating activities:		
Increase in receivables	$ (75,000)	
Increase in inventories	(100,000)	(175,000)
Net cash provided by operating activities		$ (95,000)

Note that the negative net cash provided by operating activities occurred for Hinchcliff even though it reported a positive net income. The company could easily experience a "cash crunch" because it has tied up its cash in receivables and inventory. If problems in collecting receivables occur or inventory is slow-moving or becomes obsolete, the company's creditors may have difficulty collecting on their loans.

Companies that are expanding often experience this type of "cash crunch" as they must buy increasing inventory amounts to meet increasing sales demands. This means that the cash outflow to purchase the inventory occurs before the cash inflow from the customer for sale of that product. This is often referred to as a "lead-lag" factor. The cash outflow leads (occurs first) and the cash inflow from sales lags (occurs later). The lead-lag factor requires the company to use up any excess cash that it has on hand or to borrow more funds. Refer back to Illustration 5-3 on the business operating cycle.

As mentioned earlier in the chapter, financial flexibility may be assessed by using information from the financial statements. The cash flow statement is especially good for providing this type of information.

Financial Liquidity

One ratio that is used to assess liquidity is the **current cash debt coverage ratio**. It indicates whether the company can pay off its current liabilities for the year from its operations. The formula for this ratio is shown in Illustration 5-21.

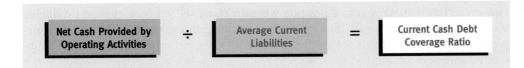

Illustration 5-21

Formula for Current Cash Debt Coverage Ratio

The higher this ratio is, the less likely it is that a company will have liquidity problems. For example, a ratio of at least 1:1 is good because it indicates that the company can meet all of its current obligations from internally generated cash flow. To compare this ratio with a benchmark number, it can be compared with the ratios for similar companies in the industry (or with the ratios of prior years for the company itself).

Financial Flexibility

A more long-run measure that provides information on financial flexibility is the **cash debt coverage ratio**. This ratio indicates a company's ability to repay its liabilities from net cash provided by operating activities without having to liquidate the assets that it uses in its operations. Illustration 5-22 presents the formula for this ratio.

Illustration 5-22

Formula for Cash Debt Coverage Ratio

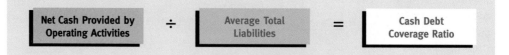

The higher this ratio, the less likely it is that the company will experience difficulty in meeting its obligations as they come due. As a result, this ratio signals whether the company can pay its debts and survive if external sources of funds become limited or too expensive.

Perspectives

Cash Flow Patterns

Refer to Illustration 5-19 showing the full statement of cash flows for Telemarketing Inc. The cash flow statement can yield some interesting results when users look at the various patterns between cash inflows and outflows for the following subtotals on the statement: operating, investing, and financing cash flows. For instance, Telemarketing Inc. has positive cash flows/cash inflows ("+") from operating activities of $10,000, negative cash flows/cash outflows ("−") from investing activities of $15,000, and positive cash flows/cash inflows ("+") from financing activities of $31,000. Together these numbers thus yield a "+" "−" "+" pattern.

Interpreting this, the company is getting its cash from operations (which is a very good sign) and also from the issuance of common shares. It is investing this cash to expand the business. The fact that the company is able to raise funds in the capital markets by issuing shares indicates that the capital markets have faith in the company's ability to prosper. The fact that the bulk of the money being used to finance the assets is generated from operations means that the company does not have to increase its solvency risk by issuing debt or further diluting its shareholders' equity by issuing more shares. Telemarketing Inc. appears to be a successful company in an expansionary mode.

Companies that generate cash from investing activities may be selling off long-term assets. This pattern generally goes with a company that is in a downsizing or restructuring mode. If the assets that are being disposed of are excess or redundant assets, then it makes sense to free up the capital that is tied up. Similarly, if the assets being disposed of relate to operations that are not profitable, disposal reflects a good management decision. However, if the company is in a position where it **must** sell off core income-producing assets (e.g., to generate cash), then it may be sacrificing future profitability and revenue-producing potential. This is obviously undesirable. Thus, cash flow patterns have significant information content.

Free Cash Flow

A more sophisticated way to examine a company's financial flexibility is to develop a free cash flow analysis. This analysis starts with net cash provided by operating activities and ends with free cash flow, which is calculated as net cash provided by operating activities less capital expenditures and dividends.[26] Free cash flow is the amount of discretionary

---

[26] In determining free cash flow, some companies do not subtract dividends, because they believe these expenditures are discretionary.

cash flow that a company has for purchasing additional investments, retiring its debt, purchasing treasury stock, or simply adding to its liquidity. This measure indicates a company's level of financial flexibility. A free cash flow analysis can answer questions such as these:

1. Is the company able to pay its dividends without the help of external financing?

2. If business operations decline, will the company be able to maintain its needed capital investment?

3. What is the free cash flow that can be used for additional investments, retirement of debt, purchases of treasury stock, or additions to liquidity?

Illustration 5-23 shows a free cash flow analysis for Nestor Corporation.

Illustration 5-23

Free Cash Flow Analysis

NESTOR CORPORATION
Free Cash Flow Analysis

Net cash provided by operating activities	$ 411,750
Less: Capital expenditures	(252,500)
Dividends	19,800
Free cash flow	$ 139,450

This analysis shows that Nestor has a positive, and substantial, net cash provided by operating activities of $411,750. Nestor reports on its statement of cash flows that it purchased equipment of $182,500 and land of $70,000 for total capital spending of $252,500. This amount is subtracted from net cash provided by operating activities because, without continued efforts to maintain and expand its facilities, it is unlikely that Nestor can continue to maintain its competitive position. Capital spending is deducted first on the analysis above to indicate it is generally the least discretionary expenditure that a company makes. Dividends are then deducted to arrive at free cash flow.

Nestor has more than enough cash flow to meet its dividend payment and therefore has satisfactory financial flexibility. Nestor used its free cash flow to redeem bonds and add to its liquidity. If it finds additional investments that are profitable, it can increase its spending without putting its dividend or basic capital spending in jeopardy. Companies that have strong financial flexibility can take advantage of profitable investments even in tough times. In addition, strong financial flexibility frees companies from worry about survival in poor economic times. In fact, those with strong financial flexibility often do better in poor economic times because they can take advantage of opportunities that other companies cannot.

Caution

As more and more complex financial instruments are created, this results in presentation issues for financial statement preparers. Many instruments have attributes of both debt and equity. This is significant for analysts since a misclassification will affect key ratios. Note disclosure of the details of the instruments helps analysts and other users in assessing a company's liquidity and solvency. This issue will be discussed further in subsequent chapters on liabilities and equities.

IFRS/PRIVATE ENTITY GAAP COMPARISON

Objective **10**

Identify differences in accounting between accounting standards for private enterprises (private entity GAAP) and IFRS.

A Comparison of IFRS and Private Entity GAAP

The differences between the IFRS and private entity GAAP sets of standards in how assets, liabilities, and shareholders' equity are accounted for and presented on the balance sheet and statement of cash flows are set out in Illustration 5-24.

	Accounting Standards for Private Enterprises (Private Entity GAAP)—*CICA Handbook* Sections 1400, 1510, 1521, 1540, and 3251	IFRS—IAS 1 and 7
Specific items to be presented in the balance sheet and statement of cash flows	For the most part, both private entity GAAP and IFRS require essentially the same items to be presented.	The following additional items are required to be presented under IFRS: Investment property Biological assets Provisions
Current vs. noncurrent liabilities	If company has refinanced debt by the issue date of the financial statements, may present as noncurrent.	If no unconditional right to defer payment of financial liability beyond one year as at balance sheet date, must show as current (including situations where the company has refinanced the debt after the balance sheet date but before issue).
Cash flow statement	Equity investments are excluded from cash and cash equivalents. Interest and dividends included in net income treated as operating activities and those booked through retained earnings treated as financing activities.	Certain preferred shares acquired within a short period of maturity date may be classified as cash and cash equivalents. IFRS allows flexibility in how to treat interest and dividends (may be classified as operating, investing or financing activities).
Cash flow per share information	Prohibited; i.e., may not disclose.	No prohibition on disclosure of this number.
Disclosure of date financial statements authorized for issue	No requirement to disclose.	Must disclose date that the financial statements were authorized for issue.

Illustration 5-24

IFRS and Private Entity GAAP Comparison Chart

Looking Ahead

Objective **11**

Identify the significant changes planned by the IASB regarding financial statement presentation.

As noted in Chapter 4, the IASB and FASB are working on financial statement presentation as a major project. The idea is to present the main financial statements in such a way as to highlight major business and financing activities. The new standard is forecast to be issued by 2011.

Appendix **5**A

Ratio Analysis: A Reference

Using Ratios to Analyze Financial Performance

Companies expose themselves to many risks in doing business. Strategically, the goal is to identify these risks and then manage them in order to take advantage of opportunities and maximize shareholder value. How do users know whether a company is managing its risks in a manner that will create the most shareholder value? Illustration 5A-1 shows

Illustration 5A-1

The Business Model and Various Related Risks That a Company Must Manage

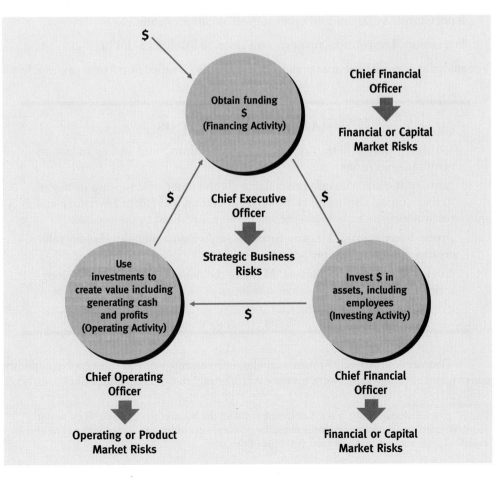

the business model that was originally introduced in Chapter 4. Now risks have been added to the model along with the key management personnel responsible for managing the risks.[27]

Financial or capital market risks are related to financing and investing activities. For example, when a company borrows funds, it might increase its solvency and liquidity risk. **Operating or product market risks** are related to operating activities. For instance, when it manufactures a drug, there is a risk that a company might not be able to produce quality products on time or successfully target the appropriate market for sale of the drug.

Information about risks is useful and much of this information is included in the annual report, both within the financial statements and in other parts. The financial statements give information about financing, investing, and operating activities and therefore provide indirect feedback on how related risks are being managed and how this in turn affects performance. A solvent company that constantly generates cash from operations has a solid business model where risks and opportunities are well managed to create value. Companies usually disclose explicit information about risks and risk management policies in the Management Discussion and Analysis section of the annual report.

Ratio analysis helps in assessing operating and financial risks by **expressing the relationship between selected financial statement data**. Qualitative information from financial statements is gathered by **examining relationships** between items on the statements and **identifying trends** in these relationships. Relationships are often expressed in terms of a percentage, a rate, or a simple proportion.

To illustrate, recently **Eastern Platinum Limited** had current assets of $48.6 million and current liabilities of $19.6 million. The relationship is determined by dividing current assets by current liabilities. The alternative means of expression are:

Percentage: Current assets are 248% of current liabilities.

Rate: Current assets are 2.48 times as great as current liabilities.

Proportion: The relationship of current assets to liabilities is 2.48:1.

For analyzing financial statements, ratios are generally classified into four types, as follows:

MAJOR TYPES OF RATIOS

Liquidity Ratios. Measure the enterprise's short-term ability to pay its maturing obligations.

Activity Ratios. Measure how effectively the enterprise is using its assets. Activity ratios also measure how liquid certain assets like inventory and receivables are; i.e., how fast the asset's value is realized by the company.

Profitability Ratios. Measure financial performance and shareholder value creation for a specific time period.

Coverage or Solvency Ratios. Measure the degree of protection for long-term creditors and investors or a company's ability to meet its long-term obligations.

WILEY PLUS

Financial Statement
Analysis Primer

In Chapter 4, profitability ratios were discussed briefly, while in this chapter, liquidity, activity, and coverage ratios were touched on. Throughout the remainder of the textbook,

---

[27] This is a brief overview only. It is meant to link risk with the business model and with the use of financial statements in communicating information about risk management. A thorough review of risk models and risk management is beyond the scope of this text.

ratios are provided to help you understand and interpret the information presented within the context of each subject area. The on-line resources available with this text look at the area of financial statement analysis, of which ratio analysis is one part. Illustration 5A-2 presents some common, basic ratios that will be used throughout the text. In practice, there are many other ratios that provide useful information and are therefore also used.

Illustration 5A-2

A Summary of Financial Ratios

RATIO	FORMULA	WHAT IT MEASURES
I. Liquidity		
1. Current ratio	$\dfrac{\text{Current assets}}{\text{Current liabilities}}$	Short-term debt-paying ability
2. Quick or acid-test ratio	$\dfrac{\text{Cash, marketable securities, and receivables (net)}}{\text{Current liabilities}}$	Immediate short-term liquidity
3. Current cash debt coverage ratio	$\dfrac{\text{Net cash provided by operating activities}}{\text{Average current liabilities}}$	Company's ability to pay off its current liabilities in a specific year from its operations
II. Activity		
4. Receivables turnover	$\dfrac{\text{Net sales}}{\text{Average trade receivables (net)}}$	Liquidity of receivables
5. Inventory turnover	$\dfrac{\text{Cost of goods sold}}{\text{Average inventory}}$	Liquidity of inventory
6. Asset turnover	$\dfrac{\text{Net sales}}{\text{Average total assets}}$	How efficiently assets are used to generate sales
III. Profitability		
7. Profit margin on sales	$\dfrac{\text{Net income}}{\text{Net sales}}$	Net income generated by each dollar of sales
8. Rate of return on assets	$\dfrac{\text{Net income}}{\text{Average total assets}}$	Overall profitability of assets
9. Rate of return on common share equity	$\dfrac{\text{Net income minus preferred dividends}}{\text{Average common shareholders' equity}}$	Profitability of owners' investment
10. Earnings per share	$\dfrac{\text{Net income minus preferred dividends}}{\text{Weighted average shares outstanding}}$	Net income earned on each common share
11. Price earnings ratio	$\dfrac{\text{Market price of shares}}{\text{Earnings per share}}$	Ratio of the market price per share to earnings per share
12. Payout ratio	$\dfrac{\text{Cash dividends}}{\text{Net income}}$	Percentage of earnings distributed as cash dividends
IV. Coverage		
13. Debt to total assets	$\dfrac{\text{Total debt}}{\text{Total assets}}$	Percentage of total assets provided by creditors
14. Times interest earned	$\dfrac{\text{Income before interest charges and taxes}}{\text{Interest charges}}$	Ability to meet interest payments as they come due
15. Cash debt coverage ratio	$\dfrac{\text{Net cash provided by operating activities}}{\text{Average total liabilities}}$	Company's ability to repay its total liabilities in a specific year from its operations
16. Book value per share	$\dfrac{\text{Common shareholders' equity}}{\text{Outstanding shares}}$	Amount each share would receive if the company were liquidated at the amounts reported on the balance sheet

The key to a refined, information-rich analysis is having a good **understanding of the business, business risks, and industry** before calculating and interpreting any ratios. Specialized industries focus on different ratios depending on the critical success factors in their business. As discussed throughout the chapter, different companies and businesses would be expected to have different types of assets and capital structures. Furthermore, they would be expected to have different types of costs, revenue streams, and business models.

Success in the retail industry, for instance, is in the ability to set prices and target customers in a way that gets maximum market penetration. Also critical is the ability to minimize inventory shrinkage (there is a high risk of theft) and keep inventory moving so that it does not become obsolete or out of fashion. A company's ability to achieve this, or its failure to do so, is reflected in the gross profit margin (a ratio). This is calculated by dividing gross profit by revenues. Companies must achieve a gross profit that is high enough to cover other costs. A stable gross profit margin is a positive sign that management is dealing with all of the above issues.

Once ratios are calculated, they must then be examined and the information interpreted. Examining ratios by themselves provides very little insight. Instead, the **ratios must be compared with or benchmarked against similar ratios, perhaps for the same company from prior periods or, alternatively, for similar companies in the same industry**.

When benchmarking is done against industry numbers, it may be necessary to create industry benchmarks if they are not available. To do this, select several companies that have a similar business model and are in the same industry. Companies that are the same size are better comparators.

Note that average amounts may be approximated by taking opening and closing balances and dividing by two.

Summary of Learning Objective for Appendix 5A

WILEY
PLUS
Glossary

KEY TERMS

activity ratios, 254
coverage ratios, 254
liquidity ratios, 254
profitability ratios, 254
ratio analysis, 254
solvency ratios, 254

12 Identify the major types of financial ratios and what they measure.

Ratios express the mathematical relationship between one quantity and another, in terms of a percentage, a rate, or a proportion. Liquidity ratios measure the short-term ability to pay maturing obligations. Activity ratios measure how effectively assets are being used. Profitability ratios measure an enterprise's success or failure. Coverage ratios measure the degree of protection for long-term creditors and investors.

Appendix **5**B

Specimen Financial Statements

Eastern Platinum Limited

The following pages contain the financial statements, accompanying notes, and other information from the first quarter 2009 financial statements of **Eastern Platinum Limited** (Eastplats).

The Business

Eastplats is in the mining, exploration, and development business, with mines in South Africa. Primarily, it mines platinum and platinum group metals (referred to in the statements as "PGM"). Prices for PGM dropped dramatically in 2008 from U.S. $1,927 per ounce to U.S. $676 per ounce. This has accounted for a sharp decrease in quarterly revenues as compared with the prior year even though the company has sold more (32,969 ounces in the first quarter of 2009 versus 27,825 in the first quarter of 2008). Since December 31, 2008, however, prices for PGM have risen by 15%.

PGM are commodities and as such, their prices reflect supply and demand. This can be a problem for mining companies, which often have significant fixed and sunk costs (often consisting of significant exploration and development costs). Note that Eastplats has been able to decrease its cash cost per ounce to U.S. $536 in March 2009 from U.S. $698 on March 2008.

At this point, we recommend that you take 20 to 30 minutes to scan the statements and notes to familiarize yourself with the contents and accounting elements. Throughout the following chapters, when you are asked to refer to specific parts of Eastplats's financials, do so. Then, when you have completed reading this book, we challenge you to reread Eastplats's financials to see how much greater and more sophisticated your understanding of them has become.

Eastern Platinum Limited

Condensed consolidated income statements

(Expressed in thousands of U.S. dollars, except per share amounts - unaudited)

	Note	March 31, 2009 (3 months)	March 31, 2008 (3 months) (Note 15)
Revenue		$ **24,903**	$ 55,795
Cost of operations			
Production costs		**17,885**	19,750
Depletion and depreciation		**3,517**	4,394
		21,402	24,144
Mine operating earnings		**3,501**	31,651
Expenses			
General and administrative		**1,636**	4,333
Share-based payment	11	**132**	1,349
		1,768	5,682
Operating profit		**1,733**	25,969
Other income (expense)			
Interest income		**494**	2,807
Finance costs		**(452)**	(8)
Foreign exchange (loss) gain		**(75)**	1,057
Profit before income taxes		**1,700**	29,825
Deferred income tax recovery (expense)		**680**	(8,247)
Net profit for the period		$ **2,380**	$ 21,578
Attributable to			
Non-controlling interest	4	$ **(784)**	$ 2,102
Equity shareholders of the Company		$ **3,164**	$ 19,476
Earnings per share			
Basic		$ **0.00**	$ 0.03
Diluted		$ **0.00**	$ 0.03
Weighted average number of common shares outstanding			
Basic		**680,526,454**	669,872,192
Diluted		**683,394,510**	718,406,612

Eastern Platinum Limited

Condensed consolidated statements of financial position
as at March 31, 2009 and December 31, 2008
(Expressed in thousands of U.S. dollars - unaudited)

	Note	March 31, 2009	December 31, 2008 (Note 15)
Assets			
Current assets			
Cash and cash equivalents		$ 7,740	$ 25,806
Short-term investments		14,226	35,257
Trade receivables		23,053	9,431
Inventories	5	3,551	3,881
		48,570	74,375
Property, plant and equipment	6	501,388	508,685
Refining contract	7	11,901	12,493
Other assets	8	1,018	1,017
		$ 562,877	$ 596,570
Liabilities			
Current liabilities			
Accounts payable and accrued liabilities		$ 14,423	$ 35,003
Provisions		1,548	1,726
Current portion of finance leases		653	649
Current loans		2,995	2,972
		19,619	40,350
Provision for environmental rehabilitation	9	5,548	5,598
Finance leases		3,249	3,261
Deferred tax liabilities		37,095	38,826
		65,511	88,035
Commitments	10		
Capital and reserves			
Issued capital	11	890,049	890,049
Equity reserve		31,959	31,827
Currency translation adjustment		(182,904)	(169,577)
Deficit		(252,602)	(255,766)
		486,502	496,533
Non-controlling interest	4	10,864	12,002
		497,366	508,535
		$ 562,877	$ 596,570

Approved by the Board and authorized for issue on May 11, 2009.

"David Cohen"
David Cohen, Director

"Robert Gayton"
Robert Gayton, Director

Eastern Platinum Limited

Condensed consolidated statement of changes in equity
(Expressed in thousands of U.S. dollars - unaudited)

	Issued Capital Shares	Amount	Equity Reserve	Currency Translation Adjustment	Deficit	Subtotal	Non-controlling Interest	Total Shareholders' Equity
Balance, January 1, 2008 (Note 15)	669,031,691	$ 868,045	$ 27,428	$ -	$ (46,385)	$ 849,088	$ 23,133	$ 872,221
Warrants exercised	2,117,400	3,936	-	-	-	3,936	-	3,936
Stock options exercised	160,000	370	(82)	-	-	288	-	288
Share-based payment	-	-	1,349	-	-	1,349	-	1,349
Currency translation adjustment	-	-	-	(96,365)	-	(96,365)	-	(96,365)
Net profit for the period	-	-	-	-	19,476	19,476	-	19,476
Non-controlling interest for the period	-	-	-	-	-	-	(1,165)	(1,165)
Balance, March 31, 2008 (Note 15)	671,309,091	$ 872,351	$ 28,695	$ (96,365)	$ (26,909)	$ 777,772	$ 21,968	$ 799,740
Warrants exercised	8,706,677	17,217	-	-	-	17,217	-	17,217
Stock options exercised	510,686	481	(145)	-	-	336	-	336
Share-based payment	-	-	3,277	-	-	3,277	-	3,277
Currency translation adjustment	-	-	-	(73,212)	-	(73,212)	-	(73,212)
Net loss for the period	-	-	-	-	(228,857)	(228,857)	-	(228,857)
Non-controlling interest for the period	-	-	-	-	-	-	(9,966)	(9,966)
Balance, December 31, 2008 (Note 15)	680,526,454	$ 890,049	$ 31,827	$ (169,577)	$ (255,766)	$ 496,533	$ 12,002	$ 508,535
Share-based payment	-	-	132	-	-	132	-	132
Currency translation adjustment	-	-	-	(13,327)	-	(13,327)	-	(13,327)
Net profit for the period	-	-	-	-	3,164	3,164	-	3,164
Non-controlling interest for the period	-	-	-	-	-	-	(1,138)	(1,138)
Balance, March 31, 2009	680,526,454	$ 890,049	$ 31,959	$ (182,904)	$ (252,602)	$ 486,502	$ 10,864	$ 497,366

Eastern Platinum Limited
Condensed consolidated statement of comprehensive loss
(Expressed in thousands of U.S. dollars - unaudited)

	March 31, 2009 (3 months)	March 31, 2008 (3 months) (Note 15)
Net profit for the period	$ 2,380	$ 21,578
Other comprehensive loss - currency translation adjustment	(13,327)	(96,365)
Comprehensive loss	$ (10,947)	$ (74,787)
Attributable to		
Non-controlling interest	$ (784)	$ 2,102
Equity shareholders of the Company	$ (10,163)	$ (76,889)

Eastern Platinum Limited

Condensed consolidated statements of cash flows

(Expressed in thousands of U.S. dollars - unaudited)

	Note	March 31, 2009 (3 months)	March 31, 2008 (3 months) (Note 15)
Operating activities			
Net profit for the period		$ 2,380	$ 21,578
Adjustments to net profit			
Depletion and depreciation		3,517	4,394
Refining contract amortization	7	254	367
Share-based payment		132	1,349
Interest income		(494)	(2,807)
Interest income received		376	1,443
Finance costs		452	8
Finance costs paid		(11)	118
Foreign exchange loss (gain)		75	(1,057)
Deferred income tax (recovery) expense		(680)	8,247
Income taxes paid		(2,422)	-
		3,579	33,640
Net changes in non-cash working capital items			
Trade receivables		(13,263)	(29,851)
Inventories		219	314
Accounts payable and accrued liabilities		(16,984)	2,362
		(26,449)	6,465
Investing activities			
Maturity of short-term investments		20,095	54,597
Purchase of other assets		(27)	(30)
Property, plant and equipment expenditures		(10,717)	(23,706)
		9,351	30,861
Financing activities			
Common shares issued for cash, net of share issue costs		-	4,224
Advance from (repayment of) current loans		41	(574)
Payment of finance leases		(13)	(412)
		28	3,238
Effect of exchange rate changes on cash and cash equivalents		(996)	(1,183)
(Decrease) increase in cash and cash equivalents		(18,066)	39,381
Cash and cash equivalents, beginning of period		25,806	18,818
Cash and cash equivalents, end of period		$ 7,740	$ 58,199
Cash and cash equivalents are comprised of:			
Cash in bank		$ 6,118	$ 17,839
Short-term money market instruments		1,622	40,360
		$ 7,740	$ 58,199

Eastern Platinum Limited
Notes to the condensed consolidated financial statements
(Expressed in thousands of U.S. dollars, except number of shares and per share amounts)

1.   Nature of operations

Eastern Platinum Limited (the "Company") is a platinum group metal ("PGM") producer engaged in the mining, exploration and development of PGM properties located in various provinces in South Africa.

2.   Basis of preparation

In February 2009, the British Columbia and Ontario Securities Commissions granted the Company exemptive relief to adopt International Financial Reporting Standards ("IFRS") with an adoption date of January 1, 2009 and a transition date of January 1, 2008.

These condensed consolidated financial statements, including comparatives, have been prepared using accounting policies consistent with International Financial Reporting Standards ("IFRS") and in accordance with International Accounting Standard ("IAS") 34 *Interim Financial Reporting*. The disclosures concerning the transition from Canadian GAAP to IFRS are included in Note 15.

The preparation of financial statements requires management to make judgments, estimates and assumptions that affect the application of policies and reported amounts of assets and liabilities, profit and expenses. The estimates and associated assumptions are based on historical experience and various other factors that are believed to be reasonable under the circumstances, the results of which form the basis of making the judgments about carrying values of assets and liabilities that are not readily apparent from other sources. Actual results may differ from these estimates.

The estimates and underlying assumptions are reviewed on an ongoing basis. Revisions to accounting estimates are recognized in the period in which the estimate is revised if the revision affects only that period or in the period of the revision and further periods if the review affects both current and future periods.

Judgments made by management in the application of IFRS that have a significant effect on the financial statements and estimates with a significant risk of material adjustment in the next year are discussed in Notes 3(e), 3(l), 9, and 14.

The standards that will be effective or available for voluntary early adoption in the financial statements for the year ending December 31, 2009 are subject to change and may be affected by additional interpretation(s). Accordingly, the accounting policies will be finalized when the first annual IFRS financial statements are prepared for the year ending December 31, 2009.

3.   Summary of significant accounting policies

The condensed financial statements have been prepared under the historical cost convention, except for the revaluation of certain financial instruments. The Company's principal accounting policies are outlined below:

(a)   Basis of consolidation

These consolidated financial statements incorporate the financial statements of the Company and the entities controlled by the Company (its subsidiaries, including special purpose entities). Control exists when the Company has the power, directly or indirectly, to govern the financial and operating policies of an entity so as to obtain benefits from its activities. The financial statements of subsidiaries are included in the consolidated financial statements from the date that control commences until the date that control ceases. All significant intercompany transactions and balances have been eliminated.

Eastern Platinum Limited
Notes to the condensed consolidated financial statements
 (Expressed in thousands of U.S. dollars, except number of shares and per share amounts)

3.   Summary of significant accounting policies (continued)

   (a)   Basis of consolidation (continued)

   Non-controlling interest in the net assets of consolidated subsidiaries are identified separately from the Company's equity. Non-controlling interest consists of the non-controlling interest at the date of the original business combination plus the non-controlling interest's share of changes in equity since the date of acquisition.

   Special Purpose Entities ("SPE's") as defined by the International Accounting Standards Board ("IASB") in SIC 12 *Consolidation – Special Purpose Entities* are entities which are created to accomplish a narrow and well-defined objective (e.g. to act as a Black Economic Empowerment ("BEE") partner). SPE's are subject to consolidation when there is an indication that the other entity controls the SPE. The Company has determined that its investment in Gubevu Consortium Holdings (Pty) Ltd. ("Gubevu") is a SPE that the Company controls. The accounts of Gubevu are consolidated with those of the Company.

   (b)   Business combinations

   Business combinations that occurred prior to January 1, 2008 were not accounted for in accordance with IFRS 3 *Business Combinations* or IAS 27 *Consolidated and Separate Financial Statements* in accordance with the IFRS 1 *First-time Adoption of International Financial Reporting Standards* exemption discussed in Note 15(a).

   Acquisitions of subsidiaries and businesses are accounted for using the purchase method. The cost of the business combination is measured as the aggregate of the fair values (at the date of exchange) of assets given, liabilities incurred or assumed, and equity instruments issued by the Company in exchange for control of the acquiree, plus any costs directly attributable to the business combination. The acquiree's identifiable assets, liabilities and contingent liabilities that meet the conditions for recognition under IFRS 3 *Business Combinations* are recognized at their fair values at the acquisition date, except for non-current assets (or disposal groups) that are classified as held for sale in accordance with IFRS 5 *Non-current Assets Held for Sale and Discontinued Operations,* which are recognized and measured at fair value less costs to sell.

   Goodwill arising on acquisition is recognized as an asset and initially measured at cost, being the excess of the cost of the business combination over the Company's interest in the net fair value of the identifiable assets, liabilities and contingent liabilities recognized. If the Company's interest in the net fair value of the acquiree's identifiable assets, liabilities and contingent liabilities exceeds the cost of the business combination, the excess is recognized immediately in profit or loss.

   The interest of non-controlling shareholders in the acquiree is initially measured at the non-controlling shareholders' proportion of the net fair value of the assets, liabilities and contingent liabilities recognized.

Eastern Platinum Limited
Notes to the condensed consolidated financial statements
(Expressed in thousands of U.S. dollars, except number of shares and per share amounts)

3. **Summary of significant accounting policies (continued)**

   (c)   *Presentation currency*

   The Company's presentation currency is the U.S. dollar ("$"). The functional currency of Eastern Platinum Limited and its South African subsidiaries is the Canadian Dollar and South African Rand ("ZAR"), respectively. These consolidated financial statements have been translated to the U.S. dollar in accordance with IAS 21 *The Effects of Changes in Foreign Exchange Rates*. These guidelines require that assets and liabilities be translated using the exchange rate at period end, and income, expenses and cash flow items are translated using the rate that approximates the exchange rates at the dates of the transactions (i.e. the average rate for the period). Subsequent to the adoption of IFRS, all resulting exchange differences are reported as a separate component of shareholders' equity titled "Cumulative Translation Adjustment".

   (d)   *Foreign currency translation*

   In preparing the financial statements of the individual entities, transactions in currencies other than the entity's functional currency (foreign currencies) are recorded at the rates of exchange prevailing at the dates of the transactions. At each statement of financial position date, monetary assets and liabilities are translated using the period end foreign exchange rate. Non-monetary assets and liabilities are translated using the historical rate on the date of the transaction. Non-monetary assets and liabilities that are stated at fair value are translated using the historical rate on the date that the fair value was determined. All gains and losses on translation of these foreign currency transactions are included in the condensed consolidated income statements.

   (e)   *Measurement uncertainty*

   The preparation of financial statements in conformity with IFRS requires management to make estimates and assumptions that affect the reported amounts of assets and liabilities and disclosures of contingent assets and liabilities at the date of the financial statements and the reported amounts of revenues and expenses during the reporting period.

   Actual results could differ from those estimates. Significant accounts that require estimates as the basis for determining the stated amounts include accounting for doubtful accounts receivable, inventories, property, plant and equipment, provision for environmental rehabilitations, share-based payment, allocation of the purchase price of acquisitions and income and mining taxes.

   Depreciation and depletion of property, plant and equipment assets are dependent upon estimates of useful lives and reserve estimates, both of which are determined with the exercise of judgement. The assessment of any impairment of property, plant and equipment is dependent upon estimates of recoverable amount that take into account factors such as reserves, economic and market conditions and the useful lives of assets. Provisions for environmental rehabilitations are recognized in the period in which they arise and are stated as the fair value of estimated future costs. These estimates require extensive judgement about the nature, cost and timing of the work to be completed, and may change with future changes to costs, environmental laws and regulations and remediation practices.

Eastern Platinum Limited

Notes to the condensed consolidated financial statements
(Expressed in thousands of U.S. dollars, except number of shares and per share amounts)

3.   Summary of significant accounting policies (continued)

(f)   *Revenue recognition*

Revenue is measured at the fair value of the consideration received or receivable. The following specific criteria must be met before revenue is recognized:

(i)   *Sale of goods*

Revenue from the sale of platinum group and other metals is recognized when all of the following conditions are satisfied:

- the specific risks and rewards of ownership have been transferred to the purchaser;
- the Company does not retain continuing managerial involvement to the degree usually associated with ownership or effective control over the metals sold;
- the amount of revenue can be measured reliably;
- it is probable that the economic benefits associated with the transaction will flow to the entity; and
- the costs incurred or to be incurred in respect of the sale can be measured reliably.

The sale of platinum group metals is provisionally priced such that the price is not settled until a predetermined future date based on the market price at that time. Revenue on these sales is initially recognized (when the conditions above are met) at the current market price. Subsequent to initial recognition but prior to settlement, sales are marked to market at each reporting date using the forward price for the period equivalent to that outlined in the contract. This mark to market adjustment is recorded in revenue.

(ii)   *Rental income*

Rental income from residential properties is recognized as other income on a straight-line basis over the term of the lease.

(iii)   *Interest income*

Interest income is recognized in the income statement as it accrues, using the effective interest method.

(g)   *Share-based payments*

The Company grants stock options to buy common shares of the Company to directors, officers, employees and service providers. The board of directors grants such options for periods of up to ten years, with vesting periods determined at its sole discretion and at prices equal to or greater than the closing market price on the day preceding the date the options were granted.

The fair value of the options is measured at grant date, using the Black-Scholes option pricing model, and is recognized over the period that the employees earn the options. The fair value is recognized as an expense with a corresponding increase in equity. The amount recognized as expense is adjusted to reflect the number of share options expected to vest.

Eastern Platinum Limited

Notes to the condensed consolidated financial statements
(Expressed in thousands of U.S. dollars, except number of shares and per share amounts)

3.   Summary of significant accounting policies (continued)

   (h)   Finance costs

   Finance costs comprise interest payable on borrowings calculated using the effective interest rate method and foreign exchange gains and losses on foreign currency borrowings.

   (i)   Income taxes

   Income tax expense consists of current and deferred tax expense. Income tax expense is recognized in the income statement.

   Current tax expense is the expected tax payable on the taxable income for the year, using tax rates enacted or substantively enacted at period end, adjusted for amendments to tax payable with regards to previous years.

   Deferred taxes are recorded using the statement of financial position liability method. Under the statement of financial position liability method, deferred tax assets and liabilities are recognized for future tax consequences attributable to differences between the financial statement carrying amounts of existing assets and liabilities and their respective tax bases. Future tax assets and liabilities are measured using the enacted or substantively enacted tax rates expected to apply when the asset is realized or the liability settled.

   The effect on future tax assets and liabilities of a change in tax rates is recognized in income in the period that substantive enactment occurs.

   A deferred tax asset is recognized to the extent that it is probable that future taxable profits will be available against which the asset can be utilized. To the extent that the Company does not consider it probable that a future tax asset will be recovered, it provides a valuation allowance against the excess.

   The following temporary differences do not result in deferred tax assets or liabilities:
   - the initial recognition of assets or liabilities that do not affect accounting or taxable profit
   - goodwill

   Deferred tax assets and liabilities are offset when there is a legally enforceable right to set off current tax assets against current tax liabilities and when they relate to income taxes levied by the same taxation authority and the Company intends to settle its current tax assets and liabilities on a net basis.

   (j)   Earnings (loss) per share

   Basic earnings (loss) per share is computed by dividing the net earnings (loss) available to common shareholders by the weighted average number of shares outstanding during the reporting year. Diluted earnings (loss) per share is computed similar to basic earnings (loss) per share except that the weighted average shares outstanding are increased to include additional shares for the assumed exercise of stock options and warrants, if dilutive. The number of additional shares is calculated by assuming that outstanding stock options and warrants were exercised and that the proceeds from such exercises were used to acquire common stock at the average market price during the reporting periods.

Eastern Platinum Limited

Notes to the condensed consolidated financial statements
(Expressed in thousands of U.S. dollars, except number of shares and per share amounts)

3.   **Summary of significant accounting policies (continued)**

(k)   *Comprehensive profit (loss)*

Comprehensive profit (loss) is the change in the Company's net assets that results from transactions, events and circumstances from sources other than the Company's shareholders and includes items that would not normally be included in net profit such as unrealized gains or losses on available-for-sale investments, gains or losses on certain derivative instruments and foreign currency gains or losses related to self-sustaining operations. The Company's comprehensive profit (loss), components of other comprehensive income, and cumulative translation adjustments are presented in the Condensed Consolidated Statements of Comprehensive Profit (Loss) and the Condensed Consolidated Statements of Shareholders' Equity.

(l)   *Property, plant and equipment*

(i)   *Mining assets*

Mining assets are recorded at cost less accumulated depreciation and accumulated impairment losses. All direct costs related to the acquisition, exploration and development of mineral properties are capitalized until the properties to which they relate are placed into production, sold, abandoned or management has determined there to be impairment. If economically recoverable ore reserves are developed, capitalized costs of the related property are reclassified as mining assets and amortized using the units-of-production method following commencement of production. Interest on borrowings incurred to finance mining assets is capitalized until the asset is capable of carrying out its intended use.

Mining properties and mining and process facility assets are amortized on a units-of-production basis which is measured by the portion of the mine's economically recoverable and proven ore reserves recovered during the period. Capital work-in-progress, which is included in mining assets, is not depreciated until the assets are ready for its intended use.

Although the Company has taken steps to verify title to the properties on which it is conducting exploration and in which it has an interest, in accordance with industry standards for the current stage of exploration of such properties, these procedures do not guarantee the Company's title. Property title may be subject to unregistered prior agreements and non-compliance with regulatory requirements.

(ii)   *Other assets*

Other assets are depreciated using the straight-line method based on estimated useful lives, which generally range from 5 to 7 years, with the exception of residential properties and mine houses whose estimated useful lives are 50 years and office buildings whose estimated useful lives are 20 years. Land is not depreciated.

Where an item of plant and equipment comprises major components with different useful lives, the components are accounted for as separate items of plant and equipment.

Eastern Platinum Limited
Notes to the condensed consolidated financial statements
(Expressed in thousands of U.S. dollars, except number of shares and per share amounts)

3. Summary of significant accounting policies (continued)

    (l) Property, plant and equipment (continued)

        (ii) Other assets (continued)

Expenditures incurred to replace a component of an item of property, plant and equipment that is accounted for separately, including major inspection and overhaul expenditures, are capitalized. Directly attributable expenses incurred for major capital projects and site preparation are capitalized until the asset is brought to a working condition for its intended use. These costs include dismantling and site restoration costs to the extent these are recognized as a provision.

The cost of self-constructed assets includes the cost of materials, direct labour and an appropriate portion of normal overheads.

The costs of day-to-day servicing are recognized in profit or loss as incurred. These costs are more commonly referred to as "maintenance and repairs."

Financing costs directly associated with the construction or acquisition of qualifying assets are capitalized at interest rates relating to loans specifically raised for that purpose, or at the average borrowing rate where the general pool of group borrowings is utilized. Capitalization of borrowing costs ceases when the asset is substantially complete.

The depreciation method, useful life and residual values are assessed annually.

        (iii) Leased assets

Leases in which the Company assumes substantially all risks and rewards of ownership are classified as finance leases. Finance leases are recognized at the lower of the fair value and the present value of the minimum lease payments at inception of the lease, less accumulated depreciation and impairment losses. Lease payments are accounted for as discussed in Note 3(s).

        (iv) Subsequent Costs

The cost of replacing part of an item within property, plant and equipment is recognized when the cost is incurred if it is probable that the future economic benefits will flow to the group and the cost of the item can be measured reliably. All other costs are recognized as an expense as incurred.

        (v) Impairment

The Company's tangible and intangible assets are reviewed for an indication of impairment at each statement of financial position date. If indication of impairment exists, the asset's recoverable amount is estimated.

An impairment loss is recognized when the carrying amount of an asset, or its cash-generating unit, exceeds its recoverable amount. A cash-generating unit is the smallest identifiable group of assets that generates cash inflows that are largely independent of the cash inflows from other assets or groups of assets. Impairment losses are recognized in profit and loss for the period. Impairment losses recognized in respect of cash-generating units are allocated first to reduce the carrying amount of any goodwill allocated to cash-generating units and then to reduce the carrying amount of the other assets in the unit on a pro-rata basis.

Eastern Platinum Limited

Notes to the condensed consolidated financial statements
(Expressed in thousands of U.S. dollars, except number of shares and per share amounts)

3.   Summary of significant accounting policies (continued)

(l)   *Property, plant and equipment (continued)*

(v)   *Impairment (continued)*

The recoverable amount is the greater of the asset's fair value less costs to sell and value in use. In assessing value in use, the estimated future cash flows are discounted to their present value using a pre-tax discount rate that reflects current market assessments of the time value of money and the risks specific to the asset. For an asset that does not generate largely independent cash inflows, the recoverable amount is determined for the cash-generating unit to which the asset belongs.

(vi)   *Reversal of impairment*

An impairment loss is reversed if there is an indication that there has been a change in the estimates used to determine the recoverable amount. An impairment loss is reversed only to the extent that the asset's carrying amount does not exceed the carrying amount that would have been determined, net of depreciation or amortization, if no impairment loss had been recognized. An impairment loss with respect to goodwill is never reversed.

(m)   *Refining contract*

The Company sells its concentrate to one customer under the terms of an off-take or refining contract. The refining contract is amortized over the life of the contract, estimated to be twelve years. An evaluation of the carrying value of the contract is undertaken whenever events or changes in circumstances indicate that the carrying amount may not be recoverable.

(n)   *Inventories*

Inventories, comprising stockpiled ore and concentrate awaiting further processing and sale, are valued at the lower of cost and net realizable value. Consumables are valued at the lower of cost and net realizable value, with replacement cost used as the best available measure of net realizable value. Cost is determined using the weighted average method and includes direct mining expenditures and an appropriate portion of normal overhead expenditure. In the case of concentrate, direct concentrate costs are also included. Net realizable value is the estimated selling price in the ordinary course of business, less the estimated costs of completion and selling expenses. Obsolete, redundant and slow moving stores are identified and written down to net realizable values.

(o)   *Short-term investments*

Short-term investments are investments which are transitional or current in nature, with an original maturity greater than three months.

(p)   *Cash and cash equivalents*

Cash and cash equivalents consist of cash on hand, deposits in banks and highly liquid investments with an original maturity of three months or less.

Eastern Platinum Limited
Notes to the condensed consolidated financial statements
(Expressed in thousands of U.S. dollars, except number of shares and per share amounts)

3.   Summary of significant accounting policies (continued)

(q)   *Financial assets*

Financial assets are classified into one of four categories:
- financial assets at fair value through profit or loss ("FVTPL");
- held-to-maturity investments;
- available for sale ("AFS") financial assets; and,
- loans and receivables.

The classification is determined at initial recognition and depends on the nature and purpose of the financial asset.

(i)   *Financial assets at FVTPL*

Financial assets are classified as FVTPL when the financial asset is held for trading or it is designated as FVTPL.

A financial asset is classified as held for trading if:
- it has been acquired principally for the purpose of selling in the near future;
- it is a part of an identified portfolio of financial instruments that the Company manages and has an actual pattern of short-term profit-taking; or
- it is a derivative that is not designated and effective as a hedging instrument.

Financial assets classified as FVTPL are stated at fair value with any resultant gain or loss recognized in profit or loss. The net gain or loss recognized incorporates any dividend or interest earned on the financial asset.

The Company has classified cash and cash equivalents as held for trading.

(ii)   *AFS financial assets*

Short-term investments held by the Company are classified as AFS and are stated at fair value. Gains and losses arising from changes in fair value are recognized directly in equity in the investments revaluation reserve. To date, these gains and losses have not been significant due to the nature of the underlying investment. As a result, the assets' carrying values approximate their fair values. Impairment losses, interest calculated using the effective interest method and foreign exchange gains and losses on monetary assets, are recognized directly in profit or loss rather than equity. When an investment is disposed of or is determined to be impaired, the cumulative gain or loss previously recognized in the investments revaluation reserve is included in profit or loss for the period.

The fair value of AFS monetary assets denominated in a foreign currency is translated at the spot rate at the statement of financial position date. The change in fair value attributable to translation differences due to a change in amortized cost of the asset is recognized in profit or loss, while all other changes are recognized in equity.

(iii)   *Effective interest method*

The effective interest method calculates the amortized cost of a financial asset and allocates interest income over the corresponding period. The effective interest rate is the rate that discounts estimated future cash receipts over the expected life of the financial asset, or, where appropriate, a shorter period.

Eastern Platinum Limited
Notes to the condensed consolidated financial statements
(Expressed in thousands of U.S. dollars, except number of shares and per share amounts)

3.   Summary of significant accounting policies (continued)

(q)   *Financial assets (continued)*

(iii)   *Effective interest method (continued)*

Income is recognized on an effective interest basis for debt instruments other than those financial assets classified as FVTPL.

(iv)   *Held-to-maturity investments*

Investments are recognized on a trade-date basis and are initially measured at fair value, including transaction costs. The Company has classified its other assets as held to maturity.

(v)   *Loans and receivables*

Trade receivables, loans, and other receivables that have fixed or determinable payments that are not quoted in an active market are classified as loans and receivables.

Loans and receivables are initially recognized at the transaction value and subsequently carried at amortized cost less impairment losses. The impairment loss of receivables is based on a review of all outstanding amounts at year end. Bad debts are written off during the year in which they are identified. Interest income is recognized by applying the effective interest rate, except for short-term receivables when the recognition of interest would be immaterial.

(vi)   *Impairment of financial assets*

Financial assets, other than those at FVTPL, are assessed for indicators of impairment at each period end. Financial assets are impaired when there is objective evidence that, as a result of one or more events that occurred after the initial recognition of the financial asset, the estimated future cash flows of the investment have been impacted.

Objective evidence of impairment could include the following:
- significant financial difficulty of the issuer or counterparty;
- default or delinquency in interest or principal payments; or
- it has become probable that the borrower will enter bankruptcy or financial reorganization.

For financial assets carried at amortized cost, the amount of the impairment is the difference between the asset's carrying amount and the present value of the estimated future cash flows, discounted at the financial asset's original effective interest rate.

The carrying amount of all financial assets, excluding trade receivables, is directly reduced by the impairment loss. The carrying amount of trade receivable is reduced through the use of an allowance account. When a trade receivable is considered uncollectible, it is written off against the allowance account. Subsequent recoveries of amounts previously written off are credited against the allowance account. Changes in the carrying amount of the allowance account are recognized in profit or loss.

Eastern Platinum Limited
Notes to the condensed consolidated financial statements
(Expressed in thousands of U.S. dollars, except number of shares and per share amounts)

3.   Summary of significant accounting policies (continued)

(q)   Financial assets (continued)

(vi)   Impairment of financial assets (continued)

With the exception of AFS equity instruments, if, in a subsequent period, the amount of the impairment loss decreases and the decrease relates to an event occurring after the impairment was recognized, the previously recognized impairment loss is reversed through profit or loss. On the date of impairment reversal, the carrying amount of the financial asset cannot exceed its amortized cost had impairment not been recognized.

(vii)   Derecognition of financial assets

A financial asset is derecognized when:
- the contractual right to the asset's cash flows expire; or
- if the Company transfers the financial asset and all risks and rewards of ownership to another entity.

(r)   Environmental rehabilitation

The Company recognizes liabilities for statutory, contractual, constructive or legal obligations associated with the retirement of property, plant and equipment, when those obligations result from the acquisition, construction, development or normal operation of the assets. The net present value of future rehabilitation cost estimates is capitalized to mining assets along with a corresponding increase in the rehabilitation provision in the period incurred. Discount rates using a pre-tax rate that reflect the time value of money are used to calculate the net present value. The rehabilitation asset is depreciated on the same basis as mining assets.

The Company's estimates of reclamation costs could change as a result of changes in regulatory requirements and assumptions regarding the amount and timing of the future expenditures. These changes are recorded directly to mining assets with a corresponding entry to the rehabilitation provision. The Company's estimates are reviewed annually for changes in regulatory requirements, effects of inflation and changes in estimates.

Changes in the net present value, excluding changes in the Company's estimates of reclamation costs, are charged to profit and loss for the period.

The costs of rehabilitation projects that were included in the rehabilitation provision are recorded against the provision as incurred. The cost of ongoing current programs to prevent and control pollution is charged against profit and loss as incurred.

(s)   Leases

(i)   The Company as lessor

Rental income from operating leases is recognized on a straight-line basis over the term of the corresponding lease. Initial direct costs incurred in negotiating and arranging an operating lease are added to the carrying amount of the leased asset and recognized on a straight-line basis over the lease term.

Eastern Platinum Limited
Notes to the condensed consolidated financial statements
(Expressed in thousands of U.S. dollars, except number of shares and per share amounts)

3.   Summary of significant accounting policies (continued)

(s)   Leases (continued)

(ii)   The Company as lessee

Assets held under finance leases are recognized as assets of the Company at the lower of the fair value at the inception of the lease or the present value of the minimum lease payments. The corresponding liability is recognized as a finance lease obligation. Lease payments are apportioned between finance charges and reduction of the lease obligation to achieve a constant rate of interest on the remaining liability. Finance charges are charged to profit or loss, unless they are directly attributable to qualifying assets, in which case they are capitalized.

Rentals payable under operating leases are expensed on a straight-line basis over the term of the relevant lease. Incentives received upon entry into an operating lease are recognized straight-line over the lease term.

(t)   Provisions

Provisions are recorded when a present legal or constructive obligation exists as a result of past events where it is probable that an outflow of resources embodying economic benefits will be required to settle the obligation, and a reliable estimate of the amount of the obligation can be made.

The amount recognized as a provision is the best estimate of the consideration required to settle the present obligation at the statement of financial position date, taking into account the risks and uncertainties surrounding the obligation. Where a provision is measured using the cash flows estimated to settle the present obligation, its carrying amount is the present value of those cash flows. When some or all of the economic benefits required to settle a provision are expected to be recovered from a third party, the receivable is recognized as an asset if it is virtually certain that reimbursement will be received and the amount receivable can be measured reliably.

(u)   Employee benefits

(i)   Employee post-retirement obligations – defined contribution retirement plan

The Company's South African subsidiaries operate a defined contribution retirement plan for its employees. The pension plans are funded by payments from the employees and the subsidiaries and payments are charged to profit and loss for the period as incurred. The assets of the different plans are held by independently managed trust funds. The South African Pension Fund Act of 1956 governs these funds.

(ii)   Leave pay

Employee entitlements to annual leave are recognized as they are earned by the employees. A provision, stated at current cost, is made for the estimated liability at period end.

(v)   Financial liabilities and equity

Debt and equity instruments are classified as either financial liabilities or as equity in accordance with the substance of the contractual arrangement.

An equity instrument is any contract that evidences a residual interest in the assets of an entity after deducting all of its liabilities. Equity instruments issued by the Company are recorded at the proceeds received, net of direct issue costs.

Eastern Platinum Limited
Notes to the condensed consolidated financial statements
(Expressed in thousands of U.S. dollars, except number of shares and per share amounts)

3.   **Summary of significant accounting policies (continued)**

(v)   Financial liabilities and equity (continued)

Financial liabilities are classified as either financial liabilities at fair value through profit or loss (FVTPL) or other financial liabilities.

(i)   Other financial liabilities

Other financial liabilities are initially measured at fair value, net of transaction costs, and are subsequently measured at amortized cost using the effective interest method, with interest expense recognized on an effective yield basis.

The effective interest method is a method of calculating the amortized cost of a financial liability and of allocating interest expenses over the corresponding period. The effective interest rate is the rate that exactly discounts estimated future cash payments over the expected life of the financial liability, or, where appropriate, a shorter period.

The Company has classified trade and other payables, short-term financial liabilities and long-term financial liabilities as other financial liabilities.

(ii)   Derecognition of financial liabilities

The group derecognizes financial liabilities when, and only when, the group's obligations are discharged, cancelled or they expire.

4.   **Non-controlling interest**

The non-controlling interests are comprised of the following:

Balance, January 1, 2008	$ 23,133
Non-controlling interests' share of profit in Barplats	2,943
Non-controlling interests' share of interest on advances to Gubevu	(841)
Foreign exchange movement	(3,267)
Balance, March 31, 2008	$ 21,968
Non-controlling interests' share of loss in Barplats	(3,660)
Non-controlling interests' share of interest on advances to Gubevu	(2,177)
Foreign exchange movement	(4,129)
Balance, December 31, 2008	$ 12,002
Non-controlling interests' share of loss in Barplats	(176)
Non-controlling interests' share of interest on advances to Gubevu	(608)
Foreign exchange movement	(354)
Balance, March 31, 2009	$ **10,864**

5.   **Inventories**

	March 31, 2009		December 31, 2008
Consumables	$ **3,312**	$	3,509
Ore and concentrate	**239**		372
	$ **3,551**	$	3,881

The Company recognized $219 of consumables inventories as an expense during the three months ended March 31, 2009 (12 months ended December 31, 2008 - $1,391).

Eastern Platinum Limited
Notes to the condensed consolidated financial statements
(Expressed in thousands of U.S. dollars, except number of shares and per share amounts)

6. Property, plant and equipment

	Mining plant and equipment	Crocodile River Mine (a)	Kennedy's Vale Project (b)	Spitzkop PGM Project (c)	Mareesburg Project (c)	Other property plant and equipment	TOTAL
Cost							
Balance as at January 1, 2008	$ 273,483	$ 149,618	$ 386,353	$ 121,443	$ 28,075	$ 118	$ 959,090
Additions							
Assets acquired	134,320	4,285	-	4,729	472	18	143,824
Assets acquired through business combination	-	12,033	53,754	-	36	-	65,823
Disposals	-	-	-	-	-	(22)	(22)
Foreign exchange movement	(87,635)	(40,794)	(106,645)	(24,459)	(5,284)	(21)	(264,838)
Balance as at December 31, 2008	$ 320,168	$ 125,142	$ 333,462	$ 101,713	$ 23,299	$ 93	$ 903,877
Additions							
Assets acquired	-	-	-	388	28	-	416
Assets under construction capitalized	10,301	-	-	-	-	-	10,301
Foreign exchange movement	(7,939)	(2,746)	(6,301)	(3,922)	(821)	(2)	(21,731)
Balance as at March 31, 2009	$ 322,530	$ 122,396	$ 327,161	$ 98,179	$ 22,506	$ 91	$ 892,863
Accumulated depreciation and impairment losses							
Balance as at January 1, 2008	$ 116,078	$ 11,932	$ 15,666	$ -	$ -	$ 24	$ 143,700
Depreciation for the period	7,842	6,768	-	-	-	52	14,662
Impairment loss	-	-	313,603	-	-	-	313,603
Foreign exchange movement	(31,017)	(3,907)	(41,832)	-	-	(17)	(76,773)
Balance as at December 31, 2008	$ 92,903	$ 14,793	$ 287,437	$ -	$ -	$ 59	$ 395,192
Depreciation for the period	2,549	967	-	-	-	1	3,517
Foreign exchange movement	(2,327)	191	(5,094)	-	-	(4)	(7,234)
Balance as at March 31, 2009	$ 93,125	$ 15,951	$ 282,343	$ -	$ -	$ 56	$ 391,475
Carrying amounts							
At January 1, 2008	$ 157,405	$ 137,686	$ 370,687	$ 121,443	$ 28,075	$ 94	$ 815,390
At December 31, 2008	$ 227,265	$ 110,349	$ 46,025	$ 101,713	$ 23,299	$ 34	$ 508,685
At March 31, 2009	$ 229,405	$ 106,445	$ 44,818	$ 98,179	$ 22,506	$ 35	$ 501,388

Eastern Platinum Limited
Notes to the condensed consolidated financial statements
(Expressed in thousands of U.S. dollars, except number of shares and per share amounts)

6. Property, plant and equipment (continued)

(a) *Crocodile River Mine ("CRM")*

The Company holds directly and indirectly 87.5% of CRM, which is located on the eastern portion of the western limb of the Bushveld Complex. The Maroelabult and Zandfontein sections are currently in production, while development of the Crocette and Kareespriut sections was temporarily suspended in the fourth quarter of 2008 due to the significant decrease in PGM prices.

(b) *Kennedy's Vale Project ("KV")*

The Company holds directly and indirectly 87.5% of KV, which is located on the eastern limb of the Bushveld Complex, near Steelpoort in the Province of Mpumalanga. It comprises PGM mineral rights on five farms in the Steelpoort Valley.

(c) *Spitzkop PGM Project and Mareesburg Project*

The Company holds directly and indirectly a 93.4% interest in the Spitzkop PGM Project and a 75.5% interest in the Mareesburg Project. The Company currently acts as the operator of both the Mareesburg Platinum Project and Spitzkop PGM Project, both located on the eastern limb of the Bushveld Complex. The development of these projects was temporarily suspended in the fourth quarter of 2008 due to the significant decrease in PGM prices.

7. Refining Contract

During the year ended June 30, 2006, the Company acquired a 69% interest in Barplats and assigned a portion of the excess of the purchase price over the fair value of the identifiable intangible assets acquired to the off-take contract governing the sales of Barplats' PGM concentrate production. The initial value of the contract was $17,939. During the year ended June 30, 2007, the Company acquired an additional 5% interest in Barplats resulting in an additional allocation to the contract of $4,802 for a total aggregate value of $22,741. During the year ended December 31, 2008, the Company acquired an additional 2.47% interest in Barplats which did not affect the aggregate value of the contract. The value of the contract is amortized over the remaining term of the contract which is 10.25 years.

Cost

Balance as at January 1, 2008	$	22,741
Foreign exchange movement		(4,784)
Balance as at December 31, 2008	$	17,957
Foreign exchange movement		(327)
Balance as at March 31, 2009	**$**	**17,630**

Accumulated depreciation

Balance as at January 1, 2008	$	4,274
Depreciation for the period		1,353
Foreign exchange movement		(163)
Balance as at December 31, 2008	$	5,464
Depreciation for the period		254
Foreign exchange movement		11
Balance as at March 31, 2009	**$**	**5,729**

Carrying amounts

At January 1, 2008	$	18,467
At December 31, 2008	$	12,493
At March 31, 2009	**$**	**11,901**

Eastern Platinum Limited
Notes to the condensed consolidated financial statements
(Expressed in thousands of U.S. dollars, except number of shares and per share amounts)

8.   Other assets

Other assets consists of a money market fund investment that is classified as held-to-maturity and serves as security for a guarantee issued to the Department of Minerals and Energy of South Africa in respect of the environmental rehabilitation liability (Note 9). Changes to other assets for the three months ended March 31, 2009 are as follows:

Balance, January 1, 2008	$ 1,247
Additional investment	-
Service fees	(16)
Interest income	122
Foreign exchange movement	(336)
Balance, December 31, 2008	$ 1,017
Additional investment	-
Service fees	(5)
Interest income	31
Foreign exchange movement	(25)
Balance, March 31, 2009	**$ 1,018**

9.   Provision for environmental rehabilitation

Although the ultimate amount of the environment rehabilitation provision is uncertain, the fair value of these obligations is based on information currently available, including closure plans and applicable regulations. Significant closure activities include land rehabilitation, demolition of buildings and mine facilities and other costs.

The liability for the environmental rehabilitation provision at March 31, 2009 is approximately ZAR52.9 million ($5,548). The liability was determined using an inflation rate of 5.78% (December 31, 2008 – 5.78%) and an estimated life of mine of 14 years for Zandfontein and Maroelabult (December 31, 2008 – 14 years), and 1 year for Kennedy's Vale (December 31, 2008 – 1 year). A discount rate of 7.09% was used (December 31, 2008 – 7.09%). A guarantee of $1,018 (December 31, 2008 - $1,017) has been issued to the Department of Minerals and Energy (Note 8). The guarantee will be utilized to cover expenses incurred to rehabilitate the mining area upon closure of the mine. The undiscounted value of this liability is approximately ZAR121 million ($12,651).

Changes to the environmental rehabilitation provision during the three months ended March 31, 2009 are as follows:

Balance, January 1, 2008	$ 6,224
Revision in estimates	554
Unwinding of interest	491
Foreign exchange movement	(1,671)
Balance, December 31, 2008	$ 5,598
Unwinding of interest	93
Foreign exchange movement	(143)
Balance, March 31, 2009	**$ 5,548**

10.   Commitments

The Company has committed to capital expenditures on projects of approximately ZAR122 million ($12,822) as at March 31, 2009.

Eastern Platinum Limited
Notes to the condensed consolidated financial statements
(Expressed in thousands of U.S. dollars, except number of shares and per share amounts)

11. Issued capital

(a) *Authorized*

- Unlimited number of preferred redeemable, voting, non-participating shares without nominal or par value

- Unlimited number of common shares with no par value

(b) *Stock options*

The Company has an incentive plan (the "2008 Plan"), approved by the Company's shareholders at its annual general meeting held on June 4, 2008, under which options to purchase common shares may be granted to its directors, officers, employees and others at the discretion of the Board of Directors.   Under the terms of the 2008 Plan, 75 million common shares are reserved for issuance upon the exercise of options. All outstanding options at June 4, 2008 granted under the Company's previous plan (the "2005 Plan") will continue to exist under the 2008 Plan provided that the fundamental terms governing such options will be deemed to be those under the 2005 Plan. Upon adoption of the 2008 Plan, options to purchase a total of 27,525,000 common shares were available for grant under the 2008 Plan, representing 75,000,000 less the 47,475,000 outstanding options at June 4, 2008 granted under the 2005 Plan.

Under the 2008 Plan, each option granted shall be for a term not exceeding five years from the date of being granted and the vesting period is determined based on the discretion of the Board of Directors. The option exercise price is set at the date of the grant and cannot be less than the closing market price of the Company's common shares on the Toronto Stock Exchange on the day immediately preceding the day of the grant of the option.

The changes in stock options during the three months ended March 31, 2009 and year ended December 31, 2008 were as follows:

	March 31, 2009		December 31, 2008	
	Number of options	**Weighted average exercise price**	Number of options	Weighted average exercise price
		Cdn$		Cdn$
Balance outstanding, beginning of period	**64,746,000**	**1.52**	46,360,000	1.93
Options granted	**80,000**	**0.32**	19,856,000	0.55
Options exercised	**-**	**-**	(845,000)	1.26
Options forfeited	**(3,350,000)**	**1.96**	(625,000)	1.76
Balance outstanding, end of period	**61,476,000**	**1.49**	64,746,000	1.52

Eastern Platinum Limited
Notes to the condensed consolidated financial statements
(Expressed in thousands of U.S. dollars, except number of shares and per share amounts)

11.   Issued capital (continued)

(b)   *Stock options (continued)*

The following table summarizes information concerning outstanding and exercisable options at March 31, 2009:

Options outstanding	Options exercisable	Exercise price	Remaining Contractual Life (Years)	Expiry date
		Cdn$		
187,500	187,500	1.00	0.41	August 26, 2009
6,725,000	6,725,000	1.70	2.15	May 24, 2011
250,000	250,000	1.70	2.66	November 27, 2011
20,237,500	20,237,500	1.82	2.94	March 7, 2012
18,356,000	16,316,000	0.32	4.72	December 18, 2013
80,000	26,667	0.32	4.87	February 11, 2014
14,350,000	13,526,667	2.31	8.52	October 5, 2017
90,000	60,000	2.50	8.71	December 12, 2017
910,000	740,000	3.38	8.90	February 20, 2018
290,000	210,000	3.38	8.99	March 27, 2018
61,476,000	58,279,334		4.80	

(c)   *Share purchase warrants*

The changes in warrants during the three months ended March 31, 2009 and year ended December 31, 2008 were as follows:

	March 31, 2009		December 31, 2008	
	Number of warrants	Weighted average exercise price	Number of warrants	Weighted average exercise price
		Cdn$		Cdn$
Balance outstanding, beginning of period	58,485,996	1.80	71,248,050	1.83
Warrants exercised	-	-	(10,824,077)	1.97
Warrants expired	(58,485,996)	1.80	(1,937,977)	2.00
Balance outstanding, end of period	-	-	58,485,996	1.80

(d)   *Share-based payment*

The fair value of each option granted is estimated at the time of the grant using the Black-Scholes option pricing model with weighted average assumptions for grants as follows:

	March 31, 2009 (3 months)	March 31, 2008 (3 months)
Risk-free interest rate	1.69%	3.05%
Expected life	3 years	3 years
Annualized volatility	78%	49%
Dividend rate	0%	0%
Grant date fair value	Cdn$0.21	Cdn$1.22

Eastern Platinum Limited
Notes to the condensed consolidated financial statements
(Expressed in thousands of U.S. dollars, except number of shares and per share amounts)

12. Related party transactions

The Company's related parties consist of companies owned by executive officers and directors as follows:

	Nature of transactions
Andrews PGM Consulting	Consulting
Buccaneer Management Inc.	Management
Jazz Financial Ltd.	Management
Maluti Services Limited	General and administrative
Xiste Consulting Ltd.	Management

The Company incurred the following expenses in connection with companies owned by key management and directors. These expenses were incurred in the normal course of operations and have been measured at the exchange amount which is determined on a cost recovery basis.

	Note	March 31, 2009 (3 months)	March 31, 2008 (3 months)
Consulting fees	(i)	$ 31	$ 17
General and administrative expenses		-	73
Management fees	(ii)	235	358
		$ 266	$ 448

i. The Company paid fees to a private company controlled by a director of the Company for consulting services performed outside of his capacity as a director.

ii. The Company paid management fees and expenses to private companies controlled by officers and directors of the Company.

iii. Amounts due to related parties are unsecured, non-interest bearing and due on demand. Accounts payable at March 31, 2009 included $Nil (December 31, 2008 - $35) which were due to private companies controlled by officers of the Company.

Eastern Platinum Limited

Notes to the condensed consolidated financial statements
(Expressed in thousands of U.S. dollars, except number of shares and per share amounts)

13.   Segmented information

(a)   Operating segment - The Company's operations are primarily directed towards the acquisition, exploration and production of platinum group metals in South Africa.

(b)   Geographic segments - The Company's assets, revenues and expenses by geographic areas for the quarters ended March 31, 2009 and March 31, 2008 are as follows:

	March 31, 2009 (3 months)		
	South Africa	Canada	Total
Property, plant and equipment	$ 501,353	$ 35	$ 501,388
Refining contract	11,901	-	11,901
Other assets	1,018	-	1,018
Total assets	544,180	18,697	562,877
Property, plant and equipment expenditures	$ 10,717	$ -	$ 10,717
Revenues	$ 24,903	$ -	$ 24,903
Production costs	(17,885)	-	(17,885)
Depletion and depreciation	(3,517)	-	(3,517)
General and administrative expenses	(758)	(878)	(1,636)
Share-based payment	(132)	-	(132)
Interest income	354	140	494
Finance costs	(452)	-	(452)
Foreign exchange (loss) gain	(94)	19	(75)
Profit (loss) before income taxes	$ 2,419	$ (719)	$ 1,700

	March 31, 2008 (3 months)		
	South Africa	Canada	Total
Property, plant and equipment expenditures	$ 23,692	$ 14	$ 23,706
Revenues	$ 55,795	$ -	$ 55,795
Production costs	(19,750)	-	(19,750)
Depletion and depreciation	(4,394)	-	(4,394)
General and administrative expenses	(2,847)	(1,486)	(4,333)
Share based payment	(687)	(662)	(1,349)
Interest income	938	1,869	2,807
Finance costs	(8)	-	(8)
Foreign exchange gain	1,057	-	1,057
Profit (loss) before income taxes	$ 30,104	$ (279)	$ 29,825

	December 31, 2008		
	South Africa	Canada	Total
Property, plant and equipment	$ 508,648	$ 37	$ 508,685
Refining contract	12,493	-	12,493
Other assets	1,017	-	1,017
Total assets	539,816	56,754	596,570

For the quarters ended March 31, 2009 and March 31, 2008, 100% of the Company's PGM production was sold to one customer.

Eastern Platinum Limited

Notes to the condensed consolidated financial statements
(Expressed in thousands of U.S. dollars, except number of shares and per share amounts)

14. Accounting estimates and judgments

(a) *Useful life of assets*

The Company engaged an independent third party engineering company in South Africa to assess the life of mine ("LOM") of Barplats Mines Limited ("Barplats") in December 2007.

At December 31, 2008 the remaining LOM for Barplats was assessed at 153 months (December 31, 2007 – 165 months). This estimate is based on proven and probable ore reserves. The change in remaining mine life will be evaluated each year as the reserves move to the proven and probable category.

(b) *Impairment of property, plant and equipment*

During the year ended December 31, 2008, the significant decline in platinum group metal prices triggered an impairment assessment which resulted in an impairment of $314 million on Kennedy's Vale. Future cash flows were discounted to present value at the weighted average cost of capital of 9%.

The foreign exchange rate utilized in the model is ZAR9.51 = US$1.00.

The average forecast prices utilized in the impairment model, in US$ per ounce, are:

	2009	2010	2011	2012	2013 +
Platinum	950	1,020	1,055	1,155	1,180
Palladium	210	225	305	385	380
Rhodium	1,000	980	2,785	2,895	2,830
Gold	870	815	650	695	680
Iridium	270	295	345	350	340
Ruthenium	190	215	240	250	245
Nickel	13,850	15,875	16,210	16,285	15,915
Copper	5,180	5,550	5,505	4,265	4,170
Chrome	380	382	400	400	400

15. IFRS

IFRS 1 *First-time Adoption of International Financial Reporting Standards* sets forth guidance for the initial adoption of IFRS. Under IFRS 1 the standards are applied retrospectively at the transitional statement of financial position date with all adjustment to assets and liabilities taken to retained earnings unless certain exemptions are applied. The Company has applied the following exemptions to its opening statement of financial position dated January 1, 2008:

(a) *Business Combinations*

IFRS 1 indicates that a first-time adopter may elect not to apply IFRS 3 *Business Combinations* retrospectively to business combinations that occurred before the date of transition to IFRS. The Company has taken advantage of this election and has applied IFRS 3 to business combinations that occurred on or after January 1, 2008.

Eastern Platinum Limited
Notes to the condensed consolidated financial statements
(Expressed in thousands of U.S. dollars, except number of shares and per share amounts)

15.   IFRS (continued)

(b)   *Cumulative translation differences*

IFRS 1 allows a first-time adopter to not comply with the requirements of IAS 21 *The Effects of Changes in Foreign Exchange Rates* for cumulative translation differences that existed at the date of transition to IFRS. The Company has chosen to apply this election and has eliminated the cumulative translation difference and adjusted retained earnings by the same amount at the date of transition to IFRS. If, subsequent to adoption, a foreign operation is disposed of, the translation differences that arose before the date of transition to IFRS will not affect the gain or loss on disposal.

(c)   *Share-based payment transactions*

IFRS 1 encourages, but does not require, first-time adopters to apply IFRS 2 *Share-based Payment* to equity instruments that were granted on or before November 7, 2002, or equity instruments that were granted subsequent to November 7, 2002 and vested before the later of the date of transition to IFRS and January 1, 2005. The Company has elected not to apply IFRS 2 to awards that vested prior to January 1, 2008.

(d)   *IAS 27 – Consolidated and Separate Financial Statements*

In accordance with IFRS 1, if a company elects to apply IFRS 3 *Business Combinations* retrospectively, IAS 27 *Consolidated and Separate Financial Statements* must also be applied retrospectively. As the Company elected to apply IFRS 3 prospectively, the Company has also elected to apply IAS 27 prospectively.

IFRS 1 also outlines specific guidelines that a first-time adopter must adhere to under certain circumstances. The Company has applied the following guidelines to its opening statement of financial position dated January 1, 2008:

(e)   *Assets and liabilities of subsidiaries and associates*

In accordance with IFRS 1, if a parent company adopts IFRS subsequent to its subsidiary or associate adopting IFRS, the assets and the liabilities of the subsidiary or associate are to be included in the consolidated financial statements at the same carrying amounts as in the financial statements of the subsidiary or associate. The Company's principal operating subsidiary, Barplats Investments Limited, adopted IFRS in 2005.

(f)   *Estimates*

In accordance with IFRS 1, an entity's estimates under IFRS at the date of transition to IFRS must be consistent with estimates made for the same date under previous GAAP, unless there is objective evidence that those estimates were in error. The Company's IFRS estimates as of January 1, 2008 are consistent with its Canadian GAAP estimates for the same date.

IFRS employs a conceptual framework that is similar to Canadian GAAP. However, significant differences exist in certain matters of recognition, measurement and disclosure. While adoption of IFRS has not changed the Company's actual cash flows, it has resulted in changes to the Company's reported financial position and results of operations. In order to allow the users of the financial statements to better understand these changes, the Company's Canadian GAAP statement of operations, statement of comprehensive profit, statement of financial position and statement of cash flows for the quarter ended March 31, 2008 and the year ended December 31, 2008 have been reconciled to IFRS, with the resulting differences explained.

Eastern Platinum Limited
Notes to the condensed consolidated financial statements
(Expressed in thousands of U.S. dollars, except number of shares and per share amounts)

15.   IFRS (continued)

    (g)   Revenue and interest income

        The Company settles its metal sales three or five months following the physical delivery of the concentrates.

        The present value of sales revenue expected to be received in three or five months is recognized on the date of sale. The difference between the present value and the future value is recognized as interest revenue over the term of settlement. In its Canadian GAAP financial statements for the year ended December 31, 2008, the Company recorded the future value as sales revenue, as opposed to recognizing the difference between the present value and the future value as interest revenue over the term of settlement. The difference in the treatment of revenue results in a timing difference in the recognition of income and is not material to these financial statements.

    (h)   Property plant and equipment

        Due to the adjustments to the provision for environmental rehabilitation discussed in Note 15(j), the cost of property plant and equipment is different in accordance with IFRS than in accordance with Canadian GAAP. As a result, even though depreciation is calculated in the same manner, the amount of depreciation differs.

    (i)   Share-based payment

        IFRS

- Each tranche of an award with different vesting dates is considered a separate grant for the calculation of fair value, and the resulting fair value is amortized over the vesting period of the respective tranches.
- Forfeiture estimates are recognized in the period they are estimated, and are revised for actual forfeitures in subsequent periods.

        Canadian GAAP

- The fair value of stock-based awards with graded vesting are calculated as one grant and the resulting fair value is recognized on a straight-line basis over the vesting period.
- Forfeitures of awards are recognized as they occur.

    (j)   Provision for environmental rehabilitation

        IFRS

- The provision for environmental rehabilitation must be adjusted for changes in the discount rate.

        Canadian GAAP

- The provision for environmental rehabilitation is not adjusted for changes in the discount rate.

    (k)   Deferred tax asset/liability

        IFRS

- All deferred tax assets and liabilities must be classified as non-current.

Eastern Platinum Limited
Notes to the condensed consolidated financial statements
(Expressed in thousands of U.S. dollars, except number of shares and per share amounts)

15.   IFRS (continued)

(k)   *Deferred tax asset/liability (continued)*

Canadian GAAP

- Deferred tax assets and liabilities can be classified as current or non-current as appropriate.

(l)   *Accounts payable, accrued liabilities and provisions*

IFRS – a provision is a liability of uncertain timing or amount. Provisions are disclosed separately from liabilities and accrued liabilities and require additional disclosure.

Canadian GAAP – Accounts payable, accrued liabilities and provisions are disclosed on the statement of financial position as a single line item.

(m)   *Other comprehensive profit (loss)*

Other comprehensive profit (loss) consists of the change in the cumulative translation adjustment ("CTA"). Due to other IFRS adjustments, the balances that are used to calculate the CTA are different in accordance with IFRS than in accordance with Canadian GAAP. As a result, CTA and other comprehensive profit (loss) are different in accordance with IFRS than in accordance with Canadian GAAP.

(n)   *Impairment*

IFRS – If indication of impairment is identified, the asset's carrying value is compared to the asset's discounted cash flows. If the discounted cash flows are less than the carrying value, the asset is impaired by an amount equal to the difference between the discounted cash flows and the carrying value.

Canadian GAAP - If indication of impairment is identified, the asset's carrying value is compared to the asset's undiscounted cash flows. If the undiscounted cash flows are less than the carrying value, the asset is impaired by an amount equal to the difference between the discounted cash flows and the carrying value.

The Company completed an impairment review of its assets at January 1, 2008 and concluded that the assets were not impaired in accordance with IFRS. At December 31, 2008, the carrying value of the Kennedy's Vale mineral property was less than the property's undiscounted cash flows, but greater than the property's discounted cash flows. As a result, the mineral property was concluded to be impaired in accordance with IFRS, but not impaired in accordance with Canadian GAAP. An impairment of $314 million and an income tax recovery of $87 million have been recorded relating to the Kennedy's Vale impairment.

(o)   *Presentation*

The presentation of the cash flow statement in accordance with IFRS differs from the presentation of the cash flow statement in accordance with Canadian GAAP.

Eastern Platinum Limited
Notes to the condensed consolidated financial statements
(Expressed in thousands of U.S. dollars, except number of shares and per share amounts)

15. IFRS (continued)

The January 1, 2008 Canadian GAAP statement of financial position has been reconciled to IFRS as follows:

	Note	Canadian GAAP	Effect of transition to IFRS	IFRS
Assets				
Current assets				
Cash and cash equivalents		$ 18,818	$ -	$ 18,818
Short-term investments		171,038	-	171,038
Trade receivables	(e)(g)	33,157	(597)	32,560
Inventories		6,888	-	6,888
		229,901	(597)	229,304
Property, plant and equipment	(e)(h)(j)	813,461	1,929	815,390
Refining contract		18,467	-	18,467
Other assets		1,247	-	1,247
		$ 1,063,076	$ 1,332	$ 1,064,408
Liabilities				
Current liabilities				
Accounts payable and accrued liabilities	(e)(l)	$ 22,967	$ (1,460)	$ 21,507
Provisions	(e)(l)	-	1,460	1,460
Current portion of long-term liability		3,837	-	3,837
Deferred tax	(k)	6,416	(6,416)	-
		33,220	(6,416)	26,804
Provision for environmental rehabilitation	(e)(j)	2,889	3,335	6,224
Finance leases		9,127	-	9,127
Deferred tax liabilities	(k)	143,616	6,416	150,032
		188,852	3,335	192,187
Capital and reserves				
Issued capital		868,045	-	868,045
Equity reserve		27,428	-	27,428
Currency translation adjustment	(b)	23,481	(23,481)	-
Deficit		(68,132)	21,747	(46,385)
		850,822	(1,734)	849,088
Non-controlling interest		23,402	(269)	23,133
		874,224	(2,003)	872,221
		$ 1,063,076	$ 1,332	$ 1,064,408

Eastern Platinum Limited
Notes to the condensed consolidated financial statements
(Expressed in thousands of U.S. dollars, except number of shares and per share amounts)

15.   IFRS (continued)

The Canadian GAAP income statement and statement of comprehensive income for the three months ended March 31, 2008 have been reconciled to IFRS as follows:

	Note	Canadian GAAP	Effect of transition to IFRS	IFRS
		3 months ended March 31, 2008		
Revenue	(g)	$ 56,408	$ (613)	$ 55,795
Cost of operations				
Production costs		19,750	-	19,750
Depletion and depreciation	(h)	4,362	32	4,394
		24,112	32	24,144
Mine operating earnings		32,296	(645)	31,651
Expenses				
General and administrative		4,333	-	4,333
Share-based payment	(i)	1,227	122	1,349
		5,560	122	5,682
Operating profit		26,736	(767)	25,969
Other income (expense)				
Interest income	(g)	2,455	352	2,807
Finance costs	(j)	(227)	219	(8)
Foreign exchange gain		1,057	-	1,057
Profit before income taxes		30,021	(196)	29,825
Deferred income tax expense	(k)	(8,248)	1	(8,247)
Net profit for the period		$ 21,773	$ (195)	$ 21,578
Attributable to				
Non-controlling interest		$ 1,811	$ 291	$ 2,102
Equity shareholders of the Company		$ 19,962	$ (486)	$ 19,476

	Note	Canadian GAAP	Effect of transition to IFRS	IFRS
		3 months ended March 31, 2008		
Net profit for the period		$ 21,773	$ (195)	$ 21,578
Other comprehensive (loss) - currency translation adjustment	(m)	(96,506)	141	(96,365)
Comprehensive loss		$ (74,733)	$ (54)	$ (74,787)
Attributable to				
Non-controlling interest		$ 1,811	$ 291	$ 2,102
Equity shareholders of the Company		$ (76,544)	$ (345)	$ (76,889)

Eastern Platinum Limited
Notes to the condensed consolidated financial statements
(Expressed in thousands of U.S. dollars, except number of shares and per share amounts)

15.   IFRS (continued)

The Canadian GAAP income statement and statement of comprehensive income for the twelve months ended December 31, 2008 have been reconciled to IFRS as follows:

| | Note | **12 months ended December 31, 2008** | | |
		Canadian GAAP	Effect of transition to IFRS	IFRS
Revenue	(g)	$ 116,198	$ (1,517)	$ 114,681
Cost of operations				
Production costs		79,961	-	79,961
Depletion and depreciation	(h)	14,599	63	14,662
		94,560	63	94,623
Mine operating earnings		21,638	(1,580)	20,058
Expenses				
Impairment	(n)	-	313,603	313,603
General and administrative	(e)	19,411	30	19,441
Share-based payment	(i)	4,290	335	4,625
		23,701	313,968	337,669
Operating loss		(2,063)	(315,548)	(317,611)
Other income (expense)				
Interest income	(g)	7,081	1,863	8,944
Finance costs	(j)	(3,551)	(174)	(3,725)
Foreign exchange gain		(2,155)	-	(2,155)
Loss before income taxes		(688)	(313,859)	(314,547)
Deferred income tax recovery	(k)	13,623	87,808	101,431
Net profit (loss) for the period		$ 12,935	$ (226,051)	$ (213,116)
Attributable to				
Non-controlling interest		$ (3,429)	$ (306)	$ (3,735)
Equity shareholders of the Company		$ 16,364	$ (225,745)	$ (209,381)

| | Note | **12 months ended December 31, 2008** | | |
		Canadian GAAP	Effect of transition to IFRS	IFRS
Net profit (loss) for the period		$ 12,935	$ (226,051)	$ (213,116)
Other comprehensive loss - currency translation adjustment	(m)	(197,052)	27,475	(169,577)
Comprehensive loss		$ (184,117)	$ (198,576)	$ (382,693)
Attributable to				
Non-controlling interest		$ (3,429)	$ (306)	$ (3,735)
Equity shareholders of the Company		$ (180,688)	$ (198,270)	$ (378,958)

Eastern Platinum Limited
Notes to the condensed consolidated financial statements
(Expressed in thousands of U.S. dollars, except number of shares and per share amounts)

15.   IFRS (continued)

The Canadian GAAP statement of financial position at March 31, 2008 has been reconciled to IFRS as follows:

	Note	March 31, 2008		
		Canadian GAAP	Effect of transition to IFRS	IFRS
Assets				
Current assets				
Cash and cash equivalents		$ 58,199	$ -	$ 58,199
Short-term investments		111,744	-	111,744
Trade receivables	(g)	56,869	(521)	56,348
Inventories		5,539	-	5,539
		232,351	(521)	231,830
Property, plant and equipment	(h)(j)	723,117	1,628	724,745
Refining contract		15,289	-	15,289
Other assets		1,082	-	1,082
		$ 971,839	$ 1,107	$ 972,946
Liabilities				
Accounts payable and accrued liabilities	(l)	$ 21,952	$ (1,236)	$ 20,716
Provisions	(l)	-	1,236	1,236
Current portion of long-term liability		4,040	-	4,040
Deferred tax liability	(k)	11,950	(11,950)	-
		37,942	(11,950)	25,992
Provision for environmental rehabilitation	(j)	2,525	2,866	5,391
Capital leases and other long-term liabilities		7,211	-	7,211
Deferred tax liability	(k)	122,662	11,950	134,612
		170,340	2,866	173,206
Capital and reserves				
Issued capital		872,351	-	872,351
Equity reserve	(i)	28,574	121	28,695
Currency translation adjustment	(m)	(73,025)	(23,340)	(96,365)
Deficit		(48,170)	21,261	(26,909)
		779,730	(1,958)	777,772
Non-controlling interest		21,769	199	21,968
		801,499	(1,759)	799,740
		$ 971,839	$ 1,107	$ 972,946

Eastern Platinum Limited
Notes to the condensed consolidated financial statements
(Expressed in thousands of U.S. dollars, except number of shares and per share amounts)

15. IFRS (continued)

The Canadian GAAP statement of financial position at December 31, 2008 has been reconciled to IFRS as follows:

	Note	December 31, 2008		
		Canadian GAAP	Effect of transition to IFRS	IFRS
Assets				
Current assets				
Cash and cash equivalents		$ 25,806	$ -	$ 25,806
Short-term investments		35,257	-	35,257
Trade receivables	(g)	9,556	(125)	9,431
Inventories		3,881	-	3,881
Deferred tax asset	(k)	1,178	(1,178)	-
		75,678	(1,303)	74,375
Property, plant and equipment	(h)(j)(n)	783,039	(274,354)	508,685
Refining contract		12,493	-	12,493
Other assets		1,017	-	1,017
		$ 872,227	$ (275,657)	$ 596,570
Liabilities				
Current liabilities				
Accounts payable and accrued liabilities	(l)	$ 36,729	$ (1,726)	$ 35,003
Provisions	(l)	-	1,726	1,726
Current portion capital leases		649	-	649
Current loans		2,972	-	2,972
		40,350	-	40,350
Non-current liabilities				
Provision for environmental rehabilitation	(j)	2,846	2,752	5,598
Capital leases		3,261	-	3,261
Deferred tax liabilities	(k)	117,234	(78,408)	38,826
		163,691	(75,656)	88,035
Capital and reserves				
Issued capital		890,049	-	890,049
Equity reserve	(i)	31,491	336	31,827
Currency translation adjustment	(m)	(173,571)	3,994	(169,577)
Deficit		(51,768)	(203,998)	(255,766)
		696,201	(199,668)	496,533
Non-controlling interest		12,335	(333)	12,002
		708,536	(200,001)	508,535
		$ 872,227	$ (275,657)	$ 596,570

Eastern Platinum Limited
Notes to the condensed consolidated financial statements
(Expressed in thousands of U.S. dollars, except number of shares and per share amounts)

15.   IFRS (continued)

The reconciliation of the statement of cash flows for the three months ended March 31, 2008:

	Note	March 31, 2008 (3 months)		
		Canadian GAAP	Effect of transition to IFRS	IFRS
Operating activities				
Net profit for the period		$ 21,773	$ (195)	$ 21,578
Adjustments to net profit				
Depreciation	(h)	4,442	(48)	4,394
Refining contract amortization	(o)	-	367	367
Share-based payment	(i)	1,227	122	1,349
Interest income	(o)	-	(2,807)	(2,807)
Interest income received	(o)	-	1,443	1,443
Finance costs	(o)	-	8	8
Finance costs paid	(o)	-	118	118
Foreign exchange gain		(1,057)	-	(1,057)
Deferred income tax expense	(k)	8,248	(1)	8,247
		34,633	(993)	33,640
Net changes in non-cash working capital items				
Trade receivables	(g)	(30,801)	950	(29,851)
Inventories		314	-	314
Accounts payable and accrued liabilities		2,362	-	2,362
		6,508	(43)	6,465
Investing activities				
Maturity of short-term investments	(o)	54,567	30	54,597
Purchase of other assets	(o)	-	(30)	(30)
Property, plant and equipment expenditures		(23,706)	-	(23,706)
		30,861	-	30,861
Financing activities				
Common shares issued for cash, net of share issue costs		4,224	-	4,224
Repayment of short-term debt	(o)	380	(954)	(574)
Other long-term liabilities	(o)	(300)	(112)	(412)
		4,304	(1,066)	3,238
Effect of exchange rate changes on cash and cash equivalents		(2,292)	1,109	(1,183)
Increase in cash and cash equivalents		39,381	-	39,381
Cash and cash equivalents, beginning of period		18,818	-	18,818
Cash and cash equivalents, end of period		$ 58,199	$ -	$ 58,199

Eastern Platinum Limited

Notes to the condensed consolidated financial statements
(Expressed in thousands of U.S. dollars, except number of shares and per share amounts)

15. IFRS (continued)

The reconciliation of the statement of cash flows for the twelve months ended December 31, 2008:

	Note	December 31, 2008 (12 months)		
		Canadian GAAP	Effect of transition to IFRS	IFRS
Operating activities				
Net profit (loss) for the period		$ 12,935	$ (226,051)	$ (213,116)
Adjustments to net profit (loss)				
Depreciation	(h)	14,877	(215)	14,662
Refining contract amortization		1,353	-	1,353
Impairment	(n)	-	313,603	313,603
Share-based payment	(i)	4,290	335	4,625
Interest income	(o)	-	(8,944)	(8,944)
Interest income received	(o)	-	10,028	10,028
Finance costs	(o)	2,845	880	3,725
Finance costs paid	(o)	-	(375)	(375)
Foreign exchange loss	(o)	5,731	(3,576)	2,155
Realized foreign exchange gain	(o)	-	(1,157)	(1,157)
Deferred income tax recovery	(k)	(13,623)	(87,808)	(101,431)
		28,408	(3,280)	25,128
Net changes in non-cash working capital items				
Trade receivables	(g)	10,765	3,266	14,031
Inventories		1,391	-	1,391
Accounts payable and accrued liabilities		12,962	-	12,962
		53,526	(14)	53,512
Investing activities				
Acquisitions, net of cash acquired		(39,589)	-	(39,589)
Maturity of short-term investments	(o)	119,318	42	119,360
Purchase of other assets	(o)	-	(42)	(42)
Property, plant and equipment expenditures		(143,373)	-	(143,373)
		(63,644)	-	(63,644)
Financing activities				
Common shares issued for cash, net of share issue costs		22,004	-	22,004
Repayment of short-term debt	(o)	(892)	892	-
Other long-term liabilities	(o)	(3,411)	(898)	(4,309)
		17,701	(6)	17,695
Effect of exchange rate changes on cash and cash equivalents		(595)	20	(575)
Increase in cash and cash equivalents		6,988	-	6,988
Cash and cash equivalents, beginning of period		18,818	-	18,818
Cash and cash equivalents, end of period		$ 25,806	$ -	$ 25,806

Note: All assignment material with an asterisk (*) relates to Appendix 5A.

Brief Exercises

(LO 1)   **BE5-1**   One of the weaknesses or limitations of the balance sheet is that it leaves out financial statement elements if they cannot be objectively recorded. Name three examples of items that are omitted because of this limitation.

(LO 2)   **BE5-2**   Koch Corporation's adjusted trial balance contained the following asset accounts at December 31, 2011: Cash $7,000; Land $40,000; Patents $12,500; Accounts Receivable $90,000; Prepaid Insurance $5,200; Inventory $30,000; Allowance for Doubtful Accounts $4,000; Temporary Investments $11,000. Prepare the current assets section of the balance sheet, listing the accounts in proper sequence. Identify which items are monetary.

(LO 2)   **BE5-3**   The following accounts are in Tsui Limited's December 31, 2011, trial balance: Prepaid Rent $1,300; Long-Term Investments in Common Shares $62,000; Unearned Fees $7,000; Land Held for Investment $139,000; and Long-Term Receivables $45,000. Prepare the long-term investments section of the balance sheet. Identify which items are financial instruments.

(LO 2)   **BE5-4**   Lowell Corp.'s December 31, 2011, trial balance includes the following accounts: Inventories $120,000; Buildings $207,000; Accumulated Depreciation—Equipment $19,000; Equipment $190,000; Land Held for Investment $46,000; Accumulated Depreciation—Buildings $45,000; Land $71,000; Machinery under Capital Leases $229,000; and Accumulated Depreciation—Machinery under Capital Leases $103,000. Prepare the property, plant, and equipment section of the balance sheet.

(LO 2)   **BE5-5**   Patrick Corporation's adjusted trial balance contained the following asset accounts at December 31, 2011: Prepaid Rent $12,000; Goodwill $50,000; Franchise Fees Receivable $2,000; Franchises $47,000; Patents $33,000; and Trademarks $10,000. Prepare the intangible assets section of the balance sheet.

(LO 2)   **BE5-6**   Included in Mai Limited's December 31, 2011, trial balance are the following accounts: Accounts Payable $251,000; Obligations under Long-Term Capital Leases $175,000; Discount on Bonds Payable $142,000; Advances from Customers $141,000; Bonds Payable $600,000; Wages Payable $127,000; Interest Payable $142,000; and Income Taxes Payable $9,000. Prepare the current liabilities section of the balance sheet. Identify which items are monetary.

(LO 2)   **BE5-7**   Use the information presented in BE5-6 for Mai Limited to prepare the long-term liabilities section of the balance sheet.

(LO 2)   **BE5-8**   Hawthorn Corporation's adjusted trial balance contained the following accounts at December 31, 2011: Retained Earnings $120,000; Common Shares $700,000; Bonds Payable $100,000; Contributed Surplus $200,000; Preferred Shares $50,000; Goodwill $55,000; and Accumulated Other Comprehensive Loss $150,000. Prepare the shareholders' equity section of the balance sheet.

(LO 6)   **BE5-9**   What is the purpose of a statement of cash flows? How does it differ from a balance sheet and an income statement?

(LO 8, 9, 12)   *****BE5-10**   Midwest Beverage Company reported the following items in the most recent year:

Net income	$40,000
Dividends paid	5,000
Increase in accounts receivable	10,000
Increase in accounts payable	7,000
Purchase of equipment	8,000
Depreciation expense	4,000
Issue of notes payable for cash	20,000

Calculate net cash provided (used) by operating activities, the net change in cash during the year, and free cash flow. Dividends paid are treated as financing activities.

(LO 8)   **BE5-11**   Ames Company reported 2011 net income of $151,000. During 2011, accounts receivable increased by $13,000 and accounts payable increased by $9,500. Depreciation expense was $44,000. Prepare the cash flows from operating activities section of the statement of cash flows.

BE5-12   Ramirez Corporation engaged in the following cash transactions during 2011:   **(LO 8)**

Sale of land and building	$196,000
Repurchase of company's own shares	25,000
Purchase of land	43,000
Payment of cash dividend	58,000
Purchase of equipment	35,000
Issuance of common shares	140,000
Retirement of bonds payable	200,000

Calculate the net cash provided (used) by investing activities.

BE5-13   Use the information from BE5-12 for Ramirez Corporation to calculate the net cash from financing activities.   **(LO 8)** Dividends paid are treated as financing activities.

BE5-14   Using the information in BE5-12, determine Ramirez's free cash flow, assuming that it reported net cash pro-   **(LO 9, 12)** vided by operating activities of $400,000.

Exercises

E5-1   **(Balance Sheet Classifications)** Several balance sheet accounts of Marcoccia Inc. follow: **(LO 2)**

1. Investment in Preferred Shares
2. Common Shares
3. Cash Dividends Payable
4. Accumulated Depreciation
5. Warehouse in Process of Construction
6. Petty Cash
7. Accrued Interest on Notes Payable
8. Deficit
9. Investments—Temporary Trading Securities
10. Income Taxes Payable
11. Unearned Subscription Revenue
12. Work-in-Process
13. Accrued Vacation Pay
14. Customer Deposits

Instructions

For each account, indicate the proper balance sheet classification. In the case of borderline items, indicate the additional information that would be required to determine the proper classification. (Refer to Illustration 5-1 as a guideline.) Also, identify which items are monetary and which are financial instruments (or both).

E5-2   **(Classification of Balance Sheet Accounts)** The classifications of Chakma Limited's balance sheet follow: **(LO 2)**

1. Current assets
2. Long-term investments
3. Property, plant, and equipment
4. Intangible assets
5. Other assets
6. Current liabilities
7. Noncurrent liabilities
8. Capital shares
9. Contributed surplus
10. Retained earnings
11. Accumulated other comprehensive income

Instructions

Indicate by number where each of the following accounts would be classified:

(a) Preferred Shares
(b) Goodwill
(c) Wages Payable
(d) Trade Accounts Payable
(e) Buildings
(f) Trading Securities
(g) Current Portion of Long-Term Debt
(h) Premium on Bonds Payable
(i) Allowance for Doubtful Accounts
(j) Accounts Receivable
(k) Demand Bank Loan
(l) Notes Payable (due next year)
(m) Office Supplies
(n) Mortgage Payable
(o) Land
(p) Bond Sinking Fund

(q) Inventory

(r) Prepaid Insurance

(s) Bonds Payable

(t) Taxes Payable

(u) Unrealized Gain on Revalued Property, Plant, and Equipment

(LO 2)   E5-3   (Classification of Balance Sheet Accounts) Assume that Phu Inc. uses the following headings on its balance sheet:

1. Current assets
2. Long-term investments
3. Property, plant, and equipment
4. Intangible assets
5. Other assets
6. Current liabilities

7. Long-term liabilities
8. Capital shares
9. Contributed surplus
10. Retained earnings
11. Accumulated other comprehensive income

Instructions

Indicate by number how each of the following should usually be classified. If an item need not be reported at all on the balance sheet, use the letter X. Indicate also whether an item is monetary and/or represents a financial instrument.

(a) Unexpired insurance

(b) Shares owned in affiliated companies

(c) Unearned subscriptions

(d) Advances to suppliers

(e) Unearned rent

(f) Copyrights

(g) Petty cash fund

(h) Sales tax payable

(i) Accrued interest on notes receivable

(j) Twenty-year issue of bonds payable that will mature within the next year (no sinking funds exist, and refunding is not planned)

(k) Machinery retired from use and held for sale

(l) Fully depreciated machine still in use

(m) Investment in bonds that will be held until maturity

(n) Accrued interest on bonds payable

(o) Salaries that company budget shows will be paid to employees within the next year

(p) Accumulated depreciation

(q) Accumulated unrealized gains on securities accounted for under the fair value through OCI model

(r) Bank demand loan

(s) Land held for speculation

(LO 2, 3, 12)   E5-4   (Preparation of Corrected Balance Sheet) Bruno Corp. has decided to expand its operations. The bookkeeper recently completed the following balance sheet in order to obtain additional funds for expansion:

BRUNO CORP.

Balance Sheet

For the Year Ended December 31, 2011

Current assets	
Cash (net of bank overdraft of $30,000)	$260,000
Accounts receivable (net)	340,000
Inventory at the lower of cost and net realizable value	401,000
Trading securities at cost (fair value $120,000)	140,000

Property, plant, and equipment	
Building (net)	570,000
Office equipment (net)	160,000
Land held for future use	175,000
Intangible assets	
Goodwill	80,000
Investment in bonds to be held until maturity	90,000
Prepaid expense	12,000
Current liabilities	
Accounts payable	195,000
Notes payable (due next year)	125,000
Pension obligation	82,000
Rent payable	49,000
Premium on bonds payable	53,000
Long-term liabilities	
Bonds payable	500,000
Shareholders' equity	
Common shares, unlimited authorized, 290,000 issued	290,000
Contributed surplus	180,000
Retained earnings	?

Instructions

(a) Prepare a revised balance sheet using the available information. Assume that the bank overdraft relates to a bank account held at a different bank than the account with the cash balance. Assume that the accumulated depreciation balance for the buildings is $160,000 and for the office equipment, $105,000. The allowance for doubtful accounts has a balance of $17,000. The pension obligation is considered a long-term liability.

*(b) What effect, if any, does the classification of the bank overdraft have on the working capital and current ratio of Bruno Corp.? What is the likely reason that the bank overdraft was given that particular classification?

Digging Deeper

E5-5 **(Correction of Balance Sheet)** The bookkeeper for Garfield Corp. has prepared the following balance sheet as at July 31, 2011: **(LO 2, 3, 12)**

GARFIELD CORP.
Balance Sheet
As at July 31, 2011

Cash	$ 69,000	Notes and accounts payable	$ 44,000
Accounts receivable (net)	40,500	Long-term liabilities	75,000
Inventories	60,000	Shareholders' equity	155,500
Equipment (net)	84,000		$274,500
Patents	21,000		
	$274,500		

The following additional information is provided:

1. Cash includes $1,200 in a petty cash fund and $12,000 in a bond sinking fund.

2. The net accounts receivable balance is composed of the following three items: (a) accounts receivable debit balances $52,000; (b) accounts receivable credit balances $8,000; (c) allowance for doubtful accounts $3,500.

3. Inventory costing $5,300 was shipped out on consignment on July 31, 2011. The ending inventory balance does not include the consigned goods. Receivables of $5,300 were recognized on these consigned goods.

4. Equipment had a cost of $112,000 and an accumulated depreciation balance of $28,000.

5. Taxes payable of $9,000 were accrued on July 31. Garfield Corp., however, had set up a cash fund to meet this obligation. This cash fund was not included in the cash balance, but was offset against the taxes payable amount.

Instructions

(a) Use the information available to prepare a corrected classified balance sheet as at July 31, 2011 (adjust the account balances based on the additional information).

*(b) What effect, if any, does the treatment of the credit balances in accounts receivable of $8,000 have on the working capital and current ratio of Garfield Corp.? What is the likely reason that the credit balances in accounts receivable were given that particular classification? What is the likely cause of the credit balances in accounts receivable?

Digging Deeper

(LO 3) E5-6 (Preparation of Classified Balance Sheet) Assume that Bhatia Inc. has the following accounts at the end of the current year:

1. Common Shares	11. Accumulated Depreciation—Buildings
2. Raw Materials	12. Cash Restricted for Plant Expansion
3. Preferred Share Investments, Long-Term	13. Land Held for Future Plant Site
4. Unearned Rent	14. Allowance for Doubtful Accounts
5. Work-in-Process	15. Retained Earnings
6. Copyrights (net)	16. Unearned Subscription
7. Buildings	17. Receivables from Officers (due in one year)
8. Notes Receivable, Short-Term	18. Finished Goods
9. Cash	19. Accounts Receivable
10. Accrued Salaries Payable	20. Bonds Payable (due in four years)

Instructions

Prepare a classified balance sheet in good form (no monetary amounts are necessary).

(LO 3, 4, 5) E5-7 (Current Assets Section of Balance Sheet) Selected accounts follow of Aramis Limited at December 31, 2011:

Finished Goods	$ 52,000	Cost of Goods Sold	$2,100,000
Revenue Received in Advance	90,000	Notes Receivable	40,000
Bank Overdraft	8,000	Accounts Receivable	161,000
Equipment	253,000	Raw Materials	187,000
Work-in-Process	34,000	Supplies Expense	60,000
Cash	50,000	Allowance for Doubtful Accounts	12,000
Short-Term Investments in Securities	31,000	Licences	18,000
Customer Advances	36,000	Contributed Surplus	88,000
Cash Restricted for Plant Expansion	50,000	Common Shares	22,000

The following additional information is available:

1. Inventories are valued at lower of cost and net realizable value using FIFO.

2. Equipment is recorded at cost. Accumulated depreciation, calculated on a straight-line basis, is $50,600.

3. The short-term investments in securities have a fair value of $29,000.

4. The notes receivable are due April 30, 2012, with interest receivable every April 30. The notes bear interest at 6%. (Hint: Accrue interest due on December 31, 2011.)

5. The allowance for doubtful accounts applies to the accounts receivable. Accounts receivable of $50,000 are pledged as collateral on a bank loan.

6. Licences are recorded net of accumulated amortization of $14,000.

Instructions

(a) Prepare the current assets section of Aramis Limited's December 31, 2011, balance sheet, with appropriate disclosures.

(b) Outline the other ways or methods that can be used to disclose the details that are required for the financial statement elements in part (a).

(LO 3) E5-8 (Current vs. Long-Term Liabilities) Toswell Corporation is preparing its December 31, 2011, balance sheet. The following items may be reported as either current or long-term liabilities:

1. On December 15, 2011, Toswell declared a cash dividend of $2.50 per share to shareholders of record on December 31. The dividend is payable on January 15, 2012. Toswell has issued 1 million common shares.

2. Also on December 31, Toswell declared a 10% stock dividend to shareholders of record on January 15, 2012. The dividend will be distributed on January 31, 2012. Toswell's common shares have a market value of $54 per share.

3. At December 31, bonds payable of $100 million are outstanding. The bonds pay 7% interest every September 30 and mature in instalments of $25 million every September 30, beginning on September 30, 2012.

4. At December 31, 2010, customer advances were $12 million. During 2011, Toswell collected $40 million of customer advances, and advances of $25 million were earned.

5. At December 31, 2011, retained earnings set aside for future inventory losses is $22 million.

6. At December 31, 2011, Toswell has an operating line of credit with a balance of $3.5 million. For several years now, Toswell has successfully met all the conditions of this bank loan. If Toswell defaults on any of the loan conditions in any way, the bank has the right to demand payment on the loan.

Instructions

For each item above, indicate the dollar amounts to be reported as a current liability and as a long-term liability, if any.

E5-9 (Current Assets and Current Liabilities) The current assets and current liabilities sections of the balance sheet **(LO 3, 12)** of Agincourt Corp. are as follows:

AGINCOURT CORP.
Balance Sheet (partial)
December 31, 2011

Cash		$ 40,000	Accounts payable	$ 61,000
Accounts receivable	$89,000		Notes payable	67,000
Allowance for doubtful accounts	7,000	82,000		$128,000
Inventories		171,000		
Prepaid expenses		9,000		
		$302,000		

The following errors have been discovered in the corporation's accounting:

1. January 2012 cash disbursements that were entered as at December 2011 included payments of accounts payable in the amount of $35,000, on which a cash discount of 2% was taken.

2. The inventory included $27,000 of merchandise that was received at December 31 but with no purchase invoices received or entered. Of this amount, $10,000 was received on consignment; the remainder was purchased f.o.b. destination, terms 2/10, n/30.

3. Sales for the first four days in January 2012 in the amount of $30,000 were entered in the sales book as at December 31, 2011. Of these, $21,500 were sales on account and the remainder were cash sales.

4. Cash, not including cash sales, collected in January 2012 and entered as at December 31, 2011, totalled $35,324. Of this amount, $23,324 was received on account after cash discounts of 2% had been deducted; the remainder was proceeds on a bank loan.

Instructions

(a) Restate the balance sheet's current assets and liabilities sections. (Assume that both accounts receivable and accounts payable are recorded gross.)

*(b) Calculate the current ratio before and after the corrections prepared in part (a). Did the restatement improve or worsen this ratio?

(c) State the net effect of your adjustments on Agincourt Corp.'s retained earnings balance.

E5-10 (Current Liabilities) Mary Pierce is the controller of Arnold Corporation and is responsible for the preparation **(LO 3, 4)** of the year-end financial statements on December 31. The following transactions occurred during the year:

1. On December 20, 2011, an employee filed a legal action against Arnold for $100,000 for wrongful dismissal. Management believes the action to be frivolous and without merit. The likelihood of payment to the employee is remote.

2. Bonuses to key employees based on net income for 2011 are estimated to be $150,000.

3. On December 1, 2011, the company borrowed $900,000 at 8% per year. Interest is paid quarterly.

4. Credit sales for the year amounted to $10 million. Arnold's expense provision for doubtful accounts is estimated to be 2% of credit sales.

5. On December 15, 2011, the company declared a $2.00 per share dividend on the 40,000 shares of common shares outstanding, to be paid on January 5, 2012.

6. During the year, customer advances of $160,000 were received; $50,000 of this amount was earned by December 31, 2011.

Instructions

For each item above, indicate the dollar amount to be reported as a current liability. If a liability is not reported, explain why.

(LO 3)   **E5-11**   **(Preparation of Balance Sheet)** The trial balance of Zeitz Corporation at December 31, 2011, follows:

	Debits	Credits
Cash	$ 205,000	
Sales		$ 7,960,000
Trading securities	153,000	
Cost of goods sold	4,800,000	
Investment in bonds to be held to maturity	299,000	
Long-term investments in shares—fair value through OCI (market $345,000)	277,000	
Short-term notes payable		98,000
Accounts payable		545,000
Selling expenses	1,860,000	
Investment gains		63,000
Land	260,000	
Buildings	1,040,000	
Dividends payable		136,000
Accrued liabilities		96,000
Accounts receivable	515,000	
Accumulated depreciation—buildings		152,000
Allowance for doubtful accounts		25,000
Administrative expenses	900,000	
Interest expense	211,000	
Inventories	687,000	
Unusual gain		160,000
Correction of prior year's error	140,000	
Long-term notes payable		900,000
Equipment	600,000	
Bonds payable		1,000,000
Accumulated depreciation—equipment		60,000
Franchise	160,000	
Common shares		809,000
Patent	195,000	
Retained earnings		218,000
Accumulated other comprehensive income		80,000
Totals	$12,302,000	$12,302,000

Digging Deeper

Instructions

(a) Prepare a classified balance sheet at December 31, 2011. Ignore income taxes.

(b) Is there any situation where it would make more sense to have a balance sheet that is not classified?

(LO 3, 8)   **E5-12**   **(Preparation of Balance Sheet)** Zezulka Corporation's balance sheet at the end of 2010 included the following items:

Current assets	$1,105,000	Current liabilities	$1,020,000
Land	30,000	Bonds payable	1,100,000
Building	1,120,000	Common shares	180,000
Equipment	320,000	Retained earnings	174,000
Accumulated depreciation—building	(130,000)	Total	$2,474,000
Accumulated depreciation—equipment	(11,000)		
Patents	40,000		
Total	$2,474,000		

The following information is available for 2011:

1. Net income was $391,000.

2. Equipment (cost of $20,000 and accumulated depreciation of $8,000) was sold for $10,000.

3. Depreciation expense was $4,000 on the building and $9,000 on equipment.

4. Patent depreciation expense was $3,000.

5. Current assets other than cash increased by $229,000. Current liabilities increased by $213,000.

6. An addition to the building was completed at a cost of $31,000.

7. A long-term investment in shares (no quoted market value) was purchased for $20,500 at the end of the year.

8. Bonds payable of $75,000 were issued.

9. Cash dividends of $180,000 were declared and paid. Dividends paid are treated as financing activities.

Instructions

(a) Prepare a balance sheet at December 31, 2011.

(b) Prepare a statement of cash flows for the year ended December 31, 2011.

E5-13 (Prepare Statement of Cash Flows) A comparative balance sheet for Carmichael Industries Inc. follows: **(LO 6, 8, 9)**

CARMICHAEL INDUSTRIES INC.
Balance Sheet

	December 31	
Assets	2011	2010
Cash	$ 21,000	$ 34,000
Accounts receivable	104,000	54,000
Inventories	220,000	189,000
Land	71,000	110,000
Equipment	260,000	200,000
Accumulated depreciation—equipment	(69,000)	(42,000)
Total	$607,000	$545,000
Liabilities and Shareholders' Equity		
Accounts payable	$ 52,000	$ 59,000
Bonds payable	150,000	200,000
Common shares	214,000	164,000
Retained earnings	91,000	22,000
Accumulated other comprehensive income	100,000	100,000
Total	$607,000	$545,000

Additional information:

1. Net income for the fiscal year ending December 31, 2011, was $129,000.

2. Cash dividends of $60,000 were declared and paid. Dividends paid are treated as financing activities.

3. Bonds payable amounting to $50,000 were retired through issuance of common shares.

4. Land was sold at its carrying amount.

Instructions

(a) Prepare a statement of cash flows using the indirect format for cash flows from operations.

(b) Comment in general on the results reported in the statement of cash flows.

E5-14 (Statement of Cash Flows—Classifications) The major classifications of activities reported in the statement of **(LO 7)** cash flows are operating, investing, and financing. For this question, assume the following:

1. The direct format is being used.

2. The indirect format is being used.

302 CHAPTER 5 Financial Position and Cash Flows

Instructions

Assume that accounting standards for private entities are followed. Classify each of the transactions in the lettered list that follows as:

1. Operating activity
2. Investing activity
3. Financing activity
4. Not reported as a cash flow

Transactions:

(a) Issuance of common shares

(b) Purchase of land and building

(c) Redemption of bonds

(d) Proceeds on sale of equipment

(e) Depreciation of machinery

(f) Amortization of patent

(g) Issuance of bonds for plant assets

(h) Payment of cash dividends

(i) Exchange of furniture for office equipment

(j) Loss on sale of equipment

(k) Increase in accounts receivable during year

(l) Decrease in accounts payable during year

(LO 8, 9) E5-15 (Prepare Statement of Cash Flows) The comparative balance sheet of Marubeni Corporation for the fiscal year ending December 31, 2011, follows:

MARUBENI CORPORATION
Balance Sheet

	December 31	
Assets	2011	2010
Cash	$ 45,000	$ 13,000
Accounts receivable	91,000	88,000
Equipment	39,000	22,000
Less: Accumulated depreciation	(17,000)	(11,000)
Total	$158,000	$112,000
Liabilities and Shareholders' Equity		
Accounts payable	$ 20,000	$ 15,000
Common shares	100,000	80,000
Retained earnings	38,000	17,000
Total	$158,000	$112,000

Net income of $34,000 was reported and dividends of $13,000 were paid in 2011. New equipment was purchased and none was sold.

Instructions

Prepare a statement of cash flows using the indirect format for cash flows from operations. Assume that the entity uses accounting standards for private enterprises.

(LO 8) E5-16 (Prepare Partial Statement of Cash Flows—Operating Activities) The income statement of Kneale Transport Inc. for the year ended December 31, 2011, reported the following condensed information:

KNEALE TRANSPORT INC.
Income Statement
Year Ended December 31, 2011

Revenue		$545,000
Operating expenses		370,000
Income from operations		175,000
Other revenues and expenses		
Gain on sale of equipment	$25,000	
Interest expense	10,000	15,000
Income before income taxes		190,000
Income taxes		42,000
Net income		$148,000

Kneale's balance sheet contained the following comparative data at December 31:

	2011	2010
Accounts receivable	$50,000	$60,000
Prepaid insurance	8,000	5,000
Accounts payable	30,000	41,000
Interest payable	2,000	750
Income taxes payable	8,000	4,500
Unearned revenue	10,000	14,000

Additional information: Operating expenses include $70,000 in depreciation expense. The company follows IFRS. Assume that interest is treated as an operating activity for purposes of the cash flow statement.

Instructions

(a) Prepare the operating activities section of the statement of cash flows for the year ended December 31, 2011, using the indirect format.

(b) Prepare the operating activities section of the statement of cash flows for the year ended December 31, 2011, using the direct format.

*E5-17   (Analysis) Use the information in E5-15 for Marubeni Corporation.   **(LO 12)**

Instructions

(a) Calculate the current ratio and debt to total assets ratio as at December 31, 2010 and 2011. Calculate the free cash flow for December 31, 2011.

(b) Based on the analysis in (a), comment on the company's liquidity and financial flexibility.

*E5-18   (Analysis) Use the information in E5-13 for Carmichael Industries.   **(LO 12)**

Instructions

(a) Calculate the current and acid-test ratios for 2010 and 2011.

(b) Calculate Carmichael's current cash debt coverage ratio for 2011.

(c) Based on the analyses in (a) and (b), comment on Carmichael's liquidity and financial flexibility.

Problems

P5-1   A list of accounts follows:

Accounts Receivable	Premium on Bonds Payable
Land	Bonds Payable
Accrued Wages	Prepaid Rent
Land for Future Plant Site	Buildings
Accumulated Depreciation—Buildings	Purchase Returns and Allowances
Loss from Flood	Cash in Bank
Accumulated Depreciation—Equipment	Purchases
Notes Payable—Current	Cash on Hand
Accumulated Other Comprehensive Income	Notes Receivable (due in five years)
Patent (net of amortization)	Commission Expense
Advances to Employees	Retained Earnings
Pension Obligations	Common Shares
Advertising Expense	Sales
Petty Cash	Copyright (net of amortization)
Allowance for Doubtful Accounts	Sales Discounts
Preferred Shares	Dividends Payable
Investment in Securities—Noncurrent	Sales Salaries Expense

Equipment	Inventory—Beginning
Taxes Payable	Unearned Subscriptions
Gain on Sale of Equipment	Inventory—Ending
Temporary Trading Securities	Unrealized Gain/Loss on Securities—fair value through OCI
Interest Receivable	
Transportation-in	

Instructions

Prepare a classified balance sheet in good form, without monetary amounts.

P5-2   Balance sheet items for Montoya Inc. follow for the current year, 2011:

Goodwill	$ 125,000	Accumulated depreciation—equipment	$ 292,000
Payroll taxes payable	177,591	Inventories	239,800
Bonds payable	300,000	Rent payable (short-term)	45,000
Discount on bonds payable	15,000	Taxes payable	98,362
Cash	360,000	Long-term rental obligations	480,000
Land	480,000	Common shares (20,000 shares issued)	200,000
Notes receivable	445,700	Preferred shares (15,000 shares issued)	150,000
Notes payable to banks (demand)	265,000	Prepaid expenses	87,920
Accounts payable	490,000	Equipment	1,470,000
Retained earnings	?	Temporary trading securities	121,000
Income taxes receivable	97,630	Accumulated depreciation—building	270,200
Unsecured notes payable (long-term)	1,600,000	Building	1,640,000

Digging Deeper

Instructions

(a) Prepare a classified balance sheet in good form. The numbers of authorized shares are as follows: 400,000 common and 20,000 preferred. Assume that notes receivable and notes payable are short-term, unless stated otherwise. Cost and fair value of temporary investments are the same.

(b) What additional disclosures would you expect to provide for the long-term rental obligations?

P5-3   The trial balance of Eastwood Inc. and other related information for the year 2011 follows:

EASTWOOD INC.
Trial Balance
December 31, 2011

	Debits	Credits
Cash	$ 41,000	
Accounts receivable	163,500	
Allowance for doubtful accounts		$ 8,700
Prepaid insurance	5,900	
Inventory	208,500	
Long-term investments in shares	339,000	
Land	85,000	
Construction work in progress	124,000	
Patents	36,000	
Equipment	400,000	
Accumulated depreciation—equipment		240,000
Unamortized discount on bonds payable	20,000	
Accounts payable		148,000
Accrued expenses		49,200
Notes payable		94,000
Bonds payable		200,000
Common shares		500,000
Accumulated other comprehensive income		45,000
Retained earnings		138,000
	$1,422,900	$1,422,900

Additional information:

1. The inventory has a net realizable value of $212,000. The FIFO method of inventory valuation is used.

2. The investments' fair value is $478,000. The fair value through other comprehensive income method is used.

3. The amount of the Construction Work in Progress account represents the costs to date on a building in the process of construction. (The company is renting factory space at the present time while waiting for the new building to be completed.) The land that the building is being constructed on cost $85,000, as shown in the trial balance.

4. The patents were purchased by the company at a cost of $40,000 and are being amortized on a straight-line basis.

5. Of the unamortized discount on bonds payable, $2,000 will be amortized in 2012.

6. The notes payable represent bank loans that are secured by long-term investments carried at $120,000. These bank loans are due in 2012.

7. The bonds payable bear interest at 11% payable every December 31, and are due January 1, 2022.

8. For common shares, 600,000 are authorized and 500,000 are issued and outstanding.

Instructions

Prepare a balance sheet as at December 31, 2011, so that all important information is fully disclosed.

P5-4   The balance sheet of Delacosta Corporation as of December 31, 2011, is as follows:

DELACOSTA CORPORATION
Balance Sheet
December 31, 2011

Assets

Goodwill (Note 2)	$ 70,000
Buildings (Note 1)	1,640,000
Inventories	312,100
Temporary trading securities (Note 4)	100,000
Land	950,000
Accounts receivable	170,000
Long-term investments in securities (Note 4)	87,000
Cash on hand	175,900
Assets allocated to trustee for plant expansion	
Cash in bank	120,000
Treasury notes, at cost and fair value	138,000
	$3,763,000

Equities

Notes payable (Note 4)	$ 600,000
Common shares, unlimited authorized, 1,000,000 issued	1,150,000
Retained earnings	706,000
Accumulated other comprehensive income	252,000
Appreciation capital (Note 1)	570,000
Income taxes payable	75,000
Reserve for depreciation of building	410,000
	$3,763,000

Note 1: Buildings are stated at cost, except for one building that was recorded at its appraised value as management determined the building to be worth more than originally paid at acquisition. The excess of the appraisal value over cost was $570,000. Depreciation has been recorded based on cost.

Note 2: Goodwill in the amount of $70,000 was recognized because the company believed that carrying amount was not an accurate representation of the company's fair value. The gain of $70,000 was credited to Retained Earnings.

Note 3: Notes payable are long-term except for the current instalment due of $100,000.

Note 4: Temporary trading securities have a fair value of $75,000 and are accounted for using the fair value through net income model. Long-term investments in securities have a fair value of $200,000 and are accounted for using the fair value through other comprehensive income model. Both investments in securities are currently recorded at cost.

Instructions

Prepare a corrected classified balance sheet in good form. The notes above are for information only. Assume that you have decided not to use the revaluation method for property, plant, and equipment.

P5-5   The balance sheet of Sargent Corporation follows for the current year, 2011:

SARGENT CORPORATION
Balance Sheet
December 31, 2011

Current assets	$ 485,000	Current liabilities	$ 380,000
Investments	640,000	Long-term liabilities	1,000,000
Property, plant, and equipment	1,720,000	Shareholders' equity	1,770,000
Intangible assets	305,000		
	$3,150,000		$3,150,000

The following additional information is available:

1. The current assets section includes the following: cash $150,000; accounts receivable $170,000, less $10,000 allowance for doubtful accounts; inventories $180,000; and unearned revenue $5,000. The cash balance is composed of $190,000, less a bank overdraft of $40,000. Inventories are stated at the lower of FIFO cost and net realizable value.

2. The investments section includes the following: notes receivable from a related company, due in 2017, $40,000; temporary trading investments in common shares of another company—fair value through net income, $80,000 (fair value $80,000); long-term investment in securities—fair value through other comprehensive income $270,000 (fair value $155,000); bond sinking fund $250,000; and patents $115,000.

3. Property, plant, and equipment includes buildings $1,040,000, less accumulated depreciation $360,000; equipment $450,000, less accumulated depreciation $180,000; land $500,000; and land held for future use $270,000.

4. Intangible assets include the following: franchise $165,000; goodwill $100,000; and discount on bonds payable $40,000.

5. Current liabilities include the following: accounts payable $140,000; notes payable, short-term $80,000, long-term $120,000; and taxes payable $40,000.

6. Long-term liabilities are composed solely of 7% bonds payable due in 2019.

7. Shareholders' equity has 70,000 preferred shares (200,000 authorized), which were issued for $450,000, and 100,000 common shares (400,000 authorized), which were issued at an average price of $10 per share. In addition, the corporation has retained earnings of $290,000 and accumulated other comprehensive income of $30,000.

Instructions

(a) Prepare a balance sheet in good form (adjust the amounts in each balance sheet classification based on the additional information).

Digging Deeper

(b) What makes the condensed format of the original balance sheet inadequate in terms of the amount of detail that needs to be disclosed under GAAP?

P5-6   Jia Inc. had the following balance sheet at the end of operations for 2010:

JIA INC.
Balance Sheet
December 31, 2010

Cash	$ 20,000	Accounts payable	$ 30,000
Accounts receivable	21,200	Long-term notes payable	41,000
Investments—fair value through net income	32,000	Common shares	100,000
Plant assets (net)	81,000	Retained earnings	23,200
Land	40,000		
	$194,200		$194,200

During 2011, the following occurred:

1. Jia Inc. sold part of its investment portfolio for $19,000. This transaction resulted in a gain of $3,400 for the firm. The company often sells and buys securities of this nature.

2. A tract of land was purchased for $18,000 cash.

3. Long-term notes payable in the amount of $17,000 were retired before maturity by paying $17,000 cash.

4. An additional $26,000 in common shares was issued.

5. Dividends totalling $9,200 were declared and paid to shareholders.

6. Net income for 2011 was $32,000 after allowing for depreciation of $12,000.

7. Land was purchased through the issuance of $30,000 in bonds.

8. At December 31, 2011, cash was $41,000; accounts receivable were $41,600; and accounts payable remained at $30,000.

Jia Inc. follows accounting standards for private entities.

Instructions

(a) Prepare a statement of cash flows for the year ended December 31, 2011.

(b) Prepare the balance sheet as it would appear at December 31, 2011.

(c) How might the statement of cash flows help the user of the financial statements?

*(d) Calculate the following ratios:
    1. Free cash flow
    2. Current cash debt coverage ratio
    3. Cash debt coverage ratio

(e) What is the cash flow pattern for Jia? Discuss any areas of concern.

**Digging
Deeper**

P5-7 Lydia Trottier has prepared baked goods for sale since 1995. She started a baking business in her home and has been operating in a rented building with a storefront since 2000. Trottier incorporated the business as MLT Inc. on January 1, 2011, with an initial share issue of 1,000 common shares for $2,500. Lydia Trottier is the principal shareholder of MLT Inc.

Sales have increased by 30% annually since operations began at the present location, and additional equipment is needed for the continued growth that is expected. Trottier wants to purchase some additional baking equipment and to finance the equipment through a long-term note from a commercial bank. Woodslee Bank & Trust has asked Trottier to submit an income statement for MLT Inc. for the first five months of 2011 and a balance sheet as at May 31, 2011.

Trottier assembled the following information from the corporation's cash basis records to use in preparing the financial statements that the bank wants to see:

1. The bank statement showed the following 2011 deposits through May 31:

Sale of common shares	$ 2,500
Cash sales	22,770
Rebates from purchases	130
Collections on credit sales	5,320
Bank loan proceeds	2,880
	$33,600

2. The following amounts were disbursed through May 31, 2011:

Baking materials	$14,400
Rent	1,800
Salaries and wages	5,500
Maintenance	110
Utilities	4,000
Insurance premium	1,920
Equipment	3,600
Principal and interest payment on bank loan	298
Advertising	424
	$32,052

3. Unpaid invoices at May 31, 2011, were as follows:

Baking materials	$256
Utilities	270
	$526

4. Customer records showed uncollected sales of $4,336 at May 31, 2011.

5. Baking materials costing $2,075 were on hand at May 31, 2011. There were no materials in process or finished goods on hand at that date. No materials were on hand or in process and no finished goods were on hand at January 1, 2011.

6. The note for the three-year bank loan is dated January 1, 2011, and states a simple interest rate of 8%. The loan requires quarterly payments on April 1, July 1, October 1, and January 1. Each payment is to consist of equal principal payments plus accrued interest since the last payment.

7. Lydia Trottier receives a salary of $750 on the last day of each month. The other employees have been paid through May 25, 2011, and are due an additional $270 on May 31, 2011.

8. New display cases and equipment costing $3,600 were purchased on January 2, 2011, and have an estimated useful life of five years. These are the only fixed assets that are currently used in the business. Straight-line depreciation is used for book purposes.

9. Rent was paid for six months in advance on January 2, 2011.

10. A one-year insurance policy was purchased on January 2, 2011.

11. MLT Inc. is subject to an income tax rate of 20%.

12. Payments and collections from the unincorporated business through December 31, 2010, were not included in the corporation's records, and no cash was transferred from the unincorporated business to the corporation.

Instructions

(a) Using the accrual basis of accounting, prepare an income statement for the five months ended May 31, 2011.

(b) Using the accrual basis, prepare a balance sheet as at May 31, 2011.

(CMA adapted)

P5-8 Aero Inc. had the following balance sheet at the end of operations for 2010:

AERO INC.
Balance Sheet
December 31, 2010

Cash	$ 20,000	Accounts payable	$ 30,000
Accounts receivable	21,200	Bonds payable	41,000
Investments—fair value through net income	32,000	Common shares	100,000
Plant assets (net)	81,000	Retained earnings	23,200
Land	40,000		
	$194,200		$194,200

During 2011, the following occurred:

1. Aero liquidated its investment portfolio at a loss of $5,000.

2. A parcel of land was purchased for $38,000.

3. An additional $30,000 worth of common shares was issued.

4. Dividends totalling $10,000 were declared and paid to shareholders.

5. Net income for 2011 was $35,000, including $12,000 in depreciation expense.

6. Land was purchased through the issuance of $30,000 in additional bonds.

7. At December 31, 2011, Cash was $70,200; Accounts Receivable was $42,000; and Accounts Payable was $40,000.

8. The fair value of the investments is equal to their cost.

Instructions

(a) Prepare the balance sheet as it would appear at December 31, 2011.

(b) Prepare a statement of cash flows for the year ended December 31, 2011. Assume dividends paid are treated as financing activities.

*(c) Calculate the current and acid-test ratios for 2010 and 2011.

*(d) Calculate Aero's free cash flow and the current cash debt coverage ratio for 2011.

(e) What is the cash flow pattern? Discuss where the cash comes from and where it goes.

(f) Use the analysis of Aero to illustrate how information in the balance sheet and statement of cash flows helps the user of the financial statements.

P5-9   In an examination of Wirjanto Corporation as at December 31, 2011, you have learned about the following situations. No entries have been made in the accounting records for these items.

1. The corporation erected its present factory building in 1995. Depreciation was calculated using the straight-line method, based on an estimated life of 35 years. Early in 2011, the board of directors conducted a careful survey and estimated that the factory building had a remaining useful life of 25 years as at January 1, 2011.

2. An additional assessment of 2010 income taxes was levied and paid in 2011.

3. When calculating the accrual for officers' salaries at December 31, 2011, it was discovered that the accrual for officers' salaries for December 31, 2010, had been overstated.

4. On December 15, 2011, Wirjanto Corporation declared a common shares dividend of $1 per share on its issued common shares outstanding, payable February 1, 2012, to the common shareholders of record on December 31, 2011.

5. Wirjanto Corporation, which is on a calendar-year basis, changed its inventory cost flow formula as at January 1, 2011. The inventory for December 31, 2010, was costed by the weighted average method, and the inventory for December 31, 2011, was costed by the FIFO method.

6. On January 15, 2012, Wirjanto's warehouse containing raw materials was damaged by a flash flood.

7. During December 2011, the former president retired and a new president was appointed.

Instructions

Describe fully how each item above should be reported in the financial statements of Wirjanto Corporation for the year 2011.

P5-10   The balance sheet of Rodges Corporation follows (in thousands):

RODGES CORPORATION
Balance Sheet
December 31, 2011

Assets

Current assets

Cash	$26,000	
Temporary trading securities—fair value through net income	18,000	
Accounts receivable	25,000	
Merchandise inventory	20,000	
Supplies inventory	4,000	
Investment in subsidiary company	20,000	$113,000
Investments		
Marketable securities – common shares		25,000
Property, plant, and equipment		
Buildings and land	91,000	
Less: Reserve for depreciation	31,000	60,000
Other assets		
Investment in bonds to be held to maturity—cost		19,000
		$217,000

Liabilities and Equity

Current liabilities

Accounts payable	$22,000	
Reserve for income taxes	15,000	
Customer accounts with credit balances	1	$ 37,001

Deferred credits

Unamortized premium on bonds payable	2,000

Long-term liabilities

Bonds payable	60,000
Total liabilities	99,001

Shareholders' equity

Common shares issued	85,000	
Earned surplus	24,999	
Cash dividends declared	8,000	117,999
		$217,000

Instructions

Evaluate the balance sheet. Briefly describe the proper treatment of any item that you find incorrect. Assume the company follows IFRS.

Writing Assignments

WA5-1   The partner in charge of the Spencer Corporation audit comes by your desk and leaves a letter he has started to the CEO and a copy of the statement of cash flows for the year ended December 31, 2010. Because he must leave on an emergency, he asks you to finish the letter by explaining (1) the difference between the net income and cash flow amounts, (2) the importance of operating cash flow, (3) the sustainable source(s) of cash flow, and (4) possible suggestions to improve the cash position.

SPENCER CORPORATION
Statement of Cash Flows
For the Year Ended December 31, 2010

Cash flows from operating activities		
Net income		$ 100,000
Adjustments to reconcile net income to net cash provided by operating activities:		
Amortization expense	$ 11,000	
Loss on sale of fixed assets	5,000	
Increase in accounts receivable (net)	(40,000)	
Increase in inventory	(35,000)	
Decrease in accounts payable	(41,000)	(100,000)
Net cash provided by operating activities		–0–
Cash flows from investing activities		
Sale of plant assets	25,000	
Purchase of equipment	(100,000)	
Purchase of land	(200,000)	
Net cash used by investing activities		(275,000)
Cash flows from financing activities		
Payment of dividends	(10,000)	
Redemption of bonds	(100,000)	
Net cash used by financing activities		(110,000)
Net decrease in cash		(385,000)
Cash balance, January 1, 2010		400,000
Cash balance, December 31, 2010		$ 15,000

Date
James Spencer III, CEO
James Spencer Corporation
125 Bay Street
Toronto, ON

Dear Mr. Spencer:

I have good news and bad news about the financial statements for the year ended December 31, 2010. The good news is that net income of $100,000 is close to what we predicted in the strategic plan last year, indicating strong performance this year. The bad news is that the cash balance is seriously low. Enclosed is the Statement of Cash Flows, which best illustrates how both of these situations occurred at the same time...

Instructions

Complete the letter to the CEO, including the four elements that the partner asked for.

WA5-2 Andrea Pafko, corporate comptroller for Khouri Industries, is trying to decide how to present property, plant, and equipment in the balance sheet. She realizes that the statement of cash flows will show that the company made a significant investment in purchasing new equipment this year, but overall she knows the company's plant assets are rather old. She feels that she can disclose one amount for the title "Property, plant, and equipment, net of amortization," and the result will be a low figure. However, it will not disclose the assets' age. If she chooses to show the cost less accumulated amortization, the assets' age will be visible. She proposes the following:

Property, plant, and equipment, net of amortization	$ 10,000,000

rather than

Property, plant, and equipment	$ 50,000,000
Less: Accumulated amortization	(40,000,000)
Net book value	$ 10,000,000

Instructions

Discuss the financial reporting issues, including any ethical issues.

WA5-3 Brookfield Properties Corporation reported net income of $164 million for the year ended December 31, 2008, which is up 192% from the prior year. The company owns, develops, and manages North American office properties and its shares trade on both the New York and Toronto stock exchanges. The company takes pride in its strong financial position and in providing a foundation for growth.

The company's balance sheet follows:

Real-World Emphasis

Consolidated Balance Sheets

December 31 (US Millions)	Note	**2008**	2007
Assets			
Commercial properties	4	**$14,901**	$15,889
Commercial developments	5	**1,225**	1,172
Residential developments	6	**1,196**	1,228
Receivables and other	7	**935**	1,056
Intangible assets	8	**637**	759
Restricted cash and deposits	9	**116**	151
Cash and cash equivalents	27	**157**	214
Assets related to discontinued operations	10	**290**	4
		$19,457	$20,473

December 31 (US Millions)	Note	2008	2007
Liabilities			
Commercial property debt	11	**$11,505**	$12,125
Accounts payable and other liabilities	12	**1,168**	1,357
Intangible liabilities	13	**707**	834
Future income tax liabilities	14	**247**	600
Liabilities related to discontinued operations	10	**217**	3
Capital securities – corporate	15	**882**	1,053
Capital securities – fund subsidiaries	16	**711**	739
Non-controlling interests – fund subsidiaries	16	**212**	216
Non-controlling interests – other subsidiaries	18	**68**	86
Preferred equity – subsidiaries	19	**313**	382
Shareholders' equity			
Preferred equity – corporate	20	**45**	45
Common equity	21	**3,382**	3,033
		$19,457	$20,473

See accompanying notes to the consolidated financial statements

Instructions

Play the role of a financial analyst and critically evaluate the balance sheet presentation. Discuss alternative presentations and recommend the presentation format that would provide the best transparency for the company's business and the message that it wants to communicate.

WA5-4 In determining if a contingent liability should be recognized or not on the balance sheet at the report date, management must decide if there is an unconditional obligation or a conditional obligation or both. Only the unconditional obligation (stand ready obligation) would be recorded.

Instructions

For each of the following cases, determine if there is an unconditional obligation and/or a conditional obligation, giving support for your answer.

(a) Food for Thought is a restaurant that held a Christmas party in early December for a customer. During the party, 30 people became violently ill, possibly from food poisoning, and had to be hospitalized. Two months later, there are still lingering effects from this illness. The restaurant is now being sued for damages. However, Food for Thought disputes the charges and does not believe that the food it served is to blame. The year-end report is just being finalized for December 31. The entity's lawyers believe that it is unlikely that the restaurant will be found liable.

(b) Encor Oil is an oil company, operating in Country A and Country B, that has caused contamination at all of its oil production sites. Encor only cleans up when it is required to do so by the country's laws. In Country A, the laws have just been amended, on December 31, 2010, to require companies to clean up any environmental contamination that they have caused in the past and, of course, any new contamination done going forward. In Country B, although new legislation is being considered with respect to environmental cleanup, nothing yet has been legislated.

(c) A manufacturer provides a three-year warranty to repair or replace any defective products that have been sold. It also, in the past, has replaced parts for some key customers where the defect was found four years after the date of sale. The company decided to replace these goods in order to maintain good relations with these customers.

WA5-5 Write a brief essay highlighting the differences between IFRS and accounting standards for private enterprises noted in this chapter discussing the conceptual justification for each.

Cases

Refer to the Case Primer to help you answer these cases.

Case Primer

CA5-1   In the late 1990s, **CIBC** helped Enron structure 34 "loans" that appeared in the financial statements as cash proceeds from sales of assets. Enron subsequently went bankrupt in 2001 and left many unhappy investors and creditors with billions of dollars lost. In December 2003, CIBC settled four regulatory investigations with the SEC, U.S. Federal Reserve, U.S. Justice Department, and Canadian Office of the Superintendent of Financial Institutions. The settlement, which amounted to U.S. $80 million, was then one of the largest regulatory penalties against a Canadian bank. The regulatory authorities felt that CIBC had aided Enron in boosting its earnings and hiding debt. CIBC set aside a $109-million reserve in early 2003 in preparation for this settlement. No additional reserves were set aside.

Real-World Emphasis

As part of the settlement, CIBC agreed to get rid of its structured financing line of business (where all of these "loans" were created). Bank management noted that the decision to get rid of the structured financing business would reduce annual earnings by 10 cents a share. The bank had previously reported annual earnings of $5.21 per share. In addition, the bank had to accept the appointment of an outside monitor whose role, among other things, would be to review the bank's compliance with the settlement. Strategically, the bank had already reduced its emphasis on corporate lending (having suffered heavy losses in 2002) in favour of an increased focus on earnings from branch banking operations.

At the end of 2003, CIBC was still owed $213 million by Enron. There were many additional Enron-related lawsuits pending against the bank, but the bank announced that the lawsuits were without merit. The bank had insurance against many of these claims and noted that it planned to vigorously defend itself.

In 2005, the bank settled a lawsuit with institutional investors, paying $2.4 billion, again setting a standard for the size of the settlement. Then in 2009, Canada Revenue Agency (CRA) challenged the bank regarding the tax deductibility of the payment. If CRA is successful in arguing that the payment is non-deductible, CIBC will have to pay just under $1 billion in taxes.

Ethics

Instructions

Discuss any financial reporting issues relating to the 2003 and 2009 financial statements. Use the conceptual framework noted in Chapter 2 for the analysis.

CA5-2   Hastings Inc. (HI) is a manufacturing company that produces stainless steel car parts. It began as a family business several years ago and all shares are owned by the Hastings family. The company's main assets are its manufacturing facility and surrounding land. The property was purchased many years ago and the carrying value reflects only a fraction of the asset's cost.

The company is aware of the need to change over to private entity GAAP for years beginning on January 1, 2011. It is also aware that it may adopt IFRS as an accounting policy choice. Several of the Hasting family members would like to take the company public in the next five to 10 years.

Because of the recent dip in the economy, the company has suffered losses over the past three years. However, as the economy has recently begun picking up, management is confident that this year will be a profitable one.

Instructions

Adopt the role of the company's auditors and discuss any financial reporting issues. Use the conceptual framework noted in Chapter 2 for the analysis.

Integrated Case

(Hint: If there are issues here that are new, use the conceptual framework to help you support your analysis with solid reasoning.)

IC5-1   Franklin Drug Ltd. (FDL) is a global public company that researches, develops, markets, and sells prescription drugs. Revenues and net income are down this year, partly because one of the company's competitors, Barker Drug Inc. (BDI), has created and is selling generic versions of two of FDL's best-selling drugs. The drugs, known as FD1 and FD2, are still protected by patents that will not expire for another three years. Normally, when a drug is patented, other drug companies are not legally allowed to sell generic versions of the drug. This practice of patenting new drugs allows the companies that develop the drugs enough time to recover their large investment in research and development of the drugs.

In recent years, however, generic drug companies have become more aggressive in producing and selling generic copies of drugs before patents expire. FDL refers to this practice as "launching the generic products at risk" because, legally, the competitors are not allowed to sell them while the patent is still in force. Currently, FDL has about $2 million in development costs capitalized on the balance sheet. It has launched a lawsuit against BDI ordering it to cease and desist selling the generic drugs. These types of lawsuits are usually long and very expensive. By the time the lawsuit is settled one way or the other, the patents will have expired. So far, legal costs incurred for the lawsuit are $300,000.

During the year, the patent on a third drug, FD3, expired and several competitor drug companies began actively marketing generic replacements. FDL still has $500,000 worth of development costs on the balance sheet. Although the increased competition may result in this asset being impaired, FDL feels that it can hold its market share based on FD3's past success in treating patients. So far, sales of FD3 have declined only 3%. On the other hand, the company's share price has declined significantly because of the uncertainty surrounding future sales. Company management is not happy with the drop in share price, because a significant portion of their remuneration is based on stock options.

The company gives volume rebates to some of its larger customers. Under the terms of the sales agreements, the more purchases that a customer makes in a certain time frame, the larger the rebate percentage is on these purchases. The length of the time frame varies. Three large contracts are currently outstanding at year end with new customers. The time frames on these contracts extend beyond year end. FDL must estimate the volume rebates by considering what the total sales will be under these contracts. The company has a history of basing this estimate on past experience.

It is now early January and the auditors are coming in for an audit planning meeting.

Instructions

In preparation for the meeting, you, as audit senior on the job, have done some preliminary research on the company. Write a memo that outlines the potential financial reporting issues.

Research and Financial Analysis

RA5-1 Eastern Platinum Limited

Real-World Emphasis

The financial statements for the three-month period ended March 31, 2009, of **Eastern Platinum Limited** appear in Appendix 5B.

Instructions

(a) What alternative formats could the company have used for its balance sheet? Which format did it adopt?

(b) Identify the various techniques of disclosure that the company could have used to disclose additional financial information that is pertinent. Which techniques does it use in its financials?

(c) Which presentation method does the company use for its statement of cash flows (direct or indirect method)? What were the company's cash flows from its operating, investing, and financing activities for the three months ended March 31, 2009? What were its trends in net cash provided by operating activities for the periods ended March 31, 2008 and 2009? Is the cash generated from operating activities significantly different from net earnings in both periods? Suggest why this might happen.

(d) Calculate the company's (1) current cash debt coverage ratio, (2) cash debt coverage ratio, and (3) free cash flow for the year ended December 31, 2008, IFRS reported numbers and January 1, 2008, IFRS reported numbers (see Note 15). What do these ratios indicate about the company's financial condition?

RA5-2 Bombardier Inc.

Real-World Emphasis

The financial statements for **Bombardier Inc.** for the year ended January 31, 2009, can be found on the company's website or at www.sedar.com.

Instructions

(a) What form of presentation has the company used in preparing its balance sheet?

(b) Calculate the ratios identified in Appendix 5A for both years that are presented in the financial statements. Make note of any ratios that cannot be calculated and why.

(c) Comment on the company's liquidity, solvency, and profitability.

(d) Review the cash flow patterns on the statements of cash flows and comment on where the company is getting its cash from and where it is spending it.

(e) Perform a "vertical analysis" of the assets. (Calculate each asset as a percentage of total assets.) How has this result changed from year to year?

RA5-3 Maple Leaf Foods Inc.

The financial statements for **Maple Leaf Foods Inc.** may be found on the company's website or at www.sedar.com.

Real-World Emphasis

Instructions

(a) Calculate the liquidity and coverage (solvency) ratios identified in Appendix 5A for both years that are presented in the financial statements.

(b) Comment on the company's financial flexibility.

(c) Review the cash flow patterns on the statements of cash flows and comment on where the company is getting its cash from and where it is spending it. (Hint: Identify the cash flow pattern and explain what information the pattern provides.)

(d) Perform a "horizontal analysis" for working capital. How has this result changed from year to year and what are the implications for the company's financial health?

RA5-4 Goldcorp Inc.

Obtain the 2001 and 2008 annual reports for **Goldcorp. Inc.** (from SEDAR www.sedar.com). Read the material leading up to the financial statements and answer the following questions:

Real-World Emphasis

(a) Explain how the company's business changed from 2000 to 2001. What significant events occurred?

(b) What was the impact on key ratios of the event(s) identified in part (a)? Include in these ratios the cash cost to produce an ounce of gold and the average selling price of gold. (This information can be found in the Management Discussion and Analysis part of the annual report.)

(c) Examine and calculate the same key ratios for 2008. Do you notice any differences? Why might this be?

RA5-5 Quebecor Inc. and Thomson Reuters Corporation

The financial statements for **Quebecor Inc.** and **Thomson Reuters Corporation** may be found on SEDAR (www.sedar.com) or the companies' websites.

Real-World Emphasis

Instructions

(a) What business is Quebecor Inc. in? Is Thomson Reuters Corporation a good benchmark for comparing against? Explain.

(b) Identify three other companies that might be used for comparisons.

(c) Calculate industry averages for these five companies for the current and debt to total assets ratios.

(d) Based on this very brief analysis, is Quebecor or Thomson Reuters in better shape in terms of liquidity and solvency? How do these companies compare with the other three companies?

(e) Review the statements of cash flows for Quebecor and Thomson Reuters for the last two years. Describe the cash flow patterns for each company.

(f) Comment on these cash flow patterns, noting changes over the past two to three years.

RA5-6 IASB's Discussion Paper: Preliminary Views on Financial Statement Presentation

From the International Accounting Standards Board website (www.iasb.co.uk), access the Discussion Paper: Preliminary Views on Financial Statement Presentation dated October 2008 (or if out in Exposure Draft, the most updated version).

Instructions

(a) What is the proposed new format for the Statement of Financial Position? Explain the different classification and categories that will be used. Identify the types of assets and liabilities to be included in each section.

(b) Why has the IASB determined that a new format is required for the presentation of a company's financial position?

(c) Discuss the advantages and disadvantages of this new presentation.

Cumulative Coverage: Chapters 3 to 5

Musical Notes Incorporated is a company involved in two different aspects of the music business. It has a chain of three stores in southwestern Ontario that sell and repair musical instruments, and another single store that sells CDs, DVDs, and other consumer entertainment products. All four stores are in leased space, and the main office is located in the largest of the three stores selling musical instruments. The company has been in business for many years, and you have just been hired as the new controller. The previous controller had been in the job since the company first opened, and had been ill for a few years, and away from the office for the past six months. As a result, the books need a thorough review in order to straighten out a few errors that have developed over the past fiscal year. The fiscal year ends January 31, 2010, and you will need to correct the errors and draft financial statements using private entity GAAP in preparation for the annual visit of the auditors. The following information has been gathered for you to work with.

The trial balance at January 31, 2010, before any adjustments are made is as follows:

Account Description	Debit	Credit
Cash	$ 53,265	
Accounts Receivable—Instruments	251,000	
Allowance for Doubtful Accounts		$ 7,200
Inventory—Instruments	8,000,000	
Inventory—CDs, DVDs, and other entertainment products	200,000	
Prepaid Insurance Expense	5,000	
Store Equipment—Instrument Division	500,000	
Accumulated Amortization—Store Equipment Instrument Division		350,000
Accounts Payable		100,000
Note Payable		100,000
Income Tax Payable		23,000
Customer Deposits—Instrument Repairs		60,000
Common Shares (10,000 shares issued and outstanding)		100
Retained Earnings		7,453,565
Sales—Instrument Division		2,500,000
Cost of Goods Sold—Instrument Division	1,200,000	
Operating Expenses—Instrument Division	150,000	
Bad Debt Expense—Instrument Division	5,000	
Insurance Expense—Instrument Division	6,600	
Sales—CD Division		250,000
Cost of Goods Sold—CD Division	350,000	
Operating Expenses—CD Division	100,000	
Income Tax Expense	23,000	

Your search through the company files has led you to the following information, which may require adjustments:

1. The CD division store is located in a shopping mall in an area of town where a number of factories have closed. The mall is virtually empty. This area of the business has been struggling for a few years due to the availability of downloadable music and movies off the Internet and recent changes to the local economy. This has resulted in a decision to close this store. It is unlikely that a buyer can be found, and the store will be closed on March 31, 2011. The only asset of this division is the inventory, and all attempts will be made to sell this by the closing date. It is expected that the company will recover the cost of the inventory as it is being carried at its current fair value. There are no liabilities related to this division.

2. The company's income tax rate is normally 20%. When the income tax was paid for 2009, the payment was debited to income tax expense.

3. The company paid a dividend of $25,000 to its shareholders in December 2009. This amount was incorrectly recorded as an operating expense of the instrument division.

4. Accounts payable at year end, which had not been recorded, were a total of $20,000 of operating expenses for the instrument division. Last year's accounts payable had been paid and were all related to operating expenses: $65,000 for the instrument division and the remaining $35,000 for the CD division. When paid, operating expense accounts had been debited.

5. During the year, one accounts receivable invoice in the amount of $5,000 for a violin had become uncollectible and was written off to bad debt expense. The company follows a policy of recording 1% of its year-end accounts receivable as an allowance for doubtful accounts. The CD division has cash sales, whereas the sales of the instrument division are 100% on credit.

6. The store equipment is being amortized using the straight-line method over 10 years, assuming no residual value. Depreciation has not been recorded for the current year.

7. Insurance is paid each November 30, and covers a 12-month period. When the invoice was paid on November 30, 2009, it was debited to insurance expense. The 2008 invoice was for $6,000.

8. Inventory listings have been provided by the store staff that indicate the inventory has been properly accounted for at year end.

9. The instrument repair department forgot to credit a customer who had paid a deposit of $500 on a repair to a bassoon. The customer invoice for $750 is included in accounts receivable.

10. The note payable is due in two equal instalments of $50,000 each, plus interest, on January 30, 2011, and 2012. The annual interest rate is 5%, and the note has been outstanding since August 1, 2009.

Instructions

Prepare the journal entries required to correct the accounts at year end. Post these journal entries to the trial balance using a 10-column worksheet, and complete the other columns of the worksheet in good form. Prepare the January 31, 2010 balance sheet and combined income statement and statement of retained earnings for Musical Notes Incorporated for the year ended January 31, 2010.

Recognizing Revenue from Reforestation

PACIFIC REGENERATION TECHNOLOGIES INC. (PRT) is the largest producer of container-grown forest seedlings in North America, with a network of nurseries across Canada and the United States and the capacity to grow more than 180 million forest seedlings a year for reforestation and other purposes. The company was founded in 1988 following the British Columbia government's privatization of several provincial forestry operations. It went public as the PRT Forest Regeneration Income Fund in July 1997.

PRT enters into service contracts with its customers, mainly forestry and logging companies, both large and small, and provincial forestry ministries. "The companies provide us with seed and we grow the seedlings for them and provide other services such as storage over the winter and shipping to the bush," says PRT's Controller Jennifer Pace. Since the company grows the seedlings as a service, most of the inventory actually belongs to customers, although it does carry a small inventory of biological assets, which it values at cost.

While the company recognizes revenue for storage and shipping when it is earned, PRT uses the percentage-of-completion method to recognize both costs and revenue for growing the seedlings. There are three big triggers in the growing process, explains Ms. Pace. First is sowing, when PRT plants the seeds in peat-filled Styrofoam blocks; second is thinning, when the growing blocks are thinned to contain only one tree per cavity; and third is lifting (or harvesting), when the trees are taken out of the blocks and prepared to ship to the customers. "Those events are considered significant and there's a percentage of the cost assigned to them," says Ms. Pace.

To determine these percentages, the company examined each of these activities as part of the total of the direct costs of running a nursery. The percentage assigned to each phase is re-evaluated every second year or if there are any significant changes that could affect costs, such as an increase in the price of the peat in which the seeds are grown.

If the trees have grown over the year, then 100% of their revenue would be recognized in that year; however, often the growth of the trees spans more than a single fiscal year. "We need to determine what percentages are not associated with that year and remove that portion of revenue," explains Ms. Pace. PRT first determines the portion of revenue for the individual tree, then takes the percentage assigned to the phase not yet complete—normally the lifting portion—off the total revenue for the current year. ■

Chapter 6

Revenue Recognition

Learning Objectives

After studying this chapter, you should be able to:

1. Understand the economics and legalities of selling transactions from a business perspective.

2. Understand the conceptual difference between an earnings approach and a contract-based approach for accounting purposes.

3. Identify and apply revenue recognition principles under the earnings approach.

4. Identify and apply revenue recognition principles under the contract-based approach.

5. Discuss issues relating to measurement and measurement uncertainty.

6. Understand how to account for sales where there is collection uncertainty.

7. Prepare journal entries for consignment sales under the earnings and contract-based approaches.

8. Apply the percentage-of-completion method under the earnings and contract-based approaches.

9. Apply the completed-contract method under the earnings and contract-based approaches.

10. Understand how to present sales transactions in the income statement.

11. Identify differences in accounting between accounting standards for private enterprises (private entity GAAP) and IFRS.

12. Understand the impact of accounting choices on key numbers/ratios.

13. Discuss current trends in standard setting for revenue recognition.

Preview of Chapter 6

When should revenue be recognized? As mentioned in the opening vignette on Pacific Regeneration Technologies Inc., it often depends on the nature of the business arrangement and whether the entity is providing a service or selling products. Revenue recognition is a complex issue, but the answer can be found by analyzing the earnings process. This chapter presents the general principles that are used in recognizing revenues for most business transactions.

The chapter is organized as follows:

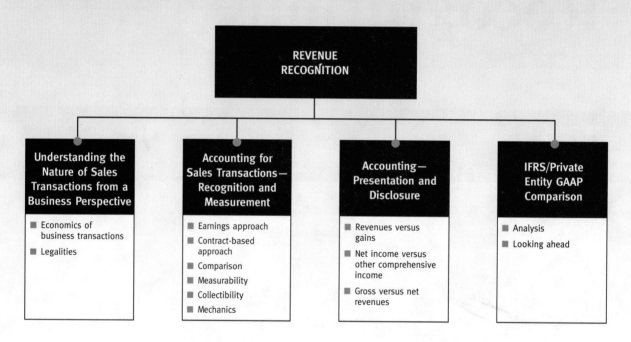

UNDERSTANDING THE NATURE OF SALES TRANSACTIONS FROM A BUSINESS PERSPECTIVE

Objective 1

Understand the economics and legalities of selling transactions from a business perspective.

Much of the complexity of accounting for revenues is rooted in the way sales transactions are structured. It is critical to understand from a *business perspective* what is being given up in the transaction and what is being received. Business people are not necessarily accountants, yet they understand how to price their products/services in order to make a profit and what they need to do to make a sale. In most selling transactions, an entity gives up one asset (for instance, inventory) in exchange for another (for instance, cash). The process of capturing this information for financial reporting purposes involves deciding when to recognize the transaction (on both the balance sheet and income statement) and how to measure and present it. Accountants must therefore understand the business an entity is engaged in, in order to account for transactions properly.[1]

---

[1] Recall that a view of the business model was presented in Chapters 4 and 5.

Let's go a little deeper and examine the economics and the legalities of a sales transaction.

Economics of Business Transactions

Certain economic attributes underlie most business transactions. We will discuss some of these below:

Basics—Are we selling goods, services or both? What is the physical nature of the transaction?

Selling transactions involve an entity transferring goods or services to its customers. The goods or services are often referred to as deliverables. It is important to focus on whether goods **or** services (or both) are being transferred.

Why does this matter for accounting purposes?   Sales of *goods* *and of services* are different.

   Goods are tangible assets. As a result, there is a definite point in time when control over the goods or the item being sold passes to the buyer. This normally coincides with the transfer of **possession**, as well as **legal title**.

   This is not the case with *services*, where the concepts of possession and legal title are irrelevant. Many contracts involve both goods and services (referred to as **multiple deliverable** or **bundled sales**), and this complicates the accounting when the goods and services are sold together as a bundle for one price. This is because possession and legal title to goods might pass before, after, or during the time when the services are rendered. Example 1 looks at a bundled sale.

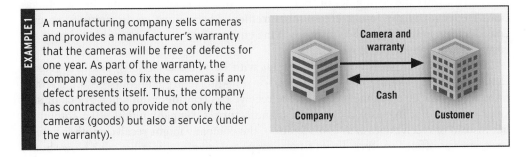

EXAMPLE 1

A manufacturing company sells cameras and provides a manufacturer's warranty that the cameras will be free of defects for one year. As part of the warranty, the company agrees to fix the cameras if any defect presents itself. Thus, the company has contracted to provide not only the cameras (goods) but also a service (under the warranty).

Camera and warranty →
← Cash

Company   Customer

   Understanding what the company is selling will help to determine when to recognize revenues. Care should be taken to identify the terms of the transaction, whether it be documented in one or more agreements or not at all. When products and services are sold and priced together as one package, as in example 1, this creates complexities in terms of determining how much revenue to recognize and when. How much should be attributed to the sale of the camera and how much to the warranty service? Obligations to deliver something in the future contribute to increased measurement uncertainty because we do not always know what will happen in the future.

Reciprocal nature—What is being received?

Most business transactions are **reciprocal**; that is, the entity gives something up and receives something in return. Once we have figured out what we are giving up, we should determine what we are getting back as consideration. Is the consideration cash or cash-like or is it another good or service?

Why does the reciprocal nature of transactions matter for accounting purposes?
If we assume that the transactions are at arm's length, i.e., they are between unrelated parties, then we may assume that the value of what is given up usually approximates the value of what is received in the transaction. Unless otherwise noted, we will generally assume that transactions are at arm's length and reciprocal. Example 2 illustrates this.

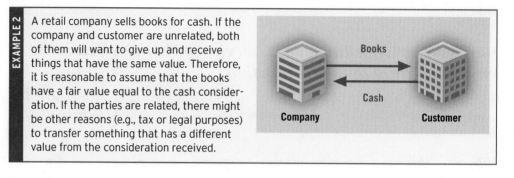

EXAMPLE 2

A retail company sells books for cash. If the company and customer are unrelated, both of them will want to give up and receive things that have the same value. Therefore, it is reasonable to assume that the books have a fair value equal to the cash consideration. If the parties are related, there might be other reasons (e.g., tax or legal purposes) to transfer something that has a different value from the consideration received.

Sales agreements normally specify what is being given up and what is being acquired as follows:

- Acquired—Consideration or rights to the consideration. The amount, nature, and timing are normally agreed upon.

- Given up—Goods/services (now or in the future). Details regarding delivery (quantities, nature of goods/services, timing, shipping terms) are agreed upon.

Recognizing and focusing on the reciprocal and arm's-length nature of transactions, as well as the detailed agreement between the customer and vendor, allows us to better capture and measure the economics of transactions in the financial statements. Just as obligations to deliver in the future create measurement uncertainty, so do rights to receive consideration in the future. For instance, if the entity sells on credit, there is a risk that the customer will not pay (credit risk).

Consideration that is non-monetary[2] (as with **barter** transactions) presents greater challenges for accounting purposes. Barter or non-monetary transactions are transactions where few or no monetary assets are received as consideration when goods or services are sold. For instance, a computer manufacturing company might sell a computer, but instead of receiving cash as consideration, the company might receive another type of asset, such as office furniture. From a business perspective, is this still a sale? How should it be measured?

Generally, a barter transaction is seen as a sale if the transaction has commercial substance. What does "commercial substance" mean? It means that the transaction is a bona fide purchase and sale and that the entity has entered into the transaction for business purposes, exchanging one type of asset or service for another different asset or service (dissimilar). After the transaction, the entity will be in a different position and its future cash flows are expected to change significantly as a result of the transaction (in terms of timing, amount, and/or riskiness).[3]

---

[2] Monetary consideration includes anything that is cash or measured in terms of cash such as a receivable. Non-monetary consideration includes other types of assets such as other inventory or fixed assets.

[3] When determining whether the cash flows have changed significantly, the "entity-specific" value is sometimes examined. The entity-specific value is the value of the assets to the company (versus the value on the open market). Because companies use assets differently, there may be synergies in one company that do not exist at another. Thus, the asset would be more valuable to the first company. The company's cash flows would be said to change significantly when the entity-specific value of the asset that is received differs from the value of the asset received (*CICA Handbook*, Part II, Section 3831.11). IAS 18.12 focuses more on whether the items sold are similar or dissimilar.

A resource company sells gold bars (which it has mined and refined) to its customers in exchange for copper. If the gold were sold for cash, it would be easy to measure. However, if it is sold in exchange for another product or service, such as copper in this case, the company must measure the value of the gold or the copper. If a market exists, then there will be evidence of the value. If no market exists (which is often the case when the consideration is a used or unique asset), then the transaction is more difficult to measure.

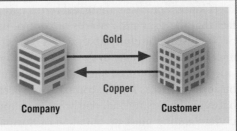

Company — Gold → Customer
Copper ←

When a reciprocal transaction occurs, the entity's risk profile changes. For instance, in example 3, before the sale, the company did not know how much it would eventually sell the gold for[4] or how much it would realize on the sale. The risk that the price of an asset will change is referred to as a **price risk**. Once the sale occurs, the company gets rid of the price risk of the gold. However, if it sells gold and receives copper as consideration, as in example 3, the company gets rid of the price risk on the gold but has taken on a price risk related to the copper.

> **Underlying Concept**
>
> The representational faithfulness concept supports full disclosure of risks and changes in risk, as they affect the entity's ability to generate future cash flows.

Concessionary terms—Are the terms of sale normal or is this a special deal?

In some cases, one party is in a better bargaining position than the other. This might occur, for instance, where supply exceeds demand. In this case, the buyer in the transaction may be able to negotiate a better deal than normal because there are so many sellers who want to sell their products and so few buyers.

Examples of concessionary terms are as follows:

> The entity agrees to a more lenient return or payment policy (including paying in instalments over an extended term or using consignment sales).
>
> The entity loosens its credit policy.
>
> The entity transfers legal title but allows the customer to take delivery at a later date (sometimes referred to as "bill and hold").
>
> The goods are shipped subject to customer acceptance conditions. Extended trial periods would be an example.
>
> The entity agrees to provide ongoing or additional services beyond the main goods/services agreed to in order to make the sale. This might include, for example, installation of an asset, ongoing servicing, or continuing fees, for instance in a franchise agreement.
>
> The seller continues to have some involvement, including a guarantee of resale (or permission to return) or guarantee of profit.

Why does this matter for accounting purposes?   Care must be taken to identify **concessionary (or abnormal) terms** in any deal as they may complicate the accounting. Concessionary terms are terms that are more lenient than usual and are meant to induce sales.

---

[4] Where the asset being sold is a commodity, prices fluctuate since they are based on supply and demand.

Concessionary or abnormal terms may create additional obligations or may reflect the fact that the risks and rewards or control has not yet passed to the customer. These situations must be carefully analyzed as they create additional recognition and measurement uncertainty. They may even indicate that no sale has taken place at all.

The question that should always be asked is whether the selling terms are normal business practices for the company or special or unusual in some way. There is a fine line between what is normal and what is abnormal. In order to do this analysis properly, an understanding must be obtained of normal business practices (this can be evidenced by looking at standard documentation of selling transactions such as contracts and/or history of past transactions).

Illustration 6-1 helps differentiate between normal selling terms and abnormal concessionary terms.

Illustration **6-1**

Normal versus Concessionary Terms

	Normal selling terms	Concessionary selling terms
Payment terms	Sell for cash or on credit. If credit, payment is usually expected within 30 to 60 days.	Any terms that are more lenient than this; e.g., • selling on credit where the buyer does not have to pay for 90 days or more, or • instalment sales where these are not normal industry practice.
Extension of credit	Sell to customers that are creditworthy.	Sales to customers that are riskier than the existing customer base.
Shipping terms including bill and hold	Ship when ordered and ready to ship.	Ship at a later date; e.g., the entity may hold the inventory in its warehouse for an extended period.
Additional services or continuing involvement in assets sold	Once shipped and legal title passes, no continuing involvement except for normal rights of return and/or standard warranties.	Extended right of return/warranty period, cash flow guarantee on future rental of building sold, profit guarantees on future resale or buyback provisions.

Example 4 illustrates a contract with concessionary terms.

EXAMPLE 4

A merchandising company sells inventory to a customer for cash. The merchandise is shipped to and stored in the warehouse of an unrelated warehousing company for a few days until after year end. Is this a sale at year end or not? It is not clear. Normally, delivery would accompany the sales order and payment. However, the merchandising company is agreeing to a non-standard selling term (i.e., to store the goods) in order to make the sale more attractive. This might mean revenue may not be recognized.

Promise to deliver and store goods

Cash

Company   Customer

Underlying Concept

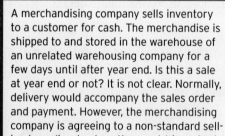

Any promise that is enforceable under law and any obligation that is imposed by law should be included in the statements under the full disclosure and transparency principles.

Legalities

Companies operate within environments governed by law—contract law, common law, securities law, etc. Laws exist to protect the rights of individuals and legal entities. It is important to understand the legal environment because rights and obligations often arise from the operation of the law.

Contract Law

Law

When an entity sells something, both the entity and the customer enter into a contract.

A contract with customers is an agreement that creates enforceable obligations and establishes the terms of the deal.[5] The contract may be written or verbal or may be evidenced by, for instance, a cash register receipt. The important thing is that two parties have promised to exchange assets and this creates a contract. There is a promissor (the seller), a promissee (the customer), and an agreement. Thus, the act of entering into a sales agreement creates legal rights and obligations.

In addition, the contract establishes the point in time when **legal title** passes (entitlement/ownership under law). When the customer takes physical **possession** of the goods straight away, legal title would normally pass at this point. If the goods are shipped, the point at which legal title passes is often evidenced by the shipping terms as follows:

FOB shipping point—means title passes at the point of shipment.

FOB destination—means title passes when the asset reaches the customer.

Why does this matter for accounting purposes? As noted above, if the entity has promised to provide goods and/or services now and/or in the future, the contract binds it and can be enforced. It creates contractual rights and obligations that may meet the definition of assets and liabilities. The contract also establishes the substantive terms of the deal, which need to be analyzed when determining if revenue has been earned. If, for instance, the contract stipulates that customers must sign invoices as evidence that they are satisfied with the goods, it may mean that no revenue may be recognized until this is done.

Other

Performance obligations may arise even if not stated in a contract. In many cases, an entity may have an implicit obligation even if it is not explicitly noted in a selling contract. This is referred to as a **constructive obligation.** A constructive obligation is an obligation that is created through past practice or by signalling something to potential customers. Constructive obligations are often enforceable under common or other law. Example 5 illustrates the concept of a constructive obligation.

EXAMPLE 5

A clothing company sells goods with a standard return policy. The policy states that the customer may return the goods within 30 days of purchase if defective. This policy is stated on the bill of sale and creates a contractual obligation. In practice, the company advertises that it stands behind its products 100%. Furthermore, it has a past history and a customary business practice

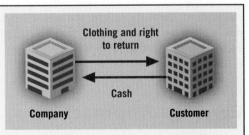

of accepting all returns for any reason and even after the 30-day period. The company probably has a constructive obligation regarding these returns; i.e., it effectively has an obligation (beyond the 30-day contractual obligation) to accept customer returns for any reason at any time because it has created an expectation.

---

[5] IASB, *Preliminary Views on Revenue Recognition in Contracts with Customers.* Discussion Paper, December 2008, par. S10.

Why does this matter for accounting purposes?   Any enforceable promise that results from the sale (whether implicit or explicit) may create a performance obligation that needs to be recognized in the balance sheet. This includes both contractual and other promises.[6]

ACCOUNTING FOR SALES TRANSACTIONS—RECOGNITION AND MEASUREMENT

Now that we understand selling transactions from a business perspective, let's look at how to account for sales transactions.

There are many definitions of revenues in the various accounting bodies of knowledge, including IFRS, private entity GAAP, and U.S. GAAP. Basically, the notion is the same under each revenue standard and that is that revenue is:

- an ***inflow of economic benefits*** (cash, receivables, or other consideration)

- arising from ***ordinary activities***.

Ordinary activities are the normal business activities of the entity. For instance, for **Magnotta Winery Corporation**, the ordinary activities are the production and sale of wine. Revenues are realized when goods and services are exchanged for cash. Realization is the process of converting noncash resources and rights into money. As noted earlier, this is referred to as the cash-to-cash cycle.

Objective 2
Understand the conceptual difference between an earnings approach and a contract-based approach for accounting purposes.

From an ***accounting perspective***, there are two conceptual views of how to account for revenues:

1. Earnings approach

2. Contract-based approach

The **earnings approach** focuses on the earnings process and how a company adds value for its customers. The **contract-based approach** focuses on the contractual rights and obligations created by sales contracts. In all cases, in order to properly account for the transaction, there should be persuasive evidence of the sales arrangement. This is important so that we know a transaction has occurred and what the terms are. Evidence might consist of a contract (written or verbal), an invoice, or other. Both of these views will be discussed below.

Earnings Approach

General Principle

Objective 3
Identify and apply revenue recognition principles under the earnings approach.

The earnings approach is the approach historically in place under Canadian GAAP and IFRS.[7] It is seen primarily as an **income statement approach to accounting for**

---

[6] Care must be taken to separate performance obligations from other obligations. For instance, if the law requires a company to pay damages to a customer if the product sold causes health problems (e.g., cigarettes), this would generally not be seen as a performance obligation (and therefore not recognized as part of the sale). It would instead be treated as a contingency.

[7] *CICA Handbook*, Part II, Section 3400.04 and IAS 11 and 18.

revenues, and so the focus is essentially on measuring revenues and costs and recognizing revenues when earned. Under this approach, revenues are recognized when:[8]

- **performance** is substantially complete, and

- **collection is reasonably assured**.[9]

Performance occurs when an entity can **measure** the revenue (and costs) and when it has substantially accomplished what it must do to be entitled to the benefits of the revenues—that is, the **earnings process must be complete or substantially complete**.[10] Both of these components are important. If the company cannot measure the transaction, then either there is too much uncertainty surrounding the transaction (for instance where there are abnormal concessionary terms), or the company has not completed all that it has to do to earn the revenues. The determination of whether the earnings process is complete or substantially complete depends on whether the entity has sold a product or provided a service (or both), so it is important to first determine what the revenue is received for.

In short, revenues are recognized when the following criteria are met:

1. **Performance is achieved,** which means
   (a) **the risks and rewards are transferred and/or the earnings process is substantially complete** (normally when a product is delivered or services are provided), and
   (b) **measurability** is reasonably assured (price is fixed/determinable).

2. **Collectibility** is reasonably assured.

Risks and rewards are discussed below and measurability and collectibility will be discussed later as they are common to both the earnings and contract-based approach.

> **Underlying Concept**
>
> The related costs must be measurable and recognized at the same time as revenues to help measure net income appropriately.

Risks and Rewards of Ownership and the Earnings Process. What does the company do to create valuable products or services that customers will pay for? How does it add value? Earnings process is a term that refers to the actions that a company takes to add value. It is an important part of the business model as it focuses on operating activities. The earnings process is unique to each company and each industry. Different industries add value in different ways. For example, companies that sell goods that they manufacture have vastly differing earnings processes than those that sell goods that they buy wholesale and sell retail. In addition, companies that are in the biotechnology business have models that are different from real estate companies. For this reason, it is important to begin with an understanding of the earnings process.

When an entity sells goods, there is often one main act or critical event in the earnings process that signals **substantial completion** or **performance**. At this point, although some uncertainty remains, its level is acceptable and revenues can be recognized under accrual accounting. In businesses that sell goods, substantial completion normally occurs at the point of delivery. This is generally when the risks and rewards of ownership (including legal title and possession) pass. If the earnings process has a critical event, it is often referred to as a discrete earnings process.

As an example, Magnotta Winery Corporation makes wine (among other products). Its business involves the steps shown in Illustration 6-2.

---

[8] Recognition is the process of including an item in the financial statements. Recognition is not the same as realization, although the two terms are sometimes used interchangeably in accounting literature and practice.

[9] *CICA Handbook*, Part II, Section 3400.04 and IAS 11 and 18.

[10] *CICA Handbook*, Part II, Section 3400.07 and IAS 11 and 18.

Illustration 6-2

*Magnotta Winery's
Earnings Process*

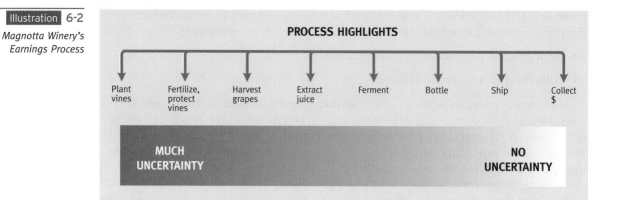

Magnotta must perform all of the acts in the illustration in order to make a profit from the sale of its wine. The entity starts with cash, invests it in inventory, sells the inventory at a price that is higher than its cost, and collects cash. At the early points of the earnings process, there is significant uncertainty about how much product will be produced and its quality. What if the vines get diseased? What if temperatures are too low or it rains too much? What if there is no market for the product? Moving along the earnings process timeline (from left to right), the conditions creating the uncertainty resolve themselves. At the far right-hand side of the earnings process, once the product is shipped and paid for, all uncertainty is eliminated about creation of the product itself, the measurability of both its costs and revenues, and the collectibility of those revenues.

The concept of risks and rewards (benefits) of ownership is a core concept in the earnings approach to revenue recognition. It helps to establish ownership and to indicate when ownership passes from one party to another.[11]

Illustration 6-3 presents some of the risks and rewards associated with the sale of wine at Magnotta.

Illustration 6-3

*Risks and Rewards of
Ownership—Case of Wine*

Risks	Rewards
— wine will age poorly and therefore decline in value — wine will be stolen/vandalized — wine will be stored improperly	— wine will age well and appreciate in value — wine can be consumed by owner or buyer — wine inventory may be used as collateral for bank loan — wine may be sold for cash

In determining who has the risks and rewards of ownership and, therefore, whether a sale has occurred at the point of delivery, it is important to look at who has possession of the goods and who has legal title. The risks and rewards usually stem from these two factors; for example, Magnotta is not entitled to sell inventory or pledge it as collateral (i.e., to reap the rewards) unless it has legal title to it, and legal title and possession expose Magnotta to risk of loss.

Because the principle is quite general, there are a wide range of practical applications. Different companies interpret these principles in different ways.[12]

---

[11] In order to recognize an asset on the balance sheet, a company must prove that it has substantially all of the risks and rewards of ownership. If these have been passed on to another party, a disposition has occurred.

[12] Because of this, and in part also because of the increased profile of revenue recognition issues with the securities commissions, companies are generally required to disclose the revenue recognition method in the notes to their financial statements. Out of a survey of 200 companies, 93% disclosed their revenue recognition policies in 2004 (*Financial Reporting in Canada*, 2005 [Toronto: CICA], Chapter 7).

What about recognizing income *before* possession and legal title to goods passes to a customer? Is there ever a situation whereby revenue might be recognized before this critical event?

In some cases, revenue may be recognized prior to the completion of production even though there is no specific customer for the asset at that point. Examples of such situations can be found in the forestry and agricultural industries when products have assured prices and ready markets. Revenue is recognized over time as the assets mature.[13]

Selling Services.   The focus is different when determining the earnings process for services. When services are provided, the focus is on **performance of the service**. The accounting is more complex where the earnings process has **numerous significant events** (**continuous earnings process**). Example 6 illustrates this.

EXAMPLE 6

An auditor accepts a contract to provide assurance to a company's shareholders about the accuracy and fairness of the company's financial position and operations. This is a service type sale and the earnings process is noted in Illustration 6-4. When does performance occur in the earnings process? Should the company wait until the audit report is signed (i.e., until the engagement is completed) before recognizing the revenue? There is no easy answer. If this is seen as a **continuous earnings process** with many significant events, including the planning and the interim work, it might make sense to recognize revenues bit by bit as each significant event is performed (as long as the revenue is collectible). Judgement is required.

An example of an earnings process for a service that is a discrete earnings process is a maintenance inspection on a car. The service is offered on the spot and is completed in a very short time. The critical event is when the mechanic hands over the inspected car and the bill.

Often a contract to set the terms of the relationship or engagement is signed up front. This contract establishes the nature of the services to be provided and their value, among other things. It also lays out the parties' rights and obligations. Illustration 6-4 depicts the earnings process for a public accounting firm.

Law

Illustration 6-4

Earnings Process of Public Accounting Firm in Providing Assurance to Client on Financial Statements

PROCESS HIGHLIGHTS

Obtain client → Plan audit → Perform interim work on controls → Attend inventory count → Perform year-end work → Sign audit report → Bill client → Collect $

---

[13] IAS 41 deals with biological assets and produce up to the point of harvest and requires that these assets be measured at fair value less estimated point of sale costs.

Long-term contracts such as construction-type contracts, including contracts for the development of military and commercial aircraft, weapons delivery systems, and space exploration hardware, frequently provide that the seller (builder) may invoice the purchaser at intervals, as various points in the project are reached. These invoices are referred to as billings. When the project has separable units, such as a group of buildings or kilometres of roadway, the passage of title and billing may occur at previously stated stages of completion, such as the completion of each building or every 10 kilometres of road. Such contract provisions provide for delivery in instalments (continuous transfer of assets).

Two methods of accounting for long-term construction and other service contracts are generally recognized:[14]

1. **Percentage-of-Completion Method.** Revenues and gross profit are recognized each period based on the construction progress—in other words, the percentage of completion. This makes the most sense in long-term service contracts when it is the service that is being provided to build something or work on something that is owned by the customer (numerous significant events).

2. **Completed-Contract Method.** Revenues and gross profit are recognized only when the contract is completed. This makes the most sense when the service consists of a single significant event or the item being built/constructed is owned by the company building/constructing it. In this latter case, it is more like building/constructing inventory and then selling it and recognizing revenues when it is complete. It may also make sense to use this method when there are measurement problems, as discussed below.

The method that **best matches the revenues to be recognized to the work performed** should be used.[15] In other words, if performance requires many ongoing acts (i.e., it is a **continuous earnings process**), the percentage-of-completion method should be used as long as the company is able to **measure** the transaction. Alternatively, the completed-contract method should be used when performance consists of a single act (i.e., it is a **discrete earnings process**) or as a default method when there is a **continuous earnings process but the progress toward completion is not measurable**. In reality, when contracts relate only to services (no assets are being constructed), the methods are not dissimilar. They both recognize revenues as the company earns them. Similarly, if there are measurement problems, and the transaction is not measurable, it makes sense not to recognize revenues until they are measurable; that is, at the end. IFRS allows recognition of recoverable revenues equal to costs incurred where the outcome is not reliably measurable.

Law Under many of these contracts, an asset is being built for a customer and the buyer and seller have obtained **enforceable rights**. The buyer has the legal right to require specific performance on the contract; the seller has the right to require progress payments that may provide evidence of the buyer's ownership interest. As a result, a continuous sale occurs as the work progresses, and revenue should be recognized accordingly. If legal title does not pass until the end of the contract, it may be more like construction of inventory, and the revenues would be recognized when the risks and rewards of the asset itself pass to the customer.

---

[14] *CICA Handbook*, Part II, Section 3400.06. IFRS currently does not mention the completed-contract method in IAS 11/18.

[15] *CICA Handbook*, Part II, Section 3400.06.

EXAMPLE 7

A construction company builds a road for the government. The road is expected to take three years to complete. Is the company selling a good (the road) or a service (construction services)? This is an excellent question. One might argue that this is very similar to producing inventory and that therefore it is a sale of goods. This might be the case if title to the road does not pass until completion. Others might argue that it is the service of constructing the road that is being provided. This might be the case if the customer is identified up front (as is the case in this example) and has legal title to the asset as it is being constructed.

Careful analysis of the economics (who has the risks and rewards and/or control over the asset?) and legalities (when does legal title pass?) of the transaction and the use of professional judgement would assist in determining this. The contract itself would articulate what is being given up and received and when legal title passes.

The presumption is that percentage-of-completion is the better method when recognizing service revenues and that the completed-contract method should be used only when the percentage-of-completion method is inappropriate.[16] The mechanics of these methods will be discussed later in the chapter.

Problems with the Earnings Approach

The following points reflect some of the problems with the earnings approach:

- Multiple and sometimes conflicting guidance (in the United States, over 100 standards exist with respect to revenue recognition).

- The earnings approach is difficult to apply, since there are different views on what the earnings process is and when revenues are earned. Both the OSC and SEC review financial statements regularly and find that there are problems with how revenues are accounted for. In addition, many large corporate frauds have involved revenue recognition.

- In many cases, the risks and rewards are split between the buyer and the seller. So it is difficult to determine definitively just who has the risks and rewards.

- It is felt that this approach requires too much subjective judgement.

- This approach does not deal with when receivables should be booked if the revenues are not yet earned.

Contract-Based Approach

General Principle

The contract-based approach reflects a more recent view of revenue recognition. The emphasis is on the balance sheet, although it is not exclusively a **balance sheet approach**. This approach focuses on measuring the rights and obligations under sales contracts and recognizes revenues when these rights and obligations change.

4 Objective
Identify and apply revenue recognition principles under the contract-based approach.

---

[16] *Accounting Trends and Techniques—2004* reports that, of the 119 of its 600 sample companies that referred to long-term construction contracts, 110 used the percentage-of-completion method and 9 used the completed-contract method.

The contract-based approach asks two questions:

1. When should the sales contract be recognized on the balance sheet?
2. When should the revenue be recognized on the income statement?

Law

Significant Change

The model focuses on the contractual and other rights and obligations created by the sales contract and analyzes the performance criteria for revenue recognition from the perspective of the customer considering whether the obligations under the contract have been fulfilled. Under this approach, the contract is recognized when:

1. **the entity becomes party to the contract,**
2. **the contractual rights are collectible/measurable,** and
3. **the performance obligation is measurable.**

Revenues are recognized when control passes/performance occurs.

When an entity becomes party to a contract, certain rights and obligations are created, including a right to receive cash now or in the future and an obligation to deliver goods or provide services now or in the future. The net amount of the contractual rights and obligations is known as the **net contract position**.

Because of reciprocity and assuming an arm's-length transaction, the initial value of the net contract position should normally be nil. As previously discussed, this generally means that the value of what is given up is equal to the value of what is received, and the value of the contractual obligation to perform is generally equal to the value of the contractual right to receive consideration. Example 8 looks at a contract to provide plumbing services.

Underlying Concept

Every time an entity enters into a contract, it alters the company. Transparency dictates that this be reflected in the statements. Even though initially the net position may be zero, this will generally change very quickly as the funds are collected or services provided.

EXAMPLE 8

A plumber agrees to provide plumbing services to a customer (a restaurant) for $500 cash payable within 30 days. Once the agreement is agreed upon by both parties, the plumber has a contractual right to receive $500 and a contractual performance obligation to provide the plumbing service.

> Plumbing service
> $500
> **Plumber**   **Restaurant**

In short, the plumber provides services and gets cash in return. The net position initially is $0 ($500 asset less $500 obligation). Once the services are performed, the obligation is extinguished, leaving the receivable of $500. Assuming that the related costs to provide the service are $250, the journal entries are as follows:

At inception of contract:

A   =   L   +   SE
0   0

Cash flows: No effect

Contractual rights/obligations	$500	
Contractual rights/obligations		$500

Should this be shown net ($0) or gross (rights and obligations shown separately as assets and liabilities) on the balance sheet? Initially, we might argue that it should be shown net, but once the service is performed, the contractual right to receive cash becomes an account receivable and should be shown in that way. The contractual right to receive cash is different from the account receivable because it is contingent upon performing the service. The receivable results from the service having been performed.

Note that until one party performs under the contract, the promise is a promise to do something in the future. If both parties agree, they could both back out of the contract and not do anything. Technically, no receivable exists until the service is performed—that is, the company is not owed anything until it performs the obligation and, unless the contract specifies otherwise, the customer does not have to pay until the service is received.

When service provided:

Contractual rights/obligations	$500	
Revenues		$500
Payroll expense	$250	
Cash		$250

A = L + SE
250   250

Cash flows: No effect

If services were provided over time, the revenue recognition would likewise be spread out over time, using the percentage-of-completion method or another allocation method that reflects the rate at which the obligation is being settled. The mechanics of accounting for long-term construction contracts under this method will be dealt with later in the chapter.

If the sale relates to goods (as opposed to services), performance occurs when the customer obtains control over the goods. This normally occurs when possession and legal title pass. This is a slightly different test than the risks and rewards test required under the earnings approach. Recall that, under the earnings approach, analysis of who has the risks and rewards requires significant judgement and may show that both seller and customer have some but not all of them.

Under the contract-based approach, the emphasis is on control as opposed to who has risks and rewards of ownership. Essentially, control passes when possession passes, but the concept of control is really rooted in a legalistic view and therefore also focuses on legal title. If you have legal title, you essentially control how an asset is used. Many feel that the "control" test will be less subjective and more conclusive than the "risks and rewards" test since only one party will have control whereas risks and rewards may be split between the parties.

To summarize, the net contract position is recognized when the entity becomes party to the contract and when the contractual rights and performance obligations are measurable (including credit risk). Revenues are recognized when control of the related assets passes (for assets sold) and when performance occurs for services.

Problems with the Contract-Based Approach

This model is consistent with the new conceptual framework being developed and therefore is conceptually sound. As it is a new model, it is in its infancy and needs to be tested. The approach does not deal with revenues that are not contract-based (i.e., recognizing revenue before the goods/services are sold to a customer). At the end of the chapter, there is a list of items that the IASB and FASB are still working on.

Comparison of the Two Approaches

Some examples and their treatments under both approaches are shown in Illustration 6-5.

	Earnings approach	Contract-based approach
Layaways	Generally do not recognize layaways as sales since legal title and possession remain with the vendor. There is some discussion on this one, however, as IFRS currently allows merchandise on layaway to be recognized as a sale if certain criteria are met (significant deposit received, past history of completion of such transactions, goods on hand and ready for delivery).	Analysis would be done to determine whether the deposit represents a contract between the vendor and seller. In essence, there is an agreement and some consideration has changed hands. Therefore, one might argue that these contractual rights and obligations should be reflected in the financial statements (valued at a net amount of $0). Since the vendor has title and possession, it would be difficult to argue that control has passed unless a significant deposit was made.
Bill and hold	Where this is not the normal business practice, ensure that these are bona fide sales transactions and not just aggressive sales that will not be consummated. Since legal title has passed, there may be an argument for recognizing sales even though possession remains with the vendor. Care would be taken to assess which party had significant risks and rewards of ownership. As long as there is a business reason for holding the goods (perhaps the customer has no space in its warehouse) and the goods are on hand ready for delivery, there may be a case to recognize the sale.	Since a contract has been entered into, the contract should be recognized (valued at a net amount of $0). Revenue would be recognized when control passes (normally when possession and legal title pass). Since the vendor still has possession, has control passed? In general, one might argue that legal title allows the customer to control the asset regardless of possession. The vendor cannot use that inventory for anything else. Therefore, one could argue that the sale should be recognized.
Warranties	Historically, warranties have been accrued as a cost if measurable (in order to match with sales revenues). This view has been changing and some entities now treat warranties as a service element of a bundled sale, i.e., the entity sells a product and a future service to maintain that product in good order (the service would be treated as unearned revenues until it is provided).	Warranties to fix assets in future represent a future performance obligation, and therefore a sale of goods with a warranty would be treated as a bundled sale. Part of the revenues would be deferred and recognized when the service is provided and the performance obligation extinguished.

Illustration 6-5

*Comparison of the
Two Approaches*

Measurability

General Principle

Objective 5

Discuss issues relating to measurement and measurement uncertainty.

Under either method, revenue should only be recognized if the transaction is measurable. Sales are generally measured at fair value, which is represented by the value of the consideration received or receivable. Where the sale is on credit and the repayment term extends over a longer period (and the receivable is non-interest-bearing or the interest rate is below market rate), the receivable should be discounted to reflect the time value of money.[17] For barter transactions, if the fair value of the consideration is not available, the fair value of the product/service sold is used as long as the sale has commercial substance and is reciprocal.[18]

Significant Change

[17] *CICA Handbook*, Part II, Section 3856.A8 and IAS 18.11. IFRS notes that the discount rate should be the more clearly determinable of (i) the prevailing rate for a similar note receivable and (ii) the imputed rate that discounts the cash flows to the current cash selling price of the item sold.

[18] *CICA Handbook*, Part II, Section 3831.06 and IAS 18.12.

Measurement Uncertainty

Measurement uncertainty results from an inability to measure the transaction or parts of the transaction. This might arise for the following reasons:

1. Inability to measure the consideration; e.g., barter transactions, price protection clauses or sales returns provisions on new products,[19]

2. Inability to measure related costs, or

3. Inability to measure the outcome of the transaction itself, e.g., where the sales are contingent upon a future event, the terms of the transaction are not sufficiently solidified, or the customer may cancel the contract (trial period).

Earlier in the chapter, we discussed the issue of concessionary terms. Concessionary terms generally make it more difficult to measure the transaction. This is the case because concessionary terms often involve longer time horizons, are unique or one-time, and include more lenient return and other policies. In addition, there is often no history of similar transactions to assist in the measurement of the uncertain items.

Care should be taken to analyze external factors such as obsolescence, business or economic cycles, the financial health of customers, and the arrival of a competitor's products that may cause the company's products to become obsolete.

In the publishing industry, the rate of return approaches 25% for hardcover books and 65% for some magazines. The high rate of return is a function of two factors: (1) the publishers want to induce sales and therefore overship, and (2) retailers have more power in the industry. **Chapters Inc.**, formed through the merger between **Smithbooks** and **Coles** in 1995, engaged in very aggressive return activities after the merger. In 2001, **Indigo Books & Music, Inc.** became Canada's largest book retailer as a result of an amalgamation between **Indigo** and Chapters Inc.

What Do the Numbers Mean?

Since this deal created an even greater concentration in the retail book industry in Canada, it was reviewed by the federal Competition Tribunal. The Tribunal concluded, among other things, that the deal could go through as long as 24 Chapters stores were sold to an unrelated party and the new company adhered to a business code of conduct. The code of conduct stipulated that returns would be limited and payments to publishers would have to be made within a reasonable time frame.

Real-World Emphasis

The domestic cigarette industry at one time used a distribution practice known as trade loading. Producers would induce their wholesale customers, known as the trade, to buy more product than they could resell. As a result, the wholesalers would return significant amounts of product in the following period. In the computer software industry, this same practice is referred to as channel stuffing. Software producers would offer deep discounts to their distributors, who would then overbuy and not be able to subsequently resell. Trade loading and channel stuffing overstate sales in one period and distort operating results. If it is used without an appropriate allowance for sales returns, channel stuffing is a classic example of booking tomorrow's revenue today. The problem is the motivating factors that underlie these transactions. It is not a problem to use aggressive selling practices as long as they are sustainable and result in revenues that are realizable. The danger is using these and similar types of transactions for the sole purpose of booking more revenues.

---

[19] Price protection clauses state that if the purchase price goes down before the customer has resold the product, the vendor will provide a cash refund. They are included to stop the customer from returning the product and repurchasing it at the lower price.

o alternative revenue recognition treatments are available where there is measure-
ncertainty:

not record a sale if it is not measurable; and

ord the sale, but attempt to measure and accrue an amount relating to the uncer-
ty as a cost or reduced revenues (e.g., sales returns and allowances may be treated
ontra sales accounts or unearned revenue/refund liabilities, with cost of sales being
sted for these potential returns).

second treatment is preferred under accrual accounting. Measurement models
used to help quantify risks and uncertainties.

Measuring Parts of a Sale

Sales involving more than one product or service create additional measurement challenges. Sales of products are dealt with differently than sales of services for revenue recognition purposes. Different services may also be accounted for differently depending on
when the related revenues are earned. In order to accommodate this, the sale needs to be
divided up or bifurcated into separate units. For instance, a cellular telephone company
might sell a phone plus a monthly service (to provide airtime). The phone and the access
are separate units for accounting purposes.

Once we establish whether there are separate units, we then allocate the overall price
to each unit. Ideally, the **relative fair value method** would be used. In this method, the
fair value of each item (referred to as stand-alone value) is determined and then the purchase price is allocated based on the relative fair values. Alternatively, the **residual value
method** could be used. In this method, the fair value of the **undelivered** item is subtracted
from the overall purchase price. The residual value is then used to value the delivered item
(in this case the telephone). The residual value method ensures that upfront revenues are
not overstated. Example 9 illustrates how to measure parts of a sale. Where stand-alone
values are estimated, the estimate should maximize the use of observable inputs.

EXAMPLE 9

Assume that Jason Inc. sells a product and a service bundled together. Assume further that
the separate deliverables meet the GAAP criteria for treatment as separate units. The fair
value of the product is $100 and the fair value of the service is $200. In order to make the
sale, Jason Inc. sold the bundle at a discount for $250. Under the fair value method, the
amount that is allocated to the product would be $83.33 and the value attributed to the
service would be $166.67. If the residual value method is used, the service would be valued
at $200 and the product at $50. The table below shows the calculations.

	Fair value method calculation	Fair value method allocation	Residual method calculation	Residual method allocation
Product	[$100 ÷ ($100 + $200) × $250]	$ 83.33	($250 − $200)	$ 50
Service	[$200 ÷ ($100 + $200) × $250]	$166.67	($250 − $50)	$200
Total		$250		$250

Once we allocate the purchase price to each unit, we then follow GAAP to see if the
revenue for each unit should be recognized. The revenue for the phone would be recognized upon delivery, and the revenue for the airtime would be recognized as the service is
provided (or the airtime is used up). Care should be taken to consider the economic value
of the services, which may change over time (e.g., under warranty contracts, the company
may have to provide more services toward the end of the period).

If it is not possible to measure each part, then revenue recognition criteria must be applied to the whole bundled sale as though it were one product or service.

Onerous Contracts

Sometimes contracts become **onerous**. The term *onerous* means that the contract is no longer profitable to the company. Where this is the case, consideration should be given to remeasuring the contract and reflecting a loss in the income statement.

Collectibility

General Principle

At the point of sale, if it is reasonably sure that collection of the receivable will ultimately occur (or it is probable that economic benefits will flow to the entity), revenues are recognized.[20] This principle applies under both approaches. Note that, as long as it is possible to estimate uncollectible amounts at the point of sale (perhaps based on historical data), the sale is booked and the potential uncollectible amount is accrued.

Alternatively, when **collectibility** cannot be reasonably assured, revenues cannot be recognized. In these cases, it is presumed that if collectibility is not established at the time of sale, then in substance no real sale has been made. Why would a company sell something to a customer who will not be able to pay for the goods? This would not make economic sense. The accounting would default to a cash basis (i.e., recognize income when cash is received). In the past, two methods—instalment sales method and cost recovery method—have been included in many accounting texts. Discussion of these can be found on the expanded discussion area on the website and in WileyPLUS.

6 Objective
Understand how to account for sales where there is collection uncertainty.

Finance

Expanded Discussion

Mechanics

Consignment

In some distribution arrangements, the vendor **retains legal title** to the goods. In such cases, the point of delivery is therefore not proof of full performance. This specialized method of marketing for certain types of products uses what is known as a **consignment**. Under this arrangement, the **consignor** (e.g., a manufacturer) ships merchandise to the **consignee** (e.g., a dealer), who acts as an agent for the consignor in selling the merchandise. Both consignor and consignee are interested in selling: the former to make a profit or develop a market, the latter to make a commission on the sales.

7 Objective
Prepare journal entries for consignment sales under the earnings and contract-based approaches.

Earnings Approach. The consignee accepts the merchandise and agrees to exercise due diligence (or care) in looking after the inventory and selling it. When the merchandise is sold, cash received from customers is then remitted to the consignor by the consignee, after deducting a sales commission and any chargeable expenses. Revenue is recognized only after the consignor receives notification of the sale. For the entire time of the consignment, the merchandise is carried as the consignor's inventory and is separately classified as Merchandise on Consignment. It is not recorded as an asset on the consignee's books.

Upon sale of the merchandise, the consignee has a liability for the net amount that it must remit to the consignor. The consignor periodically receives from the consignee a report that shows the merchandise received, merchandise sold, expenses chargeable to the consignment, and cash remitted.

---

[20] *CICA Handbook*, Part II, Section 3400.19 and IAS 18.20.

EXAMPLE 10

To illustrate consignment accounting entries, assume that Sohail Manufacturing Corp. ships merchandise costing $36,000 on consignment to Chosky Stores. Sohail pays $3,750 of freight costs and Chosky pays $2,250 for local advertising costs that are reimbursable by Sohail. By the end of the period, two-thirds of the consigned merchandise has been sold for $40,000 cash. Chosky notifies Sohail of the sales, retains a 10% commission, and remits the cash due to Sohail. The journal entries in Illustration 6-6 would be made by the consignor (Sohail) and the consignee (Chosky).

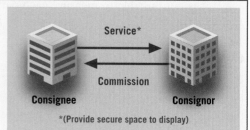

Service*

Commission

Consignee   Consignor

*(Provide secure space to display)

 Why would companies use consignment to sell their goods? The company selling the goods will often use this type of distribution mechanism to encourage consignees to take their goods and sell them. Under the consignment arrangement, the manufacturer (consignor) retains the risk that the merchandise might not sell and frees the dealer (consignee) from having to commit part of its working capital to inventory. Presumably, if the products sell very well to third parties, the consignor could push for the consignee to actually purchase the goods outright. A variety of different systems and account titles are used to record consignments, but they all share the common goal of postponing the recognition of revenue until it is known that a sale to a third party (the customer) has occurred.

Illustration 6-6

Entries for Consignment Sales

Sohail Mfg. Corp. (Consignor)			Chosky Stores (Consignee)		
Shipment of consigned merchandise					
Inventory on Consignment	36,000		No entry (record memo of		
Finished Goods			merchandise received)		
Inventory		36,000			
Payment of freight costs by consignor					
Inventory on Consignment	3,750		No entry.		
Cash		3,750			
Payment of advertising by consignee					
No entry until notified.			Receivable from Consignor	2,250	
			Cash		2,250
Sales of consigned merchandise					
No entry until notified.			Cash	40,000	
			Payable to Consignor		40,000
Notification of sales and expenses and remittance of amount due					
Cash	33,750		Payable to Consignor	40,000	
Advertising Expense	2,250		Receivable from Consignor		2,250
Commission Expense	4,000		Commission Revenue		4,000
Revenue from Consignment			Cash		33,750
Sales		40,000			
Adjustment of inventory on consignment for cost of sales					
Cost of Goods Sold	26,500		No entry.		
Inventory on Consignment		26,500			
[²/₃ ($36,000 + $3,750) = $26,500]					

Contract-Based Approach. Under the contract-based view of revenue recognition, when the consignment arrangement is first entered into, both parties have rights and obligations. In the above example, the consignor has the right to any consideration once the inventory is sold to a third-party customer. The consignor also has the obligation to provide inventory for display purposes and to pay a percentage of the consideration upon sale to a third party (as a selling commission). The consignee is the one selling the service. It agrees to display and sell the consignor's goods for a commission.

Law

Assuming an arm's-length reciprocal transaction, the net contract position would be zero on the consignee's books once the contract is agreed upon. The consignee must measure the value of the rights and obligations up front. There is measurement uncertainty here since the revenue is contingent upon making a sale. If no sale is made, then no service revenue will be earned.[21] In all likelihood, the outcome of the transaction is not reliably measurable so no entry would be booked up front for the consignee.

Significant Change

The journal entries for the consignor would be essentially the same as noted under the earnings approach assuming that the contract with the customer is entered into at the same time as the control of the goods passes to the customer.

Percentage-of-Completion Method

Earnings Approach. **The percentage-of-completion method recognizes revenues, costs, and gross profit as progress is made toward completion on a long-term contract.** If recognition of these items were deferred until the entire contract was complete, the efforts (costs) and accomplishments (revenues) of the interim accounting periods would be misrepresented. In order to apply the percentage-of-completion method, however, there has to be a basis or standard for measuring the progress toward completion at particular interim dates.

8 Objective

Apply the percentage-of-completion method under the earnings and contract-based approaches.

Measuring progress toward completion requires significant judgement. Costs, labour hours worked, tonnes produced, and other such measures are often used. The various measures are identified and classified as either input or output measures. **Input measures** (costs incurred, labour hours worked) measure the efforts that have been devoted to a contract. **Output measures** (tonnes produced, storeys of a building completed, kilometres of a highway completed) measure results. Neither of these measures can be applied to all long-term projects; instead, the measure needs to be carefully tailored to the circumstances, which means that judgement is essential.

Whichever method is used, there are some disadvantages with input and output measures. Input measures are based on an established relationship between a unit of input and productivity. If inefficiencies cause the productivity relationship to change, inaccurate measurements result. Another potential problem, called front-end loading, produces higher estimates of completion because significant costs are incurred up front. Some

Underlying Concept

Both input and output measures have measurement uncertainty.

---

[21] Upon publication of this text, the IASB and FASB were deliberating about how they would deal with measurement issues. Note that while the contract-based approach to revenue recognition requires sales contracts to be recognized when entered into, GAAP is leaning toward the other side, i.e., accounting for purchase contracts. Many purchase contracts do not get recognized on the balance sheet (unless they are onerous or are covered by derivatives accounting).

early-stage construction costs should therefore be ignored if they do not relate directly to the actual performance of the contract; these include, for example, the costs of uninstalled materials or the costs of subcontracts that have not yet been performed.

Output measures can also result in inaccurate measures if the units that are used are not comparable in time, effort, or cost to complete. For example, using storeys completed can be deceiving; completing the first storey of an eight-storey building may require more than one-eighth of the total cost because of the substructure and foundation construction.

One of the more popular input measures used to determine the progress toward completion is cost, sometimes referred to as the cost-to-cost basis. Under the cost-to-cost basis, the percentage of completion is measured by comparing costs incurred to date with the most recent estimate of the total costs to complete the contract. The formula for this is shown in Illustration 6-7.

Illustration 6-7

Formula for Percentage of Completion, Cost-to-Cost Basis—Earnings Approach

$$\frac{\text{Costs incurred to date}}{\text{Most recent estimate of total costs}} = \text{Percent complete}$$

The percentage of costs incurred out of total estimated costs is then applied to the total revenue or the estimated total gross profit on the contract to arrive at the revenue or the gross profit amounts to be recognized to date. Illustration 6-8 shows this formula.

Illustration 6-8

Formula for Total Revenue to Be Recognized to Date—Earnings Approach

| Percent complete | × | Estimated total revenue (or gross profit) | = | Revenue (or gross profit) to be recognized to date |

To find the amount of revenue and gross profit that will be recognized in each period, we would need to subtract the total revenue or gross profit that has been recognized in prior periods, as shown in Illustration 6-9.

Illustration 6-9

Formula for Amount of Current Period Revenue, Cost-to-Cost Basis—Earnings Approach

| Revenue (or gross profit) to be recognized to date | − | Revenue (or gross profit) recognized in prior periods | = | Current period revenue (or gross profit) |

Illustration of Percentage-of-Completion Method, Cost-to-Cost Basis. To illustrate the percentage-of-completion method, assume that Hardhat Construction Ltd. has a contract starting in July 2011 to construct a $4.5-million bridge that is expected to be completed in October 2013, at an estimated cost of $4 million. Illustration 6-10 shows the data for the entire construction period (note that by the end of 2012 the estimated total cost has increased from $4 million to $4,050,000). Assume that the customer has control over the asset and can make major changes to the project during construction (there is a continuous transfer of assets).

Illustration 6-10

Application of Percentage-of-Completion Method, Cost-to-Cost Basis—Earnings Approach

	2011	2012	2013
Costs to date	$1,000,000	$2,916,000	$4,050,000
Estimated costs to complete	3,000,000	1,134,000	—
Progress billings during the year	900,000	2,400,000	1,200,000
Cash collected during the year	750,000	1,750,000	2,000,000

The percent complete would be calculated as follows.

	2011	2012	2013
Costs incurred to date			
Contract price	$4,500,000	$4,500,000	$4,500,000
Less estimated cost:			
Costs to date	1,000,000	2,916,000	4,050,000
Estimated costs to complete	3,000,000	1,134,000	
Estimated total costs	4,000,000	4,050,000	4,050,000
Estimated total gross profit	$ 500,000	$ 450,000	$ 450,000
Percent complete[22]	25%	72%	100%
	$(1,000,000)	$(2,916,000)	$(4,050,000)
	$(4,000,000)	$(4,050,000)	$(4,050,000)

Based on the data above, the entries in Illustration 6-11 would be prepared to record (1) the costs of construction, (2) progress billings, and (3) collections. These entries appear as summaries of the many transactions that would be entered individually as they occur during the year.

	2011		2012		2013	
To record cost of construction:						
Construction in Process	1,000,000		1,916,000		1,134,000	
Materials, Cash, Payables, etc.		1,000,000		1,916,000		1,134,000
To record progress billings:						
Accounts Receivable	900,000		2,400,000		1,200,000	
Billings on Construction in Process		900,000		2,400,000		1,200,000
To record collections:						
Cash	750,000		1,750,000		2,000,000	
Accounts Receivable		750,000		1,750,000		2,000,000

Illustration 6-11

Journal Entries—Percentage-of-Completion Method, Cost-to-Cost Basis—Earnings Approach

In this illustration, the costs incurred to date as a proportion of the estimated total costs to be incurred on the project are a measure of the extent of progress toward completion.

The estimated revenue and gross profit to be recognized for each year are calculated in Illustration 6-12.

---

[22] Assume that this percentage represents a reasonable proxy of the amount of goods/services passed on to the customer.

Illustration 6-12

Percentage of Completion, Revenue, and Gross Profit by Year—Earnings Approach

	2011	2012	2013
Revenue recognized in:			
2011 $4,500,000 × 25%	$1,125,000		
2012 $4,500,000 × 72%		$3,240,000	
Less: Revenue recognized in 2011		1,125,000	
Revenue in 2012		$2,115,000	
2013 $4,500,000 × 100%			$4,500,000
Less: Revenue recognized in 2011 and 2012			3,240,000
Revenue in 2013			$1,260,000
Gross profit recognized in:			
2011 $500,000 × 25%	$ 125,000		
2012 $450,000 × 72%		$ 324,000	
Less: Gross profit recognized in 2011		125,000	
Gross profit in 2012		$ 199,000	
2013 $450,000 × 100%			$ 450,000
Less: Gross profit recognized in 2011 and 2012			$ 324,000
Gross profit in 2013			$ 126,000

The entries to recognize revenue and gross profit each year and to record the completion and final approval of the contract are shown in Illustration 6-13.

Illustration 6-13

Journal Entries to Recognize Revenue and Gross Profit and to Record Contract Completion—Percentage-of-Completion Method, Cost-to-Cost Basis—Earnings Approach

	2011		2012		2013	
To recognize revenue and gross profit:						
Construction in Process (gross profit)	125,000		199,000		126,000	
Construction Expenses	1,000,000		1,916,000		1,134,000	
Revenue from Long-Term Contract		1,125,000		2,115,000		1,260,000
To record completion of the contract:						
Billings on Construction in Process					4,500,000	
Construction in Process						4,500,000

Note that the gross profit that was calculated above is debited to Construction in Process, while Revenue from Long-Term Contract is credited for the amounts calculated above. The difference between the amounts that are recognized each year for revenue and gross profit is debited to Construction Expenses (similar to Cost of Goods Sold in a manufacturing enterprise), which is reported in the income statement. That amount (the difference) is the actual cost of construction incurred in that period. For example, for Hardhat Construction the actual costs of $1 million in 2011 are used to calculate both the gross profit of $125,000 and the percent complete (25%).

Costs continue to be accumulated in the Construction in Process account so that there is a record of total costs incurred (plus recognized profit) to date. The Construction in Process account represents the value of the service earned to date and would include the summary entries over the term of the construction project that are shown in Illustration 6-14.

Construction in Process				
2011 construction costs	$1,000,000	12/31/13	to close	
2011 recognized gross profit	125,000		completed	
2012 construction costs	1,916,000		project	$4,500,000
2012 recognized gross profit	199,000			
2013 construction costs	1,134,000			
2013 recognized gross profit	126,000			
Total	$4,500,000	Total		$4,500,000

Illustration 6-14

Content of Construction in Process Account—Percentage-of-Completion Method—Earnings Approach

The Hardhat illustration contains a change in estimate in the second year, 2012, when the estimated total costs increased from $4 million to $4,050,000. By adjusting the percent completed to the new estimate of total costs, and then deducting the amount of revenues and gross profit that has been recognized in prior periods from revenues and gross profit calculated for progress to date, the change in estimate is accounted for in a cumulative catch-up manner. That is, the change in estimate is accounted for in the period of change so that the balance sheet at the end of that period and the accounting in subsequent periods are the same as if the revised estimate had been the original estimate.

Financial Statement Presentation—Percentage-of-Completion. The Construction in Process and Billings accounts are presented on a net basis in the financial statements. They represent the difference between the amount that has been earned versus the amount billed. When the amount in the Construction in Process account is more than the amount in the Billings account, this excess is reported as a current asset (non-current if the contract is a longer-term contract) entitled "Recognized Revenues in Excess of Billings." The unbilled portion of the revenue recognized to date can be calculated at any time by subtracting the billings to date from the revenue recognized to date, as shown for 2011 for Hardhat in Illustration 6-15.

Amount at Dec. 31, 2011

Contract revenue recognized to date: $4,500,000 × $\dfrac{\$1,000,000}{\$4,000,000}$ = $1,125,000

Billings to date	900,000
Unbilled revenue	$ 225,000

Illustration 6-15

Calculation of Unbilled Contract—Earnings Approach

When the billings are more than the costs incurred and gross profit to date, this excess is reported as a liability entitled "Billings in Excess of Recognized Revenues." The excess signifies that the company has billed more than it has earned. Separate disclosures of the dollar amounts of billings and costs are preferred, rather than a summary presentation of the net difference.

Using data from the previous illustration, Hardhat would report the status and results of its long-term construction activities under the percentage-of-completion method as in Illustration 6-16.

HARDHAT CONSTRUCTION LTD.

Income Statement	2011	2012	2013
Revenue from long-term contracts	$1,125,000	$2,115,000	$1,260,000
Costs of construction	1,000,000	1,916,000	1,134,000
Gross profit	$ 125,000	$ 199,000	$ 126,000

Balance Sheet (12/31)		2011	2012
Current assets			
Accounts receivable		$ 150,000	$ 800,000
Inventories			
Construction in process	$1,125,000		
Less: Billings	900,000		
Recognized revenues in excess of billings		$ 225,000	
Current liabilities			
Billings ($3,300,000) in excess of recognized revenues ($3,240,000)			$ 60,000

Note 1. Summary of significant accounting policies.

LONG-TERM CONSTRUCTION CONTRACTS. The company recognizes revenues and reports profits from long-term construction contracts, its principal business, under the percentage-of-completion method of accounting. These contracts generally extend for periods in excess of one year. The amounts of revenues and profits that are recognized each year are based on the ratio of costs incurred to the total estimated costs. Costs included in construction in process include direct materials, direct labour, and project-related overhead. Corporate general and administrative expenses are charged to the periods as incurred and are not allocated to construction contracts.

Contract-Based Approach. Under the contract-based approach, when the contract is entered into, contractual rights and obligations are created.

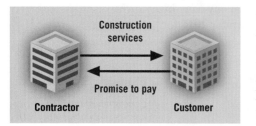

The contractor agrees to provide certain construction services and the customer agrees to pay for them at specified points in time. The net contract position would be recognized up front and measured at zero assuming an arm's-length transaction. The value of the construction services in the above example would be the contracted price as outlined in the contract, which would be equal to the agreed-upon fee. Illustration 6-17 shows the journal entries. Note that there is no need to make a journal entry for billings because the contractual rights are already recognized when the contract is entered into (although they are netted against the contract obligations for a net position of zero). Note further that there is no need for the last entry at the end of the contract since the Contract Asset/Liability account will zero itself out. Many of the calculations are the same as under the earnings approach.

Note that the above entries are based on the same percentage of completion as calculated earlier. If there are cost overruns, care must be taken to ensure that the percentage calculated is representative of the value of services passed on to the customer. With cost overruns, this might not be the case (i.e., the cost overruns do not necessarily signal that more of the job has been completed or more service has been provided), and it may make more sense to calculate the percentage another way. For instance, if 10 kilometres of highway are being built, and at the end of the first year, 4 kilometres are complete, then the job is 40% complete.

	2011		2012		2013	
To record contract rights/ obligations:						
Contract Asset/Liability	4,500,000					
Contract Asset/Liability		4,500,000				
To record cost of construction:						
Construction in Process	1,000,000		1,916,000		1,134,000	
Materials, Cash, Payables, etc.		1,000,000		1,916,000		1,134,000
To record progress billings: NA						
To record collections:						
Cash	750,000		1,750,000		2,000,000	
Contract Asset/Liability		750,000		1,750,000		2,000,000
To recognize revenue and gross profit:						
Construction Expenses	1,000,000		1,916,000		1,134,000	
Construction in Process		1,000,000		1,916,000		1,134,000
Contract Asset/Liability	1,125,000		2,115,000		1,260,000	
Revenue from Long-Term Contract		1,125,000		2,115,000		1,260,000
To record completion of the contract: NA						

Illustration 6-17

Percentage-of-Completion Method—Contract-based Approach

Significant Change

Completed-Contract Method

Earnings Approach. In the completed-contract method, revenue and gross profit are recognized when the contract is completed. Costs of long-term contracts in process and current billings are accumulated, but there are no interim charges or credits to income statement accounts for revenues, costs, and gross profit.

The main advantage of the completed-contract method is that reported revenue is based on final results rather than on estimates of unperformed work. Its major disadvantage is that it does not reflect current performance when the period of a contract is longer than one accounting period. Although operations may be fairly steady during the contract period, revenue is not reported until the year of completion, which distorts earnings.

The annual entries to record costs of construction, progress billings, and collections from customers would be identical to those illustrated under the percentage-of-completion method, but with the very important exclusion of the recognition of revenue and gross profit. For Hardhat Construction's bridge project illustrated on the preceding pages, the following entries are made in 2013 under the completed-contract method to recognize revenue and costs and to close out the inventory and billing accounts:

9 Objective

Apply the completed-contract method under the earnings and contract-based approaches.

Billings on Construction in Process	4,500,000	
Revenue from Long-Term Contracts		4,500,000
Costs of Construction	4,050,000	
Construction in Process		4,050,000

$$A = L + SE$$
$$-\$450,000 \quad +\$450,000$$

Cash flows: No effect

Illustration 6-18 compares how Hardhat would have recognized gross profit on the same bridge project under the percentage-of-completion and completed-contract methods.

Illustration 6-18

Comparison of Gross Profit Recognized—Earnings Approach

	Percentage-of-Completion	Completed-Contract
2011	$125,000	$ 0
2012	199,000	0
2013	126,000	450,000

Hardhat would report its long-term construction activities as shown in Illustration 6-19.

HARDHAT CONSTRUCTION LTD.

Income Statement	2011	2012	2013
Revenue from long-term contracts	—	—	$4,500,000
Costs of construction	—	—	4,050,000
Gross profit	—	—	450,000

Balance Sheet (12/31)		2011	2012
Current assets			
Accounts receivable		$150,000	$800,000
Construction in process	$1,000,000		
Less: Billings	900,000		
Unbilled contract costs		$100,000	
Liabilities			
Billings ($3,300,000) in excess			
of contract costs ($2,916,000)			$384,000

Note 1. Summary of significant accounting policies.

LONG-TERM CONSTRUCTION CONTRACTS. The company recognizes revenues and reports profits from long-term construction contracts, its principal business, under the completed-contract method. These contracts generally extend for periods in excess of one year. Contract costs and billings are accumulated during the periods of construction, but no revenues or profits are recognized until contract completion. Costs included in construction in process include direct material, direct labour, and project-related overhead. Corporate general and administrative expenses are charged to the periods as incurred and are not allocated to construction contracts.

Contract-Based Approach.   Under the contract-based approach, revenues are recognized as the service is provided, which may be at the end of the contract.

Where the construction of real estate or similar assets is involved and the legal title of the asset being constructed is not passed to the customer until the end of the contract, the transaction would be treated like any other inventory transaction, with the costs being accumulated in an inventory account and the sale of the asset being booked at the end of the contract. As previously mentioned, IFRS does not mention this approach explicitly although it is discussed as an option under private entity GAAP.

Significant Change

Losses on Long-Term Contracts

Earnings Approach.   Two types of losses can occur under long-term contracts:

1. **Loss in Current Period on a Profitable Contract.** This condition occurs when there is a significant increase in the estimated total contract costs during construction

but the increase does not eliminate all profit on the contract. Under the percentage-of-completion method only, the increase in the estimated cost requires an adjustment in the current period for the excess gross profit that was recognized on the project in prior periods. This adjustment is recorded as a loss in the current period because it is a change in accounting estimate (discussed in Chapter 21).

2. **Loss on an Unprofitable Contract.** Cost estimates at the end of the current period may indicate that a loss will result once the contract is completed. Under both the percentage-of-completion and completed-contract methods, the entire loss that is expected on the contract must be recognized in the current period.

Loss in Current Period.   To illustrate a loss in the current period on a contract that is expected to be profitable upon completion, assume that on December 31, 2012, Hardhat estimates the costs to complete the bridge contract at $1,468,962 instead of $1,134,000. Assuming all other data are the same as before, Hardhat would calculate the percent complete and recognize the loss as shown in Illustration 6-20. Compare these calculations with those for 2012 in Illustration 6-10. The percent complete has dropped from 72% to 66$\frac{1}{2}$% due to the increase in estimated future costs to complete the contract.

Cost to date (12/31/12)	$2,916,000
Estimated costs to complete (revised)	1,468,962
Estimated total costs	$4,384,962
Percent complete ($2,916,000/$4,384,962)	66½%
Revenue recognized in 2012	
($4,500,000 × 66½%) − $1,125,000	$1,867,500
Costs incurred in 2012	1,916,000
Loss recognized in 2012	$ 48,500

Illustration 6-20

Calculation of Recognizable Loss, 2012—Loss in Current Period

The loss of $48,500 in 2012 is a cumulative adjustment of the excessive gross profit that was recognized on the contract in 2011. Instead of restating the prior period, the prior period misstatement is absorbed entirely in the current period. In this illustration, the adjustment was large enough to result in recognition of a loss.

Hardhat would record the loss in 2012 as follows:

Construction Expenses	1,916,000	
Construction in Process (loss)		48,500
Revenue from Long-Term Contract		1,867,500

A   = L +   SE
−48,500   −48,500

Cash flows: No effect

The loss of $48,500 will be reported on the 2012 income statement as the difference between the reported revenues of $1,867,500 and the costs of $1,916,000.[23] Under the completed-contract method, no loss is recognized in 2012, because the contract is still expected to result in a profit that will be recognized in the year of completion.

---

[23] In 2013, Hardhat will recognize the remaining 33$\frac{1}{2}$% of the revenue ($1,507,500), with costs of $1,468,962 as expected, and report a gross profit of $38,538. The total gross profit over the three years of the contract would be $115,038 [$125,000 (2011) − $48,500 (2012) + $38,538 (2013)], which is the difference between the total contract revenue of $4,500,000 and the total contract costs of $4,384,962.

Loss on an Unprofitable Contract.   To illustrate the accounting for an overall loss on a long-term contract, assume that at December 31, 2012, Hardhat estimates the costs to complete the bridge contract at $1,640,250 instead of $1,134,000. Revised estimates on the bridge contract appear as follows:

	2011 Original Estimates	2012 Revised Estimates
Contract price	$4,500,000	$4,500,000
Estimated total cost	4,000,000	4,556,250*
Estimated gross profit	$ 500,000	
Estimated loss		$ (56,250)

*($2,916,000 + $1,640,250)

Under the percentage-of-completion method, $125,000 of gross profit was recognized in 2011 (see Illustration 6-12). This $125,000 must be offset in 2012 because it is no longer expected to be realized. In addition, the total estimated loss of $56,250 must be recognized in 2012 since losses must be recognized as soon as they can be estimated. Therefore, a total loss of $181,250 ($125,000 + $56,250) must be recognized in 2012.

Illustration 6-21 shows the calculation for the revenue to be recognized in 2012.

Illustration 6-21

Calculation of Revenue Recognizable, 2012— Unprofitable Contract

Revenue recognized in 2012		
Contract price		$4,500,000
Percent complete		× 64%*
Revenue recognizable to date		2,880,000
Less: Revenue recognized prior to 2012		1,125,000
Revenue recognized in 2012		$1,755,000
Cost to date (12/31/12)	$2,916,000	
Estimated cost to complete	1,640,250	
Estimated total costs		$4,556,250

*Percent complete: $2,916,000/$4,556,250 = 64%

To calculate the construction costs to be expensed in 2012, we add the total loss to be recognized in 2012 ($125,000 + $56,250) to the revenue to be recognized in 2012. This calculation is shown in Illustration 6-22.

Illustration 6-22

Calculation of Construction Expense, 2012— Unprofitable Contract

Revenue recognized in 2012 (calculated above)		$1,755,000
Total loss recognized in 2012:		
Reversal of 2011 gross profit	$125,000	
Total estimated loss on the contract	56,250	181,250
Construction cost expensed in 2012		$1,936,250

Hardhat would record the long-term contract revenues, expenses, and loss in 2012 as follows:

Construction Expenses	1,936,250	
Construction in Process (Loss)		181,250
Revenue from Long-Term Contracts		1,755,000

A   = L +   SE
−181,250   −181,250

Cash flows: No effect

As Illustration 6-23 shows, Construction in Process has a balance of $2,859,750 at the end of 2012.[24]

Illustration 6-23

Content of Construction in Process Account at End of 2012—Unprofitable Contract

Construction in Process			
2011 Construction costs	$1,000,000		
2011 Recognized gross profit	125,000		
2012 Construction costs	1,916,000	2012 Recognized loss	$181,250
Balance	2,859,750		

Under the completed-contract method, the contract loss of $56,250 is also recognized in the year in which it first became evident. The following entry is therefore made in 2012:

Loss from Long-Term Contracts	56,250	
Construction in Process (Loss)		56,250

A   = L +   SE
−56,250   −56,250

Cash flows: No effect

Just as the Billings for Construction in Process account balance cannot be higher than the contract price, neither can the balance in Construction in Process exceed the contract price. In circumstances where the Construction in Process balance is more than the Billings for Construction in Process amount, the recognized loss may be deducted on the balance sheet from the construction costs that have accumulated in Construction in Process. That is, under both the percentage-of-completion and completed-contract methods, the provision for the loss (the credit) may be combined with Construction in Process, thereby reducing the balance. In circumstances where the billings are more than the accumulated costs (as in the 2012 illustration above), the amount of the estimated loss must be reported separately on the balance sheet as a current liability. That is, under both the percentage-of-completion and completed-contract methods, the amount of the loss of $56,250, as estimated in 2012, would be taken from the Construction in Process account and reported separately as a current liability entitled Estimated Liability from Long-Term Contracts.

Contract-Based Approach.   Under the contract-based approach, losses are treated in a similar manner except under certain conditions. Recall that revenues may only be recognized under this approach as the performance obligation is extinguished.

Where there are significant losses in the current period on a profitable contract, it makes sense to recalculate the percentage of completion by looking at another proxy for

Significant Change

---

[24] If the costs in 2013 are $1,640,250 as projected, at the end of 2013 the Construction in Process account will have a balance of $1,640,250 + $2,859,750, or $4,500,000, which is equal to the contract price. When the revenue remaining to be recognized in 2013 of $1,620,000 [$4,500,000 (total contract price) − $1,125,000 (2011) − $1,755,000 (2012)] is matched with the construction expense to be recognized in 2013 of $1,620,000 [total costs of $4,556,250 less the total costs recognized in prior years of $2,936,250 (2011, $1,000,000; 2012, $1,936,250)], a zero profit results. Thus, the total loss has been recognized in 2012, the year in which it first became evident.

determining services provided (i.e., as discussed earlier, it might not make sense to use the actual costs incurred divided by total actual and estimated costs). The fact that the company has cost overruns does not necessarily mean that more of the contracted services are being provided and therefore, the performance obligation may not be extinguished. When this is the case, output measures are a better indicator of service provided and have the added quality of looking at it from the customer's perspective. The calculations would be the same but using the revised percentage, which would be based on outputs.

ACCOUNTING—PRESENTATION AND DISCLOSURE

Revenues versus Gains

What about sales of assets other than the entity's inventory? The principles discussed above do not apply only to sales of inventory, as in the case of Magnotta's wine inventory. They also apply to items that are disposed of through sales that are not part of the normal earnings process—e.g., sales of income-producing or capital assets. In these cases, a gain[25] is generated (instead of revenues). It is important to carefully establish that, in substance, a disposition has actually occurred. In certain cases, a company may sell a fixed asset and receive a note receivable that is secured by the asset itself. If very little other consideration is received, has the asset really been sold? Have the risks and rewards really passed?

Net Income versus Other Comprehensive Income

Objective 10
Understand how to present sales transactions in the income statement.

In some cases, income is generated when assets are revalued. Consider the case of investments and property, plant, and equipment measured and carried at fair value on the balance sheet. Should these gains and losses be recognized in the income statement, in other comprehensive income, or not at all? We will revisit this issue in subsequent chapters.

Ethics

Gross versus Net Revenues

What Do the Numbers Mean?

Although net income does not change if a company chooses to report revenues as the **gross** amount billed to the customer (as well as the related cost of goods sold) instead of the **net** amount retained, the revenue number changes. Since revenue is the focus of many financial statement users, this is an important issue.

Consider **Priceline.com**, the U.S. company that allows you to "name your own price" for airline tickets and hotel rooms. In its third-quarter SEC filings for 1999, Priceline reported that it earned $152 million in revenues. But that included the full amount that customers paid for tickets, hotel rooms, and rental cars. Traditional travel agencies call that amount "gross bookings," not revenues. And much like regular travel agencies, Priceline keeps only a small portion of gross bookings—namely, the spread between the customers' accepted bids and the price it paid for the merchandise. The rest, which Priceline calls "product costs," are paid to the airlines and hotels that supply the tickets and rooms. In a recent quarter, those costs came to $134 million, leaving Priceline

---

[25] Gains (as contrasted with revenues) commonly result from transactions and other events that do not involve an earnings process. For gain recognition, being earned is generally less important than being realized or realizable.

just $18 million of what it calls "gross profit" and what most other companies would call revenues. And that amount is before all of Priceline's other costs—like advertising and salaries—which netted out to a loss of $102 million. The difference is not academic: Priceline stock traded at about 23 times its reported revenues but at a mind-boggling 214 times its "gross profits."

Source: Jeremy Kahn, "Presto Chango! Sales Are Huge," *Fortune* (March 20, 2000), p. 44.

Real-World Emphasis

In analyzing this issue (which is essentially a **presentation** issue), the following factors should be considered:

1. whether the company acts as a **principal** in the transaction or an **agent or broker** (who is buying and selling an item for commission)

2. whether the company takes **title to the goods** being sold

3. whether the company has the **risks and rewards of ownership** of the goods being sold

For example, a real estate agent acts as a **broker** or **agent**, finding a house for a customer and then taking a **commission** on the sale. The agent does not take **title** to the house nor does he or she have the **risks and rewards** associated with ownership of the house. Revenues associated with the sale of a house would be recorded net as commissions. On the other hand, a company such as **Mattamy Homes Limited**, which builds houses and then sells them to customers, acts as a **principal**. It has the risks and rewards of ownership of the house before selling it (including legal title). When Mattamy sells a house, it would record the house's market value as revenue and the cost to build it as cost of goods sold.

IFRS/PRIVATE ENTITY GAAP COMPARISON

Illustration 6-20 presents a comparison of IFRS and private enterprise GAAP related to revenue recognition.

11 Objective
Identify differences in accounting between private entity GAAP and IFRS.

Analysis

Although the revenue number is used in several key ratios, the most important revenue analysis is normally a trend analysis showing changes in revenues from year to year. Due to the sensitivity and high profile of the revenues number on the income statement, there is a lot of pressure to report biased revenue numbers. Biased reporting is possible under both a principles-based accounting standards system (because there is less specific guidance) and a rules-based accounting standards system (by finding loopholes in the rules). Revenues are a key number used to judge management's job performance and they are a signal in the marketplace of sustainable growth potential. The value of firms in certain industries, such as Internet companies, is often based on revenues, since many of these firms do not generate profits in their early years. Note the differences identified between IFRS and *Handbook* Section 3400. These differences will result in completely different revenues, gross profit, and, in some cases, income numbers.

Revenue recognition is one of the main areas of misrepresentation. It is often difficult to spot such misrepresentations in financial statements, since the note disclosures are often very general. It is therefore important to carefully understand the company's underlying business and business model and to ensure that any changes in the business model are

12 Objective
Understand the impact of accounting choices on key numbers/ratios.

Ethics

	Accounting Standards for Private Enterprises (Private Entity GAAP)—*CICA Handbook*, Part II, Section 3400	IFRS—IAS 11, 18, and 41	IASB Proposed Model
Recognition	Earnings approach requires recognition when performance achieved (risks and rewards passed/services rendered and measurable) and collectible	Earnings approach requires recognition when risks and rewards passed/services rendered, no continuing involvement, measurable and collectible	Contract-based approach requires: 1. Recognition of a net contract position when contract entered into, contractual rights are measurable and collectible, and performance obligations are measurable 2. Revenue recognized upon performance of obligation (when control passed/services rendered)
	Instalment and cost recovery method mentioned in AcG 2 on franchise accounting (see expanded discussion)	No mention currently made of the instalment sales method and cost recovery methods (as alternative models when dealing with collectibility issues)	No mention currently made of the instalment sales method and cost recovery methods (as alternative models when dealing with collectibility issues). When paid over time, use discounting. Where collection issues, default to cash basis
	Percentage-of-completion and completed-contract methods allowed for long-term contracts	More detailed guidance given regarding construction accounting including percentage-of-completion method. Completed-contract method not mentioned. Where outcome of services transactions is not reliably estimable, may only recognize recoverable revenues equal to recognized expenses (sometimes referred to as the zero profit method)	Percentage-of-completion method used but wth slightly different presentation and journal entries. Completed-contract method not mentioned, but for service contracts, recognize revenue when service rendered (may be rendered at the end). Where control of asset being constructed passes at end, treat as sale of asset
	Warranty costs historically accrued as costs/obligation when revenues recognized. More recently, these may have been accounted for as bundled sales (unearned revenues)	Warranty costs historically accrued as costs/obligation when revenues recognized. More recently, these may have been accounted for as bundled sales (unearned revenues)	Sale of goods with warranties to fix goods in future treated as bundled sales (similarly, loyalty points treated as bundled sales)
Measurement	At transaction or consideration price, which is generally assumed to be fair value	At fair value, which is assumed to be transaction price unless onerous contract	At transaction price unless onerous contract. Greater emphasis on using measurement models to quantify risk/uncertainty
	Barter transactions measured at fair value when transaction has commercial substance	Barter transactions measured at fair value when products/services exchanged are dissimilar	Currently under discussion
	Accounting for biological assets not explicitly discussed	Biological assets (living animals or plants) are valued at fair value less costs to sell under IAS 41 (even before they are sold)	Biological assets (living animals or plants) are valued at fair value less costs to sell under IAS 41 (even before they are sold)
	Bundled sales bifurcated using relative fair value or residual value method	Bundled sales bifurcated using relative fair value or residual value method	Bundled sales bifurcated using relative fair value (estimate where not available)

Illustration 6-20

IFRS and Private Entity GAAP Comparison Chart

reflected appropriately in the statements. Care should also be taken to ensure that large and unusual transactions are entered into for bona fide business reasons (e.g., to add value for the shareholders) rather than to make the company's performance look better than it really is.

Looking Ahead

The IASB and FASB are currently studying a new model for revenue recognition. That model has been introduced in this chapter as the contract-based model. At the time of writing, the following issues were still on the table and being discussed:

13 Objective
Discuss current trends in standard setting for revenue recognition.

1. More detailed guidance on measurement including guidance on use of the time value of money, uncertainty due to credit risk and contingent consideration, and other issues. Note that this will likely link in with the work being done on the use of fair value accounting (a separate project).

2. Additional guidance as to how to measure the separate accounting units in multiple element arrangements/bundled sales.

3. How to identify and measure onerous contracts.

4. How to present the rights and obligations under contracts (net or gross).

5. Guidance on when to present revenues as net or gross.

Summary of Learning Objectives

WILEY PLUS
Glossary

1 Understand the economics and legalities of selling transactions from a business perspective.

It is critical to understand a transaction from a business perspective before attempting to account for it. The analysis should begin with what is being sold to the customer (goods or services) and note also the nature and amount of the consideration. When one party is in a better bargaining position than the other, it may be able to negotiate concessions such as more lenient payment terms. These concessions often complicate the accounting as they introduce measurement uncertainty in many cases.

Selling transactions are based on contractual arrangements between a buyer and a seller. Contracts create rights and obligations under law that must be considered when accounting for the transactions. In addition to contractual law, rights and obligations may exist under other forms of the law, e.g., common law or statutory law. These should also be considered.

2 Understand the conceptual difference between an earnings approach and a contract-based approach for accounting purposes.

The earnings approach focuses on the earnings process and how a company adds value whereas the contract-based approach focuses on the creation of contractual rights and obligations created by sales contracts.

3 Identify and apply revenue recognition principles under the earnings approach.

Under this approach, revenue is recognized when performance is substantially complete (risks and rewards have passed and the earnings process is substantially complete and measurable) and collection is reasonably assured.

KEY TERMS

arm's length, 322
balance sheet
    approach, 331
barter or non-monetary
    transactions, 322
billings, 330
bundled sales, 321
collectibility, 337
commercial substance, 322
completed-contract
    method, 330
concessionary (or
    abnormal) terms, 323
consideration, 322
consignment, 337
constructive
    obligation, 325
continuous earnings
    process, 329
continuous sale, 330
contract-based
    approach, 326
cost-to-cost basis, 340

4 Identify and apply revenue recognition principles under the contract-based approach.

Under this approach, there are two recognition points: (1) when to recognize the net contract position, and (2) when to recognize the related revenue in the income statement. The net contract position is first recognized when the contract is entered into. Revenue is recognized when performance occurs. This is when control passes if goods are involved or when the service is provided/performance obligation is extinguished. The accounting should also take into account measurement and collection uncertainty.

5 Discuss issues relating to measurement and measurement uncertainty.

Revenue may only be recognized when measurable. There are many reasons that measurement uncertainty exists including inability to measure the revenue itself (e.g., barter transactions or price protection clauses) and inability to measure costs or uncertainty relating to the outcome of the contract itself (contingencies). In the latter case, extreme uncertainty may indicate that the contract or business deal has not yet been completed. Where the sale involves more than one element, e.g., goods and services, then the selling price must be allocated to the respective parts of the sale using an allocation method such as the relative fair value method or residual method.

6 Understand how to account for sales where there is collection uncertainty.

Collectibility issues also create measurement uncertainty and must be considered when recognizing and measuring sales transactions. When collectibility cannot be assured and/or the related revenue is not measurable in terms of collection or credit risk, then no sale is booked.

7 Prepare journal entries for consignment sales under the earnings and contract-based approaches.

Under the earnings approach, the risks and rewards remain with the seller and, therefore, a real sale does not occur until the goods are sold to a third party. Special accounts separate inventory on consignment. Under the contract-based approach, the consignor contracts with the consignee for selling services. The consignee would book the net contract position and recognize revenues when the services are provided (upon sale to the customer). The consignor would book the sales contract when the contract is entered into by the customer and the revenues when the control to the goods passes to the customer. This would likely result in the same journal entries as under the earnings approach, assuming that the contract is entered into at the same time as when control over the goods sold is passed to the customer.

8 Apply the percentage-of-completion method under the earnings and contract-based approaches.

To apply the percentage-of-completion method to long-term contracts, a basis is needed for measuring the progress toward completion at particular interim dates. One of the most popular input measures that is used to determine the progress toward completion is the cost-to-cost basis. Using this basis, the percentage of completion is measured by comparing costs incurred to date with the most recent estimate of the total costs to complete the contract. The percentage of the total estimated costs that the costs incurred amount to is applied to the total revenue or the estimated total gross profit on the contract to arrive at the revenue or the gross profit amounts to be recognized to date. The journal entries would differ under the earnings approach as compared with the contract-based approach since the net contract position would be recognized when the contract is initially entered into under the latter. There is no need to separately account for billings under the contract-based approach.

9 Apply the completed-contract method under the earnings and contract-based approaches.

Under the earnings approach, revenue and gross profit are recognized only when the contract is completed. Costs of long-term contracts in process and current billings are accumulated, but there are no interim charges or credits to income statement accounts for revenues, costs, and gross profit. The annual entries to record costs of construction, progress billings, and collections from customers would be identical to those for the percentage-of-completion method, with one significant exception: revenue and gross profit are not recognized until the end of the contract.

Under the contract-based approach, this method is not relevant since the net contract would be booked when the contract is entered into and if a customer has been identified, the revenues would be recognized as the services were performed and control over the asset was passed to the customer. Where legal title to the asset being constructed is not passed over to the customer until the end of the contract, the transaction is treated like a sale of goods, with revenue being booked at the end when the goods are "sold." Therefore, the journal entries would be essentially the same as under the percentage-of-completion method (contract-based approach) except for the revenue recognition entries.

10 Understand how to present sales transactions in the income statement.

Transactions where the seller is acting as principal in the sale should be accounted for on a gross basis. Where the seller is acting as an agent (putting buyers and sellers together), the transaction should be booked on a net basis. Consideration should be given to whether the seller has the risks and rewards of ownership of the product being sold.

Transactions are treated as revenues when they relate to ordinary activities of the entity. They are treated as gains when they deal with ancillary activities. In general, revenues and gains are booked to net income except in very limited circumstances. These will be reviewed in later chapters.

11 Identify differences in accounting between accounting standards for private enterprises (private entity GAAP) and IFRS

The main differences are identified in the chart on page 352.

12 Understand the impact of accounting choices on key numbers/ratios.

"Revenues" is a key number on the financial statements. It is used to judge management's job performance and is an indicator of sustainable growth potential. For this reason, revenues are sometimes manipulated in the financial statements. Care should be taken to ensure that the revenues recognized reflect economic reality. Having said this, there are differing conceptual views on when and how revenues should be recognized.

13 Discuss current trends in standard setting for revenue recognition.

IASB and FASB are currently studying a new model for revenue recognition—the contract-based model, which is felt to be conceptually superior.

Brief Exercises

(LO 1) **BE6-1**   Explain the basic economics of what is being received and what is being given up in each of the following business transactions:

(a) A company sells packaging material to another company. The terms of sale require full payment upon delivery.

(b) A company sells packaging material to another company. The terms of sale require payment over one year with interest.

(c) A law firm provides legal services to an accounting firm. In lieu of payment, the accounting firm provides accounting services to the law firm.

(d) A company sells telecommunications equipment for a set fee that includes delivery, installation, 60-day trial period, three years of maintenance, and a one-year manufacturer's warranty. Payment will be received over one year without interest.

(LO 5) **BE6-2**   How should revenue be measured in each business transaction described in BE6-1?

(LO 1, 5) **BE6-3**   XYZ Company has manufactured a new product that will be marketed and sold during the current year. To encourage distributors to carry the product, XYZ will not require payment until the distributor receives the final payment from its customers. This is not a normal business practice for XYZ Company.

Should XYZ record revenue of the new product upon delivery to its distributors? Explain why or why not.

(LO 1) **BE6-4**   Explain the rights and obligations created in the following transactions:

(a) A manufacturer sells goods with terms FOB shipping point.

(b) A manufacturer sells goods with terms FOB destination point.

(c) A manufacturer sells goods with terms FOB shipping point, but routinely replaces products lost or damaged during shipping.

(LO 2, 13) **BE6-5**   Discuss how the contract-based approach to revenue recognition is consistent with the definition of revenues in the conceptual framework discussed in Chapter 2. Explain the main concepts of the earnings approach and the contract-based approach. What are the conceptual differences between the two approaches?

(LO 3) **BE6-6**   What is the earnings process for each of the following scenarios?

(a) A manufacturer that makes and sells farm equipment. The customer picks up the equipment upon purchase. In addition, there is a one-year warranty that will be honoured by another company.

(b) A company that sells books on-line and ships to the customer. Payment is made via credit cards and the company does not accept any product returns.

(c) A company that provides cable television services for residential customers. Customers sign a three-year contract.

(LO 4) **BE6-7**   For each of the scenarios noted in BE6-6 above, when would revenue be recognized under the earnings approach?

(LO 5, 13) **BE6-8**   For each of the scenarios noted in BE6-6 above, when would the net contract position be recognized and when would the revenue be recognized under the contract-based approach?

(LO 6) **BE6-9**   Explain how uncertainty about collectibility would affect your responses to BE6-7 and BE6-8 above.

(LO 5) **BE6-10**   For each of the following scenarios, how will the following circumstances affect the recognition of revenue under the earnings approach and under the contract-based approach?

(a) The anticipated revenues on a contract are $10 million but the associated costs cannot be estimated.

(b) There is a 60-day price protection clause requiring the seller to provide a cash refund to the buyer if the purchase price goes down.

(c) A new product is launched for which the manufacturer will allow unlimited returns.

BE6-11 Finch Industries shipped $550,000 of merchandise on consignment to Royal Crown Company. Finch paid **(LO 7)** freight costs of $5,000. Royal Crown Company paid $1,500 for local advertising, which is reimbursable from Finch. By year end, 75% of the merchandise had been sold for $618,750. Royal Crown notified Finch, retained a 10% commission, and remitted the cash due to Finch.

(a) Prepare all of the journal entries required by Finch for this transaction under the earnings approach.

(b) Explain how the accounting for consignment sales differs under the contract-based approach. Include a discussion of the rights and obligations under the contract in your response.

BE6-12 On August 15, 2010, Japan Ideas consigned 500 electronic play systems, costing $100 each, to YoYo Toys **(LO 7)** Company. The cost of shipping the play systems amounted to $1,250 and was paid by Japan Ideas. On December 31, 2010, an account sales summary was received from the consignee, reporting that 420 play systems had been sold for $160 each. Remittance was made by the consignee for the amount due, after deducting a 20% commission. Compute the following at December 31, 2010:

(a) The inventory value of the units unsold in the hands of the consignee.

(b) The profit for the consignor for the units sold.

(c) The amount of cash that will be remitted by the consignee.

BE6-13 Pennfield Construction Corp. began work on a $5,020,000 construction contract in 2010. During 2010, the **(LO 8)** company incurred costs of $1,600,000, billed its customer for $1,750,000, and collected $1,500,000. At December 31, 2010, the estimated future costs to complete the project total $2,500,000. Assume that Pennfield uses the percentage-of-completion method. Prepare all journal entries required for the year ended December 31, 2010, under the earnings approach.

BE6-14 Using the information provided in BE6-13, prepare all of the required journal entries for the year ended **(LO 8, 13)** December 31, 2010, under the contract-based approach. Compare your responses for BE6-13 and BE6-14 and discuss the differences between the earnings and contract-based approaches.

BE6-15 Using the data from BE6-13, assume that Pennfield cannot reliably measure the outcome of the contract. **(LO 8, 11, 13)** Explain how this transaction would be accounted for under each scenario:

(a) if Pennfield Construction Corp. is reporting under current IFRS (IAS 11 and 18).

(b) if Pennfield Construction Corp. is reporting under private entity GAAP.

BE6-16 Tompa Inc. began work on an $11.5-million contract in 2010 to construct an office building. During 2010, **(LO 9)** Tompa Inc. incurred costs of $3.3 million, billed its customers for $5.1 million, and collected $2.9 million. At December 31, 2010, the estimated future costs to complete the project total $6.0 million. Assuming that Tompa uses the completed contract method, prepare the journal entries for 2010 under the earnings approach.

BE6-17 Using the information provided in BE6-16, explain the accounting under IFRS using the following **(LO 9)** assumptions:

(a) The customer has control over the asset being constructed and can make changes during its construction.

(b) The customer does not have control over the asset being constructed and title only passes at the end of the contract.

BE6-18 Inexperienced construction company ABC Corp. signed a risky contract to build a research facility at a fixed **(LO 8)** contract amount of $2 million. The work began in early 2010 and ABC incurred costs of $900,000. At December 31, 2010, the estimated future costs to complete the project totalled $900,000. During 2011, ABC ran into trouble with weather conditions and incurred costs of $900,000 but estimated that it would need to spend $300,000 to complete the project. During 2012, ABC reluctantly completed the project, incurring further costs of $400,000.

Assuming that ABC uses the percentage-of-completion method and the earnings approach, prepare a schedule to calculate the amount of revenues and gross profit or loss to be recognized by ABC Corp. during the three years of the contract. Provide all journal entries.

BE6-19 Using the information provided in BE6-18, assume instead that ABC uses the completed-contract method and **(LO 9)** the earnings approach. Prepare a schedule to calculate the amount of revenues and gross profit or loss to be recognized by ABC Corp. during the three years of the contract and provide the journal entry for 2011.

(LO 8, 9)   **BE6-20**   Using the information provided in BE6-18, explain the implication of the loss in 2011 under the contract-based approach.

(LO 10)   **BE6-21**   Rancourt Corp. is a real estate company. Approximately 50% of sales are properties that Rancourt owns. In the remaining 50%, Rancourt brokers the transactions by finding buyers for property owned by other companies. Explain how Rancourt should present the revenues from both of these operations.

(LO 11, 13)   **BE6-22**   Compare the accounting for long-term contracts under private entity GAAP and under IFRS.

Exercises

(LO 1)   **E6-1**   **(Economics of the Transaction—Various Consumer Industries)** The following are independent situations that require professional judgement for determining when to recognize revenue from the transactions:

1. Costco sells you a one-year membership with a single, one-time upfront payment. This fee is paid at the time of signing the contract, is non-refundable, and entitles you to shop at Costco for one year.

2. DOT Home and Patio sells you patio furniture on a "no money down, no interest, and no payments for one year" promotional deal. The furniture is delivered to your home the same day.

3. The Toronto Blue Jays sell season tickets on-line to games in the Rogers Centre. Fans can purchase the tickets at any time, although the season does not officially begin until April 1. The season runs from April 1 through October each year. Payment is due in full at the time of purchase.

4. CIBC lends you money in August. The loan and interest are repayable in full in two years.

5. Students pre-register for fall classes at Seneca College in August. The fall term runs from September through December.

6. Sears sells you a sweater. In August, you place the order using Sears' on-line catalogue. The sweater is shipped and arrives in September and you charge it to your Sears credit card. In October, you receive the Sears credit card statement and pay the amount due.

7. In March, Hometown Appliances sells a washing machine with an extended warranty plan for five years. The washing machine will not be delivered to the customer until June. Payment is due upon delivery.

8. Premier Health Clubs sells you a membership with an initiation fee (which covers a medical assessment) and an ongoing monthly fee. The initiation fee is payable at the time of the medical assessment and approximates the cost of the medical assessment.

Instructions

For each scenario, identify what is being "sold": goods, services, or a combination.

(LO 2, 3)   **E6-2**   **(Revenue Recognition under Earnings Approach—Various Consumer Industries)**

Instructions

(a) Explain the principles for revenue recognition under the earnings approach.

(b) For each scenario noted in E6-1, discuss when revenue should be recognized under the earnings approach. Provide the journal entries that would be recorded to recognize the revenue under the earnings approach.

(LO 2, 4, 13)   **E6-3**   **(Revenue Recognition under Contract-Based Approach—Various Consumer Industries)**

Instructions

(a) Explain the revenue recognition principles under the contract-based approach.

(b) Compare the earnings approach and the contract-based approach.

(c) For each of the scenarios in E6-1, explain how the initial net contract position would be recognized and when the related revenue would be recognized under the contract-based approach. Provide journal entries to support your explanation.

(LO 1, 5, 6)   **E6-4**   **(Revenue Recognition—Measurement and Collection Uncertainty)** Genesis Corporation is an equipment manufacturing company.

Instructions

(a) How should revenue be recorded under the earnings and contract-based approaches if Genesis has a normal business practice of offering customers a one-year payment term?

(b) How would your response to (a) change if Genesis were a new company?

(c) How would your response to (a) change if Genesis started offering deep discounts and extending payment terms to five years?

E6-5 (Revenue Recognition under Both Approaches—Collection Uncertainty) Paradise Corporation had sales of $254,000 in fiscal 2010. Assume that $100,000 of this amount are layaway sales where the customer makes payments over time, but will only receive the goods upon final payment. **(LO 2, 6, 13)**

Instructions

(a) How would this transaction be recorded under the earnings approach?

(b) How would this transaction be recorded under the contract-based approach?

(c) Assume that customers provide a 50% deposit and the company has experience with these sales, with the majority of customers making the final payment and taking possession of their goods. How would your response change in parts (a) and (b)?

E6-6 (Bill and Hold Transaction under Both Approaches) Dave Scotland Inc. (DSI) sold inventory to a new customer, CSI, on December 20, 2010. The sale was made at a significant discount to induce the customer to switch from its regular supplier. CSI asked DSI not to ship the inventory until January 2, 2011, because CSI's warehouse was shutting down for the holidays. DSI agreed and decided to leave the inventory on its warehouse shelves with unsold inventory. It was felt that the shipment would be in the way if it was left on the shipping docks and that the shipping department could easily get the inventory ready for shipment on January 2. **(LO 2, 3, 4)**

Instructions

(a) Discuss whether the transaction should be booked as a sale in the December 31, 2010, financial statements under the earnings approach.

(b) Discuss whether the transaction should be booked as a sale in the December 31, 2010, financial statements under the contract-based approach.

E6-7 (Transactions with Customer Acceptance Provisions under Both Approaches) Consider the following unrelated situations: **(LO 1, 2, 5, 6)**

1. Book of the Week Limited sends out books to potential customers on a trial basis. If the customers do not like the books, they can return them at no cost.

2. Sea Clothing Company Inc. has a return policy that allows customers to return merchandise in good order for a full refund within 30 days of purchase.

3. Shivani Inc. sells machinery to manufacturers. Customers have the right to inspect the equipment upon delivery and may return it if certain customer-specific requirements for size and weight are not met.

Instructions

(a) Explain the implications of customer acceptance provisions for revenue transactions.

(b) Indicate the point at which these transactions may be recognized as sales under both the earnings and contract-based approaches.

(c) Review your responses to (b) and discuss the differences between the earnings and contract-based approaches.

E6-8 (Consignment Calculations under Both Approaches) On May 3, 2010, Brown Motors Limited consigned 80 motorcycles, costing $25,000 each, to Mississauga Motors Inc. The total cost of shipping the motorcycles was $5,800 and was paid by Brown Motors. On December 30, 2010, an account sales report was received from the consignee, reporting that 37 motorcycles had been sold for $33,500 each. A remittance was made by the consignee for the amount due, after deducting a commission of 6%, advertising costs of $3,200, and total inspection costs of $4,200 on the motorcycles sold. Assume that Brown Motors recognizes revenue under the earnings approach. **(LO 2, 7)**

Instructions

(a) Calculate the inventory value of the unsold units that are in the hands of the consignee.

(b) Calculate the consignor's profit on the units sold.

(c) Calculate the amount of cash that will be remitted by the consignee.

(d) Explain the accounting for consignment sales under the contract-based approach.

(LO 7) **E6-9** **(Consignment Sales)** Chang Industries ships merchandise costing $120,000 on consignment to XYZ Inc. Chang pays the freight of $5,000. XYZ Inc. is to receive a 15% commission upon sale and a 5% allowance to offset its advertising expenses. At the end of the period, XYZ notifies Chang that 75% of the merchandise has been sold for $160,000.

Instructions

Record the entries required by the two companies under the earnings-based approach, noting any differences that might exist if the contract-based approach were used.

(LO 3, 4, 10, 12) **E6-10** **(Revenue Recognition on Marina Sales with Discounts)** Seaport Marina has 500 slips that rent for $1,000 per season. Payments must be made in full at the start of the boating season, April 1. Slips may be reserved for the next season if they are paid for by December 31. Under a new policy, if payment is made by December 31, a 5% discount is allowed. The boating season ends on October 31, and the marina has a December 31 year end. To provide cash flow for major dock repairs, the marina operator is also offering a 25% discount on the fees for a second season if the second season is also paid for before December 31 of the current year.

For the fiscal year ended December 31, 2010, all 500 slips were rented at full price. Two hundred slips were reserved and paid for in advance of the 2011 boating season, and 160 slips were reserved and paid for in advance of the 2012 boating season.

Instructions

(a) Explain how revenue would be recorded for the 2011 and 2012 sales in fiscal 2010 under the earnings and contract-based approach.

(b) Prepare the appropriate journal entries for fiscal 2010.

(c) If Seaport Marina had not offered a discount of 25% for the 2012 boating season, it would have received the annual fee of $1,000 per slip on April 1, 2012. Calculate the real cost of the discount given by Seaport Marina. Express the cost as an annual percentage so that it can be compared fairly with alternative sources of financing.

(LO 5) **E6-11** **(Bundled Sales under Both Approaches)** Louis Manufacturing Inc. (LMI) purchased some telecommunications equipment in January of the current year. The equipment normally sells for $2,300. In order to induce LMI to close the deal, the salesperson offered LMI related services that normally sell for $1,000. The services allow LMI to access the Internet for the next year. The equipment and services were bundled together and LMI was charged $2,700 for the whole thing—a great deal. There is a general right of return but LMI has already taken delivery of the equipment and has started using it. All is working well and LMI is very happy with the service.

Instructions

(a) Explain how bundled sales are accounted for under the earnings and contract-based approaches.

(b) Calculate how revenue would be allocated to the separate units in the transaction under the relative fair value method.

(c) Calculate how revenue would be allocated to the separate units in the transaction under the residual method, assuming:

1. the value of the equipment is known but the value of the service is unknown.

2. the value of the Internet service is known but the value of the equipment is unknown.

(LO 8, 10) **E6-12** **(Analysis of Percentage-of-Completion Method Financial Statements)** In 2010, Aldcorn Construction Corp. began construction work on a three-year, $10-million contract. Aldcorn uses the percentage-of-completion method for financial accounting purposes. The income to be recognized each year is based on the proportion of costs incurred out of the total estimated costs for completing the contract. The financial statement presentations for this contract at December 31, 2010, are as follows:

Balance Sheet		
Accounts receivable—construction contract billings		$996,500
Construction in progress	$2,015,000	
Less contract billings	1,236,500	
Cost of uncompleted contract in excess of billings		778,500
Income Statement		
Income (before tax) on the contract recognized in 2010		$863,629

Instructions

Under the earnings approach:

(a) How much cash was collected in 2010 on this contract?

(b) What was the initial estimated total gross profit before tax on this contract?

(c) What is the relationship between the balances in the Construction in Progress and Contract Billings accounts during the contract? Is one always more than the other? Is there a predictable ratio between the two account balances during the progress of the contract?

(AICPA adapted)

E6-13 (Gross Profit on Uncompleted Contract) On April 1, 2010, Lisboa Limited entered into a cost-plus-fixed-fee **(LO 8)** contract to construct an electric generator for Martinez Corporation. At the contract date, Lisboa estimated that it would take two years to complete the project at a cost of $6.5 million. The fixed fee that is stipulated in the contract is $1.5 million. Lisboa chooses appropriately to account for this contract under the percentage-of-completion method. During 2010, Lisboa incurred costs of $2.7 million related to the project. The estimated cost at December 31, 2010, to complete the contract is $4.9 million. Martinez was billed $600,000 under the contract.

Instructions

Under the earnings approach, prepare a schedule to calculate the amount of gross profit that Lisboa should recognize under the contract for the year ended December 31, 2010. Show supporting calculations in good form.

(AICPA adapted)

E6-14 (Recognition of Profit—Percentage-of-Completion Method) In 2010, Ronaldo Construction Inc. agreed to **(LO 8)** construct an apartment building at a price of $10 million. Information on the costs and billings for the first two years of this contract is as follows:

	2010	2011
Costs incurred in the period	$2,180,000	$3,100,000
Estimated costs yet to be incurred	4,300,000	1,700,000
Customer billings in the period	3,000,000	4,000,000
Collection of billings to date	2,000,000	4,000,000

Instructions

Assume the earnings approach is used.

(a) For the percentage-of-completion method, (1) calculate the amount of gross profit to be recognized in 2010 and 2011, and (2) prepare journal entries for 2010 and 2011.

(b) For 2010 and 2011, show how the details related to this construction contract would be disclosed on the balance sheet and on the income statement.

E6-15 (Recognition of Profit—Percentage-of-Completion Method)   **(LO 8)**

Instructions

Using the information from E6-14, for the contract-based approach:

(a) Prepare a schedule of the gross profit to be recorded for each year of the contract.

(b) Prepare the journal entries under the contract-based approach for fiscal 2010.

(c) Show how the contract would be disclosed in the 2010 income statement.

(d) Compare your responses to E6-14 and E6-15 and discuss some of the differences between the earnings and contract-based approaches.   **(LO 8, 9, 13)**

E6-16 (Recognition of Profit on Long-Term Contracts and Entries) During 2010, Antoinette started a construction job with a contract price of $2.5 million. The job was completed in 2012 and information for the three years of construction is as follows:

	2010	2011	2012
Costs incurred to date	$1,050,000	$1,555,000	$1,785,000
Estimated costs to complete	850,000	175,000	–0–
Billings to date	1,000,000	1,900,000	2,500,000
Collections to date	770,000	1,810,000	2,500,000

Instructions

Under the earnings approach:

(a) Calculate the amount of gross profit that should be recognized each year under the percentage-of-completion method.

(b) Prepare all necessary journal entries for 2010, 2011, and 2012, including closing the contract accounts upon completion of the contract, assuming the percentage-of-completion method is used.

(c) Calculate the amount of gross profit that should be recognized each year under the completed-contract method.

(d) Prepare the necessary entry in 2012 to close the contract accounts and to recognize the revenues and costs upon completion, assuming the completed-contract method is used.

(e) Assume that Antoinette cannot reliably measure the outcome of the contract. Explain how this transaction would be accounted for under each scenario:

    1. If Antoinette is reporting under current IFRS (IAS 11 and 18).

    2. If Antoinette is reporting under private entity GAAP.

(LO 8, 9) **E6-17**   **(Recognition of Profit on Long-Term Contracts and Entries)**

Instructions

Using the same information as provided in E6-16, but assuming use of the contract-based approach, prepare a schedule of the gross profit to be recorded for each year of the contract and provide the journal entries for:

(a) percentage-of-completion method

(b) completed contract method

(LO 8, 9) **E6-18**   **(Recognition of Gross Profit on Long-Term Contract with Loss and Entries)** During 2010, Darwin Corporation started a construction job with a contract price of $4.2 million. Darwin ran into severe technical difficulties during construction but managed to complete the job in 2012. The following information is available:

	2010	2011	2012
Costs incurred to date	$ 600,000	$2,100,000	$4,100,000
Estimated costs to complete	3,150,000	2,100,000	–0–

Instructions

Under the earnings approach:

(a) Calculate the amount of gross profit that should be recognized each year under the percentage-of-completion method.

(b) Prepare the journal entries for 2011 to recognize the revenue from the contract, assuming the percentage-of-completion method is used. Explain the treatment of losses under the earnings approach for percentage-of-completion.

(c) Calculate the amount of gross profit or loss that should be recognized each year under the completed-contract method. Explain the treatment of losses under the earnings approach for completed-contract.

(d) Prepare the necessary entry in 2012 to close the contract accounts and to recognize the revenues and costs upon completion, assuming the completed-contract method is used.

(LO 8, 9) **E6-19**   **(Recognition of Gross Profit on Long-Term Contract with Loss and Entries)**

Instructions

Using the information provided in E6-18, but assuming use of the contract-based approach:

(a) Prepare a schedule of the gross profit to be recorded for each year of the contract.

(b) Provide the journal entries for 2010 for the percentage-of-completion method.

(c) Explain the treatment of losses on long-term contracts under the contract-based approach.

(LO 8, 9) **E6-20**   **(Recognition of Profit and Balance Sheet Amounts for Long-Term Contracts)** Venetian Construction Corp. began operations on January 1, 2010. During the year, Venetian entered into a contract with Ravi Corp. to construct a manufacturing facility. At that time, Venetian estimated that it would take five years to complete the facility at a total cost of $7.6 million. The total contract price to construct the facility is $11.9 million. During the year, Venetian incurred $3,648,000 in construction costs on the project. The estimated cost to complete the contract is $4,452,000. Venetian billed Ravi for 30% of the contract price and Ravi paid the amount.

Instructions

Assuming that Venetian Construction Corp. uses the earnings approach, prepare schedules to calculate the amount of gross profit to be recognized and the amount to be shown as cost of uncompleted contract in excess of related billings or billings on uncompleted contract in excess of related costs for fiscal 2010, under each of the following methods:

(a) completed-contract method

(b) percentage-of-completion method

Show supporting calculations in good form.

(AICPA adapted)

E6-21 **(Long-Term Contract Reporting)** Vaneeta Construction Ltd. began operations in 2010. Construction activity **(LO 9)** for the first year follows. All contracts are with different customers, and any work remaining at December 31, 2010, is expected to be completed in 2011.

Project	Total Contract Price	Billings through 12/31/10	Cash Collections through 12/31/10	Contract Costs Incurred through 12/31/10	Estimated Additional Costs to Complete
1	$3,360,000	$2,260,000	$2,040,000	$2,450,000	$1,070,000
2	2,670,000	1,220,000	1,210,000	1,126,000	504,000
3	750,000	600,000	500,000	435,000	–0–
	$6,780,000	$4,080,000	$3,750,000	$4,011,000	$1,574,000

Instructions

Under the earnings approach, prepare a partial income statement and balance sheet to indicate how the above information would be reported in the financial statements. Assume that Vaneeta Construction uses the completed-contract method.

E6-22 **(Recognition of Revenue on Long-Term Contract and Entries)** Van Horn Construction Corp. uses the **(LO 8, 9)** percentage-of-completion method of accounting. In 2010, Van Horn began work under contract #SG-OO1, which provided for a contract price of $5.2 million. Other details follow:

	2010	2011
Costs incurred during the year	$1,750,000	$1,315,000
Estimated costs to complete, as at December 31	1,050,000	–0–
Billings during the year	3,420,000	1,780,000
Collections during the year	3,350,000	1,850,000

Instructions

Under the earnings approach:

(a) What portion of the total contract price would be recognized as revenue in 2010? In 2011?

(b) Assuming the same facts as those above except that the company uses the completed-contract method of accounting, what portion of the total contract price would be recognized as revenue in 2011?

(c) Prepare a complete set of journal entries for 2010 and 2011 under the percentage-of-completion method, including the entries for closing the contract.

(d) Prepare a complete set of journal entries for 2010 and 2011 under the completed-contract method.

E6-23 **(Sales with Discounts)** On June 3, Wonka Corp. sold $27,000 of merchandise to Tony Riddell, terms 2/10, **(LO 10, 12)** n/60, FOB shipping point. An invoice totalling $1,520, terms n/30, was received by Riddell on June 8 from Flame Transport Service for the freight cost. When it received the goods on June 5, Riddell notified Wonka that merchandise costing $4,000 contained flaws that made it worthless. The same day, Wonka issued a credit memo covering the worthless merchandise and asked that it be returned at the company's expense. The freight on the returned merchandise was $150, and was paid by Wonka on June 7. On June 12, the company received a cheque for the balance due from Riddell.

Instructions

(a) Prepare journal entries on Wonka's books to record all the events noted above under each of the following bases:

1. Sales and receivables are entered at gross selling price.

2. Sales and receivables are entered net of cash discounts.

(b) Prepare the journal entry under basis 2, assuming that Riddell did not remit payment until August 5.

(c) Which method would give Wonka's general manager better reports and details for managing the business?

(LO 12)   E6-24   (Impact of Accounting Choices on Financial Statement Numbers) The Comfort-Zone Company specializes in the installation of heating, ventilation, and air conditioning in large projects such as domed stadiums, military bases, airports, and multi-storeyed buildings. Its contracts usually take two to three years to complete and, at any fiscal year end, this work-in-process (WIP) inventory represents a sizable percentage of its assets. The company is privately held and has a senior management group whose compensation is based almost entirely on the earnings results for the year. As the CFO, you have been reviewing the year-end WIP figures, which have been estimated using the percentage-of-completion method. These estimates have been provided to you by the project managers responsible for the completion of the various contracts.

This year has not been as successful or as active as previous ones and the two senior founders of the company have asked you to bring in a net income figure at least equal to the last couple of years. In your mind, you know that the project managers' estimates are somewhat fluid and you have been contemplating making the requested adjustments.

Instructions

How would you handle the request of the two senior founders?

Problems

P6-1   Soorya Enterprises sells a corporate monitoring system that includes the hardware, software, and monitoring services and annual maintenance for three years for a fixed price of $750,000. The new controller would like to understand the accounting for this transaction under both the contract-based approach and the earnings approach.

Instructions

(a) Explain the principles for recognizing revenues under the earnings and contract-based approaches. Be sure to focus on the areas of difference between the two approaches.

(b) Explain the impact of collection and measurement uncertainty for revenue recognition under the earnings and contract-based approaches.

(c) Explain how this transaction should be accounted for under the earnings and contract-based approaches.

(d) Calculate how much revenue would be recorded under the following independent assumptions:

1. The fair values of the items are known and are as follows: hardware and software are approximately $650,000; monitoring services are $150,000 for the three-year period; and the maintenance is $75,000 for the three-year period.

2. The fair value of hardware and software is not determinable but the fair value of the monitoring services is $150,000 for the three-year period and the fair value of the maintenance is $75,000 for the three-year period.

3. The fair value of the hardware and software approximates $650,000, but the fair value of the monitoring and annual maintenance cannot be established.

4. Soorya offers a delayed payment program under which payments may be made over the three-year service period of the contract.

P6-2   Daisy Construction Ltd. has entered into a contract beginning January 1, 2010, to build a parking complex. It has estimated that the complex will cost $8 million and will take three years to construct.

The complex will be billed to the purchasing company at $11 million. The details are as follows:

	2010	2011	2012
Costs to date	$3,060,000	$6,435,000	$ 9,300,000
Estimated costs to complete	4,595,000	2,656,000	–0–
Progress billings to date	4,000,000	6,300,000	11,000,000
Cash collected to date	3,500,000	5,000,000	11,000,000

Instructions

Under the earnings approach:

(a) Using the percentage-of-completion method, calculate the estimated gross profit that would be recognized during each year of the construction period.

(b) Prepare all necessary journal entries for 2010 to 2012, including the entries for closing the contract accounts upon completion, assuming the percentage-of-completion method is used.

(c) Prepare a partial comparative income statement for the fiscal years ending December 31, 2010 and 2011.

(d) Prepare a balance sheet at December 31, 2010 and 2011, that shows the accounts related to the contract and includes their classifications assuming the percentage-of-completion method is used.

(e) Calculate the estimated gross profit that would be recognized during each year of the construction period if the completed-contract method is used. Prepare a partial income statement for the fiscal year ending December 31, 2012.

(f) Prepare the necessary entry in 2012 to close the contract accounts and to recognize the revenues and costs upon completion, assuming the completed-contract method is used.

(g) Prepare a balance sheet at December 31, 2010 and 2011, that shows the accounts related to the contract and includes their classifications assuming the completed-contract method is used.

(h) Assume that Daisy Construction cannot reliably measure the outcome of the contract. Explain how this transaction would be accounted for under each scenario:

    1. If Daisy is reporting under current IFRS (IAS 11 and 18).

    2. If Daisy is reporting under private entity GAAP.

P6-3   Using the information provided in P6-2, for the contract-based approach:

Instructions

(a) Prepare a schedule of the gross profit for each year of the contract.

(b) Prepare the journal entries for 2010.

(c) Show a partial income statement for 2010.

(d) Compare your responses to P6-2 and P6-3 and discuss some of the differences between the earnings and contract-based approaches.

P6-4   Granite Construction Ltd. has entered into a contract beginning January 1, 2010, to build a bridge in Tuktoyuktuk Shores. It estimates that the bridge will cost $14.8 million and will take three years to construct.
    The bridge will be billed to the municipality at $15.5 million. The following data are for the construction period:

	2010	2011	2012
Costs to date	$ 4,500,000	$13,790,000	$15,700,000
Estimated costs to complete	10,500,000	1,934,000	–0–
Progress billings to date	4,600,000	10,000,000	15,500,000
Cash collected to date	3,000,000	9,000,000	15,500,000

Instructions

Under the earnings approach:

(a) Using the percentage-of-completion method, calculate the estimated gross profit or loss that would be recognized during each year of the construction period.

(b) Prepare all necessary journal entries for 2010 to 2012, including the entries for closing the contract accounts upon completion, assuming the percentage-of-completion method is used.

(c) Prepare a partial comparative income statement for the fiscal years ending December 31, 2010 and 2011.

(d) Prepare a balance sheet at December 31, 2010 and 2011, that shows the accounts related to the contract and includes their classifications assuming the percentage-of-completion method is used.

(e) Calculate the estimated gross profit or loss that would be recognized during each year of the construction period under the completed-contract method. Prepare any necessary entries to accrue contract losses (note the year the entry would be made) for the year ending December 31, 2010. Prepare partial income statements for the fiscal years ending December 31, 2011 and 2012.

(f) Prepare the necessary entry in 2012 to close the contract accounts and to recognize the revenues and costs upon completion, assuming the completed-contract method is used.

(g) Prepare a balance sheet at December 31, 2010 and 2011, that shows the accounts related to the contract and includes their classifications assuming the completed-contract method is used.

P6-5   Using the information in P6-4, explain the treatment of losses on long-term contracts under the contract-based approach.

P6-6   Vaughan Construction Ltd. has entered into a contract beginning in February 2010 to build two warehouses for Atlantis Structures Ltd. The contract has a fixed price of $9.5 million. The following data are for the construction period:

	2010	2011	2012
Costs for the year	$3,825,000	$4,675,000	$1,300,000
Estimated costs to complete	4,675,000	1,270,000	–0–
Progress billings to date	3,500,000	7,600,000	9,500,000
Cash collected to date	3,100,000	7,250,000	9,350,000

Instructions

Under the earnings approach:

(a) Using the percentage-of-completion method, calculate the estimated gross profit that should be recognized during each year of the construction period.

(b) Prepare all necessary journal entries for 2010 to 2012, including the entries to close the contract accounts upon completion, assuming the percentage-of-completion method is used.

(c) Prepare a partial comparative income statement for the fiscal years ending December 31, 2010 to 2012, assuming the percentage-of-completion method is used.

(d) Prepare a balance sheet at December 31, 2010 and 2011, that shows the accounts related to the contract and includes their classifications, assuming the percentage-of-completion method is used.

(e) Calculate the estimated gross profit or loss that should be recognized during each year of the construction period, assuming the completed-contract method is used. Prepare any necessary entries to accrue contract losses (note the year the entry would be made). Prepare a partial income statement for the fiscal year ending December 31, 2012.

(f) Prepare the necessary entry in 2012 to close the contract accounts and to recognize the revenues and costs upon completion, assuming the completed-contract method is used.

(g) Prepare a balance sheet at December 31, 2010 and 2011, that shows the accounts related to the contract and includes their classifications, assuming the completed-contract method is used.

P6-7   Unique Construction Inc. entered into a firm fixed-price contract with A-One Clinic on July 1, 2010, to construct a multi-storey medical office. At that time, Unique Construction estimated that it would take between two and three years to complete the project. The total contract price is $5.5 million. Unique Construction chooses appropriately to account for this contract under the completed-contract method in its financial statements and for income tax reporting. The building was deemed substantially completed on December 31, 2012.

The estimated percentage of completion, accumulated contract costs incurred, estimated costs to complete the contract, and accumulated billings to the clinic under the contract were as follows:

	Dec. 31, 2010	Dec. 31, 2011	Dec. 31, 2012
Percentage of completion	30%	71.10%	100%
Contract costs incurred to date	$1,140,000	$4,055,000	$5,800,000
Estimated costs to complete the contract	$2,660,000	$1,645,000	–0–
Billings to A-One Clinic	$1,500,000	$2,500,000	$5,500,000

Instructions

Under the earnings approach:

(a) Prepare schedules to calculate the amount to be shown as "cost of uncompleted contract in excess of related billings" or "billings on uncompleted contract in excess of related costs" at December 31, 2010, 2011, and 2012. Ignore income taxes. Show supporting calculations in good form.

(b) Prepare schedules to calculate the profit or loss that should be recognized from this contract for the years ended December 31, 2010, 2011, and 2012. Ignore income taxes. Show supporting calculations in good form.

(c) Assume a construction company had all of the information that it required to use the percentage-of-completion method for construction contracts. Why would this company want to account for contracts using the completed-contract method?

(AICPA adapted)

P6-8   Jupiter Inc. was established in 1985 by Spacey Jupiter and initially operated under contracts to build highly energy-efficient, customized homes. In the 1990s, Jupiter's two daughters joined the firm and expanded the company's activities into the high-rise apartment and commercial markets. When the company's long-time financial manager retired, Jupiter's daughters hired Meteorite Williams as controller. Meteorite, a former university friend of Jupiter's daughters, had been working for a public accounting firm for the last four years.

When he reviewed the company's accounting practices, Meteorite noticed that the company followed the completed-contract method of revenue recognition, as it always had since the years when individual home building was the company's main focus. Several years ago, most of the company's activities shifted to the high-rise and commercial building areas. From land acquisition to the completion of construction, most building contracts now cover several years. Under the circumstances, Meteorite believes that the company should follow the percentage-of-completion method of accounting. From a typical building contract, Meteorite developed the following data:

JUPITER INC.

Contract price: $10,000,000

	2010	2011	2012
Estimated costs	$2,010,000	$4,015,000	$1,675,000
Progress billings to date	2,000,000	2,500,000	5,500,000
Cash collections	1,800,000	2,300,000	5,900,000

Instructions

Under the earnings approach:

(a) Explain the difference between completed-contract revenue recognition and percentage-of-completion revenue recognition.

(b) Using the data provided for Jupiter Inc. and assuming the percentage-of-completion method of revenue recognition is used, calculate the company's revenue and gross profit for 2010 to 2012, under each of the following circumstances:

1. Assume that all costs are incurred, all billings to customers are made, and all collections from customers are received within 30 days of billing as planned.

2. Further assume that, as a result of unforeseen local ordinances and the fact that the building site was in a wetlands area, the company had cost overruns of $1.2 million in 2010 to pay for changes to the site so that it would comply with the ordinances and overcome wetlands barriers to construction.

3. Further assume that, in addition to the cost overruns of $1.2 million for this contract, inflationary factors were greater than what was anticipated when the original contract cost was set and caused an additional cost overrun of $1,240,000 in 2011. No cost overruns are expected to occur in 2012.

(CMA adapted)

P6-9   On March 1, 2010, Wilma Limited signed a contract to construct a factory building for Slate Construction Manufacturing Inc. for a total contract price of $9.4 million. The building was completed by October 31, 2012. The annual contract costs that were incurred, the estimated costs to complete the contract, and the accumulated billings to Slate Construction were as follows:

	2010	2011	2012
Contract costs incurred during the year	$1,600,000	$5,000,000	$2,200,000
Estimated costs to complete the contract at Dec. 31	4,800,000	2,084,000	–0–
Billings to Slate Construction during the year	2,000,000	5,100,000	2,300,000
Cash collections from Slate Construction during the year	1,950,000	4,900,000	2,550,000

Instructions

Under the earnings approach:

(a) Using the percentage-of-completion method, prepare schedules to calculate the profit or loss that should be recognized from this contract for the years ended December 31, 2010 to 2012.

(b) Using the completed-contract method, prepare schedules to calculate the profit or loss that should be recognized from this contract for the years ended December 31, 2010 to 2012.

(c) Prepare all necessary journal entries for 2010 to 2012, including the entries to close the contract accounts upon completion, assuming the completed-contract method is used.

P6-10

Instructions

Using the information provided in P6-9 and applying the contract-based approach:

(a) Prepare a schedule of the gross profit for each year of the contract under the percentage-of-completion method.

(b) Prepare the journal entries for 2010 and show the partial income statement.

P6-11   You have been engaged by Ashely Corp. to advise it on the proper accounting for a series of long-term contracts. Ashely began doing business on January 1, 2010, and its construction activities for the first year of operations are shown below. All contract costs are with different customers, and any work that remains to be done at December 31, 2010, is expected to be completed in 2011.

Project	Total Contract Price	Billings through 12/31/10	Cash Collections through 12/31/10	Contract Costs Incurred through 12/31/10	Estimated Additional Costs to Complete
A	$ 300,000	$200,000	$180,000	$248,000	$ 67,000
B	350,000	110,000	105,000	67,800	271,200
C	280,000	280,000	255,000	186,000	–0–
D	200,000	35,000	25,000	123,000	87,000
E	240,000	205,000	200,000	185,000	15,000
	$1,370,000	$830,000	$765,000	$809,800	$440,200

Instructions

Assuming that Ashely Corp. uses the earnings approach:

(a) Using the percentage-of-completion method, prepare a schedule to calculate gross profit or loss to be reported, unbilled contract costs and recognized profit, and billings in excess of costs and recognized profit.

(b) Prepare a partial income statement and balance sheet to show how the information would be reported for financial statement purposes.

(c) Repeat the requirements for part (a), under the completed-contract method.

(d) Using information from your answers to the previous questions, prepare a brief report that compares the conceptual features (both positive and negative) of the two revenue recognition methods.

Writing Assignments

WA6-1   The IASB is proposing a new approach to revenue recognition: the contract-based approach.

Instructions

Refer to the IASB's discussion paper "Preliminary Views on Revenue Recognition in Contracts with Customers" from December 2008, available on the IASB website at www.iasb.org. For each of the following cases, discuss how the performance obligation under the contract-based approach would be determined, and when revenue would be recognized. Point out any issues that might arise with this assessment.

(a) A telecom company offers the following plan to a customer: If the customer signs up for a three-year contract, the company will provide the Pear phone for $150 and a monthly service for a fee of $65 per month, which includes unlimited text messaging and phone calls within Canada. The customer must pay $150 at the time of signing the contract for the phone, and the initial monthly service fee of $65. For each subsequent month, the customer will be invoiced, at the beginning of the month, the $65 service fee. A further condition of this contract is that if the customer signs up for any additional services (up to three new services are currently available) with the telecom company, the company will reduce the monthly phone service fee by 10% for each new service added. And finally, the telecom company will also replace the phone if it is broken or does not work at any time during the 36 months, no questions asked. History has shown that on previous models of this Pear phone, 60% of warranty claims arose in the first six months, and the remaining warranty claims occurred evenly over the remaining 30 months. The monthly service fee is comparable to similar plans provided by the company. The Pear phone is sold separately for $600. The company also separately sells warranty programs for similar phones. The company pays commission to the salesperson at the time the contract is signed and this commission is non-refundable. The cost of the Pear phones to the company is $300 each.

(b) On January 1, 2009, Software Writer Co. signs a contract with a customer to design and construct a customized system and then to host the software system and process all the data. The total contract is for $1.2 million to design and construct the system, $500,000 for the software and any customized adaptations required, and then a monthly processing fee based on the volume of data processed, with a minimum price of $20,000 per month. The contract is to run for five years, and may be renewed at the end of five years, if both parties are agreeable. The customer will be able to renew at a price of 10% below the prevailing market price at the time. It has been decided that the customer will pay $140,000 at the signing of the contract and make progress payments of $65,000 every month throughout the two years to design and construct the system. Completion of the customized system is expected to be in 24 months. The software will be installed one month after that, and training for the personnel will run for another four months. Processing of data will begin March 1, 2011, and end December 31, 2013. Each system that the company designs is unique, and similar systems and services are not provided to other customers. The cash flows under the contract are non-refundable.

WA6-2 Franchise contracts are complex contractual arrangements with many and various parts.

Instructions

Access the Accounting Guideline (AcG) 2 – Franchise Fee Revenue from the Canadian Institute of Chartered Accountants Standards and Guidance Collection – Accounting Handbook – Accounting Guidelines. (This guideline can be accessed through Knotia, available through your school's library database.) Answer the following questions.

(a) What is a franchise?

(b) Using the information provided in the guideline, compare the accounting guidance given in this guideline for reporting and measuring the franchisee fee revenue with the general principles for revenue recognition. Address each issue separately, highlighting similarities and differences between the guidance and application of the general revenue principles.

WA6-3 The IASB is currently considering additional guidance on reporting revenues when other parties are involved in providing goods and services to a company's customer. The Board has been deliberating the conditions that must be present for a company to record revenue at the gross amount collected from the customer or the net amount the company keeps after reimbursing the other party for any related goods or services.

Instructions

Answer the following questions with respect to the gross versus net revenue issue:

(a) How can the contract-based model be applied to determine whether the revenues charged to customers should be at the gross amount collected from the customer or the net amount the company keeps after reimbursing the other party for any goods or services?

(b) What indicators might be used to signify that a company should record the revenue at the gross amount?

(c) What indicators might be used to signify that a company should record the revenue at the net amount?

(d) Apply the above discussions to the following scenario to determine if the company should report at gross or net revenue:

Office Supply Co. sells office supplies and office furniture. The company keeps catalogues from five different furniture suppliers on hand and customers make their orders from these catalogues. Once the order is received from the supplier, Office Supply Co. will take title on delivery of the shipment and the amount will go into inventory until shipped to the customer. There is no other inventory kept on hand except some showroom pieces that are not for sale. Office Supply Co. invoices the customer, and the customer must pay within 60 days of delivery and installation of the furniture. At the point of delivery to the customer's premises, the customer takes title to the furniture. The supplier sets the selling price to the customer, as detailed in the catalogue. Office Supply Co. is allowed to keep 25% of the sale price and remits the difference to the supplier. Office Supply Co. also charges for installation, and keeps this full amount. Office Supply Co. must pay the supplier for the furniture even if the customer has not yet paid. At the time of the sale, the customer is told that if there are any issues that arise after the sale dealing with damage, quality, wrong colour, wrong size, etc., they may contact Office Supply Co., which will, in turn, contact the supplier to resolve the problem.

WA6-4 The IASB proposes in its discussion paper on revenue recognition ("Preliminary Views on Revenue Recognition in Contracts with Customers," issued in December 2008) to use a single, contract-based revenue recognition standard. This proposal would eliminate IAS 18, which is a separate standard for construction contracts.

Instructions

Discuss the issues that might arise for a construction company in trying to apply the new proposed model. (Hint: Download the PricewaterhouseCoopers report "Engineering Change: Potential Impact of Revenue Recognition on the Engineering and Construction Industry" from July 2009. This is available from www.pwc.com.)

WA6-5   The IASB discussion paper on revenue recognition discusses how onerous contracts should be reported and measured.

Instructions

Refer to the IASB's discussion paper "Preliminary Views on Revenue Recognition in Contracts with Customers" from December 2008, available on the IASB website at www.iasb.org. Answer the following questions with respect to onerous contracts.

(a) What is an onerous contract? What is its significance to revenue recognition?

(b) What two triggers are being considered by the IASB to determine whether or not a contract has become onerous? What are the advantages and disadvantages of the two approaches? What trigger does the IASB currently favour?

(c) For each of the following examples, assess whether the contracts have become onerous under the two proposed triggers suggested by the IASB.

   1. A construction contract has customer consideration totalling $500,000. The company had originally estimated costs to perform under the contract to be $425,000, resulting in profits of $75,000. However, during the contract, the company had material costs increase substantially, so that the current total expected costs of the contract are now $460,000.

   2. The company is a gold producer and has entered into a contract to sell 1,000 ounces of gold (originally over a two-year period) to a customer at a price of $600 per ounce. Currently, the selling price of gold has risen to $850 per ounce. The costs to produce the gold are $250 per ounce.

WA6-6   Write a brief essay highlighting the differences between IFRS and accounting standards for private enterprises noted in this chapter, discussing the conceptual justification for each.

Cases

Refer to the Case Primer to help you answer these cases.

CA6-1   Alexi Industries has three operating divisions: Figaro Mining, Manuel Paperbacks, and Oslo Protection Devices. Each division maintains its own accounting system and accounting policies. Since this is a private company, the accounting policies chosen are generally used for management decision-making. During the year, Alexi was running short of cash due to a major expansion in Figaro Mining. Problems in the mining industry were also contributing to cash flow difficulties. Due to the buoyancy of the equity markets (markets had reached a 10-year high), prices of commodities such as gold, silver, and platinum were down. As a result, the company had approached the bank for a line of credit. Before making any adjustments, the company's draft financial statements are showing a break-even net income. The following information is available for each of the three operating divisions:

Figaro Mining

Figaro Mining specializes in the extraction of precious metals such as silver, gold, and platinum. During the fiscal year ended November 30, 2011, Figaro entered into contracts to sell metals worth $2.25 million and shipped metals worth $2 million. A quarter of the shipments were made from inventories on hand at the beginning of the fiscal year, and the remainder were made from metals that were mined during the year. Mining production totals for the year, valued at market prices, were as follows: silver $750,000; gold $1.3 million; and platinum $490,000. Figaro recognizes revenue as the metals are refined.

Manuel Paperbacks

Manuel Paperbacks sells large quantities of novels to a few book distributors that in turn sell to several national chains of bookstores. Manuel allows distributors to return up to 30% of sales, and distributors give the same terms to bookstores. While returns of individual titles fluctuate greatly, the returns from distributors have averaged 20% in each of the past five years. A total of $8 million of paperback novel sales were made to distributors during the fiscal year. On November 30, 2011, $3.2 million of fiscal 2011 sales were still subject to return privileges over the next six months. The remaining $4.8 million of fiscal 2011 sales had actual returns of 21%. Sales from fiscal 2010 totalling $2.5 million were collected in fiscal 2011, with less than 18% of sales returned. Manuel records revenue when the novels are shipped.

Oslo Protection Devices

Oslo Protection Devices works through manufacturers' agents in various cities. Orders and down payments for alarm systems are forwarded from agents, and Oslo ships the goods FOB shipping point. Customers are billed for the balance due plus actual shipping costs. The firm received orders for $6 million of goods during the fiscal year ended November 30, 2008. Down payments of $600,000 were received, and $5 million of goods were billed and shipped. Actual freight costs of $100,000 were also billed. Commissions at 10% of the product price were paid to manufacturers' agents after the goods were shipped to customers. Such goods are warranted for 90 days after shipment, and warranty returns have been about 1% of sales. Oslo also installs many of the systems as well as systems for other manufacturers. The installation is approximately 20% of the value of the sale. Oslo recognizes revenue when goods are shipped.

Instructions

Assume the role of the assistant controller and prepare a report to the controller in which you discuss any financial reporting issues related to the three divisions. The controller needs this information before his upcoming meeting with the bank. He does not want any unpleasant surprises in the meeting.

CA6-2 *Cutting Edge* is a monthly magazine that has been on the market for 18 months. It is owned by a private company and has a circulation of 1.4 million copies. Negotiations are underway to obtain a bank loan in order to update its facilities. It is producing close to capacity and expects to grow at an average of 20% per year over the next three years.

After reviewing the financial statements of *Cutting Edge*, Gary Hall, the bank loan officer, said that a loan could only be offered to *Cutting Edge* if it could increase its current ratio and decrease its debt-to-equity ratio to a specified level. Alexander Popov, the marketing manager of *Cutting Edge*, has devised a plan to meet these requirements. Popov indicates that an advertising campaign can be used to immediately increase circulation. The potential customers would be contacted after purchasing another magazine's mailing list. The campaign would include:

1. An offer to subscribe to *Cutting Edge* at three-quarters the normal price

2. A special offer to all new subscribers to receive the most current world atlas whenever requested at a guaranteed price of $2.00

3. An unconditional guarantee of a full refund for any subscriber who is dissatisfied with the magazine

Although the offer of a full refund is risky, Popov claims that few people will ask for a refund after receiving half of their subscription issues. Popov notes that other magazine companies have tried this sales promotion technique and experienced great success. Their average cancellation rate was 25%. On average, each company increased its initial circulation threefold and in the long run increased circulation to twice the level that it was before the promotion. In addition, 60% of the new subscribers are expected to take advantage of the atlas premium. Popov feels confident that the increased subscriptions from the advertising campaign will increase the current ratio and decrease the debt-to-equity ratio.

In addition to the above, Popov has just signed a large deal with a newly opened store to take delivery of the current edition of the magazine. The new customer has asked that the magazines be held by *Cutting Edge* for a couple of weeks to a month.

Instructions

Assume the role of the controller and discuss the financial reporting issues assuming GAAP is a constraint.

CA6-3 Pankratov Lakes is a new real estate development that consists of 500 recreational lakefront and lake-view lots. The entity is owned by two individuals who are also the developers. As a special incentive to the first 100 buyers of lake-view lots, the developer is offering three years of free financing on 10-year, 12% notes, no down payment, and one week at a nearby established resort (a $1,200 value). The normal price per lot is $12,000. The cost to the developer for each lake-view lot is an estimated average of $2,000. The development costs continue to be incurred and the actual average cost per lot is not known at this time. The resort promotion cost is $700 per lot. Customers must have their lot inspected before taking legal title to it. Customers who do not like the developed property after its inspection may cancel the deal.

Instructions

Discuss the issues assuming GAAP is a constraint.

CA6-4 Nimble Health and Racquet Club (NHRC) is a public company that operates eight clubs in the metropolitan area of a large city and offers one-year memberships. The members may use any of the eight facilities but must reserve racquetball court time and pay a separate fee before using the court. As an incentive to new customers, NHRC advertised that any customers who are not satisfied for any reason can receive a refund of the remaining portion of their unused membership fees. Membership fees are due at the beginning of the individual membership period; however, customers are given the option of financing the membership fee over the membership period at a 15% interest rate.

In the past, some customers had said they would like to take only the regularly scheduled aerobic classes and not pay for a full membership. During the current fiscal year, NHRC began selling coupon books for aerobic classes only to accommodate these customers. Each book is dated and contains 50 coupons that may be redeemed for any regularly scheduled aerobic class over a one-year period. After the one-year period, unused coupons are no longer valid.

During 2011, NHRC expanded into the health equipment market by purchasing a local company that manufactures rowing machines and cross-country ski machines. These machines are used in NHRC's facilities and are sold through the clubs and mail-order catalogues. Customers must make a 20% down payment when placing an equipment order; delivery is in 60 to 90 days after an order is placed. The machines are sold with a two-year unconditional guarantee. Based on experience, NHRC expects the costs to repair machines under guarantee to be 4% of sales.

NHRC is in the process of preparing financial statements as at May 31, 2011, the end of its fiscal year. James Hogan, corporate controller, expressed concern over the company's performance for the year and decided to review the preliminary financial statements prepared by Barbara Hardy, NHRC's assistant controller, for the company's bankers. After reviewing the statements, Hogan proposed that the following changes be reflected in the May 31, 2011, published financial statements:

1. Membership revenue should be recognized when the membership fee is collected.

2. Revenue from the coupon books should be recognized when the books are sold.

3. Down payments on equipment purchases and expenses associated with the guarantee on the rowing and cross-country machines should be recognized when they are paid.

Ethics

Hardy indicated to Hogan that the proposed changes are not in accordance with generally accepted accounting principles, but Hogan insisted that the changes be made. Hardy believes that Hogan wants to manipulate income to delay any potential financial problems and increase his year-end bonus. At this point, Hardy is unsure what action to take.

Instructions

Discuss the financial reporting issues.

(CMA adapted)

Real-World Emphasis

CA6-5   The following is an excerpt from the financial statements of **Viterra** (formerly Saskatchewan Wheat Pool). Among other things, the pool buys grain from farmers and sells it to the Canadian Wheat Board.

> **Notes to the 2008 Consolidated Financial Statements:**
>
> Grain inventories include both hedgeable and non-hedgeable commodities.
>
> Hedgeable and non-hedgeable grain inventories are valued on the basis of closing market quotations less freight and handling costs.
>
> Agri-products, livestock feed, and other inventories consist of raw materials, work in progress and finished goods, and are valued at the lower of cost and net realizable value.

Instructions

Discuss the financial reporting issues relating to inventory valuation and the related revenue recognition.

Integrated Cases

(Hint: If there are issues that are new, use the conceptual framework to help support your analysis with solid reasoning.)

IC6-1   Treetop Pharmaceuticals (TP) is in the business of research, development, and production of over-the-counter pharmaceuticals. During the year, it acquired 100% of the net assets of Treeroot Drugs Limited (TDL) for $200 million. The fair value of the identifiable assets at the time of purchase was $150 million (which included $120 million for patents). The company plans to sell the patents to a third party at the end of seven years even though, at that time, the remaining legal life of the patents will be five years. TP already has a commitment from a specific third party that has agreed to pay $50 million for the patents (in seven years).

In January, in an unrelated deal, the company acquired a trademark that has a remaining legal life of three years. The trademark is renewable every 10 years at little cost. TP is unsure if it will renew the trademark or not.

Because of the two acquisitions, TP was short of cash and entered into an arrangement with Drug Development Corporation (DDC) whereby DDC paid $30 million to TP upfront when the contract was signed. Under the terms, the money is to be used to develop drugs and new distribution channels. TP has already spent a considerable portion of this money. TP agreed that it will pay DDC 2% of the revenues from the subsequent sale of the drugs (which are now close to the point of commercial production).

Because of the cash shortage, the company entered into negotiations with its bank to increase its line of credit. The bank is concerned about the company's liquidity. TP's top management has graciously agreed to take stock options instead of any bonuses or raises for the next two years in order to reduce cash flow constraints.

It is now year end and TP is preparing its financial statements. It is concerned because one of its major competitors has just come out with several new drugs that will compete directly with the drugs that TDL sells. Management is worried that this may erode the market for TDL's products. In fact, TP is considering selling TDL and has contacted a consultant to help find a buyer.

Jack Kimble, the controller, is preparing for a planning meeting with TP's auditors. The auditors are analyzing TP's draft financial statements to identify critical and high-risk areas. The draft financial statements show the company as barely breaking even. The CFO has commented that the company's share price is likely to "take a tumble" since the company has always been profitable in past years and its competitors seem to be doing well. Kimble is also debating the latest news from TP's lawyers—apparently, the company is being sued in a class action lawsuit (i.e., by a significant number of people) for an illness that was allegedly caused by one of TP's main pharmaceutical products. The claim is for an amount equal to revenues from last year. At this point, the lawyers are concerned that the case against TP may be successful and they are trying to estimate the potential loss to the company.

Instructions

Adopt the role of the controller and prepare an analysis of all the financial reporting issues that TP is facing.

IC6-2   Recreational Vehicle Inc. (RVI) sells mid-sized to large, new and used motorized recreational vehicles. The company's only shareholder, Ronald Trump, manages the business. During the last two years, Canada's tourism industry has been hit hard by the appreciating Canadian dollar (most tourists are non-Canadians) and the threat of terrorism. Sales of RVs have therefore been slow.

RVI is located at the corner of two major highways, which gives it good visibility. The facilities are very old, however, and in need of upgrading. Ronald has been thinking of building a new showroom and would like to get a loan from Barrick Bank. During construction, RVI will move its business to an adjacent building that it will rent.

The loan will also be used to pay for a new electronic billboard that can be seen from the highway. The billboard will cost $1 million but will allow RVI to display many different messages, including its sales and seasonal promotions. The cost of the billboard will be defrayed by renting out space on the billboard at times during the year when RVI is not using it. RVI has had many companies interested in this and is currently involved in a bidding process to determine which companies it will take on as advertising partners. So far, 10 companies have bid for the opportunity to advertise on the billboard and RVI has charged and collected a $25,000 fee from each of them. The $25,000 fee is non-refundable and represents the amount required by RVI for the privilege to bid on the billboard space only. RVI has not decided which bids it will accept yet. It cannot accept all of the bids but plans to accept three of them.

In his years in the business, Ronald has found that many potential RV owners/customers find the cost of the vehicle to be prohibitive. The RVs normally sell for about $90,000 each. With that in mind, several years ago he came up with a unique program. Customers may buy the RV for as little as 10% down in cash as long as they also sign a marketing agreement with RVI. Under the terms of the agreement, RVI cares for the vehicle (storing it on its premises when not in use, providing repairs and maintenance), rents the vehicle to third parties, and advertises the availability of the unit. For instance, if the customer/owner decides to use the RV for only three weeks in the year, RVI will store the unit and try to rent it out the rest of the time. In return, RVI gets 40% of the rental fee. With this program in place, RVI found that sales of new RVs increased dramatically. As a result, it now has a substantial fleet which it rents out—hence the need to expand and upgrade the facilities.

Many potential RV owners/customers need financing, so RVI either provides the financing or helps negotiate a loan with Barrick Bank. Often, the customers make the loan payments out of the rental revenue that they earn under the rental program. If the customer does not make the loan payments, ownership of the RV reverts back to RVI. Ownership of several RVs has gone back to RVI in the past two years. When this happens, RVI either continues to rent the RV or tries to resell it.

The risk of theft is significant for these types of vehicles and RVI therefore ensures that owners have appropriate insurance coverage. Over the past three years, the insurance company has been complaining about excessive claims and losses. In September, it notified RVI and the RV owners that it would no longer allow the insured RVs to be rented out. Many of the owners switched insurance companies, but there are presently 10 RVs on the lot with no insurance. Ronald has not been able to get in touch with their owners.

It is now December, and Barrick Bank has loaned the company the money it needs to construct the new facilities. The old building has been demolished and the new facilities are under construction. The loan pays interest at prime plus 2% and requires that the company maintain both its profitability and a working capital ratio of 2:1. The company must provide audited financial statements to the bank at least annually.

Instructions

Adopt the role of the auditors of RVI and discuss the financial reporting issues.

Ethics

IC6-3 Communications Incorporated (CI) is a leader in delivering communications capabilities that power global commerce and secure the world's most critical information. Its shares trade on the Canadian and U.S. national stock exchanges. The company had been experiencing unprecedented growth, but then, in 2008, industry demand for the company's services and products declined dramatically due to an industry realignment, an economic downturn, and a tightening in global capital and product markets. By the end of 2010, the industry stabilized and the company began to enter a turnaround period after significant downsizing.

In 2010, employee morale was very low because of all the downsizing. Many employees were being actively recruited away from CI. Management decided to set up bonus programs for employees who stayed to see the company through the difficult times and back to profitability. Under one plan, every employee would receive a bonus in the first quarter that the company achieved enough profit to cover the bonus costs. In order to help achieve profitability, the CFO met with the managers of his divisions and established profitability targets and what he referred to as "roadmaps" that showed how these targets could be achieved. The roadmaps included statements that the profits could only be achieved through the release from the balance sheet of excess provisions (i.e., provisions for obsolete inventory and bad debts). The provisions had been overprovided for in earlier years in an effort to "manage" profits.

In 2011, the company came under scrutiny from the securities regulators and received notification from the government regarding a criminal investigation into alleged accounting irregularities. In addition, there were several class action lawsuits outstanding against the company by shareholders alleging that CI had provided misleading information to them in the financial statements for 2009 and 2010. Once news of this was released, credit rating agencies significantly downgraded their ratings of CI's securities. As a result of this negative activity, the company had not released its financial statements for 2011 and was now in breach of the stock exchange requirements to file financial statements. Although the stock exchanges had not done so, they now had the power to delist CI's shares.

The controller of CI must now finalize the financial statements and has come across the following information:

1. During the year, the company signed contracts to sell optical products which included software. Before year end, the company shipped out what it called an "interim product solution"—in other words, the optical product ordered by the company was not yet ready in its final form so the company shipped a beta or draft version of it. This interim product would then be followed shortly by the final version. Revenues were recognized upon shipment of the interim product solution as it was felt that the final version just needed minor refinements. The customers generally paid more than half of what was owed under the contract when they received the interim product solution. It was rare that customers backed out of this type of contract for any reason.

2. In 2010, CI had purchased a subsidiary of ABC Inc. and agreed to pay additional future consideration for the purchase (the consideration would take the form of additional CI shares). The additional consideration was a function of the profitability of the subsidiary. The more profitable the subsidiary, the more shares that CI would issue as consideration. Given that CI's shares are highly volatile, CI and ABC agreed that the number of shares to be issued should be based on the average price per share in the three months prior to the future issuance date of the shares. So far, the subsidiary has been performing above expectation.

3. By the end of 2011, CI was still restructuring to streamline operations and activities around its core activities. Part of the restructuring included the abandonment of the VOF (Voice Over Fibre) operations. The operations would be closed down in early 2012, and this would involve workforce reductions and abandonment of plant and equipment.

Instructions

Analyze the financial reporting issues.

Research and Financial Analysis

RA6-1 Eastern Platinum Limited

Real-World Emphasis

Eastern Platinum Limited's financial statements can be found in Appendix 5B.

Instructions

Refer to the company's financial statements and accompanying notes to answer these questions.

(a) What were the company's gross revenues for the three months ended March 31, 2009 and 2008? What is the percentage change? Why has the company seen this result?

(b) Based on your findings in (a), comment on the company's net income/loss over the period.

(c) Review the notes to the financial statements to determine the company's revenue recognition policy. Discuss the policy, considering the nature of the business and the industry.

(d) On transition to IFRS from Canadian GAAP, adjustments to revenues were required to restate revenue for the three months ended March 31, 2008, and for the year ended December 31, 2008. Explain why the company had to make these adjustments and the amounts required.

(e) The company uses the U.S. dollar to present its Canadian financial statements. Why might it do this even though its functional currencies are the Canadian dollar and the South African rand?

RA6-2 BCE Inc. and TELUS Corporation

Access **BCE Inc.'s** financial statements for the year ended December 31, 2008, from either the company's website or SEDAR (www.sedar.com). Access **TELUS Corporation's** financial statements for the year ended December 31, 2008, from either the company's website or SEDAR.

Real-World Emphasis

Instructions

Using the annual reports for BCE Inc. and TELUS, answer the following.

(a) What types of revenue does BCE have and how are they recognized?

(b) What types of revenue does TELUS have and how are they recognized?

(c) Are there any examples of when either company would report revenue at net? Why? What factors does the company consider?

(d) Explain the types of contracts where the companies have multiple deliverables. How does each company allocate the revenues on these types of contracts?

(e) Where are there similarities and differences in the companies' revenue recognition policies?

(f) Do you find one company's disclosure on revenue recognition better than another? Why?

RA6-3 EADS N.V. Construction Contracts

Access the financial statements for **EADS N.V.** (European Aeronautic Defence and Space Company) for its year ended December 31, 2008, from the company's website (www.eads.com).

Real-World Emphasis

Instructions

Answer the following questions with respect to EADS N.V.

(a) What business is EADS in?

(b) Explain how the revenue related to the construction contracts is recorded. How does the company determine when revenue should be recognized on these contracts?

(c) How does the company treat probable losses on existing contracts?

(d) What are the balance sheet amounts related to this revenue recognition? What was the aggregated amount of costs and profits recognized to date? What was the gross amount due to customers and due from customers at December 31, 2008? What do these amounts represent? (Hint: See Note 19.) Based on this information, what is the amount of the progress billings to date on these contracts in process at December 31, 2008?

RA6-4 Nortel Networks Corporation

In the recent past, there have been many cases of companies that have overstated their revenues, particularly in the United States. In Canada, **Nortel Networks Corporation** was forced to restate its revenue for the years 2004, 2005, and 2006, and years prior to 2004. In March 2007, it made an announcement as to what the final impact would be on its statements for all of these restatements.

Real-World Emphasis

Instructions

Research the issue by visiting the company website (www.nortel.com) and news sites. List the main types of misstatements related to revenues and provide the amount of each misstatement on revenues and net earnings for each applicable year. Discuss how the company had treated the revenues originally and in the restatement. How is it possible that the auditors gave the company a clean audit opinion for its original statements?

Collecting from Incommunicado Clients

TELEPHONE SERVICE COMPANY Bell Aliant is predominantly a land line provider with approximately 3 million access lines across six provinces. It serves 5.3 million customers with local, long-distance, and data line services, as well as high-speed Internet. With a staff of approximately 9,000, the company earns $3.2 billion a year under the brands Bell Aliant in Atlantic Canada and Bell in Ontario and Quebec, as well as Télébec, Northern Tel, and Kenora Municipal Telephone Services.

Bell Aliant's main sources of revenue are fees for local and long-distance phone services and high-speed and dial-up Internet services. It also receives revenue from equipment rentals and some information technology products and services provided to large enterprises.

"Our total receivables balance is around $450 million at any one month end," says Eleanor Marshall, Vice-President and Treasurer at Bell Aliant. On the balance sheet, this amount would be netted with amounts of accounts receivable the company has sold as part of its securitization program.

Bell Aliant's billing terms are regulated by the Canadian Radio-television and Telecommunications Commission (CRTC). The company bills monthly for services in arrears, and payments are due within 30 days of the billing date, which results in receivables being about 43 to 45 days outstanding, Marshall explains.

The company allows a three-day grace period beyond a bill's due date, after which late-payment charges will begin to accrue. It will then send a reminder letter to late customers with a new due date.

If the bill does not get paid, Bell Aliant will start making calls and perhaps negotiate new payment terms that might include stripping down the account to basic services. If there is still no payment, the company will suspend the account for 21 days, then reconnect for one day, and contact the client again. If there is still no payment, it will permanently disconnect the customer. The company then sends two notices to the client, and finally the bill goes to a collection agency.

"We establish provisions for bad debts long before it gets to this point," Marshall adds. Receivables are assigned to aging categories, and certain percentages, which are based on past experience, apply to each category to estimate the amount of uncollectible accounts. The company recognizes bad debt expense, which is typically about 1% of revenue, each month. ■

CHAPTER 7

Cash and Receivables

Learning Objectives

After studying this chapter, you should be able to:

1. Define financial assets, and identify items that are considered cash and cash equivalents and how they are reported.

2. Define receivables and identify the different types of receivables.

3. Account for and explain the accounting issues related to the recognition and measurement of accounts receivable.

4. Account for and explain the accounting issues related to the impairment in value of accounts receivable.

5. Account for and explain the accounting issues related to the recognition and measurement of short-term notes and loans receivable.

6. Account for and explain the accounting issues related to the recognition and measurement of long-term notes and loans receivable.

7. Account for and explain the basic accounting issues related to the derecognition of receivables.

8. Explain how receivables and loans are reported and analyzed.

9. Identify differences in accounting between accounting standards for private enterprises (private entity GAAP) and IFRS, and what changes are expected in the near future.

After studying Appendix 7A, you should be able to:

10. Explain common techniques for controlling cash.

Preview of Chapter 7

As our opening story implies, estimating the collectability of accounts receivable has important implications for accurate reporting of operating profits, net income, and assets. In this chapter, we discuss cash and receivables—two assets that are important to companies as diverse as giant BCE (the parent company of Bell Aliant) and small owner-operated private operations.

The chapter is organized as follows:

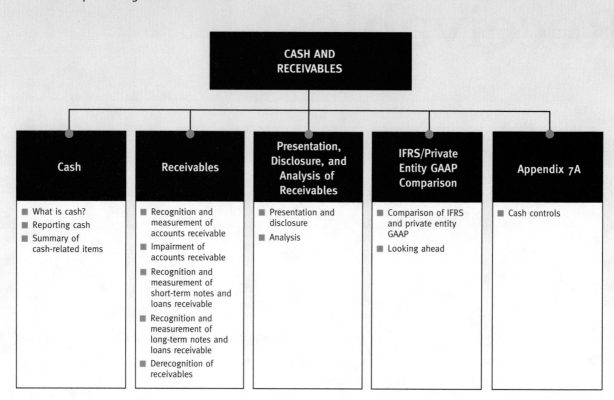

<table>
<tr><td colspan="5" align="center">CASH AND RECEIVABLES</td></tr>
</table>

Cash	**Receivables**	**Presentation, Disclosure, and Analysis of Receivables**	**IFRS/Private Entity GAAP Comparison**	**Appendix 7A**
■ What is cash? ■ Reporting cash ■ Summary of cash-related items	■ Recognition and measurement of accounts receivable ■ Impairment of accounts receivable ■ Recognition and measurement of short-term notes and loans receivable ■ Recognition and measurement of long-term notes and loans receivable ■ Derecognition of receivables	■ Presentation and disclosure ■ Analysis	■ Comparison of IFRS and private entity GAAP ■ Looking ahead	■ Cash controls

Objective 1
Define financial assets, and identify items that are considered cash and cash equivalents and how they are reported.

We now begin our detailed study of balance sheet accounts and the recognition and measurement concepts that apply to the different categories of assets, liabilities, and shareholders' equity. The first assets covered are generally the most liquid, and they are usually financial assets. A **financial asset** is any asset that is:

(i) cash;

(ii) a contractual right to receive cash or another financial asset from another party;

(iii) a contractual right to exchange financial instruments with another party under conditions that are potentially favourable to the entity; or

(iv) an equity instrument of another entity.[1]

---

[1] Based on *CICA Handbook*, Part II, Section 3856 *Financial Instruments*. The IFRS definition introduces additional complexity beyond the scope of this text related to when the entity enters into a contract that will be settled with its own shares. Private entity GAAP excludes from its definition the costs of rights to reacquire its own equity instruments.

Financial assets are also covered in other chapters of this text. Chapter 7 deals with cash and cash equivalents, and with accounts, notes, and loans receivable. Chapter 9 covers other major categories of financial assets—mainly investments in the debt and equity instruments of other companies. The financial assets in these two chapters fit parts (i), (ii), and (iv) of the definition. Chapter 9 highlights the profession's recent move away from the long-standing transactions-based historical cost model toward one that relies more and more on fair values. Chapter 2 includes a discussion of what fair value is and how it is measured. Coverage of the more complex instruments that fit part (iii) of the definition, such as derivatives, along with financial liabilities and equity, is found in Volume 2.

CASH

What Is Cash?

Cash is the most liquid asset and is the standard medium of exchange and the basis for measuring and accounting for all other items. It meets the definition of a financial asset, and is generally classified as a current asset.

Cash consists of coins, currency, and other available funds that are on deposit at a bank. Negotiable instruments such as money orders, certified cheques, cashier's cheques, personal cheques, and bank drafts are also viewed as cash. Although a company's bank may have a legal right to demand advance notice before it allows a withdrawal from a savings account, banks rarely ask for this notice and savings accounts are therefore also usually classified as cash.

It is more appropriate to classify money-market funds, certificates of deposit (CDs), and similar types of deposits and "short-term paper"[2] that allow investors to earn interest as **cash equivalents** or **short-term investments** than as cash. The reason is that there are usually restrictions or penalties on these securities when they are converted to cash. Money-market funds that give chequing account privileges, however, are usually classified as cash.

Certain items present classification problems: for example, postdated cheques from customers and IOUs are treated as receivables. It is proper to treat travel advances as receivables if the advances are to be collected from the employees or deducted from their salaries. Otherwise, it is more appropriate to classify the travel advance as a prepaid expense. Postage stamps on hand are classified as part of office supplies inventory or as a prepaid expense. Petty cash funds and change funds are included in current assets as cash because these funds are used to meet current operating expenses and to liquidate current liabilities.

---

[2] There are different types of short-term paper for investment. For example, CDs are issued by a bank as formal evidence of the bank's indebtedness. They must usually be held until maturity, although some CDs for over $100,000 are negotiable. Guaranteed investment certificates (GICs) issued by banks, trust companies, and credit unions are similar time deposits. The short-term certificates mature in 30 to 360 days and generally pay interest at the short-term rate that is in effect on the date they are issued. In money-market funds, which are a variation of the mutual fund, the yield is determined by the mix of treasury bills and commercial paper making up the fund's portfolio. Treasury bills are Canadian government obligations with 3-, 6-, and 12-month maturities; they are sold in denomination multiples of $1,000 (face value) at weekly government auctions. Commercial paper is short-term unsecured debt notes issued by corporations with good credit ratings, usually in minimum denominations of $100,000 and for terms of from 1 to 365 days.

Reporting Cash

Although the reporting of cash is fairly straightforward, there are some issues that need special attention. They concern the reporting of:

1. restricted cash
2. cash in foreign currencies
3. bank overdrafts
4. cash equivalents

Restricted Cash

Petty cash and special payroll and dividend bank accounts are examples of cash that has been set aside for a particular purpose. In most situations, these fund balances are not material and therefore are not segregated from cash when it is reported in the financial statements. When an amount is material, restricted cash is segregated from regular cash for reporting purposes. The restricted cash is separately disclosed and reported in the Current Assets section or is classified separately in the Long-Term Assets section, depending on the date of availability or of the expected disbursement.[3] In general, it should not be classified in current assets if there are restrictions that prevent it from being used for current purposes, unless the restricted cash offsets a current liability. Cash that is classified in the long-term section has often been set aside for investment or financing purposes, such as for a plant expansion, long-term debt retirement, or as collateral for a loan.

Law

Some lending institutions require customers who borrow money from them to keep minimum cash balances in their chequing or savings accounts. These minimum balances are called compensating balances and are defined as the portion of any demand deposit (or any time deposit or certificate of deposit) that a corporation keeps as support for its existing or maturing obligations with a lending institution.[4] By requiring a compensating balance, the bank gets an effective interest rate on its loan that is higher than the stated rate because it can use the restricted amount that must remain on deposit. In the United States, where banks more often require compensating balances, the accounting practice is to report in current assets any legally restricted deposits that are held as compensating balances against short-term borrowing arrangements.

To ensure that investors are not misled about the amount of cash that is available to meet recurring obligations, legally restricted balances have to be reported separately in current assets or noncurrent assets, as appropriate. In practice, many companies report this through note disclosure.

Cash in Foreign Currencies

Many companies have bank accounts in other countries, especially if they have recurring transactions in that country's currency. The foreign currency is translated into Canadian dollars at the exchange rate on the balance sheet date and, in situations where there is no restriction on the transfer of those funds to the Canadian company, it is included as cash in current assets. If there are restrictions on the flow of capital out of a country, the cash is reported as restricted. The classification of the cash as current or noncurrent is based on the circumstances and, in extreme cases, restrictions may be so severe that the foreign balances do not even qualify for recognition as assets.

---

[3] Under IFRS, if current and noncurrent asset classifications are not used on the balance sheet, separate disclosure is required of the amounts to be recovered within 12 months and more than 12 months after the balance sheet date.

[4] *Accounting Series Release No. 148*, "Amendments to Regulations S-X and Related Interpretations and Guidelines Regarding the Disclosure of Compensating Balances and Short-Term Borrowing Arrangements," Securities and Exchange Commission, November 13, 1973.

Bank Overdrafts

Bank overdrafts occur when cheques are written for more than the amount in the cash account. Overdrafts are reported in the Current Liabilities section, and companies often do this by adding the amount to what is reported as accounts payable. If the overdraft amount is material, it should be disclosed separately either on the face of the balance sheet or in the related notes.

In general, bank overdrafts should not be offset against the Cash account. A major exception is when there is available cash in another account at the same bank where the overdraft is. Offsetting in this case is appropriate.

Cash Equivalents

Cash is often reported with the asset category called cash equivalents. Cash equivalents are defined as "short-term, highly liquid investments that are readily convertible to known amounts of cash and which are subject to an insignificant risk of changes in value."[5] Companies usually hold cash equivalents for meeting upcoming cash requirements. Generally, only investments with **original maturities** of three months or less qualify under the definition. While equity investments are excluded from the private entity definition of cash equivalents, IFRS allows preferred shares that were acquired close to their maturity date to qualify. Examples of cash equivalents are treasury bills, commercial paper, and money-market funds.

In some circumstances, bank overdrafts may be deducted when the amount of cash and cash equivalents is being determined. If overdrafts are part of the firm's cash management activities, if they are repayable on demand, and if the bank balance fluctuates often between a positive and negative balance, the overdrafts may be considered part of cash and cash equivalents.

Because some companies report investments that qualify as cash equivalents in other categories of current assets, such as short-term or trading investments, it is important for entities to disclose their reporting policy in a note to the financial statements. Investments that are classified as cash equivalents are held to be sold in the very short term. These are generally reported at fair value. Their fair value at acquisition plus accrued interest to the balance sheet date often approximate fair value at the balance sheet date.

Illustration 7-1 shows the information that Ottawa-based **Zarlink Semiconductor Inc.** reports in its financial statements for the year ended March 27, 2009.

	March 27, 2009	March 28, 2008
ASSETS		
Current assets:		
Cash and cash equivalents	$45.0	$42.4
Short-term investments	–	0.2
Restricted cash and cash equivalents	13.1	17.3

2. ACCOUNTING POLICIES

(C) CASH, CASH EQUIVALENTS AND SHORT-TERM INVESTMENTS
All highly liquid investments with original maturities of three months or less are classified as cash and cash equivalents. The fair value of cash equivalents approximates the amounts shown in the financial statements. Short-term investments comprise highly liquid corporate debt instruments that are held to maturity with terms of not greater than one year. Short-term investments are carried at amortized cost, which approximates their fair value.

(D) RESTRICTED CASH AND CASH EQUIVALENTS
Restricted cash and cash equivalents consist of cash and cash equivalents used as security pledges against liabilities or other forms of credit.

Illustration 7-1

Reporting of Cash and Cash Equivalents—Zarlink Semiconductor Inc.

Real-World Emphasis

Additional Disclosures

---

[5] *CICA Handbook*, Part II, Section 1540.06(b) and IAS 7.6.

Summary of Cash-Related Items

Cash and cash equivalents include currency and most negotiable instruments. If the item cannot be converted to coin or currency on short notice, it is classified separately as an investment, receivable, or prepaid expense. Cash that is not available for paying liabilities that are currently maturing is classified in the long-term assets section. The chart below summarizes the classification of cash-related items.

Classification of Cash, Cash Equivalents, and Noncash Items		
Item	**Classification**	**Comment**
Cash	Cash	Report it as cash. If restricted, identify and report it separately as a current or noncurrent asset.
Petty cash and change funds	Cash	Report them as cash.
Short-term paper	Cash equivalents	Classify as cash equivalents if investments have a maturity of less than three months when acquired.
Short-term paper	Short-term investments	Classify as short-term investments if investments have a maturity of 3 to 12 months when acquired.
Postdated cheques and IOUs	Receivables	Classify as receivables if they are assumed to be collectible.
Travel advances	Receivables or prepaid expenses	Classify as receivables or prepaid expenses if they are collectible from employees or to be spent on travel in the future, respectively.
Postage on hand (as stamps or in postage meters)	Prepaid expenses	These may also be classified as office supplies inventory.
Bank overdrafts	Current liability	If there is a right of offset, report as a reduction of cash.
Compensating balances	Cash classified separately as a deposit that is maintained as a compensating balance	Classify as current or noncurrent in the balance sheet. Disclose details of the arrangement.

RECEIVABLES

Objective 2
Define receivables and identify the different types of receivables.

In general, receivables are claims that a company has against customers and others, usually for specific cash receipts in the future. As we saw in the introduction to this chapter, when the claim is a **contractual** right to receive cash or other financial assets from another party, the receivable is a financial asset. On a classified balance sheet, receivables are either current (short-term) or noncurrent (long-term). Current receivables are expected to be realized (converted to cash) within a year or during the current operating cycle, whichever is longer. All other receivables are classified as noncurrent.

Finance

These financial assets are generally referred to in a more specific way as loans or receivables, with loans being a type of receivable, as explained below.[6] **Loans and receivables** result from one party delivering cash (or other assets) to a borrower in exchange for a promise to repay the amount on a specified date or dates, or on demand, along with interest to compensate for the time value of money and the risk of non-payment. They are not usually acquired to be held as a cash equivalent or temporary investment of excess cash. Investments in government debt, corporate bonds, convertible debt, commercial paper, and other securities, while similar, are not loans and receivables. This is because they are traded in an active market, while loans and receivables are not.

Loans and receivables can be further described. **Trade receivables** are amounts owed by customers to whom the company has sold goods or services as part of its normal business operations; that is, they are amounts that result from operating transactions. They can be either open accounts receivable or notes receivable. Open accounts receivable are short-term extensions of credit that are based on a purchaser's **oral** promise to pay for goods and services that have been sold. They are normally collectible within 30 to 60 days, but credit terms may be longer—or shorter—depending on the industry. **Notes receivable** are **written** promises to pay a certain amount of money on a specified future date. They may arise from sales of goods and services, or from other transactions.

As the term "loan" suggests, **loans receivable** are created when one party advances cash or other assets to a borrower and receives a promise to be repaid later. Loans tend to result from financing transactions by borrowers and investing transactions by lenders. When there is a written document that gives the terms and conditions of the loan receivable, the loan is then also called a note receivable.

Nontrade receivables are created by a variety of transactions and can be written promises either to pay cash or to deliver other assets. Examples of nontrade receivables include the following:

1. Advances to officers and employees, or to subsidiaries or other companies

2. Amounts owing from a purchaser on the sale of capital assets or investments where delayed payment terms have been agreed on

3. Amounts receivable from the government: income taxes paid in excess of the amount owed, GST payments recoverable, investment tax credits, or other tax rebates receivable

4. Dividends and interest receivable

5. Claims against insurance companies for losses the company has suffered; against trucking companies or railways for damaged or lost goods; against creditors for returned, damaged, or lost goods; or against customers for returnable items (crates, containers, etc.)

Because of their special nature, nontrade receivables are generally classified and reported as separate items in the balance sheet or in a note that is cross-referenced to the balance sheet. Illustration 7-2 shows the balance sheet and separate reporting of the receivables on the financial statements of Nova Scotia–based **Empire Company Limited** for its year ended May 2, 2009.

---

[6] Some receivables are not financial assets. They are excluded when the claim does not result from a contractual commitment, such as income taxes receivable, which result from government legislation; or when the claim is not for cash or another financial asset.

Illustration 7-2
*Receivables Reporting—
Empire Company Limited*

Consolidated Balance Sheets

(in millions)	May 2, 2009	May 3, 2008
Assets		
Current		
Cash and cash equivalents	$ 231.6	$ 191.4
Receivables	318.7	291.1
Loans and other receivables (Note 6)	55.8	69.9
Income taxes receivable	4.9	—
Loans and other receivables (Note 6)	75.3	56.3

Note 6   Loans and Other Receivables

	May 2, 2009	May 3, 2008
Loans receivable	$ 65.5	$ 58.1
Mortgages receivable	21.2	26.4
Other	44.4	41.7
	131.1	126.2
Less amount due within one year	55.8	69.9
	$ 75.3	$ 56.3

LOANS RECEIVABLE

Loans receivable represent long-term financing to certain retail associates. These loans are primarily secured by inventory, fixtures and equipment, bear various interest rates and have repayment terms up to ten years. The carrying amount of the loans receivable approximates fair value based on the variable interest rates charged on the loans and the operating relationship of the associates with the Company.

Note that the following discussion of **accounts and notes receivable** assumes that they are short-term trade receivables, and that the discussion of **loans receivable** is based on long-term nontrade loans or notes. In addition, it is assumed that they all are financial assets. The basic accounting issues are discussed in the following sections: **recognition and measurement, impairment,** and **derecognition**.

Recognition and Measurement of Accounts Receivable

The general accounting standards for the recognition and initial measurement of accounts receivable are as follows:

- recognize an account receivable when the entity becomes a party to the contractual provisions of the financial instrument;

- measure the receivable initially at its fair value;[7] and

- after initial recognition, measure receivables at amortized cost.

The entity becomes a party to the contractual provisions of the financial instrument only when it has a legal claim to receive cash or other financial assets. While a commitment

---

[7] Receivables that are created by related party transactions may be an exception. Chapter 23 discusses the issues underlying related party transactions.

to sell goods or services to a customer might be made when a customer's order is received, there is usually no legal claim until one of the parties to the contract has performed under the agreement.

Recognizing receivables initially at their fair value is not as straightforward as it might seem. This is because fair value may not be the same as the exchange price that the parties agree on. The **exchange price, the amount due** from the customer or borrower, is generally indicated on a business document, usually an invoice. Two factors can make measuring the fair value of short-term receivables more complicated: (1) the availability of discounts (trade and cash discounts) and (2) the length of time between the sale and the payment due date (the interest element).

Trade Discounts

Customers are often quoted prices based on list or catalogue prices that may have trade or quantity discounts. Trade discounts are used to avoid frequent changes in catalogues, to quote different prices for different quantities purchased, or to hide the true invoice price from competitors.

Trade discounts are commonly quoted in percentages. For example, if your textbook has a list price of $90 and the publisher sells it to college and university bookstores for list less a 30% trade discount, the receivable recorded by the publisher is $63 per textbook. The normal practice is simply to deduct the trade discount from the list price and recognize the net amount as the receivable and revenue.

Cash Discounts (Sales Discounts)

Cash discounts or sales discounts are offered to encourage fast payment. They are expressed in specific terms: for example, 2/10, n/30 means there is a 2% discount if the invoice is paid within 10 days and that the gross amount is due in 30 days; while 2/10, E.O.M., n/30, means there is a 2% discount if the invoice is paid before the 10th day of the following month, with full payment due by the 30th of the following month.

Companies that buy goods or services but fail to take sales discounts are usually not using their money as effectively as they could. An enterprise that receives a 1% reduction in the sales price for paying within 10 days when the total payment is due within 30 days is basically earning 18.25% interest (0.01 divided by $^{20}/_{365}$) because of the discount—or, more technically, it is at least avoiding that rate of interest included in the undiscounted invoice price. For this reason, companies usually take the discount unless their cash is severely limited.[8]

In theory, the receivable and the associated sale should both be recognized at the net amount or fair value; that is, the present value of the future cash flows. Under this approach, sales to customers who pay within the discount period are reported at the cash price; for customers who pay after the discount period expires, the company separately reports Sales Discounts Forfeited, similar to interest income earned.

The most commonly used method of recording short-term receivables and related sales, however, is to **record the gross amounts of the receivable and sale; i.e., at the full amount assuming no discount will be taken.** Under this method, sales discounts are recognized in the accounts only when payment is received within the discount period. Sales discounts are then shown in the income statement as a deduction from sales to arrive at net sales.

---

[8] Note that 18.25% is the stated annual rate. If the compounded, or effective, rate of interest is required, the following formula is used: Rate = $[1/(1-.01)]^{365/(30-10)} - 1$. This results in an effective annual rate of 20.13%. See David B. Vicknair, "The Effective Annual Rate on Cash Discounts: A Clarification," *Journal of Accounting Education* 18 (2000), pp. 55–62.

The entries in Illustration 7-3 show the difference between the gross and net methods.

Gross Method			Net Method		
Sales of $10,000, terms 2/10, n/30:					
Accounts Receivable	10,000		Accounts Receivable	9,800	
Sales		10,000	Sales		9,800
Payment on $4,000 of sales received within discount period:					
Cash	3,920		Cash	3,920	
Sales Discounts	80		Accounts Receivable		3,920
Accounts Receivable		4,000			
Payment on $6,000 of sales received after discount period:					
Cash	6,000		Accounts Receivable	120*	
Accounts Receivable		6,000	Sales Discounts Forfeited		120
			Cash	6,000	
			Accounts Receivable		6,000*

*One net entry could be made:

Cash	6,000	
Accounts Receivable		5,880
Sales Discounts Forfeited		120

If the **gross method** is used, the accounts receivable are measured at their gross amount and any sales discounts actually taken are reported as a deduction from sales in the income statement. Proper asset valuation requires that a reasonable estimate be made of discounts that are expected to be taken after the balance sheet date and that the amount be recorded if it is material. Allowance for Sales Discounts, a contra account to Accounts Receivable on the balance sheet, is credited for such amounts and the Sales Discounts account on the income statement is increased (debited). If the **net method** is used, the receivables are already at their realizable value so no further adjustment is needed. The Sales Discounts Forfeited account is recognized as an item of "Other revenue" on the income statement.

Although the net method is theoretically preferred, it is rarely used. This is because it requires more bookkeeping for the additional adjusting entries after the discount period has passed. Using the gross method, along with the added requirement to estimate and record discounts that are expected to be taken after the balance sheet date, results in the same effect on the balance sheet and income statement.

Sales Returns and Allowances

To properly measure **sales revenues** and **receivables**, allowance accounts are normally used. Probable sales returns and price reductions are estimated and deducted as contra accounts against sales on the income statement and accounts receivable on the balance sheet. This results in net sales and the net realizable amount of accounts receivable being properly reported on the financial statements.

This procedure is followed so that the sales returns or price allowances (called sales returns and allowances) are reported in the same period as the sales that they relate to. If this adjustment is not made, however, the amount of mismatched returns and allowances is usually not material as long as the items are handled consistently from year to year. The situation changes when a company completes a few special orders for large amounts near the end of its accounting period: in this case, sales returns and allowances should be anticipated and recognized in the period of the sale to avoid distorting the current period's income statement. There are some companies that by their nature have significant returns and therefore usually have an allowance for sales returns.

As an example, assume that Astro Corporation estimates that approximately 5% of its $1 million of trade receivables outstanding will be returned or some adjustment will be made to the sales price. Leaving out a $50,000 charge could have a material effect on net income for the period. The entry to show expected sales returns and allowances is:

Sales Returns and Allowances	50,000	
Allowance for Sales Returns and Allowances		50,000

A = L + SE
−50,000   −50,000
Cash flows: No effect

The account Sales Returns and Allowances is reported as a deduction from Sales Revenue in the income statement. Allowance for Sales Returns and Allowances is an asset valuation account (contra asset) that is deducted from total accounts receivable. It is similar to the Allowance for Doubtful Accounts discussed below.

Nonrecognition of Interest Element

Ideally, receivables should be measured initially at their fair value, represented by their present value; that is, the amount of cash that would be required at the date of the sale to satisfy the outstanding claim. As mentioned in the previous section, this is equivalent to the discounted value of the cash that will be received in the future. When a company has to wait for the cash receipts, the receivable's face amount is not a good measure of its fair value.

To illustrate, assume that a company makes a sale on account for $1,000. The applicable annual interest rate is 12%, and cash is to be received at the end of four months. The receivable's present value is not $1,000 but $961.54 ($1,000 × 0.96154, Table A-2 $n = 1, i = 4\%$).[9] In other words, $1,000 to be received in four months is equivalent to $961.54 received today.

In theory, the discounted amount of $961.54 is the fair value of the receivable and sales revenue, and any additional amount received after the sale is interest revenue. **In practice, accountants generally ignore this for accounts receivable because the discount amount is not usually material when compared with the net income for the period.** Trade receivables to which normal credit terms (short-term) apply are not generally discounted.

Measurement of Accounts Receivable after Acquisition

Accounts receivable are measured in subsequent accounting periods at amortized cost. Where there is no interest element recognized, as discussed above, there is nothing to amortize, so amortized cost and cost are the same thing. For notes and loans receivable that have an interest component, the asset's carrying amount is amortized as described later in this chapter.

Impairment of Accounts Receivable

The goal in valuing accounts receivable on the balance sheet is to report them at no more than the benefits they will ultimately provide to the entity. Because of this, in addition to reductions for expected returns, allowances, or cash discounts that will be granted, all

Underlying Concept

Materiality means that an amount in question must make a difference to a decision-maker. Standard setters believe that interest and present value concepts do not need to be strictly applied if omitting them results in financial statements that are not materially different.

4 Objective
Account for and explain the accounting issues related to the impairment in value of accounts receivable.

[9] Present and future value tables are provided immediately following Chapter 12.

receivables have to be assessed for indications of uncollectibility or impairment. Loans and receivables are impaired if there has been a "significant adverse change" in either the expected timing of the future cash flows or in the amount expected to be repaid. The impairment of trade receivables is usually referred to as bad debts or **uncollectible accounts**.

Estimating Uncollectible Trade Accounts Receivable

As one accountant so aptly noted, the credit manager's idea of heaven would probably be a place where everyone (eventually) paid his or her debts.[10] Except in some segments of the retail sector, the usual method of conducting business is through extending credit to customers. This means that most companies are exposed to varying levels of credit risk: the likelihood of loss because of the failure of the other party to fully pay the amount owed. Except for cash sales, it is possible that the full amount of the sale will never be collected. Many companies set their credit policies to allow for a certain percentage of uncollectible accounts. In fact, many feel that if the percentage is not reached, sales are being lost because of credit policies that are too strict.

The **accounting issue**, therefore, is ensuring that a reasonable estimate is made of the amount of the Accounts Receivable that is unlikely to be collected. An allowance for this amount is then deducted from the receivables reported on the balance sheet. If there are only a few relatively large accounts, an analysis of each separate account can be made; but most companies have large numbers of similar accounts with smaller balances in each. How does management estimate how much may be uncollectible?

The single most important indicator used to identify impaired accounts receivable is the age of the accounts; that is, how long the amounts owed have been outstanding, especially beyond their due dates. Other factors that are taken into account include the company's past loss experience and current economic conditions. Accounts are also analyzed by grouping those with similar credit risk characteristics—perhaps by geographic location or type of industry. If one area of the country is experiencing high unemployment and depressed economic conditions, this may affect the ability of debtors in that area to pay their accounts. Or a particular industry, such as forestry or real estate, may be going through a low in the business cycle with a higher than usual incidence of tight cash, or receivership or bankruptcy.

One common method used by most companies to estimate how much of their total Accounts Receivable is probably uncollectible is the aging method. This approach allows a company to use its past experience to estimate the percentage of its outstanding receivables that will become uncollectible, without identifying specific accounts. This is referred to as the percentage-of-receivables approach. Its objective is to report receivables on the balance sheet at their net realizable value, this being the net amount expected to be received in cash. Although private entity GAAP and IFRS support measuring financial assets at the **present value of the cash that is expected to be received**, they both allow net realizable value to approximate the present value for short-term trade receivables because the effect of the time value of money is immaterial.

The percentage that is used in this approach may be a combined rate that reflects an overall estimate of the uncollectible receivables. A better approach is to set up an aging schedule, which is more sensitive to the actual status of the accounts receivable. This approach determines the age of each account receivable and applies a different percentage to each of the various age categories, based on past experience. Aging schedules are often used because they show which accounts need special attention by highlighting how long various accounts receivable have been outstanding. The schedule of Wilson & Co. in Illustration 7-4 is an example.

---

[10] William J. Vatter, *Managerial Accounting* (Englewood Cliffs, N.J.: Prentice-Hall, 1950), p. 60.

Illustration 7-4

Accounts Receivable Aging Schedule

WILSON & CO.
Aging Schedule

Name of Customer	Balance Dec. 31	Under 60 days	61–90 days	91–120 days	Over 120 days
Western Stainless Steel Corp.	$ 98,000	$ 80,000	$18,000		
Brockville Steel Company	320,000	320,000			
Freeport Sheet & Tube Co.	55,000				$55,000
Manitoba Iron Works Ltd.	74,000	60,000		$14,000	
	$547,000	$460,000	$18,000	$14,000	$55,000

Summary

Age	Amount	Percentage Estimated to Be Uncollectible	Estimate of Uncollectible Accounts
Under 60 days old	$460,000	4%	$18,400
61–90 days old	18,000	15%	2,700
91–120 days old	14,000	20%	2,800
Over 120 days	55,000	25%	13,750
Year-end balance of Allowance for Doubtful Accounts should =			$37,650

Allowance Method

This analysis indicates that Wilson & Co. expects to receive $547,000 less $37,650, or $509,350 net cash receipts from the December 31 amounts owed. That is, $509,350 is the Accounts Receivable's estimated net realizable value. The **allowance method** is used to account for this estimate of impairment. On Wilson & Co.'s December 31 balance sheet, a **contra account**, an Allowance for Doubtful Accounts (or Allowance for Uncollectible Accounts) of $37,650, is reported, as indicated in Illustration 7-5. A contra allowance account is used because the Accounts Receivable account is supported by a subsidiary ledger of each customer's balance owing and management does not know yet which specific accounts will result in non-collection and bad debt losses.

Illustration 7-5

Accounts Receivable on the Balance Sheet, Wilson & Co.

WILSON & CO. BALANCE SHEET
December 31

Current Assets	
Accounts receivable	$547,000
Less: Allowance for doubtful accounts	37,650
	$509,350

The ending balance in the allowance account should be $37,650. The appropriate entry, therefore, depends on what the balance is in the account before making the adjusting entry. Assume this is Wilson's first year of operations and that there is **no previous balance in the allowance account before this adjustment**. In this case, the entry to record the impairment for the current year is:

Bad Debt Expense	37,650	
Allowance for Doubtful Accounts		37,650

A	=	L	+	SE
−37,650				−37,650

Cash flows: No effect

To change the illustration slightly, assume that **the allowance account already has a credit balance of $800 before adjustment**. In this case, the amount to be added to the account is $36,850 ($37,650 − $800). This will bring the balance in the allowance account to $37,650. The following entry is made:

A   = L +   SE
−36,850   −36,850

Cash flows: No effect

| Bad Debt Expense | 36,850 | |
| Allowance for Doubtful Accounts | | 36,850 |

If instead the **balance in the allowance account before adjustment is a debit balance of $200**, then the amount to bring the allowance account to the correct credit balance of $37,650 is $37,850 ($37,650 desired credit balance + $200 debit balance). The balance that is already in the allowance account before the adjusting entry is made **cannot be ignored**; it has to be considered to calculate the amount needed for the adjustment.

Bad Debt Expense and the Allowance Account.   So far, we have focused on the balance in the Allowance for Doubtful Accounts. The reason for this is the emphasis in our current accounting model on ensuring good measurements of assets and liabilities. The model assumes that if assets and liabilities are measured properly, the related revenues and expenses will be as well. Let's turn now to bad debt expense.

The allowance method reports receivables at their estimated realizable value and recognizes bad debt losses as an expense in the same accounting period as when the sales on account are made. The allowance method accomplishes two things: a proper carrying value for receivables on the balance sheet, and the resulting matching of expenses and revenues in the same period. Using the allowance method, companies follow one of two accounting procedures, both of which result in the same ending balances in the Allowance and Bad Debt Expense accounts.

1. **Allowance Procedure Only**: At the end of every month, management carries out an analysis of the Accounts Receivable balances and makes an assessment of the estimated uncollectible accounts. An accounting entry is prepared, as illustrated above for Wilson & Co., adjusting the Allowance for Doubtful Accounts to its correct balance. The Bad Debt Expense account is debited or credited as necessary and at the end of the fiscal year, the total of all the entries to the expense account during the year is the bad debt expense for the year. The balance in the Allowance account is an appropriate amount because all entries were based on an analysis of the receivables.

Underlying Concept

The percentage-of-sales approach is a good illustration of using the matching concept, which relates expenses to revenues earned. The final adjustment based on the net realizable value of the receivables, however, supports the primacy of asset measurement in the model.

2. **Mix of Procedures**: At the end of every month, management estimates the company's **bad debt expense** for that month. This estimate is based on a percentage of the sales reported, and therefore is called the percentage-of-sales approach. If there is a fairly stable relationship between previous years' credit sales and bad debts, then that relationship can be turned into a percentage and used to estimate any period's bad debt expense. Because the amount of sales is known, this is a **fast and simple way** to estimate the expense each period. Each period, the Bad Debt Expense is debited and the Allowance for Doubtful Accounts is credited.

At the end of the fiscal year, however, when financial statements are issued, management still has to assess the year-end receivables to ensure that the balance in the Allowance account is appropriate. If necessary, an adjustment is then made to the Allowance account to bring it to the necessary balance, with the offsetting debit or credit made to Bad Debt Expense.

As an example, assume that every month, Dockrill Corp. estimates from past experience that about 2% of net credit sales will become uncollectible. If Dockrill Corp. has net credit sales of $400,000 in 2011, the entries made through the year to record bad debt expense in 2011 can be summarized in one entry as follows:

				A	= L +	SE
Bad Debt Expense (2% × $400,000)	8,000			−8,000		−8,000
Allowance for Doubtful Accounts		8,000				
				Cash flows: No effect		

At year end, management prepares an analysis of receivables and estimates that $9,900 will not be collectible. Therefore, the balance in the Allowance account **after adjustment** must be a credit of $9,900. The correct adjusting entry depends on the balance in the Allowance account before the adjustment is made. The balance is not likely to be a credit of $8,000, the amount of the credits to the account during the year. The Allowance is a balance sheet account and therefore would have had an opening balance, and entries to record accounts written off (as explained below) would also have been made to the account during the current year.

Assuming the balance in the Allowance for Doubtful Accounts before adjustment is $7,500 credit, then the following adjusting entry is needed:

				A	= L +	SE
Bad Debt Expense	2,400			−2,400		−2,400
Allowance for Doubtful Accounts		2,400				
($9,900 − $7,500 = $2,400)				Cash flows: No effect		

Either approach can be used. Many companies use the percentage-of-sales method for internal reporting through the year because of its ease of use, and make an adjustment at year end based on receivable balances at the balance sheet date for their external financial statements.

Accounts Written Off and the Allowance Account

Accounts Receivable Written Off. Under the allowance method, when a **specific account** is determined to be uncollectible, its balance is removed from Accounts Receivable and the Allowance for Doubtful Accounts is reduced. For example, assuming the account of Brown Ltd. of $550 is considered uncollectible, the writeoff entry is as follows:

				A	= L +	SE
Allowance for Doubtful Accounts	550			0	0	0
Accounts Receivable		550				
				Cash flows: No effect		

Note that there is no effect on the income statement **from writing off an account**, nor should there be. This is because the associated bad debt expense was **previously** recognized as an estimate **in the period of the sale**. There is also no effect on the net amount of the receivables because Accounts Receivable and its contra account are **both** reduced by equal amounts.

Collection of an Account Previously Written Off. If a collection is made on a receivable that was previously written off, the procedure is to first re-establish the receivable by reversing the writeoff entry, and **then** recognize the cash inflow as a regular receipt on account. To illustrate, assume that Brown Ltd. eventually remits $300, and indicates that this is all that will be paid. The entries to record this transaction are as follows:

A = L + SE
0   0   0

Cash flows: No effect

Accounts Receivable	300	
Allowance for Doubtful Accounts		300
(To reinstate the account written off and now determined to be collectible.)		

A = L + SE
0   0   0

Cash flows: ↑ 300 inflow

Cash	300	
Accounts Receivable		300
(To record the receipt of cash on account from Brown Ltd.)		

Effects on Accounts

Illustration 7-6

Effects on Related Accounts

Illustration 7-6 provides a summary of the transactions and events that affect the accounts related to accounts receivable.

Accounts Receivable	
Opening balance	
1. Credit sales	2. Cash received on account
5. Reinstatement of accounts previously written off	4. Accounts written off

Allowance for Doubtful Accounts	
	Opening balance
	3. Bad debt expense recognized
4. Accounts written off	5. Reinstatement of accounts previously written off
6. Year-end adjustment to reduce balance in allowance account	7. Year-end adjustment to increase balance in allowance account

Bad Debt Expense	
3. Bad debt expense recognized	
7. Year-end adjustment to increase balance in allowance account	6. Year-end adjustment to reduce balance in allowance account

Sales	
	1. Credit sales

Real-World Emphasis

What Do the Numbers Mean?

The ending balance of the Accounts Receivable account represents the total of all amounts owed to the company at the balance sheet date, except those accounts written off, of course. This amount is backed up by a subsidiary ledger of the individual customers and the amount owed by each. The ending balance of the allowance account represents management's estimate of the total accounts receivable that will not be collected. When reported together, the net amount is the estimate of the net realizable value of the total amount owed.

The allowance for doubtful accounts as a percentage of receivables varies considerably, depending on the industry and recent economic conditions. **Stantec Inc.**, a professional engineering services firm, for example, reported an allowance for doubtful accounts of 4.3% of its accounts receivable at December 31, 2008, down considerably from the 10% reported three years earlier, while **Potash Corporation of Saskatchewan Inc.**, an integrated fertilizer and related industrial and feed products company, reported an allowance of less than 1% of its trade receivables. **Canadian Tire Corporation** reported the following information about its Financial Services Division in its 2008 Annual Report.

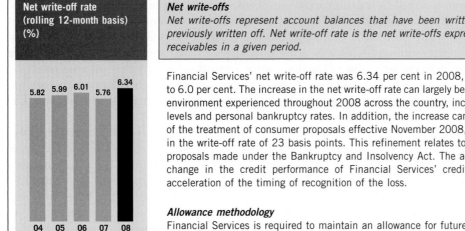

Net write-off rate (rolling 12-month basis) (%)

04	05	06	07	08
5.82	5.99	6.01	5.76	6.34

Net write-offs

Net write-offs represent account balances that have been written off, net of collections of amounts previously written off. Net write-off rate is the net write-offs expressed as a percentage of gross average receivables in a given period.

Financial Services' net write-off rate was 6.34 per cent in 2008, falling outside the target range of 5.0 to 6.0 per cent. The increase in the net write-off rate can largely be attributed to the challenging economic environment experienced throughout 2008 across the country, including job losses, higher personal debt levels and personal bankruptcy rates. In addition, the increase can be partly attributed to the refinement of the treatment of consumer proposals effective November 2008, which resulted in a one-time increase in the write-off rate of 23 basis points. This refinement relates to the immediate write-off of cardholder proposals made under the Bankruptcy and Insolvency Act. The adjustment in timing does not reflect a change in the credit performance of Financial Services' credit card receivables, but is merely an acceleration of the timing of recognition of the loss.

Allowance methodology

Financial Services is required to maintain an allowance for future write-offs that will be incurred in the receivables portfolio.

Allowance

The allowance is an estimate of the amount of receivables as at the balance sheet date that will be written off, over a set period, pursuant to Company policy. It is determined using historical loss experience of account balances based on the aging and arrears status, with certain adjustments for other relevant circumstances influencing the recoverability of the loans.

Direct Writeoff Method

Some cash-based businesses, such as corner grocery stores, do not extend credit often and therefore have very few credit transactions and small accounts receivable balances. For such businesses, **where the effect of not applying the allowance method is immaterial**, the simpler direct writeoff method is used. No estimates are made in advance and no allowance account is used. Instead, when an account is determined to be uncollectible, the specific account receivable is written off with the debit recognized as bad debt expense:

Bad Debt Expense	$$	
Accounts Receivable		$$

A = L + SE
−$$ 0 −$$
Cash flows: No effect

If amounts are later collected on an account that was previously written off, a notation is made in the customer's record, and the amount collected is recognized through entries to Cash and a revenue account entitled Uncollectible Amounts Recovered.

Cash	$$	
Uncollectible Amounts Recovered		$$

A = L + SE
+$$ 0 +$$
Cash flows: ↑ $$ inflow

Recognition and Measurement of Short-Term Notes and Loans Receivable

5 Objective
Account for and explain the accounting issues related to the recognition and measurement of short-term notes and loans receivable.

A note receivable is similar to an account receivable, with one difference: the note is supported by a formal promissory note, which is a **written** promise to pay a specific sum of money at a specific future date, and this makes a note receivable a negotiable instrument.

The note is signed by a **maker** in favour of a designated **payee** who can then legally and readily sell or transfer the note to others. **Notes always contain an interest element** because of the time value of money, but they may be classified as interest-bearing or non–interest-bearing. Interest-bearing notes have a stated rate of interest that is payable in addition to the face value of the note; zero-interest-bearing notes (or non–interest-bearing notes) also include interest, but it is equal to the difference between the amount that was borrowed (the proceeds) and the higher face amount that will be paid back. The rate may not be stated explicitly.

Companies often accept notes receivable from customers who need to extend the payment period of an outstanding account receivable. Notes are also sometimes required from high-risk or new customers. In addition, they are often used in loans to employees and subsidiaries and in sales of property, plant, and equipment. In some industries (e.g., the pleasure and sport boat industry), all credit sales are supported by notes. Most notes, however, are created by lending transactions. The basic issues in accounting for notes receivable are the same as those for accounts receivable: recognition, measurement, impairment, and disposition. This section discusses only the recognition and measurement of **short-term** notes or loans. Longer-term instruments are covered in the next section.

To illustrate the accounting for notes or loans receivable, assume that on March 14, 2011, Prime Corporation agreed to allow its customer, Gouneau Ltd., to substitute a six-month note for the account receivable of $1,000 that Gouneau was unable to pay when it came due for payment. This means that Gouneau is basically borrowing $1,000 from Prime for six months. It was agreed that the note would bear interest at a rate of 6%. Prime's entries to record the substitution and payment of the note are as follows:

A   = L   + SE
0   0   0

Cash flows: No effect

March 14, 2011		
Note Receivable	1,000	
Account Receivable		1,000

A   = L   + SE
+30   0   +30

Cash flows: ↑ 1,030 inflow

September 14, 2011		
Cash	1,030	
Note Receivable		1,000
Interest Income		30*

*$1,000 × .06 × $^{6}/_{12}$

Alternatively, a note could be accepted in exchange for lending money to an employee or subsidiary company; for example, in a **non–interest-bearing note** situation. In this case, the interest is the difference between the amount of cash that is borrowed and the face or maturity value of the note receivable. Assume that the president of Ajar Ltd. borrowed money from the company on February 23, 2011, and signed a promissory note for $5,000 repayable in nine months' time. An interest rate of 8% is appropriate for this type of loan. Instead of borrowing $5,000 and repaying this amount with 8% interest added at the maturity date, the president receives only $4,717 on February 23. The $283 difference between the $4,717 borrowed and the $5,000 repaid represents 8% interest for the nine-month period that the note is outstanding: $4,717 × 8% × $^{9}/_{12}$ = $283. Ajar's entries are as follows:[11]

---

[11] Alternatively, the entries could initially recognize the note's maturity value in Note Receivable and the discount in Discount on Note Receivable, a contra account to Note Receivable:

February 23, 2011		
Note Receivable	4,717	
Cash		4,717

A = L + SE
0   0   0

Cash flows: ↓ 4,717 outflow

November 23, 2011		
Cash	5,000	
Note Receivable		4,717
Interest Income		283*
*4,717 × .08 × $^{9}/_{12}$		

A = L + SE
+283   0   +283

Cash flows: ↑ 5,000 inflow

In both examples provided, if financial statements are prepared while the note receivable is still outstanding, interest is accrued to the balance sheet date.

Recognition and Measurement of Long-Term Notes and Loans Receivable

Since some form of promissory note is often the proof that a loan exists, the above explanation of notes receivable applies equally well to loans receivable. The examples of loans receivable that are illustrated below assume that a note is the basis for each transaction. What changes as we move from short-term to long-term notes and loans is the length of time to maturity and the importance of interest in measuring and accounting for the financial asset.

The accounting standards for the recognition and measurement of loans receivable are the same as those identified above for accounts receivable:

- recognize a loan receivable when the entity becomes a party to the contractual provisions of the financial instrument;

- when recognized initially, measure the loan receivable at its fair value;

- after initial recognition, measure loans receivable at amortized cost; and

- recognize bad debt losses on the loans receivable when they are deemed to be impaired.[12]

The **fair value** of a note or loan receivable is measured as **the present value of the cash amounts that are expected to be collected in the future, with the amounts discounted at the market rate of interest that is appropriate for a loan with similar**

6 Objective

Account for and explain the accounting issues related to the recognition and measurement of long-term notes and loans receivable.

Feb. 23	Note Receivable	5,000	
	Cash		4,717
	Discount on Note Receivable		283
Nov. 23	Cash	5,000	
	Note Receivable		5,000
	Discount on Note Receivable	283	
	Interest Income		283

The effects on the balance sheet, income statement, and cash flows are identical, regardless of the entries made. This text uses the net method in all chapters whether the instrument is an asset or a liability, as it is easier to apply and better reflects the management of the instruments on a contractual yield basis.

[12] Impairment of long-term loans is discussed in Chapter 9 along with the impairment of other financial asset investments.

Finance

credit risk and other characteristics. When the interest stated on an interest-bearing note is the same as the effective (market) rate of interest, the note's fair value is equal to its face value.[13] When the stated rate is not the same as the market rate, the note's cost (its **present value**, or **fair value**) is different from the note's **face value**. The difference between the price for the note now and its maturity value—resulting in either a discount or a premium—is then amortized over the note's life, affecting the amount of interest income that is reported. Under **IFRS**, the **effective interest method of amortization** is required, while under **private entity GAAP**, the **amortization method is not specified.** The effective interest method is illustrated further below.

Transaction costs that are incurred in acquiring a loan or note receivable, such as commissions, can be treated in one of two ways:

1. they can be recognized as an expense when they are incurred, or

2. they can be added to the fair value of the instrument, which then increases the original amount that is recognized as its "cost" at acquisition. In this case, the transaction costs are an adjustment to the discount or premium that will be amortized over the life of the loan, requiring the effective rate of interest to be recalculated.

Both private entity GAAP and IFRS agree that transaction costs associated with financial assets that are carried at amortized cost should be accounted for as explained in the second treatment above.

Under private entity GAAP, loans and receivables are accounted for at amortized cost. **Amortized cost** is the amount that was recognized when the instrument was acquired, reduced by any principal payments received, and adjusted for the amortization of any discount or premium, if appropriate, and writedowns for impairment. Under IFRS, the same accounting applies provided the note or loan has basic loan features and is managed on a contractual yield basis.[14] **Basic loan features** means that the instrument has contractual terms that result in cash flows that are payments of principal and interest. Management on a **contractual yield basis** refers to a company's business model of holding the instruments for their principal and interest flows. Let's see how this works.

Notes Issued at Face Value

To illustrate an interest-bearing note issued at face value, assume that Bigelow Corp. lends Scandinavian Imports $10,000 in exchange for a $10,000, three-year note bearing interest at 10% payable annually. The market rate of interest for a note of similar risk is also 10%. The first step is always to identify the amounts and timing of the cash flows. For our example, the following diagram shows both the interest and principal cash flows:

---

[13] The **stated interest rate**, also referred to as the **face rate** or the **coupon rate**, is the rate that is part of the note contract. The **effective interest rate**, also referred to as the **market rate** or the **yield rate**, is the rate that is used in the market to determine the note's value; i.e., the discount rate that is used to determine its present value.

[14] IFRS also allows a "fair value option" for loans and receivables in restricted circumstances and PE GAAP provides the same option for any financial instrument. These are explained in more detail in Chapter 9.

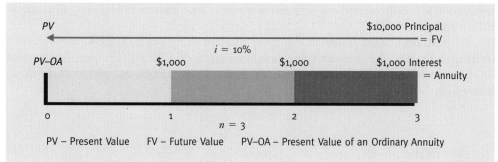

The note's present value and exchange price is calculated in Illustration 7-7.

Face value of the note	$10,000
Present value of the lump sum principal:	
$10,000 (PVF*$_{3,10\%}$) = $10,000 (0.75132) (Table A-2) $7,513	
Present value of the interest annuity:	
$1,000 (PVF*–OA$_{3,10\%}$) = $1,000 (2.48685) (Table A-4) 2,487	
Present value of the note	10,000
Difference	$ –0–

*Present Value Factors found in Tables A1–A5

Illustration 7-7

Present Value of Note—Stated and Market Rates the Same

In this case, the note's fair value, present value, and face value are the same ($10,000) **because the effective and stated interest rates are the same.** Bigelow Corp. records its acquisition of the note as follows:

Notes Receivable	10,000	
Cash		10,000

A = L + SE
0   0   0

Cash flows: ↓ 10,000 outflow

Bigelow Corp. later recognizes the interest earned each year ($10,000 × 0.10) as follows:

Cash	1,000	
Interest Income		1,000

A = L + SE
+1,000   0   +1,000

Cash flows: ↑ 1,000 inflow

Notes Not Issued at Face Value

Zero-Interest-Bearing Notes. If a zero-interest-bearing note is received in exchange for cash, its present value is usually the cash paid to the issuer. Because both the note's future amount and present value are known, the interest rate can be calculated; i.e., it is implied. The **implicit interest rate** is the rate that equates the cash paid with the amounts receivable in the future. The difference between the future (face) amount and the present value (cash paid) is a discount and this amount is amortized to interest income over the life of the note. In most cases, the implicit interest rate is the market rate. This is because the transaction is usually carried out between two parties who are at arm's length and acting in their own best interests.[15]

To illustrate, assume Jeremiah Company receives a three-year, $10,000 zero-interest-bearing note, and the present value is known to be $7,721.80. The implicit rate of interest of 9% (assumed to approximate the market rate) can be calculated as shown in Illustration 7-8.

Illustration 7-8

Determination of Implicit Interest Rate

$$PV \text{ of note} = PV \text{ of future cash flows}$$
$$PV \text{ of note} = FV \text{ of note} \times PVF_{3, ?\%} \text{ (Table A-2)}$$
$$\$7,721.80 = \$10,000 \times PVF_{3, ?\%}$$
$$PVF_{3, ?\%} = \frac{\$7,721.80}{\$10,000}$$
$$PVF_{3, ?\%} = 0.77218$$
Table A-2: Where $n = 3$ and $PVF = 0.77218$, $i = 9\%$

Thus, the implicit rate that makes the total cash to be received at maturity ($10,000) equal to the present value of the future cash flows ($7,721.80) is 9%. Note that if any two of the three variables on the second line of the equation in Illustration 7-8 are known, the third variable can be determined. For example, if the note's maturity value (**face value**) and **present value factor** (*i* and *n*) are known, the note's **present value** can be calculated.

The time diagram for the single cash flow of Jeremiah's note is as follows:

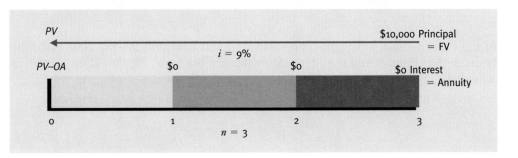

The entry to record the transaction is:

A = L + SE
0   0   0

Cash flows: ↓ 7,721.80 outflow

Notes Receivable	7,721.80	
Cash		7,721.80

Effective Interest Method of Amortization.   Under IFRS, and as applied by many private enterprises, the discount (that is, the $2,278.20 difference between the $7,721.80 provided as a loan and the $10,000 that will be repaid) is amortized each year using the **effective interest method** to recognize the interest income. This method requires that the effective interest or yield rate be calculated at the time when the investment is made. This rate is then later used to calculate interest income by applying it to the carrying amount (book

---

[15] There may be situations when the implicit interest rate is not the market rate; that is, when the fair value of the loan differs from the cash consideration. This circumstance is dealt with later in this chapter.

value) of the investment for each interest period. The note's carrying amount changes as it is increased by the amount of discount amortized. **Thus, the net carrying amount is always equal to the present value of the note's remaining cash flows (principal and interest payments) discounted at the market rate at acquisition.** Jeremiah's three-year discount amortization and interest income schedule is shown in Illustration 7-9.

Illustration 7-9

Discount Amortization Schedule—Effective Interest Method

SCHEDULE OF NOTE DISCOUNT AMORTIZATION
Effective Interest Method
0% Note Discounted at 9%

	Cash Received	Interest Income	Discount Amortized	Carrying Amount of Note
Date of issue				$ 7,721.80
End of year 1	$ –0–	$ 694.96[a]	$ 694.96[b]	8,416.76[c]
End of year 2	–0–	757.51	757.51	9,174.27
End of year 3	–0–	825.73[d]	825.73	10,000.00
	$ –0–	$2,278.20	$2,278.20	

[a] $7,721.80 × 0.09 = $694.96
[b] $694.96 − 0 = $694.96
[c] $7,721.80 + $694.96 = $8,416.76 or $10,000 − ($2,278.20 − $694.96) = $8,416.76
[d] $0.05 adjustment for rounding

Interest income at the end of the first year using the effective interest method is recorded as follows:

Notes Receivable	694.96	
Interest Income ($7,721.80 × 9%)		694.96

A   = L   +   SE
+694.96   +694.96

Cash flows: No effect

Note that the amount of the total discount, $2,278.20 in this case, represents the interest income on the note over the three years. Rather than recognize it as interest income on a straight-line basis over this period, it is recognized in increasing amounts based on the balance of the loan and previous interest earned that is still outstanding. This can be seen in Illustration 7-9. When the note comes due at the end of Year 3, the Notes Receivable account will have a balance of $10,000.00. Therefore, Jeremiah Company makes the following entry:

Cash	10,000	
Notes Receivable		10,000

A   = L   +   SE
0   0   0

Cash flows: ↑ 10,000 inflow

Straight-Line Method of Amortization. Some private entities prefer to use the straight-line method of amortizing discounts and premiums because of its simplicity. For example, in the Jeremiah Company example above, the total discount of $2,278.20 is amortized over the three-year period in equal amounts each year. Therefore, the annual amortization is $2,278.20 ÷ 3 or $759.40. The entry to record the annual interest under this method is similar to the Jeremiah example:

A = L +   SE
+759.40   +759.40

Cash flows: No effect

| Notes Receivable | 759.40 | |
| Interest Income | | 759.40 |

Underlying Concept

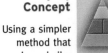

Using a simpler method that gives similar results to the effective interest method is an application of the materiality concept.

At the end of Year 3, the Notes Receivable's balance is $10,000 and the same entry is made to record the receipt of the cash.

While easier to apply, the results of using straight-line amortization do not reflect the economic reality of a loan. That is, in Year 3 Jeremiah should be reporting more interest income than in Year 1 because of the interest that also accrues on the accumulating and unpaid interest for Years 1 and 2. Under the straight-line method, equal amounts of income are reported each period.

Interest-Bearing Notes.   A note's stated rate and its effective rate are often different, as they were in the zero-interest-bearing case above. To illustrate a different situation, assume that Morgan Corp. makes a loan to Marie Co. and receives in exchange a $10,000, three-year note bearing interest at 10% annually. The market rate of interest for a note of similar risk is 12%. The time diagram for all cash flows is as follows:

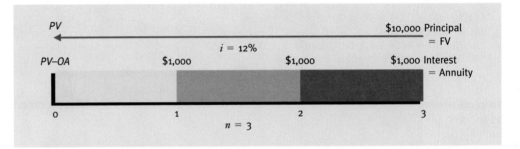

Note that the **interest cash flows are dictated by the stated rate** (10%) but that **all cash flows are discounted at the market rate** (12%) in determining the note's present value. The present value ($9,520) of the two streams of cash is calculated in Illustration 7-10.[16]

Illustration 7-10

Calculation of Present Value— Effective Rate Different from Stated Rate

Face value of the note		$10,000
Present value of the principal:		
$10,000 (PVF*$_{3,12\%}$) = $10,000 (0.71178)	$7,118	
Present value of the interest:		
$1,000 (PVF*−OA$_{3,12\%}$) = $1,000 (2.40183)	2,402	
Present value of the note		9,520
Difference		$ 480

*Present Value Factor

Because the **effective interest rate** or market interest rate (12%) is higher than the rate that the note actually pays (10%), you would expect the note's present value (also its

---

[16] Be alert to the fact that "n" equals the number of interest periods, **not one year**, and that "i" is the interest rate **for the period defined by n.** If interest were paid semi-annually in this example, n would be 6, not 3, and i would be 6%, not 12%, and these would be used to discount both the maturity amount **and** the interest flows. The interest cash flow used in the present value calculation would be $500, not $1,000.

fair value) to be less than its face value; that is, the note would be exchanged at a **discount**. This makes intuitive sense. If you were to invest in a note that promises 10% when you could get 12% elsewhere in the market at the same level of risk, you would not be willing to pay face value for the 10% note.

The receipt of the note in exchange for cash equal to its fair value is recorded by Morgan as follows:

Notes Receivable	9,520	
Cash		9,520

A = L + SE
0   0   0

Cash flows: ↓ 9,520 outflow

Over the term of the note, Morgan will receive $1,000 interest each year (a rate of 10%) and then get $480 more than the cash originally invested. This $480 (the discount) effectively increases the return on the investment from 10% to 12%. It is amortized each period and the amount of interest income that is recognized is greater than the $1,000 received each year. Morgan's three-year discount amortization and interest income schedule using the effective interest method is shown in Illustration 7-11.

SCHEDULE OF NOTE DISCOUNT AMORTIZATION
Effective Interest Method
10% Note Discounted at 12%

	Cash Received	Interest Income	Discount Amortized	Carrying Amount of Note
Date of issue				$ 9,520
End of year 1	$1,000[a]	$1,142[b]	$142[c]	9,662[d]
End of year 2	1,000	1,159	159	9,821
End of year 3	1,000	1,179	179	10,000
	$3,000	$3,480	$480	

[a] $10,000 × 10% = $1,000
[b] $9,520 × 12% = $1,142
[c] $1,142 − $1,000 = $142
[d] $9,520 + $142 = $9,662 or $10,000 − ($480 − $142) = $9,662

Illustration 7-11

Discount Amortization Schedule—Effective Interest Method

On the date of issue, the note has a present value of $9,520. Its unamortized discount—the interest income that will be spread over the three-year life of the note—is $480.

At the end of Year 1, Morgan receives $1,000 in cash, but the interest income under the effective interest method is based on the note's carrying amount and effective interest rate: $1,142 ($9,520 × 12%). The difference between $1,000 and $1,142 is the discount to be amortized, $142, and it is amortized directly to the Notes Receivable account. Morgan records the annual interest received at the end of the first year as follows:

Cash	1,000	
Notes Receivable	142	
Interest Income		1,142

A   = L +   SE
+1,142   +1,142

Cash flows: ↑ 1,000 inflow

The note's carrying amount has now been increased to $9,662 ($9,520 + $142). This process is repeated until the end of Year 3.

Under the **straight-line method,** the initial discount of $480 is amortized at a rate of $480 ÷ 3 = $160 each year with the following entry. The same entry is made each year.

Cash	1,000	
Notes Receivable	160	
Interest Income		1,160

When the stated rate is higher than the effective interest rate, the note's fair value (its present value) is more than its face value and the note is exchanged at a premium. The premium on a note receivable is recognized by recording the Note Receivable at its higher initial present value. The excess is amortized over the life of the note by crediting the Note Receivable and reducing (debiting) the amount of interest income that is recognized.

Notes Received for Property, Goods, or Services

When property, goods, or services are sold and a long-term note is received as the consideration instead of cash or a short-term receivable, there may be an issue in determining the selling price. If an appropriate market rate of interest is known for the note, or for a note of similar risk, there is no problem. The sale amount is the present value of the cash flows promised by the note, discounted at the market rate of interest. Remember that **if the stated rate and market rate are the same, the note's face value and fair value are the same.** It is when the two rates are different that the note's fair value has to be calculated by discounting the cash flows at the market rate. What if you don't know what the market rate is? In this case, one of two approaches can be used.

1. The fair value of the property, goods, or services that are given up can be used instead of the fair value of the note received. In this case, because the note's present value, the actual cash flow amounts, and the timing of the cash flows are all known, the market or yield interest rate can be calculated. This is needed in order to apply the effective interest method.

2. An appropriate interest rate can be imputed. **Imputation** is the process of determining an appropriate interest rate, and the resulting rate is called an imputed interest rate. The objective for calculating the appropriate interest rate is to approximate the rate that would have been agreed on if an independent borrower and lender had negotiated a similar transaction. The choice of a rate is affected by the prevailing rates for similar instruments of issuers with similar credit ratings. It is also affected by such factors as restrictive covenants, collateral, the payment schedule, and the existing prime interest rate.

To illustrate, assume that Oasis Corp. sold land in exchange for a five-year note that has a maturity value of $35,247 and no stated interest rate. The property originally cost Oasis $14,000. What are the proceeds on disposal of the land; that is, what selling price should be recognized in this transaction?

Situation 1: Assume that the market rate of interest of 12% is known. In this case, the proceeds from the sale are equal to the present value of the note, which is $20,000. This is a non-interest-bearing note, so the only cash flow is the $35,247 received in five periods' time: $35,247 × .56743 (Table A-2) = $20,000. The entry to record the sale is:

```
A    =  L  +    SE
+6,000          +6,000

Cash flows: No effect
```

Notes Receivable	20,000	
Land		14,000
Gain on Sale of Land ($20,000 − $14,000)		6,000

Situation 2: Assume that the market rate of interest is unknown, but the land has been appraised recently for $20,000. In this case, the property's fair value determines the amount of the proceeds and the note's fair value. The entry is the same as in Situation 1. To amortize the discount using the effective interest method, however, the implicit interest rate must be determined. This is done by finding the interest rate that makes the present value of the future cash flow amount of $35,247 equal to its present value of $20,000. The procedure is as follows: First the present value factor is calculated: $20,000 ÷ $35,247 = .56742. Table A-2 then identifies the interest rate for five periods and a factor of .56742 as 12%.

Situation 3: Assume that neither the market rate nor the land's fair value is known. In this case, a market rate must be imputed and then used to determine the note's present value. It will also be used to recognize the effective interest income over the five years and amortize the discount. If a 12% rate is estimated for Oasis, then the entry will be the same as in Situation 1. If a different rate results, the note and the gain on sale will both be different as well.

Fair Value Not Equal to Cash Consideration

Accountants need to be alert when recognizing and measuring loans receivable. Sometimes, the cash that is exchanged when the loan is made may not be the same as the fair value of the loan. In this situation, the substance of the transaction has to be determined and accounted for. Imagine a situation where a company advances $20,000 to an officer of the company, charges no interest on the advance, and makes it repayable in four years. Assuming a market rate of 6%, the fair value of the loan receivable is $15,842 ($20,000 × .79209, the PV factor for $n = 4$ and $i = 6$). Although the loan's fair value is $15,842, the officer of the company actually received $20,000. This $4,158 difference must then be recognized and accounted for according to its nature—in this case, it is likely for additional compensation. It is required to be recognized immediately in income unless it qualifies to be reported as an asset. The entry to record this transaction is as follows.

Note/Loan Receivable	15,842	
Compensation Expense	4,158	
Cash		20,000

A = L + SE
−4,158   0   −4,158

Cash flows: ↓ 20,000 outflow

Derecognition of Receivables

In the normal course of events, accounts and notes receivable are collected when they are due and then removed from the books, or derecognized. However, as credit sales and receivables have grown in size and significance, this normal course of events has evolved. **In order to receive cash more quickly from receivables, owners now often transfer accounts or loans receivable to another company for cash.**

There are various reasons for this early transfer. First, for competitive reasons, providing sales financing for customers is almost mandatory in many industries. In the sale of durable goods, such as automobiles, trucks, industrial and farm equipment, computers, and appliances, a large majority of sales are on an instalment contract basis. This means that the seller is financing the purchase by allowing the buyer to pay for it over time, usually in equal periodic payments or instalments. Many major companies in these and other industries have created wholly owned subsidiaries that specialize in receivables financing. For example, **Canadian Tire Corporation, Limited**'s Financial Services segment incorporated a federally regulated bank, **Canadian Tire Bank**. This wholly owned subsidiary manages and finances Canadian Tire's MasterCard and retail credit card and personal loan portfolios as well as other finance-related products.

Second, the **holder** may sell receivables because money is tight and access to normal credit is not available or is far too expensive or because the holder wants to accelerate its

7 **Objective**
Account for and explain the basic accounting issues related to the derecognition of receivables.

Real-World Emphasis

cash inflows. A firm may have to sell its receivables, instead of borrowing, to avoid violating the terms of its current lending agreements. In addition, the billing and collecting of receivables is often time-consuming and costly. Credit card companies such as MasterCard, Visa, and other finance companies take over the collection process and provide merchants with immediate cash in exchange for a fee to cover their collection and bad debt costs. There are also **purchasers** of receivables, who buy the receivables to obtain the legal protection of ownership rights that are given to a purchaser of assets instead of the lesser rights that a secured creditor like Visa or MasterCard has. In addition, banks and other lending institutions may be forced to purchase receivables because of legal lending limits; that is, they may not be allowed to make any additional loans but still are able to buy receivables and charge a fee for this service.

Receivables can be used to generate immediate cash for a company in two ways. Often referred to as asset-backed financing, these ways are:

1. Secured borrowings

2. Sales of receivables

Secured Borrowings

Like many other assets, receivables are often used as collateral in borrowing transactions. A creditor may require that the debtor assign or pledge receivables as security for a loan, but leave the receivables under the control of the borrowing company. The note or loan payable, a liability, is reported on the balance sheet and, if it is not paid when it is due, the creditor has the right to convert the collateral to cash; that is, to collect the receivables. Canadian banks commonly use receivables as collateral under lending agreements.

A company accounts for the collateralized assets in a secured borrowing **in the same way as it did before the borrowing**, and it accounts for the liability according to accounting policies for similar liabilities. The debtor thus recognizes interest expense on the borrowed amount, and may have to pay an additional finance charge, which is expensed. Each month, the proceeds from collecting accounts receivable are used to retire the loan obligation.

Sales of Receivables

The selling of receivables has increased significantly in recent years. One common type is a sale to a factor. **Factors** are financial intermediaries, such as a finance company, that buy receivables from businesses for a fee and then collect the amounts owed directly from the customers. Factoring receivables was traditionally associated with the garment trade in Montreal, but it is now common in other industries as well, such as furniture, consumer electronics, and automotive aftermarkets. Illustration 7-12 shows a factoring arrangement.

Illustration 7-12

Basic Procedures in Factoring

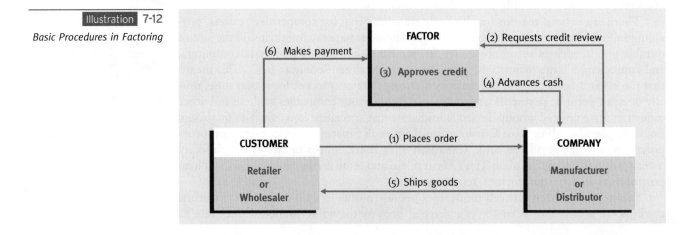

It is common today for larger companies to **transfer receivables** through a process known as securitization. Securitization is the process by which interests in financial assets are sold to a third party. It is the transformation of financial assets such as loans and receivables into securities, which are then referred to as asset-backed securities. The process takes a pool of assets that produces interest and principal payments, such as credit card receivables, mortgage receivables, or car loan receivables, and issues debt and equity interests in these pools. The resulting securities are backed by pools of assets. Almost every asset that has a payment stream (i.e., it produces payments) and has a long-term payment history is a candidate for securitization.

For example, **Canadian Tire Corporation, Limited**'s 2008 Annual Report indicates that instead of owning all of its receivables throughout the collection period, it sells interests in its customer credit card loans receivable to Glacier Credit Card Trust. **Glacier Credit Card Trust** was formed to handle receivables portfolios and is financed by the issue of debt securities to third-party investors. By this process, the receivables are transformed into securities being held by a **special purpose entity (SPE)**, the trust.

The arrangements that are made in a securitization transaction differ from company to company. Canadian Tire, for example, sells pools of these receivables for cash and some retained interest in some components of the receivables. The components it gets back include the right to the interest portion of the receivables (but not the principal), a subordinated interest in the loans sold, and a securitization reserve along with a servicing liability. Canadian Tire continues to service the receivables; that is, it manages the accounts, including the responsibility to collect the amounts due.

What is the motivation for this type of transaction? Basically, it is a financing transaction that gives companies a more attractive way to raise funds than by issuing a corporate bond or note. The credit risk for a bond or note issued by a company is higher than the credit risk of a special purpose entity that holds the company's receivables. For example, **Sears Canada Inc.**'s annual report recently reported a credit rating of AAA and R-1 (High) **for its trust securitized debt issues and commercial paper**, respectively, which are the highest possible ratings for these debt classifications. Compare these with BBB and BBB (High) ratings at the same time for Sears' **senior unsecured debt**. The higher credit rating is due to the fact that receivables transferred to an SPE are often credit enhanced[17] and the cash flows to the SPE are much more predictable than the cash flows to the operating company because there are no operating risks for an SPE. When the risk is less, the cost of financing is also less. The net result is that the company that transfers its receivables gets access to lower-cost financing that it can then use to pay off debt that has a higher cost of capital.

The differences between factoring and securitization are that **factoring** usually involves a sale to only one company, fees are relatively high, the quality of the receivables may be lower, and the seller does not usually service the receivables afterward. In a **securitization**, many investors are involved, margins are tight, the receivables are of higher quality, and the seller usually continues to service the receivables. When the company making the transfer continues to be involved in some way with the transferred assets, and measurement of the underlying transaction amounts involves some uncertainty, many disclosures are required in the financial statements.

Underlying Principles.   Before identifying the criteria that need to exist for a transaction to be treated as a sale, it is important to understand two basic concepts that underlie the decisions of standard setters. The first principle, applied in many similar situations, is that only assets that an **entity can control** should be recognized on its balance sheet. Once control is given up, the asset should no longer be recognized—it should be derecognized.

---

[17] Credit enhancements include guaranteeing payment through recourse to the company selling the receivables or third-party guarantee provisions, the use of cash reserve accounts, or overcollateralization; i.e., providing security with a greater fair value than the amount that is at risk.

Finance

The second concept, which has been applied to assets such as accounts receivable only recently, is that receivables can be disaggregated (or separated) into a variety of **financial components**. This approach makes it possible to assign values to such components as the rights to the principal cash flows and/or interest cash flows, a recourse provision, servicing rights, agreements to reacquire, and rights to returns in excess of specified limits, for example. Previous standards treated receivables as an inseparable unit that could only be "entirely sold or entirely retained."

As this text went to print, accounting standards governing the derecognition of financial assets were in a state of flux.[18] The following discussion, therefore, illustrates the key concepts involved rather than the specific detailed standards of either private entity GAAP or IFRS.

Criteria for Treatment as a Sale.   Not long ago, companies tended to account for many transactions as **sales** of receivables, even when they had a major continuing interest in and control over the transferred receivables. Doing this resulted in derecognizing accounts receivable (i.e., removing them from the balance sheet), reporting no additional debt, but often a gain on sale. The major challenge for accounting standards is to identify when a transfer of receivables qualifies for **being treated as a sale** (derecognition), and when it is merely a **secured borrowing**. Most managers would prefer to have the transaction treated for accounting purposes as a sale because this results in not having to record additional debt on the balance sheet.

In general, standard setters have concluded that the receivable or component parts of the receivable should be derecognized when control over the rights to the cash flows expires. This is troublesome in situations when the company "selling" the receivables has a continuing involvement in the asset, or when part of the consideration received from transferring the receivables is a beneficial interest in the transferred asset's benefits. A beneficial interest is basically a debt or equity claim to the cash flows of the party that acquired the receivables. Currently there are disagreements as to how to interpret and apply the control criteria and the retention of partial interests. The accounting issues are important ones because of the ability to remove significant assets from the balance sheet, and not report liabilities when substantial risks have actually been retained.

The example below illustrates the pre-2011 Canadian model. The following conditions were used to indicate whether control over the receivables has actually been transferred, supporting treatment as a sale.

1. The transferred assets are isolated from the transferor; i.e., put beyond the reach of the transferor and its creditors, even in bankruptcy or receivership.

2. The transferee (the party that receives the assets) has the right to pledge or exchange the assets (or beneficial interests) that it received.

3. The transferor does not maintain effective control over the transferred assets through an agreement to repurchase or redeem them before their maturity or an ability to unilaterally cause the holder to return specific assets.

---

[18] In 2009, the IFRS fast-tracked a replacement standard for IAS 39 *Financial Instruments—Recognition and Measurement*. This included the adoption of IFRS 9 to reduce the number of classifications and accounting methods for financial assets, an exposure draft to change the derecognition requirements for financial assets, and an exposure draft of revised standards for impairment. Much of this is a response to the global financial crisis that began in 2007. Comment letters received by the IASB indicate that there may not be general support for some of its proposed changes. In addition, the Canadian Accounting Standards Board has indicated that *Generally Accepted Accounting Principles for Private Enterprises*, released in late 2009, is likely to undergo changes related to the transfer of receivables as the IASB makes progress in this area. Only the recognition and measurement standard had been finalized as the text went to print and even this final standard is widely expected to undergo changes before its 2013 effective date. Because of this and the complexity of some of the issues, the coverage of some topics in the text is general rather than specific.

If all three conditions do not apply, the transferring company records the transfer as a secured borrowing. **Only when all three conditions are satisfied** is control over the assets assumed to be given up, and the transaction accounted for as a sale. If accounting for the transaction as a sale is appropriate but there is continuing involvement, the specific asset components retained need to be identified, as well as any liability components that were assumed. This approach is depicted in a decision tree format in Illustration 7-13. While the specific conditions for derecognition may change as revised standards for private entities and IFRS are settled, the general approach will likely be similar.

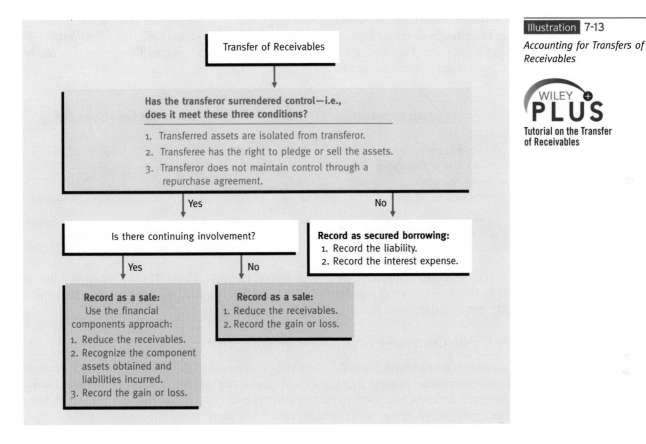

Illustration 7-13

Accounting for Transfers of Receivables

WILEY PLUS

Tutorial on the Transfer of Receivables

These transactions become more complex because of specialized contracts with different terms and conditions between companies, the securitization of receivables, and special purpose entities. The illustrations that follow are somewhat simplified to make the basic process of accounting for such transactions easier to follow.

Sale with No Continuing Involvement by Transferor. The most straightforward situation is when the receivables are sold outright to another unrelated party, such as a factor, and they are sold without recourse.

When receivables are sold without recourse, the purchaser assumes the risk of collection and absorbs any credit losses.[19] Such a transfer is an outright sale of the receivables both in form (the title is transferred) and substance (control is transferred). In non-recourse transactions, as in any sale of assets, Cash is debited for the proceeds. Accounts

---

[19] Recourse is defined as "the right of a transferee of receivables to receive payment from the transferor of those receivables for failure of debtors to pay when due, the effects of prepayments, or adjustments resulting from defects in the eligibility of the transferred receivables" (*CICA Handbook*, Part II, Section 3856 *Financial Instruments*).

Receivable is credited for the receivables' face value. The difference, reduced by any provision for probable adjustments (discounts, returns, allowances, etc.), is recognized in the account Gain or Loss on the Sale of Receivables. When appropriate, the seller uses a Due from Factor account (reported as a receivable) to account for the proceeds that are retained by a factor in order to cover probable sales discounts, sales returns, and sales allowances.

To illustrate, Crest Textiles Ltd. factors $500,000 of accounts receivable with Commercial Factors, Inc. on a **without recourse** basis. The receivables records are transferred to Commercial Factors, Inc., which takes over full responsibility for the collections. Commercial Factors assesses a finance charge of 3% of the amount of accounts receivable and withholds an initial amount equal to 5% of the accounts receivable. Illustration 7-14 shows the journal entries for both Crest Textiles and Commercial Factors for this receivables transfer without recourse.

Illustration 7-14

Entries for Sale of Receivables without Recourse

Crest Textiles Ltd.			Commercial Factors, Inc.		
Cash	460,000		Accounts (Notes)		
Due from Factor	25,000*		Receivable	500,000	
Loss on Sale of Receivables	15,000**		Due to Crest Textiles		25,000
Accounts (Notes)			Financing Revenue		15,000
Receivable		500,000	Cash		460,000

*(5% × $500,000)
**(3% × $500,000)

To recognize the outright sale of the receivables, Crest Textiles records a loss of $15,000. The factor's net income will be the difference between the financing revenue of $15,000 and the amount of any uncollectible receivables.

Sale with Continuing Involvement by Transferor

Recourse Component Retained.   If receivables are sold with recourse, the seller or transferor guarantees payment to the purchaser if the customer fails to pay. A financial components approach is used to record this type of transaction because the seller has a continuing involvement with the receivable. Each party to the sale recognizes the components (assets and liabilities) that it controls after the sale and derecognizes the assets and liabilities that were sold or extinguished.

To illustrate, assume the same information as in Illustration 7-14 for Crest Textiles and Commercial Factors except that the receivables are sold **with recourse**. Crest Textiles estimates that the recourse obligation (a liability) has a fair value of $6,000. This is the company's estimate of the cost of its agreement in the contract to pay the amount of any receivables that debtors fail to pay. To determine the loss on the sale of Crest Textiles' receivables, the net proceeds from the sale are calculated and compared with the carrying amount of the assets that were sold, as shown in Illustration 7-15. Net proceeds are cash or other assets received in a sale less any liabilities incurred.

Illustration 7-15

Calculation of Net Proceeds and Loss on Sale

Calculation of net proceeds:		
Cash received (an asset)	$460,000	
Due from factor (an asset)	25,000	$485,000
Less: Recourse obligation (a liability)		6,000
Net proceeds		$479,000

Calculation of loss on sale:	
Carrying amount of receivables	$500,000
Net proceeds	479,000
Loss on sale of receivables	$ 21,000

Illustration 7-16 shows the journal entries for both Crest Textiles and Commercial Factors for the receivables sold with a recourse component being retained.

Crest Textiles Ltd.			Commercial Factors, Inc.		
Cash	460,000		Accounts Receivable	500,000	
Due from Factor	25,000		Due to Crest Textiles		25,000
Loss on Sale of Receivables	21,000		Financing Revenue		15,000
Accounts (Notes)			Cash		460,000
Receivable		500,000			
Recourse Liability		6,000			

In this case, Crest Textiles recognizes a loss of $21,000. In addition, a liability of $6,000 is recorded to indicate the probable payment to Commercial Factors for uncollectible receivables. If all the receivables are collected, Crest Textiles would eliminate its recourse liability and increase income. Commercial Factors' net income is the financing revenue of $15,000 because it will have no bad debts related to these receivables.

Servicing and Other Components.   Often, the transferor in a securitization will retain the responsibility for servicing the receivables. This usually includes collecting the principal and interest, monitoring slow-paying accounts, and remitting cash to those who hold beneficial interests in the receivables. It may also include other specified services. If the transferor receives no reimbursement for these activities or receives less than the estimated cost of carrying them out, a **servicing liability component** is recorded. This decreases the net proceeds on disposal. Alternatively, a **servicing asset component** is recognized if the benefits of servicing (servicing fees under contract, late charges, etc.) are greater than the estimated cost of the obligation.

Other financial components that may be identified and recognized in a securitization include:

Interest-only strip receivable	The contractual right to receive some or all of the interest due on an interest-bearing receivable
Call option	The right of the transferor to repurchase similar loans or receivables from the transferee

Most of the complications associated with the accounting for the disposition of accounts receivable are related to situations when the transferor continues to have some involvement with those assets. The criteria for and extent to which those receivables should be derecognized are the major issues still being wrestled with by standard setters.

Disclosure

The need for transparency requires significant disclosures for securitized receivables that are accounted for as sales. The goal is to inform readers about the fair value measurements and key assumptions that were used, the characteristics of the securitizations, cash flows between the special purpose entity and the transferor, and the balances and risk of servicing the assets and liabilities. Illustration 7-17 in the next section of the chapter gives an example of the main securitization disclosures made by **BCE Inc.** for its year ended December 31, 2008.

PRESENTATION, DISCLOSURE, AND ANALYSIS OF RECEIVABLES

Presentation and Disclosure

Objective 8
Explain how receivables and loans are reported and analyzed.

When financial statements are prepared, the presentation of and disclosures related to receivables have to be addressed. The objective is to allow users to be able to evaluate the significance of these financial assets to the entity's financial position and performance and to allow users to assess the nature and extent of the associated risks. Aside from providing information about the accounting policies applied, entities are required to present the following data associated with loans and receivables, with more information required under IFRS than private entity GAAP:

1. The segregation and separate reporting of ordinary trade accounts, amounts owing by related parties, prepayments, and other significant amounts

2. An indication of the amounts and, where practicable, the maturity dates of accounts with a maturity of more than one year

3. Separate reporting of receivables that are current assets from those that are noncurrent

4. Separate reporting of any impaired balances, and the amount of any allowance for credit losses with, under IFRS, a reconciliation of the changes in the allowance account during the accounting period

5. Disclosure on the income statement of the amounts of interest income, impairment losses, and any reversals associated with such losses

Major disclosures are also required about the securitization or transfers of receivables, whether derecognized or not. Users are particularly interested in the risks to which the entity is exposed in general, and as a result of such transactions. Credit risk is the major concern associated with loans and receivables, so extensive qualitative and quantitative information is required under IFRS about the entity's situation, as is fair value information about loans and receivables, except for short-term trade accounts. Far less information about risk exposures and fair values is required under private entity GAAP.

Extensive excerpts from the December 31, 2008, balance sheet of the well-known Canadian communications company **BCE Inc.** and the notes cross-referenced to its balance sheet are presented in Illustration 7-17. While these disclosures are not based on current private entity GAAP or IFRS, the nature of much of the information provided is similar.[20]

Real-World Emphasis

---

[20] Students are referred to the specific requirements in *CICA Handbook*, Part II, Section 3856 *Financial Instruments* and IAS 1 *Presentation of Financial Statements*, IAS 32 *Financial Instruments: Presentation*, and IFRS 7 *Financial Instruments: Disclosures* for the detailed presentation and disclosures required.

Consolidated Balance Sheets

Illustration 7-17

BCE Inc., Disclosures of Receivables and Loans

Additional Disclosures

AT DECEMBER 31 (in $ millions)	NOTE	2008	2007
ASSETS			
Current assets			
Cash and cash equivalents		3,059	2,652
Accounts receivable	10	1,837	1,902
Future income taxes	7	86	71
Inventory	11	272	264
Prepaid and other expenses		304	274
Current assets of discontinued operations	8	20	61
Total current assets		5,578	5,224
Other long-term assets	13	2,613	3,080

NOTE 1: SIGNIFICANT ACCOUNTING POLICIES

Cash and Cash Equivalents

Cash and cash equivalents is comprised mainly of highly liquid investments with original maturities of three months or less from the date of purchase.

Securitization of Accounts Receivable

We consider a transfer of accounts receivable to be a sale when we give up control of the accounts receivable in exchange for proceeds other than our retained beneficial interest in the accounts receivable.

We determine the fair value of the accounts receivable transferred based on the present value of future expected cash flows, which we project using management's best estimates of discount rates, the weighted average life of accounts receivable, credit loss ratios and other key assumptions. We recognize a loss on the securitization, which we record in Other (expense) income. The loss is calculated by reference to the carrying amount of the transferred accounts receivable and is allocated between accounts receivable sold and our retained interest, according to their relative fair values on the day the transfer is made.

We recognize a servicing liability on the day accounts receivable are transferred when we continue to service the accounts receivable after the transfer. We amortize this liability to earnings over the expected life of the transferred accounts receivable.

NOTE 5: OTHER (EXPENSE) INCOME

FOR THE YEAR ENDED DECEMBER 31	NOTE	2008	2007
(Losses) gains on investments	13	(308)	2,414
Interest income		97	47
Securitization losses	10	(52)	(64)
Premium on redemption of Bell Aliant debt		–	–
Foreign currency gains (losses)		19	(31)
Other		(9)	39
Total other (expense) income		(253)	2,405

NOTE 10: ACCOUNTS RECEIVABLE

AT DECEMBER 31	2008	2007
Trade accounts receivable	1,405	1,403
Allowance for doubtful accounts	(132)	(127)
Allowance for revenue adjustments	(82)	(91)
Income taxes receivable	63	124
Investment tax credits	408	427
Other accounts receivable	175	166
Total accounts receivable	1,837	1,902

continued on page 412

Securitization of Accounts Receivable

At December 31, 2008, an interest of a total of $1,140 million of Bell Canada's accounts receivable had been sold to a securitization trust for cash ($1,112 million in cash at December 31, 2007) under a revolving sales agreement that expires on December 31, 2011. Bell Canada had a retained interest of $130 million in the pool of accounts receivable at December 31, 2008 ($149 million at December 31, 2007), which equals the amount of overcollateralization in the receivables sold.

At December 31, 2008, an interest of a total of $165 million of Bell Aliant's accounts receivable had been sold to a securitization trust for cash ($220 million in cash at December 31, 2007) under a revolving sales agreement that expires on July 7, 2011. Bell Aliant had a retained interest of $44 million in the pool at December 31, 2008 ($61 million at December 31, 2007).

Bell Canada and Bell Aliant continue to service these accounts receivable. The buyers' interest in the collection of these accounts receivable ranks ahead of the interests of Bell Canada and Bell Aliant, which means that Bell Canada and Bell Aliant are exposed to certain risks of default on the amount securitized. They have provided various credit enhancements in the form of overcollateralization and subordination of their retained interests.

The buyers will reinvest the amounts collected by buying additional interests in the Bell Canada and Bell Aliant accounts receivable until the agreements expire. The buyers and their investors have no further claim on Bell Canada's and Bell Aliant's other assets if customers do not pay amounts owed.

In 2008, we recognized a loss of $52 million on the revolving sale of accounts receivable for the combined securitizations, compared to losses of $64 million in 2007 and $57 million in 2006.

The following table shows balances for the combined securitizations at December 31, 2008 and the assumptions that were used in the model on the date of transfer and at December 31, 2008. A 10% or 20% adverse change in each of these assumptions would have no significant effect on the current fair value of the retained interest.

	RANGE FOR 2008	2008	2007
Securitized interest in accounts receivable		1,305	1,332
Retained interest		174	210
Servicing liability		2	2
Average accounts receivable managed		2,091	2,040
Assumptions			
Cost of funds	4.05%–4.93%	4.05%	4.74%
Average delinquency ratio	11.60%–12.97%	11.60%	12.10%
Average net credit loss ratio	0.96%–1.14%	0.96%	1.06%
Weighted average life (days)	37	37	36
Servicing fee liability	2.00%	2.00%	2.00%

The following table is a summary of certain cash flows received from and paid to the trusts during the year.

FOR THE YEAR ENDED DECEMBER 31	2008	2007
Collections reinvested in revolving sales	18,374	18,579
Decrease in sale proceeds	(27)	(6)

NOTE 13: OTHER LONG-TERM ASSETS

AT DECEMBER 31	NOTE	2008	2007
Accrued benefit asset	24	1,636	1,524
Future income taxes	7	78	126
AFS publicly-traded and privately-held securities		275	666
Investment tax credits (1)		130	239
Long-term notes and other receivables		151	234
Other		343	291
Total other long-term assets		2,613	3,080

(1) Our investment tax credits expire in varying annual amounts until the end of 2028.

NOTE 20: FINANCIAL AND CAPITAL MANAGEMENT

Credit Risk

We are exposed to credit risk from operating activities and certain financing activities, the maximum exposure of which is represented by the carrying amounts reported on the balance sheet.

We are exposed to credit risk if counterparties to our accounts receivable and derivative instruments are unable to meet their obligations. The concentration of credit risk from our customers is minimized because we have a large and diverse customer base. We regularly monitor our credit risk and credit exposure. There was minimal credit risk relating to derivative instruments at December 31, 2008. We deal with institutions that have strong credit ratings and as such we expect that they will be able to meet their obligations.

The following table provides the change in allowance for doubtful accounts for trade accounts receivable.

Balance at December 31, 2007	(127)
Additions	(66)
Use	61
Balance at December 31, 2008	(132)

For many of our customers, accounts receivable are written off directly to bad debt expense if the account has not been collected after a pre-determined period of time.

Analysis

Analysts often calculate financial ratios to evaluate the liquidity of a company's accounts receivable. To assess the receivables' liquidity, the **receivables turnover ratio** is used. This ratio measures the number of times, on average, that receivables are collected during the period. The ratio is calculated by dividing net sales by average receivables (net) outstanding during the year. Theoretically, the numerator should include only credit sales, but this information is often not available. As long as the relative amounts of credit and cash sales stay fairly constant, however, the trend indicated by the ratio will still be valid. Average receivables outstanding can be calculated from the beginning and ending balances of net trade receivables unless seasonal factors are significant. If significant, as they often are for many retail enterprises, using an average of the year's opening balance and the amounts at the end of each quarter will be more representative.

To illustrate, we use the 2008 accounts of **Canadian Utilities Limited**, a Canadian-based company in the power generation, transmission, and distribution business. Canadian Utilities reported 2008 revenue of $2,778.9 million and accounts receivable balances at December 31, 2007 and 2008, of $373.9 million and $385.5 million, respectively. Its accounts receivable turnover ratio is calculated in Illustration 7-18.

Real-World Emphasis

Accounts Receivable Turnover $= \dfrac{\text{Net Sales/Revenue}}{\text{Average Trade Receivables (net)}}$

$= \dfrac{\$2,778.9}{(\$373.9 + \$385.5)/2}$

$= $ 7.3 times, or every 50 days
(365 days $\div$ 7.3)[21]

Illustration 7-18

Calculation of Accounts Receivable Turnover

---

[21] Often the receivables turnover is converted to "days to collect accounts receivable" or "days sales outstanding"; i.e., to an average collection period. In this case, 7.3 is divided into 365 days to obtain 50 days. Several figures other than 365 could be used here; a common alternative is 360 days because it is divisible by 30 (days) and 12 (months). Please use 365 days in any assignment calculations.

The results give information about the quality of the receivables. They also give an idea of how successfully the firm collects its outstanding receivables, particularly when compared with prior periods, industry standards, the company's credit terms, or internal targets. Management would also prepare an aging schedule to determine how long specific receivables have been outstanding. It is possible that a satisfactory receivables turnover may have resulted because certain receivables were collected quickly though others have been outstanding for a relatively long time. An aging schedule would reveal such patterns.

Because the estimated expense for uncollectible accounts is subject to a degree of judgement, there is always some concern that companies can use this judgement to manage earnings. By overestimating the amount of uncollectible loans in a good earnings year, a bank, for example, can "save for a rainy day." In future less profitable periods, the bank will then be able to reduce its overly conservative allowance for its loan loss account and increase earnings as a result.[22] Remember, though, that reversals of such impairment losses should be based on specific events and circumstances occurring after the original bad debt loss was recognized.

Further analysis is often carried out on changes in the basic related accounts. Ordinarily, sales, accounts receivable, and the allowance for doubtful accounts should all move in the same direction. Higher sales should generate more receivables and an increased allowance. If sales have increased as well as receivables, but the allowance has not increased proportionately, the reader should be alert to the possibility of earnings management. If the allowance grows faster than receivables, particularly when sales have not increased, this could indicate deterioration in credit quality. Alternatively, perhaps the company has built up its allowance account so that there is a cushion for poorer performing years ahead. The answers are not always obvious, but this type of analysis can identify concerns.

With the increased practice of selling receivables through securitization transactions, especially where a company retains servicing (such as collection) responsibilities, the financial ratios have to be calculated and interpreted carefully. Consider the following:

- It is not appropriate to directly compare the turnover ratio of a company that securitizes or factors its receivables with another company that does not. This financing comes at a cost, but should provide cash flow for other value-adding purposes. Therefore, each company's situation has to be analyzed separately.

- Growth in a company's sales and growth in its receivables generally go hand in hand, but will not for a company involved in selling its receivables. Any company that begins such a program in the year should notice a significant change in the key account receivable ratios due to the lower receivable balances.

- Securitization is "off–balance sheet" because the receivables sold are removed from the current assets and because the amount "borrowed" is not reported in its liabilities. This affects liquidity ratios such as the current and quick ratios. Even though the same dollar amount is missing from the assets and liabilities, the ratios can be significantly affected.

Securitization transactions can be complex, making it necessary to be very cautious when interpreting financial statement ratios. Companies are increasingly required by regulators to provide a full discussion in the MD&A of critical issues like liquidity, especially if the company depends on such off–balance sheet financing arrangements.

---

[22] Recall from the earnings management discussion in Chapter 4 that increasing or decreasing income through management manipulation reduces the quality of financial reports.

IFRS/PRIVATE ENTITY GAAP COMPARISON

Comparison of IFRS and Private Entity GAAP

As this text went to print, accounting standards for private entities and IFRS were both in a state of flux. From an intermediate accounting perspective, the general approaches explained in the chapter are expected to continue, although the final standards that result are likely to have more specific application guidance. Private entity GAAP is designed intentionally to eliminate much of the complexity in pre-2011 financial instrument standards, and IFRS has a similar goal.

Illustration 7-19 presents the more important differences that are expected to continue, based on exposed positions to date.

9 Objective
Identify differences in accounting between private entity GAAP and IFRS, and what changes are expected in the near future.

	Accounting Standards for Private Enterprises (Private Entity GAAP)—*CICA Handbook,* Part II, Sections 1510 and 3856	IFRS—IAS 1, 32, and 39; IFRS 7
Cash and cash equivalents	Only non-equity short-term, highly liquid investments that are readily convertible to known amounts of cash and subject to an insignificant risk of change in value qualify as cash equivalents.	IFRS also allows preferred shares that are acquired close to their maturity date to qualify as a cash equivalent.
Receivables: recognition and measurement	The standard does not require use of the effective interest method of recognizing interest income and amortizing any discounts or premiums; therefore, either the straight-line method or the effective interest method may be used.	The effective interest method is required for recognizing interest income and amortizing discounts and premiums unless the investments are held for trading purposes.
Disclosures	Basic disclosures are required related to the significance of receivables to the entity's financial position and financial performance, and the financial risks to which it is exposed.	Much more detailed quantitative and qualitative disclosures are required about the receivables, interest income, and associated risks, as well as sensitivity analysis related to the measurements made.

Illustration 7-19

IFRS and Private Entity GAAP Comparison Chart

Looking Ahead

Private Entity GAAP

While most requirements set out in generally accepted accounting principles for private enterprises are not likely to change in the short term once adopted, one area that is open to change is that of the derecognition (transfer) of receivables. This issue has been contentious for many years. The Accounting Standards Board has indicated that changes are likely to be made to private entity GAAP after the IASB and FASB develop their final standards on the derecognition of financial assets and on how to account for and report continuing interests in special purpose entities. Although the IASB had issued exposure drafts on both these issues as this chapter was being finalized, there is evidence of differences of opinion and levels of acceptance of its exposed position.

The approach taken in this chapter relative to these unresolved issues has been to discuss the general approaches and not the detailed requirements.

IFRS

As indicated above, the IASB and the FASB have both been working on improvements to various issues associated with this chapter's topics. The project on the derecognition of financial assets, including loans and receivables, was expected to be completed toward the end of 2010. It was not clear what specific approach would ultimately be agreed on, but the accounting treatment for receivables transferred to a special purpose entity (SPE) that the transferring entity continues to have an interest in may change significantly. A major issue was whether or not the financial statements of the SPE should be consolidated with those of the transferor.

The IASB has fast-tracked another project on the classification and measurement of financial instruments, and its resolution may marginally affect the accounting for loans and receivables. A final standard on this issue was issued in late 2009 but some of its requirements are likely to change before its 2013 effective date. In addition, a project on developing one impairment model for all financial instruments carried at cost or amortized cost was also in progress, with a final standard due by mid-2010. It was not clear when the text went to print whether the IASB would proceed with something similar to its existing approach or whether it would move to a different model.

WILEY PLUS
Glossary

KEY TERMS

aging method, 388

aging schedule, 388

allowance method, 389

amortized cost, 396

asset-backed
    financing, 404

asset-backed
    securities, 405

bad debts, 388

bank overdrafts, 381

basic loan features, 396

beneficial interest, 406

cash, 379

cash discounts, 385

cash equivalents, 381

compensating
    balances, 380

contra account, 389

contractual yield
    basis, 396

coupon rate, 396

credit risk, 388

derecognized, 403

direct writeoff
    method, 393

discount, 401

Summary of Learning Objectives

1 Define financial assets, and identify items that are considered cash and cash equivalents and how they are reported.

Financial assets are a major type of asset defined as cash, a contractual right to receive cash or another financial asset, an equity holding in another company, or a contractual right to exchange financial instruments under potentially favourable conditions. To be reported as cash, an asset must be readily available to pay current obligations and not have any contractual restrictions that would limit how it can be used in satisfying debts. Cash consists of coins, currency, and available funds on deposit at a bank. Negotiable instruments such as money orders, certified cheques, cashier's cheques, personal cheques, and bank drafts are also viewed as cash. Savings accounts are usually classified as cash. Cash equivalents include highly liquid short-term investments (i.e., maturing less than three months from the date of purchase) that can be exchanged for known amounts of cash and have an insignificant chance of changing in value. Examples include treasury bills, commercial paper, and money-market funds. In certain circumstances, temporary bank overdrafts may be deducted in determining the balance of cash and cash equivalents.

Cash is reported as a current asset in the balance sheet, with foreign currency balances reported at their Canadian dollar equivalent at the balance sheet date. The reporting of other related items is as follows: (1) Restricted cash: Legally restricted deposits that are held as compensating balances against short-term borrowing are stated separately in Current Assets. Restricted deposits held against long-term borrowing arrangements are separately classified in noncurrent assets either in Investments or Other Assets. (2) Bank overdrafts: These are reported in the Current Liabilities section and may be added to the amount reported as accounts payable. (3) Cash equivalents: This item is often reported together with cash as "cash and cash equivalents."

2 Define receivables and identify the different types of receivables.

Receivables are claims held against customers and others for money, goods, or services. Most receivables are financial assets. The receivables are described in the following ways: (1) current or noncurrent; (2) trade or nontrade; and (3) accounts receivable or notes or loans receivable.

3 Account for and explain the accounting issues related to the recognition and measurement of accounts receivable.

Two issues that may complicate the measurement of accounts receivable are (1) the availability of discounts (trade and cash discounts) and (2) the length of time between the sale and the payment due dates (the interest element). Ideally, receivables should be measured initially at their fair value, which is their present value (discounted value of the cash to be received in the future). Receivables that are created by normal business transactions and are due in the short term are excluded from present value considerations.

4 Account for and explain the accounting issues related to the impairment in value of accounts receivable.

Short-term receivables are reported at their net realizable value—the net amount that is expected to be received in cash, which is not necessarily the amount that is legally receivable. Determining net realizable value requires estimating uncollectible receivables and any future returns or allowances and discounts that are expected to be taken. The adjustments to the asset account also affect the income statement amounts of bad debt expense, sales returns and allowances, and sales discounts. The assessment of impairment is usually based on an aged accounts receivable report, with higher percentages of uncollectible accounts indicated for older amounts outstanding. Even if a company estimates bad debt expense each period as a percentage of sales, the accounts receivable at the balance sheet date are analyzed to ensure the balance in the allowance account is appropriate.

5 Account for and explain the accounting issues related to the recognition and measurement of short-term notes and loans receivable.

The accounting issues related to short-term notes receivable are identical to those of accounts receivable. However, because notes always contain an interest element, interest income must be properly recognized. Notes receivable either bear interest on the face amount (interest-bearing) or have an interest element that is the difference between the amount lent and the maturity value (non-interest-bearing).

6 Account for and explain the accounting issues related to the recognition and measurement of long-term notes and loans receivable.

Long-term notes and loans receivable are recognized initially at their fair value (the present value of the future cash flows) and subsequently at their amortized cost. Transaction costs are capitalized. This requires amortizing any discount if the item was issued at less than its face value, or any premium if it was issued for an amount greater than its face value, using the effective interest method. The straight-line method may be used under private entity GAAP. Amortization of the discount (premium) results in a reduction of (increase in) interest income below (above) the cash amount received.

7 Account for and explain the basic accounting issues related to the derecognition of receivables.

To accelerate the receipt of cash from receivables, the owner may transfer the receivables to another entity for cash. The transfer of receivables to a third party for cash may be done in one of two ways: (1) Secured borrowing: the creditor requires the debtor to designate or pledge receivables as security for the loan. (2) Sale (factoring or securitization) of receivables: Factors are finance companies or banks that buy receivables from businesses and then collect the remittances directly from the customers. Securitization is the transfer of receivables to a special purpose entity that is mainly financed by highly rated debt instruments. In many cases, transferors have some continuing involvement with the receivables they sell. A financial components approach is used to record this type of transaction: this approach breaks the receivables down into a variety of asset and liability components, and the sold components are derecognized and accounted for separately from the retained ones.

8 Explain how receivables and loans are reported and analyzed.

Disclosure of receivables requires that valuation accounts be appropriately offset against receivables, that the receivables be appropriately classified as current or non-current, and that pledged or designated receivables be identified. As financial instruments, specific disclosures are required for receivables so that users can determine their significance to the company's financial position and performance and can assess the nature and extent of associated risks and how these risks are managed and measured. Private entities require less disclosure than those reporting under IFRS. Receivables are analyzed in terms of their turnover and age (number of days outstanding), and in terms of relative changes in the related sales, receivables, and allowance accounts.

9 Identify differences in accounting between private entity GAAP and IFRS, and what changes are expected in the near future.

The two sets of standards are very similar, with minor differences relating to what is included in cash equivalents. Private entity GAAP does not require use of the effective interest method, whereas IFRS does for financial asset investments that are not held for trading purposes. Impairment provisions and the derecogition of financial assets are two issues under study by IFRS; the eventual resolution may generate additional differences in the near future.

Appendix **7**A

Cash Controls

Management and Control of Cash

Of all assets, cash is at the greatest risk of being used or diverted improperly. Management must overcome two problems in accounting for cash transactions: (1) it must establish proper controls to ensure that no unauthorized transactions are entered into by officers, employees, or others; and (2) it must ensure that the information that is needed in order to properly manage cash on hand and cash transactions is made available. Yet even with sophisticated control devices, errors can and do happen. *The Wall Street Journal* once ran a story entitled "A $7.8 Million Error Has a Happy Ending for a Horrified Bank," which described how **Manufacturers Hanover Trust Co.** mailed about $7.8 million too much in cash dividends to its shareholders. As the headline suggests, most of the money was eventually returned.

To safeguard cash and ensure the accuracy of the accounting records for this asset, companies need effective **internal control** over cash. There are new challenges to maintaining control over liquid assets as more and more transactions are done with the swipe of a debit or credit card or through the unregulated electronic payments services like PayPal. Canadians are among the highest users of debit and credit cards in the world. The shift from cold cash to digital cash brings new challenges for the internal control systems that are designed to control this asset. The purpose of this appendix is to identify some of the basic controls related to cash.

Using Bank Accounts

Even with the increased use of electronic banking, a company may use different banks in different locations and different types of bank accounts. For large companies that operate in multiple locations, the location of bank accounts can be important. Having collection accounts in strategic locations can speed up the flow of cash into the company by shortening the time between a customer's payment mailing and the company's use of the cash. Multiple collection centres are generally used to reduce the size of a company's **collection float**, which is the difference between the amount on deposit according to the company's records and the amount of collected cash according to the bank record.

The **general chequing account** is the main bank account in most companies and often the only bank account in small businesses. Cash is deposited in and disbursed from this account as all transactions are cycled through it. Deposits from and disbursements to all other bank accounts are made through the general chequing account.

Imprest bank accounts are used to make a specific amount of cash available for a limited purpose. The account acts as a clearing account for a large volume of cheques or for a specific type of cheque. The specific and intended amount to be cleared through the imprest account, such as for a payroll, is deposited by transferring that amount from the general chequing account or other source. Imprest bank accounts are also used for

Underlying Concept

When entities have cash accounts in more than one currency, they are remeasured using the rate at the balance sheet date into a common monetary unit, typically Canadian dollars. Some Canadian companies, however, identify the U.S. dollar as their functional currency and present their statements in this unit instead.

disbursing dividend cheques, commissions, bonuses, confidential expenses (e.g., officers' salaries), and travel expenses, although increasingly these payments are being made in electronic form.

Lockbox accounts are often used by large companies with multiple locations to make collections in cities where most of their customer billing occurs. The company rents a local post office box and authorizes a local bank to pick up the remittances mailed to that box number. The bank empties the box at least once a day and immediately credits the company's account for collections. The greatest advantage of a lockbox is that it accelerates the availability of collected cash. Generally, in a lockbox arrangement, the bank microfilms the cheques for record purposes and provides the company with a deposit slip, a list of collections, and any customer correspondence. If the control over cash is improved and if the income generated from accelerating the receipt of funds is more than what the lockbox system costs, it is considered worthwhile to use it.

Companies continue to increase their use of systems that electronically transfer funds from customers and to suppliers. While these advances will make many of the controls in a system based on paper cheque transactions obsolete, companies will still always need to improve the effectiveness of the controls that are part of their information and processing systems.

The Imprest Petty Cash System

Almost every company finds it necessary to pay small amounts for a great many things, such as employee lunches, taxi fares, minor office supplies, and other miscellaneous expenses. It is usually impractical to require that such disbursements be made by cheque, but some control over them is important. A simple method of obtaining reasonable control, while following the rule of disbursement by cheque, is the petty cash system, particularly an imprest system.

This is how the system works:

1. Someone is designated as the petty cash custodian and given a small amount of currency from which to make small payments. The transfer of funds from the bank account to petty cash is recorded as follows, assuming a $300 transfer:

A = L + SE
0   0   0

Cash flows: No effect

Petty Cash	300	
Cash		300

2. As payments are made out of this fund, the petty cash custodian gets signed receipts from each individual who receives cash from the fund. If possible, evidence of the disbursement should be attached to the petty cash receipt. Petty cash transactions are not recorded in the accounts until the fund is reimbursed, and they are recorded by someone other than the petty cash custodian.

3. When the cash in the fund runs low, the custodian presents to the controller or accounts payable cashier a request for reimbursement that is supported by the petty cash receipts and other disbursement evidence. In exchange for these, the custodian receives a company cheque to replenish the fund. At this point, transactions are recorded in the accounting system based on the petty cash receipts. For example:

A = L + SE
−173   0   −173

Cash flows: ↓ 173 outflow

Office Supplies Expense	42	
Postage Expense	53	
Entertainment Expense	76	
Cash Over and Short	2	
Cash		173

4. If it is decided that the fund's balance is too high, an adjustment may be made and the surplus amount is then deposited back into the bank account. The following adjustment is made to record the reduction in the fund balance from $300 to $250:

Cash	50	
Petty Cash		50

A	=	L	+	SE
0		0		0

Cash flows: No effect

Note that **only** entries to increase or decrease the size of the fund are made **to the Petty Cash account.**

A **Cash Over and Short** account is used when the cash in the petty cash fund plus the dollar amount of the receipts does not add up to the imprest petty cash amount. When this occurs, it is usually due to an error, such as a failure to provide correct change, overpayment of an expense, or a lost receipt. If cash is short (i.e., the sum of the receipts and cash in the fund is less than the imprest amount), the shortage is debited to the Cash Over and Short account. If there is more cash than there should be, the overage is credited to Cash Over and Short. This account is left open until the end of the year, when it is closed and generally shown on the income statement as part of "other expense or revenue."

Unless a reimbursement has just been made, there are usually expense items in the fund. This means that, if accurate financial statements are wanted, the fund needs to be reimbursed at the end of each accounting period in addition to when it is nearly empty.

Under an imprest system, the petty cash custodian is responsible at all times for the amount of the fund on hand, whether the amount is in cash or signed receipts. These receipts are the evidence that the disbursing officer needs in order to issue a reimbursement cheque. Two additional procedures are followed to obtain more complete control over the petty cash fund:

1. Surprise counts of the fund are made from time to time by a superior of the petty cash custodian to determine that the fund is being accounted for satisfactorily.

2. Petty cash receipts are cancelled or mutilated after they have been submitted for reimbursement so that they cannot be used again.

Physical Protection of Cash Balances

It is not only cash receipts and cash disbursements that need to be safeguarded through internal control measures. Cash on hand and in banks must also be protected. Because receipts become cash on hand and disbursements are made from the cash in banks, adequate control of receipts and disbursements is part of protecting cash balances. Certain other procedures, therefore, are also carried out.

The physical protection of cash is such an elementary necessity that it requires little discussion. Every effort should be made to minimize the cash on hand in the office. A petty cash fund, the current day's receipts, and perhaps funds for making change should be the only funds on hand at any time. As much as possible, these funds should be kept in a vault, safe, or locked cash drawer. Each day's receipts should be transmitted intact to the bank as soon as is practical. Intact means that the total receipts are accounted for together and no part of the amount is used for other purposes. This leaves a clear trail from the receipts activity to the bank.

Every company has a record of cash received and disbursed, and the cash balance. Because of the many cash transactions, however, errors or omissions can occur in keeping this record. It is therefore necessary to periodically prove the balance shown in the general ledger. Cash that is actually present in the office—petty cash, change funds, and undeposited receipts—can be counted and compared with the company records. Cash on deposit is not available for count so it is proved by preparing a bank reconciliation, which is a reconciliation of the company's record and the bank's record of the company's cash.

Reconciliation of Bank Balances

At the end of each calendar month, the bank sends each customer a bank statement (a copy of the bank's account with the customer) together with the customer's cheques that were paid by the bank during the month, or a list of the company's payments that have been presented to and cleared by the bank during the month.[23] Less and less hard copy is being returned as banks provide companies with electronic access to this information. If no errors were made by the bank or the customer, if all deposits made and all cheques drawn by the customer reached the bank within the same month, and if no unusual transactions occurred that affected either the company's or the bank's record of cash, the balance of cash reported by the bank to the customer will be the same as the balance in the customer's own records. This rarely occurs, because of one or more of the following:

RECONCILING ITEMS

1. **Deposits in Transit.** End-of-month deposits of cash that are recorded on the depositor's books in one month are received and recorded by the bank in the following month.

2. **Outstanding Cheques.** Cheques written by the depositor are recorded when they are written but may not be recorded by (or "clear") the bank until the next month.

3. **Bank Charges.** Charges are recorded by the bank against the depositor's balance for such items as bank services, printing cheques, not-sufficient-funds (NSF) cheques, and safe-deposit box rentals. The depositor may not be aware of these charges until the bank statement is received.

4. **Bank Credits.** Collections or deposits by the bank for the depositor's benefit may not be known to the depositor until the bank statement is received. These are reconciling items as long as they have not yet been recorded on the company's records. Examples are note collections for the depositor, interest earned on interest-bearing accounts, and direct deposits by customers and others.

5. **Bank or Depositor Errors.** Errors by either the bank or the depositor cause the bank balance to disagree with the depositor's book balance.

For these reasons, differences between the depositor's record of cash and the bank's record are usual and expected. The two records therefore need to be reconciled to determine the reasons for the differences between the two amounts.

A bank reconciliation is a schedule that explains any differences between the bank's and the company's records of cash. If the difference results only from transactions not yet recorded by the bank, the company's record of cash is considered correct. But if some part

---

[23] As mentioned in the chapter, use of paper cheques continues to be a popular means of payment. However, easy access to desktop publishing software and hardware has created new opportunities for cheque fraud in the form of duplicate, altered, or forged cheques. At the same time, new fraud-fighting technologies, such as ultraviolet imaging, high-capacity barcodes, and biometrics are being developed. These technologies convert paper documents into document files that are processed electronically, thereby reducing the risk of fraud.

of the difference is due to other items, the bank's records or the company's records must be adjusted.

Two forms of bank reconciliation can be prepared. One form reconciles from the bank statement balance to the book balance or vice versa. The other form reconciles both the bank balance and the book balance to a correct cash balance. This latter form is more popular. A sample of this form and its common reconciling items is shown in Illustration 7A-1.

Balance per bank statement (end of period)		$$$
Add: Deposits in transit	$$	
Undeposited receipts (cash on hand)	$$	
Bank errors that understate the bank statement balance	$$	$$
		$$$
Deduct: Outstanding cheques	$$	
Bank errors that overstate the bank statement balance	$$	$$
Correct cash balance		$$$
Balance per company's books (end of period)		$$$
Add: Bank credits and collections not yet recorded in the books	$$	
Book errors that understate the book balance	$$	$$
		$$$
Deduct: Bank charges not yet recorded in the books	$$	
Book errors that overstate the book balance	$$	$$
Correct cash balance		$$$

Illustration 7A-1

Bank Reconciliation Form and Content

This form of reconciliation has two sections: (1) the "Balance per bank statement" and (2) the "Balance per company's books." Both sections end with the same correct cash balance. The correct cash balance is the amount that the books must be adjusted to and is the amount reported on the balance sheet. **Adjusting journal entries are prepared for all the addition and deduction items that appear in the "Balance per company's books" section**, and the bank is notified immediately about any errors that it has made.

To illustrate, Nugget Mining Company's books show a cash balance at the Ottawa National Bank on November 30, 2011, of $20,502. The bank statement covering the month of November shows an ending balance of $22,190. An examination of Nugget's accounting records and the November bank statement identified the following reconciling items:

1. A deposit of $3,680 was taken to the bank late on November 30 but does not appear on the bank statement.

2. Cheques written in November but not charged to (deducted from) the November bank statement are:

Cheque #7327	$ 150
#7348	4,820
#7349	31

3. Nugget has not yet recorded the $600 of interest collected by the bank on November 20 on Sequoia Co. bonds held by the bank for Nugget.

4. Bank service charges of $18 are not yet recorded on Nugget's books.

5. A $220 cheque for Nugget from a customer was returned with the bank statement and marked "NSF." The bank, having originally recognized this as part of one of Nugget's deposits, now deducted this bad cheque as a disbursement from Nugget's account.

6. Nugget discovered that cheque #7322, written in November for $131 in payment of an account payable, had been incorrectly recorded in its books as $311.

7. A cheque written on Nugent Oil Co.'s account for $175 had been incorrectly charged to Nugget Mining and was included with the bank statement.

Illustration 7A-2 shows the reconciliation of the bank and book balances to the correct cash balance of $21,044.

Illustration 7A-2

Sample Bank Reconciliation

NUGGET MINING COMPANY				
Bank Reconciliation				
Ottawa National Bank, November 30, 2011				
Balance per bank statement, November 30/11				$22,190
Add: Deposit in transit	(1)	$3,680		
Bank error—incorrect cheque charged to account by bank	(7)	175		3,855
				26,045
Deduct: Outstanding cheques	(2)			5,001
Correct cash balance, November 30/11				$21,044
Balance per books, November 30/11				$20,502
Add: Interest collected by the bank	(3)	$ 600		
Error in recording cheque #7322	(6)	180		780
				21,282
Deduct: Bank service charges	(4)	18		
NSF cheque returned	(5)	220		238
Correct cash balance, November 30/11				$21,044

The journal entries to adjust and correct Nugget Mining's books in early December 2011 are taken from the items in the "Balance per books" section and are as follows:

Cash	600	
Interest Income		600
(To record interest on Sequoia Co. bonds, collected by bank.)		
Cash	180	
Accounts Payable		180
(To correct error in recording amount of cheque #7322.)		
Office Expense—Bank Charges	18	
Cash		18
(To record bank service charges for November.)		
Accounts Receivable	220	
Cash		220
(To record customer's cheque returned NSF.)		

A = L + SE
+762 +180 +582

Cash flows: ↑ 542 inflow

Alternatively, one summary entry could be made with a net $542 debit to Cash, which is the difference between the balance before adjustment of $20,502 and the correct balance of $21,044. When the entries are posted, Nugget's cash account will have a balance of $21,044. Nugget should return the Nugent Oil Co. cheque to Ottawa National Bank, informing the bank of the error.

Summary of Learning Objective for Appendix 7A

Glossary

10 Explain common techniques for controlling cash.

The common techniques that are used to control cash are as follows: (1) Using bank accounts: A company can vary the number and location of banks and the types of accounts to meet its control objectives. (2) The imprest petty cash system: It may be impractical to require small amounts of various expenses to be paid by cheque, yet some control over them is important. (3) Physical protection of cash balances: Adequate control of receipts and disbursements is part of protecting cash balances. Every effort should be made to minimize the cash on hand in the office. (4) Reconciliation of bank balances: Cash on deposit is not available for counting and is proved by preparing a bank reconciliation.

KEY TERMS

bank reconciliation, 422
deposits in transit, 422
imprest system, 421
intact, 421
not-sufficient-funds (NSF) cheques, 422
outstanding cheques, 422
petty cash, 420

Note: All assignment material with an asterisk (*) relates to the appendix to the chapter.

Brief Exercises

BE7-1 Stowe Enterprises owns the following assets at December 31, 2010:   **(LO 1)**

Cash in bank savings account	48,500	Chequing account balance	30,500
Cash on hand	14,800	Postdated cheque from Yu Co.	450
Cash refund due, overpayment of income taxes	31,400	Cash in a foreign bank (CAD equivalent)	90,000

What amount should be reported as cash?

BE7-2 Civic Company made sales of $40,000 with terms 1/10, n/30. Within the discount period, it received $35,000 in   **(LO 3)** payments from customers; after the discount period, it received $5,000 in payments from customers. Assuming Civic uses the gross method of recording sales, prepare journal entries for the above transactions.

BE7-3 Use the information for Civic Company in BE7-2, but assume instead that Civic uses the net method of record-   **(LO 3)** ing sales. Prepare the journal entries for the transactions.

BE7-4 Yoshi Corp. uses the gross method to record sales made on credit. On June 1, the company made sales of   **(LO 3)** $45,000 with terms 1/15, n/45. On June 12, Yoshi received full payment for the June 1 sale. Prepare the required journal entries for Yoshi Corp.

BE7-5 Use the information from BE7-4, assuming Yoshi Corp. uses the net method to account for cash discounts.   **(LO 3)** Prepare the required journal entries for Yoshi Corp.

BE7-6 Battle Tank Limited had net sales in 2010 of $1.1 million. At December 31, 2010, before adjusting entries, the   **(LO 4)** balances in selected accounts were as follows: Accounts Receivable $250,000 debit; Allowance for Doubtful Accounts $2,800 credit. Assuming Battle Tank has examined the aging of the accounts receivable and has determined the Allowance for Doubtful Accounts should have a balance of $30,000, prepare the December 31, 2010 journal entry to record the adjustment to the Allowance for Doubtful Accounts.

BE7-7 Information for Battle Tank Limited is provided in BE7-6. Owner Instead, assume the balance in the Allowance   **(LO 4)** for Doubtful Accounts is a debit balance of $3,000. Based on this, what would be the adjustment to bad debt expense to arrive at the required balance of $30,000 in the year-end allowance?

BE7-8 Emil Family Importers sold goods to Acme Decorators for $20,000 on November 1, 2010, accepting Acme's   **(LO 5)** $20,000, six-month, 6% note. (a) Prepare Emil's November 1 entry, December 31 annual adjusting entry, and May 1 entry for the collection of the note and interest. (b) Prepare any appropriate reversing entry at January 1, 2011, and the May 1, 2011, entry for the collection of the note and interest.

(LO 5)   **BE7-9**   Aero Acrobats lent $47,530 to Afterburner Limited, accepting Afterburner's $49,000, three-month, zero-interest-bearing note. The implied interest is 12%. Prepare Aero's journal entries for the initial transaction and the collection of $49,000 at maturity.

(LO 6)   **BE7-10**   Lin Du Corp. lent $30,053 to Prefax Ltd., accepting Prefax's $40,000, three-year, zero-interest-bearing note. The implied interest is 10%. (a) Prepare Lin Du's journal entries for the initial transaction, recognition of interest each year, and the collection of $40,000 at maturity. (b) Use time value of money tables, a financial calculator, or Excel functions to prove that the note will yield 10%.

(LO 6)   **BE7-11**   Bartho Products sold used equipment with a cost of $15,000 and a carrying amount of $2,500 to Vardy Corp. in exchange for a $5,000, three-year note receivable. Although no interest was specified, the market rate for a loan of that risk would be 9%. Prepare the entries to record (a) the sale of Bartho's equipment and receipt of the note, (b) the recognition of interest each year, and (c) the collection of the note at maturity.

(LO 7)   **BE7-12**   On October 1, 2010, Alpha Inc. assigns $2 million of its accounts receivable to Alberta Provincial Bank as collateral for a $1.6-million loan evidenced by a note. The bank's charges are as follows: a finance charge of 4% of the assigned receivables and an interest charge of 13% on the loan. Prepare the October 1 journal entries for both Alpha and Alberta Provincial Bank.

(LO 7)   **BE7-13**   Landstalker Enterprises sold $750,000 of accounts receivable to Leander Factors, Inc. on a without recourse basis. The transaction meets the criteria for a sale, and no asset or liability components of the receivables are retained by Landstalker. Leander Factors assesses a finance charge of 4% of the amount of accounts receivable and retains an amount equal to 5% of accounts receivable. Prepare journal entries for both Landstalker and Leander.

(LO 7)   **BE7-14**   Use the information for Landstalker Enterprises in BE7-13 and assume instead that the receivables are sold with recourse. Prepare the journal entry for Landstalker to record the sale, assuming the recourse obligation has a fair value of $9,000.

(LO 7)   **BE7-15**   Keyser Woodcrafters sells $600,000 of receivables with a fair value of $620,000 to Keyser Trust in a securitization transaction that meets the criteria for a sale. Keyser Woodcrafters receives full fair value for the receivables and agrees to continue to service them, estimating that the fair value of this service liability component is $26,000. Prepare the journal entry for Keyser Woodcrafters to record the sale.

(LO 8)   **BE7-16**   The financial statements of **Magnotta Winery Corporation** report net sales of $24,046,671 for its year ended January 31, 2009. Accounts receivable are $260,800 at January 31, 2009, and $285,995 at January 31, 2008. Calculate the company's accounts receivable turnover ratio and the average collection period for accounts receivable in days.

(LO 8)   **BE7-17**   Refer to Illustration 7-17 in the chapter and the extra information presented in this exercise about BCE Inc. Given that the company's accounts receivable balance at December 31, 2006, was $1,864 million and 2007 sales were $17,752 million and 2008 sales were $17,698 million, calculate the company's accounts receivable turnover ratio for 2007. Did it improve in 2008?

(LO 10)   *****BE7-18**   Genesis Ltd. designated Alexa Kidd as petty cash custodian and established a petty cash fund of $400. The fund is reimbursed when the cash in the fund is at $57. Petty cash receipts indicate that funds were disbursed for $174 of office supplies and $167 of freight charges on inventory purchases. Genesis uses a perpetual inventory system. Prepare journal entries for the establishment of the fund and the reimbursement.

(LO 10)   *****BE7-19**   Use the information in BE7-18. Assume that Genesis decides (a) to increase the size of the petty cash fund to $600 immediately after the reimbursement, and (b) to reduce the size of the petty cash to $250 immediately after the reimbursement. Prepare the entries that are necessary to record the (a) and (b) transactions.

(LO 10)   *****BE7-20**   Jaguar Corporation is preparing a bank reconciliation and has identified the following potential reconciling items. For each item, indicate if it is (1) added to the balance per bank statement, (2) deducted from the balance per bank statement, (3) added to the balance per books, (4) deducted from the balance per books, or (5) not needed for the reconciliation.

    (a) Deposit in transit of $5,500

    (b) Previous month's outstanding cheque for $298 cleared the bank in the current month

    (c) Interest credited to Jaguar's account of $31

    (d) Bank service charges of $20

(e) Outstanding deposit from previous month of $876 shown by bank as deposit of current month

(f) Outstanding cheques of $7,422

(g) NSF cheque returned of $260

*BE7-21 Use the information for Jaguar Corporation in BE7-20. Prepare any entries that are necessary to make Jaguar's **(LO 10)** accounting records correct and complete.

Exercises

E7-1 **(Determining Cash Balance)** The controller for Eastwood Co. is trying to determine the amount of cash to **(LO 1)** report on the December 31, 2010, balance sheet. The following information is provided:

1. A commercial savings account with $600,000 and a commercial chequing account balance of $900,000 are held at First National Bank. There is also a bank overdraft of $35,000 in a chequing account at the Royal Scotia Bank. No other accounts are held at the Royal Scotia Bank.

2. Eastwood has agreed to maintain a cash balance of $100,000 at all times in its chequing account at First National Bank to ensure that credit is available in the future.

3. Eastwood has a $5-million investment in a Commercial Bank of Montreal money-market mutual fund. This fund has chequing account privileges.

4. There are travel advances of $18,000 for executive travel for the first quarter of next year (employees will complete expense reports after they travel).

5. A separate cash fund in the amount of $1.5 million is restricted for the retirement of long-term debt.

6. There is a petty cash fund of $3,000.

7. A $1,900 IOU from Marianne Koch, a company officer, will be withheld from her salary in January 2011.

8. There are 20 cash floats for retail operation cash registers: 8 at $75, and 12 at $100.

9. The company has two certificates of deposit, each for $500,000. These certificates of deposit each had a maturity of 120 days when they were acquired. One was purchased October 15 and the other on December 27.

10. Eastwood has received a cheque dated January 12, 2011, in the amount of $25,000 from a customer owing funds at December 31. It has also received a cheque dated January 8, 2011, in the amount of $11,500 from a customer as an advance on an order that was placed on December 29 and will be delivered February 1, 2011.

11. Eastwood holds $2.1 million of commercial paper of Sergio Leone Co., which is due in 60 days.

12. Currency and coin on hand amounted to $7,700.

13. Eastwood acquired 1,000 shares of Sortel for $3.90 per share in late November and is holding them for trading. The shares are still on hand at year end and have a fair value of $4.10 per share on December 31, 2010.

Instructions

(a) Calculate the amount of cash to be reported on Eastwood Co.'s balance sheet at December 31, 2010.

(b) Indicate the proper way to report items that are not reported as cash on the December 31, 2010, balance sheet.

E7-2 **(Determining Cash Balance)** Several independent situations follow. For each situation, determine the amount **(LO 1)** that should be reported as cash. If the item(s) is (are) not reported as cash, explain why.

1. Chequing account balance $625,000; certificate of deposit $1.1 million; cash advance to subsidiary $980,000; utility deposit paid to gas company $180.

2. Chequing account balance $500,000; overdraft in special chequing account at same bank as normal chequing account $17,000; cash held in bond sinking fund $200,000; petty cash fund $300; coins and currency on hand $1,350.

3. Chequing account balance $540,000; postdated cheque from customer $11,000; cash restricted to maintain compensating balance requirement $100,000; certified cheque from customer $9,800; postage stamps on hand $620.

4. Chequing account balance at bank $57,000; money-market balance at mutual fund (has chequing privileges) $38,000; NSF cheque received from customer $800.

5. Chequing account balance $700,000; cash restricted for future plant expansion $500,000; short-term (60-day) treasury bills $180,000; cash advance received from customer $900 (not included in chequing account balance); cash advance of $7,000 to company executive, payable on demand; refundable deposit of $26,000 paid to federal government to guarantee performance on construction contract.

(LO 2, 8) E7-3 (Financial Statement Presentation of Receivables) Norton Inc. shows a balance of $420,289 in the Accounts Receivable account on December 31, 2010. The balance consists of the following:

Instalment accounts due in 2011	$ 48,000
Instalment accounts due after 2011	44,000
Overpayments to creditors	12,640
Due from regular customers, of which $40,000 represents	
accounts pledged as security for a bank loan	165,000
Advances to employees	49,649
Advance to subsidiary company (made in 2005)	101,000
	$420,289

Instructions

Show how the information above should be presented on the balance sheet of Norton Inc. at December 31, 2010.

(LO 3) E7-4 (Determining Ending Accounts Receivable) Your accounts receivable clerk, Mitra Adams, to whom you pay a salary of $1,500 per month, has just purchased a new Cadillac. You have decided to test the accuracy of the accounts receivable balance of $86,500 shown in the ledger.

The following information is available for your first year in business:

1. Collections from customers are $198,000.

2. Merchandise purchased totalled $320,000.

3. Ending merchandise inventory is $99,000.

4. Goods are marked to sell at 40% above cost.

Instructions

Estimate the ending balance of accounts receivable from customers that should appear in the ledger and any apparent shortages. Assume that all sales are made on account.

(LO 3) E7-5 (Recording Sales Transactions) Information from Salini Computers Ltd. follows:

July	1	Sold $82,000 of computers to Robertson Corp., terms 2/15, n/30.
	5	Robertson Corp. returned for full credit one computer with an invoice price of $6,200.
	10	Salini received payment from Robertson for the full amount owed from the July transactions.
	17	Sold $160,000 in computers and peripherals to Clarkson Store, terms 2/10, n/30.
	26	Clarkson Store paid Salini for half of its July purchases.
Aug.	30	Clarkson Store paid Salini for the remaining half of its July purchases.

Instructions

(a) Prepare the entries for Salini Computers Ltd., assuming the gross method is used to record sales and cash discounts.

(b) Prepare the entries for Salini Computers Ltd., assuming the net method is used to record sales and cash discounts.

(LO 3) E7-6 (Recording Sales Gross and Net) On June 3, Arnold Limited sold to Chester Arthur merchandise having a sale price of $3,000 with terms 3/10, n/60, f.o.b. shipping point. A $90 invoice, terms n/30, was received by Chester on June 8 from John Booth Transport Service for the freight cost. When it received the goods on June 5, Chester notified Arnold that $500 of the merchandise contained flaws that rendered it worthless; the same day Arnold Limited issued a credit memo covering the worthless merchandise and asked that it be returned to them at their expense. The freight on the returned merchandise was $25, which Arnold paid on June 7. On June 12, the company received a cheque for the balance due from Chester Arthur.

Instructions

(a) Prepare journal entries on Arnold Limited's books to record all of the above transactions under each of the following independent bases:

1. Sales and receivables are entered at gross selling price.

2. Sales and receivables are entered net of cash discounts.

(b) Prepare the journal entry under basis 2, assuming that Chester Arthur did not pay until July 29.

E7-7 **(Journalizing Various Receivable Transactions)** Information on Janut Corp. follows: **(LO 3, 4, 7)**

July 1 Janut Corp. sold to Harding Ltd. merchandise having a sales price of $9,000, terms 3/10, net/60. Janut records its sales and receivables net.

3 Harding Ltd. returned defective merchandise having a sales price of $700.

5 Accounts receivable of $19,000 (gross) are factored with Jackson Credit Corp. without recourse at a financing charge of 9%. Cash is received for the proceeds and collections are handled by the finance company. (These accounts were subject to a 2% discount and were all past the discount period.)

9 Specific accounts receivable of $15,000 (gross) are pledged to Landon Credit Corp. as security for a loan of $11,000 at a finance charge of 3% of the loan amount plus 9% interest on the outstanding balance. Janut will continue to make the collections. All the accounts receivable are past the discount period and were originally subject to a 2% discount.

Dec. 29 Harding Ltd. notifies Janut that it is bankrupt and will pay only 10% of its account. Give the entry to write off the uncollectible balance using the allowance method. (Note: First record the increase in the receivable on July 11 when the discount period passed.)

Instructions

Prepare all necessary entries in general journal form for Janut Corp.

E7-8 **(Recording Bad Debts)** At the end of 2009, Perez Corporation has accounts receivable of $1.2 million and an **(LO 4)** allowance for doubtful accounts of $80,000. On January 16, 2010, Perez determined that its $16,000 receivable from Morganfield Ltd. will not be collected, and management has authorized its writeoff. On January 31, 2010, Perez received notification that the company will be receiving $0.10 for every $1.00 of accounts receivable relating to McKinley Ltd. The company had previously written off $60,000 relating to this balance.

Instructions

(a) Prepare the journal entry for Perez Corporation to write off the Morganfield receivable and any journal entry necessary to reflect the notice regarding McKinley Ltd.

(b) What is the net realizable value of Perez's accounts receivable before and after the entries in (a)? What is the book value of Perez's accounts receivable before and after the entries in (a)?

E7-9 **(Summary Entries for Accounts Receivable)** The balance sheets of Traverse Corp. on December 31, 2009 and **(LO 4)** 2010, showed gross accounts receivable of $8,450 and $9,275, respectively. The balances in Allowance for Doubtful Accounts at December 31, 2009 and 2010, after recording the bad debt expense, were $725 and $796, respectively. The income statement for Traverse for the fiscal years ending December 31, 2009 and 2010, showed bad debts expenses of $420 and $455, respectively, which is equal to 1% of sales. All sales are on account.

Instructions

Prepare summary journal entries for 2010 to record the bad debts expense, sales on account, accounts receivable writeoffs, and collections on account.

E7-10 **(Calculating Bad Debts)** At January 1, 2010, the credit balance of Andy Corp.'s Allowance for Doubtful **(LO 4)** Accounts was $400,000. For 2010, the bad debt expense entry was based on a percentage of net credit sales. Net sales for 2010 were $80 million, of which 90% were on account. Based on the latest available facts at the time, the 2010 bad debt expense was estimated to be 0.8% of net credit sales. During 2010, uncollectible receivables amounting to $500,000 were written off against the allowance for doubtful accounts. The company has estimated that at December 31, 2010, based on a review of the aged accounts receivable, the allowance for doubtful accounts was properly measured at $525,000.

Instructions

Prepare a schedule calculating the balance in Andy's Allowance for Doubtful Accounts at December 31, 2010. Prepare any necessary journal entry at year end to adjust the allowance for doubtful accounts to the required balance.

E7-11 **(Reporting Bad Debts)** The chief accountant for Dickinson Corporation provides you with the following list of **(LO 4)** accounts receivable that were written off in the current year:

Date	Customer	Amount
Mar. 31	Eli Masters Ltd.	$ 7,700
June 30	Crane Associates	6,800
Sept. 30	Annie Lowell's Dress Shop	12,000
Dec. 31	Vahik Uzerian	6,830

Dickinson Corporation follows the policy of debiting Bad Debt Expense as accounts are written off. The chief accountant maintains that this procedure is appropriate for financial statement purposes.

All of Dickinson Corporation's sales are on a 30-day credit basis. Sales for the current year total $3.2 million, and research has determined that bad debt losses approximate 2% of sales.

Instructions

(a) Do you agree with Dickinson Corporation's policy on recognizing bad debt expense? Why?

(b) By what amount would net income differ if bad debt expense was calculated using the allowance method and percentage-of-sales approach?

(c) Under what conditions is using the direct writeoff method justified?

(LO 4)   E7-12   (Calculating Bad Debts and Preparing Journal Entries) The trial balance before adjustment of Chloe Inc. shows the following balances:

	Dr.	Cr.
Accounts receivable	$105,000	
Allowance for doubtful accounts	1,950	
Sales (all on credit)		$684,000
Sales returns and allowances	30,000	

Instructions

Give the entry for bad debt expense for the current year assuming:

(a) the allowance should be 4% of gross accounts receivable.

(b) historical records indicate that, based on accounts receivable aging, the following percentages will not be collected:

	Balance	Percentage Estimated to Be Uncollectible
0–30 days outstanding	$36,000	1%
31–60 days outstanding	48,000	5%
61–90 days outstanding	12,200	12%
Over 90 days outstanding	8,800	18%

(c) Allowance for Doubtful Accounts has the same amount but it is a credit balance and the allowance should be 4% of gross accounts receivable.

(d) Allowance for Doubtful Accounts has the same amount but it is a credit balance and historical records indicate that the same percentages in (b) are to be used to determine the Allowance for Doubtful Accounts.

(LO 4)   E7-13   (Bad Debts—Aging) Anthony Co. has the following account among its trade receivables:

		Hopkins Co.			
1/1	Balance forward	850	1/28	Cash (#1710)	1,100
1/20	Invoice #1710	1,100	4/2	Cash (#2116)	1,350
3/14	Invoice #2116	1,350	4/10	Cash (1/1 Balance)	155
4/12	Invoice #2412	2,110	4/30	Cash (#2412)	1,000
9/5	Invoice #3614	490	9/20	Cash (#3614 and part of #2412)	790
10/17	Invoice #4912	860	10/31	Cash (#4912)	860
11/18	Invoice #5681	2,000	12/1	Cash (#5681)	1,250
12/20	Invoice #6347	800	12/29	Cash (#6347)	800

Instructions

Age the Hopkins Co. account and specify any items that may need particular attention at year end.

(LO 5)   E7-14   (Interest-Bearing and Non-Interest-Bearing Notes) Little Corp. was experiencing cash flow problems and was unable to pay its $105,000 account payable to Big Corp. when it fell due on September 30, 2010. Big agreed to substitute a one-year note for the open account. The following two options were presented to Little by Big Corp.:

Option 1: A one-year note for $105,000 due September 30, 2011. Interest at a rate of 8% would be payable at maturity.

Option 2: A one-year non-interest-bearing note for $113,400. The implied rate of interest is 8%.

Assume that Big Corp. has a December 31 year end.

Instructions

(a) Assuming Little Corp. chooses Option 1, prepare the entries required on Big Corp.'s books on September 30, 2010, December 31, 2010, and September 30, 2011.

(b) Assuming Little Corp. chooses Option 2, prepare the entries required on Big Corp.'s books on September 30, 2010, December 31, 2010, and September 30, 2011.

(c) Compare the amount of interest income earned by Big Corp. in 2010 and 2011 under both options. Comment briefly.

(d) From management's perspective, does one option provide better liquidity for Big at December 31, 2010? Does one option provide better cash flows than the other?

Digging Deeper

E7-15 **(Notes Receivable with Zero and Unrealistic Interest Rates)** On July 1, 2010, Agincourt Inc. made two sales: **(LO 6)**

1. It sold excess land having a fair market value of $700,000 in exchange for a four-year, non-interest-bearing promissory note in the face amount of $1,101,460. The land's carrying value is $590,000.

2. It rendered services in exchange for an eight-year promissory note having a face value of $400,000. Interest at a rate of 3% is payable annually.

The customers in the above transactions have credit ratings that require them to borrow money at 12% interest. Agincourt recently had to pay 8% interest for money it borrowed from British National Bank.

3. On July 1, 2010, Agincourt also agreed to accept an instalment note from one of its customers in partial settlement of accounts receivable that were overdue. The note calls for four equal payments of $20,000, including the principal and interest due, on the anniversary of the note. The implied interest rate on this note is 10%.

Instructions

(a) Prepare the journal entries to record the three notes receivable transactions of Agincourt Inc. on July 1, 2010.

(b) Prepare an effective-interest amortization table for the instalment note obtained in partial collection of accounts receivable. From Agincourt's perspective, what are the advantages of an instalment note compared with a non-interest-bearing note?

Digging Deeper

E7-16 **(Notes Receivable with Zero Interest Rate)** By December 31, 2009, Clearing Corp. had performed a signifi- **(LO 6, 8)** cant amount of environmental consulting services for Rank Ltd. Rank was short of cash, and Clearing agreed to accept a $200,000, non-interest-bearing note due December 31, 2011, as payment in full. Rank is a bit of a credit risk and typically borrows funds at a rate of 12%. Clearing is much more creditworthy and has various lines of credit at 9%.

Instructions

(a) Prepare the journal entry to record the transaction of December 31, 2009, for Clearing Corp.

(b) Assuming Clearing Corp.'s fiscal year end is December 31, prepare the journal entry required at December 31, 2010.

(c) Assuming Clearing Corp.'s fiscal year end is December 31, prepare the journal entry required at December 31, 2011.

(d) What are the amount and classification of the note on Clearing Corp.'s balance sheet as at December 31, 2010?

E7-17 **(Assigning Accounts Receivable)** On April 1, 2010, Ibrahim Corporation assigns $400,000 of its accounts **(LO 7)** receivable to First National Bank as collateral for a $200,000 loan that is due July 1, 2010. The assignment agreement calls for Ibrahim to continue to collect the receivables. First National Bank assesses a finance charge of 3% of the accounts receivable, and interest on the loan is 10%, a realistic rate for a note of this type.

Instructions

(a) Prepare the April 1, 2010, journal entry for Ibrahim Corporation.

(b) Prepare the journal entry for Ibrahim's collection of $350,000 of the accounts receivable during the period April 1 to June 30, 2010.

(c) On July 1, 2010, Ibrahim paid First National Bank the entire amount that was due on the loan.

(LO 7) E7-18 (Journalizing Various Receivable Transactions) The trial balance before adjustment for Sinatra Company shows the following balances.

	Dr.	Cr.
Accounts Receivable	$82,000	
Allowance for Doubtful Accounts	1,750	
Sales		$430,000

Instructions

Using the data above, prepare the journal entries required to record each of the following cases. (Each situation is independent.)

1. To obtain cash, Sinatra factors without recourse $20,000 of receivables with Stills Finance. The Finance charge is 10% of the amount factored.

2. To obtain a one-year loan of $55,000, Sinatra assigns $65,000 of specific receivable accounts to Ruddin Financial. The finance charge is 8% of the loan; the cash is received and the accounts turned over to Ruddin Financial.

3. The company wants to maintain the Allowance for Doubtful Accounts at 5% of gross accounts receivable.

4. The company wishes to increase the allowance account by $1\frac{1}{2}$% of net sales.

(LO 7, 8) E7-19 (Transfer of Receivables with Recourse) Chessman Corporation factors $600,000 of accounts receivable with Liquidity Financing, Inc. on a with recourse basis. Liquidity Financing will collect the receivables. The receivable records are transferred to Liquidity Financing on August 15, 2010. Liquidity Financing assesses a finance charge of 2.5% of the amount of accounts receivable and also reserves an amount equal to 5.25% of accounts receivable to cover probable adjustments.

Instructions

(a) What conditions must be met for a transfer of receivables to be accounted for as a sale?

(b) Assume the conditions from part (a) are met. Prepare the journal entry on August 15, 2010, for Chessman to record the sale of receivables, assuming the recourse obligation has a fair value of $6,000.

(c) What effect will the factoring of receivables have on calculating the accounts receivable turnover for Chessman? Comment briefly.

(LO 7, 8) E7-20 (Transfer of Receivables with Servicing Retained) Lute Retail Ltd. transfers $355,000 of its accounts receivable to an independent trust in a securitization transaction on July 11, 2010, receiving 96% of the receivables balance as proceeds. Lute will continue to manage the customer accounts, including their collection. Lute estimates this obligation has a liability value of $12,500. In addition, the agreement includes a recourse provision with an estimated value of $9,900. The transaction is to be recorded as a sale.

Instructions

(a) Prepare the journal entry on July 11, 2010, for Lute Retail Ltd. to record the securitization of the receivables.

(b) What effect will the securitization of receivables have on Lute Retail Ltd.'s accounts receivable turnover? Comment briefly.

(LO 8) E7-21 (Analysis of Receivables) Information follows for Jones Company:

1. The beginning of the year Accounts Receivable balance was $25,000.

2. Net sales for the year were $410,000. (Credit sales were $200,000 of the total sales.) Jones does not offer cash discounts.

3. Collections on accounts receivable during the year were $140,000.

Instructions

(a) Prepare summary journal entries to record the items noted above.

(b) Calculate Jones Company's accounts receivable turnover ratio for the year. How old is the average receivable?

(c) Use the turnover ratio calculated in (b) to analyze Jones Company's liquidity. The turnover ratio last year was 4.85.

E7-22 **(Receivables Turnover)** The **Becker Milk Company Limited**, a real estate and investment management com- **(LO 8)**
pany, reports the following information in its financial statements for the years ended April 30, 2009, 2008, and 2007:

Accounts receivable, net of		
allowance for doubtful accounts	April 30, 2009	$ 63,669
	April 30, 2008	194,017
	April 30, 2007	86,217
Revenue (note 8), year ended	April 30, 2009	3,859,039
	April 30, 2008	3,828,854
	April 30, 2007	3,460,339

**Real-World
Emphasis**

Note 8: Revenue
As of April 30, 2009, the company's largest single tenant, Alimentation Couche-Tard Inc., accounted for 85% of the
revenue. It accounted for 86% of the revenue in 2008.

Instructions

(a) Calculate the receivables turnover and days sales outstanding (or average age of receivables) for the two most recent
years provided.

(b) Comment on your results.

(c) Why do you think the information in Note 8 was provided by the company?

**Digging
Deeper**

*****E7-23** **(Petty Cash)** Kali Corp. established a petty cash fund early in 2010 to increase the company's efficiency of and **(LO 10)**
control over many of the small expenditures it makes. The company decided to set up the imprest fund at $200 and a
cheque was issued for this amount and given to the petty cash custodian.

During January, the petty cash custodian made the following disbursements and placed a receipt for each in the cash
box provided.

Tim Hortons coffee order for a management meeting	$18.62
Office supplies purchased	9.50
Courier charges paid	25.00
Travel advance to employee	100.00
Card, wrapping paper for gift for employee in hospital	9.40

The petty cash was replenished on January 22 when the amount of cash in the fund was $36.40. In June, after six months'
experience with the fund, management decided to increase it to $300.

Instructions

(a) Prepare the journal entries to establish the petty cash fund, to reimburse it on January 22, and to increase the fund
in June.

(b) Describe where the petty cash will be reported on Kali Corp.'s financial statements.

(c) Explain briefly why many companies have a policy of reimbursing the petty cash fund on each balance sheet date.

*****E7-24** **(Petty Cash)** The petty cash fund of Luigi's Auto Repair Service, a sole proprietorship, contains the following: **(LO 10)**

1. Coins and currency		$ 15.20
2. An IOU from Bob Cunningham, an employee, for a cash advance		63.00
3. A cheque payable to Luigi's Auto Repair from Pat Webber,		
an employee, marked NSF		34.00
4. Vouchers for the following:		
Stamps	$ 21.00	
Two NHL playoff tickets for Al Luigi	150.00	
A printer cartridge	14.35	185.35
		$297.55

The general ledger account Petty Cash has a balance of $300.00.

Instructions

Prepare the journal entry to record the reimbursement of the petty cash fund.

(LO 10) *E7-25 (Bank Reconciliation and Adjusting Entries) Ling Corp. deposits all receipts intact and makes all payments by cheque. The following information is available from the cash records:

April 30 Bank Reconciliation

Balance per bank	$ 7,120
Add: Deposits in transit	1,540
Deduct: Outstanding cheques	–(2,000)
Balance per books	$ 6,660

Month of May Results

	Per Bank	Per Books
Balance on May 31	$8,760	$9,370
May deposits	5,000	5,810
May cheques	4,000	3,100
May note collected (not included in May deposits)	1,000	—
May bank service charge	25	—
May NSF cheque from a customer, returned by the bank (recorded by the bank as a charge)	335	—

Instructions

(a) Keeping in mind the time lag between deposits and cheques being recorded in the books and when they are recorded by the bank, determine the amount of outstanding deposits and outstanding cheques at May 31.

(b) Prepare a bank reconciliation going from the balance per bank and balance per books to the correct cash balance.

(c) Prepare the general journal entry or entries to correct the Cash account at May 31.

(LO 10) *E7-26 (Bank Reconciliation and Adjusting Entries) Eli Corp. has just received its August 31, 2010, bank statement, which is summarized as follows:

Provincial Bank of Manitoba	Disbursements	Receipts	Balance
Balance, August 1			$ 9,369
Deposits during August		$32,200	41,569
Note collected for depositor, including $40 interest		1,040	42,609
Cheques cleared during August	$34,500		8,109
Bank service charges	20		8,089
Balance, August 31			8,089

The general ledger Cash account contained the following entries for the month of August:

Cash

Balance, August 1	10,050	Disbursements in August	34,903
Receipts during August	35,000		

Deposits in transit at August 31 are $3,800, and cheques outstanding at August 31 total $1,050. Cash currently on hand at August 31 is $310 and there were postdated cheques from customers (for September 1) in the amount of $540. The bookkeeper improperly entered one cheque in the books at $146.50. The cheque was actually written for $164.50 for supplies (expense) and cleared the bank during the month of August.

Instructions

(a) Prepare a bank reconciliation dated August 31, 2010, proceeding to a correct balance.

(b) Prepare any entries that are needed to make the books correct and complete.

(c) What amount of cash should be reported on the August 31 balance sheet?

Problems

P7-1 Dev Equipment Corp. usually closes its books on December 31, but at the end of 2010 it held its cash book open so that a more favourable balance sheet could be prepared for credit purposes. Cash receipts and disbursements for the first 10 days of January were recorded as December transactions.

The following information is given:

1. January cash receipts recorded in the December cash book totalled $38,900. Of that amount, $25,300 was for cash sales and $13,600 was for collections on account for which cash discounts of $630 were given.

2. January cash disbursements that were recorded in the December cheque register were for payments on account totalling $24,850 of accounts payable on which discounts of $520 were taken.

3. The ledger has not been closed for 2010.

4. The amount shown as inventory was determined by a physical count on December 31, 2010.

Instructions

(a) Prepare any entries that you consider necessary to correct Dev Equipment Corp.'s accounts at December 31.

(b) To what extent was Dev Equipment Co. able to show a more favourable balance sheet at December 31 by holding its cash book open? (Use ratio analysis.) Assume that the balance sheet that was prepared by the company showed the following amounts:

	Dr.	Cr.
Cash	$39,000	
Receivables	42,000	
Inventories	67,000	
Accounts payable		$45,000
Other current liabilities		14,200

P7-2 A series of unrelated situations follow:

1. Atlantic Inc.'s unadjusted trial balance at December 31, 2010, included the following accounts:

	Debit	Credit
Allowance for doubtful accounts	$ 8,000	
Sales		$1,980,000
Sales returns and allowances	60,000	
Sales discounts	4,400	

2. An analysis and aging of Central Corp.'s accounts receivable at December 31, 2010, disclosed the following:

Amounts estimated to be uncollectible	$ 160,000
Accounts receivable	1,790,000
Allowance for doubtful accounts (per books)	125,000

3. Western Co. provides for doubtful accounts based on 4.5% of credit sales. The following data are available for 2010:

Credit sales during 2010	$3,200,000
Allowance for doubtful accounts 1/1/10	37,000
Collection of accounts written off in prior years	
(customer credit was re-established)	18,000
Customer accounts written off as uncollectible during 2010	36,000

4. At the end of its first year of operations, on December 31, 2010, Pacific Inc. reported the following information:

Accounts receivable, net of allowance for doubtful accounts	$950,000
Customer accounts written off as uncollectible during 2010	24,000
Bad debt expense for 2010	92,000

5. The following accounts were taken from Northern Inc.'s unadjusted trial balance at December 31, 2010:

	Debit	Credit
Sales (all on credit)		$950,000
Sales discounts	$ 21,400	
Allowance for doubtful accounts	34,000	
Accounts receivable	610,000	

Instructions

(a) For situation 1, Atlantic estimates its bad debt expense to be 1.5% of net sales. Determine its bad debt expense for 2010.

(b) For situation 2, what is the net realizable value of Central Corp.'s receivables at December 31, 2010?

(c) For situation 3, what is the balance in Allowance for Doubtful Accounts at December 31, 2010?

(d) For situation 4, what is the balance in accounts receivable at December 31, 2010, before subtracting the allowance for doubtful accounts?

(e) For situation 5, if doubtful accounts are 7% of accounts receivable, what is the bad debt expense amount to be reported for 2010?

P7-3   Fortini Corporation had record sales in 2010. It began 2010 with an Accounts Receivable balance of $475,000 and an Allowance for Doubtful Accounts of $33,000. Fortini recognized credit sales during the year of $6,675,000 and made monthly adjusting entries equal to 0.5% of each month's credit sales to recognize bad debt expense. Also during the year the company wrote off $35,500 of accounts that were deemed to be uncollectible, although one customer whose $4,000 account had been written off surprised management by paying the amount in full in late September. Including this surprise receipt, $6,568,500 cash was collected on account in 2010.

In preparation for the audited year-end financial statements, the controller prepared the following aged listing of the receivables at December 31, 2010:

Days Account Outstanding	Amount	Probability of Collection
Less than 16 days	$270,000	97%
Between 16 and 30 days	117,000	92%
Between 31 and 45 days	80,000	80%
Between 46 and 60 days	38,000	70%
Between 61 and 75 days	20,000	50%
Over 75 days	25,000	0%

Instructions

(a) Prepare the adjusting entry to bring the Allowance for Doubtful Accounts to its proper balance at year end.

(b) Show how accounts receivable would be presented on the December 31, 2010 statement of financial position.

(c) What is the dollar effect of the year-end bad debt adjustment on the before-tax income?

P7-4   From its first day of operations to December 31, 2010, Campbell Corporation provided for uncollectible accounts receivable under the allowance method: entries for bad debt expense were made monthly based on 2.5% of credit sales; bad debts that were written off were charged to the allowance account; recoveries of bad debts previously written off were credited to the allowance account; and no year-end adjustments were made to the allowance account. Campbell's usual credit terms were net 30 days, and remain unchanged.

The balance in Allowance for Doubtful Accounts was $184,000 at January 1, 2010. During 2010, credit sales totalled $9.4 million; interim entries for bad debt expense were based on 2.5% of credit sales; $95,000 of bad debts were written off; and recoveries of accounts previously written off amounted to $15,000. Campbell upgraded its computer facility in November 2010, and an aging of accounts receivable was prepared for the first time as at December 31, 2010. A summary of the aging analysis follows:

Classification by Month of Sale	Balance in Each Category	Estimated % Uncollectible
November–December 2010	$1,080,000	8%
July–October 2010	650,000	12.5%
January–June 2010	420,000	20%
Before January 1, 2010	150,000	60%
	$2,300,000	

Based on a review of how collectible the accounts really are in the "Before January 1, 2010" aging category, additional receivables totalling $69,000 were written off as at December 31, 2010. The 60% uncollectible estimate therefore only applies to the remaining $81,000 in the category. Finally, beginning with the year ended December 31, 2010, Campbell adopted a new accounting method for estimating the allowance for doubtful accounts: it now uses the amount indicated by the year-end aging analysis of accounts receivable.

Instructions

(a) Prepare a schedule that analyzes the changes in Allowance for Doubtful Accounts for the year ended December 31, 2010. Show supporting calculations in good form. (Hint: In calculating the allowance amount at December 31, 2010, subtract the $69,000 writeoff.)

(b) Prepare the journal entry for the year-end adjustment to the Allowance for Doubtful Accounts balance as at December 31, 2010.

(AICPA adapted)

P7-5 The following information relates to Shea Inc.'s Accounts Receivable for the 2010 fiscal year:

1. An aging schedule of the accounts receivable as at December 31, 2010, is as follows:

Age	Net Debit Balance	% to Be Applied after Writeoff Is Made
Under 60 days	$172,342	1%
61–90 days	136,490	3%
91–120 days	39,924*	7%
Over 120 days	23,644	$4,200 definitely uncollectible; 20% of
	$372,400	remainder is estimated uncollectible

*The $2,740 writeoff of receivables (see item 4 below) is related to the 91–120-day category.

2. The Accounts Receivable control account has a debit balance of $372,400 on December 31, 2010.

3. Two entries were made in the Bad Debts Expense account during the year: (1) a debit on December 31 for the amount credited to Allowance for Doubtful Accounts, and (2) a credit for $2,740 on November 3, 2010, and a debit to Allowance for Doubtful Accounts because of a bankruptcy.

4. Allowance for Doubtful Accounts is as follows for 2010:

Allowance for Doubtful Accounts

11/3	Uncollectible accounts written off	2,740	1/1	Beginning balance	8,750
			12/31	5% of $372,400	18,620

5. There is a credit balance in Accounts Receivable (61–90 days) of $4,840, which represents an advance on a sales contract.

Instructions

Assuming that the books have not been closed for 2010, make the necessary correcting entries.

P7-6 The balance sheet of Reynolds Corp. at December 31, 2010, includes the following:

Notes receivable	$ 26,000	
Accounts receivable	182,100	
Less: Allowance for doubtful accounts	(17,300)	$190,800

Transactions in 2011 include the following:

1. Accounts receivable of $138,000 were collected. This amount includes gross accounts of $40,000 on which 2% sales discounts were allowed.

2. An additional $6,700 was received in payment of an account that was written off in 2010.

3. Customer accounts of $19,500 were written off during the year.

4. At year end, Allowance for Doubtful Accounts was estimated to need a balance of $21,000. This estimate is based on an analysis of aged accounts receivable.

Instructions

Prepare all necessary journal entries to reflect the information above.

(AICPA adapted)

P7-7 On October 1, 2010, Healy Farm Equipment Corp. sold a harvesting machine to Homestead Industries. Instead of a cash payment, Homestead Industries gave Healy Farm Equipment a $150,000, two-year, 10% note; 10% is a realistic rate for a note of this type. The note required interest to be paid annually on October 1, beginning October 1, 2011. Healy Farm Equipment's financial statements are prepared on a calendar-year basis.

Instructions

(a) Assuming that no reversing entries are used and that Homestead Industries fulfills all the terms of the note, prepare the necessary journal entries for Healy Farm Equipment Corp. for the entire term of the note.

(b) Repeat the journal entries under the assumption that Healy Farm Equipment Corp. uses reversing entries.

P7-8   On December 31, 2010, Zhang Ltd. rendered services to Beggy Corp. at an agreed price of $91,844.10. In payment, Zhang accepted $36,000 cash and agreed to receive the balance in four equal instalments of $18,000 that are due each December 31. An interest rate of 11% is applicable.

Instructions

(a) Prepare the entries recorded by Zhang Ltd. for the sale and for the receipts including interest on the following dates:

   1. December 31, 2010
   2. December 31, 2011
   3. December 31, 2012
   4. December 31, 2013
   5. December 31, 2014

Digging Deeper

(b) From Zhang Ltd.'s perspective, what are the advantages of an instalment note compared with a non-interest-bearing note?

P7-9   Desrosiers Ltd. had the following long-term receivable account balances at December 31, 2009:

Note receivable from sale of division	$1,800,000
Note receivable from officer	400,000

Transactions during 2010 and other information relating to Desrosiers's long-term receivables were as follows:

(a) The $1.8-million note receivable is dated May 1, 2009, bears interest at 9%, and represents the balance of the consideration received from the sale of Desrosiers's electronics division to New York Company. Principal payments of $600,000 plus appropriate interest are due on May 1, 2010, 2011, and 2012. The first principal and interest payment was made on May 1, 2010. Collection of the note instalments is reasonably assured.

(b) The $400,000 note receivable is dated December 31, 2009, bears interest at 8%, and is due on December 31, 2012. The note is due from Mark Cumby, president of Desrosiers Ltd., and is secured by 10,000 Desrosiers common shares. Interest is payable annually on December 31, and the interest payment was made December 31, 2010. The quoted market price of Desrosiers's common shares was $45 per share on December 31, 2010.

(c) On April 1, 2010, Desrosiers sold a patent to Pinot Company in exchange for a $200,000 non-interest-bearing note due on April 1, 2012. There was no established exchange price for the patent, and the note had no ready market. The prevailing rate of interest for a note of this type at April 1, 2010, was 12%. The present value of $1 for two periods at 12% is 0.79719 (use this factor). The patent had a carrying amount of $40,000 at January 1, 2010, and the amortization for the year ended December 31, 2010, would have been $8,000. The collection of the note receivable from Pinot is reasonably assured.

(d) On July 1, 2010, Desrosiers sold a parcel of land to Harris Inc. for $200,000 under an instalment sale contract. Harris made a $60,000 cash down payment on July 1, 2010, and signed a four-year, 11% note for the $140,000 balance. The equal annual payments of principal and interest on the note will be $45,125 payable on July 1, 2011, through July 1, 2014. The land could have been sold at an established cash price of $200,000. The cost of the land to Desrosiers was $150,000. Collection of the instalments on the note is reasonably assured.

Instructions

(a) For each note:
   1. Describe the relevant cash flows in terms of amount and timing.
   2. Determine the amount of interest income that should be reported in 2010.
   3. Determine the portion of the note and any interest that should be reported in current assets at December 31, 2010.
   4. Determine the portion of the note that should be reported as a long-term investment at December 31, 2010.

(b) Prepare the long-term receivables section of Desrosiers's balance sheet at December 31, 2010.

(c) Prepare a schedule showing the current portion of the long-term receivables and accrued interest receivable that would appear in Desrosiers's balance sheet at December 31, 2010.

(d) Determine the total interest income from the long-term receivables that would appear on Desrosiers's income statement for the year ended December 31, 2010.

P7-10   Logo Limited manufactures sweatshirts for sale to athletic-wear retailers. The following summary information was available for Logo for the year ended December 31, 2009:

Cash	$20,000
Trade accounts receivable (net)	40,000
Inventories	85,000
Accounts payable	65,000
Other current liabilities	15,000

Part 1

During 2010, Logo had the following transactions:

1. Total sales were $465,000. Of the total sales amount, $215,000 was on a credit basis.

2. On June 30, a $50,000 account receivable of a major customer was settled, with Logo accepting a $50,000, one-year, 11% note, with the interest payable at maturity.

3. Logo collected $160,000 on trade accounts receivable during the year.

4. At December 31, 2010, Cash had a balance of $15,000, Inventories had a balance of $80,000, Accounts Payable were $70,000, and Other Current Liabilities were $16,000.

Instructions

(a) Prepare summary journal entries to record the items noted above.

(b) Calculate the current ratio and the receivables turnover ratio for Logo at December 31, 2010. Use these measures to assess Logo's liquidity. The receivables turnover ratio last year was 4.75.

Part 2

Now assume that at year end 2010, Logo enters into the following transactions related to the company's receivables:

1. Logo sells the note receivable to Prairie Bank for $50,000 cash plus accrued interest. Given the creditworthiness of Logo's customer, the bank accepts the note without recourse and assesses a finance charge of 3.5%. Prairie Bank will collect the note directly from the customer.

2. Logo factors some accounts receivable at the end of the year. Accounts totalling $40,000 are transferred to Primary Factors, Inc., with recourse. Primary Factors retains 6% of the balances and assesses a finance charge of 4% on the transfer. Primary Factors will collect the receivables from Logo's customers. The fair value of the recourse obligation is $4,000.

Instructions

(c) Prepare the journal entry to record the transfer of the note receivable to Prairie Bank.

(d) Prepare the journal entry to record the sale of receivables to Primary Factors.

(e) Calculate the current ratio and the receivables turnover ratio for Logo at December 31, 2010. Use these measures to assess Logo's liquidity. The receivables turnover ratio last year was 4.85.

(f) Discuss how the ratio analysis in (e) would be affected if Logo had transferred the receivables in secured borrowing transactions.

P7-11   In 2010, Ibran Corp. required additional cash for its business. Management therefore decided to use accounts receivable to raise the additional cash and has asked you to determine the income statement effects of the following transactions:

1. On July 1, 2010, Ibran assigned $600,000 of accounts receivable to Provincial Finance Corporation as security for a loan. Ibran received an advance from Provincial of 90% of the assigned accounts receivable less a commission of 3% on the advance. Before December 31, 2010, Ibran collected $220,000 on the assigned accounts receivable, and remitted $232,720 to Provincial Finance. Of the latter amount, $12,720 was interest on the advance from Provincial.

2. On December 1, 2010, Ibran sold $300,000 of accounts receivable to Wunsch Corp. for $275,000. The receivables were sold outright on a without recourse basis and Ibran has no continuing interest in the receivables.

3. On December 31, 2010, an advance of $120,000 was received from First Bank by pledging $160,000 of Ibran's accounts receivable. Ibran's first payment to First Bank is due on January 30, 2011.

Instructions

Prepare a schedule showing the income statement effects of the above transactions for the year ended December 31, 2010.

P7-12   The Cormier Corporation sells office equipment and supplies to many organizations in the city and surrounding area on contract terms of 2/10, n/30. In the past, over 75% of the credit customers have taken advantage of the discount by paying within 10 days of the invoice date. However, the number of customers taking the full 30 days to pay has increased within the last year. It now appears that less than 60% of the customers are taking the discount. Bad debts as a percentage of gross credit sales have risen from the 1.5% of past years to about 4% in the current year.

The controller responded to a request for more information on the deterioration in collections of accounts receivable by preparing the following report:

THE CORMIER CORPORATION
Finance Committee Report—Accounts Receivable Collections
May 31, 2010

The fact that some credit accounts will prove uncollectible is normal. Annual bad debt writeoffs have been 1.5% of gross credit sales over the past five years. During the last fiscal year, this percentage increased to slightly less than 4%. The current Accounts Receivable balance is $1.6 million. The condition of this balance in terms of age and probability of collection is as follows:

Proportion of Total (%)	Age Categories	Probability of Collection (%)
68	not yet due	99
15	less than 30 days past due	96.5
8	30 to 60 days past due	95
5	61 to 120 days past due	91
2.50	121 to 180 days past due	70
1.50	more than 180 days past due	20

Allowance for Doubtful Accounts had a credit balance of $43,300 on June 1, 2009. The Cormier Corporation has provided for a monthly bad debt expense accrual during the current fiscal year based on the assumption that 4% of gross credit sales will be uncollectible. Total gross credit sales for the 2009–10 fiscal year amounted to $4 million. Writeoffs of bad accounts during the year totalled $145,000.

Instructions

(a) Prepare an accounts receivable aging schedule for The Cormier Corporation using the age categories identified in the controller's report to the Finance Committee. Show (1) the amount of accounts receivable outstanding for each age category and in total, and (2) the estimated amount that is uncollectible for each category and in total.

(b) Calculate the amount of the year-end adjustment that is needed to bring Allowance for Doubtful Accounts to the balance indicated by the age analysis. Then prepare the necessary journal entry to adjust the accounting records.

(c) Assuming that the economy is currently in recession, with tight credit and high interest rates:

1. Identify steps that the Cormier Corporation might consider to improve the accounts receivable situation.

2. Evaluate each step you identify in terms of the risks and costs that it involves.

(CMA adapted)

P7-13   The Patchwork Corporation manufactures sweaters for sale to athletic-wear retailers. The following information was available on Patchwork for the years ended December 31, 2009 and 2010:

	12/31/09	12/31/10
Cash	$ 20,000	$ 15,000
Accounts receivable	90,000	?
Allowance for doubtful accounts	8,500	?
Inventories	85,000	80,000
Current liabilities	80,000	86,000
Total credit sales	600,000	550,000
Collections on accounts receivable	440,000	500,000

During 2010, Patchwork had the following transactions:

1. On June 1, 2010, sales of $80,000 to a major customer were settled, with Patchwork accepting an $80,000, one-year note bearing 7% interest that is payable at maturity. The $80,000 is not included in the total credit sales amount above.

2. Patchwork factors some accounts receivable at the end of the year. Accounts totalling $60,000 are transferred to Primary Factors Inc., with recourse. Primary Factors will receive the collections from Patchwork's customers and retain 5% of the balances. Patchwork is assessed a finance charge of 6% on this transfer. The fair value of the recourse obligation is $7,000.

3. Patchwork wrote off $3,200 of accounts receivable during 2010.

4. Based on the latest available information, the 2010 allowance for doubtful accounts should have a balance at December 31, 2010, of $12,000.

Additional information:

Included in the cash balance at December 31, 2010, are the following: a chequing account with a balance of $9,600; postage stamps of $100; petty cash of $300; coins and currency on hand of $3,000; and postdated cheques from customers of $2,000.

Instructions

(a) Prepare the journal entry for the factoring of the accounts receivable to Primary Factors Inc.

(b) Based on the above transactions and additional information, determine the balances of Accounts Receivable and Bad Debt Expense at December 31, 2010.

(c) Prepare the current assets section of Patchwork's balance sheet at December 31, 2010.

(d) Calculate the current ratios for Patchwork for 2009 and 2010.

(e) Calculate the receivables turnover ratio for Patchwork for 2010. Patchwork's receivables turnover ratio for 2009 was 3.8 times.

(f) Comment on Patchwork's liquidity and ability to collect accounts receivable. Comment also on the improvement or deterioration of the current and receivables turnover ratios.

(g) Discuss the effect on the current and accounts receivable turnover ratios if Patchwork had decided to assign $40,000 of accounts receivable instead of factoring them to Primary Factors Inc. Recalculate the ratios to support your conclusions.

Digging Deeper

*P7-14 Joseph Howe is reviewing the cash accounting for Connolly Corporation, a local mailing service. Howe's review will focus on the petty cash account and the bank reconciliation for the month ended May 31, 2010. He has collected the following information from Connolly's bookkeeper:

Petty Cash

1. The petty cash fund was established on May 10, 2010, in the amount of $400.

2. Expenditures from the fund by the custodian as at May 31, 2010, were evidenced by approved receipts for the following:

Postage expense	$63.00
Envelopes and other supplies	25.00
In-house business lunch provided	99.50
Donation to local charity	35.00
Shipping charges, for goods to customers	48.50
Newspaper advertising	22.80
Taxi for sales manager to attend meeting downtown	18.75
Freight paid on incoming purchases	37.70

3. On May 31, 2010, the petty cash fund was replenished and increased to $500; currency and coin in the fund at that time totalled $47.10.

Bank Reconciliation

SCOTIA IMPERIAL BANK
Bank Statement

	Disbursements	Receipts	Balance
Balance, May 1, 2010			$9,019
Deposits		$28,000	
Note payment, direct from customer (interest of $30)		930	
Cheques cleared during May	$31,100		
Bank service charges	37		
Balance, May 31, 2010			$6,812

Connolly's general ledger Cash account had a balance of $9,300 on May 1. During the month, the company deposited $31,000 in the bank, and wrote cheques in payment of accounts payable and the payroll for $31,685. Deposits in transit at the end of the month are determined to be $3,000, cash still on hand with the company cashier is $246 (besides petty cash), and cheques outstanding at May 31 total $550.

Instructions

(a) Prepare the journal entries to record the transactions related to the petty cash fund for May.

(b) Prepare a bank reconciliation dated May 31, 2010, proceeding to a correct balance, and prepare the journal entries to make the books correct and complete.

(c) What amount of cash should be reported in the May 31, 2010, balance sheet?

*P7-15   The cash account of Villa Corp. shows a ledger balance of $3,969.85 on June 30, 2010. The bank statement as at that date indicates a balance of $4,150. When the statement was compared with the cash records, the following facts were determined:

1. There were bank service charges for June of $25.00.

2. A bank memo stated that Bao Dai's note for $900 and interest of $36 had been collected on June 29, and the bank had made a charge of $5.50 on the collection. (No entry had been made on Villa's books when Bao Dai's note was sent to the bank for collection.)

3. Receipts for June 30 of $2,890 were not deposited until July 2.

4. Cheques outstanding on June 30 totalled $2,136.05.

5. On June 29, the bank had charged Villa Corp.'s account for a customer's uncollectible cheque amounting to $453.20.

6. A customer's cheque for $90 had been entered as $60 in the cash receipts journal by Villa Corp. on June 15.

7. Cheque no. 742 in the amount of $491 had been entered in the cashbook as $419, and cheque no. 747 in the amount of $58.20 had been entered as $582. Both cheques were issued to pay for purchases of equipment.

8. In May 2010, the bank had charged a $27.50 Wella Corp. cheque against the Villa Corp. account. The June bank statement indicated that the bank had reversed this charge and corrected its error.

Instructions

(a) Prepare a bank reconciliation dated June 30, 2010, proceeding to a correct cash balance.

(b) Prepare any entries that are needed to make the books correct and complete.

*P7-16   Information related to Bonzai Books Ltd. is as follows: balance per books at October 31, $41,847.85; November receipts, $173,528.91; November disbursements, $166,193.54; balance per bank statement at November 30, $56,270.20. The following cheques were outstanding at November 30:

#1224	$1,635.29
#1230	2,468.30
#1232	3,625.15
#1233	482.17

Included with the November bank statement and not recorded by the company were a bank debit memo for $31.40 covering bank charges for the month, a debit memo for $572.13 for a customer's cheque returned and marked NSF, and a credit memo for $1,400 representing bond interest collected by the bank in the name of Bonzai Books Ltd. Cash on hand at November 30 that had been recorded and was not yet deposited amounted to $1,920.40.

Instructions

(a) Prepare a bank reconciliation to the correct balance at November 30 for Bonzai Books Ltd.

(b) Prepare any journal entries that are needed to adjust the Cash account at November 30.

*P7-17 Information follows on Quartz Industries Ltd.:

QUARTZ INDUSTRIES LTD.
Bank Reconciliation
May 31, 2010

Balance per bank statement		$30,928.46
Less: Outstanding cheques		
No. 6124	$2,125.00	
No. 6138	932.65	
No. 6139	960.57	
No. 6140	1,420.00	5,438.22
		25,490.24
Add deposit in transit		4,710.56
Balance per books (correct balance)		$30,200.80

CHEQUE REGISTER—JUNE

Date		Payee	No.	Invoice Amount	Discount	Cash
June	1	Bren Mfg.	6141	$ 237.50		$ 237.50
	1	Stempy Mfg.	6142	915.00	$ 9.15	905.85
	8	Regent Co., Inc.	6143	122.90	2.45	120.45
	9	Bren Mfg.	6144	306.40		306.40
	10	Petty Cash	6145	89.93		89.93
	17	Pretty Babies Photo	6146	706.00	14.12	691.88
	22	Hey Dude Publishing	6147	447.50		447.50
	23	Payroll Account	6148	4,130.00		4,130.00
	25	Dragon Tools, Inc.	6149	390.75	3.91	386.84
	28	Dare Insurance Agency	6150	1,050.00		1,050.00
	28	Be Smart Construction	6151	2,250.00		2,250.00
	29	M M T, Inc.	6152	750.00		750.00
	30	Lasso Co.	6153	400.00	8.00	392.00
				$11,795.98	$37.63	$11,758.35

PROVINCIAL BANK
Bank Statement
General Chequing Account of Quartz Industries—June 2010

Debits			Date	Credits	Balance
					$30,928.46
$2,125.00	$ 237.50	$ 905.85	June 1	$4,710.56	32,370.67
932.65	120.45		12	1,507.06	32,824.63
1,420.00	447.50	306.40	23	1,458.55	32,109.28
4,130.00	11.05*		26		27,968.23
89.93	2,250.00	1,050.00	28	4,157.48	28,735.78

*Bank charges

Cash received on June 29 and 30 and deposited in the mail on June 30 for the general chequing account amounted to $4,607.96. Because the Cash account balance at June 30 is not given, it must be calculated based on other information in the problem.

Instructions

Prepare a bank reconciliation to the correct balance as at June 30, 2010, for Quartz Industries.

Writing Assignments

WA7-1 The trial balance of Imotex Ltd. contains the following accounts:

1. Accounts receivable, trade

2. Accounts receivable, related company

3. Accounts receivable, to be exchanged for shares in another company

4. Note receivable, receivable in grams of a precious metal

5. Cash

6. Investment in Royal Bank common shares (long-term investment)

7. Income taxes receivable

8. Interest rate swap: contract to receive fixed rate (at 8%) and to pay variable rate (current rates are 6%) on debenture debt

9. U.S. dollar cash holdings in a U.S. subsidiary's bank account

Instructions

For 1 to 9, indicate whether the item is or is not a financial asset. Give an explanation for each of your choices.

WA7-2 IFRS provides guidance on impairment testing—in particular, what is supportable evidence of impairment of loans and receivables.

Instructions

Read IAS 39, paragraphs 58 to 64, and answer the following questions.

(a) When is a financial asset tested for impairment?

(b) What are examples of "objective evidence" that might indicate impairment?

(c) What evidence, by itself, does not indicate impairment?

(d) Are loans and receivables treated individually or as a group?

WA7-3 Soon after beginning the year-end audit work on March 10 for the 2011 year end at Arkin Corp., the auditor has the following conversation with the controller:

Controller: The year ended March 31, 2011, should be our most profitable in history and, because of this, the board of directors has just awarded the officers generous bonuses.

Auditor: I thought profits were down this year in the industry, at least according to your latest interim report.

Controller: Well, they were down, but 10 days ago we closed a deal that will give us a substantial increase for the year.

Auditor: Oh, what was it?

Controller: Well, you remember a few years ago our former president bought shares of Hi-Tek Enterprises Ltd. because he had those grandiose ideas about becoming a conglomerate? They cost us $3 million, which is the current carrying amount. On March 1, 2011, we sold the shares to Campbell Inc., an unrelated party, for $4 million. So, we'll have a gain of $686,000, which results from $1 million pre-tax minus transaction costs of $20,000 for legal fees and taxes at 30%. This will increase our net income for the year to $5.2 million, compared with last year's $4.8 million. The transaction fees were higher than normal due to the setting up of the note receivable. As far as I know, we'll be the only company in the industry to register an increase in net income this year. That should help the market value of our shares!

Auditor: Do you expect to receive the $4 million in cash by March 31, your fiscal year end?

Controller: No. Although Campbell Inc. is an excellent company, they're a little tight for cash because of their rapid growth. We have a $4-million non-interest-bearing note with $400,000 due each year for the next 10 years, which Campbell signed. The first payment is due March 1 of next year and future payments are due on the same date every year thereafter.

Auditor: Why is the note non-interest-bearing?

Controller: Because that's what everybody agreed to. Since we don't have any interest-bearing debt, the funds invested in the note don't cost us anything, and besides, we weren't getting any dividends on the Hi-Tek Enterprises shares.

Instructions

Prepare the auditor's written report to the controller on how this transaction should be accounted for, and how any corrections that are necessary will affect the reported results for the current year ended March 31, assuming that the company reports under IFRS. Make assumptions where required and make the appropriate journal entries at March 1 and March 31, 2011. What is the revised net income for the company for the year ended March 31? What changes would be necessary if the company reported under private entity GAAP?

WA7-4 Rudolph Corp. is a subsidiary of Huntley Corp. The controller believes that the yearly charge for doubtful accounts for Rudolph should be 2% of net credit sales. The president, nervous that the parent company might expect the subsidiary to sustain its 10% growth rate, suggests that the controller increase the charge for doubtful accounts to 3% yearly. The supervisor thinks that the lower net income, which reflects a 6% growth rate, will be a more sustainable rate for Rudolph.

Ethics

Instructions

(a) Should the controller be concerned with Rudolph Corp.'s growth rate in estimating the allowance? Explain your answer.

(b) Does the president's request pose an ethical dilemma for the controller? Give your reasons for why it does or does not.

WA7-5 Who would have thought that musicians David Bowie and James Brown had anything to do with accounting? Asset- or artist-backed financing vehicles have been used by these performers and others as a means of securitizing royalties and rights to other intellectual property.

Instructions

Perform an Internet search on "Bowie bonds" or on David Pullman, who created them. Write a brief report explaining how this securitization works and what similarities it has to accounts receivable securitization.

WA7-6 Write a brief essay highlighting the differences between IFRS and accounting standards for private enterprises noted in this chapter, discussing the conceptual justification for each.

Cases

Refer to the Case Primer to help you answer these cases.

Case Primer

CA7-1 Hanley Limited manufactures camera equipment. The company plans to list its shares on the Venture Exchange. To do so, it must meet all of the following initial listing requirements (among others):

1. Net tangible assets must be at least $500,000.

2. Pre-tax earnings must be $50,000.

3. The company must have adequate working capital.

Hanley has experienced significant growth in sales and is having difficulty estimating its bad debt expense. During the year, the sales team has been extending credit more aggressively in order to increase commission revenues. Under the percentage-of-receivables approach using past percentages, the estimate is $50,000. Hanley has performed an aging and estimates the bad debts at $57,000. Finally, using a percentage of sales, the expense is estimated at $67,000. Before booking the allowance, net tangible assets are approximately $550,000. The controller decides to accrue $50,000, which results in pre-tax earnings of $60,000.

Ethics

Instructions

Adopt the role of the Venture Exchange staff and decide whether the company meets the financial aspects of the initial requirements for listing on the Venture Exchange.

CA7-2 **TELUS Corporation** is one of Canada's largest telecommunications companies and provides both products and services. Its shares are traded on the Toronto and New York stock exchanges. The credit facilities contain certain covenants relating to the amount of debt the company is allowed to hold.

Real-World Emphasis

According to the 2008 Annual Report:

On July 26, 2002, TELUS Communications Inc., a wholly owned subsidiary of TELUS, entered into an agreement, which was amended September 30, 2002, March 1, 2006, November 30, 2006, March 31, 2008, and September 12, 2008, with an arm's-length securitization trust associated with a major Schedule I bank under which TELUS Communications Inc. is able to sell an interest in certain of its trade receivables up to a maximum of $650 million. This revolving-period securitization agreement had an initial term ending July 18, 2007; the November 30, 2006, amendment resulted in the term being extended to July 18, 2008; the March 31, 2008, amendment resulted in the term being extended to July 17, 2009.

As a result of selling the interest in certain of the trade receivables on a fully serviced basis, a servicing liability is recognized on the date of sale and is, in turn, amortized to earnings over the expected life of the trade receivables.

TELUS Communications Inc. is required to maintain at least a BBB (low) credit rating by Dominion Bond Rating Service or the securitization trust may require the sale program to be wound down prior to the end of the term; at December 31, 2008, the rating was A (low).

As at December 31 (millions)	2008	2007
Total managed portfolio	**$1,272**	$1,222
Securitized receivables	**(346)**	(570)
Retained interest in receivables sold	**40**	59
Receivables held	**$ 966**	$ 711

For the year ended December 31, 2008, the Company recognized composite losses of $11 million (2007 – $21 million) on the sale of receivables arising from the securitization.

Cash flows from the securitization were as follows:

Years ended December 31 (millions)	2008	2007
Cumulative proceeds from securitization, beginning of period	**$ 500**	$ 500
Proceeds from new securitizations	**150**	720
Securitization reduction payments	**(350)**	(720)
Cumulative proceeds from securitization, end of period	**$ 300**	$ 500
Proceeds from collections reinvested in revolving-period securitizations	**$3,105**	$3,947
Proceeds from collections pertaining to retained interest	**$ 382**	$ 477

The key economic assumptions used to determine the loss on sale of receivables, the future cash flows and fair values attributed to the retained interest, as further discussed in Note 1(n), were as follows:

Years ended December 31	2008	2007
Expected credit losses as a percentage of accounts receivable sold	**1.2%**	1.1%
Weighted average life of the receivables sold (days)	**33**	37
Effective annual discount rate	**3.5%**	5.0%
Servicing	**1.0%**	1.0%

Generally, the sold trade receivables do not experience prepayments.

At December 31, 2008, key economic assumptions and the sensitivity of the current fair value of residual cash flows to immediate 10% and 20% changes in those assumptions were as follows:

($ in millions)	2008	Hypothetical change in assumptions(1) 10%	20%
Carrying amount/fair value of future cash flows	**$ 40**		
Expected credit losses as a percentage of accounts receivable sold		$ –	$ 1
Weighted average life of the receivables sold (days)		$ –	$ –
Effective annual discount rate		$ –	$ –

(1) These sensitivities are hypothetical and should be used with caution. Favourable hypothetical changes in the assumptions result in an increased value, and unfavourable hypothetical changes in the assumptions result in a decreased value, of the retained interest in receivables sold. As the figures indicate, changes in fair value based on a 10% variation in assumptions generally cannot be extrapolated because the relationship of the change in assumption to the change in fair value may not be linear. Also, in this table, the effect of a variation in a particular assumption on the fair value of the retained interest is calculated without changing any other assumption; in reality, changes in one factor may result in changes in another (for example, increases in market interest rates may result in increased credit losses), which might magnify or counteract the sensitivities.

Instructions

Adopt the role of the controller of Telus and discuss the financial reporting issues.

Integrated Cases

(Hint: If there are issues here that are new, use the conceptual framework to help you support your analysis with solid reasoning.)

IC7-1 Fritz's Furniture (FF) is a mid-sized owner-operated business that was started 25 years ago by Fred Fritz. The retail furniture business is cyclical, with business dropping off in times of economic downturn, as is the case currently. In order to encourage sales, the store offers its own credit cards to good customers. FF has run into a bit of a cash crunch and is planning to go to the bank to obtain an increase in its line of credit in order to replenish and expand the furniture stock. At present, the line of credit is capped at (i.e., limited to) 70% of the credit card receivables and inventory. The receivables and inventory have been pledged as security for the loan.

Fred has identified two possible sources of the cash shortage: outstanding credit card receivables and a buildup in old inventory. He has come up with two strategies to deal with the problem:

1. Credit card receivables: For the existing receivables, Fred has found the company Factors Inc. (FI), which will buy the receivables for 93% of their face value. The two companies are currently negotiating the terms of the deal. So far, FF has agreed to transfer legal title to the receivables to FI, and FF will maintain and collect the receivables. The one term that is still being discussed is whether FI will have any recourse to FF if the amounts become uncollectible.

2. Excess inventory: A new sales promotion has been advertised in the newspaper for the past two months. Under the terms of the promotion, customers do not pay anything up front and will be able to take the furniture home and begin payments the following year. Response to the advertisement has been very good and a significant amount of inventory has been moved to date, leaving room for new inventory once the bank financing comes through.

Instructions

Assume the role of FF's bookkeeper and advise Fred about the impact of the strategies on the company's financial reporting.

IC7-2 Bowearth Limited (BL) is in the lumber business. The company sells pulp and paper products as well as timber and lumber. It has over one million acres of timberland that it either owns or leases. The company's shares trade on the Public Stock Exchange (the PSE). Net income for the past few years has been positive and increasing, and it has averaged approximately $1 million over the past five years. This year, however, due to various factors, the company is expecting to just break even.

During the year, the company announced an exclusive licensing agreement with Lindor Inc. (LI), an unrelated company. Under the terms of the agreement, the company will have exclusive sales and distribution rights for LI's technology and products. In return, it will pay LI royalties. The technology and products target the pulp and paper industry. During the first five years of the agreement, royalty payments that BL must pay to LI are 3% of sales in the first year, 2% in the second, and 1% thereafter. A minimum royalty of $500,000 must be paid regardless of the level of sales. LI has been in business many years and the technology is proven and in great demand. It is therefore very likely that BL will have to pay.

The U.S. government has recently levied anti-dumping fees of 8% on all softwood lumber shipped to the United States, as well as countervailing duties of 20%. The amounts must be paid by the company to the U.S. government in order to continue to sell in the United States. The Canadian government has challenged the right of the U.S. government to charge this amount and has appealed to the World Trade Organization. Canada feels that under the North American Free Trade Agreement (NAFTA), such charges cannot be legally levied. In the meantime, BL has been accruing and setting the amounts aside in cash deposits with the bank just in case the appeal is unsuccessful. The amounts accrued and set aside to date are approximately $3 million. The U.S. government is continuing to allow the company to ship lumber as long as the cash is set aside in the bank. To date, the appeal process is going well and the Canadian government feels that the fees/duties will at least be reduced significantly, if not completely eliminated. There are rumours that the fees/duties may be cancelled next year.

The company is currently being sued by a former major shareholder for providing misleading financial statements. The lawsuit alleges that net income was materially misstated. The case has not yet gone to court. BL feels that the case is not very strong but has nonetheless fired the president, William Waters, to be on the safe side. As a result, BL is also being sued for wrongful dismissal by its former president. Waters is suing for a lost bonus of $300,000 as well as lost future income in the amount of $10 million. BL is investigating the claim of overstated net income and, to date, has not found anything that indicates a material misstatement.

The controller, Youssef Haddad, is unsure of how to book all of the above in the financial statements (or if he even should). He has a meeting with the bank next week to discuss increasing the company's line of credit. He is hopeful that once the ruling comes down from the World Trade Organization, the increased line of credit will not be needed. In the meantime, the bank has signalled that it will be looking at the company's liquidity very closely. The auditors will also be coming in to review the statements in the next month.

Instructions

Adopt the role of Youssef Haddad and discuss the financial reporting issues.

Research and Financial Analysis

RA7-1 Maple Leaf Foods Inc.

Real-World Emphasis

Access the annual financial statements for **Maple Leaf Foods Inc.** for the year ended December 31, 2008. These statements are available from the company's website or from SEDAR (www.sedar.com).

Instructions

(a) Explain the securitization that the company is involved in (see Note 5).

(b) Calculate the accounts receivable turnover for 2008 and 2007 and the average age of the accounts receivable at December 31, 2008, and 2007, without taking the additional securitized receivables into account. Comment on your results. For the calculation of average age, use the closing balance of the formula:

$$(\text{Year end accounts receivable} / \text{sales}) \times 365$$

(c) Calculate the percentage growth in sales and accounts receivable in 2008 and 2007 without taking the securitized receivables into account. Comment on your results.

(d) Explain how the securitized receivables should be taken into account in the calculations in (a) and (b) above, or not taken into account at all. Recalculate your ratios and percentages. Did the securitizations have an effect on your assessment of the company? Explain.

RA7-2 Canadian Tire Corporation, Limited

Real-World Emphasis

Canadian Tire Corporation, Limited is one of Canada's best-known retailers. The company operates over 475 "hard-goods" retail stores through associate dealers, and over 342 corporate and franchise stores under its subsidiary Mark's Work Wearhouse, and has about 273 independently operated gasoline sites and 88 Parts Source stores. It offers financial services through its branded credit cards and now provides personal loans and a variety of insurance and warranty products.

Instructions

Access the financial statements of Canadian Tire Corporation, Limited for its year ended January 3, 2009, either on the company's website or the SEDAR website (www.sedar.com). Refer to these financial statements and their accompanying notes to answer the following questions:

(a) How does Canadian Tire define cash and cash equivalents on its balance sheet?

(b) What criteria does the company use to determine what short-term investments to include in this category?

(c) Review the financial statements and notes and identify all the assets reported by Canadian Tire that qualify as loans and receivables. Does the company disclose the amount of its allowance for doubtful accounts? What was the amount of net credit losses for the year? How does the company determine allowance for future credit losses? Be specific. What were the amounts for the writeoffs, recoveries, and provision for credit losses for the year?

(d) When is a loan impaired? How is an impaired loan valued? What happens when the loan is subsequently recovered? Be specific. Does this procedure appear reasonable?

(e) Accounting standards require companies to disclose information about their exposure to credit risk. What is credit risk? What does Canadian Tire report? What is your assessment of its exposure to credit risk?

(f) Canadian Tire uses its accounts receivable to generate cash before the receivables are due. Briefly describe the form of "transfer" activities that the company uses. Are the receivables used as security for loans, are they sold outright with no continuing interest, or does Canadian Tire have a continuing relationship with the accounts? What financial components does it retain, if any, and what are the related amounts?

(g) In part 8.1.4 of the company's Management Discussion and Analysis (page 39) in the annual report, the company discusses the current market for asset-backed commercial paper. Why is this important to the company and what impact has the credit crisis had on the company? How has the company valued these investments?

RA7-3 Eastern Platinum Limited

The interim report for the three-month period ended March 31, 2009, for **Eastern Platinum Limited** can be found in Appendix 5B.

Instructions

Using the interim financial statement of Eastern Platinum Limited and the related notes, answer the following questions.

(a) Identify all items on the company's March 31, 2009 balance sheet that qualify as cash, cash equivalents, and loans and receivables.

(b) What is included in "cash and cash equivalents?" What is included in "short-term investments?"

(c) How much was in trade receivables at March 31, 2009, and March 31, 2008? How are the trade receivables reported? What was the allowance for doubtful accounts?

(d) How does the company report loans and other receivables and what is included in this classification?

(e) How are loans and receivables tested for impairment? What factors are considered and what is the method to determine the amount of the impairment loss? How are the impairment losses reported for trade receivables? For other loans?

(f) What were the adjustments required on conversion to IFRS to the trade receivables reported at January 1, 2008, March 31, 2008, and December 31, 2008? What were the reasons for these adjustments?

RA7-4 Loblaw Companies Limited and Empire Company Limited

Instructions

From SEDAR (www.sedar.com), or the company websites, access the financial statements of **Loblaw Companies Limited** for its year ended January 3, 2009, and of **Empire Company Limited** for its year ended May 2, 2009. Review the financial statements and answer the following questions.

(a) What businesses are the companies in?

(b) Compare how the two companies report cash and cash equivalents on the statement of financial position. What is included in the cash and cash equivalents of each and what are the amounts of these? Is any restricted cash reported by either company?

(c) What types of receivables do Loblaw and Empire have and what was the reported amount for each? How does each type of receivable arise? Which types are similar or different between the companies? How are the loans and receivables reported?

(d) Explain the type of credit risk that the companies have and how this risk is managed. What was the allowance for doubtful accounts at the end of year? What percentages of the accounts receivable were past due? How was the allowance for doubtful accounts determined for each company? How does the company test for impairment? What was the bad debts expense for the year? Is the allowance adequate?

(e) Does either company dispose of receivables before their due date to generate cash? Comment on how this is done and what the company has retained.

(f) Can an accounts receivable turnover ratio be determined for either company? Why or why not?

RA7-5 Research Issue: Cash Equivalents

The IASB issued the discussion paper "Preliminary Views on Financial Statement Presentation" in October 2008, which discusses the treatment of cash equivalents, among other things.

Instructions

From the IASB website (www.iasb.org), access the discussion paper. Paragraph 3.14 of the discussion paper proposes that cash equivalents be "presented and classified in a manner similar to other short-term investments, not as part of cash." Why are cash equivalents currently grouped with cash on the statement of financial position? Why is the IASB proposing to segregate cash from cash equivalents? Do you agree or disagree with this proposed treatment? Why or why not?

Tracking Sales

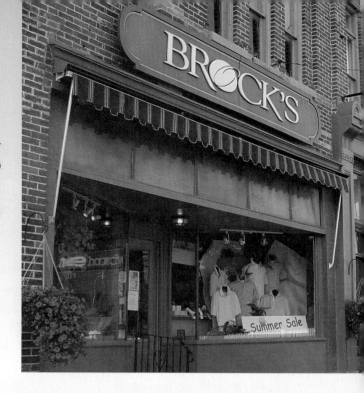

THE FIRST BROCK'S general store opened in Port Perry, Ontario, in 1881. Now the fifth generation of Brocks, sisters Marina and Juliana, run both the original store, now a large department store selling brand-name fashion and footwear, and another satellite store in Fenelon Falls in Ontario's Kawartha Lakes region.

Brock's uses the retail inventory method to estimate its inventory. Computer software keeps track of inventory by season, department, and class of item, such as sportswear or outerwear.

"We run an on-hand inventory value report at month end," Marina Brock says. "We try to get as close to a realizable value as possible, so the current season inventory is taken at full value, and then as we go back, we discount it slightly to reflect that it would be harder to sell at market value." The computer allocates the percentages of the merchandise from the current and previous seasons to get a clearer picture of the entire stock's value.

"Each sale is recorded and the cost of the goods is recorded at the time of sale," Brock explains. "It's taken out of the inventory at that time at the original cost. Everything is done on an individual transaction basis, then summarized at the end of the day."

The Brocks take a physical inventory each January, scanning each item with hand-held scanners. All returns are manually transferred out of the computer records. The computer then updates the inventory records and creates a variance, indicating the inventory's actual value versus its book value. Brock says the store's variance had usually indicated a shrinkage of about 1% of sales, due to clerical errors and shoplifting, although a new electronically tagged merchandise system has reduced the percentage of shrinkage to 0.75%.

Keeping close tabs on the value of the store's inventory helps control the investment in merchandise, which is critical to business success. The computer program Softwear POS tracks the inventory very accurately. "We know pretty much to the dollar what we've got everywhere," Brock says. ■

CHAPTER 8

Inventory

Learning Objectives

After studying this chapter, you should be able to:

1. Define inventory and identify inventory categories.
2. Identify the decisions that are needed to determine the inventory value to report on the balance sheet under a lower of cost and net realizable value model.
3. Identify the physical inventory items that should be included in ending inventory.
4. Determine the components of inventory cost.
5. Distinguish between perpetual and periodic inventory systems and account for them.
6. Identify and apply GAAP cost formula options and indicate when each cost formula is appropriate.
7. Explain why inventory is measured at the lower of cost and market, and apply the lower of cost and net realizable value standard.
8. Explain the accounting issues for purchase commitments.
9. Identify inventories that are or may be valued at amounts other than the lower of cost and net realizable value.
10. Identify the effects of inventory errors on the financial statements and adjust for them.
11. Apply the gross profit method of estimating inventory.
12. Identify the type of inventory disclosures required by accounting standards for private enterprises (private entity GAAP) and IFRS.
13. Explain how inventory analysis provides useful information and apply ratio analysis to inventory.
14. Identify differences in accounting between accounting standards for private enterprises (private entity GAAP) and IFRS, and what changes are expected in the near future.

After studying Appendices 8A and 8B, you should be able to:

15. Apply the retail method of estimating inventory.
16. Identify other primary sources of GAAP for inventory.

Preview of Chapter 8

Inventories are often a major part of a company's total assets. As the opening story indicates, accounting and reporting for this asset can have a material effect on both the income statement and balance sheet. Many decisions go into determining the final amounts to be reported for inventory on the balance sheet and for cost of goods sold on the income statement. These include determining the quantity of inventory on hand, which costs are included in inventory cost, which cost formula is used, how net realizable value is applied, and whether the cost-based model is the appropriate measurement basis for the specific inventory items.

This chapter introduces the basic issues related to the recognition, measurement, and reporting of inventory on the balance sheet and income statement, Appendix 8A explains how to determine inventory cost using the retail inventory method, and Appendix 8B identifies the primary sources of GAAP for a variety of types of inventory. Accounting for long-term construction contract inventories, a closely related topic, was examined in Chapter 6.

The chapter is organized as follows:

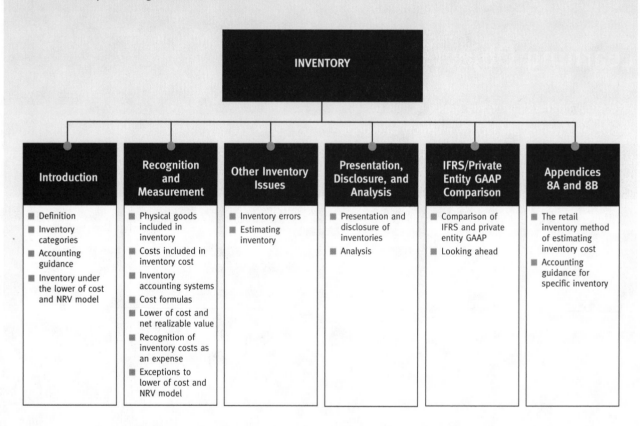

INTRODUCTION

Definition

Objective 1

Define inventory and identify inventory categories.

Inventories are defined as "assets:

    (a) held for sale in the ordinary course of business;

    (b) in the process of production for such sale; or

(c) in the form of materials or supplies to be consumed in the production process or in the rendering of services."[1]

Sometimes there is a fine line between what is inventory and what is better classified as property, plant, and equipment. Minor spare parts and servicing equipment, for example, are usually classified as inventory. Major spare parts and standby equipment, on the other hand, are recognized as capital assets if they are expected to provide benefits beyond the current accounting period. The classification issue often requires the exercise of professional judgement.

Inventory Categories

The identification, measurement, and disclosure of inventories must be done carefully because the investment in inventories is often the largest current asset of many companies, such as those in merchandising (retail) and manufacturing businesses. For example, **RONA Inc.**, a major Canadian distributor and retailer of hardware, home renovation, and garden products, reported over $900 million of inventory at March 29, 2009. This accounted for 71% of its current assets and over 33% of total assets! Like other **merchandising concerns**, RONA purchases most of its merchandise in a form that is ready for sale, and unsold units left on hand at each reporting date are usually referred to as merchandise inventory.

Potash Corporation of Saskatchewan Inc., one of Canada's most profitable companies, is an integrated fertilizer and related industrial and feed products company. It is a manufacturer. At December 31, 2008, Potash Corporation reported inventories amounting to 31.5% of its current assets. Although manufacturers produce quite different products, they normally have three types of inventory accounts: Raw Materials, Work in Process, and Finished Goods. Amounts for goods and materials that are on hand but have not yet gone into production are reported as raw materials inventory. Raw materials include the wood to make a baseball bat, for example, or the steel to make a car. These materials can be traced directly to the end product. At any point in a continuous production process, some units are not completely processed. The cost of the raw material on which production has started but is not yet complete, plus the direct labour cost applied specifically to this material and its applicable share of manufacturing overhead costs, constitutes the work-in-process inventory. The costs associated with the completed but still unsold units on hand are reported as finished goods inventory.

Illustration 8-1 shows the current assets section of Potash Corporation's December 31, 2008 statement of financial position and an excerpt from Note 4 indicating what makes up the total inventory reported. Note that this company uses the term "intermediate products" instead of work-in-process inventory. Manufacturing companies also sometimes include a manufacturing or factory supplies inventory account, as Potash Corporation does. It may be for such items as machine oils, nails, cleaning materials, and so on that are used in production but are not the primary materials being processed.

Real-World Emphasis

Consolidated Statements of Financial Position

As at December 31		in millions of US dollars except share amounts	
Notes		**2008**	2007
	Assets		
	Current assets		
	Cash and cash equivalents	$ 276.8	$ 719.5
Note 3	Accounts receivable	1,189.9	596.2
Note 4	Inventories	714.9	428.1
Note 5	Prepaid expenses and other current assets	79.2	36.7
Note 6	Current portion of derivative instrument assets	6.4	30.8
		2,267.2	1,811.3

Illustration 8-1

Manufacturing Company Current Assets and Inventory Detail—Potash Corporation of Saskatchewan Inc.

Real-World Emphasis

---

[1] *CICA Handbook*, Part II, 3031.06 and IAS 2.6.

Note 4 INVENTORIES (CONTINUED)

	2008[1]	2007
Finished products	$421.8	$186.6
Intermediate products	117.1	70.7
Raw materials	67.8	68.0
Materials and supplies	108.2	102.8
	$714.9	$428.1

[1]See change in accounting policy (Note 2)

Underlying Concept

Because inventory provides future economic benefits to the company (i.e., the revenue and ultimate cash flows from sales), it meets the definition of an asset. Inventory carrying amounts are later matched against revenue in the period when the inventory is sold.

As Illustration 8-2 shows, the flow of costs for merchandising and manufacturing companies is different. The **cost of goods manufactured** referred to in Illustration 8-2 represents the product costs of goods that are completed and transferred to Finished Goods Inventory. You are probably familiar with a statement of cost of goods manufactured (refer to a managerial accounting text for an example) that summarizes all the product costs incurred during the period that resulted in finished goods. A cost of goods manufactured statement is far more detailed than information found in published financial statements. Note that **the cost of goods manufactured during the year is similar to the cost of goods purchased in a merchandising company**. Each is the source of the cost of goods available for sale in the period.

Illustration 8-2

Flow of Costs through Manufacturing and Merchandising Companies

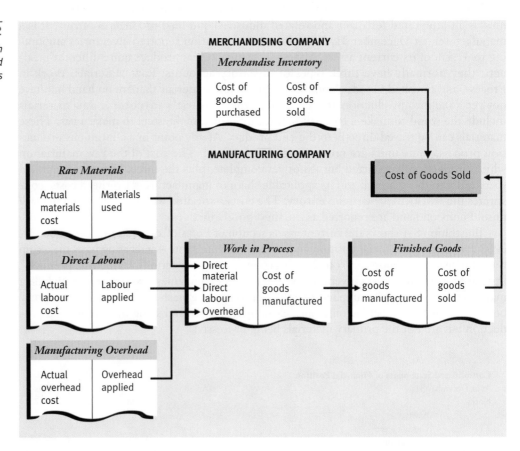

Accounting Guidance

Inventory comes in many forms. Securities held by an investment dealer, land and other property held by developers for resale, unbilled employee and partner time spent on client files in a law office or professional accounting practice, grain in silos, salmon in a fish farming operation, and long-term construction projects are all items of inventory. Some of these, however, are not covered by the basic accounting standards for inventories: *CICA Handbook*, Part II, Section 3031 for private entity GAAP or IAS 2 for international GAAP. These standards exclude some inventories entirely, and exclude others from only the measurement requirements of the standards.

In general, inventories of financial instruments, construction in progress, biological assets and agricultural products, mineral products, and inventories held by producers of agricultural and forest products and by commodity broker-traders may have special requirements. Appendix 8B summarizes where the accounting guidance is found for these forms of inventory.

Based on the fact that most types of inventory are measured and accounted for within a cost-based system referred to in this chapter as a "lower of cost and net realizable value" model, this is the method that is explained in the most detail in the following pages. However, inventories in some specialized industries, such as those involving biological assets (living plants and animals), may use a "net realizable value" model or a "fair value less costs to sell" model. These assets and approaches will be explained later in the chapter.

Inventory under the Lower of Cost and Net Realizable Value Model

Because the goods that are sold or used during an accounting period almost never correspond exactly with the goods that were bought or produced during that period, the physical inventory of items either increases or decreases. In addition, the cost of the same number of items could be higher or lower at the end of the period than at the beginning. The cost of all the goods that are available for sale or use has to be allocated between the goods that were sold or used and those that are still on hand. The cost of goods available for sale or use is the total of (1) the cost of the goods on hand at the beginning of the period and (2) the cost of the goods acquired or produced during the period. The cost of goods sold is the difference between those available for sale during the period and those on hand at the end of the period, as shown in Illustration 8-3.

Identify the decisions that are needed to determine the inventory value to report on the balance sheet under a lower of cost and net realizable value model.

Beginning inventory, Jan. 1	$100,000
Cost of goods acquired or produced during the year	800,000
Total cost of goods available for sale	**900,000**
Ending inventory, Dec. 31	200,000
Cost of goods sold during the year	**$700,000**

Illustration 8-3

Calculation of Cost of Goods Sold

Calculating the cost of ending inventory takes several steps. It can be a complex process that requires answers to each of the following questions:

1. **Which physical goods should be included as part of inventory?** Who owns inventory still in transit at the balance sheet date, or inventory on consignment? What about inventory under special sales agreements?

2. **What costs should be included as part of inventory cost?** Consider purchase discounts and vendor rebates, product versus period costs, capacity considerations in allocating overhead, and standard costs.

3. **What cost formula should be used?** Consider specific identification, average cost, or FIFO.

To determine the final value to report on the statement of financial position, one additional question has to be answered:

4. **Has there been an impairment in value of any of the inventory items?** Inventory cannot be reported on the balance sheet at more than the net cash amount that is expected to be recovered from its sale or use.

We will now explore each of these four basic issues one at a time.

RECOGNITION AND MEASUREMENT

Physical Goods Included in Inventory

Objective 3
Identify the physical inventory items that should be included in ending inventory.

Technically, purchases should be recorded when legal title to the goods passes to the buyer, as this is usually when the risks and rewards associated with ownership are transferred. In practice, however, acquisitions are generally recorded when the goods are received because it is difficult for the buyer to identify the exact time the title legally passes to the buyer for every purchase. Also, it is unlikely that a material error will result from this practice if it is done consistently. Illustration 8-4 gives the general guidelines for determining whether the seller or the buyer should report an item as inventory.

Illustration 8-4

Guidelines for Determining Who Reports the Inventory

General Rule—Who Reports the Inventory?
Inventory is the buyer's when it is received, except:

F.o.b. shipping point	– Buyer's at time of delivery to common carrier
Consignment goods	– Seller's, not buyer's
Sales with buybacks	– Seller's not buyer's
Sales with high rates of return	– Buyer's, if returns can be estimated
Sales with delayed credit terms	– Buyer's, if collectibility can be estimated

Whose inventory is it?

Goods in Transit

Law

Sometimes purchased goods are in transit—i.e., not yet received—at the end of a fiscal period. **The accounting for these goods depends on who owns them.** This can be determined by applying the "transfer of risks and rewards" test. If the goods are shipped **f.o.b. shipping point**, the risks and rewards of ownership, which usually go with having legal title, pass to the buyer when the seller delivers the goods to the common carrier (transporter), who then acts as an agent for the buyer. (The abbreviation "f.o.b." stands for "free on board.") If the goods are shipped **f.o.b. destination**, ownership and its associated risks and rewards do not pass until the goods reach the destination. "Shipping point" and "destination" are often indicated by naming a specific location; for example, f.o.b. Regina.[2]

---

[2] Terms other than "f.o.b. shipping point" or "f.o.b. destination" (e.g., "CIF" for "cost, insurance, freight") are often used to identify when legal title passes. The f.o.b. terms are used in this text to reflect that an agreement on when title passes must be reached between the buyer and seller in the purchase–sale contract. In a particular situation, the terms of the sale contract are examined to determine when the risks and rewards of ownership pass from the seller to the buyer.

Goods in transit at the end of a fiscal period that were sent f.o.b. shipping point are recorded by the buyer as purchases of the period and should be included in ending inventory. If these purchases are not recognized, the result is **understated** inventories and accounts payable in the balance sheet, and **understated** purchases and ending inventories when calculating cost of goods sold for the income statement.

The accountant normally prepares a purchase cut-off schedule for the end of a period to ensure that goods received from suppliers around the end of the year are recorded in the appropriate period. Cut-off procedures can be extensive and include the following controls:

- Curtailing and controlling the receipt and shipment of goods around the time of the count

- Marking freight and shipping documents as "before" and "after" the inventory count

- Ensuring that receiving reports on goods received before the count are linked to invoices that are also recorded in the same period

Because goods that are bought f.o.b. shipping point may still be in transit when a period ends, the cut-off schedule is not completed until a few days after the period's end since this gives time for goods in transit at year end to be received. If there is some doubt about whether or not title has passed, the accountant considers other information, such as the sales agreement's intent, the policies of the parties involved, and industry practices in coming to a conclusion.

Consigned Goods

Accounting for the sale of consigned goods was covered in Chapter 6. In terms of accounting for inventory, **it is important to recognize that goods out on consignment remain the consignor's property and are included in the consignor's inventory** at their purchase price or production cost plus the cost of handling and shipping the goods to the consignee. When the consignee sells the consigned goods, the revenue, less a selling commission and expenses incurred in accomplishing the sale, is remitted to the consignor.

Occasionally, the inventory out on consignment is shown as a separate item or is reported in notes, but unless the amount is large, there is little need for this. For the consignee, no entry is made to adjust its Inventory account for the goods it received, because the goods remain the consignor's property. In addition, the consignee should be extremely careful not to include any consigned goods in its inventory count.

Special Sales Agreements

While the transfer of legal title is a general guideline for whether the risks and rewards of ownership have passed from a seller to a buyer, **transfer of legal title and the transfer of the risks and rewards of ownership do not always go hand in hand**. For example, it is possible for legal title to pass to the purchaser but for the seller of the goods to still retain the risks of ownership. Conversely, it is also possible for legal title to remain with the seller but for the risks and rewards of ownership to be transferred to the purchaser.

Three special sale situations that were briefly referred to in Chapter 6 from the revenue side are now looked at from an inventory perspective.

Sales with Buyback Agreement. Sometimes an enterprise finances its inventory without reporting either the liability or the inventory on its balance sheet. This approach—often referred to as a **product financing arrangement**—usually involves a "sale" with either a real or implied "buyback" agreement. These are sometimes called "parking transactions" because the seller simply "parks" the inventory on another company's balance sheet for a short period of time, agreeing to repurchase it in the future. **If the risks and**

Underlying Concept

Recognizing revenue when the inventory is "parked" violates the revenue recognition principle. This principle requires that the earnings process be substantially completed, with the risks and rewards of ownership transferred to the purchaser.

rewards of ownership have not been transferred, the inventory should remain on the seller's books.

Sales with High Rates of Return.   There are often formal or informal agreements in such industries as publishing, music, toys, and sporting goods that allow a buyer to return inventory for a full or partial refund. An acceptable accounting treatment is that **if a reasonable prediction of the returns can be established**, then the goods should be considered sold and **an allowance for returns should be estimated and recognized**. Conversely, if the returns are unpredictable, the sale is not recognized and the goods are not removed from the Inventory account.

Sales with Delayed Payment Terms.   Because the risk of loss due to uncollectable accounts is higher in delayed payment sales than in other sales transactions, the seller often retains legal title to the merchandise until all payments have been received. Should the inventory be considered sold, even though legal title has not passed? The sale is recorded and the goods are removed from the seller's inventory if the cost of the outstanding risk (i.e., the bad debts) **can be reasonably estimated and matched with the related revenue**.[3] These issues are raised here to illustrate that in some cases, goods are removed from inventory even though legal title may not have passed.

Underlying Concept

Revenues should be recognized in this situation because they have been substantially earned and are reasonably estimable. The basic risks and rewards of ownership have been transferred. Collection is not the most critical event and bad debts can be reasonably estimated.

Costs Included in Inventory Cost

Objective 4
Determine the components of inventory cost.

After deciding what items are to be included in the ending inventory, the next step in calculating inventory at the lower of cost and net realizable value is to determine its cost. As mentioned previously, most inventories—like other non-financial assets—are generally recognized initially on the basis of cost. How is cost determined, and what should be included in "cost"?

Both IFRS and private entity GAAP indicate that inventory cost is made up of "all costs of purchase, costs of conversion and other costs incurred in bringing the inventories to their present location and condition."[4] This includes transportation and handling costs and other direct costs of acquisition, such as non-recoverable taxes and duties.

Purchase Discounts

When suppliers offer cash discounts to purchasers, there are two possible methods to account for the purchases: the gross method and the net method. Under the gross method, both the purchases and payables are recorded at **the gross amount of the invoice**, and any purchase discounts that are later taken **are credited to a Purchase Discount** account. This account is reported as a contra account to Purchases, as a reduction in the cost of the period's purchases.

The alternative approach, called the net method, records the purchases and accounts payable initially at an amount **net of the cash discounts**. If the account payable is paid within the discount period, the cash payment is exactly equal to the amount originally set up in the payable account. **If the account payable is paid after the discount period** is over, the discount that is lost is recorded in a **Purchase Discounts Lost account**. Recording the loss allows the company to assign responsibility for the loss to a specific employee. This treatment is considered more theoretically appropriate because it

---

[3] For revenue that is recognized using the instalment method, the inventory is removed from the balance sheet when the sale is made and the gross profit is recognized over time in proportion to the cash collected.

[4] *CICA Handbook*, Part II, Section 3031.10 and IAS 2.10.

(1) provides a correct reporting of the asset cost and related liability,[5] and (2) makes it possible to measure the inefficiency of financial management if the discount is not taken. Illustration 8-5 illustrates the difference between the gross and net methods.

Gross Method			Net Method		
Purchase cost of $10,000, terms 2/10, net 30:					
Purchases	10,000		Purchases	9,800	
Accounts Payable		10,000	Accounts Payable		9,800
Invoices of $4,000 are paid within discount period:					
Accounts Payable	4,000		Accounts Payable	3,920	
Purchase Discounts		80	Cash		3,920
Cash		3,920			
Invoices of $6,000 are paid after discount period:					
Accounts Payable	6,000		Accounts Payable	5,880	
Cash		6,000	Purchase Discounts Lost	120	
			Cash		6,000

Illustration 8-5

Entries under Gross and Net Methods

Under the gross method, purchase discounts are deducted from purchases in determining cost of goods sold. If the net method is used, purchase discounts not taken are considered a financial expense and are reported in the income statement's Other Expenses section. Many believe that the difficulty of using the more complicated net method outweighs its benefits. This may explain why the less theoretically correct, but simpler, gross method is so popular.

Underlying Concept

Not using the net method because of resultant difficulties is an example of using the cost/benefit constraint.

Vendor Rebates

Assume that Johnston Corp., with a June 30 year end, has been purchasing more and more inventory from Roster Limited in recent years. Roster offers its customers a special **vendor rebate** of $0.10 per unit on each unit purchased if the customer buys more than 100,000 units in the calendar year (i.e., from January 1 to December 31). This year, for the first time, Johnston management expects to exceed the 100,000-unit volume—60,000 units have been purchased in the first six months of the current year and forecast purchases for the next six months are over 50,000 units. Should Johnston recognize the anticipated rebate in its current year ended June 30? If so, how much should be recognized, and how does this affect the financial statements?

Cash rebates are generally a reduction of the purchase cost of inventory. If the "rebate receivable" meets both the definition of an asset and its recognition criteria, the rebate is recognized before it is received. In general:

Underlying Concept

Revenues and expenses are defined in terms of changes in assets and liabilities. Therefore, if an asset does not exist or cannot be recognized in this situation, an expense recovery cannot be recognized either.

- If the rebate is discretionary on the part of the supplier, no rebate is recognized until it is paid or the supplier becomes obligated to make a payment.

- If the rebate is **probable** and the amount can be **reasonably estimated**, the asset recognition criteria are met and the receivable can be recorded.[6] In this case, it is recognized as a reduction in the cost of purchases for the period. The amount receivable is allocated between the goods remaining in inventory, and the goods sold.

---

[5] Both *CICA Handbook*, Part II, Section 3031and IAS 2 indicate that trade discounts are deducted in determining the costs of purchase. They also indicate that, to the extent the purchase arrangement contains a financing element, the amount paid in excess of the amount payable under normal credit terms is recognized as interest expense over the period when the payable is outstanding.

[6] As indicated in Chapter 2, as work progresses on a revised conceptual framework, it is likely that the "probable" criterion of the asset definition will be removed. Instead, probability will be taken into account in the measurement of the asset.

- The amount of the receivable recognized is based on the proportion of the total rebate that is expected relative to the transactions to date.

If the rebate offered by Roster Limited is not discretionary, and if it is probable that Johnston will purchase 110,000 units by December 31 and management is able to make a reasonable estimate of the total rebate for the calendar year, Johnston recognizes the rebate as follows for its current year ended June 30.

A   = L   +   SE
+5,500   +5,500

Cash flows: No effect

Rebate Receivable	6,000	
Inventory (5,000 units)		500
Cost of Goods Sold (55,000 units)		5,500

110,000 units × $0.10 = $11,000; 60,000/110,000 × $11,000 = $6,000
or 60,000 units × $0.10 = $6,000

What Do the Numbers Mean?

Offering promotional payments is very common in the world of retail. Eager to meet their sales targets or promote their products through shelf placements and in-store advertisements, vendors have been happy to grease the palms of retailers with rebates, allowances, and price breaks. The question is, "How should retailers account for these payments?" For a while, a variety of methods were used, but some questionable practices changed that.

At one point, the Securities and Exchange Commission in the United States sued three executives of **Kmart Holding** and some Kmart vendors for their role in a $24-million accounting fraud that booked vendor allowances early. The scheme apparently allowed some Kmart managers to meet internal profit-margin targets. Similarly, **Royal Ahold**, a large Dutch supermarket operator, discovered that its U.S. Foodservice unit had improperly accounted for vendor payments, resulting in overstated earnings of at least $500 million (later revised upward to $800 million). Other subsidiaries were also found to have inflated profits for similar reasons.

Not surprisingly, standard setters issued guidelines to curb the previous flexibility in accounting for these promotional payments.

Source: C. Schneider, "Retailers and Vendor Allowances," CFO.com, August 13, 2003.

Product Costs

Product costs are costs that "attach" to inventory and are recorded in the inventory account. That is, they are capitalized. These costs are directly connected with bringing goods to the buyer's place of business and converting them to a saleable condition. They include freight charges on goods purchased, other direct costs of acquisition, and labour and other production costs that are incurred in processing the goods up to the time they are ready for sale. Under IFRS, product costs also include any eventual decommissioning or restoration costs incurred as a result of production, even though the related expenditures may not be incurred until far into the future. Under private entity GAAP, such costs are generally added to the cost of the related property, plant, and equipment. Such **asset retirement costs** are discussed more fully in Chapters 10 and 13.

Non-recoverable taxes (e.g., some provincial sales taxes) paid on goods that are purchased for resale or manufacturing purposes are a cost of inventory. Since value-added taxes (e.g., the federal Goods and Services Tax and the Harmonized Sales Tax charged in many provinces) can be recovered from the government by the purchaser, they are not included as part of the inventory's cost. Chapter 13 discusses this type of tax in more detail.

Conversion costs include direct labour and an allocation of the fixed and variable production overhead costs that are incurred in processing direct materials into finished goods. The allocation of fixed production costs is based on the company's **normal**

production capacity.[7] In this way, costs of idle capacity or low production levels do not end up in inventory, but instead are charged to expense as they are incurred. However, if production levels are abnormally high, the fixed costs are spread out over the larger number of units that is produced so that inventory is not measured at an amount higher than its cost. Actual production levels can be used if close to normal levels; and actual levels are used to charge variable costs to production.

Allocating a share of any buying costs to inventory, or expenses of a purchasing department, insurance costs in transit, or other costs that are incurred in handling the goods before they are ready for sale would be theoretically correct. This is because such costs are incurred to bring the inventories "to their present location and condition." However, on a cost/benefit basis, these items are not ordinarily included in inventory cost.

Borrowing Costs.   If interest costs are incurred to finance activities that help bring inventories to a condition and place ready for sale, they are considered by many to be as much a cost of the asset as materials, labour, and overhead.[8] Under IFRS, interest costs incurred for an inventory item that takes an extended period of time to produce or manufacture are considered **product costs**. However, if the financing relates to inventories that are manufactured or produced in large quantities and on a repetitive basis, companies can choose whether to capitalize them or not.[9] Under private entity GAAP, the only requirement is that **if interest is capitalized**, this policy and the amount that is capitalized in the current period be **disclosed**.

Standard Costs.   A company that uses a standard cost system predetermines the unit costs for material, labour, and manufacturing overhead. Usually the standard costs are based on the costs that should be incurred per unit of finished goods when the plant is operating at normal levels of efficiency and capacity. When actual costs are not the same as the standard costs, the differences are recorded in variance accounts that management can examine and follow up on by taking appropriate action to achieve greater control over costs. For financial statement purposes, **reporting inventories at standard cost is acceptable only as long as the results approximate actual cost**. Unallocated overheads are **expensed** as they are incurred.

Cost of Service Providers' Work in Process.   Companies that provide services rather than manufacture products may accumulate significant costs of work-in-process inventories. These, too, are measured at their production costs. For service providers, the major "production" costs are for service personnel and overhead costs associated with this "direct labour." Supervisory costs and other overheads are allocated using the same principles as for manufactured products.

Costs Excluded from Inventory.   Some costs are closely related to acquiring and converting a product, but they are not considered to be product costs. These include storage costs (unless they are necessary because the product must be held before the next stage of production, such as in wine production); abnormal spoilage or wastage of materials, labour, or other production costs; and interest costs when inventories that are ready for use or sale are purchased on delayed payment terms.

---

[7] Normal capacity is "the production expected to be achieved on average over a number of periods or seasons under normal circumstances, taking into account the loss of capacity resulting from planned maintenance" (*CICA Handbook*, Part II, Section 3031.13 and IAS 2.13).

[8] The reporting rules on interest capitalization have their greatest impact in accounting for property, plant, and equipment and, therefore, are discussed in detail in Chapter 10.

[9] This option also exists for qualifying inventory items measured at fair value, such as biological assets.

Selling expenses and, under ordinary circumstances, **general and administrative expenses** are not considered directly related to the acquisition or conversion of goods and, therefore, are not considered a part of inventories. Such costs are period costs. Why are these costs not considered part of inventory? Selling expenses are generally more directly related to the cost of goods sold than to the unsold inventory. In most cases, these costs are so unrelated or indirectly related to the actual production process that any allocation would be completely arbitrary.

"Basket" Purchases and Joint Product Costs

A special problem occurs when a group of units with different characteristics is purchased at a single lump-sum price; i.e., in what is called a basket purchase. Assume that Woodland Developers purchases land for $1 million and it can be subdivided into 400 lots. These lots are of different sizes and shapes but can be roughly sorted into three groups, graded A, B, and C. The purchase cost of $1 million must be allocated among the lots so that the cost of the lots that are later sold (cost of goods sold) and those remaining on hand (ending inventory) can be calculated.

It is inappropriate to use the average lot cost of $2,500 (the total cost of $1 million divided by the 400 lots) because the lots vary in size, shape, and attractiveness. When this kind of situation occurs—and it is not at all unusual—the most reasonable practice is to allocate the total cost among the various units **based on their relative sales value**. For our example, the cost allocation is shown in Illustration 8-6.

Illustration 8-6

Allocation of Costs, Using Relative Sales Value

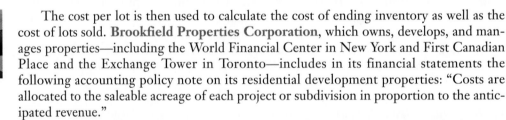

Lots	Number of Lots	Sales Price Per Lot	Total Sales Value	Relative Sales Value	Total Cost	Cost Allocated to Lots	Cost Per Lot
A	100	$10,000	$1,000,000	100/250	$1,000,000	$ 400,000	$4,000
B	100	6,000	600,000	60/250	1,000,000	240,000	2,400
C	200	4,500	900,000	90/250	1,000,000	360,000	1,800
			$2,500,000			$1,000,000	

Real-World Emphasis

The cost per lot is then used to calculate the cost of ending inventory as well as the cost of lots sold. **Brookfield Properties Corporation**, which owns, develops, and manages properties—including the World Financial Center in New York and First Canadian Place and the Exchange Tower in Toronto—includes in its financial statements the following accounting policy note on its residential development properties: "Costs are allocated to the saleable acreage of each project or subdivision in proportion to the anticipated revenue."

This method, the relative sales value method, is rational, can be applied consistently, and is commonly used whenever there is a joint cost that needs to be allocated. Other examples include when two or more products are produced at the same time and the costs for each product cannot be distinguished. The petroleum industry uses it to value (at cost) the many products and by-products obtained from a barrel of crude oil, as does the food processing industry, where different cuts of meat of varying value are "split off" from one animal carcass. When the value of a by-product is relatively minor, it is often measured at its net realizable value and deducted from the cost of the major product.

Inventory Accounting Systems

For many reasons, management is vitally interested in inventory planning and control. Whether a company manufactures or merchandises goods, it needs an accurate accounting system with up-to-date records. It may lose sales and customers if it does not stock products in the desired style, quality, and quantity. On the other side, companies must monitor inventory levels carefully to limit the risk of obsolescence and the financing costs of carrying large amounts of inventory. Inefficient purchasing procedures, faulty manufacturing techniques, or inadequate sales efforts may trap management with excessive and unusable inventories. With the use of "just-in-time" inventory order systems and better supplier relationships, inventory levels have been significantly reduced for many enterprises.

What Do the Numbers Mean?

Technology has played an important role in the development of inventory systems. Radio-frequency identification data communications systems for warehouses, for example, have helped companies such as Hospital Logistics Inc., Eli Lilly Canada Inc., and BC Hot House Foods increase the accuracy of their inventory information and the efficiency and productivity of their inventory management activities. This technology replaces bar codes and makes it possible to remotely store and retrieve data using special devices. This has resulted in reduced delivery times and levels of safety stock, lower costs, fewer errors, and increased customer and client satisfaction.

Management is well aware that the level of inventory can materially affect the amount of current assets, total assets, net income, and therefore, retained earnings. These amounts, or totals that include them, are used to calculate ratios that allow users to evaluate management's performance (e.g., calculations of bonuses) and adherence to debt restrictions (e.g., to not exceed a specified debt-to-total-asset ratio or dividend payout ratio).

For these and other reasons, companies are very interested in having an inventory accounting system that gives accurate, up-to-date information. One of two systems is commonly used for maintaining accurate inventory records: a perpetual system or a periodic system.

Perpetual System

A **perpetual inventory system** continuously tracks changes in the Inventory account. This means that the cost of all purchases and the cost of the items sold (or issued out of inventory) are recorded directly in the Inventory account as the purchases and sales occur. The accounting features of a perpetual inventory system are as follows.

5 Objective
Distinguish between perpetual and periodic inventory systems and account for them.

1. Purchases of merchandise for resale or raw materials for production are debited to Inventory rather than to Purchases.

2. Freight-in is debited and purchase returns and allowances and purchase discounts are credited to Inventory instead of being accounted for in separate accounts.

3. The cost of the items sold is recognized at the time of each sale by debiting Cost of Goods Sold and crediting Inventory.

4. Inventory is a control account that is supported by a subsidiary ledger of individual inventory records. The subsidiary records show the quantity and cost of each type of inventory on hand.

The perpetual inventory system provides a continuous record of the balances in both the Inventory account and the Cost of Goods Sold account. In a computerized record-keeping system, changes in these accounts can be recorded almost instantaneously. The popularity and affordability of computerized accounting software have made the perpetual system cost-effective for many kinds of businesses. It is now common for most retail stores, big or small, to use optical scanners at the cash register that record reductions in inventory as it is sold as part of the store's perpetual inventory system.

Periodic System

In a **periodic inventory system**, the quantity of inventory on hand is determined, as the name implies, only **periodically**. Each acquisition of inventory during the accounting period is recorded by a debit to the Purchases account. The total in the Purchases account at the end of the accounting period is added to the cost of the inventory on hand at the beginning of the period to determine the total cost of the goods available for sale during the period. The cost of ending inventory is subtracted from the cost of goods available for sale to calculate the cost of goods sold.

Note that under a periodic inventory system, the **cost of goods sold** is a **residual amount that depends on first calculating the cost of the ending inventory**. The cost of the ending inventory can be determined by physically counting and costing it. This process is referred to as "taking a physical inventory." Companies that use the periodic system take a physical inventory at least once a year.

Comparing Perpetual and Periodic Systems

To illustrate the difference between a perpetual and a periodic system, assume that Fesmire Limited had the following balances and transactions during the current year:

Beginning inventory	100 units at $ 6 = $ 600
Purchases	900 units at $ 6 = $5,400
Defective units returned to the supplier	50 units at $ 6 = $ 300
Sales	600 units at $12 = $7,200
Ending inventory	350 units at $ 6 = $2,100

The entries to record these transactions during the current year are shown in Illustration 8-7.

Illustration 8-7

Comparative Entries— Perpetual vs. Periodic

Perpetual Inventory System			Periodic Inventory System		
1. Beginning Inventory, 100 units at $6:					
The inventory account shows the inventory on hand at $600.			The inventory account shows the inventory on hand at $600.		
2. Purchase 900 units at $6:					
Inventory	5,400		Purchases	5,400	
Accounts Payable		5,400	Accounts Payable		5,400
3. Return 50 defective units:					
Accounts Payable	300		Accounts Payable	300	
Inventory		300	Purchase Returns		
			and Allowances		300
4. Sale of 600 units at $12:					
Accounts Receivable	7,200		Accounts Receivable	7,200	
Sales		7,200	Sales		7,200
Cost of Goods Sold	3,600				
(600 at $6)					
Inventory		3,600	(No entry)		
5. End-of-period entries for inventory accounts, 350 units at $6 = $2,100:					
No entry necessary.			Purchase Returns		
The account, Inventory, shows the ending			and Allowances	300	
balance of $2,100			Inventory (ending, by count)	2,100	
($600 + $5,400 − $300 − $3,600).			Cost of Goods Sold	3,600	
			Purchases		5,400
			Inventory (beginning)		600

When a **perpetual inventory system** is used and there is a difference between the perpetual inventory record and the physical inventory count, a separate entry is needed to adjust the perpetual Inventory account. To illustrate, assume that at the end of the reporting period, the perpetual Inventory account reported a balance of $4,000, but a physical count indicated $3,800 was actually on hand. The adjusting entry is:

Inventory Over and Short	200		
Inventory		200	

A   = L +   SE
−200   −200
Cash flows: No effect

The overage or shortage may be due to normal and expected shrinkage, breakage, shoplifting, or record-keeping errors, and is usually recognized as an adjustment of Cost of Goods Sold. Alternatively, the Inventory Over and Short account may be reported in the "Other revenues and gains" or "Other expenses and losses" section of the income statement. When this is done, the gross profit percentage is not distorted by the costs of shrinkage, breakage, and theft.

In a **periodic inventory system**, there is no Inventory Over and Short account. This is because there is no up-to-date inventory account that can be compared with the physical count. The amount of any inventory overage or shortage is therefore "lost" in cost of goods sold.

Supplementary System—Quantities Only

In a perfect world, companies would like a continuous record of inventory levels, their cost, and the cost of goods sold. However, even with advances in technology, it may not be cost-effective to have a complete perpetual inventory system that keeps track of both inventory quantities and their cost. Because management needs current information about inventory levels to avoid stockouts and overpurchasing, to respond to customer queries, and to help prepare monthly or quarterly financial data, many companies use a quantities only system. This system provides detailed inventory records of increases and decreases in quantities only—not dollar amounts. This memorandum record is not part of the double-entry accounting system; therefore, the company would need to use a periodic system in its main accounts.

Whether a company maintains a perpetual inventory in quantities and dollars, in quantities only, or no perpetual inventory record at all, it usually takes a physical inventory once a year. No matter what type of inventory records are used or how well-controlled the procedures for recording purchases and requisitions are, the dangers of loss and error are always present. Waste, breakage, theft, improper entry, failure to prepare or record requisitions, and similar possibilities may cause the inventory records to be different from the actual inventory on hand. Therefore, all companies need periodic verification of the inventory records by actual count, weight, or measurement, with the **counts compared with the detailed records**. The **records are then corrected** so that they agree with the quantities actually on hand.

As far as possible, the physical inventory should be taken near the end of a company's fiscal year so that correct inventory quantities are used in preparing annual accounting reports and statements. Because this is not always possible, physical inventories that are taken within two or three months of the year end are considered satisfactory as long as the **internal controls** indicate that the detailed inventory records are maintained with a fair degree of accuracy.[10]

Cost Formulas

Two issues have now been addressed in determining inventory cost: which inventory items to include, and which costs to include in, or exclude from, the product's cost. The next issue is this: if inventories need to be priced at cost and many purchases have been made at **different unit costs, which of the various cost prices should be assigned to Inventory**

6 Objective

Identify and apply GAAP cost formula options and indicate when each cost formula is appropriate.

---

[10] In recent years, some companies have developed methods of determining inventories, including statistical sampling, that are sufficiently reliable to make an annual count of each item of inventory unnecessary.

on the balance sheet and **which costs should be charged to Cost of Goods Sold** on the income statement?

Conceptually, **identifying the specific costs** of the actual items sold and those unsold seems ideal, but doing this is often too expensive or simply impossible to achieve. Consequently, companies must choose another acceptable inventory cost formula. A cost formula is a method of assigning inventory costs incurred during the accounting period to inventory that is still on hand at the end of the period (ending inventory) and to inventory that was sold during the period (cost of goods sold).

Illustration 8-8 provides data to use in the discussion of the cost formula choice. The data summarize the inventory-related activities of Call-Mart Inc. for the month of March. Note that the company experienced increasing unit costs for its purchases throughout the month.

Illustration 8-8

Data Used to Illustrate Inventory Calculation: Cost Formula Choice

	CALL-MART INC.		
Date	Purchases	Sold or Issued	Balance
Mar. 1	(beginning inventory)		
	500 @ $3.80		500 units
Mar. 2	1,500 @ $4.00		2,000 units
Mar. 15	6,000 @ $4.40		8,000 units
Mar. 19		4,000	4,000 units
Mar. 30	2,000 @ $4.75		6,000 units
	10,000	4,000	

From this information, we see that there were 10,000 units available for sale, made up of 500 units in opening inventory and 9,500 purchased during the month. Of the 10,000 available, 4,000 were sold, leaving 6,000 units in ending inventory.

The **cost of goods available for sale** is calculated as follows:

500 units @ $3.80 =	$ 1,900
1,500 units @ $4.00 =	6,000
6,000 units @ $4.40 =	26,400
2,000 units @ $4.75 =	9,500
10,000 units	$43,800

Having this information, the question now is: **which price or prices should be assigned to the 6,000 units still in inventory and which to the 4,000 units sold?** The answer depends on which cost formula is chosen.

Both IFRS and private entity GAAP recognize three acceptable cost formulas:

1. Specific identification

2. First-in, first-out (FIFO)

3. Weighted average cost

Specific Identification

When using the specific identification cost formula, each item that is sold and each item in inventory needs to be identified. The costs of the specific items that are sold are included in the cost of goods sold, and the costs of the specific items on hand are included in the ending inventory. This method is appropriate and required for goods that are not ordinarily interchangeable, and for goods and services that are produced and segregated for specific projects. It is used most often in situations involving a relatively small number of items that are costly and easily distinguishable (e.g., by their physical characteristics, serial numbers, or special markings). In the retail trade, this includes some types of jewellery, fur coats, automobiles, and some furniture. In manufacturing, it includes special orders and many products manufactured under a job cost system.

To illustrate this method, assume that Call-Mart Inc.'s inventory items are distinguishable and that the 6,000 units of ending inventory consist of 100 units from the opening inventory, 900 from the March 2 purchase, 3,000 from the March 15 purchase, and 2,000 from the March 30 purchase. The ending inventory and cost of goods sold are calculated as shown in Illustration 8-9.

Units from	No. of Units	Unit Cost	Total Cost
Beginning inventory	100	$3.80	$ 380
March 2 purchase	900	4.00	3,600
March 15 purchase	3,000	4.40	13,200
March 30 purchase	2,000	4.75	9,500
Ending inventory	**6,000**		**$26,680**
Cost of goods available for sale	$43,800		
(beginning inventory + purchases)			
Deduct: Ending inventory	26,680		
Cost of goods sold	**$17,120**		

Illustration 8-9

Specific Identification Cost Formula

Conceptually, this method appears ideal because actual costs are matched against actual revenue, and ending inventory items are reported at their specific cost. In fact, the requirement that this method **only be used for goods that are not ordinarily interchangeable** is an attempt to make sure this benefit is achieved and to prevent management from manipulating the amount of net income.

Consider what might happen if businesses were allowed to use this method more generally. Assume, for instance, that a wholesaler purchases identical plywood early in the year at three different prices. When the plywood is sold, the wholesaler can choose either the lowest or the highest price to charge to expense simply by choosing which plywood is delivered to the customer. This means that a manager can manipulate net income simply by delivering to the customer the higher- or lower-priced item, depending on whether lower or higher reported income is wanted for the period.

Another problem with the broader use of the specific identification cost formula is that allocating certain costs can become arbitrary when the inventory items are interchangeable. In many circumstances, **it is difficult to directly relate shipping charges, storage costs, discounts, and other blanket charges to a specific inventory item**. The only option, then, is to allocate these costs somewhat arbitrarily, which eliminates some of the benefits offered by the specific identification method.[11]

---

[11] A good illustration of the cost allocation problem occurs in the motion picture industry. Often actors and actresses receive a percentage of net income for a particular movie or television program. Some actors who have had these arrangements have alleged that their programs have been extremely profitable to the motion picture studios but they have received little in the way of profit-sharing. Actors contend that the studios allocate additional costs to successful projects to ensure that there will be no profits to share. Such contentions illustrate the type of problem that can emerge when contracts are based on accounting numbers that include arbitrary allocations. One way to help overcome such problems is to establish specific measurement rules on how the accounting numbers are to be determined. This should be done before the contract is signed so that all parties clearly understand what they are getting into.

Weighted Average Cost

As its name implies, an average cost formula prices inventory items based on the average cost of the goods that are available for sale during the period. The **weighted average cost formula** takes into account that the volume of goods acquired at each price is different. Assuming that Call-Mart Inc. uses a periodic inventory method, the ending inventory and cost of goods sold are calculated as indicated in Illustration 8-10.

Illustration 8-10

Weighted Average Cost Formula—Periodic Inventory

	Date	No. of Units	Unit Cost	Total Cost
Inventory	Mar. 1	500	$3.80	$ 1,900
Purchases	Mar. 2	1,500	4.00	6,000
Purchases	Mar. 15	6,000	4.40	26,400
Purchases	Mar. 30	2,000	4.75	9,500
Total goods available		10,000		$43,800

Weighted average cost per unit $\dfrac{\$43,800}{10,000} = \$4.38$

Ending inventory in units 6,000
Cost of ending inventory **6,000 × $4.38 = $26,280**

Cost of goods available for sale $43,800
Deduct ending inventory 26,280

Cost of goods sold $17,520 (= 4,000 × $4.38)

Note that the beginning inventory units and cost are both included in calculating the average cost per unit.

Another weighted-average cost method is the **moving-average cost formula**. This method is used with **perpetual** inventory records that are **kept in both units and dollars**. Use of the moving-average cost method for full perpetual records is shown in Illustration 8-11.

Illustration 8-11

Moving-Average Cost Formula—Full Perpetual Inventory

Date	Purchased	Sold or Issued	Balance*
Mar. 1	Beginning inventory		(500 @ $3.80) $ 1,900
Mar. 2	(1,500 @ $4.00) $ 6,000		(2,000 @ $3.95) 7,900
Mar. 15	(6,000 @ $4.40) 26,400		(8,000 @ $4.2875) 34,300
Mar. 19		(4,000 @ $4.2875) $17,150	(4,000 @ $4.2875) 17,150
Mar. 30	(2,000 @ $4.75) 9,500		(6,000 @ $4.4417) 26,650

*Calculation of moving-average cost per unit:
After March 2 purchase
  = Cost of units available / Units available
  = [$1,900 + (1,500 × $4.00)] / (500 + 1,500)
  = ($1,900 + $6,000) / 2,000
  = $7,900 / 2,000
  = $3.95

After March 15 purchase
  = [$7,900 + (6,000 × $4.40)] / (2,000 + 6,000)
  = $34,300 / 8,000
  = $4.2875

After March 30 purchase
  = [17,150 + (2,000 × $4.75)] / (4,000 + 2,000)
  = $26,650 / 6,000
  = $4.4417

In this method, a **new average unit cost is calculated each time** a purchase is made. This is **because the cost of goods sold at the updated average cost has to be recognized at the time of the next sale**. On March 15, after 6,000 units are purchased for $26,400, 8,000 units with a total cost of $34,300 ($7,900 plus $26,400) are on hand. The average unit cost is $34,300 divided by 8,000, or $4.2875. This unit cost is used in costing withdrawals of inventory until another purchase is made, when a new average unit cost is calculated. Accordingly, the cost of each of the 4,000 units withdrawn on March 19 is shown at $4.2875, which makes a total cost of goods sold of $17,150. On March 30, following the purchase of 2,000 units for $9,500, the total inventory cost of the 6,000 units is $26,650. The new unit cost is now $4.4417.

Justification for using the average cost method is that the costs it assigns to inventory and cost of goods sold closely follow the actual physical flow of many inventories that are interchangeable. While it is impossible to measure the specific physical flow of inventory, it is reasonable to cost items based on an average price. There are also practical reasons that support this method. It is simple to apply, objective, and not very open to income manipulation. This argument is particularly persuasive when the inventory involved is relatively homogeneous in nature. In terms of achieving financial statement objectives, an average cost method results in an average of costs being used to determine both the cost of goods sold in the income statement and ending inventory in the balance sheet.

First-In, First-Out (FIFO)

The first-in, first-out (FIFO) cost formula assigns costs based on the assumption that goods are used in the order in which they are purchased. In other words, it assumes that **the first items purchased are the first ones used** (in a manufacturing concern) **or sold** (in a merchandising concern). The inventory remaining, therefore, must come from the most recent purchases.

To illustrate, assume that Call-Mart Inc. uses a periodic inventory system, where the inventory cost is calculated only at the end of the month. **The ending inventory's cost** for the 6,000 units remaining is calculated by taking the **cost of the most recent purchase and working back until all units in the ending inventory are accounted for**. The ending inventory and cost of goods sold are calculated as shown in Illustration 8-12.

Date	No. of Units	Unit Cost	Total Cost
Mar. 30	2,000	$4.75	$ 9,500
Mar. 15	4,000	4.40	17,600
Ending inventory	6,000		$27,100
Cost of goods available for sale	$43,800		
Deduct: Ending inventory	27,100		
Cost of goods sold	$16,700		

Illustration 8-12

FIFO Cost Formula—Periodic Inventory

If a full perpetual inventory system **in quantities and dollars** is used, a cost figure is attached to each withdrawal from inventory when the units are withdrawn and sold. In the example, the cost of the 4,000 units removed on March 19 is made up first from the items in the beginning inventory, then the items purchased on March 2, and finally some from the March 15 purchases. The inventory record under FIFO and **a perpetual system** for Call-Mart Inc. is shown in Illustration 8-13, which also results in an ending inventory of $27,100 and a cost of goods sold of $16,700.

Notice that in these two FIFO examples, the cost of goods sold and ending inventory are the same. **In all cases where FIFO is used, the inventory and cost of goods sold**

Illustration 8-13

FIFO Cost Formula— Perpetual Inventory

Date	Purchased	Sold or Issued	Balance	
Mar. 1	Beginning inventory		500 @ $3.80	$ 1,900
Mar. 2	(1,500 @ $4.00) $ 6,000		500 @ 3.80 ⎱ 1,500 @ 4.00 ⎰	7,900
Mar. 15	(6,000 @ $4.40) 26,400		500 @ 3.80 ⎱ 1,500 @ 4.00 ⎬ 6,000 @ 4.40 ⎰	34,300
Mar. 19		500 @ $3.80 ⎱ 1,500 @ 4.00 ⎬ 2,000 @ 4.40 ⎰ **$16,700**	4,000 @ 4.40	17,600
Mar. 30	(2,000 @ $4.75) 9,500		4,000 @ 4.40 ⎱ 2,000 @ 4.75 ⎰	27,100

are the same at the end of the period whether a perpetual or periodic system is used. This is true because the same costs will always be first in and, therefore, first out, whether cost of goods sold is calculated as goods are sold throughout the accounting period (the perpetual system) or based on what remains at the end of the accounting period (the periodic system).

One objective of FIFO is to roughly follow the actual physical flow of goods. When the physical flow of goods really is first-in, first-out, the FIFO method approximates the use of specific identification. At the same time, it does not permit manipulation of income because the enterprise is not free to choose a certain cost to be charged to expense.

Another advantage of the FIFO method is that the ending inventory is close to its current cost. Because the costs of the first goods in are transferred to cost of goods sold, the ending inventory is made up of the cost of the most recent purchases. This approach generally provides a cost that is close to the replacement cost for inventory on the balance sheet, particularly when the inventory turnover is rapid or price changes have not occurred since the most recent purchases.

The FIFO method's basic disadvantage is that current costs are not matched against current revenues on the income statement. The oldest costs are charged against current revenue, which can lead to distortions in gross profit and net income when prices are changing rapidly.

Choice of Cost Formula

The inventory standards limit the ability of preparers to choose a cost formula. Specific identification is required when inventory is made up of goods that are not ordinarily interchangeable, and when goods and services are produced and segregated for specific projects. Otherwise, the choice is between a weighted average method and FIFO. The choice is further restricted by the requirement that companies apply the same inventory cost formula to all inventories of a similar nature and use.

The overriding objectives that underlie the inventory standards and guide management are as follows.

1. Choose an approach that corresponds as closely as possible to the physical flow of goods.

2. Report an inventory cost on the balance sheet that is representative of the inventory's recent cost.

3. Use the same method for all inventory assets that have similar economic characteristics for the entity.

These requirements are consistent with standard setters' emphasis on an asset and liability approach to the accounting model, as explained in Chapter 2. That is, assets and liabilities are the fundamental building blocks whose definition and measurement underlie the amounts and timing of revenues and expenses.

Income taxes are also a consideration. Methods that permit a lower ending inventory valuation result in lower income and reduced cash outflows for taxes. Compared with the FIFO cost formula, an average cost formula results in recent costs being reflected more in the cost of goods sold and older costs in ending inventory. In a period of rising prices, there may be tax advantages to the average cost formula.

If companies were permitted to switch from one inventory costing method to another, this would adversely affect the comparability of financial statements. Therefore, companies choose the costing formula that is most suitable to their particular circumstances and, once selected, apply it consistently from then on. If conditions indicate that another accounting policy would result in a reliable and more relevant presentation in the financial statements, a change may be made. Such a change is unusual, but is accounted for retroactively and its effect is clearly disclosed in the financial statements.

Underlying Concept

Consistent application of the same formula improves the comparability of the financial statements.

Last-In, First-Out (LIFO)

The last-in, first-out (LIFO) cost formula, no longer permitted under private entity GAAP and IFRS, assigns costs based on the assumption that the cost of the most recent purchase is the first cost to be charged to cost of goods sold. The cost assigned to the inventory remaining therefore comes from the earliest acquisitions (i.e., "first-in, still-here") and is made up of the oldest costs.

This method is no longer permitted for the following reasons. (1) In almost all situations, LIFO does not represent the actual flow of costs. (2) The balance sheet cost of ending inventory is not a fair representation of the recent cost of inventories on hand. (3) Use of LIFO can result in serious distortions of reported income, especially when old inventory cost "layers" are expensed in the period. This happens when old, low-cost inventory gets charged to cost of goods sold due to a reduction in base inventory levels.

Because the Canada Revenue Agency has never allowed companies to use LIFO to calculate their income for tax purposes, this method was not widely used in Canada. However, it is permitted under U.S. GAAP, and allowed for tax purposes there if a company also uses the method for financial reporting purposes. Canadian public companies that are listed on a U.S. stock exchange as well as a Canadian exchange are permitted to prepare their financial statements under U.S. GAAP, so it is likely that LIFO-based inventories will continue to be seen in Canada for a while yet.

Underlying Concept

The LIFO cost formula, an allowed alternative under U.S. GAAP, is not considered under private entity GAAP and IFRS to result in a faithful representation of an asset's cost.

Lower of Cost and Net Realizable Value

Rationale for Lower of Cost and Net Realizable Value (LC&NRV)

So far in the chapter, we have learned how to calculate the cost of ending inventory at the balance sheet date, determining: (1) the goods to include in ending inventory, (2) the costs to capitalize in inventory cost, and (3) the cost formulas available to allocate costs to ending inventory. The last step in applying this cost-based model is to decide whether cost is appropriate for reporting inventory on the statement of financial position.

A departure from reporting inventory at cost makes sense if the value of inventory to the entity falls below its cost. This reduction in value may be due to the inventory itself (e.g., the goods are obsolete or damaged), a reduction in selling prices, or an increase in the costs to complete and dispose of the inventory. **Cost is not appropriate if the asset's future utility (its ability to generate net cash flows) is now less than its carrying amount.** Inventories therefore are valued at the lower of cost and net realizable value.

This departure from cost is justified for two main reasons. First, readers presume that **current assets can be converted into at least as much cash as the amount reported**

7 Objective

Explain why inventory is measured at the lower of cost and market, and apply the lower of cost and net realizable value standard.

Underlying Concept

Using the lower of cost and net realizable value for measurement is an excellent example of faithful representation of asset values.

on the balance sheet; and second, **a loss of utility should be deducted from (matched with) revenues in the period in which the loss occurs**, not in the period when the inventory is sold.

For many years, inventory was valued in the cost-based system at the lower of cost and market (LCM), and there were a variety of alternative definitions of "market." The term market in LCM valuation could mean replacement cost, net realizable value, or net realizable value less a normal profit margin. Under U.S. GAAP, all these terms are still incorporated in a rule that is applied to calculate market and therefore to measure inventory on the balance sheet.

The option of choosing a meaning of "market" has been eliminated in Canada and under IFRS. The phrase lower of cost and market is still part of GAAP in Canada, but market is now strictly defined as net realizable value (NRV): the estimated selling price less the estimated costs to complete and sell the goods. Why has there been such support for this concept of market?

The use of a "replacement cost" definition of market is based on the assumption that a decline in an item's replacement cost results in a decline in its selling price. While replacement cost may be appropriate in a few specific circumstances, it is not reasonable to assume that prices will fall in the same proportion as input costs fall, or that they will fall below inventory cost, or that such market conditions exist for all products. Also, the use of a "net realizable value less a normal profit margin" definition of market value has the effect of arbitrarily shifting profits from one period to another. In effect, a very large writedown may be taken in the year the inventory's value drops, so that a normal profit can be reported in the period in which it is later sold.

If inventory is written down only to its net realizable value, a lower loss is recognized in the current period and, if the estimates are correct, the company breaks even on the sale of the item. Although the net result is the same when you add the two periods together, there is little justification for the arbitrary shifting of profit into a future period as happens when the NRV is further reduced by the profit margin. Therefore, private entity GAAP and IFRS both require the use of NRV as "market."

What Is Net Realizable Value?   Net realizable value is an estimate. Unlike inventory cost, which usually remains at a determined value, net realizable value changes over time for a variety of reasons. Inventory may deteriorate or become obsolete with time; selling prices fluctuate with changes in supply and demand; substitute products become available; and input costs to complete and sell, liquidate, or otherwise dispose of the product vary with conditions and the specific markets that the inventory is sold into.

Estimates of NRV are based on the best evidence available at and shortly after the balance sheet date. The objective is to determine the most likely (net) realizable value of the product on hand at the end of the accounting period given the specific circumstances of the particular entity. A new assessment is required at each balance sheet date. If economic circumstances change and the estimate of the net realizable value changes from the previous estimate, the revised amount is used in determining the lower of cost and NRV at the end of the next period.

Application of Lower of Cost and Net Realizable Value

The lower of cost and net realizable value (LC&NRV) standard requires that inventory be valued at cost unless NRV is lower than cost, in which case the inventory is valued at NRV. To apply this:

1. Determine the cost.

2. Calculate the net realizable value.

3. Compare the two.

4. Use the lower value to measure inventory for the balance sheet.

To demonstrate, consider the information in Illustration 8-14 for the inventory of Regner Foods Limited.

Food	Cost	Net Realizable Value	LCM
Spinach	$ 80,000	$120,000	$ 80,000
Carrots	100,000	100,000	100,000
Cut beans	50,000	40,000	40,000
Peas	90,000	72,000	72,000
Mixed vegetables	95,000	92,000	92,000
Final inventory value at LC&NRV			$384,000

Illustration 8-14

Applying the Lower of Cost and NRV

To establish the LCM value of each item of inventory, compare the net realizable value in the middle column of Illustration 8-14 with cost. The lower of the two values is then chosen. Cost is the lower amount for spinach; net realizable value is lower for cut beans, peas, and mixed vegetables; and cost and NRV are identical for carrots. The inventory amount reported on Regner Foods' balance sheet is therefore $384,000.

This analysis is usually only applied to losses in value that occur in the normal course of business from such causes as style changes, a shift in demand, or regular shop wear. Damaged or deteriorated goods are reduced directly to net realizable value. If the amount is significant, such goods may be carried in separate inventory accounts.

In Illustration 8-14 for Regner Foods, we assumed that the lower of cost and net realizable value rule is applied to each separate item of food. Indeed, **the accounting standards specify that the comparison is usually applied on an item-by-item basis**. However, the standards recognize that it may be appropriate in some circumstances to group similar or related items and then compare their cost and NRV as a group. Grouping inventory for this purpose may be appropriate, for example, for inventory items relating to the same product line in the following situations:

1. They are closely related in terms of their end use.

2. They are produced and marketed in the same geographical area.

3. They cannot be evaluated separately from other items in the product line in a practical or reasonable way.[12]

Grouping all finished goods inventory, or all products within a geographic area, or all inventory that is specific to an industry, is **not** considered appropriate.

The extent to which inventory items are grouped and their subtotals of cost and net realizable value are compared can affect the amount of inventory that is reported on the balance sheet. To illustrate, assume that Regner Foods separates its food products into "frozen" and "canned" categories.

As indicated in Illustration 8-15, if the lower of cost and NRV rule is applied to the **subtotals** of these groups, the valuation of inventory is $394,000; if it is applied to individual items, it is $384,000. The reason for the difference is that individual realizable

[12] *CICA Handbook*, Part II, Section 3031.29A and IAS 2.29.

values lower than cost are offset against realizable values higher than cost when categories are used. For example, the lower NRVs for cut beans, peas, and mixed vegetables are partially offset by the higher NRV for spinach. **The item-by-item approach** is always the more conservative (i.e., lower asset cost) method because net realizable values above cost are never included in the calculations.[13]

Illustration 8-15

Grouping Inventory Categories

	Cost	NRV	Lower of Cost and NRV by: Individual Items	Lower of Cost and NRV by: Related Products
Frozen				
Spinach	$ 80,000	$120,000	$ 80,000	
Carrots	100,000	100,000	100,000	
Cut beans	50,000	40,000	40,000	
Total frozen	230,000	260,000		$230,000
Canned				
Peas	90,000	72,000	72,000	
Mixed vegetables	95,000	92,000	92,000	
Total canned	185,000	164,000		164,000
Total			$384,000	$394,000

Recording the Lower of Cost and Net Realizable Value.   Two different methods are used for **recording** inventory at the lower market amount. The direct method records the NRV of the inventory directly in the Inventory account at the reporting date if the amount is lower than cost. No loss is reported separately in the income statement because the loss is buried in cost of goods sold. The other method does not change the Inventory account itself. Instead it keeps the Inventory account at cost and establishes a separate contra asset account to Inventory on the balance sheet. (This is very similar to Accounts Receivable and the Allowance for Doubtful Accounts.) A loss account is recognized in the income statement to record the writeoff. This second approach is referred to as the indirect method or allowance method.

The following data are the basis for Illustrations 8-16 and 8-17, which show the entries under both methods:

Inventory	At Cost	At NRV
Beginning of the period	$65,000	$65,000
End of the period	82,000	70,000

The entries in Illustration 8-16 assume the use of a **periodic** inventory system. Those in Illustration 8-17 assume a **perpetual** inventory system.

---

[13] The Canada Revenue Agency dictates that, in determining the lower of cost and NRV, the comparison should be made separately and individually in respect of each item (or each usual class of items if specific items are not readily distinguishable) in the inventory. Comparing total cost and total market is only permitted when the cost of the specific items (using specific identification, FIFO, or average cost) is not known and only an average cost is available (*CRA Interpretation Bulletin*—473R, December 21, 1998, on "Inventory Valuation," par. 3).

Ending Inventory Recorded at NRV (Direct Method)		Ending Inventory Recorded at Cost and Reduced to NRV Using an Allowance		
To transfer out beginning inventory balance:				
Cost of Goods Sold 65,000		Cost of Goods Sold 65,000		
Inventory	65,000	Inventory		65,000
To record ending inventory:				
Inventory 70,000		Inventory 82,000		
Cost of Goods Sold	70,000	Cost of Goods Sold		82,000
To write down inventory to lower NRV:				
No entry		Loss Due to Decline in NRV of Inventory*	12,000	
		Allowance to Reduce Inventory to NRV		12,000

*A debit to Cost of Goods Sold is also acceptable.

Direct Method		Indirect or Allowance Method		
To reduce inventory from cost to NRV:				
Cost of Goods Sold 12,000		Loss Due to Decline in NRV of Inventory*	12,000	
Inventory	12,000	Allowance to Reduce Inventory to NRV		12,000

*A debit to Cost of Goods Sold is also acceptable.

The advantage of identifying the loss due to the decline in net realizable value separately is that it may be reported in "Other expenses and losses," and therefore not distort the cost of goods sold for the year. It thus clearly discloses the loss resulting from the market decline in inventory prices instead of burying it in the cost of goods sold. The advantage of using an allowance account is that inventory cost numbers are retained in both the Inventory control and subsidiary ledger accounts.

Although using an allowance account makes it possible to disclose the inventory at cost and at the lower of cost and NRV on the balance sheet, it raises the problem of how to dispose of the new account balance in the following period. If the particular merchandise is still on hand, the allowance account should be retained. Otherwise, beginning inventory and cost of goods available for sale will be overstated. But **if the goods have been sold**, then the account should be closed. A new allowance account balance is then established for any decline in inventory value that exists at the end of the next accounting period.

Many accountants leave the allowance account on the books and merely adjust its balance at the next reporting date to agree with the difference between cost and the lower of cost and NRV at that time. If prices are falling, a loss is recorded. If prices are rising, a loss recorded in prior years is recovered and a gain (which is not really a gain, but **a recovery of a previously recognized loss**) is recorded, as shown in Illustration 8-18. The recovery amount is ordinarily recognized as a reduction in the cost of goods sold.

Date	Inventory at Cost	Inventory at NRV	Amount Required in Allowance Account	Allowance Account before Adjustment	Adjustment of Allowance Account Balance	Effect on Net Income
Dec. 31/10	$188,000	$176,000	$12,000 cr.	$ –0–	$12,000 increase	Loss
Dec. 31/11	194,000	187,000	7,000 cr.	12,000 cr.	5,000 decrease	Gain
Dec. 31/12	173,000	174,000	–0–	7,000 cr.	7,000 decrease	Gain
Dec. 31/13	182,000	180,000	2,000 cr.	–0–	2,000 increase	Loss

Any net "gain" can be thought of as the excess of the credit effect of closing the beginning allowance balance over the debit effect of setting up the current year-end allowance account. Recovering the loss up to the original cost is permitted, **but it may not exceed the original cost**. That is, the Allowance account cannot have a debit balance.

Evaluation of the Lower of Cost and Net Realizable Value Rule

Measuring inventories at the LC&NRV has some conceptual and practical deficiencies. Recognizing net realizable values only when they are lower than cost is an inconsistent treatment that can lead to distortions in reported income. The accounting values that are reported are not neutral and unbiased measures of income and net assets. Also, because NRV is an estimate, company management has the opportunity to over- or underestimate realizable values, depending on the results it would like to report for the period. Others feel that any accounting method that arbitrarily transfers income from one period to another reduces the quality of earnings.

On the other hand, many financial statement users appreciate the lower of cost and net realizable value requirement because they know that inventory and income are not overstated. Supporters contend that accounting measurement has not reached a level of sophistication that enables us to provide acceptably reliable (i.e., verifiable) fair values for inventory above cost.

Purchase Commitments

In many lines of business, it is common for a company to agree to buy inventory weeks, months, or even years in advance. Such arrangements may be made based on either estimated or firm sales commitments from the company's customers. Generally, title to the merchandise or materials described in these purchase commitments does not pass to the buyer until delivery. Indeed, when the commitment is made, the goods may exist only as natural resources or, in the case of commodities, as unplanted seed, or in the case of a product, as work in process.

Usually, it is incorrect for the buyer to make entries for commitments to purchase goods that have not been shipped by the seller. Ordinary orders, where the prices are determined at the time of shipment and **the buyer or seller can still cancel the order**, do not represent either an asset or a liability to the buyer. They are therefore not recorded in the books or reported in the financial statements.

Even with formal, **non-cancellable purchase contracts**, no asset or liability is recognized on the date when the contract takes effect, because it is an executory contract: in other words, neither party has performed (or fulfilled) its part of the contract.[14] However, if the amounts are abnormal in relation to the entity's normal business operations or financial position, the contract details should be disclosed in the notes to the buyer's financial statements, as shown in Illustrations 8-19 and 8-20.

---

[14] With the conceptual framework moving toward a more contract-based definition of assets and liabilities, there may be upcoming changes in this approach.

24. Commitments and Contingencies

(e) At December 31, 2008, Cameco's purchase commitments, the majority of which are fixed price uranium and conversion purchase arrangements, were as follows:

	(Millions (US))
2009	$144
2010	136
2011	153
2012	144
2013	294
Thereafter	75
Total	$946

Illustration 8-19

Disclosure of Purchase Commitments—Cameco Corporation

Real-World Emphasis

Commitments:

Contracts for the purchase of raw materials in 2012 have been executed in the amount of $600,000. The market price of such raw materials on December 31, 2011, is $640,000.

Illustration 8-20

Disclosure of Specific Purchase Commitment

In Illustration 8-20, the contracted price is lower than the market price at the balance sheet date. However, if the contracted amount was **higher than** the market price at the reporting date, management has to assess whether the entity will incur losses as a result. If the unavoidable costs of completing the contract are higher than the benefits expected from receiving contracted goods or services, a loss provision is recognized according to IAS 37 *Provisions, Contingent Liabilities, and Contingent Assets*. This is known as an **onerous contract**. Although private entity GAAP has no similar requirement, Canadian practice has been to recognize the loss and liability as well.

For example, if non-cancellable purchase contracts for delivery in 2012 have been executed at a price of $640,000, the material's market price on the company's December 31, 2011 year end is $600,000, and the purchaser does not expect to be able to recover these additional costs, the following entry is made on December 31, 2011:

Loss on Purchase Contracts	40,000	
Provision for Onerous Purchase Contracts (Liability)		40,000

A = L + SE
  +40,000 −40,000

Cash flows: No effect

The loss is included in net income under "Other expenses and losses." The Provision account is reported in the balance sheet's liability section. When the goods are delivered in 2012, the entry (in a perpetual system) is:

Inventory	600,000	
Provision for Onerous Purchase Contracts	40,000	
Accounts Payable		640,000

A = L + SE
+600,000 +600,000

Cash flows: No effect

If the price partially or fully recovers before the inventory is received, the Provision for Onerous Purchase Contracts amount is reduced. A resulting gain (Recovery of Loss) is then reported in the period of the price increase for the amount of the partial or full recovery. This accounting treatment is very similar to recognizing an impairment in inventory value by recording inventories at the lower of cost and net realizable value.

Accounting for purchase commitments (indeed, for all commitments) is unsettled and controversial. Some argue that these contracts should be reported as assets and liabilities when the contract is signed; others believe that recognition at the delivery date is more

Underlying Concept

Reporting the loss expected on the contract is questioned by some on the basis that the accrued liability on purchase contracts is not a present obligation. This demonstrates the need for good definitions of assets and liabilities.

appropriate. As work proceeds on the IFRS conceptual framework, this debate will hopefully be resolved.

Recognition of Inventory Costs as an Expense

Consistent with the matching concept, the carrying amount of inventory is recognized as an expense **in the same accounting period when the associated revenue is reported, and most often is reported as cost of goods sold**.

Writedowns to net realizable value and any recoveries of such declines in value are recognized in the accounting period when the loss or recovery takes place. Both are usually recognized along with the inventory charged to expense in the period.

Exceptions to Lower of Cost and Net Realizable Value Model

Inventories Measured at Net Realizable Value

Objective 9

Identify inventories that are or may be valued at amounts other than the lower of cost and net realizable value.

For most companies and in most situations, inventory is reported at the lower of cost and net realizable value. Some critics believe that inventory should always be valued at its **net realizable value** because that is the net amount that will be collected in cash from the inventory in the future. In certain restricted circumstances, it is possible to record inventory at its net realizable value even if that amount is above cost. The following criteria have to be met to value inventory above cost and for revenue to be recognized before the point of sale:

1. The sale is assured or there is an active market for the product and minimal risk of failure to sell.

2. The costs of disposal can be estimated.

Real-World Emphasis

Inventories of certain minerals (rare metals especially) are sometimes reported at NRV because there is often a controlled market without significant costs of disposal. A similar treatment may be used for agricultural produce after harvest and inventories of agricultural and forest products. When such inventories are measured at NRV in accordance with accounting policies common in the industry, measurement at NRV is GAAP. Changes in net realizable value are recognized in net income each period. **Viterra Inc.**, with operations in grain handling, agri-products, and agri-food processing, among others, reports such a policy in the notes to its 2008 financial statements. The note is shown in Illustration 8-21.

Illustration 8-21

Inventory Valued at Net Realizable Value—Viterra Inc.

> **Inventories:**
> Grain inventories include both hedgeable and non-hedgeable commodities. Hedgeable and non-hedgeable grain inventories are valued on the basis of closing market quotations less freight and handling costs. Agri-products, livestock feed, and other inventories consist of raw materials, work in progress and finished goods, and are valued at the lower of cost and net realizable value.

Measurement at net realizable value may also be used when cost figures are too difficult to obtain. In some cases, minor marketable by-products are produced where the costs are indistinguishable. Instead of the company attempting a costly exercise of arbitrary cost allocation, the by-products are measured at the selling price of the by-product less any costs to bring them to market.

Inventories Measured at Fair Value Less Costs to Sell

Inventories of Commodity Broker-Traders.   Another exception to the lower of cost and net realizable value measurement standard is the inventory of commodity broker-traders who measure their inventories at **fair value less costs to sell**.[15] This inventory consists of such items as grain and livestock futures contracts. Changes in the fair value less costs to sell the inventory items are recognized in net income in the period of the change.

Biological Assets and Agricultural Produce at Point of Harvest.   As they relate to agricultural activity, there is often confusion between what is a biological asset, agricultural produce, and a product that results from processing after harvest. The following excerpt of examples in Illustration 8-22, reproduced from IAS 41 *Agriculture*, helps to clarify what is included as each type of asset.

Significant Change

Illustration 8-22

Examples of Agricultural Activity Assets

Biological Assets	Agricultural Produce	Products that Result from Processing after Harvest
Sheep	Wool	Yarn, carpet
Trees in a plantation forest	Felled trees	Logs, lumber
Dairy cattle	Milk	Cheese
Pigs	Carcass	Sausages, cured hams
Vines	Grapes	Wine
Fruit trees	Picked fruit	Processed fruit

Private entity GAAP. Inventories of biological assets (living plants and animals) and products of the entity's biological assets (agricultural produce) at the point of harvest are excluded from the **measurement** requirements of private entity GAAP for inventories, but they are included for the **expense recognition** and **disclosure** requirements. This means that there is no specific guidance on how such assets should be measured. A review of the financial statements of many Canadian companies with such assets indicates that they tend to follow a lower of cost and net realizable value approach. This is reasonable considering that this valuation corresponds closely to what is the **primary source of GAAP** for similar assets.

Regardless, products resulting from further processing after harvest have to meet all the requirements of the inventory standard. They are measured at the lower of cost and NRV with whatever value they were assigned at the point of harvest recognized as their deemed cost.

IFRS. Under IFRS, accounting for biological assets and agricultural produce at the point of harvest is covered in a separate standard: IAS 41 *Agriculture*. This is a specialized industry, so at an intermediate accounting level, it is enough to know that these inventories are measured at fair value less costs to sell. For produce at the point of harvest, such as grapes or picked fruit, the "fair value less costs to sell" measure is deemed to be the inventory's "cost" for purposes of subsequent accounting (and further processing, if applicable) under IAS 2 *Inventories*.

Basic entries to account for this measurement model are set out in Illustration 8-23.[16] Assume that the enterprise is a farm that raises sheep for their wool. The sheep are biological assets, lambs born into the existing flock are biological assets, and the wool is an agricultural product.

---

[15] While fair value less costs to sell appears to be the same as net realizable value (selling price less costs to sell), it is different. NRV is an entity-specific value, whereas fair values reflect a market-based valuation.

[16] The entries to account for inventories carried at net realizable value are similar to those for assets carried at fair value less costs to sell. The changes in NRV are recognized in the Inventory account and in income in the period the NRV changes.

To record the birth of a lamb:		
Biological Asset	x	
Gain on Change in Fair Value Less Costs to Sell		x
To record general farm expenditures:		
Expenses	x	
Cash/Accounts Payable		x
To record an increase in value of lambs and other sheep:		
Biological Asset	x	
Gain on Change in Fair Value Less Costs to Sell		x
To record the wool inventory produced from the sheep:		
Agricultural Produce—Wool	x	
Fair Value of Wool Produced (Revenue)		x
To record the sale of wool produced:		
Cash/Accounts Receivable	x	
Agricultural Produce—Wool		x

The account Biological Asset, representing the fair value less selling costs of the sheep, seems to have some of the characteristics of both inventory and plant and equipment assets. However, biological assets are classified as neither. They require separate disclosure on the statement of financial position.

OTHER INVENTORY ISSUES

Inventory Errors

Objective 10

Identify the effects of
inventory errors on the
financial statements
and adjust for them.

Items that have been incorrectly included or excluded in determining the ending inventory amount create errors in both the income statement and the balance sheet. Decisions that are based on financial statement amounts affected by such errors (e.g., bonuses paid to management based on net income) would therefore be in error and comparability would also be impaired. Let's look at two cases and the effects on the financial statements.

Ending Inventory Misstated

What would happen if the beginning inventory and purchases are recorded correctly, but some items are omitted from ending inventory by mistake (e.g., they were in the warehouse but were missed in the physical count, or they were out on consignment)? The effects of this error on the financial statements at the end of the period are shown in Illustration 8-24.

Statement of Financial Position		Income Statement	
Inventory	Understated	Cost of goods sold	Overstated
Retained earnings	Understated	Net income	Understated
Working capital	Understated		
(current assets less			
current liabilities)			
Current ratio	Understated		
(Current assets divided by			
current liabilities)			

Working capital and the current ratio are understated because a portion of the ending inventory is omitted; net income is understated because cost of goods sold is overstated.

To illustrate the effect on net income over a two-year period, assume that the ending inventory of Wei Ltd. is understated by $10,000 and that all other items are stated correctly. The effect of this error is an understatement of net income in the current year and an overstatement of net income in the following year. The error affects the following year because the beginning inventory of that year is understated, thereby causing net income to be overstated. Both net income figures are misstated, but the total for the two years is correct as the two errors will be counterbalanced (offset), as shown in Illustration 8-25.

Underlying Concept

When inventory is misstated, the asset reported lacks faithful representation.

Illustration 8-25

Effect of Ending Inventory Error on Two Periods

WEI LTD.

	Incorrect Recording		Correct Recording	
	2011	2012	2011	2012
Revenues	$100,000	$100,000	$100,000	$100,000
Cost of goods sold				
Beginning inventory	25,000	20,000	25,000	30,000
Purchased or produced	45,000	60,000	45,000	60,000
Goods available for sale	70,000	80,000	70,000	90,000
Less: Ending inventory*	20,000	40,000	30,000	40,000
Cost of goods sold	50,000	40,000	40,000	50,000
Gross profit	50,000	60,000	60,000	50,000
Administrative and selling expenses	40,000	40,000	40,000	40,000
Net income	$ 10,000	$ 20,000	$ 20,000	$ 10,000

Total income for two years = $30,000   Total income for two years = $30,000

*Ending inventory understated by $10,000 in 2011; correct amount is $30,000.

If the error is discovered in 2011 just before the books are closed, the correcting entry in 2011 would be:

| Inventory | 10,000 | |
| Cost of Goods Sold | | 10,000 |

A   = L +   SE
+10,000   +10,000

Cash flows: No effect

If the error is not discovered until 2012, after the books are closed for 2011, the correcting entry in 2012 would be:

| Inventory | 10,000 | |
| Retained Earnings | | 10,000 |

A   = L +   SE
+10,000   +10,000

Cash flows: No effect

If the error is discovered after the books for 2012 are closed, **no entry is required as the error is self-correcting over the two-year period.** The inventory on the balance sheet at the end of 2012 is correct, as is the total amount of retained earnings. **However, whenever comparative financial statements are prepared that include 2011 or 2012,** the inventory and net income for those years are restated and reported at the correct figures.

If ending inventory is **overstated** at the end of 2011, the reverse effect occurs. Inventory, working capital, current ratio, and net income are overstated and cost of goods sold is understated. The error's effect on net income will be counterbalanced in the next year, but both years' net income figures are incorrect, which distorts any analysis of trends in earnings and ratios.

Purchases and Inventory Misstated

Suppose that certain goods that the company owns are **not recorded as a purchase** and are **not counted in ending inventory**. Illustration 8-26 shows the effect on the financial statements, assuming this is a purchase on account.

Illustration 8-26

Financial Statement Effects of Understated Purchases and Inventory

Statement of Financial Position		Income Statement	
Inventory	Understated	Purchases	Understated
Retained earnings	No effect	Inventory (ending)	Understated
Accounts payable	Understated	Cost of goods sold	No effect
Working capital	No effect	Net income	No effect
Current ratio	Overstated		

Omitting both the purchase of goods and the inventory results in understated inventory and accounts payable on the balance sheet, and understated purchases and ending inventory on the income statement. **Net income for the period is not affected by omitting such goods, because purchases and ending inventory are both understated by the same amount; i.e., the error offsets itself in cost of goods sold.**[17] Total working capital is unchanged, but the current ratio is overstated (assuming it was greater than 1 to 1) because equal amounts were omitted from inventory and accounts payable.

To illustrate the effect on the current ratio, assume that a company understates its accounts payable and ending inventory by $40,000. The understated and correct data are shown in Illustration 8-27.

Illustration 8-27

Effects of Purchases and Ending Inventory Errors

Purchases and Ending Inventory Understated		Purchases and Ending Inventory Correct	
Current assets	$120,000	Current assets	$160,000
Current liabilities	$ 40,000	Current liabilities	$ 80,000
Current ratio	3 to 1	Current ratio	2 to 1

The correct current ratio is 2 to 1 rather than 3 to 1. Thus, understating accounts payable and ending inventory can lead to a "window dressing" of the current ratio. In other words, it can appear better than it really is.

---

[17] To correct the error in the same year before the books are closed, and assuming inventories are adjusted before the closing entries, the following entries are needed:

Periodic Method			Perpetual Method		
Purchases	$x		Inventory	$x	
Accounts Payable		$x	Accounts Payable		$x
Inventory	$x				
Cost of Goods Sold		$x			

If purchases (on account) and ending inventory are both overstated, then the effects on the balance sheet are exactly the reverse: inventory and accounts payable are overstated, and although the dollar amount of working capital is not affected, the current ratio is understated. Cost of goods sold and net income are also unaffected because the errors offset each other. The preceding examples show some of the errors that can occur and their consequences, but there are many other types of possible errors: not recording a purchase but counting the new inventory; not recording a sale in the current period although the items have been delivered; omitting the adjusting entry to update the account Allowance for Future Returns in situations where the sales are known to have a high rate of return; failure to adjust inventory to the lower of cost and NRV; and others.

Determining correct amounts for purchases, sales, and inventory in the correct accounting period is a critical step in preparing reliable financial statements. One has only to read the financial press to learn how misstating inventory can generate high income numbers. For example, in the past some Canadian farm equipment manufacturers treated deliveries to dealers as company sales (thus reducing their inventory), even though sales to the ultimate consumer did not occur as quickly as the deliveries to the dealers. The result was a significantly inflated reported income for the manufacturers.

As Chapter 5 showed, when an error from a prior period is corrected, it is accounted for retroactively as an adjustment to retained earnings. Full disclosure requires a description of the error and a statement of the effect on the current and prior period financial statements.

Estimating Inventory

The Need for Estimates

Recall that the basic purpose of taking a physical inventory is to verify the accuracy of the perpetual inventory records, or, if there are no perpetual records, to arrive at an inventory amount. Sometimes, taking a physical inventory is impractical or impossible. In such cases, estimation methods are used to approximate inventory on hand. One such method is called the gross profit, or gross margin, method. This method is used in situations where only an estimate of inventory is needed (e.g., preparing interim reports or testing the reasonableness of the cost calculated by some other method) or where inventory has been destroyed by fire or some other catastrophe. It may also be used to provide a rough check on the accuracy of a physical inventory count. For example, the estimated amount is compared with the physical count amount to see if they are reasonably close; if they are not, the reason for the difference is investigated.

11 Objective
Apply the gross profit method of estimating inventory.

Another method that is widely used with retail inventories is the retail inventory method. Like the gross profit method, it depends on establishing a relationship between selling (retail) prices and cost. Appendix 8A discusses the retail inventory method in detail.

Applying the Gross Profit Method

The **gross profit method** is based on three premises:

1. The beginning inventory plus purchases equals the **cost of goods available for sale**.

2. Goods not included in cost of goods sold must be on hand **in ending inventory**.

3. When an estimate of cost of goods sold is deducted from the cost of goods available for sale, the result is an estimate of ending inventory.

To illustrate, assume that a company has a beginning inventory of $60,000 and purchases of $200,000, both at cost. Sales at selling price amount to $280,000. The gross profit on the selling price is 30%. Illustration 8-28 walks you through the gross margin method of estimating ending inventory.[18]

Beginning inventory (at cost)		$ 60,000
Purchases (at cost)		200,000
Goods available for sale (at cost)		260,000
Sales (at selling price)	$280,000	
Less: Gross profit (30% of $280,000)	84,000	
Sales at cost = Estimated cost of goods sold		196,000
Estimated inventory (at cost)		$ 64,000

Note that the estimated cost of goods sold could also have been calculated directly as 70% of sales; i.e., 100% less 30%. **The cost of goods sold percentage is always the complement of the gross profit percentage.**

All the information needed to estimate the inventory at cost, except for the gross profit percentage, is available in the current period's accounting records. The gross profit percentage is determined by reviewing company policies and the records of prior periods. The percentage is adjusted if the prior periods are not considered representative of the current period.

Gross Profit Percentage versus Markup on Cost

In most situations, the **gross profit percentage** is used and it is the gross profit as a percentage of the selling price. The previous illustration, for example, used a 30% gross profit on sales. Gross profit on selling price is the common method for quoting the profit for several reasons. (1) Most goods are stated on a retail basis, not a cost basis. (2) A profit quoted on the selling price is lower than one based on cost, and this lower rate gives a favourable impression to the consumer. (3) The gross profit based on selling price can never exceed 100%.[19]

In the previous example, the percentage was given to you. But how was that figure derived? To see how a gross profit percentage is calculated, assume that an article cost

---

[18] An alternative approach to estimating inventory using the gross profit percentage, considered by some to be less complicated than the method in illustration 8-28, uses the standard income statement format as follows (assume the same data as in Illustration 8-28):

Sales		$280,000		$280,000
Cost of goods sold				
Beginning inventory	$ 60,000		$ 60,000	
Purchases	200,000		200,000	
Goods available for sale	260,000		260,000	
Ending inventory	(3) ?		(3) 64,000 Est.	
Cost of goods sold		(2) ?		(2) 196,000 Est.
Gross profit on sales (30%)		(1) ?		(1)$ 84,000 Est.

Calculate the unknowns as follows: first the gross profit amount, then cost of goods sold, and then the ending inventory.

(1) $280,000 × 30% = $84,000 (gross profit on sales)
(2) $280,000 − $84,000 = $196,000 (cost of goods sold)
(3) $260,000 − $196,000 = $64,000 (ending inventory)

[19] The terms "gross profit percentage," "gross margin percentage," "rate of gross profit," and "rate of gross margin" mean the same thing: they all reflect the relationship of gross profit to the selling price. The terms "percentage markup" or "rate of markup" are used to describe the relationship of gross profit to cost. It is very important to understand the difference.

$15.00 and sells for $20.00, a gross profit of $5.00. This markup of $5.00 is one-quarter or 25% of the selling price (i.e., the retail price) but is one-third or 33¹/₃% of cost (see Illustration 8-29).

Illustration 8-29

Gross Profit Percentage vs. Percentage of Markup on Cost

$$\frac{\text{Gross profit}}{\text{Selling price}} = \frac{\$\ 5.00}{\$20.00} = 25\% \text{ of selling price} \qquad \frac{\text{Gross profit}}{\text{Cost}} = \frac{\$\ 5.00}{\$15.00} = 33^{1}/_{3}\% \text{ of cost}$$

Although gross profit is based on sales, you should understand the relationship between this ratio and the percentage of markup on cost.

For example, assume that you were told that the **markup on cost** for a specific item is 25%. What, then, is the **gross profit on selling price**? To find the answer, assume that the item's selling price is $1.00. In this case, the following formula applies:

$$\text{Cost} + \text{Gross profit} = \text{Selling price}$$
$$C + .25C = \$1.00$$
$$1.25C = \$1.00$$
$$C = \$0.80$$

The amount of gross profit is $0.20 ($1.00 − $0.80), and the rate of gross profit on selling price is 20% ($0.20/$1.00).

Alternatively, assume that you know that the **gross profit on selling price** is 20%. What is the **markup on cost**? To find the answer, again assume that the selling price is $1.00. The same formula can be used:

$$\text{Cost} + \text{Gross profit} = \text{Selling price}$$
$$C + .20\ (\$1.00) = \$1.00$$
$$C + \$0.20 = \$1.00$$
$$C = \$0.80$$

Here, as in the example above, the amount of the markup or gross profit is $0.20 ($1.00 − $0.80), and the percentage markup on cost is 25% ($0.20/$0.80). Retailers use the formulas in Illustration 8-30 to express these relationships.

Illustration 8-30

Formulas Relating to Gross Profit

1. $\text{Percent gross profit on selling price} = \dfrac{\text{Percent markup on cost}}{100\% + \text{Percent markup on cost}}$

2. $\text{Percent markup on cost} = \dfrac{\text{Percent gross profit on selling price}}{100\% - \text{Percent gross profit on selling price}}$

Using the Results

What are the disadvantages of using the gross profit method? One is that **it provides an estimate** only. Second, the gross profit method uses **past percentages** in determining the markup. Although the future may repeat the past, a current rate is usually more appropriate. Whenever fluctuations in the rate of profit occur, the percentage must be adjusted appropriately. Third, **it may be inappropriate to apply a single gross profit rate**. Often, a store or department handles merchandise with very different rates of gross profit. In these situations, the gross profit method may have to be applied by type of merchandise, or by combining merchandise with similar profit margins.

Because the result is only an estimate, the gross profit method is **not normally acceptable for financial reporting purposes**. A physical inventory is needed as an additional verification that the inventory indicated in the records is actually on hand. Nevertheless, the gross profit method is used to estimate ending inventory for **interim** (monthly and quarterly) **reporting** and for **insurance purposes** (e.g., fire losses). Note that the results of applying the gross profit method will reflect the inventory method that is used (specific identification, FIFO, average cost) because this method is based on historical records.

PRESENTATION, DISCLOSURE, AND ANALYSIS

Presentation and Disclosure of Inventories

Objective 12
Identify the type of inventory disclosures required by private entity GAAP and IFRS.

Inventories are one of the most significant assets of manufacturing and merchandising companies, and of many service enterprises. For this reason, companies are required to disclose additional information about these resources.

Some disclosures are similar to the ones required for other balance sheet items:

- the choice of accounting policies adopted to measure the inventory;

- the carrying amount of the inventory in total and by classification (such as supplies, material, work in process, and finished goods);

- the amount of inventories recognized as an expense in the period, including unabsorbed and abnormal amounts of production overheads; and

- the carrying amount of inventory pledged as collateral for liabilities.

The amount of inventory recognized as an expense is usually reported according to its function—as cost of goods sold. However, a company that chooses to present its expenses according to the nature of its costs instead of by function would present expenses for raw materials and consumables used, labour costs, and other expenses along with the change in inventories for the period.

Additional disclosures are required for inventories **under IFRS**. These include the carrying amount of inventory carried at fair value less costs to sell, and details about inventory writedowns and reversals of writedowns, such as information about what led to the reversal of any writedowns. Considerable information is required in addition for biological assets and agricultural produce at the point of harvest, such as a reconciliation of opening to ending account balances.

Real-World Emphasis

The excerpts in Illustration 8-31 are taken from the 2008 financial statements of **MEGA Brands Inc.**, a Canadian company that designs, manufactures, and markets toys, stationery, and activity products in over 100 countries. The excerpts illustrate the company's disclosure of its accounting policy choices for determining inventory cost including the cost formula used, the basis of valuation on the balance sheet, the carrying value of major categories making up the total inventory, and the cost of goods sold. In addition, the company reports its accounting policy for vendor rebates. In separate notes (not illustrated), the company provides significant information about inventory writedowns due to product recalls and replacements, and discloses that all its assets are used as security for its liabilities.

The MEGA Brands Inc. disclosures exceed those now required under private entity GAAP, and meet the requirements for disclosures under IFRS.

Illustration 8-31

*Inventory Disclosures—
MEGA Brands Inc.*

Accounting Policies:

Vendor allowance

Cash considerations received from vendors are deemed a reduction of the prices of the vendors' products or services and are accounted for as a reduction of cost of sales and related inventory when recognized in the Corporation's consolidated statement of loss and balance sheet.

Inventories

Inventories are stated at the lower of cost and net realizable value. Cost is established based on the first-in, first-out method and, as appropriate, includes material, labour and manufacturing overhead costs. Inventories of finished goods are valued at the lower of cost and net realizable value, and inventories of raw materials and supplies are valued at the lower of cost and net realizable value, which is generally defined as replacement cost, which is the best available measure of their net realizable value.

11 Inventories

	2008	2007
	$	$
Raw materials and supplies	2,724	7,882
Work in progress	7,080	14,318
Finished goods	55,416	69,481
	65,220	91,681

As at December 31, 2008, the Corporation had provided for writedowns of $14.1 million of inventories (2007 – $7.6 million).

The cost of inventories recognized as expense in 2008 included in cost of sales amounts to $315.5 million (2007 – $372.0 million).

Analysis

Inventory management is a double-edged sword. On the one hand, management wants to have a wide variety and high quantities on hand so customers have the greatest selection and always find what they want in stock. On the other hand, such a policy may result in excessive carrying costs (e.g., in investment, storage, insurance, taxes, obsolescence, and damage). Low inventory levels, however, may lead to running out of specific products (stockouts), lost sales, and unhappy customers. Financial ratios can be used to help management chart a middle course between these two dangers and to help investors assess management's performance. Common ratios that are used to evaluate inventory levels are the inventory turnover and a related measure, average days to sell (or average age of) the inventory.

The **inventory turnover ratio** measures the number of times on average that the inventory was sold during the period. This ratio helps to measure the liquidity of the investment in inventory because the faster the turnover, the sooner the company generates cash inflows from this asset. A manager may use past turnover experience to determine how long the inventory now in stock will take to be sold. This ratio is calculated by dividing the cost of goods sold by the average inventory on hand during the period.

Average inventory can be calculated from the beginning and ending inventory balances.[20] For example, **MEGA Brands Inc.** reported beginning inventory of $91,681 thousand, ending inventory of $65,220 thousand, and cost of goods sold of $315.5 million for

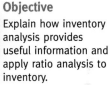

13 Objective
Explain how inventory analysis provides useful information and apply ratio analysis to inventory.

Real-World Emphasis

---

[20] Some seasonal variation is common in most companies. Fiscal year ends are usually chosen at a low activity point in the year's operations, which means that inventories in the annual financial statements are at their lowest levels in the year. Management can make adjustments to use the average monthly inventory level. External users, however, are limited to using the average between the opening and closing annual inventory balances. Public companies are required to issue reports on a quarterly basis, so external users can base the average on five inventory amounts through the year.

its 2008 fiscal year. The calculation of MEGA Brands' 2008 inventory turnover is shown in Illustration 8-32.

Illustration 8-32
Inventory Turnover Ratio

$$\text{Inventory Turnover} = \frac{\text{Cost of Goods Sold}}{\text{Average Inventory}}$$

$$= \frac{\$315{,}500}{\dfrac{\$91{,}681 + \$65{,}220}{2}}$$

$$= 4.02 \text{ times}$$

A closely related ratio is the **average days to sell inventory**, which represents the average age of the inventory on hand or the number of days it takes to sell inventory after it is acquired. For example, if MEGA Brands' inventory turns over 4.02 times per year, that means it takes, on average, 365 days divided by 4.02 or approximately 91 days to sell its investment in inventory.

Is this a good turnover ratio? If the company sells fresh fruit and vegetables, you would know that this is not a good number. However, for other products, it is not as easy to come to a firm conclusion. For example, MEGA Brands designs and manufactures a broad line of toys, stationery, and activity products, so you might expect that it would move its inventory out faster than only every three months. Each industry has its norms, however, so the industry average is one standard that the company's ratio can be compared against. Because the choice of inventory cost formula may affect the inventory reported on the balance sheet and the cost of goods sold, these differences make adjustments necessary in any inter-company comparisons. This is true not only for turnover ratios but for any analysis that includes inventory: the amount of working capital, the working capital ratio, and the gross profit percentage, for example. Internally, company management compares these numbers with its goals and objectives for the year.

There is no absolute standard of comparison for most ratios, but generally speaking, companies that are able to keep their inventory at lower levels with higher turnovers than those of their competitors, and still satisfy customer needs, are the most successful.

IFRS/PRIVATE ENTITY GAAP COMPARISON

A Comparison of IFRS and Private Entity GAAP

Objective 14
Identify differences in accounting between private entity GAAP and IFRS, and what changes are expected in the near future.

Because *CICA Handbook*, Part II, Section 3031 *Inventories* was recently (2008) converged with IAS 2 *Inventories*, there are few differences in the recognition and measurement standards for most inventories. The most significant difference relates to the fact that there is a separate international standard (IAS 41) covering biological assets and agricultural produce at the point of harvest, and these assets are not specifically covered by private entity GAAP. Illustration 8-33 identifies what the differences are between private entity GAAP and IFRS.

	Accounting Standards for Private Enterprises (Private Entity GAAP)—*CICA Handbook*, Part II, Sections 3031 and 3850	IFRS—IAS 2, 11, 23, and 41
Scope	There is no primary source of GAAP covering biological assets and agricultural produce at the point of harvest.	IAS 41 provides standards for biological assets and agricultural produce at the point of harvest.
Measurement	Asset retirement and decommissioning costs arising from production activities are added to the carrying amount of the PP&E asset.	Asset retirement and decommissioning costs arising from production activities are added to the cost of the inventory.
	Companies may choose a policy of capitalizing interest or a policy of expensing the costs. No guidance is provided on what is a qualifying asset.	Interest costs directly attributable to the acquisition, construction, or production of qualifying inventory are capitalized. Such costs may be expensed for inventory measured at fair value and for qualifying inventory produced in large quantities on a repetitive basis.
	No guidance is provided for onerous contractual obligations such as may occur with purchase commitments.	A liability and loss are required to be recognized for onerous contracts if the unavoidable costs exceed the benefits from receiving the contracted goods or services.
	No guidance is provided for measuring biological assets and agricultural produce prior to and at the point of harvest. After harvest, its carrying amount becomes the inventory's deemed cost, and subsequently it is accounted for at the lower of (the deemed) cost and NRV.	Biological assets and agricultural produce at the point of harvest are measured at fair value less costs to sell. At harvest, this becomes the inventory's deemed cost, and subsequently it is accounted for at the lower of cost and NRV.
Presentation and disclosure	Limited disclosures are required.	Additional disclosures are required, particularly about writedowns and any reversals. In addition, significant information is required about biological assets and agricultural produce.

Illustration 8-33

IFRS and Private Entity GAAP Comparison Chart

Looking Ahead

No major changes are expected in the general inventory standards in the near future. However, the IASB issued a Discussion Paper in 2009 on extractive activities related to the search for, discovery of, and extraction of minerals and oil and gas. This project is expected to result in new standards for the associated reserves and resources and therefore inventories in these industries. A final standard will take a number of years to develop, assuming the topic is added to the IASB's active agenda.

Summary of Learning Objectives

WILEY PLUS

Glossary

1 Define inventory and identify inventory categories.

Only one inventory account, Merchandise Inventory, appears in the financial statements of a merchandising concern. A manufacturer normally has three inventory accounts: Raw Materials, Work in Process, and Finished Goods. There may also be an inventory account for factory or manufacturing supplies.

2 Identify the decisions that are needed to determine the inventory value to report on the balance sheet under a lower of cost and net realizable value model.

To determine the balance sheet inventory amount, you need to decide which physical goods are included in inventory, what expenditures are included in "cost," what cost formula to apply, and finally, whether there has been any impairment in value.

KEY TERMS

allowance method, 474

asset retirement
    costs, 460

average days to sell
    inventory, 488

basket purchase, 462

consigned goods, 457

3 **Identify the physical inventory items that should be included in ending inventory.**

Generally, inventory is included on the balance sheet of the entity that has legal title to the goods; i.e., the company that has the risks and rewards of ownership. Consigned goods remain the property of the consignor. Exceptions to the general rule of legal title are made when the risks and rewards associated with ownership have been transferred and title has not.

4 **Determine the components of inventory cost.**

Inventory costs include all costs of purchase, conversion, and other costs incurred in bringing the inventories to the present location and condition necessary for sale. Such charges include freight charges on goods purchased, other direct costs of acquisition, and labour and other direct production costs incurred in processing the goods up to the time of sale. Manufacturing overhead costs are allocated to inventory based on the normal capacity of the production facilities.

5 **Distinguish between perpetual and periodic inventory systems and account for them.**

Under a perpetual inventory system, a continuous record of changes in inventory is maintained in the Inventory account. That is, all purchases into and transfers of goods out of the account are recorded directly in the Inventory account as they occur. No such record is kept under a periodic inventory system. Under the periodic system, year-end inventory is determined by a physical count, and the amount of ending inventory and cost of goods sold is based on this count. Even under the perpetual system, an annual count is needed to test the accuracy of the records.

6 **Identify and apply GAAP cost formula options and indicate when each cost formula is appropriate.**

The specific identification method is used to assign costs for items of inventory that are not ordinarily interchangeable or that are produced for specific projects. The weighted-average or first-in, first-out cost formula is used to assign costs to other types of inventory. All inventory items that have a similar nature and use to the entity apply the same cost formula.

7 **Explain why inventory is measured at the lower of cost and market, and apply the lower of cost and net realizable value standard.**

Current assets should not be reported on the balance sheet at a higher amount than the net cash that is expected to be generated from their use or sale. When this amount is less than "cost," inventory is written down and the loss in value is recognized in the same period as the decline. Net realizable value is the estimated selling price in the ordinary course of business reduced by the expected costs to complete and sell the goods. Ordinarily, each item's cost and NRV are compared and the lower value is chosen. However, items that are related to each other and have similar purposes, that are produced and marketed in the same geographical area, and that cannot be evaluated separately from other items may be grouped and the lower of the group's cost and net realizable value is chosen.

8 **Explain the accounting issues for purchase commitments.**

Generally, if purchase commitments are significant relative to the company's financial position and operations, they should be disclosed in a note to the financial statements. At the balance sheet date, if a contract requires future payments in excess of its future economic benefits, a loss is recognized, offset by a liability. This accounting treatment is similar to recognizing impairments on inventory.

9 **Identify inventories that are or may be valued at amounts other than the lower of cost and net realizable value.**

Inventories of financial instruments, construction contract work in process, biological assets related to agricultural activity, agricultural produce at the point of harvest and after harvest, inventories held by producers of agricultural and forest producers, mineral products, and inventories of commodity broker-traders all may be accounted for at other than the lower of cost and net realizable value.

10 **Identify the effects of inventory errors on the financial statements and adjust for them.**

If the ending inventory is misstated, (1) the inventory, retained earnings, working capital, and current ratio in the balance sheet will be incorrect; and (2) the cost of goods sold and net income in the income statement will be incorrect. If purchases and inventory are misstated, (1) the inventory, accounts payable, and current ratio will be incorrect; and (2) purchases and ending inventory will be incorrect.

11 **Apply the gross profit method of estimating inventory.**

Ending inventory is determined by deducting an estimate of cost of goods sold from the actual cost of goods available for sale. Cost of goods sold is estimated by multiplying net sales by the percentage of cost of goods sold to sales. This percentage is derived from the gross profit percent: 100% − gross profit percentage = cost of goods sold percentage.

12 **Identify the type of inventory disclosures required by accounting standards for private enterprises (private entity GAAP) and IFRS.**

Private entity GAAP requires disclosure of how cost is determined, inventory that is pledged as security, the amount charged to the income statement as expense in the period, and the inventories' carrying value by category. Additional information is required by IFRS, including details about inventory impairment writedowns and any recoveries, the circumstances responsible for these, and the carrying amounts and reconciliations of items measured at NRV or fair value.

13 **Explain how inventory analysis provides useful information and apply ratio analysis to inventory.**

Common ratios that are used in the management and evaluation of inventory levels are the inventory turnover and a related measure, average days to sell the inventory, often called the average age of inventory. This is useful information as excessive investment in inventory is expensive to carry, yet too little inventory results in lost sales and dissatisfied customers.

14 **Identify differences in accounting between accounting standards for private enterprises (private entity GAAP) and IFRS, and what changes are expected in the near future.**

Recent changes to both IAS 2 and *CICA Handbook* standards on inventory (Section 3031) result in Canadian and international standards being substantially harmonized. There are international but not Canadian standards on the measurement of agricultural and construction inventories, on the capitalization of borrowing costs on qualifying assets, and on onerous contracts, but no major differences in how these costs are accounted for between the two jurisdictions. No major changes are expected in the near future.

Appendix **8**A

The Retail Inventory Method of Estimating Inventory Cost

Objective **15**
Apply the retail method of estimating inventory.

Accounting for inventory in a retail operation presents several challenges. Some retailers can use the specific identification method to value their inventories. As explained in the chapter, this approach makes sense when individual inventory units are significant, such as automobiles, pianos, or fur coats. However, imagine attempting to use such an approach at Zellers or Sears—high-volume retailers that have many different types of merchandise at relatively low unit costs! It would be difficult to determine the cost of each sale, to enter cost codes on the tickets, to change the codes to reflect declines in value of the merchandise, to allocate costs such as transportation, and so on. An alternative is to estimate inventory cost when necessary by taking a physical inventory at retail prices. Also, to avoid misstating the inventory, especially in retail operations where losses due to shoplifting and breakage are common, periodic inventory counts are made at retail and are then converted to cost. Differences between the records and the physical count require an adjustment to make the records agree with the count.

In most retail businesses, there is an observable pattern between cost and selling prices. Retail prices can be converted to cost simply by multiplying them by the cost-to-retail ratio. This method, called the retail inventory method, **requires that the following information be available: (1) the total cost and retail value of the goods purchased, (2) the total cost and retail value of the goods available for sale, and (3) the sales for the period.**

Here is how it works. The sales for the period are deducted from the retail value of the goods available for sale. The result is an estimate of the ending inventory at retail (selling prices). The ratio of cost to retail for all goods is calculated by dividing the total goods available for sale at cost by the total goods available for sale at retail. The ending inventory valued at selling prices is then converted to the ending inventory at cost by applying the cost-to-retail ratio. Use of the retail inventory method is very common. For example, **Hart Stores Inc.** and **Reitmans (Canada) Limited** both report using the retail inventory method in determining inventory cost. Hart Stores' note disclosure of its policy for the year ended January 31, 2009, is shown in Illustration 8A-1.

Real-World Emphasis

Illustration 8A-1

Example of Retail Inventory Method Note—Hart Stores Inc.

Inventory

Inventory is valued at the lower of cost and net realizable value. Cost is net of cash consideration received from vendors and includes the cost of making goods available for sale. Costs such as storage costs, administrative overhead and selling costs are specifically excluded from the cost of inventory. Cost is determined using the retail method.

An example of how the retail inventory method works is shown in Illustration 8A-2.

	Cost	Retail
Beginning inventory	$14,000	$ 20,000
Purchases	63,000	90,000
Goods available for sale	$77,000	110,000
Deduct: Sales		85,000
Ending inventory, at retail		$ 25,000
Ratio of cost to retail ($77,000 ÷ $110,000)		70%
Ending inventory at cost (70% of $25,000)		$ 17,500

The retail method is approved by various retail associations and the accounting profession under both private entity GAAP and IFRS, and is allowed by the Canada Revenue Agency. **One advantage of the retail inventory method is that the inventory balance can be approximated without a physical count.** This makes the method particularly useful when preparing interim reports. Insurance adjusters use this approach to estimate losses from fire, flood, or other types of casualty.

This method also **acts as a control device** because any deviations from a physical count at year end have to be explained. In addition, the retail method **speeds up the physical inventory count at year end.** The crew taking the inventory only needs to record the retail price of each item, which is often done using a scanner. There is no need to determine each item's·invoice cost, thus saving time and expense.

Retail Method Terminology

The amounts shown in the Retail column of Illustration 8A-2 represent the original retail or selling prices (cost plus an original markup or mark-on), assuming no price changes.

Sales prices, however, are often marked up or down from the original sales price. For retailers, the term markup means an increase in the price above the original sales price. Markup cancellations are decreases in merchandise prices that had been marked up above the original retail price. Markup cancellations cannot be greater than markups. Net markups refer to markups less markup cancellations.

Markdowns are reductions in price below the original selling price. They are a common phenomenon and occur because of a decline in general price levels, special sales, soiled or damaged goods, overstocking, and competition. Markdown cancellations occur when the markdowns are later offset by increases in the prices of goods that had been marked down, such as after a one-day sale. A markdown cancellation cannot exceed the original markdown. Markdowns less markdown cancellations are known as net markdowns.

To illustrate these different concepts, assume that Designer Clothing Store recently purchased 100 dress shirts from a supplier. The cost for these shirts was $1,500, or $15 a shirt. Designer Clothing established the selling price on these shirts at $30 each. The manager noted that the shirts were selling quickly, so she added $5 to the price of each shirt. This markup made the price too high for customers and sales lagged. The manager then responded by reducing the price to $32. To this point, there has been a **markup of $5** and a **markup cancellation of $3** on the original selling price of a shirt. When the major marketing season ended, the manager set the price of the remaining shirts at $23. This price change constitutes a **markup cancellation of $2** and a **$7 markdown**. If the shirts are later priced at $24, a **markdown cancellation of $1** occurs.

Retail Inventory Method with Markups and Markdowns— Conventional Method

To determine the ending inventory figures, a decision must be made on the treatment of markups, markup cancellations, markdowns, and markdown cancellations **when calculating the ratio of cost to retail**.

To illustrate the different possibilities, consider the data for In-Fashion Stores Inc., shown in Illustration 8A-3. In-Fashion's ending inventory at cost can be calculated under two different cost-to-retail ratios.

Ratio A: Reflects a cost percentage that includes net markups but excludes net markdowns.

Ratio B: Reflects a cost ratio that incorporates both net markups and net markdowns.

Illustration 8A-3

Retail Inventory Method with Markups and Markdowns: In-Fashion Stores Inc.

Information in Records

	Cost	Retail
Beginning inventory	$ 500	$ 1,000
Purchases (net)	20,000	35,000
Markups		3,000
Markup cancellations		1,000
Markdowns		2,500
Markdown cancellations		2,000
Sales (net)		25,000

Retail Inventory Method

	Cost		Retail
Beginning inventory	$ 500		$ 1,000
Purchases (net)	20,000		35,000
Merchandise available for sale	20,500		36,000
Add:			
Markups		$ 3,000	
Less: Markup cancellations		(1,000)	
Net markups			2,000
	20,500		38,000
Cost-to-retail ratio $\dfrac{\$20,500}{\$38,000} = 53.9\%$			(A)
Deduct:			
Markdowns		2,500	
Less: Markdown cancellations		(2,000)	
Net markdowns			500
	$20,500		37,500
Cost-to-retail ratio $\dfrac{\$20,500}{\$37,500} = 54.7\%$			(B)
Deduct: Sales (net)			25,000
Ending inventory at retail			$12,500

The calculations to determine the cost of ending inventory for In-Fashion Stores are therefore:

Ending inventory at retail × Cost ratio = Ending inventory, at cost
Under **(A):** $12,500 × 53.9% = $6,737.50
Under **(B):** $12,500 × 54.7% = $6,837.50

Which percentage should be used to calculate ending inventory? The answer depends on whether you are trying to determine inventory "cost" or a more conservative lower of cost and market figure.

The conventional retail inventory method **uses the cost-to-retail ratio that includes net markups but excludes net markdowns,** as shown in the calculation of **ratio A.** It is designed to approximate **the lower of average cost and market,** with market being defined as **net realizable value less a normal profit margin.** To understand why net markups but not net markdowns are included in the cost-to-retail ratio, we must understand how a retail outlet operates. When a company has a net markup on an item, this normally indicates that the item's market value has increased. On the other hand, if the item has a net markdown, this means that the item's utility has declined. Therefore, to approximate the lower of cost and market, net markdowns are considered a current loss and are not included in calculating the cost-to-retail ratio. **This makes the denominator a larger number and the ratio a lower percentage.** With a lower cost-to-retail ratio, the result approximates a lower of cost and market amount.

To make this clearer, assume two different items were purchased for $5 each, and the original sales price was established at $10 each. One item was then marked down to a selling price of $2. Assuming no sales for the period, if markdowns are included in the cost-to-retail ratio (**ratio B** above), the ending inventory is calculated as shown in Illustration 8A-4.

Markdowns Included in Cost-to-Retail Ratio

	Cost	Retail
Purchases	$10.00	$20.00
Deduct: Markdowns		8.00
Ending inventory, at retail		$12.00
Cost-to-retail ratio $\dfrac{\$10.00}{\$12.00} = 83.3\%$		
Ending inventory at average cost ($12.00 × .833) =		$10.00

Illustration 8A-4

Retail Inventory Method Including Markdowns— Cost Method

This approach results in ending inventory at the average cost of the two items on hand without considering the loss on the one item.

If markdowns are excluded from the ratio (**ratio A** above), the result is ending inventory at the lower of average cost and market. The calculation is shown in Illustration 8A-5.

Markdowns Not Included in Cost-to-Retail Ratio

	Cost	Retail
Purchases	$10.00	$20.00
Cost-to-retail ratio $\dfrac{\$10.00}{\$20.00} = 50\%$		
Deduct: Markdowns		8.00
Ending inventory, at retail		$12.00
Ending inventory at lower of average cost and market ($12 × .50) =		$6.00

Illustration 8A-5

Retail Inventory Method Excluding Markdowns— Conventional Method (LCM)

The $6 inventory valuation includes two inventory items: one inventoried at $5 (its cost) and the other at $1 (its NRV less a normal profit margin of 50%). For the item with the market decline, the price was reduced from $10 to $2 and the cost was reduced from $5 to $1. Therefore, to approximate the lower of average cost and market, the cost-to-retail ratio is established by dividing the cost of goods available by the sum of the original retail price of these goods plus the net markups; the **net markdowns are excluded** from the ratio.

Many possible cost-to-retail ratios could be calculated. The schedule below summarizes how including or excluding various items in the cost-to-retail ratio relates to specific inventory valuation methods. Note that net purchases are always included in the ratio:

Beginning Inventory	Net Markups	Net Markdowns	Inventory Cost Formula and Valuation Method Approximated
Include	Include	Include	Average cost
Include	Include	Exclude	Lower of average cost and market (conventional method)
Exclude	Include	Include	FIFO cost
Exclude	Include	Exclude	Lower of FIFO cost and market

Using the FIFO cost formula, the estimated ending inventory (and its cost) will, by definition, come from the purchases of the current period. **Therefore, the opening inventory, at cost and retail, is excluded in determining the cost ratio.** The retail price of the opening inventory is then added to determine the total selling price of goods available for the period.

Handbook Section 3031 and IAS 2 are clear that, for purposes of determining inventory **cost**, markdowns below the original sales price are included in calculating the ratio. This means that a separate adjustment has to be made to get a **lower of cost and NRV** valuation. Why not just exclude the markdowns from the cost-to-retail ratio? As mentioned above, this results in a lower of cost and market value where market represents NRV less a normal profit margin. This concept of market is not permitted by either private entity GAAP or IFRS. If there is a significant difference between the results of applying the two ratios, an adjustment (to the lower result) representing the estimated normal profit on goods marked down below cost would be made.

Special Items

The retail inventory method becomes more complicated when such items as freight-in, purchase returns and allowances, and purchase discounts are involved. In the retail method, we treat such items as follows:

- **Freight costs** are treated as a part of the purchase cost.

- **Purchase returns** are ordinarily considered a reduction of the cost price and retail price.

- **Purchase allowances** are considered a reduction of the purchase cost column only unless normal selling prices are adjusted because of the allowance.

- **Purchase discounts** are usually considered a reduction of the purchase cost only.

In short, the treatment for the items affecting the cost column of the retail inventory approach follows the calculation of cost of goods available for sale.

Note also that it is considered proper to treat **sales returns and allowances** as adjustments to gross sales; **sales discounts to customers**, however, are not recognized when sales are recorded gross. If the Sales Discount account were adjusted in such a situation, the ending inventory figure at retail would be overvalued.

In addition, a number of special items require careful analysis.

- **Transfers-in** from another department are reported in the same way as purchases from an outside enterprise.

- **Normal shortages** (breakage, damage, theft, shrinkage) are deducted in the retail column because these goods are no longer available for sale. These costs are reflected in the selling price because a certain amount of shortage is considered normal in a retail enterprise. As a result, this amount is not considered in calculating the cost-to-retail percentage. Rather, it is shown as a deduction, similar to sales, to arrive at ending inventory at retail.

- **Abnormal shortages** are deducted from both the cost and retail columns before calculating the cost-to-retail ratio and are reported as a special inventory amount or as a loss. To do otherwise distorts the cost-to-retail ratio and overstates ending inventory.

- **Employee discounts** (given to employees to encourage loyalty, better performance, and so on) are deducted from the retail column in the same way as sales. These discounts should not be considered in the cost-to-retail percentage because they do not reflect an overall change in the selling price.

Illustration 8A-6 shows some of these concepts in more detail, using the conventional retail inventory method to determine the ending inventory at the lower of average cost and market.

	Cost	Retail
Beginning inventory	$ 1,000	$ 1,800
Purchases	30,000	60,000
Freight-in	600	–0–
Purchase returns	(1,500)	(3,000)
Totals	30,100	58,800
Net markups		9,000
Abnormal shrinkage	(1,200)	(2,000)
Totals	$28,900	65,800
Deduct:		
Net markdowns		1,400
Sales	$36,000	
Sales returns	(900)	35,100
Employee discounts		800
Normal shrinkage		1,300
Ending inventory at retail		$27,200

Cost-to-retail ratio $\dfrac{\$28,900}{\$65,800} = 43.9\%$

Ending inventory, lower of average cost and market (43.9% × $27,200) = **$11,940.80**

Illustration 8A-6

Conventional Retail Inventory Method—Special Items Included

Evaluation of Retail Inventory Method

The retail inventory method of calculating inventory is used for these reasons:

1. To permit the calculation of net income without a physical count of inventory

2. As a control measure in determining inventory shortages

3. To control quantities of merchandise on hand

4. As a source of information for insurance and tax purposes

One characteristic of the retail inventory method is that it **has an averaging effect for varying rates of gross profit**. When it is used in a business where rates of gross profit vary among departments, the method should be refined by calculating inventory separately by departments or by classes of merchandise with similar rates of gross profit. This method's reliability rests on the assumption that the mix of inventory items is similar to the mix in the total goods available for sale.

Glossary

KEY TERMS

conventional retail
   inventory method, 495
cost-to-retail ratio, 492
markdown
   cancellations, 493
markdowns, 493
markup, 493
markup cancellations, 493
net markdowns, 493
net markups, 493
retail inventory
   method, 492

Summary of Learning Objective for Appendix 8A

15 Apply the retail method of estimating inventory.

The retail inventory method is based on converting the retail price of ending inventory by a cost-to-retail percentage (derived from information in the accounting and supplementary records). To use this method, records must be kept of the costs and retail prices for beginning inventory, net purchases, and abnormal spoilage, as well as the retail amount of net markups, net markdowns, and net sales. Which items go into the numerator and denominator of the cost-to-retail ratio depends on the type of inventory valuation estimate that is wanted.

Appendix **8**B

Accounting Guidance for Specific Inventory

Illustration 8B-1 summarizes the primary sources of GAAP for most types of inventory.

16 Objective
Identify other primary sources of GAAP for inventory.

Illustration 8B-1

Inventory—Primary Sources of GAAP

Form of Inventory	Private Entity GAAP Source of Guidance	IFRS Source of Guidance
Most inventories apply a lower of cost and net realizable value model	*CICA Handbook*, Part II, Section 3031 *Inventories*	IAS 2 *Inventories*
Excluded from Section 3031 and IAS 2 but Covered by Other Primary Sources of GAAP		
Financial instruments	*CICA Handbook*, Part II, Section 3856 *Financial Instruments*	IAS 32 *Financial Instruments: Presentation*, and IAS 39 *Financial Instruments: Recognition and Measurement*
Construction contract work in process		IAS 11 *Construction Contracts*
All contracts accounted for using the percentage-of-completion method, including construction work in process	*CICA Handbook*, Part II, Section 3400 *Revenue*	
Biological assets related to agricultural activity, and agricultural product at the point of harvest		IAS 41 *Agriculture*
Industry-Specific Exclusions, from Only the Measurement Provisions of Section 3031 and IAS 2 (All disclosure requirements still apply.)		
Inventory held by producers of agricultural and forest products, agricultural produce after harvest, and mineral and mineral products	Excluded from the measurement provisions of Section 3031 if measured at net realizable value in accordance with established industry practice; otherwise, apply Section 3031	Excluded from the measurement provisions of IAS 2 if measured at net realizable value in accordance with established industry practice; otherwise, apply IAS 2
Inventory held by commodity broker-traders	Excluded from the measurement provisions of Section 3031 if measured at fair value less costs to sell; otherwise apply Section 3031	Excluded from the measurement provisions of IAS 2 if measured at fair value less costs to sell; otherwise apply IAS 2
Biological assets and harvested agricultural produce	Excluded from the measurement provisions of Section 3031. Not covered by any specific primary source of GAAP.	

Note: All assignment material with an asterisk (*) relates to the appendices to the chapter.

Brief Exercises

(LO 1, 14) BE8-1 Indicate whether the following would be considered inventory for a public company like **Honda Motor Co., Ltd.** If so, indicate the inventory category to which that item would belong.

(a) Engines purchased to make the Honda Civic

(b) Nuts and bolts purchased to attach the engine to the car body

(c) Spare parts purchased for the manufacturing equipment

(d) Standby equipment in case a machine breaks down

(e) Wages paid to assembly-line employees

(f) Rent for manufacturing facility

(g) Wages paid to supervisor

(h) Honda Civic ready to be shipped to the dealer

(i) Manufacturing plant

How would your responses change if the manufacturer followed private entity GAAP?

(LO 1) BE8-2 The following assets are included in the December 31 trial balance of Nickolas Corp.:

Cash	$ 290,000	Work in process	$100,000
Equipment (net)	1,300,000	Receivables (net)	400,000
Prepaid insurance	41,000	Patents	210,000
Raw materials	435,000	Finished goods	250,000

Prepare the current assets section of the December 31 balance sheet.

(LO 3, 4, 5) BE8-3 Fox Ltd. had beginning inventory of 50 units that cost $55 each. During September, the company purchased 150 units at $55 each, returned 6 units for credit, and sold 125 units at $75 each.

(a) Journalize the September transactions assuming that Fox Ltd. uses a perpetual inventory system.

(b) Journalize the September transactions assuming that Fox Ltd. uses a periodic inventory system.

(c) Assume that Fox uses a periodic system and prepares financial statements at the end of each month. An inventory count determines that there are 69 units of inventory remaining at September 30. Prepare the necessary adjusting entry at September 30.

(LO 4, 14) BE8-4 Alexis Corp. purchases inventory costing $4,000 on July 11 on terms 3/10, n/30, and pays the invoice in full on July 15.

(a) Prepare the required entries to record the two transactions assuming Alexis uses (1) the gross method of recording purchases, and (2) the net method of recording purchases. Assume the periodic method is used.

(b) Journalize the two transactions under (1) the gross method and (2) the net method, assuming the invoice was paid on July 31 instead of July 15.

(c) Assuming that Alexis is a private company reporting under private entity GAAP, can interest costs incurred to finance inventory be added to the cost of the inventory?

(d) Assuming that Alexis is a public company following IFRS, under what circumstances can interest costs incurred to finance inventory be added to the cost of the inventory?

(LO 3) BE8-5 Mayhelm Ltd. took a physical inventory on December 31 and determined that goods costing $250,000 were on hand. This amount included $50,000 of goods held on consignment for Delhi Corporation. Not included in the physical count were $25,000 of goods purchased from Taylor Corporation, f.o.b. shipping point; and $17,000 of goods sold to Mount Pilot Ltd. for $35,000, f.o.b. destination. Both the Taylor purchase and the Mount Pilot sale were in transit at year end. What amount should Mayhelm report as its December 31 inventory?

BE8-6   Buyers Ltd. purchases units of wood frames that have manufacturer's rebates from Traders Inc. The rebate   **(LO 4, 6)** requires Buyers to purchase a minimum number of units in a calendar year. The initial unit cost of each wood frame is $2.50 before any rebate. If more than 3,500 units are purchased, the rebate is $0.25 per unit for all units purchased beyond the base amount of 3,500 units. Buyers Ltd. has a June 30 fiscal year end. By June 30, 2010, Buyers had purchased 3,000 wood frames for the six-month period from January 1, 2010, to June 30, 2010. Buyers estimates that an additional 3,000 wood frames will be purchased from July 1, 2010, to December 31, 2010. Buyers' management is very confident that this estimate will be confirmed by future purchases from Traders.

(a) Explain the conceptual principles involved in determining if an accrual should be made for the volume rebate from Traders. Under what circumstances would an accrual not be permissible?

(b) Calculate the amount of any rebate that Buyers should accrue at June 30, 2010, assuming the rebate cannot be cancelled by Traders.

(c) Calculate the unit cost that Buyers should use in the costing of wood frames using the perpetual inventory system. (Round to four decimal places.)

BE8-7   George Enterprises Ltd. reported cost of goods sold for 2010 of $2.4 million and retained earnings of $4.2 mil-   **(LO 10)** lion at December 31, 2010. George later discovered that its ending inventories at December 31, 2009 and 2010 were overstated by $155,000 and $45,000, respectively. Determine the correct amounts for 2010 cost of goods sold and December 31, 2010, retained earnings.

BE8-8   Wholesale Plus buys 1,000 computer game CDs from a distributor that is discontinuing those games. The pur-   **(LO 4)** chase price for the lot is $7,500. Wholesale Plus will group the CDs into three price categories for resale, as follows:

Group	No. of CDs	Price per CD
1	100	$ 5
2	800	10
3	100	15

Determine the cost per CD for each group, using the relative sales value method.

BE8-9   Cortez Corp. uses a periodic inventory system. On June 24, the company sold 600 units. The following addi-   **(LO 6)** tional information is available:

	Units	Unit Cost	Total Cost
June 1 inventory	200	$12	$ 2,400
June 15 purchase	400	14	5,600
June 23 purchase	400	15	6,000
	1,000		$14,000

(a) Calculate the June 30 inventory and the June cost of goods sold using the weighted average cost formula.

(b) Calculate the June 30 inventory and the June cost of goods sold using the FIFO formula.

(c) Assume that 200 units sold on June 24 had a unit cost of $12, 300 had a unit cost of $14, and the remaining 100 units had a unit cost of $15. Calculate the June 30 inventory and the June cost of goods sold using the specific identification method.

BE8-10   Sanchez Corporation uses a perpetual inventory system. On November 19, the company sold 600 units. The   **(LO 6)** following additional information is available:

	Units	Unit Cost	Total Cost
Nov. 1 inventory	250	$12	$ 3,000
Nov. 15 purchase	400	14	5,600
Nov. 23 purchase	350	15	5,250
	1,000		$13,850

Calculate the November 30 inventory and the November cost of goods sold using

(a) the moving average cost formula, and

(b) the FIFO cost formula.

(LO 7, 14)   **BE8-11**   Jenfly Corporation has the following four items in its ending inventory:

Item	Cost	Estimated Selling Price	Estimated Disposal Costs
Jokers	$1,820	$2,100	$100
Kings	5,000	4,900	100
Queens	4,290	4,625	200
Jacks	3,200	4,210	100

(a) Assume that Jenfly is a public company using IFRS. For each of the four items, determine the value of ending inventory using the total lower of cost and net realizable value model.

(b) Would there be any difference in accounting if Jenfly were a private entity using private entity GAAP?

(LO 7)   **BE8-12**   Sahara Enterprises Ltd.'s records reported an inventory cost of $55,600 and a net realizable value of $54,000 at December 31, 2009. At December 31, 2010, the records indicated a cost of $68,700 and a net realizable value of $61,625.

(a) Assuming that Sahara Enterprises uses a perpetual inventory system, prepare the necessary December 31, 2010, entry under (1) the direct method and (2) the indirect method.

(b) Assume that at December 31, 2011, the records indicate inventory with a cost of $60,000 and a net realizable value of $60,900. Prepare the necessary December 31, 2011, entry under (1) the direct method and (2) the indirect method. Explain why a "gain" is reported under the indirect method of accounting.

(LO 8, 14)   **BE8-13**   Beaver Corp., a private entity using private entity GAAP, signed a long-term non-cancellable purchase commitment with a major supplier to purchase raw materials in 2011 at a cost of $2 million. At December 31, 2010, the raw materials to be purchased have a market price of $1,965,000.

(a) Prepare any necessary December 31, 2010, entry.

(b) In 2011, Beaver paid $2 million to obtain the raw materials, which were worth $1,915,000. Prepare the entry to record the purchase.

(c) Explain how the accounting treatment under (a) compares with the accounting treatment for public companies under IFRS.

(LO 9)   **BE8-14**

(a) Briefly explain the criteria that have to be met for inventory to be recorded above cost.

(b) Briefly explain the accounting for the following inventory items under private entity GAAP:
   1. Sheep
   2. Wool
   3. Carpet

(c) Briefly explain the accounting for the items in (b) under IFRS.

(LO 11)   **BE8-15**   Big Fish Corporation's April 30 inventory was destroyed by flood. January 1 inventory was $310,000, and purchases for January through April totalled $780,000. Sales for the same period were $1.1 million. Big Fish's normal gross profit percentage is 31%. Using the gross profit method, estimate Big Fish's April 30 inventory that was destroyed by flood.

(LO 13)   **BE8-16**   **Costco Wholesale Corporation** reported inventory of $5,039.4 million at the end of its 2008 fiscal year; $4,879.4 million at the end of its 2007 fiscal year; cost of goods sold of $63,502.7 million for the fiscal year 2008; and net sales of $70,977.5 million for fiscal year 2008. Calculate Costco's inventory turnover and the average days to sell inventory for the fiscal year 2008.

(LO 15)   ***BE8-17**   Hookfield Inc. had beginning inventory of $22,000 at cost and $30,000 at retail. Net purchases were $157,500 at cost and $215,000 at retail. Net markups were $10,000; net markdowns were $7,000; and sales were $184,500. Calculate the ending inventory at cost using the conventional retail method. Round the cost-to-retail ratio to two decimal places.

Exercises

E8-1 **(Periodic versus Perpetual Entries)** Jyoti Corporation sells one product, with information for July as follows: **(LO 5)**

July	1	Inventory	100 units at $15 each
	4	Sale	80 units at $18 each
	11	Purchase	150 units at $16.50 each
	13	Sale	120 units at $18.75 each
	20	Purchase	160 units at $17 each
	27	Sale	100 units at $20 each

Jyoti uses the FIFO cost formula. All purchases and sales are on account.

Instructions

(a) Assume Jyoti uses a periodic system. Prepare all necessary journal entries, including the end-of-month adjusting entry to record cost of goods sold. A physical count indicates that the ending inventory for July is 110 units.

(b) Calculate gross profit using the periodic system.

(c) Assume Jyoti uses the periodic system, and a count on July 31 reports only 102 units in ending inventory. How would your entries in (a) change, if at all? Explain briefly.

(d) Assume Jyoti uses a perpetual system. Prepare all July journal entries.

(e) Calculate gross profit using the perpetual system.

(f) Assume Jyoti uses the perpetual system, and a count on July 31 reports only 102 units in ending inventory. How would your entries in (d) change, if at all? Explain briefly.

E8-2 **(Determining Merchandise Amounts—Periodic)** Two or more items are omitted in each of the following tab-   **(LO 5)**
ulations of income statement data. Fill in the amounts that are missing.

	2010	2011	2012
Sales	$290,000	$_____	$410,000
Sales returns	6,000	13,000	_____
Net sales	_____	347,000	_____
Beginning inventory	20,000	32,000	_____
Ending inventory	_____	_____	_____
Purchases	_____	260,000	298,000
Purchase returns and allowances	5,000	8,000	10,000
Transportation-in	8,000	9,000	12,000
Cost of goods sold	238,000	_____	303,000
Gross profit on sales	46,000	91,000	97,000

E8-3 **(Purchases Recorded—Gross Method and Net Method)** Transactions follow for Jennings Limited: **(LO 4, 5)**

March 10	Purchased goods billed at $25,000, terms 3/10, n/60.
11	Purchased goods billed at $26,575, terms 1/15, n/30.
19	Paid invoice of March 10.
24	Purchased goods billed at $11,500, terms 3/10, n/30.

Instructions

(a) Prepare general journal entries for the transactions above, assuming that purchases are to be recorded at net amounts after cash discounts and that discounts lost are to be treated as a financial expense. Assume a periodic inventory system.

(b) Assuming there are no purchase or payment transactions other than the ones mentioned above, prepare the adjusting entry required on March 31 if financial statements are to be prepared as at that date.

(c) Prepare general journal entries for the transactions above, assuming that purchases are to be recorded using the gross method. Assume a periodic inventory system.

(d) Indicate whether there are entries required at March 31 in addition to those in (c) if financial statements are to be prepared. Explain.

(e) Which method would provide the general manager of Jennings with better information for managing the business?

(LO 3, 4, 14) **E8-4** **(Inventoriable Costs)** In an annual audit of Majestic Company Limited, you find that a physical inventory count on December 31, 2010, showed merchandise of $441,000. You also discover the following items were excluded from the $441,000:

1. Merchandise of $61,000 is held by Majestic on consignment from BonBon Corporation.

2. Merchandise costing $33,000 was shipped by Majestic f.o.b destination to XYZ Ltd. on December 31, 2010. This merchandise was accepted by XYZ on January 6, 2011.

3. Merchandise costing $46,000 was shipped f.o.b. shipping point to ABC Company on December 29, 2010. This merchandise was received by ABC on January 10, 2011.

4. Merchandise costing $73,000 was shipped f.o.b. destination from Wholesaler Inc. to Majestic on December 30, 2010. Majestic received the items on January 8, 2011.

5. Merchandise costing $51,000 was shipped by Distributor Ltd. f.o.b. shipping point on December 30, 2010, and received at Majestic's office on January 2, 2011.

6. Majestic had excess inventory and incurred additional $1,500 in storage costs due to delayed shipment in transaction (3) above.

7. Majestic incurred $2,000 for interest expense on inventory it purchased through delayed payment plans in fiscal 2010.

Instructions

(a) Based on the information provided above, calculate the amount of inventory that should appear on Majestic's December 31, 2010, balance sheet.

(b) Under what circumstances can a private company reporting under private entity GAAP capitalize interest costs incurred to finance inventory?

(c) Under what circumstances can a public company reporting under IFRS capitalize interest costs incurred to finance inventory?

(LO 3) **E8-5** **(Inventoriable Costs—Perpetual)** The Davis Machine Corporation maintains a general ledger account for each class of inventory, debiting the individual accounts for increases during the period and crediting them for decreases. The transactions that follow are for the Raw Materials inventory account, which is debited for materials purchased and credited for materials requisitioned for use:

1. An invoice for $8,100, terms f.o.b. destination, was received and entered on January 2, 2011. The receiving report shows that the materials were received on December 28, 2010.

2. Materials costing $7,300 were returned to the supplier on December 29, 2010, on f.o.b. shipping point terms. The returns were entered into Davis's general ledger on December 28 even though the returned items did not arrive at the vendor's office until January 6, 2011.

3. Materials costing $28,000, shipped f.o.b. destination, were not entered by December 31, 2010, "because they were in a railroad car on the company's siding on that date and had not been unloaded."

4. An invoice for $7,500, terms f.o.b. shipping point, was received and entered on December 30, 2010. The receiving report shows that the materials were received on January 4, 2011, and the bill of lading shows that they were shipped on January 2, 2011.

5. Materials costing $19,800 were received on December 30, 2010. No entry was made for them as of that date, because they were ordered with a specified delivery date of no earlier than January 10, 2011.

6. Materials costing $20,000 were received on December 29, 2010. The supplier's warehouse was full and the supplier asked Davis to hold these items on its behalf and has also insured these items for the period that Davis will be holding them. The purchase terms indicate that the supplier will re-purchase these items back from Davis Machine in early January 2011.

7. Materials costing $5,500 were received on December 20, 2010, that are on consignment from Able Company.

Ethics

Instructions

(a) Prepare any correcting journal entries that are required at December 31, 2010, assuming that the books have not been closed. Also indicate which entries must be reversed after closing so that the next period's accounts will be correct.

(b) Are there any ethical concerns raised by these transactions? How should Davis deal with this situation?

E8-6 **(Inventoriable Costs—Error Adjustments)** Craig Corporation asks you to review its December 31, 2010, **(LO 3, 10)** inventory values and prepare the necessary adjustments to the books. The following information is given to you:

1. Craig uses the periodic method of recording inventory. A physical count reveals $234,890 of inventory on hand at December 31, 2010, although the books have not yet been adjusted to reflect the ending inventory.

2. Not included in the physical count of inventory is $10,420 of merchandise purchased on December 15 from Browser. This merchandise was shipped f.o.b. shipping point on December 29 and arrived in January. The invoice arrived and was recorded on December 31.

3. Included in inventory is merchandise sold to Champy on December 30, f.o.b. destination. This merchandise was shipped after it was counted. The invoice was prepared and recorded as a sale on account for $12,800 on December 31. The merchandise cost $7,350, and Champy received it on January 3.

4. Included in inventory was merchandise received from Dudley on December 31 with an invoice price of $15,630. The merchandise was shipped f.o.b. destination. The invoice, which has not yet arrived, has not been recorded.

5. Not included in inventory is $8,540 of merchandise purchased from Glowser Industries. This merchandise was received on December 31 after the inventory had been counted. The invoice was received and recorded on December 30.

6. Included in inventory was $10,438 of inventory held by Craig on consignment from Jackel Industries.

7. Included in inventory is merchandise sold to Kemp, f.o.b. shipping point. This merchandise was shipped after it was counted on December 31. The invoice was prepared and recorded as a sale for $18,900 on December 31. The cost of this merchandise was $11,520, and Kemp received the merchandise on January 5.

8. Excluded from inventory was a carton labelled "Please accept for credit." This carton contains merchandise costing $1,500, which had been sold to a customer for $2,600. No entry had been made to the books to record the return, but none of the returned merchandise seemed damaged.

9. Craig has sold $12,500 of inventory to Simply Corp. on December 15, 2010. These items were shipped f.o.b. shipping point. The terms of sale indicate that Simply Corp. will be permitted to return an unlimited amount until May 15, 2011. Craig has never provided unlimited returns in the past and is not able to estimate the amount of any potential returns that Simply may make.

Instructions

(a) Determine the proper inventory balance for Craig Corporation at December 31, 2010.

(b) Prepare any adjusting correcting entries necessary at December 31, 2010. Assume the books have not been closed.

E8-7 **(Inventoriable Costs)** The following is a list of items that may or may not be reported as inventory in Dakarai **(LO 3, 4, 14)** Corp.'s December 31 balance sheet:

1. Goods out on consignment at another company's store

2. Goods sold on an instalment basis

3. Goods purchased f.o.b. shipping point that are in transit at December 31

4. Goods purchased f.o.b. destination that are in transit at December 31

5. Goods sold to another company, with Dakarai having signed an agreement to repurchase the goods at a set price that covers all costs related to the inventory

6. Goods sold where large returns are predictable

7. Goods sold f.o.b. shipping point that are in transit at December 31

8. Freight charges on goods purchased

9. Freight charges on goods sold

10. Factory labour costs incurred on goods that are still unsold

11. Interest costs incurred for inventories that are routinely manufactured in large quantities

12. Costs incurred to advertise goods held for resale

13. Materials on hand and not yet placed into production by a manufacturing firm

14. Office supplies

15. Raw materials on which a manufacturing firm has started production, but which are not completely processed

16. Factory supplies

17. Goods held on consignment from another company

18. Goods held on consignment by another company

19. Costs identified with units completed by a manufacturing firm, but not yet sold

20. Goods sold f.o.b. destination that are in transit at December 31

21. Temporary investments in shares and bonds that will be resold in the near future

22. Costs of uncleared land to be developed by a property development company

23. Cost of normal waste or spoilage of raw materials during production

24. Cost of waste and spoilage experienced above normal levels; i.e., abnormal levels of waste of raw materials

25. Costs to store excess materials inventory for a manufacturer

26. Costs to store wine as it ages for a wine producer

27. Decommissioning costs incurred as a part of the extraction of minerals

Instructions

(a) Assuming that private entity GAAP is followed, indicate which of these items would typically be reported as inventory in the financial statements. If an item should not be reported as inventory, indicate how it should be reported in the financial statements.

(b) How would your response to (a) change under IFRS?

(LO 10)   **E8-8**   **(Inventory Errors—Periodic)** Prudence Limited makes the following errors during the current year. Each error is an independent case.

Ending inventory is overstated by $1,020, but purchases are recorded correctly.

Both ending inventory and a purchase on account are understated by the same amount. (Assume this purchase of $1,500 was recorded in the following year.)

Ending inventory is correct, but a purchase on account was not recorded. (Assume this purchase of $850 was recorded in the following year.)

Instructions

Indicate the effect of each error on working capital, current ratio (assume that the current ratio is greater than 1), retained earnings, and net income for the current year and the following year.

(LO 2, 10)   **E8-9**   **(Inventory Errors)** Walker Limited has a calendar-year accounting period. The following errors were discovered in 2011:

1. The December 31, 2009, merchandise inventory had been understated by $51,000.

2. Merchandise purchased on account in 2010 was recorded on the books for the first time in February 2011, when the original invoice for the correct amount of $2,400 arrived. The merchandise had arrived on December 28, 2010, and was included in the December 31, 2010, merchandise inventory. The invoice arrived late because of a mix-up by the wholesaler.

3. Inventory, valued at $1,000, held on consignment by Walker was included in the December 31, 2010, count.

Instructions

(a) Calculate the effect of each error on the 2010 net income.

(b) Calculate the effect, if any, that each error had on the related December 31, 2010, balance sheet items.

(LO 10)   **E8-10**   **(Inventory Errors)** The net income per books of Creative Harmony Limited was determined without any knowledge of the following errors. The 2005 year was Creative Harmony's first year in business. No dividends have been declared or paid.

Year	Net Income per Books	Error in Ending Inventory	
2005	$50,000	Overstated	$ 5,000
2006	52,000	Overstated	9,000
2007	54,000	Understated	11,000
2008	56,000	No error	
2009	58,000	Understated	2,000
2010	60,000	Overstated	10,000

Instructions

(a) Prepare a work sheet to show the adjusted net income figure for each of the six years after taking into account the inventory corrections.

(b) Prepare a schedule that indicates both the original retained earnings balance reported at the end of each year and the corrected amount.

(c) Consider the trends in the increase in income from 2005 to 2010 as originally reported and as revised after the corrections. Would you suspect that the income is being manipulated by adjusting the ending balance in the inventory account?

Ethics

E8-11 **(Lower of Cost and Net Realizable Value—Effect of Error)** Orisis Corporation uses the lower of FIFO cost and net realizable value method on an individual item basis, applying the direct method. The inventory at December 31, 2010, included product AG. Relevant per-unit data for product AG follow: **(LO 7, 10, 13, 14)**

Estimated selling price	$50
Cost	45
Replacement cost	51
Estimated selling expense	19
Normal profit	14

There were 1,000 units of product AG on hand at December 31, 2010. Product AG was incorrectly valued at $35 per unit for reporting purposes. All 1,000 units were sold in 2011.

Instructions

Assume that Orisis follows the reporting under private entity GAAP and answer the following questions:

(a) Was net income for 2010 overstated or understated? By how much (ignore income tax aspects)?

(b) Was net income for 2011 overstated or understated? By how much?

(c) Indicate whether the current ratio, inventory turnover ratio, and debt-to-total assets ratio would be overstated, understated, or not affected for the years ended December 31, 2010, and December 31, 2011. Explain briefly.

(d) Assume that management did not discover the error in inventory until after the end of the fiscal year but before the closing entries were made and the financial statements were released. Should the adjustment be recorded? How would the error be treated if it were discovered after the financial statements were released?

(e) How would your responses above change if Orisis followed the reporting under IFRS?

E8-12 **(Relative Sales Value Method)** In fiscal 2010, Amacon Realty Corporation purchased unimproved land for $55,000. The land was improved and subdivided into building lots at an additional cost of $34,460. These building lots were all the same size but, because of differences in location, were offered for sale at different prices as follows: **(LO 4)**

Group	No. of Lots	Price per Lot
1	9	$3,500
2	15	4,500
3	17	2,400

Operating expenses that were allocated to this project totalled $18,200 for the year. At year end, there were also unsold lots remaining, as follows:

Group 1	5 lots
Group 2	7 lots
Group 3	2 lots

Instructions

Determine the year-end inventory and net income of Amacon Realty Corporation. Ignore income taxes.

(LO 4, 7)   **E8-13   (Cost Allocation and LC&NRV)** During 2010, Pristine Furniture Limited purchased a railway carload of wicker chairs. The manufacturer of the chairs sold them to Pristine for a lump sum of $59,850 because it was discontinuing manufacturing operations and wanted to dispose of its entire stock. Three types of chairs are included in the carload. The three types and the estimated selling price for each are as follows:

Type	No. of Chairs	Estimated Selling Price per Chair
Lounge chairs	400	$95
Armchairs	300	85
Straight chairs	700	55

Pristine estimates that the costs to sell this inventory would amount to $2 per chair. During 2010, Pristine sells 350 lounge chairs, 210 armchairs, and 120 straight chairs, all at the same prices as estimated. At December 31, 2010, the remaining chairs were put on sale: the lounge chairs at 25% off the regular price, the armchairs at 30% off, and the straight chairs at 40% off. All were expected to be sold at these prices.

Instructions

(a) What is the total cost of the chairs remaining in inventory at the end of 2010?

(b) What is the net realizable value of the chairs remaining in inventory?

(c) What is the appropriate inventory value to be reported on the December 31, 2010, balance sheet, assuming the lower of cost and NRV is applied on an individual item basis?

(LO 5, 6)   **E8-14   (FIFO and Weighted Average)** MASS Corporation is a multi-product firm. The following information concerns one of its products, the Hawkeye:

Date	Transaction	Quantity	Price/Cost
Jan. 1	Beginning inventory	1,000	$12
Feb. 4	Purchase	2,000	18
Feb. 20	Sale	2,500	30
Apr. 2	Purchase	3,000	23
Nov. 4	Sale	2,000	33

Instructions

Calculate cost of goods sold, assuming MASS uses:

(a) a periodic inventory system and FIFO cost formula.

(b) a periodic inventory system and weighted average cost formula.

(c) a perpetual inventory system and moving average cost formula.

(LO 5, 6)   **E8-15   (Alternative Inventory Methods)** Soorya Corporation began operations on December 1, 2010. The only inventory transaction in 2010 was the purchase of inventory on December 10, 2010, at a cost of $20 per unit. None of this inventory was sold in 2010. Relevant information for fiscal 2011 is as follows:

Ending inventory units:		
December 31, 2010		100
December 31, 2011, by purchase date		
—Dec. 2, 2011	100	
—July 20, 2011	30	130

During 2011, the following purchases and sales were made:

Purchases		Sales	
Mar. 15	300 units at $24	Apr. 10	200
July 20	300 units at $25	Aug. 20	300
Sept. 4	200 units at $28	Nov. 18	170
Dec. 2	100 units at $30	Dec. 12	200

The company uses the periodic inventory method.

Instructions

Determine ending inventory under (1) specific identification, (2) FIFO, and (3) weighted average cost.

E8-16 **(Calculate FIFO, Weighted Average Cost—Periodic)** The following information is for the inventory of mini **(LO 6)** radios at Cleartone Company Limited for the month of May:

Date	Transaction	Units In	Unit Cost	Total	Units Sold	Unit Price	Total
May 1	Balance	100	$4.10	$ 410			
6	Purchase	800	4.20	3,360			
7	Sale				300	$7.00	$ 2,100
10	Sale				300	7.30	2,190
12	Purchase	400	4.50	1,800			
15	Sale				200	7.40	1,480
18	Purchase	300	4.60	1,380			
22	Sale				400	7.40	2,960
25	Purchase	500	4.58	2,290			
30	Sale				200	7.50	1,500
Totals		2,100		$9,240	1,400		$10,230

Instructions

(a) Assuming that the periodic inventory method is used, calculate the inventory cost at May 31 under each of the following cost flow formulas:

1. FIFO

2. Weighted average (Round the weighted average unit cost to the nearest one-tenth of one cent.)

(b) Which method will yield the higher current ratio or gross profit?

E8-17 **(Calculate FIFO, Moving Average Cost—Perpetual)** Information is presented in E8–16 on the inventory of **(LO 7)** mini radios at Cleartone Company Limited for the month of May.

Instructions

Assuming that the perpetual inventory method is used, calculate the inventory cost at May 31 under each of the following cost flow formulas:

(a) FIFO

(b) Moving average (Round all unit costs to the nearest one-tenth of one cent.)

(c) Indicate where the inventory costs that were calculated in this exercise are different from the ones in E8–16 and explain the possible reasons why.

E8-18 **(Lower of Cost and Net Realizable Value, Periodic Method—Journal Entries)** As a result of its annual **(LO 6, 7)** inventory count, Zinck Corp. determined its ending inventory at cost and at lower of cost and net realizable value at December 31, 2010, and December 31, 2011. This information is as follows:

	Cost	Lower of Cost and NRV
Dec. 31, 2010	$321,000	$283,250
Dec. 31, 2011	385,000	351,250

Instructions

(a) Prepare the journal entries required at December 31, 2010 and 2011, assuming that the inventory is recorded directly at the lower of cost and net realizable value and a periodic inventory system is used. Assume that cost was lower than NRV at December 31, 2009.

(b) Prepare the journal entries required at December 31, 2010 and 2011, assuming that the inventory is recorded at cost and an allowance account is adjusted at each year end under a periodic system.

(c) Which of the two methods above provides the higher net income in each year?

(LO 7)   **E8-19**   **(Lower of Cost and NRV Valuation Account)** The following information is for Sandbox Enterprises Ltd.:

	Jan. 31	Feb. 28	Mar. 31	Apr. 30
Inventory at cost	$25,000	$25,100	$29,000	$23,000
Inventory at the lower of cost and net realizable value	24,500	17,600	22,600	17,300
Purchases for the month		20,000	24,000	26,500
Sales for the month		29,000	35,000	40,000

Instructions

(a) Using the above information, prepare monthly income statements (as far as the data permit) in columnar form for February, March, and April. Show the inventory in the statement at cost; show the gain or loss due to fluctuations in NRV separately. Sandbox uses the indirect or allowance method.

(b) Prepare the journal entry that is needed to establish the valuation account at January 31 and the entries to adjust it at the end of each month after that.

(LO 8, 14)   **E8-20**   **(Purchase Commitments)** At December 31, 2010, Indio Ltd. has outstanding non-cancellable purchase commitments for 45,500 litres of raw material at $3.25 per litre. The material will be used in Indio's manufacturing process, and the company prices its raw materials inventory at cost or NRV, whichever is lower.

Instructions

(a) Explain the accounting treatment for purchase commitments under private entity GAAP and IFRS.

(b) Assuming that the market price as at December 31, 2010, is $3.55 per litre, how would this commitment be treated in the accounts and statements? Explain.

(c) Assuming that the market price as at December 31, 2010, is $2.60 per litre instead of $3.55, how would you treat this commitment in the accounts and statements?

(d) Prepare the entry for January 15, 2011, when the entire shipment is received, assuming that the situation in (c) existed at December 31, 2010, and that the market price in January 2011 is $2.60 per litre. Explain your treatment.

(LO 11)   **E8-21**   **(Gross Profit Method)** Arthur Company Limited uses the gross profit method to estimate inventory for monthly reports. Information follows for the month of May:

Inventory, May 1	$ 360,000
Purchases	700,000
Freight-in	50,000
Sales	1,200,000
Sales returns	70,000
Purchase discounts	12,000

Instructions

(a) Calculate the estimated inventory at May 31, assuming that the gross profit is 25% of sales.

(b) Calculate the estimated inventory at May 31, assuming that the markup on cost is 25%. Round the gross profit percentage to four decimal places.

(LO 11)   **E8-22**   **(Gross Profit Method)** Mellon Corporation's retail store and warehouse closed for the entire weekend while the year-end inventory was counted. When the count was finished, the controller gathered all the count books and information from the clerical staff, completed the ending inventory calculations, and prepared the following partial income statement for the general manager for Monday morning:

Sales		$2,750,000
Beginning inventory	$ 650,000	
Purchases	1,550,000	
Total goods available for sale	2,200,000	
Less ending inventory	650,000	
Cost of goods sold		1,550,000
Gross profit		$1,200,000

The general manager called the controller into her office after quickly reviewing the preliminary statements. "You've made an error in the inventory," she stated. "My pricing all year has been carefully controlled to provide a gross profit of 35%, and I know the sales are correct."

Instructions

(a) How much should the ending inventory have been?

(b) If the controller's ending inventory amount was due to an error, suggest where the error might have occurred.

E8-23 **(Analysis of Inventories)** The financial statements of Forzani Corporation for Fiscal 2007 to Fiscal 2009 are as follows (in thousands): **(LO 13)**

	Fiscal 2009	Fiscal 2008	Fiscal 2007
Inventory	$ 291,497	$ 319,445	$ 302,207
Sales	1,346,758	1,331,009	1,263,955
Gross margin	483,519	478,401	451,592
Net income	29,325	47,451	35,217

Instructions

(a) Calculate Forzani's (1) inventory turnover and (2) average days to sell inventory for each of the two years ending in 2009 and 2008.

(b) Calculate Forzani's gross profit percentage and percentage markup on cost for each fiscal year.

(c) Is the growth in inventory levels over the last year consistent with the increase in sales? Explain your answer.

E8-24 **(Ratios)** Partial information follows for a Canadian manufacturing company: **(LO 13)**

	Year 10	Year 9	Year 8	Year 7
Sales	$401,244	$_____	$344,759	
Cost of goods sold	_____	286,350	263,979	
Gross margin	95,086	87,957	_____	
Ending inventory	34,511	_____	34,750	36,750
Gross profit %	_____	23.5%	_____	
Inventory turnover	_____	8.19 times	_____	
Days sales in inventory	_____	44.57 days	_____	

Instructions

(a) Enter the missing amounts where indicated for Years 8, 9, and 10 in the above schedule.

(b) Comment on the profitability and inventory management trends, and suggest possible reasons for these results.

*E8-25 **(Retail Inventory Method)** The records of Elena's Boutique report the following data for the month of September: **(LO 15)**

Sales	$118,500	Purchases (at cost)	$ 59,500
Sales returns	2,500	Purchases (at sales price)	112,600
Additional markups	10,500	Purchase returns (at cost)	2,500
Markup cancellations	1,500	Purchase returns (at sales price)	3,500
Markdowns	9,300	Beginning inventory (at cost)	32,000
Markdown cancellations	2,800	Beginning inventory (at sales price)	48,500
Freight on purchases	3,600		

Instructions

(a) Estimate the ending inventory using the conventional retail inventory method.

(b) Assuming that a physical count of the inventory determined that the actual ending inventory at retail prices at the end of September was $42,000, estimate the loss due to shrinkage and theft.

(c) Identify four reasons why the estimate of inventory may be different from the actual inventory at cost.

(LO 14) E8-26 (Biological Inventory Assets) Santa's Christmas Tree Farm Ltd. grows pine, fir, and spruce trees. The farm cuts and sells trees during the Christmas season and exports most of the trees to the United States. The remaining trees are sold to local tree lot operators.

It normally takes 12 years for a tree to grow to a suitable size and the average selling price of a tree is $24. The biggest costs to the business are pest control, fertilizer, and pruning trees over the 12-year period. These costs average $12 per tree (assume these are incurred evenly over the 12-year growing cycle).

Instructions

(a) How should this inventory be recorded under private entity GAAP?

(b) How should the costs of pest control, fertilizer, and pruning be recognized under IFRS?

(c) Assume that the fair value of each tree at the end of 2010 is $8 and the opening value was $5. Prepare the journal entries if the costs are *capitalized* each year.

(d) Assume that the fair value of each tree at the end of 2010 is $8 and the opening value was $5. Prepare the journal entries if the costs are *expensed* each year.

(LO 16) *E8-27 (Primary Sources of GAAP) There are a few primary sources of GAAP for inventory under both private entity GAAP and IFRS. Complete the table below.

Type of Inventory	Primary Guidance under Private Entity GAAP	Primary Guidance under IFRS
Equipment manufactured		
Financial derivatives held by a financial institution		
Biological assets at the point of harvest		
Harvested agricultural produce		

Problems

P8-1   The following independent situations relate to inventory accounting:

1. HOHO Co. purchased goods with a list price of $175,000, having trade discounts of 20% and 10%, and no cash discounts.

2. Francis Company's inventory of $1.1 million at December 31, 2010, was based on a physical count of goods priced at cost and before any year-end adjustments relating to the following items:

   (a) Goods shipped f.o.b. shipping point on December 24, 2010, from a vendor at an invoice cost of $69,000 to Francis Company were received on January 4, 2011.

   (b) The physical count included $29,000 of goods billed to Sakic Corp., f.o.b. shipping point, on December 31, 2010. The carrier picked up these goods on January 3, 2011.

   (c) Goods shipped f.o.b. destination received by Francis on January 5, 2011. The invoiced amount was $77,000.

   (d) Goods shipped f.o.b. destination received by Francis on December 25, 2010, that are on consignment. The invoiced amount is $83,500.

3. Messer Corp. had 1,500 units on hand of part 54169 on May 1, 2010, with a cost of $21 per unit. Messer uses a periodic inventory system. Purchases of part 54169 during May were as follows:

	Units	Unit Cost
May 9	2,000	$22.00
17	3,500	23.00
26	1,000	24.00

A physical count on May 31, 2010, shows 2,000 units of part 54169 on hand.

4. Landros Ltd., a retail store chain, had the following information in its general ledger for the year 2010:

Merchandise purchased for resale	$909,400
Interest on notes payable to vendors for the purchase of inventory	8,700
Purchase returns	16,500
Freight-in	22,000
Freight-out	17,100
Cash discounts on purchases	6,800
Storage costs incurred when warehouse became full	8,300

Instructions

Answer the following questions for the situations above and explain your answer in each case:

(a) For situation 1, how much should HOHO Co. record as the purchase cost of these goods?

(b) For situation 2, what should Francis report as its inventory amount on its 2010 balance sheet?

(c) For situation 3, using the FIFO method, what is the inventory cost of part 54169 at May 31, 2010? Using the weighted average cost formula, what is the inventory cost?

(d) For situation 4, assume that Landros is a private company reporting under private entity GAAP. What is Landros's inventoriable cost for 2010? Explain any items that are excluded.

P8-2   On February 1, 2010, SunnyTime Ltd. began selling electric scooters that it purchased exclusively from United Motors Inc. United Motors offers vendor rebates based on the volume of annual sales to its customers, and calculates and pays the rebates at its fiscal year end, December 31. SunnyTime has a September fiscal year end and uses a perpetual inventory system. The rebate offer that SunnyTime received is for a $75 rebate on each scooter that is purchased in excess of 150 units in the calendar year ending December 31. An additional rebate of $30 is given for all units purchased in excess of 175 units in the same year. By September 30, 2010, SunnyTime had purchased 190 units from United Motors and had sold all but 35. Although it only made its first purchase on February 1, 2010, SunnyTime expects to purchase a total of 250 electric scooters from United Motors by December 31, 2010. Before arriving at the estimate of 250 electric scooters, SunnyTime's management looked carefully at trends in purchases by its competitors and the strong market for sales of electric scooters in the coming months; sales are especially strong among environmentally conscious customers in suburban areas. Management is very confident the 250 electric scooters will be purchased by December 31, 2010.

Instructions

Assume that SunnyTime follows the reporting requirements under private entity GAAP:

(a) Based on the conceptual framework, discuss the reasoning that SunnyTime should use in how it treats the rebate that it expects to receive from United Motors.

(b) Would your opinion change if the rebate that is expected from United Motors had been discretionary?

(c) Discuss some of the factors that management should consider in arriving at a reasonable estimate of its amount of purchases to December 31, 2010.

(d) Calculate the amount of any accrued rebate to be recorded by SunnyTime at September 30, 2010, assuming that the rebate is not discretionary and that management has a high degree of confidence in its estimate of the amount of purchases that will occur by December 31, 2010.

(e) Record the accruals that are necessary at SunnyTime's fiscal year end of September 30, 2010.

(f) How would your response change if SunnyTime followed the reporting requirements of IFRS?

P8-3   Zoe Limited, a manufacturer of small tools, provided the following information from its accounting records for the year ended December 31, 2010:

Inventory at December 31, 2010 (based on physical count of goods in Zoe's plant, at cost, on December 31, 2010)	$1,720,000
Accounts payable at December 31, 2010	1,300,000
Total current assets	2,680,000
Total current liabilities	1,550,000
Net sales (sales less sales returns)	8,550,000

Additional information:

1. Included in the physical count were tools billed to a customer f.o.b. shipping point on December 31, 2010. These tools had a cost of $37,000 and were billed at $57,000. The shipment was on Zoe's loading dock waiting to be picked up by the common carrier.

2. Goods were in transit from a vendor to Zoe on December 31, 2010. The invoice cost was $51,000, and the goods were shipped f.o.b. shipping point on December 29, 2010. Zoe will sell these items in 2011 for $87,500. These were excluded from the inventory count.

3. Work-in-process inventory costing $38,000 was sent to an outside processor for plating on December 30, 2010. This was excluded from the inventory count.

4. Tools that were returned by customers and awaiting inspection in the returned goods area on December 31, 2010, were not included in the physical count. On January 8, 2011, these tools, costing $38,000, were inspected and returned to inventory. Credit memos totalling $48,000 were issued to the customers on the same date.

5. Tools shipped to a customer f.o.b. destination on December 26, 2010, were in transit at December 31, 2010, and had a cost of $21,000. When it was notified that the customer received the goods on January 2, 2011, Zoe issued a sales invoice for $42,000. These were excluded from the inventory count.

6. Goods with an invoice cost of $27,000 that were received from a vendor at 5:00 p.m. on December 31, 2010, were recorded on a receiving report dated January 2, 2011. The goods were not included in the physical count, but the invoice was included in accounts payable at December 31, 2010.

7. Goods that were received from a vendor on December 26, 2010, were included in the physical count. However, the vendor invoice of $56,000 for these goods was not included in accounts payable at December 31, 2010, because the accounts payable copy of the receiving report was lost.

8. On January 3, 2011, a monthly freight bill in the amount of $7,000 was received. The bill specifically related to merchandise purchased in December 2010, and half of this merchandise was still in the inventory at December 31, 2010. The freight charges were not included in either the inventory account or accounts payable at December 31, 2010.

Instructions

(a) Using the format shown below, prepare a schedule of adjustments to the initial amounts in Zoe's accounting records as at December 31, 2010. Show separately the effect, if any, of each of the eight transactions on the December 31, 2010, amounts. If the transaction has no effect on the initial amount that is shown, write "NONE."

	Inventory	Accounts Payable	Net Sales
Initial amounts	$1,720,000	$1,300,000	$8,550,000
Adjustments—increase (decrease)			
Total adjustments	_____	_____	_____
Adjusted amounts	$_____	$_____	$_____

(b) After you arrive at the adjusted balance for part (a) above, determine if the following ratios have improved or if they have deteriorated:

1. Working capital
2. Current ratio
3. Gross profit
4. Profit margin

(AICPA adapted)

Digging Deeper

P8-4   Capeland Boats Limited, which began operations in 2007, always values its inventories at their current net realizable value. Its annual inventory figure is arrived at by taking a physical count and then pricing each item in the physical inventory at current resale prices. The condensed income statements for the company's past four years are as follows:

	2007	2008	2009	2010
Sales	$850,000	$880,000	$950,000	$990,000
Cost of goods sold	560,000	590,000	630,000	650,000
Gross profit	290,000	290,000	320,000	340,000
Operating expenses	190,000	180,000	200,000	210,000
Income before taxes	$100,000	$110,000	$120,000	$130,000

Instructions

(a) Comment on the procedures that Capeland uses for valuing inventories.

(b) Prepare corrected condensed income statements using an acceptable method of inventory valuation, assuming that the inventory at cost and as determined by the corporation (using net realizable value) at the end of each of the four years is as follows:

Year	At Cost	Net Realizable Value
2007	$150,000	$160,000
2008	147,000	160,000
2009	178,000	170,000
2010	175,000	189,000

(c) Compare the trend in income for the four years using the corporation's approach to valuing ending inventory and using a method that is acceptable under GAAP.

(d) Calculate the cumulative effect of the difference in the valuation of inventory on the ending balance of retained earnings from 2007 through 2010.

(e) Comment on the differences that you observe after making the corrections to the inventory valuation over the four years.

P8-5   Some of the transactions of Wonka Corp. during August follow. Wonka uses the periodic inventory method.

Aug. 10	Purchased merchandise on account, $12,000, terms 2/10, n/30.
13	Returned $1,200 of the purchase of August 10 and received a credit on account.
15	Purchased merchandise on account, $16,000, terms 1/10, n/60.
25	Purchased merchandise on account, $20,000, terms 2/10, n/30.
28	Paid the invoice of August 15 in full.

Instructions

(a) Assuming that purchases are recorded at gross amounts and that discounts are to be recorded when taken:

1. Prepare general journal entries to record the transactions.

2. Describe how the various items would be shown in the financial statements.

(b) Assuming that purchases are recorded at net amounts and that discounts lost are treated as financial expenses:

1. Prepare general journal entries to enter the transactions.

2. Prepare the adjusting entry that is necessary on August 31 if financial statements are prepared at that time.

3. Describe how the various items would be shown in the financial statements.

(c) Which method results in a higher reported gross profit ratio? Explain.

(d) Which of the two methods do you prefer and why?

P8-6   Nazerth Limited stocks a variety of sports equipment for sale to institutions. The following stock record card for basketballs was taken from the records at the December 31, 2010, year end:

Date	Voucher	Terms	Units Received	Unit Invoice Cost	Gross Invoice Amount
Jan. 1	balance	Net 30	100	$20.00	$2,000.00
15	10624	Net 30	60	20.00	1,200.00
Mar. 15	11437	1/5, net 30	65	16.00	1,040.00
June 20	21332	1/10, net 30	90	15.00	1,350.00
Sept. 12	27644	1/10, net 30	84	12.00	1,008.00
Nov. 24	31269	1/10, net 30	76	11.00	836.00
	Totals		475		$7,434.00

A physical inventory on December 31, 2010, reveals that 100 basketballs were in stock. The bookkeeper informs you that all the discounts were taken. Assume that Nazerth Limited uses a periodic inventory system and records purchases at their invoice price less discounts. During 2010, the average sales price per basketball was $22.25.

Instructions

(a) Calculate the December 31, 2010, inventory using the FIFO formula.

(b) Calculate the December 31, 2010, inventory using the weighted average cost formula. (Round unit costs to the nearest cent.)

(c) Prepare income statements for the year ended December 31, 2010, as far as the gross profit line under each of the FIFO and weighted average methods, and calculate the gross profit rate for each. Comment.

(d) If the selling prices for the basketballs that were sold follow the same pattern as their wholesale prices from the supplier, might this have an effect on the inventory cost that is reported on the December 31, 2010, balance sheet? (Hint: Review your answers to parts [a] to [c].)

P8-7   The summary financial statements of FastMart Ltd. on December 31, 2011, are as follows:

FASTMART LTD.
Balance Sheet, December 31, 2011
Assets

Cash	$ 5,000
Accounts and notes receivable	39,000
Inventory	79,000
Property, plant, and equipment (net)	125,000
	$248,000

Liabilities and Shareholders' Equity

Accounts and notes payable	$ 75,000
Long-term debt	62,000
Common shares	60,000
Retained earnings	51,000
	$248,000

The following errors were made by the inexperienced accountant on December 31, 2010, and were not corrected:

1. The inventory was overstated by $13,000.

2. A prepaid expense of $2,400 was omitted (it was fully expensed in 2010).

3. Accrued revenue of $2,500 was omitted (it was recognized when cash was received in 2011).

4. A supplier's invoice for $1,700 for purchases made in 2010 was not recorded until 2011.

On December 31, 2011, there were further errors:

5. The inventory was understated by $17,000.

6. A prepaid expense of $750 was omitted.

7. Accrued December 2011 salaries of $1,800 were not recognized.

8. Unearned income of $2,300 was recorded in the 2011 revenue.

9. In addition, it was determined that $20,000 of the accounts payable were long-term, and that a $500 dividend was reported as dividend expense and deducted in calculating net income.

The net income reported on the books for 2011 was $53,000.

Instructions

(a) Calculate the working capital, current ratio, and debt-to-equity ratio for FastMart Ltd. based on the original balance sheet information provided above.

(b) Calculate the corrected net income for 2011.

(c) Prepare a corrected balance sheet at December 31, 2011.

(d) Using the corrected data, recalculate the ratios in part (a). Comment.

P8-8   Robin Hemming established Creative Solutions Co. as a sole proprietorship on January 5, 2010. At the company's year end of December 31, 2010, the accounts had the following balances (in thousands):

Current assets, excluding inventory	$ 10
Other assets	107
Current liabilities	30
Long-term bank loan	50
Owner's investment (excluding income)	40
Purchases during year	
Jan. 2: 5,000 @ $11	
June 30: 8,000 @ $12	
Dec. 10: 6,000 @ $16	247
Sales	284
Other expenses	40

A count of ending inventory on December 31, 2010, showed there were 4,000 units on hand.

Hemming is now preparing financial statements for the year. He is aware that inventory may be costed using the FIFO or weighted average cost formula. He is unsure of which one to use and asks for your assistance. In discussions with Hemming, you learn the following:

1. Suppliers to Creative Solutions provide goods at regular prices as long as Creative Solutions' current ratio is at least 2 to 1. If this ratio is lower, the suppliers increase their price by 10% in order to compensate for what they consider to be a substantial credit risk.

2. The terms of the long-term bank loan include the bank's ability to demand immediate repayment of the loan if the debt-to-total-assets ratio is greater than 45%.

3. Hemming thinks that, for the company to be a success, the rate of return on total assets should be at least 30%.

4. Hemming has an agreement with the company's only employee that, for each full percentage point above a 25% rate of return on total assets, she will be given an additional one day off with pay in the following year.

Instructions

(a) Prepare an income statement and a year-end balance sheet assuming the company applies:

   1. the FIFO cost formula

   2. the weighted average cost formula

(b) Identify the advantages of each formula in (a).

(c) Identify the disadvantages of each formula in (a).

(d) Which method do you recommend? Explain briefly.

(e) Considering the choice of inventory cost formulas that are available, do the ratios that Hemming uses adequately measure the financial performance of Creative Solutions?

**Digging
Deeper**

P8-9   Soorya Company determined its ending inventory at cost and at lower of cost and net realizable value at December 31, 2009, 2010, and 2011, as follows:

	Cost	Lower of Cost and Net Realizable Value
Dec. 31, 2009	$720,000	$720,000
Dec. 31, 2010	980,000	918,400
Dec. 31, 2011	950,000	880,000

Instructions

(a) Prepare the journal entries that are required at December 31, 2010 and 2011, assuming that a periodic inventory system and the direct method of adjusting to NRV are used.

(b) Prepare the journal entries that are required at December 31, 2010 and 2011, assuming that a periodic inventory system is used, with inventory recorded at cost and reduced to NRV through the use of an allowance account.

P8-10 Varma Corp. lost most of its inventory in a fire in December just before the year-end physical inventory was taken. The corporation's books disclosed the following:

Beginning inventory	$440,000	Sales	$1,350,000
Purchases for the year	850,000	Sales returns	50,000
Purchase returns	55,000	Gross margin on sales	40%

Merchandise with a selling price of $42,000 remained undamaged after the fire. Damaged merchandise with an original selling price of $30,000 had a net realizable value of $10,600.

Instructions

(a) Calculate the amount lost due to the fire, assuming that the corporation had no insurance coverage.

(b) Prepare the journal entry to record the loss and account for the damaged inventory in a separate Damaged Inventory account. In the same entry, record cost of goods sold for the year ended December 31.

(c) How would the loss be classified on the income statement of Varma Corp.?

(d) While the gross profit percentage has averaged 40% over the past five years, it has been as high as 42% and as low as 37.5%. Given this information, should a range of possible loss amounts be provided instead of a single figure? Explain.

P8-11 Arshafs Specialty Corp., a division of FH Inc., manufactures three models of gearshift components for bicycles that are sold to bicycle manufacturers, retailers, and catalogue outlets. Since beginning operations in 1969, Arshafs has used normal absorption costing and has assumed a first-in, first-out cost flow in its perpetual inventory system. Except for overhead, manufacturing costs are accumulated using actual costs. Overhead is applied to production using predetermined overhead rates. The balances of the inventory accounts at the end of Arshafs' fiscal year, September 30, 2010, follow. The inventories are stated at cost before any year-end adjustments.

Finished goods	$757,000
Work in process	192,500
Raw materials	300,000
Factory supplies	69,000

The following information relates to Arshafs' inventory and operations:

1. The finished goods inventory consists of these items:

	Cost	Net realizable value
Down tube shifter		
Standard model	$ 97,500	$ 67,000
Click adjustment model	94,500	87,000
Deluxe model	108,000	110,000
Total down tube shifters	300,000	264,000
Bar end shifter		
Standard model	133,000	120,050
Click adjustment model	79,000	108,150
Total bar end shifters	212,000	228,200
Head tube shifter		
Standard model	128,000	103,650
Click adjustment model	117,000	145,300
Total head tube shifters	245,000	248,950
Total finished goods	$757,000	$741,150

2. Half of the finished goods inventory of head tube shifters is at catalogue outlets on consignment.

3. Three-quarters of the finished goods inventory of bar end shifters has been pledged as collateral for a bank loan.

4. Half of the raw materials balance is for derailleurs acquired at a contracted price that is 20% above the current market price. The net realizable value of the rest of the raw materials is $135,500.

5. The total net realizable value of the work-in-process inventory is $105,500.

6. Included in the cost of factory supplies are obsolete items with a historical cost of $4,200. The net realizable value of the remaining factory supplies is $65,900.

7. Arshafs applies the lower of cost and net realizable value method to each of the three types of shifters in finished goods inventory. For each of the other three inventory accounts, Arshafs applies the lower of cost and net realizable value method to the total of each inventory account.

8. Consider all of the amounts presented above as being material amounts in relation to Arshafs' financial statements as a whole.

Instructions

(a) Assuming that private entity GAAP is followed, prepare the inventory section of Arshafs' statement of financial position as at September 30, 2010, including any required note(s).

(b) Regardless of your answer to (a), assume that the net realizable value of Arshafs' inventories is less than cost. Explain how this decline would be presented in Arshafs' income statement for the fiscal year ended September 30, 2010, under private entity GAAP.

(c) Assume that Arshafs has a firm purchase commitment for the same type of derailleur that is included in the raw materials inventory as at September 30, 2010, and that the purchase commitment is at a contracted price that is 15% higher than the current market price. These derailleurs are to be delivered to Arshafs after September 30, 2010. Discuss the impact, if any, that this purchase commitment would have on Arshafs' financial statements prepared for the fiscal year ended September 30, 2010, under private entity GAAP.

(d) How would your response to (c) change under IFRS?

(e) Explain and compare the disclosure requirements under private entity GAAP and IFRS.

(CMA adapted)

P8-12   The Kucharchuk Wood Corporation manufactures desks. Most of the company's desks are standard models that are sold at catalogue prices. At December 31, 2010, the following finished desks appear in the company's inventory:

Finished Desks	Type A	Type B	Type C	Type D
2010 catalogue selling price	$460	$490	$890	$1,040
FIFO cost per inventory list, Dec. 31, 2010	410	450	830	960
Estimated current cost to manufacture (at Dec. 31, 2010 and early 2011)	460	440	790	1,000
Sales commissions and estimated other costs of disposal	40	65	95	130
2011 catalogue selling price	575	650	780	1,420
Quantity on hand	15	117	113	110

The 2010 catalogue was in effect through November 2010, and the 2011 catalogue is effective as of December 1, 2010. All catalogue prices are net of the usual discounts. Generally, the company tries to obtain a 20% gross margin on the selling price and it has usually been successful in achieving this.

Instructions

(a) Assume that the company has adopted a lower of FIFO cost and net realizable value approach for the valuation of inventories and applies it on an individual inventory item basis. At what total inventory value will the desks appear on the company's December 31, 2010, balance sheet?

(b) Explain the rationale for using the lower of cost and market rule for inventories.

(c) Explain the impact if inventory was valued at lower of cost or net realizable value on a total basis.

*P8-13   The records for the Clothing Department of Isha's Discount Store are summarized as follows for the month of January:

- Inventory, January 1: at retail, $28,000; at cost, $18,000
- Purchases in January: at retail, $147,000; at cost, $110,000
- Freight-in: $6,000
- Purchase returns: at retail, $3,500; at cost, $2,700
- Purchase allowances: $2,200
- Transfers in from suburban branch: at retail, $13,000; at cost, $9,200

- Net markups: $8,000
- Net markdowns: $4,000
- Inventory losses due to normal breakage, etc.: at retail, $400
- Sales at retail: $121,000
- Sales returns: $2,400

Instructions

(a) Estimate the inventory for this department as at January 31 at (1) retail and (2) the lower of average cost and market. Round the cost-to-retail ratio to two decimal places.

(b) Assume that a physical inventory count taken at retail prices after the close of business on January 31 indicated an inventory amount that is $450 less than what was estimated in (a) part (1). What could have caused this discrepancy?

P8-14   Some of the information found on a detailed inventory card for Leif Letter Ltd. for May is as follows:

| | Received | | Issued | Balance |
Date	No. of Units	Unit Cost	No. of Units	No. of Units
May 1 (opening balance)	1,150	$2.90		1,150
2	1,050	3.00		2,200
7			700	1,500
10	600	3.20		2,100
13			500	1,600
18	1,000	3.30	300	2,300
20			1,100	1,200
23	1,300	3.40		2,500
26			800	1,700
28	1,500	3.60		3,200
31			1,300	1,900

Instructions

(a) From the above data, calculate the ending inventory based on each of the following cost formulas. Assume that perpetual inventory records are kept in units only. Carry unit costs to the nearest cent and ending inventory to the nearest dollar.

  1. First-in, first-out (FIFO)

  2. Weighted average cost

(b) Based on your results in part (a), and assuming that the average selling price per unit during May was $7.25, prepare partial income statements up to the "gross profit on sales" line. Calculate the gross profit percentage under each inventory cost formula. Comment on your results.

(c) Assume the perpetual inventory record is kept in dollars, and costs are calculated at the time of each withdrawal. Recalculate the amounts under this revised assumption, carrying average unit costs to four decimal places. Would the ending inventory amounts under each of the two cost formulas above be the same? Explain.

Writing Assignments

WA8-1   Jack McDowell, the controller for McDowell Lumber Corporation, has recently hired you as assistant controller. He wishes to determine your expertise in the area of inventory accounting and therefore asks you to answer the following unrelated questions.

Instructions

Write a memo to him that answers each of his questions.

(a) A company is involved in the wholesaling and retailing of automobile tires for foreign cars. Most of the inventory is imported, and it is valued on the company's records at the actual inventory cost plus freight-in. At year end, the warehousing costs are prorated over cost of goods sold and ending inventory. Are warehousing costs considered a product cost or a period cost?

(b) A certain portion of a company's inventory consists of obsolete items. Should obsolete items that are not currently consumed in the production of goods or services to be available for sale be classified as part of inventory?

(c) A company purchases airplanes for sale to others. However, until they are sold, the company charters and services the planes. What is the proper way to report these airplanes in the company's financial statements?

(d) A company wants to buy coal deposits but does not want the financing for the purchase to be reported on its financial statements. The company therefore establishes a trust to acquire the coal deposits. The company agrees to buy the coal over a certain period of time at specified prices. The trust is able to finance the coal purchase and then pay off the loan when it is paid by the company for the minerals. How should this transaction be reported?

WA8-2   Local Drilling Inc. is a Canadian drilling-site company. All of the company's drilling material is purchased by the head office and stored at a local warehouse before being shipped to the drilling sites. The price of drilling material has been steadily decreasing over the past few years. The drilling material is sent to various sites upon request of the site manager, where it is stored and then used in drilling. When the material is sent, managers are charged the inventory cost based on the cost assigned to the item in the head office records. At any particular time, it is estimated that about one half of the company's drilling material inventory will be at the local warehouse. Part of each site manager's performance evaluation is based on the net income reported for the site.

Instructions

With the choices of the specific identification, FIFO, and moving-average cost formulas and use of a perpetual inventory system:

(a) Which costing method would you, as a site manager, want to see used? Why?

(b) If FIFO were used, what could you, as a site manager, do that would help your performance evaluation when you request inventory? Why, and what might the implications be for the company as a whole?

(c) As the decision-maker at head office, which method would you recommend if you wanted the results to be fair for all site managers? Why?

(d) Which method would you recommend for determining the company's taxable income? Why?

(e) Which method would you recommend for financial statement purposes? Why?

WA8-3   PERO Lumber Limited is a private company. It operates in the forestry sector and owns timber lots. The company produces and sells specialty lumber to distributors and retailers. The company has a management bonus plan, which is based on net earnings and gross profits. In the past, the company has estimated decommissioning costs related to its sawmill facility and recorded them as a liability with an offsetting increase to the cost of the plant. Since the production period can be fairly long, including the curing and special treatments applied to the lumber, the company has had to borrow to finance this production process. However, historically, it has expensed this interest. Finally, the owners explained that they did have a purchase commitment to buy a minimum amount of specialty resins used to treat the lumber. This is a five-year contract at a fixed price. At the time, they were very excited about it, but now they are in the fourth year of the contract and realize that the company will not need the volumes that it committed to buy. They have now developed a new technique that is cheaper and uses a different solution to treat the wood. In fact, it looks as though the company will have to pay for items that will not be required. The owners are trying to decide whether or not to break the contract or remain with the contract and just pay for the items but not take delivery. The company has two years still remaining on this contract.

Instructions

PERO Lumber Limited has just hired you as its new controller. It is trying to decide whether to adopt IFRS or report under private entity GAAP. Provide the owners with a report that details the impact of reporting under IFRS on the company's financial results and management bonus plan, giving consideration to the issues indicated above.

WA8-4   The balance sheet valuation of inventory should represent the lower of cost and net realizable value of all inventory owned by a company. The following audit procedures are listed in the external auditor's working papers:

1. Review sales invoices after year end.

2. Review freight documents around year end.

3. Test count a sample of items during the client's physical inventory count and compare the result with the client's count sheets.

4. Review suppliers' invoices and receiving reports both before and after year end.

5. Calculate the gross profit ratio and compare it with the previous year's ratio.

6. During the client's inventory count, select a sample of items from the client's inventory count sheets and count the quantities actually on hand.

Instructions

Explain why each of these audit procedures is required.

*WA8-5   There are many forms of inventory that are not covered under the basic accounting standards for inventory: *CICA Handbook*, Part II, Section 3031 for private entity GAAP and IAS 2 for IFRS.

Instructions

For each of the following forms of inventory, briefly explain how the inventory would be reported and where guidance would be found under private entity GAAP and international GAAP. Explain the impact on the balance sheet and the income statements that would result.

(a) Securities held by an investment company

(b) Unbilled work in progress for a legal firm (i.e., employee and partner time spent on client work not yet billed)

(c) Milk from dairy cattle

(d) Sheep that are kept for wool production

(e) Construction contracts in progress

(f) Nickel resources not yet mined

*WA8-6   Harvey Corporation, your client, manufactures paint. The company's president, Vlad Harvey, has decided to open a retail store to sell his specialty paint products, as well as wallpaper and other supplies that would be purchased from other suppliers. He has asked you for information about the conventional retail method of determining the cost of inventories at the retail store.

Instructions

Prepare a report to the president explaining the retail method of valuing inventories. Your report should include these points:

(a) A description and accounting features of the method

(b) The conditions that may distort the results under the method

(c) A comparison of the advantages of using the retail method to the advantages of using cost methods of inventory pricing

(d) The accounting theory underlying the treatment of net markdowns and net markups under the method

WA8-7   Write a brief essay highlighting the differences between IFRS and accounting standards for private enterprises noted in this chapter, discussing the conceptual justification for each.

Cases

Refer to the Case Primer to help you answer these cases.

CA8-1   **Tobacco Group Inc.** (TGI) is in the consumer packaged goods industry. Its shares are widely held and key shareholders include several very large pension funds.

In the current year, 59% of the net revenues and 61% of operating income came from tobacco product sales. Because of the health risks related to the use of tobacco products, the industry is increasingly regulated by government and the company is implicated in substantial tobacco-related litigation.

During the past three years, the company entered into agreements with the government to settle asserted and unasserted health-care recovery costs and other claims. The agreements, known as the Government Settlement Agreements (GSA), call for payments by the domestic tobacco industry into a fund in the following amounts:

Current Year	$10.9 billion
Following four years	$8 billion each year
Thereafter	$9 billion each year

The fund will be used to settle claims and aid tobacco growers. Each company's share of these payments is based on its market share and TGI records its portion of the settlement costs as cost of goods sold upon shipment. These amounts may increase based on several factors, including inflation and industry volume. In the past three years, the company accrued costs of more than $5 billion each year.

Another significant lawsuit, the class action, is still in process. Last year, the jury returned a verdict assessing punitive damages against various defendants, and TGI was responsible for $74 billion. The company is contesting this and the lawsuit continues. As a result of preliminary judicial stipulations, the company has placed $500 million into a separate interest-bearing escrow account. This money will be kept by the court and distributed to the plaintiffs regardless of the outcome of the trial. The company also placed $1.2 billion into another escrow account, and this amount will be returned to the company if it wins the case.

Instructions

Assume the role of a financial analyst and discuss the related financial reporting issues. Specifically, note alternative accounting treatments for each issue and recommend how each issue should be treated in the financial statements.

CA8-2   **Findit Gold Inc.** (FGI) was created in 1996 and is 81%-owned by Findit Mining Corporation (FMC). Its shares trade on the local exchange and its objective is to become a substantial low-cost mineral producer in developing countries. FMC Mining has provided substantial financial support to FGI over the past five years as FGI is still mainly in the exploration stage. In 2010, the company decommissioned its Bulawan gold mine, which had been in production since 1996. At this point, rehabilitation and reforestation activity is the only activity in the mine.

Over the most-recent five-year period, the company carried its gold bullion inventory at net realizable value and recognized revenues on gold sales (net of refining and selling costs) at net realizable value, when the minerals were produced. Gold is a commodity that trades actively and whose price fluctuates according to supply and demand.

Instructions

Assume the role of FMC and assess the financial reporting policies relating to inventory valuation and revenue recognition. Identify any other potential financial reporting issues.

CA8-3   **Fuego Limited** (FL) is a mid-sized business that produces computer paper. During the year, raw material had been increasing significantly in price and FL was finding it difficult to compete since it could not increase its selling prices sufficiently to generate a profit. Its customers, which were primarily "big box" stores (i.e., very large stores that deal with office supplies), threatened to take their business elsewhere if FL did not hold its prices. By year end, the company had significant amounts of inventory and was negotiating with its two largest customers about a price increase. Luckily, raw material prices had begun to decline, making future sales less of a problem, but FL still needed to sell the high-priced inventory on hand in order to at least recover its costs.

Franco Fuego, the company owner, was happy that at least some progress was being made in the discussions and hoped to move the inventory out before year end. Unfortunately, during the night, he was called by the fire department. His warehouse and all the inventory had been burned to the ground. Fire department officials wanted him to see the damages and to ask him a few questions that might help them determine the cause of the fire. Apparently, they had found traces of gasoline in the warehouse. Franco immediately called his insurance company (the inventory and building were fully covered at replacement value as long as there was no foul play).

The insurance company asked whether the company records had also been destroyed. Luckily, Franco kept a backup copy in another location and so he would hopefully be able to help the insurance people determine the value. FL had been using the periodic inventory method and the last count had been at the end of the prior year. While all this was going on, Franco also needed to get draft financial statements to the bank within the next few days since the bank had been monitoring his cash flow situation carefully because his line of credit was almost fully drawn.

Instructions

Adopt the role of Franco Fuego and discuss the financial reporting issues related to the preparation of the current financial statements.

CA8-4   **Bombardier Inc.** (BI) is a manufacturer of transportation equipment, including aircraft. It has received significant financing in the past from the Canadian government. During the last several years, the company has suffered due to numerous bankruptcies in the aircraft carrier business, which, at least partly, were due to decreased demand for travel. In 2004, Paul Tellier, president and CEO, decided to streamline the company and strengthen the balance sheet in the hope of turning the company around. By 2008, income exceeded $1 billion.

Real-World Emphasis

The company is controlled by the Bombardier family and pays annual dividends. The total debt-to-equity ratio is approximately 7:1.

The following are excerpts from Bombardier's 2004 annual report:

Nature of operations and consolidated financial statement presentation

Bombardier Inc. (the "Corporation") is incorporated under the laws of Canada. Bombardier Inc., a diversified manufacturing and services company, is a manufacturer of transportation equipment, including regional and business aircraft and rail transportation equipment. It also provides financial services and asset management in business areas aligned with its core expertise.

Cost of sales – *Aerospace programs*

Average unit cost for commercial and business aircraft is determined based on the estimated total production costs for a predetermined program quantity. Program quantities are established based on Management's assessment of market conditions and foreseeable demand at the beginning of the production stage for each program, taking into consideration, among other factors, existing firm orders and options.

The average unit cost is recorded to cost of sales at the time of each aircraft delivery. Under the learning curve concept, which anticipates a predictable decrease in unit costs as tasks and production techniques become more efficient through repetition and management action, excess over-average production costs during the early stages of a program are deferred and recovered from sales of aircraft anticipated to be produced later at lower-than-average costs.

Estimates of average unit production costs and of program quantities are an integral component of average cost accounting. Management conducts quarterly reviews as well as a detailed annual review in the fourth quarter, as part of its annual budget process, of its cost estimates and program quantities, and the effect of any revisions are accounted for by way of a cumulative catch-up adjustment to income in the period in which the revision takes place.

The following are excerpts from Bombardier's 2008 annual report:

Inventories

In June 2007, the AcSB released Section 3031 "Inventories", which replaces Section 3030 "Inventories". It provides the Canadian equivalent to IAS 2 "Inventories" under IFRS. This accounting standard was adopted by the Corporation effective February 1, 2008. The Section prescribes the measurement of inventories at the lower of cost and net realizable value. It provides further guidance on the determination of cost and its subsequent recognition as an expense, including any write-downs to net realizable value and circumstances for their subsequent reversal. It also provides more restrictive guidance on the cost methodologies that are used to assign costs to inventories and describes additional disclosure requirements.

As a result, the Corporation adopted the unit cost method for its aerospace programs in replacement of the average cost method. The unit cost method is a prescribed cost method under which the actual production costs are charged to each unit produced and are recognized in income as the unit is delivered. The deferral of a portion of initial cost as EOAPC, embedded in the average cost method is not allowed under the unit cost method. In addition, as a result of the more restrictive guidance on the determination of costs, the Corporation also charged its overhead allocation policy on its aerospace programs whereby all G&A overhead costs are now expensed. In accordance with Section 3031, the Corporation has applied these changes in accounting policies by adjusting the opening retained earnings as at February 1, 2008 (prior fiscal years have not been restated).

As part of the adoption of Section 3031, customer advance payments received on account of work performed and previously deducted from aerospace program inventories have been reclassified to liabilities as advances on aerospace programs.

Also, effective February 1, 2008, the Corporation changed its G&A overhead cost allocation policy for its long-term contracts and aerospace program tooling to conform with the method applicable to its aerospace programs. Management believes that this new overhead allocation policy results in more relevant information.

Instructions

Discuss the accounting policy for accounting for inventories and cost of sales, comparing the 2004 policy with the 2008 policy.

Integrated Case

(Hint: If there are issues here that are new, use the conceptual framework to help you support your analysis with solid reasoning.)

IC8-1   Grappa Grapes Inc. (GGI) grows grapes and produces fine champagne. The company is located in a very old area of town with easy access to fertile farmland that is excellent for growing grapes. It is own by the Grappa family. The company has been in operation for 100 years and a large part of its success lies in the excellent vineyards and unique process for producing vintage wines. The winery sits at the edge of a range of hills that are composed of chalk. GGI has dug "caves" into the side of the hills at a significant cost and the chalk caves provide the perfect temperature and humidity for the maturing wines. All of the vintage wines are produced, aged, and stored in these chalk caves. People come from all over the country to visit the "caves." As a matter of fact, 25% of the company's revenues are from winery tours.

The company has had three years where it has managed to produce vintage wines. Vintage wines are of higher quality and sell for a higher price. In addition, they contribute to the prestige of the winery. Because of this success, GGI has started to sell wine "futures." Under the terms of the contract, large wholesalers pay GGI upfront and agree to take delivery of a certain number of bottles in two years at 20% off the future price. A market for trading these contracts now exists for the buyers of the futures.

During the year, in anticipation of increasing costs, the entity placed a purchase order for a significant number of oak barrels from France. The barrels are used to age the wines. Due to the declining value of the dollar during a current economic recession and the demand for wines in general over the past year, the value of the barrels has actually declined below the price locked in under the purchase commitments. The supplier is confident that this is only a temporary decline in value and that the price of the barrels will increase within the next couple of months. GGI may get out of the purchase commitment either by taking delivery of the barrels at the agreed on price or by settling net in cash for the difference between the agreed upon price and the market price (times the number of barrels ordered).

The year has been a very rainy one and some of the very old chalk caves have begun to leak and deteriorate. One of the caves holding a large number of vintage wines collapsed. It is unclear whether the wine is salvageable. The company's insurance will not cover the expected loss, although GGI has hired its lawyers to challenge this as it feels that the insurance company should cover the loss.

Instructions

Assume the role of the controller and analyze the financial reporting issues.

Research and Financial Analysis

RA8-1 Eastern Platinum Limited

Eastern Platinum Limited, as described in Note 1 to its financial statements, is a "platinum producer engaged in the mining, exploration and development of PGM [platinum group metals] properties in South Africa."

Real-World Emphasis

Eastern's financial statements for its three-month period ended March 31, 2009, are provided in Appendix 5B.

Instructions

(a) How much inventory does Eastern have at March 31, 2009 and 2008? Identify the types of inventory that Eastern reports on its March 31, 2009, balance sheet. How much was recognized as an expense in the three-month period? What comments can you make about the inventory held at the end of the reporting period? (Hint: Read the revenue recognition note.)

(b) Describe the accounting policies for inventory. Is there any additional information you would like to know? Were there any adjustments required to inventory on conversion to IFRS from Canadian GAAP?

(c) What amount of cost of goods sold is reported on the statement of income for the year ended December 31, 2008, under Canadian GAAP and IFRS? Briefly explain any differences. What is the company's gross profit percentage for 2008? Compare this with the rate for the three-month periods ended March 31, 2009, and March 31, 2008. Comment on why there are differences, if any.

(d) Explain how the company accounts for the inventory of platinum that is not yet mined.

RA8-2 Stora Enso Oyj

Stora Enso Oyj describes its business in its annual report as a "global paper, packaging and forest products company producing newsprint and book paper, magazine paper, fine paper, consumer board, industrial packaging and wood products."

Real-World Emphasis

Instructions

Access the financial statements of Stora Enso for the year ended December 31, 2008, from the company's website. Using the financial statements, answer the following questions:

(a) Describe the accounting policies that the company uses for reporting inventories. What types of expenses are included in costs? Is interest included in inventory costs?

(b) What different components are there in inventory and what is the percentage of each to the total for 2008 and 2007? Which items represent a high percentage of the inventory? How has this changed over the years? Is there any cause for concern? What was the amount reported on the income statement related to inventory items? Is it possible to calculate the days in inventory ratio?

(c) How are the inventories of the standing trees measured and reported? What types of assumptions are used to determine the reported amount of these assets? Where are these assets located? How much was harvested this year? What other changes occurred in the balance sheet and what were changes related to in 2008? How are the changes in these amounts reported and what are the impacts on earnings for the current year and previous year?

(d) Does the company use the allowance method or the direct method to record writedowns to the inventory? What were these related amounts at the 2008 year end? Were there any amounts reversed during the year?

(e) Is this disclosure useful to the reader? Is there any other information you would like to have?

RA8-3 Canadian Tire Corporation, Limited

Real-World Emphasis

Refer to the 2008 annual report of **Canadian Tire Corporation, Limited** available on SEDAR (www.sedar.com) or the company's website (www.canadiantire.ca). Note that the company provides a 10-year financial review at the end of its annual report. This summary gives relevant comparative information that is useful for determining trends and predicting the company's future results and position.

Instructions

Prepare three graphs covering the 2004 to 2008 period (express all amounts in $000). The first graph is for net earnings from continuing operations over this five-year period, the second for working capital, and the third for the current ratio. Based on the graphs, predict the values you might expect for the next fiscal period.

RA8-4 Research: Inventory Management Systems

Real-World Emphasis

Many companies, such as **HydroMississauga** and **Matsushita Electric of Canada Ltd.**, have invested in technology to improve their inventory management systems.

Instructions

Research the topic of improvements to inventory management systems, and focus in particular on two examples where companies have been able to change the way they manage this critical asset. You may choose any companies of your choice. Identify what improvements the companies have made. How do these efficiencies affect the balance sheet and income statement, if at all? Be specific.

RA8-5 Magnotta Winery Corporation

Real-World Emphasis

Access the annual financial statements of **Magnotta Winery Corporation** for the year ended January 31, 2009, on SEDAR (www.sedar.com), or the company's website (www.magnotta.com).

Instructions

Refer to these financial statements and the accompanying notes to answer the following questions.

(a) How significant are the inventories relative to total current assets? What categories of inventory does Magnotta Winery report?

(b) Identify all the accounting policies that are the basis for the inventory values reported on the January 31, 2009, balance sheet.

(c) Which category of inventory represents the highest percentage? Is this what you would expect?

(d) What was the amount recognized in expense related to inventory for 2009 and 2008? Were there any writedowns of inventory or reversals of writedowns for 2008 or 2009?

(e) What was Magnotta's inventory turnover ratio for the year ended January 31, 2009? What is the average age of the inventory? Comment briefly.

(f) Compare the gross profit ratios for the two most recent years that are reported. Comment briefly on why there might be changes from year to year.

(g) Until 2011, the company reports under Canadian GAAP. How were its vineyards measured and reported under Canadian GAAP for its 2009 year end? When the company converts to IFRS in 2011, what will be the impact on these assets? What will be the impact on balance sheet? On the income statement?

RA8-6 Loblaw Companies Limited and Empire Company Limited

Instructions

From SEDAR (www.sedar.com), or the company websites, access the financial statements of **Loblaw Companies Limited** for its year ended January 3, 2009, and of **Empire Company Limited** for its year ended May 2, 2009. Review the financial statements and answer the following questions.

Real-World Emphasis

(a) Describe the business that Loblaw and Empire operate in.

(b) What is the amount of inventory reported by Loblaw at January 3, 2009, and by Empire at May 2, 2009? What percent of total assets is invested in inventory by each company? How does this compare with the previous year?

(c) Identify the inventory policies for each company that support the inventory values reported on their respective balance sheets.

(d) How much did each company report for inventory expenses in the current and previous year? What was the writedown (or reversal of writedowns) related to inventories for the current and previous year for each company?

(e) How do the companies account for vendor allowances? Is this the appropriate treatment? How might this change if proposed changes in the framework are adopted?

(f) Calculate and compare the inventory turnover ratios and days to sell inventory for the two companies for the most current year.

(g) Comment on the results of your calculations in (f) above. Would any differences identified in any of the earlier analyses above help explain differences in the ratios between the two companies? What might be some reasons for the differences between the two companies?

RA8-7 Research: Manufacturing Inventory

Identify a company in your local community that develops a product through some form of manufacturing process. Consider a farming operation, bakery, cement supplier, or other company that converts or assembles inputs to develop a different product.

Instructions

Write a report on the company's inventory. Suggestions: Visit the manufacturing site, view a video of the operation, or speak to company management. Identify what types of costs are incurred in the manufacturing process. Determine which costs are included in inventory cost in the accounting records, and explain why some may be treated as period costs. Does the company use a periodic or a perpetual system? What cost formula does the company use? How does the company determine NRV, or does it?

Food Fortunes

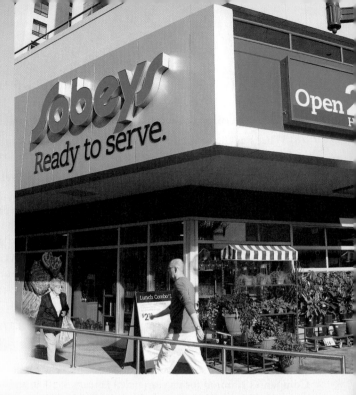

IN THE 1920S AND 1930S, when Frank Sobey was expanding his family's grocery store in Nova Scotia, he realized the company would need a real estate arm to maintain control of store locations. This became even more evident through the 1960s and 1970s, when large competitors from central Canada could easily win bids for good locations from local developers. "Frank realized he was better off if he bought the site," says Stewart Mahoney, vice-president, treasury and investor relations, at Sobeys' holding company, Empire Company Limited.

Now the Stellarton, Nova Scotia-based Empire Company, which was incorporated in 1983, has three distinct branches: a retail food branch with 100% ownership of Sobeys (with the June 2007 privatization of Sobeys, Empire took 100% ownership of the national food company, which comprises more than 1,300 stores); a real estate branch with 100% ownership of ECL Properties, a 47.4% interest in Crombie REIT, and 35.7% ownership interest in Genstar Development Partnership; and corporate investments, which include 100% ownership of Empire Theatres, as well as a 27.6% interest in

Wajax Income Fund. "All the company's various assets and revenues are matched to these three divisions," Mahoney explains.

The original investment strategy was control; however, increasing shareholder value "through income and cash flow growth and equity participation" in other businesses has become a key motivation since. For example, although Empire does not have controlling interest in Genstar, it is able to use line-by-line consolidation of the investment on its financial statements. "As they grow, we grow due to our proportionate interest in the company," Mahoney says.

Empire is evaluating the potential impact the conversion to International Financial Reporting Standards (IFRS) will have on its financial statements. The conversion from Canadian GAAP to IFRS will be applicable to the company's reporting for the first quarter of fiscal 2012, for which the current and comparative information will be prepared under IFRS. It expects the transition to affect accounting, financial reporting, internal control over financial reporting, information systems, and business processes. ■

CHAPTER 9

Investments

Learning Objectives

After studying this chapter, you should be able to:

1. Explain and apply the cost/amortized cost model of accounting for investments in debt and equity instruments, and identify how the investments are reported.

2. Explain and apply the fair value through net income model of accounting for investments in debt and equity instruments, and identify how the investments are reported.

3. Explain and apply the fair value through other comprehensive income model of accounting for investments in equity instruments, and identify how the investments are reported.

4. Identify private entity GAAP and IFRS for investments in financial assets where there is no significant influence or control.

5. Explain and apply the incurred loss, expected loss, and fair value loss impairment models, and identify private entity GAAP and IFRS requirements.

6. Explain the concept of significant influence and why the equity method is appropriate, apply the equity method, and identify private entity GAAP and IFRS requirements.

7. Explain the concept of control, the basics of consolidated financial statements, and why consolidation is appropriate, and identify private entity GAAP and IFRS requirements.

8. Explain the objectives of disclosure, and identify the major types of information that are required to be reported for investments in other companies' debt and equity instruments.

9. Identify differences in accounting between private entity GAAP and IFRS, and what changes are expected in the near future.

After studying Appendix 9A, you should be able to:

10. Recognize the classifications of financial instrument investments under Canadian GAAP prior to 2011.

Preview of Chapter 9

This chapter focuses on the different types of financial asset investments in equity and debt instruments, and the various accounting models applied in accounting for them. In some cases, the nature of the investment determines how it is accounted for and reported, so the classification of these investments is an important first step. This chapter covers a variety of investments, from those held for short-term profit-taking to those held for longer term strategic purposes. Accounting for investments in loans and receivables, also financial assets, was covered in Chapter 7. Because the international standards explained in the chapter are recent changes with effective dates extending to 2013 (with earlier adoption allowed), a summary of Canadian GAAP prior to these changes is provided in Appendix 9A.

The chapter is organized as follows:

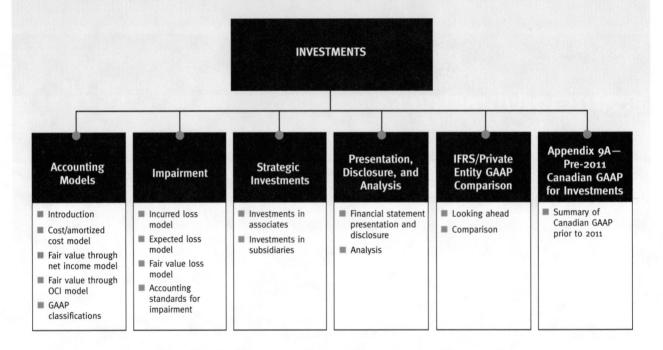

ACCOUNTING MODELS

Introduction

Recent Changes

The deficiencies of the historical cost model have been recognized for a long time, especially in accounting for financial instruments. Because of this, accounting for such instruments has been on the agendas of standard-setting bodies around the world for many years. The FASB, the IASB, and Canadian standard setters have all put accounting standards in place that require many of these assets to be accounted for at fair value, but financial reporting under these standards has encountered problems. Because only some of the instruments are recognized at fair value, the standards have had to be unnecessarily complicated, and fair value measurements under these standards did not stand up well in the world economic crisis beginning in 2007. While many of the problems are related to the more complex issues, accounting for ordinary investments in other companies' debt and equity instruments continue to be controversial.

As this text went to print, the IASB and FASB were taking a two-pronged approach to dealing with these problems. They had issued or were in the process of issuing improved guidance on how to measure fair values and simplifying the existing accounting standards. This chapter, therefore, focuses on explaining the basic accounting models used to account for investments in debt and equity securities in general, and that underlie current initiatives. Appendix 9A provides a summary of Canadian GAAP for financial asset investments prior to 2011.

Financial Assets and Investments

The broad topic of financial instruments can be complex, but coverage in this chapter is **limited to basic financial assets: investments in debt and equity instruments.**[1]

From earlier chapters, we have seen that a financial asset is "any asset that is:

a) cash;

b) an equity instrument of another entity; or

c) a contractual right:

   (i) to receive cash or another financial asset from another party; or

   (ii) to exchange financial assets or financial liabilities with another party under conditions that are potentially favourable to the entity."[2]

 Law

Companies that invest in debt instruments of another entity are creditors of the issuing company. Debt instruments include debt securities, whose prices are normally quoted in an active market, such as investments in government and corporate bonds, convertible debt, and commercial paper.

Equity instruments, on the other hand, represent ownership interests. Typical examples are common, preferred, or other capital stock or shares. They also include rights to acquire or dispose of ownership interests at an agreed-upon or determinable price, such as warrants, rights, and call or put options. An equity instrument is any contract that is evidence of a residual interest in the assets of an entity after deducting all of its liabilities.

Before looking at how to account for investments, we should address the **different motivations that companies have for investing** in debt and equity instruments issued by other companies. One motivation is **the returns provided by investments** through interest, dividends, or capital appreciation (an increase in the underlying value of the investment). Note that some types of investments provide guaranteed returns (such as term deposits), while others are riskier (such as investments in shares of other companies).

---

[1] The topic of derivatives is not included in this chapter. A derivative is a financial instrument or other contract that requires little or no initial net investment, that is settled at a future date, and whose value is derived from the level of interest rates, commodity prices, exchange rates, or some other variable. Its value therefore changes as the "underlying" variable changes. Chapter 16 discusses basic contracts such as stock options, rights and warrants, and other derivative instruments. Chapter 7 includes coverage of investments in accounts, notes, and loans receivable. Chapters 13 and 14 provide a discussion of financial liabilities, including guarantees, and Chapter 15 reviews the issue of equity securities from the issuing company's perspective. The more complex aspects of financial instruments are left to a course in advanced financial accounting.

[2] This definition is based on the definition in the IFRS *Glossary of Terms*. In addition, under IFRS a contract that can be settled in the entity's own equity instruments may be considered a financial asset under certain limited conditions.

Managers may invest for **short-term returns** or **longer term returns**, depending on their business and whether, and when, they need the cash for other purposes.

Another reason for investing in equity securities has more to do with **corporate strategy** than returns. Companies may invest in common shares of other companies because they want to have a special relationship with a supplier or customer, such as being able to access certain distribution channels or a supply of raw materials. Other investments are made so that the investor can exercise its rights to influence or control the operations of the other company, the investee. The intent is usually to establish a long-term operating relationship between the two entities. A good example of this is provided in the opening vignette to this chapter, where Empire Company explains its investments in real estate company subsidiaries.

Real-World Emphasis

In addition, consider the situation of Stantec Inc., a company that provides a comprehensive variety of professional services related to infrastructure, property, and facilities in both the public and private sectors. In 2009, Stantec acquired the shares and business of Halifax-based Jacques Whitford Limited, an engineering consulting firm, in order to strengthen the service offerings in its environmental practice as well as to increase its presence in Atlantic Canada. In the final analysis, however, strategic investments are usually made in order to increase returns to the investor's shareholders.

How investments are accounted for can depend on **the type of instrument** (debt or equity), **management's intent**, which, as noted above, may be quite different from situation to situation, the **ability to reliably measure the investment's fair value**, or the extent to which the investor can influence the activities of the investee company. The next section of this chapter explains the accounting models generally applied in accounting for straightforward investments in other companies' debt and equity instruments—**situations where the investment does not result in the investor having significant influence or control** over the other company.

After these models are explained, the chapter turns to investments where the investor can exercise significant influence over or control the strategic decisions of the investee company. For these investments, the investor's ownership interest is usually large enough to give the investor a substantial voice at the investee's boardroom table in decisions about the entity's operations, investments, and financing. This, in turn, affects how these investments are accounted for and reported.

Prices and Fair Values

Accounting for investments usually requires them to be recognized and measured initially at their fair value at acquisition. Students are reminded that Chapter 2 discusses what is meant by fair value and identifies various ways that fair value can be measured. The chapter also indicates that some methods of measuring fair value are preferred over others, with prices in an active market being the best and closest to the value we are trying to capture. We saw in previous chapters that unless there is evidence to the contrary, the price paid to acquire an asset is usually considered to be its fair value.

The price of a **debt** instrument is quoted as a percentage of its par or face value. For example, if a $25,000 face value bond is priced at 99, this means that its fair value is 99% of $25,000, or $24,750. If it is priced at 103.5, it will sell for 103.5% of $25,000, or $25,875. **Shares** that are traded on a stock exchange are usually quoted at the market price per share in dollars and cents.

Investments in shares may be acquired on margin. This means that the investor pays only part of the purchase price to acquire the shares. The rest is financed by the broker. Since the shares legally belong to the investor, the asset is recorded at the full share price and a liability to the broker for the amount that was financed is also recognized.

If financial assets are measured initially at their fair value, how should transaction costs that are directly related to the acquisition—such as fees, commissions, or transfer taxes—be accounted for?[3] The obvious choices are to expense these amounts immediately or to add them to the cost of the assets acquired. The answer is—it depends.[4] It is logical to capitalize the transaction costs associated with any investment that is accounted for using a cost-based model because transaction costs are a necessary cost of acquiring the asset. Alternatively, for assets accounted for using a fair value model, it makes more sense to expense the transaction costs. The fair value of an asset is its market price. This does not include acquisition costs. Regardless of how transaction costs are accounted for at acquisition, they are **not included** in the fair value amount at later balance sheet dates.

When a financial instrument is measured at fair value after acquisition, changes in its fair value carrying amount are called unrealized holding gains or losses. The change in value is unrealized because it has not been converted to cash or a claim to cash—the asset is still held by the entity. Such gains and losses are only realized when the asset is disposed of. Usually any unrealized holding gains and losses are separately identified from realized gains and losses on the financial statements.

With this introduction of terms, let's turn to the accounting models for a variety of investments in debt and equity securities. This next section of the chapter identifies and explains three major models of accounting for investments:

1. Cost/amortized cost model

2. Fair value through net income model (FV-NI)

3. Fair value through other comprehensive income model (FV-OCI)

The application of each of these models is summarized in Illustration 9-1.

	Cost/Amortized Cost Model	Fair Value through Net Income Model	Fair Value through OCI Model
At acquisition, measure at:	Cost (equal to fair value + transaction costs)	Fair value	Fair value
At each reporting date, measure at:	Cost or amortized cost	Fair value	Fair value
Report unrealized holding gains and losses (changes in fair value):	Not applicable	In net income	In OCI
Report realized holding gains and losses:	In net income	In net income	Transfer total realized gains/losses to net income (recycling) or directly to retained earnings

Illustration 9-1

Application of Accounting Models

[3] Brokerage commissions are usually incurred when buying and selling most securities. Commissions vary with the share value and the number of shares/units purchased, but they are often between 1% and 3% of the trade value for smaller trades. For larger trades, the commissions are often substantially lower as a percentage. Discount brokerages offer significant discounts even on smaller trades. Transactions involving mutual funds may have no commission attached to them (no-load funds) but a commission may be charged when the funds are redeemed (back-end commission).

[4] Companies also have a choice of when to recognize (and derecognize) the financial asset. This could be on the trade date, when the commitment is made to buy or sell, or on the settlement date, when the asset is delivered and title is transferred—usually a short time thereafter. When the period between these dates is the standard term for the instrument and the market—termed a regular-way purchase or sale—either trade-date or settlement-date accounting may be used. Canadian equities settle in three business days. The same policy is applied consistently to all purchases and sales that belong to the same category of financial asset and the policy that is chosen is disclosed. This chapter's illustrations assume that trade and settlement dates are the same.

Each model is described next in more detail, followed by how IFRS and PE GAAP have resolved accounting issues related to these models as this text went to print.

Objective 1

Explain and apply the cost/amortized cost model of accounting for investments in debt and equity instruments, and identify how the investments are reported.

Cost/Amortized Cost Model

The accounting standards do not always differentiate between the cost and the amortized cost models, referring to them both as amortized cost. The **amortized cost** model applies only to investments in debt instruments and long-term notes and loans receivable, while the **cost** model may be applied to investments in equity instruments (shares) of other companies. Regardless, they are both cost-based methods.

Investments in Shares of Other Entities

Underlying Concept

When shares of a company have been purchased at various times and at varying costs and only a portion of the holdings are sold, use of an average carrying value for the disposal is logical and is required under PE GAAP, but not under IFRS.

Application of the cost model to the investment one company makes in another entity's shares is straightforward:

1. Recognize the cost of the investment at the fair value of the shares acquired (or the fair value of what was given up to acquire them, if more reliable). Add to this any direct transaction costs (such as commissions) incurred to acquire the shares.

2. Unless impaired, report the investment at its cost at each balance sheet date.

3. Recognize dividend income when the entity has a claim to the dividend.

4. When the shares are disposed of, derecognize them and report a gain or loss on disposal in net income. The gain or loss is the difference between the investment's carrying amount and the proceeds on disposal.

To illustrate, assume that Kiwan Corp. (KC) purchases 1,000 shares of Hirj Co. at $4.25 per share on March 8, 2011. A 1.5% commission is charged on the transaction. On December 15, 2011, Hirj Co. directors declare a dividend of $0.10 per share to shareholders of record on December 31, 2011, payable on January 15, 2012. On July 11, 2012, KC sells 800 of the Hirj Co. shares for $5.08 per share and pays a 1.5% commission on the sale. KC has a December 31 year end. KC's entries to record these transactions and events are as follows:

A   = L +   SE
0   0   0

Cash flows: ↓ 4,314 outflow

March 8, 2011		
Investment in Hirj Co. Shares	4,314	
Cash		4,314
(1,000 × $4.25) + (1,000 × $4.25 × .015)		

A   =   L +   SE
+100   +100

Cash flows: No effect

December 31, 2011		
Dividend Receivable	100	
Dividend Income		100
(1,000 × $0.10)		

A   = L +   SE
0   0   0

Cash flows: ↑ 100 inflow

January 15, 2012		
Cash	100	
Dividend Receivable		100

July 11, 2012		
Cash	4,003	
Investment in Hirj Co. Shares		3,451
Gain on Sale of Investment		552

$(800 \times \$5.08) - (800 \times \$5.08 \times .015) = \$4,003$

$\$4,314 \times 800/1,000 = 3,451$

$\$4,003 - \$3,451 = \$552$

A	=	L	+	SE
+552				+552

Cash flows: ↑ 4,003 inflow

Investments in Debt Securities of Other Entities

When the cost model is applied to an investment in debt securities (and long-term notes and loans receivable), it is referred to as the amortized cost model. This is because any difference between the acquisition cost recognized and the face value of the security is amortized over the period to maturity.[5] Amortized cost is the amount recognized at acquisition reduced by principal repayments, where applicable, plus or minus the cumulative amortization of any discount or premium; i.e., the difference between the initial amount recognized and the maturity value. Impairment charges, discussed later in the chapter, also reduce the amortized cost. The following statements describe this method.

1. Recognize the cost of the investment at the fair value of the debt instrument acquired (or the fair value of what was given up to acquire it, if more reliable a measure). Add to this any direct transaction costs, such as commissions, incurred to acquire the investment.

2. Unless impaired, report the investment at its amortized cost as well as any outstanding interest receivable at each balance sheet date.

3. Recognize interest income as it is earned, amortizing any discount or premium at the same time by adjusting the carrying amount of the investment.

4. When the investment is disposed of, first bring the accrued interest and discount or premium amortization up to date. Derecognize the investment, reporting any gain or loss on disposal in net income. The gain or loss is the difference between the proceeds received for the security and the investment's amortized cost at the date of disposal.

WILEY PLUS

Present Value Concepts

Accounting for investments in debt securities using the amortized cost method should be familiar to you. The procedures are the same as accounting for long-term notes and loans receivable, and you may find it useful to review this section of Chapter 7 before continuing. One complication is added in this chapter: the acquisition and disposal of investments between interest payment dates.

Income under the Amortized Cost Model   Income from debt investments is usually in the form of interest. It can be received in one of two ways, depending on whether the investment is interest-bearing or non–interest-bearing. If it is **interest-bearing**, the party holding the investment on the interest payment date receives all the interest since the last interest payment date. Because debt securities can be bought and sold throughout the year, practice has developed for the purchaser to pay the seller an amount equal to the interest

---

[5] If the instrument's "cost" and face value are the same, the method is applied in the same way as for an investment in shares except that interest income is recognized instead of dividend income.

since the last interest payment date. This interest is paid to the seller over and above the agreed exchange price for the investment. If the instrument is **non–interest-bearing**, the price of the bond or other instrument adjusts to its present value at the date of the transaction and no additional amount is paid. The interest to date is incorporated in the investment's fair value.

Finance

The total income from this type of investment is the net cash flow over the time that the investment is held. In the case of investments that are held until they mature, the total income is the difference between the principal amount that is received at maturity plus all periodic interest that is received, and the amount paid to acquire the investment including the accrued interest. Because the decision to acquire and hold the investment is usually based on its yield on the date when it is purchased, the yield rate is also the most appropriate rate to measure periodic income over the term that the investment is held.

To illustrate, assume that on January 1, 2011, Robinson Limited pays $92,278 to purchase $100,000 of Chan Corporation 8% bonds.[6] Robinson accounts for this investment at amortized cost. The bonds mature on January 1, 2016, and interest is payable each July 1 and January 1. The lower-than-face-value purchase price of $92,278 provides an effective interest rate of 10%. This is a combination of the 8% interest received in cash each year and the benefit of the $7,722 discount on the bond ($100,000 – $92,278). Note that the bond is acquired on an interest payment date and there is therefore no accrued interest for Robinson to pay on January 1. Assume Robinson Limited has an August 31 year end.

Cash principal received on maturity of bond	$100,000
Add cash interest received:	
($100,000 × 0.08)/2 × 10 payments	40,000
Less cash paid to acquire the bond	(92,278)
Less cash paid for accrued interest when purchased	–0–
Total income to be recognized	$ 47,722

Because Robinson decided to purchase the bond based on its yield, the amount of income that is recognized each period should ideally reflect the yield rate. The **effective interest method**, required under IFRS unless the investment is held for trading purposes, results in recognizing interest income at a constant yield rate on the investment each period. The straight-line method of recognizing interest and amortizing the discount or premium, permitted under private entity GAAP, was explained in Chapter 7 and is briefly reviewed again below.

Illustration 9-2 shows the application of the effective interest method to Robinson's investment in the Chan bonds. The original discount is amortized exactly by the date the bond matures.

---

[6] As previously indicated, the value is determined by the investment community and is equal to the present value (PV) of the cash inflows of principal and interest payments on the bond, discounted at the market rate. This is relatively straightforward if the bond is bought or sold on its issue date or on an interest payment due date. At other times, a bond's purchase price can be estimated as follows:

PV of cash flows on the immediately preceding interest payment date   = $x

Add the increase in PV to date of sale or purchase at yield rate:

   $x × annual yield rate × portion of year since interest payment date   = y

Deduct the cash interest earned since last interest payment date:

   Face value × annual stated rate × portion of year since last interest date   = (z)

Purchase price of a bond bought or sold between interest payment dates: x + y − z

8% Bonds Purchased to Yield 10%

Date	Cash Received	Interest Income	Bond Discount Amortization	Amortized Cost of Bonds
1/1/11				$ 92,278
7/1/11	$ 4,000[a]	$ 4,614[b]	$ 614[c]	92,892[d]
1/1/12	4,000	4,645	645	93,537
7/1/12	4,000	4,677	677	94,214
1/1/13	4,000	4,711	711	94,925
7/1/13	4,000	4,746	746	95,671
1/1/14	4,000	4,783	783	96,454
7/1/14	4,000	4,823	823	97,277
1/1/15	4,000	4,864	864	98,141
7/1/15	4,000	4,907	907	99,048
1/1/16	4,000	4,952	952	100,000
	$40,000	$47,722	$7,722	

[a] $4,000 = $100,000 \times 0.08 \times 6/12$
[b] $4,614 = $92,278 \times 0.10 \times 6/12$
[c] $614 = $4,614 - $4,000$
[d] $92,892 = $92,278 + 614

The entry to record the purchase of the investment is:

Jan. 1/11	Investment in Chan Corp. Bonds	92,278	
	Cash		92,278

A   =   L   +   SE
0   0   0

Cash flows: ↓ 92,278 outflow

In practice, and as illustrated, **the discount or premium on a bond investment is not usually recognized and reported separately**, although it would also be correct.

The journal entry to record the receipt of the first semi-annual interest payment on July 1, 2011, is:

July 1/11	Cash	4,000	
	Investment in Chan Corp. Bonds	614	
	Interest Income		4,614

A   =   L   +   SE
+4,614   +4,614

Cash flows: ↑ 4,000 inflow

At its year end on August 31, 2011, Robinson recognizes the interest income that has accrued since July 1 and amortizes the discount for the two-month period:

Aug. 31/11	Interest Receivable (4,000 × 2/6)	1,333	
	Investment in Chan Corp. Bonds (645 × 2/6)	215	
	Interest Income (4,645 × 2/6)		1,548

A   =   L   +   SE
+1,548   +1,548

Cash flows: No effect

When the interest payment is received on January 1, 2012, the following entry is made, assuming that Robinson does not use reversing entries.

Jan. 1/12	Cash	4,000	
	Investment in Chan Corp. Bonds (645 × 4/6)	430	
	Interest Receivable		1,333
	Interest Income (4,645 × 4/6)		3,097

A   =   L   +   SE
+3,097   +3,097

Cash flows: ↑ 4,000 inflow

Straight-line Amortization of Bond Premium or Discount   If Robinson Limited is a private enterprise, it may decide to use straight-line amortization instead of the effective interest method. If so, the original discount of $7,722 ($100,000 − $92,278) is amortized to interest income in equal amounts from the date of acquisition to maturity, a period of 60 months. For each month of interest income recognized, 1/60 of $7,722 or $128.70 of discount is amortized. For example, the July 1, 2011 entry to recognize the receipt of the first semi-annual interest payment is:

A   = L +   SE
+4,772.20   +4,772.20

Cash flows: ↑ 4,000 inflow

July 1/11	Cash	4,000.00	
	Investment in Chan Corp. Bonds (6 × $128.70)	772.20	
	Interest Income		4,772.20

Under this approach, a constant **amount** of interest income is recognized each period instead of a constant **rate** of interest. All the other entries that involve interest income and the carrying amount of the investment will be affected in the same way when the straight-line method is used.

Financial Statement Presentation   Illustration 9-3 shows how Robinson Limited reports the items related to its investment in the Chan Corporation bonds in its **August 31, 2011** financial statements, assuming they are long-term investments and the effective interest method is used. If it is within 12 months of maturity, the investment is reported as a current asset.

Illustration **9-3**

Reporting of Investment in Chan Corp. Bonds

BALANCE SHEET

Current assets	
Interest receivable	$ 1,333
Long-term investments	
Investments in bonds, at amortized cost	$93,107[a]

INCOME STATEMENT

| Other revenue and gains | |
| Interest income | $ 6,162[b] |

[a] $92,278 + $614 + $215 = $93,107
[b] $4,614 + $1,548 = $6,162

Sale of Investments   Assume that Robinson Limited sells its investment in the Chan Corporation bonds on November 1, 2015, at 99¾ plus accrued interest. Remember that interest receivable of $1,333 (2/6 × $4,000) and discount amortization of $317 (2/6 × $952) were recognized at the company's August 31, 2015 year end. The following entry is then made on November 1, 2015, to accrue an additional two months' interest (September and October), to amortize the discount from September 1 to November 1, and bring the investment to its correct carrying amount at the date of disposal. The discount amortization for this two-month period is $317 (2/6 × $952).

A   = L +   SE
+1,650   +1,650

Cash flows: No effect

Nov. 1/15	Interest Receivable (2/6 × $4,000)	1,333	
	Investment in Chan Corp. Bonds	317	
	Interest Income (2/6 × $4,952)		1,650

The calculation of the realized gain on the sale is explained in Illustration 9-4.

Selling price of bonds ($100,000 × .9975)		$99,750
Less: Carrying amount of bonds on November 1, 2015:		
Amortized cost, July 1, 2015 (see amortization schedule)	$99,048	
Add: Discount amortized for the period July 1, 2015, to		
November 1, 2015 ($317 to August 31 + $317		
from September 1 to November 1)	634	99,682
Gain on sale of bonds		$ 68

Illustration 9-4

Calculation of Gain on Sale of Bonds

The entry to record the sale of the bonds is:

Nov. 1/15	Cash	102,416	
	Interest Receivable		2,666
	Investment in Chan Corp. Bonds		99,682
	Gain on Sale of Bonds		68

A = L + SE
+68   +68

Cash flows: ↑ 102,416 inflow

The credit to Interest Receivable is for the four months of accrued interest from July 1 to November 1, all of which the purchaser pays in cash to Robinson. The debit to Cash is made up of the selling price of the bonds, $99,750, plus the four months of accrued interest, $2,666. The credit to the Investment in Chan Corp. Bonds account is the bonds' carrying amount on the sale date, and the credit to Gain on Sale of Bonds is the excess of the selling price over the bonds' carrying amount.

Fair Value through Net Income (FV-NI) Model

When accounting standard setters first evaluated using fair value measurements for financial instruments, it was their hope that all financial instruments would be measured at fair value, with all the changes in fair values reported in net income. For a variety of reasons, this was too big a step for accounting practice to take all at once, primarily because of the difficulties in getting good measures of fair value for many financial instruments. However, the **fair value through net income (FV-NI)** method, referred to as **fair value through profit or loss (FVTPL)** in international standards, is required today for many financial assets and liabilities, including many investments in other entities' debt and equity securities.

2 Objective

Explain and apply the fair value through net income model of accounting for investments in debt and equity instruments, and identify how the investments are reported.

Measurement at Acquisition

When investments to be accounted for at fair value through net income (FV-NI) are acquired, they are recognized at their fair value, similar to all financial assets. Consistent with measurement at fair value, transaction costs incurred in acquiring such assets are expensed as incurred.

Measurement after Acquisition

The name of the method—fair value through net income—is very descriptive of how the accounting works! The carrying amount of each FV-NI investment is adjusted to its current fair value at each reporting date. All resulting holding gains and losses are reported in net income along with any dividends or interest income earned.

Income from Investments

As explained for investments carried at amortized cost, the total income on any investment is always the net cash flow from the investment: the gain or loss on the instrument itself plus any interest or dividend return. Accounting for income on an investment is the art of allocating the total income to specific accounting periods.

For FV-NI investments, periodic income is a combination of the change in an investment's carrying amount plus the interest or dividend income that has been received or is receivable for the period. For FV-NI investments in general, and especially those that are **held for trading purposes**—i.e., held to sell in the near term or to generate a profit from short-term fluctuations in price—it may not be important to report interest and dividend income separately from the holding gains or losses. Both types of income may be accounted for and reported together because this tends to mirror how such investments are managed.[7]

FV-NI Investments: Dividend and Interest Income Not Reported Separately

Assume that Investor Inc. acquires a temporary investment in $20,000 face value, 10% Sorfit Ltd. bonds on June 15 at a time when the market rate of interest on similar bonds is 8%. The bonds pay interest semi-annually on January 15 and July 15 each year. Investor Inc. pays $21,300 for the bonds, and sells them on August 31 for $21,350 when it needs the cash for operations.

Illustration 9-5 explains how income is calculated and recorded, assuming there is **no separate reporting of the types of investment income** on the income statement.

Illustration 9-5

Income on an Interest-Bearing Debt Instrument Accounted for at FV-NI, Interest Income Not Reported Separately

A = L + SE
0   0   0

Cash flows: ↓ 22,133 outflow

A   = L + SE
+167   0   +167

Cash flows: ↑ 1,000 inflow

June 15	Cost of bonds Interest since last interest payment date purchased from seller: $20,000 × 10% × 5/12	$21,300 833	
	Cash payment	$22,133	
	Temporary Investment in Bonds Interest Receivable Cash (To record purchase of Sorfit Ltd. bonds and accrued interest.)	21,300 833	 22,133

July 15	Cash
	   Investment Income
	   Interest Receivable
	     $20,000 × 10% × 6/12
	(To record receipt of semi-annual interest
	on Sorfit Ltd. bonds.)
		1,000	
			167
			833

Aug. 31	Selling price of bonds
	Interest since last interest payment
	  date sold to purchaser
	  $20,000 × 10% × 1½/12
		$21,350
		
		250	

	Cash received from purchaser	$21,600	
	Selling price of bonds Carrying value of bonds	$21,350 21,300	
	Holding gain on sale of bonds	$ 50	

[7] IFRS 7 *Financial Instruments: Disclosures* indicates in paragraph B5(e) that entities may disclose whether the net gains or losses on financial assets measured at fair value through profit or loss (i.e., FV-NI) and reported on the income statement include interest and dividend income. Private entity GAAP, on the other hand, requires separate reporting of interest income and net gains or losses recognized on financial instruments (*CICA Handbook*, Part II, Section 3856.50).

Cash		21,600	
Temporary Investment in Bonds			21,300
Investment Income ($250 + $50)			300
(To record sale of bonds, gain, and interest			
accrued since June 15.)			

A = L + SE
+300   0   +300

Cash flows: ↑ 21,600 inflow

There is no real need to use the effective interest method or to amortize any discount or premium on debt instruments that are held for a fast turnaround if interest income is not separately reported. Note that the total income reported is $167 + $300 = $467, the net cash flow on the trading transaction. This can also be calculated as follows:

Net cash flow:		
Interest received	$ 1,000	
Total cash received on disposition	21,600	
Less total cash paid on acquisition	(22,133)	
Investment income earned	$ 467	

If Investor Inc. has a June 30 year end, the interest to June 30 is accrued and the FV-NI investment is adjusted to the bond's fair value at June 30. The total of the interest accrued and holding gain or loss to June 30 is recognized as investment income. The July 15 and August 31 entries in Illustration 9-5 above would then have to take the June 30 year-end adjusting entry into account.

For a non–interest-bearing debt investment that is held for short-term trading, the investment income that is earned is the difference between the instrument's purchase price and its maturity value or the proceeds on its disposal. Treasury bills, for example, are usually traded in non–interest-bearing form. Assume that Investor Inc. pays $19,231 on March 15 for a $20,000 six-month treasury bill that matures on September 15. The investment, purchased to yield an 8% return, is designated as an FV-NI investment. Illustration 9-6 shows how to account for the investment income, assuming that interest income is not reported separately.

Mar. 15	Temporary Investment in T-Bill	19,231	
	Cash		19,231
	(To record purchase of a $20,000,		
	six-month treasury bill.)		
Sept. 15	Cash	20,000	
	Temporary Investment in T-Bill		19,231
	Investment Income/Loss		769
	(To record the proceeds on maturity		
	of a $20,000 treasury bill.)		

Illustration 9-6

Income on a Non–Interest-Bearing Debt Instrument Accounted for at FV-NI, Interest Income Not Reported Separately

Note that the investment income, which consists entirely of interest in this case, is equal to an 8% yield on the amount paid for the investment: $19,231 \times 8\% \times 6/12 = $769. If Investor Inc. needed cash prior to September 15 and sold the investment before maturity, the investment income reported is the difference between its carrying amount and the proceeds on disposal.

Investments in equity securities that are held for short-term trading profits may pay dividends. If the company does not report interest income separately, it is unlikely that it would report dividend income separately either. Because the holder of the shares on the date of record is entitled to the dividend and this date is generally a few weeks before the dividend is paid, a dividend receivable and the related income may be recognized before the cash is received. As an FV-NI investment, the shares are remeasured to their fair value at each balance sheet date with the change in fair value also recognized in the Investment Income/Loss account. When the investment is sold, its carrying amount is removed from the investment account and investment income is recognized.

To demonstrate the accounting for a portfolio of temporary investments accounted for at FV-NI with no separate reporting of interest and dividend income, assume that on December 31, 2011, Western Publishing Corporation provides the information shown in Illustration 9-7 about its temporary investments portfolio. Assume that all investments were acquired in 2011. The investments were recorded at their fair value at acquisition in an account entitled Temporary Investments, and this value is their **carrying amount** on the books before any adjustment.

<table>
<tr><td rowspan="2" style="vertical-align:top">Illustration 9-7

Calculation of Fair Value Adjustment—Temporary Investments Portfolio, December 31, 2011</td><td colspan="3" style="text-align:center">TEMPORARY INVESTMENTS PORTFOLIO
December 31, 2011</td></tr>
<tr><td>Investments</td><td>Carrying
Amount</td><td>Fair Value</td></tr>
<tr><td></td><td>Burlington Corp. shares</td><td>$ 43,860</td><td>$ 51,500</td></tr>
<tr><td></td><td>Genesta Corp. 8% bonds</td><td>184,230</td><td>175,200</td></tr>
<tr><td></td><td>Warner Ltd. shares</td><td>86,360</td><td>91,500</td></tr>
<tr><td></td><td>Total portfolio</td><td>$314,450</td><td>$318,200</td></tr>
<tr><td></td><td colspan="3">Adjustment needed to the portfolio to bring it to fair value at
December 31, 2011: $318,200 − $314,450 = $3,750 debit</td></tr>
</table>

At December 31, an adjusting entry is made to bring the investments portfolio to its year-end fair value and to record the holding gain. This entry assumes that Western Publishing has one control account in its general ledger for the entire portfolio. It would be equally correct to make a separate entry for each of the three different investments.

A = L + SE	
+3,750 +3,750	Dec. 31/11 Temporary Investments 3,750
Cash flows: No effect	Investment Income/Loss 3,750

The Investment Income/Loss account is included in net income on the income statement, and the fair values of the investments at December 31, 2011, now become the carrying amounts on the books. With a fair value measurement approach, the original cost or fair value at acquisition is not relevant.[8]

Now assume that the Genesta Corp. bonds are sold for $174,000 on February 4, 2012, their interest payment date, and that 1,000 shares of Next Ltd. are acquired for their fair value of $49,990 on September 21, 2012. The entries to record the February 4 and September 21 transactions follow. Note that the bond's carrying amount before the sale is $175,200, its fair value at the last balance sheet date.

---

[8] Certainly management's ability to earn a return and realize gains on the investments is relevant. In addition, the entity has to keep track in its files of the securities' original cost because only realized gains and losses are taxable or deductible for tax purposes.

Feb. 4/12	Cash	174,000	
	Investment Income/Loss	1,200	
	Temporary Investments		175,200

A = L + SE
−1,200   −1,200

Cash flows: ↑ 174,000 inflow

| Sept. 21/12 | Temporary Investments | 49,990 | |
| | Cash | | 49,990 |

A = L + SE
0   0   0

Cash flows: ↓ 49,990 outflow

Because the gains and losses on temporary FV-NI investments are reported in net income, the distinction between the portions that are realized and unrealized is blurred. This is not usually an issue, however, particularly for trading securities that are acquired for short-term profit-taking.

Illustration 9-8 indicates the carrying amounts and fair values of the temporary investments portfolio at December 31, 2012. As Western Publishing prepares financial statements only once a year, the carrying amounts of the Burlington and Warner shares that are still on hand are the fair values reported at December 31, 2011. The carrying amount of the Next Ltd. shares acquired during the year is their fair value at acquisition.

Illustration 9-8

Fair Value Adjustment— Temporary Investments Portfolio, December 31, 2012

TEMPORARY INVESTMENT PORTFOLIO
December 31, 2012

Investments	Carrying Amount	Fair Value
Burlington Corp. shares	$ 51,500	$ 50,500
Warner Ltd. shares	91,500	90,100
Next Ltd. shares	49,990	50,600
Total portfolio	$192,990	$191,200

Adjustment needed to bring the portfolio to fair value at
December 31, 2012: $192,990 − $191,200 = $1,790 credit

At December 31, an adjusting entry is made to bring the investments to their year-end fair values.

| Dec. 31/12 | Investment Income/Loss | 1,790 | |
| | Temporary Investments | | 1,790 |

A = L + SE
−1,790   −1,790

Cash flows: No effect

The investment loss is included in the 2012 income statement, added to the loss recognized on February 4. The portfolio is reported on the 2012 comparative statement of financial position as follows, assuming the investments were acquired for short-term trading purposes.

	2012	2011
Current assets:		
Temporary investments, at fair value	$191,200	$318,200

Terms other than "temporary investments" may be used, such as "short-term investments" or "trading securities."

Underlying Concept

Investments in financial instruments that are held for trading purposes—and therefore are generally marketable—are reported at fair value because this value is the most relevant.

FV-NI Investments: Dividend and Interest Income Reported Separately   Entities hold a variety of investments in debt and equity securities that are accounted for using the FV-NI model. Sometimes, the reporting entity may need or want to keep track of holding gains and losses separately from interest and dividend income.

Dividends Reported Separately   Accounting for dividend income separately from holding gains and losses is straightforward.

- When a dividend is received (or receivable), it is recognized in an account such as Dividend Income on FV-NI Investments.

- When the investment is adjusted to its current fair value at each reporting date, the change in value is recognized in a separate account such as Gain (or Loss) on FV-NI Investments in Shares.

It is now easier for the entity to report the dividend income separately from the fair value changes because the information has been captured in two different accounts.

Interest Reported Separately   Recognizing interest income under the effective interest method (or even the straight-line method) separately requires more complex entries than described above. This is because **any discount or premium must be amortized before the change in fair value is recognized**.

Amortizing the discount or premium changes the investment's carrying amount. Therefore, the subsequent adjustment to bring the investment to its new fair value has to take this interest adjustment into account. Two sets of information have to be kept to make this work: a schedule of the investment's amortized cost, for purposes of interest income calculations; and information on its fair value, in order to report the asset at the appropriate amount.

The bookkeeping can be handled in at least two different ways. One method keeps the investment in the accounts at its amortized cost and uses a separate valuation allowance account to bring it to its fair value at each balance sheet date. Alternatively, the investment account itself is maintained at fair value and the necessary amortized cost information is kept in records that are supplementary to the accounts. In this chapter, for purposes of explanation, the second approach is used. The authors prefer this method because it emphasizes the use of fair value measurement rather than an adjusted cost-based measure. In short, the entries are as follows.

- Recognize interest income in an account such as Interest Income on FV-NI Investments as it is earned, adjusting the book value of the investment by the amount of any discount or premium amortization.

- When the investment is adjusted to its current fair value at each reporting date, the change in value is recognized in a separate account such as Gain (or Loss) on FV-NI Debt Investments.

To illustrate the accounting for an investment in a debt instrument at FV-NI with interest income to be reported separately under the effective interest method, assume that a company purchases $100,000, 10%, five-year bonds of Graff Corporation on January 1, 2011, with interest payable on July 1 and January 1. The bond sells for $108,111, resulting in a bond premium of $8,111 and an effective interest rate of 8%. The entry to record the purchase of the bonds is:

| Jan. 1/11 | Investments in Graff Corp. Bonds | 108,111 | |
| | Cash | | 108,111 |

A = L + SE
0   0   0

Cash flows: ↓ 108,111 outflow

Illustration 9-9 shows the effect that the premium amortization has on the interest income that is reported each period. The process is identical to the amortization of debt investments explained earlier in this chapter, except this situation involves a premium instead of a discount.

10% BONDS PURCHASED TO YIELD 8%

Date	Cash Received	Interest Income	Bond Premium Amortization	Amortized Cost of Bonds
1/1/2011				$108,111
7/1/2011	$ 5,000[a]	$ 4,324[b]	$ 676[c]	107,435[d]
1/1/2012	5,000	4,297	703	106,732
7/1/2012	5,000	4,269	731	106,001
1/1/2013	5,000	4,240	760	105,241
7/1/2013	5,000	4,210	790	104,451
1/1/2014	5,000	4,178	822	103,629
7/1/2014	5,000	4,145	855	102,774
1/1/2015	5,000	4,111	889	101,885
7/1/2015	5,000	4,075	925	100,960
1/1/2016	5,000	4,040	960	100,000
	$50,000	$41,889	$8,111	

[a] $5,000 = $100,000 × 0.10 × 6/12
[b] $4,324 = $108,111 × 0.08 × 6/12
[c] $676 = $5,000 − $4,324
[d] $107,435 = $108,111 − $676

Illustration 9-9

Schedule of Interest Income and Bond Premium Amortization—Effective Interest Method

The entries to record interest income on the first interest date and at the December 31 year end are:

July 1/11	Cash	5,000	
	Investment in Graff Corp. Bonds		676
	Interest Income		4,324

A = L + SE
+4,324   +4,324

Cash flows: ↑ 5,000 inflow

Dec. 31/11	Interest Receivable	5,000	
	Investment in Graff Corp. Bonds		703
	Interest Income		4,297

A = L + SE
+4,297   +4,297

Cash flows: No effect

As a result, the company reports interest income for 2011 of $8,621 ($4,324 + $4,297).

Assume that at December 31, 2011, the fair value of the Graff Corporation bonds is $105,000. Their carrying amount at this time is $106,732 and the adjustment needed to bring the Investment account to fair value is $1,732:

Original cost and carrying amount of bonds		$108,111
Entries made to Investment in Graff Corp. Bonds account during year when recognizing interest income:		
July 1, 2011	$676 credit	
Dec. 31, 2011	703 credit	(1,379)
Carrying amount before fair value adjustment		106,732
Fair value, December 31, 2011		105,000
Fair value adjustment needed		$ 1,732 credit

The entry to adjust the investment to its fair value at December 31, 2011, is:

A   = L +   SE
−1,732   −1,732

Cash flows: No effect

Dec. 31/11 Loss on Graff Corp. Bonds (FV-NI)	1,732	
Investment in Graff Corp. Bonds		1,732

The holding loss on the bonds of $1,732 is reported in net income. At December 31, 2011, the statement of financial position reports:

Long-term Investments (assumed)	
Investment in bonds, at fair value through net income	$105,000

Fair Value through Other Comprehensive Income (FV-OCI) Model

Objective 3

Explain and apply the fair value through other comprehensive income model of accounting for investments in equity instruments, and identify how the investments are reported.

Underlying Concept

Fair value is viewed by many as being the most appropriate measure for financial assets because it best represents the value of the asset to the investor.

Although you were introduced to the concept of other comprehensive income (OCI) earlier in this text, a brief review is appropriate as we use this component of the financial statements in this chapter. Chapter 4 explained the terms associated with OCI as follows:[9]

Comprehensive income is the change in equity (or the net assets) of an entity during a period from non-owner source transactions and events. It is the total of net income and other comprehensive income.

Other comprehensive income (OCI) is made up of revenues, gains, expenses, and losses that accounting standards say are included in comprehensive income, but excluded from net income.

Accumulated other comprehensive income (AOCI) is the balance of all past charges and credits to other comprehensive income to the balance sheet date.

Illustration 9-10 shows how these financial statement categories are related.

----

[9] Private entity GAAP does not make use of OCI.

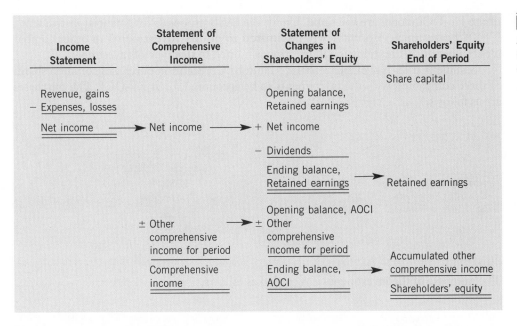

Illustration 9-10

*Net Income, OCI,
Comprehensive Income,
and AOCI*

Measurement at Acquisition

Investments accounted for at **fair value through other comprehensive income (FV-OCI)** are recognized at acquisition at their fair value. However, unlike the fair value models described above, the transaction costs tend to be added to the carrying amount of the investment. When the investment is adjusted to its fair value at the first reporting date, the transaction costs automatically end up as part of the holding gain or loss recognized in OCI at that time.

Income and Measurement after Acquisition

At each reporting date, the carrying amount of each FV-OCI investment is adjusted to its current fair value. As the name of the model implies, the changes in fair value—the holding gains and losses—are recognized in other comprehensive income. The dividend income from these investments is reported separately from the holding gains and losses because the dividend income is reported in net income, while the unrealized holding gains and losses are captured in OCI, net of income tax.[10] There are two different versions of the FV-OCI model, however, with the difference between them relating to how they treat the holding gains and losses once they are realized:

1. FV-OCI with recycling, and

2. FV-OCI without recycling.

Under the **FV-OCI model with recycling**, when the investments are disposed of and converted to cash or a claim to cash, the previously unrealized holding gains or losses to the date of disposal are transferred or "recycled" into net income.[11] Under the **FV-OCI model without recycling**, the realized gains and losses do not get recycled through net income, but are transferred directly into retained earnings. Aside from this, both versions

Underlying Concept

Recycling supports the continued use of net income as the main performance measure, while not recycling supports the concept that comprehensive income is the appropriate measure of performance.

---

[10] Intraperiod tax allocation requires that the unrealized holding gains and losses be recognized in the statement of comprehensive income, net of tax. This is explained more fully in Chapter 18. The illustrations that follow omit the related taxes to simplify the examples.

[11] In the past, changes in fair value that represent an impairment loss were transferred out of OCI and into net income. The proposed IFRS changes do not recognize these revaluations as impairment losses.

of the FV-OCI model are the same. Under the IASB proposals for financial instruments, FV-OCI investments normally will be **limited to equity investments** in other companies.[12] Therefore, the following illustration is limited to this type of investment.

Assume that on November 3, 2010, Manitoba Corporation purchases common shares of three companies, with the investments to be accounted for at FV-OCI. The purchases are as follows:

	Fair value and cost at acquisition
Nova Industries Ltd.	$259,700
Columbia Soup Corp.	317,500
St. Boniface Pulp Ltd.	141,350
Total cost	$718,550

The purchase of the investments is recorded as follows:

A = L + SE
0   0   0

Cash flows: ↓ 718,550 outflow

Nov. 3/10	Investment in Nova Industries	259,700	
	Investment in Columbia Soup	317,500	
	Investment in St. Boniface Pulp	141,350	
	Cash		718,550

Alternatively, Manitoba Corporation could use one control account for its portfolio of investments accounted for at FV-OCI and a subsidiary ledger to track each investment separately. On December 6, 2010, the company receives a cash dividend of $4,200 on its investment in the common shares of Columbia Soup. The cash dividend is recorded as follows:

A   = L +   SE
+4,200   +4,200

Cash flows: ↑ 4,200 inflow

Dec. 6/10	Cash	4,200	
	Dividend Income		4,200

Illustration 9-11 indicates the carrying amounts (and cost), fair values, and unrealized gains and losses at December 31, 2010, for Manitoba's FV-OCI investments.

Illustration 9-11

Schedule of Investments and Holding Gains/Losses—FV-OCI Equity Investments Portfolio (2010)

FV-OCI EQUITY INVESTMENTS PORTFOLIO
December 31, 2010

Investments	Carrying Amount	Fair Value	Holding Gain (Loss) for Period
Nova Industries Ltd.	$259,700	$275,000	$ 15,300
Columbia Soup Corp.	317,500	304,000	(13,500)
St. Boniface Pulp Ltd.	141,350	104,000	(37,350)
Total of portfolio	$718,550	$683,000	$(35,550)

---

[12] As this text went to print, U.S. GAAP envisaged investments in debt securities being accounted for at FV-OCI.

For Manitoba's portfolio, the gross holding gains are $15,300, and the gross holding losses are $50,850 ($13,500 + $37,350), resulting in a net unrealized loss of $35,550. The portfolio's fair value is $35,550 less than its carrying amount (and cost, in this first accounting period). The unrealized gains and losses are recorded in a Holding Gain or Loss account and are reported as part of other comprehensive income. The carrying amount of each investment is adjusted in the following entry to its fair value at the balance sheet date.[13]

Dec. 31/10	Investment in Nova Industries	15,300	
	Holding Loss on Columbia Soup (OCI)	13,500	
	Holding Loss on St. Boniface Pulp (OCI)	37,350	
	Holding Gain on Nova Industries (OCI)		15,300
	Investment in Columbia Soup		13,500
	Investment in St. Boniface Pulp		37,350

A = L + SE
−35,550   −35,550
Cash flows: No effect

A variety of terms can be used to describe the investments on the balance sheet, and they could be either current or long-term assets in nature. One possible presentation is:

Investments at fair value, with gains and losses in OCI	$683,000

Sale of FV-OCI Investments   Now assume that Manitoba sells all of its Nova Industries Ltd. common shares on January 23, 2011, receiving proceeds of $287,220. This is $12,220 more than the current carrying amount of the Investment in Nova Industries in the accounts.

While it is possible to record this event using different combinations of entries, the following series of three entries clearly accomplishes what is needed:

(a) The **first entry** adjusts the investment's carrying amount to its fair value at the date of disposal and captures the holding gain up to that date in OCI.

(b) The **second entry** removes the investment's carrying amount from the asset account and records the proceeds on disposal.

(c) The **third entry** is a reclassification adjustment that transfers the holding gain that is now realized out of OCI and into (i) net income (if FV-OCI with recycling) or (ii) to retained earnings (if FV-OCI without recycling).

Jan. 23/11	(a) Investment in Nova Industries	12,220	
	Holding Gain on Nova Industries (OCI)		12,220
	($287,220 − $275,000)		
	(b) Cash	287,220	
	Investment in Nova Industries		287,220
	($275,000 + $12,220)		

---

[13] If one control account were used instead, one summary debit to an Unrealized Loss account (OCI) for $35,550 and one credit to the control Investment account for $35,550 would be made. The subsidiary ledger would then be brought up to date for each individual investment. A subsidiary ledger would also likely be used to track the components of accumulated other comprehensive income to make it easier to later identify the realized gains and losses for each individual security.

(c) (i) if FV-OCI with recycling:			
Holding Gain on Nova Industries (OCI)		27,520	
Gain on Sale of Nova Industries			27,520
or (c) (ii) if FV-OCI without recycling:			
Holding Gain on Nova Industries (OCI)		27,520	
Retained Earnings			27,520

A = L + SE
+12,220   +12,220

Cash flows: ↑ 287,220 inflow

The amount either recycled through OCI to net income or transferred to retained earnings is the difference between the investment's original cost and the proceeds on disposal ($287,220 − $259,700). It is also the sum of all prior entries to OCI for the Nova Industries shares: a $15,300 gain on December 31, 2010, and a $12,220 gain on January 23, 2011, for a total of $27,520. All that remains in AOCI now is the unrealized net holding gains/losses on the remaining investments.

To continue with this example, assume that the information in Illustration 9-12 is provided for Manitoba's FV-OCI portfolio at December 31, 2011.

Illustration 9-12

Calculation of Holding Gain/Loss for Period—FV-OCI Equity Investments Portfolio (2011)

FV-OCI INVESTMENTS PORTFOLIO
December 31, 2011

Investments	Cost	Carrying Amount	Fair Value	Holding Gain (Loss) for Period
Columbia Soup Corp.	$317,500	$304,000	$362,550	$58,550
St. Boniface Pulp Ltd.	141,350	104,000	139,050	35,050
Total of portfolio	$458,850	$408,000	$501,600	$93,600

The entry to bring the investments to their fair value at December 31, 2011, is:

A = L + SE
+93,600   +93,600

Cash flows: No effect

Dec. 31/11	Investment in Columbia Soup	58,550	
	Investment in St. Boniface Pulp	35,050	
	Holding Gain on Columbia Soup (OCI)		58,550
	Holding Gain on St. Boniface Pulp (OCI)		35,050

Financial Statement Presentation   Illustration 9-13 indicates how Manitoba Corp.'s December 31, 2011 balance sheet and statements of income, comprehensive income, and changes in accumulated other comprehensive income are reported if the **realized** holding gains and losses are recycled to the income statement.

Illustration 9-13

Financial Statement Reporting of Equity Investments at FV-OCI

BALANCE SHEET, December 31, 2011

Long-term investments (assumed)	
Investments, at fair value with gains and losses in OCI	**$501,600**
Shareholders' equity	
Accumulated other comprehensive income	**$ 42,750**

INCOME STATEMENT, Year 2011

Other revenues and gains	
Dividend income	**$ xxx**
Gain on sale of investments in shares	**$ 27,520**

STATEMENT OF COMPREHENSIVE INCOME, Year 2011

Net income		$ x
Other comprehensive income:		
Holding gains on FV-OCI		
investments during year ($12,220 + $93,600)	$105,820	
Reclassification adjustment for realized gains	(27,520)	
Other comprehensive income		78,300
Comprehensive income		$x + 78,300

STATEMENT OF CHANGES IN SHAREHOLDERS' EQUITY: CHANGES IN ACCUMULATED OTHER COMPREHENSIVE INCOME, Year 2011

Accumulated other comprehensive income (loss), January 1, 2011	($35,550)
Other comprehensive income, 2011	78,300
Accumulated other comprehensive income (loss), December 31, 2011	$42,750

Notice two things:

1. If Manitoba Corporation's investments were accounted for at FV-OCI **without recycling**, the only financial statement shown above that would differ is the Income Statement. This is because the realized holding gain of $27,520 would have been adjusted directly to Retained Earnings instead of going through the Income Statement. Under both, the realized gain no longer appears in AOCI. Instead, it ends up in retained earnings—under one method directly, and under the other because it was reported in net income in the year.

2. The AOCI at December 31, 2011, can be calculated independently as the difference between the portfolio's carrying amount at that date, $501,600, and the original cost of the investments, $458,850.

Take your time to be sure you understand the flow of the numbers in this comprehensive example.

GAAP Classifications

Now that the three common methods of accounting for financial instruments have been explained and illustrated, how does a company decide which method is GAAP for a particular investment?[14] The correct answer is, "It depends on when you are asking."[15]

The IFRS classifications indicated in Illustration 9-14 are based on IFRS 9 *Financial Instruments* released in late 2009. These standards are not required to be implemented prior to 2013, although earlier adoption is permitted. The PE GAAP classifications are those from the private entity standards approved by the Accounting Standards Board and released in December 2009. These standards are effective January 1, 2011, with earlier adoption also allowed. Canadian GAAP in place prior to these changes are summarized in Appendix 9A.

4 Objective

Identify private entity GAAP and IFRS for investments in financial assets where there is no significant influence or control.

---

[14] This section applies only to the reporting of investments in entities when the investor company does not have significant influence, control, or joint control.

[15] As this text went to print, both FASB and the IASB were in the process of simplifying their standards. Both hoped to have revised and harmonized standards out in 2010, but as of late 2009, they had reached different tentative conclusions.

	Private Entity GAAP	IFRS
Measurement attributes	• Cost/amortized cost • Fair value	• Amortized cost • Fair value
Classification categories	**Fair value through income (FV-NI):** equity investments quoted in an active market	**Amortized cost:** if the entity's business model is to manage the instrument on the basis of yield to maturity **and** the instrument has contractual basic loan cash flows
	Cost/amortized cost: all other investments	**Fair value through net income (FV-NI):** all other financial assets
		Fair value through OCI (FV-OCI) without recycling: investments in equity instruments that are not held for the purposes of trading (special election)
Is there a fair value option?	Yes; can **designate FV-NI** category for any financial asset on initial recognition.	Yes; can **designate FV-NI** category on initial recognition for instruments that would otherwise be classified at amortized cost if it reduces or eliminates an accounting mismatch.
What to do with transaction costs	Capitalize for instruments measured at cost/amortized cost; otherwise, expense.	Capitalize for all instruments **except FV-NI**.
What to do with realized gains and losses from disposal	Recognize in net income	Recognize in net income for all instruments except for FV-OCI classified instruments where they are recognized in OCI without recycling.
What to do with interest and dividend accruals	Recognize in net income	Recognize in net income for all instruments. An exception is permitted for FV-OCI classified instruments where dividends are a return of capital, in which case they are recognized in OCI without recycling.
Is separate reporting of dividend and interest income required?	There is no requirement for dividend income. Total interest income is required to be disclosed separately.	There is no requirement for dividend income. Total interest income is required to be disclosed separately for financial asset investments that are not accounted for at FV-NI; that is, for those accounted for at amortized cost, and at FV-OCI, if any.
What to do with transfers between categories	Fair value option designation is irrevocable; otherwise the issue is not addressed.	No reclassifications are permitted except on the rare occasion that there is a change in the entity's business model.

Under **private entity GAAP**, the cost-based model is generally applied for equity investments except where active market prices are available. Because investment portfolios are usually made up of a mix of debt and equity instruments that are managed on a fair value basis, PE GAAP allows entities to choose the FV-NI model for any financial instrument. Regardless of which method is used, all interest earned and dividends received are recognized in net income.

The **IASB** decided on two measurement bases: amortized cost and fair value. Its underlying philosophy is that the amortized cost classification decision should be based on an entity's business model for managing its financial assets as well as on the contractual cash flow characteristics of the instrument.[16]

1. **Business model for managing the instrument**: The amortized cost classification does not depend on management's intent for a specific instrument, but instead, is based first on how it, or more likely, a portfolio of such instruments, is managed. If investments are managed on a contractual yield basis, changes in its fair value are not relevant. If the prospects for future cash flows are best assessed by reference to the contractual cash flows specified by the instrument, the amortized cost method is the more appropriate method of accounting for and reporting the asset.

2. **Contractual cash flow characteristics**: The instrument should have only basic loan features. This means that the financial asset has contractual terms that give rise to cash flows on specified dates that are solely payments of principal and interest on the principal outstanding.[17] Examples of such features include a fixed amount or a fixed rate of return over its life and contractual provisions of rights to unpaid amounts of principal and interest.

 Law

If an investment does not meet **both of these conditions**, it is accounted for at fair value through income. For example, if an instrument has basic loan features, but it is acquired for trading purposes or is managed on a fair value basis, it will be recognized at fair value through net income.

While the two main IFRS classifications are amortized cost and FV-NI, two other options have been included in the draft standard. One is a response to entities that acquire investments for longer term strategic purposes (but where the investor does not have significant influence or control). These shares are not held for realizing direct investment gains. Therefore, a special election may be made, on acquisition, to classify the investment as FV-OCI, without recycling realized gains and losses back through net income. In addition, the standard indicates that any dividends received from such an investment are recognized in net income unless the dividend is determined to be a return **of** capital rather than a return **on** the investment.[18]

In addition to the classifications described, IFRS also allows a **fair value option**. When an investment is first recognized, an entity may choose to measure it at FV-NI provided that this corrects an "accounting mismatch." The term "accounting mismatch" refers to a recognition or measurement inconsistency where the resulting effect in the accounts of following the standards does not represent the underlying economic situation.[19]

---

[16] There is much support among standard setters in FASB and IASB for a full fair value model with all changes in value recognized in income. This model is easy to understand and transparent, but suffers from practical problems associated with the inability to reliably measure the fair value of many financial instruments. It would also necessitate possible changes in the format and presentation of the income statement itself. Because preparers are not able to support such a major change, only incremental steps are being taken toward the goal of a full FV-NI model for all financial instruments.

[17] IASB, IFRS 9 *Financial Instruments*, November 2009, para 4.2(b).

[18] This is not really an exception: a dividend that represents a return of the investment is usually accounted for as a reduction of the investment's carrying amount rather than as dividend income. An example: AB Ltd. pays a regular dividend on June 30 each year to shareholders of record on June 15. Shareholders who purchase AB Ltd. shares just before the ex-dividend date will receive the dividend, with part of the cost of the shares really being a payment in advance for the dividend. When the dividend is received, an entry to reduce the cost of the shares better represents the substance of the transaction than to recognize it as income of the period.

[19] An example of an accounting mismatch is what happens when one financial instrument is acquired to hedge the effects of another financial instrument in order to eliminate a specific financial risk. If one is measured at amortized cost and the other at FV-NI, the holding gain or loss on one is not offset by the other and the income statement reports unwarranted variability. There is an accounting mismatch. In such a case, IFRS allow the entity to apply the FV option to the other instrument so that the gains on one "match" the losses on the other and net income is not affected.

Reclassification from one measurement category to another is not permitted under IFRS, except in the rare case that a company changes its business model in relation to its investments. In this case, an investment changed to an FV-based measure is revalued to its fair value and the gain or loss is recognized in net income. Alternatively, if the change is from fair value to another measurement, the investment's fair value at that point becomes the new carrying amount.

IMPAIRMENT

Financial asset investments are reviewed for possible impairment for the same reasons that non-financial assets are: the balance sheet value for any asset cannot be more than the future benefits the asset can bring to the organization. Since financial assets measured at fair value are already measured at their current fair value amount, it is usually only those measured at cost or amortized cost that need a method of accounting for impairment.

Both IFRS and private entity GAAP require that entities adjust for impairment at each reporting date. To the extent possible, this review is carried out at the level of individual assets. However, sometimes the information is not available on a timely basis to do this on each specific asset, so investments with similar characteristics are grouped. If an instrument, or portfolio of instruments, is determined to be impaired, the amount of the impairment loss is calculated and recognized. There are differences of opinion, however, on how such a loss should be determined and reported. Three different impairment models are explained next: an incurred loss model, an expected loss model, and a full fair value model.

Incurred Loss Model

Under the incurred loss model, investments are recognized as impaired when there is no longer reasonable assurance that the future cash flows associated with them will be either collected in their entirety or when due. Entities look for evidence that there has been a significant adverse change in the period in the expected amount of future cash flows or in the timing of those cash flows. Examples of situations that might indicate impairment include the fact that the entity that issued the debt or equity instrument:

- is experiencing significant financial difficulties,

- has defaulted on or is late making interest or principal payments,

- is likely to undergo a major financial reorganization or enter bankruptcy, or

- is in a market that is experiencing significant negative economic change.

If such evidence exists, the next step is to measure the investment's estimated realizable amounts. This is calculated as the present value of the revised amounts and timing of the future cash flows, discounted (a) at the interest rate originally used to measure the instrument when it was first recognized or (b) at a current market rate. For this reason, this method is sometimes referred to as a **discounted cash flow (DCF) model**. Alternatively, if the revised amount and timing of the cash flows cannot be reasonably determined, the realizable amount can be calculated as the current market price for the instrument, or the fair value of the net proceeds the entity would get on liquidating any collateral it is entitled to. The **impairment loss** is the difference between this revised present value calculation and the instrument's carrying amount.

To illustrate, assume a company has an investment in AB Ltd. bonds with a carrying amount of $37,500. If the present value of the discounted revised cash flows is $33,000, an impairment loss of $4,500 is indicated. The loss is recognized as follows:

Impairment Loss on Investment	4,500	
Investment in AB Ltd. Bonds		4,500

A   =   L   +   SE
−4,500   −4,500

Cash flows: No effect

Alternatively, instead of reducing the carrying amount of the investment itself, the credit could be made to an Allowance for Impairment account that is a contra account to the investment asset.

After the impairment is recorded, interest income is recognized based on the revised cash flow estimates and the **discount rate that was used to determine the present value of those flows**. Any further change in the investment's realizable value related to an event occurring after the original impairment is recognized as an adjustment of the impairment loss. It could be a further decline in value (an increased loss) or a recovery of part or all of the previous estimated impairment loss.

This impairment method is described as an incurred loss impairment model because it captures only credit losses that were triggered by events that occurred by the balance sheet date. Notice also that this model retains its cost basis when the original discount rate continues to be used to calculate the recoverable amount, but moves to a partial fair value measurement when a current interest rate is used to discount the impaired cash flows.

Expected Loss Model

Under an expected loss impairment model, estimates of future cash flows used to determine the present value of the investment are made on a continuous basis and do not rely on a triggering event to occur. Even though there may be no objective evidence that an impairment loss has been incurred, revised cash flow projections may indicate changes in credit risk associated with the issuer of the instrument. Under the expected loss model, these revised expected cash flows are discounted at the same effective interest rate used when the instrument was **first acquired**, therefore retaining a cost-based measurement.

Again similar to the incurred loss approach, the expected impairment loss is the difference between the revised present value calculation and the instrument's carrying amount. The entry to record the loss is the same as illustrated above, and an allowance account may equally well be used. This is likely under both approaches, especially if the impairment is determined for a portfolio of investments with similar risk characteristics instead of single instruments. In addition, reporting a separate allowance amount is often preferred so that the accumulated effect of changes in credit quality can be presented.

To illustrate, assume that Xia Ltd. has an investment in a $100,000 face value bond of Chan Corp. with a carrying amount of $98,900 on an amortized cost basis. All payments of interest and principal have been received on a timely basis and there are no indicators that the investment is impaired. Chan's credit rating has been reduced recently although it is still at an acceptable level. With the reduction in credit quality, the estimate of future defaults on the bond's cash flows has increased. If discounting the revised future cash flows at the original discount rate results in a valuation of $97,200, an impairment loss of $1,700 ($98,900 − $97,200) is recognized.

After the impairment is recognized, interest income continues to be recognized based on the continuously revised cash flow estimates and the original discount rate. Changes in the investment's realizable value from one period to the next are recognized as adjustments of the impairment loss. This could be an improvement and a reversal of a previous loss, or an increase in the amount already recognized.

Because the impairment loss under this model reflects both incurred losses to date and future expected credit losses, it results in earlier recognition of such losses in net income. This model is more difficult to apply, especially in continually estimating the amounts of the expected future cash flows.

Fair Value Loss Model

Under the fair value loss impairment model, the impairment loss is the difference between the asset's fair value and its current carrying amount assuming the fair value is less than the carrying amount. Its fair value is based on discounted cash flows, but in this case, the discount rate is a **current interest rate**. Because impairment is usually restricted to instruments carried at cost or amortized cost, the current carrying amount is the investment's amortized cost less any accumulated impairment losses previously recognized.

The mechanics of the accounting entry are the same as described above for the other two models. Interest income recognized after the impairment is calculated using the revised discount rate that determined the instrument's fair value or by using the original historical rate. To be consistent with the cost/amortized cost approach, the original rate is used, and the new reduced impaired value becomes the instrument's new "cost" for accounting purposes. However, using the current rate to determine the investment's new carrying amount and then calculating interest income using the historical rate is internally inconsistent and results in the discount not being appropriately amortized. Alternatively, the current interest rate that established the new "cost" could be used as the new historical rate. Reversals of the impairment loss may or may not be permitted.

Illustration 9-15, based on a paper prepared by the staff of the IASB for discussion at a May 2009 public meeting of the IASB, summarizes the three impairment loss models described.[20]

Illustration 9-15

Summary of Impairment Loss Models

For instruments carried at cost/ amortized cost	Incurred Loss Model	Expected Loss Model	Fair Value Loss Model
Recognition: Is a review of indicators necessary to trigger the impairment test?	Yes. Test is carried out only if indicated by review of evidence of impairment.	No trigger is needed. Future cash flows are continually reassessed.	Yes. Impairment indicators need to be reviewed to alert entity to change in fair value.
How the revised carrying amount is measured	Uses discounted updated expected cash flows	Uses discounted updated expected cash flows	Uses fair value
	Uses (a) original effective interest rate or (b) current market rate	Uses original effective interest rate	Uses current discount rate
How impairment loss is calculated	Uses the carrying amount less PV of cash flows	Uses the carrying amount less PV of cash flows	Uses the carrying amount less fair value
Where impairment loss is recognized	In net income	In net income	In net income
When subsequent impairments are recognized	Recognized when further triggering events occur	Recognized automatically as future cash flows are re-estimated	Recognized automatically through determination of fair value, when triggered
Basis for recognizing revenue after impairment	Based on the same interest rate used to discount the impaired cash flows	Based on the original effective interest rate	Based on either the original effective rate or current rate used to determine fair value

---

[20] IASB, Staff Paper for Agenda Item 5D: Financial Instruments – Recognition and Measurement, "Comparison between possible impairment approaches" prepared by the technical staff of the IASCF for discussion at a public meeting of the IASB, May 2009.

Whether reversals are permitted	Reversals are required if triggered by a later event, up to amortized cost	Reversals automatically happen when there is a favourable change in credit loss expectations; to limit of full contractual cash flows discounted at original interest rate	Reversals are possible, generally up to amortized cost

Accounting Standards for Impairment

The answer to the question "What are the accounting standards for impairment under IFRS?" again depends on when you are asking. As the text went to print, **IFRS** uses the incurred loss model with the cash flows discounted using the original discount rate for all financial asset investments accounted for at cost or amortized cost. A version of the full fair value model is applied to FV-OCI investments. Reversals of impairment losses are required for investments in debt instruments, but no reversals are permitted for any impairment charges recognized in net income for equity instruments accounted for at FV-OCI. However, subsequent changes in the equity investment's fair value are recognized in OCI.

Significant Change

The IASB was in the process of simplifying its standards on financial instruments in general and issuing an exposure draft on impairment issues. The proposals were as follows:

For instruments at amortized cost: Expected loss model

For instruments at fair value: No impairment model needed
    Adjust to fair value at balance sheet date

No guidance is proposed for recognizing impairment losses for investments (mostly equity investments) accounted for at FV-OCI. This appears to be a deficiency in the new standards. To the extent there are investments in this category with permanent declines in value, all the holding losses remain in accumulated OCI. If net income is the measure of performance given most attention by financial analysts and others, then it seems reasonable that impairment losses should be transferred out of this segment of equity and be reported in net income. In other words, recycling should be permitted for these non-temporary declines in value to highlight the loss.

The accounting standards that represent **private entity GAAP** have been agreed on. This GAAP has impairment provisions only for financial asset investments accounted for at cost or amortized cost. The standard uses the incurred loss model explained above, discounting the impaired cash flows using a **current market rate** rather than the original effective interest rate.

To illustrate, assume that Strickler Corp. holds a bond investment with an amortized cost carrying amount of $775,000. Although all interest and principal payments have been made on a timely basis by the bond issuer, the bond is now quoted as having a fair market value of $725,000. The issuer company has recently issued additional debt with the result that its existing debt has been downgraded to a lower, but still investment-grade, level. The older bonds currently yield 8% interest, while they were originally acquired to yield 7%. Discounting the revised expected cash flows based on new estimates of default at the original effective rate of 7% suggests a present value of expected cash flows of $745,000. No impairment losses have been recognized previously.

Under **private entity GAAP** and the incurred impairment loss model, no triggering event has occurred to justify an impairment charge, and none is recognized. Under the **IFRS** proposals and the expected loss model, the revised expected cash flows are assessed at each reporting date and discounted at the original effective rate of 7% to determine whether there is impairment. The impaired value is therefore $745,000, and an impairment loss of $775,000 − $745,000 or $30,000 is indicated. The entry to record the loss is:

A   =   L   +   SE
−30,000   −30,000

Cash flows: No effect

| Impairment Loss on Bond Investment | 30,000 | |
| Investment in Strickler Corp. Bonds | | 30,000 |

The new carrying amount of the investment is $745,000, and future interest income is recognized using the original effective interest rate of 7%, but it is based on the revised amount of $745,000 instead of $775,000.

As you can see, the choice of impairment model can result in a significant difference on a company's balance sheet and income statement, with the expected loss model recognizing credit losses earlier than the incurred loss model. Accounting for and reporting impairments is complex and unsettled, and has the most significant effect on companies in the financial services industry. This serves only as an introduction to the topic.

STRATEGIC INVESTMENTS

Accounting for investments in the common shares of another corporation after acquisition depends mostly on the relationship that exists between the investor and the investee. Relationships are classified by the level of influence that is exercised by the investor and this, in turn, is generally related to the degree of share ownership (i.e., more shares usually mean more influence). When the investment is made for strategic purposes, management usually wants to influence or control the investee's policies. Therefore, the investor is more likely to acquire a higher percentage of the outstanding voting shares.

Based on information from the company's 2008 annual report, Illustration 9-16, for example, presents the holdings of **Power Corporation of Canada**, controlled by the influential Desmarais family from Quebec. A variety of equity investments are

Illustration 9-16

Power Corporation of Canada's Holdings

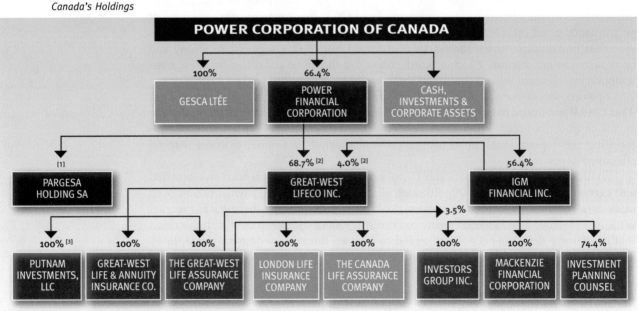

PERCENTAGES DENOTE YEAR-END EQUITY INTEREST UNLESS OTHERWISE NOTED.

[1] THROUGH ITS WHOLLY OWNED SUBSIDIARY POWER FINANCIAL EUROPE B.V., POWER FINANCIAL HELD A 50 PER CENT INTEREST IN PARJOINTCO. PARJOINTCO HELD A VOTING INTEREST OF 62.9 PER CENT AND AN EQUITY INTEREST OF 54.1 PER CENT IN PARGESA.

[2] TOGETHER, 65 PER CENT DIRECT AND INDIRECT VOTING INTEREST
[3] DENOTES VOTING INTEREST

illustrated, from the 100% ownership of **Gesca** to the 66.4% ownership of **Power Financial** and through this company to various levels of interest in other Canadian and European enterprises.

The levels of influence and types of investment are summarized in Illustration 9-17 with reference to the percentage of ownership. Note that the percentages given are guidelines only.

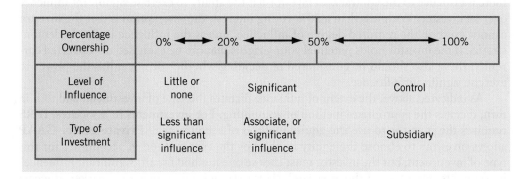

Levels of Influence and Types of Investment

The accounting standards and reporting for equity investments depend on the level of influence that dictates what type of investment a particular holding is.[21] The first part of this chapter covers how to account for investments where the investor is not able to exercise significant influence, let alone control of the investee company. Although some of those investments could have been made for strategic purposes, it was assumed earlier in the chapter that the required level of **significant influence** was not reached.

Investments in Associates

Significant Influence

When an investor has an interest of less than 20%, **it is presumed that the investor has little or no influence over the investee**. This may not be the case, however. For example, a 16% interest may allow an investor to very significantly influence decisions if the remaining shares are widely held. Alternatively, ownership of 30% of a company's shares may not give an investor company any influence at all if a 70% majority shareholder does not permit any.

Although an equity interest of less than 50% of an investee corporation does not give an investor **legal control**, it might give an investor significant influence over the strategic policies of the investee. To provide guidance, the IASB defines significant influence as "the power to participate in the financial and operating policy decisions of an entity, but not control over those policies."[22] This is similar to the private entity GAAP concept, and both indicate that an ability to exercise influence at a significant level over another company's operating, investing, and financing activities may be indicated in several ways. Examples include the following: representation on the board of directors, participation in

6 Objective

Explain the concept of significant influence and why the equity method is appropriate, apply the equity method, and identify private entity GAAP and IFRS requirements.

---

[21] Joint ventures are another type of equity investment. Since they can be incorporated companies, they can issue shares. **Joint ventures** are characterized by joint control (versus unilateral control). This is usually evidenced through a contractual agreement that states that the venturers (investors) must share key decision-making. The accounting method being proposed for joint venture entities under a 2010 IFRS revision is the equity method, although a choice between the equity method and proportionate consolidation is now permitted. PE GAAP permits a choice of the following alternative methods: proportionate consolidation, the equity method, or the cost method, with one method applied to all such investments.

[22] IASCF, IAS 28 *Investments in Associates*, para. 2.

policy-making processes, material intercompany transactions, interchange of managerial personnel, or provision of technical information.[23] Under IFRS specifically, and in general, the term associate is used to refer to the entity that the investor has significant influence over, provided it is neither a subsidiary nor a joint venture.

To ensure that the significant influence criterion is applied in a reasonably consistent manner, the standard setters concluded that an investment (direct or indirect) of 20% or more of the voting shares of another company should lead to a presumption that, unless there is evidence to the contrary, an investor has the ability to exercise significant influence over an investee. With less than a 20% voting interest, the assumption is that the investor cannot exercise the required degree of influence, unless the influence is clearly demonstrated. If the investor holds potential voting rights that can be exercised or converted currently, these also should be considered in deciding whether or not it has the power to exercise significant influence.

As indicated above, the extent of influence dictates the type of investment, and this, in turn, dictates the appropriate method of accounting. For investments in associates, **IFRS** requires the investor to use the equity method of accounting.[24] **Private entity GAAP** allows investors to choose the equity method or the cost method in accounting for this type of investment, but the investor must choose one method for all "significant influence" investments. However, if the associate's shares are quoted in an active market, the cost method cannot be used. Instead the fair value approach with gains and losses being recognized in income can be chosen. Both the cost and FV-NI models are explained earlier in this chapter, so we turn next to how the equity method works.

Equity Method Basics

Under the equity method, the investment is initially recorded at the cost of the acquired shares. After this, its carrying amount is adjusted each period for the investor's proportionate share of the changes in the investee's net assets. The equity method sounds complex at first, but it is only **the accrual basis of accounting applied to investment income**.

Under this method, **the investor recognizes investment income as the investee earns income** by debiting the Investment account and crediting Investment Income. When cash is received from the investment (i.e., the investee pays a dividend on the shares), this converts an asset that has already been recognized—the Investment—to cash. Therefore, Cash is debited and the Investment account is credited.

As indicated, the Investment account under the equity method changes to mirror the increases and decreases in the investee's book value:

- **When the associate's net assets increase** because it earns income, **the investor increases the carrying amount of its investment** for its proportionate share of the associate's increase in net assets and also **reports its share of the associate's income as investment income**.

- **When the associate's net assets decrease** because the company pays a dividend, **the investor recognizes the cash received and decreases the carrying amount of the investment** by its share of the decrease in the associate's net assets.

To illustrate the basics of the equity method, assume that Maxi Corp. purchases a 20% interest in Mini Corp. and has the ability to exercise significant influence over Mini's financial and operating policies. The entries are shown in Illustration 9-18. Note the effects on the Investment account and on the income statement.

[23] *CICA Handbook*, Part II, Section 3051.05.

[24] IAS 28 *Investments in Associates* identifies some exceptions. These include investments in associates that are held for sale and those reported by a parent that is not required to prepare consolidated financial statements.

Illustration 9-18

Application of the Equity Method Basics

On January 2, 2010, Maxi Corp. acquires 48,000 shares (20% of Mini Corp. common shares) at a cost of $10 a share.

| Investment in Mini Corp. | 480,000 | |
| Cash | | 480,000 |

For the year 2010, Mini Corp. reports net income of $200,000; Maxi Corp.'s share is 20%, or $40,000.

| Investment in Mini Corp. | 40,000 | |
| Investment Income* | | 40,000 |

At December 31, 2010, the 48,000 shares of Mini Corp. have a fair value of $12 a share, or $576,000. The investment value is not considered impaired.

No entry

On January 28, 2011, Mini Corp. announces and pays a cash dividend of $100,000; Maxi Corp. receives 20%, or $20,000.

| Cash | 20,000 | |
| Investment in Mini Corp. | | 20,000 |

For the year 2011, Mini reports a net loss of $50,000; Maxi Corp.'s share is 20%, or $10,000.

| Investment Loss* | 10,000 | |
| Investment in Mini Corp. | | 10,000 |

At December 31, 2011, the 48,000 Mini Corp. shares have a fair value of $11 a share, or $528,000. The investment value is not considered impaired.

No entry

*This entry is sometimes referred to as the equity pickup. The term refers to the fact that the investor is picking up its share of income or loss under the equity method. Another commonly used account title is Equity in Earnings of Associate Company.

Under the equity method, **the accrual basis of accounting** is applied. Maxi Corp. therefore reports investment income as Mini Corp. earns income. Revenue recognition is permitted before receiving a dividend, because of the degree of influence that the investor has over the investee's decisions, including dividend decisions. If the investee company suffers a loss, as Mini Corp. did in 2011, the investor accrues its share of the loss and reduces the carrying amount of its investment.

One of the benefits of this method is that the investor's income statement reports the economics of the situation: if the influence exerted results in the associate performing well, the investor's income statement reflects positive investment income. If the influence results in poor decisions and the associate incurs losses, the investor's income statement reflects its share of the loss. In addition, when the equity method is used, the investor cannot manipulate its own income by influencing the timing of a dividend from the associate.

Expanded Illustration of the Equity Method

There are two more complexities in applying the equity method:[25]

1. Differences between what was originally paid for the investment and the investor's share of the associate's book value need to be identified and accounted for according to the reason for the extra or smaller payment.

2. The major classifications of the income reported by the associate are retained and reported in the same way on the investor's income statement.

Underlying Concept

The equity method of accounting results in income statement amounts that more faithfully represent the underlying economic results of the investor company's management decisions.

---

[25] A third aspect involves eliminating the effects of unrealized intercompany gains and losses. This and situations where investors pay less for the shares than their proportionate interest in the identifiable net assets of the associate (i.e., "negative goodwill") are topics for an advanced accounting course.

The first item requires an understanding of what the cost of the investment represents. It is unusual for the investor to pay an amount for the investment that is exactly equal to its share of the other company's book value. The excess payment (usually it is extra) could be due to several reasons: there may be unrecorded assets; there may be assets whose fair value is greater than the carrying amount on the associate's books or liabilities whose fair value is less than book value; there may be intangibles, such as goodwill, that the associate has but that are not recognized in its books; and so on. **Any payment in excess of (or less than) the investor's share of book value is all part of the cost of the investment, and after acquisition, has to be accounted for appropriately.**

If the difference is caused by long-lived assets with fair values that are greater than book value, the amount above the asset's book value must be amortized. If it relates to inventory with a fair value in excess of its carrying amount on the associate's books, it will be recognized as an increased expense as the inventory is sold. There may also be assets with fair values that are lower than book value or liabilities with present values higher than book value. **None of these differences are on the associate's books, but they are captured as part of the purchase cost of the investment,** so it is the investment account itself and the investment income that need to be adjusted over time.

Because the equity method recognizes and reports the investor's share of the associate's income, **the type of income that is reported should remain the same.** That is, the portion that is the investor's share of the associate's discontinued operations is reported separately from the investor's share of income before discontinued operations. The same principle applies to the investor's portion of the associate's other comprehensive income, changes in accounting policy reported in retained earnings, and capital charges. The investor reports its share of all of these in the appropriate place in its financial statements.

To illustrate, assume that on January 1, 2011, Investor Company purchases 250,000 of Investee Company's 1 million outstanding common shares for $8.5 million. Investor has therefore acquired a 25% interest in Investee. The book value of Investee Company (i.e., its net assets) on this date is $30 million and Investor's proportionate share is 25% of this, or $7.5 million. Investor Company therefore has paid $1 million in excess of its share of the book value (i.e., $8,500,000 − $7,500,000).

Why did Investor pay $1 million more than its share of Investee's book value? Assume that part of the reason is because Investee's depreciable assets **are undervalued on the books** by $2.4 million. This explains $600,000 ($2,400,000 × 25%) of the excess, because Investor would only pay more in proportion to its ownership interest. Investor Company estimates the remaining life of the depreciable assets to be eight years, so the $600,000 excess payment included in the Investment account will have to be amortized over this future period.

The remaining $400,000 is unexplained and therefore is determined to be unrecorded goodwill. Investor will have to assess the carrying amount of the balance of the Investment account each year to determine whether there has been any impairment in its value. This purchase is analyzed in Illustration 9-19.

Illustration 9-19

Analysis of Acquisition of Associate Company

Cost of 25% investment in Investee Co. shares	$8,500,000
25% of book value of Investee Co. represented by investment	
25% × $30,000,000	7,500,000
Payment in excess of share of book value	1,000,000
Fair value allocation to depreciable assets	
25% × $2,400,000	600,000
Unexplained excess assumed to be goodwill	$ 400,000
Annual amortization of excess payment for capital assets	
$600,000/8-year life	$ 75,000

Investee Company later reports net income of $2.8 million for its 2011 fiscal year, including a loss on discontinued operations of $400,000. **Income before discontinued operations**, therefore, is $3.2 million. Dividends of $1.4 million are declared and paid by Investee Company on December 31, 2011. To record these transactions and events, Investor Company makes the following 2011 entries.

Jan. 1/11	Investment in Investee Company	8,500,000	
	Cash		8,500,000
	To record the acquisition of 25% of Investee Co.		

A = L + SE
0   0   0
Cash flows: ↓ 8,500,000 outflow

Dec. 31/11	Cash	350,000	
	Investment in Investee Company		350,000
	To record the dividend from Investee Co. ($1,400,000 × 0.25).		

A = L + SE
0   0   0
Cash flows: ↑ 350,000 inflow

Dec. 31/11	Investment in Investee Company	700,000	
	Loss from Discontinued		
	Operations—Investee Company	100,000	
	Investment Income		800,000
	To record investment income earned (25% × Investee Co. income).		

A = L + SE
+700,000   +700,000
Cash flows: No effect

Dec. 31/11	Investment Income	75,000	
	Investment in Investee Company		75,000
	Amortization of fair value difference, depreciable assets.		

A = L + SE
−75,000   −75,000
Cash flows: No effect

On December 31, Investor Company recognizes its 25% share of Investee Company's net income. Because its associate's income includes both continuing and discontinued operation components, 25% of each amount is reported separately by Investor Company. The account Investment in Investee Company is increased by 25% of the increase in Investee's net assets from earning net income (25% × $2,800,000). Furthermore, Investor Company paid more than book value for Investee Company's net assets and a portion of the excess amount relates to assets that are depreciable. The "extra cost" of the depreciable assets to Investor has not been recognized on the associate's books, nor has the additional depreciation. As a result, the investment income needs to be adjusted for this additional expense.

Illustration 9-20 shows the calculation of the investment in Investee Company that is presented on Investor Company's December 31, 2011 balance sheet.

Acquisition cost, January 1, 2011	$8,500,000
Add: 25% of increase in Investee's net assets from earning net income	700,000
Less: 25% of decrease in Investee's net assets from declaration/payment of dividend	(350,000)
Less: Depreciation of fair value difference related to capital assets	(75,000)
Investment in Investee Co., Dec. 31, 2011, at equity	$8,775,000

Illustration 9-20

Calculation of Investment Carrying Amount

Impairment in Value, Equity Method

Significant Change

Under both **IFRS** and **PE GAAP**, an investment that results in significant influence is assessed at each balance sheet date to determine if there are any indications that the investment may be impaired. If there are, its carrying amount is compared with the investment's **recoverable amount**: the higher of its value in use and fair value less costs to sell, both of which are discounted cash flow concepts.[26] If the carrying amount is more than the investment's recoverable amount, an impairment loss equal to the difference is recognized in net income and the investment is written down directly. This loss may be reversed if future events indicate that the recoverable amount has improved.

This impairment test is a variation of the fair value loss model described above and you will see this variation again when studying property, plant, and equipment and intangible assets.

Disposal of Investment in Associate

When the investment in the associate is sold, the balance sheet Investment account and the Investment Income account are first brought up to date as at the date of sale. This involves adjusting these accounts for the investor's share of the associate's earnings and changes in book value since the last reporting date. Then the investment's carrying value is removed from the accounts and the difference between this and the proceeds on disposal is recognized in income as a gain or loss.

Continuing with the example in Illustrations 9-19 and 9-20, assume that Investor Company sells its investment in Investee Company on January 2, 2012, for $9 million. Because the accounts are up to date in this case, the entry to record the sale is:

A   = L +   SE
+225,000   +225,000

Cash flows: ↑ 9,000,000 inflow

Cash	9,000,000	
Investment in Investee Company		8,775,000
Gain on Sale of Investment		225,000

Summary of Accounting Standards for Associates

The equity method is also known as "one-line consolidation" and is applied in ways that are related to how consolidation principles are applied. In fact, the equity method "investment income" is the same amount that is needed to increase or decrease the investor's income to the amount that would be reported if the investor had consolidated the results of the investee with those of the investor, with possible exceptions related to goodwill and investment impairment. Given this similarity, other complexities that result from such investments are left for an advanced accounting course that covers intercorporate investments.

Illustration 9-21 summarizes the accounting for investments in the equity instruments of companies in which the investor has significant influence.

---

[26] **Value in use** refers to the present value of the cash flows expected to be generated from holding the investment, discounted at an appropriate current market rate of interest.

	IFRS	Private Entity GAAP		
Measurement after recognition	Equity method	Equity method is used for all or the cost method is used for all.		If shares are quoted in an active market, cannot use cost method; may use FV-NI
		Equity method	Cost method	
Unrealized holding gains/losses	Not recognized	Not recognized	Not recognized	Recognized in net income
Investment income	Percentage of associate's income, adjusted for differences between cost and share of book value and intercompany profits	Percentage of associate's income, adjusted for differences between cost and share of book value and intercompany profits	Dividends received or receivable	Dividends received or receivable
Impairment, when assessment indicates possibility	Loss = carrying amount less recoverable amount (higher of value in use and fair value less costs to sell)	Loss = carrying amount less recoverable amount (higher of value in use and fair value less costs to sell)	Loss = carrying amount less recoverable amount (higher of value in use and fair value less costs to sell)	Not applicable
Impairment reversal	Permitted	Permitted	Permitted	Not applicable

Illustration 9-21

Accounting for Associates

Investments in Subsidiaries

When one corporation acquires control of another entity, the investor corporation is referred to as the parent and the investee corporation as the subsidiary. Control is assumed when the investor owns 50% or more of the voting shares of another company. This is because it holds a majority of the votes at the board of directors meetings of the investee company, and therefore, the investor's management virtually controls all the subsidiary's net assets and operations.

Standard setters have wrestled for many years with the best way to explain what control really is. They acknowledge that control can exist with less than 50% of the voting shares and may not exist with more than 50%. According to **PE GAAP**, control is the continuing power to determine the strategic operating, financing, and investing policies of another entity without the co-operation of others. Under **IFRS**, a new definition has recently been put forward that would allow control to extend to a broader range of investments. This definition indicates that an investor controls another if it has the power to direct the activities of the other entity to generate returns, either positive or negative, for the investor. Similar to previous descriptions, the "power to direct the activities of another" means that an investor can determine the other entity's strategic operating and financing policies. The differences in the definitions are subtle, but real, and they will become more apparent in an advanced accounting course that deals with intercorporate investments.

An investment in the common shares of a subsidiary is presented as a long-term investment on the separate financial statements of the parent, usually accounted for by either the equity or cost method. When preparing GAAP **IFRS** statements, however, an investor with subsidiaries is required to present consolidated financial statements for the group of companies under its control; that is, it **eliminates the investment account** and instead **reports all the assets and liabilities of the subsidiary on a line-by-line basis.** Under **PE GAAP**, this is a **permitted**, but **not required**, option. A parent company can choose to:

7 Objective

Explain the concept of control, the basics of consolidated financial statements, and why consolidation is appropriate, and identify private entity GAAP and IFRS requirements.

(a) consolidate all its subsidiaries, or

(b) present all of them under either the equity method or cost method.

The same choice is applied to all subsidiaries, although investments in shares that are quoted in an active market are not permitted to use the cost method. They may instead be measured and reported at FV-NI. You can see here the similarities between PE GAAP for associates and subsidiary companies. Separate reporting on the balance sheet is required for subsidiaries accounted for using the equity method and for those using the cost method. The income statement also reports the income from each group of subsidiaries accounted for on a different basis.

Real-World Emphasis

Power Corp., a Canadian public company whose corporate holdings were displayed in Illustration 9-16, consolidates its subsidiary companies, including Power Financial, and accounts for Power Financial's interest in Parjointco by the equity method. Parjointco consolidates its interest in **Pargesa Holding**.

Because we have already covered the cost, equity, and FV-NI methods, the emphasis now is on understanding consolidation. In place of the one-line long-term investment in subsidiary, the parent reports 100% of each of the assets and liabilities over which it has control. Instead of reporting investment income on the income statement, 100% of each of the revenues and expenses reported by the subsidiary is reported on a line-by-line basis with those of the parent company. That is, the parent presents consolidated financial statements. This method of reporting an investment in a controlled company is much more informative to the parent company's shareholders than a single-line balance sheet and a single-line income statement account.

Significant Change

The requirement to include 100% of the assets and liabilities and 100% of the revenues, expenses, gains, and losses under the parent's control even when the ownership is less than 100% leads to the recognition of unique balance sheet and income statement accounts. These accounts, non-controlling interest (sometimes referred to as minority interest), represent the portion of the net assets **not** owned and the portion of the consolidated net income of the entity that does **not** accrue to the parent company's shareholders. These claims to net assets and net income are **equity claims** because they represent the interests of the non-controlling **shareholders** of the subsidiary companies.

Real-World Emphasis

Illustration 9-22, taken from the 2009 Annual Report of **Marks and Spencer Group plc**, shows parts of the consolidated (group) statement of comprehensive income and balance sheet of this United Kingdom-based retail giant.

Illustration 9-22

Minority (Non-Controlling) Interests on the Statement of Comprehensive Income and Balance Sheet

Consolidated statement of recognised income and expense

	52 weeks ended 28 March 2009 £m	52 weeks ended 29 March 2008 £m
Profit for the year	**506.8**	821.0
Foreign currency translation differences	**33.1**	21.3
Actuarial (losses)/gains on retirement benefit schemes	**(927.1)**	605.4
Cash flow and net investment hedges		
– fair value movements in equity	**304.8**	(33.5)
– recycled and reported in net profit	**(206.8)**	1.3
– amount recognised in inventories	**(8.6)**	2.4
Tax on items taken directly to equity	**225.8**	(185.7)
Net (losses)/gains not recognised in the income statement	**(578.8)**	411.2
Total recognised income and expense for the year	**(72.0)**	1,232.2
Attributable to:		
Equity shareholders of the Company	**(70.8)**	1,232.9
Minority interests	**(1.2)**	(0.7)
	(72.0)	1,232.2

Consolidated balance sheet

	Notes	As at 28 March 2009 £m	As at 29 March 2008 £m
Net assets		**2,100.6**	1,964. 0
Equity			
Called-up share capital – equity	25, 26	**394.4**	396.6
Share premium account	26	**236.2**	231.4
Capital redemption reserve	26	**2,202.6**	2,199.9
Hedging reserve	26	**62.6**	(36.9)
Other reserve	26	**(6,542.2)**	(6,542.2)
Retained earnings	26	**5,728.1**	5,707.9
Total shareholders' equity		**2,081.7**	1,956.7
Minority interests in equity		**18.9**	7.3
Total equity		**2,100.6**	1,964.0

Underlying Concept

The consolidation of the financial results of different companies follows the economic entity assumption. It disregards the legal boundaries between entities. The key objective is to provide useful information to financial statement users about all the resources under the control of parent company management.

Consolidated financial statements disregard the distinction between separate legal entities and treat the parent and subsidiary corporations as an economic unit—an eco-nomic entity. After acquisition, this means that all intercompany balances and unrealized intercompany gains and losses are eliminated for reporting purposes. An entity cannot report sales or make a profit selling to itself. The preparation of consolidated financial statements is discussed in detail in advanced financial accounting.

The rules for consolidation seem very straightforward: If a company owns more than 50% of another company, it generally should be consolidated. If it owns less than 50%, it is generally not consolidated. However, with complex modern business relationships, stan-dard setters realize that this test is too artificial, and that determining who really has con-trol is often based on factors other than share ownership.

What Do the Numbers Mean?

In fact, specific guidelines have been developed that force consolidation even though share ownership is not above 50%. For example, the well-known **Enron Corporation** failure to consolidate three special-purpose entities that were effectively controlled by Enron led to a U.S. $569-million overstatement of income and a U.S. $1.2-billion over-statement of equity. In these three cases, the new GAAP would have led to consolidation. That is, the following factors indicate that consolidation should have occurred: the major-ity owner of the shares of the special-purpose entity made only a modest investment, Enron received the primary economic benefits from the activities of the entity, and the substantive risks and rewards related to the special entity's assets and debt rested directly or indirectly with Enron.

These arrangements were not unique to Enron! Many companies used non-consoli-dated special-purpose entities to "window dress" or make their financial statements look better than they really were. Such actions caused the CICA to issue separate guidance on the consolidation of variable interest entities (VIEs) where control is achieved in ways other than through ownership of voting interests. The guideline, harmonized with FASB's approach, requires a company to consolidate a variable interest entity when the com-pany is the primary beneficiary of such an entity; that is, when it will absorb a majority of a VIE's expected losses, receive a majority of its expected residual returns, or both. As this text went to print, the IASB was in the process of issuing a revised standard to change its definition of control so that if an investor meets the new definition, it will account for VIEs under its regular consolidation standards.

PRESENTATION, DISCLOSURE, AND ANALYSIS

Financial Statement Presentation and Disclosure

Investments without Significant Influence or Control

Objective 8

Explain the objectives of disclosure, and identify the major types of information that are required to be reported for investments in other companies' debt and equity instruments.

Where should a company report investments on its balance sheet? Should investments that the investor cannot exercise significant influence over or control be reported as current or long-term assets? The requirements for presentation of an investment as a current asset are the same as for other assets. In general, those classified as current are continuously turning over or circulating as working capital. As indicated in Chapter 5, **IFRS** specify that if an investment has any one of the following characteristics, it is classified as current:

- It is expected to be sold or otherwise realized within the entity's normal operating cycle or within 12 months from the balance sheet date.

- It is held primarily for trading purposes.

- It is a cash equivalent.

Under **private entity GAAP**, the conditions are similar: an investment is classified as a current asset only if it is usually realizable within 12 months from the balance sheet date (or normal operating cycle, if longer) and it can be converted to cash relatively quickly.

This means that debt and equity investments measured at cost or amortized cost and those at FV-NI could be either current or long-term assets, depending on the specific situation. Debt instruments are likely to be classified as current only if they are held to be traded or expected to mature or be sold within the following year; and equity instruments will be current only if marketable and they are expected to be converted to cash that can be used for current purposes. It is likely that under the revised IFRS issued late in 2009, investments carried at FV-OCI are most likely noncurrent assets: they are held for longer term strategic purposes, and not for current trading.

The **objective of the disclosures** required for financial assets that are investments in debt and equity instruments is generally the same under both PE and IFRS GAAP: to provide information that allows users to assess the following:

1. how significant these financial assets are to an entity's financial position and performance,

2. the nature and extent of risks that the entity faces as a result of these assets, and

3. how the entity manages these risks.

The specific standards are the best source of the many required disclosures for financial asset investments. The following section is meant to provide you with an understanding of the **types of information** that are required to be made available to users of the financial statements. Understanding the goal of the disclosures is helpful in determining and even predicting what information is reported.

- Disclose the **carrying amount of investments** in debt instruments carried at amortized cost, in equity instruments carried at cost, and in equity instruments carried at FV-NI. Also disclose the carrying amount of any investments accounted for at FV-OCI. The carrying amount of any impaired investments and related allowances for impairment, by type (method of accounting for the assets), is also separately reported.

- To enable readers to relate the **income statement effects** to the investments on the balance sheet, disclose net gains or losses recognized (by method of accounting), total interest income (under IFRS, include only interest income calculated using the effective interest method for financial assets except for those at FV-NI), interest income on impaired investments (IFRS), and impairment losses and reversals.

- For each type of **financial risk** that results from the investments, disclose what the risk exposures are, how they arise, any changes over the accounting period, and information about any concentrations of risk such as those that arise from significant investment in particular industries or foreign currency, for example. IFRS require additional information such as how risks are managed, credit risk by classification of instrument, past due and impaired investments, and sensitivity analyses for each type of market risk to which the entity is exposed.[27]

 Finance

- Under IFRS, in addition to providing such qualitative disclosures, entities also provide quantitative measures of their risk exposures and concentrations, as well as specific information that management uses internally to manage each major type of risk.

Investments in Associates

As a general rule, the significance of an investment to the investor's financial position and performance generally determines how much disclosure is required. Investments in associates are classified as noncurrent assets (unless they are held for sale) and income from these significantly influenced companies is reported as income before discontinued operations, discontinued operations, or other comprehensive income, according to its nature in the associate's financial statements. Management reports the following for associates accounted for using the equity method:

1. Separate disclosure of the investment category on the balance sheet or in the notes to the financial statements, and the method of accounting used

2. The fair value of any of these investments that has a price quoted in an active market

3. Separate disclosure of the income from investments that are accounted for using the equity method

4. Information about associates' year ends that are different from the investors

Under **IFRS**, additional information is required such as summarized financial information about the associates' assets, liabilities, revenue and net income, and any relevant contingent liabilities that may affect the investor. Under **PE GAAP**, a list of any significant investments, including a description of the investment, the names, carrying amounts, and percentage ownership held, is provided. Because private enterprises are allowed to use methods other than the equity method, they are also required to separately report the carrying amount of investments in companies subject to significant influence accounted for at cost, as well as the amount of investment income reported from these investments.

Disclosure Example

Because the standards that students will be applying have only recently been approved by the standard-setting bodies, they have not yet been applied to companies' financial

---

[27] The types of risk that are associated with financial assets in general—credit, liquidity, and market risk—are discussed more fully in Chapter 16.

statements. Illustrations from the 2008 consolidated financial statements of **Clarke Inc.** that follow, therefore, refer to the standards that were previously in place in Canada, but many of the references and disclosures should be familiar after studying this chapter. Clarke Inc. is an investment holding company with major operating subsidiaries in the trucking and other industries, and with a variety of interests in other companies.

Illustration 9-23 provides only brief and partial excerpts from the 44 pages of Clarke Inc. financial statements.

Additional Disclosures

Illustration 9-23

Financial Reporting and Disclosure of Investments— Clarke Inc.

Real-World Emphasis

CONSOLIDATED BALANCE SHEETS
(in thousands of dollars)
As at December 31

	2008 $	2007 $
ASSETS *(note 12)*		
Current		
Cash and cash equivalents	1,446	43,968
Marketable securities *(note 3)*	116,832	218,627
Receivables *(note 4)*	37,270	35,308
Income taxes receivable	2,481	1,268
Inventories *(note 5)*	3,073	13,311
Prepaid expenses	1,497	2,205
Future income tax assets *(note 6)*	28,458	6,731
Assets of discontinued operations *(note 7)*	3,622	42
Total current assets	194,679	321,460
Long-term investments *(note 8)*	16,511	15,795

CONSOLIDATED STATEMENTS OF INCOME (LOSS)
(in thousands of dollars, except per share amounts)
Years ended December 31

	2008 $	2007 $
Revenue and other income		
Sales	250,145	196,418
Investment and other income *(note 17)*	13,775	100,097
	263,920	296,515
Expenses		
Operating expenses	232,171	185,678
Other-than-temporary impairment of available for sale and significantly influenced investments *(note 3)*	146,918	4,838
Pension expense *(note 10)*	2,870	2,506
Depreciation and amortization	4,226	3,022
Interest expense *(note 18)*	13,418	13,747
	399,603	209,791
Income (loss) before equity in losses of significantly influenced investments, income taxes and non-controlling interest	(135,683)	86,724
Equity in losses of significantly influenced investments *(notes 3 and 8)*	(23,741)	(3,458)
Income (loss) before income taxes and non-controlling interest	(159,424)	83,266
Provision for (recovery of) income taxes *(note 6)*	(29,742)	23,204
Income (loss) before non-controlling interest	(129,682)	60,062
Non-controlling interest	135	—
Income (loss) from continuing operations	(129,547)	60,062
Income (loss) from discontinued operations, net of tax *(note 7)*	(8,740)	3,948
Equity in earnings from discontinued operations of significantly influenced investments, net of tax *(note 7)*	14,204	—
Net income (loss)	(124,083)	64,010

1. SUMMARY OF SIGNIFICANT ACCOUNTING POLICIES

Investments

Investment transactions are accounted for on the date the order to buy or sell is executed. Marketable securities represent investments that are capable of prompt liquidation. Investments not capable of prompt liquidation are included in long-term investments. The Company evaluates the appropriate classification of investments in fixed maturity and equity securities at the acquisition date. Effective January 1, 2007, the Company's investments are primarily classified as available for sale, except for securities purchased with the intent of resale in the near term and securities which contain embedded derivatives, both of which are classified as held for trading.

Marketable securities not subject to significant influence are recognized at fair value, which is generally the closing bid price at each consolidated balance sheet date. The Company uses the equity method of accounting for significantly influenced investments. The Company applies the equity method of accounting for investments based upon the facts and circumstances of each individual investment including representation on the investee's board of directors, material intercompany transactions, contractual veto or approval rights, participation in policy making processes and the existence or absence of other significant owners.

Transaction costs

Transaction costs related to held for trading investments are expensed as incurred. Transaction costs for all other financial instruments are capitalized and for instruments with maturity dates are then amortized over the expected life of the instrument using the effective interest rate method.

3. MARKETABLE SECURITIES

The Company's marketable securities are classified as follows:

	Amortized cost* $	December 31, 2008 Carrying value $
Shares and trust units designated as available for sale	96,698	**97,315**
Shares and trust units required to be classified as held for trading	7,190	**2,699**
Investment funds designated as available for sale	249	**249**
Shares and trust units significantly influenced (fair value - $16,569)	16,569	**16,569**
	120,706	**116,832**

* *The amortized cost of the portfolio includes the adjustment for an other-than-temporary impairment charge of $146,918 recorded in 2008 (2007 – $4,838).*

8. LONG-TERM INVESTMENTS

The Company has significant influence over certain privately held investments, by virtue of its ownership interest and management involvement and, accordingly, is using the equity method to account for these investments. As a result of the initial purchases in late 2006 and early 2007, the $1,405 difference between the cost and the underlying net book value of one of these investments has been assigned to resource properties.

The company's long-term investments consist of equity interests as follows:

	2008 $	2007 $
Investments subject to significant influence	**14,859**	14,300
Investment funds designated as available for sale	**1,652**	1,395
Private company shares, at cost which approximates fair value	**—**	100
	16,511	15,795

The private company shares are now included as available for sale with marketable securities as there is now a quoted market price for these shares.

17. INVESTMENT AND OTHER INCOME

Investment and other income is comprised of the following:

	2008 $	2007 $
Income portion of trust distributions	**21,277**	15,950
Realized gains (losses) on available for sale investments	**(5,364)**	82,205
Net realized/unrealized losses on held for trading investments	**(5,558)**	(1,543)

continued on page 572

Other realized gains (losses)	**2,375**	(802)
Interest	**980**	4,245
Dividends	**65**	42
	13,775	100,097

24. FINANCIAL INSTRUMENTS

The Company's financial instruments at December 31, 2008 included cash and cash equivalents, receivables, marketable securities, long-term investments, loans receivable, short-term indebtedness, accounts payable and accrued liabilities and long-term debt.

Risks associated with financial assets and liabilities

The Company is exposed to various financial risks arising from its financial assets and liabilities. These include market risk relating to equity prices, interest rates and foreign exchange rates, liquidity risk and credit risk. To manage these risks, the Company performs detailed risk assessment procedures at the individual investment level, under the framework of a global risk management philosophy.

Equity price risk

Equity price risk refers to the risk that the fair value of marketable securities and long-term investments will vary as a result of changes in market prices of the investments.

The carrying values of investments subject to equity price risk are, in almost all instances, based on quoted market prices as of the balance sheet dates. Market prices are subject to fluctuation and, consequently, the amount realized in the subsequent sale of an investment may significantly differ from the reported market value. Fluctuation in the market price of a security may result from perceived changes in the underlying economic characteristics of the investee, the relative price of alternative investments and general market conditions. Furthermore, amounts realized in the sale of a particular security may be affected by the relative quantity of the security being sold.

Analysis

To effectively analyze a company's performance and position, it is essential to understand the accounting and reporting for the entity's investments. Some of the key aspects that analysts watch for include the following:

1. Separation of investment results from operating results

2. The relationship between the investment asset and related returns (income)

3. Information that is lost in the process of consolidation

Because the income statement reports on management's performance in operating the company's assets, it is important to separate the results of active operating income from the investment returns, where management's role is often more passive. As gains or losses on sales of investments or special dividends can obscure a company's operating performance, these must be separately identified and assessed.

Accounting standards require disclosures that make it possible for a reader to relate the investment category on the balance sheet to the investment income reported on the income statement, and to the holding gains and losses in other comprehensive income.

Understanding the effects of the accounting methods that are used for different categories of investments is a key requirement for the analyst. If an entity has significant investments in companies that are accounted for by the equity method, for example, the analyst needs to be aware that some information is not available because the one-line investment account hides the debt and risk characteristics of the investee company that the entity is exposed to.

Consolidation of subsidiary companies also presents problems. While the financial statements reflect the combined operations of the economic entity, important information is lost through aggregating the parent's results with those of its subsidiaries. This is why segmented information, discussed in Chapter 23, has to be separately reported in the notes. Analysts also watch for major acquisitions during the current or previous year. The balance sheet contains all the assets of the subsidiary, but the income statement includes only the income earned by the subsidiary since it was acquired by the parent. Any analysis that looks at relationships between income and assets has to adjust for major acquisitions in the period(s) being examined.

IFRS/PRIVATE ENTITY GAAP COMPARISON

As indicated earlier, accounting for financial assets in general is in the midst of change. The topic coverage in this chapter is based on the newly approved Canadian standards for private entity GAAP, the IASB's approved changes to IAS 39 *Financial Instruments: Recognition and Measurement* released in late 2009 as IFRS 9 *Financial Instruments*, and the proposed impairment standards set out in an Exposure Draft released in November 2009. The differences between the current IFRS positions and the private entity set of standards are set out in Illustration 9-24 on the next page.

9 Objective

Identify differences in accounting between private entity GAAP and IFRS, and what changes are expected in the near future.

Looking Ahead

As indicated in this chapter, the IASB is working, along with the FASB, to simplify the accounting for and reporting of financial instruments. These changes will affect primarily those investments in which the investor does not have significant influence or control. The final standard to simplify the recognition and measurement of financial instruments and an exposure draft on impairment were released by the IASB just prior to the printing of this text. The new impairment standard was expected to be finalized by the end of 2010.

Two other current projects may affect investments in other companies' debt and equity instruments going forward. A new financial instrument derecognition standard was in the process of being discussed, with a final standard expected by the end of 2010. In the longer run, the FASB and IASB are working together on revisions to their conceptual frameworks. Phase D of this project relates to how the reporting entity should be defined and therefore accounted for. A discussion paper was released in 2008 on this topic and an exposure draft was in process.

A Comparison of IFRS and Private Entity GAAP

Illustration 9-24 sets out the major differences between GAAP for private entities and international accounting standards for publicly accountable enterprises.

	Accounting Standards for Private Enterprises (Private Entity GAAP)—*CICA Handbook,* Part II, Sections 1582, 1601, 1602, 3051, and 3856	IFRS—IAS 1, 27, 28, 32, and 39; IFRS 3, 7 and 9
Investments—no significant influence or control		
Measurement models	Permits only two measurement models: cost/amortized cost and FV-NI.	Identifies two measurement models: amortized cost and FV-NI. The FV-OCI model can be elected for equity investments not held for trading purposes.
Fair value option	FV-NI can be designated on initial recognition.	FV-NI can be designated on initial recognition for an instrument otherwise carried at amortized cost, but only if it reduces or eliminates an accounting mismatch.
Transaction costs	Capitalize when a cost-based measure is used.	Capitalize for all instruments except FV-NI.
Interest and dividend income	Use either straight-line or effective interest method when applicable; all to net income.	Use effective interest method when interest income is required to be reported separately; all to net income except for those at FV-OCI where dividends that are a return of investment are recognized in OCI.
Realized gains and losses	Recognize in net income.	Recognize in net income, except for those accounted for at FV-OCI.
Transfers	FV option designation is irrevocable, otherwise, the issue is not addressed.	No reclassification is permitted between measurement models unless there is a rare occurrence of a change in the entity's business model.
Impairment	Use the incurred loss model, using a current discount rate; reversals are permitted if due to a specific subsequent event.	**Existing:** There is a complex mix of models, a combination of the incurred loss model (using the original discount rate) and a fair value model; some reversals are required and others are not permitted, depending on the type of investment. **Proposed:** The expected loss model, using the original discount rate, with reversals, would be used for those measured at amortized cost.
Disclosure	Uses the same financial reporting objectives as IFRS, but more limited disclosures are required.	Requires more extensive disclosures.
Investments—in associates/significant influence		
Method of accounting	Allows an accounting policy choice of the equity method or the cost method. If shares are quoted in an active market, cannot use cost model; may use FV-NI.	Requires the equity method.
Disclosures	Requires basic disclosures, including those related to choice of model.	Requires more extensive disclosures.
Investments—in subsidiaries		
Control	Has a narrower definition of control that relies more strongly on holding more than 50% of the voting interests in another entity.	A new definition of control is expected with the emphasis to be on the power to direct another entity's activities to generate returns for the investor.
Method of reporting	Allows an accounting policy choice of consolidation or presenting all subsidiaries using the equity method or the cost method. If shares are quoted in an active market, cannot use cost model; may use FV-NI.	Use consolidation.

Illustration 9-24

IFRS and Private Entity GAAP Comparison Chart

Summary of Learning Objectives

Glossary

1 Explain and apply the cost/amortized cost model of accounting for investments in debt and equity instruments, and identify how the investments are reported.

At acquisition, the cost of the investment is recognized as its fair value plus transaction costs. If the investment is a debt instrument, any premium or discount is amortized to interest income. Holding gains are recognized only when realized, as are holding losses, unless the investment is impaired. The investment is reported at its cost or amortized cost as either a current asset or a long-term investment, depending on its maturity and management's intention to hold it.

2 Explain and apply the fair value through net income model of accounting for investments in debt and equity instruments, and identify how the investments are reported.

At acquisition, the investment is recognized at its fair value, with transaction costs being expensed. At each reporting date, the investment is revalued to its current fair value, with holding gains and losses recognized in net income. Dividend and interest income is also recognized in net income. If the investment is not held for trading purposes, any interest income is reported separately and is adjusted for discount or premium amortization. If held for trading or other current purposes, the investment is reported as a current asset.

3 Explain and apply the fair value through other comprehensive income model of accounting for investments in equity instruments, and identify how the investments are reported.

At acquisition, the investment is recognized at fair value plus transaction costs. At each reporting date, the investment is revalued to its current fair value with the holding gains or losses reported in other comprehensive income. On disposal, the accumulated holding gains or losses are either recycled to net income or transferred directly to retained earnings. Investments are reported as current or long-term assets, depending on marketability and management intent.

4 Identify private entity GAAP and IFRS for investments in financial assets where there is no significant influence or control.

Under **private entity GAAP**, all financial instrument investments are accounted for at fair value through net income or cost/amortized cost with transaction costs expensed unless using a cost-based measure. The FV-NI approach is used for equity instruments with prices quoted in an active market but there is an FV option that can be used for any other instrument. For both models, all interest and dividend income is reported in net income as are all holding gains and losses, whether realized or not. Under **IFRS**, the two major models are amortized cost and fair value through net income. Transaction costs for FV-NI investments are expensed. To use amortized cost, the investment must have characteristics of a basic loan with contractual cash flows and be managed on a yield to maturity basis. A company can opt to report equity instruments that are not held for trading as FV-OCI without recycling realized gains and losses back through net income. In addition, if there would otherwise be an accounting mismatch, investments ordinarily classified at amortized cost may be designated at FV-NI. All interest and dividend income is recognized in net income, with the effective interest method used for determining interest income, unless not separately reported, such as for those investments held for trading purposes.

5 Explain and apply the incurred loss, expected loss, and fair value loss impairment models, and identify private entity GAAP and IFRS requirements.

The three impairment loss models differ in the timing of the recognition of impairment losses and the discount rate used. Under the incurred loss approach, a triggering event is required before a loss is recognized and measured, and the revised cash flows are discounted using either the historical or a current market rate. Under the expected loss approach, no triggering event is required, and revised cash flows and impairment losses are determined on a continual basis. The discount rate is the historical or original rate. Using the fair value loss model, the expected future cash flows anticipated by the market are discounted, using a current market discount rate. Private entity GAAP applies the incurred loss model, with the cash flows discounted using a current market rate of interest. Existing IFRS use a variety of approaches, with different methods required for investments according to how they are classified, even for equity investments at FV-OCI. An exposure draft on impairment, favouring the expected loss model for amortized-cost-classified investments, was being prepared as this text went to print. No impairment model was anticipated for instruments measured at fair value.

6 Explain the concept of significant influence and why the equity method is appropriate, apply the equity method, and identify private entity GAAP and IFRS requirements.

Significant influence is the ability to have an effect on strategic decisions made by an investee's board of directors, but not enough to control those decisions. The equity method, sometimes referred to as one-line consolidation, is used because income is recognized by the investor as it is earned. The investor's income statement will reflect the performance of the investee company. Under this method, the investment account is adjusted for all changes in the investee's book value and for the amortization of any purchase discrepancy. IFRS requires use of the equity method for its associates (investees a company can significantly influence), while PE GAAP provides a policy choice: either the equity method or the cost method, except that associates with a quoted price in an active market cannot be accounted for at cost. Instead, the FV-NI model can be used.

7 Explain the concept of control, the basics of consolidated financial statements, and why consolidation is appropriate, and identify private entity GAAP and IFRS requirements.

Control relates to the ability to direct the strategic decisions of another entity and to generate returns for your own benefit or loss. When one company controls another, it controls all the net assets of that entity and is responsible for all its revenues and expenses. Therefore, all of the subsidiary's assets and liabilities, and revenues and expenses, on a line-by-line basis, are reported by the parent investor in consolidated financial statements. The interests of the non-controlling shareholders in the subsidiary company are reported separately as non-controlling interest. Under IFRS, all subsidiaries are consolidated. PE GAAP, on the other hand, allows consolidation or a choice of the equity or cost method. Investments in companies with shares traded in an active market cannot be reported using the cost method, but may use FV-NI.

8 Explain the objectives of disclosure, and identify the major types of information that are required to be reported for investments in other companies' debt and equity instruments.

The objectives of disclosure are to provide information so users can assess the significance of the financial asset investments to the entity's financial position and performance, the extent of risks to which the company is exposed as a result, and how those risks are managed. As a result, the investments are identified on the balance sheet according to how they are classified for accounting purposes, with the income statement reporting information on the returns by method of classification. Extensive disclosure is required, particularly under IFRS, on the risk exposures of the entity and how the entity manages those risks.

9 Identify differences in accounting between private entity GAAP and IFRS, and what changes are expected in the near future.

Both PE GAAP and IFRS choose from the same accounting models, with PE GAAP allowing more cost-based measures as the first choice and IFRS using FV-NI as the default category. The effective interest method is required by IFRS when calculating interest income, but PE GAAP does not require this method. Both require all realized gains and losses to be recognized in net income; however, under IFRS, they could be recognized in OCI if using FV-OCI. Different impairment models are used. PE GAAP is based on an incurred loss model, while IFRS is moving toward an expected loss model. Under IFRS, the equity method and consolidation are required for investments in associates and subsidiaries, respectively. Under PE GAAP, the same two methods are allowed; however, for investments in significantly influenced companies, entities may choose to use the cost method, and for subsidiaries, they have a choice of the equity method or cost method. In either case, if the investee's shares are traded in an active market, the cost method cannot be used.

Appendix 9A

Pre-2011 Canadian GAAP for Investments

Objective **10**

Recognize the classifications of financial instrument investments under Canadian GAAP prior to 2011.

Summary of Canadian GAAP Prior to 2011

Illustration 9A-1 is provided as a resource for students and instructors. It summarizes the accounting standards for financial asset investments (excluding those where there is significant influence or control) that were effective in Canada until January 1, 2011. Some of the changes approved in late 2009 or that are the subject of 2009 exposure drafts are not required to be applied as GAAP until 2012 and 2013, so there may be companies continuing to use the previously existing standards, very similar to IFRS, until then. It is expected that many companies will adopt the revisions earlier, and other Canadian publicly accountable companies will likely adopt them as they move into IFRS in 2011.

Illustration **9A-1**

Pre-2011 Canadian GAAP for Financial Asset Investments

	Classifications of Investment (different labels may be used on the financial statements)			
	Held for Trading (HFT)	**Held to Maturity (HTM)**	**Loans and Receivables (L&R)**	**Available for Sale (AFS)**
Investments that qualify	Those acquired for sale in the near future; **or** any investment with an FV that can be reliably estimated can be designated as HFT	Debt instruments with fixed or determinable payments and fixed maturity that the entity is able and intends to hold to maturity	Promises of others to repay on a specific date or on demand, usually with interest, amounts borrowed; excludes investments in debt securities	All others; default category
Initial measurement	At fair value	At fair value	At fair value	At fair value
Transaction costs	Expense	Choice: expense or capitalize	Choice: expense or capitalize	Choice: expense or capitalize
Subsequent measurement	At fair value	At amortized cost	At amortized cost	At fair value, if an active market quoted price; otherwise, at cost
Gains and losses from changes in fair value	Recognize in net income	N/A	N/A	Recognize in OCI, with accumulated gain or loss recycled to net income when realized
Interest income	Not addressed	Use effective interest method	Use effective interest method	Use effective interest method

	Held for Trading (HFT)	Held to Maturity (HTM)	Loans and Receivables (L&R)	Available for Sale (AFS)
Impairment model applied	N/A	Incurred loss model, using original effective interest rate	Incurred loss model, using original effective interest rate	If at FV, fair value loss model; loss is cumulative loss recognized in OCI recycled to net income
				If at cost, fair value model; loss is carrying amount less cost, recognized in net income
Impairment reversals	N/A	Reversals required for subsequent changes in realizable amounts	Reversals required for subsequent changes in realizable amounts	If at FV, no reversals for investments in equity investments, but permitted for debt securities
				If at cost, no reversals

Brief Exercises

BE9-1 Garfield Limited purchased $80,000 of five-year, 9% bonds of Chesley Corporation for $74,086, which provide **(LO 1)** an 11% return, and classified the purchase as an amortized cost model investment. Prepare Garfield's journal entries for (a) the purchase of the investment and (b) the receipt of the first year's annual interest and discount amortization.

BE9-2 Carow Corporation purchased $60,000 of five-year, 8% bonds of Harrison Inc. for $65,118, which provide a 6% **(LO 1)** return, and classified the purchase as an amortized cost model investment. The bonds pay interest semi-annually. Prepare Carow's journal entries for (a) the purchase of the investment and (b) the receipt of semi-annual interest and premium amortization for the first two interest payments that will be received.

BE9-3 On October 1, Zhang Ltd. purchased bonds with a face value of $50,000 for trading purposes, accounting for **(LO 2)** the investment at fair value through net income. The bonds were priced at $52,200 plus $2,250 for the accrued interest purchased. At December 31, Zhang received in cash the annual interest of $3,000 due December 31, and the bonds' fair value was $53,100. Prepare Zhang's journal entries for (a) the purchase of the investment and accrued interest, (b) the interest received, and (c) the fair value adjustment.

BE9-4 Duplessis Corporation purchased 300 common shares of Fallis Inc. as a short-term trading investment for **(LO 2)** $9,900 on September 8. In December, Fallis declared and paid a cash dividend of $1.75 per share. At year end, December 31, Fallis shares were selling for $35.50 per share. Prepare Duplessis Corporation's journal entries to record (a) the purchase of the investment, (b) the dividends received, and (c) the fair value adjustment.

BE9-5 Using the information from BE9-4, assume that the Fallis shares were selling for $31.45 at December 31. **(LO 2)** Prepare the fair value adjustment required at that date.

BE9-6 Hayes Company sold 10,000 shares of its investment in Kenyon Corporation common shares for $27.50 per **(LO 2)** share, incurring $1,770 in brokerage commissions. These securities were accounted for at fair value through net income and originally cost (equal to current carrying amount) $260,000. (a) Prepare the entry to record the sale of these securities. (b) How would your answer change if the securities were classified as a cost/amortized cost or fair value through other comprehensive income investment?

BE9-7 Fairbanks Corporation purchased 400 common shares of Berko Inc. for $13,200 and accounted for them using **(LO 3)** the fair value through other comprehensive income model. During the year, Berko paid a cash dividend of $3.25 per share. At year end, Berko shares were selling for $34.50 per share. Prepare Fairbanks's journal entries to record (a) the purchase of the investment, (b) the dividends received, and (c) the fair value adjustment.

BE9-8 Koga Corporation has a portfolio of shares that are accounted for using the fair value through other compre- **(LO 3)** hensive income model with a year-end fair value of $20,000 and a cost of $17,500. Assuming the portfolio's carrying amount is $18,500 before adjustment, prepare the journal entry at year end.

(LO 3)   **BE9-9**   Using the information from BE9–1, assume instead that the bonds were purchased January 1, 2010, and were accounted for using the fair value through other comprehensive income model. Prepare Garfield Limited's journal entries for (a) the purchase of the investment, (b) the receipt of the annual interest on December 31, 2010, and (c) the year-end fair value adjustment. The bonds have a year-end fair value of $75,500.

(LO 3)   **BE9-10**   The following information relates to DeCorte Corp. for 2011: net income of $672,638; unrealized holding loss of $20,380 related to investments accounted for at fair value through other comprehensive income during the year; accumulated other comprehensive income of $37,273 on January 1, 2011. Determine (a) other comprehensive income for 2011, (b) comprehensive income for 2011, and (c) accumulated other comprehensive income at December 31, 2011.

(LO 5)   **BE9-11**   Hillsborough Co. has an investment in the bonds of Schuyler Corp. with a carrying amount of $70,000. The investment is accounted for at amortized cost. Because of delays in receiving the latest interest payment from Schuyler Corp., Hillsborough reviewed its investment for impairment. Hillsborough follows private entity GAAP and it is determined that the discounted impaired cash flows using the current market rate are $63,000. (a) Prepare the journal entry, if any, to record the reduction in value. (b) Would your answer to part (a) change if the investment were accounted for using the fair value through net income model?

(LO 5)   **BE9-12**   Ramirez Company has an investment in 6%, 20-year bonds of Soto Company. The investment was originally purchased at par for $1.2 million in 2010 and it is accounted for at amortized cost. Early in 2011, Ramirez recorded an impairment on the Soto investment, due to Soto's financial distress. At that time the present value of the cash flows discounted using the original effective interest rate was $900,000, and the present value of the cash flows using the then current market rate was $910,000. In 2012, Soto returned to profitability and the Soto investment was no longer considered impaired. What entry does Ramirez make in 2012 under (a) private entity GAAP, (b) existing IFRS, which uses the incurred loss model and the historic interest rate, and (c) proposed IFRS, which uses the expected loss model for instruments at amortized cost? (d) Would your answer change if the investment were in Soto common shares instead of a debt investment?

(LO 6)   **BE9-13**   Zoop Corporation purchased for $300,000 a 30% interest in Murphy, Inc. This investment gives Zoop significant influence over Murphy. During the year, Murphy earned net income of $180,000 and paid dividends of $60,000. Assuming the purchase price was equal to 30% of Murphy's net carrying amount when it was acquired, prepare Zoop's journal entries related to this investment.

(LO 6)   **BE9-14**   Palej Corporation purchased for $630,000 a 25% interest in Orlov Corporation on January 2, 2011. At that time, the carrying amount of Orlov's net assets was $1.9 million. Any excess of cost over carrying amount can be attributed to unrecorded intangibles with a useful life of 20 years. Prepare Palej's December 31, 2011 entry to amortize the excess of cost over carrying amount.

Exercises

(LO 1, 2, 3, 4)   **E9-1**   **(Investment Classifications)** Each of the following securities is independent of the others.

1. A bond that will mature in four years was bought one month ago when the price dropped. As soon as the value increases, which is expected next month, it will be sold.

2. Ten percent of the outstanding shares of Farm Corp. were purchased. The company is planning on eventually getting a total of 30% of the outstanding shares.

3. Ten-year bonds were purchased this year. The bonds mature on January 1 of next year.

4. Bonds that will mature in five years are purchased. The company would like to hold them until they mature, but money has been tight recently and the bonds may need to be sold.

5. A bond that matures in 10 years was purchased with money that the company has set aside for an expansion project that is planned for 10 years from now.

6. Preferred shares were purchased for their constant dividend. The company is planning to hold the preferred shares for a long time.

Instructions

Identify the best accounting model classification(s) for each of the securities described above. Consider both private entity standards and the requirements of IFRS 9.

E9-2 (Entries for Cost/Amortized Cost Investments) On January 1, 2011, Jennings Corp. purchased at par 10% **(LO 1)** bonds having a maturity value of $300,000. They are dated January 1, 2011, and mature on January 1, 2016, with interest receivable on December 31 of each year. The bonds are accounted for using the amortized cost model.

Instructions

(a) Prepare the journal entry to record the bond purchase.

(b) Prepare the journal entry to record the interest received for 2011.

(c) Prepare the journal entry to record the interest received for 2012.

(d) Prepare the journal entry to record the disposal of the bond at maturity.

E9-3 (Entries for Cost/Amortized Cost Investments) On January 1, 2011, Mo'd Limited paid $537,907.40 for 12% **(LO 1)** bonds with a maturity value of $500,000. The bonds provide the bondholders with a 10% yield. They are dated January 1, 2011, and mature on January 1, 2016, with interest receivable on December 31 of each year. The bonds are accounted for using the amortized cost model.

Instructions

(a) Prepare the journal entry to record the bond purchase.

(b) Prepare a bond amortization schedule.

(c) Prepare the journal entry to record the interest received and the amortization for 2011.

(d) Prepare the journal entry to record the interest received and the amortization for 2012.

(e) Prepare the journal entry to record the disposal of the bond at maturity.

E9-4 (Cost/Amortized Cost Investments) On January 1, 2011, Phantom Corp. acquires $200,000 of Spider **(LO 1)** Products, Inc. 9% bonds at a price of $185,589. The interest is payable each December 31, and the bonds mature on December 31, 2013. The investment will provide Phantom Corp. with a 12% yield. The bonds are accounted for using the amortized cost model.

Instructions

(a) Prepare a three-year schedule of interest income and bond discount amortization.

(b) Prepare the journal entry for the interest received on December 31, 2012, including the discount amortization.

(c) Prepare the journal entries for the interest received on December 31, 2013, including the discount amortization, and for the maturity of the bond.

E9-5 (Fair Value through Net Income Investments) On December 31, 2010, Zurich Corp. provided you with the **(LO 3)** following pre-adjustment information regarding its portfolio of investments held for short-term profit-taking:

	December 31, 2010	
Investments	Carrying Amount	Fair Value
Stargate Corp. shares	$20,000	$19,000
Rodney Corp. shares	10,000	9,000
Vectorman Ltd. shares	20,000	20,600
Total portfolio	$50,000	$48,600

During 2011, Rodney Corp. shares were sold for $9,500. The fair value of the securities on December 31, 2011, was as follows: Stargate Corp. shares $19,300; Vectorman Ltd. shares $20,500.

Instructions

(a) Prepare the adjusting journal entry needed on December 31, 2010.

(b) Prepare the journal entry to record the sale of the Rodney Corp. shares during 2011.

(c) Prepare the adjusting journal entry needed on December 31, 2011.

(LO 2)   **E9-6**   **(Investment in Debt Instruments Held for Trading Purposes, Accounted for Using Fair Value through Net Income)** Ontario Corp. purchased a $100,000 face-value bond of Myers Corp. on July 31, 2010, for $105,490 plus accrued interest. The bond pays interest annually each November 1 at a rate of 9%. On November 1, 2010, Ontario Corp. received the annual interest. On December 31, 2010, Ontario's year end, *The Globe and Mail* newspaper indicated a fair value for these bonds of 104.6. Ontario sold the bonds on January 15, 2011, for $102,600 plus accrued interest. Assume Ontario Corp. follows IFRS and does not report interest income separately from gains and losses on these investments.

Instructions

(a) Prepare the journal entries to record the purchase of the bond, the receipt of interest, any adjustments required at year end, and the subsequent sale of the bonds.

(b) How many months were the bonds held by Ontario Corp. in 2010? Based on this, how much of the income reported on these bonds should be for interest received? Verify that your answer fits with the income that is reported.

(c) If these bonds were acquired to earn a return on excess funds, did the company meet its objective? If yes, how much return did Ontario Corp. earn while the bonds were held? If not, why not?

(d) How would the accounting and reporting change if Ontario Corp. followed private entity GAAP?

(LO 2)   **E9-7**   **(Fair Value through Net Income Investment Model Entries)** Lazier Corporation, a Canadian-based international company that follows IFRS, has the following securities in its portfolio of investments acquired for trading purposes and accounted for using the fair value through net income model on December 31, 2010:

Investments	Carrying Amount (before adjustment)	Fair Value
1,500 shares of David Jones Inc., common	$ 73,500	$ 69,000
5,000 shares of Hearn Corp., common	180,000	174,000
400 shares of Alessandro Inc., preferred	60,000	61,600
	$313,500	$304,600

In 2011, Lazier completed the following securities transactions:

Mar. 1   Sold the 1,500 shares of David Jones Inc. common at $41.50 per share, less fees of $500.
Apr. 1   Bought 700 shares of Oberto Ltd. common at $75 per share, plus fees of $1,300.

Lazier Corporation's portfolio of trading securities appeared as follows on December 31, 2011:

Investments	Carrying Amount	Fair Value
5,000 shares of Hearn Corp., common	$174,000	$175,000
700 shares of Oberto Ltd., common	52,500	50,400
400 shares of Alessandro Inc., preferred	61,600	57,000
	$288,100	$282,400

Assume Lazier follows IFRS and that dividend and interest income is not reported separately.

Instructions

Prepare the Lazier Corporation general journal entries for the following:

(a) The December 31, 2010 adjusting entry

(b) The sale of the David Jones Inc. shares

(c) The purchase of the Oberto Ltd. shares

(d) The December 31, 2011 adjusting entry

(LO 2, 3)   **E9-8**   **(Entries for Fair Value through Other Comprehensive Income and Fair Value through Net Income Equity Investments)** The following information is available about Kinney Corp.'s investments at December 31, 2011. This is the first year Kinney has purchased securities for investment purposes.

Securities	Cost	Fair Value
3,000 shares of Petty Corporation common shares	$40,000	$46,000
1,000 shares of Dowe Inc. preferred shares	25,000	22,000
	$65,000	$68,000

Assume that Kinney Company follows IFRS and that dividend and interest income is not reported separately.

Instructions

(a) Prepare the adjusting entry(ies), if any, at December 31, 2011, assuming the investments are acquired for trading purposes and accounted for using the fair value through net income model.

(b) Prepare the adjusting entry(ies), if any, at December 31, 2011, assuming the investments are accounted for using the fair value through other comprehensive income model.

(c) Discuss how the amounts reported in the financial statements are affected by the choice of classification.

E9-9   (Equity Securities Entries—FV-NI and FV-OCI) Arantxa Corporation made the following cash purchases of   **(LO 2, 3)** investments during 2011, the first year in which Arantxa invested in equity securities:

1. On January 15, purchased 10,000 shares of Nirmala Corp.'s common shares at $33.50 per share plus commission of $1,980.

2. On April 1, purchased 5,000 shares of Oxana Corp.'s common shares at $52.00 per share plus commission of $3,370.

3. On September 10, purchased 7,000 shares of WTA Corp.'s preferred shares at $26.50 per share plus commission of $4,910.

On May 20, 2011, Arantxa sold 4,000 of the Nirmala common shares at a market price of $35 per share less brokerage commissions of $3,850. The year-end fair values per share were as follows: Nirmala $30; Oxana $55; and WTA $28. In addition, the chief accountant of Arantxa told you that Arantxa Corporation holds these investments with the intention of selling them in order to earn short-term profits from appreciation in their prices and accounts for them using the fair value though net income model.

Assume that Arantxa Corporation follows IFRS and that dividend and interest income is not reported separately.

Instructions

(a) Prepare the journal entries to record the three investments.

(b) Prepare the journal entry for the sale of the 4,000 Nirmala shares on May 20.

(c) Prepare the adjusting entries needed on December 31, 2011.

(d) Repeat parts (a) to (c), assuming the investments will be accounted for using the fair value through other comprehensive income model. Arantxa's policy is to capitalize transaction costs on the acquisition of FV-OCI investments and reduce the proceeds on disposal.

E9-10   (Fair Value through Other Comprehensive Income Investments—Entries) On December 31, 2011, Niger   **(LO 3)** Corp. provided you with the following pre-adjustment information for its investment portfolio that is accounted for using the fair value through other comprehensive income (FV-OCI) model:

Investments	Cost and Carrying Amount	Fair Value	Unrealized Gain (Loss)
Sordle Corp. shares	$20,000	$18,500	$(1,500)
Sten Corp. shares	10,000	9,000	(1,000)
British Corp. shares	20,000	20,600	600
Total portfolio	$50,000	$48,100	$(1,900)

During 2012, Sten Corp. shares were sold for $9,400. The fair values of the shares on December 31, 2012, were as follows: Sordle Corp. shares $19,100; British Corp. shares $20,500.

Assume that Niger Corp. follows IFRS and applies the FV-OCI model with recycling.

Instructions

(a) Prepare the adjusting journal entry(ies) needed on December 31, 2011.

(b) Prepare the journal entry(ies) to record the sale of the Sten Corp. shares in 2012.

(c) Prepare the adjusting journal entry needed on December 31, 2012.

(d) Early in 2013, an announcement was made that British Corp.'s major patent that was responsible for 75% of its income had lost most of its value due to a technological improvement by a competitor. As a result, British Corp.'s share price fell to $0.20 per share or $2,000 in total for Niger's holdings. Provide the necessary adjusting entry(ies) to recognize these events.

(LO 3, 8)   E9-11   (Fair Value through Other Comprehensive Income Investment Entries and Financial Statement Presentation) At December 31, 2011, the equity portfolio of Wenger Inc., accounted for using the fair value through other comprehensive income model with recycling, was as follows:

Security	Cost and Carrying Amount	Fair Value	Unrealized Gain (Loss)
A	$17,500	$15,000	$(2,500)
B	12,500	14,000	1,500
C	23,000	25,500	2,500
Total	$53,000	$54,500	$1,500

On January 20, 2012, Wenger Inc. sold security A for $15,300.

Instructions

(a) Prepare the adjusting entry at December 31, 2011, to adjust the portfolio to fair value.

(b) Show the balance sheet presentation of the investment-related accounts at December 31, 2011. (Ignore notes presentation.)

(c) Prepare the journal entries for the 2012 sale of security A.

(LO 3)   E9-12   (Comprehensive Income Disclosure) Assume the same information as in E9–11 and that Wenger Inc. reports net income of $120,000 in 2011 and $140,000 in 2012. The adjusting entry to report the portfolio at fair value at the end of 2012 debited the investment portfolio in total by $7,000.

Instructions

(a) Prepare a statement of comprehensive income for 2011, starting with net income.

(b) Prepare a statement of comprehensive income for 2012, starting with net income.

(LO 3)   E9-13   (Fair Value through Other Comprehensive Income) Swangson Corporation has the following securities in its long-term investment portfolio accounted for at fair value through other comprehensive income (FV-OCI) on December 31, 2011:

Investment	Cost and Carrying Amount	Fair Value
1,500 shares of DJ Inc. common	$ 71,500	$ 69,000
5,000 shares of RH Corp. common	180,000	175,000
400 shares of AZ Inc. preferred	60,000	61,600
Total	$311,500	$305,600

All the investments were purchased in 2011. Swangson follows a policy of capitalizing transaction costs on the acquisition of FV-OCI investments and reducing the proceeds on disposal. Swangson Corp. follows IFRS and applies the FV-OCI model with recycling.

In 2012, Swangson completed the following transactions:

Mar. 1   Sold the 1,500 shares of DJ Inc. common at $45 per share, less fees of $1,200.
Apr. 1   Bought 700 shares of RG Corp. common at $75 per share, plus fees of $1,300.

Swangson Corporation's portfolio appeared as follows on December 31, 2012:

Investment	Carrying Amount	Fair Value
700 shares of RG Corp. common	$ 53,800	$ 50,400
5,000 shares of RH Corp. common	175,000	175,000
400 shares of AZ Inc. preferred	61,600	58,000
Total	$290,400	$283,400

Instructions

Prepare the general journal entries for Swangson for:

(a) The 2011 valuation adjusting entry

(b) The sale of the DJ Inc. shares

(c) The purchase of the RG Corp. shares

(d) The 2012 valuation adjusting entry

E9-14 **(Entries for Fair Value through Other Comprehensive Income Investments)** On January 1, 2011, Mo'd **(LO 3)** Limited paid $322,744.44 for 12% bonds with a maturity value of $300,000. The bonds provide the bondholders with a 10% yield. They are dated January 1, 2011, and mature on January 1, 2016, with interest receivable on December 31 of each year. Assume that the bonds are eligible for the special election and are accounted for at fair value through other comprehensive income. The fair values of the bonds at December 31 of each year are as follows:

2011: $320,500	2014: $310,000
2012: $309,000	2015: $300,000
2013: $308,000	

Instructions

(a) Prepare the journal entry to record the bond purchase.

(b) Prepare the journal entries to record the interest received and recognition of fair value at December 31, 2011.

(c) Prepare the journal entries to record the interest received and recognition of fair value at December 31, 2012, 2013, 2014, and 2015.

(d) Prepare the journal entry to record the disposal of the bond at maturity.

E9-15 **(Entries for Fair Value through Other Comprehensive Income Investments)** On January 1, 2012, Jovi Inc. **(LO 3)** purchased $200,000 face-value 8% bonds of Mercury Ltd. for $184,557. The bonds were purchased to yield 10% interest. Interest is payable semi-annually on July 1 and January 1 and the bonds mature on January 1, 2017. On April 15, 2015, to meet its liquidity needs, Jovi sold the bonds for $189,769 plus accrued interest. Jovi Inc. follows IFRS and applies the FV-OCI model with recycling.

Instructions

(a) Prepare the journal entry to record the bond purchase on January 1, 2012. Assume that the bonds will be accounted for at fair value through OCI.

(b) Prepare the amortization schedule for the bonds from the date of purchase to maturity.

(c) Prepare the journal entries to record the semi-annual interest received on July 1, 2012, and December 31, 2012.

(d) The fair values of the Mercury bonds are as follows:

December 31, 2012	$190,449
December 31, 2013	$186,363
December 31, 2014	$185,363

Prepare the necessary adjusting entry to bring the investment to fair value at December 31, 2012, 2013, and 2014. (Hint: You need to take the discount amortization into account.)

(e) Prepare the journal entry(ies) to record the events associated with the sale of the bonds on April 15, 2015.

E9-16 **(Fair Value through Other Comprehensive Income Securities Entries and Reporting)** Player Corporation **(LO 3, 8)** purchases equity securities costing $73,000 and accounts for them using the fair value through other comprehensive income model. At December 31, the fair value of the portfolio is $67,000. Player Corporation follows IFRS.

Instructions

Prepare the adjusting entry to report the securities properly. Indicate the statement presentation of the accounts in your entry.

E9-17 **(Impairment of Debt Investment)** Tsui Corporation owns corporate bonds at December 31, 2011, accounted **(LO 5)** for using the amortized cost model. These bonds have a par value of $800,000 and an amortized cost of $788,000. Tsui follows private entity GAAP and, after an impairment review was triggered, it is determined that the discounted impaired cash flows using the current market rate are $740,000.

Instructions

(a) Prepare any necessary journal entry(ies) related to the impairment.

(b) Given that the bonds' maturity value is $800,000, should Tsui Corporation accrete (i.e., increase) the difference between the new carrying amount and the maturity value over the life of the bonds?

(c) At December 31, 2012, assume the bonds' adjusted carrying amount is now $741,500 and the fair value of the corporate bonds is $760,000. Prepare the entry (if any) to record this information.

(d) How would your answer to the above change if the investment were accounted for using the fair value through net income model?

(LO 6) **E9-18** **(Equity Method)** Vodden Ltd. invested $500,000 in Seebach Corp. early in the current year, receiving 25% of its outstanding shares. At the time of the purchase, Seebach Corp. had a carrying amount of $1.6 million. Seebach Corp. pays out 35% of its net income in dividends each year.

Instructions

Use the information in the following T account for the investment in Seebach to answer the following questions:

Investment in Seebach Corp.

500,000	
90,000	
	31,500
	7,000

(a) How much was Vodden Ltd.'s share of Seebach Corp.'s net income for the year?

(b) How much was Vodden Ltd.'s share of Seebach Corp.'s dividends for the year?

(c) How much was Vodden Ltd.'s annual depreciation of the excess payment for capital assets?

(d) What was Seebach Corp.'s total net income for the year?

(e) What were Seebach Corp.'s total dividends for the year?

(f) Assuming that depreciable assets have a remaining useful life of 10 years, how much of the payment in excess of carrying amount was assigned to goodwill?

(LO 3, 6) **E9-19** **(Journal Entries for Fair Value and Equity Methods)** Two independent situations follow:

Situation 1

Hatcher Cosmetics acquired 10% of the 20,000 common shares of Ramirez Fashion at a total cost of $14 per share on March 18, 2011. On June 30, Ramirez declared and paid a $75,000 cash dividend. On December 31, Ramirez reported net income of $122,000 for the year. At December 31, the market price of Ramirez Fashion was $15 per share. The investment is accounted for using the fair value through other comprehensive income model.

Situation 2

Holmes, Inc. obtained significant influence over the operations of Nadal Corporation by buying 25% of Nadal's 30,000 outstanding common shares at a cost of $9 per share on January 1, 2011. The purchase price of $9 per share did not include any payment in excess of carrying amount or goodwill. On June 15, Nadal declared and paid a cash dividend of $36,000. On December 31, Nadal reported net income of $85,000 for the year.

Instructions

Prepare all necessary journal entries in 2011 for both situations.

(LO 3, 6) **E9-20** **(Fair Value and Equity Method Compared)** Gregory Inc. acquired 20% of the outstanding common shares of Handerson Inc. on December 31, 2010. The purchase price was $1,250,000 for 50,000 shares, and is equal to 20% of Handerson's carrying amount. Handerson declared and paid an $0.80 per share cash dividend on June 30 and again on December 31, 2011. Handerson reported net income of $730,000 for 2011. The fair value of Handerson's shares was $27 per share at December 31, 2011.

Instructions

(a) Prepare the journal entries for Gregory for 2010 and 2011, assuming that Gregory cannot exercise significant influence over Handerson. The investment is accounted for using the fair value through other comprehensive income model.

(b) Prepare the journal entries for Gregory for 2010 and 2011, assuming that Gregory can exercise significant influence over Handerson.

(c) What is reported for the investment in Handerson shares on the December 31, 2011 balance sheet under each of these methods? What is reported on Gregory's income statement and statement of comprehensive income in 2011 under each of these methods?

E9-21 **(Long-Term Equity Investments and Impairment)** On January 1, 2011, Warner Corporation purchased 30% **(LO 3, 6)** of the common shares of Martz Limited for $180,000. Martz Limited shares are not traded in an active market. The carrying amount of Martz's net assets was $500,000 on that date. During the year, Martz earned net income of $80,000 and paid dividends of $20,000. Any excess of the purchase cost over Warner's share of Martz's carrying amount is attributable to unrecorded intangibles with a 20-year life. The investment in Martz had a fair value of $185,000 at December 31, 2011. During 2012, Martz incurred a loss of $80,000 and paid no dividends. At December 31, 2012, the fair value of the investment was $140,000 and the recoverable amount was $148,000. Assume that Warner follows IFRS.

Instructions

(a) Prepare all relevant journal entries related to Warner's investment in Martz for 2011 and 2012, assuming this is its only investment and Warner cannot exercise significant influence over Martz's policies. Warner accounts for this investment using the fair value through other comprehensive income model (use the proposed IFRS impairment standards). Illustrate how Other Comprehensive Income is affected in 2011 and 2012.

(b) Prepare all relevant journal entries related to Warner's investment in Martz for 2011 and 2012, assuming this is its only investment and Warner exercises significant influence over Martz's policies. Identify any amounts that affect Other Comprehensive Income in 2011 and 2012. Briefly explain.

(c) How would your answer to part (b) be different if you were told that Martz's 2011 net income included a loss from discontinued operations of $10,000 (net of tax)?

E9-22 **(Determine Proper Income Reporting)** The following are two independent situations. **(LO 3, 6, 7)**

1. Bacall Inc. received dividends from its common share investments during the year ended December 31, 2011, as follows:

    (a) A cash dividend of $12,000 is received from Sleep Corporation. Bacall owns a 2% interest in Sleep.

    (b) A cash dividend of $60,000 is received from Largo Corporation. Bacall owns a 30% interest in Largo and a majority of Bacall's directors are also directors of Largo Corporation.

    (c) A cash dividend of $72,000 is received from Orient Inc., a subsidiary of Bacall.

2. On January 3, 2011, Bach Corp. purchased as a long-term investment (accounted for using fair value through other comprehensive income) 5,000 common shares of Storr Ltd. for $79 per share, which represents a 2% interest. On December 31, 2011, the shares' market price was $83 per share. On March 3, 2012, Bach sold all 5,000 shares of Storr for $102 per share.

Assume that all companies follow IFRS.

Instructions

(a) In part 1., determine how much dividend income Bacall should report in its 2011 consolidated income statement.

(b) In part 2., determine the amount of the gain or loss on disposal that should be included in net income in 2012 and in other comprehensive income. The investment in Storr Ltd. was Bach Corp.'s only investment.

E9-23 **(Equity Method with Cost in Excess of Carrying Amount)** On January 1, 2011, Jenna Limited purchased **(LO 6)** 2,500 shares (25%) of the common shares of Novotna Corp. for $355,000. At the date of acquisition, the following additional information relates to the identifiable assets and liabilities of Novotna:

	Carrying Amount	Fair Value
Assets not subject to depreciation	$ 500,000	$ 500,000
Assets subject to depreciation (10 years remaining)	800,000	860,000
Total identifiable assets	1,300,000	1,360,000
Liabilities	100,000	100,000

During 2011, Novotna reported the following information on its income statement:

Income before discontinued operations	$200,000
Discontinued operations (net of tax)	70,000
Net income	270,000
Dividends declared and paid by Novotna during 2011	120,000

Instructions

(a) Prepare the journal entry to record Jenna's purchase of the Novotna shares on January 1, 2011. Assume that any unexplained payment is goodwill.

(b) Prepare the journal entries to record Jenna's equity in the net income and dividends of Novotna for 2011. Depreciable assets are depreciated on a straight-line basis.

(LO 6)   E9-24   **(Equity Method with Cost in Excess of Carrying Amount)** On January 1, 2011, Strug Inc. purchased 40% of the common shares of Chow Corp. for $400,000. Chow Corp.'s balance sheet reported the following information at the date of acquisition:

Assets not subject to depreciation	$200,000
Assets subject to depreciation (8 years remaining)	600,000
Liabilities	100,000

Additional information:

1. Both carrying amount and fair value are the same for assets that are not subject to depreciation and for the liabilities.

2. The fair value of the assets subject to depreciation is $680,000.

3. The company depreciates its capital assets on a straight-line basis.

4. Chow reported net income of $160,000 and declared and paid dividends of $125,000 in 2011.

Instructions

(a) Prepare the journal entry to record Strug's investment in Chow Corp. Assume that any unexplained payment is goodwill.

(b) Prepare the journal entries to record Strug's equity in the net income and dividends of Chow Corp. for 2011.

(c) Assume the same facts as for parts (a) and (b), except that Chow's net income included a loss on discontinued operations of $30,000 (net of tax). Prepare the journal entries to record Strug's equity in the net income of Chow for 2011.

(d) Assume the same facts as above for parts (a) and (b), except that Chow also reports an unrealized gain of $45,000 on investments accounted for using the fair value through other comprehensive income model in Other Comprehensive Income. Explain how your answer to part (b) above would change.

Problems

P9-1   McElroy Corp. has the following portfolio of securities acquired for trading purposes and accounted for using the fair value through net income model at September 30, 2010, the end of the company's third quarter:

Investment	Cost	Fair Value
5,000 common shares of Horton Inc.	$215,000	$196,000
3,500 preferred shares of Monty Ltd.	133,000	140,000
1,000 common shares of Oakwood Inc.	180,000	179,000

On October 10, 2010, the Horton shares were sold at $54 per share. On November 2, 2010, 3,000 common shares of Patriot Corp. were purchased at $54.50 per share. McElroy pays a 1% commission on purchases and sales of all securities. At the end of the fourth quarter, on December 31, 2010, the fair values of the shares held were as follows: Monty $106,000; Patriot $132,000; and Oakwood $193,000. McElroy prepares financial statements every quarter. Assume McElroy follows IFRS.

Instructions

(a) Prepare the journal entries to record the sale, purchase, and adjusting entries related to the portfolio for the fourth quarter of 2010.

(b) Indicate how the investments would be reported on the December 31, 2010 balance sheet. State any assumptions that you have made.

P9-2   The following information relates to the 2011 debt and equity investment transactions of Yellowjackets Ltd. All of the investments were acquired for trading purposes and accounted for using the fair value through net income model. No investments were held at December 31, 2010, and the company prepares financial statements only annually, each December 31, following IFRS. Dividend and interest income are not reported separately from other investment income.

1. On February 1, the company purchased Williams Corp. 12% bonds, with a par value of $500,000, at 106.5 plus accrued interest to yield 10%. Interest is payable April 1 and October 1.

2. On April 1, semi-annual interest was received on the Williams bonds.

3. On July 1, 9% bonds of Saint Inc. were purchased. These bonds, with a par value of $200,000, were purchased at 101 plus accrued interest to yield 8.5%. Interest dates are June 1 and December 1.

4. On August 12, 3,000 shares of Scotiabank were acquired at a cost of $59 per share. A 1% commission was paid.

5. On September 1, Williams Corp. bonds with a par value of $100,000 were sold at 104 plus accrued interest.

6. On September 28, a dividend of $0.50 per share was received on the Scotiabank shares.

7. On October 1, semi-annual interest was received on the remaining Williams Corp. bonds.

8. On December 1, semi-annual interest was received on the Saint Inc. bonds.

9. On December 28, a dividend of $0.52 per share was received on the Scotiabank shares.

10. On December 31, the following fair values were determined: Williams Corp. bonds 101.75; Saint Inc. bonds 97; Scotiabank shares $60.50.

Instructions

(a) Prepare all journal entries you consider necessary for the above, including year-end adjusting entries at December 31.

(b) Identify the effect that the transactions for 2011 have on the Yellowjackets Ltd. income statement for that year.

(c) Assume instead that there were trading investments on hand at December 31, 2010, accounted for using the fair value through net income model, and that they consisted of shares with a cost of $400,000 and a fair value of $390,000. These non–dividend-paying shares were sold early in 2011 and their original cost was recovered exactly. How would your answer to part (b) be different as a result of this information?

(d) Assume that the interest income on the Saint Inc. bonds that were purchased on July 1, 2011, was separately tracked and reported. Prepare the entries that are required on July 1, December 1, and December 31, 2011, to account for this investment.

P9-3 The following amortization schedule is for an investment in Spangler Corp.'s $100,000, five-year bonds with a 7% interest rate and a 5% yield, which were purchased on December 31, 2010, for $108,660:

	Cash Received	Interest Income	Bond Premium Amortized	Amortized Cost of Bonds
Dec. 31, 2010				$108,660
Dec. 31, 2011	$7,000	$5,433	$1,567	107,093
Dec. 31, 2012	7,000	5,354	1,646	105,447
Dec. 31, 2013	7,000	5,272	1,728	103,719
Dec. 31, 2014	7,000	5,186	1,814	101,905
Dec. 31, 2015	7,000	5,095	1,905	100,000

The following schedule presents a comparison of the amortized cost and fair value of the bonds at year end:

	Dec. 31, 2011	Dec. 31, 2012	Dec. 31, 2013	Dec. 31, 2014	Dec. 31, 2015
Amortized cost	$107,093	$105,447	$103,719	$101,905	$100,000
Fair value	$106,500	$107,500	$105,650	$103,000	$100,000

Assume that Spangler follows IFRS.

Instructions

(a) Prepare the journal entry to record the purchase of these bonds on December 31, 2010, assuming the bonds are accounted for using the amortized cost model.

(b) Prepare the journal entry(ies) related to the bonds accounted for using the amortized cost model for 2011.

(c) Prepare the journal entry(ies) related to the bonds accounted for using the amortized cost model for 2013.

(d) Prepare the journal entry(ies) to record the purchase of these bonds, assuming they are accounted for using the fair value through net income model.

(e) Prepare the journal entry(ies) related to the bonds accounted for using the fair value through net income model for 2011.

(f) Prepare the journal entry(ies) related to the bonds accounted for using the fair value through net income model for 2013.

P9-4   Parnevik Corp. has the following securities (all purchased in 2011) in its investment portfolio on December 31, 2011: (1) 3,000 shares of Anderson Corp. common shares, which cost $58,500; (2) 10,000 shares of Munter Ltd. common shares, which cost $580,000; and (3) 6,000 shares of King Corp. preferred shares, which cost $255,000. Their fair values at the end of 2011 were as follows: Anderson Corp. $59,500; Munter Ltd. $569,500; and King Corp. $254,400.

In 2012, Parnevik completed the following transactions:

1. On January 15, sold 3,000 Anderson common shares at $22 per share less fees of $2,150.

2. On April 17, purchased 1,000 Castle Ltd. common shares at $33.50 per share plus fees of $1,980.

The company adds transaction costs to the cost of acquired investments and deducts them from cash received on the sale of investments. On December 31, 2012, the fair values per share of the securities were as follows: Munter $61; King $40; and Castle $29. In addition, the accounting supervisor of Parnevik tells you that even though all these securities have fair values that can be readily determined, Parnevik will not actively trade them, but is holding them for strategic purposes. Management accounts for them using the fair value through other comprehensive income model with recycling.

Instructions

(a) Prepare the entries for the sale of the Anderson Corp. investment on January 15, 2012.

(b) Prepare the entry to record the Castle Ltd. share purchase on April 17, 2012.

(c) Calculate the unrealized gains or losses and prepare any required adjusting entry(ies) for Parnevik Corp. on December 31, 2012.

(d) Indicate how all amounts will be reported on Parnevik's balance sheet, income statement, statement of comprehensive income, and the changes in the accumulated other comprehensive income portion of the statement of changes in shareholders' equity for 2012.

P9-5   Big Brother Holdings, Inc. had the following investment portfolio accounted for using the fair value through other comprehensive income model at January 1, 2010:

Investment	Quantity	Cost per Share	Fair Value at Dec. 31, 2009
Earl Corp.	1,000	$15.00	$11.50
Josie Corp.	900	20.00	16.50
Tinashe Corp.	500	9.00	7.20

During 2010, the following transactions took place:

1. On March 1, Josie Corp. paid a $2 per share dividend.

2. On April 30, Big Brother Holdings, Inc. sold 300 shares of Tinashe Corp. for $10 per share.

3. On May 15, Big Brother Holdings, Inc. purchased 50 more Earl Corp. shares at $16 per share.

4. At December 31, 2010, the shares had the following market prices per share: Earl Corp. $17; Josie Corp. $19; and Tinashe Corp. $8.

During 2011, the following transactions took place:

5. On February 1, Big Brother Holdings, Inc. sold the remaining Tinashe Corp. shares for $7 per share.

6. On March 1, Josie Corp. paid a $2 per share dividend.

7. On December 21, Earl Corp. declared a cash dividend of $3 per share to be paid in the next month.

8. At December 31, 2011, the shares had the following market prices per share: Earl Corp. $19; and Josie Corp. $21.

Assume that Big Brother Holdings, Inc. follows IFRS and is permitted to use the fair value through other comprehensive income model with recycling.

Instructions

(a) Prepare journal entries to record each of the above transactions and year-end events.

(b) Prepare the relevant parts of Big Brother Holdings, Inc.'s 2011 and 2010 comparative balance sheets, income statements, statements of comprehensive income, and statements of changes in shareholders' equity (accumulated other comprehensive income portion) to show how the investments and related accounts are reported.

P9-6 Fernandez Corp. invested its excess cash in investments accounted for using the fair value through other comprehensive income model during 2010. As at December 31, 2010, the portfolio consisted of the following common shares:

	Quantity	Cost	Fair Value
Lindsay Reuben, Inc.	1,000 shares	$ 15,000	$ 21,000
Poley Corp.	2,000 shares	40,000	42,000
Arnold Aircraft Ltd.	2,000 shares	72,000	60,000
Total		$127,000	$123,000

Assume that Fernandez follows IFRS and applies the fair value through other comprehensive income (FV-OCI) model with recycling.

Instructions

(a) What should be reported on Fernandez's December 31, 2010 balance sheet for these securities? What should be reported on Fernandez's 2010 income statement and statement of comprehensive income?

(b) On December 31, 2011, Fernandez's portfolio accounted for using the FV-OCI model consisted of the following common shares:

	Quantity	Cost	Fair Value
Lindsay Reuben, Inc.	3,000 shares	$ 48,000	$60,000
Duff Corp.	1,000 shares	16,000	12,000
Arnold Aircraft Ltd.	2,000 shares	72,000	22,000
Total		$136,000	$94,000

During 2011, Fernandez Corp. sold 2,000 shares of Poley Corp. for $38,200 and purchased 2,000 more shares of Lindsay Reuben, Inc. and 1,000 shares of Duff Corp.

What should be reported on Fernandez's December 31, 2011 balance sheet? What should be reported on Fernandez's 2011 income statement, statement of comprehensive income, and statement of changes in shareholders' equity (for AOCI)?

(c) On December 31, 2012, Fernandez's portfolio consisted of the following common shares:

	Quantity	Cost	Fair Value
Arnold Aircraft Ltd.	2,000 shares	$72,000	$82,000
Duff Corp.	500 shares	8,000	6,000
Total		$80,000	$88,000

During 2012, Fernandez Corp. sold 3,000 shares of Lindsay Reuben, Inc. for $39,900 and 500 shares of Duff Corp. at a realized loss of $2,700.

What should be reported on Fernandez's December 31, 2012 balance sheet? What should be reported on Fernandez's 2012 income statement, statement of comprehensive income, and statement of changes in shareholders' equity (for AOCI)?

(d) Assume that Fernandez is not permitted to account for these investments at FV-OCI. Identify what method of accounting would have to be used and determine, using dollar amounts, how 2010, 2011, and 2012 net income would differ from the amounts reported above.

P9-7 The following information is from a bond investment amortization schedule. Related fair values are also provided and the company prepares financial statements each December 31 following IFRS. Assume that the bonds can be accounted for using the fair value through other comprehensive income model.

	Dec. 31, 2010	Dec. 31, 2011	Dec. 31, 2012	Dec. 31, 2013
Amortized cost	$465,045	$491,150	$519,442	$550,000
Fair value	475,000	499,000	506,000	550,000

Instructions

(a) Indicate whether the bonds were purchased at a discount or at a premium. Explain.

(b) Prepare the entry to adjust the bonds to fair value at December 31, 2011.

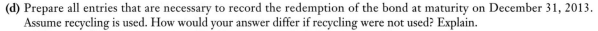

(c) Prepare the entry to adjust the bonds to fair value at December 31, 2012.

(d) Prepare all entries that are necessary to record the redemption of the bond at maturity on December 31, 2013. Assume recycling is used. How would your answer differ if recycling were not used? Explain.

Digging Deeper

(e) Assume that management has objective evidence by examining the discounted future cash flows of the investment and financial position of the investee that the investment's value is impaired at December 31, 2012, and has a fair value of only $487,500. Prepare any entries that you think are necessary to record this information based on the IFRS approach to impairment. Explain your answer.

P9-8   Octavio Corp. prepares financial statements annually on December 31, its fiscal year end. At December 31, 2011, the company has the account Investments in its general ledger that contains the following debits for investment purchases, and no credits:

Feb. 1, 2011	Chiang Corp. common shares, no par value, 200 shares	$ 37,400
April 1	Government of Canada bonds, 11%, due April 1, 2021, interest payable April 1 and October 1, 100 bonds of $1,000 par value each	100,000
July 1	Monet Corp. 12% bonds, par $50,000, dated March 1, 2011, purchased at 108 plus accrued interest to yield 11%, interest payable annually on March 1, due on March 1, 2031	56,000
Nov. 1	$60,000, six-month non–interest-bearing treasury bill that matures on May 1, 2012, bought to yield 10%	57,143

The fair values of the individual securities on December 31, 2011, were:

Chiang Corp. common shares	$ 33,800
Government of Canada bonds	124,700
Monet Corp. bonds	58,600
Treasury bill	58,350

Instructions

(a) Prepare the entries necessary to correct any errors in the Investments account, assuming that the Government of Canada bonds were being managed for their yield to maturity, and that the Monet bonds were acquired with the hope of gaining from falling interest rates. The Chiang Corp. shares were acquired with the hope of cementing the supply of raw materials in the future from this company. Assume that Octavio is interested in early adopting the recognition and measurement standards of IFRS 9. Interest income is tracked only for investments accounted for at amortized cost.

(b) Prepare the entries required to record any accrued interest, the amortization of any premium or discount, and the recognition of fair values on December 31, 2011.

(c) During 2012, the following transactions took place:

1. The treasury bill was sold on February 1, 2012, for $59,600.

2. The Government of Canada bonds were sold on July 1, 2012, for $119,200 plus accrued interest.

Prepare entries to record these transactions.

Digging Deeper

(d) Using the information from parts (a) and (b), assume that the treasury bill was not sold on February 1, 2012, but instead was held until it matured. Give the proper entry to record the disposal of the treasury bill at maturity.

(e) Assume that Octavio Corp. is a private entity and has decided instead to apply private entity GAAP. Identify which, if any, of your previous answers to parts (a) to (d) will change under this assumption. Can the company choose which standards to follow, or is it restricted by the type of company it is? Explain briefly.

P9-9   Gypsy Corporation reported the following portfolio of investments on its balance sheet at September 30, 2011, its last reporting date:

	Cost	Fair Value
Fogelberg Inc. common (5,000 shares)	$225,000	$200,000
Petra Inc. preferred (3,500 shares)	133,000	140,000
Weisberg Corp. common (1,000 shares)	180,000	179,000

On October 10, 2011, the Fogelberg Inc. shares were sold at $54 per share. In addition, 3,000 of Los Tigres Corp. common shares were acquired at $59.50 per share on November 2, 2011. A 1% commission is charged by the company's broker on all transactions and the company's policy is to capitalize all such costs. The December 31, 2011 fair values were as follows: Petra Inc. $96,000; Los Tigres Corp. $132,000; and Weisberg Corp. $193,000. Gypsy follows IFRS and all the investments are accounted for using the fair value through other comprehensive income (FV-OCI) model without recycling.

Instructions

(a) Prepare the journal entries to record the sale, purchase, and adjusting entries related to the FV-OCI investment portfolio in the last quarter of 2011.

(b) Show how all amounts will be reported on Gypsy Corporation's balance sheet, income statement, statement of comprehensive income, and statement of changes in shareholders' equity (for AOCI) for the quarter ending December 31, 2011.

(c) How would the entries in part (a) change if the securities were accounted for using the fair value through net income model, and how would your answer to part (b) be different?

P9-10   The following information relates to the debt investments of Wildcat Inc. during a recent year:

1. On February 1, the company purchased Gibbons Corp. 10% bonds with a face value of $300,000 at 100 plus accrued interest. Interest is payable on April 1 and October 1.

2. On April 1, semi-annual interest is received on the Gibbons bonds.

3. On July 1, Sampson Inc. 9% bonds were purchased. The $200,000 par-value bonds were purchased at 100 plus accrued interest. Interest dates are June 1 and December 1.

4. On September 1, Gibbons Corp. bonds with a par value of $60,000 purchased on February 1 were sold at 99 plus accrued interest.

5. On October 1, semi-annual interest is received on the remaining Gibbons Corp. bonds.

6. On December 1, semi-annual interest is received on the Sampson Inc. bonds.

7. On December 31, the fair values of the bonds purchased on February 1 and July 1 are 95 and 93, respectively.

Assume that Wildcat follows IFRS.

Instructions

(a) Prepare any journal entries that you consider necessary, including December 31 year-end entries, assuming the investments are accounted for under the recognition and measurement requirements of IFRS 9 *Financial Instruments* released late in 2009. Further assume that these investments are not managed on the basis of yield to maturity and that interest income is to be reported separately from other related investment gains and losses.

(b) Assume instead that Wildcat purchased each of these investments and manages them based on their yield to maturity. Prepare all journal entries you consider necessary, including December 31 adjusting entries.

(c) Identify whether accounting for these investments at FV-OCI is an option for Wildcat. Explain. Regardless of whether this is an option or not, prepare the transaction and adjusting entries that would be appropriate under this method.

(d) For parts (a), (b), and (c), show the December 31 presentation of the balance sheet, income statement, statement of comprehensive income, and statement of changes in shareholders' equity (for AOCI).

(e) Briefly explain what it means to manage an investment on the basis of yield to maturity and why the recommended accounting method is reasonable in such a situation.

Digging
Deeper

P9-11   Brooks Corp. is a medium-sized corporation that specializes in quarrying stone for building construction. The company has long dominated the market, and at one time had 70% market penetration. During prosperous years, the company's profits and conservative dividend policy resulted in funds becoming available for outside investment. Over the years, Brooks has had a policy of investing idle cash in equity instruments of other companies. In particular, Brooks has made periodic investments in the company's main supplier, Norton Industries Limited. Although Brooks currently owns 12% of the outstanding common shares of Norton, it does not yet have significant influence over the operations of this investee company. Brooks accounts for the investment using the fair value through other comprehensive income model without recycling.

Yasmina Thomas has recently joined Brooks as assistant controller, and her first assignment is to prepare the 2011 year-end adjusting entries for the accounts that are fair-valued for financial reporting purposes following IFRS. Thomas has gathered the following information about Brooks's relevant accounts:

1. In 2011, Brooks acquired shares of Delaney Motors Corp. and Isha Electric Ltd. for short-term trading purposes. Brooks purchased 100,000 shares of Delaney Motors for $1.4 million and the shares currently have a fair value of $1.6 million. Brooks's investment in Isha Electric has not been profitable: the company acquired 50,000 shares of Isha at $20 per share and they currently have a fair value of $720,000.

2. Before 2011, Brooks invested $22.5 million in Norton Industries and has not changed its holdings this year. This investment in Norton Industries was valued at $21.5 million on December 31, 2010. Brooks's 12% ownership of Norton Industries has a current fair value of $22,225,000.

Instructions

(a) Prepare the appropriate adjusting entries for Brooks as at December 31, 2011, to bring both classes of investments to their fair value.

(b) For both categories of investments, describe how the results of the valuation adjustments made in (a) would appear in the body of and/or notes to Brooks's 2011 financial statements.

(c) Prepare the entries for the Norton investment, assuming that Brooks owns 25% of Norton's shares and has significant influence over Norton. Norton reported income of $500,000 in 2011 and paid cash dividends of $100,000.

(d) If Brooks Corp. were a private enterprise and decided to follow PE standards, identify how your answers to parts (a), (b), and (c) above would differ.

P9-12   Kennedy Corporation has the following portfolio of investments at December 31, 2011, that are accounted for using the fair value through other comprehensive income (FV-OCI) model:

	Quantity	Percent Interest	Cost per Share	Fair Value per Share
Frank Inc.	2,000 shares	8%	$11	$16
Ellis Corp.	5,000 shares	14%	23	19
Mendota Ltd.	4,000 shares	2%	31	24

Early in 2012, Kennedy sold all the Frank Inc. shares for $17 per share, less a 1% commission on the sale. On December 31, 2012, Kennedy's portfolio consists of the following common shares:

	Quantity	Percent Interest	Cost	Fair Value per Share
Ellis Corp.	5,000 shares	14%	$23	$28
Mendota Ltd.	4,000 shares	2%	31	23
Kaptein Inc.	2,000 shares	1%	25	22

Assume that Kennedy follows the recognition and measurement requirements of IFRS 9 *Financial Instruments*, and that these investments qualify for treatment using FV-OCI.

Instructions

(a) What should be reported on Kennedy's December 31, 2011 balance sheet for this long-term portfolio accounted for using the FV-OCI model?

(b) What should be reported on Kennedy's December 31, 2012 balance sheet for the investments accounted for using the FV-OCI model? What should be reported on Kennedy's 2012 income statement for the investments accounted for using the FV-OCI model?

(c) Prepare Kennedy's 2012 statement of comprehensive income.

(d) Assuming that comparative financial statements for 2011 and 2012 are presented in 2012, draft the footnote that is necessary for full disclosure of Kennedy's transactions and investments.

P9-13   Fuentes Incorporated is a publicly traded manufacturing company in the technology industry. The company grew rapidly during its first 10 years and made three public offerings during this period. During its rapid growth period, Fuentes acquired common shares in Yukasato Inc. and Dimna Importers.

In 2000, Fuentes acquired 25% of Yukasato's common shares for $588,000 and accounts for this investment using the equity method. The book value of Yukasato's net assets at the date of purchase is $1.8 million. The excess of the purchase price over the book value of the net assets relates to assets that are subject to amortization. These assets have a remaining life of 20 years. For its fiscal year ended November 30, 2011, Yukasato Inc. reported net income of $250,000 and paid dividends of $100,000.

In 2002, Fuentes acquired 10% of Dimna Importers' common shares for $204,000 and accounts for this investment as a financial asset at fair value through other comprehensive income (FV-OCI).

Fuentes also has a policy of investing idle cash in equity securities to generate short-term profits. The following data are for Fuentes' trading investment portfolio:

TRADING INVESTMENTS (using the FV-NI model)
at November 30, 2010

	Cost	Fair Value
Craxi Electric	$326,000	$314,000
Renoir Inc.	184,000	181,000
Seferis Inc.	95,000	98,500
Total	$605,000	$593,500

INVESTMENTS (using the FV-OCI model)
at November 30, 2010

Dimna Importers	$204,000	$198,000

TRADING INVESTMENTS (USING THE FV-NI MODEL)
at November 30, 2011

	Cost	Fair Value
Craxi Electric	$326,000	$323,000
Renoir Inc.	184,000	180,000
Mer Limited	105,000	108,000
Total	$615,000	$611,000

INVESTMENTS (using the FV-OCI model)
at November 30, 2011

Dimna Importers	$204,000	$205,000

On November 14, 2011, Tasha Yan was hired by Fuentes as assistant controller. Her first assignment was to prepare the entries to record the November activity and the November 30, 2011 year-end adjusting entries for the current trading investments and the investment in common shares of Dimna Importers. Using Fuentes' ledger of investment transactions and the data given above, Yan proposed the following entries and submitted them to Edward O'Brien, controller, for review:

ENTRY 1 (NOVEMBER 8, 2011)

Cash	99,500	
Trading Investments		98,500
Investment Income		1,000

(To record the sale of Seferis Inc. shares for $99,500.)

ENTRY 2 (NOVEMBER 26, 2011)

Trading Investments	105,000	
Cash		105,000

(To record the purchase of Mer common shares for $102,200 plus brokerage fees of $2,800.)

ENTRY 3 (NOVEMBER 30, 2011)

Investment Income	3,000	
Investment Allowance		3,000

(To recognize a loss equal to the excess of cost over fair value of equity securities.)

ENTRY 4 (NOVEMBER 30, 2011)

Cash	38,500	
Investment Income		38,500

(To record the following dividends received from investments: Yukasato Inc. $25,000; Dimna Importers $9,000; and Craxi Electric $4,500.)

ENTRY 5 (NOVEMBER 30, 2011)

Investment in Yukasato Inc.	62,500	
Investment Income		62,500

(To record share of Yukasato Inc. income under the equity method, $250,000 × 0.25.)

Instructions

(a) Are there any differences between the characteristics of trading investments accounted for using the FV-NI model and investments accounted for using the FV-OCI model in general? Explain. Are there any differences in the specific case of Fuentes Incorporated's investments?

(b) The journal entries proposed by Tasha Yan will establish the value of Fuentes' equity investments to be reported on the company's external financial statements. Review each journal entry and indicate whether or not it is in accordance with the applicable accounting standards, assuming the company has adopted the recognition and measurement standards of IFRS 9 *Financial Instruments*. If an entry is incorrect, prepare the correct entry or entries that should have been made.

(c) Because Fuentes owns more than 20% of Yukasato Inc., Edward O'Brien has adopted the equity method to account for this investment. Under what circumstances would it be inappropriate to use the equity method to account for a 25% interest in the common shares of Yukasato Inc.? If the equity method is not appropriate in this case, what method would you recommend? Why?

P9-14 On January 1, 2011, Howard Corporation, a public company, acquired 10,000 of the 50,000 outstanding common shares of Kline Corp. for $25 per share. The balance sheet of Kline reported the following information at the date of the acquisition:

Assets not subject to depreciation	$290,000
Assets subject to depreciation	860,000
Liabilities	150,000

Additional information:

1. On the acquisition date, the fair value is the same as the carrying amount for the assets that are not subject to depreciation and for the liabilities.

2. On the acquisition date, the fair value of the assets that are subject to depreciation is $960,000.

3. Assets that are subject to depreciation have a remaining useful life of eight years as at January 1, 2011.

4. Kline reported 2011 net income of $100,000 and paid dividends of $30,000 in December 2011.

5. Kline's shares had a fair value of $24 per share on December 31, 2011.

Instructions

(a) Prepare the journal entries for Howard Corporation for 2011, assuming that Howard cannot exercise significant influence over Kline and accounts for the investment at fair value through other comprehensive income.

(b) Prepare the journal entries for Howard Corporation for 2011, assuming that Howard can exercise significant influence over Kline's operations.

(c) How would your answers to parts (a) and (b) change if Howard had acquired the Kline shares on July 2 instead of January 1?

Digging Deeper

(d) How would your answers to parts (a) and (b) change if Howard Corporation were a private company applying private enterprise standards?

Writing Assignments

WA9-1   Fran Song looked at the consolidated financial statements of Vixen Manufacturing Limited and shook her head. "I was asked to look at the accounting for Vixen's investments," she said, "but I can't find any investments listed on the balance sheet!" Fran has just begun her work term with Potts and Palmer, a CGA firm in public practice, and she has approached you for help.

Instructions

(a) Explain to Fran what type of investments Vixen likely holds and how they have been accounted for.

(b) Explain the rationale for the reporting standards for this type of investment.

(c) Identify what other evidence there might be on the financial statements that would indicate the existence of this type of investment.

WA9-2   Addison Manufacturing holds a large portfolio of debt securities as an investment. The fair value of the portfolio is greater than its original cost, even though some securities have decreased in value. Ted Abernathy, the financial vice-president, and Donna Nottebart, the controller, are in the process of classifying this securities portfolio in accordance with the new IFRS standard (IFRS 9) for the first time. Abernathy wants to classify all investments that have increased in value during the period as fair value through net income in order to increase net income this year. He wants to account for all the securities that have decreased in value at amortized cost.

Ethics

Nottebart disagrees. She tells Abernathy that there are no options now under IFRS. Depending on certain criteria, the debt instruments must be classified into the amortized cost category or the fair value through net income category.

Instructions

Assume for the following questions that the company has no issues related to accounting mismatches.

(a) Is Nottebart correct in that there are no choices for the classification of debt instruments?

(b) For each of the following types of debt instruments determine, by referring to the newly issued IFRS 9, if the debt security would be measured at amortized cost or fair value.

   1. A debt instrument has a variable rate of interest and matures in 2015. The variable rate is based on the prime bank lending rate and pays 2% above prime. The company has, in the past, bought and sold these bonds and not held them until maturity.

   2. A 5% bond, issued by Exnon Inc., is convertible into equity at the holder's option. If Addison decides to receive shares rather than cash, the conversion rate to be used is a price of $50 per share of Exnon Inc. Addison will likely request to convert to shares when the share price of Exnon is over $55 per share or more.

   3. A corporate bond pays interest that is linked to an inflation index. The company expects to hold onto this bond until it matures.

   4. A perpetual bond (meaning it has no maturity date), issued by Resource Inc., can be called at any point by the issuer. If the bond is called, Addison will receive the face value of the bond plus any accrued interest. In addition, interest can only be paid on the bond if Resource Inc. meets certain solvency tests, before and after the payment of the interest. The company plans to hold this debt investment in perpetuity.

WA9-3   You have just started working for Andrelli Corp. as part of the controller's group involved in current financial reporting problems. Kameela Franklin, controller for Andrelli, is interested in your accounting background because the company has several different types of investments and is wondering how to report them. The company is currently a private entity but is thinking of adopting IFRS. The following are the investments for which the controller is trying to determine what the appropriate accounting treatment would be under private entity GAAP or the new IFRS standard, which the company would adopt early.

Situation 1

The company invests excess cash in term deposits that mature in six months and bear interest at 1%. The company holds on to these investments until maturity to receive the cash flows at the maturity date.

Situation 2

Andrelli has an investment in shares of Warren Corp in which it owns 10% of the voting shares. Warren Corp is a private company and therefore the shares are not publicly traded.

Situation 3

A corporate bond investment will come due in 2016 and pays interest at a fixed rate of 8%. The company's intention is to hold this until maturity and use the cash flows from the interest payments to help fund operations.

Situation 4

The company invests in money market funds, again using excess cash. The company cashes in these investments as cash is required.

Situation 5

The company has purchased 20% of the common shares of a supplier and has been able to get three of its nominees elected to the supplier's 10-person board of directors. The supplier reported record earnings of $100,000 this year, but unfortunately was not able to pay out a dividend.

Instructions

(a) Under private entity GAAP, what is the effect on the balance sheet and earnings of each of the independent situations above?

(b) Under the proposed new standard under IFRS, what is the effect on the balance sheet and earnings of each of the independent situations above?

WA9-4 On July 1, 2010, Munns Corp. purchased for cash 25% of the outstanding shares of Huber Corporation. Both Munns and Huber have a December 31 year end. Huber Corporation, whose common shares are actively traded on the Toronto Stock Exchange, paid a cash dividend on November 15, 2010, to Munns Corp. and its other shareholders. Huber also reported net income for 2010 of $920,000.

Instructions

(a) Assuming that Munns Corp. will follow IFRS, prepare a one-page memorandum on how Munns Corp. should report the above facts on its December 31, 2010 balance sheet and its 2010 income statement, and also state what additional disclosure might be required in the notes to the financial statements. In your memo, identify and describe the method of valuation that you recommend. If additional information is needed, identify what other information would be necessary or useful. Address your memo to the chief accountant at Munns Corp. and provide reasons for your choices as much as possible.

(b) If Munns reported under private entity GAAP, what other alternatives would be available?

WA9-5 The International Accounting Standards Board (IASB) is proposing the use of the expected loss model to determine impairment losses for financial assets measured using the cost or amortized cost basis. Currently, the incurred loss model is used under IFRS and private entity GAAP.

An entity has made an investment in a debt instrument that is for $1 million and will pay interest at 5% for the next five years until 2016. The investment is bought at par, and the effective interest rate is 5%, assuming no future credit losses. In determining expected future credit losses, the effective interest rate incorporating these future expected credit losses is only 4.2%.

Instructions

Using the facts from the example above, compare and contrast the expected loss model and the incurred loss model with respect to the following issues:

(a) How is the debt investment initially recorded and the effective rate of interest determined?

(b) When is the impairment loss measured?

(c) How is the revised carrying amount measured? Where is the impairment loss recorded?

(d) When are reversals of the impairment determined and reported?

WA9-6 Write a brief essay highlighting the differences between IFRS and accounting standards for private enterprises noted in this chapter, discussing the conceptual justification for each.

Cases

Refer to the Case Primer to help you answer these cases.

CA9-1 Investment Company Limited (ICL) is a private company owned by 10 doctors. The company's objective is to manage the doctors' investment portfolios. It actually began as an investment club 10 years ago. At that time, each doctor invested equal amounts of cash and the group met every other week to determine where the money should be invested. Eventually, they decided to incorporate the company and each doctor now owns one tenth of the voting shares. The company employs two managers who look after the business full-time and make the investment decisions with input from the owners. Earnings per year after taxes now average $1.5 million. During the year, the following transactions took place:

Investment A (IA): Purchased common shares of IA for $1 million. IA allows researchers to use expensive lab equipment (which is owned by the company) on a pay-per-use basis. These shares represent 15% of the total outstanding common shares of the company. Because of its percentage ownership, ICL is allowed to appoint one member of IA's board of directors. There are three members on the board. One of the ICL owners has also been hired as a consultant to the company to advise on equipment acquisitions. The company is unsure of how long it will keep the shares. At least two of the company owners are interested in holding on to the investments for the longer term as they use the services of IA.

Investment B (IB): Purchased preferred shares of IB representing 25% of the total outstanding shares. The shares will likely be resold within two months, although no decision has yet been made.

Investment C (IC): Purchased 25% interest in voting common shares of IC for $1 million two years ago. The current carrying amount is $950,000 since the company has been in the drug development stage. IC develops drug delivery technology. In the past week, a major drug on which the company has spent large amounts (approximately $10 million) for research and development was declined by the Food and Drug Administration for sale in the United States. Most of the $10 million had previously been capitalized in the financial statements of IC. This is a significant blow to IC as it had been projecting that 50% of its future revenues would come from this drug. IC does not produce financial statements until two months after ICL's year end.

Although the investments have been mainly in private companies so far, the doctors are thinking of revising their investment strategy and investing in more public companies. They feel that the stock market is poised for recovery, and are therefore planning to borrow some funds for investment. The accountant is currently reviewing the above transactions in preparation for a meeting with the bank.

Instructions

Adopt the role of the company's accountant and analyze the financial reporting issues.

CA9-2 Cando Communications (CC) is a public company that owns and operates 10 broadcast television stations and several specialty cable channels, 10 newspapers (including the *International Post*), and many other non-daily publications. It has a 57.6% economic interest in AustraliaTV (Australia), a 45% interest in IrishTV (Republic of Ireland), and 29.9% interest in UlsterTV (Northern Ireland).

According to the notes to the annual financial statements, the company owns approximately 15% of the shares and all of the convertible and subordinated debentures of AustraliaTV. The convertible debentures are convertible into shares that would represent 50% of the total issued shares of the company at the time of conversion. In total, including the debentures, the investment in AustraliaTV yields a distribution that is equivalent to 57.5% of all distributions paid by AustraliaTV. CC has a contractual right to be represented on the board of directors and has appointed three of the board's 12 members.

The investment in IrishTV is part of a joint venture agreement with another company. Under the terms of the agreement, control of the company is shared between the two parties.

Although the company has made an attempt to influence the decisions made by UlsterTV management, it has been unsuccessful and does not have any representation on the board of directors.

Investments represent approximately $150 million (approximately 5% of total assets). Even though revenues were up by 15%, net income was only $8 million for the year end, down from $50 million the prior year.

Instructions

Adopt the role of a financial analyst and analyze the financial reporting issues.

CA9-3 Fanshaw Bank made the headlines in newspapers when it announced that it would be restating its financial statements for the year ended October 31, 2011. The restatements were the result of an investigation by the Local Securities Commission and the Superintendent of Financial Institutions. The investigation uncovered several errors, including the accounting for investments and certain transactions involving mortgage-backed securities under GAAP. While the investigation was being completed, the company issued a cautionary press release that advised investors not to rely on the previously issued financial statements.

As a result of the findings, the auditors of the past 35 years were dismissed, as was the bulk of the management team. New internal controls were put in place to ensure that the problem would not happen again. Below are the specific details for two types of transactions that were accounted for incorrectly:

1. Investments in debt securities were initially recorded at amortized cost. The investment would then be left as is or valued at fair value with gains/losses being booked either to income or other comprehensive income, depending on management's intent. No documentation was prepared.

2. The company entered into transactions called "dollar roll repurchase agreements." Under these agreements, certain mortgage-backed securities were sold and the company also signed a separate agreement to repurchase the same securities later. All of these were accounted for as secured loans.

Instructions

Adopt the role of one of the investigation team members and discuss the issues.

CA9-4 Impaired Investments Limited (IIL) is in the real estate industry. Last year, the company divested itself of some major investments in real estate and invested the funds in several instruments as follows:

1. Investments in 5% bonds: currently carried at amortized cost

2. Investments in common shares—Company A: currently carried at fair value with gains and losses booked to income

3. Investments in common shares—Company B: currently carried at fair value with gains and losses booked to other comprehensive income

During the current year, similar bonds available in the marketplace are yielding 6%. Although the company is not certain, the controller feels this may be due to greater perceived risk associated with changes in the economy and specifically the real estate industry. The investment in Company A shares is significantly below cost at year end according to market prices at year end (Company A's shares trade on a stock exchange). The investment in Company B shares is also below cost but the controller feels that this is just a temporary decline and not necessarily impairment. The shares of Company B also trade on a stock exchange.

IIL is currently a private entity but has recently contemplated going public perhaps in the next five years.

Instructions

Adopt the role of the controller and discuss the financial reporting issues related to the IIL financial statements.

Research and Financial Analysis

RA9-1 Eastern Platinum Limited

Real-World Emphasis

Refer to the interim financial statements of **Eastern Platinum Limited** for its three-month period ended March 31, 2009, found in Appendix 5B.

Instructions

(a) Review Eastern's balance sheet. Identify all financial investments that are reported. You may need to read the notes to the financial statements to get the necessary details.

(b) Does Eastern have any investments in subsidiary companies? Does it own 100% of all its subsidiaries? Can you tell this by looking at the balance sheet? At the income statement? What information is disclosed about these subsidiaries?

(c) Does Eastern exercise significant influence over any of its investment holdings? Did Eastern acquire any companies during the year? Explain the process you undertook to determine the answer to these questions.

RA9-2 Research Statement Disclosures

The standards discussed in the chapter have only recently been approved and will not need to be adopted until 2013. However, company reports prepared under the existing standards can still be useful to review to help gain an understanding of the nature of financial investments that are made, and the disclosure provided. Many of the concepts found in these notes will still be relevant for the new proposed standards.

Instructions

Find the recent financial statements of a company of your choice and answer the following questions:

(a) Identify all the types of investments in debt and equity instruments that the company has made.

(b) How has the company classified these investments? What is the impact on the balance sheet, on the income statement, and on other comprehensive income?

(c) Review the notes to the financial statements and identify all disclosures related to these investments. Do not list the details, but summarize the type of information provided by each disclosure.

RA9-3 Royal Bank of Canada

Real-World Emphasis

Refer to the 2008 financial statements and accompanying notes of **Royal Bank of Canada** (Royal) that are found on the company's website (www.royalbank.ca) or can be accessed through www.sedar.com. Note that the Royal Bank of Canada followed the standards in effect in 2009 for reporting financial investments.

Instructions

(a) What percentage of total assets is held in investments (2008 versus 2007)? Note that Royal holds a significant loan portfolio also. What is the business reason for holding loans versus securities? Comment on how the investments are classified and presented on the balance sheet.

(b) What percentage of total interest income comes from securities (2008 versus 2007)? Are there any other lines on the income statement relating to securities? What percentage of net income relates to securities (2008 versus 2007)? Calculate an approximate return on the investments in securities. Comment on the return, while looking at the nature of the securities that are being invested in.

(c) Read the notes to the financial statements that are about securities and note the valuation method.

RA9-4 Research Issue—Variable Interest Entities

Variable interest entities (VIEs) is a very complex topic and continues to be high on the agendas of the accounting standard-setting communities around the world. Part of the recent global credit crisis, as well as the fall of Enron, was a result of the use and non-consolidation of variable interest entities.

Instructions

Research and write a one- to two-page report on variable interest entities. What is a VIE? What is the accounting issue that needs resolution? How is the International Accounting Standards Board proposing to deal with this issue? Identify at least one company that has a VIE and discuss how the investment was reported.

RA9-5 Potash Corporation of Saskatchewan

Real-World Emphasis

Instructions

Gain access to the 2008 financial statements of **Potash Corporation of Saskatchewan** from the company's website (www.potashcorp.com) or www.sedar.com.

(a) Based on the information contained in these financial statements, determine each of the following for Potash:

1. Cash used in (for) investing activities during 2008 and 2007 (from the statement of cash flows)

2. Cash used for purchases of long-term investments during 2008 and 2007

3. Total investment in unconsolidated affiliates (or investments and other assets) at December 31, 2008, and 2007

(b) What conclusions about the management of investments can be drawn from the data in part (a)?

(c) Briefly identify from the notes Potash's investments reported under the equity method. Describe these investments, the amount of voting control, and the fair value of each investment. Are there any differences between the carrying value of the companies and Potash's proportionate net book value? How much cash was received from dividends and how much was reported as Potash's portion of the investee's net income? Where is this income reported?

(d) Describe each investment and the amount of voting control of the other types of investments in long-term investments. What method of accounting has the company used for these? How much cash was received from dividends related to these investments?

(e) Discuss the impairment loss that was reported by Potash for 2008 and explain the event that triggered this impairment loss to be reported.

Cumulative Coverage: Chapters 6 to 9

Suites for You Inc. is a small boutique hotel that provides 38 suites that can be rented by the day, week, or month. Food service is available through room service as well. In addition, there are two suites that have been rented on a long-term basis to corporate tenants, who have access to their suite anytime throughout the year without making a reservation. The company has a December 31 year end, and you are preparing the year-end financial statements using private entity GAAP.

The following issues require your consideration:

1. Cash

   • The company has a significant amount of U.S. cash on hand to meet the needs of its guests. At year end, there was $10,000 in U.S. cash on hand. The year-end exchange rate was 1.07, and the average rate for the year was 1.08.

- The bank statement balance at December 31 was $158,293. There were outstanding cheques of $52,375 and an outstanding deposit of $15,487. Bank charges per the bank statement were $50 for the month of December and have been recorded.

2. Accounts receivable and allowance for doubtful accounts

- The company charges $150 per night for accommodation in one of the rental suites, and guests pay at the end of their stay, with daily revenue being accrued as it is earned. At December 31, the amount outstanding from short-term guests was $10,500. At year end, the company expects to be unable to collect an amount equal to 1% of the annual sales for this type of suite. During the year, sales amounted to $1,750,000, and the balance in Allowance for Doubtful Accounts at the end of the previous year was $15,000. During the year, $12,000 in accounts were written off.

- The two corporate suites are rented for $45,000 per year. The payment for these longer term rentals is due in advance each July 1 for the following twelve months. One of these corporate suites has been in use for part of the year, but the corporate tenant went bankrupt, and was unable to pay the $45,000 fee. Hotel management had hoped the tenant would eventually be able to pay, and allowed the company to use the suite until the end of October. Since then, the hotel has been in negotiations with the bankruptcy accountant, and expects to eventually receive a settlement of $10,000. The balance will become uncollectible; no allowance for doubtful accounts has been recorded with respect to these suites as there have never been collection problems in the past.

3. Inventory

- The company has a standing weekly order at set prices with a local catering firm. If the food is not eaten before the next delivery is received, it is donated to the local women's shelter. This ensures that all meals are of appropriate quality for the guests of the hotel.

- On December 31, the following items were delivered:

Item	Unit cost	Net Realizable Value
40 chicken dinners	$5	$12
35 beef dinners	$6	$15
75 frozen vegetable servings	$1	$2
75 units of fresh fruit	$1	$2
100 desserts	$3	$5

- The invoice for the food delivery on December 31 included an additional delivery charge of $0.10 per item, totalling $32.50.

- Overnight on December 31, an ice storm resulted in a loss of electricity to the hotel building. As a result, 20 chicken and 10 beef dinners thawed, and were unusable.

4. Investments

- During the year, the company purchased 30% of the shares in Western Hotel Company, a company that owns a similar hotel property in a nearby city, for $5 million. Subsequently, Western Hotel Company paid a dividend totalling $100,000 and earned income of $250,000. You have decided to use the equity method to account for this investment.

- Suites for You Inc. also purchased common shares of SQRL as a temporary investment for $48,000. At the end of the year, these shares had a fair value of $47,000. A dividend of $500 was received during the year.

Instructions

(a) Determine the amount to be disclosed on the balance sheet under the following headings:

1. Cash and cash equivalents
2. Accounts receivable
3. Allowance for doubtful accounts
4. Inventory
5. Investment in SQRL

6. Investment in Western Hotel Company
7. Unearned revenue
8. Investment income
9. Bad debt expense

(b) What other specific note disclosures will be required based on the information provided?

The Real Value of Real Estate

HALIFAX-BASED HOMBURG INVEST INC. is a real estate investment and development company with $4 billion in property holdings in Canada, the United States, and several European countries. Among the buildings in its Canadian portfolio are Place Alexis Nihon and CN Central Station in Montreal, as well as several big-box Zellers stores across the country. In addition, it owns global and national headquarters for large corporations in Germany, the Netherlands, Lithuania, Latvia, and Estonia.

For the past 10 years, Homburg has prepared two sets of financial statements—one according to Canadian GAAP and one according to International Financial Reporting Standards (IFRS). "Most public companies in Canada have a north-south bias—they are playing to the U.S. market and have U.S. interests, whereas we are east-west—we are more Canadian and European," says Jamie Miles, Homburg's Chief Financial Officer. "When you're dealing with European investors, they want to know what it's worth today ... If you held the assets for a long time, under the cost method, the balance sheet starts to lose its relevance," he adds.

Under Canadian GAAP prior to the 2011 changeover to IFRS, real estate companies carried their real estate assets on a cost basis. Under IFRS, companies have the option to use the cost method or fair value, but they still have to disclose the fair value of these assets, that is, the price they could be sold for today. With the move to IFRS, real estate firms may have quite different financial statements.

While there may be some work to get the fair value numbers at first, once you have them, the accounting is straightforward, says Miles. "From an accounting standpoint, IFRS was never a major problem. Basically, we operate in a Canadian GAAP environment, and then we convert Canadian GAAP to IFRS. I can do that conversion in eight journal entries."

But the difference can be quite significant. Miles illustrates this point by describing Homburg's 2008 numbers. "It's the same operations, same cash flow, but under Canadian GAAP, we had no impairment on our investment properties and, under IFRS, we had a writeoff of $285 million." ■

CHAPTER 10

Property, Plant, and Equipment: Accounting Model Basics

Learning Objectives

After studying this chapter, you should be able to:

1. Identify the characteristics of property, plant, and equipment assets, and explain the importance of these long-term assets to a business enterprise.

2. Identify the costs to include in the measurement of property, plant, and equipment assets at acquisition.

3. Determine asset cost when the transaction has delayed payment terms or is a lump-sum purchase, a non-monetary exchange, or a contributed asset.

4. Identify the costs included in specific types of property, plant, and equipment.

5. Understand and apply the cost model.

6. Understand and apply the revaluation model.

7. Understand and apply the fair value model.

8. Explain and apply the accounting treatment for costs incurred after acquisition.

9. Identify differences in accounting between accounting standards for private enterprises (private entity GAAP) and IFRS, and what changes are expected in the near future.

After studying Appendix 10A, you should be able to:

10. Calculate the amount of borrowing costs to capitalize for qualifying assets.

Preview of Chapter 10

This chapter is the first of three chapters that explain the accounting, reporting, and disclosure requirements for an entity's investment in long-lived non-financial assets. Chapter 10 introduces investments in property, plant, and equipment assets and how they are accounted for at acquisition. It then sets out and explains three different accounting models that are used to measure such assets, and the accounting treatment for costs incurred after acquisition. This chapter, like those preceding it, finishes by summarizing significant differences between IFRS and private entity GAAP requirements.

Chapter 11 continues the coverage of tangible long-lived assets by explaining how these assets are accounted for after acquisition (depreciation), when their capacity to generate future cash flows is reduced (impairment), and when they are disposed of (derecognition). This chapter also addresses significant presentation and disclosure requirements. Chapter 12 zeroes in on recognition and measurement issues related to intangible long-lived assets and goodwill.

The chapter is organized as follows:

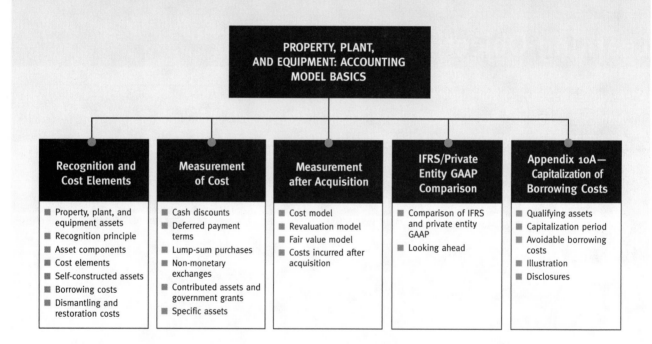

Objective 1

Identify the characteristics of property, plant, and equipment assets, and explain the importance of these long-term assets to a business enterprise.

Almost every enterprise, whatever its size or activity, invests in long-lived assets. Such long-term resources include both those that are physical assets—property, plant, and equipment—and those that are intangible. These assets provide the entity with the capacity or infrastructure to produce goods and/or provide services. Too much investment in long-lived assets results in costly overcapacity and too little investment means lost opportunities for profits and future cash flows. Both situations lower the company's rate of return. To properly assess an enterprise's potential for future cash flows, users need a solid understanding of its investment in long-term productive assets, the extent to which this investment has changed in the period, and the accounting policies applied.

RECOGNITION AND COST ELEMENTS

Property, Plant, and Equipment Assets

Property, plant, and equipment (PP&E), also commonly referred to as tangible capital assets, plant assets, or fixed assets include long-term resources such as office, factory and warehouse buildings, investment property, equipment (machinery, furniture, tools), and mineral resource properties. Consistent with the terminology in IFRS, the term "depreciation" is used in this and other chapters to refer specifically to the amortization of property, plant, and equipment; "depletion" is used for the amortization of mineral resource properties; and "amortization" is used for intangibles. In addition, the term **amortization** may be used in a general sense to refer to the allocation of the cost of any long-lived asset to different accounting periods.

Let's begin by defining the types of assets dealt with in this chapter. Property, plant, and equipment is defined in both IAS 16 *Property, Plant, and Equipment* and in the standards that apply to private enterprises, *CICA Handbook*, Part II, Section 3061, as assets that have the following characteristics:

1. **They are held for use in the production of goods and services, for rental to others, or for administrative purposes.** They are not intended for sale in the ordinary course of business.

2. **They are used over more than one accounting period** and are usually depreciated. Property, plant, and equipment provide services over many years. Through periodic depreciation charges, the cost of the investment in these assets, with the usual exception of land, is assigned to the periods that benefit from using them.

3. **They are tangible.** These assets have a physical existence or substance, which makes them different from intangible assets such as patents or goodwill.

At times there is a fine line between what is categorized as a capital asset and what is categorized as a supply inventory. Assume, for example, that a company has a substantial fleet of trucks (capital assets) and a variety of assets related to the trucks: spare tires, major motor parts, oil and grease, and truck cleaning equipment. What type of asset is each of these? The general approach is to include any items that have multiple uses and are regularly used and replaced within the accounting period as **inventory**. Major spare parts and standby or servicing equipment used only with a specific capital asset and useful for more than one period are classified as items of **property, plant, and equipment**.

What about agricultural assets such as trees in an apple orchard, grapevines in a vineyard or livestock held to produce milk, wool or additional livestock? These biological assets—living plants and animals—have all the characteristics necessary to be items of PP&E. Entities with such assets apply the same accounting principles used for other items of property, plant, and equipment if they report under private entity GAAP. However, companies applying IFRS are required to follow specific standards for biological assets that are set out in IAS 41 *Agriculture*. These are briefly described later in this chapter.

Recognition Principle

Entities incur many costs, but how do they know which ones should be recognized as an item of PP&E? Assuming the resulting item meets the definition of property, plant, and equipment, accounting standards require that the following two recognition criteria be satisfied:

Underlying Concept

This recognition principle applies to costs incurred when an asset is first acquired and later when incurring costs to upgrade, replace, or service the asset.

1. It is probable that the item's associated future economic benefits will flow to the entity.

2. Its cost can be measured reliably.

If both are met, the item is capitalized (i.e., included in the asset's cost) and recognized as a PP&E asset. Some costs, such as those for government-imposed pollution reduction equipment, may not appear to generate any net future cash inflows (future economic benefits), but are still recognized as property, plant, and equipment. This is because these expenditures are necessary in order to obtain the economic benefits from other assets.

If both recognition criteria are **not met**, the costs incurred are recognized as an expense, such as when repair and ongoing maintenance expenditures are made.

Asset Components

Significant Change

While the recognition principle is clear, the standards do not specify what level of asset should be recognized. This is referred to as a unit of measure issue. For example, if you buy or construct a building, what items should be recognized? Should it be one asset "building," or should each individual component be recognized as a separate asset, such as the foundation and frame, roof, windows, and elevators? Alternatively, can a number of smaller items, such as individual tools, be aggregated and recognized as a single asset?

The degree of **componentization** is left up to professional judgement. A primary consideration is the **significance of the individual parts** to the "whole" asset. On a cost-benefit basis, an entity would only separate out components that make up a relatively significant portion of the asset's total cost. As explained in the depreciation discussion in Chapter 11, other factors include whether items have **differing useful lives** and/or **different patterns of delivering economic benefits** to the company, making alternative depreciation methods appropriate. The significance of the items and the similarity of their life and use are also considerations in deciding whether to aggregate smaller items into a single larger asset component. While both IFRS and private entity GAAP speak to the need to recognize components, the discussion and application under IFRS are more fully developed.

Once an item of property, plant, and equipment meets the definition and recognition criteria, it is recognized at its cost. This raises two issues that need to be addressed:

1. What elements of cost are capitalized?

2. How is cost measured?

Cost Elements

Objective 2

Identify the costs to include in the measurement of property, plant, and equipment assets at acquisition.

Underlying Concept

This is an application of the cost principle that is part of the conceptual framework explained in Chapter 2.

In general, the cost of an item of property, plant, and equipment includes all expenditures needed to **acquire** the asset and bring it to its **location** and **ready it for use**. Once the item reaches this stage, no further costs are included in the asset's acquisition cost and capitalization stops.

More specifically, costs capitalized include the following:

(a) The item's purchase price net of trade discounts and rebates, plus any non-refundable purchase taxes (such as many provincial sales taxes) and duties.

(b) The expenditures necessary to bring the asset to its required location and condition to operate as management intended. These include employee costs needed to acquire or construct the asset; delivery and handling costs; site preparation, installation, and assembly costs; net material and labour costs incurred to ensure it is working properly; and professional fees.

(c) The estimate of the costs of obligations associated with the asset's eventual disposal. This includes, for example, some or all of the costs of the asset's decommissioning and site restoration.

Costs that are not capitalized as part of the PP&E asset include initial operating losses, the costs of training employees to use the asset, and costs associated with a reorganization of operations. Also excluded are administration and general overhead costs and the costs of opening a new facility, introducing a new product or service, and operating in a new location.

Although this general principle is the same under both IFRS and private entity GAAP, it is applied somewhat differently under each and this may result in different outcomes. Consider a situation where a company, after clearing land and while waiting for construction to begin, either incurs net costs or generates net income from using the property as a parking lot. Should these net costs or revenue be added to or deducted from the cost of the building, or should they be recognized immediately in net income?

IFRS	Private Entity GAAP
Capitalization of costs stops when the asset is in place and ready to be used as management intended, even if it has not begun to be used or is used at less than a desirable capacity level.	Capitalization of costs stops when an asset is substantially complete and ready for productive use as determined in advance by management in relation to factors such as reaching a given level of productive capacity, occupancy level, period of time, or other industry-specific consideration.
The principle of being a necessary cost to acquire and get in place and ready for use is strictly applied. The temporary use of land as a parking lot and its net cost or revenue is not necessary to develop the asset being constructed; therefore it cannot be included in the asset cost. The net cost or revenue is recognized in income when incurred or earned.	Any net revenue or costs generated prior to substantial completion and readiness for use are included in the asset's cost. Therefore, the net parking lot cost or revenue is debited or credited to the asset account.

Three specific cost issues are more fully discussed below:

- costs incurred when assets are constructed internally rather than purchased outright,

- associated borrowing costs, and

- site restoration or asset retirement costs.

Self-Constructed Assets

Often, companies construct their own assets. Even after deciding what components will be separately recognized, determining the cost of self-constructed assets such as machinery or buildings can be a challenge. Without a firm purchase or contract price, the company has to review numerous expenditures that were incurred to arrive at its cost.

The costs of materials and direct labour used in construction are not difficult to identify and measure; they can be traced directly to actual work orders and materials used in the constructed assets. However, allocating the indirect costs of manufacturing may create special problems. These indirect costs, called **overhead** or **burden**, include power, heat, light, insurance, property taxes on factory buildings and equipment, factory supervisory labour, depreciation of fixed assets, and supplies. Which of the following accounting choices is appropriate?

Underlying Concept

A company determines the cost of a self-constructed asset by applying the same general principles as for an acquired asset.

1. Assign a portion of all overhead to the construction project.

2. Assign no fixed overhead to the cost of the constructed asset.

Although the standards for manufactured inventories (see Chapter 8) require that a portion of all production overhead costs be applied to an inventory asset, the principle for PP&E assets is different. For these assets, only **directly attributable costs**—costs directly related to the specific activities involved in the construction process—are capitalized. Therefore, no fixed overhead is usually charged to the PP&E asset account.[1] Whether the entity also makes similar assets for resale or uniquely for its own purposes, care has to be taken to ensure that no abnormal amount of wasted inputs and related excess costs were experienced. If so, these are expensed in the period.

Borrowing Costs

Underlying Concept

The accounting treatment for borrowing costs under IFRS is consistent with the general asset recognition principle.

Significant Change

What Do the Numbers Mean?

Entities often acquire or construct capital assets that take substantial time to get ready for their intended use. To finance any interim expenditures that have to be made, a company may have to increase its bank loans, otherwise borrow money, or use existing company funds that could be used for other purposes. Do the financing or borrowing costs that are incurred for this purpose meet the criteria to be capitalized as part of the asset's cost, or should they be expensed in the period incurred?

Not surprisingly, IAS 23 *Borrowing Costs* considers any **avoidable** borrowing costs to be "expenditures directly attributable to bringing the asset to its required location and condition to operate as management intended." Such amounts are therefore added to the cost of the PP&E asset.

Appendix 10A explains how **borrowing costs** are defined, how to determine which are **avoidable**, and how to determine the **amount to capitalize**.

Until Canadian publicly accountable entities adopt IFRS in 2011, they have a choice of whether to capitalize interest for qualifying assets or report all interest as an expense in the income statement as incurred. Interest capitalization can have a substantial effect on the financial statements. When the earnings of **Jim Walter Corporation** dropped from $1.51 to $1.17 per share, the building manufacturer looked for ways to regain its profitability and was able to pick up an additional 11 cents per share by capitalizing the interest on coal mining projects and several plants under construction.

How can statement users determine the effect of interest capitalization on a company's bottom line? The amount of interest capitalized in the period has to be disclosed in the notes to the financial statements. For example, **ClubLink Corporation**, a major Canadian owner, operator, and developer of golf clubs across the country, once reported $2,391,000 of capitalized interest, an amount equal to 25% of the interest expense deducted on its income statement. The following year's numbers were lower: about 12%.

Private entity GAAP permits management to choose between a policy of capitalizing interest and expensing such costs. Regardless, the policy chosen and amount capitalized are required to be disclosed.

Dismantling and Restoration Costs

In some industries, when a company acquires and uses its long-lived assets, it takes on obligations that need to be met when the assets are eventually retired. For example, a nuclear facility must be decommissioned at the end of its useful life, mine sites must be

---

[1] If a company is involved in a significant amount of self-construction activity, some of its fixed costs may be considered "directly attributable."

closed and dismantled and the property restored, and landfill sites have significant closure and post-closure costs associated with the end of their operations.

In order to be able to use the long-lived asset companies often assume responsibility for the costs associated with dismantling the item, removing it, and restoring the site at the end of its useful life. These asset retirement costs meet the recognition criteria for capitalization and are added to the PP&E asset cost.

Once again, while this general principle underlies both IFRS and private entity GAAP, it is applied differently under each. The differences relate to the types of obligations and activities undertaken.

Significant Change

Law

	IFRS	**Private Entity GAAP**
Category of obligations	Recognizes costs of both legal and constructive obligations, such as when an entity creates an expectation in others through its own actions that it will meet this obligation.	Recognizes costs associated with legal obligations only.
Category of activities	Costs include only those related to the acquisition of the asset, not those related to the use of the asset in the production of goods or services (product costs).	Costs include both retirement obligations resulting from the acquisition of the asset and its subsequent use in producing inventory, such as the mining of coal.

Under both IFRS and private entity GAAP, the original cost estimates and any changes in them are capitalized in the asset account and a credit is made to an asset retirement or restoration liability. Because the actual expenditures will often not be incurred for a number of years, the obligation provision and the asset are both measured using the present value of the future costs. There is a fuller discussion of provisions and liability recognition and measurement issues in Chapters 2 and 13, but you should be aware that the cost of property, plant, and equipment will often include such a charge when the asset is acquired.

MEASUREMENT OF COST

Now that you have a general idea of what is included in "cost," the second step is to determine how it is measured. In general, **cost** is measured by the amount of cash or cash equivalents paid or the fair value of the other consideration given to acquire an asset when it is acquired.[2]

Cost, therefore, is the **cash cost** when the asset is recognized. This amount may not always be obvious. The paragraphs that follow discuss how several common issues are resolved when cash is not exchanged at the date of acquisition:

(a) Cash discounts not taken

(b) Deferred payment terms

(c) Lump-sum purchases

(d) Non-monetary exchanges—share-based payment

(e) Non-monetary exchanges—asset exchanges

(f) Contributed assets and government grants

3 Objective

Determine asset cost when the transaction has delayed payment terms or is a lump-sum purchase, a non-monetary exchange, or a contributed asset.

---

[2] Sometimes a standard will specify that another amount will be the asset's **deemed cost**. The deemed cost is the amount recognized under the specific requirements of a particular standard, such as IFRS 2 *Share-based Payments*, for example.

Cash Discounts

When cash discounts for prompt payment are offered on purchases of plant assets, how should the discount be handled? If the discount is taken, it is definitely a reduction in the asset's purchase price. It is not recognized as a Purchase Discount (see Chapter 8), because purchase discounts relate only to inventory purchases that are included in the cost of goods sold. What is not clear, however, is whether the asset's cost should be reduced even if the discount is not taken. There are two points of view on this matter.

Under one approach, the net-of-discount amount is considered the asset's cost, **regardless of whether the discount is taken or not**. The rationale for this view is that an asset's cost is its cash or cash equivalent price. The discount, if it is lost, is the cost of not paying at an earlier date and should be recognized according to its nature as a financing or interest expense. Supporters of the **other approach** argue that the discount should not always be deducted from the asset's cost, because the terms may be unfavourable or because it might not be prudent for the company to take the discount. Both methods are used in practice. Recognition of the asset at its lower "cash cost" is preferred, at least on conceptual grounds.

Deferred Payment Terms

Underlying Concept

This measure is consistent with the IAS 16 definition of cost which includes the fair value of other consideration given to acquire an asset at the time of its acquisition or construction.

Finance

Plant assets are often purchased on long-term credit arrangements through the use of notes, mortgages, bonds, or equipment obligations. The cost of an asset whose payment is deferred beyond normal credit terms is its **cash price equivalent.** Any difference between this fair value and the total payments made is recognized as **interest.** That is, the asset's cost is the **present value of the consideration** that is exchanged at the transaction date.

For example, equipment purchased today in exchange for a $10,000, non-interest-bearing note that is payable four years from now is not recorded at $10,000 because four years far exceeds normal credit terms. Assuming the cash price is not known, the **present value of the note is the transaction's exchange price** and the asset's "cash cost." If 12% is an appropriate interest rate, the equipment is recognized at a cost of $6,355.20 [$10,000 × 0.63552; see Table A-2 for the present value of a single sum, PV = $10,000 $(PVF_{4,12})$].

When no interest rate is stated, or if the specified rate is unreasonable, an appropriate interest rate is imputed. The objective is to approximate the interest rate that the buyer and seller would negotiate in a similar arm's-length borrowing transaction. Factors to consider in determining an appropriate interest rate are the borrower's credit rating, the note's amount and maturity date, and prevailing interest rates. If the acquired asset's cash exchange price can be determined, it is used as the basis for measuring the asset's cost and identifying the interest element.

To illustrate, assume that Sutter Corporation purchases a specially built robot spray painter for its production line. The company issues a $100,000, five-year, non-interest-bearing note to Wrigley Robotics Ltd. for the new equipment when the prevailing market interest rate for obligations of this nature is 10%. Sutter is to pay off the note in five $20,000 instalments made at the end of each year. Assume that the fair value of this specially built robot cannot readily be determined. Therefore, it has to be approximated by establishing the note's fair value (its present value). This calculation and the entries at the purchase and payment dates are as follows:

At date of purchase		
Equipment	75,816	
Notes Payable		75,816
Present value of note = $20,000 (PVF – OA$_{5,\,10\%}$)		
= $20,000 (3.79079) (Table A-4)		
= $75,816		

$A = L + SE$
$+75,816\ \ +75,816$

Cash flows: No effect

The $24,184 difference between the asset's cash cost of $75,816 and the $100,000 cash that is eventually payable (($20,000 × 5) is the discount or interest on the $75,816 amount borrowed.

At end of first year		
Interest Expense	7,582	
Notes Payable		7,582
Notes Payable	20,000	
Cash		20,000

$A = L + SE$
$+7,582\ \ -7,582$

Cash flows: No effect

$A = L + SE$
$-20,000\ \ -20,000$

Cash flows: ↓ 20,000 outflow

Interest expense under the effective interest method (as required by IFRS and allowed by private entity GAAP) is $7,582 [($75,816) × 10%]. The entries at the end of the second year to record interest and to pay off a portion of the note are as follows:

At end of second year		
Interest Expense	6,340	
Notes Payable		6,340
Notes Payable	20,000	
Cash		20,000

$A = L + SE$
$+6,340\ \ -6,340$

Cash flows: No effect

$A = L + SE$
$-20,000\ \ -20,000$

Cash flows: ↓ 20,000 outflow

Interest expense in the second year is calculated by applying the 10% interest rate to the net book value of the outstanding Notes Payable. At the end of the first year, the Notes Payable account was reduced to $63,398 ($75,816 + $7,582 − $20,000) and this was the note's carrying amount throughout the second year. The second year's interest expense is $63,398 × 10%, or $6,340.

If interest is not taken into account in such deferred payment contracts, the asset would be recorded at an amount that is higher than its fair value. In addition, no interest expense would be reported in any of the periods involved.

Lump-Sum Purchases

There is a special problem in determining the cost of specific capital assets when they are purchased together for a single lump-sum price. When this occurs, and it is not at all unusual, the practice is to allocate the total cost among the various assets based on their relative fair values. The assumption is that costs will vary in direct proportion to those values.

Underlying Concept

This is the same approach that is applied to a basket purchase of inventory.

To determine the individual fair value of the parts making up the total purchase, any of the following might be used: an appraisal for insurance purposes, the assessed valuation for property taxes, estimates of replacement costs, or simply an independent appraisal by an engineer or other appraiser. Which approach is most appropriate will depend on the specific situation. When a property is acquired consisting of a building and the land it sits on, the relative property tax value of each is often used. Estimates of replacement cost or independent appraisal might be used to determine the relative values of the components making up the building acquired.

To illustrate, assume that a company decides to purchase several assets of a smaller company in the same business for a total price of $80,000. The assets purchased are as follows:

	Seller's Book Value	Asset Fair Value
Inventory	$30,000	$ 25,000
Land	20,000	25,000
Building	35,000	50,000
	$85,000	$100,000

The allocation of the $80,000 purchase price based on the relative fair values is shown in Illustration 10-1. Note that the assets' carrying amounts on the seller's books are not representative of their fair values. **They are irrelevant.**

Illustration 10-1

Allocation of Purchase Price— Relative Fair Value Basis

		Asset Cost
Inventory	$\dfrac{\$25,000}{\$100,000} \times \$80,000 =$	$20,000
Land	$\dfrac{\$25,000}{\$100,000} \times \$80,000 =$	$20,000
Building	$\dfrac{\$50,000}{\$100,000} \times \$80,000 =$	$40,000
		$80,000

Depending on the situation and the company's accounting policies, the $40,000 cost allocated to the building may have to be further broken down and allocated to more specific components of the building, such as the basic structure, the roof, and the windows. If so, once the relative fair values of each is determined, the process of allocation is carried out using the same approach that is explained above.

Non-Monetary Exchanges

Share-Based Payments

When property, plant, and equipment assets are acquired and the company issues its own shares in payment, the cost of the asset is based either on the fair value of the shares given up or the fair value of the assets acquired. But which should be used?

IFRS 2 *Share-based Payment*[3] indicates that the fair value of the asset acquired should be used to measure its acquisition cost, and it presumes that this value can be determined except in rare cases. If the asset's fair value cannot be determined reliably, then its fair value and cost are determined by using the fair value of the shares given in exchange. If the company shares are widely traded, their fair value should be a good indication of the current cash-equivalent price of the PP&E asset acquired.[4] Private entity GAAP is more flexible, indicating only that the more reliable of the fair value of the goods received or the equity instruments given up is the asset cost. As private company shares are not widely traded, the asset value is more likely to be used.

To illustrate, assume that a hardware company decides to purchase land next to its current property in order to expand its carpeting and cabinet operation. Instead of paying cash for the land, it issues 5,000 no par value common shares to the seller. Assuming a recent appraisal valued the land at $62,000, the following entry is made:

Land	62,000	
Common Shares		62,000

A = L + SE
+62,000   +62,000

Cash flows: No effect

If no fair value can be reliably determined for the land, and assuming the company's shares have been widely traded with a fair market value of $12 per share, the land is assigned a cost equal to the fair value of the shares, or $5,000 \times \$12 = \$60,000$.

Asset Exchanges

When non-monetary assets such as property, plant, and equipment **are acquired for cash or other monetary assets**, the cost of the acquired asset is measured by the fair value (present value) of the cash or other monetary assets that are given up. Monetary assets are money or claims to future cash receipts that are fixed or determinable in amount and timing. Cash and accounts and notes receivable are the most common types of monetary assets. Non-monetary assets, on the other hand, are assets that are not claims to fixed or determinable cash flows. Examples include inventory, long-lived plant assets, and equity investments in other companies.

When non-monetary assets such as property, plant, and equipment **are disposed of and the company receives monetary assets in exchange**, a gain or loss on disposal is recognized in income. The gain is recognized in income because it is realized—i.e., it has been converted to cash or a claim to cash—and the entity's economic situation has clearly changed in terms of its future cash flows.

However, when an existing **non-monetary asset is exchanged for a new non-monetary asset such as an item of property, plant, and equipment**, the proper accounting is not necessarily obvious. There are two underlying issues:

---

[3] IFRS 2 *Share-based Payment* is considerably more complex than is indicated here. The recognition and measurement guidance depends on what is being acquired as well as whether the payment is in shares directly or in cash with the amount based on the price of the shares, or whether there is a choice of cash-based settlement or settlement in shares.

[4] The term "fair value" will be replaced by "market-based value" in this part of IFRS 2 if the provisions of the exposure draft *Fair Value Measurement* (ED/2009/5) are accepted. A market-based value is "the price that would be received or paid to sell an asset, transfer a liability, or exchange an equity instrument... ." It assumes an orderly transaction between market participants. A final standard is expected to be released in 2010.

1. What should be the cost of the non-monetary asset acquired?

2. Should a gain or loss on disposal be recognized on the non-monetary asset that was given up?

Some argue that the new asset's cost should be determined by its **fair value**, or by the fair value of the assets given up, and that a **gain or loss should be recognized** on the disposal of the old asset. Others believe that the cost of the new asset should be determined by the **carrying amount** of the assets given up, with **no gain or loss recognized**. Still others favour an approach that would **recognize losses** in all cases, but **defer gains** in special situations.

Underlying Concept

The FASB standard defines a non-monetary exchange as an exchange where no more than 25% of the consideration is monetary. There is no such threshold in the Canadian or international standard, where the transaction's economic substance has to be assessed.

General Principle—The Fair Value Standard.   International and Canadian standard setters have been in agreement for a number of years on the preferred answer to these choices. The general principle is that **non-monetary transactions are accounted for on the same basis as monetary transactions**: thus, the cost of the PP&E asset acquired—by giving up a non-monetary asset or a combination of monetary and non-monetary assets—is determined by the fair value of the assets given up unless the fair value of the asset received can be more reliably measured. Any gains or losses that result are recognized in income.

Why is the accounting like this? Although cash or a claim to cash is not received or is relatively minor in non-monetary exchanges, the earnings process related to the "old" asset is usually substantially complete. The specific values to the entity of the assets that are received generally are different from those of the assets that are given up. That is, the company's economic circumstances change as a result of the exchange.

The general standard that **non-monetary exchanges are measured at fair value** is applied, therefore, **unless one of the following conditions is true**:

1. The transaction lacks commercial substance.

2. Fair values are not reliably measurable.

In these situations, as explained below, the exchange is recorded **at the carrying amount of the asset(s) given up**, including any cash or other monetary assets.

Underlying Concept

Under PE GAAP, a third condition is stated, but it could be interpreted as an example of a transaction that lacks commercial substance.

1. Commercial Substance.   In following the general standard, the entity basically derecognizes (i.e., takes out of the accounts) the carrying value of the asset(s) given up, recognizes the fair value of the asset(s) received in exchange, and then reports the difference as a gain (or loss) in net income. Because the company's underlying economic situation has changed as a result of the transaction—in other words, the transaction has commercial or economic substance—income is permitted to be reported. However, if the company is in the same economic position after the exchange as it was before, there is little or no justification for reporting increased asset values or income.[5]

What does commercial substance really mean? Simply, it means that there is a **significant change** in the company's expected future cash flows and therefore its value. The exchange transaction has commercial substance if:

1. The amount, timing, or risk of future cash flows associated with the asset(s) received is different from the configuration of cash flows for the asset(s) given up; or

2. The specific value of the part of the entity affected by the transaction has changed as a result. For example, a company may benefit from significant cost savings from economies of scale made possible by acquiring and using the asset.

In either case, the change must be **significant relative to the fair values of the exchanged assets**. This often requires using professional judgement.

---

[5] For example, if a company exchanges inventory held for sale for other similar merchandise for sale in order to complete a sale to a customer, it would be difficult to justify the claim that the company's economic position has changed significantly. In fact, private enterprise standards list this situation as a third exception to the use of fair value in a non-monetary exchange.

2. *Ability to Measure Fair Values.* As might be expected, the exchange cannot be recorded at fair value if the fair value of neither the asset given up nor the asset received can be reliably measured. Also, this exception helps reduce the risk that entities can assign arbitrarily high values to assets exchanged as a way of engineering and reporting gains.

An overriding caution: When an asset is acquired, **it cannot be recognized at more than its fair value**. In an exchange when fair values cannot be used the cost of the new asset is based on the carrying amount of the asset(s) given up. If the carrying amount of the asset(s) given up in the exchange is more than the fair value of the asset(s) received, the new asset has to be recorded at its lower fair value amount and a loss is recognized.

Accounting for asset exchanges is summarized in Illustration 10-2. This is followed by examples to illustrate the appropriate entries.

Does the exchange meet both criteria: it has commercial substance, and fair values can be reliably determined?	
Yes	**No**
Apply the fair value standard:	Exception to the fair value standard:
Cost of asset(s) received = fair value of what is given up, or what is acquired, if more reliably measurable.	Cost of asset(s) received = carrying amount of asset(s) given up.
Difference between carrying amount and fair value of asset(s) given up is recognized in income as a gain or loss.	No gain is recognized. Loss is recognized if fair value of asset(s) acquired is less than the carrying amount of the asset(s) given up.

Illustration 10-2

Accounting for Asset Exchanges

When assets are exchanged or traded in, the transaction often requires a payment or receipt of cash or some other monetary asset. When the transaction's monetary component—or **boot**, as it is sometimes called—is significant, there is less need to question whether the transaction has commercial substance. As the percentage gets smaller, the transaction becomes primarily a non-monetary exchange and the need to evaluate whether or not the transaction has commercial substance increases.

Asset Exchange—Example 1. Assume that Information Processing, Inc. trades in its used machine for a new model. The machine given up has a book value of $8,000 (original cost of $12,000 less $4,000 accumulated depreciation) and a fair value of $6,000. It is traded for a new model that has a list price of $16,000. In negotiations with the seller, a trade-in allowance of $9,000 is finally agreed on for the used machine.

Note that the amount agreed on as a **trade-in allowance is not necessarily the used asset's fair value.** In many cases, such as with automobiles, the trade-in allowance is essentially used to change the new asset's selling price without reducing its list price.

The cash payment that is needed and the cost of the new machine are calculated in Illustration 10-3. Because the cash paid is significant relative to the fair value of the total consideration, the change in the configuration of the company's future cash flows justifies a conclusion that this transaction has commercial substance.

Fair value of assets given up	
Fair value of cash given up = list price less trade-in allowance	$16,000 − $9,000 = $ 7,000
Fair value of machine given up	6,000
Cost of new machine = fair value of assets given up	$13,000

Illustration 10-3

Calculation of Cost of New Machine

Ethics

The journal entry to record this transaction is:

Equipment (new)	13,000
Accumulated Depreciation (old)	4,000
Loss on Disposal of Equipment	2,000
Equipment (old)	12,000
Cash	7,000

A　=　L　+　SE
−2,000　　　　　−2,000

Cash flows: ↓ 7,000 outflow

The loss on the disposal of the used machine is verified in Illustration 10-4.

Illustration 10-4

Calculation of Loss on Disposal of Used Machine

Fair value of used machine	$6,000
Carrying amount of used machine	8,000
Loss on disposal of used machine	$2,000

Asset Exchange—Example 2.　Cathay Corporation exchanges several used trucks plus cash for vacant land that might be used for a future plant site. The trucks have a combined carrying amount of $42,000 (cost of $64,000 less $22,000 of accumulated depreciation). Cathay's purchasing agent, who has had previous dealings in the second-hand market, indicates that the trucks have a fair value of $49,000. In addition to the trucks, Cathay pays $4,000 cash for the land.

This exchange has commercial substance because the pattern and timing of cash flows from the investment in land are very different from those of the trucks. In addition, fair values can be determined. Assuming that the land's fair value is not known, or its fair value is not as reliable as that of the trucks, the cost of the land is calculated as indicated in Illustration 10-5.

Illustration 10-5

Calculation of Land's Acquisition Cost

Cost of land = fair value of assets given up:	
Fair value of trucks exchanged	$49,000
Fair value of cash given up	4,000
Acquisition cost of the land	$53,000

The journal entry to record the exchange is:

Land	53,000
Accumulated Depreciation	22,000
Trucks	64,000
Cash	4,000
Gain on Disposal of Trucks	7,000

A　=　L　+　SE
+7,000　　　　　+7,000

Cash flows: ↓ 4,000 outflow

The gain is the difference between the trucks' fair value of $49,000 and their carrying amount of $42,000. Now, if the trucks' fair value was $39,000 instead of $49,000, the land's cost would be $43,000 ($39,000 + $4,000) and a loss on the exchange of $3,000 ($42,000 − $39,000) would be reported.

Asset Exchange—Example 3.　Westco Limited owns a number of rental properties in Western Canada as well as a single property in Ontario. Management has decided to concentrate its business in the west and to dispose of its one property outside this area. Westco agrees to exchange its Ontario property for a similar commercial property outside Lethbridge owned by Eastco Limited, a company with many properties east of Manitoba. The two properties are almost identical in size, rentals, and operating costs. Eastco agrees to the exchange but requires a cash payment of $30,000 from Westco to equalize and complete the transaction. Illustration 10-6 sets out information about these two properties.

	Westco Ltd. Property	Eastco Ltd. Property
Carrying amounts:		
Building	$ 520,000	$540,000
Accumulated depreciation	100,000	145,000
	$ 420,000	$395,000
Fair value	$ 615,000	$645,000
Cash paid	$ 30,000	
Cash received		$ 30,000

Illustration 10-6

Property Exchange—Westco and Eastco

Assume an evaluation by both Westco and Eastco management indicates that there is an insignificant difference in the configuration of future cash flows and that commercial substance is not indicated. What entry would be made by each company to record this asset exchange? Remember that fair values do not apply in this situation and that the cost of the assets acquired by each company is recognized at the carrying amount of the assets given up by each. Because the companies are recognizing amounts equal to the book value of what is given up, no gain or loss is recorded by either.

Westco Ltd. entry		
Building (new)	450,000	
Accumulated Depreciation (old)	100,000	
Building (old)		520,000
Cash		30,000

A = L + SE
0 = 0 + 0
Cash flows: ↓ 30,000 outflow

Eastco Ltd. entry		
Building (new)	365,000	
Accumulated Depreciation (old)	145,000	
Cash	30,000	
Building (old)		540,000

A = L + SE
0 = 0 + 0
Cash flows: ↑ 30,000 inflow

Westco recognizes its new asset (the building) at the carrying amount of the assets given up. It gave up cash with a book value of $30,000 and a building with a book value of $420,000, for a total of $450,000. Eastco recognizes its new assets at the carrying amount of what it gave up, i.e., $395,000. Of this, $30,000 was cash received, leaving $365,000 to be recognized as the new building's cost. As both companies remain in the same economic position after the exchange as before, there is no reason to recognize any change in asset values and related gain or loss on the exchange.

Remember to check whether the fair value of the asset acquired is less than the cost assigned to it. Assets cannot be recognized at more than their fair value, so the asset would have to be recorded at the lower fair value amount and a loss equal to the difference recognized.

Contributed Assets and Government Grants

Companies sometimes receive contributions of assets as donations, gifts, or government grants. Such contributions are referred to as non-reciprocal transfers because they are transfers of assets in one direction only—nothing is given in exchange. The grants may be in the form of land, buildings, or equipment, or cash to acquire such assets, or even as the forgiveness of a debt. There are two important accounting issues for non-reciprocal transfers:

1. How should the asset be measured at acquisition?

2. What account should be credited?

When assets are acquired as a donation, a strict cost concept dictates that the asset's acquisition cost is zero. A departure from the cost principle is justified, however, because the only costs that are incurred (legal fees and other relatively minor expenditures) do not form a reasonable basis of accounting for the assets received. To record nothing is to ignore the economic reality of an increase in the entity's resources. Therefore, accounting standards generally require that **the asset's fair value be used to establish its "cost" on the books.**[6]

Having established the asset's acquisition cost, a further question remains about the credit entry in the transaction. Is it income, or is it contributed capital? Two general approaches have been used to record the credit in this type of transaction.

The capital approach considers donated assets as contributed capital financing and they are therefore accounted for with a credit directly to Contributed Surplus—Donated Capital. This approach is only appropriate, however, for a donation from an owner, and such donations are rare. The income approach reflects contributions in **net income** because the contribution is a non-owner source of the change in net assets.[7]

Accounting standards generally take the position that government assistance should be recognized in income, either as revenue or as a reduction of expense. If the contributed assets are expected to be used over several future periods, as in the case of a grant for a building or equipment, then the effect on income is spread out over the future periods that benefit from having received the grant. When assets or funds to acquire assets are received from federal, provincial, territorial, or municipal governments, GAAP requires that recipients defer and recognize the amount received over the periods that the related assets are used. This is accomplished in one of two ways:

(a) by reducing the asset cost and therefore future depreciation by the amount of government assistance received (the cost reduction method); or

(b) by recording the amount of assistance received as a deferred credit and amortizing it to revenue over the life of the related asset (the deferral method).

To illustrate the **cost reduction method**, assume that a company receives a grant of $225,000 from the federal government to upgrade its sewage treatment facility. The entry to record the receipt of the grant under this method is as follows:

A	=	L	+	SE			
0		0		0			

Cash flows: ↑ 225,000 inflow

Cash	225,000	
Equipment		225,000

---

[6] IAS 20 *Accounting for Government Grants and Disclosure of Government Assistance* indicates that while government grants in the form of non-monetary assets are usually measured at their fair value, an entity may record both the asset and the grant at a nominal amount.

[7] While a credit to Other Comprehensive Income (OCI) may seem like a valid option, accounting standards tend to be prescriptive about what can bypass net income and be recognized directly in OCI. This option is not provided in either IFRS or Canadian private entity standards for government grants.

This results in the equipment being carried on the books **at cost less the related government assistance**. Assuming a 10-year life and straight-line depreciation, the annual depreciation expense for the equipment is reduced by $22,500 and net income therefore is increased by this amount each year.

Alternatively, the **deferral method** credits a deferred revenue account with the grant amount. This amount is then recognized in income each year **on the same basis that is used to amortize the underlying asset**. The entries to record the receipt of the grant and its amortization for the first year under the **deferral method** are as follows:

Cash	225,000	
Deferred Revenue—Government Grants		225,000
Deferred Revenue—Government Grants	22,500	
Revenue—Government Grants		22,500

A = L + SE
+225,000 +225,000

Cash flows: ↑ 225,000 inflow

A = L + SE
−22,500 +22,500

Cash flows: No effect

A weakness of the cost reduction method is that it reports assets at less than their fair value to the entity. This issue is resolved if the deferral method is used, but this method also has a weakness. The deferral method is not consistent with the conceptual framework because the Deferred Revenue account does not usually meet the definition of a liability.

Note that a donation **of land** by a government may be deferred and taken into income over future periods because few government grants are provided without some conditions having to be met. If the requirement is to build and operate a manufacturing plant on the land over a specific period of time, then the grant is taken into income over the same period. Only when there is no way to associate the grant with future periods is it taken directly into income when received.

Government grants that are awarded to a company **for incurring certain current expenditures**, such as those related to payroll, are recognized in income in the same period as the related expenses. If grants or donations that have been received have a condition attached to them that requires a future event to occur—such as being required to maintain a specified number of employees on the payroll—the contingency is reported in the notes to the financial statements.

Entities are required to provide extensive disclosure about the amounts, terms and conditions, and accounting treatment they use for government assistance they have received. Readers can then evaluate the effect of such assistance on the entity's financial position and performance.

Specific Assets

Land

Land costs typically include (1) the purchase price; (2) closing costs, such as title to the land, legal fees, and recording fees; (3) costs incurred to condition the land for its intended use, such as grading, filling, draining, and clearing; (4) the costs of assuming any liens, such as taxes in arrears or mortgages or encumbrances on the property; and (5) any additional land improvements that have an indefinite life.

When land has been purchased to construct a building, all costs that are incurred up to the excavation for the new building are considered land costs. **Removal of old buildings, clearing, grading, and filling are considered land costs because these costs are necessary to get the land in condition and ready for its intended purpose.** Any proceeds that are obtained in the process of getting the land ready for its intended use—such as amounts received for salvaged materials from the demolition of an old building or the sale of timber that has been cleared—are treated as reductions in the land cost.

4 Objective

Identify the costs included in specific types of property, plant, and equipment.

Underlying Concept

The acquisition cost of each specific asset is determined by applying the recognition and cost principles explained earlier in the chapter.

Special amounts assessed for local improvements—such as pavements, street lights, and sewers and drainage systems—are usually charged to the Land account because they are relatively permanent and are maintained and replaced by the local government. In addition, it is also proper to charge permanent improvements that are made by the owner, such as landscaping, to the Land account. Improvements with limited lives—such as private driveways, walks, fences, and parking lots—are recorded separately as Land Improvements so they can be amortized over their estimated lives.

Generally, land is considered part of property, plant, and equipment. If the major purpose of acquiring and holding land is for capital appreciation or rentals or an undetermined future use, it is classified as investment property, a special category of PP&E discussed below. If the land is held by a real estate company for resale, or is held by land developers or subdividers, it is classified as inventory.

Buildings

One accounting issue relates to the cost of an old building that is on the site of a planned new building. Is the cost to remove the old building a cost of the land or of the new building? The standards indicate that, if land is purchased with an old building on it that will not be used, then the demolition cost less its salvage value is a cost of getting the land ready for its intended use. The costs relate to the land rather than to the new building.

On the other hand, if a company razes (tears down) an old building that it owns and previously used in order to construct a new building on the same land, the costs of demolition net of any cost recoveries are expensed as disposal costs of the old building, thus increasing any loss on disposal of the old asset. The remaining book value of the old building is included in depreciation expense in its final year of use.

Under private entity GAAP, an exception is made when a building is torn down to redevelop rental real estate. In this case, the remaining carrying amount of the building and the net costs of removing it can be capitalized as part of the redeveloped property, but only to the extent the costs can be recovered from the project in the future.

Leasehold Improvements

What is the proper accounting for capital expenditures that are made on property that is being leased or rented? Long-term leases ordinarily specify that any leasehold improvements revert to the lessor at the end of the lease. If the lessee constructs new buildings on leased land or reconstructs and improves existing buildings, the lessee has the right to use those facilities during the life of the lease, but they become the property of the lessor when the lease expires. The lessee charges the facilities' cost to a separate capital asset account, Leasehold Improvements, and the cost is amortized as an operating expense over the remaining life of the lease or the useful life of the improvements, whichever is shorter.

Equipment

The term "equipment" in accounting includes delivery equipment, office equipment, machinery, furniture and fixtures, furnishings, factory equipment, and similar tangible capital assets. The cost of such assets includes the purchase price, freight and handling charges that are incurred, insurance on the equipment while it is in transit, the cost of special foundations if they are required, assembling and installation costs, and costs of making any adjustments to the equipment to make it operate as intended. The Goods and Services Tax (GST), Harmonized Sales Tax (HST), or Quebec Sales Tax (QST) that is paid on the acquired assets is a recoverable tax eligible for an Input Tax Credit. It is not included in the assets' acquisition cost.

Investment Property

Investment property, or rental real estate, is a separate category of PP&E that may be accounted for after acquisition in a special way by entities applying international standards. It is defined as property held to generate rentals and/or appreciate in value rather than to sell in the ordinary course of business or to use in production, administration, or supplying goods and services.[8] It includes property that is currently under construction for investment purposes as well.

Investment property, covered in international standards by IAS 40, is different from owner-occupied property, to which IAS 16 *Property, Plant, and Equipment* applies. Complexities arise when one property is used partly as an investment property and is partly owner-occupied. In general, if the two parts could be sold separately (or leased as a finance lease separately) then the two parts should be accounted for separately. Another area of difficulty arises when an owner provides a variety of services in connection with an investment property. If providing the services exposes the owner to the normal risks of running a business (as distinct from investment risk), the classification as an investment property may not be appropriate. Consider a situation where a company rents out office space to tenants and provides furnished units and secretarial support in addition to the space. Judgement is often needed to determine whether the services provided are such a significant component of the arrangement that the property is actually "owner-occupied" space and not investment property.

The cost of investment property under IFRS and private entity GAAP is determined following the same principles as used for PP&E. Also, if the property continues to be accounted for at cost, the components of the property are accounted for separately for purposes of depreciation.

Natural Resource Properties

Mineral resources, sometimes called wasting assets, generally refer to minerals and oil and gas resources that do not regenerate. Mineral resource properties are capitalized costs associated with the acquired rights, and the exploration, evaluation, and development of these minerals. Unlike buildings and machinery, natural resource properties are consumed physically over the period of use and do not retain their original physical characteristics. Regardless, many of the accounting problems associated with these assets are similar to those for other capital assets.

How is the acquisition cost of a mineral resource property determined? For example, a company like Petro-Canada needs to spend large amounts to find oil and gas reserves, and projects often end in failure. Furthermore, there are long delays between the time it incurs costs and the time it obtains benefits from any extracted resources. The acquisition cost of natural resource property normally includes some costs from each of four stages: (1) acquisition of the deposit, (2) exploration for and evaluation of reserves, (3) development, and (4) decommissioning and site restoration. In general, the capitalized costs of acquisition, exploration, development, and restoration make up the depletion base of the natural resource. As its name implies, the depletion base is the amount that later will be amortized (through a depletion charge) and form a significant portion of the cost of the mined or extracted inventory. Through depletion, the costs of the long-term mineral resource capital asset become part of the cost of the inventory that is produced—very similar to the direct materials cost of a manufactured product.

---

[8] Investment property includes land or buildings or part of a building or both under IAS 40, and could be property held under a finance lease or directly owned.

Accounting for natural resources is a specialized area, especially as Canadian companies move to IFRS. Because of the complex nature of this industry, additional coverage is beyond the scope of an intermediate text. It should be noted, however, that many of the issues that need to be resolved are familiar ones: they involve bringing accounting practice into greater consistency with general standards for asset recognition and measurement, cost allocation, and impairment testing. Not surprisingly, these issues are complicated by the uncertainties associated with estimating the volume and fair values of reserves and resources.

Biological Assets

Under private entity GAAP, the general principles established for PP&E assets are also followed for biological assets. Under IFRS, however, separate standards are set out in IAS 41 *Agriculture* for assets related to agricultural activity. Examples of such assets that are long-lived, tangible and used in production include fruit trees, grapevines, and livestock held to produce wool, milk, or additional livestock assets. These and other biological assets are measured initially, and at every balance sheet date, at **fair value less costs to sell**, with changes in value recognized in the income statement as the values change. The accounting is similar to the fair value model explained later in this chapter. In the rare situation that no reliable fair value measure can be determined, then the asset is measured at cost less accumulated depreciation and impairment losses.

MEASUREMENT AFTER ACQUISITION

Significant Change

After recognizing the cost of property, plant, or equipment assets at acquisition, companies may have a choice of how to account for them after this point. Three different models have been identified and are currently used: a **cost model** (CM), a **revaluation model** (RM), and a **fair value model** (FVM). However, the GAAP choice of model depends on the type of asset and whether international or private entity standards are being applied. This is summarized in Illustration 10-7.

Illustration 10-7

Accounting Model Choices

	Private Entity GAAP			IFRS		
	CM	RM	FVM	CM	RM	FVM
Investment property	✔			✔		✔
Other property, plant, and equipment assets	✔			✔	✔	

For example, under IFRS a company must choose whether to measure all of its **investment property** under the cost model or all under the fair value model, with few exceptions. All **other items defined as PP&E** are separated into classes and a decision is made whether to apply the cost model or the revaluation model to each class. The same method must be used for **all assets in each class**. Common classes of assets include:

Underlying Concept

Historical costs are **verifiable** and therefore considered more reliable. On the other hand, they often do not **faithfully represent** the value of the asset to the business and therefore are considered a less reliable measure. This is an example of a qualitative characteristic trade-off.

– land   – motor vehicles   – aircraft
– land and buildings – machinery   – furniture and fixtures
– office equipment   – ships

Not surprisingly, the revaluation model can only be applied to assets whose fair value can be reliably measured. This method is used by relatively few companies, but is included as an IFRS alternative and is used by companies that operate in countries with relatively high rates of inflation, making the revaluation measure more relevant than historical cost. This leaves the cost model as the most commonly used method under IFRS and the only one acceptable under private entity GAAP. Let us now review how each of these models works.

Cost Model

The cost model (CM) is by far the most widely used model to account for PP&E, and you are probably familiar with the basics of how it works. This model measures property, plant, and equipment assets after acquisition **at their cost less accumulated depreciation and any accumulated impairment losses**. Details about depreciation and impairment are explained in Chapter 11.

5 Objective
Understand and apply the cost model.

Revaluation Model

The choice of a revaluation model (RM) is new to most Canadian companies. Under this approach, property, plant, and equipment assets **whose fair value can be measured reliably** are carried after acquisition **at their fair value at the date of the revaluation less any subsequent accumulated depreciation and any subsequent impairment losses**. The discussion of depreciation and impairment under this model is also deferred to Chapter 11.

    A revaluation is not required at each reporting date, but must be carried out often enough that the carrying amount reported is not materially different from the assets' fair value. Some assets need to be remeasured only every three years or so, but for assets whose values change rapidly, an annual revaluation may be needed. Between revaluation dates, **depreciation is taken** on the revalued amount.

    What is fair value, and how do companies determine this value for their PP&E assets? Fair value is "the price that would be received to sell an asset or paid to transfer a liability in an orderly transaction between market participants at the measurement date."[9] Professional valuators use active market or market-related evidence to the extent possible, but may have to revert to other methods if equipment, for example, is very specialized.[10]

    Before walking through an example of how the RM works, one issue needs to be resolved. If you regularly revalue or change the asset's carrying amount, what do you do with the increases and decreases in the carrying amount? The changes are accounted for as follows.

6 Objective
Understand and apply the revaluation model.

Underlying Concept

IAS 29 sets out how companies reporting in the currency of a hyper-inflationary economy should restate their financial statements.

Expanded Discussion

If the asset's carrying amount is **increased (debited)**	If the asset's carrying amount is **decreased (credited)**
The amount is recorded as a credit to Revaluation Surplus, an equity account, unless the increase reverses a revaluation decrease previously recognized in income. If so, recognize the increase in income to the extent of the prior decrease.	The amount is recorded as a debit to Revaluation Surplus, an equity account, to the extent of any credit balance associated with that asset. This account cannot have a debit (i.e., a negative) balance. Any remaining amount is recognized in income.

The amounts debited or credited to the Revaluation Surplus account are reported in the statement of comprehensive income as other comprehensive income (OCI) items. Over the life of the asset, the effect of the treatment described is that there is no **net increase** in net income from revaluing the asset.

    When revaluing an asset, two methods of accounting for the balance in the accumulated depreciation account are permitted. (a) The account may be adjusted proportionately, or (b) its balance is eliminated. The proportionate approach adjusts both the carrying amount of the asset and the accumulated depreciation, so that the net balance is

---

[9] IASCF, IASB *Fair Value Measurement* Exposure Draft (ED/2009/5), Appendix A, p. 32, 2009.

[10] Chapter 2 includes a discussion of the meaning of fair value and ways in which fair values are determined.

the fair value of the asset at the revaluation date.[11] The second method eliminates the balance in the accumulated depreciation account, writing it off against the asset itself. The asset is then adjusted to its new revalued amount. The second, and simpler, method is illustrated in the example that follows.

Revaluation Model Example

Convo Corp. (CC) purchases a building in early January 2010 and the cost of the basic structure of $100,000 is classified in an account called Building. CC accounts for this class of asset using the revaluation model, revalues the class every three years, and uses straight-line depreciation. The building structure is expected to have a useful life of 25 years with no residual value. CC has a December 31 fiscal year end. The asset's fair value at December 31, 2012, is $90,000 and at December 31, 2015, it is $75,000.

Illustration 10-8 walks us through the depreciation for the first three years and the revaluation entries needed at December 31, 2012, assuming the balance in the Accumulated Depreciation account is eliminated.

Illustration 10-8

Convo Corp. 2010 to 2012 and December 31, 2012, Adjustment

Annual depreciation in each of 2010, 2011, and 2012:

$$\frac{\$100,000 - \$0}{25 \text{ years}} = \$4,000$$

December 31, 2012

	Before Revaluation	Adjustments	After Revaluation
Building	$100,000	$(12,000)	$90,000
		2,000	
Accumulated depreciation $4,000 × 3	(12,000)	12,000	–0–
Carrying amount	$ 88,000	$ 2,000	$90,000

A   =   L   +   SE
0   0   0

Cash flows: No effect

Entries, December 31, 2012:

Accumulated Depreciation	12,000	
Building		12,000
To eliminate the accumulated depreciation.		

A   =   L   +   SE
+2,000   +2,000

Cash flows: No effect

Building (90,000 – 88,000)	2,000	
Revaluation Surplus (OCI)		2,000
To adjust the Building account to fair value.		

Balance sheet presentation, December 31, 2012:

Long-term assets:
Building	$90,000
Less accumulated depreciation	–0–
	$90,000

---

[11] This method is easy to apply when fair values are based on an index of specific prices, such as a construction price index. It also has the benefit of providing additional information to users about the relative age of the assets because the accumulated depreciation continues.

A new depreciation rate needs to be calculated because there has been a change in the asset's carrying amount. This calculation and the revaluation adjustment amounts on December 31, 2015, are provided in Illustration 10-9.

Illustration 10-9

Convo Corp. 2013 to 2015 and December 31, 2015, Adjustment

Annual depreciation in each of 2013, 2014, and 2015:

$$\frac{\$90,000 - \$0}{22 \text{ years}} = \$4,091$$

December 31, 2015

	Before Revaluation	Adjustments	After Revaluation
Building	$90,000	$(12,273)	$75,000
		(2,727)	
Accumulated depreciation			
$4,091 × 3	(12,273)	12,273	–0–
Carrying amount	$77,727	$ (2,727)	$75,000

Entries, December 31, 2015:

Accumulated Depreciation	12,273	
Building		12,273
To eliminate the accumulated depreciation.		

A = L + SE
0   0   0

Cash flows: No effect

Revaluation Surplus (OCI)	2,000	
Revaluation Loss (to income)	727	
Building		2,727
To adjust the Building account to fair value.		

A = L + SE
−2,727   −2,727

Cash flows: No effect

Balance sheet presentation, December 31, 2015:

Long-term assets:	
Building	$75,000
Less accumulated depreciation	–0–
	$75,000

Notice that the Revaluation Surplus account can only be reduced to zero. The remaining loss in value is recognized as a loss in the income statement. Once again, the depreciation rate going forward has to be recalculated. The $75,000 carrying amount is now allocated over the remaining 19 years of useful life, so the new rate is $75,000/19 = $3,947 each year.

Revaluation Surplus Account

What happens to the revaluation surplus account? A company has two choices. One option is to transfer amounts from the account directly into Retained Earnings every period. The amount transferred is the difference between the depreciation expense based on the revalued carrying amount and the expense based on the original cost. Alternatively, the balance in the Revaluation Surplus could remain there until the asset is retired or disposed of. At that point, the balance is transferred directly to Retained Earnings, again, without going through the income statement.

Notice that the amounts in the Revaluation Surplus account are not "recycled" through net income as the asset is depreciated, impaired, or disposed of. The revaluation model, therefore, is closer to a current cost measurement approach where holding gains and losses are equity adjustments, than to a true fair value model.

Illustration 10-10 provides the accounting entries assuming that Convo Corp. sells the building in the example above on **January 2, 2013**, for $93,000.

Illustration 10-10

Revaluation Surplus Adjustment on Disposal of Asset

A   =   L   +   SE
+3,000   +3,000

Cash flows: ↑ 93,000 inflow

A   =   L   +   SE
0   0   0

Cash flows: No effect

Cash	93,000	
Building		90,000
Gain on Sale		3,000
To record the proceeds on sale of the building.		

Revaluation Surplus (OCI)	2,000	
Retained Earnings		2,000
To transfer the Revaluation Surplus in OCI related to the building sold to Retained Earnings.		

Fair Value Model

Objective 7
Understand and apply the fair value model.

As indicated above, investment property is the only tangible capital asset that may be accounted for under the fair value model (FVM). Under this approach, the investment property is recognized on the statement of financial position after acquisition at its fair value. Changes in its value are reported in net income in the period of the change, and no depreciation is recognized over the life of the asset. Once this method is chosen instead of the cost model, the property continues to be measured at fair value until it is disposed of, becomes owner-occupied, or is developed for sale in the ordinary course of business. The example that follows illustrates how the FV model is applied. Note that although biological assets are measured at **fair value less costs to sell** instead of **fair value**, the example provided for investment property below applies also to accounting for the changes in value of biological assets.

Fair Value Model Example

Erican Corp. (EC) acquired a small 10-store shopping mall in eastern Canada for $1 million on February 2, 2011. The mall qualifies as investment property under IAS 40 *Investment Property*. At this time, nine of the stores were leased with remaining lease terms of two to four years. In addition to the purchase price, EC had to pay a $40,000 property transfer fee and legal fees of $3,000, and the company decided to paint the empty store at a cost of $2,000 before advertising it for rent. The acquisition was financed by assuming a $730,000 mortgage from the previous owner, who also turned over $37,000 of tenant damage deposits. The remainder of the transaction was settled in cash. On December 31, 2011, the fair value of the shopping centre property was determined to be $1,040,000; on December 31, 2012, it was $1,028,000, and on December 31, 2013, it had risen to $1,100,000. EC has a December 31 year end and applies the fair value method to all its investment property.

The summary entry to record the acquisition of the property is as follows.

February 2, 2011		
Investment Property—Shopping Mall	1,043,000	
Maintenance Expense	2,000	
Mortgage Payable		730,000
Tenant Deposits Liability		37,000
Cash		278,000

A = L + SE
+765,000 +765,000 −2,000

Cash flows: ↓ 278,000 outflow

The acquisition cost includes the transfer and legal fees, while the incidental painting is a period expense. The mortgage and the tenant deposits are both liabilities and they reduce the amount of cash EC has to pay on the date of acquisition. Because the building is not being amortized, the land and the building may be reported together as illustrated in the entry. On each December 31 balance sheet date, the investment property is remeasured to its new fair value with the following entries being made. Note that transaction costs are not included in the asset's fair value.

December 31, 2011		
Loss in Value of Investment Property	3,000	
Investment Property—Shopping Mall		3,000
($1,043,000 − $1,040,000)		
December 31, 2012		
Loss in Value of Investment Property	12,000	
Investment Property—Shopping Mall		12,000
($1,040,000 − $1,028,000)		
December 31, 2012		
Investment Property—Shopping Mall	72,000	
Gain in Value of Investment Property		72,000
($1,100,000 − $1,028,000)		

A = L + SE
−3,000   −3,000

−12,000   −12,000

+72,000   +72,000

Cash flows: No effect

The gains and losses are recognized directly in income. They are not reported in other comprehensive income.

It is important to recognize that the fair value of investment property must be **disclosed in the financial statements, even if the cost model is used**. Therefore all companies with such properties need to develop appropriate methods to measure fair value.

Costs Incurred after Acquisition

After plant assets are installed and ready for use, additional costs are incurred for anything from ordinary servicing and repairs to periodic overhauls, significant additions, or replacement of components. The major problem is allocating these costs to the proper time periods. Is the cost expensed in the current period, or capitalized and recognized over the future periods benefiting?

Accounting standards take the position that the recognition criteria for these costs should be the same when an asset is acquired and subsequently. If future economic benefits are expected to result from an expenditure, then the cost is capitalized, assuming it can

8 Objective
Explain and apply the accounting treatment for costs incurred after acquisition.

Underlying Concept

Applying the same principle both at acquisition and at a point after acquisition makes for more consistent accounting for similar events.

Underlying Concept

Expensing long-lived staplers, pencil sharpeners, and wastebaskets is an application of the materiality constraint.

What Do the Numbers Mean?

be measured reliably. For a cost after acquisition to be included as part of an asset's cost, the assumption is that there has been **an increase** in the future economic benefits, **not merely a restoration** of the asset to normal operating efficiency.

Day-to-day servicing costs and other maintenance-type expenditures do not meet the asset recognition criteria and are expensed in the period incurred. These costs tend to keep an asset in its proper working condition; they do not add significantly to the asset's future cash-generating ability.

It is not uncommon, however, for companies to expense costs below an arbitrary minimum amount even if they meet the capitalization criteria. For example, an entity may adopt a rule that expenditures below, say, $500 or $5,000 or even higher (depending on the size of the company) are always expensed. Although this treatment may not be correct conceptually, a cost-benefit assessment and materiality justify it.

The distinction between a capital expenditure (an asset) and a revenue expenditure (an expense) is not always clear-cut, and **this accounting choice can have a significant effect on reported income**. If costs are capitalized as assets on the balance sheet, the income statement is freed from charges that would otherwise reduce the bottom line and earnings per share in that period.

The "managing" of earnings has been behind many of the well-publicized accounting scandals of recent years. WorldCom executives accounted for billions of dollars of current operating costs as capital additions. Adelphia Communications Corp. aggressively deferred operating items as assets on its balance sheet. Closer to home, **Livent** carried out similar actions in Canada. There is also the case of Toronto-based Atlas Cold Storage Income Trust, the second-largest cold storage firm in North America, which announced that expenditures of approximately $3.6 million were inappropriately recorded as additions to capital assets during the previous year. Atlas also adjusted the financial statements of another prior year for an additional $1.6 million of expenditures that had been recognized as assets. While these examples look like situations where management set out intentionally to exaggerate profits and mislead investors, decisions are made on a daily basis where the distinction between whether an expenditure should be capitalized or expensed is not always clear-cut.

Generally, companies incur four major types of expenditures related to existing assets.

MAJOR TYPES OF EXPENDITURES

Additions   Increase or extension of existing assets.

Replacements, major overhauls, and inspections   Substitution of a new part or component for an existing asset, and performing significant overhauls or inspections of assets whether or not physical parts are replaced.

Rearrangement and reinstallation   Movement of assets from one location to another.

Repairs   Servicing expenditures that maintain assets in good operating condition.

Additions

Additions present no major accounting problems. By definition, any **addition to plant assets is capitalized** because a new asset has been acquired. Adding a wing to a hospital or an air conditioning system to an office, for example, increases the service potential of that facility. These costs are capitalized and then recognized as expenses in the future periods that benefit from the asset's use.

One problem that does arise in this area is the accounting for any changes related to an existing structure as a result of the addition. Is the cost incurred to tear down an old wall to make room for an addition a cost of the addition or a disposal cost of the portion of the existing asset that is being eliminated? In theory, it is a disposal cost of a part of the existing asset. From a practical standpoint, however, if the wall is a minor portion of the cost of the original asset, most companies would keep the carrying amount of the old wall in the accounts and include the cost to tear down the wall in the cost of the addition.

Replacements, Major Overhauls, and Inspections

Replacements are substitutions of one asset or asset component for another, often resulting from a general policy to modernize or rehabilitate a building, piece of equipment, or interior of an aircraft, for example. Costs of major overhauls, reconditioning, or inspections are similar to replacements in that they recur and are often needed in order to permit continued use of an asset.

Costs such as those for the replacement of significant parts, or the periodic inspection, overhaul, or reconditioning of major assets, often meet the capitalization criteria. If so, they are, in effect, asset acquisitions. As such, the costs are capitalized and added to the asset's carrying amount. Because it is a replacement of something already incorporated in the asset's cost or of an item recognized as a separate component, the depreciated carrying amount of the original part or inspection is removed. If the original cost of the replaced part or previous overhaul is not known, it has to be estimated. The current cost of the part or overhaul can be used to help estimate the original cost of what is being replaced. Once the original cost is determined, it and the associated accumulated depreciation are both removed from the accounts.

Let's work through the examples described in Illustrations 10-11 and 10-12.

Significant Change

Illustration 10-11

Asset Replacement

> **Situation 1—Asset Replacement**   Ace Manufacturing Ltd. (AML) incurred $27,000 in costs for roofing work on its factory: $26,000 to replace the previous roof installed when the building was first built, and $1,000 to repair and replace a few shingles on the garage extension as a result of a recent storm. The factory building was constructed 15 years ago.
>
> **Assumption (a):** The original roof was identified as a separate component of the building (Building—Roof) when it was constructed. It cost $16,000 and has been depreciated on a straight-line basis over a 20-year life.
>
> **Assumption (b):** The original roof was not recognized as a separate component of the building and its original cost is not known. The building has been depreciated on a straight-line basis assuming a 40-year useful life. Construction costs in the area have doubled since the factory was completed 15 years ago.

In **Situation 1(a),** $26,000 of the roofing costs meets the capitalization criteria and $1,000 does not. The first entry below accounts for the $27,000 expenditure, and the second one removes the original roof's carrying amount and recognizes the associated loss.

Repair Expense	1,000	
Building—Roof (new)	26,000	
Cash		27,000

A   = L +   SE
−1,000   −1,000

Cash flows: ↓ 27,000 outflow

Accumulated Depreciation (old)	12,000	
Loss on Disposal of Roof	4,000	
Building—Roof (old)		16,000
($16,000/20 years × 15 years = $12,000)		

A   = L +   SE
−4,000   −4,000

Cash flows: No effect

Under **Situation 1(b)**, the exact cost and accumulated depreciation are not known, but can be estimated. If construction costs have doubled in the area since the building was acquired, a reasonable estimate of the roof's original cost might be 50% of $26,000, or $13,000. The first entry below records the $27,000 expenditure assuming the roof is not accounted for after replacement as a separate component. This is a reasonable decision if AML estimates that the new roof will not have to be replaced before the building's useful life is over. If the new roof has a useful life of only 15 years, however, then it should be recognized as a separate asset. The numbers in the second entry below are different than in 1(a) because the old roof was being depreciated over a 40-year life as part of the building.

A	=	L	+	SE			
−1,000				−1,000			

Cash flows: ↓ 27,000 outflow

Repair Expense	1,000	
Building	26,000	
Cash		27,000

A	=	L	+	SE			
−8,125				−8,125			

Cash flows: No effect

Accumulated Depreciation	4,875	
Loss on Disposal of Roof	8,125	
Building		13,000
($13,000/40 years × 15 years = $4,875)		

Illustration 10-12

Overhaul Costs

Situation 2—Overhaul   Beta Corp. (BC) maintains a fleet of specialized trucks. BC has an operating policy of taking its trucks out of service and giving them a significant overhaul after every 50,000 km of use. The overhaul is a requirement for maintaining the company's insurance coverage. When Truck #B14, acquired two years previously for $63,000, completed its first 50,000 km of service, it was taken off the road and given its first major overhaul. The overhaul cost BC $9,000. When Truck #B14's odometer reading was 92,100 km, the truck was experiencing difficulties and BC management decided to take it in for an early overhaul. This time, the servicing costs totalled $11,000. The useful life of a truck is assumed to be 300,000 km.

Assumption (a): When the truck was acquired, the cost of the benefits to be restored by the overhaul after 50,000 km was estimated to be $8,000, based on current overhaul costs. Therefore the truck was recognized at its cost of $63,000 − $8,000 = $55,000, and the overhaul service component was recognized separately at a cost of $8,000.

Assumption (b): No separate asset components were recognized initially for the truck, but one will be recognized separately when the first full overhaul is carried out.

In **Situation 2(a)**, the same approach is used for the overhaul as for the replacement of the roof in Situation 1(a). The first entry below records the $9,000 overhaul expenditure, and the second one removes the original overhaul component's cost and accumulated depreciation from the accounts. The third entry recognizes the asset cost of the overhaul at 92,100 km, and the fourth entry removes the cost of the first overhaul and its accumulated depreciation to the date of the second one. The first actual overhaul costs of $9,000 were being depreciated at a rate of $9,000 ÷ 50,000 = $0.18 per km. When the truck reached 92,100 km, it had travelled an additional 92,100 − 50,000 = 42,100 km.

A	=	L	+	SE
0				0

Cash flows: ↓ 9,000 outflow

A	=	L	+	SE
0				0

Cash flows: No effect

First overhaul		
Truck Overhaul #B14 (1)	9,000	
Cash		9,000
Accumulated Depreciation (old)	8,000	
Truck Overhaul #B14 (old)		8,000
($8,000/50,000 km × 50,000 km = 8,000)		

Second overhaul		
Truck Overhaul #B14 (2)	11,000	
Cash		11,000
Accumulated Depreciation (1)	7,578	
Loss on Overhaul	1,422	
Truck Overhaul #B14 (1)		9,000
(42,100 km × $0.18/km = 7,578)		

A = L + SE
0   0
Cash flows: ↓ 11,000 outflow

A   = L +   SE
−1,422   −1,422
Cash flows: No effect

Under **Situation 2(b)**, because no "overhaul" component was recognized separately when the truck was acquired, a representative cost and carrying amount have to be determined for it at the time of the 50,000 km servicing. If truck service bay costs have increased 10% over the two-year period since the truck was acquired, this might imply an original cost of $9,000/1.10, or $8,182. The first entry below records the overhaul cost as a separate asset component and the second entry removes the appropriate amount from the truck's book value. Remember that the cost of the truck, and therefore any unrecognized overhaul component, was being depreciated over the full useful life of the truck in this situation.

First overhaul		
Truck Overhaul #B14 (1)	9,000	
Cash		9,000
Accumulated Depreciation	1,364	
Loss on Overhaul	6,818	
Truck #B14 (1)		8,182
($8,182/300,000 km × 50,000 km = 1,364)		

A = L + SE
0   0
Cash flows: ↓ 9,000 outflow

A   = L +   SE
−6,818   −6,818
Cash flows: No effect

Now recognized separately, the Truck Overhaul asset is depreciated over the next 50,000 km at a rate of $9,000/50,000 km, or $0.18 per km. When Truck #B14's odometer reads 92,100 km and it is taken out of service again, the depreciation accumulated on the overhaul service asset is $0.18 × 42,100 km, or $7,578. The two entries required for the second overhaul are exactly the same as under Situation 2(a) above. The first entry below recognizes the cost of the second overhaul and the second entry removes the old overhaul's carrying amount and recognizes a loss.

Second overhaul		
Truck Overhaul #B14 (2)	11,000	
Cash		11,000
Accumulated Depreciation (1)	7,578	
Loss on Overhaul	1,422	
Truck Overhaul #B14 (1)		9,000
(42,100 km × $0.18/km = 7,578)		

A = L + SE
0   0
Cash flows: ↓ 11,000 outflow

A   = L +   SE
−1,422   −1,422
Cash flows: No effect

When an entity uses the revaluation model or the fair value model, the basic principle for replacements and overhauls continues to apply. If the **revaluation model** is used, the cost of the "new" asset component, part, or overhaul is added to the asset's carrying amount, and the carrying amount of the replaced asset component or part is removed, with a gain or loss recognized on disposal. When the **fair value model** is applied to investment property, the property's fair value may already reflect the reduced value of the part to be replaced. This fact may not be known or it may be difficult to reasonably determine the carrying amount of the part being replaced. A practical solution, therefore, is to add the cost of the replacement part or overhaul to the asset and then reassess and adjust the asset to its fair value after the replacement.

Accounting for replacements, and major overhauls or inspections as illustrated in Situations 1 and 2 above, is required by international financial reporting standards, with the entries being a direct application of general PP&E principles. Canadian practice in the past, and private entity GAAP going forward, have not required such a strict application of general principles, although this may change over time as we enter an IFRS world.

For now, private entity GAAP removes the net book value of a part and capitalizes the replacement only if the cost and accumulated depreciation of the old part are known. When the carrying amount cannot be determined, and when major overhauls or renovations are carried out, practice differs depending on the circumstances. If the asset's useful life is extended, the Accumulated Depreciation account is often debited, on the basis that the renewal is "recovering" part of the past depreciation. If the quantity or quality of the asset's service potential or productivity is increased, the cost of the improvement is usually capitalized as part of the asset's cost.

Rearrangement and Reinstallation

Rearrangement and reinstallation costs that are intended to benefit future periods are different from additions, replacements, and major overhauls. An example is the rearrangement and reinstallation of a group of machines to facilitate future production. If the original installation cost and the accumulated depreciation taken to date on it can be determined, the rearrangement and reinstallation cost could be handled as a replacement. These amounts, however, are rarely known and may be difficult to estimate. In this case, because the asset's cost at acquisition already includes installation costs, any additional costs incurred to rearrange or reinstall it are recognized as an expense of the current period.

If the amounts are material, private entity GAAP may capitalize such costs on the basis that the original cost of installation is not known, and is likely to have been depreciated to a significant extent.

Repairs

Ordinary repairs are expenditures that are made to maintain plant assets in good operating condition; they are charged to an expense account in the period in which they are incurred, based on the argument that there is no increase in a PP&E asset. Replacing minor parts, the ongoing lubricating and adjusting of equipment, repainting, and cleaning are examples of maintenance charges that occur regularly and are treated as ordinary operating expenses.[12]

BP p.l.c., an international integrated oil and gas giant, reported net property, plant, and equipment of U.S. $103,200 million on its December 31, 2008, statement of financial position. Illustration 10-13 includes excerpts from Note 1 to BP's financial statements that explain the acquisition costs of these assets. BP engages in oil and gas exploration and production activities, operates refineries and service stations, and provides a variety of petrochemical products. The company's financial statements are prepared under IFRS.

Underlying Concept

This is an example of how the asset-liability approach to our accounting model works. If the cost is not an asset, it is an expense.

Real-World Emphasis

---

[12] Note that, to the extent these ordinary expenditures are classified as factory overhead, the costs are included as an inventory (product) cost before being charged to the income statement as an expense—cost of goods sold.

BP Annual Report and Accounts 2008
Notes on financial statements

1. Significant accounting policies continued

Oil and natural gas exploration and development expenditure

Oil and natural gas exploration and development expenditure is accounted for using the successful efforts method of accounting.

Exploration expenditure

Geological and geophysical exploration costs are charged against income as incurred. Costs directly associated with an exploration well are initially capitalized as an intangible asset until the drilling of the well is complete and the results have been evaluated. These costs include employee remuneration, materials and fuel used, rig costs, delay rentals and payments made to contractors. If hydrocarbons are not found, the exploration expenditure is written off as a dry hole. If hydrocarbons are found and, subject to further appraisal activity, which may include the drilling of further wells (exploration or exploratory-type stratigraphic test wells), are likely to be capable of commercial development, the costs continue to be carried as an asset. All such carried costs are subject to technical, commercial and management review at least once a year to confirm the continued intent to develop or otherwise extract value from the discovery. When this is no longer the case, the costs are written off. When proved reserves of oil and natural gas are determined and development is sanctioned, the relevant expenditure is transferred to property, plant and equipment.

Development expenditure

Expenditure on the construction, installation or completion of infrastructure facilities such as platforms, pipelines and the drilling of development wells, including unsuccessful development or delineation wells, is capitalized within property, plant and equipment and is depreciated from the commencement of production as described below in the accounting policy for Property, plant and equipment.

Property, plant and equipment

Property, plant and equipment is stated at cost, less accumulated depreciation and accumulated impairment losses. The initial cost of an asset comprises its purchase price or construction cost, any costs directly attributable to bringing the asset into operation, the initial estimate of any decommissioning obligation, if any, and, for qualifying assets, borrowing costs. The purchase price or construction cost is the aggregate amount paid and the fair value of any other consideration given to acquire the asset. The capitalized value of a finance lease is also included within property, plant and equipment. Exchanges of assets are measured at fair value unless the exchange transaction lacks commercial substance or the fair value of neither the asset received nor the asset given up is reliably measurable. The cost of the acquired asset is measured at the fair value of the asset given up, unless the fair value of the asset received is more clearly evident. Where fair value is not used, the cost of the acquired asset is measured at the carrying amount of the asset given up. The gain or loss on derecognition of the asset given up is recognized in profit or loss. Expenditure on major maintenance refits or repairs comprises the cost of replacement assets or parts of assets, inspection costs and overhaul costs. Where an asset or part of an asset that was separately depreciated is replaced and it is probable that future economic benefits associated with the item will flow to the group, the expenditure is capitalized and the carrying amount of the replaced asset is derecognized. Inspection costs associated with major maintenance programmes are capitalized and amortized over the period to the next inspection. Overhaul costs for major maintenance programmes are expensed as incurred. All other maintenance costs are expensed as incurred.

IFRS AND PRIVATE ENTITY GAAP COMPARISON

Objective 9

Identify differences in accounting between private entity GAAP and IFRS, and what changes are expected in the near future.

A Comparison of IFRS and Private Entity GAAP

Illustration 10-14 sets out the major differences between GAAP for private entities and international accounting standards for publicly accountable enterprises.

	Accounting Standards for Private Enterprises (Private Entity GAAP)—*CICA Handbook*, Part II, Sections 3061, 3110, 3800, 3831, 3850, and AcG-16	IFRS—IAS 16, 20, 23, 37, 40, and 41; IFRS 6
Scope	The costs of mining and oil and gas properties are considered items of PP&E, with specific application guidance covering the full cost method of accounting in the oil and gas industry covered in AcG-16.	The cost of mineral rights and reserves, including oil, natural gas, and similar non-regenerative resources, are not covered specifically as PP&E in IAS 16; only the costs of the exploration for and evaluation of mineral resources are addressed in IFRS 6.
	Investment property and biological assets are considered items of PP&E and HB 3061 applies.	Investment property is considered an item of PP&E, but a separate IFRS—IAS 40—applies to it. Biological assets are accounted for by standards in IAS 41 for agricultural assets.
Recognition	Uses general recognition principle in Section 1000 based on measurability and probability of future economic benefits to be received. Less guidance is provided.	Recognition criteria are incorporated in IAS 16 and used for costs both at and after initial recognition—same criteria, based on measurement reliability and probability that associated future economic benefits will flow to the entity.
Components	Indicates that the costs of significant separable component parts are allocated to those parts when practicable, but practice has not been to carry this out to the same extent as required internationally.	Requires the parts of PP&E with relatively significant costs to be depreciated separately. There is no mention made of practicability. Practice under IAS 16 results in more componentization than under HB 3061.
Measurement at recognition	Initial measurement is at cost.	Initial measurement is at cost, but more detail is provided on how cost is measured.
	Any net revenue/expense from using an item of PP&E prior to substantial completion and readiness for use is included in the asset's cost.	Net revenue or expense derived from an item of PP&E prior to its being in place and ready for use as intended is taken into income, on the basis that it was not needed to acquire the asset and bring it to its location and use.
	Capitalization of costs at acquisition stops when the asset is substantially complete and ready for productive use, as predetermined by management with reference to productive capacity, occupancy level, passage of time, or other industry considerations. This is a more flexible approach than under IFRS.	Capitalization of costs in the initial carrying amount stops when the item is in the location and condition necessary for it to be used as management intended, even if it has not begun to be used or is used at less than desired capacity. No initial operating losses or costs of relocation or reorganization of the asset(s) are capitalized.
	Interest costs directly attributable to the acquisition, construction, or development of items of PP&E may be capitalized if that is the accounting policy used by the entity.	Borrowing costs directly attributable to the acquisition, construction, or development of qualifying assets are capitalized.
	Only the cost of legal obligations related to site restoration and asset retirement is capitalized. Changes in the estimate of the cost are also capitalized in the asset.	The cost of legal and constructive obligations related to asset retirement is capitalized, measured under IAS 37 *Provisions, Contingent Liabilities, and Contingent Assets.* Increases in the cost of the obligation related to the production of inventory are specifically excluded.

	Accounting Standards for Private Enterprises (Private Entity GAAP)—*CICA Handbook*, Part II, Sections 3061, 3110, 3800, 3831, 3850, and AcG-16	IFRS—IAS 16, 20, 23, 37, 40, and 41; IFRS 6
Measurement after acquisition	Only one model—the cost model—applies to all items of PP&E.	All investment property is accounted for under either the cost model or fair value model. Each class of items of other PP&E is accounted for under the cost model or the revaluation model. The cost model continues to be used to the greatest extent.
Costs incurred after acquisition	Betterments are capitalized and costs that are incurred to maintain service potential are expensed. Increased service potential means increased physical output or service capacity, lower operating costs, an increase in useful life, or an increase in quality of output. For betterments and major replacements, if the cost of the previous part is known, its carrying amount is removed. If not, and depending on the circumstances, the asset account, its accumulated depreciation, or an expense could be charged with the cost.	All expenditures that meet the recognition criteria for an item of PP&E are capitalized. Does not specifically refer to betterments, but does refer to replacement parts that meet the recognition criteria. These are capitalized and the replaced part's carrying amount is removed, whether originally recognized as a separate component or not.
	The redevelopment of rental real estate qualifies as a betterment, with the book value of the existing building included in the cost of the redeveloped property, if recoverable.	The carrying amount of the building being redeveloped would not be carried forward as part of the cost of the new asset.
	Overhauls are not specifically addressed and are usually expensed when incurred.	Major inspections or overhauls that allow the continued use of an asset are treated similarly to replacements.

Illustration 10-14

IFRS versus Private Entity GAAP Comparison Chart

Looking Ahead

When Canadian publicly accountable entities apply IFRS for the first time, they are permitted to revalue items of PP&E to fair value at the transition date. This amount becomes the assets' deemed cost at that point. Many Canadian companies have expressed their intention to take advantage of this transition exemption, even though they are likely to apply the cost model going forward.

An ongoing project related to the IASB's research agenda is particularly important to many companies in Canada. It deals with the development of comprehensive accounting standards for the extractive industries, such as mining and oil and gas. The project's objective is to eventually issue a replacement standard for IFRS 6 *Exploration and Evaluation of Mineral Resources*. The project expects to cover all financial reporting issues associated with upstream extractive activities, reserves, and resources from the exploration for, discovery of, and extraction of minerals and oil and gas. The IASB issued a Discussion Paper on key issues in 2009 and expects to make a decision in 2010 on whether to add this project to its active agenda.

A major project that is expected to be finalized and issued as a new standard just prior to the adoption of IFRS by Canadian publicly accountable entities relates to fair value measurement guidance. The objective of the standard is to provide a single definition of fair value for all IFRSs, a source of guidance for how fair value is measured, and what disclosures are needed so users can understand how the values are determined and the extent to which they are used.

Glossary

Summary of Learning Objectives

KEY TERMS

additions, 630

asset retirement costs, 611

biological assets, 607

boot, 617

capital approach, 620

capital expenditure, 630

capitalized, 608

commercial
substance, 616

cost, 608

cost model (CM), 625

cost reduction
method, 620

deferral method, 620

depletion base, 623

fair value, 625

fair value model
(FVM), 628

fixed assets, 607

income approach, 620

inspections, 631

investment property, 623

leasehold
improvements, 622

lump-sum price, 613

major overhauls, 631

mineral resources, 623

mineral resource
properties, 623

monetary assets, 615

non-monetary assets, 615

non-reciprocal
transfers, 620

ordinary repairs, 634

plant assets, 607

property, plant, and
equipment, 607

rearrangement and
reinstallation
costs, 634

replacements, 631

revaluation model
(RM), 625

revenue expenditure, 630

self-constructed
assets, 609

1 Identify the characteristics of property, plant, and equipment assets, and explain the importance of these long-term assets to a business enterprise.

Property, plant, and equipment assets are tangible assets held for use in the production of goods and services, for rental to others, or for administrative purposes, and have a useful life of more than one accounting period. This type of asset provides an entity with its operating capacity and infrastructure, but also adds to fixed costs. For this reason, it is important that a company invest enough in PP&E to meet its potential, but not so much that it has to bear the related costs of overcapacity.

2 Identify the costs to include in the measurement of property, plant, and equipment assets at acquisition.

PP&E costs that provide probable future economic benefits to the entity and that can be measured reliably are recognized. Asset components should be recognized separately to the extent their costs are significant and/or the related assets have different useful lives or patterns of depreciation. Asset costs include all necessary costs directly attributed to acquiring the asset, bringing it to its location, and making it ready for use. These include direct material, direct labour, and variable overhead costs for self-constructed PP&E assets, borrowing costs for those taking substantial time to get ready for use, and dismantling and restoration costs required as a result of the asset's acquisition. Once the asset is in place and ready for use, costs are no longer capitalized.

3 Determine asset cost when the transaction has delayed payment terms or is a lump-sum purchase, a non-monetary exchange, or a contributed asset.

Cost means the asset's cash equivalent cost. When payment is deferred beyond normal credit terms, the excess paid over cash cost is interest. When a number of assets are acquired in a basket purchase, the cost is allocated based on the relative fair value of each. When PP&E assets are acquired and paid for by issuing the entity's shares, cost is usually determined as the fair value of the asset. When acquired in an exchange of assets, cost is the fair value of the assets given up, unless the fair value of the assets received can be more reliably measured. However, if the transaction lacks commercial substance or fair values cannot be reliably determined, the assets acquired are measured at the book value of the assets given up. This amount cannot exceed the fair value of the assets acquired. Assets contributed to a company are measured at fair value and credited to contributed surplus if donated by a shareholder. This is rare. If contributed by government, the contribution is accounted for under the income approach whereby the amount credited flows through the income statement, usually as the asset is used by the entity.

4 Identify the costs included in specific types of property, plant, and equipment.

Land: Includes all expenditures made to acquire land and to make it ready for use. Land costs typically include the purchase price; closing costs, such as title to the land, legal fees, and registration fees; costs incurred to condition the land for its intended use, such as grading, filling, draining, and clearing; the assumption of any liens, mortgages, or encumbrances on the property; and any additional land improvements that have an indefinite life. Buildings, including investment property: Includes all expenditures related directly to their acquisition or construction. These costs include materials, labour, and direct overhead costs that are incurred during construction and professional fees and building permits. Equipment: Includes the purchase price, freight, and handling charges that are incurred; insurance on the equipment while it is in transit; the cost of special foundations if they are required; assembling and installation costs; and the costs incurred in calibrating the equipment so that it can be used as intended. Mineral resource properties: Four types of costs may be included in establishing the cost of mineral resource assets. These are (a) acquisition costs, (b) exploration and evaluation costs, (c) development costs, and (d) site restoration and asset retirement costs.

5   Understand and apply the cost model.

The cost model is appropriate for all classes of PP&E, including investment property. Under this model, the assets are carried at cost less accumulated depreciation and any accumulated impairment losses.

6   Understand and apply the revaluation model.

The revaluation model may be applied to any class of PP&E except investment property, provided its fair value can be measured reliably. Under this model, the assets are carried at their fair value at the revaluation date less any subsequent accumulated depreciation and any subsequent accumulated impairment losses. While held, net increases in fair value are not reported in income, but are accumulated in a revaluation surplus account in equity. Net losses are reported in income once the revaluation surplus has been eliminated.

7   Understand and apply the fair value model.

The fair value model can be applied only to investment property and the choice between cost and fair value must be made for all investment property reported. Under this model, all changes in fair value are recognized in net income. No depreciation is recognized.

8   Explain and apply the accounting treatment for costs incurred after acquisition.

Day-to-day servicing, repair, and maintenance costs, and costs of rearrangement and relocation, are expensed as incurred. PP&E expenditures that provide future economic benefits and whose costs can be reliably measured are capitalized. The cost of additions, replacements, and major overhauls and inspections are capitalized and the carrying amount of the replaced asset or the previous overhaul or inspection is removed from the accounts.

9   Identify differences in accounting between private entity GAAP and IFRS, and what changes are expected in the near future.

In general, the accounting for PP&E assets is very similar under both IFRS and private entity GAAP because the principles underlying both are very similar. However, under IFRS, practice remains closer to the principles identified. This is seen, for example, in accounting for components and major overhauls and inspections; incidental revenues and expenses before asset use; and borrowing costs. IFRS permits application of a revaluation model and a fair value model, neither of which is acceptable under private entity GAAP. The IASB is researching activities related to the extractive industry with the objective of developing accounting standards to cover the exploration for, and the development and extraction of, minerals and oil and gas resources and assets. In addition, a new standard on fair value measurement is expected to be finalized in 2010.

Appendix **10**A

Capitalization of Borrowing Costs

Objective **10**

Calculate the amount of borrowing costs to capitalize for qualifying assets.

Chapter 10 introduces some of the issues for the capitalization of borrowing costs, underscoring the underlying principle that "borrowing costs that are directly attributable to the acquisition, construction, or production of a qualifying asset form part of the cost of that asset." Other borrowing costs are expensed. This appendix continues the discussion in more detail and illustrates the recognition guidance in IAS 23 *Borrowing Costs*. Private entities that choose a policy of capitalizing interest costs for relevant PP&E assets are also likely to apply this guidance.

In the past, many Canadian publicly traded companies followed a policy of capitalizing interest, applying the U.S. accounting standard in FAS No. 34. While both the international and FASB standards require capitalization and their general approach is similar, **there are application differences between SFAS 34 and IAS 23** that could produce different results in practice. These relate to the definitions of borrowing and interest costs, what is included as a qualifying asset, the treatment of income earned on the temporary investment of amounts borrowed, the capitalization rate, and the timing of the beginning and ending of capitalization.

Borrowing costs are defined as "interest and other costs that an entity incurs in connection with the borrowing of funds." The cost of equity financing is specifically excluded. Interest and other costs include interest expense that results from applying the effective interest method, finance charges on finance leases, and exchange adjustments on foreign currency borrowings if they are viewed as adjustments to interest costs.

Four issues need to be considered in determining the amount of borrowing costs to be capitalized and how to report them:

1. Which assets qualify?

2. The capitalization period

3. Avoidable borrowing costs—the amount eligible to capitalize

4. What disclosures are needed?

Qualifying Assets

To qualify for inclusion in the cost of an asset, the borrowing costs must:

1. be "directly attributable to the acquisition, construction, or production" of a qualifying asset; and

2. meet both recognition criteria—it is probable that associated future economic benefits will flow to the entity, and the cost can be measured reliably.

Qualifying assets must require **substantial time to get ready** for their intended use or sale. This may include inventories; items of property, plant, and equipment; investment properties; or intangible assets.

Borrowing costs for qualifying assets measured at fair value and inventories that are produced in large quantities on a repetitive basis **may be capitalized**, but it is not required.

Examples of assets that **do not qualify**, aside from financial assets, include (1) assets that are already in use or ready for their intended use when acquired; (2) those produced over a short period of time; and (3) assets not undergoing activities necessary to get them ready for use, such as land that is not being developed and assets that are not being used because of obsolescence, excess capacity, or needed repairs.

Capitalization Period

The capitalization period is the time over which interest must be capitalized. It **begins** on the **commencement date,** which is when **all three** of the following conditions are met:

1. Expenditures for the asset have been made.

2. Activities that are necessary to get the asset ready for its intended use or sale are in progress, including necessary pre-construction administrative and technical work.

3. Borrowing costs are being incurred.

Capitalization **ends** when substantially all the activities needed to prepare the asset for its intended use or sale are complete. This is usually when the physical activities associated with construction are finished, even if minor matters are still outstanding. If a project is finished in stages so that the parts completed can be used while activities continue on the remainder, capitalization stops on the parts that are substantially complete. If active development of a project is on hold, capitalization of the borrowing costs is **suspended**. Note that this does not refer to temporary delays needed as part of the development process.

Let's apply this to different situations associated with land. What if land was purchased with the intention of developing it for a particular use? If the land is purchased as a site for a structure (such as a plant site), the borrowing costs that are capitalized **during the construction period** are part of the cost of the plant, not of the land. Borrowing costs on the land while held and awaiting the start of construction are expensed. If land is being developed for sale as lots, the borrowing cost is part of the developed land's acquisition cost. However, borrowing costs involved in purchasing land that is held for speculation are not capitalized, because the asset is ready for its intended use.

Avoidable Borrowing Costs

To qualify for capitalization, the costs must be **directly attributable** to a project; i.e., they must be avoidable borrowing costs. When an entity borrows funds to finance a specific qualifying asset, the avoidable costs are the actual borrowing costs that would not have been incurred if the expenditures for the qualifying asset had not been made. These costs are reduced by the investment income earned on any temporary investment of these monies.

Avoidable costs are more difficult to calculate when a company's borrowings are not directly related to specific assets or projects. Some companies borrow funds using a variety of debt instruments to support their general financing requirements. In this case, the calculation is not as straightforward and professional judgement is often needed to determine which costs were avoidable.

In general, the following steps are taken to calculate the borrowing costs to capitalize:

1. Determine the expenditures on the qualifying asset.

2. Determine the avoidable borrowing costs on the asset-specific debt.

3. Determine the avoidable borrowing costs on the non-asset-specific debt.

4. Determine the borrowing costs to capitalize.

Step 1. Determine the expenditures on the qualifying asset

The **expenditures on the qualifying asset** means the weighted-average accumulated expenditures—the construction expenditures weighted by the amount of time (fraction of a year or accounting period) in which borrowing costs could be incurred. The expenditures include amounts paid for by cash or other asset or an interest-bearing liability, including previously capitalized borrowing costs. The expenditures are reduced by any progress payments received from a customer (in the case of construction of an inventory item) and by any grants received, such as from one or more levels of government.

To illustrate, assume a 17-month bridge construction project with current-year payments to the contractor of $240,000 on March 1; $480,000 on July 1; and $360,000 on November 1. The weighted-average accumulated expenditures for the year ended December 31 are calculated in Illustration 10A-1.

Illustration 10A-1

Calculation of Weighted-Average Accumulated Expenditures

| | Expenditures | | | Capitalization | | Weighted-Average Accumulated |
Date		Amount	×	Period*	=	Expenditures
Mar. 1		$ 240,000		10/12		$200,000
July 1		480,000		6/12		240,000
Nov. 1		360,000		2/12		60,000
		$1,080,000				$500,000

*Months between the date of expenditure and the date when interest capitalization stops or year end arrives, whichever comes first (in this case, December 31)

The costs incurred are weighted by the amount of time that borrowing costs could have been incurred on each expenditure in the year. For the March 1 expenditure, 10 months of borrowing cost could be associated with the expenditure; for the expenditure on July 1, only 6 months of interest could have been incurred; and for the November 1 expenditure, there would only be 2 months.

Step 2. Determine the avoidable borrowing costs on the asset-specific debt

In this example, there is no asset-specific borrowing and therefore, no asset-specific borrowing costs. If there were, remember that the borrowing costs on this debt would have to be reduced by the investment income on any temporary investment of the funds.

Step 3. Determine the avoidable borrowing costs on the non-asset-specific debt

The next step entails (a) calculating an appropriate capitalization rate and (b) applying it to the weighted-average expenditures financed by general debt. The rate is a weighted-average borrowing rate on the general borrowings. Assume that the borrowings identified in Illustration 10A-2 were all outstanding for the full year.

Illustration **10A-2**

*Calculation of
Capitalization Rate*

	Principal	Borrowing costs[13]
12%, 2-year note	$ 600,000	$ 72,000
9%, 10-year bonds	2,000,000	180,000
7.5%, 20-year bonds	5,000,000	375,000
	$7,600,000	$627,000

Because each debt instrument was outstanding for the full year, each principal amount is already weighted by 12/12. The interest also represents a full 12 months of borrowing costs. The weighted-average capitalization rate on the general-purpose debt is calculated as follows:

$$\frac{\text{Total borrowing costs}}{\text{Weighted-average principal outstanding}} = \frac{\$627,000}{\$7,600,000} = 8.25\%$$

The avoidable borrowing cost is the total weighted-average amount of accumulated expenditures (from step 1) reduced by the weighted average expenditures financed by asset-specific debt from step 2, multiplied by the capitalization rate: ($500,000 − $0) × 8.25% = $41,250.

Step 4. Determine the borrowing costs to capitalize

This step adds the eligible borrowing costs on asset-specific borrowings of $0 (step 2) and those on general borrowings of $41,250 (step 3) for a total of $41,250. This is the amount of cost to capitalize unless the actual borrowing costs incurred in the year are less than this. The lower amount is used.

An example that incorporates both asset-specific and general borrowings is explained next.

Illustration

Assume that on November 1, 2010, Shalla Corporation contracted with Pfeifer Construction Co. Ltd. to have a building constructed for its own use for $1.4 million on land costing $100,000. The land is acquired from the contractor and its purchase price is included in the first payment. Shalla made the following payments to the construction company during 2011:

January 1	March 1	May 1	December 31	Total
$210,000	$300,000	$540,000	$450,000	$1,500,000

---

[13] Unlike investment income earned on the temporary investment of asset-specific borrowings, IAS 8 *Borrowing Costs* does not speak to whether investment income earned on general-purpose debt should reduce the borrowing costs eligible to be capitalized or not. The principles set out in this IFRS and the company-specific circumstances would have to be assessed to determine the best approach in each case.

Construction of the building began very early in January and it was completed and ready for occupancy on December 31, 2011. Shalla had the following debt outstanding at December 31, 2011:

Specific Construction Debt	
15%, 3-year note to finance construction of the building, dated December 31, 2010, with interest payable annually on December 31	$750,000
Other Debt	
10%, 5-year note payable, dated December 31, 2007, with interest payable annually on December 31	$550,000
12%, 10-year bonds issued December 31, 2004, with interest payable annually on December 31	$600,000

Step 1. Determine the expenditures on the qualifying asset. The weighted-average accumulated expenditures during 2011 are calculated in Illustration 10A-3.

Illustration 10A-3

Calculation of Weighted-Average Accumulated Expenditures

	Expenditures			Current Year Capitalization		Weighted-Average Accumulated
Date		Amount	×	Period	=	Expenditures
Jan. 1		$ 210,000		12/12		$210,000
Mar. 1		300,000		10/12		250,000
May 1		540,000		8/12		360,000
Dec. 31		450,000		0		0
		$1,500,000				$820,000

Note that the expenditure made on December 31, the last day of the year, gets a zero weighting in the calculation. It will have no borrowing cost assigned to it.

Step 2. Determine the avoidable borrowing costs on the asset-specific debt. The asset-specific construction debt of $750,000 was outstanding for the full year and is therefore weighted for a full 12 months. Therefore, the avoidable borrowing cost on this debt is $750,000 × 15% = $112,500.

Step 3. Determine the avoidable borrowing costs on the non-asset-specific debt. Illustration 10A-4 shows the calculation of this borrowing cost. It is the weighted-average accumulated expenditures financed by general borrowings multiplied by the capitalization rate.

Illustration 10A-4

Calculation of Avoidable Borrowing Cost on General Debt

Total weighted-average accumulated expenditures	$820,000	
Less financed by specific construction loan	750,000	
Weighted-average accumulated expenditures financed by general borrowings	$ 70,000	
Capitalization rate calculation:	Principal	Borrowing Cost
10%, 5-year note: $550,000 × 12/12	$ 550,000	$ 55,000
12%, 10-year bonds: $600,000 × 12/12	600,000	72,000
	$1,150,000	$127,000

Capitalization rate = $\dfrac{\text{Borrowing cost on general debt}}{\text{Weighted principal outstanding}} = \dfrac{\$127,000}{\$1,150,000} = 11.04\%$

Avoidable borrowing cost on general debt: $70,000 × 11.04% = $7,728

Step 4. Determine the borrowing costs to capitalize. Use the lower of the total avoidable borrowing costs **eligible** for capitalization (result of 2 and 3 above) and the **actual** borrowing costs incurred. The calculations are shown in Illustration 10A-5.

Avoidable costs on asset-specific debt	$112,500
Avoidable costs on general debt	7,728
Total avoidable borrowing costs	$120,228

Illustration 10A-5

Calculation of Total Avoidable and Actual Borrowing Costs

Total actual borrowing costs for the period:		
Construction note	$750,000 × 0.15 =	$112,500
5-year note	$550,000 × 0.10 =	55,000
10-year bonds	$600,000 × 0.12 =	72,000
Actual borrowing costs		$239,500

The amount of borrowing costs capitalized, therefore, is $120,228.

The journal entries made by Shalla Company during 2011 are as follows:

Jan. 1	Land	100,000	
	Building (or Construction in Process)	110,000	
	Cash		210,000
Mar. 1	Building	300,000	
	Cash		300,000
May 1	Building	540,000	
	Cash		540,000
Dec. 31	Building	450,000	
	Cash		450,000
Dec. 31	Building	120,228	
	Interest Expense		120,228

The capitalized borrowing costs of $120,228 are added to the building's acquisition cost and are amortized as part of its depreciation charge; i.e., they will be recognized in expense over the useful life of the asset and not over the term of the debt.

Disclosures

Only two disclosures are required for borrowing costs: the amount capitalized and the capitalization rate.

Illustration 10A-6 provides an example of **Royal Dutch Shell Plc's** disclosures in its 2008 financial statements. Royal Dutch Shell is a vertically integrated energy giant with operations worldwide, including Canada. The amounts reported are expressed in millions of U.S. dollars.

2
ACCOUNTING
POLICIES   **PROPERTY, PLANT AND EQUIPMENT AND INTANGIBLE ASSETS**
            [A] Recognition in the Consolidated Balance Sheet

Interest in capitalised, as an increase in property, plant and equipment, on major capital projects during construction.

5
INTEREST AND
OTHER INCOME AND
INTEREST EXPENSE
[B] INTEREST EXPENSE

			$ million
	2008	2007	2006
Interest incurred	1,371	1,235	1,296
Accretion expense (see Note 21)	680	540	417
Less: interest capitalised	(870)	(667)	(564)
Total	1,181	1,108	1,149

The interest rate applied in determining the amount of interest capitalised in 2008 was 5.0% (2007: 5.0%; 2006: 4.0%).

Glossary

Summary of Learning Objective for Appendix 10A

KEY TERMS

avoidable borrowing
    costs, 641
borrowing costs, 640
capitalization period, 641
capitalization rate, 642
qualifying assets, 641
weighted-average
    accumulated
    expenditures, 642

10 Calculate the amount of borrowing costs to capitalize for qualifying assets.

The avoidable borrowing costs related to the financing of eligible expenditures on qualifying assets are capitalized to the extent they are less than the total borrowing costs incurred in the period.

Note: All assignment material with an asterisk (*) relates to the appendix to the chapter.

Brief Exercises

BE10-1 Passos Brothers Inc. purchased land at a price of $57,000. Closing costs were $1,400. An old building was removed at a cost of $28,200. What amount should be recorded as the land cost? **(LO 2, 4)**

BE10-2 Okanagan Utilities Ltd. incurred the following costs in constructing a new maintenance building during the fiscal period. What costs should be included in the cost of the new building? **(LO 2, 4)**

(a) Direct labour, $73,000

(b) Allocation of the president's salary, $54,000

(c) Material purchased for the building, $82,500

(d) Interest on the loan to finance construction until completion, $2,300

(e) Allocation of plant overhead based on labour hours worked on the building, $29,000

(f) Architectural drawings for the building, $7,500

BE10-3 Petri Corporation purchased equipment for an invoice price of $40,000, terms 2/10, n/30. (a) Record the purchase of the equipment and the subsequent payment, assuming the payment was made within the discount period. (b) Repeat (a), but assuming the company's payment missed the discount period. **(LO 3)**

BE10-4 Chavez Corporation purchased a truck by issuing an $80,000, four-year, non-interest-bearing note to Equinox Inc. The market interest rate for obligations of this nature is 12%. Prepare the journal entry to record the truck purchase. **(LO 3)**

BE10-5 Martin Corporation purchased a truck by issuing an $80,000, 12% note to Equinox Inc. Interest is payable annually and the note is payable in four years. Prepare the journal entry to record the truck purchase. **(LO 3)**

BE10-6 Hamm Inc. purchased land, a building, and equipment from Spamela Corporation for a cash payment of $306,000. The assets' estimated fair values are land $95,000; building $250,000; and equipment $110,000. At what amounts should each of the three assets be recorded? **(LO 3)**

BE10-7 Wizard Corp. obtained land by issuing 2,000 of its no par value common shares. The land was recently appraised at $85,000. The common shares are actively traded at $41 per share. Prepare the journal entry to record the land acquisition. **(LO 3)**

BE10-8 Kristali Corporation traded a used truck (cost $23,000, accumulated depreciation $20,700) for another used truck worth $3,700. Kristali also paid $300 cash in the transaction. Prepare the journal entry to record the exchange, assuming the transaction lacks commercial substance. **(LO 3)**

BE10-9 Sloan Ltd. traded a used welding machine (cost $9,000, accumulated depreciation $3,000) for office equipment with an estimated fair value of $5,000. Sloan also paid $2,000 cash in the transaction. Prepare the journal entry to record the exchange. The equipment results in different cash flows for Sloan, compared with those the welding machine produced. **(LO 3)**

BE10-10 Bulb Ltd. traded a used truck for a new truck. The used truck cost $30,000 and had accumulated depreciation of $27,000. The new truck was worth $35,000. Bulb also made a cash payment of $33,000. Prepare Bulb's entry to record the exchange, and state any assumptions that you have made. **(LO 3)**

BE10-11 Swanton Corp. recently purchased a building to house its manufacturing operations in Moose Jaw for $470,000. The company agreed to lease the land that the building stood on for $14,000 per year from the industrial park owner, and the municipality donated $140,000 to Swanton as an incentive to locate in the area and acquire the building. Prepare entries to record the cash that was exchanged in each of the transactions, assuming the cost reduction method is used. **(LO 3)**

BE10-12 Use the information for Swanton Corp. in BE10-11. Prepare the entries to record the three cash transactions, assuming the deferral method is used. **(LO 3)**

(LO 3)   **BE10-13**   Dubois Inc. received equipment as a donation. The equipment has a fair market value of $55,000. Prepare the journal entry to record the receipt of the equipment under each of the following assumptions:

(a) The equipment was donated by a shareholder.

(b) The equipment was donated by a retired employee.

(LO 4)   **BE10-14**   Khan Corporation acquires a coal mine at a cost of $400,000. Development costs that were incurred total $100,000, including $12,300 of depreciation on movable equipment to construct mine shafts. Based on construction to date, the obligation to restore the property after the mine is exhausted has a present value of $75,000. Prepare the journal entries to record the cost of the natural resource.

(LO 6)   **BE10-15**   Revalue Assets Inc. has a manufacturing plant with an initial cost of $100,000. At December 31, 2011, the date of revaluation, accumulated depreciation amounted to $55,000. The fair value of the asset, by comparing it with transactions in similar assets, is assessed to be $65,000. Prepare the journal entries to revalue the assets under the revaluation model using the asset adjustment method.

(LO 7)   **BE10-16**   TrueValue Investment Properties Inc. and its subsidiaries have provided you with a list of the properties they own:

(a) Land held by TrueValue for undetermined future use

(b) A vacant building owned by TrueValue and to be leased out under an operating lease

(c) Property held by a subsidiary of TrueValue, a real estate firm, in the ordinary course of its business

(d) Property held by TrueValue for use in the manufacturing of products

Advise TrueValue and its subsidiaries as to the proper presentation and measurement options for the above properties under both IFRS and private entity GAAP.

(LO 8)   **BE10-17**   Identify whether the following costs should be treated as a capital expenditure or a revenue expenditure when they are incurred.

(a) $13,000 paid to rearrange and reinstall machinery

(b) $200 paid for a tune-up and oil change on a delivery truck

(c) $200,000 paid for an addition to a building

(d) $7,000 paid to replace a wooden floor with a concrete floor

(e) $2,000 paid for a major overhaul that extends the useful life of a truck

(f) $700,000 paid for relocating company headquarters

(LO 8)   **BE10-18**   Big Wheels Inc. has acquired a large transport truck at a cost of $90,000 (with no breakdown of the component parts). The truck's estimated useful life is 10 years. At the end of the seventh year, the powertrain requires replacement. It is determined that it is not economical to put any more money or time into maintaining the old powertrain. The remainder of the transport truck is in good working condition and is expected to last for the next three years. The cost of a new powertrain is $40,000. Should the cost of the new powertrain be recognized as an asset or as an expense? How should the transaction be measured and recorded?

(LO 2, 10)   ***BE10-19**   Brent Hill Company is constructing a building. Construction began on February 1 and was completed on December 31. Expenditures were $1.5 million on March 1; $1.2 million on June 1; and $3 million on December 31. Calculate Brent Hill's weighted-average accumulated expenditures that would be used for capitalization of borrowing costs.

(LO 2, 10)   ***BE10-20**   Brent Hill Company (see BE10-19) borrowed $1 million on March 1 on a five-year, 12% note to help finance the building construction. In addition, the company had outstanding all year a $2-million, five-year, 13% note payable and a $3.5-million, four-year, 15% note payable. Calculate the appropriate capitalization rate on general borrowings that would be used for capitalization of borrowing costs.

(LO 2, 10)   ***BE10-21**   Use the information for Brent Hill Company from BE10-19 and BE10-20. Calculate the company's avoidable borrowing costs.

Exercises

E10-1 (Cost Elements and Asset Componentization) The following assets have been recognized as items of prop- **(LO 1)**
erty, plant, and equipment.

1. Head office boardroom table and executive chairs

2. A landfill site

3. Wooden pallets in a warehouse

4. Forklift vehicles in a manufacturing plant

5. Stand-alone training facility for pilot training, including a flight simulator and classrooms equipped with desks, whiteboards, and electronic instructional aids

6. Large passenger aircraft used in commercial flights

7. Medical office building

8. Computer equipment

Instructions

For each of the items listed:

(a) Identify what specific costs are likely to be included in the acquisition cost.

(b) Explain whether any components of this asset should be given separate recognition, and why.

E10-2 (Purchase and Cost of Self-Constructed Assets) Wen Corp. both purchases and constructs various pieces of **(LO 2, 3)**
equipment that it uses in its operations. The following items are for two different pieces of equipment and were recorded
in random order during the calendar year 2011:

Purchase	
Cash paid for equipment, including sales tax of $8,000 and GST of $6,000	$114,000
Freight and insurance cost while in transit	2,000
Cost of moving equipment into place at factory	3,100
Wage cost for technicians to test equipment	4,000
Materials cost for testing	500
Insurance premium paid on the equipment during its first year of operation	1,500
Special plumbing fixtures required for new equipment	8,000
Repair cost on equipment incurred in first year of operations	1,300
Cash received from provincial government as incentive to purchase equipment	25,000

Construction	
Material and purchased parts (gross cost $200,000; failed to take 2% cash discount)	$200,000
Imputed interest on funds used during construction (equity/share financing)	14,000
Labour costs	190,000
Overhead costs (fixed $20,000; variable $30,000)	50,000
Profit on self-construction	30,000
Cost of installing equipment	4,400

Instructions

Calculate the total cost for each of these two pieces of equipment. If an item is not capitalized as an equipment cost, indicate how it should be reported.

E10-3 (Treatment of Various Costs) Farrey Supply Ltd. is a newly formed public corporation that incurred the fol- **(LO 2, 3, 9)**
lowing expenditures related to land, buildings, machinery, and equipment:

Legal fees for title search		$ 520
Architect's fees		2,800
Cash paid for land and dilapidated building on it		112,000
Removal of old building	$20,000	
Less: Salvage	5,500	14,500
Surveying before construction		370
Interest on short-term loans during construction		7,400

continued on page 650

Excavation before construction for basement	$ 19,000
Machinery purchased (subject to 2% cash discount, which was not taken)	65,000
Freight on machinery purchased	1,340
Storage charges on machinery, made necessary because building was still under construction when machinery was delivered	2,180
New building constructed (building construction took six months from date of purchase of land and old building)	485,000
Assessment by city for drainage project	1,600
Hauling charges for delivery of machinery from storage to new building	620
Installation of machinery	2,000
Trees, shrubs, and other landscaping after completion of building (permanent in nature)	5,400
Municipal grant to promote locating in the municipality	(8,000)

Instructions

(a) Determine the amounts that should be included in the cost of land, buildings, and machinery and equipment. Indicate how any amounts that are not included in these accounts should be recorded.

(b) Assume that the company was not a public company, and that it elected to use private entity GAAP. How would that affect the solution provided in part (a)?

(LO 2, 3) E10-4   (Entries for Asset Acquisition, Including Self-Construction) The following are transactions related to Hood Limited:

(a) The City of Piedmont gives the company five hectares of land as a plant site. This land's market value is determined to be $81,000.

(b) Hood issues 13,000 no par value common shares in exchange for land and buildings. The property has been appraised at a fair market value of $990,000, of which $180,000 has been allocated to land, $567,000 to the structure of the buildings, $162,000 to the building services (wiring, plumbing, heating, air conditioning, elevators), and $81,000 to the interior coverings in the buildings (flooring, etc.). The Hood shares are not listed on any exchange, but a block of 100 shares was sold by a shareholder 12 months ago at $65 per share, and a block of 200 shares was sold by another shareholder 18 months ago at $58 per share.

(c) No entry has been made to remove amounts for machinery constructed during the year that were charged to the accounts Materials, Direct Labour, and Factory Overhead and should have been charged to plant asset accounts. The following information relates to the costs of the machinery that was constructed:

Construction materials used	$15,000
Direct materials used in calibrating the equipment	375
Factory supplies used	900
Direct labour incurred	34,000
Additional variable overhead (over regular) caused by construction of machinery, excluding factory supplies used	2,700
Fixed overhead rate applied to regular manufacturing operations	60% of direct labour cost
Cost of similar machinery if it had been purchased from outside suppliers	84,000

Instructions

Prepare journal entries on the books of Hood Limited to record these transactions. Assume that Hood Limited uses IFRS.

(LO 2, 4) E10-5   (Acquisition Costs of Equipment) Lili Corporation acquires new equipment at a cost of $100,000 plus 8% provincial sales tax and 5% GST. (GST is a recoverable tax.) The company paid $1,700 to transport the equipment to its plant. The site where the equipment was to be placed was not yet ready and Lili Corporation spent another $500 for one month's storage costs. When installed, $300 of labour and $200 of materials were used to adjust and calibrate the machine to the company's exact specifications. The units produced in the trial runs were subsequently sold to employees for $400. During the first two months of production, the equipment was used only at 50% of its capacity. Labour costs of $3,000 and material costs of $2,000 were incurred in this production, while the units sold generated $5,500 of sales. Lili paid an engineering consulting firm $11,000 for its services in recommending the specific equipment to purchase and for help during the calibration phase. Borrowing costs of $1,100 were incurred because of the one-month delay in installation.

Instructions

Determine the capitalized cost of the equipment and explain why the remainder of the costs have not been capitalized.

E10-6 (Directly Attributable Costs) DAC Manufacturing Inc. is installing a new plant at its production facility. It has **(LO 2, 4)** incurred these costs:

1. Cost of the manufacturing plant (cost per supplier's invoice plus taxes)	$2,500,000
2. Initial delivery and handling costs	200,000
3. Cost of site preparation	600,000
4. Consultants used for advice on the acquisition of the plant	700,000
5. Interest charges paid to supplier of plant for deferred credit	200,000
6. Estimated dismantling costs to be incurred after seven years	300,000
7. Operating losses before commercial production	400,000

Instructions

Advise DAC Manufacturing Inc. on the costs that can be capitalized in accordance with IAS 16.

E10-7 (Acquisition Costs of Realty) The following expenditures and receipts are related to land, land improvements, **(LO 2, 4)** and buildings that were acquired for use in a business enterprise. The receipts are in parentheses.

(a) Money borrowed to pay a building contractor (signed a note), $(275,000)

(b) A payment for construction from note proceeds, $275,000

(c) The cost of landfill and clearing, $8,000

(d) Delinquent real estate taxes on property, assumed by a purchaser, $7,000

(e) A premium on a six-month insurance policy during construction, $6,000

(f) Refund of one month's insurance premium because construction was completed early, $(1,000)

(g) An architect's fee on a building, $22,000

(h) The cost of real estate purchased as a plant site (land $200,000; building $50,000), $250,000

(i) A commission fee paid to a real estate agency, $9,000

(j) The installation of fences around a property, $4,000

(k) The cost of razing and removing a building, $11,000

(l) Proceeds from the salvage of a demolished building, $(5,000)

(m) Interest paid during construction on money borrowed for construction, $13,000

(n) The cost of parking lots and driveways, $19,000

(o) The cost of trees and shrubbery that were planted (non-permanent in nature, to be replaced every 20 years), $14,000

(p) Excavation costs for new building, $3,000

(q) The GST on an excavation cost, $150

Instructions

Identify each item by letter and list the items in columnar form, as shown below. Using the column headings that follow, write the letter for each item in the first column and its amount under the column heading where it would be recorded. All receipt amounts should be reported in parentheses. For any amounts that should be entered in the Other Accounts column, also indicate the account title.

Item	Land	Land Improvements	Building	Other Accounts

E10-8 (Acquisition Costs of Realty) Glesen Corp. purchased land with two old buildings on it as a factory site for $460,000. The property tax assessment on this property was $350,000: $250,000 for the land and the rest for the build- **(LO 2, 4)** ings. It took six months to tear down the old buildings and construct the factory.

The company paid $50,000 to raze the old buildings and sold salvaged lumber and brick for $6,300. Legal fees of $1,850 were paid for title investigation and drawing up the purchase contract. Payment to an engineering firm was made for a land survey, $2,200, and for drawing the factory plans, $82,000. The land survey had to be made before final plans could be drawn. The liability insurance premium that was paid during construction was $900. The contractor's charge for construction was $3,640,000. The company paid the contractor in two instalments: $1,200,000 at the end of three months and $2,440,000 upon completion. The architects and engineers estimated the cost of the building to be 55% attributable to the structure, 35% attributable to the building services (wiring, plumbing, heating, air conditioning), and the remainder attributable to the roof structure as each of these elements is expected to have a different useful life. Interest costs of $170,000 were incurred to finance the construction.

Instructions

Determine the land and building costs as they should be recorded on the books of Glesen Corp. Assume that the land survey was for the building.

(LO 2, 4) **E10-9** **(Natural Resource—Oil)** Oil Products Limited leases property on which oil has been discovered. The lease provides for an immediate payment of $550,000 to the lessor before drilling has begun and an annual rental of $42,000. In addition, the lessee is responsible for cleaning up the waste and debris from drilling and for the costs associated with reconditioning the land for farming when the wells are abandoned. It is estimated that the cleanup and reconditioning obligation has a present value of $31,000.

Instructions

Determine the amount that should be capitalized in the Oil Property asset account as a result of the lease agreement.

(LO 2, 3, 10) ***E10-10** **(Asset Acquisition)** Hayes Industries Corp. purchased the following assets and also constructed a building. All this was done during the current year.

Assets 1 and 2

These assets were purchased together for $100,000 cash. The following information was gathered:

Description	Initial Cost on Seller's Books	Depreciation to Date on Seller's Books	Book Value on Seller's Books	Appraised Value
Machinery	$100,000	$50,000	$50,000	$90,000
Office Equipment	60,000	10,000	50,000	30,000

Asset 3

This machine was acquired by making a $10,000 down payment and issuing a $30,000, two-year, zero-interest-bearing note. The note is to be paid off in two $15,000 instalments made at the end of the first and second years. It was estimated that the asset could have been purchased outright for $35,000.

Asset 4

A truck was acquired by trading in an older truck that has the same value in use. The newer truck has options that will make it more comfortable for the driver; however, the company remains in the same economic position after the exchange as before. Facts concerning the trade-in are as follows:

Cost of truck traded	$100,000
Accumulated depreciation to date of sale	40,000
Fair market value of truck traded	80,000
Cash received	10,000
Fair market value of truck acquired	70,000

Asset 5

Office equipment was acquired by issuing 100 no par value common shares. The shares had a market value of $11 per share.

Construction of Building

A building was constructed on land that was purchased last year at a cost of $150,000. Construction began on February 1 and was completed November 1. The payments to the contractor were as follows:

Date	Payment
Feb. 1	$120,000
June 1	360,000
Sept. 1	480,000
Nov. 1	100,000

To finance construction of the building, a $600,000, 12% construction loan was taken out on February 1. During the beginning of the project, Hayes invested the portion of the construction loan that was not yet expended and earned investment income of $4,600. The loan was repaid on November 1. The firm had $200,000 of other outstanding debt during the year at a borrowing rate of 8% and a $350,000 loan payable outstanding at a borrowing rate of 6%.

Instructions

Record the acquisition of each of these assets.

E10-11 (Acquisition Costs of Trucks) Jackson Corporation operates a retail computer store. To improve its delivery **(LO 3)** services to customers, the company purchased four new trucks on April 1, 2011. The terms of acquisition for each truck were as follows:

1. Truck #1 had a list price of $17,000 and was acquired for a cash payment of $15,900.

2. Truck #2 had a list price of $18,000 and was acquired for a down payment of $2,000 cash and a non-interest-bearing note with a face amount of $16,000. The note is due April 1, 2012. Jackson would normally have to pay interest at a rate of 10% for such a borrowing, and the dealership has an incremental borrowing rate of 8%.

3. Truck #3 had a list price of $18,000. It was acquired in exchange for a computer system that Jackson carries in inventory. The computer system cost $13,500 and is normally sold by Jackson for $17,100. Jackson uses a perpetual inventory system.

4. Truck #4 had a list price of $16,000. It was acquired in exchange for 1,000 common shares of Jackson Corporation. The common shares are no par value shares with a market value of $15 per share.

Instructions

Prepare the appropriate journal entries for Jackson Corporation for the above transactions. If there is some uncertainty about the amount, give reasons for your choice.

E10-12 (Correction of Improper Cost Entries) Plant acquisitions for selected companies are as follows: **(LO 3)**

1. Bella Industries Inc. acquired land, buildings, and equipment from a bankrupt company, Torres Co., for a lump-sum price of $700,000. At the time of purchase, Torres' assets had the following book and appraisal values:

	Book Value	Appraisal Value
Land	$200,000	$150,000
Buildings	250,000	350,000
Equipment	300,000	300,000

To be conservative, Bella Industries decided to take the lower of the two values for each asset it acquired. The following entry was made:

Land	150,000	
Buildings	250,000	
Equipment	300,000	
Cash		700,000

Bella Industries expects the building structure to last another 20 years; however, it expects that it will have to replace the roof in the next five years. Torres Co. indicated that, on initial construction of the building, the roof amounted to 20% of the value of the building. In meetings with contractors, due to the unique design and materials required to replace the roof, the contractors stated that the roof structure is currently worth 15% of the value of the building purchase.

2. Hari Enterprises purchased store equipment by making a $2,000 cash down payment and signing a $23,000, one-year, 10% note payable. The purchase was recorded as follows:

Store Equipment	27,300	
Cash		2,000
Note Payable		23,000
Interest Payable		2,300

3. Kim Company purchased office equipment for $20,000, terms 2/10, n/30. Because the company intended to take the discount, it made no entry until it paid for the acquisition. The entry was:

Office Equipment	20,000	
Cash		19,600
Purchase Discounts		400

4. Kaiser Inc. recently received land at zero cost from the Village of Chester as an inducement to locate its business in the village. The appraised value of the land was $27,000. The company made no entry to record the land because it had no cost basis.

5. Zimmerman Company built a warehouse for $600,000. It could have contracted out and purchased the building for $740,000. The controller made the following entry:

Warehouse	740,000	
Cash		600,000
Profit on Construction		140,000

Instructions

Digging Deeper

(a) Prepare the entry that should have been made at the date of each acquisition. Round to the nearest dollar.

(b) Prepare the correcting entry that is required in each case to correct the accounts. In other words, do not simply reverse the incorrect entry and replace it with the entry in part (a).

(c) List the accounting principle, assumption, or constraint from the conceptual framework that has been violated in each case.

(LO 3) E10-13   (Entries for Equipment Acquisitions) Geddes Engineering Corporation purchased conveyor equipment with a list price of $50,000. Three independent cases that are related to the equipment follow. Assume that the equipment purchases are recorded gross.

1. Geddes paid cash for the equipment 15 days after the purchase, along with 5% GST and provincial sales tax of $3,210. The vendor's credit terms were 1/10, n/30.

2. Geddes traded in equipment with a book value of $2,000 (initial cost $40,000), and paid $40,500 in cash one month after the purchase. The old equipment could have been sold for $8,000 at the date of trade, but was accepted for a trade-in allowance of $9,500 on the new equipment.

3. Geddes gave the vendor a $10,000 cash down payment and a 9% note payable with blended principal and interest payments of $20,000 each, due at the end of each of the next two years.

Instructions

Digging Deeper

(a) Prepare the general journal entries that are required to record the acquisition and payment in each of the three independent cases above. Round to the nearest dollar.

(b) Compare the treatment of the cash discount in item 1 above with the accounting for purchase discounts for inventories using the net method in Chapter 8.

(LO 3) E10-14   (Entries for Acquisition of Assets) Information for Zoe Ltd. follows:

1. On July 6, Zoe acquired the plant assets of Desbury Company, which had discontinued operations. The property's appraised value was:

Land	$ 400,000
Building—Structure	1,000,000
Building—Services	200,000
Machinery and equipment	800,000
Total	$2,400,000

Zoe gave 12,500 of its no par value common shares in exchange. The shares had a market value of $168 per share on the date of the property purchase.

2. Zoe had the following cash expenses between July 6 and December 15, the date when it first occupied the building:

Repairs to building	$105,000
Construction of bases for machinery to be installed later	135,000
Driveways and parking lots	122,000
Remodelling of office space in building, including new partitions and walls	61,000
Special assessment by city on land	18,000

On December 20, Zoe purchased machinery for $260,000, subject to a 2% cash discount, and paid freight on the machinery of $10,500. The machine was dropped while being placed in position, which resulted in repairs costing $12,000. The company paid the supplier within the discount period.

Instructions

(a) Prepare the entries for these transactions on the books of Zoe Ltd.

(b) Prepare the entry for the purchase and payment of the machinery in item 2, assuming the discount was not taken.

E10-15 **(Purchase of Equipment with Non-Interest-Bearing Debt)** Mohawk Inc. decided to purchase equipment **(LO 3)** from Central Ontario Industries on January 2, 2011, to expand its production capacity to meet customers' demand for its product. Mohawk issued an $800,000, five-year, non-interest-bearing note to Central Ontario for the new equipment when the prevailing market interest rate for obligations of this nature was 12%. The company will pay off the note in five $160,000 instalments due at the end of each year of the note's life.

Instructions

(Round to nearest dollar in all calculations.)

(a) Prepare the journal entry(ies) at the date of purchase.

(b) Prepare the journal entry(ies) at the end of the first year to record the payment and interest, assuming that the company uses the effective interest method.

(c) Prepare the journal entry(ies) at the end of the second year to record the payment and interest.

(d) Assuming that the equipment has a 10-year life and no residual value, prepare the journal entry that is needed to record depreciation in the first year. (The straight-line method is used.)

E10-16 **(Purchase of Equipment with Debt)** On September 1, 2011, Reta Corporation purchased equipment for **(LO 3)** $30,000 by signing a two-year note payable with a face value of $30,000 due on September 1, 2013. The going rate of interest for this level of risk was 8%. The company has a December 31 year end.

Instructions

(a) Calculate the cost of the equipment assuming the note is as follows:

  1. An 8% interest-bearing note, with interest due each September 1.

  2. A 2% interest-bearing note, with interest due each September 1.

  3. A non-interest-bearing note.

(b) Record all journal entries from September 1, 2011, to September 1, 2013, for the three notes in (a). Ignore depreciation of the equipment.

(CGA-Canada adapted)

E10-17 **(Asset Exchange, Monetary Transaction)** Cannondale Company purchased an electric wax melter on April **(LO 3)** 30, 2012, by trading in its old gas model and paying the balance in cash. The following data relate to the purchase:

List price of new melter	$15,800
Cash paid	10,000
Cost of old melter (five-year life, $700 residual value)	11,200
Accumulated depreciation on old melter (straight-line)	6,300
Second-hand market value of old melter	5,200

Instructions

Assuming that Cannondale's fiscal year ends on December 31 and depreciation has been recorded through December 31, 2011, prepare the journal entry(ies) that are necessary to record this exchange. Give reasons for the accounting treatment you used.

(LO 3) E10-18   (Non-Monetary Exchange) Starr Company Limited exchanged equipment that it uses in its manufacturing operations for similar equipment that is used in the operations of Ping Company Limited. Starr also paid Ping $1,500 in cash. The following information pertains to the exchange:

	Starr Co.	Ping Co.
Equipment (cost)	$31,000	$34,000
Accumulated depreciation	22,000	16,000
Fair value of equipment	15,500	17,000
Cash paid	1,500	

Instructions

(a) Prepare the journal entries to record the exchange on the books of both companies if the exchange is determined to have commercial substance.

(b) Repeat part (a), assuming the exchange is determined not to have commercial substance.

(c) List some of the factors that the accountant would need to consider in order to determine whether the transaction has commercial substance.

(LO 3) E10-19   (Non-Monetary Exchanges) Carver Inc. recently replaced a piece of automatic equipment at a net price of $4,000, f.o.b. factory. The replacement was necessary because one of Carver's employees had accidentally backed his truck into Carver's original equipment and made it inoperable. Because of the accident, the equipment had no resale value to anyone and had to be scrapped. Carver's insurance policy provided for a replacement of its equipment and paid the price of the new equipment directly to the new equipment manufacturer, minus the deductible amount paid to the manufacturer by Carver. The $4,000 that Carver paid was the amount of the deductible that it has to pay on any single claim on its insurance policy. The new equipment represents the same value in use to Carver. The used equipment had originally cost $65,000. It also had a book value of $45,000 at the time of the accident and a second-hand market value of $50,800 before the accident, based on recent transactions involving similar equipment. Freight and installation charges for the new equipment cost Carver an additional $1,100 cash.

Instructions

(a) Prepare the general journal entry to record the transaction to replace the equipment that was destroyed in the accident.

(b) Repeat part (a), but assume that the new equipment will result in significant savings to Carver since the new equipment is more efficient and requires less staff time to operate.

(LO 3) E10-20   (Non-Monetary Exchanges) Jamil Jonas is an accountant in public practice. Not long ago, Jamil struck a deal with his neighbour Ralph to prepare Ralph's business income tax and GST returns for 2011 in exchange for Ralph's services as a landscaper. Ralph provided labour and used his own equipment to perform landscaping services for Jamil's personal residence for which he would normally charge $500. Jamil would usually charge $650 for the number of hours spent completing Ralph's returns but considers the transaction well worth it since he really dislikes doing his own landscaping.

Instructions

How would each party record this transaction? Prepare the journal entries for both Jamil's and Ralph's companies.

(LO 3) E10-21   (Government Assistance) Lightstone Equipment Ltd. wanted to expand into New Brunswick and was impressed by the provincial government's grant program for new industry. After being sure that it would qualify for the grant program, it purchased property in downtown Saint John on June 15, 2011. The property cost $235,000 and Lightstone spent the next two months gutting the building and reconstructing the two floors to meet the company's needs. The building has a useful life of 20 years and an estimated residual value of $65,000. In late August, the company moved into the building and began operations. Additional information follows:

1. The property was assessed at $195,000, with $145,000 allocated to the land.

2. Architectural drawings and engineering fees related to the construction cost $18,000.

3. The company paid $17,000 to the contractor for gutting the building and $108,400 for construction. Lightstone expects that these improvements will last for the remainder of the life of the building.

4. The provincial government contributed $75,000 toward the building costs.

Instructions

(a) Assuming that the company uses the cost reduction method to account for government assistance, answer the following:

1. What is the cost of the building on Lightstone Equipment's balance sheet at August 31, 2011, its fiscal year end?

2. What is the effect of this capital asset on the company's income statement for the company's year ended August 31, 2012?

(b) Assuming the company uses the deferral method to account for government assistance, answer the following:

1. What is the cost of the building on Lightstone Equipment's balance sheet at August 31, 2011?

2. What is the effect of this capital asset on the company's income statement for the company's year ended August 31, 2012?

(c) Compare the balance sheet and income statement presentations for the two alternative treatments for government assistance for the fiscal year ended August 31, 2012.

Digging Deeper

E10-22 (Measurement after Acquisition—Revaluation Model) A partial balance sheet of Bluewater Ltd. on December 31, 2010, showed the following property, plant, and equipment assets after recording depreciation for that fiscal year: **(LO 6)**

Building—Structure	$300,000	
Less: accumulated depreciation	100,000	$200,000
Manufacturing equipment	$120,000	
Less: accumulated depreciation	40,000	80,000

The company has adopted the revaluation model for its building structure and equipment. Bluewater uses straight-line depreciation for its building structure (remaining useful life of 20 years, no residual value) and for its manufacturing equipment (remaining useful life of 8 years, no residual value). The use of the revaluation model has resulted in the recognition in prior periods of an asset revaluation surplus for the building structure of $14,000. Bluewater aggregates all of the assets accounted for under the revaluation model into one revaluation surplus account. On December 31, 2010, an independent appraiser assessed the fair value of the building structure to be $160,000 and that of the equipment to be $90,000.

Instructions

(a) Prepare the necessary general journal entry(ies), if any, to revalue the building and the manufacturing equipment as at December 31, 2010.

(b) Prepare the entries to record depreciation expense for the year ended December 31, 2011.

E10-23 (Measurement after Acquisition—Revaluation Model) On January 1, 2011, ABC Company acquires a building at a cost of $100,000. The building is expected to have a 25-year life and no residual value. The asset is accounted for under the revaluation model and revaluations are carried out every three years. On December 31, 2013, the fair value of the building is appraised at $90,000, and on December 31, 2016, its fair value is $75,000. **(LO 6)**

Instructions

(Round to the nearest dollar in all calculations.)

(a) Prepare the entry(ies) required on December 31, 2011.

(b) Prepare the entry(ies) required on December 31, 2012.

(c) Prepare the entry(ies) required on December 31, 2013.

(d) Prepare the entry(ies) required on December 31, 2014.

(e) Prepare the entry(ies) required on December 31, 2016.

E10-24 (Measurement after Acquisition—Fair Value Model versus Cost Model) Plaza Holdings Inc., a listed company in Canada, ventured into construction of a mega shopping mall in Edmonton, which is rated as the largest shopping mall in North America. The company's board of directors, after much market research, decided that instead of selling the shopping mall to a local investor who had approached them several times during the construction period with excellent offers that he steadily increased during the year of construction, the company would hold this property for the purposes of capital appreciation and earning rental income from mall tenants. Plaza Holdings retained the services of a real estate company to find and attract many important retailers to rent space in the shopping mall, and within months of completion at the end of 2011, the shopping mall was fully occupied. **(LO 5, 7)**

According to the company's accounting department, the total construction cost of the shopping mall was $50 million. The company used an independent appraiser to determine the mall's fair value annually. According to the appraisal, the fair values of the shopping mall at the end of 2011 and at each subsequent year end were:

2011	$50 million
2012	$60 million
2013	$63 million
2014	$58 million

The independent appraiser felt that the useful life of the shopping mall was 20 years and its residual value was $5 million.

Instructions

Describe the impact on the company's income statement and prepare the necessary journal entries for 2012, 2013, and 2014 if it decides to treat the shopping mall as an investment property under IAS 40:

(a) Using the fair value model.

(b) Using the cost model.

Note that the mall's rental income and expenses would be the same under both options, and thus can be omitted from the analysis for this exercise.

(LO 5, 7) **E10-25   (Measurement after Acquisition—Fair Value Model)** Nevine Corporation owns and manages a small 10-store shopping centre and classifies the shopping centre as an investment property. Nevine has a May 31 year end and initially recognized the property at its acquisition cost of $10.8 million on June 2, 2010. The acquisition cost consisted of the purchase price of $10 million, costs to survey and transfer the property of $500,000 and legal fees for the acquisition of the property of $300,000. Nevine determines that approximately 25% of the shopping centre's value is attributable to the land, with the remainder attributable to the building. The following fair values are determined:

Date	Fair Value
May 31, 2011	$10,500,000
May 31, 2012	$10,400,000
May 31, 2013	$11,000,000

Nevine expects the shopping centre building to have a 35-year useful life and a residual value of $1.1 million. Nevine uses the straight-line method for depreciation.

Instructions

(a) Assume that Nevine decides to apply the cost model. What journal entries, if any, are required each year, and how will the investment property be reported on each year-end balance sheet?

(b) Assume that Nevine decides to apply the fair value model. Prepare the journal entries, if any, required at each year end. In addition, explain how the property would be reported if Nevine prepared a balance sheet shortly after acquisition in 2010.

(LO 8) **E10-26   (Analysis of Subsequent Expenditures)** On January 1, 2011, the accounting records of Robinson Limited included a debit balance of $15 million in the building account and of $12 million in the related accumulated depreciation account. The building was purchased in January 1971 for $15 million, and was estimated to have a 50-year useful life with no residual value. Robinson uses the straight-line depreciation method for all its property, plant, and equipment. During 2011, the following expenditures relating to the building were made:

1. The original roof of the building was removed and replaced with a new roof. The old roof cost $1 million and the new roof cost $2.5 million. It is expected to have a 15-year useful life.

2. The ongoing frequent repairs on the building during the year cost $57,000.

3. The building's old heating system was replaced with a new one. The new heating system cost $700,000 and is estimated to have a seven-year useful life and no residual value. The cost of the old heating system is unknown.

4. A natural gas explosion caused $44,000 of damage to the building. This major repair did not change the estimated useful life of the building.

Instructions

Prepare the journal entries to record the expenditures related to the building during 2011.

(CGA-Canada adapted)

E10-27 **(Analysis of Subsequent Expenditures)** The following transactions occurred during 2011. Assume that (LO 8) depreciation of 10% per year is charged on all machinery and 5% per year on buildings, on a straight-line basis, with no estimated residual value. Assume also that depreciation is charged for a full year on all fixed assets that are acquired during the year, and that no depreciation is charged on fixed assets that are disposed of during the year.

Jan. 30	A building that cost $132,000 in 1994 was torn down to make room for a new building structure. The wrecking contractor was paid $5,100 and was permitted to keep all materials salvaged.
Mar. 10	A new part costing $2,900 was purchased and added to a machine that was purchased in 2009 for $16,000. The new part replaced an original machine part, and resulted in a 25% increase in the efficiency of the equipment. The old part's cost was not separable from the original machine's cost.
Mar. 20	A gear broke on a machine that cost $9,000 in 2006, and the gear was replaced at a cost of $85. The replacement does not extend the machine's useful life.
May 18	A special base that was installed for a machine in 2005 when the machine was purchased had to be replaced at a cost of $5,500 because of defective workmanship on the original base. The cost of the machinery was $14,200 in 2005. The cost of the base was $3,500, and this amount was charged to the Machinery account in 2005.
June 23	One of the buildings was repainted at a cost of $6,900. It had not been painted since it was constructed in 2007.

Instructions

(a) Prepare general journal entries for the transactions. (Round to nearest dollar.)

(b) Assume that on March 20, the gear replacement extends the machine's useful life. How would your journal entry change?

E10-28 **(Analysis of Subsequent Expenditures)** Plant assets often require expenditures subsequent to acquisition. It (LO 8) is important that they be accounted for properly. Any errors will affect both the balance sheets and income statements for several years.

Instructions

For each of the following items, indicate whether the expenditure should be capitalized (C) or expensed (E) in the period when it was incurred:

1. _____ A betterment
2. _____ Replacement of a minor broken part on a machine
3. _____ An expenditure that increases an existing asset's useful life
4. _____ An expenditure that increases the efficiency and effectiveness of a productive asset but does not increase its residual value
5. _____ An expenditure that increases the efficiency and effectiveness of a productive asset and its residual value
6. _____ An expenditure that increases a productive asset's output quality
7. _____ An overhaul to a machine that increases its fair market value and its production capacity by 30% without extending the machine's useful life
8. _____ Ordinary repairs
9. _____ A major overhaul
10. _____ Interest on borrowing that is necessary to finance a major overhaul of machinery that extends its life
11. _____ An expenditure that results in a 10%-per-year production cost saving
12. _____ Costs of a major overhaul that brings the asset's condition back to "new," with no change in the estimated useful life

*E10-29 **(Capitalization of Borrowing Costs)** On December 31, 2010, Omega Inc. borrowed $3 million at 12% (LO 2, 10) payable annually to finance the construction of a new building. In 2011, the company made the following expenditures related to this building structure (unless otherwise noted): March 1, $360,000; June 1, $600,000; July 1, $1.5 million (of which $400,000 was for the roof); December 1, $1.5 million (of which $700,000 was for the building services including wiring, heating, air conditioning, and plumbing). Additional information follows:

1. Other debt outstanding:

   $4-million, 10-year, 13% bond, dated December 31, 2004, with interest payable annually

   $1.6-million, six-year, 10% note, dated December 31, 2008, with interest payable annually

2. The March 1, 2011, expenditure included land costs of $150,000.

3. Interest revenue earned in 2011 on the unused idle construction loan amounted to $49,000.

Instructions

(a) Determine the interest amount that could be capitalized in 2011 in relation to the building construction.

(b) Prepare the journal entry to record the capitalization of borrowing costs and the recognition of interest expense, if any, at December 31, 2011.

(LO 2, 10) *E10-30   **(Capitalization of Borrowing Costs)** The following three situations involve the capitalization of borrowing costs.

Situation 1

On January 1, 2011, Oksana Inc. signed a fixed-price contract to have Builder Associates construct a major head office facility at a cost of $4 million. It was estimated that it would take three years to complete the project. Also on January 1, 2011, to finance the construction cost, Oksana borrowed $4 million that is repayable in 10 annual instalments of $400,000, plus interest at the rate of 10%. During 2011, Oksana made deposit and progress payments totalling $1.5 million under the contract; and the weighted-average amount of accumulated expenditures was $800,000 for the year. The excess amount of borrowed funds was invested in short-term securities, from which Oksana realized investment income of $25,000.

Situation 2

During 2011, Midori Ito Corporation constructed and manufactured certain assets and incurred the following interest cost in connection with these activities:

Borrowing Costs Incurred	
Warehouse constructed for Ito's own use	$30,000
Special-order machine for sale to unrelated customer, produced according to customer's specifications	9,000
Inventories routinely manufactured, produced on a repetitive basis	8,000

All of these assets required an extended time period for completion.

Situation 3

Fleming, Inc. has a fiscal year ending April 30. On May 1, 2011, Fleming borrowed $10 million at 11% to finance construction of its own building. Repayments of the loan are to begin the month after the building's completion. During the year ended April 30, 2012, expenditures for the partially completed structure totalled $7 million. These expenditures were incurred evenly throughout the year. Interest that was earned on the part of the loan that was not expended amounted to $650,000 for the year.

Instructions

(a) For situation 1, what amount should Oksana report as capitalized borrowing costs at December 31, 2011?

(b) For situation 2, assuming the effect of interest capitalization is material, what is the total amount of borrowing costs to be capitalized?

(c) For situation 3, how much should be shown as capitalized interest on Fleming's financial statements at April 30, 2012?

(CPA adapted)

(LO 2, 10) *E10-31   **(Capitalization of Borrowing Costs)** In early February 2011, Huey Corp. began construction of an addition to its head office building that is expected to take 18 months to complete. The following 2011 expenditures relate to the addition:

Feb. 1	Payment #1 to contractor	$120,000
Mar. 1	Payment to architect	24,000
July 1	Payment #2 to contractor	60,000
Dec. 1	Payment #3 to contractor	180,000
Dec. 31	Asset carrying amount	$384,000

On February 1, Huey issued a $100,000 three-year note payable at a rate of 12% to finance most of the initial payment to the contractor. No other asset-specific debt was entered into. Details of other interest-bearing debt during the period are provided in the table below:

Other debt instruments outstanding—2011	Principal amount
7% 10-year bonds, issued June 15, 2005	$500,000
6% 12-year bonds, issued May 1, 2011	$300,000
9% 15-year bonds, issued May 1, 1996, matured May 1, 2011	$300,000

Huey's fiscal year end is December 31.

Instructions

What amount of interest should be capitalized according to IAS 23?

Problems

P10-1 At December 31, 2010, certain accounts included in the property, plant, and equipment section of Golden Corporation's balance sheet had the following balances:

Land	$310,000
Buildings—Structure	883,000
Leasehold Improvements	705,000
Machinery and Equipment	845,000

During 2011, the following transactions occurred:

1. Land site No. 621 was acquired for $800,000 plus a commission of $47,000 to the real estate agent. Costs of $33,500 were incurred to clear the land. In clearing the land, topsoil and gravel were recovered and sold for $11,000.

2. Land site No. 622, which had a building on it, was acquired for $560,000. The closing statement indicated that the land's assessed tax value was $309,000 and the building value's was $102,000. Shortly after acquisition, the building was demolished at a cost of $28,000. A new building was constructed for $340,000 plus the following costs:

Excavation fees	$38,000
Architectural design fees	15,000
Building permit fee	2,500
"Green roof" design and construction (to be retrofitted every seven years)	36,000
Imputed interest on funds used during construction (share financing)	8,500

The building was completed and occupied on September 30, 2011.

3. A third tract of land (No. 623) was acquired for $265,000 and was put on the market for resale.

4. During December 2011, costs of $89,000 were incurred to improve leased office space. The related lease will terminate on December 31, 2013, and is not expected to be renewed.

5. A group of new machines was purchased under a royalty agreement. The terms of the agreement require Golden Corporation to pay royalties based on the units of production for the machines. The machines' invoice price was $111,000; freight costs were $3,300; installation costs were $3,600; and royalty payments for 2011 were $15,300.

Instructions

(a) Prepare a detailed analysis of the changes in each of the following balance sheet accounts for 2011: Land, Leasehold Improvements, Buildings—Structure, Buildings—Roof, and Machinery and Equipment. Ignore the related accumulated depreciation accounts.

(b) List the items in the situation that were not used to determine the answer to part (a) above, and indicate where, or if, these items should be included in Golden's financial statements.

(c) Using the terminology from the conceptual framework in Chapter 2, explain why the items in part (b) were not included in the accounts Land, Leasehold Improvements, Buildings (the Structure and Roof accounts), and Machinery and Equipment.

(AICPA adapted)

DD

Digging Deeper

P10-2 Selected accounts included in the property, plant, and equipment section of Webb Corporation's balance sheet at December 31, 2010, had the following balances:

Land	$ 300,000
Land Improvements	140,000
Buildings	1,100,000
Machinery and Equipment	960,000

During 2011, the following transactions occurred:

1. A tract of land was acquired for $150,000 as a potential future building site.

2. A plant facility consisting of land and a building was acquired from Knorman Corp. in exchange for 20,000 of Webb's common shares. On the acquisition date, Webb's shares had a closing market price of $37 per share on the Toronto Stock Exchange. The plant facility was carried on Knorman's books at $110,000 for land and $320,000 for the building at the exchange date. Current appraised values for the land and building, respectively, are $230,000 and $690,000.

3. Items of machinery and equipment were purchased at a total cost of $400,000. Additional costs were incurred as follows:

Freight and unloading	$13,000
Sales taxes	20,000
GST	24,000
Installation	26,000

4. Expenditures totalling $95,000 were made for new parking lots, streets, and sidewalks at the corporation's various plant locations. These expenditures had an estimated useful life of 15 years.

5. A machine that cost $80,000 on January 1, 2003, was scrapped on June 30, 2011. Double-declining-balance depreciation had been recorded based on a 10-year life.

6. A machine was sold for $20,000 on July 1, 2011. Its original cost was $44,000 on January 1, 2008, and it was depreciated on the straight-line basis over an estimated useful life of seven years, assuming a residual value of $2,000.

Instructions

(a) Prepare a detailed analysis of the changes in each of the following balance sheet accounts for 2011: Land, Land Improvements, Buildings, and Machinery and Equipment. (Hint: Ignore the related accumulated depreciation accounts.)

(b) List the items in the transactions above that were not used to determine the answer to (a), and show the relevant amounts and supporting calculations in good form for each item. In addition, indicate where, or if, these items should be included in Webb's financial statements.

Digging Deeper

(c) How will the land in item 1 be accounted for when it is used as a building site?

(AICPA adapted)

P10-3 Kiev Corp. was incorporated on January 2, 2011, but was unable to begin manufacturing activities until July 1, 2011, because new factory facilities were not completed until that date. The Land and Building account at December 31, 2011, was as follows:

Jan. 31, 2011	Land and building	$166,000
Feb. 28, 2011	Cost of removal of building	9,800
May 1, 2011	Partial payment of new construction	60,000
May 1, 2011	Legal fees paid	3,770
June 1, 2011	Second payment on new construction	40,000
June 1, 2011	Insurance premium	2,280
June 1, 2011	Special tax assessment	4,000
June 30, 2011	General expenses	36,300
July 1, 2011	Final payment on new construction	10,000
July 1, 2011	Payment for plumbing, furnace, air conditioning system	30,000
Dec. 31, 2011	Asset write-up	43,800
		405,950
Dec. 31, 2011	Depreciation for 2011 at 1%	4,060
	Account balance	$401,890

The following additional information needs to be considered:

1. To acquire land and a building, the company paid $80,400 cash and 800 of its no par value, $8, cumulative preferred shares. The fair market value was $107 per share.

2. The costs for removing old buildings amounted to $9,800, and the demolition company kept all the building materials.

3. Legal fees covered the following:

Cost of organization	$ 610
Examination of title covering purchase of land	1,300
Legal work in connection with construction contract	1,860
	$3,770

4. The insurance premium covered the building for a two-year term beginning May 1, 2011.

5. The special tax assessment covered street improvements that are permanent in nature.

6. General expenses covered the following for the period from January 2, 2011, to June 30, 2011:

President's salary	$32,100
Plant superintendent's wages covering supervision of new building	4,200
	$36,300

7. Because of a general increase in construction costs after entering into the building contract, the board of directors increased the building's value by $43,800. It believed that such an increase was justified to reflect the current market at the time when the building was completed. Retained Earnings was credited for this amount.

8. The estimated life of the building structure is 50 years. The depreciation for 2011 on the building structure was 1% of the asset value (1% of $405,950, or $4,060). The estimated useful life of the building services (heating system, plumbing, air conditioning) is 20 years. No depreciation has been recorded on the building services.

Instructions

Prepare the entries to reallocate the proper balances into the Land, Building, and Accumulated Depreciation accounts at December 31, 2011.

(AICPA adapted)

P10-4   On June 28, 2011, in relocating to a new town, Kerr Corp. purchased a property consisting of two hectares of land and an unused building for $225,000 plus taxes in arrears of $4,500. The company paid a real estate broker's commission of $12,000 and legal fees on the purchase transaction of $6,000. The closing statement indicated that the assessed values for tax purposes were $175,000 for the land and $35,000 for the building. Shortly after acquisition, the building was demolished at a cost of $24,000.

Kerr Corp. then entered into a $1.3-million fixed-price contract with Maliseet Builders, Inc. on August 1, 2011, for the construction of an office building on this site. The building was completed and occupied on April 29, 2012, as was a separate maintenance building that was constructed by Kerr's employees. Additional costs related to the property included:

Plans, specifications, and blueprints	$25,000
Architects' fees for design and supervision	82,000
Landscaping	42,000
Extras on contract for upgrading of windows	46,000
External signage on the property	23,000
Advertisements in newspaper and on television announcing opening of the building	10,600
Gala opening party for customers, suppliers, and friends of Kerr	18,800
Costs of internal direct labour and materials for maintenance building	67,000
Allocated plant overhead based on direct labour hours worked on maintenance building	10,000
Allocated cost of executive time spent on project	54,000
Interest costs on debt incurred to pay contractor's progress billings up to building completion	63,000
Interest costs on short-term loan to finance maintenance building costs	3,200

As an incentive for Kerr to locate and build in the town, the municipality agreed not to charge its normal building permit fees of approximately $36,000. This amount was included in the $1.3-million contract fee. The building and the maintenance building are estimated to have a 40-year life from their dates of completion and will be depreciated using the straight-line method.

Kerr has an April 30 year end, and the company accountant is currently analyzing the new Building account that was set up to capture all the expenditures and credits explained above that relate to the property.

Instructions

(a) Prepare a schedule that identifies the costs that would be capitalized and included in the new Building account on the April 30, 2012 balance sheet, assuming the accountant wants to comply with private entity GAAP, but tends to be very conservative in nature; in other words, she does not want to overstate income or assets. Briefly justify your calculations. How would your answer change if Kerr were to comply with IFRS?

(b) Prepare a schedule that identifies the costs that would be capitalized and included in the new Building account on the April 30, 2012 balance sheet, assuming the accountant wants to comply with private entity GAAP, but is aware that Kerr needs to report increased income to support a requested increase in its bank loan next month. Briefly justify your calculations.

(c) Comment on the difference in results for (a) and (b) above. Calculate the total expenses related to the building under both scenarios. What else should be considered in determining the amount to be capitalized?

P10-5 Vidi Corporation made the following purchases related to its property, plant, and equipment during its fiscal year ended December 31, 2011. The company uses the straight-line method of depreciation for all its capital assets.

1. In early January, Vidi issued 140,000 common shares with a market value of $6 per share (based on a recent sale of 1,000 shares on the Toronto Stock Exchange) in exchange for property consisting of land and a warehouse. The company's property management division estimated that the market value of the land and warehouse were $600,000 and $300,000, respectively. The seller had advertised a price of $860,000 or best offer for the land and warehouse in a commercial retail magazine. Vidi paid a local real estate broker a finder's fee of $35,000.

2. On March 31, the company acquired equipment on credit. The terms were a $7,000 cash down payment plus payments of $5,000 at the end of each of the next two years. The implicit interest rate was 12%. The equipment's list price was $17,000. Additional costs that were incurred to install the equipment included $1,000 to tear down and replace a wall, and $1,500 to rearrange existing equipment to make room for the new equipment. An additional $500 was spent to repair the equipment after it was dropped during installation.

During the year, the following events also occurred:

3. A new motor was purchased for $50,000 for a large grinding machine (original cost of the machine, $350,000; accumulated depreciation at the replacement date, $100,000). The motor will not improve the quality or quantity of production; however, it will extend the grinding machine's useful life from the current 8 years to 10 years.

4. On September 30, the company purchased a small building in a nearby town for $125,000 to use as a display and sales location. The municipal tax assessment indicated that the property was assessed for $95,000, which consists of $68,000 for the building and $27,000 for the land. The building had been empty for six months and required considerable maintenance work before it could be used. The following costs were incurred in 2011: previous owner's unpaid property taxes on the property for the previous year, $900; current year's (2011) taxes, $1,000; reshingling of roof, $2,200; cost of hauling refuse out of the basement, $230; cost of spray cleaning the outside walls and washing windows, $750; cost of painting inside walls, $3,170; and incremental fire and liability insurance for 15 months, $940.

5. The company completely overhauled the plumbing system in its factory for $55,000. The original plumbing costs were not known.

6. On June 30, the company replaced a freezer with a new one that cost $20,000 cash (market value of $21,000 for the new freezer less trade-in value of old freezer). The cost of the old freezer was $15,000. At the beginning of the year, the company had depreciated 60% of the old freezer; that is, 10% per year of use.

7. The company painted the factory exterior at a cost of $12,000.

Instructions

(a) Prepare the journal entries that are required to record the acquisitions and/or costs incurred in the above transactions.

(b) If there are alternative methods to account for any of the transactions, indicate what the alternatives are and your reason for choosing the method that you used.

*P10-6 Inglewood Landscaping began constructing a new plant on December 1, 2011. On this date, the company purchased a parcel of land for $184,000 cash. In addition, it paid $2,000 in surveying costs and $4,000 for title transfer fees. An old dwelling on the premises was demolished at a cost of $3,000, with $1,000 being received from the sale of materials.

Architectural plans were also formalized on December 1, 2011, when the architect was paid $30,000. The necessary building permits costing $3,000 were obtained from the city and paid for on December 1 as well. The excavation work began during the first week in December and payments were made to the contractor as follows:

Date of Payment	Amount of Payment
Mar. 1	$240,000
May 1	360,000
July 1	60,000

The building was completed on July 1, 2012.

To finance the plant construction, Inglewood borrowed $600,000 from a bank on December 1, 2011. Inglewood had no other borrowings. The $600,000 was a 10-year loan bearing interest at 10%.

Instructions

(a) Calculate the balance in each of the following accounts at December 31, 2011, and December 31, 2012. Assume that Inglewood complies with IFRS.

1. Land

2. Buildings

3. Interest Expense

(b) Identify what the effects would be on Inglewood's financial statements for the years ending December 31, 2011 and 2012, if its policy was to expense all interest costs as they are incurred.

*P10-7 Wordcrafters Inc. is a book distributor that had been operating in its original facility since 1985. The increase in certification programs and continuing education requirements in several professions has contributed to an annual growth rate of 15% for Wordcrafters since 2005. Wordcrafters' original facility became obsolete by early 2011 because of the increased sales volume and the fact that Wordcrafters now carries audio books and DVDs in addition to books.

On June 1, 2011, Wordcrafters contracted with Favre Construction to have a new building constructed for $5 million on land owned by Wordcrafters. Wordcrafters made the following payments to Favre Construction:

Date	Amount
July 30, 2011	$1,200,000
Jan. 30, 2012	1,500,000
May 30, 2012	1,300,000
Total payments	$4,000,000

Construction was completed and the building was ready for occupancy on May 27, 2012. Wordcrafters had no new borrowings directly associated with the new building but had the following debt outstanding at May 31, 2012, the end of its fiscal year:

14½%, five-year note payable of $2 million, dated April 1, 2008, with interest payable annually on April 1

12%, 10-year bond issue of $3 million sold at par on June 30, 2004, with interest payable annually on June 30

The company is an international distributor and thus complies with IFRS.

Instructions

(a) Calculate the weighted-average accumulated expenditures on Wordcrafters' new building during the capitalization period.

(b) Calculate the avoidable interest on Wordcrafters' new building.

(c) Wordcrafters Inc. capitalized some of its interest costs for the year ended May 31, 2012:

1. Identify the item(s) relating to interest costs that must be disclosed in Wordcrafters' financial statements.

2. Calculate the amount of the item(s) that must be disclosed.

(CMA adapted)

P10-8 The production manager of Chesley Corporation wants to acquire a different brand of machine by exchanging the machine that it currently uses in operations for the brand of equipment that others in the industry are using. The brand being used by other companies is more comfortable for the operators because it has different attachments that allow the operators to adjust the controls for a variety of arm and hand positions. The production manager has received the following offers from other companies:

1. Secord Corp. offered to give Chesley a similar machine plus $23,000 in exchange for Chesley's machine.

2. Bateman Corp. offered a straight exchange for a similar machine with essentially the same value in use.

3. Shripad Corp. offered to exchange a similar machine with the same value in use, but wanted $8,000 cash in addition to Chesley's machine.

The production manager has also contacted Ansong Corporation, a dealer in machines. To obtain a new machine from Ansong, Chesley would have to pay $93,000 and also trade in its old machine. Chesley's equipment has a cost of $160,000, a net book value of $110,000, and a fair value of $92,000. The following table shows the information needed to record the machine exchange between the companies:

	Secord	Bateman	Shripad	Ansong
Machine cost	$120,000	$147,000	$160,000	$130,000
Accumulated depreciation	45,000	71,000	75,000	–0–
Fair value	69,000	92,000	100,000	185,000

Digging Deeper

Instructions

(a) For each of the four independent situations, assume that Chesley accepts the offer. Prepare the journal entries to record the exchange on the books of each company. (Round to the nearest dollar.) When you need to make assumptions for the entries, state the assumptions so that you can justify the entries.

(b) Suggest scenarios or situations where different entries would be appropriate. Prepare the entries for these situations.

P10-9 During the current year, Garrison Construction trades in two relatively new small cranes (cranes no. 6RT and S79) for a larger crane that Garrison expects will be more useful for the particular contracts that the company has to fulfill over the next couple of years. The new crane is acquired from Pisani Manufacturing, which has agreed to take the smaller equipment as trade-ins and also pay $17,500 cash to Garrison. The new crane cost Pisani $165,000 to manufacture and is classified as inventory. The following information is available:

	Garrison Const.	Pisani Mfg.
Cost of crane #6RT	$130,000	
Cost of crane #S79	120,000	
Accumulated depreciation, #6RT	15,000	
Accumulated depreciation, #S79	18,000	
Fair value, #6RT	120,000	
Fair value, #S79	87,500	
Fair market value of new crane		$190,000
Cash paid		17,500
Cash received	17,500	

Instructions

(a) Assume that this exchange is considered to have commercial substance. Prepare the journal entries on the books of (1) Garrison Construction and (2) Pisani Manufacturing. Pisani uses a perpetual inventory system.

(b) Assume that this exchange is considered to lack commercial substance. Prepare the journal entries on the books of (1) Garrison Construction and (2) Pisani Manufacturing. Pisani uses a perpetual inventory system.

(c) Assume that you have been asked to recommend whether it is more appropriate for the transaction to have commercial substance or not to have commercial substance. Develop arguments that you could present to the controllers of both Garrison Construction and Pisani Manufacturing to justify both alternatives. Which arguments are more persuasive?

P10-10 On July 1, 2011, Lucas Ltd. acquired assets from Jared Ltd. The assets had the following fair values on the transaction date:

Manufacturing plant (building #1)	$400,000
Storage warehouse (building #2)	210,000
Machinery and equipment (in building #1)	75,000
Machinery and equipment (in building #2)	45,000

The buildings are owned by the company and the land that the buildings are situated on is owned by the local municipality and is provided free of charge to the owner of the buildings as a stimulus to encourage local employment.

In exchange for the acquisition of these assets, Lucas Ltd. issued 146,000 common shares with a fair value of $5 per share. Lucas Ltd. decided to measure the buildings at fair value and the machinery and equipment at cost. At the time of acquisition, both buildings were considered to have an expected remaining useful life of 10 years, the machinery in building #1 was expected to have a remaining useful life of 3 years, and the machinery in building #2 was expected to have a useful life of 9 years. Lucas uses straight-line depreciation.

At December 31, 2011, Lucas's fiscal year end, Lucas recorded the correct depreciation amounts for the six months that the assets were in use. An independent appraisal concluded that the assets had the following fair values:

Manufacturing plant (building #1)	$387,000
Storage warehouse (building #2)	178,000

At December 31, 2012, Lucas once again retained an independent appraiser and determined that the fair value of the assets was:

Manufacturing plant (building #1)	$340,000
Storage warehouse (building #2)	160,000

Instructions

(a) Prepare the journal entries required for 2011 and 2012.

(b) Assume that the asset revaluation surplus for the buildings was prepared based on a class-by-class basis rather than on an individual asset basis as required by IAS 16. Prepare the journal entries required for 2011 and 2012 that relate to the buildings (ignore the machinery accounts since they are accounted for using the cost model).

(c) Comment on the effects on the 2011 income statement with respect to the different revaluation methods presented in parts (a) and (b).

P10-11   Zhang Mining Corp. received a $760,000 low bid from a reputable manufacturer for the construction of special production equipment that Zhang needs as part of its expansion program. However, because Zhang's own plant was not operating at capacity, it decided to use the space available and construct the equipment itself. Zhang recorded the following production costs related to the construction:

Services of consulting engineer	$ 40,000
Work subcontracted	36,000
Materials	280,000
Plant labour normally assigned to production	152,000
Plant labour normally assigned to maintenance	172,000
Total	$680,000

Management prefers to record the equipment cost under the incremental cost method. Approximately 40% of the company's production is devoted to government supply contracts that are all based in some way on cost. The contracts require that any self-constructed equipment be allocated its full share of all costs that are related to its construction.

The following information is also available:

1. The production labour was for partial fabrication of the plant equipment. Skilled personnel were required and were assigned from other projects. The maintenance labour represents idle time of non-production plant employees who would have stayed on the payroll whether or not their services were used.

2. Payroll taxes and employee fringe benefits are approximately 35% of labour costs and are included in the manufacturing overhead cost. Total manufacturing overhead for the year was $6,084,000, which included the $172,000 of maintenance labour that was used to construct the equipment.

3. Manufacturing overhead is approximately 60% variable and is applied based on production labour costs. Production labour costs for the year for the corporation's normal products totalled $8,286,000.

4. General and administrative expenses include $27,000 of allocated executive salary cost and $13,750 of postage, telephone, supplies, and miscellaneous expenses that have been directly identified with the equipment construction.

Instructions

(a) Prepare a schedule that calculates the amount that should be reported as the full cost of the constructed equipment to meet the government contract requirements. Any supporting calculations should be in good form.

(b) Prepare a schedule calculating the incremental cost of the constructed equipment.

(c) What is the greatest amount that should be capitalized as the equipment cost? Why?

(AICPA adapted)

P10-12   Adamski Corporation manufactures ballet shoes and is experiencing a period of sustained growth. In an effort to expand its production capacity to meet the increased demand for its product, the company recently made several acquisitions of plant and equipment. Tanya Mullinger, newly hired with the title Capital Asset Accountant, requested that Walter Kaster, Adamski's controller, review the following transactions:

Transaction 1

On June 1, 2011, Adamski Corporation purchased equipment from Venghaus Corporation. Adamski issued a $20,000, four-year, non–interest-bearing note to Venghaus for the new equipment. Adamski will pay off the note in four equal instalments due at the end of each of the next four years. At the transaction date, the prevailing market interest rate for obligations of this nature was 10%. Freight costs of $425 and installation costs of $500 were incurred in completing this transaction. The new equipment qualifies for a $2,000 government grant.

Transaction 2

On December 1, 2011, Adamski purchased several assets of Haukap Shoes Inc., a small shoe manufacturer whose owner was retiring. The purchase amounted to $210,000 and included the assets in the following list. Adamski engaged the services of Tennyson Appraisal Inc., an independent appraiser, to determine the assets' fair market values, which are also provided.

	Haukap Book Value	Fair Market Value
Inventory	$ 60,000	$ 50,000
Land	40,000	80,000
Building	70,000	120,000
	$170,000	$250,000

During its fiscal year ended May 31, 2012, Adamski incurred $8,000 of interest expense in connection with the financing of these assets.

Transaction 3

On March 1, 2012, Adamski traded in four units of specialized equipment and paid an additional $25,000 cash for a technologically up-to-date machine that should do the same job as the other machines, but much more efficiently and profitably. The equipment that was traded in had a combined carrying amount of $35,000, as Adamski had recorded $45,000 of accumulated depreciation against these assets. Adamski's controller and the sales manager of the supplier company agreed that the new equipment had a fair value of $64,000.

Instructions

(a) Tangible capital assets such as land, buildings, and equipment receive special accounting treatment. Describe the major characteristics of these assets that differentiate them from other types of assets.

(b) For each of the three transactions described above, determine the value at which Adamski Corporation should record the acquired assets. Support your calculations with an explanation of the underlying rationale.

(c) The books of Adamski Corporation show the following additional transactions for the fiscal year ended May 31, 2012:

   1. Acquisition of a building for speculative purposes

   2. Purchase of a two-year insurance policy covering plant equipment

   3. Purchase of the rights for the exclusive use of a process used in the manufacture of ballet shoes

For each of these transactions, indicate whether the asset should be classified as an item of property, plant, and equipment. If it should be, explain why. If it should not, explain why not, and identify the proper classification.

(CMA adapted)

P10-13 Donovan Resources Group has been in its plant facility for 15 years. Although the plant is quite functional, numerous repair costs are incurred to keep it in good working order. The book value of the company's plant is currently $800,000, calculated as follows:

Original cost	$1,200,000
Accumulated depreciation	400,000
	$ 800,000

During the current year, the following expenditures were made to the plant:

(a) Because of increased demand for its product, the company increased its plant capacity by building a new addition at a cost of $270,000.

(b) The entire plant was repainted at a cost of $23,000.

(c) The roof was made of asbestos cement slate; for safety purposes, it was removed at a cost of $4,000 and replaced with a wood shingle roof at a cost of $61,000. The original roof's cost had been $40,000 and it was being depreciated over an expected life of 20 years.

(d) The electrical system was completely updated at a cost of $22,000. The cost of the old electrical system was not known. It is estimated that the building's useful life will not change as a result of this updating.

(e) A series of major repairs was made at a cost of $47,000, because parts of the wood structure were rotting. The cost of the old wood structure was not known. These extensive repairs are estimated to increase the building's useful life.

Instructions

Indicate how each of these transactions would be recorded in the accounting records.

Writing Assignments

WA10-1 Highstreet Inc. is a distributor of electronic equipment. In January 2009, the company purchased a new building for its warehousing and head office requirements for a total cost of $5 million. It is now August 27, 2009, and the company has just completed renovations costing an additional $2 million and will be moving in on August 31. During these eight months, the company was able to rent out a portion of the building to a company next door for storage. Net storage revenue of $100,000 was earned during this renovation period. The elevator has just been inspected for a total cost of $150,000 and the next inspection will occur in five years as required. Based on a property inspection that was completed prior to the purchase, the inspector reported that the roof would likely last another 7 years, and the heating and air conditioning system would likely have to be replaced in 10 years. The company has determined that the roof is worth about 10% of the total original cost of the building and the heating and air conditioning system is worth about 15%. The company expects the building's useful life will be 30 years.

Instructions

(a) Assuming Highstreet follows private entity GAAP, discuss how the costs of the building should be initially recorded. Also discuss how any additional subsequent costs should be recorded and the related depreciation costs.

(b) Assuming Highstreet follows IFRS, discuss how the costs of the building should be initially recorded. Also discuss how any additional subsequent costs should be recorded and the related depreciation.

WA10-2 Gomi Medical Labs, Inc. began operations five years ago producing a new type of instrument it hoped to sell to doctors, dentists, and hospitals. The demand for the new instrument was much higher than had been planned for, and the company was unable to produce enough of them to meet demand. The company was manufacturing its product on equipment that had been built at the start of its operations.

To meet demand, more efficient equipment was needed. The company decided to design and build the equipment because the equipment currently available on the market was unsuitable for producing this product.

In 2009, a section of the plant was devoted to developing the new equipment and special employees were hired. Within six months, a machine, developed at a cost of $714,000, increased production dramatically and reduced labour costs substantially. Thrilled by the new machine's success, the company built three more machines of the same type at a cost of $441,000 each.

Instructions

(a) In general, what costs should be capitalized for self-constructed equipment?

(b) Discuss whether the capitalized cost of self-constructed assets should include the following:

1. The increase in overhead that results from the company's own construction of its fixed assets

2. A proportionate share of overhead on the same basis as what is applied to goods that are manufactured for sale

(c) Discuss the proper accounting treatment of the $273,000 cost amount ($714,000 − $441,000) that was higher for the first machine than the cost of the subsequent machines.

WA10-3 Hotel Resort Limited is a company that builds world-class resorts in tourist areas around the globe. When the company decided to build a resort in Yellowknife, the federal government agreed to provide a forgivable loan in the amount of $50 million to help fund the construction of the tourist facilities anticipated to cost about $700 million. The loan will be forgiven provided the tourist facility is operated for at least 15 years. If the resort is closed or sold before 15 years have elapsed, the amount of the loan must be repaid in full, along with interest at the prevailing market rate.

In addition, the federal government also agreed to provide annual funding to cover 70% of the related costs of payroll and room and board for 50 summer students provided the students were hired to work for four full months. The company would receive this annual funding once it proved the costs incurred for these students.

Instructions

Prepare a memo that would be suitable to present to the Hotel Resort Limited board of directors in which you explain how the receipt of the government funding is expected to affect the company's reported total assets and earnings. Also, draft the related note disclosure that would be required.

WA10-4   You have two clients in the construction industry that are considering exchanging machinery with each other. Ames Construction has decided to market its services to clients who need major construction projects, but it has a significant inventory of equipment that is more appropriate for smaller home renovations. Jung Corp.'s strategic plan, on the other hand, has recently changed to focus on home renovations, additions, and repairs. Jung would like to sell off the equipment it used in constructing larger apartment buildings and condominiums over the past few years and acquire equipment that is more suitable for its new strategy. A deal has been reached between the owner-managers of both companies to exchange a group of machinery and equipment. The fair values determined for the equipment are reliable in both cases. The details of the transaction are as follows:

	Ames Construction	Jung Corp.
Original cost	$100,000	$150,000
Accumulated depreciation	40,000	80,000
Market value	85,000	95,000
Cash received (paid)	(10,000)	10,000

Instructions

Write a memo to the accountants of both Ames Construction and Jung Corp. with your recommendation on how this transaction should be recorded on the books of each company. If there are any choices available to them, identify what they are. Be sure to explain the rationale for your recommended treatment.

Ethics

WA10-5   A machine's invoice price is $40,000. Various other costs relating to the acquisition and installation of the machine—including transportation, electrical wiring, a special base, and so on—amount to $7,500. The machine has an estimated life of 10 years, with no residual value at the end of that period.

The owner-manager of the company that you work for as an accountant suggests that the incidental costs of $7,500 be charged to expense immediately for the following reasons:

- If the machine is ever sold, these costs cannot be recovered in the sale price.

- The inclusion of the $7,500 in the machinery account on the books will not necessarily result in a closer approximation of this asset's market price over the years, because demand and supply levels could change.

- Charging the $7,500 to expense immediately will reduce income taxes.

Instructions

Prepare a memo to the owner-manager that addresses each of the issues assuming that the company follows private entity GAAP.

(AICPA adapted)

WA10-6   Write a brief essay highlighting the differences between IFRS and accounting standards for private enterprises noted in this chapter, discussing the conceptual justification for each.

Case

Case Primer

Refer to the Case Primer to help you answer these cases.

CA10-1   Real Estate Investment Trust (RE) was created to hold hotel properties. RE currently holds 15 luxury and first-class hotels in Europe. The entity is structured as an investment trust, which means that the trust does not pay income taxes on the earnings from the assets that it holds directly; instead, income taxes are paid by the unitholders—those who own ownership units in the trust. The other key feature of the trust is that 85% to 90% of the distributable income is required to be paid to unitholders every year. The units of RE trade on the national stock exchange.

Distributable income is calculated as net income (according to GAAP) before special charges less a replacement reserve, which is an amount set aside to refurbish assets. RE distributed 127% and 112% of its distributable income in 2011 and 2010, respectively. Management calculates distributable income since this calculation is not defined by GAAP. As at the end of 2011, property and equipment was $1.7 billion compared with $1.9 billion in total assets. Net income for the year was $55 million.

According to the notes to the financial statements, RE accounts for its property, plant, and equipment at amortized cost.

Instructions

Assume the role of the entity's auditors, and discuss any financial reporting issues. RE changed over to IFRS in 2011.

Integrated Cases

(Hint: If there are issues here that are new, use the conceptual framework to help you support your analysis with solid reasoning.)

IC10-1 TransAlta Corporation (TC) is a power generation and wholesale marketing company. The company's goals were stated in its annual report as follows:

Real-World Emphasis

> Financial strength through a strong balance sheet, investment-grade credit ratings and a balanced approach to capital allocation.

Property, plant, and equipment consist of coal-fired, gas-fired, hydro, and renewable generation assets with a 2008 carrying value of $6 billion (total assets $7.48 billion). The following are excerpts from the notes to the financial statements:

Asset Retirement Obligations ("ARO")

The Corporation recognizes ARO in the period in which they are incurred if a reasonable estimate of a fair value can be determined. The associated asset retirement costs are capitalized as part of the carrying amount of the long-lived asset. The ARO liability is accrued over the estimated time period until settlement of the obligation and the asset is depreciated over the estimated useful life of the asset. Reclamation costs for mining assets are recognized on a unit-of-production basis. TransAlta has recorded an ARO for all generating facilities for which it is legally required to remove the facilities at the end of their useful lives and restore the plant and mine sites to their original condition. For some hydro facilities, the Corporation is required to remove the generating equipment, but is not legally required to remove the structures. TransAlta has recognized legal obligations arising from government legislation, written agreements between entities, and case law. The asset retirement liabilities are recognized when the ARO is incurred. Asset retirement liabilities for coal mines are incurred over time, as new areas are mined, and a portion of the liability is settled over time as areas are reclaimed prior to final pit reclamation.

Accounting for Emission Credits and Allowances

Purchased emission allowances are recorded on the balance sheet at historical cost and are carried at the lower of weighted average cost and net realizable value. Allowances granted to TransAlta or internally generated are recorded at nil. TransAlta records an emission liability on the balance sheet using the best estimate of the amount required to settle the Corporation's obligation in excess of government-established caps and targets. To the extent compliance costs are recoverable under the terms of contracts with third parties, these amounts are recognized as revenue in the period of recovery. Proprietary trading of emissions allowances that meet the definition of a derivative are accounted for using the fair value method of accounting.

Allowances that do not satisfy the criteria of a derivative are accounted for using the accrual method.

Subsequent Events – Sundance Unit 4 Derate

On Feb. 10, 2009, TransAlta reported the first quarter financial impact of an extended derate at Unit 4 of the Sundance thermal plant ("Unit 4"). The facility experienced an unplanned outage in December 2008 related to the failure of an induced draft ("ID") fan. At that time, Unit 4, which has a capacity of 406 MW, had been derated to approximately 205 MW. The repair of the ID fan components by the original equipment manufacturer took longer than planned, and therefore, Unit 4 did not return to full service until Feb. 23, 2009. As a result of the extended derate, first quarter production was reduced by 328 GWh and net income declined by $17 million. TransAlta has given notice of a High Impact Low Probability Event to the PPA (power purchase agreement) Buyer and the Balancing Pool, which if successful, will protect the Corporation from the financial loss and related penalties. The available penalties that TransAlta expects to recover in net income are anticipated to be $14 million.

Instructions

Adopt the role of a financial analyst and evaluate the different financial reporting choices that are available to the company for the above-noted items.

IC10-2   Iskra Vremec and Colin McFee are experienced scuba divers who have spent many years in the salvage business. About a year ago, they decided to start their own company to recover damaged and sunken vessels and their cargoes off the east coast of Canada. They incorporated Atlantic Explorations Limited (AEL) on February 1, 2010. Iskra (president) and Colin (vice-president) each own 30% of AEL's shares. The remaining 40% of the shares were purchased by a group of 10 investors who contributed $50,000 each so that AEL could acquire the necessary equipment and cover other start-up costs.

AEL carries on two types of activities. The first is a commercial salvage operation. The second is treasure hunting. To date, commercial salvage operations have generated all of AEL's revenues. The demand for these services is strong, and there are few competitors due to the unpredictable nature of the business and the long hours. Colin manages the commercial salvage operations. Customers pay in three instalments, including an upfront fee, a fee payable approximately midway through the contract, and a fee at the end once the items in question have been salvaged (found and brought to land). If the item is never found or AEL cannot bring the item to the surface and to land, then the final payment is not made.

Iskra spends most of her time locating and recovering underwater artifacts and, where possible, sunken treasure. Her research shows that numerous vessels carrying gold, silver, and other valuables to the "Old World" were wrecked off the shores of Nova Scotia. AEL has permits to investigate three target areas. As compensation for the permits, AEL agrees to remit 1% of the fair value of any treasure found. These funds are to be invested in the local economy by AEL (subject to government approval). The company also pays an upfront fee that allows it to search a given area. There has been a discovery in the first of these target areas.

It is now September 5, 2010. AEL has engaged your auditing firm to provide advice on the accounting for the ongoing operations and the discovery that AEL has just made. You (as audit manager) and Alex Green, the partner assigned to the engagement, met with Colin and Iskra.

During your meeting, Iskra said that she believes that finding treasure is like winning a lottery as all revenues would accrue to AEL and thus should be treated accordingly. If this discovery proves to be as substantial as preliminary results suggest, AEL will require additional financing of $1.5 million to acquire the equipment and on-shore laboratory, and lease a specially equipped vessel needed to salvage the wreck and its treasures. The bank has said that it is not willing to advance further funds. However, Iskra and Colin know of other individuals who are interested in investing in AEL.

AEL receives grants from the government to assist in the process of finding treasure and salvaging sunken vessels. Iskra and Colin have just found out that they are likely to receive a grant in connection with the recent discovery.

Instructions

Draft a memo for auditor Alex Green, analyzing all financial reporting issues and providing recommendations.

(CICA adapted)

Research and Financial Analysis

RA10-1 Magna International Inc.

Access the financial statements of Magna International Inc. for the company's year ended December 31, 2008. These are available at www.sedar.com or the company's website. Review the information that is provided and answer the following questions about the company.

Real-World Emphasis

Instructions

(a) What business is Magna International in?

(b) What types of tangible capital assets does Magna report? Do these assets form a significant portion of the company's total assets at December 31, 2008?

(c) Identify all the accounting policies disclosed in the notes to the financial statements that explain how the company determines the cost of its property, plant, and equipment.

(d) How much did Magna spend on new capital asset acquisitions in 2007 and 2008 (excluding business acquisitions)? Identify where the company obtained the funds to invest in these additions.

(e) Explain how the company accounts for government assistance.

RA10-2 Stora Enso Oyj

Access the annual financial statements of Stora Enso Oyj for the company's year ended December 31, 2008. These are available at the company's website, www.storaenso.com. Review the information that is provided and answer the following questions about the company.

Real-World Emphasis

Instructions

(a) What major business(es) is Stora Enso Oyj in?

(b) What type of biological assets does the company have? Identify the accounting policies disclosed in the notes to the financial statements that explain how the company accounts for these assets.

(c) What was the amount in the biological assets account at December 31, 2008 and 2007, owned directly by Stora Enso? What caused this account balance to change from 2007 to 2008? Be specific.

(d) How is fair value of the biological assets determined? What kinds of estimates are required to determine fair value?

(e) What was the impact on the net earnings for 2008 and 2007 related to the biological assets valuation?

RA10-3 Empire Company Limited and Loblaw Companies Limited

Companies in the same line of business usually have similar investments and capital structures, and an opportunity for similar rates of return. One of the key performance indicators that is used to assess the profitability of companies is the return on assets ratio. This ratio results from two key relationships—the profit margin and the total asset turnover—and in general terms can be written as follows:

Real-World Emphasis

Return on assets = Total asset turnover (or Sales / Total assets) × Profit margin (or Income / Sales)

This says that profitability depends directly on how many sales dollars are generated for each dollar invested in assets (total asset turnover) and on how costs are controlled for each dollar of sales (profit margin). An increase in either ratio results in an increase in the return on assets. As property, plant, and equipment is often the largest single asset on the balance sheet, companies need to have strategies to manage their investment in such assets.

Instructions

Access the financial statements of two companies that are in the food distribution business: **Empire Company Limited** for the year ended May 2, 2009, and **Loblaw Companies Limited** for the year ended January 3, 2009. These are available at www.sedar.com or each company's website. Review the financial statements and answer the following questions.

(a) At each company's year end, determine the percentage of property, plant, and equipment to total assets.

(b) Calculate each company's fixed asset turnover, total asset turnover, and profit margin (using net income) for the most recent year.

(c) Determine the return on assets for each company. Which company is more profitable?

(d) Which company appears to use its total assets more effectively in generating sales? Its fixed assets?

(e) Are there any differences in accounting policies that might explain the differences in the fixed asset turnover ratios?

(f) Examine the leasing note for each company. How might the amount of assets that are leased impact the above asset turnover ratios?

(g) Which company has better control over its expenses for each dollar of sales? How do you explain the asset turnover ratios and the profit ratio comparisons?

RA10-4 Homburg Invest Inc.

Real-World Emphasis

Homburg Invest Inc., a Canadian company, currently reports under Canadian GAAP and IFRS. The reports prepared under Canadian GAAP (currently being used by Homburg) are similar to what would result from applying private entity GAAP. For Homburg, the most significant differences between the two reporting standards relate to its fixed assets.

Instructions

Access the financial statements of Homburg Invest Inc. under both bases of accounting for its year ended December 31, 2008, from the company's website, www.homburgcanada.com. Review the statements that are presented and answer the following questions.

(a) What business is Homburg Invest Inc. in? What two sets of accounting standards does it report under? Why does the company report under two different sets of generally accepted accounting principles?

(b) Identify the single most significant accounting difference, and indicate the effect that this has on the income statements. Be specific. What is the impact of these differences on the income statement? Balance sheet?

(c) Which set of financial statements do you think comes closer to meeting the objectives of financial reporting? Discuss briefly.

(d) Using the IFRS-prepared financial statements, explain how the company determined fair values for the investment properties. What methods were used and what were the key assumptions required?

RA10-5 Extractive Industry

Real-World Emphasis

Access the financial statements of **BHP Billiton plc** for the company's year ended December 31, 2008. Access the financial statements of **Delphi Energy Corp** for the company's year ended December 31, 2008. These are available at the companies' websites. Review the information that is provided and answer the following questions about the companies.

Instructions

(a) What business is BHP Billiton plc in? What business is Delphi Energy Corp in?

(b) How does BHP Billiton account for exploration, evaluation, and development expenditures related to its mineral reserves and resources? What specific costs are included?

(c) How does Delphi account for exploration, evaluation, and development expenditures related to its mineral reserves and resources? What specific costs are included?

(d) Using the two companies as examples, discuss the similarities and differences between the successful efforts method and the full cost method.

(e) One method for reporting these assets that is being contemplated by IFRS is the fair value method. What assumptions would be required to determine the fair value of mineral or oil and gas reserves? What are some drawbacks to using the fair value method to value these types of assets?

(f) From a user's perspective, which method(s) discussed above would provide the most faithful presentation and/or relevant information?

RA10-6 Research Issue: Tangible Capital Assets

In groups, and as explained by your instructor, choose eight different companies, taking one company from each of the following industry groups: Consumer products—autos and parts; Consumer products—biotechnology/pharmaceuticals; Film production; Financial services—investment companies and funds; Industrial products—steel; Merchandising—specialty stores; Metals and minerals—integrated mines; and Utilities—telephone utilities. An excellent source is the SEDAR website at www.sedar.com. If you search the database by industry group for financial statements for the most recent 12-month period, you will be able to choose from the large number of public companies on the site.

Instructions

(a) For each company, determine the relative importance of its tangible capital assets to its total assets invested, and the percentage that depreciation or amortization expense is of total expenses.

(b) For each company, determine the percentage of total assets that is financed by long-term debt.

(c) What industries require the highest relative investment in tangible capital assets?

(d) Is there any relationship between the investment in tangible capital property and financing by long-term debt? Comment.

(e) How might the strategies of companies with significant investments in fixed assets or property, plant, and equipment differ from the strategies of companies that have very little investment in such assets?

Rolling Stock

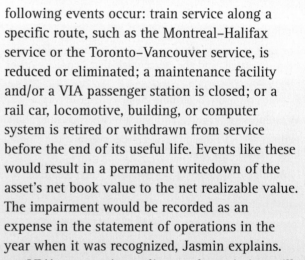

VIA RAIL CANADA operates 503 intercity trains each week, using a fleet of 75 locomotives and 454 passenger cars. It carries more than 4.6 million passengers a year. These trains run over 12,500 kilometres of track and serve more than 450 Canadian communities. These are no small numbers, and neither are the numbers required to allocate the cost of these trains to the Crown corporation.

Corporate comptroller Patricia Jasmin says VIA Rail follows the standard accounting theory for depreciating its tangible capital assets, such as the trains. Of the total capital assets of $1,382.5 million, VIA Rail's trains, or "rolling stock," amounted to $774.4 million in 2008. Of that amount, $517.6 million had been depreciated to date, leaving a net book value of $333.4 million.

VIA Rail calculates the depreciation of tangible capital assets on a straight-line basis at rates high enough to depreciate the cost of the assets, less their residual value, over their estimated lives. The corporation maintains detailed subsidiary records for each car's cost and accumulated depreciation, Jasmin explains.

The impairment of property, plant, and equipment occurs at VIA when one or all of the following events occur: train service along a specific route, such as the Montreal–Halifax service or the Toronto–Vancouver service, is reduced or eliminated; a maintenance facility and/or a VIA passenger station is closed; or a rail car, locomotive, building, or computer system is retired or withdrawn from service before the end of its useful life. Events like these would result in a permanent writedown of the asset's net book value to the net realizable value. The impairment would be recorded as an expense in the statement of operations in the year when it was recognized, Jasmin explains.

VIA's accounting policy on depreciation will not change after the transition to IFRS; however, the implementation of IFRS will result in the recognition of components within an asset. For example, a VIA locomotive will be segregated into three major components with different useful lives: the main engine, with a 10-year useful life; the technical systems, with a 15-year useful life; and the locomotive car body, with a 25-year useful life. Thus, during its useful life, each locomotive will be depreciated on three different depreciation streams instead of only one. ■

CHAPTER 11

Depreciation, Impairment, and Disposition

Learning Objectives

After studying this chapter, you should be able to:

1. Explain the concept of depreciation.

2. Identify and explain the factors to consider when determining depreciation charges.

3. Identify how depreciation methods are selected.

4. Calculate depreciation using the straight-line, decreasing charge, and activity methods and recognize the effects of using each.

5. Explain the accounting issues for depletion of mineral resources.

6. Explain and apply the accounting procedures for a change in depreciation rate.

7. Explain the issues and apply the accounting standards for capital asset impairment under both IFRS and accounting standards for private enterprises (private entity GAAP).

8. Explain and apply the accounting standards for long-lived assets that are held for sale.

9. Account for the derecognition of property, plant, and equipment.

10. Describe the types of disclosures required for property, plant, and equipment.

11. Analyze a company's investment in assets.

12. Identify differences in accounting between accounting standards for private enterprises (private entity GAAP) and IFRS, and what changes are expected in the near future.

After studying Appendix 11A, you should be able to:

13. Calculate capital cost allowance in straightforward situations.

Preview of Chapter 11

As noted in the opening story, capital assets can be a major investment for companies. Given this fact, and given also the alternatives that exist for charging these costs to operations, the potential for impairment in their values, and the argument by some critics that financial statement readers do not need to be concerned with these non-cash expenses, it is important to have a firm understanding of this chapter's topics. In addition, the appendix outlines key aspects of the capital cost allowance system that is required for income tax purposes.

The chapter is organized as follows:

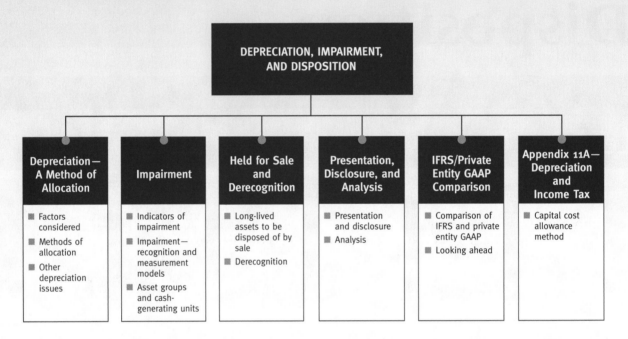

DEPRECIATION—A METHOD OF ALLOCATION

Objective 1
Explain the concept of depreciation.

Most individuals at one time or another purchase and trade in an automobile. The automobile dealer and the buyer typically discuss what the old car's trade-in value is. Also, they may talk about what the new car's trade-in value will be in several years. In both cases, the decline in value is generally referred to as depreciation.

To accountants, however, depreciation is not a matter of valuation. Depreciation—or amortization, as it is also called—**is a means of cost allocation**. It is the process of allocating the depreciable amount of a property, plant, and equipment (PP&E) asset to expense in a systematic manner to those periods expected to benefit from its use. As explained in this chapter, the depreciable amount is the asset's cost less its residual amount, although there could be a substitute value used instead of cost, such as that used when the revaluation model is applied.

It is true that an asset's value changes between the time it is purchased and the time it is sold or scrapped. Companies use a cost allocation approach rather than a valuation approach, however, because objectively measuring the changes in their assets' values every reporting period is often difficult and usually costly.

As referred to above, the terms **amortization** and **depreciation** are almost interchangeable. Amortization refers to the general process of allocating the carrying amount of any long-lived asset to the accounting periods that benefit from its use. It can also specifically refer to this process for **intangible assets. Depreciation** is reserved for property, plant, and equipment, and depletion is used only with natural resource assets.

Underlying Concept

Although fair valuing long-lived assets at each reporting date may provide more relevant information to users, its reliability, particularly when evaluated on a cost-benefit basis, supports the widely continued use of amortized cost.

Factors Considered in the Depreciation Process

Before calculating the dollar amount of depreciation expense, a company has to answer four basic questions:

2 Objective
Identify and explain the factors to consider when determining depreciation charges.

1. What asset components are depreciated separately?

2. What is the asset's depreciable amount?

3. Over what period is the asset depreciated?

4. What pattern best reflects how the asset's economic benefits are used up?

As you might expect, judgement and estimates are needed to answer these questions. This means that the resulting **depreciation can only ever be an estimate**. A perfect measure of expense for each period is impossible.

Asset Components

As referred to in Chapter 10, and as indicated in the opening vignette to this chapter, management has to develop a componentization policy; that is, to guide decisions on which fixed asset components to recognize separately. What individual parts of multi-component assets, such as a building, should be pulled out and recorded separately? And when should numerous small PP&E assets, such as small tools, be combined and accounted for together? Determining the unit of account is the first step in the depreciation process.

Significant Change

The following principles guide the componentization decision:

- Identify each part of a PP&E asset whose cost is a significant portion of the total asset cost as a separate component.

- Group together significant components with similar useful lives and patterns of providing economic benefits.

- Add together the costs of the remaining parts of the asset, none of which is individually significant. These may be depreciated as a single component, taking into account the nature of the different parts.

- Group together individual minor assets to depreciate as one component based on the similarity of their useful life and pattern of consumption.

British Airways plc reports, for example, that the cabin interior modifications of its aircraft fleet are recognized and depreciated separately from the aircraft itself. **Air Canada** indicates that aircraft reconfiguration costs are separately recognized and depreciated over a much shorter period of time than the aircraft and flight equipment.

Real-World Emphasis

Both IFRS and private entity GAAP require entities to recognize separate components for the purpose of depreciation, but the international standards are more fully developed and more strictly applied.

Depreciable Amount

The amount of an asset that is to be depreciated—its depreciable amount—is the difference between the asset's cost (or revalued amount, if the revaluation model is being used) and its residual value.[1] The residual value is defined as the estimated amount a company would **receive today** on disposal of the asset, less any related disposal costs, if the asset were at the **same age and condition it is expected to be in at the end of its useful life**.[2] It is the amount the company depreciates the asset to over its useful life. For example, Illustration 11-1 shows that if an asset has a cost (or net revalued amount) of $10,000 and a residual value of $1,000, only $9,000 of its cost is depreciated.

Illustration   11-1

Calculation of Amount to Be Depreciated

Original cost (or amount substituted for "cost")	$10,000
Less: residual value	1,000
Depreciable amount	$ 9,000

In some cases, the residual value may be so low as to be immaterial. Some long-lived assets, however, have substantial net realizable values at the end of their useful lives to a specific enterprise. As long as the residual value is less than the asset's carrying amount, depreciation is recognized on the asset. If the residual value increases so it is more than the asset's carrying amount, no depreciation is taken until this situation reverses. It is important that the residual value be reviewed on a regular basis, but particularly whenever changes in the environment occur that might affect its estimate. Under international GAAP, this review is required at least at each year end.

A more technical and conservative policy is sometimes required, such as under private entity GAAP. To ensure that charges to the income statement are adequate, the depreciation charge is based on the higher of two amounts:

1. The cost less salvage value over the life of the asset; and

2. The cost less residual value over the asset's useful life.

The salvage value—the estimate of the asset's net realizable value at the end of its life, rather than its value at the end of its useful life to the entity—is usually an insignificant amount. In practice, the residual value is most commonly used.

Depreciation Period

Next, a company estimates the useful life of the asset. An asset's useful life is the period during which the asset is expected to be available for use by the entity. Alternatively, useful life can be stated in terms of the number of units of product or service that the asset is expected to produce or provide over this period.

Depreciation begins when the asset is available for use; that is, when it is in place and in the condition necessary for it to be able to operate as management intends. The **depreciation process ends** when the asset is derecognized (removed from the accounts), or when it is classified as held for sale, if earlier. **Depreciation continues** even if the asset is idle or has been taken out of service, unless it is fully depreciated, of course.

Useful or service life and physical life are often not the same. A piece of machinery may be physically capable of producing a specific product for many years past its useful

---

[1] After acquisition, it is the asset's **net carrying amount** and residual value that determine the depreciable amount.

[2] This is the IAS 16 *Property, Plant, and Equipment* definition. The *CICA Handbook*, Part II, Section 3061 *Property, Plant, and Equipment* definition refers only to the asset's net realizable value at the end of its useful life to an entity. They are not inconsistent.

life in a particular organization, but the equipment may not be used for all of those years due to **economic factors** such as obsolescence. The "economic useful life" of VIA Rail's fleet described in the opening vignette is likely determined through discussions with engineering and manufacturing specialists. New processes or techniques or improved machines may provide the same product or service at lower cost or with higher quality. Changes needed in the product or service itself may shorten an asset's service life. Environmental factors and asset management policies also influence asset retirement decisions.

Physical factors set the outside limit for an asset's service life. Physical factors relate to such things as decay or wear and tear that result from use of the asset and the passage of time. Whenever the asset's physical nature is the main factor that determines its useful life, a company's maintenance policies play a vital role—the better the maintenance, the longer the life of the asset.[3] An asset's **legal life** may also limit its useful life to a specific entity. For example, the benefits of leasehold improvements end when the lease term is over.

To illustrate these concepts, consider a new nuclear power plant. Which is most important in determining its useful life: physical factors, economic factors, or its legal life? The limiting factors seem to be (1) ecological considerations, (2) competition from other power sources, and (3) safety concerns. Physical and legal life do not appear to be primary factors affecting the plant's useful life. While the plant's physical life may be far from over, the plant may be obsolete in 10 years.

The estimate of useful life is often not easy to determine. In some cases, arbitrary lives are selected; in others, sophisticated statistical methods are used. The main basis for estimating an asset's useful life is often judgement and the company's past experience with similar assets. In an industrial economy such as Canada's, where research and innovation are so prominent, economic and technological factors have as much effect on the service lives of tangible assets as do physical factors, if not more.

Underlying Concept

Depreciation is a good example of how the matching concept is applied when there is no direct relationship between revenues and costs.

Methods of Allocation (Depreciation)

Basis for the Choice

3 Objective
Identify how depreciation methods are selected.

The last major issue in the depreciation process is deciding **which depreciation method is most appropriate**. The underlying principle is that the resulting depreciation should reflect the pattern in which the asset benefits are expected to be used up by the entity. This suggests that the concern is with the pattern in which the physical capacity, wear and tear, technical obsolesence, or legal life are used up as the asset provides service to the company. Four possible patterns are identified in Illustration 11-2.

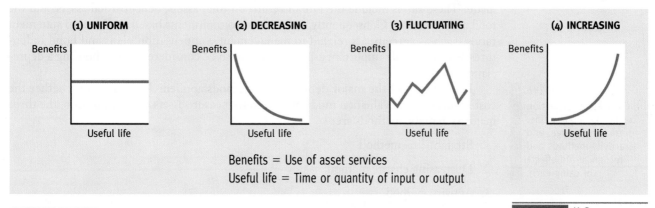

Benefits = Use of asset services
Useful life = Time or quantity of input or output

[3] The airline industry illustrates the type of problem found in estimations. In the past, aircraft were assumed not to wear out; they just became obsolete. However, some jets have been in service for as long as 20 years, and maintenance of these aircraft has become increasingly expensive. As a result, some airlines now replace aircraft, not because of obsolescence, but because of physical deterioration.

Illustration 11-2

Possible Benefit Patterns for Assets

Pattern (1) is for an asset that provides roughly the same level of benefits in each year of its life. A warehouse could be an example. For such assets, a straight-line method is rational because it results in a constant depreciation expense each period. An airplane may be an example of an asset with a decreasing benefit pattern (2). When it is new, it is constantly in service on major routes. As it gets older, its operating efficiency declines—it may be repaired more often and used for more peripheral routes. Depreciation expense should therefore decline each year. The use of a truck, in terms of kilometres driven, may fluctuate considerably from period to period, yielding a benefit pattern that varies, such as that in pattern (3). An increasing benefit pattern (4) is seldom applicable because few assets provide more service potential or generate higher value cash flows as they age.

Because of the difficulty in some cases in identifying the pattern in which benefits are received, the **simplicity** of each method may be considered. If so, some argue that a straight-line method should be used. However, others may think that the method used for income tax purposes should be used for book purposes because it **eliminates some record-keeping costs**. Canadian companies are required to use the capital cost allowance approach for tax purposes (explained in Appendix 11A), so they may decide to also use this for financial reporting purposes. While this is common for smaller companies, larger companies use different methods for tax purposes and for financial reporting. This is reasonable because the objectives of financial reporting differ from those of calculating income tax. One result of using different methods for financial reporting than for tax is that the entity's financial statement amounts for property, plant, and equipment and for income before taxes will be different from the tax value of capital assets and from taxable income. The financial accounting consequences of such differences are explored in Chapter 18.

Management sometimes appears to choose a depreciation method based on the **perceived economic consequences** of the amounts that will be reported. Companies that want to appear more profitable change from the declining-balance method to a straight-line approach. Because share value tends to be related to reported income, management feels that such a change favourably affects the firm's market value. In fact, research in this area has found just the opposite, with companies that switch to more liberal accounting policies experiencing declines in share values. One explanation is that changes like this signal that the company is in trouble and also lead to scepticism about management's attitudes and behaviour.

What Do the Numbers Mean?

The choice of a depreciation method affects both the balance sheet (i.e., the carrying amount of property, plant, and equipment) and the income statement (i.e., the depreciation expense). It follows, therefore, that various ratios are affected by the choice that is made. These ratios include the rate of return on total assets, debt-to-total assets, and the total asset turnover. Consequently, contractual commitments based on financial statement ratios, such as agreements related to management compensation plans and bond indentures, are potentially important aspects that tend to be considered when choosing a depreciation method.

Objective 4

Calculate depreciation using the straight-line, decreasing charge, and activity methods and recognize the effects of using each.

How is each of the major depreciation methods applied? Regardless of whether the cost model or the revaluation model is chosen to measure assets after acquisition, the three major systematic methods are:

1. Straight-line method

2. Decreasing charge method

3. Activity method

To illustrate these choices, assume that a company purchases a crane for heavy construction purposes. Illustration 11-3 presents the relevant data on the purchase of the crane.

Cost of crane	$500,000
Estimated useful life	5 years
Productive life	30,000 hours
Estimated residual value	$ 50,000

Illustration 11-3

Data Used to Illustrate Depreciation Methods

Straight-Line Method

Under the straight-line method, depreciation is considered **a function of the passage of time.** This is the most widely used method in practice. Not only is it straightforward to apply, it is often the most conceptually appropriate method as well. When creeping obsolescence is the main reason for a limited service life, the decline in usefulness is likely constant from period to period. The depreciation expense for the crane under the straight-line method is calculated in Illustration 11-4.

Underlying Concept

If the benefits flow evenly over time, there is justification for using the straight-line basis of allocation.

Illustration 11-4

Depreciation Calculation, Straight-Line Method—Crane Example

$$\frac{\text{Cost less residual value}}{\text{Estimated service life}} = \text{Depreciation charge}$$

$$\frac{\$500,000 - \$50,000}{5 \text{ years}} = \$90,000$$

One objection to the straight-line method is that it relies on two assumptions: (1) that the asset actually does deliver equal economic benefits each year, and (2) that maintenance expense is about the same each period (assuming constant revenue flows). If these assumptions are not valid, some argue that this method will not give a rational matching of expense with the periods that benefit from the asset.

One issue with this method (and often some of the others) is the distortion that develops in a rate of return analysis (income ÷ assets). Illustration 11-5 indicates how the rate of return increases, assuming constant revenue flows, because the asset's book value decreases. The increasing trend in the rate of return can be very misleading as a basis for evaluating the success of operations because the increase is only due to the accounting method used, and not to improvements in underlying economic performance.

Year	Depreciation Expense	Undepreciated Asset Balance (net book value)	Income (after depreciation expense)	Rate of Return (income ÷ assets)
0		$500,000		
1	$90,000	410,000	$100,000	24.4%
2	90,000	320,000	100,000	31.2%
3	90,000	230,000	100,000	43.5%
4	90,000	140,000	100,000	71.4%
5	90,000	50,000	100,000	200.0%

Illustration 11-5

Depreciation and Rate of Return Analysis—Crane Example

Decreasing Charge Method

Decreasing charge methods, often called diminishing balance methods or accelerated amortization, create a higher depreciation expense in the earlier years and lower charges in later periods. The justification for this approach is that many assets offer their greatest benefits in the early years, so that this method best reflects their pattern of use. Another argument is that repair and maintenance costs are often higher in later periods, and an accelerated method therefore provides a fairly constant total expense (for depreciation plus repairs and maintenance). When a decreasing charge approach is used by

Underlying Concept

The matching concept does not justify a constant charge to income. If the benefits from the asset decline as it ages, then a decreasing expense better reflects how its benefits are consumed.

Canadian companies, it is usually a version of what is called the declining-balance method.[4]

Declining-Balance Method   The declining-balance method uses a depreciation rate (expressed as a percentage and called the declining-balance rate) that stays constant throughout the asset's life, assuming there is no change in estimate. This rate is applied each year to the declining book value (cost less accumulated depreciation and any accumulated impairment losses) to calculate depreciation expense. For assets accounted for by the revaluation method, the rate is applied to the revalued asset amount less the total of any accumulated depreciation and accumulated impairment losses.

The rate is usually calculated as a multiple of the straight-line rate.[5] For example, the double-declining-balance rate for an asset with a 10-year life is 20% (the straight-line rate of 100% ÷ 10, or 10%, multiplied by 2). For an asset with a 20-year life, the triple-declining-balance rate is 15% (the straight-line rate of 100% ÷ 20, or 5%, multiplied by 3), while the double-declining-balance rate would be 10% (100% ÷ 20, or 5%, multiplied by 2).

Unlike other methods, **the asset's residual value is not deducted** in calculating depreciation expense. Instead, the declining-balance method applies the appropriate rate to the asset's carrying amount at the beginning of each period. Since the asset's book value is reduced each period by the depreciation charge, the rate is applied to a lower and lower carrying amount each period, resulting in a depreciation charge that gets smaller each year. This process continues until the asset's carrying amount is reduced to its estimated residual value. **When the residual value is reached, the asset is no longer depreciated.**

Illustration 11-6 shows how to apply the double-declining-balance method, using the crane example.

Year	Book Value of Asset, Beginning of Year	Rate on Declining Balance[a]	Depreciation Expense	Balance of Accumulated Depreciation	Net Book Value, End of Year
1	$500,000	40%	$200,000	$200,000	$300,000
2	300,000	40%	120,000	320,000	180,000
3	180,000	40%	72,000	392,000	108,000
4	108,000	40%	43,200	435,200	64,800
5	64,800	40%	14,800[b]	450,000	50,000

[a] (100% ÷ 5) × 2
[b] Limited to $14,800 because the book value is never reduced below the residual value.

[4] There is another systematic decreasing charge approach, called the sum-of-the-years'-digits method, but it is rarely used in Canada. Under this method, the depreciable amount is multiplied each year by a decreasing fraction. The **denominator** of the fraction equals the sum of the digits of an asset's useful life. For example, the sum of the digits of the life of an asset with a five-year life is $1 + 2 + 3 + 4 + 5 = 15$. The **numerator** decreases year by year and the denominator stays constant. Because this is a decreasing charge approach, depreciation expense is $5/15$ of the depreciable amount in the first year, $4/15$ of the depreciable amount in the second year, $3/15$ in the third, $2/15$ in the fourth, and $1/15$ in the fifth year. At the end of the asset's useful life, its net book value is equal to the estimated residual value. Similarly, for an asset with a 10-year life, the sum of the years' digits, 1 through 10, equals 55. Depreciation in the first year is $10/55$ of the depreciable amount, in the second year it is $9/55$, and so on.

[5] The straight-line rate (%) is equal to 100% divided by the estimated useful life of the asset that is being depreciated. A pure form of the declining-balance method (sometimes called the fixed percentage of book value method) has also been suggested as a possibility, but it is not used very much. This approach finds a rate that depreciates the asset to exactly its residual value at the end of its expected useful life. The formula for determining this rate is as follows:

$$\text{Depreciation rate} = 1 - \sqrt[n]{\frac{\text{Residual value}}{\text{Acquisition cost}}}$$

The life in years is n. Once the rate is calculated, it is applied to the asset's declining book value from period to period.

Activity Method

The **activity method**, often called the **units of production method** or a **variable charge approach**, calculates depreciation **according to usage or productivity** instead of the passage of time. The asset's life is defined in terms of either the output it provides (units produced), or the input required (the number of hours it operates). Conceptually, a better cost association results from using output instead of an input measure such as hours used, but both are widely accepted and used.

The crane's usage in hours is relatively easy to measure. If it is used for 4,000 hours the first year, the depreciation charge is calculated as shown in Illustration 11-7.

$$\frac{\text{Cost less residual value}}{\text{Total estimated hours}} = \text{Depreciation expense per hour}$$

$$\frac{\$500,000 - \$50,000}{30,000 \text{ hours}} = \$15 \text{ per hour}$$

First year depreciation expense: 4,000 hours × \$15 = \$60,000

Illustration 11-7

Depreciation Calculation, Activity Method—Crane Example

When the asset's economic benefits are consumed by usage, activity, or productivity, the units of production method results in the best measure of periodic expense. Companies that adopt this approach have low depreciation during periods of low usage, high charges during high usage, and zero depreciation expense when the asset is available, but idle.

This method's major limitation is that it is appropriate in only a few situations. For example, a building usually suffers a great amount of steady deterioration from the weather (a function of time) regardless of how it is used. In addition, when an asset's useful life is affected by economic or functional factors that have nothing to do with its usage, the activity method is not appropriate. If a company is expanding rapidly, a particular building may soon become obsolete for its intended purpose. The level of activity is irrelevant.

Depletion.   One industry where the activity method is particularly relevant is the extractive industry. Chapter 10 explains generally that the costs of oil and gas reserves and mineral deposits are capitalized into mineral resource assets. The amortization of the cost of these reserves as the wells or ore bodies are put into production is known as **depletion**. The resulting **depletion expense** is a product cost, and therefore is a part of the direct cost of the minerals or petroleum products (inventory) produced during the period.

5 Objective
Explain the accounting issues for depletion of mineral resources.

The accounting issues associated with the depletion of mineral resources are similar to those encountered with the amortization of other types of property, plant, and equipment. They include:

1. Determining the pattern of depletion (amortization) to be used

2. The difficulty in estimating the asset's useful life

Natural resource companies also have to deal with the associated issue of liquidating dividends as discussed below.

Pattern of depletion.   Once the depletion base (i.e., the cost of the mineral resource asset to be amortized) is established, the next decision is to determine how these capitalized costs will be allocated to accounting periods. Normally, **depletion is calculated using an activity approach, such as the units-of-production method**. This approach is used because of the close association of the resulting expense with the asset benefits consumed in the period. Under this method, the cost of the resource asset is divided by the estimated recoverable reserves (the number of units that are estimated to be in the resource deposit) to obtain a cost per unit of production. The cost per unit is then multiplied by the number of units extracted during the period to determine the depletion charge.

For example, assume a mining company acquired the right to use 1,000 hectares of land in the Northwest Territories to mine for gold. The lease cost is $50,000, the related exploration and evaluation costs are $100,000, and development costs incurred in opening the mine are $850,000, all of which have been capitalized. Total costs related to the mine before the first ounce of gold is extracted are, therefore, $1 million. The company estimates that the mine will provide approximately 100,000 ounces of gold. The depletion rate is determined in Illustration 11-8.

<table>
<tr><td>Illustration 11-8

Calculation of Depletion Rate</td><td>$$\frac{\text{Total cost} - \text{residual value}}{\text{Total estimated units available}} = \text{Depletion cost per unit}$$

$$\frac{\$1,000,000}{100,000} = \$10 \text{ per ounce}$$</td></tr>
</table>

If 25,000 ounces are extracted in the first year, the depletion for the year is $250,000 (25,000 ounces at $10). The entry to record the depletion is:

<table>
<tr><td>A = L + SE
0   0   0

Cash flows: No effect</td><td>Inventory (Depletion Expense)
    Accumulated Depletion</td><td>250,000</td><td>
250,000</td></tr>
</table>

The depletion charge for the extracted resource (in addition to labour and other direct production costs) is initially charged (debited) to inventory. When the resource is sold, the inventory costs are transferred to cost of goods sold and matched with the period's revenue. The remaining mineral resource is reported with property, plant, and equipment as a non-current asset, as follows:

<table>
<tr><td>Gold mine (at cost)
Less: Accumulated depletion</td><td>$1,000,000
250,000</td><td>
$750,000</td></tr>
</table>

The equipment used in extracting the resource may also be amortized on a units-of-production basis, especially if the equipment's benefits and useful life are directly related to the quantity of ore extracted from that specific deposit. If the equipment is used on more than one job and at more than one site, other cost allocation methods may be more appropriate.

Estimating recoverable reserves.   Companies often change the estimate of the resource's useful life; that is, the amount of the recoverable reserves. This may result from new information or from the availability of more sophisticated production processes. Natural resources such as oil and gas deposits and some rare metals are the greatest challenges. Estimates of these reserves are in large measure "knowledgeable guesses."

Accounting for a change in the estimate of reserves is the same as for a change in the useful life of an item of plant and equipment. The procedure, explained later in this chapter, is to revise the depletion rate by dividing the costs remaining on the books less any residual value by the new estimate of the recoverable reserves. Past depletion is not adjusted. This approach has much merit since the required estimates are so uncertain.

Nexen Inc., a Canadian company involved in the oil and gas industry, reports in its 2008 Form 10-K that "the process of estimating reserves is complex," with estimates based on geological, geophysical, engineering, and economic information.[6] The company also indicates that, while the factors and assumptions underlying the estimates are reasonable based on the information available, the "estimates may change substantially as additional data from ongoing development activities and production performance becomes available and as economic conditions impacting oil and gas prices and costs change."

This caveat, combined with the **Simmons & Company International** illustration of the Value Pyramid below, underscores the measurement uncertainty associated with resource quantities and therefore the depletion expenses recognized by companies in the industry.

What Do the Numbers Mean?

Real-World Emphasis

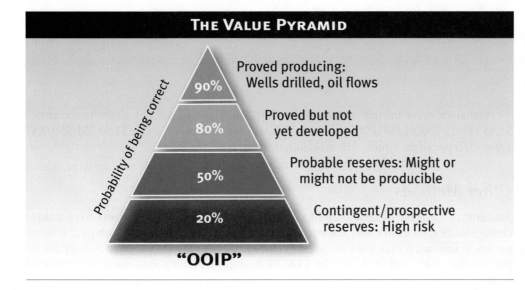

THE VALUE PYRAMID

Probability of being correct

90% — Proved producing: Wells drilled, oil flows

80% — Proved but not yet developed

50% — Probable reserves: Might or might not be producible

20% — Contingent/prospective reserves: High risk

"OOIP"

"OOIP" refers to the original oil in place, and determining this is the starting point in the calculation of reserves. After this, the amount of the OOIP that is technically and economically recoverable is then estimated. The percentages indicated in each layer of the pyramid give you some idea of the likelihood of these estimates being correct. The bottom line is that estimating oil and gas reserves may be more an art than a science!

Source: Simmons and Company International. From a presentation given by Matthew R. Simmons to the Standing Group on the Oil Market of the International Energy Agency in Paris, France, March 16, 2004, available at: http://www.simmonsco-intl.com/files/IEA-SOM.pdf, accessed June 2, 2009.

Liquidating dividends.   A company may own a property from which it plans to extract mineral resources, and have this as its only major asset. If the company does not expect to purchase more properties, it may decide to distribute to shareholders a portion or all of their capital investment by paying a liquidating dividend, which is a dividend greater than the amount of accumulated net income. These dividends are usually equal to the

---

[6] A Form 10-K is an annual report filed by public companies in the U.S., as required by the Securities Exchange Commission (SEC). It contains audited financial statements and management commentary.

accumulated amount of net income (after depletion) **plus the amount of depletion that has been charged**.

The major accounting issue is to distinguish between dividends that are a return **of capital** and those that are not. A company issuing a liquidating dividend reduces the appropriate Share Capital account for the portion of the dividend that is related to the original investment instead of reducing Retained Earnings, because the dividend is a return of part of the investor's original contribution.

To illustrate, assume Callahan Mining Corp. has a retained earnings balance of $1,650,000, accumulated depletion on mineral properties of $2.1 million, and common share capital of $5.4 million. Callahan's board declares and pays a dividend of $3 per share on the 1 million shares outstanding. The company records the dividend as follows:

A   = L +   SE
−3,000,000   −3,000,000

Cash flows: ↓ 3,000,000 outflow

Retained Earnings	1,650,000	
Common Shares	1,350,000*	
Cash		3,000,000
*($3,000,000 − $1,650,000)		

Callahan must inform shareholders that the $3 dividend per share represents a $1.65 ($1,650,000/1,000,000) per share **return on investment** and a $1.35 ($1,350,000/1,000,000) per share liquidating dividend, or **return of capital**.

Other Methods

WILEY
PLUS
Expanded Discussion

Sometimes, because of cost-benefit considerations or because the assets have unique characteristics, an entity may choose not to use one of the more common depreciation methods. Instead, it may use the method required by the Canada Revenue Agency for tax purposes as explained in Appendix 11A, or develop its own tailor-made amortization method.

What Do the Numbers Mean?

Some companies try to imply that amortization is not a cost. For example, in their press releases, they often draw more attention to earnings before interest, taxes, depreciation, and amortization (referred to as EBITDA) or pro forma earnings other than net income under GAAP. Some companies like the EBITDA figure because it "dresses up" their earnings numbers, and they promote it using the argument that the excluded costs are not operating costs or that amortization and depreciation are non-cash charges. Regardless, when all is said and done, companies must generate enough cash from revenues to cover all their costs, as the amounts they borrow to finance long-term asset acquisitions have to be repaid. Investors need to understand the differences between these various indicators of financial performance.

Consider **Aliant Inc.**'s review of its results for a recent year. EBITDA was reported at $941.6 million, while net income under GAAP amounted to $177.6 million. In the same year, **Hollinger International Inc.** reported EBITDA of U.S. $111.4 million and a GAAP net loss of U.S. $238.8 million! Because of concerns that investors may be confused or misled by non-GAAP earnings measures, the Canadian Securities Administrators, which is the umbrella group for provincial regulators, issued specific guidance for certain disclosures that are associated with non-GAAP earnings measures. These include requiring that entities present a reconciliation of their non-GAAP measure(s) with audited GAAP results.

While reporting EBITDA and other pro forma numbers has not been prohibited, it appears that the new requirements have made some companies less enthusiastic about reporting these results as prominently as they previously did.

Other Depreciation Issues

Two additional depreciation issues remain:

1. How should depreciation be calculated for partial periods?

2. How are revisions to depreciation rates made and reported?

Depreciation and Partial Periods

Plant assets are rarely purchased on the first day of a fiscal period or disposed of on the last day of a fiscal period, except in accounting texts! A practical question therefore is, "How much depreciation should be charged for partial periods?"

Assume, for example, that an automated drill machine with a five-year life is purchased for $45,000 (no residual value) on June 10, 2011. The company's fiscal year ends December 31, and depreciation is charged for $6^2/_3$ months during the year. The total depreciation for a full year, assuming the straight-line method, is $9,000 ($45,000 ÷ 5). The depreciation for the first, partial year is therefore:

$$\$9,000 \times \frac{6^2/_3}{12} = \$5,000$$

Rather than making a precise allocation of cost for a partial period, many companies set a policy to simplify the process. One variation is to take no depreciation in the year of acquisition and a full year's depreciation in the year of disposal. For example, depreciation is calculated for the full period on the opening balance in the asset account, and none for acquisitions in the year. Another variation is to charge a full year's depreciation on assets that are used for a full year and charge a half year of amortization in the years of acquisition and disposal. Alternatively, the company may charge a full year's depreciation in the year of acquisition and none in the year of disposal.

Although not conceptually "correct," companies may adopt one of these fractional-year policies in allocating cost to the first and last years of an asset's life if the method is applied consistently and the resulting effect on the financial statements is not material. **VIA Rail Canada**, for example, follows a policy of beginning depreciation in the month after a train is put into service and continuing it up to the month of disposal. For the illustrations and problem material in this text, depreciation is calculated based on the nearest full month, unless something different is stated. Illustration 11-9 shows depreciation allocated under five different fractional-year policies using the straight-line method on an automated drill machine purchased for $45,000 on June 10, 2011.

Real-World Emphasis

Machine Cost = $45,000	Depreciation Allocated Each Year over 5-Year Life*					
Fractional-Year Policy	2011	2012	2013	2014	2015	2016
1. Nearest fraction of a year	$5,000[a]	$9,000	$9,000	$9,000	$9,000	$4,000[b]
2. Nearest full month	5,250[c]	9,000	9,000	9,000	9,000	3,750[d]
3. Half year in period of acquisition and disposal	4,500	9,000	9,000	9,000	9,000	4,500
4. Full year in period of acquisition, none in period of disposal	9,000	9,000	9,000	9,000	9,000	0
5. None in period of acquisition, full year in period of disposal	0	9,000	9,000	9,000	9,000	9,000

[a]6.667/12 ($9,000)   [b]5.333/12 ($9,000)   [c]7/12 ($9,000)   [d]5/12 ($9,000)
*Rounded to nearest dollar

Illustration 11-9

Fractional-Year Depreciation Policies, Straight-line Method

The partial period calculation is relatively simple when a company uses the straight-line method. But how is partial period depreciation handled when an accelerated method is used? To illustrate, assume that an asset was purchased for $10,000 on July 1, 2011, with an estimated useful life of five years. The depreciation expense for 2011, 2012, and 2013 using the double-declining-balance method is shown in Illustration 11-10.

Illustration 11-10

Calculation of Partial Period Depreciation, Double-Declining-Balance Method

1st full year	(40% × $10,000) = $4,000
2nd full year	(40% × 6,000) = 2,400
3rd full year	(40% × 3,600) = 1,440

Depreciation July 1, 2011, to December 31, 2011:

6/12 × $4,000 = $2,000

Depreciation for 2012:

6/12 × $4,000 = $2,000
6/12 × $2,400 = 1,200
$3,200

Depreciation for 2013:

6/12 × $2,400 = $1,200
6/12 × $1,440 = 720
$1,920

Alternatively:

Depreciation for 2011: (40% × $10,000) × 6/12 = $2,000
   Asset carrying amount now = $10,000 − $2,000 = $8,000
Depreciation for 2012: (40% × $8,000) = $3,200
   Asset carrying amount now = $8,000 − $3,200 = $4,800
Depreciation for 2013: (40% × $4,800) = $1,920
   Asset carrying amount now = $4,800 − $1,920 = $2,880

As you can see, the depreciation amount is identical whether you proceed through yearly "layers" of depreciation or whether you simply apply the rate to the asset's carrying amount at the first of each year.

Revision of Depreciation Rates

Objective 6

Explain and apply the accounting procedures for a change in depreciation rate.

When a plant asset is acquired, depreciation rates are carefully determined based on past experience with similar assets and other pertinent information. Depreciation is only an estimate, however, and the estimates of the expected pattern of consumption of the asset's benefits, useful life, and residual value need to be reviewed regularly and at least at each fiscal year end under IFRS. A change in any one of these variables requires that either the depreciation method or the rate also be changed. Unexpected physical deterioration, unforeseen obsolescence, or changes in the extent or way in which the asset is used may make the asset's useful life less than originally estimated. Improved maintenance procedures, a revision of operating policies, or similar developments may prolong its life beyond what was expected.

When a change in estimate takes place, accounting standards **do not permit companies to go back and "correct" the records, nor to make a "catch-up" adjustment** for any accumulated difference. Instead, a company accounts for a change in estimate **prospectively; i.e., in the period of change and in the future, if applicable.** This is because estimates are such an inherent part of the accounting process. As new information becomes available, the changes are incorporated into current and future measurements.

For example, assume that machinery that cost $90,000 was estimated originally to have a 20-year life and a $10,000 residual value. It has already been depreciated for eight years. In year nine, the asset's total life is now expected to be 30 years with a residual value of only $2,000. Depreciation has been recorded on the asset at the rate of 1/20 ($90,000 – $10,000), or $4,000 each year, by the straight-line method, but now a new depreciation schedule has to be prepared for the asset. The new schedule uses the undepreciated costs that remain on the books, along with the most recent estimates of the asset's residual value and remaining useful life. If another depreciation method is more appropriate for the current circumstances, then it will be applied going forward.

Continuing with our example, Illustration 11-11 shows the charges for depreciation in the current and subsequent periods based on revised calculations, assuming the straight-line method is still appropriate.

Machinery cost	$90,000
Less: Accumulated depreciation to date: 8 × $4,000/year	32,000
Carrying amount of machinery at end of 8th year	58,000
Less estimated residual value	2,000
Costs to be depreciated	$56,000

Revised depreciation = $56,000 ÷ (30 − 8) years remaining life = $2,545 per year

Illustration 11-11

Calculation of Depreciation after Revision of Estimated Life and Residual Value

The entry to record depreciation in each of the remaining 22 years is:

Depreciation Expense	2,545	
Accumulated Depreciation—Machinery		2,545

A	= L +	SE
−2,545		−2,545

Cash flows: No effect

If the double-declining-balance method had been used initially, the change in estimated life would result in a new depreciation rate to be applied to the book value in the current (ninth) and subsequent years.[7] In this example, a revised remaining life of 22 years results in a revised 100%/22 or 4.55% straight-line and a 9.09% double-declining rate. As this method initially ignores residual value in determining depreciation expense, a change in residual value is ignored in the revised calculation.

TransAlta Corporation, a Canadian power generation and wholesale marketing company operating in Canada, the United States, Mexico, and Australia, recently provided information about a change in the estimated useful life of some of its equipment components. The information, disclosed in Illustration 11-12, also reports the change in its depreciation expense.

Real-World Emphasis

---

[7] To determine the undepreciated carrying amount to date when using the double-declining-balance method, the following formula can be used:

Book value = $C(1 - r)^n$, where C = cost of asset; r = depreciation rate; and n = number of full years from the asset's acquisition date. For example, if the machinery in the illustration had been depreciated using the double-declining-balance method instead of the straight-line method, C = $90,000; r = 2 × (100% ÷ 20) = 10%; and n = 8.

The asset's carrying amount at the end of year 8, therefore, is $90,000(1 − 0.10)^8$, or $38,742.

Illustration 11-12

*Change in Estimate of Useful
Life and Depreciation Expense*

TransAlta Corporation

1. Summary of Significant Accounting Policies

T. Accounting Changes

Change in Estimate of Certain Components at Centralia Thermal

During 2007, test burns were conducted to determine what equipment modifications are needed to be performed to optimize this consumption of third party delivered coal. During 2007, a technical plan was completed including which components needed to be replaced to ensure continued maximum output from Centralia Thermal. These equipment modifications are scheduled to occur during planned maintenance outages in 2008 and 2009. As a result, the estimated useful life of the component parts that are to be replaced during these planned outages has been reduced and this change in estimate in useful life will be recognized over the period up to the related maintenance outage.

As a result, depreciation expense increased $5.5 million in 2007 compared to 2006. In 2008 and 2009 depreciation expense will increase by $13.6 million and $2.6 million, respectively, compared to 2006.

IMPAIRMENT

Objective 7

Explain the issues and apply the accounting standards for capital asset impairment under both IFRS and private entity GAAP.

As indicated in Chapter 10, property, plant, and equipment (PP&E) assets are measured after acquisition by applying the cost model, the revaluation model, or the fair value model. If an **investment property is measured at fair value** and its usefulness to the company is significantly reduced (i.e., the asset becomes impaired), the remeasurement of the asset to fair value automatically recognizes this reduction and the associated loss is recognized in income.

Assets measured under the **cost or revaluation model**, however, are not automatically adjusted to fair value. Instead, they are reported at cost (or at fair value at the most recent revaluation date) less accumulated depreciation. Is this amount the appropriate balance sheet value? Or should PP&E assets be valued at **the lower of cost and net realizable value** as most inventory assets are?

It is important to report inventory on the balance sheet at no more than the net cash the entity expects to receive on its disposal because, as a **current asset**, it is expected to be converted into cash within the operating cycle. Property, plant, and equipment assets, however, are **not held to be directly converted into cash**. They are ordinarily **used in operations over the long term**. For this reason, the same "lower of cost and net realizable value" measure is not appropriate for PP&E assets. However, it is important that any impairment in value be recognized.

Real-World Emphasis

Even when long-lived capital assets become partially obsolete, accountants have been reluctant to reduce their carrying amount. This is because it is often difficult to arrive at a measure for property, plant, and equipment that is not subjective and arbitrary. For example, **Falconbridge Ltd.** at one time had to decide whether all or a part of its property, plant, and equipment in a nickel-mining operation in the Dominican Republic should be written off. The project had been incurring losses because nickel prices were low and operating costs were high. Only if nickel prices increased by about 33% would the project be reasonably profitable. Whether it was appropriate to recognize an impairment loss depended on the future price of nickel. Even if a decision were made to write down the asset, the amount to be written off would not be obvious. This same issue faced most Canadian companies in the oil and gas industry in 2008 and 2009 as the price of a barrel of oil dropped by about 70%.

How do accountants handle this problem? The first step in accounting for impairments is for management to be alert to events and circumstances that might indicate that a long-lived asset is impaired; i.e., that its carrying amount is higher than its future economic benefits to the company.

Indicators of Impairment

Illustration 11-13 provides examples of possible evidence of impairment.

Illustration 11-13

Potential Indicators of Impairment

External Indicators

There has been a significant reduction in the asset's market value.

A significant change in the technological, market, economic, or legal environment has affected or may adversely affect the entity.

Market rates of return have increased, with a negative effect on the asset's value and recoverable amount.

The book value of the entity's net assets is more than the company's market capitalization.

Internal Indicators

There is evidence of obsolescence or physical damage of an asset.

Significant changes with adverse effects have taken place or are expected to take place in how the asset is used.

Internal reports about the asset indicate its performance is or will be worse than expected.

Costs incurred for an asset's acquisition or construction significantly exceed the amount originally expected.

There may be other factors that suggest that an asset's carrying amount is overstated. The objective is to be open to the possibility of impairment with changes in the internal and external environment. Even if an impairment loss is not evident, a change may be needed in the estimate of the asset's useful life or residual value, or in the depreciation method applied.

International standards require that assets be assessed for indications of impairment at the end of each reporting period, while **private entity GAAP** requires this assessment only when events and changes in circumstances indicate that an asset's carrying amount may not be recoverable. When such an assessment indicates that an asset's carrying amount may not be recoverable, the asset is tested for impairment. Two different approaches to impairment accounting are described next.

Impairment—Recognition and Measurement Models

Just as there are different models for measuring capital assets, there are also different models for measuring impairment losses for these assets. One approach, a cost recovery impairment model, concludes that a long-lived asset is impaired only if an entity cannot recover the asset's carrying amount from using the asset and eventually disposing of it. Another approach, a rational entity impairment model, assumes that an entity makes rational decisions in managing its long-term assets. A company is likely to continue to use an asset if its use and later disposal earn a higher return than if it is currently disposed of. If current disposal generates a higher return, then management is likely to take this action. This model, therefore, incorporates both these values in the impairment decision.

Cost Recovery Impairment Model

If events or changes in circumstances indicate that an asset's carrying amount may not be recoverable, the cost recovery impairment model uses a recoverability test to determine whether an impairment loss needs to be recognized. Two basic assumptions underlie this approach:

1. The asset will continue to be used in operations.

2. As long as the dollars of cost remaining are expected to be recovered by future inflows of dollars, the asset's carrying amount will be recovered and no impairment is evident.

An estimate is made of the future net cash flows that are expected from the use of the asset and its eventual disposal. These cash flows are not discounted. If these **undiscounted** future cash flows are **less than the asset's carrying amount**, the asset is considered impaired. Conversely, if the **undiscounted** future net cash flows are **equal to or greater than the asset's carrying amount**, no impairment has occurred. Essentially, the recoverability test is a **screening device** to determine whether an asset is impaired.

If the recoverability test indicates that an asset held for use is impaired, an impairment loss is calculated. It is the amount by which the asset's carrying amount exceeds its fair value. This is **not the same** as the difference between its carrying amount and its recoverable amount in the recoverability test. Fair value under this model is the price that would be agreed upon in an arm's-length transaction between knowledgeable, willing parties who are under no compulsion to act, and by its nature is a discounted or present value measure. It is best measured by quoted market prices in active markets, but if there is no active market—which is often the case—other valuation methods are used.

WILEY PLUS
Present Value Concepts

Example A: Cost Recovery Impairment Model   Step 1: Because of changes in how equipment is being used, it is reviewed for possible impairment.

Step 2: Based on the possibility of impairment, carry out a **recoverability test**. The asset's carrying amount is $600,000 ($800,000 cost less $200,000 accumulated depreciation). The expected future undiscounted net cash flows from the use of the asset and its later disposal are estimated to be $650,000, and the asset's fair value is $525,000. The recoverability test indicates that the $650,000 of expected net cash flows from the asset exceeds its carrying amount of $600,000. As a result, **no impairment is evident** and no further steps are required.

Example B: Cost Recovery Impairment Model   Assume the same facts as in Example A above, except that the expected future net cash flows from the equipment are $580,000 instead of $650,000.

Step 1: Because of changes in how equipment is being used, it is reviewed for possible impairment.

Step 2: Based on the possibility of impairment, carry out a recoverability test. The **recoverability test** indicates that the $580,000 of expected net cash flows from the asset is less than its carrying amount of $600,000. Therefore, the asset is considered impaired.

Step 3: Measure and record the impairment loss. If the asset's fair value is $525,000, the impairment loss is calculated as shown in Illustration 11-14.

Illustration 11-14	
Carrying amount of the equipment	$600,000
Fair value of equipment	525,000
Impairment loss	$ 75,000

Illustration 11-14

Calculation of Impairment Loss—Cost Recovery Model

The entry to record the impairment loss is as follows:

A = L + SE		Loss on Impairment	75,000	
−75,000 −75,000		Accumulated Impairment Losses		75,000

Cash flows: No effect

Notice that the entry credits an Accumulated Impairment Losses account rather than Accumulated Depreciation or the capital asset account itself. Any one of these credits may be and is used in practice. Regardless of which account is credited, the adjusted carrying amount becomes the asset's new "cost" and the writedown is charged to expense. As the asset is considered to have a new cost basis, no reversal of the impairment charge is permitted. After the impairment loss is recorded, the depreciation method chosen for the asset is reviewed, as are the remaining useful life and residual value. Revised depreciation amounts are then calculated.

Both private entity and U.S. GAAP use the cost recovery impairment model.

Rational Entity Impairment Model

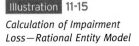
Significant Change

Another approach to the recognition and measurement of impairment losses is the **rational entity impairment model**. This approach assumes that an entity makes rational decisions in managing its long-term assets and therefore it compares the asset's book value with a recoverable amount **that differs depending on the circumstances**. If management can earn a higher return from using an asset than from selling it, the company will continue to use it. However, if a higher return is possible from selling the asset, then the rational decision is to sell it. This model, therefore, compares the asset's carrying amount with its recoverable amount, defined as the **higher of its value in use and its fair value less costs to sell**. If the recoverable amount is less than its book value, the **impairment loss** is equal to the difference. Illustration 11-15 indicates how the loss is calculated.

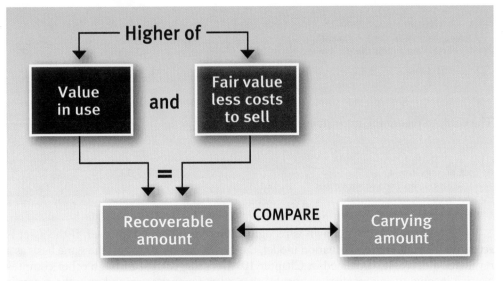

Illustration 11-15

Calculation of Impairment Loss—Rational Entity Model

If recoverable amount > carrying amount: no impairment loss

If recoverable amount < carrying amount: impairment loss = difference

Unlike the cost recovery impairment method, there is **no pre-screening test** to determine whether an asset is impaired. Instead, the carrying amount is compared directly with a fair-value-based recoverable amount that is always a discounted present value measure.

Value in use is the present value of the future cash flows expected to be derived from the asset's use and subsequent disposal. **Fair value less costs to sell** is the current amount expected to be received from the sale of the asset in an orderly transaction between market

Present Value Concepts

participants less any incremental costs directly related to the disposal.[8] Disposal costs might include legal costs, transaction taxes, and removal costs, for example, but exclude finance costs and income tax expense.

Example C: Rational Entity Impairment Model   Step 1: As a result of its annual assessment of property, plant, and equipment for indications of impairment, an entity determines that equipment with a carrying amount of $45,000 (cost of $60,000; accumulated depreciation of $15,000) may be impaired due to technological obsolescence.

Step 2: The entity calculates the asset's recoverable amount to be $47,500. This is the higher of its value in use of $47,500 and its fair value less costs to sell of $40,000. Because the recoverable amount is more than the asset's book value, there is no impairment loss to be recognized.

Example D: Rational Entity Impairment Model   Assume the same facts as in Example C, except that the asset's value in use is determined to be $37,500 and its fair value less costs to sell is $40,000.

Step 1: As a result of its annual assessment of property, plant, and equipment for indications of impairment, an entity determines that equipment with a carrying amount of $45,000 (cost of $60,000; accumulated depreciation of $15,000) may be impaired due to technological obsolescence.

Step 2: The entity calculates the asset's recoverable amount to be $40,000. This is the higher of its value in use of $37,500 and its fair value less costs to sell of $40,000. Now an impairment loss of $5,000 is indicated, as calculated in Illustration 11-16.

Illustration 11-16

Calculation of Impairment Loss—Rational Entity Model

Carrying amount of the equipment	$45,000
Recoverable amount of the equipment	40,000
Impairment loss	$ 5,000

The entry to record the impairment loss is as follows:

A   = L +   SE
−5,000   −5,000

Cash flows: No effect

Loss on Impairment	5,000	
Accumulated Impairment Losses		5,000

Significant Change

The loss from the writedown is recognized in net income. However, if the asset is accounted for under the revaluation model, the loss is accounted for on the same basis as a revaluation decrease, explained in Chapter 10: it is charged first through other comprehensive income to any revaluation surplus that exists for that asset, and only the excess is recognized in income. After the impairment loss is recognized, the depreciation method, remaining useful life, and residual value are reviewed, and revised depreciation amounts are determined.

Under the rational entity method, it is important to keep track separately of any impairment losses recognized because, unlike the cost recovery approach, a portion of **the impairment loss may be reversed in the future**. The recoverable amount is considered to be based on estimates that may change in the future. At each reporting date, information that mirrors the original indicators of impairment is assessed to determine whether a

---

[8] This definition is based on the expected amendment to IAS 36 *Impairment of Assets* assuming approval of the IASB's *Fair Value Measurement* Exposure Draft (ED/2009/5). Chapter 2 of this text provides a fuller discussion of fair values and how they are measured.

previously recognized impairment loss still exists. If the estimates used to determine the asset's value in use and fair value less costs to sell have changed, then a reversal of the impairment can be recognized.

The reversal amount, however, is limited. The specific asset cannot be increased in value to more than what its book value would have been, net of depreciation, if the original impairment loss had never been recognized.

The method described here as the rational entity model is the one applied under IFRS. What is the core difference between this and the cost recovery impairment method? The IFRS approach better reflects the economic circumstances underlying the asset's usefulness to the entity, capturing both the declines and recoveries in value. The cost recovery approach waits until circumstances indicate that conditions are very bad before recognizing an impairment—with no later recognition of any recovery.

Asset Groups and Cash-Generating Units (CGU)

The discussion above assumes that recoverable amounts can be determined for each individual asset. However, many assets do not generate cash flows on their own, but only in combination with other assets. In this case, the cash flows based on a single asset's value in use cannot be independently determined. Instead, the asset has to be identified with an asset group or cash-generating unit (CGU) and it is the group whose cash flows are tested for impairment. An asset group or CGU is the "smallest identifiable group of assets that generates cash inflows that are largely independent of the cash flows from other assets or groups of assets."[9] IAS 36 *Impairment of Assets* provides the examples summarized in Illustration 11-17.

Illustration 11-17

Examples of Cash-Generating Units

Situation	Asset Group or CGU
A mining company owns a private railway to support its mining activities. The railway could be sold for scrap value only. It does not generate cash inflows that are largely independent of those from the mine's other assets. [IAS 36.67]	It is not possible to estimate the recoverable amount of the private railway alone because its value in use cannot be determined and is probably different from its scrap value. Therefore, the entity estimates the recoverable amount of the CGU to which the private railway belongs. This is the mine as a whole.
A bus company provides services under contract with a municipality that requires minimum service on each of five separate routes. The assets devoted to each route and the cash flows from each are known. One of the routes operates at a significant loss. [IAS 36.68]	Because the company does not have the option to reduce service on any one bus route, the lowest level of identifiable cash flows that are largely independent of the cash inflows from other assets or groups of assets is the cash flows generated by the five routes together. The CGU for each route is the bus company as a whole.

These examples should help provide a basic understanding of what an asset group or CGU is and how each is generally determined. **Both the cost recovery and the rational entity impairment models are then applied as explained above to the groups of assets rather than individual assets.** Any resulting impairment loss is then allocated on a pro rata basis (based on relative carrying amounts) to the long-lived assets in the asset group. However, no individual asset is reduced below its fair value (cost recovery model),

[9] IASF, IAS 36.6. This is almost identical to *CICA Handbook*, Part II, Section 3063.03. Both private entity GAAP Section 3063 and IAS 36 include liabilities in the asset group if cash flows from the group are the only source of cash to meet the obligation.

or the highest of its fair value less costs to sell, its value in use, or zero (under the rational entity model). This is illustrated in the following example.

Example E: Asset Group or CGU   Uni Corp. (UC) is a manufacturer that produces parts for residential telephone sets. Recent indications are that the market for this product is likely to decline significantly and UC is testing equipment used in the production process for impairment. The following assets are used only in the manufacture of these parts:

	Cost	Accumulated Depreciation	Carrying Amount
Tools and dies	$1,000	$ 600	$ 400
Specialized equipment	5,000	3,500	1,500
General equipment	3,000	1,800	1,200
	$9,000	$5,900	$3,100

The tools and dies and specialized equipment cannot be used elsewhere and have no resale value, while the general equipment could be sold today for $1,500. UC plans to continue producing the parts for two more years to fill a commitment to its customer. The net future cash flows from the next two years' production of these parts and the disposal of the equipment are estimated to be $3,200, and the present value of these cash flows is $2,600.

Impairment Loss—Cost Recovery Model   Because the tools and dies and specialized equipment cannot generate cash flows on their own, they are combined into an asset group with the general equipment. The carrying amount of the asset group is $3,100. The cost recovery model applies a recoverability test to determine if there is impairment. The book value of $3,100 is compared with the undiscounted future cash flows expected from the use and later disposal of the asset group of $3,200. Because the book value can be recovered, there is no impairment, and no loss is recognized. As mentioned above, if an impairment loss is indicated, it is allocated only to the long-lived assets in the group that are held for use. The allocation is based on the assets' relative carrying amounts, although no asset is written down below its fair value, if known.

Impairment Loss—Rational Entity Model   Under this model, the carrying amount of the cash-generating group of $3,100 is compared with the CGU's recoverable amount. The recoverable amount is $2,600—the higher of the CGU's value in use of $2,600 and its fair value less costs to sell of $1,500.

Carrying amount of CGU	$3,100
Recoverable amount	2,600
Impairment loss	$ 500

The impairment loss is then allocated to the individual assets in the group, but no individual asset can be reduced below the highest of (1) its value in use, (2) its fair value less costs to sell, or (3) zero. In this case, the only determinable amount is the general equipment's fair value less costs to sell of $1,500. Because this asset's book value is already less than this, the $500 loss is therefore allocated only to the tools and dies and specialized equipment.

Allocation:	Carrying Amount	Proportion	Loss Allocation
Tools and dies	$ 400	4/19	$105
Specialized equipment	1,500	15/19	395
Total	$1,900		$500

The entry to record the impairment is:

Impairment Loss	500	
Accumulated Impairment Losses, Tools and Dies		105
Accumulated Impairment Losses, Specialized Equipment		395

A	=	L	+	SE
−500				−500

Cash flows: No effect

HELD FOR SALE AND DERECOGNITION

Long-Lived Assets to Be Disposed of by Sale

What happens if a company intends to dispose of its long-lived assets by sale instead of continuing to use them? Because this is relevant information for financial statement readers, such an asset is classified as **held for sale**, is remeasured at the lower of its carrying amount and fair value less costs to sell, and is reported separately. A "fair value less costs to sell" measurement is used if this is less than its book value because it corresponds better to the amount of cash a company expects to generate from the asset. The usefulness of this measurement is increased by the strict criteria for classifying a long-lived asset as held for sale, including the requirement that the asset be disposed of within a short period of time. These criteria were presented in Chapter 4 in the section on discontinued operations.

Assets that are held for sale **are not depreciated while they are held**. The explanation is that it would be inconsistent to amortize assets that are not in use, that are likely to be sold, and that are carried at the equivalent of the lower of (amortized) cost and net realizable value. In many respects, these assets are closer to inventory than capital assets.

After being classified as a held-for-sale asset, such an asset continues to be carried at the lower of amortized cost and fair value less costs to sell. Further losses are recognized if the net amount expected from the asset continues to drop. Gains (i.e., loss recoveries) are recognized for any increases in net realizable value, but these are limited to the amount of the cumulative losses previously recognized.

How these assets and gains and losses are reported is governed by the need for users to understand the effects of discontinued operations and disposals of non-current assets. If the long-lived asset is a component of an entity that meets the criteria for being reported as a discontinued operation, the losses and any recoveries are reported as part of discontinued operations on the income statement. Otherwise, they are reported in income from continuing operations. Practice differs on how the PP&E assets held for sale are reported on the balance sheet. Private entity GAAP allows these assets to be reclassified as a current asset only if they are sold before the financial statements are completed, and the proceeds to be received qualify as a current asset. Otherwise, they are reported separately as non-current assets. Under IFRS, most non-current assets that meet the stringent requirements for classification as held for sale also meet the criteria for recognition as current assets. In all cases, they are reported separately from other assets on the balance sheet with note disclosure of the major classes of assets making up the total.

8 Objective

Explain and apply the accounting standards for long-lived assets that are held for sale.

Derecognition

Sale of Property, Plant, and Equipment

Objective 9
Account for the derecognition of property, plant, and equipment.

Unless an asset has been classified as held for sale, depreciation is taken until the date the asset is derecognized; i.e., the time when all accounts related to the asset are removed from the accounts. An item of property, plant, and equipment is usually derecognized on the date of disposal, but it could be taken off the books earlier if management thinks it will provide no further economic benefits, from either use or disposal. Ideally, when it is derecognized, the asset's carrying amount is the same as its disposal value, but this is rarely the case. Therefore, a gain or loss is usually reported.

Under the cost and fair value models, the gain or loss on derecognition is shown on the income statement along with other items that arise from ordinary business activities. However, a gain or loss from the disposal of long-lived assets included in a discontinued business is reported in the discontinued operations section of the statement.

Underlying Concept

The "ideal" treatment of the change in value suggested here is more consistent with a physical concept of capital maintenance.

What happens to the gain or loss on disposal if the asset was accounted for under the revaluation model? The internally consistent answer to this question is that there would not be a gain or loss on disposal. Ideally, the asset would be revalued to its fair value at the date of disposal with the change in value accounted for in the same way as all previous revaluations. If so, there would be no difference between the proceeds on disposal and the carrying amount to recognize on the income statement. Any remaining balance in the Revaluation Surplus account would be adjusted directly to Retained Earnings. However, IAS 16 *Property, Plant, and Equipment* does not address this issue, stating only that gains or losses on derecognition are reported in income. A company could, then, recognize the difference between the asset's most recent carrying amount and the proceeds of disposal on the income statement.

To illustrate the disposal of an asset that is held for use, assume that a machine costing $18,000 has been used for nine years and depreciated at a rate of $1,200 per year. If the machine is sold in the middle of the tenth year for $7,000, the entry to record the half-year's depreciation up to the sale date is:

A = L + SE
−600   −600

Cash flows: No effect

Depreciation Expense	600	
Accumulated Depreciation—Machinery		600

The entry for the asset's sale is:

A = L + SE
+400   +400

Cash flows: ↑ 7,000 inflow

Cash	7,000	
Accumulated Depreciation—Machinery	11,400	
[($1,200 × 9) + $600]		
Machinery		18,000
Gain on Disposal of Machinery		400

There is a gain on sale because the $7,000 proceeds on disposal is $400 more than the machinery's book value of $6,600 ($18,000 − $11,400).

If an asset is classified as **held for sale**, it is carried at its fair value less costs to sell. In this case, the net proceeds from the sale should be close to the asset's carrying amount and it is likely that only minor gains or losses would be recognized when the actual disposal occurs.

Involuntary Conversion

Significant Change

Sometimes an asset's service ends through an involuntary conversion, such as fire, flood, theft, or expropriation. When this happens, the gains or losses are calculated in the same way as they are for the sale of an item of property, plant, and equipment. Unlike U.S. and pre-2011 Canadian GAAP, neither IFRS nor private entity GAAP recognizes extraordinary items as a separate section in the income statement.

To illustrate, assume that a company is forced to sell its plant and property that stand directly in the path of a planned major highway. For several years, the provincial government has tried to purchase the land on which the plant stands, but the company has always resisted. The government ultimately exercises its right to expropriate and its actions have been upheld by the courts. In settlement, the company receives $500,000, which is much higher than the $100,000 book value of the plant (cost of $300,000 less accumulated depreciation of $200,000) and the $100,000 book value of the land. The following entry is made:

Cash	500,000	
Accumulated Depreciation—Plant Assets	200,000	
Plant Assets		300,000
Land		100,000
Gain on Expropriation of Land and Plant Assets		300,000

A = L + SE
+300,000   +300,000
Cash flows: ↑ 500,000 inflow

Similar treatment is given to other types of involuntary conversions. The difference between any amount that is recovered, such as through insurance, and the asset's carrying amount is reported as a gain or loss.

Donations of Capital Assets

When a company donates or contributes an asset, the gift is recorded as an expense and is measured at the asset's fair value. The difference between its fair value and its carrying amount is recognized as a gain or loss. To illustrate, assume that Kline Industries donates property with a fair value of $110,000 to the City of Saskatoon for a city park. The land's book value is $30,000 and the small building is carried at its cost of $95,000 and accumulated depreciation to the contribution date of $45,000. The entry to record the donation is:

Contribution (or Donations) Expense	110,000	
Accumulated Depreciation—Building	45,000	
Building		95,000
Land		30,000
Gain on Disposal of Land and Building		30,000

A = L + SE
−80,000   −80,000
Cash flows: No effect

Miscellaneous Issues

If an asset is scrapped or abandoned without any cash recovery, the entity recognizes a loss that is equal to the asset's book value. If the asset can be sold for scrap, the gain or loss is the difference between its scrap value and its book value. If a fully depreciated asset is still used, both the asset and its accumulated depreciation remain on the books.

PRESENTATION, DISCLOSURE, AND ANALYSIS

Presentation and Disclosure

Objective 10

Describe the types of disclosures required for property, plant, and equipment.

A significant amount of information needs to be reported about a company's property, plant, and equipment so that users of financial statements can assess the existence and measurement of, and changes in, such assets. The following is a summary of the types of disclosures that are generally required:[10]

- an entity's investment in property, plant, and equipment, in investment property, and in biological assets;

- changes in that investment and in the accumulated depreciation and impairment;

- the nature and circumstances relating to impairment losses (and any reversal, if applicable);

- how net income is affected by the changes related to depreciation, impairment, and impairment reversals;

- the policies, models, and choices made in measuring PP&E, such as depreciation rates and methods and government grants;

- the existence and amounts of restrictions related to the assets;

- the effects related to each of continuing and discontinued operations;

- changes in assets as a result of fair value remeasurements;

- the carrying amount and other details of capital assets that are not being used because they are under construction or held for sale;

- cash inflows and outflows associated with the exploration and evaluation of mineral resources;

- the fair value of investment property assets;

- assumptions underlying fair-value-related measurements; and

- any outstanding related contingencies.

The requirement for separate disclosure of both the cost and accumulated depreciation gives financial statement readers more information than if only the net book value is disclosed. As an example, consider two companies, each having capital assets with a carrying amount of $100,000. The first company's assets cost $1 million and have accumulated depreciation of $900,000 charged against them. The second company, on the other hand, has assets with a cost of $105,000, and accumulated depreciation of $5,000. With the additional data, information is provided about the size of the original investment in property, plant, and equipment and its relative age. Information about depreciation rates and methods, and accounting policy choices are important disclosures as these result in material charges to the income statement, many of which are the largest non-cash expenses recognized by most companies.

Illustration 11-18 provides excerpts from the disclosures for **Cadbury plc**'s property, plant, and equipment, including its assets held for sale on the December 31, 2008, balance

Additional Disclosures

Real-World Emphasis

---

[10] Refer to the specific IFRS and private entity GAAP standards for complete coverage of the specific disclosures. Because the users of private entity financial statements can generally request additional information if needed, there are many fewer required disclosures under private entity GAAP than under IFRS.

sheet. The company is based in England and reports amounts in millions of pounds sterling (£). You are probably familiar with some of Cadbury's products!

Balance Sheets at 31 December 2008

		Group		Company
		2008	2007	2008
Notes		£m	£m	£m
	Assets			
	Non-current assets			
16	Property, plant and equipment	1,761	1,904	—
		5,990	8,667	7,762
	Current assets	2,635	2,600	210
21	Assets held for sale	270	71	—
	Total assets	8,895	11,338	7,972

1. Nature of operations and accounting policies *continued*

Impairment review

The Group carries out an impairment review of its tangible and definite life intangible assets when a change in circumstances or situation indicates that those assets may have suffered an impairment loss. Impairment is measured by comparing the carrying amount of an asset or of a cash-generating unit with the 'recoverable amount', that is the higher of its fair value less costs to sell and its 'value in use'. 'Value in use' is calculated by discounting the expected future cash flows, using a discount rate based on an estimate of the rate that the market would expect on an investment of comparable risk.

(q) Property, plant and equipment and leases

Assets are recorded in the balance sheet at cost less accumulated depreciation and any accumulated impairment losses.

Depreciation is charged (excluding freehold land and assets in course of construction) so as to writeoff the cost of assets to their residual value, over their expected useful lives using the straight-line method. The principal rates are as follows:

Freehold buildings and long leasehold properties	2.5%
Plant and machinery	7%–10%
Vehicles	12.5%–20%
Office equipment	10%–20%
Computer hardware	12.5%–33%

Assets in the course of construction are not depreciated until they are available for use, at which time they are transferred into one of the categories above and depreciated according to the rates noted.

Short leasehold properties are depreciated over the shorter of the estimated life of the asset and the life of the lease.

In specific cases different depreciation rates are used, e.g. high-speed machinery, machinery subject to technological changes or any machinery with a high obsolescence factor.

(t) Assets held for sale and discontinued operations

Assets classified as held for sale are measured at the lower of carrying value and fair value less costs to sell.

5. Non-trading items

		Re-presented
	2008	2007
	£m	£m
Net (loss)/profit on disposal of subsidiaries and brands	(6)	17
Profit on sale of investments	3	—
Profit on disposal of land and buildings	4	—
Loss on impairment of land and buildings	—	(12)
Write down to recoverable value of asset held for sale	—	(41)
Gain on rebuild of buildings	—	38
	1	2

16. Property, plant and equipment
(i) Group
(a) Analysis of movements

	Land and buildings £m	Plant and equipment £m	Assets in course of construction £m	Total £m
Cost				
At 31 December 2007	**732**	**2,578**	**283**	**3,593**
Exchange rate adjustments	74	256	45	375
Additions	7	51	417	475
Finalisation of fair value of acquisitions	(7)	(5)	—	(12)
Transfers on completion	93	249	(342)	—
Disposals	(9)	(87)	—	(96)
Demerger of Americas Beverages	(197)	(465)	(90)	(752)
Transfers to assets held for sale	(47)	(187)	(19)	(253)
At 31 December 2008	**646**	**2,390**	**294**	**3,330**
Accumulated depreciation				
At 31 December 2007	**(151)**	**(1,538)**	**—**	**(1,689)**
Exchange rate adjustments	(22)	(158)	—	(180)
Depreciation for the year	(19)	(175)	—	(194)
Disposals	3	64	—	67
Demerger of Americas Beverages	45	248	—	293
Transfers to assets held for sale	6	128	—	134
At 31 December 2008	**(138)**	**(1,431)**	**—**	**(1,569)**
Carrying amount				
At 31 December 2007	581	1,040	283	1,904
At 31 December 2008	**508**	**959**	**294**	**1,761**

The value of land not depreciated is £117 million (2007: £183 million).

21. Assets held for sale
(i) Group

	2008 £m	2007 £m
At the beginning of the year	**71**	**22**
Additions	270	71
Disposals	(71)	(22)
At the end of the year	**270**	**71**

The additions to assets held for sale in the year relate primarily to the Australia Beverages business, whose assets include £145 million non-current assets and £122 million current assets. Liabilities directly associated with Australia Beverages are £97 million.

Analysis

Objective **11**
Analyze a company's investment in assets.

Because property, plant, and equipment and their depreciation are so significant on most companies' balance sheets and income statements, it is important to understand the nature of these long-lived assets, and to ensure that management is generating an acceptable rate of return on their investment in them.

Depreciation and Replacement of Assets

Depreciation is similar to other expenses in that it reduces net income, but is different in that **it does not involve a current cash outflow**. A common misconception about depreciation is that it provides funds to replace capital assets.

To illustrate that depreciation does not provide funds for replacing plant assets, assume that a business starts operating with plant assets of $500,000 with a useful life of five years. The company's balance sheet at the beginning of the period is:

| Plant assets | $500,000 | Owners' equity | $500,000 |

Now if we assume the company earns no revenue over the five years, the income statements are as follows:

	Year 1	Year 2	Year 3	Year 4	Year 5
Revenue	$ –0–	$ –0–	$ –0–	$ –0–	$ –0–
Depreciation	(100,000)	(100,000)	(100,000)	(100,000)	(100,000)
Loss	$(100,000)	$(100,000)	$(100,000)	$(100,000)	$(100,000)

The balance sheet at the end of the five years is:

| Plant assets | $–0– | Owners' equity | $–0– |

This extreme example shows that depreciation in no way provides funds to replace assets. Funds for the replacement of assets usually come from new asset inflows represented by revenues. By setting selling prices high enough to recover out-of-pocket costs plus depreciation expense, companies do generate cash flows to help finance replacements. If management wants to accumulate a replacement fund, however, it has to set aside the cash specifically for this purpose.

Efficiency of Asset Use and Return on Investment

Investors are interested in information that tells them how efficiently management uses the long-lived assets it has invested in. Incurring capital costs provides the company with a certain level of operating capacity, and usually creates the need for significant amounts of fixed costs far into the future.

Which ratios provide information about the usage of the assets? Assets can be analyzed in terms of both activity (turnover) and profitability. How efficiently a company uses its assets to generate revenue is measured by the asset turnover ratio. This ratio is calculated by dividing net revenue or sales by average total assets for the period. The resulting number represents the dollars of revenue produced by each dollar invested in assets. **For a given level of investment in assets, a company that generates more revenue per dollar of investment is more efficient and likely to be more profitable.** While this may not be true if the percentage profit on each dollar of revenue is lower than another company's, the asset turnover ratio is one of the key components of return on investment.[11]

To illustrate, the following data are provided from the 2008 financial statements of **Loblaw Companies Limited**. Loblaw is Canada's largest food distributor, with more than 1,000 corporate and franchised stores across the country. Its asset turnover ratio is calculated in Illustration 11-19.

 Real-World Emphasis

---

[11] The higher the proportion of property, plant, and equipment to total assets, the more this turnover ratio says about the efficiency of capital asset use. Analysts often calculate separate turnover ratios for each major type of asset reported on the balance sheet and analyze each.

LOBLAW COMPANIES LIMITED
(in millions)

Revenues	$30,802
Total assets, January 3, 2009	13,985
Total assets, December 27, 2007	13,674
Net income	545

Illustration 11-19

Asset Turnover Ratio

$$\text{Asset turnover} = \frac{\text{Net revenue}}{\text{Average total assets}}$$

$$= \frac{\$30,802}{\dfrac{\$13,985 + \$13,674}{2}}$$

$$= 2.23$$

The asset turnover ratio shows that **Loblaw** generated $2.23 of revenue for each dollar invested in assets during 2008. Asset turnover ratios vary considerably among industries. For the same year, **Research in Motion**, a technology company, had a ratio of 1.63 times, and a capital-asset-heavy company like **Canadian Pacific Railway Limited** had a ratio of only 0.33 times.

Using the profit margin ratio together with the asset turnover ratio makes it possible to determine another key indicator, the rate of return earned on total assets. By using the Loblaw data shown above, the profit margin ratio and the rate of return on total assets are calculated as in Illustration 11-20.

Illustration 11-20

Profit Margin

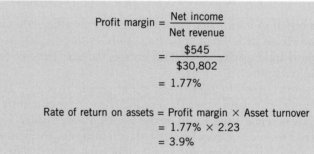

$$\text{Profit margin} = \frac{\text{Net income}}{\text{Net revenue}}$$

$$= \frac{\$545}{\$30,802}$$

$$= 1.77\%$$

$$\text{Rate of return on assets} = \text{Profit margin} \times \text{Asset turnover}$$

$$= 1.77\% \times 2.23$$

$$= 3.9\%$$

The profit margin indicates how much is left over from each sales dollar after all expenses are covered. In the Loblaw example, a profit margin of 1.77% indicates that 1.77 cents of profit remained from each $1 of revenue generated. By combining the profit margin with the asset turnover, it is possible to calculate the rate of return on assets for the period. This makes sense. The more revenue that is generated per dollar invested in assets, the better off the company is. Also, the more of each sales dollar that is profit, the better off the company should be. Combined, the ratio provides a measure of the profitability of the company's investment in assets. To the extent that long-lived assets make up a significant portion of total assets, fixed asset management has a definite effect on profitability.

The rate of return on assets (ROA) can also be calculated directly by dividing net income by average total assets. Continuing with the same example, Illustration 11-21 shows the calculation of this ratio.

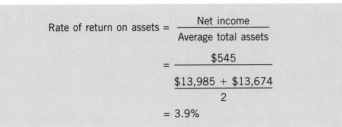

Illustration 11-21

Rate of Return on Assets

The 3.9% rate of return calculated in this way is the same as the 3.9% rate calculated by multiplying the profit margin by the asset turnover. The rate of return on assets is a good measure of profitability because it combines the effects of cost control (profit margin) and asset management (asset turnover).

A more sophisticated calculation adds back the after-tax interest expense to net income so that the results are not skewed by how the assets are financed. The ratio can then be used more legitimately for inter-company comparisons. An adjustment should also be made when there are significant assets measured at fair values, with the changes in value bypassing the income statement by being reported directly in Other Comprehensive Income (OCI). To be comparable, either the net income should be compared with the reported assets reduced by the related Accumulated OCI, or total comprehensive income should be compared with the total assets as reported.

Care must be taken in interpreting the numbers, however. A manager who is interested in reporting a high return on assets can achieve this in the short run by not investing in new plant and equipment and by cancelling expenditures such as those for research and development and employee training—decisions that will result in lower long-term corporate value. In the short run, the result is a higher return on investment because the net income number (the numerator) will be higher and the total asset number (the denominator) will be lower.

IFRS AND PRIVATE ENTITY GAAP COMPARISON

A Comparison of IFRS and Private Entity GAAP

In general, the concept of depreciation and how is it applied is almost identical under private entity GAAP and IFRS, and the same is true for non-current assets held for sale. It is also true, however, that there are minor differences not covered in this chapter that require a thorough reading of the specific detailed standards.

The most significant differences between these two GAAPs in Chapter 11 relate to the impairment models, as can be seen in Illustration 11-22.

12 Objective
Identify differences in accounting between private entity GAAP and IFRS, and what changes are expected in the near future.

	Accounting Standards for Private Enterprises (Private Entity GAAP)—CICA Handbook, Part II, Sections 1505, 3061, 3063, and 3475	IFRS—IAS 16, 36, 40, and 41; IFRS 5
Depreciation process	Practice has been not to recognize asset components to the same extent as under IFRS.	Componentization is more common, with parts of assets recognized separately and depreciated over different periods of time.
	Depreciation is the larger of: (a) cost less salvage value over asset's life, and (b) cost less residual value over asset's useful life.	Depreciation is the allocation of the cost (or other amount) less the residual value over the asset's useful life, including any idle period.
Impairment	Evaluation of impairment is required only when events and changes in circumstances indicate that the carrying amount may not be recoverable.	In addition, an assessment of indicators of impairment is required at least at each reporting date.
	Cost recovery approach to impairment is applied. An asset or asset group is impaired only if the entity cannot recover the carrying amount with the net future undiscounted cash flows from use and later disposal.	Rational entity approach is applied. Asset or cash-generating unit is impaired only if the carrying amount is more than the higher of the value in use and the fair value less costs to sell. These are discounted cash flows.
	"Recoverable amount" is used to mean the undiscounted net future cash flows from use and eventual disposal.	"Recoverable amount" is defined as the higher of value in use and the fair value less costs to sell.
	Once an asset is written down to its impaired value, this becomes the asset's new cost and no reversal of the writeoff is allowed.	An impairment loss is reversed if there is a change in the estimates used to calculate recoverable amount. It is limited in amount.
Held for sale	Long-lived assets classified as held for sale are classified as current only if sold before the date the financial statements are completed and the proceeds will be received within the period defined for an asset to be a current asset.	Non-current assets (according to IAS 1) may be reclassified as current assets only when they meet the criteria to be classified as held for sale. This requires that the asset (or disposal group) be available for immediate sale in its present condition and its sale must be highly probable.
Disclosures	A reconciliation of the opening to ending balances of the carrying amounts of each class of PP&E asset is not required.	A reconciliation of the opening to ending balances of the carrying amounts of each class of PP&E asset is required, along with the same reconciliation for its associated accumulated depreciation and accumulated impairment losses.
	Because the cost model is the only accepted model, there are no disclosure requirements related to revaluation and fair value measurement models.	Extensive disclosures are required for investment property measured under the fair value model. Even where the cost model is used for investment property, its fair value must be disclosed.

Illustration 11-22

IFRS versus Private Entity GAAP Comparison Chart

Looking Ahead

Few changes are expected in the near future to standards covering the majority of property, plant, and equipment. There are two exceptions: fair value measurement in general and accounting standards related to the upstream extractive activities undertaken by companies in the mining and oil and gas industries.

The IASB issued an Exposure Draft entitled *Fair Value Measurement* in 2009 that, when approved, will provide a single definition of fair value and guidance on how it should be measured when referred to in any of the international standards. The definition of fair value is identical to the one in FAS 157, FASB's fair value standard, and the guidance provided is substantially the same. A final IFRS is expected in 2010.

A Discussion Paper based on the IASB's extractive activities research project is due to be released in 2009. The Board expects to make a decision in late 2010 about whether to add this topic to its active agenda. If added then, it is likely to take at least two to three years from that date to develop a final standard.

Summary of Learning Objectives

1 Explain the concept of depreciation.

Depreciation is the process of allocating the cost of property, plant, and equipment assets in a systematic and rational manner to the periods that are expected to benefit from their use. The allocation of the cost of intangible capital assets is termed "amortization," and the allocation of the costs of mineral resource assets is termed "depletion." "Amortization" is also the generic term that applies to depreciation and depletion as well.

2 Identify and explain the factors to consider when determining depreciation charges.

Four factors involved in determining depreciation expense are (1) the recognition of the appropriate asset components, (2) the amount to be depreciated (depreciable amount), (3) the estimated useful life, and (4) the pattern and method of depreciation.

3 Identify how depreciation methods are selected.

The depreciation method chosen should amortize an asset in a pattern and at a rate that correspond to the benefits received from that asset. The choice often involves the use of professional judgement. Tax reporting, simplicity, perceived economic consequences, and impact on ratios are examples of factors that influence such judgements in practice.

4 Calculate depreciation using the straight-line, decreasing charge, and activity methods and recognize the effects of using each.

The straight-line method assumes that an asset provides its benefits as a function of time. As such, cost less residual value is divided by the useful life to determine the depreciation expense per period. The decreasing charge method provides for a higher depreciation charge in the early years and lower charges in later periods. For this method, a constant rate (e.g., double the straight-line rate) is multiplied by the net book value (cost less accumulated depreciation and accumulated impairment losses) at the start of the period to determine each period's expense. The main justification for this approach is that the asset provides more benefits in the earlier periods. The activity method assumes that the benefits provided by the asset are a function of use instead of the passage of time. The asset's life is considered in terms of either the output that it provides or an input measure, such as the number of hours it works. The depreciation charge per unit of activity (depreciable amount divided by estimated total units of output or input) is calculated and multiplied by the units of activity produced or consumed in a period to determine the depreciation expense.

5 Explain the accounting issues for depletion of mineral resources.

After the depletion base has been established through accounting decisions related to the acquisition, exploration and evaluation, development, and restoration obligations associated with mineral resources, these costs are allocated to the natural resources

Glossary

KEY TERMS

accelerated
  amortization, 683
activity method, 685
amortization, 679
asset group, 697
asset turnover ratio, 705
cash-generating unit
  (CGU), 697
componentization, 679
cost recovery impairment
  model, 693
declining-balance
  method, 684
decreasing charge
  methods, 683
depletion, 679
depreciable amount, 680
depreciation, 678
derecognized, 700
diminishing balance
  methods, 683
double-declining-balance
  method, 684
fair value, 694
impaired, 693
impairment loss, 694
impairments, 692
liquidating dividend, 687
profit margin ratio, 706
rate of return on assets
  (ROA), 707
rational entity impairment
  model, 693
recoverability test, 693
recoverable amount, 695
residual value, 680
salvage value, 680
straight-line method, 683
sum-of-the-years'-digits
  method, 684

that are removed. Depletion is normally calculated using the units-of-production method. In this approach, the resource's cost less residual value, if any, is divided by the number of units that are estimated to be in the resource deposit, to obtain a cost per unit of product. The cost per unit is then multiplied by the number of units withdrawn in the period to calculate the depletion expense.

6   Explain and apply the accounting procedures for a change in depreciation rate.

Because all the variables in determining depreciation are estimates—with the exception, perhaps, of an asset's original cost—it is common for a change in those estimates to result in a change in the depreciation amount. When this occurs, there is no retroactive change and no catch-up adjustment. The change is accounted for in the current and future periods.

7   Explain the issues and apply the accounting standards for capital asset impairment under both IFRS and accounting standards for private enterprises (private entity GAAP).

A capital asset is impaired when its carrying amount is not recoverable. The cost recovery method (private entity GAAP) defines recoverable as the undiscounted cash flows from the asset's use and later disposal. If impaired, the asset is written down to its fair value, and this loss cannot be reversed later if the asset's value recovers. The rational entity model (IFRS) defines recoverable amount as the higher of the asset's value in use and fair value less costs to sell. Both these values are discounted cash flow amounts. If the recoverable amount subsequently improves, the impairment losses recognized are reversed.

8   Explain and apply the accounting standards for long-lived assets that are held for sale.

Assets held for sale are no longer depreciated. They are remeasured to their fair value less costs to sell at each balance sheet date. Recoveries in value may be recognized to the extent of previous losses. Held-for-sale items of property, plant, and equipment are separately reported as non-current assets unless they meet the definition of current assets. Under private entity GAAP, assets held for sale are only permitted to be reported in current assets if sold before the financial statements are completed and the proceeds on sale are expected within 12 months from the balance sheet date (or operating cycle, if longer).

9   Account for the derecognition of property, plant, and equipment.

Depreciation continues for PP&E assets until they are classified as held for sale or derecognized. At the date of disposal, all accounts related to the retired asset are removed from the books. Gains and losses from the disposal of plant assets are shown on the income statement in income before discontinued operations, unless the conditions for reporting as a discontinued operation are met. For property, plant, and equipment donated to an organization outside the reporting entity, the donation is reported at its fair value with a gain or loss on disposal recognized.

10   Describe the types of disclosures required for property, plant, and equipment.

The type of information required to be disclosed for property, plant, and equipment is governed by the information needs of users. Because users of private entities' financial information are often able to seek further specific information from a company, there are fewer required disclosures than for public companies reporting under IFRS. The required disclosures include those relating to measurement, changes in account balances and the reasons for the changes, information about how fair values are determined, and many others.

11 **Analyze a company's investment in assets.**

The efficiency of use of a company's investment in assets may be evaluated by calculating and interpreting the asset turnover rate, the profit margin, and the rate of return on assets.

12 **Identify differences in accounting between accounting standards for private enterprises (private entity GAAP) and IFRS, and what changes are expected in the near future.**

In most major ways, international and Canadian accounting standards for the depreciation of property, plant, and equipment are similar. Significant differences do exist, however, in the extent of componentization for depreciation, the impairment models applied, and the extent of disclosure. The impairment differences relate to how it is determined whether an asset is impaired, how the impairment is measured, and the ability to recognize recoveries in value.

Appendix 11A

Depreciation and Income Tax

Capital Cost Allowance Method

Objective 13
Calculate capital cost allowance in straightforward situations.

Law

For the most part, issues related to the calculation of income taxes are not discussed in a financial accounting course. However, because the concepts of tax depreciation are similar to those of depreciation for financial reporting purposes and because the tax method is sometimes adopted for book purposes, an overview of this subject is presented here.

Canadian businesses use the capital cost allowance method to determine depreciation in calculating their taxable income and the tax value of assets, regardless of the method they use for financial reporting purposes. Because companies use this method for tax purposes, some—particularly small businesses—also use it for financial reporting, judging that the benefits of keeping two sets of records are less than the costs of doing this.[12] While keeping only one set of records may be cost-effective, it may not provide a rational measure of expense under GAAP. Therefore, many companies keep a record of capital cost allowance for tax purposes and use another method to determine depreciation for financial reporting purposes.

The capital cost allowance method is similar to the declining-balance approach covered in the chapter, except for the following:

1. Instead of being labelled "depreciation expense," it is called capital cost allowance (CCA).

2. The *Income Tax Act* (Income Tax Regulations, Schedule II) specifies the rate to be used for an asset class. This rate is called the capital cost allowance (CCA) rate. The *Income Tax Act* identifies several different classes of assets and the maximum CCA rate for each class. To determine which class a particular asset falls into, it is necessary to examine the definition of each asset class and the examples given in the Act. Illustration 11A-1 provides examples of various CCA classes, the maximum rate for the class, and the types of assets it includes.

Illustration 11A-1

Examples of CCA Classes

Class	Rate	Examples of Assets Included in the Class
1	4%	• a bridge, canal, or building, including component parts such as plumbing, elevators, sprinkler systems
4	6%	• railway, tramway, or trolley bus system
6	10%	• frame, log, stucco on frame, galvanized iron, or corrugated metal building; greenhouse; oil or water storage tank

---

[12] The widespread availability of accounting software capable of maintaining detailed records for property, plant, and equipment; the related depreciation expense; and accumulated depreciation under a variety of methods has significantly reduced the cost of record keeping and the possibility of errors.

Illustration 11A-1 continued

Class	Rate	Examples of Assets Included in the Class
8	20%	• manufacturing or processing machinery or equipment not included in other specified classes
10	30%	• automotive equipment, contractor's movable equipment, including portable camp buildings, processing equipment
16	40%	• taxicab, coin-operated video game
33	15%	• timber resource property
42	12%	• fibre optic cable

Source: Excerpts from Schedule II of the Income Tax Regulations

3. CCA is calculated separately for each asset class and can be claimed only on year-end amounts in each class. Assuming there have been no net additions (purchases less disposals, if any) to a class during a year, the maximum CCA allowed is the undepreciated capital cost (UCC) at year end multiplied by the CCA rate for the class. In a year when there is a net addition (regardless of when it occurs), the maximum CCA on the net addition is one half of the allowed CCA rate multiplied by the amount of the net addition. This is often referred to as the half-year rule. The CCA for the net addition plus the CCA on the remaining UCC is the total CCA for the asset class. If there is only one asset in a class, the maximum CCA allowed in the acquisition year is the acquisition cost multiplied by one half of the CCA rate, even if the asset was purchased one week before year end. No CCA is allowed in the year of disposal for this single asset, even if it is sold just before year end.

4. The government, through the *Income Tax Act*, requires that any benefits that a company receives from government grants and investment tax credits for the purpose of acquiring a capital asset reduce the cost basis of the capital asset for tax purposes. For investment tax credits, the capital cost of the asset and the UCC of the class of asset are reduced in the taxation year following the year of acquisition.

5. CCA can be taken even if it results in a UCC balance that is less than the estimated residual value.

6. Companies are not required to take the maximum rate, or even any CCA, in a particular year, although they normally would as long as they have taxable income. If a company takes less than the maximum CCA in a specific year, it cannot add the remainder to the amount claimed in a subsequent year. In any year, the maximum that can be claimed is limited to the UCC times the specified CCA rate.

Basic CCA and UCC Example

To illustrate depreciation calculations under the CCA system, assume the following facts for a company's March 28, 2010, acquisition of manufacturing equipment, its only asset in this CCA class:

Cost of equipment	$500,000	CCA class	Class 8
Estimated useful life	10 years	CCA rate for Class 8	20%
Estimated residual value	$ 30,000		

Illustration 11A-2 shows how to calculate the CCA for the first three years and the UCC at the end of each of the three years.[13]

---

[13] CCA is subject to rules set by government legislation and can therefore change from time to time. Furthermore, various provincial governments can have different rules for determining CCA for purposes of calculating the income on which provincial taxes are based. The examples in this chapter are based on the federal income tax regulations for 2009.

Illustration 11A-2

CCA Schedule for Equipment

Class 8—20%	CCA	UCC
January 1, 2010		0
Additions during 2010		
Cost of new asset acquisition		$500,000
Disposals during 2010		0
CCA 2010: $500,000 × ½ × 20%	$50,000	(50,000)
December 31, 2010		**$450,000**
Additions less disposals, 2011		0
		$450,000
CCA, 2011: $450,000 × 20%	$90,000	(90,000)
December 31, 2011		**$360,000**
Additions less disposals, 2012		0
		$360,000
CCA, 2012: $360,000 × 20%	$72,000	(72,000)
December 31, 2012		**$288,000**

The **undepreciated capital cost (UCC)** at any point in time is known as the capital asset's **tax value** or **tax basis**. Note that the asset's carrying amount on the balance sheet will be different from its tax value whenever the depreciation method for financial reporting is not the tax method. The significance of this difference to financial reporting is explained in Chapter 18.

Illustration 11A-3 is a continuation of Illustration 11A-2. It incorporates the following transactions:

1. In 2013, the company bought another Class 8 asset for $700,000.

2. In 2014, the company sold for $300,000 the equipment that it purchased in 2010.

3. In 2015, the company sold the remaining Class 8 asset for $500,000. There are no Class 8 assets remaining.

Illustration 11A-3

CCA Schedule for Class 8

Class 8—20%		CCA	UCC
December 31, 2012			**$288,000**
Additions less disposals, 2013			
Cost of new asset			700,000
			$988,000
CCA, 2013			
$288,000 × 20% =	$57,600		
$700,000 × ½ × 20% =	70,000	$127,600	(127,600)
December 31, 2013			**$860,400**
Additions less disposals, 2014			
Manufacturing equipment			
purchased in 2010 (lesser of			
original cost of $500,000 and			
proceeds of disposal of $300,000)			(300,000)
			$560,400
CCA, 2014: $560,400 × 20% =		$112,080	(112,080)
December 31, 2014			**$448,320**
Additions less disposals, 2015			
2013 asset acquisition (lesser of			
original cost of $700,000 and			
proceeds of disposal of $500,000)			(500,000)
			$ (51,680)
Recaptured CCA, 2015		$ (51,680)	51,680
December 31, 2015			**$ 0**

Additions to an Asset Class

The purchase of another Class 8 asset in 2013 resulted in a **net addition** of $700,000 to the undepreciated capital cost at the end of 2013. Consequently, the balance of the UCC at the end of 2013 prior to calculating CCA is made up of this $700,000 plus the $288,000 UCC of the original equipment. The capital cost allowance for 2013 is therefore 20% of $288,000 ($57,600) plus one half of 20% of the net addition of $700,000 ($70,000) for a total of $127,600.

If a government grant of $35,000 had been received in 2013 to help finance the acquisition of this asset, the addition in 2013 would be reported net of the government grant; i.e., at $700,000 − $35,000 = $665,000. If the 2013 acquisition were eligible instead for an investment tax credit (ITC) of $35,000, the tax legislation specifies that the ITC reduces the asset's capital cost and the UCC of the class of assets **in the year following** the year of acquisition.[14] Assuming the Class 8 asset acquired in 2013 in Illustration 11A-3 was eligible for a $35,000 ITC, the $700,000 addition is recognized in 2013, and the UCC is reduced by the $35,000 ITC in 2014 along with the $300,000 proceeds on the original manufacturing equipment. The CCA claimed in 2014 is reduced accordingly.

Retirements from an Asset Class, Continuation of Class

While the CCA class is increased by the cost of additions, it is reduced **by the proceeds on the asset's disposal**, not by the asset's cost. However, if the proceeds on disposal are more than the asset's original capital cost, the class is reduced by the cost only. There is a good reason for this. If the proceeds on disposal are more than the original cost, there is a capital gain on the disposal. Capital gains are taxed differently than ordinary business income; thus, the portion that is a capital gain must be identified as being that. Cost, therefore, is the maximum amount to be deducted from the CCA class. It is not common for most depreciable assets to be sold for more than their cost.

In 2014, the company sells the original manufacturing equipment for $300,000. Since this is less than its $500,000 capital cost, there is no capital gain on disposal. Therefore, Class 8 is reduced by the proceeds on disposal of $300,000, and the CCA for the year is calculated on the remaining balance in the class.

Retirements from an Asset Class, Elimination of Class

When an asset's disposal eliminates the asset class, either because there are no more assets remaining in the class or because the disposal results in the elimination of the UCC balance of the class, the following may result:

1. There may be a recapture of capital cost allowance, with or without a capital gain.

2. There may be a terminal loss, with or without a capital gain. This occurs only when the last asset in the class is disposed of and a UCC balance still exists in the class after deducting the appropriate amount on the asset disposal.

A recapture of CCA occurs when, after deducting the appropriate amount from the class on disposal of an asset, a negative amount is left as the UCC balance. The negative balance is the amount of CCA that must be "recaptured" and included in the calculation of taxable income in the year. It is taxed at the normal income tax rates. When this situation occurs, it suggests that too much CCA was deducted throughout the lives of the assets, and the taxing of the recaptured capital cost allowance therefore adjusts for this. This is what occurred in 2015 in our example. When the proceeds of disposal were deducted from the UCC, the UCC became negative. The excess of $51,680 is therefore added back and included in taxable income in 2015.

---

[14] The rationale is that the ITC is not calculated until after the company's year end, when the tax return is completed and filed.

As indicated above, if an asset is sold for more than its cost, a capital gain results. This may occur whether or not the class is eliminated. For tax purposes, a capital gain is treated differently from a recapture of CCA. Essentially, the **taxable** capital gain (i.e., the amount subject to tax) is only a portion of the capital gain as defined above.[15] The taxable capital gain is included with other taxable income.

If the Class 8 asset purchased in 2013 had been sold in 2015 for $750,000, a capital gain and a recapture of CCA would have resulted. The capital gain would be $50,000, but only 50% or $25,000 would be the taxable capital gain. In this case, Class 8 would be reduced by $700,000 and the recapture would be $251,680 ($700,000 less the $448,320 UCC).

A terminal loss occurs when a positive balance remains in the class after the appropriate reduction is made to the CCA class from the disposal of the last asset. This remaining balance is a terminal loss that is deductible in full when calculating taxable income for the period. If the remaining equipment had been sold in 2015 for $300,000, a terminal loss of $148,320 would have resulted (the UCC of $448,320 less the $300,000 proceeds).

This example illustrating the basic calculations of capital gains, taxable capital gains, recaptured capital cost allowance, and terminal losses has necessarily been simplified. In essence, the tax rate on taxable capital gains is specified by tax law, which may change from time to time and have other implications (e.g., a refundable dividend tax on hand). Similarly, the tax rate that applies to recaptured CCA is affected by the particular circumstances of the type of taxable income that is being reported, of which the recaptured amount is a component. These and other technical aspects, including definitions, are beyond the scope of this text. The reader is warned that specialist knowledge of tax law is often required to determine income taxes payable.

Summary of Learning Objectives for Appendix 11A

KEY TERMS

capital cost allowance (CCA), 712

capital cost allowance method, 712

capital gain, 716

half-year rule, 713

recapture, 715

tax basis, 714

tax value, 714

terminal loss, 716

undepreciated capital cost (UCC), 714

13 Calculate capital cost allowance in straightforward situations.

"Capital cost allowance" (CCA) is the term used for depreciation when calculating taxable income in income tax returns. The CCA method is similar to the declining-balance method except that rates are specified for asset classes and the amount claimed is based on year-end balances. The half-year rule is applied to net additions in the year, which means that only 50% of the normal rate is permitted. For an asset class, retirements are accounted for under specific rules that govern the calculation of taxable income. Capital gains occur if the proceeds on disposal are more than the asset's original cost. When an asset class is eliminated, a terminal loss or recapture of capital cost allowance can occur. When a CCA class ends in a negative balance, a recapture of CCA occurs.

---

[15] The percentage of the capital gain that is taxable has varied in recent years. In 2008, the inclusion rate—the taxable portion—was 50%.

Note: All assignment material with an asterisk (*) relates to the appendix to the chapter.

Brief Exercises

BE11-1   Chong Corp. purchased a machine on July 1, 2011, for $24,000. Chong paid $200 in title fees and a legal fee of **(LO 2)** $125 related to the machine. In addition, Chong paid $500 of shipping charges for delivery, and $475 was paid to a local contractor to build and wire a platform for the machine on the plant floor. The machine has an estimated useful life of six years and a residual value of $3,000. Determine the depreciable amount of Chong's new machine. Chong uses straight-line depreciation.

BE11-2   Odyssey Ltd. purchased machinery on January 1, 2011, for $60,000. The machinery is estimated to have a resid- **(LO 3, 4)** ual value of $6,000 after a useful life of eight years. (a) Calculate the 2011 depreciation expense using the straight-line method. (b) Calculate the 2011 depreciation expense using the straight-line method, but assuming the machinery was purchased on September 1, 2011.

BE11-3   Use the information for Odyssey Ltd. in BE11-2. (a) Calculate the 2011 depreciation expense using the double- **(LO 3, 4)** declining-balance method. (b) Calculate the 2011 depreciation expense using the double-declining-balance method, but assuming the machinery was purchased on October 1, 2011.

BE11-4   Andeo Corporation purchased a truck at the beginning of 2011 for $48,000. The truck is estimated to have a **(LO 4)** residual value of $3,000 and a useful life of 275,000 km. It was driven 52,000 km in 2011 and 65,000 km in 2012. Calculate depreciation expense for 2011 and 2012.

BE11-5   Use the information for Odyssey Ltd. in BE11-2. (a) Calculate the 2011 depreciation expense using the sum-of- **(LO 3, 4)** the-years'-digits method. (b) Calculate the 2011 depreciation expense using the sum-of-the-years'-digits method, but assuming the machinery was purchased on April 1, 2011.

BE11-6   Ironweed Corporation acquires a mine at a cost of $500,000. Capitalized development costs total $125,000. **(LO 5)** After the mine is exhausted, $75,000 will be spent to restore the property, after which it can be sold for $157,500. Ironweed estimates that 5,000 tonnes of ore can be extracted. Assuming that 900 tonnes are extracted in the first year, prepare the journal entry to record depletion.

BE11-7   Chuckwalla Limited purchased a computer for $7,000 on January 1, 2010. Straight-line depreciation is used for **(LO 6)** the computer, based on a five-year life and a $1,000 residual value. In 2012, the estimates are revised. Chuckwalla now feels the computer will be used until December 31, 2013, when it can be sold for $500. Calculate the 2012 depreciation.

BE11-8   Qilin Corp., a small company that follows Canadian private entity GAAP, owns machinery that cost $900,000 **(LO 7)** and has accumulated depreciation of $360,000. The expected future net cash flows from the use of the asset are anticipated to be $500,000. The equipment's fair value is $400,000. Using the cost recovery impairment model, prepare the journal entry, if any, to record the impairment loss.

BE11-9   Use the information for Qilin Corp. given in BE11-8. By the end of the following year, the machinery's fair **(LO 7)** value has increased to $490,000. Assuming the machinery continues to be used in production, prepare the journal entry required, if any, to record the increase in its fair value.

BE11-10   Hambrecht Corp., a publicly traded multinational manufacturer, is preparing its financial statements for the **(LO 7)** fiscal year ending November 30, 2011. Certain specialized equipment was scrapped on January 1, 2012. At November 30, 2011, this equipment was being used in production by Hambrecht and had a carrying amount of $5 million. The asset's value in use at November 30, 2011, was determined to be $6 million, and its fair value less costs to sell was estimated to be $50,000 (the scrap value). What is the recoverable amount of the equipment at November 30, 2011?

BE11-11   Greentree Properties Ltd. is a publicly listed company following IFRS. Assume that on December 31, 2011, the **(LO 7)** carrying amount of land on the balance sheet is $500,000. Management determines that the land's value in use is $425,000 and that the fair value less costs to sell is $400,000. (a) Using the rational entity impairment model, prepare the journal entry required, if any, to record the impairment loss. (b) Due to an economic rebound in the area, by the end of the following year, the land has a value in use of $550,000 and the fair value less costs to sell is $480,000. Prepare the journal entry required, if any, to record the increase in its recoverable amount.

BE11-12   Riverbed Ltd. is a manufacturer of computer network equipment and has just recently adopted IFRS. The **(LO 7)** wireless division is a cash-generating unit that has the following carrying amounts for its net assets: land, $20,000; buildings, $30,000; and equipment, $10,000. The undiscounted cash flows from the use and eventual disposal of the wireless division are $65,000 and the present value of these cash flows is $47,000. The land could be sold immediately for $35,000; however, the buildings and the equipment are specialized and cannot be used elsewhere and thus have no resale value. Allocate the impairment loss to the net assets of the wireless division using (a) the cost recovery model for private entity GAAP and (b) the rational entity model for IFRS.

(LO 9) **BE11-13** Volumetrics Corporation owns machinery that cost $20,000 when purchased on January 1, 2009. Depreciation has been recorded at a rate of $3,000 per year, resulting in a balance in accumulated depreciation of $9,000 at December 31, 2011. The machinery is sold on September 1, 2012, for $10,500. Prepare journal entries to (a) update depreciation for 2012 and (b) record the sale.

(LO 9) **BE11-14** Use the information presented for Volumetrics Corporation in BE11-13, but assume the machinery is sold for $5,200 instead of $10,500. Prepare journal entries to (a) update depreciation for 2012 and (b) record the sale.

(LO 11) **BE11-15** In its 2010 annual report, Winkler Limited reports beginning-of-the-year total assets of $1,923 million, end-of-the-year total assets of $2,487 million, total revenue of $2,687 million, and net income of $52 million. (a) Calculate Winkler's asset turnover ratio. (b) Calculate Winkler's profit margin. (c) Calculate Winkler's rate of return on assets (1) using the asset turnover and profit margin, and (2) using net income.

(LO 13) ***BE11-16** Fong Limited purchased an asset at a cost of $45,000 on March 1, 2011. The asset has a useful life of seven years and an estimated residual value of $3,000. For tax purposes, the asset belongs in CCA Class 8, with a rate of 20%. Calculate the CCA for each year, 2011 to 2014, assuming this is the only asset in Class 8.

Exercises

(LO 1, 3) **E11-1** **(Match Depreciation Method with Assets)** The following assets have been acquired by various companies over the past year:

1. Boardroom table and chairs for a corporate head office

2. Dental equipment in a new dental clinic

3. Long-haul trucks for a trucking business

4. Weight and aerobic equipment in a new health club facility

5. Classroom computers in a new community college

Instructions

For each long-lived asset listed above, (a) identify the factors to consider in establishing the useful life of the asset, and (b) recommend the pattern of depreciation that most closely represents the pattern of economic benefits received by the entity that owns the asset. Defend your position.

(LO 2, 3, 4) **E11-2** **(Terminology, Calculations—Straight-Line, Double-Declining-Balance)** Diderot Corp. acquired a property on September 15, 2010, for $220,000, paying $3,000 in transfer taxes and a $1,500 real estate fee. Based on the provincial assessment information, 75% of the property's value was related to the building and 25% to the land. It is estimated that the building, with proper maintenance, will last for 35 years, at which time it will be torn down. Diderot, however, expects to use it for 10 years only as it is not expected to suit the company's purposes after that. The company should be able to sell the property for $95,000 at that time, with $40,000 of this amount being for the land.

Instructions

Assuming a December 31 year end, identify all of the following:

(a) The building's cost

(b) The building's depreciable amount

(c) The building's useful life

(d) Depreciation expense for 2010, assuming the straight-line method

(e) Depreciation expense for 2011, assuming the double-declining-balance method

(f) The building's carrying amount at December 31, 2011, assuming the double-declining-balance method

E11-3 **(Depreciation Calculations—Straight-Line, Double-Declining-Balance)** Jiang Company Ltd. purchases **(LO 4)** equipment on January 1, 2011, at a cost of $387,000. The asset is expected to have a service life of 12 years and a residual value of $39,000.

Instructions

(a) Calculate the amount of depreciation for each of 2011, 2012, and 2013 using the straight-line method.

(b) Calculate the amount of depreciation for each of 2011, 2012, and 2013 using the double-declining-balance method. (In performing your calculations, round percentages to the nearest one-hundredth and round dollar amounts to the nearest dollar.)

E11-4 **(Depreciation—Conceptual Understanding)** Hubbub Company Ltd. acquired a plant asset at the beginning of **(LO 4)** Year 1. The asset has an estimated service life of five years. An employee has prepared depreciation schedules for this asset using two different methods to compare the results of using one method with the results of using the other. Assume that the following schedules have been correctly prepared for this asset using (1) the straight-line method and (2) the double-declining-balance method.

Year	Straight-line	Double-Declining-Balance
1	$12,000	$30,000
2	12,000	18,000
3	12,000	10,800
4	12,000	1,200
5	12,000	–0–
Total	$60,000	$60,000

Instructions

Answer the following questions.

(a) What is the cost of the asset that is being depreciated?

(b) What amount, if any, was used in the depreciation calculations for the residual value for this asset?

(c) Which method will produce the higher net income in Year 1?

(d) Which method will produce the higher charge to income in Year 4?

(e) Which method will produce the higher carrying amount for the asset at the end of Year 3?

(f) Which method will produce the higher cash flow in Year 1? In Year 4?

(g) If the asset is sold at the end of Year 3, which method would yield the higher gain (or lower loss) on disposal of the asset?

E11-5 **(Depreciation Calculations—Straight-Line, Double-Declining-Balance; Partial Periods)** Gambit **(LO 3, 4)** Corporation purchased a new plant asset on April 1, 2011, at a cost of $769,000. It was estimated to have a service life of 20 years and a residual value of $71,180. Gambit's accounting period is the calendar year.

Instructions

(a) Calculate the depreciation for this asset for 2011 and 2012 using the straight-line method.

(b) Calculate the depreciation for this asset for 2011 and 2012 using the double-declining-balance method.

***E11-6** **(Depreciation Calculations—Four Methods; Partial Periods)** Iroko Corporation purchased a new machine **(LO 3, 4, 13)** for its assembly process on August 1, 2011. The cost of this machine was $136,400. The company estimated that the machine will have a trade-in value of $14,200 at the end of its service life. Its useful life was estimated to be six years and its working hours were estimated to be 18,000 hours. Iroko's year end is December 31. (Round depreciation per unit to three decimal places.)

Instructions

Calculate the depreciation expense under each of the following:

(a) Straight-line depreciation for 2011

(b) The activity method for 2011, assuming that machine use was 800 hours

(c) The double-declining-balance method for 2012

(d) The capital cost allowance method for 2011 and 2012 using a CCA rate of 25%

(LO 3, 4)   **E11-7**   **(Depreciation Calculations—Five Methods; Partial Periods)** Jupiter Wells Corp. purchased machinery for $315,000 on May 1, 2010. It is estimated that it will have a useful life of 10 years, residual value of $15,000, production of 240,000 units, and 25,000 working hours. During 2011, Jupiter Wells Corp. uses the machinery for 2,650 hours and the machinery produces 25,500 units.

Instructions

From the information given, calculate the depreciation charge for 2011 under each of the following methods, assuming Jupiter has a December 31 year end. (Round to three decimal places.)

  (a) Straight-line

  (b) Units-of-output

  (c) Working hours

  (d) Declining-balance, using a 20% rate

  (e) Sum-of-the-years'-digits

(LO 3, 4)   **E11-8**   **(Different Methods of Depreciation)** Jared Industries Ltd. presents you with the following information:

Description	Date Purchased	Cost	Residual Value	Life in Years	Depreciation Method	Accumulated Depreciation to Dec. 31, 2010	Depreciation for 2011
Machine A	Dec. 2, 2009	$142,500	$16,000	10	(a)	$39,900	(b)
Machine B	Aug. 15, 2008	(c)	21,000	5	Straight-line	29,000	(d)
Machine C	July 21, 2007	75,400	23,500	8	Double-declining-balance	(e)	(f)

Instructions

Complete the table for the year ended December 31, 2011. The company depreciates all assets for a half year in the year of acquisition and the year of disposal.

(LO 4)   **E11-9**   **(Depreciation for Fractional Periods)** On March 10, 2012, Lucas Limited sold equipment that it purchased for $192,000 on August 20, 2005. It was originally estimated that the equipment would have a life of 12 years and a residual value of $16,800 at the end of that time, and depreciation has been calculated on that basis. The company uses the straight-line method of depreciation.

Instructions

  (a) Calculate the depreciation charge on this equipment for 2005 and for 2012, and the total charge for the period from 2006 to 2011, inclusive, under each of the following six assumptions for partial periods:

   1. Depreciation is calculated for the exact period of time during which the asset is owned. (Use 365 days for your base.)

   2. Depreciation is calculated for the full year on the January 1 balance in the asset account.

   3. Depreciation is calculated for the full year on the December 31 balance in the asset account.

   4. Depreciation for a half year is charged on plant assets that are acquired or disposed of during the year.

   5. Depreciation is calculated on additions from the beginning of the month following their acquisition and on disposals to the beginning of the month following the disposal.

   6. Depreciation is calculated for a full period on all assets in use for over half a year, and no depreciation is charged on assets in use for less than half a year. (Use 365 days for your base.)

  (b) Briefly evaluate the above methods in terms of basic accounting theory and how simple the methods are to apply.

(LO 4, 6, 9)   **E11-10**   **(Depreciation Calculations—Revaluation Model)** Jamoka Corporation is a public company that manufactures farm implements such as tractors, combines, and wagons. Jamoka uses the revaluation model allowed in IAS16. One of the items in the property, plant, and equipment section on Jamoka's balance sheet is equipment that was revalued to $100,000 at December 31, 2009. This equipment is expected to have a remaining useful life of five years, with benefits being received evenly over that period. Management has estimated the residual value to be $10,000.

Consider the following two situations:

Situation 1: At December 31, 2010, no formal revaluation is performed as management determines that the carrying amount of the assets is not materially different from the fair value.

Situation 2: At December 31, 2010, a formal revaluation is performed and the independent external appraisers assess the equipment's fair value to be $89,000. During the revaluation process, it is determined that the remaining useful life is four years and the residual value is $11,000.

At December 31, 2011, no formal revaluation is performed as management determines that the assets' carrying amount is not materially different from their fair value. The equipment is sold on March 31, 2012, for $62,000.

Instructions

Consider the following independent situations.

(a) Prepare the journal entries required, if any, under situation 1 described above for: (1) the fiscal year ended December 31, 2010; (2) the fiscal year ended December 31, 2011; and (3) the disposal of the equipment on March 31, 2012.

(b) Prepare the journal entries required, if any, under situation 2 described above for: (1) the fiscal year ended December 31, 2010; (2) the fiscal year ended December 31, 2011; and (3) the disposal of the equipment on March 31, 2012.

E11-11 (Depletion Calculations—Timber) Rachel Timber Inc., a small private company that follows Canadian private **(LO 5)** entity GAAP, owns 9,000 hectares of timberland purchased in 1999 at a cost of $1,400 per hectare. At the time of purchase, the land without the timber was valued at $420 per hectare. In 2000, Rachel built fire lanes and roads, with a life of 30 years, at a cost of $84,000 and separately capitalized these costs. Every year, Rachel sprays to prevent disease at a cost of $3,000 per year and spends $7,000 to maintain the fire lanes and roads. During 2001, Rachel selectively logged and sold 700,000 cubic metres of the estimated 3.5 million cubic metres of timber. In 2002, Rachel planted new seedlings to replace the cut trees at a cost of $100,000.

Instructions

(a) Determine the depletion charge and the portion of depletion included in the cost of timber sold for 2001.

(b) Rachel has not logged since 2001. Assuming that Rachel logged and sold 900,000 cubic metres of timber in 2012, and the timber cruiser (i.e., the appraiser) had estimated a total resource of 5 million cubic metres, determine the cost of timber sold that relates to the depletion for 2012.

(c) How would Rachel account for the maintenance costs of the fire lanes and roads and the spraying of the timberland?

(d) Discuss the depreciation methods that Rachel could use to depreciate the cost of the fire lanes and roads.

(e) Explain how your answers for parts (a) to (d) would differ if Rachel were a public company and followed IFRS.

Digging Deeper

E11-12 (Depletion Calculations—Oil) Marmon Drilling Limited leases property on which oil has been discovered. **(LO 5)** Wells on this property produced 21,000 barrels of oil during the current year and it was sold at an average of $45 per barrel. The total oil resources of this property are estimated to be 250,000 barrels.

The lease provided for an immediate payment of $500,000 to the lessor (owner) before drilling began and an annual rental of $27,500. Development costs of $625,000 were incurred before any oil was produced, and Marmon follows a policy of capitalizing these preproduction costs. The lease also specified that each year the lessor would be paid a premium of 5% of the sales price of every barrel of oil that was removed. In addition, the lessee is to clean up all the waste and debris from drilling and to pay the costs of reconditioning the land for farming when the wells are abandoned. It is estimated that the present value of the obligations at the time of the lease for the cleanup and reconditioning for the existing wells is $30,000.

Instructions

(a) From the information given, provide the journal entry made by Marmon Drilling Limited to record depletion for the current year assuming that Marmon applies Canadian private entity GAAP.

(b) Assuming that the oil property was acquired at the beginning of the current year, provide the entry to record the acquisition of the asset and the annual rental payment.

E11-13 (Depletion Calculations—Minerals) At the beginning of 2011, Kao Company, a small private company, **(LO 5)** acquired a mine for $850,000. Of this amount, $100,000 was ascribed to the land value and the remaining portion to the minerals in the mine. Surveys conducted by geologists have indicated that approximately 12 million units of the ore appear to be in the mine. Kao incurred $170,000 of development costs associated with this mine prior to any extraction of minerals. It also determined that the fair value of its obligation to prepare the land for an alternative use when all of the mineral has been removed was $40,000. During 2011, 2.5 million units of ore were extracted and 2.2 million of these units were sold.

Instructions

Calculate the following information for 2011 (rounding your answers to two decimal places):

(a) The depletion cost per unit

(b) The total amount of depletion for 2011 (and prepare the required journal entry, if any)

(c) The total amount that is charged as an expense for 2011 for the cost of minerals sold during 2011 (and prepare the required journal entry, if any)

(LO 2, 6, 9) **E11-14** **(Depreciation Calculation—Replacement, Trade-in)** Hawkins Corporation bought a machine on June 1, 2008, for $31,800, f.o.b. the place of manufacture. Freight costs were $300, and $500 was spent to install it. The machine's useful life was estimated at 10 years, with a residual value of $1,900.

On June 1, 2009, a part that was designed to reduce the machine's operating costs was added to the machine and cost $1,980. On June 1, 2012, the company bought a new machine with a greater capacity for $35,000, delivered. A trade-in value was received on the old machine equal to its fair value of $19,000. Removing the old machine from the plant cost $75, and installing the new one cost $1,300. It was estimated that the new machine would have a useful life of 10 years, with a residual value of $4,000.

Instructions

Assuming that depreciation is calculated on the straight-line basis, determine the amount of any gain or loss on the disposal of the first machine on June 1, 2012, and the amount of depreciation that should be provided during the company's fiscal year, which begins on June 1, 2012.

(LO 6) **E11-15** **(Depreciation—Change in Estimate)** Machinery purchased for $56,000 by Wong Corp. in 2007 was originally estimated to have an eight-year life with a residual value of $4,000. Depreciation has been entered for five years on this basis. In 2012, it is determined that the total estimated life (including 2012) should have been 10 years, with a residual value of $4,500 at the end of that time. Assume straight-line depreciation.

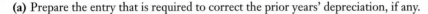

Instructions

(a) Prepare the entry that is required to correct the prior years' depreciation, if any.

(b) Prepare the entry to record depreciation for 2012.

Digging Deeper

(c) Repeat part (b) assuming Wong Corp. uses the double-declining-balance method of depreciation.

(LO 6) **E11-16** **(Depreciation Calculation—Addition, Change in Estimate)** In 1983, Lincoln Limited completed the construction of a building at a cost of $1.8 million; it occupied it in January 1984. It was estimated that the building would have a useful life of 40 years and a residual value of $400,000.

Early in 1994, an addition to the building was constructed at a cost of $750,000. At that time, no changes were expected in its useful life, but the residual value with the addition was estimated to increase by $150,000. The addition would not be of economic use to the company beyond the life of the original structure.

In 2012, as a result of a thorough review of its depreciation policies, company management determined that the building's original life should have been estimated at 30 years. Because the district where the building is has been going through a large-scale renewal, with older buildings being torn down and new ones built, it is now expected that the company's building and addition are unlikely to have any residual value at the end of the 30-year period.

Instructions

(a) Using the straight-line method, calculate the annual depreciation that would have been charged from 1984 through 1993.

(b) Calculate the annual depreciation that would have been charged from 1994 through 2011.

(c) Prepare the entry, if necessary, to adjust the account balances because of the revision of the estimated life in 2012.

(d) Calculate the annual depreciation to be charged beginning with 2012.

(LO 6) **E11-17** **(Depreciation Replacement—Change in Estimate)** Finlay Limited constructed a building at a cost of $2.8 million and has occupied it since January 1991. It was estimated at that time that its life would be 40 years, with no residual value. In January 2011, a new roof was installed at a cost of $370,000, and it was estimated then that the building would have a useful life of 25 years from that date. The cost of the old roof was $190,000 and was capitalized in the Building account at that time.

Instructions

(a) What amount of depreciation was charged annually for the years 1991 through 2010? (Assume straight-line depreciation.)

(b) What entry should be made in 2011 to record the roof replacement?

(c) Prepare the entry in January 2011 to record the revision in the building's estimated life, if necessary.

(d) What amount of depreciation should be charged for the year 2011?

E11-18 **(Error Analysis and Depreciation)** Gibbs Inc. purchased a machine on January 1, 2011, at a cost of $60,000. **(LO 2, 4)** The machine is expected to have an estimated residual value of $5,000 at the end of its five-year life. The company capitalized the machine and depreciated it in 2011 using the double-declining-balance method of depreciation. The company has a policy of using the straight-line method to depreciate equipment but the company accountant neglected to follow company policy when he used the double-declining-balance method. Net income for the year ended December 31, 2011, was $53,000 as the result of depreciating the machine incorrectly.

Instructions

Using the method of depreciation that the company normally follows, prepare the correcting entry and determine the corrected net income.

E11-19 **(Error Analysis and Depreciation)** Wettlauffer Company Ltd. shows the following entries in its Equipment **(LO 2, 4)** account for 2011; all amounts are based on historical cost.

	Equipment				
1/1	Balance	134,750	6/30	Cost of equipment sold	
8/10	Purchases	32,000		(purchased prior to 2011)	23,000
8/12	Freight on equipment purchased	700			
8/25	Installation costs	2,700			
11/10	Repairs	500			

Instructions

(a) Prepare any correcting entries that are necessary.

(b) Assuming that depreciation is to be charged for a full year on the ending balance in the asset account, calculate the proper depreciation charge for 2011 under both methods listed below. Assume an estimated life of 10 years, with no residual value. The machinery included in the January 1, 2011 Equipment balance was purchased in 2009.

   1. Straight-line

   2. Declining-balance (assume twice the straight-line rate)

E11-20 **(Impairment—Cost Recovery and Rational Entity Models)** The information that follows relates to equip- **(LO 7)** ment owned by Gaurav Limited at December 31, 2011:

Cost	$9,000,000
Accumulated depreciation to date	1,000,000
Expected future net cash flows (undiscounted)	7,000,000
Expected future net cash flows (discounted, value in use)	6,350,000
Fair value	6,200,000

Assume that Gaurav will continue to use this asset in the future. As at December 31, 2011, the equipment has a remaining useful life of four years. Gaurav uses the straight-line method of depreciation.

Instructions

(a) Assume that Gaurav is a private company that follows Canadian private entity GAAP and uses the cost recovery impairment model.

   1. Prepare the journal entry, if any, to record the impairment of the asset at December 31, 2011.

   2. Prepare the journal entry, if any, to record depreciation expense for 2012.

   3. The equipment's fair value at December 31, 2012, is $6.5 million. Prepare the journal entry, if any, to record this increase in fair value.

(b) Repeat the requirements in (a) above assuming that Gaurav is a public company that follows IFRS and uses the rational entity impairment model.

E11-21 **(Impairment—Cost Recovery and Rational Entity Models)** Assume the same information as in E11-20, **(LO 7, 8)** except that at December 31, 2011, Gaurav discontinues use of the equipment and intends to dispose of it in the coming year by selling it to a competitor. It is expected that the disposal cost will be $50,000.

Instructions

(a) Assume that Gaurav is a private company that follows Canadian private entity GAAP and uses the cost recovery impairment model.

    1. Prepare the journal entry, if any, to record the impairment of the asset at December 31, 2011.

    2. Prepare the journal entry, if any, to record depreciation expense for 2012.

    3. Assume that the asset was not sold by December 31, 2012. The equipment's fair value (and recoverable amount) on this date is $6.5 million. Prepare the journal entry, if any, to record this increase in fair value. It is expected that the cost of disposal is still $50,000.

    4. Identify where, and at what amount, this asset will be reported on the December 31, 2012 balance sheet.

(b) Repeat the requirements in (a) above assuming that Gaurav is a public company that follows IFRS and uses the rational entity impairment model.

(LO 7) **E11-22** **(Impairment—Cost Recovery Model)** The management of Luis Inc., a small private company that uses the cost recovery impairment model, was discussing whether certain equipment should be written down as a charge to current operations because of obsolescence. The assets had a cost of $900,000, and depreciation of $400,000 had been taken to December 31, 2011. On December 31, 2011, management projected the undiscounted future net cash flows from this equipment to be $300,000 and its fair value to be $230,000. The company intends to use this equipment in the future.

Instructions

(a) Prepare the journal entry, if any, to record the impairment at December 31, 2011.

(b) Where should the gain or loss on the writedown, if any, be reported in the income statement?

(c) At December 31, 2012, the equipment's fair value increased to $260,000. Prepare the journal entry, if any, to record this increase in fair value.

(d) Assume instead that the undiscounted future net cash flows from the equipment on December 31, 2011, were expected to be $510,000 and its fair value was $450,000 on this date. Prepare the journal entry, if any, to record the impairment at December 31, 2011.

(e) Assume instead that the future net cash flows from the equipment are $45,000 per year for each of the next 10 years and that there is no active market for the equipment. Luis Inc. uses a 10% discount rate on its cash flow estimates. Prepare the journal entry, if any, to record impairment at December 31, 2011.

Digging Deeper

(f) Discuss why impairment is tested using undiscounted future cash flows rather than the present value of future cash flows.

(LO 7) **E11-23** **(Impairment—Cash-Generating Units)** A mining company owns a significant mineral deposit in its northern territory. Included in the assets is a road system that was constructed to give company personnel access to the mineral deposit for maintenance and later extraction activities. The road system cannot be sold independently.

Instructions

How should the road system's recoverable amount be determined?

(LO 7) **E11-24** **(Impairment—Rational Entity Model and Cash-Generating Units)** Green Thumb Landscaping Limited has determined that its lawn maintenance division is a cash-generating unit. The carrying amounts of the assets in the division at December 31, 2011, are as follows:

Land	$ 25,000
Building	50,000
Equipment	30,000
Trucks	15,000
	$120,000

The lawn maintenance division has been assessed for impairment and it is determined that the recoverable amount is $108,000, indicating that the unit has incurred an impairment loss of $12,000.

Instructions

(a) Determine the allocation of the impairment loss to the assets in the lawn maintenance division and prepare the journal entry, if any, to record the impairment at December 31, 2011, assuming that none of the individual assets in the division have a determinable recoverable amount on their own.

(b) Determine the allocation of the impairment loss to the assets in the lawn maintenance division and prepare the journal entry, if any, to record the impairment at December 31, 2011, assuming the only individual asset in the division that has a determinable recoverable amount on its own is the building, which has a fair value less cost to sell of $46,000.

E11-25   (Entries for Disposition of Assets) Consider the following independent situations for Kwok Corporation: **(LO 9)**

Situation 1: Kwok purchased equipment in 2005 for $120,000 and estimated a $12,000 residual value at the end of the equipment's 10-year useful life. At December 31, 2011, there was $75,600 in the Accumulated Depreciation account for this equipment using the straight-line method of depreciation. On March 31, 2012, the equipment was sold for $28,000.

Situation 2: Kwok sold a piece of machinery for $10,000 on July 31, 2012. The machine originally cost $38,000 on January 1, 2004. It was estimated that the machine would have a useful life of 12 years with a residual value of $2,000.

Situation 3: Kwok sold office equipment that had a carrying amount of $3,500 for $5,200. The office equipment originally cost $12,000 and it is estimated that it would cost $16,000 to replace the office equipment.

Instructions

Prepare the appropriate journal entries to record the disposition of the property, plant, and equipment assets assuming that Kwok's fiscal year end is December 31 and that Kwok only prepares financial statements and adjusts the accounts annually.

E11-26   (Entries for Disposition of Assets) On December 31, 2011, Grey Inc. owns a machine with a carrying amount   **(LO 9)** of $940,000. The original cost and accumulated depreciation for the machine at this date are as follows:

Machine	$1,300,000
Accumulated depreciation	360,000
	$ 940,000

Depreciation is calculated at $60,000 per year on a straight-line basis.

Instructions

A set of independent situations follows. For each situation, indicate the journal entry to record the transaction. Make sure that depreciation entries are made to update the machine's carrying amount before its disposal.

(a) A fire completely destroys the machine on August 31, 2012. An insurance settlement of $430,000 was received for this casualty. Assume the settlement was received immediately.

(b) On April 1, 2012, Grey sold the machine for $1,040,000 to Dwight Company.

(c) On July 31, 2012, the company donated this machine to the Dartmouth City Council. The machine's fair value at the time of the donation was estimated to be $1.1 million.

E11-27   (Disposition of Assets) On April 1, 2011, Lombardi Corp. was awarded $460,000 cash as compensation for the   **(LO 9)** forced sale of its land and building, which were directly in the path of a new highway. The land and building cost $60,000 and $280,000, respectively, when they were acquired. At April 1, 2011, the accumulated depreciation for the building amounted to $165,000. On August 1, 2011, Lombardi purchased a piece of replacement property for cash. The new land cost $160,000 and the new building cost $410,000.

Instructions

(a) Prepare the journal entries to record the transactions on April 1 and August 1, 2011.

(b) How would the transaction be shown on the income statement for 2011?

Digging
Deeper

E11-28   (Ratio Analysis) The 2010 annual report of Trocchi Inc. contains the following information (in thousands):   **(LO 11)**

	Dec. 31, 2010	Dec. 31, 2009
Total assets	$1,071,348	$ 787,167
Total liabilities	626,178	410,044
Consolidated sales	3,374,463	2,443,592
Net earnings	66,234	49,062

Instructions

(a) Calculate the following ratios for Trocchi Inc. for 2010:

1. Asset turnover ratio

2. Rate of return on assets

3. Profit margin on sales

(b) How can the asset turnover ratio be used to calculate the rate of return on assets?

(c) Briefly comment on the results for the ratios calculated in part (a).

(LO 13)   ***E11-29**   **(CCA)** During 2011, Laiken Limited sold its only Class 3 asset. At the time of sale, the balance of the undepreciated capital cost for this class was $37,450. The asset originally cost $129,500.

**Digging
Deeper**

Instructions

(a) Indicate what the amounts would be for recaptured CCA, capital gains, and terminal losses, if any, assuming the asset was sold for proceeds of (1) $132,700, (2) $51,000, and (3) $22,000.

(b) Assume the tax rates are scheduled to increase for 2011. What strategy could Laiken Limited use to reduce its taxes payable that are due to the recapture on the disposal of the asset?

(LO 13)   ***E11-30**   **(Book vs. Tax Depreciation)** Barnett Inc. purchased computer equipment on March 1, 2010, for $31,000. The computer equipment has a useful life of five years and a residual value of $1,000. Barnett uses a double-declining-balance method of depreciation for this type of capital asset. For tax purposes, the computer is assigned to Class 10 with a 30% rate.

Instructions

(a) Prepare a schedule of depreciation covering 2010, 2011, and 2012 for financial reporting purposes for the new asset purchase. The company follows a policy of taking a full year's depreciation in the year of purchase and none in the year of disposal.

(b) Prepare a schedule of CCA and UCC for this asset covering 2010, 2011, and 2012, assuming it is the only Class 10 asset owned by Barnett.

(c) How much depreciation is deducted over the three-year period on the financial statements? In determining taxable income? What is the carrying amount of the computer equipment on the December 31, 2012 balance sheet? What is the tax value of the computer equipment at December 31, 2012?

Problems

P11-1   Phoenix Corp. purchased Machine no. 201 on May 1, 2011. The following information relating to Machine no. 201 was gathered at the end of May:

Price	$85,000
Credit terms	2/10, n/30
Freight-in costs	$ 800
Preparation and installation costs	$ 3,800
Labour costs during regular production operations	$10,500

It was expected that the machine could be used for 10 years, after which the residual value would be zero. Phoenix intends to use the machine for only eight years, however, and expects to then be able to sell it for $1,500. The invoice for Machine no. 201 was paid on May 5, 2011. Phoenix has a December 31 year end.

Instructions

(a) Calculate the depreciation expense for the years indicated using the following methods. (Round to the nearest dollar.)

1. Straight-line method for the fiscal years ended December 31, 2011 and 2012

2. Double-declining-balance method for the fiscal years ended December 31, 2011 and 2012

*(b) Calculate the capital cost allowance for the 2011 and 2012 tax returns, assuming a CCA class with a rate of 25%.

(c) The president of Phoenix tells you that because the company is a new organization, she expects it will be several years before production and sales reach optimum levels. She asks you to recommend a depreciation method that will allocate less of the company's depreciation expense to the early years and more to later years of the assets' lives. Which method would you recommend? Explain.

(d) In your answer to part (c) above, how would cash flows to the new company be affected by the choice of depreciation method? How would current and potential creditors interpret the choice of depreciation method?

P11-2 On June 15, 2008, a second-hand machine was purchased for $77,000. Before being put into service, the equipment was overhauled at a cost of $5,200, and additional costs of $400 for direct material and $800 for direct labour were paid in fine-tuning the controls. The machine has an estimated residual value of $5,000 at the end of its five-year useful life. The machine is expected to operate for 100,000 hours before it will be replaced and is expected to produce 1.2 million units in this time. Operating data for the next five fiscal years are as follows:

Year	Hours of Operation	Units Produced
2008	10,000	115,000
2009	25,000	310,000
2010	25,000	294,000
2011	30,000	363,000
2012	10,000	118,000

The company has an October 31 year end.

Instructions

(a) Calculate the depreciation charges for each fiscal year under each of the following depreciation methods:

   1. Straight-line method

   2. Activity method: based on output

   3. Activity method: based on input

   4. Double-declining-balance method

   *5. CCA, Class 8, 20%

(b) What is the carrying amount of the machine on the October 31, 2011 balance sheet under the first four methods above?

(c) Compare your answers in (b) with the asset's tax value at the same date.

(d) What happens if the actual hours of operation or units produced do not correspond to the numbers that were estimated in setting the rate?

P11-3 Comco Tool Corp. records depreciation annually at the end of the year. Its policy is to take a full year's depreciation on all assets that are used throughout the year and depreciation for half a year on all machines that are acquired or disposed of during the year. The depreciation rate for the machinery is 10%, applied on a straight-line basis, with no estimated scrap or residual value.

The balance of the Machinery account at the beginning of 2011 was $172,300; the Accumulated Depreciation on Machinery account had a balance of $72,900. The machinery accounts were affected by the following transactions that occurred in 2011:

Jan. 15 Machine no. 38, which cost $9,600 when it was acquired on June 3, 2004, was retired and sold as scrap metal for $600.

Feb. 27 Machine no. 81 was purchased. The fair value of this machine was $12,500. It replaced two machines, nos. 12 and 27, which were traded in on the new machine. Machine no. 12 was acquired on February 4, 1999, at a cost of $5,500 and was still carried in the accounts although it was fully depreciated and not in use. Machine no. 27 was acquired on June 11, 2004, at a cost of $8,200. In addition to these two used machines, $9,000 was paid in cash.

Apr. 7 Machine no. 54 was equipped with electric controls at a cost of $940. This machine, originally equipped with simple hand controls, was purchased on December 11, 2007, for $1,800. The new electric controls can be attached to any one of several machines in the shop.

   12 Machine no. 24 was repaired at a cost of $720 after a fire caused by a short circuit in the wiring burned out the motor and damaged certain essential parts.

July 22 Machines 25, 26, and 41 were sold for $3,100 cash. The purchase dates and cost of these machines were as follows:
   No. 25   May 8, 2003 $4,000
   No. 26   May 8, 2003   3,200
   No. 41   June 1, 2005   2,800

Instructions

(a) Record each transaction in general journal form.

(b) Calculate and record depreciation for the year. None of the machines currently included in the balance of the account were acquired before January 1, 2002.

P11-4   On January 1, 2011, Dayan Corporation, a small manufacturer of machine tools, acquired new industrial equipment for $1.1 million. The new equipment had a useful life of five years and the residual value was estimated to be $50,000. Dayan estimates that the new equipment can produce 12,000 machine tools in its first year. It estimates that production will decline by 1,000 units per year over the remaining useful life of the equipment.

The following depreciation methods may be used: (1) straight-line, (2) double-declining-balance; and (3) units-of-output. For tax purposes, the CCA class is Class 10—30%.

Instructions

(a) Which of the three depreciation methods would maximize net income for financial statement reporting purposes for the three-year period ending December 31, 2013? Prepare a schedule showing the amount of accumulated depreciation at December 31, 2013, under the method you chose.

*(b) Over the same three-year period, how much capital cost allowance would have been written off for tax purposes?

(c) Prepare a graph that covers the five-year period and has separate chart lines for each of the three depreciation methods and for the CCA method. Which pattern of depreciation do you feel best reflects the benefits that are provided by the new equipment? Explain briefly.

P11-5   The following data relate to the Plant Assets account of Keller Inc. at December 31, 2010:

	A	B	C	D
Original cost	$46,000	$58,000	$68,000	$73,000
Year purchased	2005	2006	2007	2008
Useful life	10 years	17,000 hours	15 years	10 years
Residual value	$3,900	$4,450	$8,000	$4,700
Depreciation method	straight-line	activity	straight-line	double-declining
Accumulated depreciation through 2010[a]	$21,050	$31,600	$12,000	$26,280

[a]In the year an asset is purchased, Keller does not record any depreciation expense on the asset. In the year an asset is retired or traded in, Keller takes a full year's depreciation on the asset.

The following transactions occurred during 2011:

1. On May 5, Asset A was sold for $16,500 cash. The company's bookkeeper recorded this retirement as follows:

Cash	16,500	
Asset A		16,500

2. On December 31, it was determined that Asset B had been used 3,200 hours during 2011.

3. On December 31, before calculating depreciation expense on Asset C, Keller management decided that Asset C's remaining useful life should be nine years as of year end.

4. On December 31, it was discovered that a plant asset purchased in 2010 had been expensed completely in that year. The asset cost $31,000 and had a useful life of 10 years when it was acquired and had no residual value. Management has decided to use the double-declining-balance method for this asset, which can be referred to as "Asset E." Ignore income taxes.

Instructions

Prepare any necessary adjusting journal entries required at December 31, 2011, as well as any entries to record depreciation for 2011.

P11-6   Soon after December 31, 2011, the auditor of Morino Manufacturing Corp. asked the company to prepare a depreciation schedule for semi trucks that showed the additions, retirements, depreciation, and other data that affected the company's income in the four-year period from 2008 to 2011, inclusive. The following data were obtained.

Balance of Semi Trucks account, January 1, 2008:	
Truck no. 1, purchased Jan. 1, 2005, cost	$18,000
Truck no. 2, purchased July 1, 2005, cost	22,000
Truck no. 3, purchased Jan. 1, 2007, cost	30,000
Truck no. 4, purchased July 1, 2007, cost	24,000
Balance, January 1, 2008	$94,000

The account Semi Trucks—Accumulated Depreciation had a correct balance of $30,200 on January 1, 2008 (includes depreciation on the four trucks from the respective dates of purchase, based on a five-year life, no residual value). No charges had been made against the account before January 1, 2008.

Transactions between January 1, 2008, and December 31, 2011, and their record in the ledger were as follows:

July 1, 2008   Truck no. 3 was traded for a larger one (no. 5). The agreed purchase price (fair value) was $34,000. Morino Manufacturing paid the automobile dealer $15,000 cash on the transaction. The entry was a debit to Semi Trucks and a credit to Cash, $15,000.

Jan. 1, 2009   Truck no. 1 was sold for $3,500 cash. The entry was a debit to Cash and a credit to Semi Trucks, $3,500.

July 1, 2010   A new truck (no. 6) was acquired for $36,000 cash and was charged at that amount to the Semi Trucks account. (Assume truck no. 2 was not retired.)

July 1, 2010   Truck no. 4 was so badly damaged in an accident that it was sold as scrap for $700 cash. Morino Manufacturing received $2,500 from the insurance company. The entry made by the bookkeeper was a debit to Cash, $3,200, and credits to Miscellaneous Income, $700, and Semi Trucks, $2,500.

Entries for depreciation were made at the close of each year as follows: 2008, $20,300; 2009, $21,100; 2010, $24,450; 2011, $27,800.

Instructions

(a) For each of the four years, calculate separately the increase or decrease in net income that is due to the company's errors in determining or entering depreciation or in recording transactions affecting the trucks. Ignore income tax considerations.

(b) Prepare one compound journal entry as at December 31, 2011, to adjust the Semi Trucks account to reflect the correct balances according to your schedule, and assuming that the books have not been closed for 2011.

P11-7   Linda Monkland established Monkland Ltd. in mid-2010 as the sole shareholder. The accounts on June 30, 2011, the company's year end, just prior to preparing the required adjusting entries, were as follows:

Current assets		$100,000
Capital assets		
Land	$40,000	
Building	90,000	
Equipment	50,000	180,000
Current liabilities		40,000
Long-term bank loan		120,000
Share capital		90,000
Net income prior to depreciation		30,000

All the capital assets were acquired and put into operation in early July 2010. Estimates and usage information on these assets were as follows:

Building: 25-year life, $15,000 residual value
Equipment: Five-year life, 15,000 hours of use, $5,000 residual value. The equipment was used for 1,000 hours in 2010 and 1,400 hours in 2011 up to June 30.

Linda Monkland is now considering which depreciation method or methods would be appropriate. She has narrowed the choices down for the building to the straight-line or double-declining-balance method, and for the equipment to the straight-line, double-declining-balance, or activity method. She has requested your advice and recommendation. In discussions with her, the following concerns were raised:

1. The company acquires goods from suppliers with terms of 2/10, n/30. The suppliers have indicated that these terms will continue as long as the current ratio does not fall below 2 to 1. If the ratio falls lower, no purchase discounts will be given.

2. The bank will continue the loan from year to year as long as the ratio of long-term debt to total assets does not exceed 46%.

3. Linda Monkland has contracted with the company's manager to pay him a bonus equal to 50% of any net income in excess of $14,000. She prefers to minimize or pay no bonus as long as conditions of agreements with suppliers and the bank can be met.

4. In order to provide a strong signal to attract potential investors to join her in the company, Ms. Monkland believes that a rate of return on total assets of at least 5% must be achieved.

Instructions

(a) Prepare a report for Linda Monkland that (1) presents tables, (2) analyzes the situation, (3) provides a recommendation on which method or methods should be used, and (4) justifies your recommendation by considering her concerns and the requirement that the method(s) used be considered generally acceptable accounting principle(s).

(b) What other factors should you discuss with Ms. Monkland to help her in choosing appropriate depreciation methods for her business?

(c) Do any ethical issues arise if a depreciation method is chosen in order to manipulate the financial results in a way that will satisfy the constraints listed above? Explain.

Ethics

Digging Deeper

P11-8 Khamsah Mining Ltd. is a small private company that purchased a tract of land for $720,000. After incurring exploration costs of $83,000, the company estimated that the tract will yield 120,000 tonnes of ore having enough mineral content to make mining and processing profitable. It is further estimated that 6,000 tonnes of ore will be mined in the first and last years and 12,000 tonnes every year in between. The land is expected to have a residual value of $30,000.

The company built necessary bunkhouses and sheds on the site at a cost of $36,000. It estimated that these structures would have a physical life of 15 years but, because they must be dismantled if they are to be moved, they have no residual value. The company does not intend to use the buildings elsewhere. Mining machinery installed at the mine was purchased second-hand at a cost of $60,000. This machinery cost the former owner $150,000 and was 50% depreciated when it was purchased. Khamsah Mining estimated that about half of this machinery will still be useful when the present mineral resources are exhausted but that dismantling and removing it would cost about as much as it is worth at that time. The company does not intend to use the machinery elsewhere. The remaining machinery is expected to last until about one-half the present estimated mineral ore has been removed and will then be worthless. Cost is to be allocated equally between these two classes of machinery.

Khamsah also spent another $126,400 in opening up the mine so that the ore could be extracted and removed for shipping. The company estimates that the site reclamation and restoration costs that the company is responsible for by contract when the mine is depleted have a present value of $53,600. Khamsah follows a policy of expensing exploration costs and capitalizing development costs.

Instructions

(a) As chief accountant for the company, you are to prepare a schedule that shows the estimated depletion and depreciation costs for each year of the mine's expected life.

(b) Prepare the journal entry(ies) to record the transactions for the acquisition of the mining property and related assets during the first year. Also prepare entries to record depreciation and depletion for the first year. Assume that actual production was 5,000 tonnes. Nothing occurred during the year to cause the company engineers to change their estimates of either the mineral resources or the life of the structures and equipment.

(c) Assume that 4,500 tonnes of product were processed and sold during the first year of the mine's expected life. Identify all costs mentioned above that will be included in the first-year income statement of Khamsah Mining Ltd.

P11-9 Conan Logging and Lumber Company, a small private company that follows Canadian private entity GAAP, owns 3,000 hectares of timberland on the north side of Mount Leno, which was purchased in 1998 at a cost of $550 per hectare. In 2010, Conan began selectively logging this timber tract. In May of 2010, Mount Leno erupted, burying the timberland of Conan under 15 centimetres of ash. All of the timber on the Conan tract was downed. In addition, the logging roads, built at a cost of $150,000, were destroyed, as well as the logging equipment, with a carrying amount of $300,000.

At the time of the eruption, Conan had logged 20% of the estimated 500,000 cubic metres of timber. Prior to the eruption, Conan estimated the land to have a value of $200 per hectare after the timber was harvested. Conan includes the logging roads in the depletion base.

Conan estimates it will take three years to salvage the downed timber at a cost of $700,000. The timber can be sold for pulp wood at an estimated price of $3 per cubic metre. The value of the land is unknown, but must be considered nominal due to future uncertainties.

Instructions

(a) Determine the depletion cost per cubic metre for the timber that was harvested prior to the eruption of Mount Leno.

(b) Prepare the journal entry to record the depletion before the eruption.

(c) Determine the amount of the estimated loss before income taxes and show how the losses of roads, machinery, and timber and the timber salvage value should be reported in Conan's financial statements for the year ended December 31, 2010.

P11-10 Darby Sporting Goods Inc. has been experiencing growth in the demand for its products over the last several years. The last two Olympic Games greatly increased the popularity of basketball around the world. As a result, a European sports retailing consortium entered into an agreement with Darby's Roundball Division to purchase basketballs and other accessories on an increasing basis over the next five years.

To be able to meet the quantity commitments of this agreement, Darby had to obtain additional manufacturing capacity. A real estate firm located an available factory in close proximity to Darby's Roundball manufacturing facility, and Darby agreed to purchase the factory and used machinery from Encino Athletic Equipment Company on October 1, 2009. Renovations were necessary to convert the factory for Darby's manufacturing use.

The terms of the agreement required Darby to pay Encino $50,000 when renovations started on January 1, 2010, with the balance to be paid as renovations were completed. The overall purchase price for the factory and machinery was $400,000. The building renovations were contracted to Malone Construction at $100,000. The payments made as renovations progressed during 2010 are shown below. The factory was placed in service on January 1, 2011.

	Jan. 1	Apr. 1	Oct. 1	Dec. 31
Encino	$50,000	$90,000	$110,000	$150,000
Malone		30,000	30,000	40,000

On January 1, 2010, Darby secured a $500,000 line of credit with a 12% interest rate to finance the purchase cost of the factory and machinery, and the renovation costs. Darby drew down on the line of credit to meet the payment schedule shown above; this was Darby's only outstanding loan during 2010.

Bob Sprague, Darby's controller, will capitalize the maximum allowable interest costs for this project, which he has calculated to be $21,000. Darby's policy regarding purchases of this nature is to use the appraisal value of the land for book purposes and prorate the balance of the purchase price over the remaining items. The building had originally cost Encino $300,000 and had a carrying amount of $50,000, while the machinery originally cost $125,000 and had a carrying amount of $40,000 on the date of sale. The land was recorded on Encino's books at $40,000. An appraisal, conducted by independent appraisers at the time of acquisition, valued the land at $290,000, the building at $105,000, and the machinery at $45,000.

Angie Justice, chief engineer, estimated that the renovated plant would be used for 15 years, with an estimated residual value of $30,000. Justice estimated that the productive machinery would have a remaining useful life of five years and a residual value of $3,000. Darby's depreciation policy specifies the 200% declining-balance method for machinery and the 150% declining-balance method for the plant. One half year's depreciation is taken in the year the plant is placed in service and one half year is allowed when the property is disposed of or retired.

Instructions

(a) Determine the amounts to be recorded on the books of Darby Sporting Goods Inc. as at December 31, 2010, for each of the following properties acquired from Encino Athletic Equipment Company: (1) land, (2) building, and (3) machinery.

(b) Calculate Darby Sporting Goods Inc.'s 2011 depreciation expense, for book purposes, for each of the properties acquired from Encino Athletic Equipment Company.

(c) Discuss the arguments for and against the capitalization of interest costs.

P11-11 Roland Corporation uses special strapping equipment in its packaging business. The equipment was purchased in January 2010 for $10 million and had an estimated useful life of eight years with no residual value. In early April 2011, a part costing $875,000 and designed to increase the efficiency of the machinery was added. The machine's estimated useful life did not change with this addition. By December 31, 2011, new technology had been introduced that would speed up the obsolescence of Roland's equipment. Roland's controller estimates that expected undiscounted future net cash flows on the equipment will be $6.3 million, the expected discounted future flows on the equipment will be $5.8 million, and the fair value of the equipment is $5.6 million. Roland intends to continue using the equipment, but estimates that its remaining useful life is now four years. Roland uses straight-line depreciation. Assume that Roland is a private company that follows Canadian private entity GAAP.

Instructions

(a) Prepare the journal entry, if any, to record the impairment at December 31, 2011.

(b) Prepare any journal entries for the equipment at December 31, 2012. The fair value of the equipment at December 31, 2012, is estimated to be $5.9 million.

(c) Repeat the requirements for (a) and (b), assuming that Roland intends to dispose of the equipment, but continues to use it while it waits for a satisfactory offer, and that it has not been disposed of as at December 31, 2012.

(d) Repeat the requirements for (a) and (b), assuming that Roland designates the equipment as "held for sale." Due to matters beyond Roland's control, a potential sale falls through in 2012 and the equipment is still on hand at December 31, 2012.

(e) For each situation in (b), (c), and (d), indicate where the equipment will be reported on the December 31, 2011 and 2012 balance sheets.

(f) Repeat parts (a) and (b) assuming instead that Roland is a public company that follows IFRS.

P11-12   The following is a schedule of property dispositions for Shangari Corp.:

SCHEDULE OF PROPERTY DISPOSITIONS

	Cost	Accumulated Depreciation	Cash Proceeds	Fair Market Value	Nature of Disposition
Land	$40,000	—	$31,000	$31,000	Expropriation
Building	15,000	—	3,600	—	Demolition
Warehouse	70,000	$16,000	74,000	74,000	Destruction by fire
Machine	8,000	2,800	900	7,200	Trade-in
Furniture	10,000	7,850	—	3,100	Contribution
Automobile	9,000	3,460	2,960	2,960	Sale

The following additional information is available:

Land

On February 15, land that was being held mainly as an investment was expropriated by the city. On March 31, another parcel of unimproved land to be held as an investment was purchased at a cost of $35,000.

Building

On April 2, land and a building were purchased at a total cost of $75,000, of which 20% was allocated to the building on the corporate books. The real estate was acquired with the intention of demolishing the building, which was done in November. Cash proceeds that were received in November were the net proceeds from the building demolition.

Warehouse

On June 30, the warehouse was destroyed by fire. The warehouse had been purchased on January 2, 2007, and accumulated depreciation of $16,000 had been reported. On December 27, the insurance proceeds and other funds were used to purchase a replacement warehouse at a cost of $90,000.

Machine

On December 26, the machine was exchanged for another machine having a fair market value of $6,300. Cash of $900 was also received as part of the deal.

Furniture

On August 15, furniture was contributed to a registered charitable organization. No other contributions were made or pledged during the year.

Automobile

On November 3, the automobile was sold to Jared Dutoit, a shareholder.

Instructions

Indicate how these items would be reported on the income statement of Shangari Corp. Assume that Shangari follows private entity GAAP, but also indicate if the reporting would be treated differently under IFRS.

(AICPA adapted)

P11-13   Sung Corporation, a manufacturer of steel products, began operations on October 1, 2009. Sung's accounting department has begun preparing the capital asset and depreciation schedule that follows. You have been asked to assist in completing this schedule. In addition to determining that the data already on the schedule are correct, you have obtained the following information from the company's records and personnel:

1. Depreciation is calculated from the first day of the month of acquisition to the first day of the month of disposition.

2. Land A and Building A were acquired together for $820,000. At the time of acquisition, the land had an appraised value of $90,000 and the building had an appraised value of $810,000.

3. Land B was acquired on October 2, 2009, in exchange for 2,500 newly issued common shares. At the date of acquisition, the shares had a fair value of $30 each. During October 2009, Sung paid $16,000 to demolish an existing building on this land so that it could construct a new building.

4. Construction of Building B on the newly acquired land began on October 1, 2010. By September 30, 2011, Sung had paid $320,000 of the estimated total construction costs of $450,000. It is estimated that the building will be completed and occupied by July 2012.

5. Certain equipment was donated to the corporation by a local university. An independent appraisal of the equipment when it was donated estimated its fair value at $30,000 and the residual value at $3,000.

6. Machine A's total cost of $164,900 includes an installation expense of $600 and normal repairs and maintenance of $14,900. Its residual value is estimated at $6,000. Machine A was sold on February 1, 2011.

7. On October 1, 2010, Machine B was acquired with a down payment of $5,740 and the remaining payments to be made in 11 annual instalments of $6,000 each, beginning October 1, 2010. The prevailing interest rate was 8%. The following data were determined from present-value tables and are rounded:

PV of $1 at 8%		PV of an Ordinary Annuity of $1 at 8%	
10 years	0.463	10 years	6.710
11 years	0.429	11 years	7.139
15 years	0.315	15 years	8.559

SUNG CORPORATION
Capital Asset and Depreciation Schedule
For Fiscal Years Ended September 30, 2010, and September 30, 2011

Assets	Acquisition Date	Cost	Residual Value	Depreciation Method	Estimated Life in Years	Depreciation Expense, Year Ended September 30 2010	2011
Land A	Oct. 1, 2009	$ (1)	N/A	N/A	N/A	N/A	N/A
Building A	Oct. 1, 2009	(2)	$40,000	Straight-line	(3)	$17,450	(4)
Land B	Oct. 2, 2009	(5)	N/A	N/A	N/A	N/A	N/A
Building B	Under construction	$320,000 to date	—	Straight-line	30	—	(6)
Donated equipment	Oct. 2, 2009	(7)	3,000	150% declining-balance	10	(8)	(9)
Machine A	Oct. 2, 2009	(10)	6,000	Double-declining-balance	8	(11)	(12)
Machine B	Oct. 1, 2010	(13)	—	Straight-line	20	—	(14)

N/A = Not applicable

Instructions

For each numbered item in the schedule, give the correct amount. Round each answer to the nearest dollar.

P11-14 **Situation 1:** Ducharme Corporation purchased electrical equipment at a cost of $12,400 on June 2, 2007. From 2007 through 2010, the equipment was depreciated on a straight-line basis, under the assumption that it would have a 10-year useful life and a $2,400 residual value. After more experience and before recording 2011's depreciation, Ducharme revised its estimate of the machine's useful life downward from a total of 10 years to eight years, and revised the estimated residual value to $2,000.

On April 29, 2012, after recording part of a year's depreciation for 2012, the company traded in the equipment on a newer model, and received a $4,000 trade-in allowance although its fair value was only $2,800. The new asset had a list price of $15,300 and the supplier accepted $11,300 cash for the balance. The new equipment was depreciated on a straight-line basis, assuming a seven-year useful life and a $1,300 residual value.

Situation 2: Malcolm Limited acquired a truck to deliver and install its specialized products at the customer's site. The vehicle's list price was $45,000, but customization added another $10,000 of costs. Malcolm took delivery of the truck on September 30, 2010, with a down payment of $5,000, signing a four-year, 8% note for the remainder, payable in equal payments of $14,496 beginning September 30, 2011.

Malcolm expected the truck to be usable for 500 deliveries and installations. After that, the product's technology would have changed and made the vehicle obsolete. In late July 2013, the truck was destroyed when a concrete garage collapsed. Malcolm used the truck for 45 deliveries in 2010, 125 in 2011, 134 in 2012, and 79 in 2013. The company received a cheque for $12,000 from the insurance company and paid what remained on the note.

Situation 3: A group of new machines was purchased on February 17, 2011, under a royalty agreement with the following terms: The purchaser, Keller Corp., is to pay a royalty of $1 to the machinery supplier for each unit of product that is produced by the machines each year. The machines are expected to produce 200,000 units over their useful lives. The machines' invoice price was $75,000, freight costs were $2,000, unloading charges were $1,500, and royalty payments for 2011 were $13,000.

Keller uses the units-of-production method to depreciate its machinery.

Instructions

(a) For situation 1, determine the amount of depreciation expense reported by Ducharme for each fiscal year for the years ending December 31, 2007, to December 31, 2012.

(b) For situation 2, prepare all entries that are needed to record the events and activities related to the truck, including the depreciation expense on the truck each year. Assume that Malcolm uses an activity approach to depreciate the truck, and bases it on deliveries.

(c) For situation 3, prepare journal entries to record the purchase of the new machines, the related depreciation for 2011, and the royalty payment.

*P11-15   Munro Limited reports the following information in its tax files covering the five-year period from 2008 to 2012. All assets are Class 10 with a 30% maximum CCA.

2008   Purchased assets A, B, and C for $20,000, $8,000, and $1,200, respectively.
2009   Sold asset B for $7,000; bought asset D for $4,800.
2010   Purchased asset E for $5,000; received an investment tax credit of $1,000.
2011   Sold asset A for $9,900 and asset C for $1,800.
2012   Asset D was destroyed by fire and was uninsured; asset E was sold to an employee for $500.

Instructions

(a) Prepare a capital cost allowance schedule for Class 10 assets covering the 2008 to 2012 period.

(b) Identify any capital gains, terminal losses, or recapture of CCA and indicate how each would be taxed.

*P11-16   Kitchigami Limited was attracted to the Town of Mornington by the town's municipal industry commission. Mornington donated a plant site to Kitchigami, and the provincial government provided $180,000 toward the cost of the new manufacturing facility. The total cost of plant construction came to $380,000 and it was ready for use in early October 2011. Kitchigami expects the plant to have a useful life of 15 years before it becomes obsolete and is demolished. The company uses the straight-line method of depreciation for buildings and is required to include the plant in Class 6 (10% rate) for tax purposes.

Instructions

(a) Prepare the entry(ies) that are required in 2011 to record the payment to the contractor for the building and the receipt of the provincial government assistance. Assume that the company treats the assistance as a reduction of the asset's cost. Also prepare any adjusting entries that are needed at the company's year ends, December 31, 2011 and 2012.

(b) Repeat (a), but assume instead that the company treats the government assistance as a deferred credit.

(c) If Kitchigami reports 2012 income of $79,000 before depreciation on the plant and government assistance, what income before tax will the company report assuming (a) above? Assuming (b) above?

(d) What is the building's tax value at December 31, 2012?

Writing Assignments

WA11-1   Prophet Manufacturing Limited was organized on January 1, 2009. During 2009, it used the straight-line method of amortizing its plant assets in its reports to management.

As the company's controller, on November 8 you are having a conference with Prophet's officers to discuss the depreciation method to be used for income tax and for reporting to shareholders. Fred Peretti, president of Prophet, has suggested using a new method that he feels is more suitable than the straight-line method for the company's current needs during what he foresees will be a period of rapid expansion of production and capacity. The following is an example in which the proposed method is applied to a capital asset with an original cost of $248,000, an estimated useful life of five years, and a residual value of approximately $8,000:

Year	Years of Life Used	Fraction Rate	Depreciation Expense	Accumulated Depreciation at Year End	Book Value at Year End
1	1	Jan. 15	$16,000	$ 16,000	$232,000
2	2	Feb. 15	32,000	48,000	200,000
3	3	Mar. 15	48,000	96,000	152,000
4	4	Apr. 15	64,000	160,000	88,000
5	5	May 15	80,000	240,000	8,000

The president favours the new method because of the following claims that he has heard about it:

1. It will increase the funds that are recovered during the years near the end of the assets' useful life when maintenance and replacement disbursements are high.

2. It will result in increased writeoffs in later years when the company is likely to be in a better operating position.

Instructions

Draft a response to Fred Peretti that explains the purpose of depreciation, and whether the method that has been suggested qualifies as a generally accepted accounting method. Identify the circumstances, if any, that would make using the method reasonable and those, if any, that would make using it unreasonable. Also respond to his statement that depreciation charges recover or create funds.

WA11-2   Lian Tang, HK Corporation's controller, is concerned that net income may be lower this year. He is afraid that upper-level management might recommend cost reductions by laying off accounting staff, himself included. Tang knows that depreciation is a major expense for HK. The company currently uses the same method for financial reporting as it uses for tax purposes—i.e., a declining-balance method—and he is thinking of changing to the straight-line method.

Tang does not want to highlight the increase in net income that would result from this change. He thinks, "Why don't I just increase the estimated useful lives and the residual values of the property, plant, and equipment? They are only estimates anyway. This will decrease depreciation expense and increase income. I may be able to save my job and those of my staff."

Ethics

Instructions

Discuss. Make sure that you identify the objectives of depreciation, who the stakeholders are in this situation, what disclosures are required, whether any ethical issues are involved, and what Tang should do.

WA11-3   Nickel Strike Mines is a nickel mining company with mines in northern Ontario, Colombia, and Australia. It is a publicly traded company and follows IFRS, and has historically used units of production as its depreciation policy for all its mines. During 2009, the price of nickel declined significantly, even below the costs of production for the Ontario mines. Consequently, the company has had the Ontario mines closed since early January 2009. It has continued to produce in its Colombian and Australian mines. It is now December 2009 and the controller is trying to decide what accounting issues there are related to the Ontario mines. Since it was a very bad year for the company, and investors are expecting the worst, the controller is considering switching to the declining-balance method of depreciation for the Ontario mine only. This would create a significant depreciation charge for 2009, but in the future, the depreciation costs related to the mine would decrease, resulting in higher net income. In addition, since there were no units produced in the Ontario mine for the year, no depreciation is taken. The controller believes that this is wrong, and that some amount of depreciation should be recorded.

Additionally, the controller is also considering taking as large an impairment loss as possible on all the mines. The controller will do this by assuming a very low nickel price, which will cause the recoverable amounts to be below carrying values for all mines. This impairment loss should likely reverse in the following years, since nickel prices are expected to climb dramatically over the next year, as supplies diminish and as demand from Asian countries increases. With the reversal of the impairment in 2010, this would show a significant improvement in the company's net income.

Instructions

You are a Nickel Strike Mines board member and have just heard the controller's comments on these issues. Comment on the controller's suggestions. Include in your discussion how the impairment test would be completed and the assumptions required. Also discuss the note disclosure that would be required related to all of these issues.

WA11-4   Realtor Inc. is a company that owns five large office buildings that are leased out to tenants. Most of the leases are for 10 years or more with renewal clauses for an additional 5 years. Currently, the company is a private company. Recently Rita Mendoza was hired as a new controller. Ms. Mendoza has suggested to Habib Ganem, the owner and sole shareholder of the company, that perhaps the company should consider switching to IFRS. She explained that under private entity GAAP, the buildings are recorded at cost and then depreciated and tested for impairment when events occur. However, under IFRS, she explained, the buildings could be classified as investment properties and adjusted to fair value every year. In addition, there is no impact on the income statement since no depreciation is recorded on the investment properties. Finally, Ms. Mendoza stated that there is no impairment testing required for investment properties under IFRS so there would never be any impairment losses to be recognized.

Mr. Ganem was intrigued with this idea. He had just been looking at the calculation of the bank loan covenants and had found that the company's debt to asset ratio was very close to the maximum that would be allowed. He wanted to take this year's annual financial statement, once completed, to the bank and ask for revisions on the covenants, since he was also looking at some new properties to possibly purchase. He particularly liked the idea of no depreciation having to be recorded on these assets, which would also improve the company's times interest earned covenant ratio (calculated as Earnings before taxes and interest / Interest expense). Mr. Ganem decided he might call his banker to discuss this change and get her thoughts.

Instructions

You are the loans officer at the bank. What comments would you make to Mr. Ganem about the controller's suggestions? In particular, explain the impact on the balance sheet and the income statement under both the cost model and the fair value model and the resulting impact on the existing covenants. From a banker's point of view, which method for reporting the investment properties would be most useful? Make a final recommendation to Mr. Ganem.

WA11-5   Puma Paper Company Ltd. operates a 300-tonne per-day kraft pulp mill and four sawmills in New Brunswick. The company is expanding its pulp mill facilities to a capacity of 1,000 tonnes per day and plans to replace three of its older, less efficient sawmills with an expanded facility in three years' time. The fourth mill did not operate for most of 2011 (current year), and there are no plans to reopen it before the new sawmill facility becomes operational.

In reviewing the depreciation rates and in discussing the residual values of the sawmills that are to be replaced, it was noted that if present depreciation rates were not adjusted, substantial amounts of plant costs on these three mills would not be depreciated by the time the new mill is operational.

Instructions

What is the proper accounting for the four sawmills at the end of 2011 under private entity GAAP? Under IFRS?

WA11-6   Howeven Inc. is a Canadian company that is publicly traded and will have to adopt IFRS by 2011. It is a manufacturing company with extensive investments in property, plant, and equipment. The company currently has a profit sharing plan that is based on 30% of the earnings after depreciation, but before interest and taxes. There is also a debt to fixed asset covenant ratio that must be maintained for the bank loan.

The controller has been learning about IFRS and has determined that there are three different treatments that the property, plant, and equipment can have on transition to IFRS.

1. The first is to continue using the cost model as the company currently has been doing. The company currently uses the straight-line method of depreciation for all of its assets.

2. The second option is that the company, on transition at January 1, 2011, can elect to revalue all of its property, plant, and equipment to fair value. This is a one-time increase in value that is allowed for first-time adopters of IFRS. The company would still use the cost model to depreciate this new value (which becomes the deemed cost) in subsequent years.

3. The third option is to adopt the revaluation model for the plant and property assets. The company would continue to use the cost model for the equipment, as fair market values are not readily available for this type of asset.

The controller has estimated the following numbers at January 1, 2011 (debt is expected to be $1,700 million):

	Remaining Useful Life	Carrying Value	Estimated Fair Value at Jan. 1, 2011
Property and plant	25 years	$2,500 million	$3,250 million
Equipment	10 years	$1,300 million	$1,400 million

Instructions

You are the Vice President Finance and must prepare a memo to the board explaining these options. Using the numbers in the table to assist you, discuss the implications of the three options on the balance sheet, income statement, bonuses, and the debt to fixed asset covenant.

WA11-7 Write a brief essay highlighting the differences between IFRS and accounting standards for private enterprises noted in this chapter, discussing the conceptual justification for each.

Integrated Cases

Refer to the Case Primer to help you answer these cases.

(Hint: If there are issues here that are new, use the conceptual framework to help you support your analysis with solid reasoning.)

WILEY PLUS
Case Primer

IC11-1   ClubLoop Corporation (CL) is a large owner, operator, and developer of golf clubs and resorts. The company is privately owned by several wealthy individuals. During the current year, according to the draft financial statements, revenues increased by 7.2% and net operating income increased by 13% to $22.5 million. Net income dropped from $2.9 million to $822,000. The decrease was largely due to two events, a change in accounting policy and costs related to the settlement of a lawsuit.

One of the company's objectives is to always ensure that capital resources are readily available to meet approved capital expenditures and to take advantage of growth opportunities. According to the draft year-end financial statements, the company has current assets of $12 million and current liabilities of $28 million, resulting in a working capital deficit. Included in the current liabilities are long-term debts that are currently due. The company is working with the financial institutions in question to renew or replace these facilities. CL has received unsolicited expressions of interest from several financial institutions concerning these facilities and management believes that these facilities will be replaced—hopefully before the current financial statements are issued.

The company owns most of the land on which CL's golf courses are developed. Currently, the company follows a rigorous "weed and feed" program in order to keep the grass on the golf courses in top shape. The chemicals in these fertilizers, herbicides, and insecticides are felt by some people in the local community to be toxic to the environment. The company has met with several community groups and has agreed to study the issue further. In a current meeting of the board of directors, the CEO committed the company to spending $1 million to limit any potential damage. As at year end, none of this amount has yet been spent. There is a concern that the community groups are going to launch legal proceedings and the company feels that this move will help CL's position if there ends up being a lawsuit. Part of the money is for landscaping to limit the spread of the sprayed chemicals and part of it is for advertising to promote the company as a good corporate citizen.

The company is currently developing new golf courses. All direct costs related to the acquisition, development, and construction of these properties, including interest and management costs, are capitalized. For one of the new locations, which was just purchased and developed in the current year, the company has run into a small problem. After CL spent several million dollars on development, the planned golf course is being blocked by environmental groups. The costs to develop the land have been capitalized as previously mentioned, on the basis that they would be recoverable from future membership revenues. However, the company has now decided to sell the land to a real estate developer.

CL's stock-based compensation plan consists of stock options. The company does not recognize any expense for this plan when stock options are issued to employees. It has been company policy to repurchase any shares issued under these stock option plans, although this year the company has indicated that it might not do this since it is planning to redesign the stock-based compensation system.

On July 1, the government tax department issued notices of assessment to the company regarding a dispute over the recognition of revenues. Although the outcome of an appeal of the assessment cannot be determined, the company believes that it will owe $8.7 million if its appeal is unsuccessful.

Instructions

Adopt the role of the company's auditor and prepare an analysis of the financial reporting issues.

IC11-2   Talisman Energy Inc. (TE) is an international company whose main business activities are the exploration, development, production, and marketing of crude oil, natural gas, and natural gas liquids. Its strategy is to continue to develop its North American gas business while expanding internationally. Wherever it makes sense to do so, the company owns and operates key assets and infrastructure and plans to grow through exploration and acquisition. The company is a public company.

Real-World Emphasis

TE follows what is known as the successful efforts method of accounting for exploration and development costs. Under this method, the costs related to drilling exploratory wells are written off to "dry hole expense" when they are determined to be unsuccessful. Until that time, they are included in property, plant, and equipment as non-depleted capital. In its 2008 statements, the company reported $19.5 billion for PP&E including $5.1 billion that was not being depleted (since it was still in pre-exploration, exploration, or development stages). Of the $5.1 billion, $2.1 billion was from development activities. Net income for the year was $3.5 billion.

TE monitors its oil and gas reserves, and reserve estimates are made using available geological and reservoir data, as well as production performance data. The reserves affect the income statement through depletion charges since property, plant, and equipment that relate to oil and gas production are amortized using the units-of-production method over proved, developed reserves.

Instructions

Adopt the role of company management and discuss the financial reporting issues. Note that as a public entity, TE must follow IFRS for years beginning January 2011. For discussion purposes, however, consider the accounting for property, plant, and equipment under both IFRS and private entity GAAP. Compare and contrast the treatments under private entity GAAP and IFRS.

(Hint: Research the accounting standards by reviewing *CICA Handbook*, Part II, Section 3061 and IFRS 6.)

IC11-3   Eastern Platinum Limited (EPL) is a metals and minerals company whose shares trade on the TSX. The company obtained permission from the British Columbia Securities Commission and the Ontario Securities Commission to early adopt IFRS effective January 1, 2009. The March 31, 2009 unaudited quarterly statements are replicated in Chapter 5.

Real-World Emphasis

Instructions

Review note 15 to the statements and discuss the respective merits of the accounting policies under Canadian GAAP (policies prior to changeover) and under IFRS for the following items:

(a) Revenue and interest income

(b) Property, plant, and equipment: provision for environmental rehabilitation

(c) Impairment

Note the impact on the December 31, 2008 restated income statement.

Research and Financial Analysis

RA11-1 Canadian Tire Corporation, Limited

Canadian Tire Corporation, Limited is one of Canada's best-known retailers. Obtain a copy of Canadian Tire's financial statements for the year ended December 31, 2008, through SEDAR at www.sedar.com or on the company's website. To answer the following questions, you may also want to include the 10-year financial review that is produced as supplementary information in the annual report.

Real-World Emphasis

Instructions

(a) How significant is Canadian Tire's investment in property, plant, and equipment compared with its investment in other assets? Compare this with sample companies in other industries, such as financial services, utilities, and technology. Comment.

(b) Calculate the company's total asset turnover for 2008, 2007, and 2006.

(c) Calculate the company's profit margin for the same three years.

(d) Calculate the company's return on assets for the same three years by using the ratios calculated in (b) and (c) above.

(e) Based on your calculations in (d), suggest ways in which Canadian Tire might increase the return that it earns on its investment in assets.

RA11-2 Brookfield Asset Management Inc.

Brookfield Asset Management Inc. is a publicly traded Canadian company that converted to IFRS on January 1, 2010. Before conversion, in its reports to shareholders, it outlined the estimated impact that this would have on its statements.

Real-World Emphasis

Instructions

From the company's website, access the annual report for the year ended December 31, 2008. Using the report, specifically the section entitled "Part 6 – International Financial Reporting Standards" and the notes to the statements, answer the following questions.

(a) What business is Brookfield in?

(b) What policies does the company currently use to report commercial properties, power generation, timberlands, transmission assets, and development and other properties? Include in this discussion the depreciation and impairment testing policies. What is the current amount of depreciation expense that is shown on the income statement?

(c) What policies is the company considering adopting for each of its capital asset categories? What will be the estimated impact of this change on the balance sheet and income statement? What method and assumptions has the company used to determine fair values for each class of assets?

(d) What other methods are available to determine fair value? Which methods are most reliable from a user's perspective? Review the exposure draft on fair value measurement (or the standard if this has been released) from IASB to determine what level of fair value measurement the company has used to determine fair values.

RA11-3 Canadian National Railway Company and Canadian Pacific Railway Limited

Two well-known company names in the transportation industry in Canada are Canadian National Railway Company and Canadian Pacific Railway Limited. Go to either SEDAR (www.sedar.com) or to each company's website to gain access to the financial statements of these companies for their years ended December 31, 2008.

Real-World Emphasis

Instructions

(a) How significant are the investments made by these companies in property, plant, and equipment? Express the size of these investments as a percentage of total assets.

(b) Compare the types of property, plant, and equipment that each company reports.

(c) Do the companies follow similar policies in what they capitalize as part of property, plant, and equipment?

(d) What methods of depreciation are used by each company?

(e) For assets that are similar at both companies, compare their useful lives and/or rates of depreciation. Are these similar or would applying them result in differences in the reported results for each year? Explain briefly.

RA11-4 Lufthansa and Air Canada

Real-World Emphasis

Lufthansa and **Air Canada** are both global airline companies. Lufthansa reports under IFRS and Air Canada reports under Canadian GAAP. Access the financial statements of Lufthansa for its year ended December 31, 2008, and Air Canada for its year ended December 31, 2008, from each company's website.

Instructions

(a) What amounts are reported on the balance sheet for capital assets for Lufthansa and Air Canada at December 31, 2008? What percentage of total assets is invested in these types of assets by each company?

(b) For Lufthansa: What types of capital assets does the company report? What is included in costs? Is interest capitalized? What depreciation methods are used by Lufthansa? How are residual values estimated for aircraft?

(c) For Air Canada: What types of capital assets does the company report? What is included in costs? Is interest capitalized? What depreciation methods are used by Air Canada? How are residual values estimated for aircraft?

(d) Compare and contrast the above accounting policies for the two companies. Where are there significant differences? What will be the impact on the balance sheet and net earnings based on these differences?

(e) For Lufthansa, how are the assets tested for impairment? Were any impairment losses recorded for the year, and if so, how much? What did these relate to? Was there any reversal of impairment losses from previous years?

(f) For Air Canada, how have the assets been tested for impairment and were there any impairment losses for 2008?

(g) Does Lufthansa have assets held for sale? How much has been reclassified to this account and where is it presented on the balance sheet? What does it relate to? Does Air Canada have any assets designated as held for sale?

RA11-5 Homburg Invest Inc.

Real-World Emphasis

Usually an international comparison assignment involves comparing two similar companies that are reporting under different GAAP. If possible, it would be better to compare the same company's financial reports prepared on two different bases. **Homburg Invest Inc.**, a Canadian company, does exactly that, and notes that the most significant differences relate to its fixed assets.

Instructions

Access the financial statements of Homburg Invest Inc. under both bases of accounting for its year ended December 31, 2008, from the company's website (www.homburgcanada.com). Review the statements and answer the following questions.

(a) What business is Homburg Invest Inc. in? What two sets of accounting standards does it report under and why?

(b) Compare the accounting policies used to report investment properties and development properties under IFRS and Canadian GAAP. What are the effects of these differences on the balance sheet, income statement, and statement of cash flows? Be specific.

(c) Calculate the following ratios for the company's year ended December 31, 2008, under both Canadian GAAP and IFRS:

1. Total asset turnover

2. Profit margin

3. Return on assets

(d) Comment on the results obtained in part (c). In your opinion, which set of ratios provides a better assessment of the company's profitability? Explain.

(e) Based on your findings, write a short hypothetical memo to the chief financial officer (CFO) of a Canadian company in the same business as Homburg. You need to alert the CFO to the possible effects that the company will experience when Canadian financial accounting requirements are changed to IFRS, which will occur in 2011.

RA11-6 Research Topic: Deferred Maintenance

A topic that concerns not-for-profit organizations and relates to their long-lived assets is the matter of "deferred maintenance." Canadian schools and universities in particular are concerned with this issue.

Instructions

(a) Research the topic of deferred maintenance well enough so that you understand the term. Explain the concept in 50 words or less.

(b) Interview the chief financial officer of your college or university or a not-for-profit or government organization to discuss the issue. Can you determine from an organization's financial statements if it has a deferred maintenance problem? Should you be able to? Discuss.

A Canadian Staple's Intangible Value

NINE OUT OF TEN ADULT CANADIANS shop at Canadian Tire every year, and 40% of Canadians shop there every week, the company website boasts. In fact, the location of Canadian Tire's 475 retail stores allows it to serve more than 90% of the Canadian population. This market reach translates into "near-universal brand awareness." Indeed, the Canadian Tire logo, the instantly recognizable red triangle with the green maple leaf, is a significant intangible asset for the company. However, that specific asset doesn't have any capitalized asset value on Canadian Tire's balance sheet.

"If we had done a lot of work to create that triangle as a brand, [it would have been capitalized]," explains Huw Thomas, Canadian Tire's Executive Vice-President, Financial Strategy and Performance. The creation of the brand's value happened over a long period, and Canadian Tire didn't capitalize any costs associated with that process. "If we had," Thomas continues, "we would have the potential for the creation of further intangibles, because the brand obviously has significant value. But current accounting (and IFRS) doesn't have you carry the value of assets like that on your balance sheet."

Intangible assets that have been purchased, however, are carried on the balance sheet. For example, Canadian Tire's acquisition of the Mark's Work Wearhouse chain includes the capitalization of intangibles, such as that company's well-established brand name.

On a large acquisition such as Mark's Work Wearhouse, Canadian Tire calculates the fair value of the various assets it has acquired, including any trademarks. "You create models as to what that trademark might be worth looking into the future, and then the difference between the total amount that you've paid, less the fair value of the net assets you've acquired, represents goodwill," explains Thomas. "That becomes an asset that sits on the balance sheet, and every year you have to assess whether the goodwill amount has become impaired."

In 2009, Canadian Tire adopted the new *CICA Handbook* Section 3064, "Goodwill and Intangible Assets." Its most significant impact was reclassifying the cost of software that is not integral to computer hardware from property, plant, and equipment to intangible assets. Another change, required by the conversion to IFRS, is that borrowing costs on qualifying software assets the company has developed will now have to be capitalized as part of the cost of the software. ■

CHAPTER 12

Intangible Assets and Goodwill

Learning Objectives

After studying this chapter, you should be able to:

1. Define and describe the characteristics of intangible assets.

2. Identify and apply the recognition and measurement requirements for purchased intangible assets.

3. Identify and apply the recognition and measurement requirements for internally developed intangible assets.

4. Explain how intangible assets are accounted for after initial recognition.

5. Identify and explain the accounting for specific types of intangible assets.

6. Explain and account for impairments of limited-life and indefinite-life intangible assets.

7. Explain the concept of goodwill and how it is measured and accounted for after acquisition.

8. Identify the types of disclosure requirements for intangible assets and goodwill and explain the issues in analyzing these assets.

9. Identify differences in accounting between accounting standards for private enterprises (private entity GAAP) and IFRS.

After studying Appendix 12A, you should be able to:

10. Explain and apply basic approaches to valuing goodwill.

Preview of Chapter 12

As the opening vignette indicates, the valuation of intangible assets is not always clear cut. Because of the difficulty in determining which costs actually result in adding value to an asset such as a "brand," it is one of the assets whose value is recognized only when it is acquired in a purchase and sale transaction. This chapter explains the basic conceptual and reporting issues related to intangible assets and their close relative, goodwill.

The chapter is organized as follows:

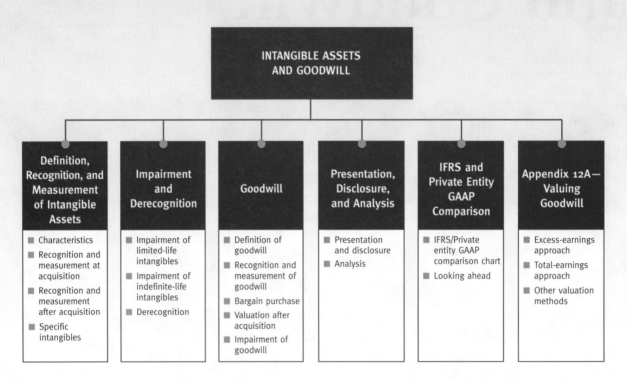

DEFINITION, RECOGNITION, AND MEASUREMENT OF INTANGIBLE ASSETS

Characteristics

Objective 1
Define and describe the characteristics of intangible assets.

Lululemon athletica inc. and Roots Canada's most important asset is not store fixtures—it's the brand image. The major asset of Coca-Cola is not its plant facilities—it's the secret formula for making Coke. Sympatico's most important asset is not its Internet connection equipment—it's the subscriber base. We have an economy that is increasingly dominated by information and service providers, and their major assets are often intangible in nature. Identifying and measuring these intangibles is often difficult, and as a result many intangibles have not been captured on companies' balance sheets.

What are intangible assets? Broadly defined, **intangible assets** are identifiable non-monetary assets that lack physical substance. Intangible assets must have these three characteristics—**identifiability, non-physical existence**, and a **non-monetary nature**—so that only appropriate assets are recognized as intangibles.

1. **Intangible assets are identifiable**. An asset is identifiable if it has at least one of the following characteristics:

   Law

   - it results from contractual or other legal rights; or
   - it is separable—it can be separated or divided from the entity and sold, transferred, licensed, rented, or exchanged, either by itself or in combination with another contract, identifiable asset, or liability.[1]

For example, the right to lease space at favourable rates arises from contractual arrangements and the right may or may not be transferable to others. A subscription list of a successful newspaper or magazine has value in contributing to future revenue streams and is saleable. These are examples of identifiable intangibles that are given separate recognition. Note also, in order to recognize these items as assets, the company has to be able to control access to the future benefits and restrict others' access. One way to control access to the benefits is having legally enforceable rights; another is having the ability to enter into exchange transactions related to the intangible.

Goodwill and some other non-physical items of value, on the other hand, are not separable from the rest of the entity, and control over the future benefits does not result from contractual or legal rights. For example, the synergies of a combined sales force or a superior management team can be identified as having value. However, these items cannot be recognized separately as intangible assets because they cannot be separated from the entity in order to exchange them with others, nor can they be controlled through contractual or other legal rights. They are therefore considered part of goodwill.

While it is important to distinguish one identifiable intangible from another, financial reporting objectives are not well met if every identifiable intangible is recognized separately. At a minimum, the ones that have similar characteristics (such as continuity, stability, and risk) are grouped and recognized together. Because knowledge-based and high-technology companies with large investments in such "soft" assets are an important part of our modern economy, how accounting treats such intangibles is a major issue.

2. **Intangible assets lack physical substance.** Unlike assets such as property, plant, and equipment (PP&E), the value of intangible assets comes from the rights and privileges that are granted to the company using them. Sometimes it is difficult to tell whether a particular asset is tangible and is therefore an item of PP&E, or whether it is intangible and covered by accounting standards for intangible assets. Consider the example of computer software and licensing rights to films. What is the asset? Is it the intangible software and the licensing rights, or is it the related tangible hardware and film? In general, if the intangible component is needed for the physical component to work, it is treated as an item of PP&E. If the intangible component is not an integral part of the physical object, then it is classified separately as an intangible asset.

3. **Intangible assets are non-monetary.** Assets such as accounts receivable and long-term loans lack physical substance, but they are not classified as intangible assets. They are monetary assets whose value comes from the right (or claim) to receive fixed or determinable amounts of money in the future. Intangible assets do not contain any such right or claim.

In most cases, items that meet the definition of an intangible asset provide economic benefits over a period of years. The benefits may be in the form of revenue from selling products or services, a reduction in future costs, or other economies. They are normally classified as long-term assets. Examples include such widely varied assets as patents, copyrights, franchises or licensing agreements, trademarks or trade names, secret formulas,

---

[1] GAAP for *Business Combinations* in *CICA Handbook*, Part II, Section 1582.02A(k) and IFRS 3, Appendix A.

computer software, technological know-how, prepayments, and some development costs. Specific intangibles are discussed later in the chapter.

Recognition and Measurement at Acquisition

Objective 2

Identify and apply the recognition and measurement requirements for purchased intangible assets.

The **recognition criteria** for intangible assets are identical to those for PP&E assets and both are **measured at cost** at acquisition. For example, each type of asset can be recognized only when it meets the same two recognition criteria:

1. It is probable that the entity will receive the expected future economic benefits.

2. The asset's cost can be measured reliably.

In applying these criteria, however, management has to take into account the reality that there is often more uncertainty about the future economic benefits associated with intangible assets than with tangible capital assets.

Purchased Intangibles

Underlying Concept

The cost concepts introduced in Chapter 10 for property, plant, and equipment are also appropriate for determining the cost of purchased intangible assets.

Intangible assets may be purchased outright, they can be acquired as part of a business combination, or they can be developed internally.

As indicated above, intangible assets purchased from another party are **measured at cost**. Because the amount paid is based on the company's expectations about receiving future economic benefits from the asset, the "probability" criterion for recognition is met. Cost includes the acquisition cost and all expenditures directly associated with making the intangible ready for its intended use—for example, the purchase price, legal fees, and other direct costs to bring it into working condition. Costs that are **not capitalized** are similar to those for property, plant, and equipment assets: those related to product introduction and promotion, conducting business in a new location or with new types of customers, and administration and general overhead. Expenditures incurred after the asset is ready for use as intended and initial operating losses are also excluded.

Lastly, similar to other long-lived assets, when direct costs that meet the recognition criteria are incurred after acquisition of the intangible asset, these costs are accounted for as additions or replacements and are capitalized. This is not as common with intangibles, however.

Cost, as was seen in earlier chapters, is the cash cost.

- If there are **delayed payment terms**, any portion of the payments that represents interest is recognized as a financing expense rather than as part of the asset cost.

- If the intangible asset is **acquired for shares**, cost is the asset's fair value.[2] In rare circumstances, if this cannot be determined, then the shares' fair value is used. Private entity GAAP is not as prescriptive. It allows the more reliable of the fair value of the asset or of the shares to be used.

- If the intangible asset is acquired by giving up **non-monetary assets**, the cost of the intangible is the fair value of what is given up or the fair value of the intangible received, whichever one can be measured more reliably. This assumes that the transaction has **commercial substance** and that fair values can be reliably measured. You may want to review the section in Chapter 10 that discusses this situation and provides examples of transactions and entries for non-monetary exchanges.

---

[2] IFRS 2 *Share-based Payment* is considerably more complex than is indicated here. In addition, the term "fair value" will be replaced by "market-based value" in this part of IFRS 2 if the provisions of the *Fair Value Measurement* (ED/2009/5) exposure draft are accepted. A market-based value is "the price that would be received or paid to sell an asset, transfer a liability, or exchange an equity instrument... ." It assumes an orderly transaction between market participants. A final standard was expected in 2010.

- If the intangible asset is acquired as a government grant, the asset's fair value usually establishes its cost on the books. IFRS does permit a company to recognize a zero or nominal dollar cost in this case. Any other direct costs of acquisition are capitalized into the asset cost, however.

Intangibles Purchased in a Business Combination

When a company purchases an intangible asset as a single asset, such as an acquisition of a specific trademark or patent, the accounting is relatively clear. When several intangibles are bought together in a "basket purchase," the accounting is more complex because the cost has to be allocated to each intangible based on its relative fair value.

A further complication happens when intangibles are acquired in a **business combination**—when one entity acquires control over one or more businesses. This can take place either by directly purchasing the net assets of the business or by acquiring the equity interests (i.e., the shares) that control the entity and its net assets. An issue arises because of the variety of assets and liabilities that make up a complete and ongoing business. Even the fact that the business is fully operational instead of being just in the planning stages adds value to it. The entity has to account for all the assets that are acquired, regardless of whether or not they are recognized in the acquired business's accounting records. Many of the assets acquired that contribute to the value of the business are intangible, but only those that are **identifiable** can be separately recognized. Intangibles acquired that are not identifiable assets are considered part of goodwill.

The acquisition cost assigned to each of the identifiable intangible assets acquired as part of a business combination is its fair value.[3] All such assets acquired in this way are recognized, even though they may have been internally generated by the business itself and not eligible for capitalization under the standards for internally generated intangible assets. Examples include brand names, patents, customer relationships, and **in-process research and development (R&D)**. In-process R&D comes about when one company acquires the business of another company, and one of the identifiable assets acquired is the research work and findings of the acquired company. When the research work and findings meet the requirements for reporting as an asset separate from goodwill, they are recognized as an identifiable intangible.

Internally Developed Intangible Assets

It is a more challenging task to decide which costs should be capitalized and recognized as intangible assets when an entity develops such assets internally. The difficulty involves both recognition and measurement issues:

1. Has an identifiable asset been created that will generate expected future cash flows?

2. What costs should be capitalized? Were the costs incurred just day-to-day operating costs or expenditures related to internally generated goodwill (which are expensed), or were they really additional costs of identifiable assets? How reliably can cost be measured?

How costs associated with internally generated intangible assets should be accounted for has been a controversial issue for many years. The following alternatives have been suggested:

   (a) Recognize the costs as internally generated intangible assets when certain criteria are met, and expense all others.

   (b) Recognize all costs of internally generated intangible assets as expense.

Underlying Concept

The basic attributes of intangibles, the uncertainty of their future benefits, and their uniqueness have discouraged valuing them at more than their cost.

3 Objective
Identify and apply the recognition and measurement requirements for internally developed intangible assets.

Underlying Concept

The Financial Accounting Standards Board (FASB) in the United States has chosen option (b).

---

[3] If control over the assets is acquired through the acquisition of voting shares, the fair value of all the identifiable assets and liabilities (identifiable net assets) is assigned as their cost through the consolidation process. Please refer to Chapter 2 for a discussion of how fair values are determined.

(c) Recognize expenditures on all internally generated intangible assets as an expense, with certain specified exceptions.

(d) Allow a choice between the accounting treatments in (a) and (b) above.[4]

Significant Change

The IASB decided on option (a) in IAS 38 *Intangible Assets* while option (d) was selected in *CICA Handbook*, Part II, Section 3064 *Goodwill and Intangible Assets* for private enterprises. Option (a) is illustrated in the next section. Note that the IFRS requirements for recognizing "self-constructed" intangibles are more stringent than those for property, plant, and equipment assets. This is because of the recognition and measurement uncertainties referred to above.

Identifying Research and Development Phase Activities.   To deal with the uncertainty of whether an asset should be recognized, the process of generating the intangible is broken down into two parts: a **research phase** and a **development phase**.

Research is the planned investigation undertaken with the hope of gaining new scientific or technical knowledge and understanding. The investigation may or may not be directed toward a specific practical aim or application.

Development, on the other hand, is the translation of research findings or other knowledge into a plan or design for new or substantially improved materials, devices, products, processes, systems, or services before starting commercial production or use.[5]

The research phase and the development phase are interpreted in the accounting standards as broader terms than implied in the definitions of research and development provided. Examples of activities in each of these phases are set out in Illustration 12-1.

Illustration 12-1

Examples of Research Stage Activities and Development Stage Activities

Activities in the Research Stage	Activities in the Development Stage
Obtaining new knowledge	Designing, constructing, and testing prototypes and models prior to production or use
Searching for, evaluating, and selecting ways to use research findings or knowledge in general	Designing tools, jigs, moulds, and dies involving new technology
Investigating possible alternatives for existing materials, products, processes, systems, and services	Designing, constructing, and operating pilot plants that are not economically feasible for commercial production
Formulating, designing, evaluating, and choosing possible alternatives for existing materials, products, processes, systems, and services	Designing, constructing, and testing chosen alternatives for new or improved materials, products, processes, systems, and services[6]

If there is uncertainty about which phase a particular activity relates to when internally creating an intangible asset, it is classified as a **research phase** activity.

Accounting for Research Phase Costs.   The accounting standards are very clear that no costs incurred on research or the research phase of an internal project meet the criteria for recognition as an asset. **All such costs are recognized as expenses when they are incurred**. However, if a company has its own research facility consisting of buildings, laboratories, and equipment that are used for general research activities, it accounts for these assets as capitalized property, plant, and equipment. The depreciation and other costs that are related to such facilities are accounted for as research-related expenses.

---

[4] IAS 38. BCZ29.

[5] *CICA Handbook*, Part II, Section 3064.08.

[6] *CICA Handbook*, Part II, Section 3064.39 and .42; IAS 38.56 and .59.

Sometimes entities conduct research activities for other companies **under a contractual arrangement**. In this case, the contract usually specifies that all direct costs, certain specific indirect costs, and a profit element will be reimbursed to the entity performing the research work. Because reimbursement is expected, such research costs are recorded as inventory or a receivable.

Accounting for Development Phase Costs.

An intangible asset can be recognized from the development stage of an internal project, but only when an entity can demonstrate its technical and financial feasibility and the company's intention and ability to generate future economic benefits from it. **All six of the following specific conditions need to be demonstrated** in order to capitalize costs incurred in the development phase:

1. Technical feasibility of completing the intangible asset

2. The entity's intention to complete it for use or sale

3. The entity's ability to use or sell it

4. Availability of technical, financial, and other resources needed to complete it, and to use or sell it

5. The way in which the future economic benefits will be received; including the existence of a market for the asset if it will be sold, or its usefulness to the entity if it will be used internally

6. The ability to reliably measure the costs associated with and attributed to the intangible asset during its development

Because all six criteria must be met, this means that an entity capitalizes development phase costs **only when the future benefits are reasonably certain**. This means that internally generated intangible assets are recognized only in limited situations, and projects may be quite far along in the development stage before all six criteria are met. **Only then do the costs begin to be capitalized**. No expenditures incurred prior to this point and previously expensed are added to the asset's cost, even if the expenditures were in the same accounting period.

Although contrary to the usual principles-based approach, several items are specifically identified as not being recognized as internally generated intangible assets. These include brands, mastheads (the front-page or cover banner design of newspapers and magazines), publishing titles, customer lists, and other similar items. They are excluded on the basis that costs incurred to develop them cannot be distinguished from general business development costs.

Costs Included and Excluded.

The cost of an internally generated intangible begins to be accumulated at the date when the six criteria in the development process are met. From this point forward, the types of expenditures that are capitalized are familiar: all directly attributable costs needed to create, produce, and prepare the intangible asset to operate in the way intended by management. Examples of such direct costs include:

1. Materials and services used or consumed

2. Direct costs of personnel, such as salaries, wages, payroll taxes, and related employee benefit costs

3. Fees needed to register a legal right

4. Amortization of other intangibles needed to generate the new asset

5. Interest or borrowing costs[7]

Underlying Concept

The requirement that all research-type and most development-type costs be expensed as they are incurred is an example of the old conflict between relevance and reliability, with verifiability or reliability carrying more weight in this case.

---

[7] Under private entity GAAP, this would be included only if it is the accounting policy chosen by the entity. See Chapter 10 for a fuller discussion of the capitalization of borrowing costs.

Specifically **excluded** as capitalized costs are selling, administrative, and other general overhead costs that cannot be directly linked to preparing the asset for use, costs incurred to train employees, and initial operating losses after the intangible is ready for use.

Significant Change

With the exception of any start-up costs that can be capitalized as property, plant, and equipment, the costs of start-up activities such as legal and other costs of incorporation (**organization costs**); pre-opening costs associated with new facilities or businesses; and pre-operating costs for launching new operations, products, or processes are all expensed. Relocation and reorganization costs, and those associated with advertising and promotional activities including mail order catalogues, are also not capitalized.[8]

To illustrate the accounting treatment of activities associated with intangible items and research and development phases, assume that a company develops, produces, and markets laser machines for medical, industrial, and defence uses. The types of expenditures related to its laser machine activities, along with the recommended IFRS accounting treatment, are listed in Illustration 12-2.

Illustration 12-2

Sample Expenditures and Their Accounting Treatment

Type of Expenditure	Accounting Treatment
1. Construction of long-range research facility (three-storey, 100,000-m² building) for use in current and future projects	Capitalize as PP&E assets; depreciate as a research-type expense.
2. Acquisition of research-related equipment for use on current project only	Capitalize as PP&E asset; depreciate as a research-type expense.
3. Purchase of materials to be used on current and future R&D projects	Capitalize as inventory; expense as a research-type expense as consumed.
4. Salaries of research staff designing new laser bone scanner	Expense immediately as a research-type expense.
5. Research costs incurred under contract for customer and billable monthly	Expense as operating expense in period of related revenue recognition.
6. Material, labour, and overhead costs of prototype laser scanner	Capitalize as intangible asset if development criteria are all met; otherwise expense.
7. Costs of testing prototype and design modifications	Capitalize as intangible asset if development criteria are all met; otherwise expense.
8. Legal fees to obtain patent on new laser scanner	Capitalize as patent (intangible asset) provided asset meets recognition criteria; amortize to cost of goods manufactured as used.
9. Executive salaries	Expense as operating expense (general and administrative).
10. Cost of marketing research related to promotion of new laser scanner	Expense as operating expense (selling).
11. Engineering costs incurred to advance the laser scanner to full production stage	Capitalize as intangible asset if development criteria are all met; otherwise expense.
12. Costs of successfully defending patent on laser scanner	Capitalize as intangible asset (patent); amortize to cost of goods manufactured as used.
13. Commissions to sales staff marketing new laser scanner	Expense as operating expense (selling).

---

[8] Unlike IAS 38 *Intangible Assets*, private entity GAAP does not make specific reference to mail order catalogues.

Prepayments

The discussion so far indicates that if expenditures for intangibles do not qualify for recognition as an intangible asset or as part of goodwill in a business combination, they must be recognized as an expense when incurred. In some cases, however, a prepaid asset—a prepaid expense—can be recognized initially. A prepayment is recognized as an asset only when an entity pays for **goods** before their delivery (or other right of access) or for **services** before receiving those services. The asset is the right to receive the goods or services. When received, this asset no longer exists and the costs are expensed.

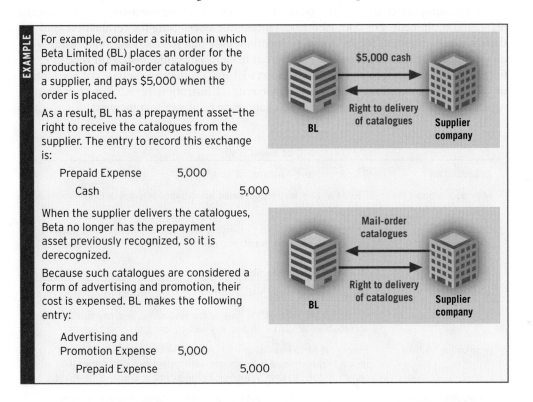

EXAMPLE

For example, consider a situation in which Beta Limited (BL) places an order for the production of mail-order catalogues by a supplier, and pays $5,000 when the order is placed.

As a result, BL has a prepayment asset–the right to receive the catalogues from the supplier. The entry to record this exchange is:

Prepaid Expense	5,000	
Cash		5,000

When the supplier delivers the catalogues, Beta no longer has the prepayment asset previously recognized, so it is derecognized.

Because such catalogues are considered a form of advertising and promotion, their cost is expensed. BL makes the following entry:

Advertising and Promotion Expense	5,000	
Prepaid Expense		5,000

$5,000 cash — BL → Supplier company
Right to delivery of catalogues — BL ← Supplier company

Mail-order catalogues — BL ← Supplier company
Right to delivery of catalogues — BL → Supplier company

Recognition and Measurement after Acquisition

Unlike items of property, plant, and equipment, which commonly have parts added to them or replaced, most intangible assets do not. The nature of intangibles is such that costs incurred after the asset has been acquired are normally made to maintain the asset's benefits and therefore do not meet the recognition criteria for capitalization. Although there are exceptions, most after-acquisition costs are expensed.

Two models have been put forward for measuring intangible assets after initial recognition: a **cost model (CM)** and a **revaluation model (RM)**. The cost model is the most widely used approach by far, and under private entity GAAP, it is the only method allowed.

Why is the RM not widely used? The reason is simply that it can be applied only to intangible assets that have a fair value determined in an active market.[9] This limits its use to situations where the items are homogeneous (interchangeable), there is a good supply of willing buyers and sellers, and the prices are available to the public. An active securities market, such as the Toronto Stock Exchange, exists for equity securities, but active markets do not ordinarily exist for intangible assets. Most intangible assets, such as patents, brands,

4 Objective
Explain how intangible assets are accounted for after initial recognition.

Significant Change

---

[9] See Chapter 2 for a fuller discussion of fair value measurement.

and trademarks, grant unique rights to the entity that holds them. This results in unique pricing when such assets are bought and sold. There are some exceptions. Examples include the prices of quotas for a variety of agricultural products for which the government sets production limits, such as milk or eggs, or for transferable taxi licences in some jurisdictions, so a company could opt to account for these under the revaluation model.

When the RM is chosen for an intangible asset, all the assets in the same class must also apply the same method. Examples of classes include copyrights, patents, computer software, secret recipes, and designs. If there is no active market for the other assets in the class, then the cost model is applied to these assets.

Accounting under these two models is the same for intangible assets as for property, plant, and equipment. For both PP&E and intangible assets using the revaluation method, there is no requirement for an annual revaluation, only that the carrying amount reported on the balance sheet not be materially different from its fair value. Instead of repeating the full coverage of this topic provided in Chapters 10 and 11, the two methods of accounting for limited-life intangible assets are summarized in Illustration 12-3.[10] You may want to review the specific examples in the earlier chapters to reinforce that material.

Illustration 12-3

Cost Model and Revaluation Model for Intangible Assets

Cost Model (CM)	
At acquisition	Recognized and measured at cost.
After acquisition	Carried at cost less accumulated amortization and any accumulated impairment losses.
On disposal	Difference between asset's carrying amount and proceeds on disposal is gain or loss reported in net income.

Revaluation Model (RM)	
At acquisition	Recognized and measured at cost.
After acquisition	Carried at fair value at the date of the revaluation less any subsequent accumulated amortization and any subsequent impairment losses.
Revaluation increase	Record credit to Revaluation Surplus (Other Comprehensive Income) unless this reverses a previous decrease recognized in income. If so, recognize the increase in income to the extent of the prior decrease.
Revaluation decrease	Record debit to Revaluation Surplus (Other Comprehensive Income) to extent there is a balance associated with the same asset. Any remaining amount is recognized in income.
Revaluation	Apply either the **proportional method** (both asset and accumulated amortization balances continue and are adjusted so that net amount is asset's new fair value) or the **asset adjustment method** (accumulated amortization is closed to asset account and begins again at zero; asset is revalued to new amount).
On disposal	Either (a) bring asset to its fair value at the date of disposal, account for the revaluation increase or decrease as above, and recognize no gain or loss on disposal; or (b) recognize a gain or loss on disposal in net income equal to the difference between the proceeds on disposal and the asset's carrying amount on the date of disposal.
Revaluation Surplus account balance	Either transfer amounts directly to Retained Earnings each period (equal to the difference between amortization expense determined on the cost model basis and amortization expense determined on the revaluation model basis), or wait until asset is disposed of and transfer balance remaining in the account directly to Retained Earnings.

---

[10] For indefinite-life intangible assets, the same accounting applies except that the amortization amounts would be nil ($0) amounts.

As suggested above, intangibles are a diverse mix of assets. Some intangibles have values based on rights that are given legally by contract, statute, or similar means. Examples include a Tim Hortons franchise or licences granted by the federal government to cable companies. Some of these rights have finite or limited legal lives that can be easily renewed; others have lives that are not renewable, and others are renewable only at a significant cost. Some can be sold while others may not be exchangeable. Internally developed intangibles may have a wide range of useful lives. Other intangibles may be granted in perpetuity and have an indefinite life. An indefinite life does not mean "infinite"—that the asset will last forever. Instead, it means that, after looking at all relevant factors, there appears to be no foreseeable limit to how long the asset will generate positive net cash flows to the entity.

Accounting standards used to require all intangible assets to be amortized over a period of not more than 40 years. While this simplified the accounting, the reality is that intangibles are diverse, and the approach to their measurement after acquisition should be based on their specific characteristics. Under current standards, if an intangible asset has a finite, or limited, useful life, it is amortized over that useful life. If instead the intangible has an indefinite life, no amortization is taken. Financial reporting is better served by retaining the asset in the accounts until it is determined to be impaired or its life becomes limited.

Limited-Life Intangibles

An intangible asset with a finite or limited life is amortized by systematic charges to expense over its useful life whether the cost model or revaluation model is used. The factors to consider in determining the useful life are similar to the factors for long-lived property, plant, and equipment, and include:

1. The expected use of the asset by the entity, and the expected useful life of other assets that may affect the useful life of the intangible asset (such as mineral rights to depleting assets).

2. Any legal, regulatory, or contractual provisions that may either limit the useful life or allow renewal or extension of the asset's legal or contractual life without the entity having to pay a substantial cost. (If the renewal cost is significant, then the expenditure for the renewal may be the cost of a new intangible asset.)

3. The effects of obsolescence, demand, competition, and other economic factors. Examples include the stability of the industry, known technological advances, and legislative action that results in an uncertain or changing regulatory environment.

4. The level of maintenance expenditure that is needed to obtain the expected future cash flows from the asset.[11]

Amortization expense for a limited-life asset should ideally reflect the pattern in which the asset's economic benefits are used up, if that pattern can be reliably determined. For example, assume that Second Wave, Inc. has purchased a licence to manufacture a limited quantity of a gene product called Mega. Because the life of the licence is reduced with each unit produced, the cost of the licence is amortized following the pattern of production of Mega—a units of production approach. If the pattern cannot be determined, the straight-line method is used. The amortization charges are usually reported **as expenses**, and the credits are made to **accumulated amortization** accounts. Note that in the Second Wave, Inc. example, the amortization is likely a product cost that is first included in inventory and then expensed on the income statement as part of the cost of goods sold when the product is sold.

---

[11] *CICA Handbook*, Part II, Section 3064.60.

The amount to amortize for an intangible asset is its carrying amount less residual value. Uncertainties about residual values for intangibles are greater than they are for items of property, plant, and equipment. Because of this, an intangible asset's residual value is assumed to be zero. This assumption can be overturned only if the asset is expected to be of use to another entity and a third party commits to purchase the asset at the end of its useful life, or if there is an observable market for the asset that is expected to still exist at the end of its useful life to the entity.[12]

There are other similarities between the accounting for limited-life intangibles and property, plant, and equipment assets, as indicated in Illustration 12-4.

Illustration 12-4

Accounting for Intangible Assets with a Limited Life

Transaction or Event	Accounting Treatment for Intangible Assets with a Limited Life	Same as for Most PP&E Assets?
Amortization begins...	...when the asset is in the location and condition to be able to be used as management intends	Yes
Amortization stops...	...at the earlier of when it is derecognized or classified as held for sale	Yes
Review of useful life and amortization method	Private entity GAAP: at least annually	PP&E is reviewed "regularly"
	IFRS: at least at the end of each financial year	Yes
Change in estimate of useful life, residual value, amortization method	Accounted for prospectively—as a change in accounting estimate	Yes

Indefinite-Life Intangibles

An intangible asset with an indefinite life **is not amortized**. For example, assume that Double Clik, Inc. acquires a trademark that is used to distinguish a leading consumer product from other such products. The trademark is renewable every 10 years at minimal cost. After evaluating all relevant factors, the evidence indicates that this trademark product will generate net cash flows for an indefinite period of time. It, therefore, has an indefinite life.

Because of the potential effect on the financial statements, it is important for management to review whether events and circumstances continue to support the assessment of an indefinite life. This is required every accounting period. If the useful life is later considered to be limited instead of indefinite, the change is considered as a change in estimate and past results are not affected. Such an assessment may also indicate that the asset's carrying amount is impaired. The accounting treatment for impairment is discussed later in this chapter.

Specific Intangibles

Objective 5
Identify and explain the accounting for specific types of intangible assets.

The many different types of intangibles are sometimes classified into the following five major categories:[13]

1. Marketing-related intangible assets

2. Customer-related intangible assets

---

[12] *CICA Handbook*, Part II, Section 3064.58 and IAS 38.100.

[13] This classification framework is used in IFRS 3 *Business Combinations:* Illustrative Examples IE16–IE44 to describe identifiable intangible assets acquired in a business combination. This same classification was previously used in superseded *CICA Handbook* Section 1581 *Business Combinations*, Appendix A.

3. Artistic-related intangible assets

4. Contract-based intangible assets

5. Technology-based intangible assets

Marketing-Related Intangible Assets

Marketing-related intangible assets are used mainly in the marketing or promotion of products or services and derive their value from the contractual or legal rights that they contain. Examples are trademarks or trade names, newspaper mastheads, Internet domain names, and non-competition agreements.

A very common form of marketing-related intangible asset is a trademark. A **trademark** or **trade name** is a word, symbol, or design, or combination of these, that is used to distinguish the goods or services of one person or entity from those of others. The terms **brand** and **brand name** are similar but often refer to a group of assets such as a trade name and its related formulas, recipes, and technology. The right to use a trademark, trade name, or brand name in Canada is granted by Industry Canada and the registration system is administered by its Trade-marks Office.[14] In order to obtain and maintain this right, the owner must have made prior and continuing use of it. Trade names like Kraft Dinner, Pepsi-Cola, and Kleenex and brand names such as President's Choice and Canadian Tire create immediate product recognition in our minds, which makes them more marketable. As indicated in this chapter's opening story, company names themselves also identify qualities and characteristics that the companies have worked hard and spent much on developing.[15]

 Law

If a mark or name is **purchased**, its capitalizable cost is the purchase price and other direct costs of acquisition. If it is **developed** by the enterprise itself and its future benefits to the company are reasonably assured, the costs may be capitalized, but only from the point in time when all six of the required capitalization criteria are met in its development phase. These costs may include lawyers' fees, registration fees, design costs, consulting fees, successful legal defence costs, expenditures related to securing the mark or name, and other direct development costs. When a trademark, trade name, or brand name's total cost is insignificant or all six capitalization criteria have not been met, the costs are expensed.

What Do the Numbers Mean?

Hoping to promote the management of brands in the same financially robust way as other long-term investments, Brand Finance plc published a report entitled *Canada's Most Valuable Brands 2009*.[16] The study uses a "royalty relief" approach to value the brands of major companies; that is, the authors determine how much a company would have to pay to license the brand from a third party, and the brand's value is the present value of that hypothetical stream of payments.

In spite of the upheaval in global financial services in 2008, the most valuable Canadian brand, according to this report, belonged to the **Royal Bank of Canada**, with an estimated worth of almost $5.4 billion. Other major Canadian banks were numbers 3, 6, 9, and 10 on the list. The RBC brand, however, does not appear as an asset on the Royal Bank's balance sheet. Why not? Brand value is a function of marketing, advertising, and public relations spending, including customer loyalty and retention programs, which all result in an increased volume of business, retail sales, and shipments. This type of cost is expensed as it is incurred because it cannot be directly related to future benefits.

---

[14] Canadian Intellectual Property Office: <www.cipo.ic.gc.ca>.

[15] To illustrate how various intangibles might arise from a specific product, consider what the creators of the highly successful game Trivial Pursuit did to protect their creation. First, they copyrighted the 6,000 questions that are at the heart of the game. Then they shielded the Trivial Pursuit name by applying for a registered trademark. As a third mode of protection, the creators obtained a design patent on the playing board's design because it represents a unique graphic creation.

[16] <www.brandfinance.com>.

In a similar 2005 report, Brand Finance contended that "long-term investment decisions about future promotional expenditures, and the host of other activities that combine to build brand value" are better made when management can articulate the arguments in financial terms, as is done for most other investments.

Trademark registrations in Canada last for 15 years, and are renewable at a reasonable cost. Although the legal life of such assets **may be unlimited**, in practice they may only provide benefits to the enterprise over a **finite** period. Trademarks can, however, be determined to provide benefits to an enterprise indefinitely. A brand such as Coca-Cola, worth billions of dollars, may reasonably be expected to have an indefinite useful life. In this case, the intangible asset is not amortized.

Customer-Related Intangible Assets

Customer-related intangible assets result from interactions with outside parties and their value may be derived from legal-contractual rights, or because they are separable. Examples include customer lists, order or production backlogs, and customer contracts or non-contractual relationships.

To illustrate, assume that We-Market Inc. acquires the customer list of a large newspaper for $6 million on January 1, 2011. The customer list is a database that includes names, contact information, order history, and demographic information for a list of customers. We-Market expects to benefit from the information on the acquired list for three years, and it believes that these benefits will be spread evenly over the three years. In this case, the customer list is a limited-life intangible that should be amortized on a straight-line basis over the three-year period.

The entries to record the purchase of the customer list and its amortization at the end of each year are as follows:

A = L + SE
0   0   0

Cash flows: ↓ 6,000,000 outflow

January 1, 2011		
Customer List	6,000,000	
Cash		6,000,000

December 31, 2011, 2012, 2013		
Amortization Expense—Customer List	2,000,000	
Accumulated Amortization—Customer List		2,000,000

A = L + SE
−2,000,000   −2,000,000

Cash flows: No effect

This example assumes that the customer list has no residual value. But what if We-Market determines that it can sell the list for $60,000 to another company at the end of three years? In that case, the residual value is subtracted from the cost in order to determine the amortizable amount.

Artistic-Related Intangible Assets

Artistic-related intangible assets involve ownership rights to plays, literary works, musical works, pictures, photographs, and video and audiovisual material. These ownership rights are protected by copyrights and have value because of the legal-contractual nature of the rights.

A copyright is the exclusive right to copy a creative work or allow someone else to do so. It is a federally granted right that applies to all original literary, dramatic, musical, and artistic works, whatever the mode or form of expression. A copyright is acquired automatically when an original work is created, but it can also be registered with the federal Copyright Office. The right is granted for the life of the creator plus 50 years, and gives the owner or heirs the exclusive right to reproduce, sell, communicate, or translate an artistic or published work. Copyrights are not renewable. Like trade names, they may be assigned or sold to other individuals.[17] The costs of acquiring and defending a copyright may be capitalized, but research costs that are associated with them are expensed as they are incurred.

Generally, the copyright's useful life is shorter than its legal life. Its useful life depends on the unique facts and circumstances of each case. Consumer habits, market trends, and prior experience all play a part. Because it is so difficult to determine how many periods will benefit from a copyright, companies often choose to write these costs off over a fairly short period of time.

What Do the Numbers Mean?

Copyrights can be valuable. When Michael Jackson died in mid-2009, he was in dire financial trouble. However, he did have one asset that was extremely valuable: a 50% interest in the Sony Corp./ATV Music Publishing joint venture set up in 1995. The partnership owns copyrights to the lyrics and music of tens of thousands of songs by such artists as the Beatles, Roy Orbison, Hank Williams, and Jimi Hendrix. The venture is said to have total revenues of approximately $350 million and be worth in excess of $1 billion! Altogether, Sony/ATV Music Publishing owns or administers in excess of 750,000 copyrights for a variety of the Who's Who in the music industry today.

Contract-Based Intangible Assets

Law

Contract-based intangible assets are the value of rights that come from contractual arrangements. Examples are licensing arrangements, lease agreements, construction permits, broadcast rights, and service or supply contracts. A very common form of contract-based intangible asset is a franchise.

When you drive down the street in an automobile purchased from a Toyota dealer, fill your tank at the corner Petro-Canada station, grab a coffee at Tim Hortons, eat lunch at McDonald's, cool off with a Baskin-Robbins cone, work at a Coca-Cola bottling plant, live in a home purchased through a Royal Le Page real estate broker, or vacation at a Holiday Inn resort, you are dealing with franchises. A **franchise** is a contractual arrangement under which the franchisor grants the franchisee the right to sell certain products or services, to use certain trademarks, trade names, or brands, or to perform certain functions, usually within a designated geographic area. **Licensing agreements** work in a similar way.

After having developed a unique concept or product, the franchisor protects it through a patent, copyright, trademark, or trade name. The franchisee then acquires the right to take advantage of the franchisor's idea or product by signing a franchise agreement. Another type of franchise is the arrangement that is commonly entered into by a municipality or other government body and a business enterprise that uses public property. In this case, a privately owned enterprise is given permission to use public property in performing its services. Examples are the use of public waterways for a ferry service, the use of public land for telephone or electric lines, the use of city streets for a bus line, or the use of the airwaves for radio or TV broadcasting. Such operating rights are frequently referred to as **licences** or **permits**, and are obtained through agreements with government departments or agencies.

Franchises and licences may be granted for a definite period of time, for an indefinite period of time, or in perpetuity. The enterprise that acquires the franchise or licence recognizes an intangible asset account titled either Franchise or Licence on its books as soon as there are costs (such as a lump-sum payment in advance or legal fees and other expenditures) that are identified with the acquisition of the operating right. The cost of a franchise or licence **with a limited life** is amortized over the lesser of its legal or useful life. A franchise **with an indefinite life**, **or a perpetual franchise**, is amortized if its **useful life** is deemed to be limited. Otherwise, it is not amortized.

---

[17] Canadian Intellectual Property Office: <www.cipo.ic.gc.ca>.

Annual franchise fees paid under a franchise agreement are entered as operating expenses in the period in which they are incurred. They do not represent an asset to the enterprise since they do not relate to future rights.

Another contract-related intangible asset is a favourable lease. A lease or leasehold is a contractual understanding between a lessor (property owner) and a lessee (property renter) that grants the lessee the right to use specific property, owned by the lessor, for a certain period of time in return for specific, usually periodic, cash payments. A lease contract is an intangible asset to the extent that the terms are more favourable than the usual market terms for such an arrangement. It could be an asset to the lessor or the lessee.[18]

Technology-Based Intangible Assets

Law

Technology-based intangible assets relate to innovations or technological advances. Examples are patented technology and trade secrets that are granted by the federal government's Patent Office. Patents are granted for products and processes that are new, workable, and ingenious. A patent gives the holder the right to exclude others from making, selling, or using a product or process for a period of 20 years from the date the patent application is filed with the Patent Office. Fortunes can be made by holding patents, as companies such as RIM, Bombardier, IMAX, Polaroid, and Xerox can attest.[19]

If a patent is purchased from an inventor or other owner, the purchase price represents its cost. Other costs that are incurred in connection with securing a patent, including legal fees and unrecovered costs of a successful lawsuit to protect the patent, are capitalized as part of the patent cost. Most research and development costs incurred that result in an internally generated patent are expensed. Only directly attributable costs incurred in the development phase after the six capitalization criteria are met can be included as part of the asset's cost. For this reason, most research and development costs related to developing a product, process, or idea that is subsequently patented are expensed as they are incurred.

The cost of a patent is amortized over its legal life or its useful life to the entity, whichever is shorter. If a patent is owned from the date it is granted, and it is expected to be useful during its entire legal life, it is amortized over 20 years. If it is expected to be useful for a shorter period, its cost is amortized to expense over that shorter period. Changing demand, new inventions replacing old ones, inadequacy, and other factors often limit the useful life of a patent to less than its legal life. For example, the useful life of patents in the pharmaceutical industry is often less than the legal life because of the testing and approval period that follows their issuance. A typical drug patent has five to 11 years knocked off its 20-year legal life. Why? A drug manufacturer spends one to four years on animal tests, four to six years on human tests, and two to three years for government agencies to review the tests—all after the patent is issued but before the product goes on the pharmacist's shelves.

Legal fees and other costs that are associated with a successful defence of a patent are capitalized as part of the asset's cost because lawsuits establish the patent holder's legal rights. Such costs are amortized along with other acquisition costs over the remaining useful life of the patent.

---

[18] Accounting for lease contracts themselves is in the midst of change. Under existing standards, a lease that transfers the risks and rewards of ownership to the lessee is usually treated as an item of property, plant, and equipment, not an intangible asset. This is likely to change before long. With a change in concept to a lease being a "right of use" asset, it is likely that most lease contracts will fall within the intangible asset category.

[19] Consider the opposite result: Sir Alexander Fleming, who discovered penicillin, decided not to use a patent to protect his discovery. He hoped that companies would produce it more quickly to help save sufferers. Companies, however, refused to develop it because they did not have the protection of a patent and, therefore, were afraid to make the investment.

Patent amortization follows a pattern that is consistent with the benefits that are received, if that pattern can be reliably determined. This could be based on time or on units produced. To illustrate, assume that on January 1, 2011, Harcott Ltd. either pays $180,000 to acquire a patent or incurs $180,000 in legal costs to successfully defend an internally developed patent. Further, assume that the patent has a remaining useful life of 12 years and is amortized on a straight-line basis. The entries to record the $180,000 expenditure on January 1, 2011, and the amortization at the end of each year are as follows:

January 1, 2011		
Patents	180,000	
Cash		180,000

A = L + SE
0   0   0

Cash flows: ↓ 180,000 outflow

December 31, 2011		
Patent Amortization Expense	15,000	
Accumulated Amortization, Patents		15,000

A = L + SE
−15,000   −15,000

Cash flows: No effect

Although a patent's useful life may be limited by its legal life, small modifications or additions may lead to a new patent and an extension of the life of the old patent.[20] In this case, the entity can apply the unamortized costs of the old patent to the new patent if the new patent provides essentially the same benefits. Alternatively, if a patent's value is reduced because, for example, demand drops for the product, the asset is tested for impairment.[21]

What Do the Numbers Mean?

Coca-Cola has managed to keep the recipe for the world's best-selling soft drink under wraps for more than 100 years. How has it done so? The company offers almost no information about its lifeblood. The only written copy of the formula is in a bank vault in Atlanta, Georgia. This handwritten sheet is not available to anyone except by vote of the Coca-Cola board of directors.

Why is science unable to offer some clues? Coke contains 17 to 18 ingredients. These include the usual caramel colour and corn syrup, as well as a blend of oils known as 7X—rumoured to be a mix of orange, lemon, cinnamon, and others. Distilling natural products like these is complicated since they are made of thousands of compounds. Although the original formula contained trace amounts of cocaine, this is one ingredient that you will not find in today's Coke. When was it removed? That is a secret, too. Some experts indicate that the power of this formula and related brand image account for almost U.S. $63 billion, or roughly 12% of Coke's U.S. $538 billion share value.

Source: Adapted from Reed Tucker, "How Has Coke's Formula Stayed a Secret?" *Fortune* (July 24, 2000), p. 42; and David Kiley, "Best Global Brands," *Business Week* (August 6, 2007), p. 59.

Another common technology-based intangible relates to computer software costs, either for internal use or for sale as a product. Costs that are incurred in the development of software as a potential product **for sale** or those directly attributable to the development, betterment, or acquisition of computer software **for internal use** are covered by the same capitalization criteria required for other intangible assets.

---

[20] The Canadian Intellectual Property Office website <www.cipo.ic.gc.ca> indicates in its "A Guide to Patents, Part 1" that 90% of patents are for improvements to existing patented inventions.

[21] Eli Lilly's well-known drug Prozac, which is used to treat depression, accounted for 43% of the company's U.S. sales in 1998. The patent on Prozac expired in 2001 and the company was unable to extend its protection with a second-use patent for the use of Prozac to treat appetite disorders. Sales of Prozac went down substantially in 2001 as generic equivalents entered the market.

Deferred Charges

In the past and sometimes still seen today are assets referred to as deferred charges. This term has been used to describe different types of items that have debit balances, such as deferred development costs, pre-operating and start-up costs, and organization costs.

However, use of the term "deferred charges" is disappearing as standard setters no longer recognize deferred costs as assets unless the resulting costs meet the definition and recognition criteria for an asset. And even when they do meet the definition, the assets are more properly described as internally developed intangibles.[22] For example, the former *CICA Handbook* section on research and development costs, the standard for one of the most common types of deferred charges, has been eliminated completely and replaced with new Section 3064 *Goodwill and Intangible Assets*. It and IAS 38 *Intangible Assets* have taken the position that if a wide variety of costs incurred meet the development phase capitalization criteria identified above on page 749, then they are internally developed intangible assets.

Deferred charges also used to include such items as debt discount and issue costs. Because long-term debt is a financial liability that is usually carried at amortized cost, the debt discount and issue costs are now deducted from the related liability. Long-term prepayments for insurance, rent, taxes, and other down payments may still be referred to as "deferred charges," but the term is expected to be used less and less over time.

IMPAIRMENT AND DERECOGNITION

Objective 6
Explain and account for impairments of limited-life and indefinite-life intangible assets.

Similar to property, plant, and equipment, the carrying amounts of intangible assets and goodwill have to be reviewed to ensure that they do not exceed the economic benefits the assets are expected to provide in the future. If an item is determined to be impaired, its carrying amount will have to be written down and an impairment loss recognized.

Impairment of Limited-Life Intangibles

Tutorials: Impairment

The same impairment models and standards that apply to **long-lived tangible assets** also apply to **limited-life intangibles**.[23] As indicated in Chapter 11, long-lived assets that a company intends to hold and use are assessed for potential impairment as follows:

Private entity GAAP	Whenever events and circumstances indicate the carrying value may not be recoverable
IFRS	At the end of each reporting period

The internal and external sources of information that may indicate an intangible asset is impaired are the same factors described in Illustration 11-13 in Chapter 11 for items of property, plant, and equipment. However, evidence of physical damage is understandably much less important in the assessment of an intangible asset! If an assessment indicates

---

[22] Section 3070 *Deferred Charges* was removed from the *CICA Handbook* in 2005. Now, even the one recommendation that was transferred from Section 3070 to Section 1510 no longer exists in private entity GAAP.

[23] *CICA Handbook*, Part II, Section 3063 *Impairment of Long-lived Assets* and IAS 36 *Impairment of Assets*.

there may be impairment, the asset is formally tested by applying the appropriate impairment model.

A summary of the two models and how they are applied is provided in Illustration 12-5. Remember that the cost recovery impairment model is used for **private entity GAAP**, and the rational entity impairment model is incorporated in **IFRS**. A review of pages 693 to 697 in Chapter 11 might help to reinforce your understanding of the details of each model.

Illustration 12-5

Summary of Impairment Models for Limited-life Intangible Assets

Cost Recovery Impairment Model	
Concept	Assumes asset will continue to be used; it is impaired only if the asset's carrying amount is not recoverable from the future undiscounted cash flows from use and eventual sale.
Recoverability test	If undiscounted future cash flows ≥ carrying amount, asset is not impaired. If undiscounted future cash flows < carrying amount, asset is impaired. Proceed to calculate impairment loss.
Impairment loss	Asset's carrying amount − fair value = impairment loss; fair value is a discounted cash flow, market-based concept.
Entry to record loss	Impairment Loss $ Accumulated Impairment Losses $
Subsequent amortization	Review carrying amount to be amortized, useful life, and pattern of amortization and determine new periodic rate.
Reversal of impairment loss	Reversal not permitted. The fair value to which the asset is written down becomes the asset's new cost basis.
If no single-asset identifiable cash flows	Combine with other assets into an asset group, test for impairment and, if impaired, calculate impairment loss using same approach as for an individual asset. Allocate loss only to long-lived assets, based on their relative carrying amounts, within limits.

Rational Entity Impairment Model	
Concept	Assumes management will use the asset or dispose of it currently, whichever results in a higher return to the entity. It is impaired only if its carrying amount is not recoverable from the more profitable/less costly of the two options.
Recoverability test	No separate test.
Impairment loss	Calculate recoverable amount = **higher of** value in use **and** fair value less costs to sell, both of which are discounted cash flow concepts. If recoverable amount ≥ carrying amount, no impairment loss. If recoverable amount < carrying amount, impairment loss = the difference.
Entry to record loss under cost model	Impairment Loss $ Accumulated Impairment Losses $
Subsequent amortization	Review carrying amount to be amortized, useful life, and pattern of amortization and determine new periodic rate.
Reversal of impairment loss	Reversal of loss is required if estimates underlying recoverable amount have changed. Reversal amount is limited.
If no single-asset identifiable cash flows	Combine with other assets into a cash-generating group and calculate impairment loss using same approach as for an individual asset. Allocate loss to assets based on their relative carrying amounts, within limits.

Impairment of Indefinite-Life Intangibles

Accounting for the impairment of intangible assets with an **indefinite life** is a little different than explained above for limited-life intangibles. These differences and the reasons for them are discussed below.

Private Entity GAAP

An intangible asset with an indefinite life still needs to be tested for impairment only when events and circumstances indicate there might be impairment, but now the test is different. The impairment test for an indefinite-life asset is a **fair value test**. This test compares the **fair value** of the intangible asset with the asset's carrying amount. If its fair value is less than the carrying amount, an impairment loss equal to the difference is recognized.

Why is there a different standard for indefinite-life intangibles? This one-step test is used because it would be relatively easy for many indefinite-life assets to meet the recoverability test. That is, the undiscounted cash flows would extend many years into the future and the total cash to be recovered tends to add up to a large sum. However, the dollars received in periods far into the future have a much lower value today. **As a result, the separate recoverability test is not used**, and the test compares the carrying amount directly with the asset's fair value—a discounted cash flow concept.

To illustrate, assume that Space Corp. (SC) purchases a broadcast licence for $1,150,000, and that the licence is renewable every 10 years if the company provides appropriate service and does not violate the rules and regulations of the Canadian Radio-television and Telecommunications Commission (CRTC). The licence is then renewed with the CRTC twice at a minimal cost, and because cash flows are expected to last indefinitely, the licence is reported as an indefinite-life intangible asset. Assume that SC is beginning to question whether the asset might be impaired because advertising revenues are expected to drop with changing demographics in the area covered by the licence. The following information has been gathered about the benefits of the licence:

Undiscounted future net cash flows expected from its use	$1,800,000
Discounted future net cash flows, or fair value	$ 950,000

Is the licence impaired? Yes, because the carrying amount of $1,150,000 is more than its fair value of $950,000, an impairment loss of $1,150,000 − $950,000 = $200,000 is indicated.

Space Corp. may either set up and credit an accumulated impairment loss account for the licence or credit the asset account itself. The licence is now reported at a net amount of $950,000, and this is its new "cost" for subsequent accounting.

IFRS

There is only a minor difference in the IFRS standard for impairment for indefinite-life intangibles than for those with limited lives. For example, assets with an indefinite life are tested for impairment by comparing their carrying amount and recoverable value **on an annual basis whether or not there is any indication of impairment**. Why a stronger standard for these assets? The answer lies in the fact that no expense is being charged against income for such assets on a regular basis. For this reason, the assumption of a continuing recoverable value in excess of book value needs to be regularly tested.

Derecognition

An intangible asset is derecognized when it is disposed of or when its continuing use or disposal are not expected to generate any further economic benefits. Similar to property, plant, and equipment assets, a gain or loss is recognized at this time, equal to the difference between the asset's carrying amount and the proceeds on disposal, if any. The gain or loss on disposal is recognized in income in the period of disposal.

Goodwill

While companies capitalize certain costs that are incurred to develop identifiable assets such as patents and copyrights, the amounts that are capitalized are generally not significant. Material amounts of intangible assets are recorded, however, when companies purchase intangible assets, particularly in situations where another business is being purchased in a business combination. In this latter case, goodwill is also often recognized as an asset. In fact, this is the only time that goodwill is ever recognized!

Objective
7 Explain the concept of goodwill and how it is measured and accounted for after acquisition.

Definition of Goodwill

In a business combination where **one company purchases 100% of another business**, the fair value of what is given up by the acquiring entity (the acquirer) is allocated to the various assets and liabilities it receives.[24] All identifiable assets acquired and liabilities assumed (the identifiable net assets) are recognized at their fair values at the acquisition date. The difference between the fair value of the consideration transferred to acquire the business and the fair value amounts assigned to the identifiable net assets is the amount recognized as goodwill. This is shown in Illustration 12-6.

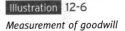

Significant Change

Fair value of consideration transferred—any one or a combination of cash, other assets, notes payable at a later date, common or preferred shares, or other equity instruments, or contingent consideration

− **Fair value of all identifiable assets acquired and liabilities assumed,** whether or not previously recognized by the acquired entity

= **GOODWILL**

Illustration 12-6

Measurement of goodwill

Goodwill is "an asset representing the future economic benefits arising from other assets acquired in a business combination that are not individually identified and separately recognized."[25] As you can tell from Illustration 12-6, it is an unidentified excess or residual amount, and it can only be calculated in relation to the business as a whole. The only way it can be sold is to sell the business.

---

[24] When less than a 100% interest is acquired or the controlling interest is acquired in stages, the calculation of goodwill is more complex. This is because a choice is permitted in how the non-controlling shareholders' interest is calculated and prior holdings are revalued. This topic is left to a course in advanced financial accounting.

[25] *CICA Handbook,* Part II, 1582.02A(j) and IFRS 3 Appendix A.

Recognition and Measurement of Goodwill

Recognition of Internally Generated Goodwill

Goodwill that is generated internally is not capitalized in the accounts. Measuring the components of goodwill is simply too complex, and associating costs incurred with future benefits is too difficult. In fact, the future benefits of goodwill may have no relationship to the costs that were incurred to develop it. To add to the complexity, goodwill may even exist when there have been no specific expenditures to develop it. In addition, because no transaction has taken place with outside parties, a great deal of subjectivity—even misrepresentation—might be involved in trying to measure it.

Purchased Goodwill

As previously indicated, goodwill is recognized only when a business combination occurs, because the value of goodwill cannot be separated from a business as a whole. The problem of determining the proper values to assign to identifiable intangible assets in a business combination is complex because of the many different types of intangibles that might be acquired. Because goodwill is a residual amount, every dollar that is assigned to other assets, including identifiable intangible assets, is one less dollar assigned to goodwill.

To illustrate, assume that Multi-Diversified, Inc. decides that it needs a parts division to supplement its existing tractor distributorship. The president of Multi-Diversified is interested in buying Tractorling Ltd., a small company near Edmonton that has an established reputation and is looking to sell its business. Illustration 12-7 shows Tractorling's current balance sheet.

Illustration 12-7

Tractorling Ltd. Balance Sheet

TRACTORLING LTD.
Balance Sheet
December 31, 2011

Assets		Liabilities and equity	
Cash	$ 25,000	Current liabilities	$ 55,000
Receivables	35,000	Share capital	100,000
Inventories	42,000	Retained earnings	100,000
Property, plant, and equipment (net)	153,000		
Total assets	$255,000	Total liabilities and equity	$255,000

After considerable negotiation, Tractorling Ltd.'s shareholders decide to accept Multi-Diversified's offer of $400,000. The two companies might agree on a $400,000 cash payment, or $400,000 in value of Multi-Diversified's shares, or on a number of other forms of consideration. How should goodwill, if any, be measured?

The answer is not obvious. The fair values of Tractorling's identifiable assets and liabilities are not disclosed in its cost-based balance sheet. It is likely, though, that as the negotiations progressed, Multi-Diversified had a detailed investigation done of Tractorling's underlying assets to determine their fair values. Such an investigation may be done through a purchase audit by Multi-Diversified's auditors, or an independent appraisal from some other source. Illustration 12-8 shows the results.

Illustration 12-8

Fair Values of Tractorling Ltd.'s Identifiable Net Assets

Fair Values, December 31, 2011	
Cash	$ 25,000
Receivables	35,000
Inventories	62,000
Property, plant, and equipment (net)	265,000
Patents	18,000
Liabilities	(55,000)
Fair value of identifiable net assets	$350,000

Differences between the current fair value and carrying amount are more common among long-term assets, although there can also be significant differences in the current asset category. Cash is obviously not a problem in terms of its value and receivables are normally fairly close to their current valuation, although adjustments do sometimes need to be made because of inadequate bad debt provisions. The fair values of liabilities also are usually close to their recorded book values. However, if interest rates have changed since long-term liabilities were issued, their current value determined using current interest rates may be quite different from their carrying amount. A careful analysis must also be done to ensure that there are no unrecorded liabilities.

Returning to our example, the $20,000 difference between the fair value and carrying amount of Tractorling's inventories ($62,000 − $42,000) could be due to several factors. One explanation might be that Tractorling acquired significant inventories when the prices were lower and uses specific identification or an average cost valuation, in which ending inventory is made up of inventory at older costs.

In many cases, the values of long-lived assets such as property, plant, and equipment and intangibles may have increased substantially over the years. This difference could be due to inaccurate estimates of useful lives, continual expensing of small expenditures (say, amounts less than $500), or substantial increases in replacement costs. Alternatively, there may be assets that have not been recognized in the company's books. In Tractorling's case, land was acquired many years ago and its fair value has increased significantly, and internally developed patents have not been recognized in the accounts, yet they have a fair value of $18,000.

Since the investigation indicates that the fair value of the identifiable net assets is $350,000, why would Multi-Diversified pay $400,000? Tractorling might point to the company's established reputation, good credit rating, top management team, well-trained employees, and so on as factors that make the value of the business as a whole greater than $350,000. Multi-Diversified places a premium on the future earning power of these attributes as well as the company's current basic asset structure. At this point in the negotiations, Tractorling's total fair value, and price, may be due to many factors; the most important may be sheer skill at the bargaining table.

Multi-Diversified labels the difference between the fair value of the consideration paid of $400,000 and the fair value of the identifiable net assets of $350,000 as goodwill. Goodwill is viewed as the unidentifiable values plus the value of the identifiable intangibles that do not meet the criteria for separate recognition. The procedure for valuation shown in Illustration 12-9 is referred to as a master valuation approach, because goodwill is assumed to cover all the values that cannot be specifically associated with any identifiable tangible or intangible asset. Note that this method of accounting for a business combination is a fair value approach rather than one based on the cost of the acquisition and cost allocation. For example, acquisition-related costs associated with a business combination are expensed as incurred and not capitalized as they would be in a cost-based system.

Illustration 12-9
Determination of Goodwill—Master Valuation Approach

Fair value of consideration transferred:		$400,000
Fair value of identifiable net assets:		
Cash	$ 25,000	
Receivables	35,000	
Inventories	62,000	
Property, plant, and equipment	265,000	
Patents	18,000	
Liabilities	(55,000)	350,000
Value assigned to goodwill:		$ 50,000

Multi-Diversified's entry to record the purchase of Tractorling's net assets, assuming the consideration is $400,000 cash, is as follows:[26]

A = L + SE
+55,000 +55,000

Cash flows: ↓ 375,000 outflow

Cash	25,000	
Receivables	35,000	
Inventories	62,000	
Property, plant, and equipment	265,000	
Patents	18,000	
Goodwill	50,000	
Liabilities		55,000
Cash		400,000

Bargain Purchase

A **bargain purchase**, resulting in what is sometimes called **negative goodwill**, arises when the total of the fair value of the identifiable net assets acquired is higher than the fair value of the consideration transferred for those net assets. This situation is a result of market imperfection (a poor decision by the seller) because the seller would be better off to sell the assets individually than in total. However, situations do occur when the value of what is given up is less than the value of the identifiable net assets that are acquired, and this requires that a goodwill "credit" be accounted for.

Significant Change

How should this credit be handled in the accounts? Should it be taken to Retained Earnings directly, to Other Comprehensive Income, to net income in the year of purchase, or amortized to income over a reasonable future period? The accounting standards over the past 35 years have taken a variety of approaches to this "bonus," which shows the difficulty there has been in coming to terms with its conceptual nature.

Current standards require the excess to be recognized **as a gain in net income** in the same period that the combination takes place. However, this cannot be done without a

---

[26] In reality, the Cash amounts would be netted and only $375,000 would be transferred. If Multi-Diversified gained control over Tractorling by purchasing all of that company's shares instead of buying all the individual assets and liabilities making up the business, the entry would be:

Investment in Shares of Tractorling	400,000	
Cash		400,000

When Multi-Diversified prepares consolidated financial statements, the Investment account is removed from the balance sheet and is replaced with the underlying assets and liabilities that the Investment balance represents. Regardless of the transaction's legal form, the goodwill appears on the investor's GAAP balance sheet.

thorough reassessment of all the variables, values, and measurement procedures used that resulted in this gain. If a gain still results from the re-examination, then it is recognized in income. While some critics do not agree with the recognition of a gain **on the acquisition of assets**, this treatment is not applied lightly and appears to be a practical approach to a situation that rarely occurs.

Valuation after Acquisition

Once goodwill has been recognized in the accounts, how should it be treated in subsequent periods? Three basic approaches have been suggested:

1. **Charge goodwill immediately to expense.** Supporters of this approach justify an immediate writeoff because the accounting for goodwill is then consistent whether purchased or created internally. Goodwill created internally is not recognized as an asset. They also argue that amortization of purchased goodwill leads to double counting, because net income is reduced by amortization of the purchased goodwill as well as by the internal expenditure that is made to maintain or increase its value. Perhaps the best rationale for charging goodwill against income directly is that identifying the periods over which the future benefits are to be received is so difficult that the result is purely arbitrary.

2. **Amortize goodwill over its useful life.** Others believe that goodwill has value when it is acquired, but that its value eventually disappears. Therefore the asset should be charged to expense over the periods that are affected. To the extent that goodwill represents a wasting asset, this method provides a better matching of the costs of the benefits to revenues than other methods, even though the useful life may be difficult to determine.

3. **Retain goodwill indefinitely unless a reduction in value occurs.** Others believe that goodwill can have an indefinite life and should be kept as an asset until a decline in value occurs. Some form of goodwill should always be an asset because the current costs to maintain or enhance the purchased goodwill are being expensed. Also, unless there is strong evidence that a decline in its value has occurred, a writeoff of goodwill is arbitrary and leads to distortions in net income.

Underlying Concept

Standard setters have had difficulty determining the most appropriate method of accounting for goodwill after acquisition. Until recently, companies in the United Kingdom were allowed to write off goodwill immediately against equity. In 1998, British companies were required to capitalize and amortize goodwill. With the move to IFRS, they now apply a non-amortization and test-for-impairment policy.

Not so long ago, companies were required to amortize goodwill over a period no longer than 40 years. This has changed. Goodwill acquired in a business combination **is now considered to have an indefinite life and is no longer amortized**. Although goodwill may decrease over time, predicting the actual life of goodwill and an appropriate pattern of amortization is extremely difficult. Therefore, it is carried on the statement of financial position at the amount originally recognized in the combination less any subsequent impairment losses. **Income statements are not charged with any amounts paid for the goodwill until the asset is considered impaired.**

Real-World Emphasis

What Do the Numbers Mean?

The method of accounting for goodwill can have a significant effect on a company's income statement because goodwill is often a major asset on its balance sheet. **Quebecor Inc.**, for example, reported income of $91.9 million in a recent year. **If the accounting standard for goodwill had not changed**, the company would have had an additional $123.3 million of amortization expense (after tax and non-controlling interest) related to goodwill. It would have reported a loss of $31.4 million. In addition, because companies were also required to review their existing goodwill and recognize any impairments as an adjustment to their opening balance of retained earnings when the new standard was first applied, Quebecor recognized a goodwill impairment loss of $2.163 billion—a charge that bypassed the income statement completely!

Impairment of Goodwill

Significant Change

Goodwill is not an identifiable asset and cannot generate cash flows independently of other assets. Because it can be acquired only in combination with other assets making up a business, it has to be assigned to a reporting or cash-generating unit (CGU) in order to be tested for impairment. Other than this specific feature that focuses on the reporting unit or cash generating unit, impairment accounting for goodwill is similar to that for intangibles with an indefinite life. Applying the standards in this area can be complex, but a summary of the basic elements is provided in Illustration 12-10.

Illustration 12-10

Summary of Accounting for Impairment of Goodwill

	Private Entity GAAP	IFRS
Apply impairment test...	...when events or changes in circumstances indicate	...annually, and whenever there is an indication that CGU may be impaired
At acquisition date, assign goodwill...	...to a reporting unit: an operating segment or one level below	...to cash-generating unit: lowest level where goodwill is monitored for management purposes, and no larger than an operating segment
There is an impairment loss...	...when carrying amount of reporting unit including goodwill > fair value of reporting unit. Loss = amount of excess	...when carrying amount of unit including goodwill > recoverable amount. Loss = amount of excess. Recoverable amount is the higher of value in use and fair value less costs to sell
Impairment loss is allocated...	...to goodwill as a goodwill impairment loss; impairment test for other assets in group is done before goodwill impairment test	...first to goodwill, then remainder to other assets on a relative carrying amount (proportionate) basis
Goodwill impairment reversal...	...is not permitted	...is not permitted

To illustrate, assume that Coburg Corporation has three divisions. One division, Pritt Products, was purchased four years ago for $2 million and has been identified as a reporting unit. Unfortunately, it has experienced operating losses over the last three quarters and management is reviewing the reporting unit to determine whether there has been an impairment of goodwill. The carrying amounts of Pritt Division's net assets, including the associated goodwill of $900,000, are listed in Illustration 12-11.

Illustration 12-11

Pritt Reporting Unit—Carrying Amount of Net Assets Including Goodwill

Cash	$ 200,000
Receivables	300,000
Inventory	700,000
Property, plant, and equipment (net)	800,000
Goodwill	900,000
Less: Accounts and notes payable	(500,000)
Net assets, at carrying amounts	$2,400,000

Situation 1: The fair value of the Pritt Division reporting unit as a whole is estimated to be $2.8 million. Management determines that the unit's value in use is $2.9 million and that the company would incur direct costs of $50,000 if the unit were sold.

Under **private entity GAAP**, the goodwill is not impaired. The asset group's $2.4-million book value is less than its fair value of $2.8 million. Under **IFRS**, goodwill is not considered impaired either. The recoverable amount of the unit is $2.9 million—the higher of its value in use ($2.9 million) and its fair value less costs to sell ($2.8 million – $50,000)—and this exceeds the unit's carrying amount of $2.4 million.

Situation 2: The fair value of the Pritt Division cash-generating unit as a whole is $1.9 million, its value in use is $2.1 million, and the direct cost of selling the unit is $50,000.

Under **private entity GAAP**, an impairment loss is indicated:

Carrying amount of unit, including goodwil	$2,400,000
Fair value of unit	1,900,000
Goodwill impairment loss	$ 500,000

The entry to record the loss is:

Impairment Loss—Goodwill	500,000	
Accumulated Impairment Losses, Goodwill		500,000

A = L + SE
−500,000   −500,000
Cash flows: No effect

Alternatively, the Goodwill account itself could have been credited. Either way, its carrying amount is now reduced to $400,000 (i.e., $900,000 – $500,000). Under **IFRS**, an impairment loss is also indicated:

Carrying amount of unit, including goodwill		$2,400,000
Recoverable amount of unit: higher of		
Value in use	$2,100,000	
and		(2,100,000)
Fair value less costs to sell	$1,850,000	
Goodwill impairment loss		$ 300,000

The entry to record the loss is:

Impairment Loss—Goodwill	300,000	
Accumulated Impairment Losses, Goodwill		300,000

A = L + SE
−300,000   −300,000
Cash flows: No effect

Because there is a requirement to report the gross amount of goodwill and accumulated impairment losses at the end of the period, it is better to credit the Accumulated Impairment Losses account so that this information is retained. Its net carrying amount is now $600,000 (i.e., $900,000 – $300,000).

Illustration 12-12 summarizes the impairment tests for various intangible assets.

	Impairment Test	
Type of Asset	**Private entity GAAP**	**IFRS**
Limited-life intangible	Recoverability test; if failed, write down to fair value	Compare carrying amount with recoverable amount
Indefinite-life intangible	Compare carrying amount with fair value	Compare carrying amount with recoverable amount
Goodwill	Compare carrying amount of reporting unit with its fair value	Compare carrying amount of CGU with its recoverable amount

Illustration 12-12

Summary of Intangible Asset Impairment Tests

PRESENTATION, DISCLOSURE, AND ANALYSIS

Real-World Emphasis

A recent survey indicates that the most common types of intangible assets reported are broadcast rights, publishing rights, trademarks, patents, licences, customer lists, non-competition agreements, franchises, and purchased R&D.[27] These, along with goodwill, have become an increasingly large proportion of companies' reported assets, making intangibles an important contributor to entity performance and financial position. For example, **Corus Entertainment Inc.**, a Canadian-based media and entertainment company, reported indefinite-life broadcast licences and goodwill at August 31, 2008, that amounted to 65.5% of its total assets. Nine months later, the company recognized $175 million of impairment losses on these two classes of assets, about 13% of their August 31, 2008 book value.

Presentation and Disclosure

Overview

Objective 8

Identify the types of disclosure requirements for intangible assets and goodwill and explain the issues in analyzing these assets.

Significant Change

While there are few required disclosures on the face of the statement of financial position and the statement of comprehensive income, a significant amount of information is required in the notes to the financial statements, particularly those prepared under IFRS. As seen in previous chapters, private entity GAAP disclosures are considerably curtailed on the basis that most users of their financial statements can request additional information as needed. The goal of disclosure for publicly accountable entities is basically to allow readers to understand the significance of intangibles and goodwill to the operations of the business. To that end, this section summarizes some of the major disclosures required.

For each class of intangible asset, and separately for internally generated intangibles and other intangible assets, the following information is required:

- whether their lives are indefinite or finite (limited), useful life, methods and rates of amortization, and the line where amortization is included on the statement of comprehensive income

- the carrying amount of intangible assets with an indefinite life, and the reasons supporting an assessment of an indefinite life

- a reconciliation of the opening and ending balances of their carrying amount and accumulated amortization and impairment losses, separately identifying each reason for an increase or decrease

- impairment losses and reversals of impairment losses and where they are reported in the statement of comprehensive income

For each material impairment loss recognized or reversed in the period:

- the circumstances that led to its recognition, the amount recognized, the nature of the asset or cash-generating unit, and information about how the recoverable amount was determined

---

[27] Nadi Chlala, Diane Paul, Louise Martel, and Andrée Lavigne, *Financial Reporting in Canada, 2007* (CICA, 2007), p. 343, and Clarence Byrd, Ida Chen, and Joshua Smith, *Financial Reporting in Canada, 2005* (CICA, 2005), p. 256.

For each cash-generating unit or group of units that has a significant amount of goodwill or intangible assets with an indefinite life:

- how the unit's recoverable amount was determined, as well as assumptions underlying the calculation of the recoverable amount

For intangible assets measured using the revaluation model:

- their carrying amount, the carrying amounts if the revaluation model had not been applied, the date of the revaluation, the amount of the associated revaluation surplus and changes in that account, and the methods and assumptions used in estimating fair values

This list identifies only some of the disclosures. The best source of the specific requirements is the standards themselves.

Illustration of Disclosures

Excerpts from the financial statements of **Dorel Industries Inc.** for its year ended December 30, 2008, are provided in Illustration 12-13. These disclosures are similar to current private entity GAAP. This Canadian company, reporting in thousands of U.S. dollars, designs, manufactures or sources, and markets and distributes a diverse portfolio of consumer products in the United States, Canada, and Europe. The intangible assets, goodwill, and deferred charges make up about 45% of the company's reported assets at December 30, 2008.

It is interesting to read the company's Management Discussion and Analysis in its annual report for this same year. Management identifies the impairment testing of goodwill and certain other indefinite-life intangible assets **as one of its most critical accounting policies**. The company considers that these would have the most material effect on the financial statements if the policies were to change or be applied in a different manner.

Additional Disclosures

Illustration 12-13

Notes on Intangible Assets

Real-World Emphasis

NOTE 2 – SIGNIFICANT ACCOUNTING POLICIES (Cont'd)

Intangible Assets

Intangible assets are recorded at cost:

Trademarks

Trademarks acquired as part of business acquisitions and registered trademarks are considered to have an indefinite life and are therefore not subject to amortization. They are tested annually for impairment or more frequently when events or changes in circumstances indicate that the trademarks might be impaired. The impairment test compares the carrying amount of the trademarks with its fair value.

Customer Relationships

Customer relationships acquired as part of business acquisitions are amortized on a straight-line basis over a period of 15 to 25 years.

Supplier Relationship

Supplier relationship acquired as part of a business acquisition is amortized on a straight-line basis over a period of 10 years.

Patents

Patents are amortized on a straight-line basis over their expected useful lives ranging from 4 years to 18 years.

Software Licence

Software licence is amortized on a straight-line basis over its expected useful life of 10 years.

Impairment or Disposal of Long-Lived Assets

The Company reviews its long-lived assets and amortizable intangible assets for impairment whenever events or changes in circumstances indicate that the carrying amount of a long-lived asset may not be recoverable. Determination of recoverability is based on an estimate of undiscounted future net cash flows resulting from the use of the assets and its eventual disposition. An impairment loss is recognized when the carrying amount of the assets exceeds the fair value. Such evaluations for impairment are significantly affected by estimates of future prices for the Company's product, economic trends in the market and other factors. Quoted market values are used whenever available to estimate fair value. When quoted market values are unavailable, the fair value of the long-lived asset is generally based on estimates of discounted expected net cash flows. Assets held for sale are reflected at the lower of their carrying amount or fair values less cost to sell and are not depreciated while classified as held for sale. Assets held for sale are included in other assets on the balance sheet.

NOTE 8- INTANGIBLE ASSETS

	December 30, 2008		
	Cost	Accumulated Amortization	Net
Trademarks	$275,085	$ —	$275,085
Customer relationships	97,401	14,783	82,618
Supplier relationship	1,500	75	1,425
Patents	22,576	13,525	9,051
Software licence	668	—	668
	$397,230	$28,383	$368,847

In 2008, the aggregate amount of amortizable intangible assets acquired amounted to $1,992 (2007 − $1,830) of which $140 (2007 − $8) is unpaid at year-end. The aggregate amortization expense of intangible assets amounted to $6,738 (2007 − $4,632).

Real-World Emphasis

Illustration 12-14

Excerpts from IFRS Disclosures, Unilever Group

The goodwill and intangible asset disclosures in Illustration 12-14 are excerpts from the 2008 financial statements of the **Unilever Group**, an international conglomerate operating in about 100 countries around the world. You may be familiar with many of their brandnames, such as Dove, Lipton, Hellmann's, Bertolli, and Knorr—just a few of their products in their broad-based markets. Unilever follows IFRS and reports in euros (€). Intangible assets and goodwill are significant investments to Unilever, which reports worldwide spending of €927 million on research and development in 2008!

1 Accounting information and policies (continued)

Goodwill

Goodwill (being the difference between the fair value of consideration paid for new interests in group companies and the fair value of the Group's share of their net identifiable assets and contingent liabilities at the date of acquisition) is capitalised. Goodwill is not amortised, but is subject to an annual review for impairment (or more frequently if necessary). Any impairment is charged to the income statement as it arises.

For the purpose of impairment testing, goodwill acquired in a business combination is, from the acquisition date, allocated to each of the Group's cash generating units, or groups of cash generating units, that are expected to benefit from the synergies of the combination, irrespective of whether other assets or liabilities of the acquired business are assigned to those units or groups of units. Each unit or group of units to which the goodwill is allocated represents the lowest level within the Group at which the goodwill is monitored for internal management purposes, and is not larger than a segment based on either the Group's primary or the Group's secondary reporting format.

Intangible assets

On acquisition of group companies, Unilever recognises any specifically identifiable intangible assets separately from goodwill, initially measuring the intangible assets at fair value as at the date of acquisition. Separately purchased intangible assets are initially measured at cost. Finite-lived intangible assets mainly comprise patented and non-patented technology, know-how and software.These assets are capitalised and amortised on a straight-line basis in the income statement over the period of their expected useful lives, or the period of legal rights if shorter, none of which exceeds ten years. Periods in excess of five years are used only where the Directors are satisfied that the life of these assets will clearly exceed that period.

Indefinite-lived intangibles are not amortised, but are subject to an annual review for impairment (or more frequently if necessary). Any impairment is charged to the income statement as it arises.

Unilever monitors the level of product development costs against all the criteria set out in IAS 38. These include the requirement to establish that a flow of economic benefits is probable before costs are capitalised. For Unilever this is evident only shortly before a product is launched into the market. The level of costs incurred after these criteria have been met is currently insignificant.

9 Goodwill and intangible assets

Indefinite-lived intangible assets principally comprise those trademarks for which there is no foreseeable limit to the period over which they are expected to generate net cash inflows. These are considered to have an indefinite life, given the strength and durability of our brands and the level of marketing support. Brands that are classified as indefinite have been in the market for many years, and the nature of the industry we operate in is such that brand obsolescence is not common, if appropriately supported by advertising and marketing spend. Finite-lived intangible assets, which primarily comprise patented and non-patented technology, know-how, and software, are capitalised and amortised in operating profit on a straight-line basis over the period of their expected useful lives, none of which exceeds ten years. The level of amortisation for finite-lived intangible assets is not expected to change materially over the next five years.

At cost less amortisation and impairment	€ million 2008	€ million 2007
Goodwill	11 665	12 244
Intangible assets:	4 426	4 511
Indefinite-lived intangible assets	3 886	3 921
Finite-lived intangible assets	206	273
Software	334	317
	16 091	16 755

Movements during 2008	€ million Goodwill	€ million Indefinite-lived intangible assets	€ million Finite-lived intangible assets	€ million Software	€ million Total
Cost					
1 January 2008	13 182	4 134	621	501	18 438
Acquisitions of group companies	60	90	1	—	151
Disposals of group companies	(129)	—	—	—	(129)
Additions	—	1	—	146	147
Disposals	—	—	(3)	(33)	(36)
Currency retranslation	(496)	(81)	(20)	(34)	(631)
Reclassification as held for sale	—	(37)	(1)	—	(38)
31 December 2008	12 617	4 107	598	580	17 902
Amortisation and impairment					
1 January 2008	(938)	(213)	(348)	(184)	(1 683)
Disposal of group companies	12	—	—	—	12
Amortisation for the year	—	—	(59)	(109)	(168)
Impairment	—	(37)	(1)	—	(38)
Disposals	—	—	2	33	35
Currency retranslation	(26)	(8)	13	14	(7)
Reclassification as held for sale	—	37	1	—	38
31 December 2008	(952)	(221)	(392)	(246)	(1 811)
Net book value 31 December 2008	11 665	3 886	206	334	16 091

There are no significant carrying amounts of goodwill and intangible assets that are allocated across multiple cash generating units (CGUs).

Impairments charge in the year

The impairments charged in 2008 principally related to a non-core savoury business in the Americas which was subsequently classified as held for sale. There were no impairments in 2007.

Significant CGUs

The goodwill and indefinite-lived intangible assets (predominantly Knorr and Hellmann's) held in the global savoury and dressings CGU, comprising €10.6 billion (2007: €11.1 billion) and €3.1 billion (2007: € 3.2 billion) respectively, are considered

continued on page 774

significant in comparison to the total carrying amounts of goodwill and indefinite-lived intangible assets at 31 December 2008. No other CGUs are considered significant in this respect.

During 2008, we conducted an impairment review of the carrying value of these assets. Value in use of the global savoury and dressings CGU has been calculated as the present value of projected future cash flows. A pre-tax discount rate of 10% was used.

The following key assumptions were used in the discounted cash flow projections for the savoury and dressings CGU:
• a longer-term sustainable growth rate of 4%, adjusted for market fade, used to determine an appropriate terminal value multiple;
• average near-term nominal growth for the major product groups within the CGU of 6%; and
• average operating margins for the major product groups within the CGU ranging from 15% to 19%.

The growth rates and margins used to estimate future performance are based on past performance and our experience of growth rates and margins achievable in our key markets as a guide. We believe that the assumptions used in estimating the future performance of the savoury and dressings CGU are consistent with past performance.

The projections covered a period of ten years as we believe this to be a suitable timescale over which to review and consider annual performance before applying a fixed terminal value multiple to the final year cash flows of the detailed projection. Stopping the detailed projections after five years and applying a terminal value multiple thereafter would not result in a value in use that would cause impairment.

The growth rates used to estimate future performance beyond the periods covered by our annual planning and strategic planning processes do not exceed the long-term average rates of growth for similar products.

We have performed sensitivity analysis around the base case assumptions and have concluded that no reasonably possible changes in key assumptions would cause the recoverable amount of the global savoury and dressings CGU to be less than the carrying amount.

Analysis

Missing Values?

The requirement that most research and development phase costs incurred for internally developed intangibles be expensed immediately is a conservative, practical solution that ensures consistency in practice and uniformity among companies. But the practice of immediately writing off expenditures that are made in the expectation of benefiting future periods cannot always be justified on the grounds that it is good accounting theory.

Real-World Emphasis

During the 1990s, the conventional financial-accounting model was increasingly criticized for its inability to capture many of the attributes that give a business value. In November 1997, for example, **Microsoft** had a total book value of U.S. $10.8 billion, while its market capitalization (the market value of its outstanding shares) was U.S. $166.5 billion. Why such a significant difference?

The answer is that financial accounting does not capture and report many of the assets that contribute to future cash flows, and this is seen by some critics as the greatest challenge facing the accounting profession today. Many of the missing values belong to unrecognized, internally developed intangible assets known as knowledge assets or intellectual capital. These include the value of key personnel (not only Bill Gates, but the many creative and technologically proficient employees in general), the investment in products from research and development and their potential, organizational adaptability, customer retention, strategic direction, brands, flexible and innovative management, customer service capability, and effective advertising programs, to name only a few types of knowledge assets. When a company is not allowed to capitalize many of these expenditures, this removes from its balance sheet what may be its most valuable assets.

Underlying Concept

These decisions represent some of the older trade-offs between relevance and reliability. With a growing emphasis on faithful representation over verifiability, standard setters may be taking another look at existing standards.

These indicators of longer-term value that are created in an organization will ultimately result in realized values through future transactions and, therefore, are relevant information for financial statement readers. Companies increasingly disclose more of this "soft" information in annual reports outside the financial statements, in news releases, and in interviews with market analysts. While some observers believe that standard setters should work to ensure that more of these intangibles are captured on the balance sheet, others believe that new frameworks for reporting performance need to be developed together with—or that they should even replace—the current financial reporting model.

Our conventional accounting model captures the results of past transactions. This has been considered a very significant benefit as it is what makes it possible to verify the reported measures and therefore add to the reliability of the financial statements. In most cases, the intellectual capital and knowledge assets identified above cannot be measured in financial terms with enough reliability to give them accounting recognition. Some cannot be included as assets because of the enterprise's inability to control access to the benefits. Investments that are made in employee education and development, for example, can walk out the door when employees leave the company to work elsewhere. Others argue that the amount of costs charged to expense in each accounting period is about the same whether there is immediate expensing or capitalization followed by amortization because most companies continuously invest in a variety of research, development, and other activities.

Others opposed to increased capitalization of costs point to the decline in market value of technology shares in particular, from early 2000 to 2001. Microsoft, for example, lost over 60% of its value over this period, supporting the arguments of many that the historical cost model still has much to recommend it! The "truth," of course, lies somewhere in between. While inflated market values are not reliable enough to support the recognition of previously unrecognized intangible asset value, the historical-cost, transactions-based model certainly fails to capture many of the things that lie at the heart of corporate value. Much research is being carried out in the search for solutions to the discrepancies between what gets reported as having value on the financial statements and what the capital markets perceive as having value and reflect in share prices.

Comparing Results

When comparing the operating results of companies—either of one company over time or between companies—it is important to pay close attention not only to which set of GAAP each applies, but also to how deferred charges, intangible assets, and goodwill have been accounted for and how any changes in related accounting policies have been handled. This is important because the standards for intangibles have changed significantly in recent years and may continue to change. The **Quebecor Inc.** example earlier in the chapter showed the effect that one change in accounting principle had on the company's results. The "big bath" writedown that Quebecor took by writing down goodwill that it had previously reported as an asset means that these asset costs will never flow through the company's income statement, and future operating statements are freed from these costs.[28] Care has to be taken when calculating and interpreting any ratios that include earnings and asset numbers, especially when the results of different years are being compared.

Real-World Emphasis

IFRS and Private Entity GAAP Comparison

A Comparison of IFRS and Private Entity GAAP

With a few specific exceptions, private entity and international GAAP are very similar. Illustration 12-15 identifies the relevant standards that apply to intangible assets and goodwill for both and the areas of difference that exist.

9 Objective

Identify differences in accounting between private entity GAAP and IFRS.

---

[28] A "big bath" in accounting refers to a situation when a company decides that if a loss has to be reported, it might as well report a very large loss. Any loss is seen as negative and the advantage of reporting a bigger loss is that fewer costs remain in the accounts to be reported as future expenses.

	Accounting Standards for Private Enterprises (Private Entity GAAP)—*CICA Handbook*, Part II, Sections 1582, 3063, 3064, 3475, and 3831	IFRS—IAS 23, 36, and 38; IFRS 3
Measurement at acquisition	Interest costs directly attributable to the acquisition, construction, or development of an intangible asset once it meets the criteria to be capitalized may be capitalized or expensed, depending on the entity's accounting policy.	Borrowing costs directly attributable to the acquisition, construction, or development of qualifying assets are capitalized.
	Costs associated with the development of internally generated intangible assets that meet the six specific conditions in the development stage may be capitalized or expensed, depending on the entity's accounting policy.	Costs associated with the development of internally generated intangible assets are capitalized when six specific conditions are met in the development stage.
Measurement after acquisition	Intangible assets are accounted for according to the cost model.	Intangible assets are accounted for under the cost model or the revaluation model. The latter is used only when the asset has an active market fair value.
Impairment of intangible assets	Test both limited- and indefinite-life intangibles for potential impairment whenever events and changing circumstances indicate the carrying value may not be recoverable.	Assess limited-life intangible assets for potential impairment at the end of each reporting period; for those with an indefinite life, this includes calculating the (IFRS) recoverable amount and comparing it with book value.
	For limited-life intangibles, apply the cost recovery impairment model.	For limited-life intangibles, apply the rational entity impairment model.
	For indefinite-life intangibles, impairment test is comparison of carrying amount with asset's fair value; loss is equal to the difference when fair value is lower.	For indefinite-life intangibles, apply the rational entity impairment model.
	Impairment losses are not reversed.	Impairment losses are reversed for economic changes.
Impairment of goodwill	Similar to impairment of indefinite-life intangible assets. See also Illustration 12-10.	Similar to impairment of indefinite-life intangible assets, except that there is no reversal of an impairment loss for goodwill. See also Illustration 12-10.
Disclosures	Basic disclosures are required about the balance of intangible assets and goodwill on the balance sheet with additional details by classes and whether or not they are amortized. Details explaining each impairment loss and where each is reported on the income statement are also required.	Significant disclosures are required including detailed reconciliations between opening and ending balances for each type of intangible and goodwill. Considerable information is also required whenever fair values are used to explain how they are determined, as well as background information about impairment losses on goodwill and intangibles.

Illustration 12-15

IFRS and Private Entity GAAP Comparison Chart

Looking Ahead

Whether recognized or not, intangible assets are an increasingly important aspect of what gives an entity value, and existing standards do not do an adequate job of reporting these assets to users of the financial statements. Current standards significantly restrict the intangibles that can be recognized, and after acquisition only intangibles with fair values determined in an active market can use the revaluation model under IFRS. Also, there are inconsistent treatments of intangible assets developed internally and those acquired in a business combination, as well as for internally developed property, plant, and equipment assets.

A proposal for a joint (with the FASB) comprehensive recognition-based project was considered recently by the IASB, but it was not added to its agenda because of other projects competing for time and resources. It is unlikely that there will be changes in the intangible asset standards in the short to medium term.

The IASB's fair value measurement project, aimed at converging international and U.S. GAAP, may affect the measurement guidance in this standard. The final standard was expected in 2010.

Summary of Learning Objectives

Glossary

1   Define and describe the characteristics of intangible assets.

Intangible assets have three characteristics: (1) they are identifiable; (2) they lack physical substance; and (3) they are non-monetary in nature.

2   Identify and apply the recognition and measurement requirements for purchased intangible assets.

A purchased intangible asset is recognized when it is probable that the entity will receive the expected future economic benefits and when its cost can be measured reliably. It is measured initially at cost. When several intangibles, or a combination of intangibles and other assets, are acquired in a business combination, the cost of each intangible asset is its fair value. When acquired in a business combination, the identifiable intangibles are recognized separately from the goodwill component.

3   Identify and apply the recognition and measurement requirements for internally developed intangible assets.

No costs are capitalized unless they meet the general recognition criteria concerning future benefits and measurability. Costs incurred in the research phase of developing an intangible asset internally are expensed. Costs incurred in the development phase of a project are also expensed unless the entity can demonstrate that it meets six stringent criteria. These criteria are designed to provide evidence that the asset is technically and financially feasible and that the company has the intent and ability to generate future economic benefits from it. Under private entity GAAP, entities have a choice whether to capitalize or expense costs that meet the six criteria.

4   Explain how intangible assets are accounted for after initial recognition.

Under private entity GAAP, intangible assets are accounted for using the cost model, whereas IFRS also allows the revaluation model to be used if the asset's fair value is determined in an active market. This is not often used. An intangible with a finite or limited useful life is amortized over its useful life to the entity. Except in unusual and specific circumstances, the residual value is assumed to be zero. The amount to report for amortization expense should reflect the pattern in which the asset is consumed or used up if that pattern can be reliably determined. Otherwise a straight-line approach is used. An intangible with an indefinite life is not amortized until its life is determined to no longer be indefinite. All intangibles are tested for impairment.

5   Identify and explain the accounting for specific types of intangible assets.

Major types of intangibles include the following: (1) marketing-related intangibles that are used in the marketing or promotion of products or services; (2) customer-related intangibles that are a result of interactions with outside parties; (3) artistic-related intangibles that involve ownership rights to such items as plays and literary works; (4) contract-related intangibles that represent the value of rights that arise from contractual arrangements; and (5) technology-related intangible assets that relate to innovations or technological advances.

KEY TERMS

acquirer, 763
active market, 751
artistic-related intangible assets, 756
bargain purchase, 766
brand, 755
brand name, 755
business combination, 747
computer software costs, 759
contract-based intangible assets, 757
copyright, 756
cost recovery impairment model, 761
customer-related intangible assets, 756
deferred charges, 760
development, 748
development phase, 748
economic benefits, 745
favourable lease, 758
finite life, 753
franchise, 757
goodwill, 763
identifiable, 745
identifiable net assets, 763
impaired, 760
indefinite life, 753
in-process research and development (R&D), 747
intangible assets, 744
intellectual capital, 774
knowledge assets, 774
lease, 758
leasehold, 758
licences, 757
licensing agreements, 757

6 Explain and account for impairments of limited-life and indefinite-life intangible assets.

Under private entity GAAP, impairment is determined and applied by using the cost recovery impairment model. Impairment for *limited-life* intangible assets is based first on a recoverability test. If the carrying amount is higher than its net recoverable amount (undiscounted), then an impairment loss must be measured and recognized, based on the asset's fair value. No reversals of such losses are permitted. The procedures are the same as for property, plant, and equipment. *Indefinite-life* intangibles use only a fair value test. **Under IFRS**, the rational entity impairment model is used. An intangible asset is impaired only if its carrying amount is higher than its recoverable amount. The recoverable amount is defined as the greater of the asset's value in use and its fair value less costs to sell. The impairment loss is the difference between the carrying amount and the recoverable amount, if lower. The loss is reversed subsequently if economic conditions change and the recoverable amount increases. The same approach is used for both limited-life and indefinite-life intangible assets.

7 Explain the concept of goodwill and how it is measured and accounted for after acquisition.

Goodwill is unique because, unlike all other assets, it can be identified only with the business as a whole. It is not an identifiable asset. Goodwill is recorded only when a business is purchased. To calculate goodwill in a 100% acquisition, the fair value of the identifiable assets that are acquired and liabilities that are assumed is compared with the fair value of the consideration transferred for the acquired business. The difference is goodwill. After acquisition, it is not amortized but is regularly assessed for impairment. The goodwill has to be assigned to a cash-generating group or reporting unit and the group is tested for impairment. Under **private entity GAAP**, a goodwill impairment loss is recognized if the fair value of the asset group is lower than the group's carrying amount, and the loss is equal to the difference. Under **IFRS**, there is a goodwill impairment loss if the recoverable amount of the cash-generating unit is less than its carrying amount. The loss is equal to the difference and is applied to goodwill first. Under **both**, goodwill impairment losses are not reversed.

8 Identify the types of disclosure requirements for intangible assets and goodwill and explain the issues in analyzing these assets.

Disclosures under **private entity GAAP** are limited because users can access additional information. Under **IFRS**, significant details are required to be disclosed. The disclosures allow a reader to determine how amounts invested in classes of intangibles (and goodwill) have changed over the period, with substantial information provided when fair values are used, such as under the revaluation model and all impairment calculations. For intangibles that are not amortized, companies must indicate the amount of any impairment losses that have been recognized as well as information about the circumstances that led to the writedown. Goodwill must be separately reported, as are the major classes of intangible assets. Because it is difficult to measure intangibles, some resources, such as intellectual capital and other internally developed intangible assets, do not get captured on the balance sheet. Other intangibles are recognized, but with a relatively high level of measurement uncertainty. For these reasons and because of recent changes in the accounting policy related to intangibles, care must be taken in the analysis of financial statement information related to earnings and total assets.

9 Identify differences in accounting between private entity GAAP and IFRS.

There are few, but significant, differences between private entity GAAP and IFRS regarding intangible assets and goodwill. One major difference relates to the accounting treatment for costs incurred in the development phase of internally generated intangible assets that meet the six stringent criteria for capitalization. Under private entity GAAP, entities can choose a policy of whether to capitalize these costs or expense all costs associated with internally generated intangibles. Under IFRS, these costs are capitalized. The other major difference relates to the impairment models applied: the cost recovery model for private entity GAAP, and the rational entity model for IFRS.

Appendix 12A

Valuing Goodwill

Objective 10
Explain and apply basic approaches to valuing goodwill.

In this chapter, we discussed the method of measuring and recording goodwill when one entity acquires 100% of another business **as the excess of the fair value of the consideration given up by the acquirer over the fair value of the identifiable assets acquired and liabilities assumed in a business acquisition.** Determining the fair value of the consideration transferred and the fair value of the assets and liabilities acquired is an inexact process; and therefore, so is the calculation of the amount of goodwill. As the chapter suggests, it is usually possible to determine the fair value of specifically identifiable assets, but the question remains, "How does a buyer value intangible factors such as superior management, a good credit rating, and so on?"

Excess-Earnings Approach

Finance

One widely used method to estimate the amount of goodwill in a business is the **excess-earnings approach**. This approach works as follows:

1. Calculate the average annual "normalized" earnings that the company is expected to earn in the future.

2. Calculate the annual average earnings that the company would be expected to earn if it generated the same return on investment as the average firm in the same industry. The return on investment is the percentage that results when income is divided by the net assets or shareholders' equity invested to generate that income.

3. Calculate the excess annual earnings: the difference between what the specific company and the average firm in the industry are expected to earn in the future. The ability to generate a higher income indicates that the business has an unidentifiable value that provides this greater earning power. This ability to earn a higher rate of return than the industry is considered to be the heart of what goodwill really is.

4. Estimate the value of the goodwill based on the future stream of excess earnings.

This approach is a systematic and logical way to calculate goodwill because its value is directly related to what makes a company worth more than the sum of its parts. The Tractorling Ltd. example referred to in Illustration 12-8 will be used again now to explain each of the four steps above. We begin with the first step:

1. **Calculate the average annual "normalized" earnings that the company is expected to earn in the future.** Because the past often provides useful information about the future, the past earnings are a good place to start in estimating a company's likely future earnings. Going back three to six years is usually adequate.

Assume that Tractorling's net income amounts for the last five years and the calculation of the company's average earnings over this period are as given in Illustration 12A-1.

Illustration 12A-1

Calculation of Average Past Earnings

Earnings History—Tractorling Limited

2006	$ 60,000
2007	55,000
2008	110,000[a]
2009	70,000
2010	80,000
Total for 5 years	$375,000

Average earnings $375,000 ÷ 5 years = $75,000

[a]Includes gain on discontinued operation of $25,000

Based on the average annual earnings of $75,000 and the fair value of the company's identifiable net assets of $350,000 from Illustration 12-8, a return on investment of approximately 21.4% is initially indicated: $75,000 ÷ $350,000. Before we go further, however, we need to know whether $75,000 is representative of Tractorling's **future earnings**. A company's past earnings need to be analyzed to determine whether any adjustments are needed in estimating expected future earnings. This process is often called "normalizing earnings" and the income that results is termed normalized earnings.

First, **the accounting policies applied should be consistent with those of the purchaser**. For example, assume that the purchasing company measures earnings using the FIFO cost formula rather than average cost, which Tractorling uses. Further assume that the use of average cost had the effect of reducing Tractorling's net income by $2,000 each year below a FIFO-based net income. In addition, Tractorling uses accelerated depreciation while the purchaser uses straight-line. As a result, the reported earnings are $3,000 lower each year than they would have been on a straight-line basis.

Second, because the purchaser will pay current prices for the company, **future earnings should be based on the net assets' current fair values** rather than the carrying amount on Tractorling's books. That is, differences between the assets' carrying amounts and fair values may affect reported earnings in the future. For example, internally developed patent costs not previously recognized as an asset would be recognized on the purchase of Tractorling. This asset will need to be amortized, say, at the rate of $1,000 per year.

Finally, because we are trying to estimate future earnings, **amounts that are not expected to recur should be adjusted out of our calculations**. The 2008 gain on discontinued operations of $25,000 is an example of such an item. Illustration 12A-2 shows the analysis that can now be made of what the purchaser expects the annual future earnings of Tractorling to be.

Illustration 12A-2

Calculation of Normalized Earnings

Average past earnings of Tractorling (from Illustration 12A-1)		$75,000
Add		
Adjustment for change from average cost to FIFO	$2,000	
Adjustment for change from accelerated to straight-line depreciation	3,000	5,000
		80,000
Deduct		
Gain on discontinued operation ($25,000 ÷ 5)	5,000	
Patent amortization on straight-line basis	1,000	6,000
Expected future annual earnings of Tractorling		$74,000

Note that it was necessary to divide the gain on the discontinued operation of $25,000 by five years to adjust it correctly. The whole $25,000 was included in the total income earned over the five-year history, but only one-fifth of it, or $5,000, is included in the average annual earnings.[29]

2. **Calculate the annual average earnings that the company would generate if it earned the same return as the average firm in the industry.** Determining the industry's average rate of return earned on net assets requires an analysis of companies that are similar to the enterprise being examined. An industry average may be determined by examining annual reports or data from statistical services. Assume that a rate of 15% is found to be average for companies in Tractorling's industry. **This is the level of earnings that is expected from a company without any goodwill.** In this case, the estimate of what Tractorling's earnings would be if based on the norm for the industry is calculated in Illustration 12A-3.

Illustration 12A-3

Tractorling's Earnings at the Average Rate for the Industry

Fair value of Tractorling's identifiable net assets	$350,000
Industry average rate of return	15%
Tractorling's earnings if no goodwill	$ 52,500

The net assets' fair value—not their carrying amount—is used to calculate Tractorling's level of earnings at the industry average rate of return. Fair value is used because the cost of the net identifiable assets to any company that is interested in purchasing Tractorling will be their fair value, not their carrying amount on Tractorling's books. This makes fair value the relevant measure.

3. **Calculate the company's excess annual earnings.** The next step is to calculate how much of the company's expected earnings exceed the industry norm. This is what gives the company value in excess of the fair value of its identifiable net assets. Tractorling's excess earnings are determined in Illustration 12A-4.

Illustration 12A-4

Calculation of Excess Earnings

Expected future earnings of Tractorling	$74,000
Tractorling's earnings if no goodwill	52,500
Tractorling's excess annual earnings	$21,500

4. **Estimate the value of the goodwill based on the excess earnings.** Because the excess earnings are expected to continue for several years, they are discounted back to their present value to determine how much a purchaser would pay for them now. A discount rate must be chosen, as well as the length of the discount period.

---

[29] If you find this unclear, try the following approach: Start with the total earnings of $375,000 over the past five years and make the necessary adjustments. First add 5 × $2,000 for the average cost/FIFO adjustment and 5 × $3,000 for the depreciation, and then deduct 5 × $1,000 for the patent amortization and $25,000 for the gain on discontinued operations. The adjusted total five-year earnings of $370,000 are then divided by 5 to get the expected future annual earnings. The result is $74,000.

Discount Rate

The choice of discount rate is relatively subjective.[30] The lower the discount rate, the higher the goodwill value and vice versa. To illustrate, assume that the excess earnings of $21,500 are expected to continue indefinitely. If the excess earnings are capitalized at a rate of 25% in perpetuity, for example, the results are as indicated in Illustration 12A-5.

Capitalization at 25%

$$\frac{\text{Excess earnings}}{\text{Capitalization rate}} = \frac{\$21,500}{0.25} = \$86,000$$

Illustration 12A-5

Capitalization of Excess Earnings at 25% in Perpetuity

As indicated in Illustration 12A-6, if the excess earnings are capitalized in perpetuity at a somewhat lower rate, say 15%, a much higher goodwill figure results.[31]

Capitalization at 15%

$$\frac{\text{Excess earnings}}{\text{Capitalization rate}} = \frac{\$21,500}{0.15} = \$143,333$$

Illustration 12A-6

Capitalization of Excess Earnings at 15% in Perpetuity

What do these numbers mean? In effect, if a company pays $86,000 over and above the fair value of Tractorling's identifiable net assets because the company generates earnings above the industry norm, and Tractorling actually does generate these excess profits in perpetuity, the $21,500 of extra earnings per year represents a 25% return on the amount invested; i.e., there is a $21,500 return on the $86,000 invested.

If the purchaser invests $143,333 for the goodwill, the extra $21,500 represents a 15% return on investment: $21,500 relative to the $143,333 invested.

Because it is uncertain—risky—that excess profits will continue, a conservative or risk-adjusted rate (higher than the normal rate) tends to be used. Factors that are considered in determining the rate are the stability of past earnings, the speculative nature of the business, and general economic conditions.

---

[30] The following illustrates how the capitalization or discount rate might be calculated for a small business:

A Method of Selecting a Capitalization Rate

	%
Long-term Canadian government bond rate	8
Add: Average premium return on small company shares over government bonds	8
Expected total rate of return on small publicly held shares	16
Add: Premium for greater risk and illiquidity	6
Total required expected rate of return, including inflation component	22
Deduct: Consensus long-term inflation expectation	5
Capitalization rate to apply to current earnings	17

From Warren Kissin and Ronald Zulli, "Valuation of a Closely Held Business," *The Journal of Accountancy*, June 1988, p. 42.

[31] Why do we divide by the capitalization or discount rate to arrive at the goodwill amount? Recall that the present value of an ordinary annuity is equal to:

$$P\overline{n}|i = [1 - 1 \div (1 + i)^n] \div i$$

When a number is capitalized in perpetuity, $(1 + i)^n$ becomes so large that $1/(1 + i)^n$ essentially equals zero, which leaves $1/i$ or, as in the case above, $21,500/0.25$ or $21,500/0.15$.

Discount Period

Determining the period over which excess earnings are expected to continue is perhaps the most difficult problem in estimating goodwill. The perpetuity examples above assume that the excess earnings will last indefinitely. Usually, however, the excess earnings are assumed to last a limited number of years. The earnings are then discounted over the shorter period.

Assume that the company interested in purchasing Tractorling's business believes that the excess earnings will last only 10 years and, because of general economic uncertainty, chooses 25% as an appropriate rate of return. The present value of a 10-year annuity of excess earnings of $21,500 discounted at 25% is $76,766.[32] This is the amount that a purchaser should be willing to pay above the fair value of the identifiable net assets—i.e., for goodwill—given the assumptions stated.

Total-Earnings Approach

There is another way to estimate goodwill that is similar and that should increase your understanding of the process and resulting numbers. Under this approach—the total-earnings approach—the value of the company as a whole is determined, based on the total expected earnings, not just the excess earnings. The fair value of the identifiable net assets is then deducted from the value of the company as a whole. The difference is goodwill. The calculations under both approaches are provided in Illustration 12A-7, assuming the purchaser is looking for a 15% return on the amounts it will invest in Tractorling, and the earnings are expected to continue into perpetuity.

Illustration 12A-7

Total Earnings Approach to the Calculation of Goodwill

Assumptions:	Expected future earnings	$74,000
	Normal or industry-level earnings	$52,500
	Expected excess future earnings	$21,500
	Discount rate	15%
	Discount period	perpetuity, ∞

Excess-Earnings Approach:

Goodwill = present value of the annuity of excess future earnings
= present value of annuity of $21,500 ($n = \infty$, $i = 0.15$)
$$= \frac{\$21,500}{0.15} \qquad = \underline{\$143,333}$$

Total-Earnings Approach:

Goodwill = difference between the fair value of the company and the fair value of its identifiable net assets

Fair value of company = present value of the annuity of future earnings
= present value of annuity of $74,000 ($n = \infty$, $i = 0.15$)
$$= \frac{\$74,000}{0.15} \qquad = \underline{\$493,333}$$

---

[32] The present value of an annuity of $1 received in a steady stream for 10 years in the future discounted at 25% is $3.57050. The present value of an annuity of $21,500, therefore, is $21,500 × 3.57050 = $76,765.75.

Fair value of identifiable net assets	=	present value of the annuity of industry-level earnings	
	=	present value of annuity of $52,500 (n = ∞, i = 0.15)	
	=	$\dfrac{\$52,500}{0.15}$	= (350,000)
Goodwill	=		$143,333

Other Valuation Methods

There are several other methods of valuing goodwill: some are very basic and others are very sophisticated. The methods illustrated here are some of the least complex approaches. Others include simply multiplying excess earnings by the number of years that the excess earnings are expected to continue. Often referred to as the **number of years method**, it is used to provide a rough measure of goodwill. The approach has the advantage only of simplicity; it does not consider the time value of money because the future cash flows are not discounted.

An even simpler method is one that relies on multiples of average yearly earnings that are paid for other companies in the same industry. If Skyward Airlines was recently acquired for five times its average yearly earnings of $50 million, or $250 million, then Worldwide Airways, a close competitor with $80 million in average yearly earnings, would be worth $400 million.

Another method (similar to discounting excess earnings) is the **discounted free cash flow method**, which involves projecting the company's free cash flow over a long period, typically 10 or 20 years. The method first projects into the future a dozen or so important financial variables, including production, prices, non-cash expenses such as amortization, taxes, and capital outlays—all adjusted for inflation. The objective is to determine the amount of operating cash flow that will be generated over and above the amount needed to maintain existing capacity. The present value of the free cash flow is then calculated. This amount represents the value of the business.

 Finance

For example, if Magnaputer Ltd. is expected to generate $1 million a year of free cash flow for 20 years, and the buyer's rate-of-return objective is 15%, the buyer would be willing to pay about $6.26 million for Magnaputer. (The present value of $1 million to be received for 20 years discounted at 15% is $6,259,330.) The goodwill, then, is the difference between the $6.26 million and the fair value of the company's identifiable net assets.

In practice, prospective buyers use a variety of methods to produce a valuation curve or range of prices. But the actual price that ends up being paid may be more a factor of the buyer's or seller's ego and negotiating skill.

Valuation of a business—determining how much to pay for it—and its inherent goodwill is at best a highly uncertain process.[33] The estimated value of goodwill depends on a number of factors, all of which are tenuous and subject to bargaining. It ends up accounted for as the difference between the fair value of what you give up to acquire the business and the fair value of the identifiable net assets acquired.

---

[33] Business valuation is a specialist field. The Canadian Institute of Chartered Business Valuators oversees the granting of the specialist designation, Chartered Business Valuator (CBV), to professionals who meet the education, experience, and examination requirements.

Summary of Learning Objective for Appendix 12A

Glossary

KEY TERMS

discounted free cash flow method, 785

excess-earnings approach, 780

normalized earnings, 781

number of years method, 785

total-earnings approach, 784

10 Explain and apply basic approaches to valuing goodwill.

One method of valuing goodwill is the excess-earnings approach. Using this approach, the value of goodwill is based on discounting expected future earnings in excess of the industry average to their present value. Another method involves determining the total value of the business by capitalizing total earnings, and then deducting the fair values of the identifiable net assets. The number of years method of valuing goodwill simply multiplies the excess earnings by the number of years of expected excess earnings. Another method of valuing goodwill is the discounted free cash flow method, which projects the future operating cash that will be generated over and above the amount needed to maintain current operating levels. The present value of the free cash flows is today's estimate of the firm's value.

Note: All assignment material with an asterisk (*) relates to the appendix to the chapter.

Brief Exercises

(LO 1, 2, 3) **BE12-1** For each independent scenario outlined below, discuss whether the three criteria required for an asset to be classified as an intangible are fulfilled:

(a) Software purchased specifically for a manufacturing machine that cannot operate without that software.

(b) Purchased software that is not essential to the related ancillary hardware equipment (e.g., hotel reservation system).

(c) Internally developed software for eventual sale to customers.

(d) Software purchased for eventual resale to customers.

(LO 4) **BE12-2** Latupatula Corporation purchases a patent from MaFee Corp. on January 1, 2012, for $87,000. The patent had a remaining legal life of 16 years. Prepare Latupatula's journal entries to record the 2012 patent purchase and amortization.

(LO 2, 3, 4) **BE12-3** Use the information in BE12-2 and assume that in January 2014, Latupatula spends $26,000 successfully defending a patent suit. In addition, Latupatula now feels the patent will be useful only for another seven years. Prepare the journal entries to record the 2014 expenditure and amortization.

(LO 2, 3, 4, 9) **BE12-4** Swinson, Inc., a private company, incurred $15,000 in materials and $12,000 in direct labour costs between January and March 2010 for developing a new product. In May 2010, the criteria required to capitalize development costs were met. A further $45,000 was spent for materials, $15,000 for direct labour costs, $2,000 for borrowing costs, and $72,000 for legal fees. Discuss any options that may be available to Swinson for recording these expenditures. In addition, prepare the appropriate journal entries.

(LO 2, 3) **BE12-5** Bountiful Industries Ltd. had one patent recorded on its books as at January 1, 2010. This patent had a book value of $365,000 and a remaining useful life of eight years. During 2010, Bountiful incurred research costs of $140,000 and brought a patent infringement suit against a competitor. On December 1, 2010, Bountiful received the good news that its patent was valid and that its competitor could not use the process Bountiful had patented. The company incurred $106,000 to defend this patent. At what amount should the patent be reported on the December 31, 2010 balance sheet, assuming monthly straight-line amortization of patents?

(LO 2) **BE12-6** Azure Industries Ltd. acquired two copyrights during 2010. One copyright was on a textbook that was developed internally at a cost of $18,000. This textbook is estimated to have a useful life of three years from September 1, 2010, the date it was published. The second copyright is for a history research textbook and was purchased from University Press on December 1, 2010, for $29,400. This textbook has an indefinite useful life. How should these two copyrights be reported on Azure's balance sheet as at December 31, 2010?

(LO 3) **BE12-7** Using the data provided in BE12-6, assume that Azure spent $12,500 in January 2011 to promote and launch the textbooks under its new publishing banner. Explain the accounting for these costs.

BE12-8 WEBDESIGN Ltd. decided that it needed to update its computer programs for its supplier relationships. It **(LO 2, 3)** purchased an off-the-shelf program and modified it internally to link it to WEBDESIGN's other programs. The following costs may be relevant to the accounting for the new software:

Net carrying amount of old software	$1,100
Purchase price of new software	5,900
Training costs	4,550
General and administrative costs	3,750
Direct cost of in-house programmer's time spent on conversion	1,720

Prepare journal entries to record the software replacement.

BE12-9 Darrien Corporation purchased a trade name, customer list, and manufacturing equipment for a lump sum of **(LO 2, 3, 5)** $800,000. The fair market values of each asset are $280,000, $290,000, and $320,000, respectively. There were initial operating losses of $14,500 during the first four months after the assets were put into use. Prepare the journal entry to record the treatment of these costs.

BE12-10 ABC Company has a trademark with a carrying value of $83,750. As part of an impairment test on January 1, **(LO 6, 9)** 2011, due to a change in customer tastes, ABC gathered the following data about the trademark for purposes of an impairment test: Fair value is $45,000; Fair value less disposal costs is $40,000; Value in use is $95,200; and Undiscounted cash flows are $125,000.

Assume that ABC is reporting under private entity GAAP. Determine if the trademark is impaired on January 1, 2011.

BE12-11 Use the data provided in BE12-10. How would your response change if ABC were a public company reporting **(LO 6, 9)** under IFRS?

BE12-12 Sunny Valley Inc. purchased an Internet domain name by issuing a $220,000, five-year, 12%, non-interest- **(LO 2)** bearing note to Cloudy Corp. The note is repayable in five annual payments of $44,000 each. Prepare the journal entry to record the purchase of the intangible asset.

BE12-13 Indicate whether the following items are capitalized or expensed in the current year: **(LO 2, 3)**

(a) The purchase cost of a patent from a competitor

(b) Product research costs

(c) Organization costs

(d) Costs that are incurred internally to create goodwill

(e) Legal costs to successfully support trademark

(f) Pre-operating costs to launch new products

(g) Relocation of manufacturing activities

(h) Corporate reorganization costs

BE12-14 Brilliant Minds Inc. incurred the following costs associated with its research facilities. Indicate whether these **(LO 1, 2, 3)** items are capitalized or expensed in the current year:

(a) Executive salaries

(b) Costs of testing prototypes

(c) Market research to prepare for the product launch

(d) Sales commissions

(e) Salaries of research staff investigating alternatives for existing products

BE12-15 Green Earth Corp. has capitalized software costs of $980,000 on a product to be sold externally. During its first **(LO 3, 4)** year, sales of this product totalled $380,000. Green Earth expects to earn $1,560,000 in additional future revenue from this product, which is estimated to have an economic life of four years. Calculate the amount of software amortization, assuming that amortization is based on the pattern in which Green Earth receives benefits from the software program.

BE12-16 On September 1, 2010, Luigi Corporation acquired Edinburgh Enterprises for a cash payment of $863,000. **(LO 7)** At the time of purchase, Edinburgh's balance sheet showed assets of $900,000, liabilities of $460,000, and owners' equity of $440,000. The fair value of Edinburgh's assets is estimated to be $1,160,000. Calculate the amount of goodwill acquired by Luigi.

(LO 7, 9)   **BE12-17**   Using the data from BE12-16, assume that Luigi Corporation is a public company and the goodwill was allocated entirely to one cash-generating unit (CGU). Two years later, the CGU's carrying amount is $3,500,000, the value in use is $3,850,000, and the fair value less costs to sell is $4,250,000. Determine if the goodwill is impaired.

(LO 7, 9)   **BE12-18**   Use the data from BE12-16, assuming that Luigi Corporation is a private entity. Explain how goodwill will be tested for impairment. If the carrying amount of the unit (including goodwill) is $3,613,000 and its fair value is $3,550,000, determine the amount of impairment, if any, under private entity GAAP.

(LO 10)   ***BE12-19**   Nigel Corporation is interested in purchasing Lau Car Company Ltd. The total of Lau's net income amounts over the last five years is $750,000. During one of those years, Lau reported a gain on discontinued operations of $94,000. The fair value of Lau's net identifiable assets is $690,000. A normal rate of return is 15%, and Nigel wants to capitalize excess earnings at 20%. Calculate the estimated value of Lau's goodwill.

Exercises

(LO 2, 5, 9)   **E12-1**   **(Classification Issues—Intangibles)** The following is a list of items that could be included in the intangible assets section of the balance sheet:

1. An investment in a subsidiary company
2. Timberland
3. The cost of an engineering activity that is required to advance a product's design to the manufacturing stage
4. A lease prepayment (six months of rent paid in advance)
5. The cost of equipment obtained under a capital lease
6. The cost of searching for applications for new research findings
7. Costs incurred in forming a corporation
8. Operating losses incurred in the start-up of a business
9. Training costs incurred in the start-up of a new operation
10. The purchase cost of a franchise
11. Goodwill generated internally
12. The cost of testing in the search for product alternatives
13. Goodwill acquired in the purchase of a business
14. The cost of developing a patent
15. The cost of purchasing a patent from an inventor
16. Legal costs incurred in securing a patent
17. Unrecovered costs of a successful legal suit to protect the patent
18. The cost of conceptual formulation of possible product alternatives
19. The cost of purchasing a copyright
20. Product development costs
21. Long-term receivables
22. The cost of developing a trademark
23. The cost of purchasing a trademark
24. The cost of an annual update on payroll software
25. A five-year advertising contract for rights of advertising by a top hockey player in Canada
26. Borrowing costs specifically identifiable with an internally developed intangible asset

Instructions

(a) Indicate which items on the list would be reported as intangible assets on the balance sheet.

(b) Indicate how, if at all, the items that are not reportable as intangible assets would be reported in the financial statements.

(c) Identify any differences between PE GAAP and IFRS with respect to capitalization of such items as intangible assets.

E12-2   (Classification Issues—Intangibles) Selected account information follows for Richmond Inc. as at December   **(LO 2, 5, 7)**
31, 2010. All the accounts have debit balances.

Cable Television Franchises	Film Contract Rights
Music Copyrights	Customer Lists Acquired in a Business Combination
Research Costs	Prepaid Expenses
Goodwill	Covenants Not to Compete
Cash	Brand Names
Discount on Notes Payable	Notes Receivable
Accounts Receivable	Investments in Affiliated Companies
Property, Plant, and Equipment	Organization Cost
Leasehold Improvements	Land
Annual Franchise Fee Paid	Excess of Purchase Price over Fair Value of Identifiable
In-Process Research and Development Acquired	Net Assets, X Corp.
in a Business Combination	

Instructions

Identify which items should be classified as intangible assets. For the items that are not classified as intangible assets, indicate where they would be reported in the financial statements.

E12-3   (Classification Issues—Intangibles) Berlinni Inc. has the following amounts included in its general ledger at   **(LO 2, 5, 7)**
December 31, 2010:

Organization costs	$ 34,000
Purchased trademarks	17,500
Discount on bonds payable	23,000
Development phase activities (meet all criteria)	29,000
Deposits with advertising agency for ads to promote goodwill of company	8,000
Excess of cost over fair value of identifiable net assets of acquired subsidiary	81,000
Cost of equipment acquired for research and development projects;	
the equipment has an alternative future use	125,000
Costs of researching a secret formula for a product that is expected to be	
marketed for at least 20 years	75,000
Payment for a favourable lease; lease term of 10 years	15,000

Instructions

(a) Based on the information, calculate the total amount for Berlinni to report as intangible assets on its balance sheet at December 31, 2010.

(b) If an item should not be included in intangible assets, explain the proper treatment for reporting it.

E12-4   (Intangible Amortization) Selected information follows for Mount Olympus Corporation for three independ-   **(LO 2, 3, 4)**
ent situations:

1. Mount Olympus purchased a patent from Bakhshi Co. for $1.8 million on January 1, 2010. The patent expires on January 1, 2020, and Mount Olympus is amortizing it over the 10 years remaining in its legal life. During 2012, Mount Olympus determined that the patent's economic benefits would not last longer than six years from the date of acquisition.

2. Mount Olympus bought a perpetual franchise from Carmody Inc. on January 1, 2010, for $650,000. Its carrying amount on Carmody's books at January 1, 2010, was $750,000. Assume that Mount Olympus can only provide evidence of clearly identifiable cash flows for 25 years, but thinks the franchise could have value for up to 60 years.

3. On January 1, 2010, Mount Olympus incurred development costs (meeting all required criteria) of $375,000. Mount Olympus is amortizing these costs over five years.

Instructions

(a) In situation 1, what amount should be reported in the balance sheet for the patent, net of accumulated amortization, at December 31, 2012?

(b) In situation 2, what amount of amortization expense should be reported for the year ended December 31, 2012?

(c) In situation 3, what amount, if any, should be reported as unamortized development costs as at December 31, 2012?

(LO 2, 3, 4) **E12-5** **(Correct Intangible Asset Account)** As the recently appointed auditor for Daleara Corporation, you have been asked to examine selected accounts before the six-month financial statements of June 30, 2010, are prepared. The controller for Daleara Corporation mentions that only one account is kept for intangible assets. The entries in Intangible Assets since January 1, 2010, are as follows:

INTANGIBLE ASSETS

			Debit	Credit	Balance
Jan.	4	Research costs	1,050,000		1,050,000
	5	Legal costs to obtain patent	45,000		1,095,000
	31	Payment of seven months' rent on property leased by Daleara (February to August)	49,000		1,144,000
Feb.	11	Proceeds from issue of common shares		310,000	834,000
Mar.	31	Unamortized bond discount on bonds payable due March 31, 2014	14,000		848,000
Apr.	30	Promotional expenses related to start-up of business	157,000		1,005,000
June	1	Development stage costs (meet all required criteria)	215,000		1,220,000
	30	Operating losses for first six months	316,000		1,536,000

Instructions

Prepare the entry or entries that are necessary to correct this account. Assume that the patent has a useful life of 10 years.

(LO 2, 3, 4, 5) **E12-6** **(Recognition and Amortization of Intangibles)** Thinesha Limited organized late in 2010 and set up a single account for all intangible assets. The following summary shows the entries in 2011 (all debits) that have been recorded in Intangible Assets since then:

Jan.	2	Purchased patent (8-year life)	$ 320,000
Apr.	1	Purchased goodwill (indefinite life)	310,000
July	1	Purchased franchise with 10-year life; expiration date July 1, 2021	250,000
Aug.	1	Payment for copyright (5-year life)	140,000
	1	Purchased trademark (3-year life)	15,000
	1	Purchased customer list (2-year life)	10,000
Sept.	1	Research costs	239,000
			$1,284,000

Instructions

(a) Prepare the necessary entries to clear the Intangible Assets account and to set up separate accounts for distinct types of intangibles.

(b) Make the entries as at December 31, 2011, for any necessary amortization so that all balances are accurate as at that date.

(c) Provide the asset amounts reported on the December 31, 2011 balance sheet.

(LO 2, 3, 4, 5) **E12-7** **(Accounting for Trade Name)** In early January 2010, Murano Corporation applied for and received approval for a trade name, incurring legal costs of $45,000. In January 2011, Murano incurred $24,300 of legal fees in a successful defence of its trade name.

Instructions

(a) Management determines that this asset has a definite useful life. Identify the variables that must be considered in determining the appropriate amortization period for this trade name.

(b) Calculate amortization for 2010; carrying amount at December 31, 2010; amortization for 2011; and carrying amount at December 31, 2011, if the company amortizes the trade name over its 15-year legal life.

(c) Repeat part (b), assuming a useful life of five years.

(d) Assume the trade name is assessed as having an indefinite life upon initial acquisition. Explain the accounting implications.

E12-8 **(Accounting for Patents, Franchises, and R&D)** PrideTalk Corp., reporting under private entity GAAP, has **(LO 3, 4,** provided the following information on its intangible assets: **5, 9)**

1. A patent was purchased from Marvin Inc. for $1.2 million on January 1, 2010. PrideTalk estimated the patent's remaining useful life to be 10 years. The patent was carried in Marvin's accounting records at a carrying amount of $1,350,000 when Marvin sold it to PrideTalk.

2. During 2011, a franchise was purchased from Burr Ltd. for $290,000. As part of the deal, Burr must also be paid 5% of revenue from the franchise operations. Revenue from the franchise for 2011 was $1.4 million. PrideTalk estimates the franchise's useful life to be 10 years and takes a full year's amortization in the year of purchase.

3. PrideTalk incurred the following research and development costs in 2011:

Materials and equipment	$ 81,000
Personnel	111,000
Indirect costs	55,000
	$247,000

On January 1, 2011, because of recent events in the field, PrideTalk estimates that the remaining life of the patent purchased on January 1, 2010, is only five years from January 1, 2011.

Instructions

(a) Prepare a schedule showing the intangibles section of PrideTalk's balance sheet at December 31, 2011. Show supporting calculations in good form.

(b) Prepare a schedule showing the income statement effect for the year ended December 31, 2011, as a result of the facts above. Show supporting calculations in good form.

(c) Explain how the accounting would differ if PrideTalk were a public company.

(AICPA adapted)

E12-9 **(Internally Generated Intangibles)** From time to time, Gators Corp. embarks on a research program when a **(LO 3, 4, 5)** special project seems to offer possibilities. In 2010, the company spent $414,000 on a research project, but by the end of 2010 it was impossible to determine whether any benefit would come from it.

Instructions

(a) What account should be charged for the $414,000, and how should it be shown in the financial statements for fiscal 2010?

(b) The research project is completed in 2011, and a successful patent is obtained. The research phase costs to complete the project are $80,000. The administrative and legal expenses incurred in obtaining patent number 481-761-0092 in 2011 total $15,000. The patent has an expected useful life of five years. Gators Corp. will now begin investigating applications that use or apply the knowledge obtained on this project. Record these costs in journal entry form. Also, record patent amortization for a full year in 2011.

(c) In 2012, the company successfully defended the patent in lengthy litigation at a cost of $12,400. The victory extended the patent's life to December 31, 2019. What is the proper way to account for this cost? Also, record patent amortization (full year) in 2012.

(d) By early September 2012, and at an additional cost of $123,000, Gators Corp. had a product design that was technologically and financially feasible. Additional engineering and consulting costs of $78,000 were incurred in October 2012 to advance the design of the new product to the manufacturing stage. Discuss the proper accounting treatment for the 2012 costs incurred.

E12-10 **(Internally Generated Intangibles)** Parastu Corp. incurred the following costs during 2010 in connection **(LO 3, 4)** with its research and development phase activities:

Cost of acquired equipment for use in research and development projects over the next five years (straight-line amortization used)	$240,000
Materials consumed in research projects	61,000
Materials consumed in the development of a product committed for manufacturing in first quarter 2011	32,000
Consulting fees paid in the last quarter of 2010 to outsiders for research and development projects, including $4,500 for advice related to the $32,000 of materials used above	95,000
Personnel costs of persons involved in research and development projects	108,000

Indirect costs reasonably allocated to research and development projects	$25,000
General borrowing costs on the company's line of credit	12,000
Training costs for a new customer service software	17,500

Instructions

(a) Calculate the amount to be reported as research and development expense by Parastu on its income statement for 2010. Assume the equipment is purchased at the beginning of the year.

(b) Explain the treatment of training costs and borrowing costs that are incurred after the required criteria for capitalization as internally generated assets are fulfilled.

(LO 3, 4, 6, 9) **E12-11** **(Internally Developed Intangibles)** During 2010, Saskatchewan Enterprises Ltd., a private entity, incurred $4.7 million developing a new software product called Dover. Of this amount, $1.8 million was spent before establishing that the product was technologically and financially feasible. Dover was completed by December 31, 2010, and will be marketed to third parties. Saskatchewan expects a useful life of eight years for this product, with total revenues of $12 million. During 2011, Saskatchewan realized revenues of $2.7 million from sales of Dover.

Instructions

(a) Assuming Saskatchewan reports under PE GAAP, prepare the journal entries that are required in 2010 to record the above.

(b) Prepare the entry to record amortization at December 31, 2011.

(c) At what amount should the software costs be reported in the December 31, 2011 balance sheet?

(d) Could the net realizable value of this asset at December 31, 2011, affect your answer? Explain how limited-life assets are tested for impairment.

(e) How would your response to (d) change if Saskatchewan Enterprises Ltd. were a public company?

(LO 6, 9) **E12-12** **(Impairment Testing)** At the end of 2010, Paris Corporation owns a licence with a remaining life of 10 years and a carrying amount of $530,000. Paris expects future net (undiscounted) cash flows from this patent to total $535,000. The patent's fair value is $425,000 and disposal costs are estimated to be nil. The discounted cash flows (i.e., value in use) would be $475,000.

Instructions

(a) Determine if the licence is impaired at the end of 2010 if Paris Corporation is a publicly accountable enterprise. Prepare any entries that are necessary.

(b) Assume the recoverable amount is calculated to be $450,000 at the end of 2011. Prepare any journal entries needed related to impairment at the end of 2011 under IFRS.

(LO 6, 9) **E12-13** **(Impairment Testing)** Use the information in E12-12.

Instructions

(a) Determine if the licence is impaired under private entity GAAP at the end of 2010.

(b) Assume the recoverable amount is calculated to be $300,000 at the end of 2011. Prepare the journal entry to record any reversal at the end of 2011 under PE GAAP.

(LO 6, 9) **E12-14** **(Impairment Testing)** Use the information in E12-12 and assume that the licence was granted in perpetuity and has an indefinite life. Explain the accounting and prepare any journal entries under IFRS.

(LO 6, 9) **E12-15** **(Impairment Testing)** Use the information in E12-12 and assume that the licence was granted in perpetuity and has an indefinite life. Explain the accounting and prepare any journal entries under PE GAAP.

(LO 6, 9) **E12-16** **(Intangible Impairment)** The following information is for a copyright owned by Venetian Corp., a private entity, at December 31, 2010:

Cost	$4,300,000
Carrying amount	2,150,000
Expected future net cash flows (undiscounted)	2,000,000
Fair value	1,600,000

Assume that Venetian Corp. will continue to use this copyright in the future. As at December 31, 2010, the copyright is estimated to have a remaining useful life of 10 years.

Instructions

(a) Prepare the journal entry, if any, to record the asset's impairment at December 31, 2010.

(b) Prepare the journal entry to record amortization expense for 2011 related to the copyright.

(c) The copyright's fair value at December 31, 2011, is $2.2 million. Prepare the journal entry, if any, that is necessary to record the increase in fair value.

(d) Using the information from part (a), discuss whether the copyright would be amortized in 2010 before the impairment test. Would the asset be tested for impairment before or after amortizing the copyright?

Digging
Deeper

E12-17 **(Intangible Impairment)** Refer to the information provided in E12-16, but now assume that Venetian Corp. is   **(LO 6, 9)** a publicly accountable entity. The copyright's value in use is $1,850,000 and the selling costs are $100,000.

Assume that Venetian Corp. will continue to use this copyright in the future. As at December 31, 2010, the copyright is estimated to have a remaining useful life of 10 years.

Instructions

(a) Prepare the journal entry, if any, to record the asset's impairment at December 31, 2010.

(b) Prepare the journal entry to record amortization expense for 2011 related to the copyright.

(c) The copyright's fair value at December 31, 2011, is $2.2 million. Prepare the journal entry, if any, that is necessary to record the increase in fair value.

E12-18 **(Accounting for Goodwill)** Fred Moss, owner of Medici Interiors Inc., is negotiating for the purchase of   **(LO 7)** Athenian Galleries Ltd. The condensed balance sheet of Athenian follows in an abbreviated form:

ATHENIAN GALLERIES LTD.
Balance Sheet
As at December 31, 2010

Assets		Liabilities and Shareholders' Equity		
Cash	$118,000	Accounts payable		$ 92,000
Land	70,000	Long-term notes payable		351,000
Building (net)	244,000	Total liabilities		443,000
Equipment (net)	185,000	Common shares	$200,000	
Copyright (net)	98,000	Retained earnings	72,000	272,000
Total assets	$715,000	Total liabilities and shareholders' equity		$715,000

Medici and Athenian agree that the land is undervalued by $40,000 and the business equipment is overvalued by $12,000. Athenian agrees to sell the business to Medici for $382,000.

Instructions

Prepare the entry to record the purchase of the business's net assets on Medici's books.

E12-19 **(Accounting for Goodwill)** On July 1, 2010, Zoe Corporation purchased the net assets of Soorya Company by   **(LO 7, 9)** paying $415,000 cash and issuing a $50,000 note payable to Soorya Company. At July 1, 2010, the balance sheet of Soorya Company was as follows:

Cash	$ 75,000	Accounts payable	$300,000
Receivables	102,000	Soorya, capital	239,000
Inventory	98,000		$539,000
Land	50,000		
Buildings (net)	75,000		
Equipment (net)	90,000		
Trademarks (net)	49,000		
	$539,000		

The recorded amounts all approximate current values except for land (worth $60,000), inventory (worth $125,000), and trademarks (worthless). The receivables are shown net of an allowance for doubtful accounts of $12,000. The amounts for buildings, equipment, and trademarks are shown net of accumulated amortization of $14,000, $23,000, and $47,000, respectively.

Instructions

(a) Prepare the July 1, 2010 entry for Zoe Corporation to record the purchase.

(b) Assume that Zoe is a private entity and tested its goodwill for impairment on December 31, 2011. Management determines that the new unit's carrying value (including goodwill) was $500,000 and the unit's fair value was $450,000.

(c) Repeat part (a), assuming that the purchase price was $204,000, all paid in cash.

(d) Based on part (a), assume now that Zoe is a public entity and tested its goodwill for impairment on December 31, 2011. The unit's values are as follows:

Carrying amount	$500,000
Value in use	475,000
Fair value	450,000
Disposal costs	25,000

Determine if there is any impairment and prepare any necessary entry on December 31, 2011.

(LO 7, 9) **E12-20** **(Goodwill Impairment)** The following is net asset information (including associated goodwill of $200 million) for the Reinert Division of Klaus, Inc.:

NET ASSETS
as of December 31, 2010
(in millions)

	Book Value	Fair Value
Cash	$ 50	$ 50
Receivables	216	159
Property, plant, and equipment (net)	2,618	2,817
Goodwill	206	
Less: Notes payable	(2,700)	(2,700)
Net assets	$ 390	

The purpose of this division (also identified as a reporting unit) is to develop a nuclear-powered aircraft. If successful, travelling delays that are associated with refuelling could be greatly reduced. Many other benefits would also occur.

To date, management has not had much success and is deciding whether a writedown is appropriate at this time. Management has prepared the following estimates:

1. Fair value of the future undiscounted net cash flows approximate $400 million.

2. Future value in use approximates $385 million.

3. A sale would yield $346 million and selling costs would approximate $5 million.

Instructions

(a) Using PE GAAP, prepare the journal entry, if any, to record the impairment at December 31, 2010.

(b) Using PE GAAP, at December 31, 2011, it is estimated that the division's fair value increased to $400 million. Prepare the journal entry, if any, to record this increase in fair value.

(c) Using IFRS, prepare the journal entry, if any, to record the impairment at December 31, 2010.

(d) Using IFRS, at December 31, 2011, it is estimated that the division's fair value increased to $400 million. Prepare the journal entry, if any, to record this increase in fair value.

(LO 10) ***E12-21** **(Calculate Normalized Earnings)** Rotterdam Corporation's pre-tax accounting income of $725,000 for the year 2010 included the following items:

Amortization of identifiable intangibles	$147,000
Depreciation of building	115,000
Loss from discontinued operations	44,000
Unusual, non-recurring gains	152,000
Profit-sharing payments to employees	65,000

Ewing Industries Ltd. would like to purchase Rotterdam Corporation. In trying to measure Rotterdam's normalized earnings for 2010, Ewing determines that the building's fair value is triple the book value and that its remaining economic life is double the life that Rotterdam is using. Ewing would continue the profit-sharing payments to employees, with the payments being based on income from continuing operations before amortization and depreciation.

Instructions

Calculate the 2010 normalized earnings amount of Rotterdam Corporation that Ewing would need to determine so that it could calculate goodwill.

*E12-22   (Calculate Goodwill) Net income figures for Belgian Ltd. are as follows: **(LO 10)**

2006—$75,000	2009—$87,000
2007—$53,000	2010—$69,000
2008—$84,000	

Future income is expected to continue at the average of the past five years. The company's identifiable net assets are appraised at $460,000 on December 31, 2010. This business is to be acquired by Mooney Corp. early in 2011. The normal rate of return on net assets for the industry is 7%.

Instructions

What amount should be paid for goodwill, and for the company as a whole, if:

(a) goodwill is equal to average excess earnings capitalized at 23%?

(b) a perpetual 18% return is expected on any amount paid for goodwill?

(c) goodwill is equal to five years of excess earnings?

(d) goodwill is equal to the present value of five years of excess earnings capitalized at 18%?

*E12-23   (Calculate Goodwill) Aswan Corporation is interested in acquiring Richmond Plastics Limited. Richmond   **(LO 10)** has determined that its excess earnings have averaged approximately $175,000 and feels that such an amount should be capitalized over an unlimited period at a 15% rate. Aswan feels that because of increased competition, the excess earnings of Richmond Plastics will continue for seven years at the most and that a 12% discount rate is appropriate.

Instructions

(a) How far apart are the positions of these two parties?

(b) Is there really a difference in the two approaches being used by the parties to evaluate Richmond Plastics' goodwill? Explain.

*E12-24   (Calculate Goodwill) As the president of Victoria Recording Corp., you are considering purchasing Moose   **(LO 10)** Jaw CD Corp., whose balance sheet is summarized as follows:

Current assets	$ 400,000	Current liabilities	$ 350,000
Plant and equipment (net)	750,000	Long-term liabilities	600,000
Other assets	325,000	Common shares	425,000
		Retained earnings	100,000
Total	$1,475,000	Total	$1,475,000

The current assets' fair value is $150,000 higher than their carrying amount because of inventory undervaluation. All other assets and liabilities have book values that approximate their fair value. The normal rate of return on net assets for the industry is 15%. The expected annual earnings for Moose Jaw CD Corp. are $125,000.

Instructions

Assuming that the excess earnings are expected to continue for five years, how much would you be willing to pay for goodwill, and for the company? (Estimate goodwill by the present value method.)

*E12-25   (Calculate Fair Value of Identifiable Assets) Louvre Inc. bought a business that is expected to give a 25%   **(LO 10)** annual rate of return on the investment. Of the total amount paid for the business, $75,000 was deemed to be goodwill, and the rest was attributed to the identifiable net assets. Louvre Inc. estimated that the annual future earnings of the new business would be equal to the average ordinary earnings per year of the business over the past three years. The total net income over the past three years was $375,000. This amount included a loss on discontinued operations of $25,000 in one year and an unusual and non-recurring gain of $95,000 in one of the other two years.

Instructions

Calculate the fair value of the identifiable net assets that Louvre Inc. purchased in this transaction.

Problems

P12-1   Monsecours Corp. incorporated on June 28, 2010, and set up a single account for all its intangible assets. The following summary discloses the debit entries that were recorded during 2010 and 2011 in that account:

INTANGIBLE ASSETS

July 1, 2010	8-year franchise; expiration date of June 30, 2018	$ 35,000
Oct. 1	Advance payment on leasehold (2-year lease)	25,000
Dec. 31	Net loss for 2010 including incorporation fee, $1,000; related legal fees of organizing, $5,000; expenses of recruiting and training staff for start-up of new business, $3,800	17,000
Feb. 15, 2011	Patent purchased (10-year life)	65,400
Mar. 1	Direct costs of acquiring a 5-year licensing agreement	86,000
Apr. 1	Goodwill purchased (indefinite life)	287,500
June 1	Legal fee for successful defence of patent (see above)	13,350
Dec. 31	Costs of research department for year	75,000
31	Royalties paid under licensing agreement (see above)	2,775

The new business started up on July 2, 2010. No amortization was recorded for 2010 or 2011. The goodwill purchased on April 1, 2011, includes in-process research and development valued at $175,000. The company estimates that this amount will help it generate revenues over a 10-year period.

Instructions

Prepare the necessary entries to clear the Intangible Assets account and to set up separate accounts for distinct types of intangibles. Make the entries as at December 31, 2011, and record any necessary amortization so that all balances are appropriate as at that date. State any assumptions that you need to make to support your entries.

P12-2   Gelato Corporation, a private entity reporting under PE GAAP, was incorporated on January 3, 2010. The corporation's financial statements for its first year of operations were not examined by a public accountant. You have been engaged to audit the financial statements for the year ended December 31, 2011, and your audit is almost complete. The corporation's trial balance is as follows:

GELATO CORPORATION
Trial Balance
December 31, 2011

	Debit	Credit
Cash	$ 57,000	
Accounts receivable	87,000	
Allowance for doubtful accounts		$ 1,500
Inventories	60,200	
Machinery	82,000	
Equipment	37,000	
Accumulated amortization		26,200
Patents	128,200	
Leasehold improvements	36,100	
Prepaid expenses	13,000	
Goodwill	30,000	
Licensing agreement No. 1	60,000	
Licensing agreement No. 2	56,000	
Accounts payable		93,000
Unearned revenue		17,280
Common shares		300,000
Retained earnings, January 1, 2011		173,020
Sales		720,000
Cost of goods sold	475,000	
Selling and general expenses	180,000	
Interest expense	29,500	
Totals	$1,331,000	$1,331,000

The following information is for accounts that may still need adjustment:

1. Patents for Gelato's manufacturing process were acquired on January 2, 2011, at a cost of $87,500. An additional $35,000 was spent in July 2011 and $5,700 in December 2011 to improve machinery covered by the patents and was charged to the Patents account. Amortization on fixed assets was properly recorded for 2011 in accordance with Gelato's practice, which is to take a full year of amortization for property on hand at June 30. No other amortization was recorded. Gelato uses the straight-line method for all amortization and amortizes its patents over their legal life, which was 17 years when the patent was granted. Accumulate all amortization expense in one income statement account.

2. At December 31, 2011, management determined that the net (undiscounted) future cash flows that are expected from use of the patent would be $80,000, the value in use was $75,000, the resale value of the patent was approximately $55,000, and disposal costs would be $5,000.

3. On January 3, 2010, Gelato purchased licensing agreement no. 1, which management believed had an unlimited useful life. Licences similar to this are frequently bought and sold. Gelato could only clearly identify cash flows from agreement no. 1 for 15 years. After the 15 years, further cash flows are still possible, but are uncertain. The balance in the Licensing Agreement No. 1 account includes the agreement's purchase price of $57,000 and expenses of $3,000 related to the acquisition. On January 1, 2011, Gelato purchased licensing agreement no. 2, which has a life expectancy of five years. The balance in the Licensing Agreement No. 2 account includes its $54,000 purchase price and $6,000 in acquisition expenses, but it has been reduced by a credit of $4,000 for the advance collection of 2012 revenue from the agreement. In late December 2010, an explosion caused a permanent 60% reduction in the expected revenue-producing value of licensing agreement no. 1. In January 2012, a flood caused additional damage that rendered the agreement worthless.

4. The balance in the Goodwill account results from legal expenses of $30,000 that were incurred for Gelato's incorporation on January 3, 2010. Although management assumes that the $30,000 cost will benefit the entire life of the organization, it decided late in 2011 that these costs should be amortized over a limited life of 30 years. No entry has been made yet.

5. The Leasehold Improvements account includes the following: (a) There is a $15,000 cost of improvements that Gelato made to premises that it leases as a tenant. The improvements were made in January 2010 and have a useful life of 12 years. (b) Movable assembly-line equipment costing $15,000 was installed in the leased premises in December 2011. (c) Real estate taxes of $6,100 were paid by Gelato in 2011, but they should have been paid by the landlord under the terms of the lease agreement.

   Gelato paid its rent in full during 2011. A 10-year non-renewable lease was signed January 3, 2010, for the leased building that Gelato uses in manufacturing operations. No amortization has been recorded on any amounts related to the lease or improvements.

6. Included in selling and general expenses are the following costs incurred to develop a new product. Gelato hopes to establish the technical, financial, and commercial viability of this project in fiscal 2012.

Salaries of two employees who spend approximately 50% of their time on research and development initiatives (this amount represents their full salary)	$110,000
Materials consumed	35,000

Instructions

(a) Prepare an eight-column work sheet to adjust the accounts that require adjustment and include columns for an income statement and a balance sheet. A separate account should be used for the accumulation of each type of amortization. Formal adjusting journal entries and financial statements are not required.

(b) Prepare Gelato's balance sheet and income statement for the year ended December 31, 2011, in proper form.

(c) Explain how the accounting would differ if Gelato were reporting under IFRS.

(AICPA adapted)

P12-3   Information for Canberra Corporation's intangible assets follows:

1. On January 1, 2010, Canberra signed an agreement to operate as a franchisee of Hsian Copy Service, Inc. for an initial franchise fee of $75,000. Of this amount, $35,000 was paid when the agreement was signed and the balance is payable in four annual payments of $10,000 each, beginning January 1, 2011. The agreement provides that the down payment is not refundable and no future services are required of the franchisor. The present value at January 1, 2010, of the four annual payments discounted at 8% (the implicit rate for a loan of this type) is $33,121. The agreement also provides that 5% of the franchisee's revenue must be paid to the franchisor each year. Canberra's revenue from the franchise for 2010 was $800,000. Canberra estimates that the franchise's useful life will be 10 years. (Hint: Refer to the Expanded Discussion on Franchises posted to the student website to determine the proper accounting treatment for the franchise fee and payments.)

2. Canberra incurred $45,000 of experimental costs in its laboratory to develop a patent, and the patent was granted on January 2, 2010. Legal fees and other costs of patent registration totalled $13,600. Canberra estimates that the useful life of the patent will be six years.

3. A trademark was purchased from Shanghai Company for $28,600 on July 1, 2007. Expenditures to successfully defend the trademark in litigation totalled $8,160 and were paid on July 1, 2010. Canberra estimates that the trademark's useful life will be 15 years from the acquisition date.

Assume that Canberra reports using PE GAAP.

Instructions

(a) Prepare a schedule showing the intangible assets section of Canberra's balance sheet at December 31, 2010. Show supporting calculations in good form.

(b) Prepare a schedule showing all expenses resulting from the transactions that would appear on Canberra's income statement for the year ended December 31, 2010. Show supporting calculations in good form.

(c) How would your response change under IFRS?

(AICPA adapted)

P12-4   Meridan Golf and Sports was formed on July 1, 2010, when Steve Powerdriver purchased Old Master Golf Corporation. Old Master provides video golf instruction at kiosks in shopping malls. Powerdriver's plan is to make the instruction business part of his golf equipment and accessory stores. Powerdriver paid $650,000 cash for Old Master. At the time of purchase, Old Master's balance sheet reported assets of $550,000 and liabilities of $100,000 (so shareholders' equity was $450,000). The fair value of Old Master's identifiable assets was estimated to be $700,000. Included in the assets was the Old Master trade name with a fair value of $15,000 and a copyright on some instructional books with a fair value of $25,000. The trade name had a remaining life of five years and can be renewed indefinitely at nominal cost. The copyright had a remaining life of 40 years.

Instructions

Assume that Meridan Golf and Sports is a private company reporting under PE standards.

(a) Prepare the intangible assets section of Meridan Golf and Sports at December 31, 2010. How much amortization expense is included in Meridan's income for the year ended December 31, 2010? Show all supporting calculations.

(b) Prepare the journal entry to record the amortization expense for 2011. Prepare the intangible assets section of Meridan Golf and Sports at December 31, 2011. (No impairments need to be recorded in 2011.)

(c) At the end of 2012, Powerdriver is evaluating the results of the instructional business. Due to fierce competition from Internet sites and television, the Old Master reporting unit has been losing money and has a carrying value (including goodwill) of $450,000; the fair value is estimated to be $430,000.

Powerdriver has collected the following information about the company's intangible assets:

Intangible Asset	Expected Cash Flows (undiscounted)	Fair Value
Trade name	$11,000	$ 8,000
Copyright	30,000	25,000

Prepare the required journal entries, if any, to record impairments on Meridan's intangible assets. (Assume that amortization for 2012 has been recorded.) Show supporting calculations.

P12-5   Use the data provided in P12-4. Assume instead that Meridan Golf and Sports is a public company. The relevant information for the impairment test on December 31, 2012, is as follows:

	Carrying Value	Future net cash flows (undiscounted)	Value in Use	FV – Selling Costs
Trade name	15,000	11,000	7,000	7,500
Copyright	23,438	30,000	27,000	24,000
Cash-generating unit to which goodwill was allocated	450,000	470,000	440,000	420,000

Provide the calculations for the impairment test and any associated journal entry.

P12-6   In late July 2010, Mona Ltd., a private company, paid $2 million to acquire all of the net assets of Lubello Corp., which then became a division of Mona. Lubello reported the following balance sheet at the time of acquisition:

Current assets	$ 415,000	Current liabilities	$ 300,000
Noncurrent assets	1,335,000	Long-term liabilities	265,000
		Shareholders' equity	1,185,000
	$1,750,000		$1,750,000

It was determined at the date of the purchase that the fair value of the identifiable net assets of Lubello was $1,700,000. Over the next six months of operations, the new division had operating losses. In addition, it now appears that it will generate substantial losses for the foreseeable future. At December 31, 2010, the Lubello Division reports the following balance sheet information:

Current assets	$ 462,000
Noncurrent assets (including goodwill recognized in purchase)	2,400,000
Current liabilities	(703,500)
Long-term liabilities	(530,000)
Net assets	$1,628,500

It is determined that the fair value of the Lubello Division is $1,850,000.

Assume that Mona Ltd reports using PE GAAP.

Instructions

(a) Calculate the amount of goodwill, if any, that should be recognized in late July 2010.

(b) Determine the impairment loss, if any, to be recognized on December 31, 2010.

(c) Assume that the fair value of the Lubello Division on December 31, 2010, is $1.5 million. Determine the impairment loss, if any, that would be recognized.

(d) Prepare the journal entry to record the impairment loss, if any, in (b) and (c) and indicate where the loss would be reported in the income statement.

(e) Explain how the accounting would differ under IFRS.

P12-7   On September 1, 2010, Madonna Lisa Corporation, a public company, acquired Jaromil Enterprises for a cash payment of $763,000. At the time of purchase, Jaromil's balance sheet showed assets of $850,000, liabilities of $430,000, and owners' equity of $420,000. The fair value of Jaromil's identifiable assets is estimated to be $1,080,000.

(a) Calculate the amount of goodwill acquired by Madonna Lisa.

(b) Assume that the goodwill was allocated entirely to one cash-generating unit (CGU) as indicated below. The CGU's value in use at the balance sheet date was $3,850,000 and the fair value less costs to sell was $4,250,000. Determine if the goodwill is impaired.

	Plant A CGU
Assets (other than goodwill)	$4,500,000
Goodwill	113,000
Total carrying value of CGU	$4,613,000

(c) Explain how a future reversal of impairment is accounted for under IFRS.

P12-8   Six examples follow of purchased intangible assets. They are reported on the consolidated balance sheet of Phelp Enterprises Limited and include information about their useful and legal lives.

Intangible 1a is the trade name for one of the company's subsidiaries. The trade name has a remaining legal life of 16 years, but it can be renewed indefinitely at a very low cost. The subsidiary has grown quickly, has been very successful, and its name is well known to Canadian consumers. Phelp management has concluded that it can identify positive cash flows from the use of the trade name for another 25 years, and assumes the cash flows will continue even longer.

Intangible 1b is the trade name as identified in 1a, but assume instead that Phelp Enterprises expects to sell this subsidiary in three years since the subsidiary operates in an area that is not part of Phelp's core activities.

Intangible 2 is a licence granted by the federal government to Phelp that allows Phelp to provide essential services to a key military installation overseas. The licence expires in five years, but is renewable indefinitely at little cost. Because of the profitability associated with this licence, Phelp expects to renew it indefinitely. The licence is very marketable and will generate cash flows indefinitely.

Intangible 3 is a magazine subscription list. Phelp expects to use this subscriber list to generate revenues and cash flows for at least 25 years. It has determined the cash flow potential of this intangible by analyzing the subscribers' renewal history, the behaviour of the group of subscribers, and their responses to questionnaires.

Intangible 4 is a non-competition covenant. Phelp acquired this intangible asset when it bought out a major owner-managed competitor. The seller signed a contract in which he agreed not to set up or work for another business that was in direct or indirect competition with Phelp. The projected cash flows resulting from this agreement are expected to continue for at least 25 years.

Intangible 5 is medical files. One of Phelp's subsidiary companies owns several medical clinics. A recent purchase of a retiring doctor's practice required a significant payment for the practice's medical files and clients. Phelp considers that this base will benefit the business for as long as it exists, providing cash flows indefinitely.

Intangible 6 is a favourable lease. Phelp acquired a sublease on a large warehouse property that requires annual rentals that are 50% below competitive rates in the area. The lease extends for 35 years.

Instructions

For each intangible asset and situation described above, do the following:

(a) Identify the appropriate method of accounting for the asset subsequent to acquisition, and justify your answer.

(b) Provide an example of a specific situation that would cause you to test the intangible asset for impairment.

P12-9   Guiglano Inc. is a large, publicly held corporation. The following are six selected expenditures that were made by the company during the current fiscal year ended April 30, 2010. The proper accounting treatment of these transactions must be determined in order to ensure that Guiglano's annual financial statements are prepared in accordance with generally accepted accounting principles.

1. Guiglano spent $3 million on a program that is designed to improve relations with its dealers. Dealers responded well to the project and Guiglano's management believes that it will therefore result in significant future benefits. The program was conducted during the fourth quarter of the current fiscal year.

2. A pilot plant was constructed during 2009–10 at a cost of $5.5 million to test a new production process. The plant will be operated for approximately five years. After the five years, the company will make a decision about the economic value of the process. The pilot plant is too small for commercial production, so it will be dismantled when the test is over.

3. During the year, Guiglano began a new manufacturing operation in Newfoundland, its first plant east of Montreal. To get the plant into operation, the following costs were incurred: (a) $100,000 to make the building fully wheelchair-accessible; (b) $41,600 to outfit the new employees with Guiglano uniforms; (c) $12,700 for the reception to introduce the company to others in the industrial mall where the plant is located; and (d) $64,400 in payroll costs for the new employees while they were being trained.

4. Guiglano purchased Eagle Company for $6 million cash in early August 2009. The fair value of Eagle's net identifiable assets was $5.2 million.

5. The company spent $14 million on advertising during the year: $2.5 million was spent in April 2010 to introduce a new product to be released during the first quarter of the 2011 fiscal year; and $200,000 was used to advertise the opening of the new plant in Newfoundland. The remaining expenditures were for recurring advertising and promotion coverage.

6. During the first six months of the 2009–10 fiscal year, $400,000 was expended for legal work on a successful patent application. The patent became effective in November 2009. The patent's legal life is 20 years and its economic life is expected to be approximately 10 years.

Instructions

For each of the six items presented, determine and justify the following:

(a) The amount, if any, that should be capitalized and included on Guiglano's statement of financial position prepared as at April 30, 2010.

(b) The amount that should be included in Guiglano's statement of income for the year ended April 30, 2010.

(CMA adapted)

P12-10　During 2008, Medicine Hat Tools Ltd., a Canadian public company, purchased a building site for its product development laboratory at a cost of $61,000. Construction of the building was started in 2008. The building was completed in late December 2009 at a cost of $185,000 and placed in service on January 2, 2010. The building's estimated useful life for depreciation purposes is 15 years. The straight-line method of depreciation is used and there is no estimated residual value. After the building went into service, several projects were begun and many are still in process.

Management estimates that about 50% of the development projects will result in long-term benefits (i.e., at least 10 years) to the corporation. The other projects either benefited the current period or were abandoned before completion. A summary of the different projects, their number, and the direct costs that were incurred for development activities in 2010 appears in the following table.

Upon recommendation of the research and development group, Medicine Hat Tools Ltd. acquired a patent for manufacturing rights at a cost of $102,500. The patent was acquired on April 1, 2009, and has an economic life of 10 years.

	Number of Projects	Salaries and Employee Benefits	Other Expenses (Excluding Building Depreciation Charges)
Development of viable products (management intent and capability, financial technical and commercial viability criteria were met)	15	$125,000	$ 81,000
Abandoned projects or projects that benefit the current period only	10	87,000	21,000
Projects in process—results uncertain	5	52,500	18,500
Total	30	$264,500	$120,500

Instructions

(a) If generally accepted accounting principles are followed, how should the items above that relate to product development activities be reported on the company's income statement and balance sheet at December 31, 2010? Be sure to give account titles and amounts, and briefly justify your presentation.

(b) Outline the criteria that would have to be met for any costs to qualify as deferred development costs.

(CMA adapted)

*P12-11　Macho Inc. has recently become interested in acquiring a South American plant to handle many of its production functions in that market. One possible candidate is De Fuentes SA, a closely held corporation, whose owners have decided to sell their business if a proper settlement can be obtained. De Fuentes' balance sheet is as follows:

Current assets	$125,000
Investments	55,000
Plant assets (net)	405,000
Total assets	$585,000
Current liabilities	$ 85,000
Long-term debt	105,000
Share capital	225,000
Retained earnings	170,000
Total equities	$585,000

Macho has hired Yardon Appraisal Corporation to determine the proper price to pay for De Fuentes SA. The appraisal firm finds that the investments have a fair market value of $75,000 and that inventory is understated by $40,000. All other assets and liabilities have book values that approximate their fair values. An examination of the company's income for the last four years indicates that the net income has steadily increased. In 2010, the company had a net operating income of $110,000, and this income should increase by 15% each year over the next four years. Macho believes that a normal return in this type of business is 15% on net assets. The asset investment in the South American plant is expected to stay the same for the next four years.

Instructions

(a) Yardon Appraisal Corporation has indicated that the company's fair value can be estimated in several ways. Prepare estimates of the value of De Fuentes SA, with the value based on each of the following independent assumptions:

1. Goodwill is based on the purchase of average excess earnings over the next four years.
2. Goodwill is equal to the capitalization of average excess earnings of De Fuentes SA at 30%.
3. Goodwill is equal to the present value of the average excess earnings over the next four years discounted at 15%.
4. The value of the business is based on the capitalization of future excess earnings of De Fuentes SA at 16%.

(b) De Fuentes SA is willing to sell the business for $1 million. What advice should Yardon Appraisal give Macho in regard to this offer?

(c) If Macho were to pay $850,000 to purchase the assets and assume the liabilities of De Fuentes SA, how would this transaction be reflected on Macho's books?

*P12-12   The president of Plain Corp., Joyce Lima, is thinking of purchasing Balloon Bunch Corporation. She thinks that the offer sounds fair but she wants to consult a professional accountant to be sure. Balloon Bunch Corporation is asking for $85,000 in excess of the fair value of the identifiable net assets. Balloon Bunch's net income figures for the last five years are as follows:

2006—$67,000	2009—$80,000
2007—$50,000	2010—$72,000
2008—$81,000	

The company's identifiable net assets were appraised at $400,000 on December 31, 2010.

You have done some initial research on the balloon industry and discovered that the normal rate of return on identifiable net assets is 15%. After analyzing such variables as the stability of past earnings, the nature of the business, and general economic conditions, you have decided that the average excess earnings for the last five years should be capitalized at 20% and that the excess earnings will continue for about six more years. Further research led you to discover that the Happy Balloon Corporation, a competitor of similar size and profitability, was recently sold for $450,000, five times its average yearly earnings of $90,000.

Instructions

(a) Prepare a schedule that includes the calculation of Balloon Bunch Corporation's goodwill and purchase price under at least three methods.

(b) Write a letter to Joyce Lima that includes all of the following:

1. An explanation of the nature of goodwill
2. An explanation of the different acceptable methods of determining the fair value of goodwill. (Include with your explanation of the different methods the rationale for how each method arrives at a goodwill value.)
3. Advice for Joyce Lima on how to determine her purchase price.

Writing Assignments

WA12-1   Kolber Manufacturing Limited designs, manufactures, and distributes safety boots. In January 2009, Kolber purchased another business that manufactures and distributes safety shoes, to complement its existing business. The total purchase price was to be $10 million in cash immediately and another $5 million in cash one year from now. The company's current interest cost is 6%. The assets and liabilities purchased included accounts receivable, finished goods inventories, land and plant, manufacturing equipment and office equipment, accounts payable, and a loan that is secured by the manufacturing equipment. In addition, a trademark was purchased (which has six years remaining on its current legal life), as well as existing customer relationships (although there are no outstanding contracts with these customers), and a noncompete agreement with the existing owners that they will not start any similar business for the next five years. The company reports under IFRS.

Instructions

You are the controller of Kolber and have been given the task of recording the purchase in the company's books.

(a) Outline how you might go about determining how to allocate the purchase price to the **intangible assets** and any goodwill purchased. In addition, consider how each of these assets is subsequently reported and what the impact will be on net earnings in subsequent years given your decisions now.

(b) If this company reported under private entity GAAP, explain how the impairment test for goodwill would differ from the IFRS method.

(To assist you with this question, you may want to read the following article: "From Intangible to Tangible," by Andrew Michelin, *CA Magazine*, June/July 2008.)

(AICPA adapted)

WA12-2 Weaver Limited is a company that is a distributor of hard-to-find computer supplies such as hardware parts and cables. It sells and ships products all over the world. Recently the board of directors approved the plan and a budget for the company to design its own website. The website has two sections. One is for general information and can be accessed by anyone. On this part of the site, the company has information about what it does, and pictures of all the products sold. The other part of the website is only accessible by logging in. Here customers are given passwords to enter the site and can place their orders, which are then reviewed by the order clerks and sent on to shipping. The IT manager has been put in charge of managing the website project, keeping track and approving all the costs incurred.

The company has incurred the following costs to develop the site: the IT manager's salary for the six months required to supervise the project; legal fees to register the domain name; consulting costs for a feasibility study; purchase of the hardware; software developers to develop the code for the application, installation, and testing of the software; graphic artist to design the layout and colour for the web pages; photographers to take pictures of the products to be shown on the site; staff time to upload all the information to the site, including the company and product descriptions and the data required to place an order, including prices, data entry screens, and shipping options. Finally, the company has incurred costs to train the employees on using the software. Ongoing costs include updating product prices and content, adding new functions, and backing up the data.

Instructions

You are an external auditor and have been hired by Weaver to explain how these costs should be reported. Using IAS 38 and SIC 32 – Intangible Assets – Web Site Costs (an Interpretation under International Financial Reporting Standards), discuss the treatment of these costs, referring to the general principles in IAS 38 to support your analysis. Explain how the company must report costs incurred once the website is operating.

WA12-3 On June 30, 2010, your client, Bearcat Limited, was granted two patents for plastic cartons that it had been producing and marketing profitably for the past three years. One patent covers the manufacturing process and the other covers related products.

Bearcat executives tell you that these patents represent the most significant breakthrough in the industry in the past 30 years. The products have been marketed under the registered trademarks Evertight, Duratainer, and Sealrite. Licences under the patents have already been granted by your client to other manufacturers in Canada and abroad and are producing substantial royalties.

On July 1, Bearcat began patent infringement actions against several companies whose names you recognize as substantial and prominent competitors. Bearcat's management is optimistic that these suits will result in a permanent injunction against the manufacture and sale of the infringing products and collection of damages for loss of profits caused by the alleged infringement.

The financial vice-president has suggested that the patents be recorded at the discounted value of expected net royalty receipts.

Instructions

(a) What is the meaning of "discounted value of expected net receipts"? Explain.

(b) How would the value in (a) be calculated for net royalty receipts?

(c) What is the accounting basis of valuation for Bearcat's patents under private entity GAAP? Under IFRS?

(d) The financial VP has suggested the patents be recorded at the discounted value of expected net royalty receipts. Discuss whether or not this would be allowed under IFRS.

(e) What recognition, if any, should be made of the infringement litigation in the financial statements for the year ending September 30, 2010? Discuss.

(AICPA adapted)

*WA12-4   Echo Corp., a retail propane gas distributor, has increased its annual sales volume to a level that is three times greater than the annual sales of a dealer that it purchased in 2008 in order to begin operations. The board of directors of Echo Corp. recently received an offer to negotiate the sale of the company to a large competitor. As a result, the majority of the board wants to increase the stated value of goodwill on the balance sheet to reflect the larger sales volume that it developed through intensive promotion and the product's current market price. A few of the board members, however, would prefer to eliminate goodwill from the balance sheet altogether in order to prevent possible misinterpretations. Goodwill was recorded properly in 2008.

Instructions

(a) Discuss the meaning of the term "goodwill."

(b) Why are the book and fair values of Echo Corp.'s goodwill different?

(c) Discuss the appropriateness of each of the following:
1. Increasing the stated value of goodwill prior to the negotiations
2. Eliminating goodwill completely from the balance sheet

(AICPA adapted)

WA12-5   Appendix A of IAS 38 provides nine examples of acquired intangibles and how their useful lives should be assessed. The examples are as follows:

1. An acquired customer list

2. An acquired patent that expires in 15 years

3. An acquired copyright that has a remaining legal life of 50 years

4. An acquired broadcasting licence that expires in five years

5. A broadcasting licence that is not renewed by the licensing authority

6. An acquired airline route between two European cities that expires in three years

7. An acquired trademark used to identify and distinguish a consumer product that has been a market leader for the last eight years

8. A trademark acquired 10 years ago that distinguishes a leading consumer product

9. A trademark for a line of products that was acquired several years ago in a business combination

Instructions

Take one of the examples above, as assigned by your instructor. Apply the general principles of IAS 38 to support the guidance given. Present your findings to the class.

WA12-6   Write a brief essay highlighting the differences between IFRS and accounting standards for private enterprises noted in this chapter, discussing the conceptual justification for each.

Case

Refer to the Case Primer to help you answer this case.

CA12-1   Acquisitions Limited (AL) is a privately owned business that operates in the biotechnology business and has recently been on an acquisitions binge. It is now nearing year end and the company has been signalling to its bankers that the current year has been a good year with substantial revenue growth. At present, the controller is preparing the adjustment for the year-end financial statements in preparation for a meeting with the bank next week. The bank is worried that the company has been overpaying for the acquired businesses and wants to be certain that its profitability and cash flows will not be harmed.

The following intangible assets have been acquired in several acquisitions:

Health-care industry contact lists: The company plans to use these lists for sales purposes and expects that it will be able to benefit from the information on the lists for two to three years.

Patents for drug delivery systems: The legal life remaining is 12 years; however, due to the competitive nature of this branch of research, the protection will only last approximately 8 years. The vendor has agreed to buy back the patent for approximately 50% of the value in five years. AL has committed to resell.

A trademark for certain over-the-counter allergy drugs: The legal life remaining on the trademark is three years but it is renewable every five years at little cost. AL is planning to add these drugs to its stable of core revenue-producing drugs and has already invested significant amounts in advertising. Research in the area of treating allergies has led AL scientists to believe that there will not be a better drug or cure for allergies in the near to mid term.

AL has also started up an on-line distribution business. So far, the company has relocated 40 employees, developed a new website and database, and spent significant amounts on training and advertising. It is now December 15 and preparations to get ready have been ongoing for six months. Management originally estimated that it would take seven months to be up and running. AL is already serving its first few customers in the new business although there are still many little problems to work out. It is estimated that the business will break even in about five more months.

Instructions

Adopt the role of the company's auditors and do a critical evaluation of the financial reporting choices that are available to the company.

Integrated Cases

(Hint: If there are issues here that are new, use the conceptual framework to help you support your analysis with solid reasoning.)

IC12-1   The following is an excerpt from **Biovail Corporation**'s (BC) Annual Report for a recent year:

Real-World
Emphasis

> Biovail Corporation is a full-service pharmaceutical company that applies its proprietary drug delivery technologies in developing "oral controlled-release" products throughout North America. Biovail applies its proprietary drug delivery technologies to successful drug compounds that are free of patent protection to develop oral controlled-release pharmaceutical products. Branded oral controlled-release products improve on existing formulations, providing better therapeutic and economic benefits.
>
> Biovail engages in the formulation, clinical testing, registration, manufacturing, sales and marketing of these oral controlled-release products throughout North America. To date, Biovail technologies have been used to develop 18 products that have been sold in more than 55 countries. Biovail's proven technologies are being applied to over 20 new products currently under development.

In 2003 and 2004, several class action lawsuits were launched against the company for misleading investors. Among other things, the lawsuits alleged that the company's growth in revenues was mainly due to acquisitions.

On October 1, 2003, a large shipment of the company's Wellbutrin XL drug was involved in a fatal multi-vehicle traffic accident that killed eight people. BC's truck was rear-ended in the accident, suffering $10,000 in damages, but no product spilled on the ground. The shipment was on its way to GlaxoSmithKline. BC stated that it had to take the drug back to the plant for inspection to be on the safe side. The insurance would only cover the actual manufacturing costs, estimated at somewhere between $2 and $4 million, if the entire order were to be destroyed.

Ethics

The company stated that the loss caused it to miss its expected quarterly profit target. On October 3, the company announced that it would have to lower revenue expectations by up to 22% for the third quarter, citing the traffic accident as contributing significantly to this by about $15–$20 million.

A week later, Banc of America Securities LLC issued a research report that included commentary by three forensic accountants who reviewed BC's financial reporting and raised a list of concerns over "aggressive accounting." As a result of the report, many investors sold their shares, driving the price of stock down significantly. The company responded to the comment in the report by announcing that it was considering a lawsuit against the analyst for what BC termed irresponsible comments.

Other analysts noted that a substantial portion of Biovail's earnings in the first half of the year came from one-time items. Sixty percent of the company's assets were represented by intangibles and goodwill. Net income for the nine months ended September 30, 2003, was approximately U.S. $75 million.

Instructions

Adopt the role of BC's controller and discuss the financial reporting issues.

IC12-2   Dr. Gary Morrow, a former surgeon, is the president and owner of Morrow Medical (MM), a private Ontario company whose focus is on the design and implementation of various medical and pharmaceutical products. With the recent success of various products put to market by MM, Dr. Morrow has decided that this would be a good opportunity to sell his company and retire to the Arizona desert. Dr. Morrow has located a potential buyer of the business and an agreement has been put in place that would see MM being sold at five times the December 31, 2010, net income. The potential buyer is extremely interested in an MM product that is currently in the development stage—the MM Surgical Drill.

During 2010, MM launched into production a special latex glove for use during surgery. This glove is laced with a special anti-bacterial agent, that significantly reduces the risk of infection during surgery. This product had been in the development phase since 2007, and in early 2009, it was approved by Health Canada for production and use.

Dr. Morrow was pleased with the initial demand for the product after trial runs conducted by surgeons during late 2009. After the success of the trial testing, MM successfully landed contracts with several hospitals in the province and early feedback from hospitals was favourable. Dr. Morrow was surprised, however, with how small the quantity of orders placed by hospitals actually was. He was certain that hospitals would quickly run out of the gloves and was beginning to fear that they would buy a competitor's product.

Since Dr. Morrow wanted to prevent hospitals from buying elsewhere, as it would result in a loss of sales for MM, for each purchase order received from a hospital, Dr. Morrow shipped several more units than were ordered. He was certain that all of the extra inventory would eventually be consumed and this was MM's way of avoiding the hospitals' running out of inventory. To prevent hospitals from returning the extra inventory, he allowed them eight months to either pay for the entire shipment or return any unused gloves in excess of the initial amount that was ordered. Dr. Morrow's first priority is always getting the product out of the warehouse and into the hospitals. Orders are generally filled and shipped within two days of the receipt of a purchase order. Because MM is dealing with hospitals, there is little concern over collectibility.

During 2008, under the supervision of Dr. Morrow, MM began the research and development of a special surgical drill (the MM Surgical Drill mentioned above) that would allow for more precise handling by surgeons than any other drill currently in the market. The development of this product grew from various market surveys conducted in hospitals throughout Ontario that showed that surgeons were unhappy with the drills that were currently available on the market.

The following costs were incurred in 2010:

Cost of setting up production lab	$ 30,000
Testing of Surgical Drill	100,000
Design of the moulds involved in Surgical Drill technology	17,500
Testing to evaluate product alternatives	12,000
Marketing and promotion costs in connection with launching the surgical gloves$	15,000

Dr. Morrow intends to capitalize all of these costs for the December 31 year end. In addition, $25,000 of tool design costs that were expensed in 2009 will be capitalized in 2010.

MM has the technical resources available to complete the Surgical Drill project and, since testing to date has been successful, management intends to bring this product to market in early 2012. MM has been faced with cash flow problems in the last few months but hopes that once MM is sold, additional funding will be available to see this product into its production stage.

In early 2010, an engineer testing the Surgical Drill was severely injured as a result of a product malfunction. This glitch was subsequently identified and fixed. MM was recently served with legal papers naming it responsible for the injuries that were sustained. The claim is for $500,000. MM lawyers' best estimate of what the company will end up paying is $100,000 to $200,000. As the trial does not begin until 2008, MM has no intention of recording this in its December 31, 2010, financial statements.

Instructions

Adopt the role of the auditor hired by MM's potential buyer and analyze the financial reporting issues.

Research and Financial Analysis

RA12-1 British Airways

Access the annual report for **British Airways plc** for the year ended March 31, 2009, from the company's website. Use the notes to the financial statements to answer the following questions.

Real-World Emphasis

Instructions

(a) Does British Airways plc report any intangible assets in its 2009 financial statements and accompanying notes? Identify all intangibles, describe their nature, their reported balance sheet amounts at March 31, 2009, and the accounting policies that are applied to these assets. Be sure to discuss any changes in these policies and how they were reported and the impact on the 2009 statements. Finally, discuss any discrepancies with IFRS standards.

(b) Note 6 to the financial statements indicates that the company entered into one business combination in 2009, the acquisition of the French airline L'Avion. Identify the following amounts for the L'Avion acquisition:

1. The fair value of L'Avion.

2. The carrying value and the fair value of identifiable net assets.

3. The type of identifiable intangible assets that were acquired and their related carrying value and fair value.

4. Initial goodwill value on acquisition. Identify what the goodwill was attributed to.

(c) What additions were made to the landing rights for 2009? How are the identifiable intangible assets tested for impairment?

(d) How is goodwill tested for impairment? Provide details on the methods and key assumptions used by the company. What was the recoverable amount determined? Do these appear reasonable? Were there any impairment losses recorded in 2009? What assumptions would make the recoverable amount equal to the carrying amount for the network airline operations?

(e) Why is all of the information provided in (d) helpful to users?

RA12-2 Rights to Use Sports Celebrities' Names

Since 1996, **Nike, Inc.** has had a partnership with Tiger Woods, one of the world's greatest athletes. Nike has been able to gain the rights to use Tiger Woods's name in advertising promotions and on Nike Golf apparel, footwear, golf balls, and golf equipment.

Real-World Emphasis

Instructions

Conduct research on the Internet to determine the nature of the agreements Nike has with Tiger Woods. How does Nike pay for the rights to use Tiger Woods's name? Using Nike, Inc.'s most recent annual report, determine how Nike reports this cost. Does it qualify as an intangible asset under IAS 38?

RA12-3 Comparative Analysis

Instructions

Go to the SEDAR website (www.sedar.com) and choose two companies from each of four different industry classifications. Choose from a variety of industries such as real estate and construction, food stores (under merchandising), biotechnology and pharmaceuticals (under consumer products), publishing (under communications and media), etc. From the companies' most recent financial statements, identify the intangibles, the total assets, and the accounting policies for each type of intangible that is reported.

(a) What net amounts were reported for intangible assets by each company? What are the amounts of accumulated amortization reported by these companies for the intangible assets? Have any impairment losses been reported in the current period?

(b) What percentage of total assets does each company have invested in intangible assets?

(c) Does the type of intangible assets differ depending on the type of industry? Does the relative size of the investment in this category of asset differ among industries? Comment.

(d) Do the policies differ by type of intangible? By type of industry?

(e) Describe the type of disclosure provided for those companies that reported impairment losses.

RA12-4 L'Oréal

Real-World Emphasis

L'Oréal is the world's largest cosmetic company, with brands such as its own name, Redken, Maybelline, Lancôme, and Ralph Lauren, just to name a few.

Instructions

Access L'Oréal's annual financial statements for the year ended December 31, 2008, from the company's website and answer the following questions with respect to the intangible assets.

(a) Identify all types of intangibles that are reported by L'Oréal and their related amounts. You may have to refer to the notes to the financial statements to complete your list. How much was added to each intangible asset during the year? Are intangible assets a significant portion of the company's total assets?

(b) For each intangible asset that you identified, indicate the accounting policy that L'Oréal follows.

(c) Describe how L'Oréal's management tests for impairment of intangibles. Be specific on the methods and assumptions used. Are these reasonable? Is there any other information you would like to have as a user? Was there any impairment losses reported in 2008?

(d) Does L'Oréal report any R&D assets? Explain. What were the company's expenditures on R&D for its year ended December 31, 2008?

(e) How does L'Oréal account for advertising costs?

(f) Read Note 2 to the financial statements and describe the amounts of the intangible assets acquired.

RA12-5 Regulated Assets

Instructions

Read the article "Recognizing Assets" by John Browne, *CA Magazine*, December 2008. Answer the following questions.

(a) What are regulatory assets? Which types of companies have these assets?

(b) What are the current accounting issues with respect to reporting and measuring these assets?

(c) Do these assets qualify as intangible assets under IAS 38?

Cumulative Coverage: Chapters 10 to 12

Fit Fixtures Incorporated (FFI) is a manufacturer of exercise equipment such as treadmills, stair climbers, and elliptical machines. The company has a December 31 year end and uses private entity GAAP. As at December 31, 2009, the company had the following balances in its capital asset accounts:

Account Title	Description	Cost at December 31, 2009	Accumulated Depreciation/ Amortization at Dec. 31, 2009	Depreciation/ Amortization Method and Rate
Land	Land on which manufacturing facility is located	$1,500,000	$ nil	Not applicable
Factory building	Manufacturing facility in Ontario	$10,875,000	$1,057,500	Residual value = $5,000,000 Straight-line depreciation over 25 years
Equipment	Used in manufacturing	$23,756,000	$17,179,022	Declining-balance, 25%
Office equipment	Used by office staff	$3,000,000	$2,688,960	Declining-balance, 40%
Vehicles	Delivery trucks, vehicles used by sales and office staff	$500,000	$315,680	Declining-balance, 20%
Goodwill	Purchased in 2005 when the company took over the business of its predecessor	$500,000	$ nil	Not applicable
Customer list	Purchased in 2005 when the company took over the business of its predecessor	$250,000	$112,500	Straight-line over 10 years

The accounting staff member who normally looks after the capital asset accounts was on maternity leave for the year, and the company put all transactions in a temporary account called Asset Additions and Disposals, which has a current balance of $2,844,000. The company policy on calculating depreciation for partial periods of ownership is to take 50% of the normal amount of depreciation in the year of addition and none in the year of disposal. Due to the maternity leave, no depreciation or amortization expense has been taken yet in 2010. FFI does not currently capitalize interest costs.

1. The company completed construction of a new plant in Saskatchewan on December 15, 2010, to help it better meet the needs of its customers west of Ontario. The costs associated with this construction project were as follows:

Land	$ 500,000
Construction contract: building life, 20 years, residual value $50,000	1,500,000
Manufacturing equipment	See point 4.
Office equipment	250,000
Avoidable interest calculated at 8% on financing of project from inception until put in use	75,000

2. FFI purchased a used computer at an auction for $2,500. This purchase included a printer that needed a new drum. The cost of the new drum purchased was $500. The computer was to be used in the manufacturing plant, and the printer in the office. The used computer's fair market value was $2,000 if purchased separately. The printer was worth $1,000 without a drum and $1,500 with the drum replaced.

3. In June 2010, FFI sold a delivery truck for $10,000. The truck originally cost $25,000, and accumulated depreciation on the truck to December 31, 2009, was $10,000. The sale was recorded as a debit to Cash and a credit to Asset Additions and Disposals.

4. The equipment purchased for the new plant was purchased on a deferred payment contract signed December 1. FFI issued a $5,000,000, five-year, non-interest-bearing note payable to the equipment supplier at a time when the annual market rate of interest was 6%. The note will be repaid with five equal payments made on December 1 of each year, beginning in 2011. The equipment's fair market value cannot be readily determined. No entry has been made for the equipment.

5. Due to an office redesign in the Ontario building, FFI traded some old office equipment for different office equipment with a similar life and value in use. The fair value of the equipment disposed of was $5,000. The cost of this equipment was $7,000, and the accumulated depreciation on the equipment at December 31, 2009, was $3,000. This transaction was not recorded in the books of account. No entry was made to record the exchange.

6. Shortly after the new factory was complete, vandals attacked the building and significant damage was done. The costs to correct the damage, which were not covered by insurance, included:

New paint to cover graffiti	$ 4,000
Glass for broken windows	10,000
Improved security system	25,000

7. During the year, the company developed a new piece of exercise equipment that had a built-in video game. It was the policy to amortize development costs on a straight-line basis over three years, with 50% of the normal amount in the year of development. The costs associated with product development included:

Costs to determine how a video game would work with exercise equipment	$ 50,000
Design, testing, and construction of prototype equipment	350,000
Determining the best production process for the new equipment	40,000
Advertising costs to alert customers about the new product	47,000

8. The customer list has lost value, and will not provide benefits through to 2015, as was originally predicted. It is now expected to provide undiscounted future cash flows of $50,000 in total over the next two years. There are no estimated costs to sell the list as it will not be sold, and the value in use is $46,000. Goodwill has a recoverable value of $700,000 as at December 31, 2010.

Instructions

It is year end, and you have been asked to assist the company in preparing the financial statements.

(a) Create all necessary journal entries and the Capital Assets section of the balance sheet at December 31, 2010.

(b) If the company were using IFRS, what changes would be required to your answer?

Table A-1

FUTURE VALUE OF 1
(FUTURE VALUE OF A SINGLE SUM)

$$FVF_{n,\,i} = (1+i)^n$$

(n) periods	2%	2½%	3%	4%	5%	6%	8%	9%	10%	11%	12%	15%
1	1.02000	1.02500	1.03000	1.04000	1.05000	1.06000	1.08000	1.09000	1.10000	1.11000	1.12000	1.15000
2	1.04040	1.05063	1.06090	1.08160	1.10250	1.12360	1.16640	1.18810	1.21000	1.23210	1.25440	1.32250
3	1.06121	1.07689	1.09273	1.12486	1.15763	1.19102	1.25971	1.29503	1.33100	1.36763	1.40493	1.52088
4	1.08243	1.10381	1.12551	1.16986	1.21551	1.26248	1.36049	1.41158	1.46410	1.51807	1.57352	1.74901
5	1.10408	1.13141	1.15927	1.21665	1.27628	1.33823	1.46933	1.53862	1.61051	1.68506	1.76234	2.01136
6	1.12616	1.15969	1.19405	1.26532	1.34010	1.41852	1.58687	1.67710	1.77156	1.87041	1.97382	2.31306
7	1.14869	1.18869	1.22987	1.31593	1.40710	1.50363	1.71382	1.82804	1.94872	2.07616	2.21068	2.66002
8	1.17166	1.21840	1.26677	1.36857	1.47746	1.59385	1.85093	1.99256	2.14359	2.30454	2.47596	3.05902
9	1.19509	1.24886	1.30477	1.42331	1.55133	1.68948	1.99900	2.17189	2.35795	2.55803	2.77308	3.51788
10	1.21899	1.28008	1.34392	1.48024	1.62889	1.79085	2.15892	2.36736	2.59374	2.83942	3.10585	4.04556
11	1.24337	1.31209	1.38423	1.53945	1.71034	1.89830	2.33164	2.58043	2.85312	3.15176	3.47855	4.65239
12	1.26824	1.34489	1.42576	1.60103	1.79586	2.01220	2.51817	2.81267	3.13843	3.49845	3.89598	5.35025
13	1.29361	1.37851	1.46853	1.66507	1.88565	2.13293	2.71962	3.06581	3.45227	3.88328	4.36349	6.15279
14	1.31948	1.41297	1.51259	1.73168	1.97993	2.26090	2.93719	3.34173	3.79750	4.31044	4.88711	7.07571
15	1.34587	1.44830	1.55797	1.80094	2.07893	2.39656	3.17217	3.64248	4.17725	4.78459	5.47357	8.13706
16	1.37279	1.48451	1.60471	1.87298	2.18287	2.54035	3.42594	3.97031	4.59497	5.31089	6.13039	9.35762
17	1.40024	1.52162	1.65285	1.94790	2.29202	2.69277	3.70002	4.32763	5.05447	5.89509	6.86604	10.76126
18	1.42825	1.55966	1.70243	2.02582	2.40662	2.85434	3.99602	4.71712	5.55992	6.54355	7.68997	12.37545
19	1.45681	1.59865	1.75351	2.10685	2.52695	3.02560	4.31570	5.14166	6.11591	7.26334	8.61276	14.23177
20	1.48595	1.63862	1.80611	2.19112	2.65330	3.20714	4.66096	5.60441	6.72750	8.06231	9.64629	16.36654
21	1.51567	1.67958	1.86029	2.27877	2.78596	3.39956	5.03383	6.10881	7.40025	8.94917	10.80385	18.82152
22	1.54598	1.72157	1.91610	2.36992	2.92526	3.60354	5.43654	6.65860	8.14028	9.93357	12.10031	21.64475
23	1.57690	1.76461	1.97359	2.46472	3.07152	3.81975	5.87146	7.25787	8.95430	11.02627	13.55235	24.89146
24	1.60844	1.80873	2.03279	2.56330	3.22510	4.04893	6.34118	7.91108	9.84973	12.23916	15.17863	28.62518
25	1.64061	1.85394	2.09378	2.66584	3.38635	4.29187	6.84847	8.62308	10.83471	13.58546	17.00000	32.91895
26	1.67342	1.90029	2.15659	2.77247	3.55567	4.54938	7.39635	9.39916	11.91818	15.07986	19.04007	37.85680
27	1.70689	1.94780	2.22129	2.88337	3.73346	4.82235	7.98806	10.24508	13.10999	16.73865	21.32488	43.53532
28	1.74102	1.99650	2.28793	2.99870	3.92013	5.11169	8.62711	11.16714	14.42099	18.57990	23.88387	50.06561
29	1.77584	2.04641	2.35657	3.11865	4.11614	5.41839	9.31727	12.17218	15.86309	20.62369	26.74993	57.57545
30	1.81136	2.09757	2.42726	3.24340	4.32194	5.74349	10.06266	13.26768	17.44940	22.89230	29.95992	66.21177
31	1.84759	2.15001	2.50008	3.37313	4.53804	6.08810	10.86767	14.46177	19.19434	25.41045	33.55511	76.14354
32	1.88454	2.20376	2.57508	3.50806	4.76494	6.45339	11.73708	15.76333	21.11378	28.20560	37.58173	87.56507
33	1.92223	2.25885	2.65234	3.64838	5.00319	6.84059	12.67605	17.18203	23.22515	31.30821	42.09153	100.69983
34	1.96068	2.31532	2.73191	3.79432	5.25335	7.25103	13.69013	18.72841	25.54767	34.75212	47.14252	115.80480
35	1.99989	2.37321	2.81386	3.94609	5.51602	7.68609	14.78534	20.41397	28.10244	38.57485	52.79962	133.17552
36	2.03989	2.43254	2.88928	4.10393	5.79182	8.14725	15.96817	22.25123	30.91268	42.81808	59.13557	153.15185
37	2.08069	2.49335	2.98523	4.26809	6.08141	8.63609	17.24563	24.25384	34.00395	47.52807	66.23184	176.12463
38	2.12230	2.55568	3.07478	4.43881	6.38548	9.15425	18.62528	26.43668	37.40434	52.75616	74.17966	202.54332
39	2.16474	2.61957	3.16703	4.61637	6.70475	9.70351	20.11530	28.81598	41.14479	58.55934	83.08122	232.92482
40	2.20804	2.68506	3.26204	4.80102	7.03999	10.28572	21.72452	31.40942	45.25926	65.00087	93.05097	267.86355

Time Value of Money

Table A-2

PRESENT VALUE OF 1

(PRESENT VALUE OF A SINGLE SUM)

$$PVF_{n,i} = \frac{1}{(1+i)^n} = (1+i)^{-n}$$

(n) periods	2%	2½%	3%	4%	5%	6%	8%	9%	10%	11%	12%	15%
1	.98039	.97561	.97087	.96156	.95238	.94340	.92593	.91743	.90909	.90090	.89286	.86957
2	.96117	.95181	.94260	.92456	.90703	.89000	.85734	.84168	.82645	.81162	.79719	.75614
3	.94232	.92860	.91514	.88900	.86384	.83962	.79383	.77218	.75132	.73119	.71178	.65752
4	.92385	.90595	.88849	.85480	.82270	.79209	.73503	.70843	.68301	.65873	.63552	.57175
5	.90583	.88385	.86261	.82193	.78353	.74726	.68058	.64993	.62092	.59345	.56743	.49718
6	.88797	.86230	.83748	.79031	.74622	.70496	.63017	.59627	.56447	.53464	.50663	.43233
7	.87056	.84127	.81309	.75992	.71068	.66506	.58349	.54703	.51316	.48166	.45235	.37594
8	.85349	.82075	.78941	.73069	.67684	.62741	.54027	.50187	.46651	.43393	.40388	.32690
9	.83676	.80073	.76642	.70259	.64461	.59190	.50025	.46043	.42410	.39092	.36061	.28426
10	.82035	.78120	.74409	.67556	.61391	.55839	.46319	.42241	.38554	.35218	.32197	.24719
11	.80426	.76214	.72242	.64958	.58468	.52679	.42888	.38753	.35049	.31728	.28748	.21494
12	.78849	.74356	.70138	.62460	.55684	.49697	.39711	.35554	.31863	.28584	.25668	.18691
13	.77303	.72542	.68095	.60057	.53032	.46884	.36770	.32618	.28966	.25751	.22917	.16253
14	.75788	.70773	.66112	.57748	.50507	.44230	.34046	.29925	.26333	.23199	.20462	.14133
15	.74301	.69047	.64186	.55526	.48102	.41727	.31524	.27454	.23939	.20900	.18270	.12289
16	.72845	.67362	.62317	.53391	.45811	.39365	.29189	.25187	.21763	.18829	.16312	.10687
17	.71416	.65720	.60502	.51337	.43630	.37136	.27027	.23107	.19785	.16963	.14564	.09293
18	.70016	.64117	.58739	.49363	.41552	.35034	.25025	.21199	.17986	.15282	.13004	.08081
19	.68643	.62553	.57029	.47464	.39573	.33051	.23171	.19449	.16351	.13768	.11611	.07027
20	.67297	.61027	.55368	.45639	.37689	.31180	.21455	.17843	.14864	.12403	.10367	.06110
21	.65978	.59539	.53755	.43883	.35894	.29416	.19866	.16370	.13513	.11174	.09256	.05313
22	.64684	.58086	.52189	.42196	.34185	.27751	.18394	.15018	.12285	.10067	.08264	.04620
23	.63416	.56670	.50669	.40573	.32557	.26180	.17032	.13778	.11168	.09069	.07379	.04017
24	.62172	.55288	.49193	.39012	.31007	.24698	.15770	.12641	.10153	.08170	.06588	.03493
25	.60953	.53939	.47761	.37512	.29530	.23300	.14602	.11597	.09230	.07361	.05882	.03038
26	.59758	.52623	.46369	.36069	.28124	.21981	.13520	.10639	.08391	.06631	.05252	.02642
27	.58586	.51340	.45019	.34682	.26785	.20737	.12519	.09761	.07628	.05974	.04689	.02297
28	.57437	.50088	.43708	.33348	.25509	.19563	.11591	.08955	.06934	.05382	.04187	.01997
29	.56311	.48866	.42435	.32065	.24295	.18456	.10733	.08216	.06304	.04849	.03738	.01737
30	.55207	.47674	.41199	.30832	.23138	.17411	.09938	.07537	.05731	.04368	.03338	.01510
31	.54125	.46511	.39999	.29646	.22036	.16425	.09202	.06915	.05210	.03935	.02980	.01313
32	.53063	.45377	.38834	.28506	.20987	.15496	.08520	.06344	.04736	.03545	.02661	.01142
33	.52023	.44270	.37703	.27409	.19987	.14619	.07889	.05820	.04306	.03194	.02376	.00993
34	.51003	.43191	.36604	.26355	.19035	.13791	.07305	.05340	.03914	.02878	.02121	.00864
35	.50003	.42137	.35538	.25342	.18129	.13011	.06763	.04899	.03558	.02592	.01894	.00751
36	.49022	.41109	.34503	.24367	.17266	.12274	.06262	.04494	.03235	.02335	.01691	.00653
37	.48061	.40107	.33498	.23430	.16444	.11579	.05799	.04123	.02941	.02104	.01510	.00568
38	.47119	.39128	.32523	.22529	.15661	.10924	.05369	.03783	.02674	.01896	.01348	.00494
39	.46195	.38174	.31575	.21662	.14915	.10306	.04971	.03470	.02430	.01708	.01204	.00429
40	.45289	.37243	.30656	.20829	.14205	.09722	.04603	.03184	.02210	.01538	.01075	.00373

Table A-3

FUTURE VALUE OF AN ORDINARY ANNUITY OF 1

$$FVF\text{-}OA_{n,\,i} = \frac{(1+i)^n - 1}{i}$$

(n) periods	2%	2½%	3%	4%	5%	6%	8%	9%	10%	11%	12%	15%
1	1.00000	1.00000	1.00000	1.00000	1.00000	1.00000	1.00000	1.00000	1.00000	1.00000	1.00000	1.00000
2	2.02000	2.02500	2.03000	2.04000	2.05000	2.06000	2.08000	2.09000	2.10000	2.11000	2.12000	2.15000
3	3.06040	3.07563	3.09090	3.12160	3.15250	3.18360	3.24640	3.27810	3.31000	3.34210	3.37440	3.47250
4	4.12161	4.15252	4.18363	4.24646	4.31013	4.37462	4.50611	4.57313	4.64100	4.70973	4.77933	4.99338
5	5.20404	5.25633	5.30914	5.41632	5.52563	5.63709	5.86660	5.98471	6.10510	6.22780	6.35285	6.74238
6	6.30812	6.38774	6.46841	6.63298	6.80191	6.97532	7.33592	7.52334	7.71561	7.91286	8.11519	8.75374
7	7.43428	7.54743	7.66246	7.89829	8.14201	8.39384	8.92280	9.20044	9.48717	9.78327	10.08901	11.06680
8	8.58297	8.73612	8.89234	9.21423	9.54911	9.89747	10.63663	11.02847	11.43589	11.85943	12.29969	13.72682
9	9.75463	9.95452	10.15911	10.58280	11.02656	11.49132	12.48756	13.02104	13.57948	14.16397	14.77566	16.78584
10	10.94972	11.20338	11.46338	12.00611	12.57789	13.18079	14.48656	15.19293	15.93743	16.72201	17.54874	20.30372
11	12.16872	12.48347	12.80780	13.48635	14.20679	14.97164	16.64549	17.56029	18.53117	19.56143	20.65458	24.34928
12	13.41209	13.79555	14.19203	15.02581	15.91713	16.86994	18.97713	20.14072	21.38428	22.71319	24.13313	29.00167
13	14.68033	15.14044	15.61779	16.62684	17.71298	18.88214	21.49530	22.95339	24.52271	26.21164	28.02911	34.35192
14	15.97394	16.51895	17.08632	18.29191	19.59863	21.01507	24.21492	26.01919	27.97498	30.09492	32.39260	40.50471
15	17.29342	17.93193	18.59891	20.02359	21.57856	23.27597	27.15211	29.36092	31.77248	34.40536	37.27972	47.58041
16	18.63929	19.38022	20.15688	21.82453	23.65749	25.67253	30.32428	33.00340	35.94973	39.18995	42.75328	55.71747
17	20.01207	20.86473	21.76159	23.69751	25.84037	28.21288	33.75023	36.97371	40.54470	44.50084	48.88367	65.07509
18	21.41231	22.38635	23.41444	25.64541	28.13238	30.90565	37.45024	41.30134	45.59917	50.39593	55.74972	75.83636
19	22.84056	23.94601	25.11687	27.67123	30.53900	33.75999	41.44626	46.01846	51.15909	56.93949	63.43968	88.21181
20	24.29737	25.54466	26.87037	29.77808	33.06595	36.78559	45.76196	51.16012	57.27500	64.20283	72.05244	102.44358
21	25.78332	27.18327	28.67649	31.96920	35.71925	39.99273	50.42292	56.76453	64.00250	72.26514	81.69874	118.81012
22	27.29898	28.86286	30.53678	34.24797	38.50521	43.39229	55.45676	62.87334	71.40275	81.21431	92.50258	137.63164
23	28.84496	30.58443	32.45288	36.61789	41.43048	46.99583	60.89330	69.53194	79.54302	91.14788	104.60289	159.27638
24	30.42186	32.34904	34.42647	39.08260	44.50200	50.81558	66.76476	76.78981	88.49733	102.17415	118.15524	184.16784
25	32.03030	34.15776	36.45926	41.64591	47.72710	54.86451	73.10594	84.70090	98.34706	114.41331	133.33387	212.79302
26	33.67091	36.01171	38.55304	44.31174	51.11345	59.15638	79.95442	93.32398	109.18177	127.99877	150.33393	245.71197
27	35.34432	37.91200	40.70963	47.08421	54.66913	63.70577	87.35077	102.72314	121.09994	143.07864	169.37401	283.56877
28	37.05121	39.85990	42.93092	49.96758	58.40258	68.52811	95.33883	112.96822	134.20994	159.81729	190.69889	327.10408
29	38.79223	41.85630	45.21885	52.96629	62.32271	73.63980	103.96594	124.13536	148.63093	178.39719	214.58275	377.16969
30	40.56808	43.90270	47.57542	56.08494	66.43885	79.05819	113.28321	136.30754	164.49402	199.02088	241.33268	434.74515
31	42.37944	46.00027	50.00268	59.32834	70.76079	84.80168	123.34587	149.57522	181.94343	221.91317	271.29261	500.95692
32	44.22703	48.15028	52.50276	62.70147	75.29883	90.88978	134.21354	164.03699	201.13777	247.32362	304.84772	577.10046
33	46.11157	50.35403	55.07784	66.20953	80.06377	97.34316	145.95062	179.80032	222.25154	275.52922	342.42945	644.66553
34	48.03380	52.61289	57.73018	69.85791	85.06696	104.18376	158.62667	196.98234	245.47670	306.83744	384.52098	765.36535
35	49.99448	54.92821	60.46208	73.65222	90.32031	111.43478	172.31680	215.71076	271.02437	341.58955	431.66350	881.17016
36	51.99437	57.30141	63.27594	77.59831	95.83632	119.12087	187.10215	236.12472	299.12681	380.16441	484.46312	1014.34568
37	54.03425	59.73395	66.17422	81.70225	101.62814	127.26812	203.07032	258.37595	330.03949	422.98249	543.59869	1167.49753
38	56.11494	62.22730	69.15945	85.97034	107.70955	135.90421	220.31595	282.62978	364.04343	470.51056	609.83053	1343.62216
39	58.23724	64.78298	72.23423	90.40915	114.09502	145.05846	238.94122	309.06646	401.44778	523.26673	684.01020	1546.16549
40	60.40198	67.40255	75.40126	95.02552	120.79977	154.76197	259.05652	337.88245	442.59256	581.82607	767.09142	1779.09031

Time Value of Money

Table A-4

PRESENT VALUE OF AN ORDINARY ANNUITY OF 1

$$PVF\text{-}OA_{n,\,i} = \frac{1 - \dfrac{1}{(1+i)^n}}{i}$$

(n) periods	2%	2½%	3%	4%	5%	6%	8%	9%	10%	11%	12%	15%
1	.98039	.97561	.97087	.96154	.95238	.94340	.92593	.91743	.90909	.90090	.89286	.86957
2	1.94156	1.92742	1.91347	1.88609	1.85941	1.83339	1.78326	1.75911	1.73554	1.71252	1.69005	1.62571
3	2.88388	2.85602	2.82861	2.77509	2.72325	2.67301	2.57710	2.53130	2.48685	2.44371	2.40183	2.28323
4	3.80773	3.76197	3.71710	3.62990	3.54595	3.46511	3.31213	3.23972	3.16986	3.10245	3.03735	2.85498
5	4.71346	4.64583	4.57971	4.45182	4.32948	4.21236	3.99271	3.88965	3.79079	3.69590	3.60478	3.35216
6	5.60143	5.50813	5.41719	5.24214	5.07569	4.91732	4.62288	4.48592	4.35526	4.23054	4.11141	3.78448
7	6.47199	6.34939	6.23028	6.00205	5.78637	5.58238	5.20637	5.03295	4.86842	4.71220	4.56376	4.16042
8	7.32548	7.17014	7.01969	6.73274	6.46321	6.20979	5.74664	5.53482	5.33493	5.14612	4.96764	4.48732
9	8.16224	7.97087	7.78611	7.43533	7.10782	6.80169	6.24689	5.99525	5.75902	5.53705	5.32825	4.77158
10	8.98259	8.75206	8.53020	8.11090	7.72173	7.36009	6.71008	6.41766	6.14457	5.88923	5.65022	5.01877
11	9.78685	9.51421	9.25262	8.76048	8.30641	7.88687	7.13896	6.80519	6.49506	6.20652	5.93770	5.23371
12	10.57534	10.25776	9.95400	9.38507	8.86325	8.38384	7.53608	7.16073	6.81369	6.49236	6.19437	5.42062
13	11.34837	10.98319	10.63496	9.98565	9.39357	8.85268	7.90378	7.48690	7.10336	6.74987	6.42355	5.58315
14	12.10625	11.69091	11.29607	10.56312	9.89864	9.29498	8.24424	7.78615	7.36669	6.98187	6.62817	5.72448
15	12.84926	12.38138	11.93794	11.11839	10.37966	9.71225	8.55948	8.06069	7.60608	7.19087	6.81086	5.84737
16	13.57771	13.05500	12.56110	11.65230	10.83777	10.10590	8.85137	8.31256	7.82371	7.37916	6.97399	5.95424
17	14.29187	13.71220	13.16612	12.16567	11.27407	10.47726	9.12164	8.54363	8.02155	7.54879	7.11963	6.04716
18	14.99203	14.35336	13.75351	12.65930	11.68959	10.82760	9.37189	8.75563	8.20141	7.70162	7.24967	6.12797
19	15.67846	14.97889	14.32380	13.13394	12.08532	11.15812	9.60360	8.95012	8.36492	7.83929	7.36578	6.19823
20	16.35143	15.58916	14.87747	13.59033	12.46221	11.46992	9.81815	9.12855	8.51356	7.96333	7.46944	6.25933
21	17.01121	16.18455	15.41502	14.02916	12.82115	11.76408	10.01680	9.29224	8.64869	8.07507	7.56200	6.31246
22	17.65805	16.76541	15.93692	14.45112	13.16800	12.04158	10.20074	9.44243	8.77154	8.17574	7.64465	6.35866
23	18.29220	17.33211	16.44361	14.85684	13.48857	12.30338	10.37106	9.58021	8.88322	8.26643	7.71843	6.39884
24	18.91393	17.88499	16.93554	15.24696	13.79864	12.55036	10.52876	9.70661	8.98474	8.34814	7.78432	6.43377
25	19.52346	18.42438	17.41315	15.62208	14.09394	12.78336	10.67478	9.82258	9.07704	8.42174	7.84314	6.46415
26	20.12104	18.95061	17.87684	15.98277	14.37519	13.00317	10.80998	9.92897	9.16095	8.48806	7.89566	6.49056
27	20.70690	19.46401	18.32703	16.32959	14.64303	13.21053	10.93516	10.02658	9.23722	8.45780	7.94255	6.51353
28	21.28127	19.96489	18.76411	16.66306	14.89813	13.40616	11.05108	10.11613	9.30657	8.60162	7.98442	6.53351
29	21.84438	20.45355	19.18845	16.98371	15.14107	13.59072	11.15841	10.19828	9.36961	8.65011	8.02181	6.55088
30	22.39646	20.93029	19.60044	17.29203	15.37245	13.76483	11.25778	10.27365	9.42691	8.69379	8.05518	6.56598
31	22.93770	21.39541	20.00043	17.58849	15.59281	13.92909	11.34980	10.34280	9.47901	8.73315	8.08499	6.57911
32	23.46833	21.84918	20.38877	17.87355	15.80268	14.08404	11.43500	10.40624	9.52638	8.76860	8.11159	6.59053
33	23.98856	22.29188	20.76579	18.14765	16.00255	14.23023	11.51389	10.46444	9.56943	8.80054	8.13535	6.60046
34	24.49859	22.72379	21.13184	18.41120	16.19290	14.36814	11.58693	10.51784	9.60858	8.82932	8.15656	6.60910
35	24.99862	23.14516	21.48722	18.66461	16.37419	14.49825	11.65457	10.56682	9.64416	8.85524	8.17550	6.61661
36	25.48884	23.55625	21.83225	18.90828	16.54685	14.62099	11.71719	10.61176	9.67651	8.87859	8.19241	6.62314
37	25.96945	23.95732	22.16724	19.14258	16.71129	14.73678	11.77518	10.65299	9.70592	8.89963	8.20751	6.62882
38	26.44064	24.34860	22.49246	19.36786	16.86789	14.84602	11.82887	10.69082	9.73265	8.91859	8.22099	6.63375
39	26.90259	24.73034	22.80822	19.58448	17.01704	14.94907	11.87858	10.72552	9.75697	8.93567	8.23303	6.63805
40	27.35548	25.10278	23.11477	19.79277	17.15909	15.04630	11.92461	10.75736	9.77905	8.95105	8.24378	6.64178

Table A-5

PRESENT VALUE OF AN ANNUITY DUE OF 1

$$PVF-AD_{n,\,i} = 1 + \frac{1-\dfrac{1}{(1+i)^{n-1}}}{i}$$

(n) periods	2%	2½%	3%	4%	5%	6%	8%	9%	10%	11%	12%	15%
1	1.00000	1.00000	1.00000	1.00000	1.00000	1.00000	1.00000	1.00000	1.00000	1.00000	1.00000	1.00000
2	1.98039	1.97561	1.97087	1.96154	1.95238	1.94340	1.92593	1.91743	1.90909	1.90090	1.89286	1.86957
3	2.94156	2.92742	2.91347	2.88609	2.85941	2.83339	2.78326	2.75911	2.73554	2.71252	2.69005	2.62571
4	3.88388	3.85602	3.82861	3.77509	3.72325	3.67301	3.57710	3.53130	3.48685	3.44371	3.40183	3.28323
5	4.80773	4.76197	4.71710	4.62990	4.54595	4.46511	4.31213	4.23972	4.16986	4.10245	4.03735	3.85498
6	5.71346	5.64583	5.57971	5.45182	5.32948	5.21236	4.99271	4.88965	4.79079	4.69590	4.60478	4.35216
7	6.60143	6.50813	6.41719	6.24214	6.07569	5.91732	5.62288	5.48592	5.35526	5.23054	5.11141	4.78448
8	7.47199	7.34939	7.23028	7.00205	6.78637	6.58238	6.20637	6.03295	5.86842	5.71220	5.56376	5.16042
9	8.32548	8.17014	8.01969	7.73274	7.46321	7.20979	6.74664	6.53482	6.33493	6.14612	5.96764	5.48732
10	9.16224	8.97087	8.78611	8.43533	8.10782	7.80169	7.24689	6.99525	6.75902	6.53705	6.32825	5.77158
11	9.98259	9.75206	9.53020	9.11090	8.72173	8.36009	7.71008	7.41766	7.14457	6.88923	6.65022	6.01877
12	10.78685	10.51421	10.25262	9.76048	9.30641	8.88687	8.13896	7.80519	7.49506	7.20652	6.93770	6.23371
13	11.57534	11.25776	10.95400	10.38507	9.86325	9.38384	8.53608	8.16073	7.81369	7.49236	7.19437	6.42062
14	12.34837	11.98319	11.63496	10.98565	10.39357	9.85268	8.90378	8.48690	8.10336	7.74987	7.42355	6.58315
15	13.10625	12.69091	12.29607	11.56312	10.89864	10.29498	9.24424	8.78615	9.36669	7.98187	7.62817	6.72448
16	13.84926	13.38138	12.93794	12.11839	11.37966	10.71225	9.55948	9.06069	8.60608	8.19087	7.81086	6.84737
17	14.57771	14.05500	13.56110	12.65230	11.83777	11.10590	9.85137	9.31256	8.82371	8.37916	7.97399	6.95424
18	15.29187	14.71220	14.16612	13.16567	12.27407	11.47726	10.12164	9.54363	9.02155	8.54879	8.11963	7.04716
19	15.99203	15.35336	14.75351	13.65930	12.68959	11.82760	10.37189	9.75563	9.20141	8.70162	8.24967	7.12797
20	16.67846	15.97889	15.32380	14.13394	13.08532	12.15812	10.60360	9.95012	9.36492	8.83929	8.36578	7.19823
21	17.35143	16.58916	15.87747	14.59033	13.46221	12.46992	10.81815	10.12855	9.51356	8.96333	8.46944	7.25933
22	18.01121	17.18455	16.41502	15.02916	13.82115	12.76408	11.01680	10.29224	9.64869	9.07507	8.56200	7.31246
23	18.65805	17.76541	16.93692	15.45112	14.16300	13.04158	11.20074	10.44243	9.77154	9.17574	8.64465	7.35866
24	19.29220	18.33211	17.44361	15.85684	14.48857	13.30338	11.37106	10.58021	9.88322	9.26643	8.71843	7.39884
25	19.91393	18.88499	17.93554	16.24696	14.79864	13.55036	11.52876	10.70661	9.98474	9.34814	8.78432	7.43377
26	20.52346	19.42438	18.41315	16.62208	15.09394	13.78336	11.67478	10.82258	10.07704	9.42174	8.84314	7.46415
27	21.12104	19.95061	18.87684	16.98277	15.37519	14.00317	11.80998	10.92897	10.16095	9.48806	8.89566	7.49056
28	21.70690	20.46401	19.32703	17.32959	15.64303	14.21053	11.93518	11.02658	10.23722	9.54780	8.94255	7.51353
29	22.28127	20.96489	19.76411	17.66306	15.89813	14.40616	12.05108	11.11613	10.30657	9.60162	8.98442	7.53351
30	22.84438	21.45355	20.18845	17.98371	16.14107	14.59072	12.15841	11.19828	10.36961	9.65011	9.02181	7.55088
31	23.39646	21.93029	20.60044	18.29203	16.37245	14.76483	12.25778	11.27365	10.42691	9.69379	9.05518	7.56598
32	23.93770	22.39541	21.00043	18.58849	16.59281	14.92909	12.34980	11.34280	10.47901	9.73315	9.08499	7.57911
33	24.46833	22.84918	21.38877	18.87355	16.80268	15.08404	12.43500	11.40624	10.52638	9.76860	9.11159	7.59053
34	24.98856	23.29188	21.76579	19.14765	17.00255	15.23023	12.51389	11.46444	10.56943	9.80054	9.13535	7.60046
35	25.49859	23.72379	22.13184	19.41120	17.19290	15.36814	12.58693	11.51784	10.60858	9.82932	9.15656	7.60910
36	25.99862	24.14516	22.48722	19.66461	17.37419	15.49825	12.65457	11.56682	10.64416	9.85524	9.17550	7.61661
37	26.48884	24.55625	22.83225	19.90828	17.54685	15.62099	12.71719	11.61176	10.67651	9.87859	9.19241	7.62314
38	26.96945	24.95732	23.16724	20.14258	17.71129	15.73678	12.77518	11.65299	10.70592	9.89963	9.20751	7.62882
39	27.44064	25.34860	23.49246	20.36786	17.86789	15.84602	12.82887	11.69082	10.73265	9.91859	9.22099	7.63375
40	27.90259	25.73034	23.80822	20.58448	18.01704	15.94907	12.87858	11.72552	10.75697	9.93567	9.23303	7.63805

Company Index

Subject Index

Credits

References to the *CICA Handbook* are reprinted (or adapted) with permission from The Canadian Institute of Chartered Accountants, Toronto, Canada. Any changes to the original material are the sole responsibility of the author (and/or publisher) and have not been reviewed or endorsed by the CICA.

Extracts adapted from *Financial Accounting: Assets* (FA2) and *Financial Accounting: Liabilities and Equities* (FA3) published by the Certified General Accountants Association of Canada © 2001 to 2008 CGA-Canada. Reproduced with permission.

CMA Canada adapted material is adapted with the permission of The Society of Management Accountants of Canada.

All images are copyright© iStockphoto unless otherwise noted.

Page 88: Courtesy XBRLSpy/Diane Mueller.
Page 151: Courtesy XBRL Canada.
Page 218: Photo courtesy of Eastern Platinum Ltd.
Page 318: Courtesy Pacific Regeneration Technologies.
Page 376: Cindy Wilson/Telegraph-Journal.
Page 393: Courtesy Canadian Tire Corporation, Limited.
Page 450: Courtesy Brock's.
Page 528: Courtesy Empire Company Ltd.
Page 604: Courtesy Homburg Invest Inc.
Page 676: Courtesy Via Rail / Matthew G. Wheeler.
Page 687: Simmons & Company International.
Page 742: Courtesy Canadian Tire Corporation, Limited.